S0-ASM-360

VAULT
TOP LAW FIRMS

SPECIAL
ADVERTISING
SECTION

EXPANDING OUR REACH

Orrick prides itself on service to the community. We view it as fundamental to the way we work as a firm in offices around the world, and as individuals in our own neighborhoods.

Our sense of community responsibility is fueled by individual passion. We reach out and take action to help those with the greatest need, and in situations where we can make the greatest impact. From arts and education to legal services and community building, Orrick provides much more than just financial assistance. Through superior leadership, legal counsel and volunteer support, Orrick gives a voice to organizations and individuals in need around the world.

To learn more about Orrick and our community responsibility efforts, **please visit** www.orrick.com/community.

ASIA | EUROPE | NORTH AMERICA

BEIJING   HONG KONG   SHANGHAI   TAIPEI   TOKYO
LONDON   MILAN   MOSCOW   PARIS   ROME
LOS ANGELES   NEW YORK   ORANGE COUNTY   PACIFIC NORTHWEST
SACRAMENTO   SAN FRANCISCO   SILICON VALLEY   WASHINGTON DC

ORRICK

WWW.ORRICK.COM

Orrick, Herrington & Sutcliffe LLP | 666 Fifth Avenue | New York, NY 10103-0001 | United States | tel +1-212-506-5000
Attorney advertising. As required by New York law, we hereby advise you that prior results do not guarantee a similar outcome.

Why settle?

Three parties in three cases that could not settle - a company being sued for $135 million in a case that was pending for 17 years; a man, forced out of the company he founded, seeking punitive damages; a company suing for breach of a multi-year, multi-million-dollar contract - each hired Quinn Emanuel the week before trial, and each won.

Time and again, Quinn Emanuel has been called in to try a case after a traditional business litigation firm failed to settled. You see, we live to try cases. It's our purpose and our passion. And we're good at it. The result? Top clients who don't settle come to Quinn Emanuel. Top lawyers too. How about you?

quinn emanuel trial lawyers

Los Angeles   New York   San Francisco   Silicon Valley

The media's watching Vault!
Here's a sampling of our coverage.

"With reviews and profiles of firms that one associate calls 'spot on',
[Vault's] guide has become a key reference for those who want to know
what it takes to get hired by a law firm and what to expect once they
get there."
- *New York Law Journal*

"The best place on the web to prepare for a job search."
- *Fortune*

"Vault is indispensable for locating insider information."
- *Metropolitan Corporate Counsel*

"[Vault's guide] is an INVALUABLE Cliff's Notes to prepare for
interviews."
- *Women's Lawyer's Journal*

"For those hoping to climb the ladder of success, [Vault's] insights are
priceless."
- *Money Magazine*

"[Vault guides] make for excellent starting points for job hunters and
should be purchased by academic libraries for their career sections
[and] university career centers."
- *Library Journal*

TAKE A CLOSER LOOK.

For more than a century, Hogan & Hartson has combined professional excellence and industry leadership with a culture of respect and collegiality. At any given moment, hundreds of major national and multi-national clients are relying on our lawyers to resolve critical business disputes, structure complex transactions, protect key intellectual assets, and navigate complicated regulatory and administrative hurdles. But we believe that the success of our law firm as an institution should also be measured by the success of our individual lawyers—not only as attorneys, but as people. We are proud to offer our new lawyers the guidance and resources they need to develop their practices and to grow as professionals and as leaders. We invite you to learn more about our team-oriented culture, and to take a closer look at a law firm that will exceed your expectations.

To learn more about Hogan & Hartson, visit:
www.hhlaw.com/careers

HOGAN & HARTSON L.L.P.
555 13TH STREET, NW
WASHINGTON, DC 20004
T. 202.637.5600 | F. 202.637.5910

HOGAN & HARTSON

www.hhlaw.com

BALTIMORE BEIJING BERLIN BOULDER BRUSSELS BUDAPEST CARACAS COLORADO SPRINGS
DENVER GENEVA HONG KONG LONDON LOS ANGELES MIAMI MOSCOW MUNICH
NEW YORK NORTHERN VIRGINIA PARIS SHANGHAI TOKYO WARSAW WASHINGTON, DC

VAULT GUIDE TO THE

TOP 100
LAW FIRMS

© 2007 Vault Inc.

McKee Nelson LLP
Attorneys at Law
This is where business is going.
Find out why.
#9-Best in Informal Training
#9-Associate/Partner Relations
#9-Best in Diversity/GLBT
#3-Best in Compensation
#8-Tax Law
#15-Quality of Life/ Best Firms to Work For
#9-Best in Overall Diversity
With more than 170 lawyers in offices in Washington, DC and New York, NY, McKee Nelson LLP is a recognized leader, representing corporations and financial institutions in the areas of structured finance, tax litigation, tax planning, corporate finance and M&A, securities, and white collar/investigations and enforcement.
Visit us at www.mckeenelson.com.

VAULT GUIDE TO THE
TOP 100
LAW FIRMS

**BRIAN DALTON, J.D.
AND THE STAFF OF VAULT**

© 2007 Vault Inc.

Copyright © 2007 by Vault Inc. All rights reserved.

All information in this book is subject to change without notice. Vault makes no claims as to the accuracy and reliability of the information contained within and disclaims all warranties. No part of this book may be reproduced or transmitted in any form or by any means, electronic or mechanical, for any purpose, without the express written permission of Vault Inc.

Vault, the Vault logo, and "the most trusted name in career information™" are trademarks of Vault Inc.

For information about permission to reproduce selections from this book, contact Vault Inc., 150 W. 22nd St., 5th Floor, New York, NY 10011, (212) 366-4212.

Library of Congress CIP Data is available.

ISSN: 1549-8484
ISBN 13: 978-1-58131-488-5
ISBN 10: 1-58131-488-4

Printed in the United States of America

Acknowledgments

Thank you to all the Vault sales, graphics, editorial and IT staff for writing, selling, designing and programming the guide.

Special thanks to Claire Blechman, Vera Djordjevich, Anne Holmes, Laurie Pasiuk and Kristina Tsamis.

As always, the book is dedicated to the more than 18,800 associates and 167 law firms who took time out of their busy schedules to complete our survey.

Will a random choice decide your future?
NOT IF WE CAN HELP IT.

It's risky to choose a career specialty based on the strength of a law school class and some initial interviews. At Winston & Strawn, you don't have to. We will help you find the right path without getting pigeonholed early in your career. Even after you've joined the firm, you'll have a range of opportunities. The only decision you need to make now is choosing Winston. Everything else will follow.

WINSTON & STRAWN LLP

Chicago Geneva London Los Angeles Moscow New York Paris San Francisco Washington, DC   www.winston.com

Table of Contents

Visit the Vault Law Channel, the complete online resource for law careers, featuring firm profiles, message boards, the Vault Law Job Board, and more. www.vault.com/law

VAULT CAREER LIBRARY

ix

We are diverse in all respects —
background, political persuasion, family life, interests and
experience, age, gender, lifestyles, personalities —
everything, in fact, except our intense commitment to
representing the interests of our clients, serving the
community, and respecting each other.

JENNER & BLOCK

CHICAGO   DALLAS   NEW YORK   WASHINGTON, DC

For more information please email
legalrecruiting@jenner.com

Jenner & Block LLP
www.jenner.com

THE VAULT 100: FIRMS 1-50   87

Visit the Vault Law Channel, the complete online resource for law careers, featuring firm profiles, message boards, the Vault Law Job Board, and more. www.vault.com/law

VAULT CAREER LIBRARY   xi

Paul Hastings

Choose Your Path

Paul Hastings provides guidance to the world's leading financial institutions, multinational corporations, Fortune 500 companies and other organizations. Wherever our clients operate, the collective discipline and individual creativity of our lawyers is the fulcrum for an integrated approach to problem-solving and transactional efficiency. Visit the Paul Hastings web site to learn more about our people, our practice and our accomplishments. The Careers section will introduce you to our benefits, diversity, employment opportunities, pro bono, professional development, summer programs and contact information. Get started early...we look forward to hearing from you.

37 Practice Areas and 84 Lawyers Ranked Among the Best in the United States *Chambers USA 2007*

Top-ranked Practice Areas and Attorneys in Litigation, Employment and International Arbitration *The Legal 500 US Volume III: Litigation 2007*

Leading Firm for Diversity/Top 5 Family-Friendly Firm *Minority Law Journal Diversity Scorecard and Multicultural Law Magazine/Yale Law Women*

18 Offices Worldwide | Paul, Hastings, Janofsky & Walker LLP | www.paulhastings.com

Visit the Vault Law Channel, the complete online resource for law careers, featuring firm profiles, message boards, the Vault Law Job Board, and more. www.vault.com/law

VAULT CAREER LIBRARY   xiii

Associate with us.
Linklaters

Linklaters advises the world's leading companies, financial institutions and governments on their most challenging transactions and assignments. With offices in major business and financial centers, we deliver an outstanding service to our clients anywhere in the world.

Amsterdam	Bratislava	Dubai	Luxembourg	New York	Shanghai
Antwerp	Brussels	Frankfurt	Madrid	Paris	Singapore
Bangkok	Bucharest	Hong Kong	Milan	Prague	Stockholm
Beijing	Budapest	Lisbon	Moscow	Rome	Tokyo
Berlin	Cologne	London	Munich	São Paulo	Warsaw

www.linklaters.com

Linklaters LLP is a limited liability partnership.

Visit the Vault Law Channel, the complete online resource for law careers, featuring firm profiles, message boards, the Vault Law Job Board, and more. www.vault.com/law

VAULT CAREER LIBRARY

xv

DEWEY BALLANTINE LLP

OUT OF THE MANY,
YOU WILL CHOOSE **ONE**

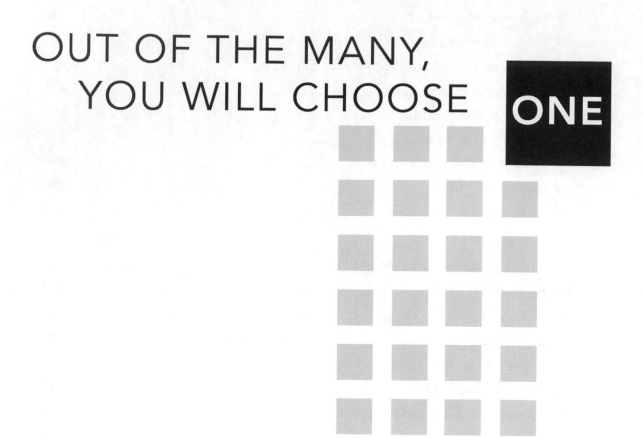

Our nation's motto, *E pluribus unum*, means "out of many, one." This also expresses the spirit of Dewey Ballantine. In our talents, opportunities, practices, and even locations, we are many—but in our standard of excellence, our commitment to common guiding principles, and our collegial tradition, we are one. Dewey Ballantine is a firm where you'll find that your greatest aspirations are rewarded with exceptional opportunities.

www.deweyballantine.com

New York • Washington, D.C. • Los Angeles • East Palo Alto • Austin
Charlotte • London • Warsaw • Frankfurt • Milan • Rome • Beijing

THE BEST OF THE REST
547

Visit the Vault Law Channel, the complete online resource for law careers, featuring firm profiles, message boards, the Vault Law Job Board, and more. www.vault.com/law

VAULT CAREER LIBRARY

xvii

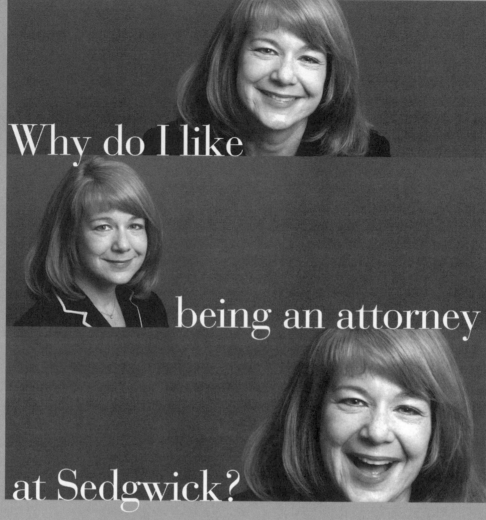

Why do I like being an attorney at Sedgwick?

**Stephanie Sheridan
Partner, San Francisco**

Stephanie is a trial lawyer and a founding member of the Sedgwick Women's Forum, a group dedicated to fostering professional growth and networking opportunities for women in the law.

Austin
Bermuda*
Chicago
Dallas
Houston
London
Los Angeles
New York
Newark
Orange County
Paris
San Francisco
Zurich
www.sdma.com

BECAUSE TODAY I WALKED THE DOGS, RESOLVED A PROBLEMATIC MATTER FOR MY CLIENT, INTERVIEWED AN ATTORNEY CANDIDATE, FILED A MOTION, MET WITH MY ASSOCIATE-MENTEE, SAW A CLIENT AT OUR YOGA CLASS, AND GOT HOME IN TIME TO PLAN A WEEKEND SURFING TRIP WITH MY HUSBAND. **JUST SOME OF THE MANY REASONS WHY I LIKE BEING AN ATTORNEY AT SEDGWICK.**

**Sedgwick
women's forum**

Fostering professional growth
and networking opportunities
for women in the law

*Affiliated office.

Visit the Vault Law Channel, the complete online resource for law careers, featuring firm profiles, message boards, the Vault Law Job Board, and more. **www.vault.com/law**

VAULT CAREER LIBRARY

xix

© 2007 Vault Inc.

Visit the Vault Law Channel, the complete online resource for law careers, featuring firm
profiles, message boards, the Vault Law Job Board, and more. **www.vault.com/law**

VAULT CAREER LIBRARY   **xxi**

LEGAL RECRUITER FIRM DIRECTORY   647

DIVERSITY PROGRAMS DIRECTORY   661

PRO BONO PROGRAMS DIRECTORY   707

APPENDIX   737

Visit the Vault Law Channel, the complete online resource for law careers, featuring firm
profiles, message boards, the Vault Law Job Board, and more. **www.vault.com/law**

V\ULT CAREER LIBRARY   **xxiii**

Wondering what it's like to work at a specific employer?

Read what **EMPLOYEES** have to say about:

- Workplace culture
- Compensation
- Hours
- Diversity
- Hiring process

Read employer surveys on THOUSANDS of top employers.

V ULT
> the most trusted name in career information™

Go to www.vault.com

Introduction

Welcome to the tenth edition of the *Vault Guide to the Top 100 Law Firms*, the most comprehensive, candid, up-to-date guide to the most prestigious law firms. This year, our guide is bigger and better, with more law firm profiles than ever before. We rank 100 of the nation's top firms, and offer 100 law firm profiles incorporating quotes and opinions from thousands of associates. The guide also provides a glimpse of more than 60 additional firms, with contact and salary information, office locations, notable perks, major practice areas and more, including the ever-popular "Buzz" section, in which associates offer observations about firms other than their own.

Vault's associate survey continues to attract more and more respondents, which makes our rankings even more comprehensive and adds greater depth to our profiles. For our eighth edition, we cracked 15,000 respondents. Last year over 16,300 associates took our survey. This year we did even better, with over 18,800 responses. The survey polled associates at more than 167 of the most prestigious firms in the country and asked them to rank their peer law firms based on prestige. (Associates were asked only to rank those firms with which they were familiar.) We took those scores and calculated the Vault Top 100. We also asked associates to comment on and rank their own firm in terms of general satisfaction, hours, compensation, diversity, treatment by partners and selectivity in hiring. As always, it's the associates who give us the Vault Top 100, not Vault's editors or law firm management.

We're at it year after year, surveying associates and bugging law firm recruiting directors and hiring partners, for one reason: to provide lawyers and law students with an insider's view of what it's like to work at the nation's most prestigious law firms. But why do we bother ranking the Top 100 firms? Why does law firm prestige matter? A job is a job, after all, and many law firms not profiled in this guide pay as well as any firm on our list. Still, prestige matters plenty. Working for a prestigious law firm means being exposed to a greater variety and volume of work, as well as more prominent and high-profile cases and deals. It can also mean working with some particularly gifted and accomplished lawyers from whom you can learn a great deal. Most importantly, working for a prestigious firm will give you instant credibility in the job market and mark you as someone to be taken seriously throughout your career.

But prestige isn't everything. Choosing the right firm may mean looking beyond prestige to such issues as compensation, hours, perks, practice specialties, partnership chances, diversity and corporate culture. In our Best 20 Firms to Work For, we rank the firms that associates find the most amenable to an enjoyable lawyerly existence.

This year, for the first time, we have included a special appendix that details the personnel policies for the majority of the firms we profile. In previous years, official firm policies on maternity leave, vacation, flex-time and other matters have been a source of confusion as we've sought to define them based on the survey responses. For our tenth edition of the Guide, we've gone straight to the source—the firms themselves—and clarified the official details.

Of course, the smart law firm job candidate will still use every resource at his or her disposal—and we think there's no better resource for finding a law firm job than the *Vault Guide to the Top 100 Law Firms*. Use our prestige, departmental, quality of life and diversity rankings to identify the firms that are most attractive to you, then read our profiles to get the inside scoop on your target firms. Armed with knowledge, confidence and a strong handshake, you can't go wrong.

Brian Dalton
Vault Inc.
New York, N.Y.

Visit the Vault Law Channel, the complete online resource for law careers, featuring firm profiles, message boards, the Vault Law Job Board, and more. **www.vault.com/law**

VAULT CAREER LIBRARY

1

Use the Internet's
MOST TARGETED
job search tools.

Vault Job Board

Target your search by industry, function, and experience level, and find the job openings that you want.

VaultMatch Resume Database

Vault takes match-making to the next level: post your resume and customize your search by industry, function, experience and more. We'll match job listings with your interests and criteria and e-mail them directly to your in-box.

VAULT
> the most trusted name in career information™

The State of the Law

Big business as usual

Here in Manhattan, it's back to the future: The Police are playing Madison Square Garden and a legion of smug corporate lawyers are toasting leveraged buyouts in bars across town.

A global rise in transactional and M&A work, which saw $3.7 trillion in deals in 2006, was the key to many law firms reporting double-digit profits. Still, the revenue upswing has been somewhat imbalanced: the firms lolling in corporate work are buoying industry turnover, even as bankruptcy and litigation shops are barely dog-paddling. Also complicating the profit picture is a rise in law firm overhead. The boom in markets has firms scrambling, grasping for talent and plumping salaries to levels unimaginable even a year earlier. As firms augment their rosters, and as they pursue globalisation, they face the costs of new office space and foreign expansion. Pricey technology upgrades and increased interest rates are also having an effect.

The fact is that while firms are presenting impressive numbers, the pressure to continue doing so is fierce. And with ever more scrutiny on their bottom line, some law firms are taking drastic measures, i.e. severing moderately profitable practices, or reshuffling their equity partner line-up—as Mayer, Brown did in March 2007. In a memo announcing the sacking of 45 partners, Mayer, Brown gave voice to law firms' new (cold-blooded?) practicality: "Being a partnership need not be antithetical to being a well-run business."

Billers can't be choosers

And then (sigh!) there are the clients—better informed and more demanding, or "pesky." Nowadays clients are well aware of their market power, and well aware of their options, thanks to legal media rankings and "Best of" categories. As they streamline preferred advisor lists, corporations are forcing firms to strut their merits; even the most august of white shoe firms are increasingly held to the new-fangled metrics of quality, price and efficiency. A penny-pinching corporate climate has GCs facing pressure to rein in legal spending, pushing hard for discounts, and questioning yearly fee-hikes they once accepted without comment. And whereas law firms were once able to command high fees in dispute resolution, GCs are now talking dispute prevention—less messy, true, but less lucrative for outside advisors. Firms are also facing strong pressure to standardize fees for routine work, and move away from the hourly model. Barclays (which spends £100 million on legal issues per year), Deutsche Bank and Goldman Sachs have all implemented e systems to monitor legal spending in real time, enabling them to track trends and target costs more effectively. For some, clients' new activism is proving a bit annoying: as one partner grumbles to *The Lawyer*, "If it's automatic billing, why can't we have automatic payment?"

A vindication of the rights of ~~man~~ minions

In 1517, a law school dropout named Martin Luther marched up to a church in Wittenberg and nailed a list to the door. Four hundred and fifty years later, we have Christian rock. In April 2007, a 125-member organization called Law Students Building a Better Legal Profession e-mailed hiring partners and coordinators at the AmLaw 100. The group asked, nicely, that firms foster better working conditions by pledging to abide by certain core principles, i.e. balanced hours policies and clear work expectations. While the petition provoked some disapproving commentary on legal blogs (and words like "whine," "spoiled" and "blackball"), it underscores a change in the balance of power. According to the Law School Admission Council, since 2005 law school applications have been on the decline. The talent shortage has reached such proportions that even new grads are emboldened to ask for assurances before signing away—and, it seems, before interviewing or being offered the job.

The shortage has BigLaw recruiters going boldly where they have never gone before, taking their OCI roadshow to the halls of lesser-ranked law schools. In 2006, Northeastern, University of Pittsburgh and Loyola all had inaugural visits from top firms. Firms which once deigned to interview only the top 20 percent of a class are now considering the top 25 and even 35 percent.

Visit the Vault Law Channel, the complete online resource for law careers, featuring firm profiles, message boards, the Vault Law Job Board, and more. www.vault.com/law

VAULT CAREER LIBRARY

3

Prejudices are slipping as firms weigh the option of hiring prestige-school grads with poorer grades, versus lesser-ranked schools' high-performers. Those who were half-hearted at Harvard, beware: Brooklyn Law's finest are taking your jobs.

You catch more flies with money

In January 2007, New York City's Simpson Thacher seized first-mover advantage: it released a memo to all associates in its Manhattan office, informing them that the firm was raising their base salaries by $15,000. The incoming class, squirts just out of law school, would earn a bountiful $160,000 for their rookie season—more than many seasoned lawyers earn in cities across America. The raises caught everyone off guard, not least Simpson Thacher associates, who scratched their noggins and tried to recall if they had actually asked for them. BigLaw partners across the city were exasperated: Wasn't it just eleven months ago that we upped the kids' allowance to $145,000? And gave them iPods, in-house massage therapists, Pepperidge Farm and Snapple? Still, within a matter of weeks, all major New York firms had matched the new figure—making it perfectly clear that the inmates have taken over the asylum.

How do I love thee? Let me count the ways

In tandem with (considerable) pay raises, associate retention initiatives are also increasing—like a dog with a bone, law firms are on heightened alert. And it's not just other firms they're leery of, it's hedge funds and clients. In addition to handling more work in-house and cutting back on outside advisors, GCs are raiding the law firm ranks, nicking associates weary of the long hours and work-life balance. Considering the financial investment that firms make in training new associates and the fact that recruits do not begin "earning their keep" for several years, associate attrition is costly; NALP estimates that replacing ex-associates with lateral hires costs firms $300,000 per person.

In this climate of knavery and thievery, the care and emotional feeding of associates has taken on new importance. In February 2007, partners across Sullivan & Cromwell sat through a PowerPoint charm school, which reminded them to incorporate such obscure jargon as "thank you" and "good job" into their daily speech. Diversity issues are attacked with new vigor, and firms are beefing up training and development programs to ease the long journey to partnerhood. And nowadays, when harried associates complain of cancelled vacations and imminent divorces, firms listen. Part-time and flex-time options are rising, as are matched 401(k) retirement plans (once uncommon for associates), dog-walking, concierge services and elder care. DLA Piper offers a hybrid car reimbursement of $2,000, while Nixon Peabody dangles $10,000 referral carrots. And smaller firms that can't afford to match each and every pay hike are taxing their creativity to come up with inventive perks and events (Build-a-Burrito!) that bolster culture—and loyalty. The battle to keep associates happy covers issues large and small: *legalweek* reports that in March 2007, 200 Freshfields associates in the London office met with management to discuss issues such as "remuneration, appraisals and career development"—oh, and could they do something about that distracting "80s chic" carpeting? Mere hours after the meeting adjourned, workmen were called in, and the offending carpet replaced with a "more muted" style. Yes dear, anything you say dear.

Payback's a b*tch

The 2006 Democratic changeover in Congress marks the first time in 12 years that Dems have rocked both houses—and certain left-leaning law firms are lovin' it. A Covington & Burling memo (sans happy faces, which were implicit) notes that election results are likely to "energize Democratic members predisposed to support aggressive investigations"; a WilmerHale missive gambles that is "a safe bet that there will be a good deal of hearing and investigative activity in the 110th Congress." Indeed many firms are banking on aggressive inquiries and ruthless examination of Bush Administration activities, e.g. Iraq redevelopment fraud, as well as private sector issues like hedge fund oversight. White collar defense practices are receiving greater love and attention, and the once-niche practice of representing clients embroiled in Congressional investigations is not-so-niche anymore. Post-election, D.C. firms Venable and Dickstein Shapiro promptly brought on ex-D.C. staffers with investigative committee experience. Congressional investigators, start your engines.

V/AULT CAREER LIBRARY

© 2007 Vault Inc.

I spy with my little PI

In 2006, Hewlett-Packard found itself in a sticky situation regarding its use of pretexting. (Yeah, we didn't know either. It's just a fancypants form of lying. "Pretexting: the act of creating and using an invented scenario [the pretext] to persuade a target to release information or perform an action; usually done over the telephone and often involving prior research and the use of pieces of known information, e.g., for impersonation purposes, date of birth, Social Security Number, last bill amount, etc."). While ferreting out the identity of a boardroom leak, HP chairwoman Patricia Dunn authorised private investigators to use false information in order to obtain the phone records of company directors and journalists. A boardmember tattled, and HP's executive committee was hauled before Congress with some splainin' to do. As outside advisor to HP, Larry Sonsini of Wilson Sonsini Goodrich and Rosati also came under scrutiny. Though Sonsini was cleared of wrongdoing, in September 2006 HP let its external counsel go (while emphasizing that "Hewlett-Packard and Wilson Sonsini continue to enjoy a strong relationship"); both Dunn and HP's longtime GC Ann Baskins eventually resigned.

YouTube? SueTube!

IP lawyers were wondering when it was all gonna blow. After Google bought YouTube for $1.65 billion in October 2006, most figured that next up would be a tidal wave of copyright infringement lawsuits. Bring it, said Google: one of its first acts of business, post-purchase, was to establish a $500 million YouTube defense fund. Good thing they planned ahead. Among the throng suing over unauthorized clips are Viacom, owner of Comedy Central and MTV; England's top-tier soccer league; music publisher Bourne Co. (owner of the 1972 instrumental hit *The Popcorn Song* ... obvious why they'd want to protect that); a man who videotaped the beating of a trucker during the 1992 Los Angeles riots; and a one-time mandolin player for the Grateful Dead. Oh, and Thailand. In May 2007, the Thai government joined the queue, announcing a lawsuit over clips that ridicule the Thai King.

Plaintiffs charge that Google/YouTube deliberately promotes copyright infringement by refusing to take "real" steps to stop the uploading of unauthorized clips. Google smirks that YouTube is protected by a 1998 U.S. copyright law exemption, which shields online services from claims stemming from the actions of their customers, and maintains that YouTube stays within the law by removing copyrighted material when owners protest.

They paved my paradise and put up a parkin' lot

... with a pink hotel, a boutique and a swingin' hot spot. Yes, Kelo vs. City of New London, the controversial 2005 Supreme Court decision which enables the government to take over privately-owned property for private use, as long as the general benefits to the community can be termed "public use," is still a contentious topic. In addition to mass outrage, Kelo sparked a flurry of hastily-drafted state reform: in the two years since the law's passing, over 80 percent of states passed laws limiting eminent domain powers. Florida banned the usage of eminent domain to fix blighted areas, South Dakota now prohibits its use for transfer of private property to a non-governmental entity, and South Carolina disallows private-to-private transfers. Proceeding more cautiously are Colorado and Kentucky, which narrowed their definitions of "public use" but refused to define "blighted." The issue has even made bedfellows of bickering pols, liberal Dems who argue that eminent domain statutes disproportionately affect minorities and the poor, and libertarian-leaning conservatives who, given their political druthers, would rather flip Big Gov the finger.

As for Susette Kelo, the Connecticut resident who had her home yanked to make way for a Pfizer-riffic office park, well, her "holiday greetings" to members of the New London City Council ran along these lines: "Your houses, your homes, your family, your friends, may they live in misery that never ends."

Trials and tribe-ulations

Many Native American tribes are now profitable enough to need the same investment and business services as major corporations; as the GC for a California clan puts it, tribes now "need the same type of legal representation as any Fortune 500 company." Top law firms have been more than happy to accommodate them—after all, casinos run by Native American tribes

Visit the Vault Law Channel, the complete online resource for law careers, featuring firm profiles, message boards, the Vault Law Job Board, and more. www.vault.com/law

VAULT CAREER LIBRARY

5

saw revenues of nearly $23 billion in 2005, and tribes are already moving beyond entertainment to financial services, real estate development and insurance.

Formally established in 2005, Orrick's tribal finance unit now numbers 18 practitioners; other firms that have created tribal finance units are Holland & Knight, Akin Gump, Dorsey & Whitney, Pillsbury Winthrop, and Sonnenschein Nath & Rosenthal. These specialized practice units must be able to juggle federal, state, local and tribal laws, as well as the demands of deep pocket investors, business partners and banks. Matters involving Indian tribes can be more complex than other corporate entities, as they are sovereign nations with, um, a rather bitter history with the U.S. government. And a lot rides on a successful outcome: when tribes go to trial over preservation of nationhood and sovereignty issues, verdicts affect Native Americans en masse.

Something wiki this way comes

The law community, which took to blawgs and online legal tabloids with mischievous gusto, has been an early adopter of wikis, the most egalitarian of infosources. In 2007 legal wikis are mushrooming everywhere. Wikis have proven popular by enabling lawyers to pool knowledge quickly—an invaluable capability in an info-saturated, time sensitive industry—and because it's fun to go around correcting people. Congresspedia, for example, is a research tool which shares information about members of Congress, Death Penalty Wiki sustains a collaboratively-edited log of death penalty cases, while WikiPatents encourages large-scale public comment on issued patents and pending applications. Also on the upswing are legal podcasts, i.e. a joint effort between *The NewsHour with Jim Lehrer* and *The National Law Journal* which offers enhanced coverage of the U.S. Supreme Court.

Special forces

Legal temp agencies have been around for decades, farming out lawyers who step in during bulky litigation or antitrust cases (for a warts-and-all look at the legal temp life, check out *temporaryattorney.blogspot.com*). In the last years these services have been augmented by "elite" agencies, whose members are typically graduates of top schools or ex-members of renowned firms. One such agency, New York-based Axiom, opened their doors in 2000 with one employee; seven years later, the firm employs 150, tallies $30 million in revenue, and has opened a second location in San Francisco. For some elite temps, the decision to do agency work may be temporary,. as they juggle family obligations like relocation or illness. For others, it is a conscious lifestyle choice. In addition to the greater flexibility in workload and hours, pay isn't too shabby; these mercenaries can earn as much as $250,000 per year, roughly the salary of a fourth-year associate at a major Manhattan firm. But the ultra-ambitious should look elsewhere; the downside to such work is lack of ascension, a scarcity of career milestones or interesting projects, and certainly no partner track. Hmm … sounds a bit like… oh drop it.

The Return of the Headquarter-less Horsemen

The recent spate of law firm mergers is giving rise to a new phenomenon: headquarter-less BigLaw firms. When Kirkpatrick & Lockhart Nicholson Graham merged with Preston Gates & Ellis in 2007, management agreed that the new entity would have no designated headquarters. Firms that also insist that they have no home base are Jones Day, founded in Cleveland, Pittsburgh-based Reed Smith, and Chicago-native Sidley Austin. There can be, of course, valid reasons for this: Jones Day bases its managing partner in D.C., and its largest office is in New York, while Reed Smith recently merged with firms in the U.K. and Chicago. Rapidly-expanding firms huff that they are merely trying to build cultural cohesion between offices, but doubters speculate that firms' insistence on shedding hometown associations has more to do with being perceived as small potatoes, or "not Big Apple."

Bill, Padding & Howe

Along with disowning their hometowns, firms are still hacking the unwieldy and unattractive bits off their names. Howrey Simon Arnold & White is now plain Howrey, while Orrick Herrington & Sutcliffe jousts with Oprah to be the big "O." Off went the ampersand (Baker Botts, Jones Day) and in came snazzy bullet points Doherty • Long • Wagner)—and, in some misguided cases,

© 2007 Vault Inc.

punky little stars (Provost * Umphrey). And as Crummy Gibbons & O'Neill discovered, while undergoing its butterfly transformation to Gibbons Del Deo, sometimes a rose by any other name is less likely to elicit mockery. As one legal marketing consultant puts it, there is a "natural tendency among Americans to abbreviate." And with websites in mind, the focus is on punchy, short, and easily recognizable. Though name changes can be costly and difficult to implement, they may also pay off in big ways: Colonel Sanders helped us forget that his poultry paddles in vats of hissing fat via a much-derided but ultimately successful 1991 rebranding—and KFC profits soared. So hang in there, name-changing law firm. Dewgoode, Befayre & Prosper.

Oil and water

Corporate firms have traditionally turned away contingency work—dunno, there's something about championing damage claims that tends to tick Big Business clients off. But in recent years, firms that earn their daily brioche defending companies from similar claims have been joining hands with the Forces of Evil, or crossing over to the your-asbestos-laced-insulation-gave-this-whole-community-incurable-respiratory-problems side. Upon examination, the crossover trend isn't really surprising: plaintiffs cases, while long-drawn and risky, can end in torrents of dough. Also fuelling the trend is patent litigation: last year, Washington's Wiley Rein earned more than $200 million suing BlackBerry-manufacturer Research in Motion. In 1989, a partner at Minneapolis' Faegre & Benson, which normally represents corporations, convinced the firm to take on a contingency basis the case of Alaskan fishermen who lost their livelihood due to the Exxon Valdez oil spill. Seventeen years and several rounds of appeal later, a federal appeals court awarded the fisherman $2.5 billion in damages, of which Faegre & Benson will see some $100 million in fees.

Faegre & Benson now finds itself with a pleasant problem—how to split the takings? Like the majority of its BigLaw ilk, Faegre & Benson weighs yearly productivity when allocating compensation; firms that specialize in plaintiff's work, on the other hand, often let lawyers reap the rewards from their own cases. But it isn't always that simple: in large scale, long-running contingency cases, other partners are also carrying the financial load, accepting risk and swallowing costs for years. Before the final payout, Faegre & Benson had only collected some $1.5 million in Exxon Valdez fees, compared to its $28 million in costs. So when a check finally comes, divvying the windfall becomes a careful exercise in diplomacy.

Sticking it to Motorola? Priceless

While Linda Evangelista and those of her ilk "do not get out of bed for less that $10,000 day," flamboyant plaintiffs litigator Willie Gary has a tad more self-esteem. A $10 billion trade secrets case involving telecom giant Motorola ended in a mistrial after two Motorola witnesses defied a sequestration order and boned up on plaintiff testimony before taking the stand. The presiding judge called Motorola's actions "intentional, deliberate, blatant, willful, and contumacious," and acknowledged that it "affected the outcome of the trial." Hoppin' mad Gary pulled out his calculator, tabulated what Motorola's actions had cost him, and submitted a request for $93 million—$11,000 per hour for 2,200 hours of work (to put this in perspective, his co-counsels asked for $3.1 million and $1.3 million). Due to a contingency-fee arrangement, Gary justified, "Had we won the case, we would have gotten $4 billion in fees." Attorneys testifying in support of Gary's fee request noted that he is one of the top litigators in the country, and likened him to Yankees star Alex Rodriguez ("Not every litigator is in the Rodriguez classification"). Though a Florida circuit court judge bypassed a request that Motorola pay some $100 million in sanctions and restitution for Gary's client, he did award Gary and other plaintiffs lawyers a quarter of their asked-for $96 million in fees and costs. Well, you can't always get what you want—but if you try sometimes, you just might find, you get $23 million.

Visit the Vault Law Channel, the complete online resource for law careers, featuring firm profiles, message boards, the Vault Law Job Board, and more. www.vault.com/law

VAULT CAREER LIBRARY   7

Smart in your world®
Arent Fox

Write a great essay.
Start a great relationship.
On us.

ARENT FOX OFFERS $15,000 SCHOLARSHIPS TO MINORITY FIRST YEAR LAW STUDENTS.
APPLICATION PERIOD RUNS DECEMBER 1, 2007 THROUGH JANUARY 1, 2008.
VISIT WWW.ARENTFOX.COM/FIRM/DIVERSITY/INDEX.CFM?FA=SCHOLARSHIP FOR DETAILS.

A Guide to this Guide

If you're wondering how our entries are organized, read on. Here's a handy guide to the information you'll find packed into each entry of this book.

THE BUZZ

When it comes to other law firms, our respondents certainly like to dish. We asked them to share their opinions and observations about firms other than their own. We've collected a sampling of these comments in "The Buzz."

When selecting The Buzz, we included quotes representative of the common outsider's perceptions of the firms, even if (in our opinion) the quotes did not accurately describe the firm. In the interest of fairness, we chose four Buzz comments for each firm—two positive and two negative (or, at least, not positive).

Please keep in mind when reading The Buzz that it's often more fun for outsiders to trash than praise a competing law firm. Nonetheless, we have found The Buzz to be another valuable means of gauging a firm's reputation in the legal field.

FIRM FACTS

Locations: A listing of the firm's offices, with the headquarters bolded. You may see firms with no bolded location. This means that these are self-proclaimed decentralized firms without an official headquarters.

Major Departments/Practices: Practice areas that employ a significant portion of the firm's headquarters' attorneys as reported by the firms.

Base Salary: The firm's base salary at its headquarters. Base salaries at other offices are given when available. Pay is for 2007, except where noted.

Notable Perks: A listing of perks and benefits outside the norm. For example, we do not list health care, as every firm we surveyed offers health care plans.

Uppers and Downers: Good points and bad points about working at the firm, as gleaned from associate interviews and surveys. Uppers and downers are the perceptions of insiders and not based on statistics.

Employment Contact: The person that the firm identifies as the primary contact to receive resumes or to answer questions about the recruitment process. More than one contact is sometimes given. In some instances, we refer the reader to the firm's web site.

THE STATS

No. of attorneys: The total number of attorneys at the firm in all offices as of Spring 2007. Sometimes the number is an estimate.

No. of offices: The firm's total number of offices worldwide.

Summer associate offers: The firmwide number of second-year law students offered full-time associate positions by the firm, compared to the firmwide number of second-year law students who worked at the firm in 2006 as summer associates.

Chairman, Managing Partner, etc.: The name and title of the leader of the firm. Sometimes more than one name is provided.

Visit the Vault Law Channel, the complete online resource for law careers, featuring firm profiles, message boards, the Vault Law Job Board, and more. **www.vault.com/law**

VAULT CAREER LIBRARY

9

RANKING RECAP

A summary of all categories in which the firm ranked particularly well, including departmental, geographic, quality of life and diversity rankings.

QUALITY OF LIFE METERS

Our meters are based on the responses of more than 18,800 law firm associates. Survey participants were asked to rate their firm in a variety of categories on a 1 to 10 scale. The firm's score in each category is simply the average (mean) of the scores its associates gave in that area. We have highlighted the following categories for our meters:

Satisfaction: Associates rank their satisfaction with their firm on a scale from "unsatisfactory" to "entirely fulfilling."

Hours: Associates rank how they feel about their hours on a scale from "overwhelming" to "very livable." Please note that the hours score is based on the subjective perceptions of associates, not on the actual hours they work.

Training: Associates rank their satisfaction with the level of formal and informal training their firm provides.

Diversity: Associates rank their satisfaction with all diversity issues, including the situations of minority group members, women, gays and lesbians. Again, the diversity score is based on the subjective perceptions of associates, not on actual diversity statistics.

Associate/Partner Relations: Associates rank how well they feel they are treated and mentored by the partners at their firm.

Please note that some firms that did not participate in our survey are not rated by our quality of life meters. In most cases, Vault contacted associates independently at firms that did not participate in our survey. If a sufficiently representative sampling of associates completed our survey, the non-participating firm was rated by our quality of life meters.

THE PROFILES

You'll notice two types of firm profiles—long ones and short ones. What's the deal? Firms ranked No. 1 through 50 in the Vault prestige ranking received long profiles, and shorter profiles were reserved for the firms that ranked No. 51 to 100. Both the long and short profiles are divided into three sections: The Scoop, Getting Hired and Our Survey Says.

The Scoop: The firm's history, clients, recent deals, recent firm developments and other points of interest.

Getting Hired: The qualifications the firm looks for in new associates, tips on interviewing, and other notable aspects of the hiring process.

Our Survey Says: Actual quotes from surveys of current associates at the firm on various topics related to law firm life, including the firm's assignment system, feedback, partnership prospects, levels of responsibility, summer associate program, culture, hours, pay, training and much more. Some profiles also contain brief "firm responses" to associate criticism or clarification of points of confusion expressed in the profile. Vault editors sometimes modified associate quotes to correct grammar or spelling.

© 2007 Vault Inc.

BEST OF THE REST

In addition to the 50 long and 50 short profiles, we've also included information on additional law firms that did not make our Top 100 list this year. This additional information is in the form of one-page "stats" entries containing information on salary, office locations, major departments/practices, firm size and more.

Visit the Vault Law Channel, the complete online resource for law careers, featuring firm profiles, message boards, the Vault Law Job Board, and more. **www.vault.com/law**

VAULT CAREER LIBRARY

11

LATERAL LINK

JOIN OUR EXCLUSIVE NETWORK OF ELITE ATTORNEYS & GAIN IMMEDIATE ACCESS TO PREMIER LEGAL JOBS

Our web-based platform and experienced search consultants will help you find new opportunities that match your skills and interests

· ·

OUR UNIQUE BENEFITS INCLUDE:

$10,000 Placement Bonus to Attorneys for Law Firm Transitions

Automatic e-mail alerts on new job openings

Professional consultants to manage the process

Online Career Library with Free Access to Vault Guides

OUR EMPLOYER CLIENTS:

- International Law Firms
- Lifestyle Law Firms
- Fortune 1000 Companies
- Sports and Entertainment Companies
- Investment Banks
- Hedge Funds
- Non-Profit Companies

OUR REGIONS:

United States:
- Atlanta
- Boston
- California
- Charlotte
- Chicago
- New York
- Pacific Northwest
- Philadelphia
- Texas
- Washington, DC

International:
- Beijing, Hong Kong, London, Paris, Shanghai, Singapore & Tokyo

CONTACT US:

www.laterallink.com

Toll Free:
(866) 374-5829

Email Questions:
generalhelp@laterallink.com

"The Professional Placement Network for Elite Attorneys"

THE VAULT
PRESTIGE
RANKINGS

Milbank. Leading the way.

© 2006 MILBANK, TWEED, HADLEY & McCLOY LLP

International Firm of the Year
Legal Week

European Law Firm of the Year
International Financial Law Review

North American Project Finance Firm of the Year
Chambers and Partners

Satellite Law Firm of the Year
Satellite Finance

Private Equity Law Firm of the Year
JUVE

Law Firm of the Year
Global Water Intelligence

For additional information, visit ***www.milbank.com***.

Milbank

NEW YORK   LOS ANGELES   WASHINGTON, D.C.   LONDON   FRANKFURT   MUNICH   TOKYO   HONG KONG   SINGAPORE

The Ranking Methodology

TOP 100

The king still reigns. Fours years after snagging the top slot, Wachtell, Lipton, Rosen & Katz (No. 2 in Vault's rankings for the first five years) has maintained its stranglehold on the No. 1 spot for prestige. Cravath, Swaine & Moore is No. 2 for the fifth straight year. Sullivan & Cromwell also stayed right where it was, coming in at No. 3 for the tenth (!) straight year. Overall, the top five has remained true to last year's rankings. The only change in the top 10 is the flip-flopping of Covington & Burling and Kirkland & Ellis. Covington vaulted over Kirkland to reclaim the No. 10 spot.

How does Vault come up with its list of the Top 100 firms in the country? The first step is to compile a list of the most renowned law firms in the land by reviewing the feedback we receive from previous surveys, consulting our previous lists, poring over legal newspapers, talking to lawyers in the field and checking out other published rankings. This year, we asked these 167 law firms to distribute a password-protected online survey to their associates. Over 18,800 attorneys returned anonymous surveys to Vault. Associates from all over the country and the world responded. We heard from lawyers in New York, Los Angeles, San Francisco, Palo Alto, Chicago, Boston, Philadelphia, Houston, Dallas, Washington, D.C., Miami, Cleveland, Seattle, Orlando, Phoenix and Atlanta, among many other domestic locations—not to mention London, Paris and beyond. The online survey asked attorneys to score each of the 167 law firms on a scale of 1 to 10 based on how prestigious it is to work for the firm. Associates were asked to ignore any firm with which they were unfamiliar and were not allowed to rank their own firm.

We collected all the surveys and averaged the score for each firm. The firms were then ranked in order, starting with the highest average prestige score as No. 1 on down to determine the Vault Top 100. Remember that in the Top 100, Vault is not assessing firms by profit, size, lifestyle, number of deals or quality of service—we are ranking the most prestigious law firms based on the perceptions of currently practicing lawyers at peer firms.

Think it's easy getting over 18,800 associates to take our survey? Think again. Lawyers are busy people, and many are stressed out as it is without having to take 30 minutes out of their day to work on a non-billable project—especially with the increased emphasis on racking up billable hours. Despite it all, an incredible amount of associates came through for us and helped us produce the Vault Top 100. Associates, many thanks for your insight and patience.

Visit the Vault Law Channel, the complete online resource for law careers, featuring firm profiles, message boards, the Vault Law Job Board, and more. **www.vault.com/law**

VAULT CAREER LIBRARY   15

The Vault 100   2008

The 100 most prestigious law firms

2008 RANK	LAW FIRM	PRESTIGE SCORE	2007 RANK	2006 RANK	2005 RANK	LARGEST OFFICE/ HEADQUARTERS
1	Wachtell, Lipton, Rosen & Katz	8.780	1	1	1	New York, NY
2	Cravath, Swaine & Moore LLP	8.732	2	2	2	New York, NY
3	Sullivan & Cromwell LLP	8.224	3	3	3	New York, NY
4	Skadden, Arps, Slate, Meagher & Flom[1]	8.197	4	4	4	New York, NY
5	Davis Polk & Wardwell	8.126	5	5	5	New York, NY
6	Simpson Thacher & Bartlett LLP	8.116	6	6	6	New York, NY
7	Cleary, Gottlieb, Steen & Hamilton LLP	7.759	7	8	7	New York, NY
8	Latham & Watkins LLP	7.712	8	7	8	Los Angeles, CA
9	Weil, Gotshal & Manges LLP	7.672	9	9	9	New York, NY
10	Covington & Burling LLP	7.510	11	10	10	Washington, DC
11	Kirkland & Ellis LLP	7.492	10	11	11	Chicago, IL
12	Debevoise & Plimpton LLP	7.468	13	13	14	New York, NY
13	Paul, Weiss, Rifkind, Wharton & Garrison[2]	7.444	12	17	13	New York, NY
14	Shearman & Sterling LLP	7.240	15	12	12	New York, NY
15	Wilmer Cutler Pickering Hale and Dorr LLP	7.237	14	14	21	Washington, DC
16	Williams & Connolly LLP	7.234	17	16	16	Washington, DC
17	Sidley Austin LLP	7.232	16	15	15	Chicago, IL
18	Gibson, Dunn & Crutcher LLP	7.158	18	18	17	Los Angeles, CA
19	O'Melveny & Myers LLP	7.105	20	20	19	Los Angeles, CA
20	White & Case LLP	7.092	21	22	20	New York, NY
21	Arnold & Porter LLP	7.012	19	19	18	Washington, DC
22	Jones Day	6.932	22	21	22	Washington, DC
23	Morrison & Foerster LLP	6.898	23	23	23	San Francisco, CA
24	Milbank, Tweed, Hadley & McCloy	6.752	28	25	25	New York, NY
25	Clifford Chance LLP	6.747	26	27	27	New York, NY

NR = Not Ranked   1 Skadden, Arps, Slate, Meagher & Flom LLP and Affiliates
2. Paul, Weiss, Rifkind, Wharton & Garrison LLP

2008 RANK	LAW FIRM	PRESTIGE SCORE	2007 RANK	2006 RANK	2005 RANK	LARGEST OFFICE/ HEADQUARTERS
26	Cadwalader, Wickersham & Taft LLP	6.648	31	36	35	New York, NY
27	Hogan & Hartson LLP	6.622	24	29	30	Washington, DC
28	Mayer, Brown, Rowe & Maw LLP	6.615	27	26	29	Chicago, IL
29	Fried, Frank, Harris, Shriver & Jacobson[1]	6.588	29	28	28	New York, NY
30	Ropes & Gray LLP	6.566	25	24	26	Boston, MA
31	Paul, Hastings, Janofsky & Walker	6.545	30	32	33	Los Angeles, CA
32	Willkie Farr & Gallagher LLP	6.352	37	37	32	New York, NY
33	Akin Gump Strauss Hauer & Feld LLP	6.343	33	31	34	Washington, DC
34	Winston & Strawn LLP	6.316	35	34	38	Chicago, IL
35	Dewey Ballantine LLP	6.313	32	30	31	New York, NY
36	Wilson Sonsini Goodrich & Rosati	6.308	34	35	36	Palo Alto, CA
37	Linklaters	6.301	44	47	42	London, UK
38	Orrick, Herrington & Sutcliffe LLP	6.244	38	38	43	San Francisco, CA
39	Freshfields Bruckhaus Deringer LLP	6.204	42	42	NR	London, UK
40	Proskauer Rose LLP	6.195	39	44	42	New York, NY
41	King & Spalding LLP	6.183	36	33	37	Atlanta, GA
42	Morgan, Lewis & Bockius LLP	6.099	41	41	41	Philadelphia, PA
43	Quinn Emanuel[2]	6.080	NR	NR	NR	Los Angeles, CA
44	Baker & McKenzie	6.079	43	45	45	Chicago, IL
45	Baker Botts LLP	6.061	40	40	39	Houston, TX
46	Boies, Schiller & Flexner LLP	6.026	45	39	40	Armonk, NY
47	Munger, Tolles & Olson LLP	6.004	52	49	46	Los Angeles, CA
48	Dechert LLP	5.973	51	55	60	Philadelphia, PA
49	Irell & Manella LLP	5.952	56	58	53	Los Angeles, CA
50	McDermott, Will & Emery	5.946	47	46	48	Chicago, IL

1 Fried, Frank, Harris, Shriver & Jacobson LLP
2. Quinn Emanuel Urquhart Oliver & Hedges LLP

Visit the Vault Law Channel, the complete online resource for law careers, featuring firm profiles, message boards, the Vault Law Job Board, and more. www.vault.com/law

VAULT CAREER LIBRARY   17

The 100 most prestigious law firms

2008 RANK	LAW FIRM	PRESTIGE SCORE	2007 RANK	2006 RANK	2005 RANK	LARGEST OFFICE/ HEADQUARTERS
51	Jenner & Block LLP	5.940	48	50	52	Chicago, IL
52	LeBoeuf, Lamb, Greene & MacRae LLP	5.925	54	53	51	New York, NY
53	Allen & Overy LLP	5.922	60	60	59	London, UK
54	DLA Piper	5.913	49	65	46	Chicago/DC
55	Cahill Gordon & Reindel LLP	5.913	55	56	47	New York, NY
56	Fish & Richardson PC	5.868	63	62	75	Boston, MA
57	Fulbright & Jaworski LLP	5.863	50	43	44	Houston, TX
58	Pillsbury Winthrop Shaw Pittman LLP	5.825	46	48	49	San Francisco, CA
59	Goodwin Procter LLP	5.807	53	54	63	Boston, MA
60	Cooley Godward LLP	5.794	57	52	50	Palo Alto, CA
61	Alston & Bird LLP	5.742	59	57	57	Atlanta, GA
62	Heller Ehrman LLP	5.690	62	59	54	San Francisco, CA
63	Vinson & Elkins LLP	5.676	58	51	56	Houston, TX
64	Bingham McCutchen LLP	5.641	66	67	70	Boston, MA
65	Sonnenschein Nath & Rosenthal LLP	5.635	61	61	58	Chicago, IL
66	Greenberg Traurig, LLP	5.631	65	71	77	Miami, FL
67	Kaye Scholer LLP	5.591	67	64	55	New York, NY
68	Holland & Knight LLP	5.498	64	63	64	Tampa, FL
69	Steptoe & Johnson LLP	5.403	69	68	65	Washington, DC
70	Foley & Lardner LLP	5.360	68	66	71	Milwaukee, WI
71	K&L Gates[1]	5.358	74	79	74	Pittsburgh, PA
72	Chadbourne & Parke LLP	5.239	73	72	62	New York, NY
73	Hunton & Williams LLP	5.230	70	70	68	Richmond, VA
74	Nixon Peabody LLP	5.153	75	80	87	Boston, MA
75	Thacher Proffitt & Wood LLP	5.137	81	NR	NR	New York, NY

NR = Not Ranked   1 Kirkpatrick & Lockhart Preston Ellis Gates LLP

© 2007 Vault Inc.

2008 RANK	LAW FIRM	PRESTIGE SCORE	2007 RANK	2006 RANK	2005 RANK	LARGEST OFFICE/ HEADQUARTERS
76	Bryan Cave LLP	5.095	77	76	80	St. Louis, MO
77	Schulte Roth & Zabel LLP	5.080	76	82	79	New York, NY
78	Perkins Coie LLP	5.058	72	75	72	Seattle, WA
79	Stroock & Stroock & Lavan LLP	5.022	78	77	76	New York, NY
80	Patton Boggs LLP	5.015	71	74	73	Washington, DC
81	Howrey LLP	5.002	80	69	66	Washington, DC
82	Reed Smith LLP	4.967	82	86	99	Pittsburgh, PA
83	Crowell & Moring LLP	4.951	79	78	83	Washington, DC
84	McGuireWoods LLP	4.858	86	84	94	Richmond, VA
85	Hughes Hubbard & Reed LLP	4.833	85	90	86	New York, NY
86	Arent Fox PLLC	4.813	88	93	98	Washington, DC
87	Katten Muchin Rosenman LLP	4.801	84	83	93	Chicago, IL
88	Finnegan, Henderson, Farabow, Garrett[1]	4.801	89	85	81	Washington, DC
89	Dorsey & Whitney LLP	4.768	83	81	84	Minneapolis, MN
90	Thelen Reid Brown Raysman & Steiner LLP	4.717	91	87	90	New York, NY
91	Baker & Hostetler	4.660	90	95	81	Cleveland, OH
92	Kramer Levin Naftalis & Frankel LLP	4.658	97	BofR	96	New York, NY
93	Venable LLP	4.636	96	100	95	Washington, DC
94	Squire, Sanders & Dempsey LLP	4.599	87	91	97	Cleveland, OH
95	Kelley Drye & Warren LLP	4.597	98	94	91	New York, NY
96	Dickstein Shapiro LLP	4.595	95	BofR	81	Washington, DC
97	Fenwick & West LLP	4.545	94	88	85	Mountain View, CA
98	Kilpatrick Stockton LLP	4.538	93	89	98	Atlanta, GA
99	Mintz, Levin, Cohn, Ferris, Glovsky[2]	4.496	92	92	92	Boston, MA
100	Manatt, Phelps & Phillips, LLP	4.459	BofR	NR	NR	Los Angeles, CA

1 Finnegan, Henderson, Farabow, Garrett & Dunner, L.L.P.
2 Mintz, Levin, Cohn, Ferris, Glovsky and Popeo PC

Visit the Vault Law Channel, the complete online resource for law careers, featuring firm profiles, message boards, the Vault Law Job Board, and more. www.vault.com/law

VAULT CAREER LIBRARY 19

REGIONAL RANKINGS

Sometimes all you care about is how a firm stacks up against its peers in a particular region of the country. That's where our regional rankings come in. We took only the votes from associates in each regional area to determine the regional prestige rankings.

This year's guide categories are: Boston, Northern California, Southern California, Chicago, the Midwest, New York City, the Pacific Northwest, Pennsylvania/Mid-Atlantic, Atlanta, Miami, Texas and Washington, D.C.

Starting with the 2006 edition of the guide, we have expanded the pool of eligible firms to include all firms with offices in a particular region, rather than those firms "headquartered" there. We believe this approach is more appropriate in light of the increasing trend toward decentralization among large law firms.

New York City

RANK	FIRM	SCORE	2007 RANK
1	Wachtell, Lipton, Rosen & Katz	9.020	1
2	Cravath, Swaine & Moore	8.806	2
3	Davis Polk & Wardwell	8.374	4
4	Simpson Thacher & Bartlett LLP	8.285	5
5	Sullivan & Cromwell LLP	8.243	3
6	Skadden, Arps, Slate, Meagher & Flom LLP and Affiliates	8.157	6
7	Cleary, Gottlieb, Steen & Hamilton	7.803	7
8	Debevoise & Plimpton LLP	7.680	9
9	Paul, Weiss, Rifkind, Wharton & Garrison LLP	7.625	8
10	Weil, Gotshal & Manges LLP	7.598	10
11	Latham & Watkins LLP	7.174	12
12	Shearman & Sterling LLP	7.001	11
13	White & Case LLP	6.851	13
14	Kirkland & Ellis	6.723	14
15	Willkie Farr & Gallagher LLP	6.508	16
16	Sidley Austin LLP	6.502	15
17	Milbank, Tweed, Hadley & McCloy	6.425	17
18	Fried, Frank, Harris, Shriver & Jacobson LLP	6.352	19
19	Cadwalader, Wickersham & Taft	6.200	20
20	Covington & Burling	6.177	18

© 2007 Vault Inc.

Boston

RANK	FIRM	SCORE	2007 RANK
1	Ropes & Gray LLP	8.170	1
2	Wilmer Cutler Pickering Hale and Dorr LLP	8.102	2
3	Skadden, Arps, Slate, Meagher & Flom LLP and Affiliates	7.357	4
4	Goodwin Procter	7.294	3
5	Bingham McCutchen	6.749	5
6	Fish & Richardson PC	6.064	8
7	Foley Hoag LLP	6.006	6
8	Choate, Hall & Stewart	5.874	7
9	Mintz Levin Cohn Ferris Glovsky and Popeo	5.757	9
10	Goulston & Storrs	5.551	NR

Washington, DC

RANK	FIRM	SCORE	2007 RANK
1	Williams & Connolly LLP	8.406	1
2	Covington & Burling LLP	8.214	2
3	Wilmer Cutler Pickering Hale and Dorr LLP	8.109	3
4	Arnold & Porter LLP	7.838	4
5	Skadden, Arps, Slate, Meagher & Flom LLP and Affiliates	7.833	5
6	Latham & Watkins LLP	7.714	8
7	Hogan & Hartson	7.620	7
8	Kirkland & Ellis LLP	7.525	6
9	Gibson, Dunn & Crutcher	7.399	9
10	Sidley Austin LLP	7.174	10
11	O'Melveny & Myers	6.982	11
12	Jones Day	6.917	12
13	Mayer, Brown, Rowe & Maw LLP	6.787	13
14	Akin Gump Strauss Hauer & Feld	6.629	14
15	Fried, Frank, Harris, Shriver & Jacobson LLP	6.324	NR

Visit the Vault Law Channel, the complete online resource for law careers, featuring firm profiles, message boards, the Vault Law Job Board, and more. www.vault.com/law

VAULT CAREER LIBRARY   21

Thank You.

To our Associates.
For your dedication which continues to be a source of recognition and respect for our firm worldwide.

Chicago   Hong Kong   London   Los Angeles   Munich   New York .

KIRKLAND & ELLIS LLP
www.kirkland.com

Chicago

RANK	FIRM	SCORE	2007 RANK
1	Kirkland & Ellis LLP	8.735	1
2	Sidley Austin LLP	8.337	2
3	Skadden, Arps, Slate, Meagher & Flom LLP and Affiliates	8.262	3
4	Mayer, Brown, Rowe & Maw LLP	8.035	4
5	Winston & Strawn LLP	7.789	5
6	Latham & Watkins LLP	7.785	6
7	Jenner & Block LLP	7.372	7
8	Jones Day	7.110	8
9	McDermott, Will & Emery	6.895	9
10	Baker & McKenzie	6.617	10

Midwest

RANK	FIRM	SCORE	2007 RANK
1	Jones Day	8.228	1
2	Squire, Sanders & Dempsey	6.888	2
3	Baker & Hostetler	6.560	3
4	Foley & Lardner LLP	6.417	4
5	Bryan Cave	6.163	6
6	Sonnenschein Nath & Rosenthal LLP	6.149	5
7	Barnes & Thornburg	5.954	8
8	Thompson Hine	5.674	7
9	Baker & Daniels	5.365	9
10	Frost Brown Todd LLC	5.140	10

Visit the Vault Law Channel, the complete online resource for law careers, featuring firm profiles, message boards, the Vault Law Job Board, and more. www.vault.com/law

VAULT CAREER LIBRARY

23

Northern California

RANK	FIRM	SCORE	2007 RANK
1	Latham & Watkins LLP	7.770	1
2	Morrison & Foerster LLP	7.578	2
3	Skadden, Arps, Slate, Meagher & Flom LLP and Affiliates	7.577	3
4	Orrick, Herrington & Sutcliffe	7.270	4
5	O'Melveny & Myers	7.233	6
6	Gibson, Dunn & Crutcher LLP	7.131	5
7	Wilson Sonsini Goodrich & Rosati	7.022	7
8	Weil, Gotshal & Manges LLP	6.927	10
9	Heller Ehrman LLP	6.891	8
10	Davis Polk & Wardwell	6.818	9

Southern California

RANK	FIRM	SCORE	2007 RANK
1	Latham & Watkins LLP	8.189	1
2	Skadden, Arps, Slate, Meagher & Flom LLP and Affiliates	8.018	4
3	O'Melveny & Myers	8.005	3
4	Munger, Tolles & Olson LLP	7.810	5
5	Gibson, Dunn & Crutcher LLP	7.797	2
6	Irell & Manella LLP	7.750	6
7	Morrison & Foerster LLP	7.321	7
8	Kirkland & Ellis	7.105	9
9	Quinn Emanuel Urquhart Oliver & Hedges LLP	7.065	NR
10	Paul, Hastings, Janofsky & Walker	6.972	8

Pacific Northwest

RANK	FIRM	SCORE	2007 RANK
1	Heller Ehrman LLP	6.699	2
2	Perkins Coie LLP	6.506	1
3	K&L Gates	6.395	3
4	Davis Wright Tremaine LLP	6.172	4
5	Stoel Rives LLP	5.239	5

© 2007 Vault Inc.

Miami

RANK	FIRM	SCORE	2007 RANK
1	White & Case LLP	7.658	2
2	Weil, Gotshal & Manges LLP	7.242	1
3	Greenberg Traurig, LLP	7.131	3
4	Hunton & Williams LLP	7.007	5
5	Hogan & Hartson	6.603	4
6	Morgan, Lewis & Bockius	6.601	6
7	Holland & Knight	6.344	7
8	Squire, Sanders & Dempsey LLP	5.597	9
9	Shook, Hardy & Bacon LLP	5.551	10
10	Carlton Fields	5.516	8

Atlanta

RANK	FIRM	SCORE	2007 RANK
1	King & Spalding LLP	8.066	2
2	Alston & Bird	7.505	1
3	Jones Day	6.678	3
4	Sutherland Asbill & Brennan LLP	6.549	4
5	Kilpatrick Stockton LLP	6.491	5
6	Paul, Hastings, Janofsky & Walker	6.319	8
7	Troutman Sanders	6.289	6
8	Hunton & Williams LLP	5.837	7
9	Powell Goldstein LLP	5.722	9
10	McKenna Long & Aldridge LLP	5.716	10

Visit the Vault Law Channel, the complete online resource for law careers, featuring firm profiles, message boards, the Vault Law Job Board, and more. **www.vault.com/law**

VAULT CAREER LIBRARY

25

Morgan Lewis

As business opportunities grow in size and complexity, relationships built on trust and respect are more important than ever.

Close working relationships define the Morgan Lewis culture and service philosophy.

We're in this together. Your team and ours.

Morgan, Lewis & Bockius LLP
J. Gordon Cooney, Jr., Managing Partner
1701 Market Street, Philadelphia PA 19103
215.963.5000

www.morganlewis.com

Pennsylvania and Mid-Atlantic

RANK	FIRM	SCORE	2007 RANK
1	Morgan, Lewis & Bockius	8.113	1
2	Dechert	7.852	2
3	Jones Day	6.974	3
4	Drinker Biddle & Reath LLP	6.626	4
5	Reed Smith	6.536	7
6	Pepper Hamilton	6.464	6
7	Blank Rome LLP	6.258	8
8	Ballard Spahr Andrews & Ingersoll, LLP	6.180	5
9	Duane Morris	5.969	9
10	Hogan & Hartson	5.780	10

Texas

RANK	FIRM	SCORE	2007 RANK
1	Baker Botts LLP	8.031	1
2	Weil, Gotshal & Manges LLP	8.013	2
3	Vinson & Elkins LLP	7.760	3
4	Fulbright & Jaworski	7.512	4
5	Jones Day	6.971	5
6	Akin Gump Strauss Hauer & Feld	6.941	7
7	Gibson, Dunn & Crutcher	6.827	6
8	Andrews & Kurth	6.564	9
9	Bracewell & Giuliani, LLP	6.525	10
10	Wilson Sonsini Goodrich & Rosati	6.313	8

Visit the Vault Law Channel, the complete online resource for law careers, featuring firm profiles, message boards, the Vault Law Job Board, and more. **www.vault.com/law**

VAULT CAREER LIBRARY   27

Use the Internet's
MOST TARGETED
job search tools.

Vault Job Board

Target your search by industry, function, and experience level, and find the job openings that you want.

VaultMatch Resume Database

Vault takes match-making to the next level: post your resume and customize your search by industry, function, experience and more. We'll match job listings with your interests and criteria and e-mail them directly to your in-box.

> the most trusted name in career information™

DEPARTMENTAL RANKINGS

In order to arrive at the following departmental rankings, associates were able to vote for up to three firms in their practice area, but were not permitted to vote for their own firm. Associates who identified themselves as corporate attorneys were allowed only to vote in corporate-related categories (securities, M&A, etc.); litigators were allowed only to vote in the litigation category, and so on. We indicate the top firms in each area, as well as the total percentage of votes cast in favor of the firm. (Each associate surveyed chose three firms; the maximum percentage of votes per firm is 33.3 percent.)

This year's departmental categories are: Antitrust, Bankruptcy/Creditors' Rights, Corporate, Intellectual Property, International Law, Labor and Employment, Litigation, Mergers and Acquisitions, Real Estate, Securities, Tax and Technology.

Antitrust

RANK	FIRM	% OF VOTES	2007 RANK
1	Arnold & Porter LLP	12.14	1
2	Cleary, Gottlieb, Steen & Hamilton	11.95	2
3	Howrey LLP	9.68	3
4 (tie)	Freshfields Bruckhaus Deringer LLP	7.21	5
4 (tie)	Skadden, Arps, Slate, Meagher & Flom LLP and Affiliates	7.21	7
5	Jones Day	5.69	4
6	Latham & Watkins LLP	3.80	8
7 (tie)	Wilmer Cutler Pickering Hale and Dorr LLP	3.61	6
7 (tie)	Simpson Thacher & Bartlett LLP	3.61	NR
8	Gibson, Dunn & Crutcher	3.23	10

Bankruptcy & Creditors' Rights

RANK	FIRM	% OF VOTES	2007 RANK
1	Weil, Gotshal & Manges LLP	25.64	1
2	Kirkland & Ellis	20.42	2
3	Skadden, Arps, Slate, Meagher & Flom LLP and Affiliates	18.65	3
4	Akin Gump Strauss Hauer & Feld	4.66	4
5	Milbank, Tweed, Hadley & McCloy	4.00	6
6	Davis Polk & Wardwell	2.44	7
7	Cadwalader, Wickersham & Taft	1.89	8 (tie)
8	Wachtell, Lipton, Rosen & Katz	1.78	8 (tie)
9	Jones Day	1.55	5
10	Willkie Farr & Gallagher LLP	1.11	NR

Visit the Vault Law Channel, the complete online resource for law careers, featuring firm profiles, message boards, the Vault Law Job Board, and more. www.vault.com/law

VAULT CAREER LIBRARY

29

GO FOR THE GOLD!

GET VAULT GOLD MEMBERSHIP AND GET ACCESS TO ALL OF VAULT'S AWARD-WINNING LAW CAREER INFORMATION

◆ Access to **500+ extended insider law firm profiles**

◆ Access to **regional snapshots** for major non-HQ offices of major firms

◆ Complete access to **Vault's exclusive law firm rankings**, including quality of life rankings, diversity rankings, practice area rankings, and rankings by law firm partners

◆ Access to **Vault's Law Salary Central**, with salary information for 100s of top firms

◆ Receive **Vault's Law Job Alerts** of top law jobs posted on the Vault Law Job Board

◆ Access to complete **Vault message board archives**

◆ **15% off** all Vault Guide and Vault Career Services purchases

For more information go to
www.vault.com/law

VAULT
> the most trusted name in career information™

Corporate

RANK	FIRM	% OF VOTES	2007 RANK
1	Wachtell, Lipton, Rosen & Katz	15.74	1
2	Cravath, Swaine & Moore	13.42	2
3	Skadden, Arps, Slate, Meagher & Flom LLP and Affiliates	13.23	3
4	Simpson Thacher & Bartlett LLP	9.84	5
5	Sullivan & Cromwell LLP	9.72	4
6	Davis Polk & Wardwell	5.08	6
7	Cleary, Gottlieb, Steen & Hamilton	3.21	8
8	Latham & Watkins LLP	3.13	7
9	Weil, Gotshal & Manges LLP	1.87	10
10	Clifford Chance LLP	1.79	NR

Intellectual Property

RANK	FIRM	% OF VOTES	2007 RANK
1	Fish & Richardson PC	20.34	1
2	Finnegan, Henderson, Farabow, Garrett & Dunner	15.42	2
3	Kirkland & Ellis	7.02	3
4	Morrison & Foerster LLP	3.75	4
5	Kenyon & Kenyon	3.12	NR
6	Jones Day	3.05	7
7	Weil, Gotshal & Manges LLP	2.99	6
8	Howrey LLP	2.89	5
9	Ropes & Gray LLP	2.67	10
10	Fitzpatrick, Cella, Harper & Scinto	2.23	NR

Visit the Vault Law Channel, the complete online resource for law careers, featuring firm profiles, message boards, the Vault Law Job Board, and more. www.vault.com/law

VAULT CAREER LIBRARY   31

ELT - Specialists in Ethics & Legal Compliance Training

- 700 satisfied clients
- 2,000,000 learners
- Millions of dollars saved
- 8 years of market-tested success

With the power of more than 600 employment attorneys behind you, you are certain to prevent harassment and discrimination in your workplace.

We specialize in comprehensive harassment training courses that exceed Federal Supreme Court, EEOC, California AB 1825, and Connecticut requirements. ELT's courses are consistently updated to ensure optimal compliance with these evolving standards guaranteeing you always have the most cutting-edge course.

ELT

www.elt-inc.com

info@elt-inc.com

PARTNERS WITH

SHRM
SOCIETY FOR HUMAN
RESOURCE MANAGEMENT

LITTLER MENDELSON, P.C.
THE NATIONAL EMPLOYMENT & LABOR LAW FIRM®

International Law

RANK	FIRM	% OF VOTES
1	White & Case LLP	10.32
2	Freshfields Bruckhaus Deringer LLP	8.71
3	Sidley Austin LLP	7.10
4	Wilmer Cutler Pickering Hale and Dorr LLP	6.77
5	Allen & Overy	5.81

Labor & Employment

RANK	FIRM	% OF VOTES	2007 RANK
1	Morgan, Lewis & Bockius	13.19	3
2	Littler Mendelson, PC	12.26	1
3	Paul, Hastings, Janofsky & Walker	12.19	2
4	Jackson Lewis	8.55	6
5	Seyfarth Shaw	8.13	4
6	Proskauer Rose LLP	7.06	5
7	Jones Day	2.14	7
8	O'Melveny & Myers	1.92	8 (tie)
9	Akin Gump Strauss Hauer & Feld	1.64	8 (tie)
10	Winston & Strawn LLP	1.43	NR

Litigation

RANK	FIRM	% OF VOTES	2007 RANK
1	Williams & Connolly LLP	6.91	2
2	Paul, Weiss, Rifkind, Wharton & Garrison LLP	6.83	1
3	Cravath, Swaine & Moore	6.82	3
4	Kirkland & Ellis	6.03	4
5	Skadden, Arps, Slate, Meagher & Flom LLP and Affiliates	5.35	5
6	Wachtell, Lipton, Rosen & Katz	3.57	8
7	Davis Polk & Wardwell	3.56	6
8	Quinn Emanuel Urquhart Oliver & Hedges LLP	3.52	NR
9	Latham & Watkins LLP	3.46	7
10	Simpson Thacher & Bartlett LLP	2.83	NR

Visit the Vault Law Channel, the complete online resource for law careers, featuring firm profiles, message boards, the Vault Law Job Board, and more. www.vault.com/law

VAULT CAREER LIBRARY   33

Your journey begins

At Freshfields Bruckhaus Deringer,
we give you the world

www.freshfields.com/usrecruiting

- International Law Firm of the Year 2007, PLC Which Lawyer?
- Competition Law Firm of the Year 2007, Who's Who Legal Awards
- Global Arbitration Firm of the Year 2007, Who's Who Legal Awards
- #2 International Law, Vault 2008
- #2 Overall Diversity, Vault 2008
- #10 M&A, Vault 2008
- #4 Diversity with Respect to Women, Vault 2008

New York Washington London Hong Kong

Amsterdam Barcelona Beijing Berlin Bratislava Brussels Budapest Cologne Dubai Düsseldorf Frankfurt
Hamburg Hanoi Ho Chi Minh City Madrid Milan Moscow Munich Paris Rome Shanghai Tokyo Vienna

Mergers & Acquisitions

RANK	FIRM	% OF VOTES	2007 RANK
1	Wachtell, Lipton, Rosen & Katz	21.33	1
2	Skadden, Arps, Slate, Meagher & Flom LLP and Affiliates	17.05	2
3	Simpson Thacher & Bartlett LLP	11.08	5
4	Cravath, Swaine & Moore	10.31	3
5	Sullivan & Cromwell LLP	10.05	4
6	Davis Polk & Wardwell	2.90	6
7	Cleary, Gottlieb, Steen & Hamilton	2.27	9
8	Clifford Chance LLP	2.01	10
8	Latham & Watkins LLP	2.01	7
9	Weil, Gotshal & Manges LLP	1.89	NR
10	Freshfields Bruckhaus Deringer LLP	1.58	NR

Real Estate

RANK	FIRM	% OF VOTES	2007 RANK
1	DLA Piper	9.08	2
2	Fried, Frank, Harris, Shriver & Jacobson LLP	7.03	1
3	Skadden, Arps, Slate, Meagher & Flom LLP and Affiliates	6.76	4
4	Greenberg Traurig, LLP	5.39	7
5	Cadwalader, Wickersham & Taft	4.91	5
6	Paul, Hastings, Janofsky & Walker	4.64	3
7	Allen Matkins Leck Gamble & Mallory LLP	4.03	6
8	Holland & Knight	2.59	8
9	Mayer, Brown, Rowe & Maw LLP	2.05	NR
10 (tie)	Dechert	1.98	NR
10 (tie)	Goulston & Storrs	1.98	NR
10 (tie)	Simpson Thacher & Bartlett LLP	1.98	NR

Visit the Vault Law Channel, the complete online resource for law careers, featuring firm profiles, message boards, the Vault Law Job Board, and more. **www.vault.com/law**

VAULT CAREER LIBRARY   **35**

Securities

RANK	FIRM	% OF VOTES	2007 RANK
1	Sullivan & Cromwell LLP	11.19	1
2	Cravath, Swaine & Moore	10.77	2
3	Skadden, Arps, Slate, Meagher & Flom LLP and Affiliates	10.54	3
4	Simpson Thacher & Bartlett LLP	9.16	5
5	Davis Polk & Wardwell	8.50	4
6	Cleary, Gottlieb, Steen & Hamilton	6.79	7
7	Wachtell, Lipton, Rosen & Katz	6.36	6
8	Latham & Watkins LLP	3.80	9
9	Shearman & Sterling LLP	2.54	8
10	Clifford Chance LLP	2.06	NR

Tax

RANK	FIRM	% OF VOTES	2007 RANK
1	Cleary, Gottlieb, Steen & Hamilton	11.44	1
2	Skadden, Arps, Slate, Meagher & Flom LLP and Affiliates	10.65	2
3	Cravath, Swaine & Moore	6.8	3
4	Sullivan & Cromwell LLP	6.41	5
5	Davis Polk & Wardwell	6.02	4
6	Baker & McKenzie	4.83	6
7	McKee Nelson LLP	4.64	8
8	Wachtell, Lipton, Rosen & Katz	4.34	7
9	Simpson Thacher & Bartlett LLP	3.85	10
10	McDermott, Will & Emery	3.35	9

Technology

RANK	FIRM	% OF VOTES	2007 RANK
1	Wilson Sonsini Goodrich & Rosati	12.57	1
2	Morrison & Foerster LLP	9.71	4
3	Cooley Godward	8.00	3
4	Fenwick & West LLP	7.43	2
5	Fish & Richardson PC	5.71	NR

© 2007 Vault Inc.

THE VAULT
PARTNER
SURVEY

© 2007 Vault Inc.

THE VAULT PARTNER SURVEY

What can we say about partners? They're the brawn, the squinted eye, the pricked ear. They carry the keys to the firm in their superiorly tailored trousers. They're the watchdogs, the power brokers, the policymakers and upholders of the law (obviously), the celebrated men and women at the top of the attorney food chain. These are no-time-to-talk hustlers and bustlers, always on the move and skipping meals (and rapport with underlings) to get there. They're the fearless and the feared, or the worshipped gurus, graciously attracting the associate masses who seek direction, assurance and enlightenment. But to all, they're the ones in charge: brown-nosers, start your engines.

Partners aren't shareholders and owners for naught. In essence, they oversee all deals, cases and cash flow. They make sure associates are pulling their weight and not using legal documents for trashcan basketball. From selecting cases, to assigning associate bonuses, to dealing with thorny clients, partners are the guardians of the firm's livelihood and public image. And for all their expertise, innumerable sacrifices and sky-scraping stress, they bring home enough bacon to satisfy even the hungriest flock.

After years spent polling only associates, we realized something: partners are people too, and probably have interesting things to say. We thought long and hard about it, and—kaboom!—our partner surveys were born. Let's face it, these guys (and gals, naturally) possess infinite wisdom and know-how when it comes to their vocation, and what better way to help our law-hungry readers than by going straight to the top of the pile? So, here we are for the third time, beseeching partners in quest of the gritty lowdown.

This time around, nearly 1,000 partners stepped up to help us out. Just like associates, partners were asked to rate firms in terms of prestige, on a scale from 1 to 10. Rating their own firm was a no-no, and they were asked to rank only the firms with which they were familiar. In addition, we asked them to rank other firms' aptitude in several practice areas—Antitrust, Bankruptcy/Creditors' Rights, Corporate, Intellectual Property, International, Labor and Employment, Litigation, Mergers and Acquisitions, and Securities. We also asked some open-ended questions about becoming a partner, and what to expect upon arrival to the role. We asked how new partners become the chosen ones at their firm, what advice they'd give an associate aching for a chance to make partner, and grilled them about the pros and cons of partnership, including the job's most important functions.

MAKING IT BIG

So, what does it take to fill a partner's big, no-nonsense shoes? We invited these heavy hitters to cough up some pointers for hopeful, wannabe partners, and they gladly obliged.

Pay attention, because here's the key to success: "do good work in a variety of areas." Well, okay, maybe we need a little more. A relatively prolix partner advises to "seek out work, pay attention to detail, take ownership of projects/cases, gain trust of partners, do not be afraid to express an opinion, stay in touch with college and law school friends, begin to develop business as a senior associate." Okay, that's better. Some insiders insist that "common sense and good humor" can pave the way to the top, while others encourage aspirants to "become indispensable to clients" and "demonstrate the ability to perform with minimal supervision." One partner recommends that associates "should show creativity—come up with the idea or find the case that will make a difference," though another simply prizes the ability to "bring in new business [and] aim for it from the start," because "you can tell very quickly whether someone is partnership material."

Other sources hint at stellar connections and camaraderie with the firm's key players. "Establish relationships with influential partners," we're told, and "make lots of friends in high places." Some say it's all about the hours: "Bill 2,000 hours each of the two years before you are considered," one direct partner counsels. Seeking mentors is a big tip for some.

At the end of the day, it's all about first-class performance. "The primary criteria is rock-solid lawyering," a partner remarks. Another agrees, concluding that "high-quality work is the single most important factor."

Visit the Vault Law Channel, the complete online resource for law careers, featuring firm profiles, message boards, the Vault Law Job Board, and more. **www.vault.com/law**

VAULT CAREER LIBRARY

39

2008 ASSOCIATE PRESTIGE RANKING		2008 PARTNER PRESTIGE RANKING	
1	Wachtell, Lipton, Rosen & Katz	1	Cravath, Swaine & Moore
2	Cravath, Swaine & Moore	2	Wachtell, Lipton, Rosen & Katz
3	Sullivan & Cromwell LLP	3	Sullivan & Cromwell LLP
4	Skadden, Arps, Slate, Meagher & Flom LLP[1]	4	Davis Polk & Wardwell
5	Davis Polk & Wardwell	5	Skadden, Arps, Slate, Meagher & Flom LLP[1]
6	Simpson Thacher & Bartlett LLP	6	Simpson Thacher & Bartlett LLP
7	Cleary, Gottlieb, Steen & Hamilton	7	Cleary, Gottlieb, Steen & Hamilton
8	Latham & Watkins LLP	8	Latham & Watkins LLP
9	Weil, Gotshal & Manges LLP	9	Williams & Connolly LLP
10	Covington & Burling	10	Weil, Gotshal & Manges LLP
11	Kirkland & Ellis	11	Debevoise & Plimpton LLP
12	Debevoise & Plimpton LLP	12	Covington & Burling
13	Paul, Weiss, Rifkind, Wharton & Garrison LLP	13	Paul, Weiss, Rifkind, Wharton & Garrison LLP
14	Shearman & Sterling LLP	14	Kirkland & Ellis
15	Wilmer Cutler Pickering Hale and Dorr LLP	15	Shearman & Sterling LLP
16	Williams & Connolly LLP	16	Gibson, Dunn & Crutcher
17	Sidley Austin LLP	17	Wilmer Cutler Pickering Hale and Dorr LLP
18	Gibson, Dunn & Crutcher	18	Arnold & Porter LLP
19	O'Melveny & Myers	19	O'Melveny & Myers
20	White & Case LLP	20	Milbank, Tweed, Hadley & McCloy
21	Arnold & Porter LLP	21	Fried, Frank, Harris, Shriver & Jacobson LLP
22	Jones Day	22	Sidley Austin LLP
23	Morrison & Foerster LLP	23	Cahill Gordon & Reindel LLP
24	Milbank, Tweed, Hadley & McCloy	24	White & Case LLP
25	Clifford Chance LLP	25	Cadwalader, Wickersham & Taft

1 Skadden, Arps, Slate, Meagher & Flom LLP and Affiliates

PRESTIGE RANKINGS

On the prestige front, associates and partners stayed pretty close to last year's picks. Once again, partners place bigwig Cravath, Swaine & Moore in the first-place spot, while associates continue to root for the smaller but fierce Wachtell, Lipton, Rosen & Katz. Whereas silver medals go to the opposing group's first pick (an even swap), both partners and associates round out their top three, yet again, with the exalted Sullivan & Cromwell. Next, they perform another switcheroo—partners prize Davis, Polk & Wardwell, while associates fawn over the high-rolling Skadden, Arps, Slate, Meagher & Flom.

Moving beyond the top spots, we have Simpson & Thacher dropping a notch with partners this year, with Kirkland & Ellis following suit on the associate list, creating passage for Covington & Burling to sneak its way into the associate top 10. Where Williams & Connolly flaunts ninth-place status on the partner side, associates push the D.C.-based firm to No. 17, opening a surprising gap in an otherwise tight race.

© 2007 Vault Inc.

Even though partners and associates have similar perspectives on prestige, what accounts for the sometimes marked discrepancies? Well, we can't be sure, but we suppose it might have something to do with different criteria and priorities. Since partners have their heads in more industry-wide, upper-management matters, factors such as practice breadth, partner income and case/client reputation may carry more weight with regard to a firm's status. As for associates, more immediate-seeming concerns—a firm's quality of life, asssociate retention pattern, salary structure—could sway their rankings. When taking these components into consideration, slightly divergent views make perfect sense.

DEPARTMENTAL RANKINGS

When it comes to which firms are best in particular practice areas, partners and associates agree to disagree. In fact, the groups only reach harmony on two fronts—DLA Piper dominates real estate and Wachtell wears the M&A crown. (In fact, both groups agree all the way down to No. 6 on the M&A list.)

In other departments, though never agreeing on first places, associates and partners at least come to a general consensus about top spots. Concerning the international practice area, however, the two lists appear as if someone spilled rankings onto the floor and haphazardly pieced them back together. Settling into the No. 2 spot for associates is Freshfields, while partners strongly disagree, sliding the firm into 11th place. As for the top spots: White and Case take the lead for associates, but rank No. 5 for partners; on the flipside, partners pick Clifford Chance as the international alpha firm, while associates place the firm back at No. 7.

Visit the Vault Law Channel, the complete online resource for law careers, featuring firm profiles, message boards, the Vault Law Job Board, and more. **www.vault.com/law**

VAULT CAREER LIBRARY

41

PARTNER PRESTIGE RANKINGS

Partner Prestige

RANK	FIRM	SCORE	2007 RANK
1	Cravath, Swaine & Moore	9.063	1
2	Wachtell, Lipton, Rosen & Katz	8.960	2
3	Sullivan & Cromwell LLP	8.712	3
4	Davis Polk & Wardwell	8.578	4
5	Skadden, Arps, Slate, Meagher & Flom LLP and Affiliates	8.401	6
6	Simpson Thacher & Bartlett LLP	8.283	5
7	Cleary, Gottlieb, Steen & Hamilton	8.038	7
8	Latham & Watkins LLP	8.030	8
9	Williams & Connolly LLP	7.850	9
10	Weil, Gotshal & Manges LLP	7.742	11
11	Debevoise & Plimpton LLP	7.723	13
12	Paul, Weiss, Rifkind, Wharton & Garrison LLP	7.646	10
13	Kirkland & Ellis	7.637	14
14	Covington & Burling	7.628	12
15	Gibson, Dunn & Crutcher	7.510	18
16	Shearman & Sterling LLP	7.505	16
17	Wilmer Cutler Pickering Hale and Dorr LLP	7.377	15
18	Arnold & Porter LLP	7.268	19
19	O'Melveny & Myers	7.252	17
20	Milbank, Tweed, Hadley & McCloy	7.239	23
21	Fried, Frank, Harris, Shriver & Jacobson LLP	7.213	25
22	Cahill Gordon & Reindel LLP	7.128	22
23	Sidley Austin LLP	7.121	21
24	White & Case LLP	7.055	20
25	Cadwalader, Wickersham & Taft	6.997	NR

© 2007 Vault Inc.

PARTNER DEPARTMENTAL RANKINGS

Partner Antitrust

RANK	FIRM	% OF VOTES	2007 RANK
1	Jones Day	19.44	4 (tie)
2	Arnold & Porter LLP	16.67	2
3	Howrey LLP	13.89	4 (tie)
4 (tie)	Cleary, Gottlieb, Steen & Hamilton	11.11	1
4 (tie)	Wilmer Cutler Pickering Hale and Dorr LLP	11.11	3

Partner Bankruptcy/Creditors' Rights

RANK	FIRM	% OF VOTES	2007 RANK
1	Kirkland & Ellis	28.57	2
2	Weil, Gotshal & Manges LLP	24.29	1
3	Skadden, Arps, Slate, Meagher & Flom LLP and Affiliates	22.86	3
4	Cadwalader, Wickersham & Taft	4.29	NR

Partner Corporate

RANK	FIRM	% OF VOTES	2007 RANK
1	Cravath, Swaine & Moore	18.03	1
2	Wachtell, Lipton, Rosen & Katz	13.24	4
3	Davis Polk & Wardwell	10.70	3
4	Sullivan & Cromwell LLP	10.42	2
5	Skadden, Arps, Slate, Meagher & Flom LLP and Affiliates	9.58	5

Visit the Vault Law Channel, the complete online resource for law careers, featuring firm profiles, message boards, the Vault Law Job Board, and more. www.vault.com/law

VAULT CAREER LIBRARY

43

Partner Intellectual Property

RANK	FIRM	% OF VOTES	2007 RANK
1	Finnegan, Henderson, Farabow, Garrett & Dunner	22.73	1
2	Fish & Richardson PC	15.91	2
3	Kirkland & Ellis	11.36	3
4	Jones Day	5.30	NR
5 (tie)	Irell & Manella LLP	4.55	NR
5 (tie)	Wilmer Cutler Pickering Hale and Dorr LLP	4.55	NR

Partner Labor and Employment

RANK	FIRM	% OF VOTES	2007 RANK
1	Paul, Hastings, Janofsky & Walker	20.39	1
2	Morgan, Lewis & Bockius	18.45	2
3	Seyfarth Shaw	16.5	3
4	Littler Mendelson, PC	9.71	4
5	Proskauer Rose LLP	5.83	5

Partner Litigation

RANK	FIRM	% OF VOTES	2007 RANK
1	Kirkland & Ellis	10.68	2
2	Williams & Connolly LLP	9.8	1
3	Paul, Weiss, Rifkind, Wharton & Garrison LLP	8.50	3
4	Cravath, Swaine & Moore	7.84	4
5	Skadden, Arps, Slate, Meagher & Flom LLP and Affiliates	4.79	NR

VAULT CAREER LIBRARY

© 2007 Vault Inc.

Partner Mergers and Acquisitions

RANK	FIRM	% OF VOTES	2007 RANK
1	Wachtell, Lipton, Rosen & Katz	27.35	1
2	Skadden, Arps, Slate, Meagher & Flom LLP and Affiliates	18.39	2
3	Simpson Thacher & Bartlett LLP	13.0	5
4	Cravath, Swain & Moore	12.56	3
5	Sullivan & Cromwell LLP	7.17	4

Partner Real Estate

RANK	FIRM	% OF VOTES
1	DLA Piper	12.82
2	Paul, Hastings, Janofsky & Walker	8.55
3 (tie)	Fried, Frank, Harris, Shriver & Jacobson LLP	5.13
3 (tie)	Goulston & Storrs	5.13
4 (tie)	Willkie Farr & Gallagher LLP	4.27
4 (tie)	Allen Matkins Leck Gamble & Mallory LLP	4.27

Partner Securities

RANK	FIRM	% OF VOTES	2007 RANK
1	Davis Polk & Wardwell	15.38	2
2	Sullivan & Cromwell LLP	14.62	1
3	Cravath, Swaine & Moore	11.15	3
4	Skadden, Arps, Slate, Meagher & Flom LLP and Affiliates	8.85	5
5	Latham & Watkins LLP	6.92	NR

Visit the Vault Law Channel, the complete online resource for law careers, featuring firm profiles, message boards, the Vault Law Job Board, and more. www.vault.com/law

VAULT CAREER LIBRARY

45

Partner Tax

RANK	FIRM	% OF VOTES
1	Skadden, Arps, Slate, Meagher & Flom LLP and Affiliates	12.70
2	Cleary, Gottlieb, Steen & Hamilton	9.52
3 (tie)	Davis Polk & Wardwell	7.94
3 (tie)	Sullivan & Cromwell LLP	7.94
4 (tie)	Sutherland Asbill & Brennan LLP	6.35
4 (tie)	Mayer, Brown, Rowe & Maw LLP	6.35

© 2007 Vault Inc.

Visit the Vault Law Channel, the complete online resource for law careers, featuring firm profiles, message boards, the Vault Law Job Board, and more. **www.vault.com/law**

VAULT CAREER LIBRARY 47

Stay Ahead of the Market

Sutherland Asbill & Brennan LLP
ATTORNEYS AT LAW

Sutherland Rankings

Best of the Rest

#4 Best in Atlanta

#4 Tied Best in Tax Law, Partner

#12 Best to Work For

#20 Satisfaction

#15 Hours

#20 Associate-Partner Relations

#2 Best in Formal Training

#13 Best in Informal Training/Mentoring

#19 Best in Pay

#10 Best in Pro Bono

But don't just rely on our numbers.
Visit www.sablaw.com to learn more
about life at Sutherland.

Source: 2008 Vault Guide

Atlanta ▪ Austin ▪ Houston ▪ New York ▪ Tallahassee ▪ Washington DC   **www.sablaw.com**

THE VAULT
QUALITY
OF LIFE
RANKINGS

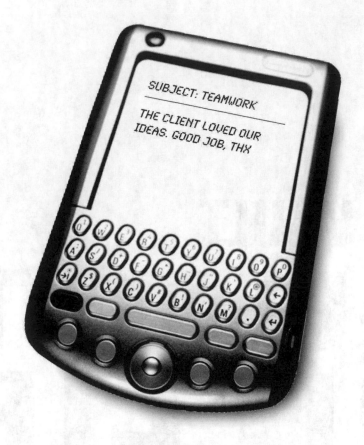

SYNC UP

At DLA Piper, our success depends on our most important asset—our people. Join us and you will be part of a values-based culture that emphasizes teamwork and respect, diversity, community involvement, and continuous learning in an exciting global environment.

DLA Piper's 3,400 lawyers work together across 25 countries from 63 offices throughout the United States, Europe, Asia, and the Middle East.

To apply or learn more about opportunities at our law firm, please contact a recruiter listed at www.dlapiper.com/us/careers/summer/contactus.

www.dlapiper.com   DLA Piper US LLP   **EVERYTHING MATTERS**

Ben Boyd, National Hiring Partner, DLA Piper US LLP | 1200 Nineteenth Street, NW, Washington, DC 20036-2412
Ron S. Holliday, Tampa Managing Partner, DLA Piper US LLP | 101 East Kennedy Boulevard, Tampa, Florida 33602-5149

DLA Piper US LLP practices law in the United States and France, and together with other related entities is a member of DLA Piper, a global legal services organization.
DLA Piper US LLP is an Equal Opportunity Employer. AA-M/F/D/V

QUALITY OF LIFE RANKINGS

METHODOLOGY

Associates were asked to rate their firm on a 1 to 10 scale for each of several quality of life categories. The firm's score in each quality of life category is simply the average of the scores its associates gave in that area. It is important to note that those firms without a high enough aggregate of associates completing the survey were ineligible to appear in these rankings.

THE BEST 20 FIRMS TO WORK FOR

Which are the best firms to work for? For some, this is a far more important consideration than prestige. To determine our Best 20 firms, we analyzed our initial list of 167 firms using a formula that weighed the most relevant categories for an overall quality of life ranking. Each firm's overall score was calculated using the following formula:

40 percent satisfaction

10 percent hours

10 percent pay

10 percent associate/partner relations

10 percent diversity (women, minorities and GLBT)

10 percent formal training

5 percent informal training

5 percent pro bono

Like our Top 100 rankings, our Best 20 is meant to reflect the subjective opinion of associates. By its nature, the list is based on the perceptions of insiders—some of whom may be biased in favor (or against) their firm.

Visit the Vault Law Channel, the complete online resource for law careers, featuring firm profiles, message boards, the Vault Law Job Board, and more. **www.vault.com/law**

VAULT CAREER LIBRARY   51

BY NEVER BELIEVING OUR JOB IS DONE, WE'VE CREATED A FIRM WHERE OPPORTUNITY THRIVES.

For the last five years, Vault has ranked MoFo number one in Diversity.
The Minority Law Journal consistently ranks us among the most diverse firms
in the country. We're one of the "100 Best Companies to Work For" according to
Fortune magazine. Now, for the third year in a row, Morrison & Foerster has been
named to *The American Lawyer's A-List*. An exceedingly proud moment – especially
after leaping from eleventh to sixth on the list in just a year. But around here, there
is always room to raise the glass ceiling a little higher and open the doors a little wider.
We like the trend. We plan to continue it. In a firm where nearly half of our associates are
women, and people of color account for nearly a third of our associates,
opportunity thrives. And grows. See how your aspirations may align with ours.

www.mofo.com

MORRISON | FOERSTER

BEST 20 LAW FIRMS TO WORK FOR

Average score = 7.66

RANK	FIRM	SCORE	2007 RANK
1	McKee Nelson LLP	8.484	15
2	Patterson Belknap Webb & Tyler LLP	8.463	NR
3	Hughes Hubbard & Reed LLP	8.462	8
4	Fish & Richardson PC	8.452	17
5	Quarles & Brady LLP	8.403	NR
6	Morrison & Foerster LLP	8.349	2
7	Baker & Daniels	8.343	NR
8	Patton Boggs LLP	8.305	NR
9	Finnegan, Henderson, Farabow, Garrett & Dunner LLP	8.287	1
10	Dickstein Shapiro LLP	8.280	4
11	Faegre & Benson LLP	8.250	NR
12	Sutherland Asbill & Brennan LLP	8.233	13
13	Clifford Chance LLP	8.178	NR
14	Davis Polk & Wardwell	8.168	16
15	Jenner & Block LLP	8.160	NR
16	Weil, Gotshal & Manges LLP	8.148	18
17	Manatt, Phelps & Phillips, LLP	8.143	9
18	Carlton Fields	8.142	NR
19	Paul, Hastings, Janofsky & Walker	8.129	NR
20	Ropes & Gray LLP	8.094	11

Top three firms to work for

1. McKee Nelson LLP

McKee Nelson makes a major leap from its No. 15 spot last year, to the very top of the "Best Firms to Work For." With warm associate-partner relations, sky-high compensation, and super-satisfied associates, it's a wonder this young firm didn't get here sooner.

This is a firm that takes its work very seriously. "We're the best at what we do," one McKee associate asserts simply. But they're also among the happiest doing it. "McKee Nelson is an intense work environment," another associate explains. "On the other hand, it's a very human place that values and recognizes the individual and fundamentally wants to develop the potential of each associate." The firm is filled with "really bright, yet really fun associates," another insider offers. Bright, fun, and invested in their firm as well: "Most partners and associates are very committed to the success of the firm and not just to their individual practices," says one source. "There is thus a unique sense of firm spirit at McKee."

That unique firm spirit is infectious. "There isn't competition between associates here," states a source. "Its an environment that's more about getting the job done than stepping over another associate on your way to partner. Also, the firm is still making

Visit the Vault Law Channel, the complete online resource for law careers, featuring firm profiles, message boards, the Vault Law Job Board, and more. www.vault.com/law

VAULT CAREER LIBRARY   53

a name for itself and evolving, so it's great to be part of something new that is still willing to do things differently." The McKee spirit even extends past the end of the work day: "Associates in the D.C. office (even the married ones) socialize often with each other, even on weekends. We are a very close bunch." The love here is strong: "I was trying to think about it," muses an associate, "and there isn't a single person I don't like."

Associates at McKee also appreciate the assignments they're given and the attention paid to them by the partners. One McKee associate relishes "challenging work, great people to work with [and] as much responsibility as you can handle." Along with the responsibility comes plenty of guidance: "Partners seem to always welcome the opportunity to mentor and groom associates into becoming better attorneys," believes an insider. Another agrees, "I receive informal training on a daily basis from top partners at our firm, including the managing partner."

As much as they like the work, it seems that associates at McKee are encouraged not to do too much of it: "When it gets busy, it gets really busy. But when there is down time, partners tell you to hurry up and go home!" Clearly, this is a firm that knows how to take care of its associates, and in more ways than one. "One of the best things about McKee is that they don't nickel and dime their employees," asserts this staffer. Perks range from "little things like car rides home and free dinners, to big thing like plush parties and a Rolls Royce of a benefits package." From another happy employee: "McKee Nelson always pays top of the market and is never stingy on pay." The firm has also learned that an easy way to an associate's heart is through his or her stomach, and accordingly provides "huge Friday breakfast spreads, a Thursday afternoon treat cart that brings around cookies or ice cream and every kind of beverage in coolers all over the office."

While it's hard to predict how the culture might change as the firm continues to grow, for now, the grass is about as green as it gets at McKee Nelson. The firm has "top level work, top practitioners in the field [and a] great office atmosphere," one associate sums up, which leaves him feeling "entirely fulfilled."

2. Patterson Belknap Webb & Tyler LLP

"If you want to work in a New York law firm, this is the place to be," insists an associate at Patterson Belknap Webb & Tyler, a newcomer making a very impressive debut to the "Best to Work For" list. At Patterson, associates get good work and lots of TLC. "I receive close mentorship from partners, including senior partners, at every step of the way," affirms one associate, adding, "I've had client contact and interesting, substantive work from my first week here." Another attorney notes the "very interesting cases that are unique in the New York market" including "smaller IP and commercial cases." Although not all the work is delicious, the firm does what it can to keep things interesting: "No matter where you are, litigation involves some boring and tedious work, so you do that at Patterson also. However, the firm administration makes a concerted effort to balance your work load so [that] each attorney is exposed to many different types of cases and at different stages. The firm really cares about each attorney's development."

The upshot is that associates here get their hands dirty, and love it. A senior associate boasts, "I just finished a five-week trial with two partners and four associates and all the associates were given opportunities to present and cross witnesses and argue motions." A first-year beams, "I spend most of my time working directly with partners and clients" and "I get to make real decisions." Another states: "The partners empower associates and give them great autonomy. Direct and timely feedback is given."

So the work is great at Patterson. But another great thing about life here is that associates do stuff other than work. "I feel like I am respected and trusted by partners, given challenging and rewarding work, and—most importantly—room to be human and have a life," says one associate. A life … remember what that was like? At Patterson, they do. The place is "more family-oriented than most firms," attests this attorney, "since people want to get on home to their families, there's less expectation of face time and crazy billables." This firm doesn't ask for associates' outside hours on top of their workday. Instead, "associates are treated like adults and their personal lives are given healthy respect." Elaborates one insider: "Patterson takes the practice of law very seriously, but lawyers are generally very relaxed with one another. We leave each other alone outside of work for the most part—which makes for more interesting colleagues, because most people seem to have a life!" Life, it appears, goes on.

It's a credit to the firm that, in its focus on professionalism and efficiency, Patterson does not neglect to share its legal talent with those who need it. "The culture of the firm is very focused on pro bono, and this focus appears to be rather genuine and not

© 2007 Vault Inc.

cynically motivated." Indeed, the firm's commitment earned it a first-place finish in this year's pro bono rankings, and seems of a piece with the generally humane culture here. One Patterson associate offers this summary: "At Patterson, there is a purposeful attempt, with observable success, not to be the barbarous place most New York City law firms seem determined to be." For not joining the barbarous hordes, Patterson Belknap wins this year's silver.

3. Hughes Hubbard & Reed LLP

Hughes Hubbard "really cares about all of its employees and strives to make associates happy." All that striving is paying off. As one attorney claims, "The people are wonderful to be around, the firm's culture is open and never stuffy, the work is fun and challenging, the hours are generally good." The firm also has a commitment to diversity, and a strong pro bono ethic, as evidenced by its quality of life rankings. What more could an associate ask for?

Fellowship is in the air at Hughes Hubbard & Reed—just wander the hallways and you'll notice it: "As you walk around the halls, anyone you see, no matter what seniority, has a friendly greeting for each other." Such friendly interaction seems to be a hallmark of this firm. One attorney explains: "For a New York law firm HHR is fairly laid back, not in terms of work or hours, but in terms of how people interact. It is not uncommon to see partners and associates joking around." Of course, joking around with other lawyers is no fun if the other lawyers are bores. At Hughes Hubbard, this is not generally a problem: "The firm is full of lawyers with personalities, which I wasn't convinced existed when I was in law school. Everyone's very smart and committed, but they're also quirky and fun to be around." Asked to name a strong point of the firm, another attorney exclaims: "The people! The associates are personable and friendly and understand that you value your life outside the firm."

Lest you worry that lawyers here do nothing but pal around and make chitchat, rest assured: sometimes those conversations are about work. What's more surprising is that sometimes the person doing the talking is an associate, while the person doing the listening is a partner. "Associates are granted a high level of responsibility early on, which provides the opportunity to develop new skills and take on new tasks. There are always 'more-senior' associates and partners willing to provide feedback." Explains another associate: "Every partner I have worked with has wanted to know what I think. They are willing to accept disagreement as to approach and can be convinced that there is a better way than their initial reaction."

And associates here don't have to tiptoe around before knocking on a partner's door for help. The partners are eager to offer it: "Overall our partners are great and want to provide guidance and training to the associates; they are also interested in maintaining personal relationships with associates that transcend the workplace reporting structure." One well-cared-for insider reports, "My partner mentor takes me to lunch at least once a month and regularly e-mails me to see how I am doing or to offer to read something before I send it out to a partner or senior associate." As for the hours, "the corporate traffic manager and other attorneys try to be flexible to be sure the work gets done without anyone getting stuck holding the bag all the time," insiders say. In other words, this firm has got your back; and for that, it's also got this year's big bronze.

Visit the Vault Law Channel, the complete online resource for law careers, featuring firm profiles, message boards, the Vault Law Job Board, and more. www.vault.com/law

VAULT CAREER LIBRARY

55

OVERALL SATISFACTION

Average score = 7.70

RANK	FIRM	SCORE	2007 RANK
1	Fish & Richardson PC	8.750	9
2	McKee Nelson LLP	8.680	NR
3	Hughes Hubbard & Reed LLP	8.600	NR
4	Quarles & Brady LLP	8.507	NR
5	Baker & Daniels	8.500	13
6	Patterson Belknap Webb & Tyler LLP	8.460	NR
7	Williams & Connolly LLP	8.436	4
8	Patton Boggs LLP	8.393	NR
9	Faegre & Benson LLP	8.390	NR
10	Finnegan, Henderson, Farabow, Garrett & Dunner LLP	8.357	12
11 (tie)	Morrison & Foerster LLP	8.356	10
11 (tie)	Paul, Hastings, Janofsky & Walker LLP	8.356	NR
12	Manatt, Phelps & Phillips, LLP	8.281	6
13	Carlton Fields	8.264	5
14	Dickstein Shapiro LLP	8.202	16
15	Jenner & Block LLP	8.147	NR
16	Munger, Tolles & Olson LLP	8.123	NR
17	Davis Polk & Wardwell	8.122	NR
18	Locke Liddell & Sapp	8.114	NR
19	Clifford Chance LLP	8.109	NR
20	Sutherland Asbill & Brennan LLP	8.075	NR

Top three in overall satisfaction

1. Fish & Richardson PC

It looks like Fish & Richardson has mastered the formula. Challenging work + great people + lots of money = some seriously blissed out employees. Let's start with the work: lawyers here relish the duties they're given. "I love the amount of responsibility the firm gives me—and I'm a first-year!" exclaims one attorney. Adds another, "I am continually asked to work on high-level, critical matters that stretch what I consider my present capabilities, but not to the breaking point." And how about the people? One associate reports, "We have a tight-knit group of attorneys and paralegals that are great to work with, and very laid-back." They ain't stupid, either: "There are some brilliant people working at Fish & Richardson. Working with them is truly a learning experience, and very fulfilling." Throw platinum compensation packages into the mix, and you have lawyers who sound like they've been knocking back happy pills. "Morale is very high. I think all the associates feel blessed to be here," believes one. Another associate beams: "Overall, this is a fantastic place to work—I love coming in every day!" Perhaps most remarkably, some lawyers at Fish find themselves happier now than before they were lawyers: "I can safely say that this is one of the best

© 2007 Vault Inc.

cultures, and I've worked in both law and a prior profession as an accountant." Another associate says: "I am very happy I made the career switch from engineering." A law firm that makes people happy to be lawyers? No wonder Fish is No. 1.

2. McKee Nelson LLP

At McKee Nelson, "The partners get it." "It" being how to keep their associates happy. At this firm, higher-ups tend to associates with so much care, you'd think they were prize orchids. As one young flower explains, "The culture is one in which mentoring relationships spring up organically, and I feel that the partners take a great interest in my professional development." Another adds: "I am learning a new skill with great senior associates and partners who are eager to teach." Associates here "get hands-on experience right away and learn a lot." One bright-eyed first-year gushes, "The work is really interesting and I feel like I have learned so much in a short time, but the nice thing is that it feels just like the tip of the iceberg and that I could practice in this area for 100 years and still be learning." In sum, "McKee Nelson really takes care of its associates" to the point where "associates very rarely leave to work at another firm."

3. Hughes Hubbard & Reed LLP

Wander the offices of Hughes Hubbard & Reed, second runner-up for satisfaction, and you'll notice an inspiring thing: Lawyers who seem to enjoy the practice of law. Summing up a common sentiment, one senior associate notes, "I have been given excellent work on interesting cases with high levels of responsibility." In case you think they save the best work for senior associates, listen to this first-year: "Despite my being a young associate, I feel involved in all aspects of the life of the firm: recruiting, meeting clients, representing the firm at seminars. I am also impressed by the quality of work I get: While some may be considered tedious, most is interesting." And here's the other thing to know about Hughes Hubbard: They care. They really do! "The people I work with are intelligent, caring, and very supportive of junior associates," explains one attorney. Another testifies that Hughes provides "great responsibility, but also lots of respect. More importantly, a willingness to brainstorm to see if we can collectively find the best answer, rather than simply executing someone else's strategy." This kind of respectful collaboration breeds very loyal associates. As this insider claims: "I can't imagine working anywhere else."

Visit the Vault Law Channel, the complete online resource for law careers, featuring firm profiles, message boards, the Vault Law Job Board, and more. **www.vault.com/law**

VAULT CAREER LIBRARY   57

HOURS

Average score = 7.01

RANK	FIRM	SCORE	2007 RANK
1	Patterson Belknap Webb & Tyler LLP	8.270	12
2	Fish & Richardson PC	8.129	NR
3	Allen Matkins Leck Gamble & Mallory LLP	8.074	NR
4	Baker & Daniels	8.061	17
5	Quarles & Brady LLP	8.040	NR
6	Winstead Sechrest & Minick	8.027	11
7	Morgan & Finnegan, LLP	7.917	NR
8	Moore & Van Allen	7.913	NR
9	Faegre & Benson LLP	7.902	NR
10	Patton Boggs LLP	7.893	NR
11	Manatt, Phelps & Phillips, LLP	7.879	6
12	Thompson Hine	7.864	9
13	Venable	7.810	20
14	Mintz Levin Cohn Ferris Glovsky and Popeo PC	7.805	15
15	Sutherland Asbill & Brennan LLP	7.745	NR
16	Dickstein Shapiro LLP	7.738	NR
17	Sedgwick, Detert, Moran & Arnold	7.727	3
18	Thompson & Knight	7.710	NR
19	Barnes & Thornburg	7.683	NR
20	Wiley Rein LLP	7.611	4

Top three in hours

1. Patterson Belknap Webb & Tyler LLP

Patterson Belknap Webb & Tyler recognizes that a bleary-eyed associate does not a good lawyer make. Accordingly, "The firm's billable hour philosophy supports the notion that it does not want attorneys burning out, and thereby not servicing the client as effectively and efficiently as possible." The firm "asks for 1,850 billable per year—and a total of 2,100 for all hours put together." Lawyers here meet those demands without pulling too many unnecessary all-nighters. "The firm encourages efficiency, so I tend to bill most of the time I'm here," says one associate. Furthermore, "At least for senior associates, the firm respects individual lawyers' judgments about whether they can take on new work (of course taking account of the overall workload at the firm)." And flex-time is not fiction: "Flex-time is for real: associates and partners, men and women." As one working father says, "as the parent of young children, I appreciate the flexibility afforded me by the firm as far as when and where I work my hours." Patterson Belknap pulls off a New York practice without freefalling into hours madness, and thus earns first place in our 2007 associate survey.

© 2007 Vault Inc.

2. Fish & Richardson PC

"As big law firms go, I think Fish is as good as it gets," muses an associate at Fish & Richardson. This law firm respects its attorneys enough to untether them from their desks. "There's no face time requirement—I can work from home or from the train on the way home and no one would know the difference," explains one source. In other words, the firm "provides you with the responsibility to manage your time and projects." F&R also recognizes commitments outside of the office, and "works with people to accommodate weddings, children and other personal situations." Agrees this insider, "The firm's leave policies are very generous." One parent reports that "the firm has been very supportive of my non-traditional work hours ever since I had my daughter." As for the hours requirement, everything's above board: "The firm has a 1,900-hour requirement, which is not too onerous, and most people you ask say 1,900 is 1,900—there's no hidden requirement to work more."

3. Allen Matkins Leck Gamble & Mallory LLP

Sanity seems the order of the day at California's Allen Matkins Leck Gamble & Mallory. "I leave by 7:00 p.m. most nights and that is amazing," beams one attorney, happy with her good fortune. "At my old firm, that was unheard of." Another associate declares, "I feel I am in control of the number of hours I work." Lawyers at Allen Matkins can make plans for the weekend … and keep them. "I find most weekends are free unless you need or want to work to increase hours loads," explains an associate. The firm requires 1,950 billable hours annually, and awards full bonuses at 2,150. And no reading between the lines is required: "1,950 still means 1,950!" The firm is also flexible: One associate reports that "due to personal/family reasons, I have requested that they allow me to cut back to 80 percent starting soon, and Allen Matkins has been completely supportive." All in all, "hours are not unreasonable, and most partners and senior associates are happy for you to leave early/take time off when work is slow." This accommodating attitude earns Allen Matkins the third place spot on our pedestal.

Visit the Vault Law Channel, the complete online resource for law careers, featuring firm profiles, message boards, the Vault Law Job Board, and more. **www.vault.com/law**

VAULT CAREER LIBRARY 59

PAY

Average score = 8.10

RANK	FIRM	SCORE	2007 RANK
1	Wachtell, Lipton, Rosen & Katz	9.756	4
2	Fish & Richardson PC	9.692	16
3	McKee Nelson LLP	9.542	3
4	Brown Rudnick Berlack Israels LLP	9.323	NR
5	Ropes & Gray LLP	9.261	17
6	Cadwalader, Wickersham & Taft	9.184	NR
7	LeBoeuf, Lamb, Greene & MacRae, LLP	9.150	NR
8	Cleary, Gottlieb, Steen & Hamilton LLP	9.125	NR
9	Clifford Chance LLP	9.120	7
10	Skadden, Arps, Slate, Meagher & Flom LLP and Affiliates	9.113	NR
11	Kirkland & Ellis	9.071	NR
12	Willkie Farr & Gallagher LLP	9.023	9
13	Paul, Weiss, Rifkind, Wharton & Garrison LLP	9.012	10
14	Linklaters	9.000	NR
15	Dewey Ballantine	8.962	NR
16	Simpson Thacher & Bartlett LLP	8.947	18
17	Fried, Frank, Harris, Shriver & Jacobson LLP	8.942	NR
18	Finnegan, Henderson, Farabow, Garrett & Dunner LLP	8.907	NR
19	Sullivan & Cromwell LLP	8.899	NR
20	Morrison & Foerster LLP	8.859	NR

Top three in pay

1. Wachtell, Lipton, Rosen & Katz

"We make more than you." It's not a taunt, it's a fact of life. Wachtell is the perennial compensation leader, and except for last year, has placed No. 1 on this scale every time we've surveyed associates. The firm has an industry-wide reputation to maintain, and salary always settles in above the New York market rate, establishing a "totally different scale" that none dare match. Compensation is "light years ahead of the next best firm," and "top salary and outstanding bonuses" help keep lawyers at Wachtell and out of the lucrative hedge fund industry. Bottom line: "We get paid vastly more than associates at any other large law firm in the world. The firm has made very clear its absolute commitment to keeping it that way."

2. Fish & Richardson PC

Why did Fish & Richardson associates rate their compensation so highly this year? Well, the firm "was one of the first to jump on the new raises. Their willingness sent a very positive message to associates." A lot of firms matched quickly, but what really impressed F&R associates (and vaulted the firm to second on this ranking scale) was that not only did their firm raise, it offered the New York rate to everyone. At the time, Fish & Richardson was "one of the few firms that have raised to that level in our

© 2007 Vault Inc.

California offices," and it still leads in markets like Dallas and Delaware, where associates say compensation is "incredible" and "exceeds my expectations," respectively. As for bonuses, they are "a combination of billable hours and subjective analysis of your work at the firm." A litigator finds it fair that "if you work harder than average, you will be compensated as such," though a Boston associate assures you that "there is no pressure to bill over minimum." And overall, "Fish remains the national market leader for compensating IP associates."

3. McKee Nelson LLP

At McKee Nelson, firm management makes things very clear: "The partnership has simply stated that we will remain at the top of the market and compensation will never be the reason an associate leaves." In practical terms, that means that: "anytime there is a salary increase, McKee Nelson matches it. In addition, bonuses are also among the highest paid and there are many fringe benefits." New York rates set the standard, even for the Washington office; "associates are basically paid at the top of the New York scale in both the New York and D.C. offices. Bonuses are performance-based and generous." Just how generous? The firm "will often pay bonuses above the market rate," one insider confirms. All in all, associates at No. 3 McKee have little to grumble about. As one source sums up, "Our firm pays top dollar and rewards good performance with good bonuses. It's nice not to have to worry about that."

Visit the Vault Law Channel, the complete online resource for law careers, featuring firm profiles, message boards, the Vault Law Job Board, and more. **www.vault.com/law**

VAULT CAREER LIBRARY   **61**

ASSOCIATE/PARTNER RELATIONS

Average score = 8.11

RANK	FIRM	SCORE	2007 RANK
1	McKee Nelson LLP	9.146	9
2	Patterson, Bellknap, Webb & Tyler LLP	9.086	8
3	Fish & Richardson LLP	8.954	19
4	Munger, Tolles & Olson LLP	8.926	1
5	Wachtell, Lipton, Rosen & Katz	8.911	15 (tie)
6	Baker & Daniels	8.875	NR
7	Locke Liddell & Sapp	8.837	NR
8	Quarles & Brady LLP	8.797	NR
9	Williams & Connolly LLP	8.759	3
10	Carlton Fields	8.750	13
11	Faegre & Benson LLP	8.683	NR
12	Morrison & Foerster LLP	8.861	NR
13	Dorsey & Whitney LLP	8.672	NR
14	Dickstein Shapiro LLP	8.654	NR
15	Haynes & Boone	8.641	NR
16	Hughes Hubbard & Reed LLP	8.640	18
17	Moore & Van Allen	8.630	NR
18	Patton Boggs LLP	8.623	NR
19	Davis Polk & Wardwell LLP	8.610	NR
20	Sutherland Asbill & Brennan LLP	8.609	NR

Top three firms in Associate/Partner Relations

1. McKee Nelson LLP

In the space of one year, how do you climb from No. 9 in the rankings for associate/partner relations, all the way to No. 1? If you ask McKee Nelson, maybe all you need is love. "I love the partners," one dewy-eyed first-year confesses. The feeling is widespread, and runs both ways. McKee Nelson is "a unique firm, truly, in terms of partner/associate relationships," believes one insider. "The respect here is clearly mutual, and I am thoroughly impressed by the collegial nature the firm has maintained since its inception." Another first-year feels that working regularly with partners is "one of the best parts of my job." Associates at this firm are anything but cogs in the machine: "The partners recognize that the associates are critical to the success of the firm. The associates are always made to feel valued and are given the sense that the partners are investing a lot of time and money in them." And at McKee Nelson, partners and associates not only work together, they play together: "There is significantly more socializing and camaraderie among partners and associates than was the case at my prior firm," a source confides.

© 2007 Vault Inc.

2. Patterson Belknap Webb & Tyler LLP

Making another great leap forward in associate/partner relations is Patterson Belknap Webb & Tyler, which takes the silver by cutting through the red tape. "There is not the crippling protocol of reporting upwards that appears to be the norm at many firms," reports an associate. Instead, "cases are lightly staffed, and associates interact frequently with partners." It's one for all and all for one at Patterson Belknap: "No 'us versus them,' or very little, from either partners or associates." Indeed, "Associates are treated as capable attorneys and their contributions are sought and respected." A content first-year confesses, "I have never been treated disrespectfully. In fact, even as a very junior associate, I find the most senior and renowned partners value what I have to say, allow me to speak to the client, etc. It is really quite a pleasant surprise." Moreover, associates are kept informed in an elegant fashion: "there was recently a salary raise and the head of litigation took associates out to dinner in groups to inform them of potential bonus changes and solicit their opinions."

3. Fish & Richardson PC

The award for most improved might go to Fish & Richardson, which rockets 17 slots to come in at third place. According to a New York associate, "The firm has a wonderful environment." The reasons? "No screamers. Responsibility is pushed to low levels early, but there is still great partner support and accessibility." At Fish, partners let associates keep a hand on the steering wheel, at least where their own careers are concerned: "While associates don't have the same level of input on firm management as at other firms, we have a lot of say in the type of work and cases we want to take, and the type of contribution we make." As with any good relationship, the keys seem to be quality time and communication: "The partners really listen to what the associates have to say, they give us meaningful work, and they socialize and are friendly with us." And associates here don't have to read partners' minds: "Fish is very good at communication and transparency. The standards may be high, but at least the associates know what the standards are."

Visit the Vault Law Channel, the complete online resource for law careers, featuring firm profiles, message boards, the Vault Law Job Board, and more. **www.vault.com/law**

VAULT CAREER LIBRARY   **63**

FORMAL TRAINING

Average score = 7.15

RANK	FIRM	SCORE	2007 RANK
1	Kirkland & Ellis	8.907	1
2	Sutherland Asbill & Brennan LLP	8.848	17
3	Ropes & Gray LLP	8.603	6
4	Clifford Chance LLP	8.490	11
5	Weil, Gotshal & Manges LLP	8.483	7
6	Hughes, Hubbard & Reed LLP	8.400	8
7	Shook, Hardy & Bacon L.L.P	8.320	5
8	Cravath, Swaine & Moore LLP	8.289	3
9	Cooley Godward Kronish LLP	8.273	4
10	Davis, Polk & Wardwell LLP	8.219	13
11	Sedwick, Detert, Moran & Arnold LLP	8.216	9
12	Finnegan, Henderson, Farabow, Garrett & Dunner LLP	8.209	2
13	Latham & Watkins	8.115	12
14	Linklaters	8.046	14
15	Patton Boggs LLP	8.037	NR
16	Jones Day	8.011	15
17	Jenner & Block LLP	7.985	NR
18	Littler Mendelson, PC	7.958	NR
19	Dorsey & Whitney LLP	7.952	19
20	Dewey Ballantine	7.912	NR

Top three in formal training

1. Kirkland & Ellis

For the third straight year, Kirkland & Ellis leads the field for formal training. The firm's offerings leave at least one attorney in a state of disbelief: "Unbelievably effective training programs from the top dogs. I cannot believe how seriously they take training and how much time and effort big wigs at the firm dedicate to teaching the younger associates, both formally and informally." What one insider calls "the jewel of the firm's litigation training" is KITA, a program where "every year, all litigation associates conduct a full mock trial with partners serving as judges and instructors, and hired jurors." KITA, it seems, is a blast. It is "a lot of fun. It reminds you why you wanted to be a litigator in the first place." The corporate department is not left out—"We have training once or twice a week, very extensive," a corporate associate reports. "I have yet to hear of another large law firm that invests as much time and money into training its associates," declares a proud Kirkland insider.

© 2007 Vault Inc.

2. Sutherland Asbill & Brennan LLP

Making a bold break into the No. 2 spot, Sutherland Asbill & Brennan LLP provides a training program that "must be one of the best in the country." In this firm, "each practice group routinely hosts training classes on a diverse array of substantive legal topics." Sutherland provides an "excellent format for internal training programs which are varied, extensive and very easy to attend (lunchtime sessions)." In addition to substantive legal training, the firm offers "career development programs aimed at instilling business goals at an early stage." Overall, "I would find it hard to imagine a law firm that is more committed to professional development than Sutherland," says an associate. "The training program is organized, focused, and supported."

3. Ropes & Gray LLP

A little obsession can be a good thing. Third place finisher Ropes & Gray "is almost obsessed with training, and there are opportunities all over the place." In other words: "There is training out the wazoo here. The training programs are also very, very good, as attorneys put a lot of effort into creating them and keeping them up-to-date." Think of a topic, and Ropes has got a training session for it, according to the insider who says: "I can't imagine a subject not offered as part of a formal training program." New associates attend a week-long "boot camp," which one attorney calls "invaluable—if not for its substantive content, at least for exposing me to some issues I hadn't thought about before joining the firm (like how to manage a document production or review)." Overall, insiders seem to feel "There can simply be no rival in this area."

Visit the Vault Law Channel, the complete online resource for law careers, featuring firm profiles, message boards, the Vault Law Job Board, and more. **www.vault.com/law**

VAULT CAREER LIBRARY

65

INFORMAL TRAINING/MENTORING

Average score = 7.26

RANK	FIRM	SCORE	2007 RANK
1	Quarles & Brady LLP	8.649	NR
2	Locke Liddell & Sapp	8.465	12
3	Baker & Daniels LLP	8.400	15
4	McKee Nelson LLP	8.265	9
5	Carlton Fields	8.177	4
6	Finnegan, Henderson, Farabow, Garrett & Dunner LLP	8.140	3
7	Paul, Hastings, Janofsky & Walker LLP	8.138	NR
8	Dickstein & Shapiro LLP	8.128	NR
9	Faegre & Benson LLP	8.077	NR
10	Fish & Richardson PC	8.062	NR
11	Saul Ewing LLP	8.057	14
12	Morrison & Foerster LLP	8.042	10
13	Sutherland Asbill & Brennan LLP	7.989	NR
14	Shook, Hardy & Bacon LLP	7.980	NR
15	Barnes & Thornburg LLP	7.974	6
16	Haynes & Boone	7.931	NR
17	Dorsey & Whitney LLP	7.921	NR
18	Patterson, Bellknap, Webb & Tyler LLP	7.917	NR
19	Brown Rudnick Berlack Israels LLP	7.906	NR
20	Manatt, Phelps & Phillips, LLP	7.855	NR

Top three in informal training/mentoring

1. Quarles & Brady LLP

It's a fresh new threesome at the top of the informal training charts this year. Quarles & Brady leapt into first place for 2008, after finishing out of the top 20 in 2007. "Almost without exception, Quarles & Brady's partners consider informal training and mentoring for associates a part of their jobs." One associate says, "I have received outstanding informal training and mentoring. Every partner I have approached for advice has been willing to provide help and guidance when needed." Moreover, "partners generally do a good job of explaining the rationale behind strategic tactics and changes that are made to work." In addition to informal guidance, the firm provides a formal mentoring program to keep associates on track. Associates get "a skill mentor" to help them "gain work to develop their skill set," as well as "marketing mentors who groom associates for partnership responsibilities." The mentoring system has been called "very successful," in part because the firm recognizes mentors' contributions. "Mentors get credit for mentoring hours and are therefore eager to help." One associate says that "people take ownership for informal mentoring and training within each practice group and across associate classes. I couldn't be happier with this aspect of the firm."

© 2007 Vault Inc.

2. Locke Liddell & Sapp LLP

"The majority of my training, and a true strength of Locke Liddell, is in the firm's informal mentoring program," attests an associate at this year's silver medal firm. "I'm very happy with the level of informal mentoring," reports another. Indeed, if associates at Locke Liddell & Sapp ever find themselves stuck, they need not look far to find a mentor. Explains one source: "Locke provides each of its associates with a partner and senior associate mentor. I have been extremely satisfied with the level of attention I have received from my mentor." Informally, senior attorneys make sure that knowledge flows downhill: "The 'open-door' policy and the approachability of the partners, as well as the great personalities in the firm, make the informal mentoring opportunities invaluable." Prepare for the onslaught: "If you pair up with the right senior associates and partners early, you learn more than you can handle."

3. Baker & Daniels LLP

At Baker & Daniels, the lines of communication are open. Insiders tell us that "Senior lawyers tend to be approachable and, when asked, willingly share ideas for improving legal skills and dealing with particular problems." Associates here find that questions don't go unanswered for long. Finds one source, "All of the members—partners and more senior associates—of my team have reached out to me to provide training and mentoring. Outside my team, many partners are more than willing to answer any questions I may have." It helps that Baker & Daniels partners don't place themselves on pedestals and "are generally very open-door, and very willing to spend time with associates to help mentor them and ensure their progress in their careers." In fact, there is an "extensive amount of great people at B&D" to provide guidance.

Visit the Vault Law Channel, the complete online resource for law careers, featuring firm profiles, message boards, the Vault Law Job Board, and more. **www.vault.com/law**

VAULT CAREER LIBRARY   **67**

PRO BONO

Average score = 8.12			
RANK	**FIRM**	**SCORE**	**2007 RANK**
1	Patterson Belknap Webb & Tyler LLP	9.686	1
2	Hughes Hubbard & Reed LLP	9.583	NR
3	Manatt, Phelps & Phillips, LLP	9.526	4
4 (tie)	Patton Boggs LLP	9.500	8
4 (tie)	Debevoise & Plimpton LLP	9.500	2
5	Quarles & Brady LLP	9.451	NR
6	Morgan, Lewis & Bockius	9.318	NR
7	Kramer Levin Naftalis & Frankel	9.308	NR
8	Carlton Fields	9.289	3
9	Dickstein Shapiro LLP	9.276	NR
10	Sutherland Asbill & Brennan LLP	9.258	12
11	Jenner & Block LLP	9.231	NR
12	Kilpatrick Stockton	9.205	7
13	Arnold & Porter LLP	9.203	NR
14	Paul, Weiss, Rifkind, Wharton & Garrison LLP	9.199	10
15	Morrison & Foerster LLP	9.171	6
16	Covington & Burling	9.153	18
17 (tie)	Foley Hoag LLP	9.146	19
17 (tie)	Howrey LLP	9.146	NR
18	Weil, Gotshal & Manges LLP	9.140	20
19	Saul Ewing LLP	9.135	NR
20	Arent Fox PLLC	9.107	NR

Top three in pro bono

1. Patterson Belknap Webb & Tyler LLP

How seriously does king-of-the-pro-bono-hill Patterson Belknap Webb & Tyler take its public service duties? So seriously that "pro bono work is basically mandatory." Indeed, every single attorney at this New York firm hit the boards on pro bono matters in 2006—the third year in a row the firm passed this benchmark. And no fewer than half a dozen Patterson Belknap attorneys have been honored for their commitment with the New York State Bar Association "President's Pro Bono Service Award." Interestingly, the leader in pro bono satisfaction does not count pro bono toward billable hours—but then again, "There is no minimum billables requirement for getting a bonus." So Patterson associates put their shoulder to the wheel, representing such clients as the Legal Aid Society, Brooklyn Legal Services Corp., and the Manhattan District Attorney's Office, to name just a few. This is Patterson Belknap's second year on top, after coming from nowhere to win Vault's 2007 pro bono crown.

© 2007 Vault Inc.

2. Hughes Hubbard & Reed LLP

At Hughes Hubbard & Reed, how many pro bono hours count toward billables? "How many you got?" answers one associate. It's this kind of attitude that causes the firm's associates here to place their firm at No. 2 for pro bono in this year's survey. Opinions differ, but the actual answer to the question of how many pro bono hours count toward billables is likely "200, but if you're working on something big, they'll count more than that." Any way you slice it, associates here have their hands full working in partnership with groups such as the National Congress of American Indians, Doctors of the World, Volunteer Lawyers for the Arts, the Legal Aid Society, and Human Rights First. One associate claims, "I work on as many pro bono cases as possible, within reason." With commitment like this, perhaps it's no surprise the firm won "The President's Pro Bono Service Award" from the New York State Bar Association in 2006.

3. Manatt, Phelps & Phillips, LLP

Manatt Phelps & Phillips moves proudly into the top three this year, but at least one associate seems to believe it deserves the No. 1 slot. "The commitment is second to none," says this insider. "Partners highly encourage it and lots of associates take advantage of the offerings." The firm's commitment is reflected in the number of pro bono hours that count toward billable hours requirements: all of them, without limit. As one insider marvels, "It's amazing." In fact, "Each attorney must bill a minimum of 20 or 30 hours a year" of pro bono. The firm has utilized those man hours in connection with a number of interesting projects. Manatt set up a legal services clinic to attend to the needs of homeless veterans, and the firm helps refugee children in Special Immigrant Juvenile Status cases. In addition, Manatt provided legal help to two public charter schools in lower-income parts of Los Angeles. Manatt has also set out to engage its non-legal employees in community service projects such as its "Manatt Empowering DC Youth" program. Impressive work indeed, and worthy of this year's winner's circle.

Visit the Vault Law Channel, the complete online resource for law careers, featuring firm profiles, message boards, the Vault Law Job Board, and more. **www.vault.com/law**

VAULT CAREER LIBRARY

69

OFFICE SPACE

Average score = 7.49

RANK	FIRM	SCORE	2007 RANK
1	Cleary, Gottlieb, Steen & Hamilton LLP	8.898	2
2	Lord Bissell & Brook	8.839	4
3	Winston & Strawn LLP	8.800	1
4	Dewey Ballantine	8.580	6
5	Thacher Profitt & Wood LLP	8.540	5
6	Finnegan, Henderson, Farabow, Garrett & Dunner LLP	8.476	3
7	Brown Rudnick Berlack Israels LLP	8.452	NR
8	Holland & Hart	8.370	NR
9	Jones Day	8.360	NR
10	Moore & Van Allen	8.333	NR
11	Powell Goldstein LLP	8.222	NR
12	King & Spalding LLP	8.159	NR
13	Dorsey & Whitney	8.141	NR
14	Dickstein Shapiro LLP	8.114	NR
15	Barnes & Thornburg	8.105	NR
16	Arnold & Porter LLP	8.102	16
17	Vinson & Elkins LLP	8.077	NR
18	Kramer Levin Naftalis & Frankel	8.076	11
19	Fenwick & West LLP	8.069	NR
20	Wilmer Culter Pickering Hale and Dorr LLP	8.046	NR

Top three in office space

1. Cleary Gottlieb Steen & Hamilton LLP

Thrice the runner-up, this year Cleary overcame the competition to top the best office space category. The firm's qualifications are solid: "beautiful," "comfortable," "modern" offices that some associates consider "the best law firm offices in Manhattan" and "the nicest space in D.C. that I've ever seen." It's a big plus that in New York, "every associate has large windows" because the most impressive feature of that particular office is the "unparalleled" view. "My office looks out on the harbor, the Statue of Liberty, Ellis Island, and the Verrazano Bridge," brags one junior associate. What's more, Cleary associates love that they don't have to share. From the top down, and around the globe, "Everyone has their own office (including summer associates and first-years)!" Associates say this is no mere happenstance, but rather a longstanding tradition. A New Yorker says "I don't know anyone who has ever shared an office here." When associates venture away from their desks, they are met with "fresh flowers," "excellent catering" and a "fantastic" art collection. "Our art is gallery- or even museum-class," gushes a corporate lawyer. A litigator attests, "there's a Warhol and a Rauschenberg in the hall outside my office."

© 2007 Vault Inc.

2. Lord, Bissell & Brook LLP

Thanks to a brand-new office space in Chicago, last year Lord Bissell & Brook came out of nowhere to place fourth in this category. It appears that associates' love for their new digs is no fleeting romance, as this year the firm advanced even further, placing No. 2 in office space. After 30 years on LaSalle Street, the firm is now in a new 51-story building at 111 South Wacker Drive, where it occupies 6 floors and 175,000 square feet. The Wacker Drive building is "brand new," "high-tech" and "well-designed for associate work." A Sacramento associate thinks he has it pretty good on the West Coast too, with a "full gym and swimming pool in the building. Can't beat that. " It remains to be seen how Lord Bissell's upcoming merger with Locke Liddell will affect the firm's office situation, but for now, associates like what they see.

3. Winston & Strawn LLP

By the numbers, Winston & Strawn may have come in third, but its associates still think the office space is No. 1—"best in the city, bar none." This source is unequivocal: "No one has better offices. Period." According to another, the firms has the "best decor/office space of any firm I have ever set foot in." Associates love the "swanky" and "spacious" offices. and that it's easy to tell that "art and architecture is a priority here," manifested by the "modern art, marble, and clean lines." There's so much marble, in fact, that Winston's space is affectionately dubbed the "heaven floor" and "red wine at parties makes the management nervous about stains." Associates are also in love with the "fabulous views," which include the Bay Bridge in San Francisco and Lake Michigan in Chicago. The only downside is that you'll have to wait nine months for a view of your own. Exterior offices are reserved for second-years and up.

Visit the Vault Law Channel, the complete online resource for law careers, featuring firm profiles, message boards, the Vault Law Job Board, and more. **www.vault.com/law**

VAULT CAREER LIBRARY   71

SELECTIVITY

Average score = 8.06

RANK	FIRM	SCORE	2007 RANK
1	Wachtell, Lipton, Rosen & Katz	9.844	4
2	Munger, Tolles & Olson LLP	9.482	1
3	Williams & Connolly LLP	9.370	2
4	Cravath, Swaine & Moore LLP	9.310	8
5	Irell & Manella LLP	9.283	5
6	Covington & Burling	9.250	6
7	Davis Polk & Wardwell	9.110	3
8	Sullivan & Cromwell LLP	9.011	12
9	Gibson, Dunn & Crutcher	8.929	7
10	Cleary, Gottlieb, Steen & Hamilton LLP	8.874	9
11	Wilmer Culter Pickering Hale and Dorr LLP	8.824	16
12	Skadden, Arps, Slate, Meagher & Flom LLP and Affiliates	8.724	17
13	Fish & Richardson P.C.	8.720	20
14	Debevoise & Plimpton LLP	8.718	14
15	Ropes & Gray LLP	8.679	11
16	Finnegan, Henderson, Farabow, Garrett & Dunner LLP	8.667	NR
17	Kirkland & Ellis	8.614	NR
18	Simpson Thacher & Bartlett LLP	8.613	13
19	Moore & Van Allen	8.590	NR
20	Latham & Watkins LLP	8.585	18

Top three in selectivity

1. Wachtell Lipton Rosen & Katz

Wachtell didn't become the most prestigious firm in the country by letting any less than the most elite grace its rolls. It is no hyperbole to say that it is "nearly impossible to get a job here." According to those who have been judged and found worthy, if you belong at Wachtell, "you know who you are." Although the firm "says it's getting less grade-focused," astronomical marks are still par for the course. "It seems like you need to have almost straight-As at one of a handful of top schools just to get an interview," observes a litigator. The bulk of that handful, and recent incoming classes, represents the Big Four, "Harvard, Yale, Columbia and NYU." A Duke graduate who overcame the statistics cautions, "If you're not from the above-named schools, I would say your chances are poor if you're not among the top 10 students in your class." Even with an ace transcript, there's still the crucial matter of fit. An interest in a particular niche practice or a compatible personality goes a long way, as does a willingness to work long and hard on it. "We do deals and want people who want to do deals, and who want to work hard," offers a midlevel. No kidding. At a firm known for its legendary hours as much as its stratospheric prestige, the best candidates are "clearly smart and committed." "You also have to be a passionate person," explains a junior associate, "or else you will never

© 2007 Vault Inc.

make it, and so we look for people who have clearly been passionate about something in their life." One last hurdle to clear: the Wachtellians have to like you in person. "You have to interview well. Remember, we'll be spending a lot of time together."

2. Munger, Tolles & Olson LLP

You might have done everything right—right school, right grades, right extracurriculars—but it still might not be enough to land a job at Munger, Tolles & Olson. "I've been astounded at some of the people we've turned away—Harvard, Yale and Stanford grads, law review, amazing grades, clerkships," reveals a midlevel. A Harvard grad reminds us, "This is always considered one of the hardest places to get hired, and rightly so." Last year, Munger topped our selectivity charts.

What makes Munger such a competitive gig? For starters, the firm has an unusual hiring process. "The whole firm participates in the decision of whether to accept a certain candidate," and "all decisions are by firmwide consensus," so "the scrutiny is intense." Candidates should take for granted that "grades are critical," and the most serious consideration/recruiting efforts are reserved for the "top of the class at top-tier law schools." Beyond that, Munger loves clerks. "Every single associate in the San Francisco office (and a large proportion of L.A. associates) has done a federal clerkship, most on the appellate level," reports a litigator. When building that Munger-friendly resume, "journal/law review, moot court and clerkship experience are major pluses," but not free passes. One litigator tells a story: "Firm lore has it that a Supreme Court clerk was once turned away after failing to impress lawyers during the interview process." There is some truth to this, according to a San Francisco associate: "We have dinged Supreme Court clerks because they seemed like they would not work well with others." Further positive traits the firm looks for include "articulate candidates with strong initiative."

3. Williams & Connolly LLP

A Georgetown grad at Williams & Connolly believes "it's a miracle I got hired. It's like getting into astronaut school." An apt difficulty comparison, but this firm is not in the market for space cadets. To be successful, candidates "have to be personable and instill confidence." "We look for driven, ambitious, gregarious, go-get-'em types," adds a litigator.

You thought Munger liked clerks? At Washington institution Williams & Connolly, many new hires are coming fresh off their appellate clerkship gigs. While a definite plus, the bounty of clerks is more a function of the type of lawyers the firm attracts, and not a hiring requirement. What is required is "to seem genuinely interested in the firm," and not just because it's prestigious—"you need to want to litigate." So "study up on the firm and be able to thoughtfully explain why you want to work here," advises a senior insider. Desire alone will not produce an offer, however; you still need the resume to back it up. "The firm hires almost entirely from the very best law schools, and almost entirely from the top of the class at these schools," observes a senior associate. And a second-year elaborates, "We have no specific GPA cutoff, but your grades must be extremely good to get a foot in the door."

Visit the Vault Law Channel, the complete online resource for law careers, featuring firm profiles, message boards, the Vault Law Job Board, and more. **www.vault.com/law**

VAULT CAREER LIBRARY

73

THE VAULT
DIVERSITY
RANKINGS

Diverse
by design.

For many, the bringing together of different elements into one perfect composition is the essence of good design. At Littler Mendelson, such an approach is an integral part of our practice. It takes diverse talents, ideas and perspectives to solve the problems posed by today's varied and multicultural workplaces. To learn more about Littler Mendelson, our practice, and our commitment to diversity, please visit us online at www.littler.com.

Littler's rankings in **The Vault Guide to the Top 100 Law Firms** 2008 Edition:

#2 – Best in Labor and Employment
#4 – Best in Overall Diversity
#4 – Best in Diversity—Minorities
#8 – Best in Diversity—GLBT
#11 – Best in Diversity—Women

LITTLER MENDELSON, P.C.
THE NATIONAL EMPLOYMENT & LABOR LAW FIRM®
630 Attorneys + 43 National Offices = One Integrated Solution
www.littler.com

Employment and Class Action Litigation | Unfair Competition and Trade Secrets | Employee Benefits | Labor Management Relations
HR Risk Management and Corporate Compliance | Workplace Safety | Global Migration

THE VAULT DIVERSITY RANKINGS

This is the sixth year that Vault has included a separate section for our diversity rankings. Associates were asked to rate their firm's commitment to diversity with respect to women, with respect to minorities and with respect to gays and lesbians. They were asked to think about efforts the firm has undertaken to recruit and/or retain female, minority or gay associates. To determine our Best 20 Law Firms for Diversity, we used a formula that weights the average score in all three categories equally.

Like our other rankings, the diversity rankings reflect the opinions and perceptions of associates.

Dickstein Shapiro—last year's No. 2—moved up a spot to No. 1 for Overall Diversity. Thus ends a five-year run by Morrison & Foerster as the top firm in the category.

Visit the Vault Law Channel, the complete online resource for law careers, featuring firm profiles, message boards, the Vault Law Job Board, and more. **www.vault.com/law**

VAULT CAREER LIBRARY

77

BEST 20 LAW FIRMS FOR DIVERSITY

Average score = 7.80

RANK	FIRM	SCORE	2007 RANK
1	Dickstein Shapiro LLP	9.190	2
2 (tie)	Hughes Hubbard & Reed LLP	8.921	4
2 (tie)	Freshfields Bruckhaus Deringer LLP	8.921	3
3	Carlton Fields	8.877	NR
4 (tie)	McKee Nelson LLP	8.869	9
4 (tie)	Littler Mendelson, PC	8.869	NR
5	Jenner & Block LLP	8.853	6
6	Morrison & Foerster LLP	8.829	1
7	Pillsbury Winthrop LLP	8.644	NR
8	Manatt, Phelps & Phillips, LLP	8.635	15
9	Davis Polk & Wardwell	8.633	NR
10	Weil, Gotshal & Manges LLP	8.625	NR
11	Patterson Belknap Webb & Tyler LLP	8.621	17
12	Fish & Richardson PC	8.618	NR
13	Cleary, Gottlieb, Steen & Hamilton LLP	8.610	7
14	Finnegan, Henderson, Farabow, Garrett & Dunner LLP	8.572	5
15	Paul, Weiss, Rifkind, Wharton & Garrison LLP	8.563	16
16	Sonnenschein Nath & Rosenthal LLP	8.560	NR
17	Quarles & Brady LLP	8.492	12
18	Foley Hoag LLP	8.451	NR
19	Arnold & Porter LLP	8.442	13
20	Sullivan & Cromwell LLP	8.428	NR

Top three in Diversity

1. Dickstein Shapiro LLP

Dickstein Shapiro caps off strong rankings in diversity with regard to both minorities and women by gaining this year's overall diversity crown, usurping former longtime diversity champ Morrison & Foerster. With its commitment to openness, Dickstein is trying hard to buck the generally discouraging trend among law firms. Insiders report that the firm is "committed to hiring and retaining minorities" and has been "aggressive" in recruiting women and welcoming them to leadership posts. In fact, out of three total firm offices, two are led by female managing partners. The inclusive attitude extends to gay and lesbian attorneys as well. "The firm is very welcoming of LGBT attorneys," insiders say. There are "gay partners [and] gay associates at all levels" and the latter are "well respected and often promoted to partner." For minorities, the "Diversity Counsel makes a strong effort in recruiting to hire diverse candidates." Notably, "Dickstein has a generous diverse lawyer scholarship program for law students who clerk at the firm." When it comes to inclusiveness, Dickstein Shapiro remains "a clear leader." Indeed, the results of our associate survey couldn't be any clearer: Dickstein is king of the hill.

© 2007 Vault Inc.

2. Hughes Hubbard & Reed

After just missing the top three last year, Hughes Hubbard & Reed leapfrogs into the No. 2 slot for overall diversity. The whole here is indeed greater than the sum of its parts—the firm bests its third place finishes in both diversity with regard to minorities and diversity with regard to women. According to associates, the firm has made a concerted effort to increase the diversity of its work force, and its openness is unquestionable. "The firm is extraordinarily welcoming of all people, including gays and lesbians," offers an associate. "There are many openly gay associates at the firm," some of which are "senior and very well-respected." The firm is reportedly good at retaining female associates, and remains focused on recruiting minorities as well. Hughes' "outstanding history" with regard to accepting women includes appointing the first woman chairperson of a New York law firm. Meanwhile, minorities are the sincere focus of Hughes recruiters, and "it is difficult to see what more the firm could be doing" in that regard.

3. Freshfields Bruckhaus Deringer LLP

Although it medaled in only one of our diversity categories—a third place finish in diversity with regard to GLBT diversity—Freshfields Bruckhaus Deringer nevertheless holds tight to its No. 3 slot in overall diversity. Insiders report that "almost half of the Freshfields New York City partners are women," and overall, there is "very much a cultural mix." An African-American source reports, "As an associate in the minority at this firm, I do not feel that my work opportunities are unequal to my professional counterparts." All in all, it's pretty simple: "Freshfields is diverse and race is not an issue." Additionally, "the firm is very welcoming to gays and lesbians," who enjoy domestic partner benefits. For mothers, there is a "generous maternity policy." Freshfields' "focus on diversity" inspires associates to claim "our firm provides equal opportunity for everyone."

Visit the Vault Law Channel, the complete online resource for law careers, featuring firm profiles, message boards, the Vault Law Job Board, and more. **www.vault.com/law**

VAULT CAREER LIBRARY   79

DIVERSITY ISSUES WITH RESPECT TO WOMEN

Average score = 7.86

RANK	FIRM	SCORE	2007 RANK
1	Carlton Fields	9.250	4
2	Dickstein Shapiro LLP	9.222	2
3	Hughes Hubbard & Reed LLP	9.130	3
4	Freshfields Bruckhaus Deringer LLP	8.920	5
5	Davis Polk & Wardwell	8.837	NR
6	Patton Boggs LLP	8.809	NR
7	Thompson Hine	8.800	NR
8	Sonnenschein Nath & Rosenthal LLP	8.787	NR
9	Pillsbury Winthrop LLP	8.771	NR
10	Quarles & Brady LLP	8.757	16
11	Littler Mendelson, PC	8.750	NR
12	Weil, Gotshal & Manges LLP	8.735	NR
13	Manatt, Phelps & Phillips, LLP	8.729	NR
14	McKee Nelson LLP	8.692	NR
15	Baker & Daniels	8.690	NR
16	Haynes and Boone	8.674	NR
17	Ballard Spahr Andrews & Ingersoll, LLP	8.633	NR
18	Jenner & Block LLP	8.600	NR
19	Fish & Richardson PC	8.491	NR
20	Morrison & Foerster LLP	8.470	6

Top three in diversity issues with respect to women

1. Carlton Fields

"The brightest women in the city"—that is how one insider describes Carlton Fields, which advances from fourth to first place this year in our rankings. The firm has strength in numbers: "There are a number of female attorneys (at least 30 percent, if not higher)," reports an associate. "The last six out of seven summer associate interviewees were all women, so the firm actively recruits female attorneys." Furthermore, the firm takes pains to accommodate the family demands of its employees, and is thus "among the very best in town in terms of alternative work schedules and supporting working mothers," boasts an associate. Happily, the partnership is not an old boy's club: "There are also a number of female partners to provide mentoring (at least one in every practice group I believe)," a male insider observes. In fact, one attorney declares that "women are in leadership positions as a matter of course."

© 2007 Vault Inc.

2. Dickstein Shapiro LLP

"As a woman, I am very pleased here," grins a Dickstein Shapiro associate, and perhaps this should come as no surprise. The "firm is run by women," one insider claims. The "managing partner is a woman and prominent partners in my practice area are all women," agrees this litigator. "Women partners head the L.A. and N.Y. offices!" exclaims another associate. Flexibility is also a Dickstein Shapiro selling point: "The firm is particularly open to alternative schedule arrangements, for example, for working mothers. Many women have recently been promoted to partner, including those on part-time schedules." There is apparently no stigma for part-timers here: "Women often take maternity leave beyond the three-month paid leave provided, and many women work part-time and are respected and treated the same as full-time associates." Furthermore, recruitment of women appears strong—"in the last few years, most of the first-year IP associates have been women."

3. Hughes Hubbard & Reed LLP

When women come to Hughes Hubbard & Reed, they stay—so say insiders at the No. 3 firm in our rankings. "The attrition rate doesn't seem to be as high for women as at peer firms," notes one associate. Another "sees more women staying here long-term than at other firms." Why do women stick around? "The firm is extremely flexible with regard to maternity leave and part-time schedules." In fact, "a part-time female attorney was just made partner." In addition, "HHR has many women partners," and "there are a lot of women in the upper ranks of the corporate department." To top things off, "The chairperson of our firm is a wonderful woman, Candace Beinecke, and she was the first woman chairperson of a New York law firm." All in all, says one Hughes Hubbard insider, "I couldn't be more pleased with the way the firm respects its women and minority associates."

Visit the Vault Law Channel, the complete online resource for law careers, featuring firm profiles, message boards, the Vault Law Job Board, and more. **www.vault.com/law**

VAULT CAREER LIBRARY

81

DIVERSITY ISSUES WITH RESPECT TO MINORITIES

Average score = 7.46

RANK	FIRM	SCORE	2007 RANK
1	Dickstein Shapiro LLP	9.073	2
2	Carlton Fields	8.800	6 (tie)
3	Hughes Hubbard & Reed LLP	8.739	1 (tie)
4	Littler Mendelson, PC	8.672	NR
5	Morrison & Foerster LLP	8.667	1 (tie)
6	McKee Nelson LLP	8.528	NR
7	Finnegan, Henderson, Farabow, Garrett & Dunner LLP	8.500	4
8	Thompson & Knight	8.480	NR
9	Manatt, Phelps & Phillips, LLP	8.467	NR
10	Fish & Richardson PC	8.464	NR
11	Freshfields Bruckhaus Deringer LLP	8.455	14
12	Paul, Weiss, Rifkind, Wharton & Garrison LLP	8.440	11
13	Jenner & Block LLP	8.414	18
14	Weil, Gotshal & Manges LLP	8.387	NR
15	Haynes and Boone	8.366	NR
16	Davis Polk & Wardwell	8.360	NR
17	Cleary, Gottlieb, Steen & Hamilton LLP	8.358	10
18	Fenwick & West LLP	8.333	NR
19	Pillsbury Winthrop LLP	8.287	NR
20	Patterson Belknap Webb & Tyler LLP	8.269	17

Top three in diversity issues with respect to minorities

1. Dickstein Shapiro LLP

Firms, take note: Put diversity on top of your agenda, and you could find yourself at the top of the diversity rankings, as did Dickstein Shapiro. "The hiring, retention, promotion and mentoring of diverse attorneys is a top priority," offers one source. "The firm is focused and prides itself on pushing for diversity within the firm." Specifically, "We have a Diversity Counsel in our office and the firm makes a strong effort in recruiting to hire diverse candidates. I think our office is diverse across the board." Indeed, "The firm absolutely goes out of its way to recruit diverse candidates and provide a welcoming environment for them. For example, Dickstein has a generous diverse lawyer scholarship program for diverse law students who clerk at the firm." And we can't overlook the paper trail. "The constant barrage of e-mails relating to the diversity committee, diversity hiring and diversity events are proof enough of the firm's commitment."

© 2007 Vault Inc.

2. Carlton Fields

Carlton Fields attacks the diversity question by throwing its support behind programs and affinity groups. This firm "is actively seeking to increase its diversity with respect to minorities, and there have been specific firmwide initiatives on this matter." For example, the firm sports "a standing diversity committee," and the Tampa office helps to sponsor a "Carlton Fields Diversity Fellow." And that's not all: "Additionally, we have the Minority Lawyer Network (MLN), which is one of two affinity groups at the firm (the other being the Women's Initiative Network). The MLN is an opportunity for minority lawyers to get to know each other, network, market the firm's diversity to corporate counsel and raise issues that need to be addressed within the firm." Clearly, diversity "is extremely important to the firm."

3. Hughes Hubbard & Reed LLP

Though Hughes Hubbard & Reed lost its first place slot this year, it stays in the top three. According to one Hughes Hubbard associate, "With regard to both women and minorities, the law firm is extremely open." HHR's diversity efforts have been years in the making: "The firm has, for some years, made a priority of hiring and retaining minorities It is difficult to see what more the firm could be doing." Another insider also speaks to the firm's history with regard to diversity: "The firm has an outstanding history of acceptance of women and minorities, and that carries on today."

Visit the Vault Law Channel, the complete online resource for law careers, featuring firm profiles, message boards, the Vault Law Job Board, and more. **www.vault.com/law**

VAULT CAREER LIBRARY

83

DIVERSITY ISSUES WITH RESPECT TO GAYS AND LESBIANS

Average score = 8.12

RANK	FIRM	SCORE	2007 RANK
1	Jenner & Block LLP	9.544	3
2	Irell & Manella LLP	9.478	1
3	Freshfields Bruckhaus Deringer LLP	9.389	5
4	McKee Nelson LLP	9.387	4
5	Morrison & Foerster LLP	9.351	2
6	Dickstein Shapiro LLP	9.274	8
7	Cleary, Gottlieb, Steen & Hamilton LLP	9.234	6
8	Littler Mendelson, PC	9.184	NR
9	Patterson Belknap Webb & Tyler LLP	9.160	9
10	Foley Hoag LLP	9.087	14
11	Sullivan & Cromwell LLP	9.006	19 (tie)
12	Arent Fox PLLC	8.969	12
13	Fish & Richardson PC	8.899	NR
14	Paul, Weiss, Rifkind, Wharton & Garrison LLP	8.897	11
15	Hughes Hubbard & Reed LLP	8.895	NR
16	Alston & Bird	8.893	NR
17	Arnold & Porter LLP	8.889	19 (tie)
18	Pillsbury Winthrop LLP	8.874	NR
19	Crowell & Moring LLP	8.857	NR
20	LeBoeuf, Lamb, Greene & MacRae, LLP	8.829	NR

Top three in diversity issues with respect to gays and lesbians

1. Jenner & Block LLP

After a four-year hiatus, Jenner & Block finally regains its No. 1 position in diversity issues with respect to gays and lesbians. The firm's stellar ranking lends credence to one associate's boast that "Jenner is the leading firm in the country for gays and lesbians." Indeed, associates at Jenner & Block enthusiastically agree that this firm "is probably one of the most welcoming, receptive and effective in achieving diversity for gays and lesbians." This insider is unequivocal: "I am gay and Jenner is absolutely the best place I could be. There is a great support system and everyone is incredibly open and friendly." Furthermore, Jenner & Block "is on the forefront of many GLBT issues." Another associate gushes, "I have never seen a firm more accepting of gays and lesbians. In this regard, as in many others, Jenner is top-notch." With such a great atmosphere, perhaps it is no surprise that "there is a huge number of openly gay men and women here at Jenner." As one insider cutely sums up, "Jenner is great to the gays."

© 2007 Vault Inc.

2. Irell & Manella LLP

His firm's second-place finish notwithstanding, one Irell associate believes, "I doubt there is another firm that is more welcoming to gays and lesbians." Indeed, Irell & Manella is so accepting of the GLBT set that one associate reports, "I have heard it said that attorneys come to Irell to come out." The firm, of course, puts its money where its mouth is: "Domestic partner benefits are available as much as at any firm in America." According to a (mostly) pleased associate, "This is an exceptionally great place to work if you're gay (unless you want to spend time with your significant other)." The practically unanimous verdict? Irell is "traditionally a gay-friendly firm and remains so."

3. Freshfields Bruckhaus Deringer LLP

Freshfields Bruckhaus Deringer comes back out with this year's third-place finish in GLBT diversity. According to this insider, the firm "is very welcoming to gays and lesbians and there are and have been several gays and lesbians who are openly out, including partners." At Freshfields, being "openly out" is pretty normal. "I am aware of several colleagues who are comfortable being openly gay in the firm," reports an associate. The firm "provides domestic partner benefits" and likewise "equal opportunity for everyone." Overall, "sexual orientation is not an issue," explains another. As one insider somewhat mischievously puts it: "Several partners are openly gay, just as several others are openly hetero."

Visit the Vault Law Channel, the complete online resource for law careers, featuring firm profiles, message boards, the Vault Law Job Board, and more. **www.vault.com/law**

VAULT CAREER LIBRARY   85

When you're deciding where to practice law, one place to consider is the courthouse.

Did you know there are lititgation partners who have never thanked and excused a juror, made an opening statement, or asked to approach a witness? It's more common than you'd imagine.

Quinn Emanuel is the largest firm in the country devoted exclusively to business litigation, but what really sets us apart is that we try cases. Lots of them. To verdict and judgement. And because we win, clients bring us more of the cases they know will go to trial.

So while there are many fine litigation departments, people see Quinn Emanuel as something more - trial lawyers.

How do you see yourself?

quinn emanuel trial lawyers

Los Angeles   New York   San Francisco   Silicon Valley

THE VAULT 100:
FIRMS 1 - 50

1

PRESTIGE
RANKING

Wachtell, Lipton, Rosen & Katz

51 West 52nd Street
New York, NY 10019-6150
Phone: (212) 403-1000
www.wlrk.com

LOCATION

New York, NY

MAJOR DEPARTMENTS & PRACTICES

Antitrust
Corporate
Executive Compensation & Benefits
Litigation
Real Estate
Restructuring & Finance
Tax
Trusts & Estates

THE STATS

No. of attorneys: 199
No. of offices: 1
Summer associate offers: 19 out of 19 (2006)
Executive Committee Co-Chairs: Edward D. Herlihy &
    Daniel A. Neff
Executive Partner: Meyer G. Koplow
Hiring Partner: By committee

BASE SALARY (2007)

1st year: $165,000
Summer associate: $3,100/week

UPPERS

- "Unmatched" responsibility
- "Unbeatable pay scale"
- "Close working relationship" with partners

DOWNERS

- "Hours, hours and hours"
- "Sleep deprivation"
- "The pressure is unrelenting"

NOTABLE PERKS

- "Hard to enumerate. The firm is extremely generous across the board"
- "Pantry on every floor with unlimited soda and cookies"
- "Fully subsidized health care"
- Frozen yogurt machine

THE BUZZ
WHAT ATTORNEYS AT OTHER FIRMS ARE SAYING ABOUT THIS FIRM

- "Far and away the gold standard"
- "I'll never see you again, but well done"
- "Star of the transactional world"
- "Only for those who live for law"

© 2007 Vault Inc.

RANKING RECAP

Regional Rankings
#1 - New York

Practice Area Rankings
#1 - Corporate
#1 - Mergers & Acquisitions
#6 - Litigation
#7 - Securities
#8 - Bankruptcy
#8 - Tax

Partner Rankings
#1 - Mergers & Acquisitions
#2 - Overall Prestige
#2 - Corporate

Quality of Life
#1 - Pay
#1 - Selectivity
#5 - Associate/Partner Relationships

EMPLOYMENT CONTACT

Ms. Elizabeth F. Breslow
Director of Recruiting & Legal Personnel
Phone: (212) 403-1334
Fax: (212) 403-2000
E-mail: efbreslow@wlrk.com

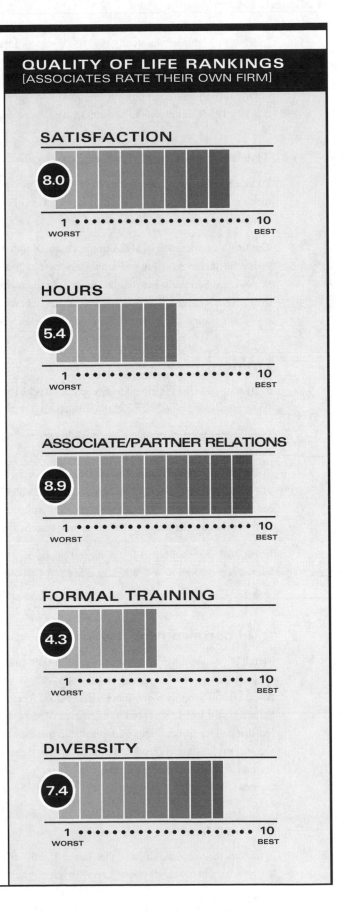

QUALITY OF LIFE RANKINGS
[ASSOCIATES RATE THEIR OWN FIRM]

SATISFACTION
8.0
1 WORST .... 10 BEST

HOURS
5.4
1 WORST .... 10 BEST

ASSOCIATE/PARTNER RELATIONS
8.9
1 WORST .... 10 BEST

FORMAL TRAINING
4.3
1 WORST .... 10 BEST

DIVERSITY
7.4
1 WORST .... 10 BEST

Visit the Vault Law Channel, the complete online resource for law careers, featuring firm profiles, message boards, the Vault Law Job Board and more. **www.vault.com/law**

VAULT CAREER LIBRARY   89

THE SCOOP

In New York, this is what really matters: Wachtell, Lipton, Rosen & Katz posts the highest earnings-per-partner in the world. In 2006, that figure averaged $3.79 million. Q: How doth one make such silly money? A: Close a chunk of the world's major mergers and acquisitions, handle high-stakes antitrust and shareholder litigation, restructure well-known (and sometimes notorious) corporations, engineer multibillion-dollar real estate deals, and just be all-around badass. Of course, it helps that there are only 195 Wachtellians to share cake with.

The princes and the poison pill

Founded in 1965 by four princes of NYU's law review—Herbert Wachtell, Martin Lipton, Leonard Rosen and George Katz— the firm still operates from a single Manhattan office. Forty years later, Wachtell and Lipton remain partners, while Rosen continues to serve his firm as counsel.

The firm's prominence in M&A might be traced to Marty Lipton's 1982 invention of the "poison pill." The innovative defense to hostile takeovers allows shareholders of a targeted company to acquire additional shares cheaply, rendering a potential takeover prohibitively expensive. Such innovation extended to the firm's billing philosophy. In the 1980s, it became the first firm to link its M&A fees to an end result, and its own effectiveness in achieving that result. The fee structure Wachtell devised is now the aspiration for law firms doing big-ticket M&A work.

Eminent in M&A

In 2006, total value for global M&A activity reached almost $4 trillion (beating the previous record, set in 2000, by $500 billion). Wachtell advised on 62 completed transactions, for an aggregate of $397.287 billion.

Listing all of Wachtell's major deals would seriously strain our word count, but here's a sampler platter: The firm has represented Goldman Sachs in the $22 billion privatization of Kinder Morgan; Apollo and Texas Pacific Group in their $28 billion acquisition of Harrah's; ConocoPhillips in its $34 billion purchase of Burlington Resources; MBNA in its $35 billion acquisition by Bank of America; Caremark in its $22 billion merger with CVS and its $25 billion unsolicited bid by Express Scripts; the New York Stock Exchange during its $10 billion merger with Euronext and its transition to a publicly traded company; SUPERVALU in its $17.4 billion acquisition of Albertsons; and Lucent Technologies in its $14 billion combination with Alcatel.

In 2000, the firm took part in the largest public offering in U.S. history—the $10.6 billion IPO of AT&T Wireless. Four years later, it represented AT&T Wireless in its $40.7 billion acquisition by Cingular, the largest cash acquisition in history. In 2005, Wachtell represented Lazard, privately held for 157 years, as the bank welcomed a whole new family of shareholders.

It all came out in the wash

March 2006 saw a weighty victory for the firm's antitrust corps, as the Justice Department finally approved Whirlpool's $1.79 billion takeover of Wachtell client Maytag. After an eight-month investigation into antitrust issues, the government decided that despite the new entity's dominant market share (critics put the number at 70 percent), rival companies GE, Electrolux, LG and Samsung still had some room to maneuver. The new firm will now rank as the world's largest appliance maker. In its report, the Justice Department determined that the transaction was not likely to risk consumer welfare, due to strong competition and the cost savings a merger would engender. The department theorized that any effort by the new company to raise prices on its washers and dryers "likely would be unsuccessful," as at least five other companies are well established in the United States. At the news, Maytag's stock leapt for joy, climbing 25 percent.

At long last

A mammoth insurance dispute that began shortly after the September 11 terrorist attacks is now over. World Trade Center leaseholder and Wachtell client Larry Silverstein held 99-year leases on the WTC starting in 2001, and was in the process of

© 2007 Vault Inc.

finalizing the terms of property insurance policies that provided for $3.54 billion in coverage on a "per occurrence" basis. In 2001, Silverstein filed suit against over 20 of his insurers, arguing that the events of September 11th were in fact two separate occurrences, and that insurers were obligated under the terms of his policies to recompense him accordingly. A Southern District of New York court disagreed as to three of the insurers, finding that they had bound coverage under a particular insurance form that defined what happened as a single occurrence. Silverstein appealed the District Court's grant of summary judgment for these three insurers, but the U.S. Second Circuit Court of Appeals upheld the district court's order in 2003. Two jury trials were held in 2004 to determine the coverage obligations of the remaining insurers. In the first trial, several of the insurers were found to have bound coverage on the same "one occurrence" form. But in the second trial, the jury found that, under the forms used by all of the remaining insurers, the parties intended to treat what happened as two occurrences. In October 2006, the Second Circuit affirmed both jury verdicts. In total, Wachtell's litigators succeeded in obtaining over $4.6 billion of insurance coverage for Silverstein. Then, in November 2006—in what some observers have called the most complex real estate deal in human history— the firm's real estate department successfully negotiated a new master development agreement for the World Trade Center site with the Port Authority and other government representatives. To top it off, in May 2007, all outstanding disputes with the insurers were finally settled, with the insurers agreeing to pay more than 97 percent of the total amount of coverage available.

In the past, Wachtell litigators have defended the board of Walt Disney Corp. against dissident members of the Disney family; counseled the New York Stock Exchange in litigation against nonconforming minority exchange members; and represented Sirius Satellite Radio in litigation brought by CBS Radio regarding the hiring of shock jock Howard Stern.

Give 'em an inch, they'll take a golf course

It looks like the city council of North Hills, New York, could use a little grammar review—particularly the proper usage of possessive structures and with especial focus on the word "mine." After the controversial 2005 Supreme Court decision in Kelo v. New London, which ruled that a city may exercise its right of eminent domain for private development purposes, the Long Island township felt emboldened to condemn the exclusive Deepdale golf club, in an attempt to convert the club into a public golf course open to all North Hills residents. The club is ranked 36th in *Golf Connoisseur*'s 100 most prestigious golf courses, and counts among its past and present members President Eisenhower, the Duke of Windsor, Sean Connery, Michael Bloomberg and Sidney Poitier. Deepdale came out swingin' (sorry) and turned to Wachtell litigators. Two separate lawsuits were filed, a multipronged public relations campaign was mounted, and the result was that the New York State Legislature adopted a statute stopping the Village's efforts dead in its tracks. Deepdale members can now putt in peace.

Tommy's guns

When fashion house Tommy Hilfiger came under investigation by the Manhattan U.S. Attorney's Office, it too sought out Wachtell litigators. After a yearlong criminal tax investigation, the Manhattan U.S. Attorney's Office announced on August 10, 2005, that it had determined criminal tax charges were not warranted and entered into a non-prosecution agreement with Hilfiger's American subsidiary, in which the company agreed to pay $18.1 million in back taxes and interest. The retailer has moved to dismiss a shareholder suit filed after the U.S. attorney's investigation was disclosed, using the argument that charges were never filed against the chain. The company was acquired in spring 2006 by private equity fund Apax Partners Worldwide. Other firms that Wachtell has represented in shareholder and derivative actions include Sears, Morgan Stanley, Bausch & Lomb, Avon and Lazard.

Achtung! Beware the pouncing hedge fund

In March 2006, firm founder Martin Lipton provided corporate clients with a Hedge Fund Attack Response Checklist, which addressed his concerns about a Court of Appeals decision to vacate SEC hedge fund registration requirements. In the three-page memo, Lipton contended that an increase in hedge fund "activism" poses a threat to corporate America, and outlined step-by-step preventive measures that could protect a "target's ability to control its own destiny."

Visit the Vault Law Channel, the complete online resource for law careers, featuring firm profiles, message boards, the Vault Law Job Board and more. www.vault.com/law

VAULT CAREER LIBRARY

91

Though the memo engendered some snickering in legal blogs, such zealous customer care could explain why Lipton headed *New York Magazine*'s 2006 list of the most influential lawyers in New York. The magazine described Lipton as "still the city's most sought-after deal lawyer at 74, with potential rivals for the title either less active (Skadden's Joseph Flom) or still behind him (Sullivan & Cromwell's Rodgin Cohen)."

Black sheep and cheeky monkeys

Among younger BigLaw associates, the firm's most famous alumnus may be its most irreverent. In 2005, the identity of David Lat, creator of the *Underneath Their Robes* legal blog (and now editor of the equally impudent and compulsively readable *Abovethelaw.com*) was revealed in a *New Yorker* article. The unmasked avenger is a former federal prosecutor and ex-Wachtell associate; starting in 2000, Lat spent two-and-a-half years at the firm, working on commercial litigation and M&A.

GETTING HIRED

We're not worthy ... oh, wait, yes we are

If you belong at Wachtell, as one insider puts it, "You know who you are." This is, after all, the single most selective law firm in the nation. Recruiters will come to you if you're at Boalt, Chicago, Columbia, Harvard, Howard, NYU, Penn, Stanford, UCLA, UTexas or Yale. Muses one third-year, "There's no specific GPA cutoff, but if you're not from the above-named schools, I would say your chances are poor if you're not among the top-10 students in your class." Stellar grades are merely the minimum expected, and while a finance background is certainly helpful, "the key is not coming across as someone who wants to be a politico or an appellate litigator or something other than what we do. We do deals and want people who want to do deals. And who want to work hard." Stresses a colleague, "You also have to be a passionate person, or else you will never make it here, and so we look for people who have clearly been passionate about something in their life." The firm will even go so far as "attempting to dissuade candidates, in an effort to weed out those who are not interested in hard work." They'll work you, all right, but Wachtell on your resume can color an entire career. "It is nearly impossible to get a job here," says one blunt fourth-year. "If you get one, take it."

OUR SURVEY SAYS

The ethic is work

"Culture? Who has time for culture?" sighs one insider. "Asking to describe our firm's culture socially or politically is a little silly," grumbles a seasoned source. "Our culture is about one thing: work." Well, no surprises there—Wachtell's round-the-clock productivity is legendary. Still, one newbie clarifies, "Since the firm is generally viewed as being aggressive, people tend to think that the people who work here are also aggressive. In fact, most of the people are incredibly pleasant to work with. This isn't to necessarily say that I want to spend time with them socially, but the time we spend in the office is incredibly productive and sometimes even enjoyable." Indeed, this crew may be all about the deal, but the vast majority rate Wachtell a pleasant, collaborative, informal environment. Defends one first-year, "Everyone is working very hard all the time, but contrary to rumors, people do talk about their personal lives and engage in 'normal conversation' while at work." Agrees a midlevel litigator, "The firm is intensely focused on providing the highest level services possible, but the atmosphere is a remarkable mixture of intensity and informality—people are driven ... but are also very friendly, laid-back and informal with one another, including in associate/partner relationships." A third-year sees it differently, describing the scene as "very professional and rarely boring, but also distant and isolated. This is not a particularly friendly environment."

Bittersweet musings from a midlevel: "I love the work and generally like the people. I get enormous responsibility and am generally pleased that I came here. But I'm trying to get out because this job consumes everything else in your life. It's an interesting job but unsustainable as a career." It didn't take this first-year long to cotton on, either—"Headline-making, exciting

© 2007 Vault Inc.

and intellectually stimulating work, but it never stops!" One long-termer has this to say: "It sounds trite, but if you're going to be a lawyer, there is simply no other place to do it."

Just like the girl with the curl

The hours, smiles one second-year ruefully, are "just like the girl with the curl. When they're bad, they're very, very bad." Colleagues testify that "we pretty much work 24/7/365" and "our hours are brutal. This is a firm where working past 1 a.m. is the norm, where all-nighters are frequent, and where the reaction to your closing a deal after a week of all-nighters is 'Good, now you have time to work all weekend on another deal.'" For one first-year, "A typical Wachtell workday begins at 10 a.m. and ends at around 10 p.m. Typically, you get one full day off per week, as there is always something to do before the next week starts. However, the good thing about the firm is that if you're up for a closing, which normally requires two to three days of not sleeping, or sleeping in the firm somewhere, you typically get the next day off to recover." A midlevel estimates that "rough spots can last for two to three weeks."

"I find that the sheer sense of accomplishment, the commitment of everyone else in the firm, and the engaging nature of the work usually make the long hours a source of satisfaction rather than a detraction," shares one third-year. "That said, there were a couple crunch periods in the last year (which was a crushingly busy one in the M&A market) where it got very hard to keep going." And sometimes ellipses speak louder than words: "The hours can be grueling, but if you want to be the best …"

You catch more flies with money

Just the facts, ma'am: "We get paid vastly more than associates at any other large law firm in the world. The firm has made very clear its absolute commitment to keeping it that way." Yup, acknowledges one junior associate, "The compensation is in a class of its own." A senior colleague agrees that compensation is indeed "light years ahead of the next best firm. Totally different scale." Salary is the highest out the gate, and "bonuses are determined by partnership vote and are loosely correlated to the performance of the firm in that year. Generally, bonuses are at a single percentage of salary for all classes, but that does vary at times."

A senior level insists that all the zeros on that bonus check are relative: "We make a lot of money compared to other lawyers, but that is not our peer group. We should make more relative to the partners given the value that we add." Nods a litigator, "The partners have been doing even better vis-à-vis their peers at other firms than the associates have." And don't forget, adds one midlevel, Wachtell "needs to continue paying much more than other firms to retain us, or else we will go to other firms, hedge funds, etc."

Some are more equal than others

All animals are created equal, but some animals are more equal than others. At Wachtell, "we are all partners (except in pay and title)." With Wachtell's low headcount and massive deal load, associates are simply too involved and too integral to be mere underlings. All levels report remarkably collegial and equitable relations with higher-ups. Marvels one litigator, who still counts his blessings, "Partners are incredibly respectful of associates and their opinions on legal issues. This also extends to the social realm—partners and associates forge very close relationships and many associates here count many of the partners as friends." What he said, agrees a colleague: "Very close contact, friendly and human interaction, open and amicable discussions." A first-year gushes: "From day one, everyone treats you as a full member of the team. I am very confident that there are few associates at other firms at my level that have the relationships with the partners that I do. That's what makes us who we are." A litigator makes it clear that "one of the firm's most admirable characteristics is an attitude of intellectual democracy. If a summer associate has a good idea, a senior partner will listen." But make no mistake, "This is not a 'friendly' firm and people are blunt if they're unhappy about something. And there are some jerks. Generally, though, the partners are nice people and they highly value associates' contributions. I feel like I get a lot of respect from partners here and I appreciate that." One corporate does say that while he was generally very pleased with his relationships to higher-ups, he "knocked down the score a bit because of the

Visit the Vault Law Channel, the complete online resource for law careers, featuring firm profiles, message boards, the Vault Law Job Board and more. **www.vault.com/law**

VAULT CAREER LIBRARY   93

total lack of information about firmwide decisions. I don't think this is a big deal to most associates here, but it might be nice to have some insight into how the firm is run."

CliffsNotes

"There's a quote I often use, from the movie *The Big Kahuna*. A nervous neophyte says to his seasoned colleague, 'I guess I'll just have to jump in the water and see if I can swim.' The response: 'I don't think you understand the situation. We're about to throw you off a cliff and see if you can fly.'" And that's Wachtell training, "Very much learning by doing, and incredibly effective in getting you up the learning curve—and flying—in a matter of days, or even hours." Agrees a third-year, "You do the deals yourself, with oversight and insight from partners. You learn quickly here and rapidly become a self-sufficient and capable lawyer." And even though such early responsibility can be daunting, "I've never had a partner who wasn't willing to take time to walk me through the problem, the concerns and the possible solutions." Even better, says a litigator, Wachtell "makes sure associates don't do the same thing over and over but instead develop a wider skill set." Formal training is scant, but "even when there's a seminar, I almost never have time to attend," notes one second-year. "What's formal training?" asks a senior-level. Scoffs one long-termer, "If you leave here less than an amazing lawyer, then there's something wrong with you. We learn on the job and we are always on the job. We learn from the best."

Pepperidge Farm and pantyhose

If heaven has perks, five bucks says Wachtell's are better. Associates tell us that "the firm in general doesn't blink an eye at paying any expense that makes it easier for us to do work." Evangelizes one second-year, "If it's a perk, we have it. Free car rides home after 8; free meals (breakfast, lunch and dinner); free drinks and Pepperidge Farm cookies; moving expenses; gym membership; free health care and dental; fly first-class everywhere; pretty much any piece of equipment or junk for your office you could think to request; the best support staff; frozen yogurt machine; six kinds of diet soda; extra socks and pantyhose should you need them; greeting cards if you miss your mom's birthday." A perk in itself is the "general feeling that the firm trusts you in use of the generous support services—[there is] no overbearing accounting department." From another source, "I could go on and on about [perks], and the fact that they handle taxes for nannies and maids, but the truth is the best perk is that you are treated like a grown-up, perhaps even a partner, from the second you walk in the door."

© 2007 Vault Inc.

"If you leave here less than an amazing lawyer, there's something wrong with you."

— *Wachtell, Lipton, Rosen & Katz associate*

Visit the Vault Law Channel, the complete online resource for law careers, featuring firm profiles, message boards, the Vault Law Job Board and more. **www.vault.com/law**

VAULT CAREER LIBRARY

95

2

PRESTIGE
RANKING

Cravath, Swaine & Moore LLP

Worldwide Plaza
825 Eighth Avenue
New York, NY 10019-7475
Phone: (212) 474-1000
www.cravath.com

LOCATIONS

New York, NY (HQ)
London

MAJOR DEPARTMENTS & PRACTICES

Corporate
Executive Compensation & Benefits
Litigation
Tax
Trusts & Estates

THE STATS

No. of attorneys: 458
No. of offices: 2
Summer associate offers: 102 out of 102 (2006)
Presiding Partner: Evan R. Chesler
Hiring Partners:
  Corporate: William V. Fogg
  Litigation: Michael T. Reynolds

BASE SALARY (2007)

1st year: $160,000
2nd year: $170,000
3rd year: $185,000
4th year: $210.000
5th year: $230,000
6th year: $250,000
7th year: $265,000
Summer associate: $3,077/week

UPPERS

• Stellar reputation
• "Unparalleled" formal training
• "Top-of-the-market pay

DOWNERS

• "It is possible to get stuck on an uninteresting case for a long time"
• "Unpredictable hours"
• "Associates share offices for much too long"

NOTABLE PERKS

• "Everyone gets a laptop"
• Subsidized Equinox memberships
• "Tickets to the Met at about 75% off!!"
• "The cafeteria on the 48th floor is fantastic (at least as cafeterias go)"

THE BUZZ
WHAT ATTORNEYS AT OTHER FIRMS ARE SAYING ABOUT THIS FIRM

• "The definition of prestige"
• "Pretentious, but rightfully so"
• "If you can make it there, you can make it anywhere"
• "Night of the Living Dead"

© 2007 Vault Inc.

RANKING RECAP

Regional Rankings
#2 - New York

Practice Area Rankings
#2 - Corporate
#2 - Securities
#3 - Litigation
#3 - Tax
#4 - Mergers & Acquisitions

Partner Rankings
#1 - Overall Prestige
#1 - Corporate
#3 - Mergers & Acquisitions
#3 (tie) - Tax
#3 - Securities
#4 - Litigation

Quality of Life
#4 - Selectivity
#8 - Formal Training

EMPLOYMENT CONTACT

Ms. Lisa A. Kalen
Associate Director of Legal Personnel & Recruiting
Phone: (212) 474-3215
Fax: (212) 474-3225
E-mail: lkalen@cravath.com

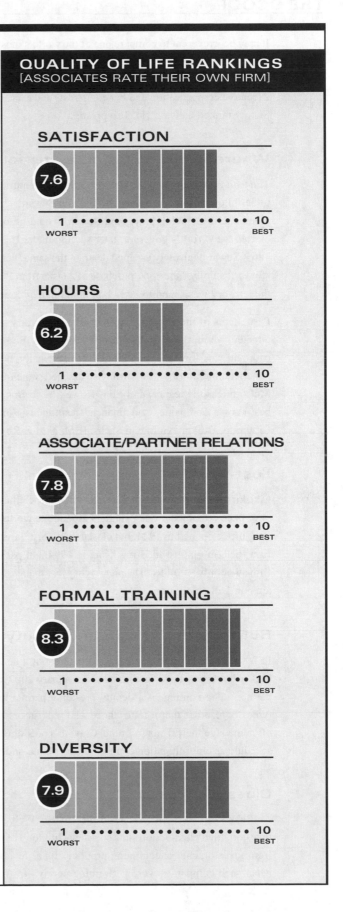

QUALITY OF LIFE RANKINGS
[ASSOCIATES RATE THEIR OWN FIRM]

SATISFACTION
7.6
1 WORST — 10 BEST

HOURS
6.2
1 WORST — 10 BEST

ASSOCIATE/PARTNER RELATIONS
7.8
1 WORST — 10 BEST

FORMAL TRAINING
8.3
1 WORST — 10 BEST

DIVERSITY
7.9
1 WORST — 10 BEST

Visit the Vault Law Channel, the complete online resource for law careers, featuring firm profiles, message boards, the Vault Law Job Board and more. **www.vault.com/law**

VAULT CAREER LIBRARY   97

THE SCOOP

It may be irreverent to compare one of the world's most respected law firms with a beloved West Coast burger chain, but Cravath, Swaine & Moore and In-N-Out Burger have essentially the same formula for success: streamline the menu, then execute very, very well. Though the firm has only two offices, 458 lawyers and a concentrated list of services (litigation, tax, corporate, executive compensation and benefits, trusts and estates), it has the unqualified esteem of its legal peers—in 2007, Vault's Partner Survey ranked Cravath No. 1 in prestige.

Where ignorance is bliss, 'tis folly to be wise

The firm now known as Cravath is nearly two centuries old. In 1819, Richard Blatchford opened a law office in New York City, to be followed four years later by William Seward's branch office in Auburn, N.Y. Blatchford and Seward were also founding members of the Whig party, and Seward would go on to hold office in both state and national government. In 1838, he was elected New York's governor, later serving in the U.S. Senate. President Lincoln appointed him Secretary of State in 1861; in 1865, Seward narrowly escaped death in the same plot that took Lincoln's life. High school students will best remember him for "Seward's Folly," the 1867 purchase of Alaska from Russia for some $7.2 million. Well, Seward redefined "folly": 30 years later, the territory was found to be rich in gold (and, of course, oil).

Past clients of the firm include several 19th century greats, such as *New York Tribune* publisher and famed abolitionist Horace Greeley, whom the firm defended in a libel suit filed by *Last of the Mohicans* author James Fenimore Cooper (Greeley lost the case and was forced to pay $200. Of the penalty, he would shrug, "We rather like the idea of being so generous a patron of American literature.") The firm also assisted some of the era's greatest inventors: Samuel Morse (the electric telegraph), Cyrus McCormick (the reaper) and Elias Howe (the sewing machine). Modern clients include governments, and some of the world's best-known companies and financial institutions: American Express, Bristol-Myers Squibb, JPMorgan Chase, Credit Suisse, Citigroup, DuPont, Goldman Sachs, IBM, Nestlé, Royal Dutch Shell, Time Warner, Unilever and Xerox.

Lost satellites

Like kindred spirit Wachtell, Cravath's dominance illustrates that it isn't necessary to have a shop on every corner. Though there have been attempts to open shutters around the world, the firm's propensity is to pull the plug on less profitable operations. A D.C. office opened in 1924, but closed in 1946; a Paris office existed from 1927 until 1934, and again from 1963 until 1981. The firm tried an outpost in Hong Kong in 1994, but packed up less than a decade later. A London office, established in 1973, is Cravath's only satellite. Despite having just the single foreign office, approximately one-fifth of the firm's 100-largest clients are non-U.S. institutions.

But they didn't shoot no deputy

In 2006, Cravath announced the appointment of a new deputy presiding partner, C. Allen Parker of the firm's corporate group. Parker became second-in-command in January 2007, at the same time Evan R. Chesler succeeded Robert D. Joffe as presiding partner. The naming of a deputy presiding partner at this early juncture is an unusual step for conservative Cravath, which typically reserves that role for those who will succeed the presiding partner within the year. However, while other firm leaders often manage their firms full time, Cravath's presiding partners still maintain robust practices. Chesler is no exception; his busy schedule as chief litigation counsel to several major clients has necessitated some backup in firm administration.

Class dismissed

As Babs sang so mellifluously in the 1980s, "We've got nothing to be guilty of," so sang Cravath's client, Citigroup, when investors filed class-action suits accusing Citigroup of offering secret incentives to brokers and advisors, extracting improper fees from investors and encouraging propriety funds to invest in companies that were also their investment banking clients—even when such companies were performing poorly. In August 2006, a federal judge dismissed the class-action claim, stating that

© 2007 Vault Inc.

plaintiffs did not have a right to file actions against funds in which they had no shares, and that claims could not proceed because the plaintiffs had failed to plead loss causation.

Trials and tribulations

In May 2006, the firm's litigation department was able to give client Merck some good news, when a shareholder derivatives action against the pharma giant was dismissed due to lapses in protocol. A U.S. District judge found that the plaintiffs failed to comply with a federal court rule that required shareholders to demand corrective action prior to filing a suit. The derivatives action alleged that Merck scientists were aware for nearly a decade that their drug Vioxx might have cardiovascular risks, but that the company breached its fiduciary duties and intentionally marketed it while making no mention of the negative research. The dismissal of the shareholder suit should come as some consolation to Merck—it's feeling the sting of a recent $13.5 million New Jersey verdict over Vioxx, and there are some 11,500 product viability cases pending round the nation.

In September 2006, a class-action suit against Cravath-represented QUALCOMM was also dismissed. The suit, brought by Broadcom Corporation, asserted that QUALCOMM engaged in anticompetitive conduct regarding technology and chipsets for its cell phones.

Of late the firm is figuring in the tribulations of famed tech attorney Larry Sonsini (of Wilson, Sonsini, Goodrich & Rosati). In September 2006, Cravath served as Sonsini's counsel during a House Committee hearing on the Hewlett-Packard wiretapping scandal. Sonsini, HP's corporate counsel, was questioned as to whether he had prior knowledge of events, in particular the company's use of "pretexting" to gather information on a possible company leak.

Double double, trademarks and trouble

Cravath's IP litigation team is also back in court, defending handbag manufacturer Dooney & Bourke in the ongoing trademark infringement case brought by luxury retailer Louis Vuitton Malletier. Louis Vuitton accused Dooney & Bourke of ripping off a multicolored, modernized version of its ubiquitous logo, which the company had developed in 2002. In 2004, a lower court dismissed the case, finding that in a side-by-side comparison, there was no likelihood that the Dooney bag could logically be mistaken for the Vuitton. However, in a July 2006 reversal of the lower court's ruling, a 2nd Circuit Court of Appeals found that side-by-side comparisons of items, "in lieu of focusing on actual market conditions," are not enough to determine whether a trademark has been infringed upon; the ultimate issue remains the likelihood of consumer confusion, and "the law requires only confusing similarity, not identity."

Personal shopper

In 2006, Cravath's M&A prowess continued unimpeded. In October, Cravath managed affairs for Royal Dutch Shell in its C$7.7 billion acquisition of Shell Canada, and assisted wireless operator Crown Castle in its $5.8 billion purchase of Global Signal. In June 2006, the firm counseled Johnson & Johnson in its $16.6 billion acquisition of Pfizer's consumer health care business, and in January 2006, the firm handled gambling technology company GTECH Holdings' $4.8 billion sale to Italian gambling company Lottomatica. Cravath also figured in longtime client IBM's 2006 buying spree, drafting the acquisition deals for such companies as Internet Security Systems ($1.3 billion), FileNet ($1.6 billion), Palisades Technology Partners and Webify Solutions.

Financing powerhouse

The firm's securities practice is rolling in transactions as well. Cravath participated in over $400 billion worth of securities offerings in the past two years. Clients included First Solar (in a $450 million initial public offering), Credit Suisse and Citigroup (the firm represented the bans when they were the initial purchasers of $6 billion worth of debt issue by Freescale Semiconductor) and Goldman Sachs and Morgan Stanley (which the firm represented in connection with the innovative €4 billion initial global offering of KKR Private Equity Investors, L.P.). The firm also represented Goldman Sachs, Credit Suisse, JPMorgan, Morgan Stanley and other underwriters in connection with Warner Chilcott's $1 billion initial public offering.

Visit the Vault Law Channel, the complete online resource for law careers, featuring firm profiles, message boards, the Vault Law Job Board and more. **www.vault.com/law**

VAULT CAREER LIBRARY   99

The firm's commercial banking practice had another outstanding year. Cravath represented JPMorgan Chase in connection with $1.385 billion of credit facilities to finance Apollo Partners' acquisition of the GE Advanced Materials business, and $3.865 billion of credit facilities for Golden Gate Private Equity's acquisition of SSA Global Technologies and Systems Union Group plc. Cravath was involved in the largest LBO ever completed in the technology sector, representing (who else?) Citigroup and Credit Suisse as the arrangers of $4.25 billion in multicurrency credit facilities that were used to finance part of the $17.6 billion acquisition of Freescale Semiconductor by a consortium of private equity funds led by The Blackstone Group.

GETTING HIRED

No time limits, no dithering

While Cravath has a clear preference for candidates coming from the Ivies, the firm can be open to (slightly) lower-ranked schools as well. "This place is lousy with Harvard and Columbia people, but they pursue people from the top 15 to 20 schools, plus Fordham," says a junior New York litigator. "Other than the usual high credentials, I think the firm looks for confident, street-smart types who are able to figure things out quickly without having every little issue explained to them." Or, as a less generous insider puts it, "I think Cravath is willing to hire from too many schools … but I think if you are the best in your class, and have a great personality, you have a shot here." Then again, an associate who graduated from a top law school reports, "I can't figure out how we choose people because everyone I interview is way more qualified than I am."

As for the specifics of the interview process itself, one recent interviewee advises applicants to expect a "full-day interview process, where you meet with four or five partners and at least three associates." She adds, "Interviews are not planned in advance so you can't research the people interviewing you. There is no time limit for individual interviews—an interview with any given partner could last for 15 minutes or two hours." Unlike some firms, candidates should not assume anything: "We ding people on callbacks all the time," one insider cautions. When it comes to making a decision, the firm does not dither: "The offer usually comes on the spot at the end of the day."

OUR SURVEY SAYS

"I'll learn more in two years than most associates will learn in six"

On the whole, Cravath associates report a high degree of satisfaction with their jobs. "I enjoy working here much more than I thought I would," reports a junior tax attorney. "I feel like I am respected for my intelligence and challenged just enough." Or, as a junior litigator puts it, "It is a stressful environment due to the constant pressure to produce perfect work product befitting the self-described 'best law firm in the world.' But the challenge is what I signed up for—I'll learn more in two years than most associates will learn in six, and I'll learn how to do things the right way." Another enthusiastic junior associate says, "I have terrific mentors here, both on a personal and professional level. These relationships have contributed a great deal to my high level of satisfaction with, and sense of loyalty to, my firm." A corporate attorney adds, "As a junior associate, I've been surprised at the amount of substantive work that I've been entrusted to complete." There are, of course, a couple of grumblers, but this is about as bad as their complaints get: "The work is very unpredictable, as with most firms, and feedback is difficult to come by."

Associates call Cravath "collegial," "respectful," "formal," "polite," "friendly," and "not very social." As one junior associate reports, "I don't know how much socializing goes on since people work such long and unpredictable hours. But I think the firm has an agreeable, cordial environment." Another insider advises, "Other than having lunch with other associates and attending summer events, I rarely socialize with my colleagues, but I have a friendly relationship with many of them. The standard of work is quite high, but people are overall less intense than I expected." And a junior litigator adds, "Social events are there if you want it. First-years get together every Friday, teams go to drinks every one to three months."

© 2007 Vault Inc.

Specific v. General

Individually, Cravath partners garner strong praise, for the most part. Institutionally, well, the firm has some work to do. "My partners are definitely a perfect 10—and while I do not think they are the exception, they are probably not the rule, either," advises a tax expert. However, a banking associate warns, "Obviously, it varies greatly depending on the partner, and there are some partners who are really great to associates, but there is a general feeling of ambivalence on the part of partners towards associates" An ERISA specialist adds, "Relations are generally formal and polite but not overly friendly. Associates do not participate in firmwide decisions." A midlevel corporate associate voices a similar opinion, though a little more plaintively: "Associates are never allowed to participate in firmwide decisions. It is the partners and then everyone else."

Associates universally agree that Cravath's formal training program ranks among the firm's strongest suits. "Almost daily there is some area of training being offered by partners who practice in the field—typically these sessions are useful 'in the trenches'," says a junior tax attorney. A junior litigator adds, "The firm offers many training programs, all conducted by partners. They take it fairly seriously." Of course, there is such a thing as too much of a good thing. A corporate associate opines, with respect to the entirely optional training program, "There's probably more formal training than we need."

Guidance must be sought

The firm also excels at informal training, associates report, though finding a mentor can requires an associate to be a little more assertive. "Mentoring is easily available if you look for it, and most people take the time to explain what you need to be doing and why," says a junior associate. Another junior associate reports, "It probably varies widely by partner, but the firm puts a lot of effort into making sure associates are given early responsibility and substantive, varied experience in their area." A junior M&A expert adds, "Most partners, and most senior associates, take the time to provide instruction when the matter at hand provides the opportunity." In late 2006, the firm announced a formal mentoring program to supplement the mentoring that already takes place at the practice group or team level.

Associates call the firm's compensation merely "market" rate, with a huge carrot at the end of the partner-track stick: "Our partners are the second-highest compensated of any major law firm in the city." The typical complaints about pay sound something like, "Especially given the recent increases, I have no complaint about what I make. It's certainly more than I could make doing anything else. But I still can't get over how damn expensive the New York City area is. Not the firm's fault I guess." Or this: "I'm probably being overpaid—but could be paid slightly more." Or this: "Compensation is great. But, there's always Wachtell."

"The only thing that prevents this job from being perfect"

The firm's hours are relatively flexible—there's no billable hours requirement!—but it's a stretch to call them reasonable, Cravath's associates report. "Face time is unimportant," according to a corporate specialist. "The only thing that matters is getting your work done." A midlevel warns, however, that the hours-burden only increases. "I work all the time," he sighs. "Cravath does not hire laterals, so there are not a lot of 'senior' associates still around." As a pragmatist puts it, "It is what it is. I had a two-month period where I billed 80 to 90 hours a week, and for the last month it has been more like 40 to 45. I think it's unrealistic not to expect long hours when you get paid as much as we do." A corporate finance expert adds, "The only thing that prevents this job from being perfect is that it demands too many hours. But that's true for almost any big NYC firm. I at least have found that I'm not working long hours on busy work or at someone else's command. I have integral roles in my deals so I'm almost always working on substantive tasks that I know I need to complete in order to keep a deal on track."

Associates consider Cravath's pro bono policy very liberal, or perhaps even libertarian—the firm pays little attention to how much, or how little, effort is devoted to such issues, associates say. "Nobody cares about how many hours you're billing unless you're extremely low" advises a junior associate. Or as another newbie puts it, one can devote "unlimited" time towards pro bono work, as the cases are "treated like any other client matter." A junior banking associate says the firm's hands-off attitude implicitly discourages volunteer work. "All of the hours count, but I know very few associates who have done any pro bono (at least very few compared to my first-year friends at other law firms). I think it should be a requirement." A junior litigator agrees,

Visit the Vault Law Channel, the complete online resource for law careers, featuring firm profiles, message boards, the Vault Law Job Board and more. **www.vault.com/law**

VAULT CAREER LIBRARY   **101**

adding, "There is no hours requirement, so it's not really applicable. Commitment to pro bono really varies (like everything here) by partner."

Don't like to share

Many associates call their offices surprisingly drab and worn, though the sentiment appears to be far from universal. They also complain about having to share offices. "The office generally is very nice, but the associates' offices are cramped, especially for associates who share offices," complains a junior associate. A third-year says, "Some of the double offices are too small and should only be singles." And a litigator adds, "Associates share offices for much too long for a firm like Cravath—generally two years." As a second-year (less gently) puts it, Cravath has "pretty nice offices, but first- and second-year associates have to share, which sucks." On the other hand, a first-year reports, "The offices here are excellent—based on my memories of interviewing elsewhere, I would say much larger than average—with giant picture windows. Mine overlook the Hudson and Central Park." A midlevel adds, "Generally after the first year or two, associates have their own offices. Views are quite good. Some of the offices are starting to look a little worn, but are generally kept up well."

© 2007 Vault Inc.

"My partners are definitely a perfect 10."

— Cravath, Swain & Moore associate

Visit the Vault Law Channel, the complete online resource for law careers, featuring firm profiles, message boards, the Vault Law Job Board and more. **www.vault.com/law**

VAULT CAREER LIBRARY

103

3

PRESTIGE RANKING

Sullivan & Cromwell LLP

125 Broad Street
New York, NY 10004
Phone: (212) 558-4000
www.sullcrom.com

LOCATIONS

New York, NY (HQ)
Los Angeles, CA
Palo Alto, CA
Washington, DC
Beijing
Frankfurt
Hong Kong
London
Melbourne
Paris
Sydney
Tokyo

MAJOR DEPARTMENTS & PRACTICES

Estates & Personal
General Practice/Corporate
Litigation
Tax

THE STATS

No. of attorneys: 646
No. of offices: 12
Summer associate offers: 121 out of 121 (2006)
Managing Partner: H. Rodgin Cohen
Hiring Partner: Keith A. Pagnani

BASE SALARY (2007)

1st year: $160,000
Summer associate: approximately $3,077/week

UPPERS

- Top-flight pay and benefits
- Significant opportunities for junior lawyers
- Superb training program

DOWNERS

- Recent negative publicity
- Long hours
- Occasional grunt work

NOTABLE PERKS

- On-site emergency day care
- Associate entertainment allowance
- Weekly lunches with Rodge Cohen, the firm's chairman
- On-site gym

THE BUZZ
WHAT ATTORNEYS AT OTHER FIRMS ARE SAYING ABOUT THIS FIRM

- "Classy, sophisticated, smart, meritocracy"
- "Stuffy"
- "Charney bad rap is undeserved"
- "Too old school"

© 2007 Vault Inc.

RANKING RECAP

Regional Rankings

#5 - New York

Practice Area Rankings

#1 - Securities

#4 - Tax

#5 - Corporate

#5 - Mergers & Acquisitions

Partner Rankings

#2 - Securities

#3 - Overall Prestige

#3 (tie) - Tax

#4 - Corporate

Quality of Life

#8 - Selectivity

Diversity

#11 - Diversity with Respect to GLBT

#20 - Overall Diversity

EMPLOYMENT CONTACT

Ms. Patricia J. Morrissy

Phone: (212) 558-3518

Fax: (212) 558-3588

E-mail: morrissyp@sullcrom.com

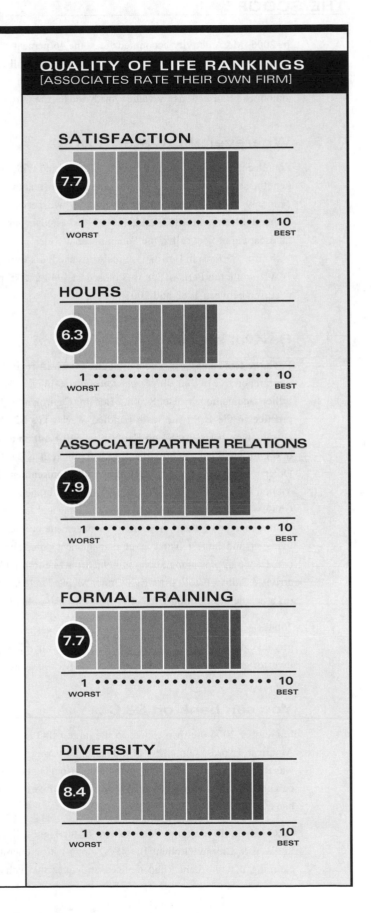

QUALITY OF LIFE RANKINGS
[ASSOCIATES RATE THEIR OWN FIRM]

SATISFACTION

7.7   1 WORST ... 10 BEST

HOURS

6.3   1 WORST ... 10 BEST

ASSOCIATE/PARTNER RELATIONS

7.9   1 WORST ... 10 BEST

FORMAL TRAINING

7.7   1 WORST ... 10 BEST

DIVERSITY

8.4   1 WORST ... 10 BEST

Visit the Vault Law Channel, the complete online resource for law careers, featuring firm profiles, message boards, the Vault Law Job Board and more. www.vault.com/law

VAULT CAREER LIBRARY   105

THE SCOOP

In 2006, M&A activity accounted for some 46 percent of global investment banking fee revenue. And when the bankers are happy, everyone's happy, right?—especially those Wall Street firms that head up the class in corporate work. In 2006 S&C continued to lead the M&A league tables, and was ranked first by Bloomberg among law firms representing principals in announced transactions by value worldwide for the third consecutive year.

Wherever the water floweth

Founded in 1879 by Algernon Sydney Sullivan and William Nelson Cromwell, Sullivan & Cromwell has the distinction of having kept the same name for 125 years. Equally consistent over the last century is the firm's impact on the domestic and international economy. No exaggeration: as the courtier whispering in J.P. Morgan's ear, the firm weighed in on the formation of Edison General Electric in 1882, and, in 1901, assisted in the creation of U.S. Steel. It also helped secure financing for a little landscaping project called the Panama Canal. Such international involvement led to some of the first international offices for a U.S. firm. Offices in Berlin, Buenos Aires and Paris were opened in the early 20th century (the Berlin office was closed prior to WWII while the Paris office was closed in 1940 and reopened in 1962), and further expansion in Europe, Australia and Asia occurred between 1983 and 2001.

Revival season

Pitch the tents and corral the neighbors, the M&A revival's come to town. Sullivan & Cromwell scooped its share of the pie, working on five of The Wall Street Journal's 10-biggest deals for 2006. The firm served as AT&T's legal advisor during its $72.7 billion acquisition by BellSouth. Led by Chairman H. Rodgin Cohen, S&C remained the preeminent financial institutions practice in the U.S.: the team handled Wachovia's $25.5 billion offer for Golden West Financial and the representation of Birmingham-based AmSouth Bank in its $10.4 billion merger with hometown neighbor Regions Financial in May 2006. The new entity will have approximately $140 billion in assets and operate 2,000 branches across 16 Midwestern and Southern states. Other recent activities for the firm include representing The Bank of New York in both its $16.5 billion pending merger with Mellon Financial and its $3.1 billion sale of its branch network to, and acquisition of the corporate trust business of JPMorgan Chase—creating the largest securities servicing and asset management firm globally—and representing Merrill Lynch in the $9.8 billion merger of their investment management business, MLIM, with BlackRock—creating the largest U.S. fixed-income manager and largest listed asset management company in the world. Across the pond, the firm challenges Magic Circle dominance by upstaging such eminent firms as Freshfields Bruckhaus Deringer, and Slaughter and May. One Euro deal that arriviste Sullivan stole from right under Magic Circle noses: representing Spanish energy company Endesa in its battle to fend off a hostile multibillion-euro offer from Spanish utility Gas Natural.

2006 was also a record year for private equity investment. M&A head James Morphy and his merry band featured in the largest private equity deal of the year, the $21.2 billion buyout of hospital chain HCA. In July 2006, the Tennessee chain agreed to an investor group's takeover bid. In 2005, HCA's 190 hospitals generated $25 billion in revenue.

You can bank on S&C ...

In October 2006 the firm shared in the largest IPO in history. Sullivan & Cromwell represented Goldman Sachs, Allianz and American Express in the IPO of Industrial and Commercial Bank of China (ICBC), China's largest state-owned bank. The IPO was the first concurrent listing on the Hong Kong and Chinese exchanges; on the first day of trading, ICBC's share price rose 15 percent, valuing the bank at $139 billion. U.S. investors ponied up $21.9 billion, helping make ICBC the world's fifth-largest bank.

S&C helped its banking clients to two of the biggest litigation victories scored by the defense bar in recent years. In 2002, Sullivan & Cromwell client Barclays, along with numerous other banks, was sued in a class action by Enron's shareholders, claiming that the banks had devised structures that helped Enron hide losses. The shareholders, led by the University of

© 2007 Vault Inc.

California, were seeking some $40 billion, and alleged that Barclays and the others had helped Enron mask its financial woes. In September 2006, Andrew Fastow, former CFO of Enron, gave testimony (in an attempt to get a reduced criminal sentence), and tried to implicate the banks in the energy company's meltdown. As the case headed toward trial several banks (including JPMorgan Chase, Citibank and CIBC) settled for a record-breaking $6.6 billion. Barclays and certain others refused to settle. That strategy paid off. In July 2006, the judge dismissed the case against Barclays, ruling that no valid legal claim had been stated against the bank. Although the court later allowed plaintiffs to re-plead against Barclays, an appeal filed by Barclays and two other banks was decided in favor of Barclays and the others. Just three weeks before the trial was scheduled to begin, the Fifth Circuit Court of Appeals ruled that the trial could not go forward because the claims were legally baseless.

One more to take to the bank

S&C recorded another big win for the 55 investment banks named as defendants in the mammoth IPO securities litigation. Shareholders in 310 dot-com companies that undertook IPOs during the tech boom of 1999-2000 filed more than 1,000 lawsuits in 2001, alleging that the investment banks and dot-com companies pumped up the companies' stock prices in a giant manipulation scheme. As defense counsel to Goldman Sachs and liaison counsel to the investment banks, an S&C team led by partner Vince DiBlasi coordinated the complex defense. In a landmark decision in December 2006, the federal court of appeals in New York ruled that the litigation could not proceed as a class action and imposed rigorous standards on future securities class-action suits. In the related IPO antitrust litigation, in which plaintiffs contend that the defendants' same conduct during the dot-com boom constituted violations of the federal and state antitrust laws, the U.S. Supreme Court recently handed down an important victory to S&C and its client Goldman Sachs and the other investment banks, blocking plaintiffs' antitrust claims. The Supreme Court's June 2007 decision reversed the Second Circuit's previous ruling, and agreed with the underwriters that "to allow an antitrust lawsuit would threaten serious harm to the efficient functioning of the securities markets."

Time to play ball!

Sullivan & Cromwell is representing the New York Giants and their owners, the Mara and Tisch families, in their ongoing $1.5 billion joint venture development with the ownership of the New York Jets of a new football stadium and related sports and retail developments in the New Jersey Meadowlands. This partnership represents the first time that the owning families of two National Football League teams will jointly finance and build a stadium to be the home for two NFL teams, the Giants and the Jets. S&C, led by Vice Chairman Joseph Shenker and partner Ivan Deutsch in New York, acted as counsel to the Giants and the team's co-owners, the Mara and Tisch families, in negotiating the ground lease and related development and lease agreements with the State of New Jersey, in negotiating the Jets joint venture arrangement, and in related agreements with the NFL.

Why, thank you kindly

Your magnolia-mouthed Southern granny had it right: you catch more flies with honey. Espousing this philosophy, in February 2006 Sullivan & Cromwell partners viewed a slide presentation on the care and emotional feeding of associates. Among other suggestions, the presentation recommended that partners acknowledge associates' efforts with such odd phrases as "thank you" and "good work." Attrition rates at most big New York firms, including S&C, ran high in 2005, but this trend has been reversed at S&C in 2006, perhaps in part because of the firm's morale-boosting efforts, which include weekly associate lunches with Rodge Cohen, the firm's chairman; $1,000 entertainment budgets for senior associates to entertain more junior associates; and greater attention to the performance review process, including the introduction of 360° reviews, where associates provide feedback on working with partners and senior associates to the practice group heads. Recent "town halls" with firm leaders have focused on enhancing internal communications with associates about firm finances and strategy.

Sources at the firm say that the wealth is shared with associates in places where other firms will nickel and dime, at significant cost to the firm. In fact, S&C is at the top of the industry when it comes to support staff levels on a per-lawyer basis. For example, the ratio of lawyer to secretary is low in an industry where many firms have three or four (and sometimes more) attorneys per secretary. At S&C, it's generally 2:1. Another example: unlike most of its peer firms, S&C offers a $100,000 down-payment loan assistance program to associates. Other seemingly little things add up—S&C associates don't have to worry about fiddling around punching client matter numbers into copy machines or telephones, or sharing printers—"Clients don't choose S&C because they're worried about the cost of a copy" as a firm source puts it.

Doing unto others

On average, Sullivan & Cromwell lawyers devote nearly 40,000 hours a year to pro bono and public service. Recent pro bono activities for the firm include staffing a legal clinic for New York Presbyterian Hospital, which provides estate planning for AIDS victims, and representing the Council of New York in its efforts to enforce the Equal Benefits Law, which prohibits discrimination against and provides for marital benefits to same-sex domestic partners. Pro bono highlights for the firm include landmark case Bivens v. Six Unknown Agents, the 1971 Supreme Court case that established damages for illegal searches; working with The Legal Aid Society to prevent prisoner abuse and force system reform at Rikers Island; and obtaining political asylum for a Cote d'Ivoire citizen who was arrested and tortured due to his political beliefs and Djioula Muslim ethnicity.

It's not quite boiling bunnies ...

... but when Aaron Charney boiled his hard drive in February 2007, legal gawkers scratched their heads. In a case obsessively covered by cyberscribes (for a full rundown, we recommend David Lat's *Abovethelaw.com*, as well as *The New York Observer*'s terrific coverage), ex-S&C associate Charney sued his former firm in January 2007, alleging harassment and discrimination. Soon after, blawgs were ablaze with reports of Charney and S&C talking settlement—and then Charney went and poured a kettle on his hard drive. And bashed it to bits with a hammer. (What do you deduce from this, Watson?) As of this writing, Sullivan v. Charney shows no signs of coming to a conclusion anytime soon ... nor becoming any less of a legal soap opera.

GETTING HIRED

Top school not required, but top grades are

Snobbery is not the norm at Sullivan & Cromwell. "Sullivan & Cromwell will take anyone, from any school, if they can prove they are smart enough to hack it and willing to work," reports one attorney. "My class was tremendously diverse with lawyers from Yale to Rutgers to New York Law School." "Although most Sullivan & Cromwell lawyers are from the elite law schools, [the firm] definitely considers top candidates from other law schools," agrees a source. Of course, the lower your school is in the ranking, the better your credentials need be. "If you attended a 'lesser' school, you will have to be in the top two or three in your class," warns a contact. "But if you demonstrate that you are capable, it doesn't matter where you come from." Another insider notes that "if you aren't from a top school, journal experience is basically a must." Additionally, while grades are important regardless of where you're from, "strong character and a history of achievement can override a lousy semester."

Once you're past the grade hurdle, try to present yourself well. The firm "stresses collegiality and fitting in, which simply means no jerks or potential jerks." "Once you're at the office, it's entirely a question of personality," concurs a source. "We like friendly, non-pretentious people who exhibit good judgment." Don't expect a cakewalk, either. "The interviewers go behind pat questions and actually grill applicants on substantive issues," advises a lawyer. "During the interview process, we look for people who are sharp—people who can discuss an issue intelligently and will come across well to clients," notes a contact.

OUR SURVEY SAYS

The mixed bag

For the most part, Sullivan & Cromwell associates are happy with life at their firm, though there are numerous qualifiers. "Sullivan & Cromwell provides the best work, great colleagues, more responsibility and experience than I could get at any other place," brags a midlevel associate. "What more could one want? Well, maybe a little more sleep, but what other big firm lawyer wouldn't want that?" "I like my work. I like the people I work with. I like the level of responsibility I have," says one source. "I don't like how much work I have." Indeed, the workload is an issue. "The work is stimulating and the people generally are nice," states a senior associate. "The workload is heavy however, and the unpredictability of the workload can be wearing." There are other quirks. "Associates are given much responsibility and client interaction from the beginning, which is challenging and rewarding," notes one attorney. "On the negative side, there is not much consideration given to associates' personal life."

There seems to be a correlation between associate satisfaction and the amount of responsibility given to associates. "The amount of responsibility you get as a junior lawyer is unique among other comparable firms," says one source. "As a third-year associate, I am often the senior associate on a deal and I often find myself negotiating against partners at other firms." Another insider shares a similar experience, reporting that "I'm a second-year negotiating deals against sixth-years at other firms." The firm's system helps perpetuate that. "The assigning partners take great effort to take into account associates' preference in terms of assignment," says a corporate lawyer. "Most associates can get the work they want to do in the long term."

Pros through and through

Sullivan & Cromwell associates use one adjective to describe themselves and their firm: professional. "I would describe the firm's culture as very professional," says a midlevel. "But this doesn't mean stuffy or formal. It means everybody's eye is on making the finished work product as perfect as it can be." "The culture can only be described as professional," echoes another source. "Everyone respects one another and enjoys working together." The word keeps popping up. "Sullivan & Cromwell is a very professional environment," reports another associate. "Everyone with whom I've interacted has been cordial and respectful." Some are pleasantly surprised at how pleasant professional can be. "The firm's culture is definitely not what I anticipated—and I mean that in the best way possible," says a junior associate. "The Currier & Ives décor incorrectly reinforces an impression that Sullivan & Cromwell remains a 'white shoe' firm. While undoubtedly there are traditions that the firm is attempting to maintain—as an aside, why wouldn't you want to hold onto some customs with a history as remarkable as Sullivan & Cromwell's—there is no doubt that S&C has long ago developed into much more than a 'white shoe' firm." That "much more" appears to embody teamwork from the top all the way down. "The firm's culture could not be better," gushes a contact. "The partners are friendly, always available and helpful. The other associates are smart and interesting people. The support staff is amazing—loyal and hardworking people."

The professional culture extends beyond your tenure at S&C—the firm really big deals the alumni network. There's an annual reception for alumni, a web site for alumni, and other events involving alumni that keep it all in the family. Which helps when you're looking to network with heavy hitters.

Money bags

Associates "can't complain about salary" because "Sullivan & Cromwell appears to pay higher than other firms for senior classes." There's less jockeying for bonuses, too, as they are "lock-step, although there are grumbling from associates about wanting to go to some non-hours-based merit system." "I make gobs of money," says an international associate. "Base salary doesn't begin to tell the story: benefits, COLA, currency adjustment, bonus, etc." American lawyers get lots of extras, too. "In addition to our salaries and bonuses being top of the market, we are also very well taken care of otherwise—good health benefits, gym membership, free food in the kitchens, etc.," reports one junior associate. "I love that we do not have to meet a minimum billable requirement to get a bonus," states another attorney. "I think it is much fairer and allows you to spend the time you need on assignments without inflating or taking on stupid work just to churn time." Some associates are philosophical about all the money being thrown around. "If I'm looking at my compensation from an outside point of view and comparing compensation for people my age in different jobs, I should be very satisfied," says one lawyer. "But being in this profession and looking at the profits per lawyer that this firm generates, I should be paid more."

Visit the Vault Law Channel, the complete online resource for law careers, featuring firm profiles, message boards, the Vault Law Job Board and more. www.vault.com/law

VAULT CAREER LIBRARY   109

Killer hours

Like working? You'll love Sullivan & Cromwell. "The hours are great, if by 'great' you mean that you love billing a minimum of 12 hours a day for at least six days a week," says one lawyer who lays on the sarcasm pretty thick. "The hours are brutal," complains another insider. "And with the newer BlackBerry culture, you are truly on call 24/7/365 and expected to respond." At least you won't have to be around for no good reason. "While we are expected to work until the job is done, there is no emphasis on face time here, and there are no minimum billable requirements," says a source. "So while that means that there have certainly been some weekends and late nights, there are also days when I am able to stroll out the door at 5 p.m. because I have finished my work." Weekends are common. "Every weekend my goal is to not come into the office on the weekend," says a litigator, who estimates that "I hit that goal about 50 percent of the time." Maybe the worst part: no one seems to know when they'll be required to put in weekend hours (or overtime, etc.). "The lack of predictability is irritating, but this must be common to all Wall Street law firms," observes a lawyer. According to firm sources, the average associate client billable annual total is 1,950.

Back to school

Learning the ropes is not a problem at Sullivan & Cromwell. "The firm has a solid two-week orientation program and offers several first-year and second-year associate courses during the year in addition to other trainings. The firm has emphasized the importance of the training programs and has asked for feedback from junior associates to revamp the orientation to make it more useful." The feedback we're getting is virtually entirely positive. "The firm really has quite an excellent training program in place," notes a source. "Classes are offered every week to help you brush up on, or learn for the first time, various topics." "The formal training programs—especially the hands-on litigation training programs—are top notch," says a litigator. The training opportunities make it easy for lawyers to fulfill their CLE requirements. "The formal training program is amazing. Within days of arriving at the firm, I fulfilled all my New York CLE requirements," reports one junior associate.

According to the firm, "S&C subscribes to the belief that associates learn best by doing. The premise is that associates will become better lawyers and develop more quickly if exposed to substantive legal work and given real responsibilities at junior levels. To make this model work, S&C relies on a culture of knowledge sharing and 'on-the-job' training across all levels."

The efforts are there

Insiders say Sullivan & Cromwell is doing its best when it comes to diversity, with some improved results. The firm has instituted several programs aimed at retention of top women and minority associates as they climb through the ranks for consideration as partner. The recent installation of a former Assistant United States Attorney (and Sullivan & Cromwell alum) as its director of diversity, is deemed a great success as the firm has begun to see these efforts bear fruit. For example, although Sullivan & Cromwell and peer firms have about the same percentage of women partners (13 to 14 percent), since 2000 the firm has made 16 women partners, representing 23 percent of the overall partners made during such period. "The female partners are a force within the firm, and generally believe that recruiting and retaining other women is very important," says one attorney. "There are women's cocktail parties and monthly coffee breaks to discuss issues for mothers at the firm, [and] there are a lot of female associates and a number of highly visible female partners," notes another contact. "But there seem to be very few female partners who had kids as associates, and there's still a sense that most female associates leave after they have kids." Additionally, "there are a ton of diversity programs aimed at recruiting and retaining minorities." And in the broader sense, even the partnership is surprisingly diverse, with 56 law schools and 34 countries represented among them, and where 61 percent of the partners are under the age of 50. In fact, 48 percent of the partners were named in the past 10 years. Still, "the number of minority lawyers is alarmingly low, but I don't really understand why because I think there is a huge effort put into recruiting minority lawyers and into making them feel comfortable at the firm." Also, the firm is "one of the most welcoming workplaces for gays and lesbians imaginable," according to one associate. "I know a lot of openly gay associates and partners, and have never seen anyone take issue with their sexuality," reports a lawyer. "That being said, there is always the possibility of some bad apples in the bunch that I have not had exposure to." With regard to the Charney lawsuit, a source summed up the general view, saying that "I have always been proud of the firm in this regard, which is why the lawsuit alleging otherwise is so hard to stomach."

© 2007 Vault Inc.

"As a third-year associate, I am often the senior associate on a deal and I often find myself negotiating [with] partners at other firms"

—*Sullivan & Cromwell associate*

Visit the Vault Law Channel, the complete online resource for law careers, featuring firm profiles, message boards, the Vault Law Job Board and more. **www.vault.com/law**

VAULT CAREER LIBRARY   111

Skadden, Arps, Slate, Meagher & Flom LLP and Affiliates

Four Times Square
New York, NY 10036
Phone: (212) 735-3000
www.skadden.com

LOCATIONS

New York, NY (HQ)

Boston, MA • Chicago, IL • Houston, TX • Los Angeles, CA • Palo Alto, CA • San Francisco, CA • Washington, DC • Wilmington, DE • Beijing • Brussels • Frankfurt • Hong Kong • London • Moscow • Munich • Paris • Singapore • Sydney • Tokyo • Toronto • Vienna

MAJOR DEPARTMENTS & PRACTICES

Alternative Dispute Resolution • Antitrust • Appellate Litigation & Legal Issues • Asia • Australia & New Zealand • Banking & Institutional Investing • Brazil • Canada • China • Communications • Complex Mass Torts & Insurance Litigation • Consumer Financial Services Enforcement & Litigation • Corporate • Corporate Compliance Programs • Corporate Finance • Corporate Governance • Corporate Restructuring • Derivative Financial Products, Commodities & Futures • Employee Benefits & Executive Compensation • Energy Project Finance & Development • Energy Regulatory • Environmental • Environmental (International) • Environmental Litigation • Europe • European Union/International Competition • Financial Institutions Practice • Financial Services • Franchise Law • Gaming • Government Contract Disputes • Government Enforcement Litigation • Health Care • Health Care Enforcement & Litigation • Health Care Fraud & Abuse • Hong Kong Law • India • Information Technology & E-Commerce • Insurance • Intellectual Property & Technology • International Arbitration • International Law & Policy • International Tax • International Trade • Investment Management • Israel • Italy • Japan • Labor & Employment Law • Latin America • Lease Financing • Life Sciences • Litigation • Mergers & Acquisitions • Outsourcing • Patent and Technology Litigation & Counseling • Political Law • Private Equity • Private Investment Funds • Pro Bono • Public Policy • Real Estate • Real Estate Investment Trusts • Russia & CIS • Securities Enforcement & Compliance • Securities Litigation • Sports • Structured Finance • Tax • Tax Controversy & Litigation • Trademark, Copyright, Advertising and Internet Litigation & Counseling • Trusts & Estates • UCC & Secured Transactions • Utilities Mergers & Acquisitions • White Collar Crime

THE BUZZ
WHAT ATTORNEYS AT OTHER FIRMS ARE SAYING ABOUT THIS FIRM

- "Tops in every market"
- "500-pound Gorilla"
- "The best for clients"
- "Way too intense"

THE STATS

No. of attorneys: Approximately 2,000
No. of offices: 22
Summer associate offers: 184 out of 188 (2006)
Executive Partner: Robert C. Sheehan
Hiring Partner: Howard L. Ellin

BASE SALARY (2007)

1st year: $160,000
2nd year: $170,000
3rd year: $185,000
4th year: $210,000
5th year: $230,000
6th year: $250,000
7th year: $265,000
8th year: $280,000
9th year: $290,000
Summer associate: $3,100/week

UPPERS

- International corporate powerhouse
- "Incredible resources, including technology, human and other"
- Improving training

DOWNERS

- Losing its status as a market leader in compensation
- Typically grueling hours
- Type-A personalities can be off-putting to Types B-Z

NOTABLE PERKS

- Technology allowance ($3,000 first year, $1,000/per year after that)
- Flexible return from maternity leave program
- Free on-site gym (New York)
- Bar and moving expenses

© 2007 Vault Inc.

RANKING RECAP

Regional Rankings

#2 - Southern California
#3 - Northern California
#3 - Chicago
#3 - Boston
#5 - Washington, DC
#6 - New York

Practice Area Rankings

#2 - Mergers & Acquisitions
#2 - Tax
#3 - Bankruptcy
#3 - Corporate
#3 - Real Estate
#3 - Securities
#4 (tie) - Antitrust
#5 - Litigation

Partner Rankings

#1 - Tax
#2 - Mergers & Acquisitions
#3 - Bankruptcy
#4 - Securities
#5 - Litigation
#5 - Overall Prestige

Quality of Life

#10 - Pay
#12 - Selectivity

EMPLOYMENT CONTACT

Ms. Carol Lee H. Sprague
Director, Associate/Alumni Relations & Attorney Recruiting
Phone: (212) 735-2076
E-mail: csprague@skadden.com

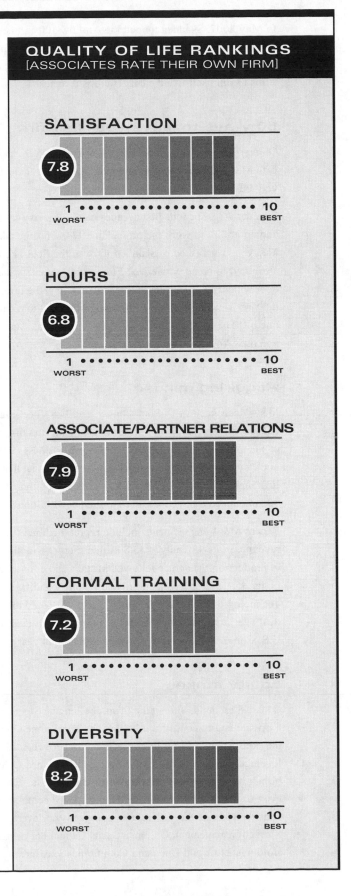

QUALITY OF LIFE RANKINGS
[ASSOCIATES RATE THEIR OWN FIRM]

SATISFACTION
7.8
1 WORST — 10 BEST

HOURS
6.8
1 WORST — 10 BEST

ASSOCIATE/PARTNER RELATIONS
7.9
1 WORST — 10 BEST

FORMAL TRAINING
7.2
1 WORST — 10 BEST

DIVERSITY
8.2
1 WORST — 10 BEST

Visit the Vault Law Channel, the complete online resource for law careers, featuring firm profiles, message boards, the Vault Law Job Board and more. www.vault.com/law

VAULT CAREER LIBRARY   113

THE SCOOP

In May 2007, Skadden topped the AmLaw 100 for the 21st time. In 1999, it was the first law firm to break the billion-dollar mark; these days, netting over $1.85 billion annually, in terms of revenue it is the largest law firm in the United States. Over the past four decades Skadden has earned recognition not just for its pioneering corporate practice, but for being one of the first law firms to run itself like the corporations it represents.

50 ways to leave your law firm

On April Fool's Day 1948, three New York lawyers let the screen door slam on the firm now known as Dewey Ballantine. The firm Marshall Skadden, Les Arps and John Slate founded would become New York's largest, redefining the tactics as well as the very business of law.

Skadden Arps spent its first decades handling proxy cases and tender offers—while building a reputation for aggressive strategies and an ability to work the press. In 1974, a hostile takeover of battery maker ESB by International Nickel set a new tone for M&A, and unorthodox Skadden took to the field like a natural. The firm's notorious no-more-Mr.-Nice-Guy posture can be attributed to name partner Joe Flom, who started at Skadden three months after its founding and whose name would grace the door a mere 13 years later. Flom, still active in the firm, participated in most of the major M&A deals of the 70s and 80s, forging the firm's hard-nosed style. In recognition of Flom's imprint on the legal industry, in 1999 *The American Lawyer* named him one of "The Lawyers of the Century." Other stars and alumni of the 2,000-lawyer firm include famed litigator Robert Bennett and New York Governor Eliot Spitzer.

Acquiring minds

M&A deals such as DuPont-Conoco and U.S. Steel-Marathon Oil—and most notably the 1989 takeover of RJR Nabisco, then the second-largest LBO of all time—launched the firm into the top rung of American law firms. Though the market slowdown of the early 90s did affect the firm's core business (1992 and 1993 were the only years that Skadden did not top the Am Law 100), by 2000 the firm was back in form. In a deal that broke the merger record set by Time Warner just one month before, the firm represented Mannesmann during its $183 billion acquisition by Britain's Vodafone. In 2006, the firm represented clients in 90 announced transactions, each valued at $1 billion or more.

Recent M&A engagements include representation of Luxembourg-based Arcelor, the world's largest steel company in terms of revenue, in its "friendly" $33.8 billion merger with the Netherlands-based Mittal Steel, the world's largest steel maker in terms of production. The truce followed Mittal's earlier unsolicited bid of $22.8 billion. The firm also represented Guidant Corporation in its $27 billion acquisition by Boston Scientific Corporation, Alcatel in its $13.4 billion merger-of-equals with Lucent Technologies Inc., and BlackRock, Inc. in its $9.8 billion merger with Merrill Lynch Investment Managers LP, the largest M&A deal ever in the asset management industry. For deals of this scope, in 2006 *Corporate Board Member* named Skadden "Best U.S. Corporate Law Firm" for the sixth straight year.

Equity stakes

Of late Skadden is among the firms challenging Simpson Thacher's lead in private equity. In September 2006, Skadden advised a private equity consortium led by The Blackstone Group L.P., The Carlyle Group, Permira Funds and Texas Pacific Group in the consortium's $17.6 billion acquisition of Freescale Semiconductor. And in July 2006, the firm had a role in the largest leveraged buyout in history: Skadden represented Credit Suisse, financial advisor to hospital chain HCA, during HCA's $33 billion buyout by private equity firms Bain Capital, KKR, Merrill Lynch Global Private Equity and HCA co-founder Thomas F. Frist Jr. The firm also represented the special committee of the board of directors of Kinder Morgan Inc. in connection with its consideration of the $22 billion going-private leveraged buyout sponsored by Richard D. Kinder, other members of Kinder Morgan management, Goldman Sachs Capital Partners, American International Group, Inc., The Carlyle Group and Riverstone Holdings LLC; and Univision Communications Inc. in its $13.7 billion leveraged buyout by Broadcasting Media Partners Inc.,

© 2007 Vault Inc.

a consortium that includes private equity firms Madison Dearborn Partners, LLC, Providence Equity Partners Inc., Thomas H. Lee Partners, L.P., TPG, Inc. and Saban Capital Group.

Litigation nation

The 1990s recession forced the firm to diversify and fortify other practice areas: these days, M&A is just one of the things Skadden does well. The Skadden brand now carries serious weight in such practice areas as restructuring, IP, white-collar defense and commercial litigation.

Litigation wins for the firm include a *National Law Journal* "Top Defense Win" of the year, in which Skadden won the dismissal of a billion-dollar securities fraud action brought against client DaimlerChrysler by financier Kirk Kerkorian's investment company, Tracinda. In April 2005, the U.S. District Court for the District of Delaware dismissed the federal securities and common law fraud claims brought by Tracinda, which claimed that the 1998 business combination of Daimler-Benz and Chrysler was falsely represented to be a "merger of equals." The case was the largest securities claim ever tried in federal court, involving compensatory damage claims of more than $1.35 billion.

Skadden's victory before the U.S. Supreme Court on behalf of Merrill Lynch in Dabit v. Merrill Lynch was the latest installment of the firm's successful defense of Merrill in more than 150 shareholder actions relating to the content of certain analyst reports. In the case, Skadden persuaded the Supreme Court that the Securities Litigation Uniform Standards Act (SLUSA) preempts private securities class actions brought under state law by individuals who assert claims as "holders" of securities and who do not allege that they purchased or sold securities during the period in question. Had such cases been allowed to proceed, the potential would have existed for a companion "holder" state law securities class case along with every federal securities class action brought.

In August 2006 the firm's noted mass torts division won a summary judgment for insurer State Farm in a nationwide class action. In Hill v. State Farm, plaintiffs alleged that between 1983 and 1998, State Farm's dividends to its policyholders were rather puny in relation to the size of its surplus. The plaintiffs sought a determination of what surplus would have been reasonable (a figure they put at $47 billion), and to compel State Farm to distribute the amount to policyholders across the nation. Skadden argued that business judgment provisions barred the plaintiffs' claims, and that the plaintiffs' insurance policies clearly stated that State Farm's board of directors had discretion to determine the amount of dividends. The court found that the plaintiffs had failed to show that State Farm's board of directors had not exercised proper business judgment with regard to surplus and dividends, and held that there were acceptable rationales for State Farm's decision to stockpile surplus.

The firm also earned a victory before the 11th Circuit Court of Appeals in October 2006, in which it secured the dismissal of a securities class-action complaint against NDCHealth Corporation. The complaint alleged that NDCHealth had engaged in wrongful revenue recognition practices, which caused the company's financial statements to be misleading and artificially inflated the price of NDCHealth's common stock. A District Court had initially dismissed the complaint as inadequate with regard to the Federal Rules of Civil Procedure and the Private Securities Reform Act, and the Eleventh Circuit agreed.

You get what you don't pay for

The firm has found some legal resolution in a billing skirmish with the owner and publisher of the Pulitzer Prize-winning *San Juan Star*, Puerto Rico's largest English language newspaper. A Manhattan Supreme Court justice upheld Skadden's claim that publisher Gerard Angulo owed it $1.24 million in legal fees, and in January 2005 ordered Angulo to turn over his shares in the newspaper's controlling companies in order to satisfy the judgment. The firm began representing Angulo during his dispute with a former partner in 1993; in the dispute, Angulo won the right to buy out his partner, as well as $1 million in consulting fees. While his case was ongoing, Angulo paid approximately $1 million in legal fees, but Skadden claimed that Angulo slowed payments after his result was upheld by an appeals court in 1998. The publisher's legal malpractice suit against the firm, charging that he was fraudulently overbilled, was dismissed.

Visit the Vault Law Channel, the complete online resource for law careers, featuring firm profiles, message boards, the Vault Law Job Board and more. **www.vault.com/law**

VAULT CAREER LIBRARY **115**

GETTING HIRED

Many tiers, at long as you fit the mold

Snobbery just doesn't exist at Skadden—at least not when it comes to the law schools from which the firm recruits. "Skadden cares less about the name of your law school and more about whether you will actually be a good lawyer," reports one insider. "Consequently, it will often take a student from a less prestigious law school." "It seems like they are more willing to take top students from lower-ranked schools than to take average students from higher-ranked schools," notes another lawyer. The firm does have wide-ranging expectations, looking for "grades, personality—and an interesting back story doesn't hurt either." Personality is key. "The firm is looking for overachieving individuals who work hard but can also communicate well with clients and be a good ambassador for the firm," reports a corporate lawyer.

The process itself can be surprisingly grueling, and prospective Skaddenites can take nothing for granted. "[The] interview process can be lengthy for laterals—stick to it if you really want to get in," advises an attorney who joined the firm via that route. Those wishing to get an offer should be on for everyone they meet. "Arrogance by candidates is looked down upon by most associates who do the interviewing—and associates have a large voice in deciding who gets summer associate offers," warns a source. "Negative evaluations from just one or two associates has doomed a candidate, even if he/she hits it off with the partner he/she meets with."

OUR SURVEY SAYS

Best of times, worst of times

With a firm as big as Skadden, it's hard to get a consensus about anything, much less get a feel for the firm as a whole. Opinions vary, but a few broad themes shine through. "The work is steady, high profile, sophisticated and interesting, which makes working at Skadden bearable," says one junior associate. "I love the fact that I work on high-level transactions and research every day," gushes another young associate. "Every day when I leave I feel like I've learned something. The downsides are the hours (to be expected) and sometimes I lose learning opportunities because the components of a transaction or problem are over my head and there's no real time to play meaningful catch-up." "Everything about my job is wonderful," says another enthusiastic insider. "I'm learning interesting things every day, working with great people, and (the biggest surprise, given the New York City BigLaw stories) feeling respected." Perhaps it's important to know what you're getting into. "No place is perfect, but Skadden, despite some of the rumors out there, is a great place to work," notes an attorney. "It may not be everyone's cup of tea, but if you don't mind a lot of type-A personalities and want to work on some of the biggest legal deals in the world, this is the place."

But it's not the place for everyone. "The honeymoon period wore off quickly," fumes a first-year. "I am already actively looking at exit opportunities. The No. 1 one gripe is utter lack of control over your schedule. Often you never know whether it could be one of those lucky nights where you get to leave at 8 or whether you'll be here until the next morning." "Although initially a great place to work, as associates advance here, the absence of partner or educational opportunities and lack of retention strategies becomes difficult," notes another lawyer. Tedium is a problem. "After an initial honeymoon period, you realize that every day is the same," says another contact (who is discussing Skadden, not actual marriage). "I think this is about as fulfilling a law firm experience as I could expect, but nevertheless not terribly exciting to me," notes a midlevel.

Pride in their work

Skadden associates say that, to a large extent, the firm's culture revolves around its desire to do good work for its clients. "It's all about the quality of work product," states one source. "Skadden charges more, so there's a sense, even among associates, that the quality of our product needs to be better than other firms. Internal criticism can get rough, even brutal, at times, but always in the spirit of making the product as good as it needs to be." Another insider agrees, warning that "in general, the partners here are not warm and fuzzy types who bring out the marching band for every new associate. Skadden is top notch in terms of professionalism and work ethic." Still, that doesn't mean the culture is one to be feared. "The firm culture is perfect for me," says a lawyer. "This is a very pleasant environment and the junior associates are definitely a cohesive bunch." "You can truly be yourself at the firm—there are jocks, nerds, beauty queens," says a high school-minded L.A. attorney. The firm does do a good job of easing associates into the mix. "There's a perfect balance between informal and professional," observes a junior associate. "I don't know of another firm where first-years feel so comfortable and integrated." "It is a very collegial atmosphere," notes another contact. "I have no problem dropping into another associate's office with questions."

Leader no more

Associates lament that Skadden is no longer the compensation leader it once was. "Most of the associates at Skadden were hired when Skadden was the market leader in salary for its peer group," recalls an insider. "It is significant that Simpson led the push of first-year salaries to $160,000 and Skadden only matched." "Skadden will not be undersold, but the firm's delay in announcing last year's bonus (until mid-December after other top firms had set total compensation threshold) was race-to-the-bottom embarrassing," gripes another lawyer. The firm requires "only a minimal threshold [of 1,600 hours] for a full bonus." Skadden's compensation system, while it may have its glitches, does help the firm's culture. "The market lock-step salary and bonus compensation system keeps an objective and fair framework in what can be a subjective assignment system that cannot possibly give every associate equal experience," reports a lawyer. "This eliminates any feelings of animosity between associates that inevitably surfaces at other firms." So the animosity comes from elsewhere. "With salaries and bonuses like this, you really can't complain," states a senior associate. "The lack of a matching 401(k) is a sore point with some associates, but come on—we make a ton of money." "Our bonuses should have been bigger given the level of profits our partners achieved last year," fumes another senior lawyer.

No floor, no ceiling

Oh, the hours you'll work. "The hours are what you would expect at any large New York law firm," says one attorney. "The one huge plus is that there is no face time here. If you don't have some reason to be in the office there is no reason you have to stay late and no partners checking on you to see if you do." The target numbers don't seem to mean much. "Skadden claims to have a 1,600-hour target I think everyone must hit that by August," says a first-year. In reality, "there is no minimum billable so the hours are dependent on the amount of work available." That can have its good and bad points. "In a slow year, this policy is a boon as associates billing over a set number of billable hours (very low) will get the full benefit of the salary and bonus. On the flip side, on a busy year there is no potential cap to the number of hours worked." Different departments deal with the hours crunch in different ways. "Corporate work anywhere is feast and famine, but I've found that Skadden is very serious about eliminating any unnecessary hours from your time," says a corporate lawyer. "There's no face time at all and you're encouraged to pass grunt work down to support staff, as appropriate, to keep you efficient and happy." "The hours are [to be] expected with high-level litigation cases," reports a litigator. "The office requires late arrival/early departure/absence memos be e-mailed when you are not in the office, but it does not seem to be an issue if you are accessible via cell or BlackBerry."

Mucho training

Skadden's training "gets an A-plus, and organizers are continually improving it." "The firm has implemented a formal training regime that I think is very useful and spans a wide range of topics," says a source. "While the training is extensive, they have done a good job with spreading it over several days to make attendance manageable." Sometimes the training gets better (and more helpful) as time passes. The firm offers "lots of training in the beginning. I don't know how helpful it is for first-years, but they make second-years do it again too," says a junior associate. "It's much more helpful after a year of experience because you have a context to put the training in." "We receive a thorough training program that touches different aspects of lawyering, including writing, research and substantive corporate law," notes another lawyer. Some complain that the firm is "not so committed to making sure associates are actually able to attend. I've had to miss several training sessions I was looking forward to due to work obligations."

Visit the Vault Law Channel, the complete online resource for law careers, featuring firm profiles, message boards, the Vault Law Job Board and more. www.vault.com/law

VAULT CAREER LIBRARY   117

Trying, but still needs to go the extra mile

Diversity at Skadden is on par with many big law firms—which includes all the efforts, and many of the problems maintaining numbers. The firm "[tries] to provide accommodations [for female associates], particularly with respect to children, but there just aren't enough women partners here and it's tough to find a good mentor who has dealt with these types of issues." Others disagree to a certain extent, saying "there are numerous female mentors, and a number of female associates have children, though it is unclear whether that stops your advancement." As far as minority associates go, "I think we are certainly trying, but retention seems to remain an issue." "In terms of hiring, mentoring and promotion opportunities, minorities fare as well as any other associate. I believe that the partners would like to see more diversity in their own ranks," observes a contact.

© 2007 Vault Inc.

"I don't know of another firm where first-years feel so comfortable and integrated."

— *Skadden associate*

Visit the Vault Law Channel, the complete online resource for law careers, featuring firm profiles, message boards, the Vault Law Job Board and more. www.vault.com/law

VAULT CAREER LIBRARY

119

Davis Polk & Wardwell

450 Lexington Avenue
New York, NY 10017
Phone: (212) 450-4000
www.dpw.com

LOCATIONS

New York, NY (HQ)
Menlo Park, CA • Washington, DC • Beijing • Frankfurt •
Hong Kong • London • Madrid • Paris • Tokyo

MAJOR DEPARTMENTS AND PRACTICES

Capital Markets • Credit • Environmental • Executive
Compensation/Employee Benefits • Insolvency &
Restructuring • Intellectual Property • Litigation • Mergers &
Acquisitions • Private Equity • Real Estate • Trusts &
Estates

THE STATS

No. of attorneys: 600+
No. of offices: 10
Summer associate offers: 132 out of 132 (2006)
Managing Partner: John R. Ettinger
Hiring Partner: Nicholas A. Kronfeld

BASE SALARY (2007)

1st year: $160,000
2nd year: $170,000
3rd year: $185,000
4th year: $210,000
5th year: $230,000
6th year: $250,000
Summer associate: $3,077/week

UPPERS

- "High-profile" work
- "Genteel" environment
- "Top-of-the-market" compensation

DOWNERS

- "Typical" BigLaw hours
- "Market followers, not market leaders" in compensation
- "Too bureaucratic"

NOTABLE PERKS

- "The best perk is the cafeteria"
- "Heavily subsidized gym memberships"
- "Great" Mets and Yankees tickets
- Moving expenses, including broker's fee

THE BUZZ
WHAT ATTORNEYS AT OTHER FIRMS ARE SAYING ABOUT THIS FIRM

- "Perfect in every way"
- "Prestigious but boring"
- "Classy; values collegiality"
- "Not fooling anyone with the 'nice-guy' image"

© 2007 Vault Inc.

RANKING RECAP

Regional Rankings
#3 - New York
#10 - Northern California.

Practice Area Rankings
#5 - Securities
#5 - Tax
#6 - Bankruptcy
#6 - Corporate
#6 - Mergers & Acquisitions
#7 - Litigation

Partner Rankings
#1 - Securities
#3 - Corporate
#3 (tie) - Tax
#4 - Overall Prestige

Quality of Life
#7 - Selectivity
#10 - Formal Training
#14 - Best Firms to Work For
#17 - Overall Satisfaction
#19 - Associate/Partner Relationships

Diversity
#5 - Diversity with Respect to Women
#9 - Overall Diversity
#16 - Diversity with Respect to Minorities

EMPLOYMENT CONTACT

Ms. Sharon L. Crane
Director of Legal Recruiting
Phone: (212) 450-4143
Fax: (212) 450-3143
E-mail: sharon.crane@dpw.com

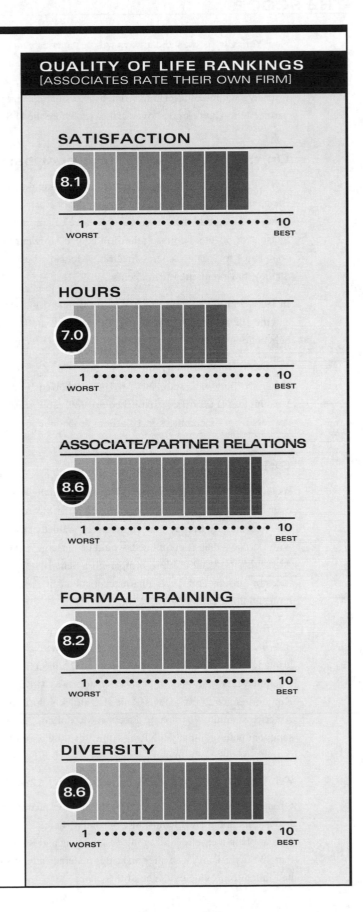

QUALITY OF LIFE RANKINGS
[ASSOCIATES RATE THEIR OWN FIRM]

SATISFACTION
8.1
1 WORST — 10 BEST

HOURS
7.0
1 WORST — 10 BEST

ASSOCIATE/PARTNER RELATIONS
8.6
1 WORST — 10 BEST

FORMAL TRAINING
8.2
1 WORST — 10 BEST

DIVERSITY
8.6
1 WORST — 10 BEST

Visit the Vault Law Channel, the complete online resource for law careers, featuring firm profiles, message boards, the Vault Law Job Board and more. www.vault.com/law

VAULT CAREER LIBRARY   121

THE SCOOP

New York City is, was and always will be America's money vortex—it's no surprise that Davis Polk & Wardwell, founded in the city over 150 years ago, has finance in its DNA. The firm boasts one of the nation's best and most comprehensive corporate departments, with impressive teams in capital markets, M&A, bankruptcy and tax. Unusual for Wall Street, the firm also offers extensive white-collar criminal defense. Its highly regarded litigation practice also has deep roots—in his long career, name partner John Davis argued over 250 cases before the U.S. Supreme Court.

On the coattails of the robber barons

Davis Polk & Wardwell dates back to 1849, making it one of the oldest law firms in the United States. Original founder Francis Bangs made his name opposing the legendary Boss Tweed and his ring of corruption. Bangs' successor, Francis Stetson, was quick to recognize the growing importance of corporate work. In 1887 banker and industrialist J. Pierpont Morgan selected Stetson for his chief counsel; the firm helped Morgan restructure the Pennsylvania Railroad, and knit together several electrical companies to create General Electric. Morgan's businesses, in their modern day incarnations JPMorgan Chase and Morgan Stanley, have remained firm clients.

In 1921, John Davis and Frank Polk joined the firm. Davis was solicitor general of the United States, ambassador to the U.K. and the 1924 Democratic nominee for president. Polk would lead the U.S. delegation to the Paris Peace Conference in 1921 and help negotiate the Treaty of Versailles. In 1949, in recognition of banking law expert Allen Wardwell, the firm took on its current name.

A Paris office was established in 1962, followed by a London office in 1973; interestingly, the firm's first U.S. satellite, a Washington, D.C., office established in 1980, came after the firm was well settled overseas. Today Davis Polk employs over 600 lawyers from 41 countries in 10 offices around the world.

Going corporate

As always, Davis Polk's corporate lawyers found themselves in the middle of many of the megadeals and offerings that transpired over the past year or so. For example, on the M&A front, over the course of one week in April, Davis Polk advised on four headline-making transactions cumulatively valued at over $150 billion: Dutch bank ABN AMRO's proposed $91 billion merger with Barclays that, if completed, would be the largest-ever merger in the banking industry, as well as the $21 billion sale of ABN AMRO's U.S. bank holding company, La Salle Bank, to Bank of America; Sallie Mae's proposed $25 billion acquisition by an investor group; and U.K. pharmaceutical giant AstraZeneca's proposed $15.6 billion acquisition of MedImmune, a U.S. biotechnology company.

The firm's activity in big capital markets offerings was equally brisk, particularly in Asia. In what is the largest-ever initial public offering, the firm advised Industrial and Commercial Bank of China, China's largest bank, on its $21.9 billion IPO. The firm also advised Japan's Aozora Bank on its $3.2 billion IPO and Tokyo Stock Exchange listing—the largest IPO by a Japanese issuer in eight years. Another IPO success story was U.K. financial service group Standard Life's IPO—the largest in the United Kingdom since 2000. Davis Polk also struck gold in high-yield debt offerings, advising on the $6 billion offering by North American mining company Freeport-McMoRan, the second-largest in history, and the €4.5 billion offering by Dutch semiconductor company NXP,the largest-ever by a European issuer.

At least somebody's winning the drug wars

Of late, the firm has managed some big wins in pharma suits. In September 2006, a U.S. district court judge ruled in favor of Davis Polk client Hoffmann-LaRoche and co-defendant Glaxo-Smith-Kline, denying a preliminary injunction request by Procter & Gamble in a case regarding false advertising and Roche's osteoporosis drug Boniva. In a January 2006 lawsuit, P&G claimed that TV advertising, web sites and sales materials advertising for Boniva were false and misleading, but the court held that P&G had failed to provide evidence of this claim.

© 2007 Vault Inc.

In other Big Pharma wins, the firm successfully defended Astra-Zeneca in an antitrust class action arising out of a 1993 patent infringement case involving breast cancer drug tamoxifen citrate, invented by Astra-Zeneca's predecessor company. New Jersey-based Barr Laboratories had contended the original patent was invalid; the two companies reached a settlement where Barr received a cash payment and a nonexclusive distributorship to sell tamoxifen. In 2000, seven years after the settlement, over 30 federal and state class-action complaints were filed protesting the agreement. In November 2005 the Second Circuit affirmed dismissal of the case, ruling that there was no plausible evidence that the agreement had restrained competition.

Getting Delta airborne

In what has become the feel-good story of the bankruptcy bar, Davis Polk advised its longtime client Delta in what many experts have called one of the most efficient and least litigious large corporate Chapter 11 cases ever. Davis Polk led 20 firms representing the airline, which emerged from bankruptcy in April 2007 and is now flying high again. Among other things, Delta secured over $2.5 billion during its bankruptcy, successfully defended against a $10 billion hostile takeover attempt by USAirways and restructured hundreds of contracts and other relationships yielding billions of dollars in savings.

Live at the Mets

Late-breaking news in the firm's ongoing representation of the New York Mets baseball franchise concerns a naming rights agreement for the new stadium. The firm is representing the Mets in legal matters concerning Citigroup's sponsorship of the stadium; the 45,000-seat facility, to be completed in time for the opening of the 2009 major league baseball season, will be named Citi Field. In 2005, the firm won a dismissal of litigation for the Mets in a suit brought by SportsChannel, which alleged that the Mets had violated a 1996 agreement to license the pay TV rights to its games to SportsChannel for a fixed term.

Pro bono triumph

On January 30, 2007, Davis Polk won an acquittal on all charges in the jury trial of pro bono client Lonnie Jones, who was charged with murder in the second degree and sentenced to 37 years to life. Jones first became Davis Polk's client in 2003, when the firm took on the appeal of his murder conviction. After extensive investigation, Davis Polk was able to prove that the prosecution's main eyewitness at the trial had fabricated her account and intentionally misidentified Jones as the shooter. The court reversed the conviction and ordered a new trial. At the new trial, Jones was found not guilty, resulting in his immediate release after having spent more than five years in prison.

In another big pro bono win, Davis Polk worked on a landmark federal lawsuit that sought to improve the treatment and housing conditions for inmates with mental illness throughout the New York state prison system. After five years of litigation and two weeks of trial, the parties negotiated a settlement, subject to court approval, that will provide for major improvements in psychiatric treatment for mentally ill New York State inmates.

Going in house

How much do you like your clients? Enough to go work for them? Some of Davis Polk's senior partners have done just that, leaving to take in-house positions at major firm clients. Recent examples include: Dennis Hersch, one of the leaders of Davis Polk's M&A group, who took an in-house post as global chairman of M&A at longtime client JP Morgan, and Eric Grossman, who made a similar move to Morgan Stanley, where he is now global head of litigation.

Visit the Vault Law Channel, the complete online resource for law careers, featuring firm profiles, message boards, the Vault Law Job Board and more. **www.vault.com/law**

VAULT CAREER LIBRARY

123

GETTING HIRED

"One of the toughest offers to land"

Associates in the firm's New York headquarters believe Davis Polk to be "one of the toughest offers to land in the city." The general consensus is that top grades from top schools are a given; successful candidates must also engender that ethereal quality known as "fit."

As one first-year puts it, "Davis Polk is huge on 'personality fit.' It's not uncommon for a student to have offers from Sullivan & Cromwell and Cravath, only to be turned down by Davis Polk. Credentials get you in the door, but your degree of 'Davis Polk-ness' gets you the offer." An associate on the hiring committee advises, "Most of the people I interviewed for positions and liked did not get called back, and those who get called back do not get offers. Grades are REALLY important. Riding the curve at a good school is NOT enough, and if you go to a second-tier school, be at the top of your class, or save your interview bid. You would be wasting your time." A senior associate adds, "Top grades and an exceptional resume might get you in the door but call-back interviews make or break you. We have a very high percentage of people that do not receive offers after callbacks. You have to be a well-rounded, interesting person that seems like they are truly interested in coming to work at Davis Polk and contribute. Not to mention it really helps if you are the kind of person we'd like to share a drink with after work."

OUR SURVEY SAYS

As good as it gets?

Associates say Davis Polk is about as good as it gets for law firm life. As one senior associate boasts, "I have interesting work, and the people I work with are great. If I didn't love my job I would not have stayed here as long as I have." A midlevel associate says, "Any level of dissatisfaction comes from factors associated with working at a large international firm generally, not my firm specifically." Another midlevel adds, "If I liked being a lawyer more, I would have a higher satisfaction score. As far as law firms go, Davis Polk can't be beat—there's no other law firm that I would like to be at."

Indeed, a senior associate says that the firm has grown more attractive the longer she's worked there. "I never thought I'd still be at a firm four-plus years out of law school," she says. "However, when you feel like you are learning a lot, enjoy what you do and love the people you are working with, it is pretty hard to leave, especially when I compare my experience and satisfaction to other midlevel and senior associates at New York law firms. And I must not be alone in my opinion because the senior associate class in the litigation department at Davis Polk is huge!" However, one senior associate offers a very contrary view. "My job satisfaction has decreased each year that I have been at Davis Polk," he warns. "For junior lawyers, I think the firm is a great place to work on high-profile matters, try different practice areas and build a set of skills. As I have progressed in seniority, however, I have noticed it is more difficult to work with new partners and to develop senior-level skills, such as arguing cases in front of a judge and taking primary responsibility for interfacing with a client."

Beyond polite

Associates call Davis Polk "polite," "civil," "helpful," "respectful" and "calm." A junior New York litigator brags, "The culture here is really fantastic—I couldn't be more pleased. Everyone is incredibly friendly, and we have a lot of fun. People have their office doors open and there is a lot of socializing and chatting during the day. But at the same time, people are very focused, driven and incredibly smart. I find that it's a great balance." A midlevel M&A expert reports, "The culture is very professional, partners are very good to work with, and associates get a lot of responsibility early on. On the whole, it is a great place to work, and the fact that the culture elsewhere might not be as good makes me hesitant to think about leaving." As one insider puts it, "The best way to describe most people at the firm may be genteel. I think that results in a pleasant culture and, beyond being polite, people generally seem to like one another. Socializing is there if you want it, but not required." And a bankruptcy

© 2007 Vault Inc.

specialist adds, "I find the people to be quite friendly and interesting. Most lawyers try to get home as early as possible and don't spend a lot of time socializing out of the office together."

Associates agree that the firm's partners are, by and large, "respectful" and "pleasant." Institutionally, however, the firm does not always let information trickle all the way down to the associates. A senior New York associate advises, "Treatment really depends on the partners, but overall associates are treated with respect." A junior New Yorker says, "Partners are very respectful and appreciative of associate efforts. I've never seen a partner act unprofessionally." A corporate attorney adds, "On an individual level, most partners treat even the most junior associates with great respect. They express thanks for a job well done and tend to give good feedback. The firm has an associates committee and upward review, but the firm's partnership isn't particularly transparent." Or, as a junior litigator puts it, "In my experience, partners have always treated associates very well in working situations. While I would like for there to be more transparency into firmwide decisions, associates are generally informed of these after the fact."

Lawyering 101

Davis Polk's associates also uniformly praise the firm's "very extensive" formal training program. A first-year explains, "In addition to a weeklong training session for incoming associates, corporate rotators attend training sessions at least monthly." A midlevel litigator from New York advises, "I think we have a good balance-enough training, but not too much." A midlevel explains the specifics. "Lawyering 101, 301 and 501 (for first-, third- and fifth-years) are the most formal of the training programs, but consistent CLE lunches, breakfasts and other trainings (as well as learn-as-you-do experience) make the training here pretty well rounded." Of course, there is probably not a single complaint-free legal training program in the country, Davis Polk's included. One tax specialist complains that the firm's program is "mostly useless." He opines, "Considering the deal-flow, there needs to be more emphasis on practical training."

As for mentoring, a New York litigator raves, "I have found that more often than not the partners that I work for take the time to explain the larger picture and the greater implications of a decision. In my opinion, that is the most important kind of training. Training in the abstract can be helpful, but it is hard to retain the information outside of any particular context." But as one banking expert puts it, "Partners tend to be somewhat detached in their attitude toward associates. Yet, there are partners with whom it is possible to discuss matters that are unrelated to billable client work and who are very supportive." Another Big Apple litigator adds, "I would like for there to be a bit more of this, but to this end, the firm recently revamped its mentoring program entirely so that each incoming first-year is assigned both an associate mentor and a partner mentor, with regularly scheduled events. All of this is, of course, in addition to traditional organic mentoring."

The money's fair, and the hours are what you should expect

Associates say that Davis Polk consistently pays exactly "top of the market" rates, no higher, no lower, no matter. "It's what everyone receives at this stage in New York, so I can't complain," says a first-year. "Exactly on par with other top-tier firms," chimes in a fourth-year. A tax attorney adds, "The raise helped. Honestly, we are being overpaid for what we do, but it is NOT enough considering the family sacrifices the hours take. Don't give me a raise, give me fewer hours." And yet, it's possible to find associates who are looking for more money. "DPW generally pays market, and the recent pay bumps have finally caught us back up to inflation since 2001. Still, firms are having record years that put the dot-com boom to shame, and the cost of living in New York City is continuing to rise (particularly if you're renting, which many of us associates must do when a two-bedroom costs $1.2 million), and so I'm hopeful that salaries will continue to rise."

The hours are what you should anticipate at a top-tier firm, associates suggest. "They are what I expected, but that doesn't mean I like working after my kids go to sleep," says a senior litigator. That said, a banking associate reports, "The firm is fairly flexible to accommodate special arrangements and it has a friendly policy regarding flexible work schedules. There is also great respect for associates' vacations. As far as I know, it is very rare that an associate would be asked to reschedule a vacation." And a first-year adds, "I am pleasantly surprised by my hours. I do a solid 10-hour day most days, which is fair considering the amount we're getting paid."

Visit the Vault Law Channel, the complete online resource for law careers, featuring firm profiles, message boards, the Vault Law Job Board and more. www.vault.com/law

VAULT CAREER LIBRARY 125

VAULT TOP 100

6 PRESTIGE RANKING

Simpson Thacher & Bartlett LLP

425 Lexington Avenue
New York, NY 10017
Phone: (212) 455-2000
www.simpsonthacher.com

LOCATIONS

New York, NY (HQ)

Los Angeles, CA • Palo Alto, CA • Washington, DC •
Beijing • Hong Kong • London • Tokyo

MAJOR DEPARTMENTS & PRACTICES

Antitrust/Competition • Banking & Credit • Bankruptcy •
Capital Markets & Securities • Corporate • Corporate
Governance • Environmental • Executive Compensation &
Employee Benefits • Exempt Organizations • Government
Investigations/Business Crimes • Insurance/Reinsurance •
Intellectual Property • International Arbitration •
International Practice • Investment Management • Labor •
Litigation • Mergers & Acquisitions • Personal Planning •
Private Equity • Pro Bono • Product Liability & Mass Tort •
Real Estate • Securities/Shareholder Litigation • Structured
Finance • Tax

THE STATS

No. of attorneys: 786
No. of offices: 8
Summer associate offers: 147 out of 147 (2006)
Chairman of Executive Committee: Philip T. Ruegger
Administrative Partners: Gary I. Horowitz, Steven C. Todrys
Hiring Partners:
  New York: John W. Carr, Lynn K. Neuner, Ken Ziman
  Los Angeles: Chet Kronenberg
  Palo Alto: Alexis Coll-Very

BASE SALARY (2007)

1st year: $160,000
2nd year: $170,000
3rd year: $185,000
4th year: $210,000
5th year: $230,000
6th year: $250,000
7th year: $265,000
8th year: $280,000
9th year: $290,000
Summer associate: $3,077/week

UPPERS

• *The* market leader for pay raises
• "Variety and prestige of clients"
• Free rein on the type and amount of pro bono work

DOWNERS

• "Working at a law firm is not fun"
• Long, unpredictable hours
• "Poor information dissemination"

NOTABLE PERKS

• "Great" cafeteria
• Plenty of sponsored social events
• Subsidized gym membership
• Frequent free sports and events tickets

THE BUZZ
WHAT ATTORNEYS AT OTHER FIRMS ARE SAYING ABOUT THIS FIRM

• "Thanks for the raises!"
• "See daylight much?"
• "Swimming in private equity cash"
• "Prestige, but no life"

RANKING RECAP

Regional Rankings

#4 - New York

Practice Area Rankings

#3 - Mergers & Acquisitions

#4 - Corporate

#4 - Securities

#7 (tie) - Antitrust

#9 - Tax

#10 - Litigation

#10 - Real Estate

Partner Rankings

#4 - Mergers & Acquisitions

#5 - Corporate

#6 - Overall Prestige

Quality of Life

#16 - Pay

#18 - Selectivity

EMPLOYMENT CONTACT

Ms. Dee Pifer
Director Legal Employment
Phone: (212) 455-2698
Fax: (212) 455-2502
E-mail: dpifer@stblaw.com

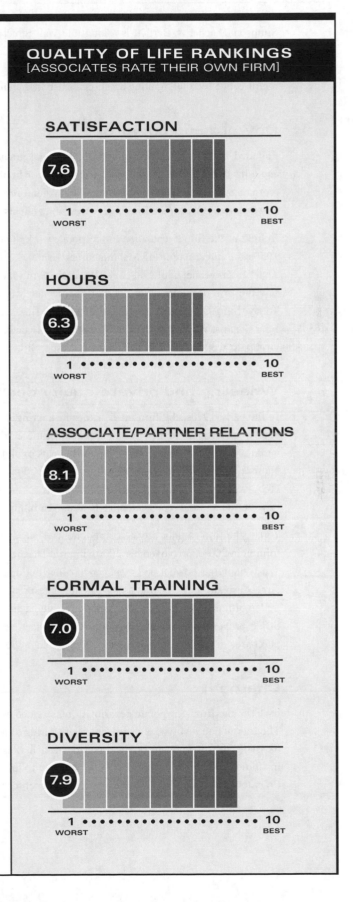

QUALITY OF LIFE RANKINGS
[ASSOCIATES RATE THEIR OWN FIRM]

SATISFACTION

7.6

1 WORST   10 BEST

HOURS

6.3

1 WORST   10 BEST

ASSOCIATE/PARTNER RELATIONS

8.1

1 WORST   10 BEST

FORMAL TRAINING

7.0

1 WORST   10 BEST

DIVERSITY

7.9

1 WORST   10 BEST

Visit the Vault Law Channel, the complete online resource for law careers, featuring firm profiles, message boards, the Vault Law Job Board and more. www.vault.com/law

VAULT CAREER LIBRARY   127

THE SCOOP

Simpson Thacher & Bartlett is a longtime Wall Street workhorse, housing elite teams in M&A, banking, capital markets and securities law. The firm is a bit more versatile than many of its peers, boasting formidable prowess in private equity, litigation and intellectual property as well. Oh, and in January 2007, the firm rang in the New Year by bumping starting salaries to a munificent $160,000, igniting a national salary matching frenzy.

Onward and upward

Founded in 1884 by three Columbia law school graduates, Simpson Thacher & Bartlett has throughout its 123-year history capitalized on financial and industrial trends. In the late 19th and early 20th centuries, the firm assisted in railroad reorganizations, the creation of mining and natural resource companies, and the expansion of the public utility system. By the close of World War I, the firm was representing clients in Europe, Asia and South America.

In light of the firm's reputation for corporate work, it's interesting that Simpson Thacher's banking practice only took off in the 1950s. Representation of Manufacturers Hanover Trust Company eventually reached a high of 30 percent of Simpson & Thacher's revenue; until 1988, over 100 of the firm's lawyers worked out of the Manufacturers Trust office. The 1980s and 1990s saw the firm develop one of the world's premier M&A practices, with a unique strength in private equity leveraged buyouts. Today, Simpson Thacher represents JPMorgan (the successor to Manufacturers Hanover), Lehman Brothers, Goldman Sachs, Bear Stearns, Wachovia, UBS and Travelers. Private equity clients include Kohlberg Kravis Roberts (KKR) and The Blackstone Group, as well as Hellman & Friedman, Vestar, Silverlake and First Reserve, among others.

Wheeling and private equity dealing

In the early 1970s, the firm made a fortune-altering decision when it took on representation of newly created KKR, a private equity consortium founded by ex-staffers of Bear Stearns. Simpson Thacher went on to handle the vast majority of KKR's deals, and represent KKR in one of the largest buyouts of all time, the $31 billion purchase of RJR Nabisco in 1989; legal fees for the Nabisco deal alone hit some $30 million. In July 2006 the firm managed KKR's $33 billion leveraged buyout of hospital operator HCA—a deal that broke the RJR Nabisco record and subsequently represented KKR and TPG in their $45 billion leveraged buyout of TXU and represented KKR in its $26 billion leveraged buyout of First Data.

Today, the firm's major private equity clients, KKR and The Blackstone Group, contribute over 15 percent of its revenue ($800 million in 2006). In November 2006 Simpson Thacher managed Blackstone's $36 billion acquisition of Equity Office Properties Trust, the largest owner and manager of office buildings in the Unites States—a transaction *The Wall Street Journal* called the largest private equity buyout as well as the largest real estate deal in history. In March 2006, the firm represented Blackstone in a $5.6 billion acquisition of CarrAmerica Realty, a publicly traded real estate investment trust. The Carr portfolio includes 285 office properties, totaling 26.8 million square feet. Since mid-2004, the firm has represented The Blackstone Group in 11 purchases of public real estate companies, for an aggregate of $76 billion.

Charge it

In 2006, the firm's corporate department represented MasterCard in the largest IPO completed in the United States since 2004. The transaction involved a significant restructuring of the company's capital structure and corporate governance that broadened its ownership to include public investors and a MasterCard charitable foundation in addition to the company's financial institution customers. *Thomson Financial* ranked Simpson Thacher No. 1 in 2006 as issuer's counsel for U.S. IPOs and global IPOs for U.S. issuers and No. 1 as issuer's counsel for U.S. high-yield debt.

© 2007 Vault Inc.

Yen again ...

Internationally, the firm is a market leader in Japan and Korea and has recently opened an office in Beijing to supplement its offices in Hong Kong and Tokyo. Simpson Thacher has advised on some of China's most sophisticated transactions, including the representation of China Life Insurance Company, China's largest insurer, in a consortium to acquire Guangdong Development Bank Co., Ltd. for $3.1 billion. This transaction is the largest acquisition to date of a majority stake in a Chinese financial institution and the outcome of one of the largest takeover battles in China's history. The firm also represented the underwriters in connection with the $3.3 billion IPO and Hong Kong listing of H shares of Shenhua Energy Company Limited, China's largest coal producer; and advised Suntech Power Holdings Co., Ltd., a leading solar energy company headquartered in China, in connection with its Rule 144A offering of $500 million convertible notes, the largest-ever convertible offering of a non-state owned company out of China. The firm has also worked on several share offerings of Focus Media, a leading Chinese media company based in Shanghai. The firm has long been active in European private equity and acquisition finance and completed the largest 2006 M&A transaction in Eastern Europe in representing Barr Pharmaceuticals in acquiring PLIVA; and has worked on over 25 IPOs in Latin America in since 2005.

I scream, you scream, we all scream for YouTube

In October 2006 Simpson Thacher's Palo Alto office nailed a glossy new economy deal when it represented Google in its largest acquisition to date, that of privately held YouTube. YouTube, the hugely popular web-based media company that allows users to watch and share original video clips, generates 100 million viewings daily. Though YouTube had originally raised only $11.5 million in VC funding, Google shelled out $1.65 billion in the all-stock transaction—a payout that harkens back to the golden purses of the dot-com daze. YouTube was advised by Silicon Valley tech-firm Wilson Sonsini Goodrich & Rosati; both Simpson Thacher and Wilson Sonsini had been involved in Google's own 2004 IPO, with Simpson Thacher representing underwriters Morgan Stanley and Credit Suisse First Boston.

Holding court

With over 300 lawyers, Simpson Thacher boasts one of the top litigation departments in the nation, handling matters across a broad spectrum of legal disciplines. For insurer Swiss Re, the firm won a huge victory in a case involving payouts related to the September 11 terrorist attacks. In 2001 World Trade Center leaseholder Larry Silverstein filed suit against his insurers, arguing that the attacks constituted two separate occurrences, and thus entitled him to collect $7 billion, twice the "per occurrence" amount listed on his insurance policies. In May 2004, a jury denied his claims and rendered a verdict in favor of several insurers, one of which was Swiss Re. Silverstein appealed, but in October 2006 a Second Circuit Court of Appeals affirmed the earlier verdict. *The National Law Review* named Simpson Thacher's role in the case one of the "Top Defense Wins" of 2004.

A little from column A, a little from column B

For commercial and securities litigation, Simpson has consistently placed in the first rank by Chambers and Partners, with numerous partners highlighted for individual recognition. Simpson's litigators have enabled some of the largest transactions handled by their corporate colleagues to go forward by defeating and resolving shareholder litigation, such as the $45 billion TXU buyout and the previously mentioned Equity Office Properties acquisition. On a confidential basis, the firm has handled numerous internal and SEC investigations regarding the backdating of stock options. And the firm's international arbitration practice is booming. Simpson represents Korean conglomerate Hanwha and Japanese company Orix in a multibillion-dollar insurance arbitration relating to the ownership of Korea Life Insurance. In the Caribbean, the firm represents the Dominican Republic in disputes involving hundreds of millions of dollars brought by foreign investors in connection with the country's effort to privatize its electricity infrastructure. The firm recently scored a big victory in Uruguay on behalf of rating agency Moody's Investors Service, which had been sued by investors claiming that they relied on Moody's ratings when investing in bonds issued by one of Uruguay's largest private banks. The Uruguayan court dismissed the plaintiffs' claims against Moody's in a series of 35+ cases—an important, precedent-setting win for the company.

Visit the Vault Law Channel, the complete online resource for law careers, featuring firm profiles, message boards, the Vault Law Job Board and more. **www.vault.com/law**

VAULT CAREER LIBRARY   129

Antitrust in me

Led by the former head of the Bureau of Competition at the Federal Trade Commission, Simpson Thacher's antitrust practice is booming. The firm provides regulatory guidance on the splashiest headline-making deals, like Sirius Satellite Radio's $13 billion merger of equals with XM satellite radio and DoubleClick's $3.1 billion acquisition by Google. Simpson's antitrust litigators are in the thick of things as well, scoring victories for MasterCard in litigation over Visa's anticompetitive practices and defeating price-fixing allegations brought by independent video retailers against Viacom and Paramount. With so many successes under its belt, it's no surprise that Simpson's antitrust practice has been ranked No. 1 by *Chambers USA* for three years running.

Friend of the court

The firm has also tallied some notable victories in pro bono litigation. In October 2006 the New Jersey Supreme Court held it unconstitutional to discriminate against same-sex couples with regard to the rights and obligations of marriage. The Court ordered remedial action that either opens the institution of marriage to same-sex couples or broadens the state's existing Domestic Partnership Act to include all the legal benefits and obligations of marriage. Simpson Thacher represented a number of civil rights groups as amici curiae. Together with the Center for Constitutional Rights, the firm acts as pro bono counsel for Guantánamo detainees from Saudi Arabia in connection with legal challenges to their detention. Pursuant to a court order, two Simpson Thacher associates have traveled to Guantánamo several times for attorney-client meetings.

Impressive IP

The firm is involved in cutting edge intellectual property matters, representing clients such as Travelers in its buyback of the "red umbrella" logo; Intel in a major patent infringement case involving challenges to its core microprocessor designs; and Peter Morton, a founder of the Hard Rock Café and the Hard Rock Hotel and Casino in Las Vegas, in a trademark licensing dispute. The IP group also represents America Online, DoubleClick, Google, Sirius Satellite Radio, 3Com, Virgin Mobile and Warner Music in a variety of IP litigation and/or transactional matters.

GETTING HIRED

They want to hear "your success stories and your disappointment stories"

Simpson Thacher's hiring attorneys try to dig a little deeper than the surface, associates report. They assume the transcript will be stellar, but try to get a little bit more. "Like any other top-notch firm, my firm searches for the best talent available," says a junior banking associate. "One thing that makes this firm different is that the firm does not focus entirely on a person's GPA. They like to see if the candidate is talented as a whole, not only grade-wise. They like to hear about your life story, how you got where you are at, your success stories and disappointment stories, any information that can paint a whole picture of you as a person and future professional." As a corporate attorney puts it, "Simpson is mostly looking to ensure that you are someone they would want to be stuck with at 3 a.m. in a data room. They're looking for personable, interesting people who, while being workhorses, are more than just brains."

Associates say that Simpson limits its recruiting to top-five schools, as well as the New York-area schools such as Fordham and Brooklyn Law. "Simpson focuses the bulk of its efforts on the Princeton Review top-five law schools and New York City schools outside of the top five," says a New York associate (whose school falls into neither of those two categories). Another New Yorker stresses the geographic component. "Simpson is very active in New York-area law schools, i.e., Columbia, NYU, Fordham."

© 2007 Vault Inc.

OUR SURVEY SAYS

Unique work. Uniquely demanding clients.

Simpson's associates fall somewhere between generally satisfied and downright enthusiastic about their jobs. A senior associate brags, "I can't imagine a better law firm to work at than Simpson Thacher. The clients are top notch and the work is as good as it gets, because we are not retained for run-of-the-mill or ordinary cases." However, here's how another associate spins that same quality. "The work is satisfactory in that we won't take just any deal—size, complexity and status matter. Thus, you won't get bored continually doing the same structures over and over. However, this makes clients more demanding. Your 'quality of life' goes way down." A corporate finance associate reports that the "top-notch capital market practice with its exceptional bank and equity firm client base makes each deal unique and the work exciting."

We'd hang out together if we ever had a free minute ...

Associates characterize the firm's culture as "friendly," "genteel," "relaxed," "reserved," "very polite," "pleasant" and "amazing." A banking associate says, "The people here are friendly and I haven't encountered any screamers. No one has time to socialize, but I believe we have the best people working here." A junior litigator adds, "Simpson is surprisingly a pretty social place. The cafeteria is usually full during lunch. There is no frat-like pressure to socialize at the end of the day, but associates still have plenty of opportunities to do so if they wanted to. For the most part, everyone is extremely nice. At least on the litigation side, associates seem excited about the work they are doing and the partners they work with." This litigator provides a slightly different take, saying, "The firm is not very social on the whole. However, smaller groups within the firm seem to socialize. There is not much interaction outside work. The atmosphere is very collegial and business is taken seriously."

Respect and reliance

The partners' reviews are mostly off the charts. A midlevel New Yorker says that she feels a "high degree of respect from partners, not just through interaction, but also in their reliance of associate work product." Another junior New Yorker reports, "My experience in the banking group is that partners are friendly, encouraging, helpful and show respect to their associates. Even in these busy times, the partners let us know how thankful they are for what we are doing. The group aims at having group events that are well attended by partners. The management as a whole tries hard to get the associates involved." Over in the tax department, one attorney adds, "I can only speak to the tax department, but I find that associate/partner relations are relatively good." However, one litigator warns, "Partners treat associates very well, but we don't interact with them all that much. And, if they're workaholics, you have to be one, too. They respect family and personal commitments, but not just having 'free time.' You need a good excuse."

Formal training: Catch-22

Associates say the firm's formal training program is sometimes too much and sometimes too little. On a good day, "The training could be better," says a junior banking attorney. "As juniors, we receive some formal training when we start, but it is not enough to meet our needs." A junior litigator complains, "The firm's litigation training program for new associates needs work. There is a LOT of training and it is spread out over the first few new months of working. Sometimes three times a week. But it is extremely boring because it is often out of context and not interactive. The fact that training takes place several times a week after we have started working cuts into our days and requires us to stay later than we would have otherwise had to in order to finish everything up." An M&A attorney piles on, adding, "Simpson provides little, if any, training for corporate associates. Litigation associates receive extensive mandatory training." The firm has recently revamped its training programs. In 2007, the firm introduced a training program for midlevel litigation associates and the corporate department hired a manager of training.

Visit the Vault Law Channel, the complete online resource for law careers, featuring firm profiles, message boards, the Vault Law Job Board and more. **www.vault.com/law**

VAULT CAREER LIBRARY 131

Hit-or-miss

Alas, insiders report that Simpson Thacher's mentoring program varies greatly based on the mentors assigned. A banking associate suggests, "Simpson could also improve their informal mentoring. As a junior we are placed in a group that has three mentors. This is okay, but when everyone is so busy it would be better to have an individual mentor to which you would feel less intimidated in asking questions." A litigator agrees, reporting, "There is very little in the way of training from partners. Partners just expect you to figure out what to do." Another litigator adds, "Mentoring is pretty variable. There is a mentoring program, but each 'mentor' chooses the level of involvement with his mentee. One mentor usually has several mentees. Some mentors are very helpful, answering questions and organizing events, while others are completely M.I.A. The mentoring program is completely left up to the discretion of the mentor."

Market leader = universal happiness? Not quite ...

A junior litigator raves, "Having Simpson lead the way on the new wave of raises is definitely a point of pride for the new associates. It's funny to have associates from other firms calling me to thank the Simpson partners for them for their inevitable raises."

One might think that Simpson's status as the first firm to institute the latest round of raises—thus bringing the rest of the market along with it—would be the end of the compensation story. One would be wrong. Simpson's associates have any number of complaints about their pay. A banking associate warns, "The compensation is great for someone who just graduated law school. I think in order to retain midlevels, the firm could increase the midlevel compensation." Another insider says, "Our firm provides the best compensation for BigLaw attorneys outside of Wachtell. It is pretty good, but I would like the option of cashing out unused vacation time and it would be nice if the firm made a matching contribution into associates' 401(k) plans like most companies do." And sounding a theme common to attorneys who work alongside investment bankers, one corporate attorney complains, "Simpson is tops in compensation, but the industry in general is under-compensating deal attorneys."

BigLaw means BigHours (no BigSurprise)

Simpson's associates say that the hours are as long as you might imagine, but not as bad as you might fear, and that the partners' general flexibility cushions the blow. "Big firm with big firm hours, which is to be expected," says a junior litigator. "But absolutely no pressure for face time." A banking expert advises, "The firm has great policies in place. There is flex-time for attorneys, which allows attorneys a day where they can work from home. My friend is a flex-time attorney and is allowed every Friday to work from home so she can spend time with her kids. The firm is also flexible when requesting leaves of absence, etc. The hours are long, as expected." As for specifics, a junior litigator reports, "I expected long hours. Right now my hours range between 9:30 a.m. and 10 p.m., with work on most weekends. Many people here seem to work flex-time or part-time, but still work hard."

© 2007 Vault Inc.

"Having Simpson lead the way
on the new wave of raises is
definitely a point of pride."

—Simpson, Thacher & Bartlett associate

Visit the Vault Law Channel, the complete online resource for law careers, featuring firm
profiles, message boards, the Vault Law Job Board and more. **www.vault.com/law**

VAULT CAREER LIBRARY   **133**

Cleary Gottlieb Steen & Hamilton LLP

One Liberty Plaza
New York, NY 10006
Phone: (212) 225-2000

2000 Pennsylvania Avenue, NW
Washington, DC 20006
Phone: (202) 974-1500
www.cgsh.com

LOCATIONS

New York, NY • Washington, DC • Beijing • Brussels •
Cologne • Frankfurt • Hong Kong • London • Milan •
Moscow • Paris • Rome

MAJOR DEPARTMENTS & PRACTICE AREAS

Antitrust & Competition—European • Antitrust &
Competition—US • Asian Practice • Banking & Financial
Institutions • Bankruptcy & Restructuring • Belgian Law •
Corporate Governance • Derivatives • Employee Benefits •
Energy • English Law • Environmental Law • French Law •
German Practice • Intellectual Property • International Trade •
Italian Law • Latin America • Leveraged Finance • Litigation &
Arbitration • Mergers, Acquisitions & Joint Ventures • Private
Clients & Charitable Organizations • Private Equity •
Privatizations • Pro Bono • Project Finance & Infrastructure •
Real Estate • Russian Practice • Securities & Capital Markets
• Securities Enforcement • Sovereign Governments &
International Institutions • Structured Finance • Tax

THE STATS

No. of attorneys: 850+
No. of offices: 12
Summer associate offers:
  Firmwide: 109 out of 109 (2006)
  Washington, DC: 18 out of 18 (2006)
Managing Partner: Mark A. Walker
Hiring Partners:
  New York: David Leinwand
  Washington, DC: Michael A. Mazzuchi

THE BUZZ
WHAT ATTORNEYS AT OTHER FIRMS ARE SAYING ABOUT THIS FIRM

- "Charmed Elite"
- "Associate burnout"
- "Fantastic internationally"
- "Left-wing sweatshop"

UPPERS

- International work
- Accessible partners
- Great firm culture

DOWNERS

- "Hours—like any other big law firm"
- "Uneven work allocation"
- Shortage of midlevels

NOTABLE PERKS

- "Overseas rotation program"
- "Weekly wine and cheese parties held on Fridays"
- "All associates get their own offices (even summer associates)"
- "Free gym membership anywhere in town"

© 2007 Vault Inc.

RANKING RECAP

Regional Rankings

#7 - New York

Practice Area Rankings

#1 - Tax

#2 - Antitrust

#6 - Securities

#7 - Corporate

#7 (tie) - International Law

#7 - Mergers & Acquisitions

Partner Rankings

#2 - Tax

#4 (tie) - Antitrust

#7 - Overall Prestige

Quality of Life

#1 - Office Space

#8 - Pay

#10 - Selectivity

Diversity

#7 - Diversity with Respect to GLBT

#13 - Overall Diversity

#17 - Diversity with Respect to Minorities

EMPLOYMENT CONTACTS

Now York

Ms. Norma F. Cirincione

Director of Legal Personnel

Phone: (212) 225-3150

Fax: (212) 225-3159

E-mail: nyrecruit@cgsh.com

Washington, DC

Ms. Georgia Emery Gray

Director of Legal Personnel

Phone: (202) 974-1804

Fax: (202) 974-1999

E-mail: dcrecruit@cgsh.com

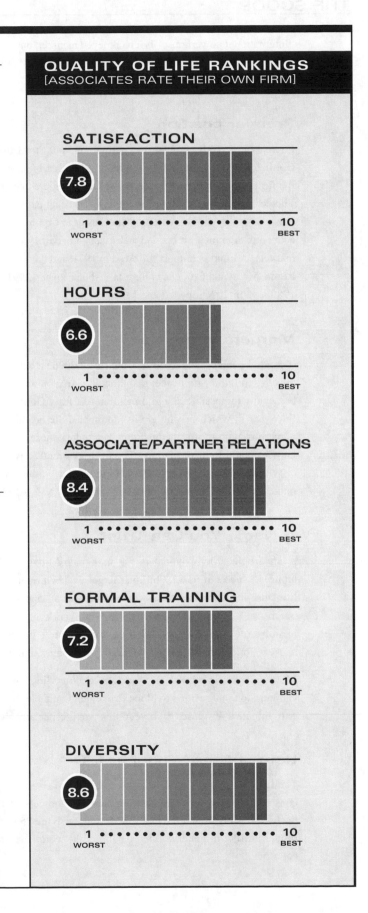

QUALITY OF LIFE RANKINGS
[ASSOCIATES RATE THEIR OWN FIRM]

SATISFACTION

7.8

1 WORST .... 10 BEST

HOURS

6.6

1 WORST .... 10 BEST

ASSOCIATE/PARTNER RELATIONS

8.4

1 WORST .... 10 BEST

FORMAL TRAINING

7.2

1 WORST .... 10 BEST

DIVERSITY

8.6

1 WORST .... 10 BEST

Visit the Vault Law Channel, the complete online resource for law careers, featuring firm profiles, message boards, the Vault Law Job Board and more. www.vault.com/law

VAULT CAREER LIBRARY   135

THE SCOOP

"International powerhouse" is a hackneyed moniker, but heck, if the cliché fits anyone, it's Cleary Gottlieb. Ten out of the firm's 12 offices are overseas, and the firm employs over 850 lawyers from more than 50 countries. Such breadth naturally gives the firm first dibs on many foreign deals, but its two U.S. offices score their share of major, home-field engagements.

Premier position

Founded in 1946 by four former partners in Wall Street firm Root Clark Buckner and Ballantine, the success of today's Cleary Gottlieb Steen & Hamilton lies in its prescient, early foray into Europe. Supplementing its New York and D.C. offices, in 1949 the firm set up shop in Paris, making the strategic choice to hire local lawyers who were partially trained in the United States. The decision to award these foreign lawyers equal partnership gave Cleary Gottlieb a unique advantage in terms of international presence. With the formation of the European Community in 1967, the firm was well situated; having anticipated the eventual economic alignment, it opened a Brussels office in 1960. The firm would then play a leading role in the burgeoning Eurodollar markets. A London outpost followed in 1971, and the firm added English law capabilities in 1997. Offices in Frankfurt, Moscow, Rome, Milan and Cologne were established between 1991 and 2004. As to Asia, the firm has had an office in Hong Kong since 1980 and, in 2006, opened another in Beijing.

Mergers of equals

It would be impossible to discuss the firm's 2006 activities without mentioning its role in Mittal Steel's grand-slam €18.6 billion unsolicited bid for rival steel manufacturer Arcelor, an acquisition that united the world's two largest steel companies. It would be equally impossible to avoid mention of Cleary Gottlieb's participation in a number of the world's largest leveraged buyouts. In a year in which private equity dominated the headlines, the firm represented firms, such as TPG and Warburg Pincus, in numerous high-profile acquisitions, including those of Harrah's Entertainment, Qantas Airways, Freescale Semiconductor, Univision and Neiman Marcus. The firm is currently advising TPG and the private equity arm of Goldman Sachs in the purchase of wireless operator Alltel, and is representing Warburg Pincus in its acquisition of Bausch & Lomb. For 2006, Bloomberg ranked the firm second for global private equity M&A deals.

A Name You Can Trust

Aside from its involvement in the mammoth Mittal/Arcelor merger, 2006 saw Cleary Gottlieb representing Maytag on the antitrust aspects of its $2.7 billion merger with Whirlpool. Automaker Toyota also had reason to thank Cleary Gottlieb antitrust litigators in 2006: in February the firm won an appeal affirming the dismissal of class-action claims brought by new car purchasers. In a suit supported by New York's attorney general, plaintiffs asserted that a conspiracy among automobile manufacturers inflated U.S. car prices by preventing the import of less expensive Canadian cars. The appeals court asserted that, as New York antitrust law allows for triple damages, it therefore doesn't permit class-action claims by plaintiffs seeking penalty.

More recently, in May 2007, the U.S. antitrust litigation team scored another major victory in defeating the Federal Trade Commission in its efforts to block firm client Equitable Resources from merging with Peoples Natural Gas. As the FTC and DOJ only litigate a few cases each year, this win is especially significant.

Home of the Whopper IPO

Though the company's prime consumers, teenagers across America, couldn't care less, Burger King's May 2006 IPO was of considerably more excitement to its new shareholders. Cleary Gottlieb advised underwriters JPMorgan, Citigroup, Goldman Sachs and Morgan Stanley in a transaction involving 25 million shares of common stock listed on the NYSE. It was the largest restaurant IPO in history; Burger King is the world's second-largest fast-food restaurant chain, with 11,109 restaurants in 65 countries.

© 2007 Vault Inc.

The firm, which Bloomberg ranked the No. 1 issuers' counsel in global IPOs for 2006, also had a hand in the July 2006 IPO of clothing retailer J.Crew, the third-largest clothing retailer in the U.S. Following the installation of a new CEO and president in early 2003, J.Crew began repositioning its business, and Cleary Gottlieb represented the company in complex debt equity restructurings connected to the planned IPO. Other U.S. IPOs in which the firm was involved in 2006 include those of Mastercard and Chipotle Mexican Grill.

Outside of the U.S., Cleary Gottlieb also had a hand in groundbreaking matters. The firm represented Rosneft in its $10 billion IPO and London Stock Exchange listing in July 2006, and was counsel to Lotte Shopping Co. in its $3.5 billion IPO on the Korea Exchange and London Stock Exchange—the largest IPO ever by a Korean company.

Rituals of courtship

International and national litigators also had a busy 2006. Internationally, firm litigators continued to defend the Republic of Argentina against numerous bondholder lawsuits in New York, Italy and Germany, including by successfully defeating challenges to Argentina's debt exchange offer, a victory that permitted the cancellation of over $60 billion of nonperforming sovereign debt, and by defeating numerous efforts to attach sovereign assets. The firm also prevailed in invoking the Foreign Sovereign Immunities Act in two Fifth Circuit appeals to defend the Republic of Congo from creditors seeking rights to oil royalty payments. It also successfully represented Italian airline Alitalia in proceedings brought by its biggest domestic competitor, Air One, which sought to block Alitalia's auction-block purchase of low cost carrier Volare, and won a trial victory in Florida state court for Del Monte, defeating claims of fraud, breach of fiduciary duty and breach of contract.

Sayonara SEC

In 2006, the firm welcomed back some returning heroes. Alan Beller, a former director and senior counselor in the Securities and Exchange Commission, rejoined the firm as a partner, focusing on securities, corporate governance and other corporate law matters. Beller's return followed that of Giovanni Prezioso, former general counsel of the Commission, who served during the implementation of the Sarbanes-Oxley Act, the most significant reform of the U.S. securities laws since the Great Depression, and one that dramatically changed the way public companies operate. In their Cleary Gottlieb homecoming, both Beller and Previoso join David Becker, Prezioso's predecessor as SEC general counsel. Managing Partner Mark Walker asserts that the ex-SEC triumverate "will allow us to offer our clients around the world an even higher level of service in the corporate and securities areas."

With the returns of Beller and Prezioso, Cleary Gottlieb's rock-solid white-collar and enforcement practice now boasts five former federal prosecutors and two former SEC general counsels, as well as a former general counsel of the FDIC and former senior officials of the Justice Department's Antitrust Division and the FTC. The firm regularly advises individuals and corporations in criminal investigations and enforcement proceedings related to money laundering, price fixing, banking law issues, accounting issues, insider trading, antitrust, political corruption, false claims, financial irregularities and the Foreign Corrupt Practices Act. Perhaps most importantly, Cleary Gottlieb also advises clients on how to avoid becoming the target of a government investigation.

Regular clients include major financial institutions, banking organizations and large insurance companies. Recently, Cleary Gottlieb advised the nonmanagement directors of Riggs Bank in a money laundering investigation, and Doral Financial Corporation in civil litigation and SEC, NYSE and Federal Reserve Bank of New York investigations regarding its earnings statement. The firm is also counsel to independent directors of Verisign in an internal investigation relating to options backdating.

Out of Africa

Cleary Gottlieb attorneys have worked on a broad spectrum of pro bono cases, including representing individuals in search of asylum, offering educational opportunities for students in underserved school districts, representing Hurricane Katrina survivors with appeals to FEMA, protecting the rights of domestic violence survivors, and partnering with not-for-profit organizations on

Visit the Vault Law Channel, the complete online resource for law careers, featuring firm profiles, message boards, the Vault Law Job Board and more. www.vault.com/law

VAULT CAREER LIBRARY   137

community development and affordable housing projects. In 2006, *The American Lawyer* ranked the firm No. 5 across the nation for pro bono activity.

The firm recently secured the release of Zakirjan Hassam, an ethnic Uzbek born in the former Soviet Union, who had been declared a non-enemy combatant but was nonetheless detained at Guantánamo Bay for over four years. Mr. Hassam has since been released to the government of Albania, where he was granted asylum with the firm's help. Clearly Gottlieb has also assisted immigrants from Africa's most troubled nations. Firm lawyers won political asylum for a couple who fled Rwanda after suffering persecution at the hands of the Kagame regime. Complicating the asylum petition was the fact that the clients were born in the Democratic Republic of Congo, though they carried only Rwandan citizenship; to win asylum, the firm had to prove that the couple faced persecution in both Rwanda and the Congo.

One of the firm's most high-profile cases was its representation of nonprofit AUTONOMY, Inc. in its fight to uphold Oregon's Death with Dignity Act, which permits physician-aided suicide for terminally ill patients. The Bush administration went on the attack, citing inconsistency with the federal Controlled Substances Act, but in 2006 the U.S. Supreme Court upheld the law, ruling that a federal drug law could not be used to prosecute doctors who facilitated the deaths of terminally ill patients by prescribing overdoses.

In another ongoing, high-profile case, the firm's Washington, D.C., office has joined in the investigation of Washington, D.C.-based businesses that were allegedly recruiting homeless individuals and paying them less than minimum wage to evict people from rental homes. The effort was spearheaded by a D.C.-based associate, who learned of the allegations in an article in *Street Sense*, a monthly local newspaper written and sold on the street by the homeless. Cleary Gottlieb has since filed a federal class-action suit on behalf of local homeless coalitions against six of the companies.

GETTING HIRED

(Not-so-secret) formula: School + Grades + Social Skills = Offer

Cleary's associates generally agree as to what it takes to land a job here: A candidate must have top 10 percent (or so) grades from a top-10 (or so) school, as well as, of course, top-notch social skills. As one midlevel corporate attorney puts it, "If you are not in the top 10 percent of your class at Harvard, Yale, Georgetown, Stanford, NYU, Columbia or a few other schools, have been on law review and have some international experience of some type, you are fighting a very uphill battle. The upside is, when you get in, you're in, and you're surrounded by incredible people." A junior antitrust specialist adds, "Cleary is a difficult place to get a job. They love to cherry-pick from the top students at the nation's top schools. However, they are also willing to recruit at other schools, and resumes are always welcome [...] to be honest, grades are important, but so are social skills. Cleary wants smart people who can interact with one another, and with clients."

A second-year suggests, "Cleary is looking for academically strong candidates, but also real people who would be enjoyable to work with and usually someone with international experience or interests." Or, as one (straight to the point) first-year puts it, "I have been told by the person heading up our recruiting that we are 'grade snobs.' So basically, go to a top law school and get great grades."

OUR SURVEY SAYS

Somewhere between "Happy" and "Very Happy"

Associate satisfaction at Cleary Gottlieb seems to range from "happy" to "very happy." A junior New Yorker, for example, reports, "I am generally satisfied with the work I do and the people I work with. There are times that it can be a bit stressful and there is a tendency to expect almost too much, but for the most part I like the challenge and colleagues." A midlevel litigator says, "I am very happy with my combination of exciting litigation work and pro bono representations. I find my work always

© 2007 Vault Inc.

challenging and interesting, and I am continually growing as an attorney with new experiences." And a midlevel adds, "The structured finance work is usually intellectually stimulating. You are doing deals, so there is of course a fair amount of mundane tasks that need to be done, but at the core you are asked to understand and apply very complex concepts as you incorporate the financial terms into documents that work. There's a fair amount of negotiation at times, which also keeps things interesting, and most partners allow the midlevel associates to take on a fair amount of the substantive responsibilities in these areas."

Associates call Cleary Gottlieb "open," "relaxed," "unpretentious" and "very collegial." The consensus seems to be that attorneys love to hang out and socialize, and would do so more often if they didn't have to work so much. "The culture is friendly, but people are busy," says a New York corporate attorney. "Most of the socializing takes place not around the water-cooler or in the cafeteria, but during firm-sponsored parties." A labor expert adds, "Cleary is an extremely social, generous firm—I love the parties and the events! All my friends at other law firms are always impressed by events hosted by Cleary, whether it's in the office or at an outside venue."

A crabby minority

Associates say that the firm's partners rank somewhere between good and about as good as it gets. As one corporate associate puts it, "I find most partners to be very respectful of associates. There are a couple of exceptions, but it's not different from anywhere else." Another attorney from the New York headquarters reports, "It depends on the partner, of course, but I've heard few complaints." A junior corporate New Yorker agrees, adding, "There is a bad apple in every bunch, but I am convinced that I would have a much worse quality of life at any peer firm, as the partners and senior attorneys have been, with few exceptions, very thoughtful in terms of protecting my time and looking out for me." And a midlevel litigator adds, "Largely, the partners are very respectful and friendly, often taking an interest in us as people. Certainly, there are a few crabby partners, but they are clearly in the minority." However, a few associates warn about the lack of firmwide communication. "Partnership and firmwide management decisions are a closed book," one senior litigator complains. "There has been an effort recently at greater transparency, but the efforts and result have been minimal."

"Almost too much"

Associates say that the firm makes every effort with its formal training program, but that that's not the best way to learn how to practice law. There's "almost too much training—the firm invests a huge amount of resources in it, including an annual three-day NITA training for junior litigators," reports a New York litigator. A corporate-finance expert advises, "The training is good here. There are frequent CLEs and opportunities to learn about different areas of the law." A D.C. attorney praises his office's offerings. "The firm offers numerous training opportunities," he says. "In addition, associates are encouraged to enroll in CLEs offered outside of the office if a course of interest is offered by another organization." However, another corporate finance associate warns, "Tons of training opportunities, not a ton of time to take advantage of them." So, as one New Yorker succinctly suggests, associates simply "learn by doing."

Although the firm may offer "too much" formal training, that's not the problem with the firm's informal training efforts, associates generally agree. "From partners it is not very extensive," complains one junior associate. "It does not come very naturally and often feels very strained and awkward, no doubt discouraging partners from spontaneous mentoring." A banking expert adds, "The firm is making efforts to implement a mentoring program, but without a clear vision for what they are supposed to accomplish." There are, however, a number of associates who consider mentoring to be one of the firm's true strengths. "The informal training I receive—learning from partners and trial-by-fire—is fantastic," says a midlevel litigator. "I really feel that the partners, by working with me on projects and by giving me substantial responsibility, I learn more and more every day."

Exceeds what any human is worth?

Cleary Gottlieb's associates give the firm's compensation plan nearly perfect scores. A junior labor attorney boasts, "I love Cleary's lock-step system and that everyone works hard together, with the confidence that we will always be paid at the best rates." A Manhattan litigator reports, "Our pay matches the top of the New York market. It's not a leader in setting the salary,

Visit the Vault Law Channel, the complete online resource for law careers, featuring firm profiles, message boards, the Vault Law Job Board and more. www.vault.com/law

VAULT CAREER LIBRARY 139

but it will follow Sullivan & Cromwell and Cravath." The pay is even better for associates in the firm's other offices. A D.C. attorney says, "We're top of the market for New York, but work in D.C., so it's excellent in comparison to the D.C. market. Of course, we work as much as our investment banking clients, but they make a ton more money then we do. Put it this way, the compensation is only enough when viewed in comparison with my other options." As one thankful litigator puts it, "I know that we get paid the exact same as our peer firms and that we are never a salary-increase leader, but my compensation far exceeds what any human is worth."

Hours and hours and more hours and no surprise there

Cleary Gottlieb's associates call the firm's hours among the longest in the business, though many of them seem to take that in stride. "There are ups and downs—with an understanding that after an up you should have some down," reports a midlevel New Yorker. A corporate attorney advises, "The hours can be rough, but it is what I thought it would be." A corporate expert adds, "There are many things to deal with during the day and the tendency to see a 6 p.m. e-mail with some urgent task is annoying. That said, most people respect your time and previous plans and allow you to get out of the office if necessary." A number of associates commend the firm for its part-time and flexible-schedule efforts, though they add that there remains room for improvement. As one antitrust specialist puts it, "Cleary is working through its position on part-time work schedules. The policy is flexible on paper, but it has some kinks on a practical level."

© 2007 Vault Inc.

"All my friends at other law firms are always impressed by events hosted by Cleary."

—*Cleary, Gottlieb, Steen & Hamilton associate*

Visit the Vault Law Channel, the complete online resource for law careers, featuring firm profiles, message boards, the Vault Law Job Board and more. **www.vault.com/law**

VAULT CAREER LIBRARY

141

8

Latham & Watkins LLP

Although Latham & Watkins is a global firm without any one particular office serving as headquarters, for ease of communications correspondence can be sent to:

633 West Fifth Street, Suite 4000
Los Angeles, CA 90071
Phone: (213) 485-1234
www.lw.com

LOCATIONS

Chicago, IL • Costa Mesa, CA • Los Angeles, CA • Menlo Park, CA • Newark, NJ • New York, NY • Reston, VA • San Diego, CA • San Francisco, CA • Washington, DC • Barcelona • Brussels • Frankfurt • Hamburg • Hong Kong • London • Madrid • Milan • Moscow • Munich • Paris • Shanghai • Singapor • Tokyo

MAJOR DEPARTMENTS & PRACTICES

Corporate (including Communications, Company Representation, Corporate Finance/Securities, Equity Capital Markets, Health Care, Life Sciences, Mergers & Acquisitions, Private Equity, Technology Transactions, Venture & Technology) • **Environment, Land & Resources** (including Environmental Litigation, Environmental Regulatory, Environmental Transactional Support, Land Use) • **Finance** (including Banking, Bankruptcy, Private Equity Finance, Project Development & Finance, Real Estate, Structured Finance & Securitization) • **Litigation** (including Antitrust & Competition, Appellate, Communications, Employment Law, Entertainment, Sports & Media, Government Contracts, Health Care, Life Sciences, Insurance Coverage, Intellectual Property, Media & Technology, International Dispute Resolution, Product Liability & Mass Torts, Securities Litigation & Professional Liability, White Collar & Government Investigations) • **Tax** (including Benefits & Compensation, International Tax, REITS, Tax Controversy, Tax-exempt Organizations, Transactional Tax)

THE STATS

No. of attorneys: 1,900 +
No. of offices: 24
Summer associate offers: 271 out of 276 (2006)
Chairman & Managing Partner: Robert M. Dell
Global Recruiting Chair: John C. Tang

 ## THE BUZZ
WHAT ATTORNEYS AT OTHER FIRMS ARE SAYING ABOUT THIS FIRM

- "One of the best, excellent international work"
- "A bit like Degrassi"
- "Innovative, agile, very well managed"
- "Where the beautiful people go"

BASE SALARY (2007)

1st year: $160,000
Summer associate: $3,080/week

UPPERS

- Great partner/associate relations
- Great compensation
- "Early responsibility—you ask for it, you get it"

DOWNERS

- Tough, unpredictable hours
- "Growth makes it hard to know attorneys in other offices"
- "Relatively few perks"

NOTABLE PERKS

- Biannual business meeting at resort for the entire firm
- "Luxurious" attorney retreats
- Business development budget of $250 per client outing for even junior associates
- "Robust mobile network access capabilities"

© 2007 Vault Inc.

RANKING RECAP

Regional Rankings

#1 - Northern California
#1 - Southern California
#6 - Chicago
#6 - Washington, DC
#11 - New York

Practice Area Rankings

#6 - Antitrust
#7 (tie) - Technology
#8 - Corporate
#8 (tie) - Mergers & Acquisitions
#8 - Securities
#9 - Litigation

Partner Rankings

#5 - Securities
#8 - Overall Prestige

Quality of Life

#13 - Formal Training
#20 - Selectivity

EMPLOYMENT CONTACT

Ms. Debra Perry Clarkson
Director of Global Recruiting
Phone: (858) 523-5400
Fax: (858) 523-5450
E-mail: debra.clarkson@lw.com

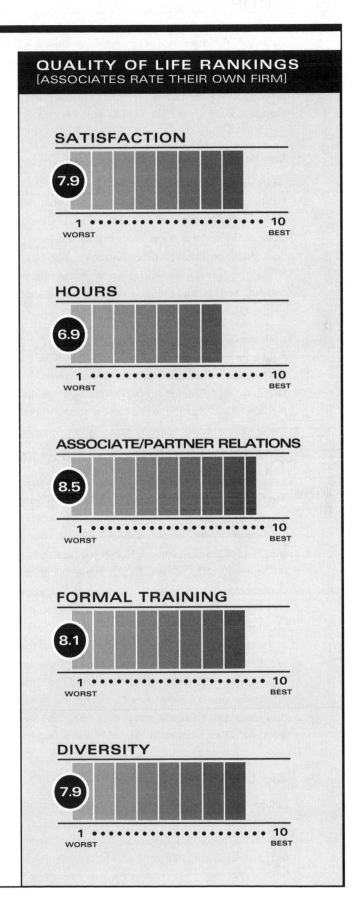

QUALITY OF LIFE RANKINGS
[ASSOCIATES RATE THEIR OWN FIRM]

SATISFACTION
7.9
1 WORST ... 10 BEST

HOURS
6.9
1 WORST ... 10 BEST

ASSOCIATE/PARTNER RELATIONS
8.5
1 WORST ... 10 BEST

FORMAL TRAINING
8.1
1 WORST ... 10 BEST

DIVERSITY
7.9
1 WORST ... 10 BEST

Visit the Vault Law Channel, the complete online resource for law careers, featuring firm profiles, message boards, the Vault Law Job Board and more. **www.vault.com/law**

VAULT CAREER LIBRARY   **143**

THE SCOOP

Latham & Watkins is one of the world's premier law firms, serving the domestic and cross-border needs of an impressive roster of clients. With more than 1,900 attorneys in 24 offices around the world, the firm practices in all the major jurisdictions of the United States, the EU and Asia, as well as regularly representing companies doing business in Latin America and Africa. In addition to corporate work, the firm is a leader in environmental law, finance, litigation and tax services—founding partner Dana Latham was a former commissioner of the Internal Revenue Service.

Latham goes global

Beginning as a small Los Angeles law firm in 1934, Latham & Watkins was well positioned to take advantage of Southern California's swiftly escalating postwar industrialization and population growth. By 1969, the firm employed 42 lawyers—a healthy practice, but still undeniably local. Over the ensuing three decades, Latham & Watkins aggressively and steadily expanded around the globe. So successful was the expansion that the New York office is now the firm's largest, with a little black book that lists almost all of its downtown, Wall Street neighbors as clients. In 2006, Latham sits secure as one of the world's largest law firms, a bona fide member of the clique that includes Clifford Chance, Baker McKenzie, DLA Piper—and that's without cheati ... um, engaging in any mergers. Annual firm revenue is among the highest. In 2007, for the second consecutive year, Latham ranked No. 2 in the AmLaw 100, with firm revenue at $1.624 billion and profits per partner exceeding $1.8 million.

And, as might be expected of a firm of Latham's stature, firm alumni have some weighty titles and responsibilities: Bruce Babbitt, former governor of Arizona and U.S. Secretary of the Interior; Michael Chertoff, Secretary of Homeland Security; Christopher Cox, SEC chair; Beth Wilkinson, general counsel to Fannie Mae; Alice Fisher, chief of the Department of Justice's Criminal Division; and J. Thomas Rosch, Commissioner of the Federal Trade Commission. The new crop isn't too shabby either: joining the firm's D.C., San Diego and San Francisco offices in fall 2006 were six U.S. Supreme Court clerks.

A lawyer in every port ... and landlocked financial center

Expansion continues to be a priority—in late 2006, Latham opened offices in Madrid and Barcelona, recruiting highly regarded M&A partner Jose Luis Blanco to lead the firm's Spanish operations. The expansion in Spain continued the firm's European growth to 10 offices, following on the 2005 Munich office opening. The German practice is now three offices and more than 100 lawyers strong, and a frequent recipient of accolades from the German legal press. A vigorous global project finance practice is run out of London; banking, leveraged finance, high-yield and private equity are also key drivers of the London office—and the firm has beefed up its U.K. litigation capabilities. In Paris, strengths include private equity, capital markets and litigation; the firm employs more than 120 lawyers and counts among its clients Goldman Sachs, BNP Paribas, AXA and LVMH. Latham also augmented its capabilities in Asia in 2005 by opening shutters in Shanghai, and has seen growth in its Indian, Philippine and Malaysian practices. The firm's Shanghai and Hong Kong offices presently consist of a handful of trailblazers setting up camp in the new frontier of Chinese corporate work, and the firm is optimistic about the array of IPOs, M&A and project finance work to come. Latham has already had success with Asian deals, having worked on a number of Chinese IPOs listing in the States—including that of search engine baidu.com, "The Chinese Google." The firm also had a hand in The Carlyle Group's acquisition of Xugong Group Construction Machinery, China's largest machinery manufacturer; the deal was hailed as a breakthrough for the Chinese private equity industry. In 2006, Latham added a Latin American practice in New York (luring a six-lawyer practice from rival O'Melveny & Myers, led by market leader Jose Fernandez).

Big business as usual

Latham & Watkins' transactional practices consistently rank at the top of *The American Lawyer* Corporate Scorecard. For the second consecutive year, Latham earned the highest number of top-10 rankings in the Corporate Scorecard—in 2007, Latham secured 14 top-10 rankings. Reflecting this leadership position, Latham's corporate and finance teams work on market-defining and groundbreaking transactions. For example, in October 2006, the firm figured in three biotech collaborations valued at $1.3 billion. Two deals involve drug discovery company Plexxikon: a potential $706 million multiproduct collaboration with Basel-based Roche, focused on the development of cancer treatments, and a potential $100 million collaboration with French pharmaceutical company Servier, focused on the treatment of cardiovascular disease. A third deal saw biopharma Intermune forge a $530 million global collaboration with Roche to develop and commercialize protease inhibitors for the treatment of hepatitis C virus.

In 2006, the firm was involved in a merger that will create an extensive global derivatives exchange. Latham & Watkins represents the Chicago Board of Trade in a cash/stock election transaction with the Chicago Mercantile Exchange, a deal expected to close by midyear 2007. The merged company, valued at approximately $25 billion, will be named CME Group.

Other stellar M&A activity for the firm includes longtime client Harrah's Entertainment, Inc., which recently accepted a buyout offer from private equity firms Texas Pacific Group and Apollo Management in an all-cash transaction valued at approximately $27.8 billion. The firm previously handled Harrah's $10 billion acquisition of gaming rival Caesars in 2005, which made Harrah's the world's largest casino company

Enron ... and on ... and on ...

When Enron fell, lawsuits mushroomed, and many an executive or affiliated company found itself with some "splainin" to do. Accounting firm Arthur Andersen was no exception: in June 2002, a federal jury in Houston convicted the firm of "corruptly persuading" its employees to destroy Enron-related documentation. Arthur Andersen maintained that all was in accordance with its standard document retention policy, and Latham led the firm's successful 2005 appeal before the Supreme Court. Then-Chief Justice Rehnquist drafted the Court's unanimous opinion, which held that the conviction rested on a misinterpretation of the witness tampering statute, which requires proof of conscious wrongdoing as well as a sufficient connection between a defendant's conduct and any future proceeding. The consequent dismissal of the case was, according to *Legal Times*, "the biggest victory for businesses this term."

Keepin' up the good works

In 2006, Latham personnel—including more than 1,240 Latham attorneys as well as summer associates, paralegals and other professional staff—provided more than 161,000 hours of free legal services around the globe, valued in excess of $56 million. Since 2000, Latham personnel have provided more than 860,000 hours of pro bono, totaling almost $260 million in free legal services.

Pro bono work in 2006 included a high-profile case in Los Angeles, where a young man with no record of gang affiliation and no criminal record was convicted of murder and attempted murder stemming from a gang related shooting. After several habeas petitions, seven years of advocacy and an eight-day evidentiary hearing presented by the Latham team, the California Court of Appeal concluded that errors and omissions of trial counsel had deprived the young man of a fair trial. His conviction was vacated in its entirety. Latham continues to assist in preparing the case for retrial and ensuring that justice ultimately is served. The story was captured in a documentary film that won top honors at the Los Angeles Film Festival.

The firm was also recently honored by the Humane Society of the United States (HSUS) for outstanding pro bono litigation on behalf of animals. In May 2006, Latham secured a sweeping victory on the Humane Society's behalf in the U.S. District Court for the District of Columbia in connection with HSUS's challenge to the government's decision to issue numerous invasive research permits that would have had the effect of killing, without any meaningful environmental review, many endangered and threatened Steller sea lions.

In a rare example of M&A pro bono, Latham completed an extensive affiliation transaction for adventure-education organization Outward Bound, which united under the national organization six chartered schools and urban centers in locations across the country. The affiliation process, completed in 2005, involved managing complex 501(c)3 rules, nonprofit corporation codes in various jurisdictions, and governance and fiduciary issues.

And it was a case of classic, camera-ready pro bono: in Texas, a state that has executed over 355 inmates since reinstating the death penalty in the 1970s, freeing a man condemned to die is no mean feat. But in 2004, Latham & Watkins attorney James

Visit the Vault Law Channel, the complete online resource for law careers, featuring firm profiles, message boards, the Vault Law Job Board and more. **www.vault.com/law**

VAULT CAREER LIBRARY   **145**

Blank managed to do just this for pro bono client Ernest Willis, on Texas' death row since 1987; Willis was the first Texas death row inmate released since 1997. IP attorney Blank, who first came across the case as a summer intern at Mudge Rose, had been working on the case his entire career, carting it with him when he came aboard at Latham. (A group of more than 30 IP and product liability litigators joined Latham from Mudge Rose Guthrie Alexander & Ferdon, one of New York's old-line firms, in 1995.) In addition to finding constitutional defects in the government's case, Blank and the Latham team argued that Willis had no motive to burn the house nor harm the women that were killed in the blaze. Persuaded, a district court granted habeas relief, and Texas' attorney general decided not to appeal. Lesson learned? Never underestimate the intern.

Heard through the grapevine ...

In 2006, a survey of Fortune 500 general counsel by *Corporate Counsel* magazine selected Latham as a "Go-To Law Firm." Latham & Watkins also received the 2006 "Client Choice Award for Excellence in Client Service" in the U.S. category from the *International Law Office*, and placed sixth in the 2006 *Legal Business* Global 50, a league table representing the top-50 law firms in the world, as ranked by turnover. In *The American Lawyer's* midlevel associates survey, Latham ranked No. 1 among "national" firms and firms with more than 500 lawyers, and placed No. 1 in associate satisfaction among the most profitable firms. Latham also placed in *The American Lawyer*'s A-List, which recognizes the top-20 U.S. firms based on results in four categories: revenue per lawyer, pro bono, associate satisfaction and diversity. And in Chambers & Partners' 2006 standings, the firm garnered 18 No. 1 national and regional rankings; 56 of the firm's practice areas were recognized, up from 46 in 2005.

GETTING HIRED

"Not just people who are brilliant"

A D.C. insider reports that Latham is "looking for people with very intimidating resumes—3.3 or above GPA from the top-10 law schools, and amazing conversation/personal skills." A first-year associate advises, "The ranking of schools and GPA cutoff are inversely related, i.e., you need a higher GPA at the lower-ranked schools (law review is almost required), and a lower GPA is acceptable (law review is not required) at the higher-ranked schools." She adds, "The firm generally hires friendly and sociable people." A junior litigator agrees, adding, "There is a lot of talk at Latham about the need to maintain our culture of mentally sharp but friendly people through effective recruiting practices. Within the universe of high academic achievers at top-20 schools, a lot of effort is expended to weed out the insufferable ones. I think, on the whole, these efforts succeed."

A New Yorker emphasizes the importance of a candidate's social skills: "We take almost every interviewee to a meal, which provides vastly more insight into the interviewee's personal skills and helps enforce the rule that we only hire people we would actually want to work with, not just people who are brilliant. I feel assured that junior-level input is as valued as senior level, and I really think the recruiting staff 'gets it' and takes care of recruits while not just spoiling them." An Angeleno adds, "In short, you need (1) good grades from a great school and (2) a universally friendly and social personality. The firm does look at diversity significantly when making hiring decisions."

OUR SURVEY SAYS

"My third and last firm"

Latham & Watkins' associate satisfaction reviews definitely tip toward the positive side of the scale. For new associates, happiness is strongly correlated to their feelings about the firm's system of assigning newbies to new departments—or, more specifically, not assigning them at all. "The 'Unassigned Program,' in which new associates are not assigned to any one department for two years, has its advantages and disadvantages," reports a first-year. A junior associate professes, "I am very happy here. My experience tends to compare very favorably with that of almost any other junior lawyer I know." Another junior associate says, "As at any other elite firm, hours are long and work is hard, but I am largely surrounded by great people." A

© 2007 Vault Inc.

senior associate adds that Latham employs "the best group of partners and associates—and this is said with knowledge, as this is my third and last firm."

90% friendly

Latham's associates praise the firm's "great spirit of team play and collegiality," calling the firm's culture "very friendly" and "quite social." A junior IP expert reports, "The culture generally is quite laid-back. Attorneys interact and socialize together across all levels of seniority. There is very little artificial hierarchy." Another (unassigned) junior associate says, "There are various events for the lawyers to socialize together—happy hours, holiday parties, lunch meetings. Not everyone attends, though, because they are often busy." A Chicagoan adds, "Latham is a firm where you can spend the whole day bouncing from office to office chatting it up with your friends and colleagues. At the same time, Latham is the type of place where you can get in, get your work done and go home. I would say that most people are somewhere in between those two extremes." Or, as this first-year puts it, "Lawyers always have the opportunity to socialize outside of work but never feel pressure to do so. All in all, we are a cohesive office and 90 percent of my colleagues are friendly and supportive."

Partners pretty perfect

Associates give the firm's partners a big, fat, passionate and (nearly) unanimous thumbs-up. "The partners I've worked for are uniformly interesting, quirky and kind," says a second-year. "In my view, people with bitter or self-aggrandizing personalities tend to be weeded out as they get more senior." A first-year adds, "I've been completely comfortable with partners in the firm. Almost too comfortable—I find myself viewing them more as friends than superiors."

Associates participate actively

Even "firmwide decisions"—the bane of associates at big firms everywhere seem to involve associate input, sources report. "All important aspects of associate work at the firm are managed by committees where associates participate actively," says a New York attorney. "Associates therefore participate and are informed of firmwide decisions." Another insider adds, "The associates' committee provides a nice buffer between the partnership and the associates. There are, of course, a lot of different personalities amongst the partnership but, generally speaking, my experience has only been positive."

Training: usually useful

Latham's associates call the firm's formal training offerings top of the line, though they also feel there's room for the firm to improve. There is "lots and lots of training—constant MCLE's, and 'academies' for all associates at a particular level," says a senior litigator. A first-year reports, "Training is great. The 'first-year academy' is top notch, and the mandatory core curriculum can't be beat." However, a junior litigator adds, "The firm places a great deal of emphasis on training for junior associates and has a detailed course of mandatory training sessions for the first year (in addition to non-mandatory, but highly encouraged packages, such as deposition training). Not all of it is useful. Too often, a training session is a too-detailed PowerPoint filled with boilerplate."

Likewise, associates call the firm's informal training generally great, though occasionally spotty. A junior litigator raves, "The senior associates and partners seem to truly care about the younger associates' career development." A Chicagoan adds, "The mentoring program is great here, both on an informal and formal level. The true learning takes place informally—through extensive evaluation and feedback on our work product and the way we handle ourselves with clients and colleagues." That said, a New Yorker warns, "The individual must pursue informal training and mentoring, at his or her own initiative." Another first-year adds, "There is a formal mentoring program, but it doesn't seem to work in practice. It works when mentors have time for lunch. Informal training is almost nil. Partners and associates don't have time: it's all about billables, and informal training isn't billable."

Visit the Vault Law Channel, the complete online resource for law careers, featuring firm profiles, message boards, the Vault Law Job Board and more. **www.vault.com/law**

VAULT CAREER LIBRARY   **147**

Long hours, but you knew that

At Latham, the hours requirements can be—surprise—long and daunting. However, associates call them (more or less) manageable and the partners (more or less) flexible. "I billed 2,400 hours as a first-year associate and expect to bill around 2,300 in my second year," says a Chicago attorney. "Since I'm young and single, it's quite easy to manage. I am not sure how attorneys who are parents manage such a workload, though." According to the firm, "Latham prides itself on facilitating as best as possible efficient remote work arrangements as well as designing and making available comprehensive benefits to assist working parents balance the work/life equation. And unlike many of our peers, who have raised their minimum billables to 1,950 hours, Latham's expectations remain 1,900." A first-year New Yorker warns, "It is nearly impossible to control the number of hours spent in the office, or even the efficiency with which time in the office is spent. Assignments for first-year associates, or requests from supervisors, sometimes arrive in the evening, after often spending a full day with no work to do." Another insider adds, "We have professional discretion to determine when we are in the office. Yet, hours are hours, and the reality that billable hour goals need to be met holds true at Latham."

© 2007 Vault Inc.

"The partners I've worked for are uniformly interesting, quirky and kind."

—*Latham & Watkins associate*

Visit the Vault Law Channel, the complete online resource for law careers, featuring firm
profiles, message boards, the Vault Law Job Board and more. **www.vault.com/law**

VAULT CAREER LIBRARY   **149**

9

PRESTIGE
RANKING

Weil, Gotshal & Manges LLP

767 Fifth Avenue
New York, NY 10153
(212) 310-8000
www.weil.com

LOCATIONS

New York, NY (HQ)
Austin, TX • Boston, MA • Dallas, TX • Houston, TX •
Miami, FL • Providence, RI • Silicon Valley, CA •
Washington, DC • Wilmington, DE • Brussels • Budapest •
Frankfurt • Hong Kong • London • Munich • Paris •
Prague • Shanghai • Warsaw

PRACTICE AREAS

Business Finance & Restructuring
Corporate
Litigation/Regulatory
Tax

THE STATS

No. of attorneys: 1,200+
No. of offices: 19
Summer associate offers: 73 out of 73 (2006)
Chairman: Stephen J. Dannhauser
Hiring Partner: Penny Reid

BASE SALARY (2007)

1st year: $160,000
2nd year: $170,000
3rd year: $185,000
4th year: $210,000
5th year: $230,000
6th year: $250,000
7th year: $265,000
Summer associate: $3,077/week

UPPERS

- "Exciting work"
- "Friendly and fun atmosphere"
- Firm's "strong commitment" to pro bono

DOWNERS

- "Lack of clarity on partnership opportunities"
- Unpredictable schedule
- "Can be tight with money"

NOTABLE PERKS

- $2,000 technology stipend (for first- and second-years)
- Gym membership reimbursements
- "Numerous tickets to sporting events, theater, opera,etc."
- "My floor has a 'cookie party' every Thursday"

THE BUZZ
WHAT ATTORNEYS AT OTHER FIRMS ARE SAYING ABOUT THIS FIRM

- "Bankruptcy 'R Us"
- "Insane hours"
- "Great reputation; great bonus scale"
- "Testosterone Island"

© 2007 Vault Inc.

RANKING RECAP

Regional Rankings
#2 - Texas
#2 - Miami
#8 - Northern California
#10 - New York

Practice Area Rankings
#1 - Bankruptcy
#7 - Intellectual Property
#9 - Corporate
#9 - Mergers & Acquisitions

Partner Rankings
#2 - Bankruptcy
#10 - Overall Prestige

Quality of Life
#5 - Formal Training
#16 - Best Firms to Work For
#18 - Pro Bono

Diversity
#10 - Overall Diversity
#12 - Diversity with Respect to Women
#14 - Diversity with Respect to Minorities

EMPLOYMENT CONTACTS

Ms. Petal Modeste
Director, Legal Recruiting
Phone: (212) 833-3669
Fax: (212) 310-8007

Ms. Naima Walker-Fierce
Director, Legal Recruiting
Phone: (212) 310-6799
Fax: (212) 310-8007

Ms. Nancy Gray
Associate Director, Legal Recruiting
Phone: (212) 735-4554
Fax: (212) 310-8007
E-mail: recruit@weil.com

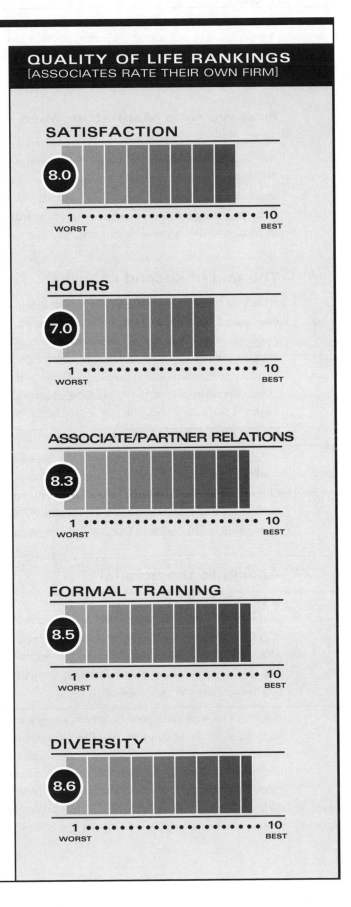

QUALITY OF LIFE RANKINGS
[ASSOCIATES RATE THEIR OWN FIRM]

SATISFACTION
8.0
1 WORST • • • • • • • • • • • • • • • • • 10 BEST

HOURS
7.0
1 WORST • • • • • • • • • • • • • • • • • 10 BEST

ASSOCIATE/PARTNER RELATIONS
8.3
1 WORST • • • • • • • • • • • • • • • • • 10 BEST

FORMAL TRAINING
8.5
1 WORST • • • • • • • • • • • • • • • • • 10 BEST

DIVERSITY
8.6
1 WORST • • • • • • • • • • • • • • • • • 10 BEST

Visit the Vault Law Channel, the complete online resource for law careers, featuring firm profiles, message boards, the Vault Law Job Board and more. www.vault.com/law

VAULT CAREER LIBRARY   151

THE SCOOP

A powerhouse in corporate restructuring, private equity and litigation, Weil, Gotshal & Manges is undoubtedly one of the world's leading law firms—and is, apparently, just getting started. In 2006, the firm hurdled eight spots to reach a No. 11 ranking on *The American Lawyer*'s "A-List."

First we take Manhattan, then we take Berlin

Weil was founded in New York in 1931, and now houses its headquarters on a prize chunk of Manhattan real estate—a Fifth Avenue office with views over Central Park. With more than 1,200 lawyers scattered throughout Europe, the U.S. and Asia, the firm bases half of its 19 offices overseas and has a tradition of jumping on expansion opportunities, i.e., heading off to Warsaw shortly after the fall of the Iron Curtain. Recent additions to the real estate portfolio are offices in Munich, Shanghai and Hong Kong; the Shanghai office, though young, has already had a hand in some weighty deals, like Chinese tech company Lenovo's acquisition of IBM's global PC business.

The god of second chances

"The God I believe in is the god of second chances," said one William Jefferson Clinton, and certainly Weil Gotshal's roster of bankruptcy/insolvency clients would have to agree. The firm fields one of the most respected and effective restructuring departments in the world, and has figured in the high-profile reshufflings of Enron and WorldCom. Of late, the firm is helping Silicon Graphics climb out of the Chapter 11 hole. In September 2006, Weil Gotshal obtained judicial approval of Silicon Graphics' reorganization plan from a U.S. Bankruptcy Court. The ruling authorized a $115 million exit financing package, which Silicon Graphics will use to pay off debts and provide cash for operations. Silicon Graphics, one of many firms regaining its footing in the wake of the giddy dot-com days, was formed in 1981 by the founder of Netscape and a group of computer science students from Stanford University.

In February 2007, a Texas bankruptcy court threw out in summary judgment a legal malpractice suit filed by one of the firm's former clients. Weil Gotshal had represented The National Benevolent Association, a social services arm of the Disciples of Christ Christian Church, during its 2004 bankruptcy proceedings; in filing the $40 million suit, the association later claimed that the firm should have recommended less financially disruptive measures. The National Benevolent Association paid Weil Gotshal approximately $10 million in fees, but the firm is presently suing for the remaining $1 million owed.

Adding to the arsenal

In the States, Weil Gotshal is top tier in private equity, advising on such deals as the $15 billion Hertz buyout in September 2005—the third-largest private equity transaction in history, after the famed RJR Nabisco buyout in 1989 and the July 2006 sale of hospital company HCA. In June 2006 Weil orchestrated one of the largest management buyouts ever: the $100-per-share MBO of Houston-based natural gas pipeline operator and distributor Kinder Morgan. Involving investment partners such as D.C.-based Carlyle Group and the Goldman Sachs Group of New York, the deal is estimated to be worth a total of $22 billion in purchased equity and assumed debt.

It is Weil's avowed intention to become as strong a force in European private equity as it is in the States. In pursuit of this aim, and after a whirlwind courtship, the firm's London office won the hand of 18-year Lovells veteran and private equity partner Marco Compagnoni (rumored to have brought with him business amounting to some £5 million per year). The February 2006 coup increased Weil's private equity capability in London to five partners. Recent private equity engagements for the London office include acting for European Capital on its November 2006 acquisition of Whitworths Limited, the U.K.'s leading supplier of dried fruit and nut-based products. This is the first deal the London office has completed for European Capital, though its U.S. affiliate, American Capital, is a longtime Weil client.

© 2007 Vault Inc.

Ford focus

After posting large net losses in recent quarters, including $5.8 billion in the third quarter of 2006 alone, Ford Motor Company—the world's third-largest automaker and an icon of American industry—took bold and decisive action to address its cash-flow situation and to fund its ongoing restructuring in response to changing market conditions, including the company's decision to seek out additional financing—over $18 billion in total—to ensure the smooth implementation of the company's plan to return to profitability. Weil clients J.P. Morgan Securities Inc., Citigroup Global Markets Inc. and Goldman Sachs Credit Partners L.P. acted as lead arrangers in the financing, which is the largest corporate debt financing in history. To secure the financing and close the deal, Ford pledged a substantial portion of its assets as collateral for the first time in its 103-year history. Weil's banking and finance team took the lead in the negotiations, providing its clients with the security of knowing that the deal terms offer enough protection in the event of a default, while also providing Ford with the financial flexibility it needs going forward, a not-so-insignificant feat considering the value of the loan's collateral.

Where the M&A action is

Weil's corporate work goes beyond private equity and corporate finance. In 2006, the firm served as counsel to Vivendi Universal S.A. in its acquisition of Matsushita's 7.7 percent stake in Universal Studios Holding I Co. (USHI) for $1.154 billion. USHI owns Universal Music Group, Universal Interactive and 20 percent of NBC Universal. Through this transaction, Vivendi Universal increased its control and ownership in USHI from 92.3 percent to 100 percent. Vivendi Universal is a leader in media and telecommunications with activities in music, interactive games, television and film, and fixed and mobile telecommunications.

Weil continues to make headlines with its representation of long-standing client GE. In May 2007, Weil counseled GE in the company's sale of GE Plastics to Saudi Basic Industries Corporation, one of the world's 10 largest petrochemicals manufacturers. The deal is valued at $11.6 billion.

MasterCard, MasterLitigators

In November 2006 Weil successfully moved to dismiss all claims brought against client MasterCard by internet payment service provider Paycom Billing Service. Paycom alleged MasterCard violated federal antitrust laws with its rules and policies relating to "excessive chargeback" activity. The district court dismissed Paycom's claims, and the Second Circuit Court of Appeals affirmed the decision, finding that Paycom lacked antitrust standing and had not sufficiently alleged concerted activity.

In September 2006, Weil litigators won a victory for client Yeda Research & Development in a patent dispute covering the use of ImClone's anticancer drug Erbitux. Yeda argued that three Israeli scientists were the actual inventors, and not the individuals named on the patent. In a 140-page decision, the U.S. District Court for New York ruled in favor of Yeda, and directed the U.S. Patent and Trademark Office to make a complete substitution of inventors, removing the individuals originally named on the patent and effectively granting Yeda ownership.

Their finest hours

Weil Gotshal's bono efforts have garnered recognition from organizations such as the Legal Aid Society of New York, the NAACP and legal publication *The Lawyer*. A revised pro bono policy, which encourages that firm lawyers perform a minimum of 50 hours of pro bono each year and that all new attorneys take on at least one pro bono matter during their first two years at the firm, went into effect in 2006.

On behalf of pro bono client Human Rights Watch, Weil submitted a successful amicus curiae brief defending the right of a human rights monitor not to reveal its sources, for fear of reprisals against those sources or their families. The brief was submitted in December 2005 in an ongoing trial of three soldiers of the Armed Forces Revolutionary Council, which is being heard in the Special Court for Sierra Leone. Following submission of the brief, the Appeals Chamber of the Special Court reversed an earlier decision and ruled that, in appropriate circumstances, human rights monitors can refuse to name their sources

Visit the Vault Law Channel, the complete online resource for law careers, featuring firm profiles, message boards, the Vault Law Job Board and more. **www.vault.com/law**

VAULT CAREER LIBRARY   **153**

when giving evidence. The successful brief was a joint initiative between the firm's New York and London offices; the London team handled international and European aspects, while the New York team dealt with U.S. precedents concerning the rights of journalists and informants.

The firm also acted as pro bono counsel for a United Nations World Food Programme initiative that created the world's first weather-derivative transaction for humanitarian emergencies. As part of an effort to finance natural disaster aid more quickly and efficiently, the U.N. program signed a deal with French insurer Axa Re. The contract provides $7.1 million in emergency funding in the event of extreme drought. The derivative is based upon a calibrated index of rainfall data gathered from 26 weather stations across Ethiopia. In the experimental project, payment would be triggered if data between March to October 2006 indicates that rainfall was below historic averages, pointing to the likelihood of widespread crop failure. Weil's structured finance and derivatives attorneys worked closely with U.N. World Food Programme executives and the World Bank Commodity Risk Management Group to structure the novel deal.

GETTING HIRED

Local flavor

Traditionally, Weil Gotshal has been relatively less grade-fixated, and very accepting of recruits from regional schools. Reports one third-year, "The primary criteria are intelligence and a good work ethic. They don't care much about academic pedigree, but of course that doesn't hurt." A Big Apple colleague believes that "competitiveness really depends on one's vantage. Weil is not competitive for a Harvard Law grad who can tie his tie or walk in heels, but it is harder to get hired here from schools outside of the *U.S. News* Top 25, although plenty of people are from those schools." A junior associate in Silicon Valley thinks that Weil is "pretty picky ... you're going to need to be a good student at a good law school to get a serious look from us. Though we've rejected candidates with stellar resumes because they came across as a poor fit for our group, and accepted people with lesser qualifications because they seemed like they would fit in." A D.C. associate thinks his office is "grade obsessed" and "concentrates a lot on local schools." Advice from a midlevel in Dallas: "Summers and first-years tend to come from Texas law schools; laterals from NYC BigLaw." In Miami, "They look for a strong GPA and journal work. Also, a commitment to the city in which the office is located. Most offices don't tend to recruit candidates at the lower tiered schools, but the Miami office has and continues to. A fifth-year in New York grumbles that the firm "should be more selective"; other insiders report that the firm has been upping hiring standards across its offices, and "is trying to attract more candidates from nationally recognized schools."

OUR SURVEY SAYS

Got a date yet for the bankruptcy ice cream social?

At Weil, work comes first, and associates prefer it that way. Though many do report that some of their closest friends are within the firm, after-work socialization isn't expected; as a senior insider describes it, "socializing is made on a personal basis." In Dallas, "attorneys are a bit older and more family-focused than is typical in NYC BigLaw ... most people have families they want to spend their free time with. That said, the social climate here is relaxed and friendly. It just doesn't generate as much nightlife as in New York." A senior level in the international group tells us that "the D.C. office on the whole is laid-back, politically left of center, and people do socialize together when given the opportunity. Work usually takes precedence, but the willingness to socialize is there. Specific practice groups, however, tend to socialize together." The West Coast reports that "the Silicon Valley office is laid-back in comparison to the other offices." In New York, "lawyers do tend to socialize together—we go for lunches together both as part of formal mentoring events and casually as colleagues. Some people go for happy hours after work, and the various different groups have different social events like the bankruptcy ice cream social every week, bankruptcy dinner once a week, M&A dinners and cocktail party. Overall it's a pretty social firm, yet there is no real pressure to socialize outside the firm if you'd rather have your own life and just want to do your work." A Boston associate believes that

© 2007 Vault Inc.

"regional offices tend to have much more cross-departmental socialization. New Yorkers tends to stick within departments," but that overall, Weil boasts a "very social, collegial atmosphere."

It comes with the territory, and the pay

Asserts a corporate associate in New York, "The culture of this firm has changed for the better. You need a tremendous work ethic to be successful here, but your efforts will not go unrecognized. The old image of a sweatshop has been all but eradicated here." Agrees a junior associate in Manhattan, "Overall, the hours are not as bad as everyone makes them out to be. The tough part is having very little, if any, control over my schedule. But it comes with the territory. This is a service business." Adds a fellow newbie, "It's no 9-to-5 job, but it's no 9-to-5 salary either. Things haven't been any worse than expected though, except for the occasional very, very late nights or long weekends." Shrugs an antitrust lawyer in D.C., "I get paid a lot. I should expect to work a lot." A banking associate in New York thinks Weil is "ahead of the curve on flex-time and part-time work schedules. It makes Herculean efforts to make them work, and they do work for a number of people here." In Silicon Valley, "hours are reasonably flexible, at least in the sense of letting associates control which hours they spend at their desks. I am routinely able to arrive early and leave early." An eighth-year agrees that "the firm tries as much as possible to allow flex-time and part-time, although sometimes it is difficult under the circumstances." A New York litigator has this to say: "Hours are unpredictable, as expected. However, those that do high-quality work are 'rewarded' with more work, which in my observation is a factor that has led many star associates to leave the firm."

Vroom vroom ... follower of the pack

Weil faithfully follows the firms that set the New York market, but "only aims to match, never to be a market leader." To the delight of first-years ("We get paid at the top-market rate, so no complaints whatsoever"), Weil followed Simpson's lead and raised salaries in January 2007. While Manhattanites are content, though not terribly impressed, with the figure on their checks, that same figure gets a different reception in, say, Texas. A midlevel crows, "Top of New York scale, but with zero state income taxes and two-thirds of NYC's cost of living." A litigator in Dallas, however, believes that "there are serious trade-offs for being paid that much. The expectations with respect to hours, responsiveness, and the degree to which you are expected to put your life on hold are very high." Some have found the recent salary hike to be bittersweet. Says an M&A associate in New York, "After the recent hike in salaries, partners appear to have less respect for an associate's personal space and weekends—it's expected that we work through weekend after weekend." And as for bonuses, a fourth-year in New York notes that "people can earn more than the standard bonus for distinguished work, but this seems to cause more problems, as people who do not receive it are unhappy with the system." A midlevel in Manhattan sees it differently: "Weil is a great place for high-achievers. It rewards 'distinguished' associates with merit bonuses that are [at least] $10,000 higher than market rate."

Feelin' the love

"I'm very satisfied with the level of respect that I receive from the partners," says a litigator in Manhattan. "I believe that they keep the associates informed of management decisions, value associate input and treat associates well." A colleague in the same office finds the vibe "very positive ... good working relationships, associates' opinions on client matters are taken seriously, positive learning experience." A fifth-year in Houston agrees that "associates are generally well respected, though it varies from partner to partner. Some make you feel almost like equals, others not so much. But it's more of the former than the latter." He does, however, regret the "negligible associate participation in firmwide decisions." From a New York litigator: "All partners I've worked with have been respectful of my time, personal life and skills. Partners usually ask my availability before giving me an assignment; they don't just assume you can get it done. When I've done good work, it's been recognized and appreciated. Also, the firm takes associate feedback of partners very seriously and is about to roll out a similar feedback system for senior associates." Of course there are outlier partners, but a finance attorney says that "I know there have been steps taken to reign in 'bad' behavior by partners in other groups and that the firm as a whole is working hard and has succeeded in improving in this area."

Visit the Vault Law Channel, the complete online resource for law careers, featuring firm profiles, message boards, the Vault Law Job Board and more. **www.vault.com/law**

VAULT CAREER LIBRARY   155

Getting schooled

"The firm has A LOT of training. If there is any complaint, it would be that there is too much," grumbles one first-year in the Big Apple. A fifth-year in Houston reports that "if you are looking for formal litigation training, Weil is a hard place to beat." In Silicon Valley, an insider observes that "the firm dedicates a great deal of its resources to flying associates around, hiring trainers, getting partners involved in training, etc." But a skeptic in New York has this to say: "There's a lot of training, but its utility is sometimes dubious. For example, jury training for bankruptcy attorneys makes little sense. We almost never encounter juries." A Houston associate's grievance is that "the firm uses the excuse that it offers so many programs to be very inflexible in paying for outside CLE."

Bagels and Weight Watchers—a perk conspiracy?

Weil perks are the "standard New York extras": car rides after 8:30 p.m., SeamlessWeb, moving expenses, emergency day care. A "$2,000 technology stipend each year for first- and second-year associates" is much appreciated, and there is a "gym membership stipend up to $750 per year." In Washington, there are "laptops with few restrictions, a mentoring budget, Weight Watchers at work, Friday night in-office happy hour." In Boston, it's "jeans on Fridays!" One New Yorker sulks, "There's nothing really cool—we don't have an in-house shoeshine guy like Cravath," though many consider the New York office's Central Park views to be a perk in itself. Some outposts score "free soft drinks and popcorn," and Miami's happy with "bagels on payday."

© 2007 Vault Inc.

"Partners usually ask my availability before giving me an assignment ... When I've done good work, it's recognized and appreciated."

—Weil, Gotshal & Manges associate

Visit the Vault Law Channel, the complete online resource for law careers, featuring firm profiles, message boards, the Vault Law Job Board and more. **www.vault.com/law**

VAULT CAREER LIBRARY

157

Covington & Burling LLP

1201 Pennsylvania Avenue, NW
Washington, DC 20004-2401
Phone: (202) 662-6000
www.cov.com

LOCATIONS

New York, NY
San Francisco, CA
Washington, DC
Brussels
London

MAJOR DEPARTMENTS & PRACTICES

Antitrust • Arbitration/ADR • Communications • Corporate,
Securities, Insolvency & Real Estate • Employee Benefits •
Employment • Energy • Environment • Financial Institutions
• Food & Drug • Government Investigations • Health Care •
Information Technology, Privacy & E-Commerce • Insurance
• Intellectual Property • International • Legislative •
Life Sciences • Litigation (Trial & Appellate) • M&A •
New Media & Content • Patent Advice & Litigation • Sports
• Tax • Trade • Transportation • White Collar Defense

THE STATS

No. of attorneys: 650
No. of offices: 5
Summer associate offers: 93 out of 93 (2006)
Chair, Management Committee: Stuart C. Stock
Hiring Partners:
  Washington, DC: Paul V. Rodgers & Michael X.
    Imbroscio
  New York, NY: P. Benjamin Duke, Carey Roberts &
    Carolyn Taylor
  San Francisco, CA: Kenneth D. Ebanks

BASE SALARY (2007)

New York, NY; Washington, DC; San Francisco, CA
1st year: $160,000
2nd year: $170,000
3rd year: $185000
4th year: $210,000
5th year: $230,000
6th year: $250,000
7th year: $265,000
8th year: $280,000
Summer associate: $3,080/week

UPPERS

• Top-of-the-market compensation
• Top-of-the-line partners
• "The firm is extremely supportive of pro bono"

DOWNERS

• Poor institutional communication
• "I don't like feeling tethered to my BlackBerry"
• "The quality of the secretarial help varies widely"

NOTABLE PERKS

• "Fantastic" gym
• On-site child care center in Washington
• "Frequent lunches with interesting speakers"
• Recent office retreats at extremely nice resorts

THE BUZZ
WHAT ATTORNEYS AT OTHER FIRMS ARE SAYING ABOUT THIS FIRM

• "Excellent and now diverse"
• "Niche player"
• "Coveted pedigree"
• "Good, but extremely pretentious"

© 2007 Vault Inc.

RANKING RECAP

Regional Rankings
#2 - Washington, DC
#20 - New York

Partner Rankings
#12 - Overall Prestige

Quality of Life
#6 - Selectivity
#16 - Pro Bono

EMPLOYMENT CONTACTS

Washington, DC
Ms. Ellen Purvance
Director, Legal Personnel Recruiting
Phone: (202) 662-6200
Fax: (202) 662-6291
E-mail: legal.recruiting@cov.com

New York, NY
Ms. Nicole Adams
Director of Legal Recruitment
Phone: (212) 841-1066
Fax: (212) 841-1010
E-mail: nadams@cov.com

San Francisco, CA
Ms. Gabrielle Hall
Human Resources Manager
Phone: (415) 591-6000
Fax: (415) 591 6091
E-mail: ghall@cov.com

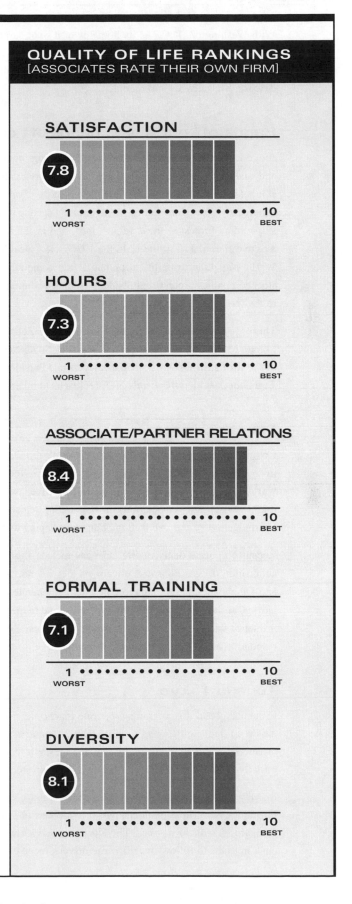

QUALITY OF LIFE RANKINGS
[ASSOCIATES RATE THEIR OWN FIRM]

SATISFACTION
7.8
1 WORST — 10 BEST

HOURS
7.3
1 WORST — 10 BEST

ASSOCIATE/PARTNER RELATIONS
8.4
1 WORST — 10 BEST

FORMAL TRAINING
7.1
1 WORST — 10 BEST

DIVERSITY
8.1
1 WORST — 10 BEST

Visit the Vault Law Channel, the complete online resource for law careers, featuring firm profiles, message boards, the Vault Law Job Board and more. **www.vault.com/law**

VAULT CAREER LIBRARY   **159**

THE SCOOP

With Washington, D.C., as its hometown, it's not surprising that Covington & Burling is an old hand at governmental affairs, habitually handling regulatory, antitrust, enforcement and investigative issues. But governmental work is just one Covington strength: the firm's 650 lawyers advise on some 25 practice areas, including corporate, transactional, technology, white-collar defense, life sciences and media.

Hands off our ships, hands off our steel

Judge J. Harry Covington and Edward B. Burling founded their firm in Washington, D.C., in 1919. One of the firm's first cases, and one that would build the fledgling firm's reputation, was an international arbitration in The Hague between Norwegian shipholders and the United States government. World War I legislation had led to the creation of the U.S. Shipping Board Emergency Fleet Corporation, a government agency that had the power to acquire vessels by requisition and seizure. Norwegian shipholders protested these requisitions, and in the successful arbitration Covington litigators helped them recover the then-massive sum of $12 million. In the 1930s, New Deal legislation led the firm to a strong regulatory practice, and by the close of World War II, antitrust litigation had also become key. During the Korean War, Covington & Burling successfully represented steel companies protesting President Truman's commandeering of all national steel mills and assembly plants deemed necessary to the war effort.

These days representative clients include AstraZeneca, Eastman Kodak, Estée Lauder, GlaxoSmithKline, IBM, JP Morgan, Merck, Microsoft, Pfizer, Procter & Gamble, Société Générale and Verizon. Alumni of the firm include the late Chuck Ruff, one of the firm's earliest white-collar lawyers and President Clinton's White House Counsel during impeachment proceedings; Paul Tagliabue, who led the firm's NFL representation before becoming NFL commissioner; and numerous law professors.

Exact sciences

Covington & Burling now ranks as the world's top life sciences firm. In January 2006 and April 2007, it was awarded first place in the *Practical Law Company*'s "Life Sciences Industry" and "Life Sciences Regulatory" rankings, which are based on a worldwide survey of industry and private practice lawyers. In its extremely broad life sciences and regulatory practices, lawyers might assist trade associations in negotiating legislation for emerging technologies, i.e., gene therapy, cell processing and pharmogenetics, and counseling companies hoping to bring their products to the United States and European markets.

Recent corporate deals in life sciences include the November 2006 representation of Abbott Laboratories in its announced acquisition of Kos Pharmaceuticals via a cash tender offer of $3.7 billion. In July 2006, Covington advised Novartis Vaccines and Diagnostics in its plans to construct and operate a cell-culture influenza vaccines manufacturing facility in Holly Springs, North Carolina. The facility, the first of its kind in the United States, will significantly boost manufacturing capacity for seasonal influenza vaccine doses over the traditional chicken egg-based method of producing such doses—thereby increasing ability to respond to an influenza epidemic or pandemic, e.g., avian flu.

Tune in Tokyo

In January 2006, Covington's corporate practice advised Sony NetServices on its partnership with Vodafone to offer 3G mobile music service to customers in more than 20 countries. Vodafone Radio DJ, a subscription service, allows customers to listen to interactive radio channels and download music to their 3G handsets and personal computers. The Vodafone radio service was initially offered in Western Europe, and then expanded worldwide.

In May 2006, the firm's technology, media and communications practice helped Kangaroo Media ink a six-year deal with Formula One. The agreement will provide fans at Formula One racing events access to live race video, audio and data via a Kangaroo handheld device. The Kangaroo service will combine the race telecast with live in-car camera and audio channels, enabling fans to follow their favorite drivers, receive race telemetry, and be privy to communications between drivers and their teams.

© 2007 Vault Inc.

They fight crime too

In January 2006, Covington "special forces" contributed to a police raid that resulted in the arrest of eight individuals for alleged data theft and financial fraud. Working together with Microsoft and the Bulgarian National Services to Combat Organized Crime (NSCOC), the firm's Global Internet Enforcement Team helped identify the group, which is accused of creating false Microsoft web pages for the purpose of financial fraud. By inviting unwitting users to "update their personal information," the group was able to collect victims' financial data, and make illegal money transfers and purchases. The Global Internet Enforcement Team includes internet investigators with specialized skills and legal expertise pertaining to cyber crime. Their skill in fighting such crime stems from long experience in internet monitoring and enforcement on behalf of IP holders worldwide. In recognition of the team's unique skills, the firm was awarded "Best Achievement in Protecting IP on the Internet" at the 2005 WORLDleader's European IP Awards.

Stolen Stoli?

Or so the Russian government claimed in a 2006 lawsuit against Covington client Spirits International (SPI). Covington IP litigators defended SPI's U.S. rights to the famous Stolichnaya vodka brand, one of the world's best selling vodkas. In a suit filed against Spirits International (SPI) and its U.S. distributor, Allied Domecq, the Russian government claimed that it was the lawful owner of all U.S. rights in Stolichnaya trademarks, and accused the defendants of trademark and copyright infringement. In March 2006, a U.S. District Court in New York dismissed all claims against SPI but one (the sole remaining claim does not involve ownership rights of the Stolichnaya brand, but asserts that Allied's marketing of the vodka as "Russian" is improper, because the vodka is bottled in Latvia, though it is manufactured in Russia). In the last years, the Putin-led government has pursued similar litigation around the world, attempting to reclaim IP rights that were sold off during the demise of the Soviet Union and the onset of perestroika.

Covington is also representing Bacardi in litigation over the Havana Club trademark, a dispute that has its roots in the Cuban government's 1960 confiscation of the Arechabala family's Havana Club rum business.

Match called

In June 2006 Covington antitrust lawyers helped win a U.S. Court of Appeals affirmation upholding the legality of The Match, the nationwide system that matches medical residents with hospitals offering positions in their particular specialties. In 2004, three medical residents filed a class action against the National Resident Matching Program, its sponsoring organizations and 29 teaching hospitals, maintaining that the organizations engaged in antitrust activities in order to depress wages; Covington antitrust litigators defended seven of the 29 defendant institutions. The plaintiffs sought higher wages and lower work hours through enforcement of federal antitrust laws. In August 2004, their petition was denied, following the passage of last-minute federal legislation that shielded The Match from antitrust claims. The June 2006 decision upholds the legality of the 2004 statute. At the time the suit was filed, medical residents worked approximately 90 hours per week, for an average salary of $40,000. Medical residents' hours were subsequently capped at an average of 80 hours a week.

Pro bono plaudits

Covington is well known for its pro bono activism. In 2006, *The American Lawyer*'s Pro Bono Survey ranked the firm No. 1; the firm has achieved a first place ranking seven times in the last 12 years. The D.C. Bar Association awarded Covington its 2006 Thurgood Marshall Award, for "commitment to excellence in the fields of civil rights and individual liberties." And the Human Rights Campaign presented the firm with its 2006 National Ally of Justice Award.

Covington lawyers are presently representing Yemeni nationals being held at Guantánamo Bay, and have obtained favorable rulings regarding these clients' rights under the Fifth Amendment and the Geneva Convention. A court ruled in March 2005 that the U.S. government could not transfer the firm's clients from Guantánamo Bay to foreign custody without first giving the prisoners a chance to challenge the move in court. The firm is also handling nine capital cases: three in Alabama, two in Mississippi, two in Florida, one in Maryland and one in Virginia.

Visit the Vault Law Channel, the complete online resource for law careers, featuring firm profiles, message boards, the Vault Law Job Board and more. **www.vault.com/law**

VAULT CAREER LIBRARY   **161**

Putting on the £s

The London office of Covington & Burling has become one of the few U.S. firms to bill in sterling. The change was introduced formally in October 2005, but gathered momentum in January 2006. Gross revenue in London had dropped from £17.1 million in 2004 to £15.9 million for 2005; the firm admits that generating revenue in dollars while incurring expenses and overhead in sterling has been problematic. The currency switchover will temper the firm's exposure to exchange rate fluctuations and a weak dollar.

GETTING HIRED

Degree of difficulty

A couple of words come up repeatedly when Covington associates discuss their firm's hiring practices: "Difficult," and "Harvard." For example, one senior associate from the firm's D.C. headquarters says that the hiring attorneys seek out students at the "top of the class, journal, and no unusual career paths. Harvard, Harvard, Harvard." Another D.C. associate advises, "Covington concentrates on Harvard, though less so than in the past. Generally limited to Law Review members from top-10 schools." A D.C. litigator recommends, "Go to Harvard or Yale, or be the very best somewhere else. The firm has made a tremendous effort to diversify the schools at which it recruits. There will always be a heavy Harvard/Yale crowd here, but the ranks of junior associates are now more frequently filled with top people from other schools." Another D.C. litigator adds, "In recent years, the firm has recruited more from outside the traditional Harvard-Yale-Michigan-Chicago-Stanford set and looked to schools in the next 'tier,' such as William & Mary, Iowa, etc. However, to be considered from a school in the next tier, a candidate really needs to have exceptional credentials."

As for specific qualities, a junior associate advises, "Associates at Covington tend to have worked before law school and have unique academic backgrounds." Another junior associate says, "there is no GPA-specific cutoff, but like at all of its peer firms, the higher the GPA the greater a candidate's prospects. References are vital here in a way that I don't think is true at other peer firms." A senior D.C. associate concludes, "Anyone who is pompous or supercilious is weeded out early during the interview process."

OUR SURVEY SAYS

Great expectations fulfilled?

In general, it seems Covington lives up to the heightened expectations of its young attorneys, who could have chosen similar jobs at most any other major law firm. "I never expected to be at a firm for this long," says a seventh-year from the D.C. office. "Covington has far surpassed the expectations that I had for law firm life when I was evaluating career options in law school." A midlevel Washingtonian adds, "The work is more interesting than just about any you'll find in a law firm elsewhere. Also, the firm is extremely supportive of pro bono." Even the ostensibly ambivalent associates sound, for the most part, positive. "I don't think that I would find work at any law firm 'entirely fulfilling,'" says a senior D.C. litigator. "Covington is a more satisfying and rewarding firm to work at than the overwhelming majority of other options. I do interesting and challenging work with nice people." One added bonus of working at Covington (at least in the D.C. office): private offices. "Each associate gets their own office, which is quite nice," boasts a first-year. There are, of course, the occasional gripers. "The work has gotten more mundane, and less interesting, as time has worn on here," complains another senior D.C. litigator.

"Reserved does not equal unfriendly"

At Covington, it's about as "collegial," "respectful," "friendly" and "social" as a top-tier firm can be. "Covington lawyers are friendly and eminently civil to one another," reports a D.C. litigator. "We do socialize, and we enjoy each other's company."

© 2007 Vault Inc.

Another D.C. litigator adds, "People are friendly, although people do not socialize together in large groups as much as at some firms. I count work colleagues among my friends, but rarely go out for drinks after work with them—more likely that they'd be included in a social gathering with a wider circle of friends. The firm tends to be a quiet place." That said, a recent lateral transfer adds, "Covington is a bit formal and reserved, especially at first. As a lateral, I was struck by the degree of polite formality in the firm's culture. Since I've settled in, I've come to the conclusion that the firm is actually a very friendly place. Reserved does not equal unfriendly, just reserved. And in some ways the formality operates to protect associates from the bad behaviors allowed elsewhere." As for formal social opportunities, a D.C. second-year advises, "There is an in-house happy hour nearly every Friday, providing ample opportunity to get to meet your co-workers. However, attendance at these happy hours is less than I would have expected. The firm has recently instituted a program called 'Covington Nights Out' which allows associates the opportunity to socialize at bars and restaurants in the D.C. area." The "Nights Out" program also operates in New York and San Francisco.

We heart partners

The associates' reviews of the firm's partners fall just a step or two short of being actual love letters. "The partners are highly respectful of associates," says a D.C. seventh-year. "We are consistently told that the associates are the true life-blood of the firm. The firm now has an associate advisory committee, which is making a tangible contribution to associate life." A corporate associate reports, "Firm management is concerned about associate retention overall and has taken several steps to improve associate life, including partner interaction. The D.C. corporate group has terrific partners that treat associates with respect." However, a number of associates complain about being kept out of firmwide decisions or not receiving sufficient feedback. "Both individual partners and the firm as a whole could do a better job of keeping associates informed about management policies and cases," suggests a third-year. A senior associate adds, "Most of the partners are nice. But there are substantial minorities who cannot be bothered to keep track of what an associate is doing or what he has done. And feedback must be a no-no for many of them."

Covington's associates rate the firm's formal training program somewhere between passable and good. "There are a number of formal training programs, including a NITA trial advocacy program, deposition training, writing seminars, etc.," advises a senior D.C. litigator. A senior corporate attorney reports, "They are working on it, but the formal training is currently not well organized and thus suffers from inconsistency. Mid- and senior-level associates get none, unless they have CLE requirements (which the firm pays for if required, but D.C. does not require)." A banking associate adds, "The litigation training is excellent, and the corporate department has recently upgraded their training efforts. Formal training in the regulatory areas, however, could be improved." The firm notes that it is aware of the need for improvement in this area, and in fact has just hired a director of professional development, who will build a department dedicated to professional training.

Ad hoc but strong mentoring

Associates call the firm's mentoring offerings "ad hoc," but generally strong. "I have had absolutely wonderful mentors since joining the firm," reports a D.C. litigator. "Each one mentors in different ways, but the consistent practice is that they all have taken a keen interest in ensuring that I have opportunities to develop the full panoply of litigation skills." As a D.C. corporate attorney puts it, "I've been fortunate to have a couple of partners who look out for me. But that can just be happenstance, at times." Another D.C. corporate attorney says, "Mentoring is pretty good; training from senior lawyers is spotty." And a newbie adds, "Not too much one-on-one partner contact to date. Several of the more senior associates do a good job of training."

Judged on an hourly basis, Covington lawyers would rank among the profession's highest paid, a number of associates boast. As one senior D.C. associate reports, "Including bonuses, we pay at the top of the D.C. market." As a junior D.C. associate puts it, "For the hours required, the compensation is quite good. While there is a disparity in salaries and bonuses between here and large New York firms, the demands are clearly less than at those New York factories." This feeling, though, is far from unanimous. A second-year complains, "Covington is not a salary leader. This is especially disappointing given the overall reputation of the firm in D.C. and nationwide." A senior attorney reports, "I wish the bonus formula were clearer. I'm not certain

Visit the Vault Law Channel, the complete online resource for law careers, featuring firm profiles, message boards, the Vault Law Job Board and more. www.vault.com/law

VAULT CAREER LIBRARY   163

we get credit for the countless non-billable hours." A midlevel piles on, adding, "C&B never will be a market leader. Bonuses are historically below market."

"Part of your overall contribution to the firm"

Associates say the firm's generous, flexible pro bono policy would be hard to improve upon. A D.C. insider advises, "Pro bono work is part of your overall contribution to the firm that is considered for purposes of your yearly bonus." A D.C. corporate attorney adds, "There is no set formula at Covington—the bonus is not hours-based—so it's hard to tell how many pro bono hours 'count' for bonus purposes. Firm management has indicated that significant pro bono undertakings are factored into the bonus process." Or, as a junior associate describes it, "This is not very relevant for our firm because we have no billable hours requirement and our bonuses are not tied to billable hours, which are lock-step by year. So while we don't refer to pro bono hours as 'billable,' there is also no institutional disincentive to doing pro bono work."

"I never expected to be at a firm for this long. Covington has far surpassed the expectations that I had for law firm life."

—*Covington & Burling associate*

Visit the Vault Law Channel, the complete online resource for law careers, featuring firm profiles, message boards, the Vault Law Job Board and more. **www.vault.com/law**

VAULT CAREER LIBRARY   **165**

11

PRESTIGE RANKING

Kirkland & Ellis LLP

Aon Center
200 East Randolph Drive
Chicago, IL 60601
Phone: (312) 861-2000
www.kirkland.com

LOCATIONS

Chicago, IL
Los Angeles, CA
New York, NY
San Francisco, CA
Washington, DC
Hong Kong
London
Munich

MAJOR DEPARTMENTS & PRACTICES

Corporate/Transactional
Intellectual Property
Litigation
Real Estate
Restructuring
Tax

THE STATS

No. of attorneys: 1,200+
No. of offices: 8
Summer associate offers: 179 out of 183 (2006)
Management Committee Chair: Thomas D. Yannucci
Hiring Partners:
  Chicago: Sallie G. Smylie
  Los Angeles: Melissa D. Ingalls
  New York: Joshua N. Korff
  San Francisco: David A. Breach
  Washington, DC: Craig S. Primus
  London: Matthew H. Hurlock
  Munich: Frank Becker
  Hong Kong: David Patrick Eich

THE BUZZ
WHAT ATTORNEYS AT OTHER FIRMS ARE SAYING ABOUT THIS FIRM

- "The top firm in the country"
- "Not for the faint of heart"
- "Possibly the future of associate compensation"
- "Don't play well with others"

BASE SALARY (2007)

All Offices
1st year: $160,000
2nd year: $170,000
3rd year: $185,000
4th year: $210,000
5th year: $230,000
6th year: $250,000
Summer associate: $3,077/week

UPPERS

- The free-market work distribution system
- Top-of-the-market—or higher—compensation
- World-class cases and clients

DOWNERS

- The free-market work distribution system
- "Hours that can bring tears to your eyes"
- Overworked partners

NOTABLE PERKS

- Generous maternity and paternity leave policies
- Free breakfast, free Starbucks coffee
- Free dinner after 7 p.m. (as opposed to the industry-standard 8 p.m.)
- Free cab rides to work (before 7 a.m.)

© 2007 Vault Inc.

RANKING RECAP

Regional Rankings
#1 - Chicago
#8 - Southern California
#8 - Washington, DC
#14 - New York

Practice Area Rankings
#2 - Bankruptcy
#3 - Intellectual Property
#4 - Litigation

Partner Rankings
#1 - Bankruptcy
#1 - Litigation
#3 - Intellectual Property
#14 - Overall Prestige

Quality of Life
#1 - Formal Training
#11 - Pay
#17 - Selectivity

EMPLOYMENT CONTACT

Chicago
Ms. Betsy Zukley
Attorney Recruiting Manager
Phone: (312) 861-2054
Fax: (312) 861-2200
E-mail: attorney_recruiting@kirkland.com

See web site for recruiting managers in other offices

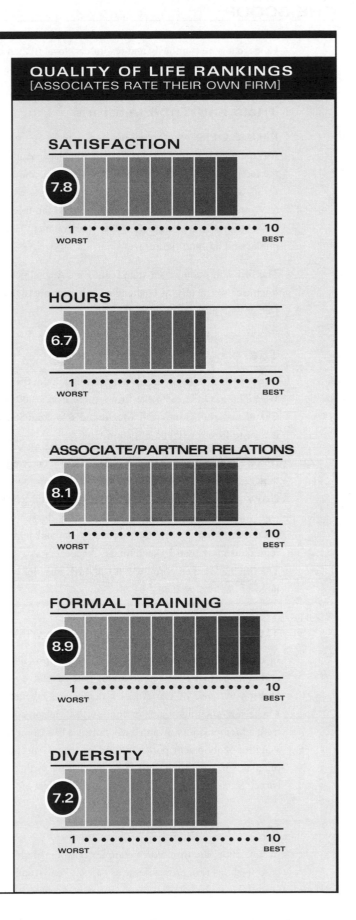

QUALITY OF LIFE RANKINGS
[ASSOCIATES RATE THEIR OWN FIRM]

SATISFACTION
7.8
1 WORST — 10 BEST

HOURS
6.7
1 WORST — 10 BEST

ASSOCIATE/PARTNER RELATIONS
8.1
1 WORST — 10 BEST

FORMAL TRAINING
8.9
1 WORST — 10 BEST

DIVERSITY
7.2
1 WORST — 10 BEST

Visit the Vault Law Channel, the complete online resource for law careers, featuring firm profiles, message boards, the Vault Law Job Board and more. **www.vault.com/law**

VAULT CAREER LIBRARY   **167**

THE SCOOP

Chicagoans are (famously and resolutely) loyal to their own, so within its hometown, Kirkland & Ellis ranks tops for prestige—but the firm's reputation in litigation, intellectual property, restructuring and corporate work stretches far beyond Chitown.

Trials and *Tribune*-ations

Kirkland & Ellis was formed nearly a century ago by attorneys Stewart G. Shephard and Robert R. McCormick. McCormick was the grandson of *Chicago Tribune* founder Joseph Medill; in 1920, McCormick left his law firm to take over as publisher of the family paper. With McCormick at the helm, and as the nation soldiered through the Depression, the *Tribune* became known for its uninhibited and crusading editorial policy—which led, naturally, to a series of defamation lawsuits. To defend his paper, McCormick relied upon his former firm and the litigation and First Amendment prowess of Weymouth Kirkland and Howard Ellis. Ellis was a champion of the "fair comment" defense, a privilege that protects published or spoken opinions directed at public officials and figures.

The firm still maintains a significant First Amendment practice, led by none other than Kirkland & Ellis head honcho Thomas Yannucci. Ironically, as challengers to media intrusion and negative coverage, these days clients often sit on the other side of the free press fence.

There's no place like home

Most of Kirkland's activity is concentrated in the firm's five U.S. offices (Chicago, New York, San Francisco, Los Angeles and Washington, D.C.), with the firm's more than 1,000 attorneys serving such American biggies as 3M, Bank of America, Dow Chemical, Kraft, Honeywell, McDonald's, Morgan Stanley, Time Warner, Verizon and Whirlpool. For the Fortune 250, Kirkland is a go-to firm for IP and litigation work.

Despite its largely American base, the firm is venturing overseas. A Munich office, operational since 2005, has enabled the firm to access the profitable German market and join the various foreign firms presently jostling for position; in 2006, activities in Germany contributed to a 12 percent increase in the firm's revenue. The firm's London office already has well-regarded private equity and leveraged finance practices. But the big expansion news is, of course, the new Hong Kong office. Opened in fall 2006, the office is Kirkland's first in Asia, and will focus on transnational private equity funds; Kirkland & Ellis currently represents more than 70 such funds. A recent private equity deal was the August 2006 acquisition of Caudwell Communications. The firm handled all corporate, tax and IP issues for client Providence Equity Partners in the £1.46 billion transaction, the firm's largest U.K. deal to date.

The case of the busy inventor

In one of 2005's most impressive IP wins, firm litigators changed stripes, representing an individual inventor instead of a corporation. In a 2001 suit involving patents related to spinal regeneration and minimally invasive surgery technology, Kirkland took on the case of Los Angeles doctor and inventor Gary Michelson. Medical device company Medtronic Inc. had sued Michelson, alleging breach of contract; Michelson countersued, alleging patent infringement. In late 2004, after a three-month trial, a Memphis jury awarded Michelson a handsome $510 million. It gets better: the verdict forced Medtronic to reconsider the viability of its patent portfolio (and its then 45 percent market share). After considerable calculation, and with considerable pragmatism, Medtronic agreed to purchase a further 500 of prolific Michelson's patents—for $1.35 billion. The settlement earned Michelson the No. 258 spot on *Forbes'* list of the 400 richest Americans—and Kirkland & Ellis received rightful acclaim.

In light of the facts

In June 2006, the firm won a complex patent infringement victory for lighting company Osram Sylvania. Plaintiff Ole Nilssen, described in a firm press release as "a well-known and litigious inventor," alleged that Osram had infringed upon 11 of his patents and sought more than $100 million in damages. Arguing that Nilssen had submitted false affidavits, misclaimed small entity status and failed to disclose related litigation, Kirkland litigators propounded a defense of inequitable conduct. Under this argumentation, they were able to win an Illinois court's declaration that the patents were unenforceable.

Sort it out amongst yourselves

In February 2006, the Supreme Court ruled in favor of Kirkland client Buckeye Check Cashing Co. in a case regarding the enforceability of arbitration clauses in contracts. Respondents in the Buckeye case had sought to avoid a contractual obligation to settle disputes via arbitration by claiming that the contracts containing such arbitration clauses were voided due to illegalities. Though the Florida Supreme Court accepted this argument, Kirkland took the case to the U.S. Supreme Court, arguing that under the Federal Arbitration Act, a court's role is limited to deciding whether the parties assented to arbitration; all else, including the legality of the contract itself, must be decided by an arbitrator. In a 7-1 decision, the Supreme Court agreed.

Water damages

In the first Hurricane Katrina insurance case to go to trial, the firm got client Nationwide Mutual out of some hot water. Pascagoula residents and hurricane victims Paul and Julie Leonard sought over $160,000 in flood-related damages from insurer Nationwide, but a judge for the U.S. District Court for the Southern District of Mississippi upheld the enforceability of the standard water damage exclusion in Nationwide's homeowners' insurance policy. The court further found that the Leonards had known that separate flood insurance was available, but did not purchase it. The eight-day bench trial was closely watched by both insurance companies and ravaged Gulf Coast communities.

Banking on bankruptcy

Kirkland may find itself justifying its billing, as a judge in the Chapter 11 proceedings of Kirkland client and auto parts maker Collins & Aikman is expected to examine the company's more than $100 million in bankruptcy advisers' fees. With 14,000 employees, Collins & Aikman is one of the largest auto suppliers in North America; the company entered Chapter 11 in May 2005. Creditor Third Avenue Value Fund, which owns Collins & Aikman bonds with a face value of $250 million, asked a federal bankruptcy judge overseeing the case to appoint a fee examiner. Third Avenue's fee objections stem from Collins & Aikman's plans to sell itself off in its entirety or in parts; Third Avenue charges that fees billed by lawyers, restructuring bankers and other professionals could have been avoided had the company reached that conclusion sooner. Kirkland & Ellis billed $18.4 million in fees as of August 2006; law firm Akin Gump billed $4.8 million through August. Under federal bankruptcy law, professional advisers must prove that fees and expenses are both "reasonable" and a "benefit to the estate," but a reorganization doesn't have to be successful for such fees to be paid.

Suffer the little children

In August 2006, an Oxford, Mississippi jury returned a defense victory for Kirkland client NL Industries. The plaintiffs in the case were 14 children alleging brain damage, cardiovascular disease, kidney ailments and peripheral neuropathy as a result of lead poisoning from NL manufactured paints in their apartments. In their successful rebuttal, Kirkland lawyers propounded a "gene defense," implying that the children's learning disabilities and health problems were genetically-based. Additional defense arguments focused on alternate sources of lead in the children's vicinity, i.e., in the soil samples of the apartment complex where the children lived. The closely monitored case was of interest to a number of paint manufacturers facing similar lawsuits, and was the second such trial of a former manufacturer of lead-based paints; the first one, held in Baltimore and also defended by Kirkland attorneys, was heralded by the *National Law Journal* as a 2000 "Defense Win of the Year."

Thank your lucky Starr

Notable pro bono wins for the firm include saving the life of a convicted murderer the day before his execution. In November 1998, Robin M. Lovitt was convicted and sentenced to death for a murder that occurred during the robbery of a pool hall in

Visit the Vault Law Channel, the complete online resource for law careers, featuring firm profiles, message boards, the Vault Law Job Board and more. www.vault.com/law

VAULT CAREER LIBRARY   169

Arlington, Va. In November 2005, Kirkland lawyers, including former Whitewater investigator and firm partner Kenneth Starr, won Lovitt a last-minute grant of clemency from Virginia Gov. Mark R. Warner. The firm's argument hinged on missing DNA evidence that, due to advanced forensic techniques, might have exonerated their client; initial DNA tests had been inconclusive. A court clerk testified that after the first trials, he had destroyed the evidence to create space in the evidence room.

Junior Kirkland associates recently cut their legal teeth on a case brought in from the Central District of California Civil Rights Panel. As a member of this panel, Kirkland periodically receives requests from judges in the district to represent pro se plaintiffs who have brought Eighth Amendment cruel and unusual punishment claims. In January 2007, the Kirkland trial team won a federal court jury verdict in favor of their client, California Department of Corrections inmate Maurice Sanders. Specifically, an eight-member jury unanimously found that eight correctional officers violated 42 U.S.C. Section 1983 by acting with deliberate indifference toward Mr. Sanders while he was housed in a special unit reserved for high-risk inmates. Notably, every attorney on the trial team participated in the courtroom proceedings. While partner Robyn Bladow and senior associate Becca Wahlquist handled voir dire, opening, closing and most of the examinations, both Nadia Janjua (third-year associate) and Shaun Paisley (first-year associate) handled additional cross examinations.

Patron of the smarts

In February 2006, Kirkland & Ellis, as well as individual partners, pledged over $7 million to the University of Chicago Law School. In recognition of the donation, the top five percent of Chicago law school students will be known as Kirkland & Ellis Scholars. More than 10 percent of Kirkland lawyers are Chicago graduates. In addition, the firm's diversity committee sponsors a fellowship program that provides law student recipients with a $15,000 stipend and a salaried summer associate position at one or more of the firm's domestic offices. Seventeen fellows will summer with Kirkland in 2007.

GETTING HIRED

Jump on in, roll up your sleeves

"The firm recruits the best, and I'm sure there are GPA cutoffs, but no one seems to know what they are," says a first-year from Chicago. "Getting in is the toughest part. Once you're here, the sky is the limit." Or, as another junior associate puts it, "There is definitely a GPA cutoff and a preference for upper-tier schools. In addition, there is some prejudice among some partners toward associates from lower-tier schools, which is difficult, but that kind of situation is exactly why we have the free-market system at Kirkland."

A Chicago litigator says that the firm's insatiable need for new associates has opened Kirkland's doors just a little wider. "On the one hand, we are desperately looking to bring in more associates. But on the other hand, we still continue to insist on fairly high credentials, although not as high as a few years ago. I believe most grade cutoffs are a B+, with most people coming from the Ivy schools, Chicago, Stanford and Duke, and the rest from the D.C.-area schools." A corporate associate adds, "Our firm is both critical and open-minded. We recruit all over the place and welcome all sorts of candidates, but also look for someone who wants to work here and do the kind of work we do, and that seems to like how we operate." A D.C. litigator elaborates on the desired Kirkland personality type: "We want someone who is going to jump in, roll up his or her sleeves, and dig into a case. We concentrate on the top members of the top schools, but regardless of numbers, the candidate needs to be able to think on his or her feet and also be personable and someone the clients will want to interact with."

© 2007 Vault Inc.

OUR SURVEY SAYS

Amazing deal flow

At Kirkland, associates' feelings for their firm closely correspond to their feelings about the firm's free-market work distribution system, which most associates seem to love. As one enthusiastic litigator puts it, "I appreciate the freedom we have to determine our own case load, choose our cases and thereby choose the people we work with." A corporate associate reports, "I find the work here very interesting. The deal-flow is amazing—there are new and interesting transactions coming in on a daily basis. There's tremendous opportunity for training and growth. Responsibility is given early on to those who prove themselves." A junior litigator advises, "If you want to be at a large law firm doing commercial litigation, I don't think there is a better place than Kirkland." And a positively zealous first-year adds, "As far law firms go, one cannot find a better firm than Kirkland & Ellis. Although it has problems endemic to firms in general, it has resolved several major issues that generally decrease the quality of life of the associates."

"Kirkland is not for the weak"

Associates call Kirkland "friendly," "courteous," "professional" and "aggressive." They also almost uniformly agree that while collegial, the firm is not the least bit "social," though they also agree that that's not necessarily a bad thing. A junior associate reports, "There is not a lot of socialization, due primarily to the firm not requiring face time. When people are done with their work they leave the office." Another junior Chicago associate advises, "This is not a place where people tend to socialize outside of the office. That said, people are generally friendly and enjoy working with each other." On the other hand, one Chitown litigator puts a different spin on the firm's lack of socializing. "The firm culture is fiercely competitive, and some days it feels like I've been thrown to the sharks, where the pushiest person is the person who gets what they want and gets their ideas across," she warns. "Kirkland is not for the weak."

Look at the size of my bonus

Associates call the firm's partners respectful and pleasant, if a little distant and hands-off. "Partners are generally very respectful of associates," suggests a midlevel litigator. "You must be proactive, however, if you want mentoring." A corporate attorney reports, "Once you find your group, you are set. By third or fourth year, associates have found the partners they like to work with (and vice-versa) and form smaller teams, most of whom get along very well—since they get to choose each other under the free-market system rather than being assigned." As for the partnership as a whole, he says, "The partnership does its best to make associates happy, both financially (our bonuses were enormous last year!) and by being responsive to associate input (e.g., there have been quite a few technology upgrades in the last year)." A representative Chicago associate adds, "My experience has been that partners treat associates with the utmost respect."

"Unmatched" training

Kirkland's associates describe the firm's formal training program as "ideal," "unmatched" and "the best." A midlevel business and finance specialist calls the firm's training "incredible" for both "general practice matters or for specific practice groups." Another midlevel adds, "Kirkland is currently instituting a comprehensive knowledge management database in its corporate group (which is being contributed to by the entire group) and provides extensive training for new associates." That said, there are a number of complainers. A junior litigator advises, "It is extensive, but not very useful. The firm spends a lot of money on a mock trial program, but will not write off an associate's time sitting in at a deposition, which is infinitely more useful." And a midlevel Chicago associate gripes, "The firm has a formal training program, but I have found it to be a waste of time. I think the on-the-job training is much more effective."

The firm's informal training and mentoring get more mixed reviews. The consensus: it's great, when you can find it. "Mentoring is available, and indispensable, but you must seek it out," suggests one litigator. A corporate associate warns, "If you are lucky

Visit the Vault Law Channel, the complete online resource for law careers, featuring firm profiles, message boards, the Vault Law Job Board and more. www.vault.com/law

VAULT CAREER LIBRARY   171

and find a partner to mentor you, then they do 'protect' you in the Kirkland 'jungle.' But, even the best mentors you can find are incredibly overworked, pretty much all the time. So you take your mentoring when you can, in five-minute increments, if that. There's no such thing as sitting and talking about your career path with someone—no such planning or development ever occurs here, to my knowledge." Another litigator complains that mentoring is "extremely minimal." She adds, "Most partners feel it is not their responsibility to provide informal training; you'll get it eventually, I guess. Some senior associates are nice and take it upon themselves to look after younger associates, but usually only to a degree." Obviously, not everyone agrees. One newbie provides a sunnier perspective: "Not only has the firm developed wonderful formal training programs, they have developed a culture of training and developing young associates as well. In my experience, senior associates and partners take the time to be sure that the younger associates understand new concepts we may encounter."

No complaint$

On the other hand, associates have no complaints about Kirkland's compensation system. A Chicago litigator calls his pay "The best in the market by far—I have no complaints whatsoever." A corporate associate advises, "Kirkland pays the most in Chicago. Period. Before this year's pay increases (which introduced a significant discrepancy between New York and Chicago), we got paid more than anyone except Wachtell. In winter of 2006, there were people in my [third-year] class getting six-figure bonuses." Another corporate associate adds, "The firm recently revamped the bonus structure to be much more favorable than in the past (and even in the past it was very competitive)."

The firm's hours may be brutal, associates say, but they are also surprisingly flexible—a product of the firm's vaunted "free-market" system. "The reward for doing good work is more work, that's for sure," advises an associate in the Chicago corporate department. "But it is in your control to some degree—while I am not that happy with the number of hours that I spend at the office, a lot of it is my fault. Under the free-market system, it's really up to you how much you work." He adds that the firm's "part-time policy is outstanding. Each participant basically creates a proposal and it is approved. (They've never rejected a proposal.) So part-time people set their own schedules." A new dad reports, "I took six weeks of paternity leave and got no guff for it whatsoever." Another dad adds, "I am able to work from wherever I need to—at work or at home. I have two small kids, so this has been one of the best aspects of my job."

How much is too much?

Associates call the firm's pro bono policy generous, up to a point. Here's how a litigator describes the firm's policy: "There's no cap (although I imagine someone would say something if ALL you billed were pro bono hours)." A midlevel says, "At Kirkland, pro bono cases are given the same attention and resources as other client matters." On the other hand, another third-year adds, "Yes, pro bono hours count as billables. One for one, in fact, but the partners do not want associates to work on pro bono matters 'too much.' But because there is no policy and everyone acts 'PC' and talks about how great pro bono is, no one knows what 'too much' is until you get a bad review."

Associates call the offices in the Chicago headquarters old and a little dingy, but say that they are soon to be replaced. "Our offices are okay. Some floors in our building are starting to show their age," tells a junior litigation attorney. As a less generous associate puts it, "The Chicago office looks like it hasn't been remodeled since the 1970s (although, the firm is moving to a new office space in 2009)." A Chicago litigator adds, "I have the space I need to do my job. I'd rather have the firm spend its money on me, not on my office."

© 2007 Vault Inc.

"The deal-flow is amazing—there are new and interesting transactions coming in on a daily basis."

— *Kirkland & Ellis associate*

Visit the Vault Law Channel, the complete online resource for law careers, featuring firm profiles, message boards, the Vault Law Job Board and more. **www.vault.com/law**

VAULT CAREER LIBRARY   **173**

12

PRESTIGE
RANKING

Debevoise & Plimpton LLP

919 Third Avenue
New York, NY 10022
Phone: (212) 909-6000
www.debevoise.com

LOCATIONS

New York, NY (HQ)
Washington, DC
Frankfurt
Hong Kong
London
Moscow
Paris
Shanghai

MAJOR DEPARTMENTS & PRACTICES

Corporate
Litigation
Tax
Trusts & Estates

THE STATS

No. of attorneys: 660
No. of offices: 8
Summer associate offers: 95 out of 95 (2006)
Managing Partner: Martin Frederic Evans
Hiring Partner: Jennifer J. Burleigh

BASE SALARY (2007)

1st year: $160,000
2nd year: $170,000
3rd year: $185,000
4th year: $210,000
5th year: $230,000
6th year: $250,000
7th year: $265,000
Summer associate: $3,077/week

UPPERS

- Collegial and polite culture
- "Mostly reasonable" hours
- "Great" training program

DOWNERS

- Too many document reviews/internal investigations
- High stress
- Non-matching 401(k)

NOTABLE PERKS

- Monthly "Lawyers' Tea"
- Annual firm outing at New York country club
- Subsidized gym membership
- Bar and moving expenses (even for in-city moves)

THE BUZZ
WHAT ATTORNEYS AT OTHER FIRMS ARE SAYING ABOUT THIS FIRM

- "Best of the white shoe NYC firms"
- "Tendency to overlawyer"
- "Bulletproof"
- "Good reputation, but I rarely see D&P listed in deal journals"

© 2007 Vault Inc.

RANKING RECAP

Regional Rankings
#8 - New York

Practice Area Rankings
#10 - International Law

Partner Rankings
#11 -Overall Prestige

Quality of Life
#4 (tie) - Pro Bono
#14 - Selectivity

EMPLOYMENT CONTACT

Ms. Sandra E. Herbst
Director of Legal Recruiting
Phone: (212) 909-6657
E-mail: recruit@debevoise.com

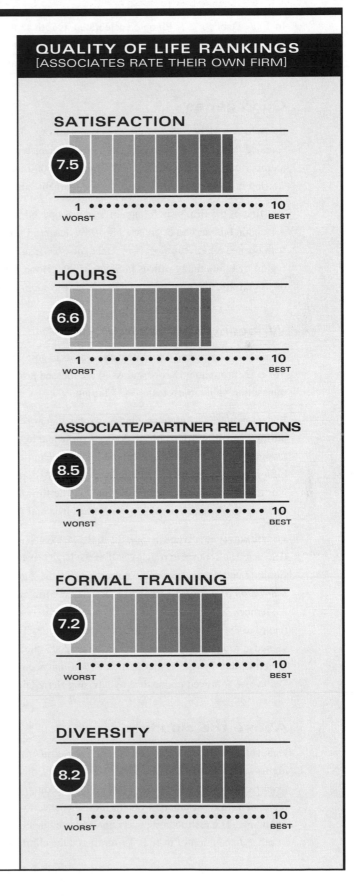

Visit the Vault Law Channel, the complete online resource for law careers, featuring firm profiles, message boards, the Vault Law Job Board and more. **www.vault.com/law**

VAULT CAREER LIBRARY   175

THE SCOOP

In 2006, Debevoise & Plimpton celebrated its 75th anniversary. The firm's 660 lawyers represent clients in all principal practice areas, including complex acquisition and financing transactions, litigation and arbitration, tax, employee benefits, and trusts and estates. Clients of the firm bridge the alphabet backwards, from Yahoo! to American Airlines.

Good genes

Eli Whitney Debevoise—a direct descendent of, you guessed it, the inventor of the cotton gin—and William E. Stevenson founded their firm in New York in 1931. Debevoise wasn't the only one with an interesting background; Stevenson had been a member of the gold-winning 1924 Olympic 1,600-meter relay team. Francis T.P. Plimpton, whose name graced the masthead starting in 1933, was the father of famed journalist and writer George Plimpton.

The first of the firm's six foreign offices was opened in Paris in 1964, handling matters pertaining to French, U.K. and U.S. law. A London bureau was established in 1989. Eastern Europe came in 1992, with the creation of a Moscow office, and in 2001, the firm opened a Frankfurt location. Debevoise has also had a presence in Asia from the 1980s, and signifies its commitment to the region by maintaining offices in Shanghai and Hong Kong. Still, the firm's Midtown New York headquarters handles the bulk of its activity, and houses some 475 of the firm's 660 lawyers.

Wheeling and dealing

Debevoise's corporate department remains its largest, and M&A its biggest practice. Thirty-two of the firm's partners (20 in New York, 12 throughout Europe and Asia) are focused primarily on M&A; in 2006, the firm handled more than 165 deals with a total transaction value in excess of $435 billion.

Recent matters include managing Verizon's January 2006 $8.5 billion acquisition of MCI; the firm has also counseled Verizon during the spin-off of its Idearc domestic print and internet yellow pages directories. In November 2006, the firm advised Phelps Dodge on its merger with Freeport-McMoRan Copper & Gold Inc. (FCX). FCX will acquire Phelps Dodge for roughly $25.9 billion in cash and stock; the combined company will result in the world's largest publicly traded copper company and the largest North American-based mining company. The firm had previously represented Phelps Dodge during its proposed $40 billion acquisition of Canadian mining companies Inco and Falconbridge.

Private equity involvement took off in the last years, and Debevoise has handled its share of deals. Between 2000 and 2006, the firm acted as counsel to roughly half of the large private funds raised in the United States, and topped the list for both U.S. Private Equity Fund Formation and Transactions in the *International Financial Law Review* 1000 (2007 edition). *Private Equity International* awarded Debevoise "Best Law Firm (Deals) in North America" in its 2006 Global Private Equity Awards. In November 2006, the firm advised Bear Stearns in connection with its financing arrangements with The Blackstone Group with regard to the agreement by Equity Office Properties Trust to be aquired by Blackstone Real Estate Partners. The transaction was valued at roughly $36 billion. In December 2005, the firm advised Clayton, Dubilier & Rice, Inc., The Carlyle Group and Merrill Lynch Global Private Equity in their $15 billion acquisition of The Hertz Corporation from Ford Motor Company. A year later, Debevoise followed up the deal by advising Hertz Global Holdings, Inc. during its $1.26 billion IPO.

Above the clouds

Debevoise has played a central role in the restructuring of the U.S. airline industry, representing a variety of major carriers in highly sophisticated restructurings. Most recently, on April 30, 2007, Delta Air Lines, Inc. and several of its subsidiaries emerged from bankruptcy. During the 19-month proceeding, the firm served as Delta's special aircraft counsel, advising Delta and its regional airline subsidiary, Comair, Inc., in connection with the restructuring of its aircraft fleet and billions of dollars in related financing. The restructuring was unprecedented in size and complexity, involving the refinancing of over 275 aircraft, the return or other disposition of over 140 aircraft and the elimination of four aircraft types from Delta's fleet.

© 2007 Vault Inc.

Trouble at the top

Led by Mary Jo White, the former U.S. Attorney for the Southern District of New York, Debevoise litigators have represented approximately 850 clients worldwide over the past two years, including Siemens AG's Audit Committee in connection with a worldwide investigation into possible corrupt payments to government officials. The firm was retained by a special committee of the board of Merck to review the company's actions before the September 30, 2004 withdrawal of Vioxx. Additionally, Debevoise represented Candlewood Timber Group in a trial arising out of Pan American's excavation activities in an Argentine rainforest, and the Association of American Publishers and five publishing houses in a copyright infringement action challenging Google's plan to build a virtual digital library.

What price art?

Well, if it is a Klimt, and you are cosmetics maven Ronald S. Lauder, let's say $135 million. In June 2006, Debevoise & Plimpton represented Lauder, the president and co-founder of the Neue Galerie New York, and the Neue Galerie in the museum's agreement to acquire a spectacular Gustav Klimt painting, *Adele Bloch-Bauer I* (1907). The painting, which had been stolen from the Bloch-Bauer family by the Nazis in 1938 and had been restituted to Maria Altmann and the heirs of the family by the Austrian government, made its debut at the Neue Galerie in New York as part of a display of masterworks by Klimt.

A helping hand

Over the years Debevoise has been especially recognized for its pro bono program. In 2006, the firm was a recipient of the Pro Bono Publico Award by the American Bar Association. Pro bono representation for the firm includes handling habeas corpus proceedings for a death row inmate in Georgia, successfully litigating the rights of 51 Mexican nationals on death row in the United States before the International Court of Justice and participating in related litigation including arguments before the Supreme Court of the United States. The firm is also representing Yemeni and Sudanese detainees at Guantánamo Bay, filing habeas petitions for the detainees' release and to improve the conditions of detention. In 2006, Debevoise lawyers devoted over 6,600 hours to representing asylum-seekers from around the world in their bids to obtain refugee status and settle permanently in the United States. Debevoise lawyers provide legal assistance to inner-city micro-enterprises in partnership with the New York Alliance for New Americans, the Business Outreach Center and the Neighborhood Entrepreneur Law Project, and also provide general corporate, tax, employment and intellectual property advice to a host of not-for-profit community service and arts organizations.

GETTING HIRED

No automatons need apply

Debevoise has a high opinion of its prospective associates. "We like to think that only the smartest of the smart should apply," sniffs one lawyer. "The firm will only hire candidates who can be put in front of a client, have a high GPA and are generally intelligent," says a senior associate. "The firm prefers that their lawyers look good, are on the intellectual side, went to fancy schools, are a bit preppy and work hard (without acting or being slavish)." A colleague adds, "We want smart, dedicated, committed people who will be nice individuals to work with." The first step to getting hired: getting into a great law school. "The firm generally hires associates from a small handful of prestigious law schools, such as Harvard, Yale, Columbia, and NYU," observes a source. "The firm strongly favors persons with high GPAs, law review experience, and a demonstrated work ethic. The firm also favors people with financial, business, or accounting backgrounds, and also people who have unusual or interesting backgrounds (such as having previously worked in the arts) or areas of study."

Some insiders say Debevoise cares a little too much about grades. "I wish the firm was more flexible about the cutoff GPA," says a lawyer. "I don't think GPA is the only indicator of talent." The firm seems to agree at least some of the time. "Supposedly this firm is super competitive to get in, but my law school grades were very mediocre. But I had work experience before law

Visit the Vault Law Channel, the complete online resource for law careers, featuring firm profiles, message boards, the Vault Law Job Board and more. **www.vault.com/law**

VAULT CAREER LIBRARY   177

school," notes a lawyer. All told, "You need to have done very well at a top law school and also stand out based on your interests, personality, etc. They don't just want automatons."

OUR SURVEY SAYS

Nice work, if you can get it

At Debevoise, you can be a happy lawyer, provided you get the kind of work that's going to make you happy. Make sense? Let a set of dueling litigators explain. "I have yet to have a boring assignment," says one of our sources. "I'm surprised by the level of responsibility being given to me, I both admire and enjoy the company of my colleagues, and I'm proud of the work we do." So things are great for everyone, right? "The litigation department has too many internal investigations and not enough actual litigation work," gripes another litigation associate. So which is it?

Maybe a little of both. Some associates report getting loads of fantastic work, while some are flat-out bored. But most like Debevoise overall. "Junior corporate associates are given as much responsibility as they can handle and can be directly involved in interesting, substantive aspects of the deals," says one second-year. "The work can be terribly tedious, but my colleagues are the best—amazing attorneys, with respect for their colleagues and wonderful senses of humor (for the most part)," says another insider. Even lodging a complaint doesn't seem to help. A source who gets "a lot of routine work" goes on to report that, "You tell the partners that you are not very interested in certain aspects of your work but your input seems to have been ignored and got you nowhere." Most Debevoise associates just chalk it up to the vagaries of big-firm life. One junior attorney is "not so satisfied with the type of work, but that can't be avoided by a first-year at a big firm." Overall, many, if not most, agree that "the practice of law at Debevoise is satisfying and fulfilling."

Polite, congenial, but not a cocktail party

Debevoise's culture earns kudos, even if it's not a party firm. "The firm's culture places value on politeness and respect and law as an intellectual pursuit," reports one litigation associate. "Debevoise has an open and supportive culture," says a midlevel colleague. "The lawyers here are supportive and sensitive to the quality of life and professional development of associates. Collaboration and open communication are encouraged among associates, counsel and partners." "The people here, lawyers, staff, etc. are all very nice and professional," echoes another associate. Don't come to Debevoise expecting to do keg stands, or to have to endure forced socialization. The firm "is not a frat house—if you want to socialize, great, if you have other commitments, fine, no penalty." Indeed, the firm's culture is quite the opposite of *Animal House*. "The Debevoise culture is both genteel and nerdy," observes a lawyer. The firm "has a strong civic-minded culture, and for the most part cares about the right things." A source reports, "I like everyone that I work with, and feel liked and respected in turn."

(Almost) everyone gets a say

"The partners I've worked with at Debevoise have been great to work for," says a New York lawyer. "They work hard and expect us to work hard too, but they are good at expressing their appreciation for our hard work and provide feedback—more so than I would have expected." Sometimes, associates feel like they're back in law school. "I recently had a top-billing partner spend more than 15 hours speaking one-on-one with me over a two-day period just discussing the law, teaching me as a professor would, with no client to bill for this time," reports one well-educated first-year. Not all partners are that helpful, of course. "Partners are hit-or-miss, like everywhere else. Most [are] nice and decent, but there are occasional socially dysfunctional people," says a source. "Everyone will be nice to you, no papers thrown in your face and no yelling, but few care if you have to cancel vacation or even notice if you have been working every weekend for weeks on end," complains another contact. While "there are many committees on which associates are given representation," some want more of a say. "The partnership occasionally informs associates about firmwide matters, but they do not participate in firmwide decisions," says a senior associate.

© 2007 Vault Inc.

New York minutes (and hours and hours)

Associates praise Debevoise's hours expectations, if faintly. "For a big New York law firm, the hours are reasonable," says a contact. "The firm respects attorneys' private lives." "My work hours are generally long but relatively stable and predictable," reports a senior associate. "I usually have my weekends free of work. However, there are times when a matter or case requires a period of intense work very late into the evening and on the weekends." Those times are oh-so-gratifying to workaholics. "While the hours are sometimes difficult, they are not always so, and I tend to be a workaholic anyway," notes one worker bee. "Slow periods infuriate me, so it's fortunate that I've seen very few of them." Some are less pleased about the lack of slow periods. "The hours are the same as all but the most notorious sweatshops, although they are flexible— both as a matter of policy and culture—to accommodate other obligations as well as social commitments that are important to you. Some matters have soft minimum required weekly billables associated with them, which is definitely a drag," complains a litigator. "There are weeks I feel that I never leave and then there are weeks when I am out of here by 6 p.m.," notes an M&A lawyer who sighs, "It could be worse."

Thanks for the raise. What took you so long?

Back up the money truck. "We are paid at the high end of the compensation scale for New York law firms," says a first-year making $160,000. "I am very satisfied by my compensation in terms of salary and bonuses," gushes a senior associate. "The firm always matches the prevailing salary and bonus amounts for each class, but generally the firm waits to see what other large firms in the market are doing with regard to compensation before making any changes." While that's a common complaint among associates at many firms, it especially rankles at Debevoise. "The firm took an embarrassingly long time to announce it was matching the recent pay raise," gripes a source. "By the time they announced, it felt insulting that they had waited so long." At least "Debevoise's lock-step compensation system contributes to the firm's collegial atmosphere."

It's like law school never ended

No one need worry about being untutored at Debevoise. "There is a constant stream of training, which is generally very relevant and helpful," says a second-year. The training starts early. "The first-year training program is growing and mandatory," notes one attorney. "The firm seems to value it. Some programs are useful, others are stale but the effort is appreciated." Some people can't get into the classroom soon enough. "I think the initial training that you receive as a first-year should be earlier," says a contact. But it's not just first-years who get the benefit of Debevoise's commitment to training. "The firm's litigation department has established a program of monthly training programs for associates on advanced topics in litigation practice," reports a senior litigation associate. "These sessions are usually helpful and informative."

BigLaw diversity

Though "Debevoise is at or near the top of the pack of New York BigLaw firms when it comes to diversity," insiders concede "that still leaves quite a bit to be desired." "The firm has taken significant steps in the hiring, promotion, and mentoring of women associates, notes a source. "Women are very well represented in the junior classes, and the firm has recently signed a contract with an emergency child care center." There seems to be a retention problem for minority associates. "The issue is not hiring. It's retention," says an African-American lawyer. "It's doing the things necessary to get people to stay or at least get the most out of their time here. It feels like at least half of the black associates have left since I've been here." The firm is known for being welcoming to gay associates. "Debevoise is a great firm at which to be an openly gay attorney," says one such associate. "It is a total nonissue. My partner is invited to firm events and treated with respect, and we have a large number of gay attorneys and summer associates."

Visit the Vault Law Channel, the complete online resource for law careers, featuring firm profiles, message boards, the Vault Law Job Board and more. **www.vault.com/law**

VAULT CAREER LIBRARY   **179**

13

PRESTIGE RANKING

Paul, Weiss, Rifkind, Wharton & Garrison LLP

1285 Avenue of the Americas
New York, NY 10019
Phone: (212) 373-3000
www.paulweiss.com

LOCATIONS

New York, NY (HQ)
Washington, DC
Beijing
Hong Kong
London
Tokyo

MAJOR DEPARTMENTS & PRACTICES

Antitrust • Bankruptcy & Corporate Reorganization •
Communications & Technology • Corporate • Employment
Discrimination • Entertainment • Environmental • Executive
Compensation & Employee Benefits • Finance • Intellectual
Property • Investment Funds • Litigation • Mergers &
Acquisitions • Patent & Other Scientific Litigation • Personal
Representation • Private Equity Transactions • Real Estate •
Securities & Capital Markets • Securities Enforcement •
Tax • White Collar Defense

THE STATS

No. of attorneys: 550
No. of offices: 6
Summer associate offers: 92 out of 92 (2006)
Firm Chair: Alfred D. Youngwood
Hiring Partner: Kelley A. Cornish

BASE SALARY (2007)

1st year: $160,000
Summer associate: $3,100/week

UPPERS

• Some of the best cases and transactions
• Some of the highest salaries
• No "face time" expectations

DOWNERS

• Some of the longest hours
• Narrow partnership track
• Document review for junior litigators

NOTABLE PERKS

• "Excellent offices, great location"
• Wednesday overtime "supper club"
• Women's networking and mentoring groups
• Paid paternity leave (one month)

THE BUZZ
WHAT ATTORNEYS AT OTHER FIRMS ARE SAYING ABOUT THIS FIRM

• "Sharp, savvy litigators"
• "Pushy, aggressive"
• "Go Ted Wells!"
• "Scorched Earth"

© 2007 Vault Inc.

RANKING RECAP

Regional Rankings
#9 - New York

Practice Area Rankings
#2 - Litigation

Partner Rankings
#3 - Partner Litigation
#13 - Overall Prestige

Quality of Life
#13 - Pay
#14 - Pro Bono

Diversity
#12 - Diversity with Respect to Minorities
#14 - Diversity with Respect to GLBT
#15 - Overall Diversity

EMPLOYMENT CONTACT

Pamela H. Nelson
Legal Recruitment Director
Phone: (212) 373-2548
Fax: (212) 373-2205
E-mail: pnelson@paulweiss.com

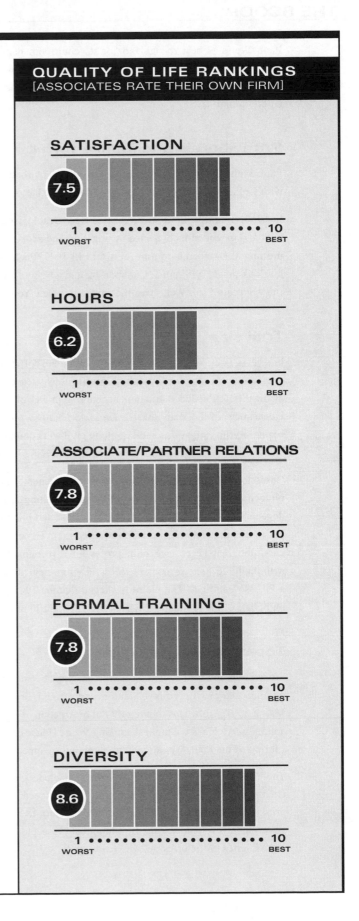

QUALITY OF LIFE RANKINGS
[ASSOCIATES RATE THEIR OWN FIRM]

SATISFACTION
7.5
1 WORST — 10 BEST

HOURS
6.2
1 WORST — 10 BEST

ASSOCIATE/PARTNER RELATIONS
7.8
1 WORST — 10 BEST

FORMAL TRAINING
7.8
1 WORST — 10 BEST

DIVERSITY
8.6
1 WORST — 10 BEST

Visit the Vault Law Channel, the complete online resource for law careers, featuring firm profiles, message boards, the Vault Law Job Board and more. www.vault.com/law

VAULT CAREER LIBRARY   181

THE SCOOP

Paul, Weiss is best recognized for its courtroom dazzle, and is the 2006 recipient of *The American Lawyer*'s "Litigation Department of the Year" award. However, the firm's prolific corporate department more than holds its own, regularly handling multibillion-dollar mergers and complex transactional work. The firm is also known for its expertise in telecom and entertainment law.

With liberals and justice for all

Paul, Weiss, Rifkind, Wharton & Garrison has its roots in a pre-World War I general practice. In 1923, Louis Weiss joined up with Columbia Law School classmate John F. Wharton to create one of the first firms where Jews and gentiles worked together.

In 1950, Simon Rifkind—who drafted New Deal legislation in the 1930s and served as a federal judge in the 1940s—joined the firm and extended its presence in litigation and added big money clients. In 1957, Adlai Stevenson became the first of several prominent Democrats to join the firm. In 1949, Paul, Weiss (don't forget that comma!) was the first New York firm to hire a black associate, William T. Coleman Jr., a magna cum laude graduate of Harvard Law School and a former Supreme Court clerk. In later years Paul, Weiss was the first major New York law firm to make a woman partner, tax attorney Carolyn Agger.

Trial size

For years Paul, Weiss has valiantly defended the coffers and reputations of some of the world's largest financial institutions and companies. Among the firm's high-profile defense cases were shareholder class actions against Citigroup, securities class actions against Merck's Medco unit, and accounting probes of AIG, Adecco and Fannie Mae. In naming Paul, Weiss its 2006 "Litigation Department of the Year" award, *The American Lawyer* noted that "in a time period in which business scandal ... criminal and regulatory investigations and tag-along civil suits dominated headlines, no law firm handled cases with higher stakes than Paul, Weiss—and no law firm was as successful at saving its clients' businesses." High praise indeed.

Cases for 2006 include a November win for Genentech against a researcher who claimed that he had an oral contract with the biotech giant for a percentage of profits resulting from the sale of its successful drug Lucentis, which combats macular degeneration, the leading cause of eye disease and blindness in people over 60. In a suit seeking over $1 billion in lost fees, the plaintiff claimed that his research was central to Genentech's development of the drug, and that he had provided it only upon the condition that he receive both professional recognition and one percent of the profits of any viable drug that Genentech manufactured. The firm also successfully represented the Andrew Lloyd Webber Art Foundation in a suit over the ownership of a Picasso painting. The plaintiff alleged that the 1903 painting "The Absinthe Drinker," which Christie's was offering for sale on behalf of the foundation, was in fact the rightful property of the plaintiff's ancestors.

Top-dollar white collar

Since 2005, the firm's white-collar defense practice has had its hands full defending Cheney's chief of staff, Scooter Libby, who was accused of lying to investigators and a grand jury during the probe into a CIA agent's leaked name to the news media. In March 2007, Libby was found guilty of obstruction of justice, giving false statements to the FBI and two counts of perjury against a grand jury. He is the highest-ranking White House official to be convicted of a felony since the Iran-Contra trials of the 1980s. Libby and his Paul, Weiss team are pursuing an appeal.

The firm's other high-profile defendants include Credit Suisse banker Frank Quattrone. Paul, Weiss won an appeal of Quattrone's conviction on obstruction of justice and witness tampering charges and subsequently negotiated a deferred-prosecution agreement that enabled him to return to his investment banking career. As reported by *The New York Times*, "The government's retreat was the first time that prosecutors had dropped such a prominent case without seeking a penalty and came after a series of victories by Mr. Quattrone."

© 2007 Vault Inc.

Right on the money

Corporate Board Member magazine ranked the firm as one of the top-20 corporate law firms in the country for 2006. Among the firm's M&A deals was Time Warner's acquisition of nearly all of bankrupt cable operator Adelphia Communications' remaining assets; Time Warner shelled out $12.5 billion in cash and 16 percent of Time Warner Cable stock. Paul, Weiss also closed the $3.2 billion merger of Intelsat and PanAmSat to create the largest commercial satellite operator in the United States. In the real estate field, the firm guided MeriStar Hospitality Corporation, one of the nation's largest hotel real estate investment trusts, through its $2.6 billion sale to The Blackstone Group and helped an investor group complete a deal to develop more than six million square feet of office space in four new towers at the World Trade Center site, including the signature Freedom Tower.

Oh, Canada!

The firm's highly regarded Canada practice took the lead in representing Teck Cominco in a hostile takeover bid for Inco Ltd., a Canadian mining and metals company and was retained by petroleum company Shell Canada in a tender offer for its shares by its parent, Royal Dutch Shell. Royal Dutch Shell successfully offered to purchase the 22 percent of Shell Canada's shares that it did not own for $45 per share, or approximately C$8.2 billion.

This deal runs on Dunkin'

On the corporate finance side, Paul, Weiss received a "Dealmaker of the Year" award from *The American Lawyer* for its work in helping Lehman Brothers develop and close a $1.7 billion securitization of the revenue-generating assets of Dunkin' Brands, franchise-holder of the Dunkin' Donuts, Baskin-Robbins and Dunkin' Deli brands. Proceeds from the securitization will be used to repay debt incurred in connection with Dunkin' Brands' LBO by private equity firms The Carlyle Group, Bain Capital and Thomas H. Lee Partners, which acquired the franchise-holder for $2.425 billion. And the firm's global securities lawyers helped Swiss Re launch the second phase of a $3.8 billion financing, which included a $1 billion rights offering/global offering, followed by a $2 billion hybrid capital offering—half offered in the form of securities of a repackaging vehicle for European investors and half through a Jersey partnership structure for U.S investors—intended to qualify for regulatory capital treatment. Swiss Re used the proceeds, together with cash and securities, to fund its $7.6 billion acquisition of GE Insurance Solutions.

The firm's restructuring lawyers had a major success as they helped develop a plan of reorganization for Foamex International Inc., a leading North American producer of flexible polyurethane and advanced polymer foam products. The plan, which will be funded with up to $790 million of new debt financing and $150 million of new equity financing to be raised through a rights offering to the company's shareholders, provides for the payment in full of all valid creditor claims and allows stockholders to retain their ownership interests. Foamex expects to emerge from chapter 11 in 2007.

Telecom-tubbies

Recent telecom and media deals for the firm include representing Hutchison Telecommunications in the $11.1 billion sale of its 67 percent interest in Hutchison Essar, one of India's largest cellular telephone service providers, to U.K.-based Vodafone and The Carlyle Group in its $5.6 billion offer to purchase Taiwan-based Advanced Semiconductor Engineering, Inc., the largest semiconductor packaging and testing company in the world. If completed, this will be the first leveraged buyout of a listed company in Taiwan and the largest private equity acquisition in Asia to date. The firm also represented The Carlyle Group in its acquisition of a majority of shares in Taiwan's largest cable TV operator, Eastern Multimedia, and the sale of its interest in Taiwan Broadband Company to Macquarie Bank.

The firm's entertainment experience comes to the fore in its frequent involvement in major music, film and television deals. Paul, Weiss represented Warner Music in its acquisition of entertainment company Ryko Corporation from an investment group led by JPMorgan Partners, acquiring Ryko's catalog, which includes the works of such artists as Frank Zappa, Joe Jackson and Soul Asylum. The firm represented David Geffen, Jeffrey Katzenberg and Steven Spielberg in connection with the sale of DreamWorks SKG, Inc. to Paramount Pictures. The deal, valued at $1.6 billion, will bring Paramount several key assets, including an ongoing partnership with DreamWorks' founders Mr. Geffen and Mr. Spielberg, an exclusive worldwide distribution

Visit the Vault Law Channel, the complete online resource for law careers, featuring firm profiles, message boards, the Vault Law Job Board and more. www.vault.com/law

VAULT CAREER LIBRARY   183

agreement with DreamWorks animation, and all of DreamWorks' current projects. In addition, the firm handled the tax structuring for Viacom as it split into Viacom Inc. and CBS in one of the largest splits of equals in history.

Goodbye Gitmo

In February, two more Paul, Weiss pro bono clients were released from Guantánamo Bay. Of the firm's original 13 pro bono clients, five have been transferred back to their home country of Saudi Arabia, where they were briefly incarcerated and then released. The firm continues to work for the release of their eight remaining clients. Paul, Weiss lawyers also represented on a pro bono basis five donor countries—France, the United Kingdom, Norway, Brazil and Chile—in connection with their negotiations with the World Health Organization to establish the UNITAID program, through a referral by firm client the William J. Clinton Foundation. UNITAID's mission is to drive down the prices of drugs to combat HIV/AIDS, malaria and tuberculosis in developing countries. The program is funded by an innovative levy imposed by the donor countries on airline tickets.

GETTING HIRED

The more fun you're having ...

Although the firm has a fondness for the Ivies, the hiring partners also look for top students from lower-ranked schools, associates report. Either way, a little personality goes a long way. "The firm is very Harvard-Yale-Columbia-NYU-Stanford-focused for recruiting," says a second-year New Yorker. "Beyond that, you basically have to be extraordinary or fill a special niche." He adds, "On the other hand, I get the sense everyone realizes that the woman who is top of her class at Brooklyn Law or Fordham is almost certainly a much better candidate than someone with a 3.4 from Harvard. If you are smart and can carry on a good conversation, you are in good shape during recruiting season. The way I see it, the more fun you have doing interviews, the better your chances." As one junior litigator puts it, "This firm likes people with the full package: excellent law school, excellent experiences while in law school (journal, moot court, etc.), excellent grades, interesting life experiences and, most importantly, people who are interesting and well spoken. I've been told that after the first-round interview grades are not looked at for the most part. At that point, people here are trying to figure out if you seem like someone they want to work with."

OUR SURVEY SAYS

No surprises here

Associates generally love their jobs at Paul, Weiss—but those who don't, really don't. A junior associate reports, "The reputation is true. A generally better group of people than most law firms." A second-year says there are "long hours, but substantive responsibility early in terms of client contact, court papers, depositions and independence." He adds that the "structure is relatively flat, although that may depend on the size of the case and the individuals staffed to the case." Another junior associate appreciates the firm's "incredibly smart people" and "interesting cases," as well as the "high levels of responsibility at an early stage." On the other hand, a dispirited insider adds, "Satisfaction with the work—but not satisfied with my quality of life. You get to work with the best, but unless you are the absolute best, you will not get promoted to partner." And a junior litigator adds, "The work is fantastic, but the hours are grueling."

Associates call the firm's culture "nice," "friendly," "polite," "dynamic" and "energetic." As one fairly typical insider puts it, "The culture is relaxed and casual, but also professional." A midlevel litigator describes his colleagues as "generally brilliant, progressive and, unsurprisingly, a bit socially awkward. Good people who work way too much."

Respectful partners—for, ahem, the most part

Associates give the firm high scores for associate/partner relations, with some notable exceptions. A junior litigator is typical when she says, "I've worked with some incredibly wonderful partners, and some who are less cuddly but nonetheless human.

That's all I ask." A second-year echoes and expands on that sentiment, saying, "The partnership has been very active to keep associates in the loop, especially lately, about the firm. The partners generally treat associates and others with respect, although some are known to be, ahem, less nice than most. I have personally had nothing but extraordinary treatment from partners, particularly those I work with on a near-daily basis. This includes availability, open communication, constructive feedback and praise." A real estate specialist adds, "Although demanding in terms of workload and responsibility, partners are respectful and understanding." That said, a cynical junior litigator warns, "They don't like us really—but they try."

A bountiful harvest of training

Associates call the firm's formal training program plentiful. Perhaps too plentiful. As a junior New York litigator reports, "There is more training than you know what to do with. They need less classroom-style trainings, though, and more hands-on activities early on." A senior bankruptcy expert adds, "The firm has an extensive formal training curriculum. It is, to some extent, only as good as the commitment each associate brings to the training to learn. Having time to attend also becomes an issue, and having the opportunity to translate what we learn into real world experience is not always possible."

Junior associates report that, for the most part, mentoring is a true strong point at Paul, Weiss. A real estate attorney advises, "Partners are open to questions and will take time to help you understand." A litigator adds, "Everyone here has something to teach. Mentoring comes naturally to people here. There is no shortage of advice." As one first-year reports, "The firm (i.e., the managing partners) feels that the current mentoring system is insufficient and is trying to improve it. I think it is not bad as is, but would not mind seeing it improve."

Few make more

Everyone agrees that there are very few places to make more money as an associate than at the market leader Paul, Weiss. The question remains, is it enough? (Is it ever in BigLaw?) Here's how an IP associate sums up the firm's compensation plan: "Our compensation is at the highest level in the country for young associates, other than Wachtell and certain other small, specialized firms," he says. "That said, we work very hard." Still, especially lately, New York firms have really stepped up by raising base salaries $35,000 in less than a year. If bonuses next year do not suffer as a result (and they did not this year after the initial $15,000 rise in base salary), it is hard to complain. Paul, Weiss does not have an incentive bonus. Everyone at the same level by calendar year of law school graduation gets the same bonus. A junior litigator notes, "Paul, Weiss was the second firm to raise salaries this year," following Simpson Thacher. Or, as a corporate describes it, "Paul, Weiss matched this year's salary increase within 24 hours of Simpson's announcement. I appreciate that bonuses are lock-step, and not based on hours—though accruing enough billable hours is usually not the problem."

No need to hang around and be seen

The general consensus is that associates would gladly accept less pay if it meant working fewer hours. A second-year states, "Time at the office is flexible, but there is a tremendous amount of work and it takes time. That means many weekends in the office, as necessary, to do a good job. However, the self-directed motivation for the lawyers here to do their best work drives the long hours." As this first-year puts it, "No face time whatsoever. When there's work to be done, I'm working. When I don't need to be doing work, I feel no pressure to pad my hours. There's generally work so this isn't much of an issue, but I never feel like I'm just hanging around to be seen." A bankruptcy attorney reports that "the firm, in theory, is very generous with its flex-time program." "In practice, adhering to a flex-time schedule proves extremely difficult."

Visit the Vault Law Channel, the complete online resource for law careers, featuring firm profiles, message boards, the Vault Law Job Board and more. **www.vault.com/law**

VAULT CAREER LIBRARY   185

14

PRESTIGE
RANKING

Shearman & Sterling LLP

599 Lexington Avenue
New York, NY 10022
Phone: (212) 848-4000
www.shearman.com

LOCATIONS

New York, NY (HQ)

Menlo Park, CA • San Francisco, CA • Washington, DC •
Abu Dhabi • Beijing • Brussels • Düsseldorf • Frankfurt •
Hong Kong • London • Mannheim, Germany • Munich •
Paris • Rome • São Paulo • Shanghai • Singapore • Tokyo •
Toronto

MAJOR DEPARTMENTS & PRACTICES

Antitrust • Asset Management • Bankruptcy &
Reorganization • Capital Markets • Derivatives • Corporate
Governance • Environmental • Executive Compensation &
Employee Benefits • Finance • Financial Institutions
Advisory • Intellectual Property • International Arbitration •
International Tax • International Trade • Latin America •
Litigation • Mergers & Acquisitions Private Clients • Project
Development & Finance • Property • Sports • Structured
Finance • Tax • White Collar

THE STATS

No. of attorneys: Approximately 1,000
No. of offices: 20
Summer associate offers: 100 out of 100 (2006)
Senior Partner: Rohan S. Weerasinghe
Hiring Partners: John Cannon & Antonia Stolper

BASE SALARY (2007)

New York, NY
1st year: $160,000
2nd year: $170,000
3rd year: $185,000
4th year: $210,000
5th year: $230,000
6th year: $250,000
7th year: $265,000
8th year: $280,000
9th year: $290,000+
Summer associate: $3,077/week

UPPERS

• Compensation is top-of-the-market
• "Global scope of practice. High-profile deals"
• "Friendly, respectful work environment"

DOWNERS

• "Work is (let's not kid ourselves) boring and stressful"
• Mentoring is hard to come by
• "Long hours (it's the nature of the beast)"

NOTABLE PERKS

• Free language classes
• Possibility of international rotation
• Midlevel retention bonus
• Associate Sabbatical Program

THE BUZZ
WHAT ATTORNEYS AT OTHER FIRMS ARE SAYING ABOUT THIS FIRM

• "Very prestigious in finance"
• "Workaholics"
• "M&A bluechip"
• "Self-important"

© 2007 Vault Inc.

RANKING RECAP

Regional Rankings
#12 - New York

Practice Area Rankings
#7 (tie) - International Law
#9 - Securities

Partner Rankings
#15 - Overall Prestige

EMPLOYMENT CONTACT

Ms. Trisha Weiss
Professional Recruiting
Phone: (212) 848-8977
E-mail: trisha.weiss@shearman.com

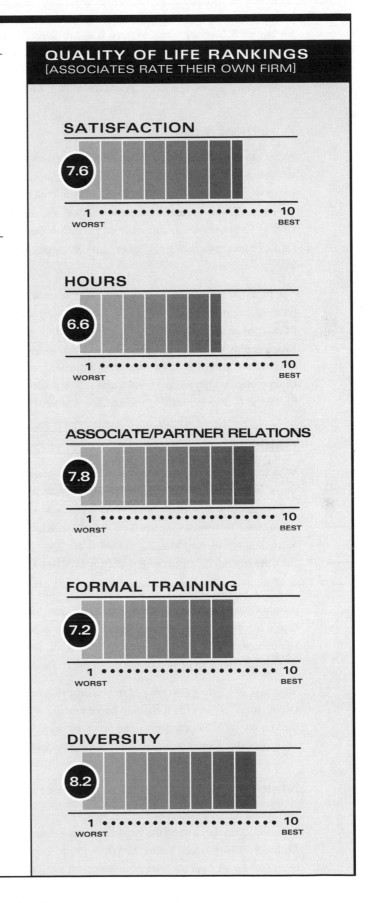

QUALITY OF LIFE RANKINGS
[ASSOCIATES RATE THEIR OWN FIRM]

SATISFACTION
7.6
1 WORST .... 10 BEST

HOURS
6.6
1 WORST .... 10 BEST

ASSOCIATE/PARTNER RELATIONS
7.8
1 WORST .... 10 BEST

FORMAL TRAINING
7.2
1 WORST .... 10 BEST

DIVERSITY
8.2
1 WORST .... 10 BEST

Visit the Vault Law Channel, the complete online resource for law careers, featuring firm profiles, message boards, the Vault Law Job Board and more. www.vault.com/law

VAULT CAREER LIBRARY   187

THE SCOOP

Shearman & Sterling seems to have it all: prestige (it's consistently rated near the top of the heap in every survey of legal professionals), history (it was founded more than 130 years ago), superstar practices (it's one of the top corporate law firms in the country) and international reach (16 non-U.S. offices). All told, this superfirm has approximately 1,000 lawyers in 20 offices in the United States, Europe, Asia and the Middle East.

A firm of titans

Shearman & Sterling first strapped on its white shoes in 1873, when renowned litigator Thomas Shearman founded a partnership with corporate lawyer John Sterling. (Sterling, a Yale grad, left $15 million to the university upon his death in 1918. The university was so impressed it reportedly considered renaming itself "Sterling University." Instead, Yale built a library, law and grad school facilities and other buildings with the money.) The firm's early clients include financier and railroad baron Jay Gould, the Rockefeller family, railroad executives George and Donald Smith and the early predecessor of what is now Citibank. One of Shearman & Sterling's key early engagements was a 1903 case that established the intellectual property right in a business' name.

The firm first branched out overseas in 1963, when it opened an office in Paris. Shearman & Sterling has kept that international momentum going and currently has 16 offices outside the United States. The firm's German practice is especially strong—one of its co-managing partners is based in Düsseldorf, and Shearman & Sterling has four offices in Germany. The firm's global footprint makes it a player in cross-border business transactions as well as international disputes. In fact, internationally inclined law students probably know Shearman & Sterling as the chief sponsor of the Philip C. Jessup International Law Moot Court Competition, which pits over 500 teams of law students from around the world against each other in staged legal drama for the Shearman & Sterling Jessup Cup, which was won in 2007 by the University of Sydney.

DealS&S

With such a broad reach, it's not surprising that Shearman & Sterling has been involved in so many of the biggest deals in recent times, including as lead counsel to DaimlerChrysler AG on the May 2007 sale of 80.1 percent of the shares in the future Chrysler Holding LLC to an affiliate of the private equity house Cerebrus Capital Management, L.P. That same month, the firm advised Saudi Basic Industries Corp. on the $11.6 billion acquisition of General Electric's plastics division. Earlier in the year, Shearman & Sterling represented Marafiq, the utility company for Jubail and Yanbu in Saudi Arabia, on the development of the landmark Jubail Independent Water and Power Project. The $3 billion Jubail IWPP is one of the largest facilities of its kind in the world.

In July 2006, the firm advised the board of directors of HCA Inc. in the health care company's leveraged buyout. A handful of private equity firms acquired HCA for $33 billion, which was, at the time, the second-largest leveraged buyout in history. The firm's mergers and acquisitions group also was legal advisor to Allianz AG in its cross-border merger with Italian insurer Riunione Adriatica di Sicurta to create Allianz SE, the first European company (SE) on the EuroStoxx50, and to Toronto-based ATI Technologies in its sale to Advanced Micro Devices, Inc. for approximately $5.4 billion.

Shearman & Sterling also advised on the financing for the $4.8 billion acquisition of the U.S.-based lotteries and gaming group Gtech Holdings Corp. by the Italian-based lotteries group Lottomatica. This 2006 transaction was the largest-ever acquisition in the U.S. by an Italian company. The firm went on to help set a record in November when it advised the underwriters for the IPO of Industrial & Commercial Bank of China. The deal was the largest ever IPO, and raised $22 billion for China's largest bank.

Making a case ... and a difference

In March 2007, Shearman & Sterling won a major legal victory for its client Merrill Lynch in the Enron securities class-action litigation, considered to be the largest securities class action in U.S. history. In the case, still pending at date of publication, the firm successfully argued before the Fifth Circuit Court of Appeals that the certified class could not proceed against Merrill Lynch because Merrill Lynch's alleged conduct did not satisfy the requirements for primary liability under Section 10(b) of the

© 2007 Vault Inc.

Securities Exchange Act of 1934. Trial has been stayed pending plaintiffs' efforts to seek review of the Court of Appeals' decision in the U.S. Supreme Court.

Not all of Shearman & Sterling's litigation victories were won in the courtroom, however. In April 2006, the firm negotiated settlements in two class-action lawsuits filed by investors in Nortel Networks Corp. Investors sued the company after it restated earnings for the years 2000 through 2003; Shearman settled the claims in both of the suits, and won the dismissal of claims in other actions. In a more hotly contested lawsuit, the firm won the dismissal of claims against electronics manufacturer Nokia. Investors were upset when Nokia missed sales forecasts for the first quarter of 2004, and sued the company and its executives, claiming they misrepresented Nokia's prospects. A federal judge dismissed the claim in April 2006, finding that the company didn't act with bad intent in making its sales estimates.

The firm won an international arbitration victory for client Lahmeyer International Pally Power Services in December 2006. Lahmeyer sought arbitration after Rural Power Co., a state-run Bangladeshi power company, reneged on an agreement to run a power plant in Bangladesh. A panel of arbitrators sitting in Singapore found that Rural Power had breached the agreement, awarding Lahmeyer $20 million. Of course, international arbitration victories are nothing new for Shearman & Sterling. That same December, Chambers Global ranked the firm first in international arbitration for the second consecutive year. Chambers also singled out Shearman & Sterling's public international law practice as the best in the business, the first time the firm has been so honored.

Shearman & Sterling lawyers also devote significant time and effort to pro bono matters. The firm is highly regarded for its assistance to the office of the prosecutor at the International Criminal Tribunal for Rwanda (ICTR), and for its work organizing and leading several trial advocacy seminars in Arusha, Tanzania, for the staff offices. Attorneys from firm offices around the globe have participated in these programs. In other pro bono matters, Shearman & Sterling's representation of current and former employees alleging a racially hostile environment at Tyson Foods' Ashland, Alabama plant resulted in a November 2006 settlement of nearly $1 million in favor of the plaintiffs.

GETTING HIRED

"International credentials really help"

Shearman & Sterling's recruiting efforts reflect its stature and its international practice. A second-year New Yorker says that the hiring partners scour from the "Ivy Leagues to top-20 schools" looking for "candidates with interest in international relations and foreign languages" and "open minds." Another second-year describes the firm as "very competitive, but not too snobby or doctrinaire about GPA cutoffs, law review, etc." A business and finance expert adds, "The firm is still under a reputation hit from a few years back so it is a good time to come here—the work is the same and it is as busy as ever. International credentials really help." A junior litigator offers up similar advice. "Shearman continues, as always, to focus on candidates from the top-14 schools, although as the recruiting market gets increasingly competitive, the firm (like most of its peers) also looks to other national law schools and even some local schools to fill its summer class ranks," he says. "An ideal candidate would be a friendly, cosmopolitan person who is a good student at a top law school or a great student at another national school. International experience and foreign language skills are extremely helpful, as well. The firm also has been aggressive in its recruiting at the top Canadian law schools." One insider paints this sunny picture: "I think we genuinely allow good, quality people to self-select—and we look widely in the U.S., Canada, Australia and around the world. We are looking for a package. Luckily for us, smart jerks want to go to [other BigLaw firms] so we end up with the smart but reasonable people."

Visit the Vault Law Channel, the complete online resource for law careers, featuring firm profiles, message boards, the Vault Law Job Board and more. www.vault.com/law

VAULT CAREER LIBRARY   189

OUR SURVEY SAYS

"I realize how good I have it here"

Shearman & Sterling's associates say that, recent reports of low morale notwithstanding, they are generally content with their jobs. "Even as a first-year, you have substantial responsibility and client contact," boasts a New York M&A expert. "However, you need to show initiative and willingness to work to get interesting work." Another M&A attorney adds, "I am very happy with the availability of my colleagues and their seeming interest in my own professional development. Questions are encouraged and answers are proffered. There is a real interest in diversity issues—in addition to the longstanding diversity committee, affinity groups exist to better address more specific concerns. Along the same lines, associate committees address those concerns that relate to associate morale and welfare in general." Associate-run affinity groups for women, African-Americans, and GLBT attorneys focus on recruiting, mentoring and associate life. A litigator boasts, "The more I talk with my friends at the other top firms in New York City, the more I realize how good I have it here at Shearman. I have gotten to do a wide variety of interesting work (including several high-profile international matters) right from the start while many of my friends at other firms were essentially locked in a closet doing document review for months on end." The typical complaint sounds something like this: "It is a law firm, but as far as they go it is not bad."

One big pizza party?

Associates call Shearman "friendly," "collaborative" and "very social." Indeed, as one associate describes it, Shearman sounds like the fun floor in a cool dorm. "We do socialize a lot, help each other with work and also have social gatherings like a Pizza Party every other Friday," shares a finance specialist. A junior associate reports, "I find that 'firm' culture for Shearman is determined by which department you are working in. The M & A department expects you to work hard, but also provides social activities every other Friday for the lawyers to relax and interact. I have also been pleasantly surprised to find that almost all of the associates and partners are willing to work together to provide flexibility with regard to non-law firm commitments and an external social life." An antitrust attorney adds, "If you want to socialize with co-workers, there are plenty of opportunities to do so and plenty of co-workers who would like to do so. There is no pressure to do so, however."

Civilized partners

Shearman's associates give the firm's partners high marks for civility and concern. "I think the partners treat everyone very professionally," reports a midlevel litigator. "I don't have any complaints at all. There are a couple of partners that I would prefer not to work with, but from my experience, that is just a standard work environment. You are not going to be best friends with everyone. The vast majority of partners are great." Another litigator adds, "I think that associate/partner relations are fine in my department. On some teams I work closely with the partner(s), on others less frequently. I have never heard a partner raise his or her voice to an associate. I have a great deal of respect for the partners I work with, both professionally and personally, and, speaking generally, I think that they respect us." A New Yorker says, "I could not ask for better in this department. In all of my interactions so far, the partners were respectful without crossing the line into a false sense of familiarity." And this point is underscored by an M&A associate: "The partners are very respectful and actually come by your office to thank you for the hard work you do." Also, insiders report it is typical of the firm's culture that "partners take associates to lunch frequently."

Formal training improving

Shearman's formal training offerings get generally good scores, and its recently instituted litigation program seems to have the firm's young trial attorneys kind of excited. A junior business and finance attorney reports, "Excellent training, with more training programs than you can imagine and regular team meetings to address things you do in your daily practice." A litigator adds, "The firm just launched a new training program that seems to be well thought out. It is in the beginning stages, though, so it is a little early to tell." Another litigator adds, "A new training program unveiled for 2007 looks very promising in providing increased training to the litigation department, which could also lead toward more actual experience in the courtroom." However,

© 2007 Vault Inc.

a corporate associate warns that there are "lots of CLE courses, but some of them aren't all that helpful. Team meetings are often at levels above a junior's head, or don't mean much unless you have seen it in practice."

Mentoring's mixed

Associates say that the firm's long hours make partners less accessible for meaningful mentoring. As one Big Apple insider puts it, "There could probably be more informal training and mentoring, but people are busy so it is understandably difficult." Another junior New Yorker advises, "If you don't ask, a partner typically will not spend the time to teach you. Associates will, though." Another insider adds, "The partners will talk to me about the overall deal, but as a first-year, I work with the midlevel associates most of the time." That said, there are a number of associates who call the firm's informal training exemplary. An employee benefits attorney says, "Many partners go out of their way to make sure you understand the material." And a junior litigator adds, "I feel that I have gotten a great deal of useful informal training and mentoring from the partners and senior associates on my cases. Since Shearman's litigation department is somewhat smaller than its counterparts at the other top firms, work (especially depositions and court appearances) is done at a somewhat higher level than elsewhere."

Above the market rate

Shearman & Sterling pays salaries and bonuses that are at the top of the market and then sweetens the deal. A midlevel reports, "Shearman pays a retention bonus to fourth-years, putting compensation above market." An insider asks rhetorically, "Would I accept more pay? Yes. Am I going to cry about what I am receiving now? No." Of course, at most any law firm (outside of Wachtell), there are associates that are dissatisfied with their compensation. Here's one from Shearman: "Unfortunately, law firms across the city compensate their associates within a very narrow range. In general, for the hours we work—and also the responsibility—we are underpaid, particularly when you consider our sisters and brothers in finance. But the pay is good, definitely livable, and Shearman does keep up with the herd when it comes to compensation." An employee benefits attorney adds, "It would be great if the firm offered 401(k) matching, even if I had to reduce my base."

"Hours are not that bad"

Shearman associates arrive expecting to work ungodly hours and then, it seems, are pleasantly surprised, for the most part. "For me, the hours are far better than the horror stories I heard, but they do vary department to department and person to person," says a junior litigator. A midlevel litigator reports, "Even when it is busy, I go home at 7 to see my family and put my kids to bed and then do work from home. That seems very fair to me." A colleague adds, "It depends on the department, but there are ups and downs in the work hours. You might be extremely busy for a couple of weeks and then have nothing to do for a while. The partners are good about giving some 'rest time' after intense deals."

Visit the Vault Law Channel, the complete online resource for law careers, featuring firm profiles, message boards, the Vault Law Job Board and more. **www.vault.com/law**

VAULT CAREER LIBRARY   **191**

Wilmer Cutler Pickering Hale and Dorr LLP

60 State Street
Boston, MA 02109
Phone: (617) 526-6000

1875 Pennsylvania Avenue, NW
Washington, DC 20006
Phone: (202) 663-6000
www.wilmerhale.com

LOCATIONS

Baltimore, MD • Boston, MA • New York, NY • Palo Alto, CA • Washington, DC • Beijing • Berlin • Brussels • London • Waltham

MAJOR DEPARTMENTS & PRACTICES

Antitrust & Competition • Aviation • Bankruptcy & Commercial • Communications & E-commerce • Corporate • Defense, National Security & Government Contracts • Environmental • FDA • Financial Institutions • Intellectual Property • International Arbitration • International Trade, Investment & Market Access • Labor & Employment • Litigation • Private Client • Public Policy & Strategy • Real Estate • Securities • Tax

THE STATS

No. of attorneys: 1,118
No. of offices: 10
Summer associate offers: 137 out of 138 (2006)
Chairs, Management Committee: William F. Lee & William J. Perlstein
Hiring Partners:
  Boston: Colleen Superko
  New York: Fraser L. Hunter Jr. & Stuart R. Nayman
  Palo Alto: Curtis Mo
  Washington, DC: Andre Owens & Erika Robinson

BASE SALARY (2007)

1st year: $160,000
2nd year: $170,000
3rd year: $185,000
4th year: $210,000
5th year: $230,000
6th year: $250,000
7th year: $265,000
Summer associate:
    Boston; Washington, DC; Palo Alto: $2,800/week
    New York: $3,100/week

UPPERS

• "Interesting/engaged/diverse people"
• "Exciting top-end work in the policy/appellate spheres"
• "Impressive client space"

DOWNERS

• "The opposite of 'leanly staffed' cases"
• "Document reviews abound"
• "IT still playing catch-up"

NOTABLE PERKS

• In-building gym
• Frequent firm socials
• "Great" parental leave policy
• "Aeron desk chairs in *every* office"

THE BUZZ
WHAT ATTORNEYS AT OTHER FIRMS ARE SAYING ABOUT THIS FIRM

• "Wonderful appellate practice"
• "Merger hasn't made them any more prestigious"
• "Great culture, intellectual"
• "Losing culture"

© 2007 Vault Inc.

RANKING RECAP

Regional Rankings
#2 - Boston
#3 - Washington, DC

Practice Area Rankings
#4 - International Law
#7 (tie) - Antitrust

Partner Rankings
#4 (tie) - Antitrust
#17 - Overall Prestige

Quality of Life
#11 - Selectivity
#20 - Office Space

EMPLOYMENT CONTACTS

Washington and Baltimore
Ms. Elizabeth Miller
DC Legal Recruiting & Personnel Director
Phone: (202) 247-4294
E-mail: dc.legalrecruiting@wilmerhale.com

Boston and Waltham, MA
Ms. Karen Rameika
Legal Recruitment Manager
Phone: (617) 526-5565
E-mail: boston.legalrecruiting@wilmerhale.com

New York, NY
Ms. Bess Frank
Legal Personnel & Recruitment Manager
Phone: (212) 295-8825
Fax: (212) 841-1010
E-mail: ny.legalrecruiting@wilmerhale.com

Palo Alto, CA
Ms. Heather Hayes
Legal Personnel & Recruitment Project Manager
Phone: (617) 526-6808
E-mail: paloalto.legalrecruiting@wilmerhale.com

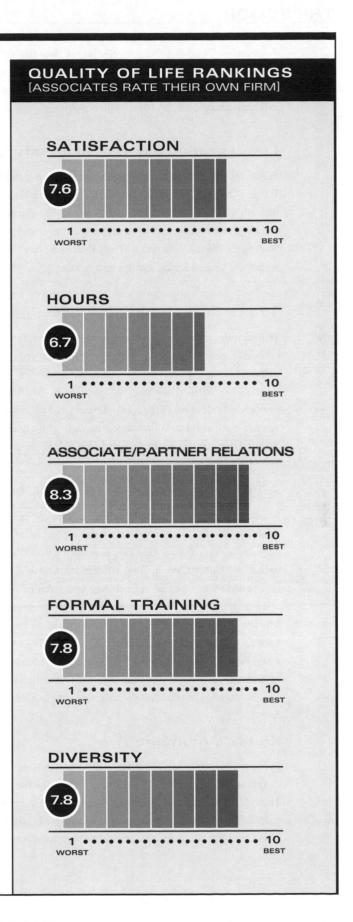

QUALITY OF LIFE RANKINGS
[ASSOCIATES RATE THEIR OWN FIRM]

SATISFACTION
7.6
1 WORST — 10 BEST

HOURS
6.7
1 WORST — 10 BEST

ASSOCIATE/PARTNER RELATIONS
8.3
1 WORST — 10 BEST

FORMAL TRAINING
7.8
1 WORST — 10 BEST

DIVERSITY
7.8
1 WORST — 10 BEST

Visit the Vault Law Channel, the complete online resource for law careers, featuring firm profiles, message boards, the Vault Law Job Board and more. www.vault.com/law

VAULT CAREER LIBRARY   193

THE SCOOP

WilmerHale is one of the nation's largest law firms and a constant on *The American Lawyer*'s A-list. The firm maintains internationally respected litigation, corporate and IP practices, and following the successful management of internal probes at Enron and WorldCom, among others, its securities and regulatory practices have risen to even greater prominence. In 2006, WilmerHale crossed the $800 million barrier—biting at the heels of the nation's highest-grossing law firms.

I now pronounce you successfully merged

When Washington, D.C.'s Wilmer Cutler Pickering and Boston's Hale and Dorr joined together in 2004, the result was megafirm Wilmer Cutler Pickering Hale and Dorr. In this union of two Northeastern bluebloods, no one should grouse that they married beneath them. Each firm brought to the table a sturdy pedigree: proven governmental ties, and vigorous corporate, regulatory and litigation practices. Post-merger, the firm is still growing. In 2006, personnel increased by 10 percent, with the D.C. office posting the highest headcount of any firm in the city. Today WilmerHale numbers over 1,000 lawyers, staffing offices in 10 cities across the United States, Europe and Asia.

Those folks mean business

WilmerHale's 250-strong corporate team juggles all manner of IPOs, venture capital, private equity, M&A, strategic alliance and corporate governance work. The group has served as counsel on more than 250 public offerings in the past five years, and managed more than 750 venture financings, including multimillion-dollar deals in the life sciences and IT sector. In the past five years alone, WilmerHale has worked on more than 800 M&A transactions valued in excess of $400 billion. The firm serves as primary outside counsel for approximately 125 public companies in the U.S. and Europe, and in the Eastern U.S., represents more venture-backed startups than any other law firm. In 2006, *Chambers Guide to America's Leading Business Lawyers* named 89 WilmerHale lawyers as leaders in their field.

All patents are created equal, but some are more equal than others

Should all patents be treated equally in terms of enforceability? WilmerHale IP litigators and client MercExchange certainly think so. While it has been fairly standard for patent holders to be granted injunctions when a patent is infringed, a May 2006 Supreme Court ruling is changing that assumption. Patent holding company (or "patent troll") MercExchange filed a suit against online auctioneer eBay in 2001, alleging that eBay's "buy-it-now" feature infringed upon patents that MercExchange holds. A jury found in favor of MercExchange and awarded it $35 million, and a federal court granted MercExchange's request for an injunction against eBay, agreeing that one of the protections afforded patent holders is the right to exclude. eBay claimed that MercExchange's patent was wrongly affirmed, and took the case to the Supreme Court. In 2006 the Court remanded the case back to a lower court, concluding that in validating MercExchange's injunction request, the lower court had not "fairly" applied a number of factors prescribed by federal law. MercExchange's case is in good hands: with over 120 lawyers holding scientific or technological degrees, WilmerHale's IP practice ranks as one of the best in the country. In January 2006, *The American Lawyer* named the firm "Intellectual Property Department of the Year."

Kodak's moment

In November 2006, a WilmerHale IP litigation team achieved a victory for client Eastman Kodak and fellow defendant Altek Corporation. In October 2004, visual technology company Ampex filed a patent infringement complaint with the International Trade Commission (ITC) and the Federal Court in Delaware, asserting that Kodak's digital cameras infringed upon an Ampex patent. Though Ampex eventually dropped its ITC complaint, the case was litigated in federal court for over 12 months. In May 2006, WilmerHale filed a successful motion for summary judgment in Kodak's favor.

© 2007 Vault Inc.

Cell division

WilmerHale has represented Broadcom Corporation, a global leader in semiconductors for wired and wireless communications, in numerous widely-watched patent cases against QUALCOMM INC. Three of those cases have gone to trial since 2006, and Broadcom has prevailed in each. In December 2006, the U.S. International Trade Commission determined that QUALCOMM's next generation, or "3G," cellular chips infringe a Broadcom patent for important power-saving technology. Then, in January 2007, a jury in San Diego federal court returned a verdict that Broadcom did not infringe two QUALCOMM patents for video compression, and the judge in that case further found, by clear and convincing evidence, that QUALCOMM had waived its right to enforce those same patents by failing to comply with its obligations before a standards body responsible for a next-generation video standard called H.264. Most recently, in May 2007, a jury in Santa Ana federal court returned a verdict that QUALCOMM had willfully infringed three Broadcom patents covering a variety of cellular and video processing technology, and awarded Broadcom damages of approximately $20 million.

Stalled at the Second Circuit

While the IPO era made many rich, it certainly made some investors angry. WilmerHale is one of the firms leading the defense of underwriters such as Credit Suisse and Citigroup Global Markets in investor litigation charging the banks with artificially inflating the value of newly issued internet stocks through misinformation, undisclosed compensation and analyst conflicts. In March 2005, a Southern District judge in New York dismissed one class action, finding that listed IPO prices were not misleading and that claimants had failed to prove loss causation. And in another victory for the defendants, in December 2006 a federal appeals court overturned class certification in six key cases; a New York U.S. District Judge had consolidated thousands of suits into 310 class actions, and then certified six of them to move forward. The December ruling makes it difficult for the plaintiffs to pursue their claims, as without class certification, thousands of individual cases would have to be litigated separately.

Houston, we have a leak

The HP ruckus is still drawing quite a crowd. WilmerHale has joined the law firms jumping into the melee, representing key figure and initial "leak" George Keyworth; Keyworth resigned from HP's board in September 2006 after being outed as the secret source of a CNET news story. To find the boardroom leak, HP investigators posed as directors and journalists in order to trick phone companies into divulging call logs, a tactic that has landed the company in a legal pickle. A congressional panel is presently probing Hewlett-Packard's actions, and the culpability of its general counsel.

Nude developments in ISP accountability

WilmerHale's Washington office is representing Yahoo in a $3 million lawsuit filed by an Oregon woman, who is suing the ISP for failing to fulfill a promise to remove nude pictures of her from the Web. The plaintiff claims that an ex-boyfriend pretending to be her posted pictures of her in a fake Yahoo profile, causing strangers to show up at her workplace "looking for dates." The case is on appeal in a Ninth U.S. Circuit Court. In their defense, Yahoo has cited the 1997 Communications Decency Act, which holds that ISPs are not accountable for content posted by third parties. However, the plaintiff's lawyers argue that when a Yahoo representative told their client that the photos would be removed, they "undertook an affirmative duty," a claim allowed under Oregon state law.

You say potato, I say graffiti artiste

Together with the Urban Justice Center, Wilmer Hale litigators have taken to the streets, defending the rights of roadside vendors who sell graffiti-adorned garments. In an effort to combat urban congestion, in 1997, New York City's General Vendors Law mandated that all vendors must be licensed, unless they sell items that "communicate some idea or concept," e.g., paintings, photos, prints, sculptures, which are covered by the First Amendment. Though the firm won a district court injunction barring the city from enforcing licensing requirements on street artists, in January 2006 a Second Circuit Court of Appeals ruled that the licensing requirement did not infringe upon the free speech rights of vendors who sell graffiti-adorned items of clothing. In their

Visit the Vault Law Channel, the complete online resource for law careers, featuring firm profiles, message boards, the Vault Law Job Board and more. www.vault.com/law

VAULT CAREER LIBRARY   195

decision, the court found that if an item does possess a "non-expressive purpose", the court must then determine if the item's non-expressive purpose is dominant. In a case concerning graffiti-adorned baseball hats, the court judged the hats' utilitarian purposes to be dominant over their purposes as an instrument of communication.

Thou shalt not covet thy neighbor's lawyers

2006 saw two former WilmerHale partners turn general counsel to Citigroup and AIG Inc. Now partner Stephen M. Cutler, back from a six-year stint as the SEC's director of enforcement, is once again bidding the firm adieu. In February 2007 Cutler leaves WilmerHale, where he has been since his return from the SEC in 2005, to serve as general counsel to JPMorgan Chase. Cutler was a partner and co-chair of the firm's securities department in the Washington, D.C. office. Prior to joining the SEC in 1999, Mr. Cutler spent 11 years at Wilmer, Cutler and Pickering.

In other comings and goings, Washington partner Andrew Vollmer has been named the SEC's deputy general counsel, while Charles E. Davidow, co-chair of the firm's securities litigation and enforcement group, joined the Washington office of New York's Paul, Weiss, Rifkind, Wharton & Garrison. In November 2006 the firm's D.C. office welcomed pharmaceutical regulatory practitioner James N. Czaban to its growing FDA department. Recently, the firm successfully recruited Bob Gunther, a noted IP trial lawyer, to join the New York office from Latham & Watkins, where he served as vice chair of the litigation department.

Going above and beyond

Wilmer Hale has consistently ranked at or near the top of *The American Lawyer*'s annual pro bono rankings, and in 2006 received pro bono awards from the Massachusetts Bar Association as well as the *The National Law Journal*. Recent pro bono activities include representing a Virginia death row inmate in his claim that the prosecution's failure to disclose key evidence had violated his constitutional rights; in August 2006 a Fourth Circuit court agreed that the inmate was entitled to a hearing on the suppression of evidence charges. In February 2006, the firm went to court on behalf of disabled plaintiffs in order to force the city of Richmond, Virginia, to fund a five-year plan for eliminating barriers to access in Richmond schools. At least 56 Richmond schools have architectural defects that prevent persons with disabilities from participating in activities held at school facilities.

GETTING HIRED

Lather, rinse, repeat

Well, they're honest: "Getting hired here is difficult. The firm has so many Ivy League grads, they tend to favor the same. It's hard to get that interview." One midlevel categorizes the firm as "pretty snobby," as another grumbles, "Harvard and Yale, Yale and Harvard. Repeat until ill." In Boston, "the firm focuses on the top law schools and local schools"; in New York, "you pretty much have to be top tenth of the class, do journal and have some other notable achievements." While one D.C. source is "not sure about a GPA cutoff," he can testify that "nearly every person in my summer associate class was on law review at school. (There are) many attorneys from Harvard, Yale, Columbia, and other top-10 schools." A colleague in the same office concurs that "there really aren't firm numbers cutoffs, but your resume better be unusually good if you're coming from a law school outside the top 15." Nevertheless, "a top performing student from a lower-ranked school who reaches out to the firm might have a shot, especially as a 3L hire or lateral instead of as a summer associate." And once you get an interview, "The firm looks past numbers and focuses on people, including diversity of interests, personality and initiative." One source active in the hiring process points out that "when I interviewed initially, and when I have interviewed candidates myself, the conversations have mainly focused on the candidates' interests and experiences." According to one litigator, the firm "used to be harder. It's still hard, but now they're hiring more, and experiencing more turnover. More slots = more chances to get in."

© 2007 Vault Inc.

OUR SURVEY SAYS

Dorky charmers, sexy legal nerds

"WilmerHale tends to attract the type of person who enjoyed law school and enjoys the intellectual aspects of legal practice," reports one Washington source. "The typical WilmerHale lawyer is a politically liberal, academic type, hardworking, a bit nerdy. I get the impression that a lot of folks here are happy, but see themselves ending up in the public sector or as professors down the line," speculates a New Yorker. Another associate calls his officemates "intellectual, hardworking and diligent people who are not showoffs or flashy." Smiles another Big Apple insider, "We are pretty dorky, but in a charming way." In the eyes of one litigator, WilmerHale lawyers are "extremely professional without being pompous. People are exceptionally bright and generally nice and interesting—albeit not always the most socially adept. But to the extent that there is any sense of competitiveness, it seems geared more toward quality (legal-nerd sexiness) of work than toward quantity (billable-hours machismo)." Nevertheless, the firm's 2004 merger has some associates worried about "the management push toward a business model that will make us an indistinguishable big firm." Observes one insider, "Since the merger, associates feel more commodified than they used to."

As for culture, "It's definitely not a party-house." Observes one Washington first-year, "Attorneys are more into their lives outside the firm than socializing with their co-workers. Most people leave by 7:30 to have dinner with their families, and then work from home." Still, "It's a very friendly, cooperative office, with opportunities to socialize." In Boston, there's "happy hour every Friday at 5," while the Manhattan office hosts "a Thursday night 'pizza and wings' gathering called the Chowder and Marching Society." Notes a midlevel in Washington, "Junior associates tend to make friends with others in their class. However, partners don't regularly socialize with associates." In general, "There are some social people, and some very unsocial people. Overall, most people just do their own thing."

Depends on the ebb and flow

For BigLaw, hours at WilmerHale are "pretty reasonable." As one D.C. lower-level describes it, "Hours tend to come all at once. I might work 16-hour days for three weeks, and then have nothing to do for two weeks." A Manhattan source feels that "the expectations are not as intense as other New York firms, but still it is not a lifestyle firm." Agrees a litigator in the same office, WilmerHale is "one of the better firms in New York City in this regard, but (there's) room for improvement." What helps is that the "firm is very flexible about work being done at home, telecommuting, in other offices, etc. It is not a face time firm." A D.C. rookie explains that "I work a lot of hours, but I do appreciate that the firm is pretty flexible about the hours I work. I can control my time to a reasonable extent, considering how junior I am." Observes another newbie, "So long as you get your work done, there really aren't people 'checking up' on you. Some weeks are great; some weeks I'm at the office until 11 p.m. or later all week. It just depends on the ebb and flow of the work. But it's nothing I didn't expect as a first-year associate at a large firm." Still, though the "firm is flexible," "2,000 hours is the base expectation." Complains one source, "That feels too high for comfort for an IP attorney."

Rest easy—vacations are safe. Notes one Washington midlevel, "Partners often expect associates to be available for weekend work, but don't interfere with family commitments or vacation plans that the associate has already informed them of." Assures one Boston source, "And the other lawyers are very understanding if you're going out of town or need to take some time off."

Street fashion

WilmerHale is a "big firm that follows the street slavishly"—so associates in its New York offices weren't biting their nails, waiting to see if the firm would match the January 2007 increases. Beams one source, "No complaints about compensation. The firm matches market. And everyone gets the same rate as long as they meet a minimum threshold." A midlevel in New York reports, "Our compensation is excellent, considering the fact this place is not a sweat shop. You can have a life and still make a great salary." Non-New York offices have since matched their respective markets as well.

Visit the Vault Law Channel, the complete online resource for law careers, featuring firm profiles, message boards, the Vault Law Job Board and more. **www.vault.com/law**

VAULT CAREER LIBRARY   **197**

Regarding bonuses, "The bonus system has been quite generous and, even better, transparent. It is tied to hours and unlimited pro bono hours are counted toward it." A first year litigator points out that "first-year bonuses are guaranteed. After that, I believe the goal is around 2,000 hours. But there are a number of factors in the calculus, including pro bono and career development work, etc. I think if you're around 2,000, you get the bonus for sure, and even if you're under (so long as you've made a contribution to the firm in other ways that year)."

Ask not of others what ye wouldn't do

At WilmerHale, "Partners treat associates with a great deal of respect and generally would not ask an associate to do any more work than the partners themselves are already doing." A newbie is impressed that "even the most senior, famous, seemingly unapproachable partners can actually be approached and listen to, and value, associate input." As associates report, save for "a few idiosyncratic exceptions," "day-to-day partner relations are generally very good" and "partners (are) very respectful and interested in getting associates involved." Of course, in some groups "there is still quite a bit of hierarchy and protocol, particularly in more 'elite' practice areas like securities litigation and appellate litigation."

What could be improved? "Communication from partners to associates with regard to firmwide issues. If you are not working with an in-the-know partner, you may not hear about things for weeks."

Your mediocrity is truly outstanding

"Mentoring at the firm is mixed," reports one insider. "A handful of partners and counsel are very good at providing informal feedback and advice, but the vast majority avoid it. Formal feedback to lower-level associates is almost always positive, even if they are doing a mediocre job." An associate seconds this: "Partners rarely provide constructive criticism or feedback until the evaluations, conducted twice yearly. Associates aren't often included in discussions or meetings to gain an understanding of the bigger picture of a case. For example, an associate who has drafted a research memo or a team of associates who have reviewed documents may never learn how their research (or documents identified as important) were used in a motion, presentation to regulators, or some other context." This junior associate just wants a little quality time: "We have partner mentors who take us out to lunch once (with other associates they are mentoring), and then they give us a six-month evaluation. It would be nice to have more one-on-one interaction with a partner-mentor, in a casual setting."

© 2007 Vault Inc.

VAULT CAREER LIBRARY

"We are pretty dorky, but in a charming way."

—*WilmerHale associate*

Visit the Vault Law Channel, the complete online resource for law careers, featuring firm profiles, message boards, the Vault Law Job Board and more. www.vault.com/law

VAULT CAREER LIBRARY   199

Williams & Connolly LLP

The Edward Bennett Williams Building
725 Twelfth Street, N.W.
Washington, DC 20005
Phone: (202) 434-5000
www.wc.com

LOCATION

Washington, DC

MAJOR DEPARTMENTS & PRACTICES

Administrative Law • Antitrust • Appellate • Arbitration •
Business Transactions & Tax • Criminal Defense •
Employment & Labor • Federal Programs & National Defense
• First Amendment & Media • General Civil Litigation •
Health Care & Medical Products • Intellectual Property •
Product Liability, Torts & Medicine • Professional Liability
Defense • Securities & Financial Services Litigation • Sports

THE STATS

No. of attorneys: 230
No. of offices: 1
Summer associate offers: "Because nearly all of our summer
associates obtain judicial clerkships, formal offers are only
extended after the clerks receive permission from judges to
request offers. Typically, all summer associates who
request offers are welcomed for permanent employment."
Managing Partner: By committee
Hiring Partner: Glenn J. Pfadenhauer

BASE SALARY (2007)

Washington, DC
1st year: $165,000
Summer associate: $3,100/week

UPPERS

• "The most interesting, most important litigation"
• Collaborative team environment
• Great client base

DOWNERS

• No bonuses
• "More and more gigantic cases"
• Little formal training

NOTABLE PERKS

• Free lunch in the firm dining room
• Tickets to D.C. sporting events
• Starbucks coffee machines
• Bar and moving expenses

THE BUZZ
WHAT ATTORNEYS AT OTHER FIRMS ARE SAYING ABOUT THIS FIRM

• "The envy of every other litigation practice in the
country"
• "Sink-or-swim mentality"
• "These guys are the best. Period"
• "Not nice but very good at what they do"

© 2007 Vault Inc.

RANKING RECAP

Regional Rankings
#1 - Washington, DC

Practice Area Rankings
#1 - Litigation

Partner Rankings
#2 - Litigation
#9 - Overall Prestige

Quality of Life
#3 - Selectivity
#7 - Overall Satisfaction
#9 - Associate/Partner Relations

EMPLOYMENT CONTACT

Ms. Donna M. Downing
Attorney Recruiting Manager
Phone: (202) 434-5605
Fax: (202) 434-5029
E-mail: ddowning@wc.com

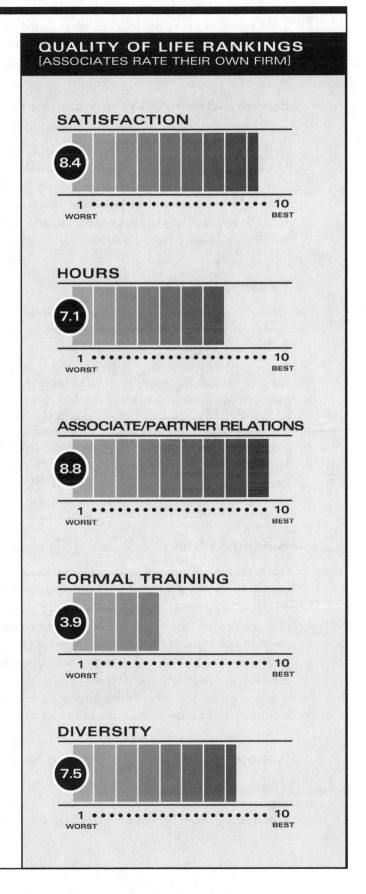

QUALITY OF LIFE RANKINGS
[ASSOCIATES RATE THEIR OWN FIRM]

SATISFACTION
8.4
1 WORST •••••••••••••••••••• 10 BEST

HOURS
7.1
1 WORST •••••••••••••••••••• 10 BEST

ASSOCIATE/PARTNER RELATIONS
8.8
1 WORST •••••••••••••••••••• 10 BEST

FORMAL TRAINING
3.9
1 WORST •••••••••••••••••••• 10 BEST

DIVERSITY
7.5
1 WORST •••••••••••••••••••• 10 BEST

Visit the Vault Law Channel, the complete online resource for law careers, featuring firm
profiles, message boards, the Vault Law Job Board and more. www.vault.com/law

VAULT CAREER LIBRARY   201

THE SCOOP

There's something to be said for doing one thing, and doing it well. Really, really well. Williams & Connolly LLP doesn't act like most law firms, seeking worldwide expansion and a full list of practices. Instead, Williams & Connolly focuses on its preeminent litigation practice, and operates one office (in Washington, D.C.) with approximately 230 attorneys.

Edward Bennett Williams, super lawyer

The patriarch of the Williams & Connolly family was Edward Bennett Williams, whose client list includes just about everyone famous in the D.C. area, and some from beyond the Beltway. Williams represented Frank Sinatra, Hugh Hefner, Senator Joseph McCarthy, Jimmy Hoffa, *The Washington Post* and the Reverend Sun Myung Moon. In 1967, Williams teamed with Paul Connolly, formerly a student of his at Georgetown's law school, to form Williams & Connolly. The firm has continued Edward Bennett Williams' tradition of representing high-profile clients, including Oliver North, John Hinckley Jr. (President Reagan's would-be assassin), Juan Miguel Gonzalez (father of Cuban refugee Elián González), and Bill and Hillary Clinton in numerous investigations during Clinton's presidency.

Passing the torch

Obviously, Williams & Connolly is a courtroom fixture. For instance, the firm is representing JMIC Life Insurance Co. in a class-action suit. A Georgia man purchased credit life insurance from JMIC, the proceeds of which would go to satisfy a car loan if the man died before paying it off. If he decided to pay off the loan early, he would be entitled to a refund of the unearned premium upon notice to the company; he claims he gave notice, but JMIC denied his refund request. The man filed a lawsuit and sought class-action status. JMIC countered by saying it hadn't had a chance to pay off the claim before the lawsuit was filed because it never received any notice the loan had been paid. A Georgia court denied JMIC's motion for summary judgment, a ruling upheld by the Georgia Court of Appeals in August 2006.

It was bad deals on wheels for a Colorado car dealership (and Williams & Connolly client) in a lawsuit filed under the Truth in Lending Act (TILA). Customers of the dealership filed the suit alleging that it concealed finance charges in violation of the TILA and sought class-action status; in August 2006, a federal judge dismissed some of the claims, saying the disputed finance charges placed some of the transactions outside the maximum jurisdictional amount under the statute. The remaining claims are pending.

Saving KPMG

One of the firm's recent success stories is its representation of accounting giant KPMG, which tapped Williams & Connolly to develop and oversee a compliance and ethics program after it was indicted for pushing illegal tax shelters. The program helped KPMG avoid the "death penalty"—a conviction that would bar KPMG from representing publicly traded companies in the U.S. (The death penalty effectively killed Arthur Andersen after the accounting firm was convicted of criminal charges related to its representation of Enron.) A federal judge approved KPMG's progress under the program in January 2007; if the firm stays on its best behavior until September 2008, it will be completely free of the criminal indictment. Williams & Connolly was less successful in its representation of Walter A. Forbes, former chairman of travel-services provider Cendant Corp., who was accused of conspiracy and filing false financial reports for misstating earnings at CUC International (which later merged with Cendant). A federal jury in Connecticut convicted Forbes of the crimes in November 2006; an appeal is pending.

Behind the pulpit and playing on Grass(o)

Williams & Connolly has represented the Roman Catholic Archdiocese of Washington in lawsuits filed by former parishioners alleging abuse by priests when the plaintiffs were minors. The Archdiocese reached a $1.3 million settlement with 18 men who alleged separate acts of abuse over a 20-year period starting in 1962.

© 2007 Vault Inc.

Moving up the East Coast, the firm continues to represent Richard A. Grasso, former chairman of the New York Stock Exchange (NYSE) who retired in August 2003. A deferred compensation plan gave him approximately $140 million on his retirement. The numbers raised eyebrows (to put it mildly), and then-New York State Attorney General Eliot Spitzer (who later rode his fame to the governorship) sued Grasso in 2004 to get some of that money back. A New York state judge found that Grasso had thwarted attempts by the NYSE's board to oversee his compensation and ordered him to return at least $100 million. Williams & Connolly has disputed that order and, to boot, has asked that the judge be forced to recuse himself. The Appellate Division recently agreed with the firm that the attorney general did not have authority to bring four of the causes of action at issue. The case is still pending.

A sporting chance

One other accomplishment we have yet to mention about Superlawyer Edward Bennett Williams: he used to own the Washington Redskins and Baltimore Orioles (which he bought in 1979). These days, former partner Larry Lucchino continues his former firm's sports connection—post W&C, he's now a part-owner and CEO of the Boston Red Sox. Those lawyers still left out of the owners' box, and slugging away at Williams & Connolly, have represented players, owners, players' associations and teams in matters ranging from stadium construction and contract negotiations to marketing deals. Watch ESPN for any significant amount of time and you're guaranteed to hear about dozens of Williams & Connolly clients.

Right-handed pitcher Chris Young signed with the Padres this year, hopefully for the long haul. After being traded three times in his career, Young wanted a contract that would give him security. His lawyers, Williams & Connolly partners Lon Babby and Damon Jones, came through with a four-year, $14.5 million contract which, while not a no-trade agreement, would cost the team a pretty penny to let him go. Firm negotiations on the behalf of Larry Brown, former Knicks coach, were less favorable. He left the franchise with only $18.5 million of the $41 million left on his contract. To be fair though, the Knicks had a damning case against him for a variety of offenses.

GETTING HIRED

Wanted: a plus factor

"It is extremely difficult to get an offer" at Williams & Connolly, reports one source. "We look for driven, ambitious, gregarious, go-get-'em types." There is "no specific GPA cutoff, but your grades must be extremely good to get a foot in the door." It helps to know a little bit about Williams & Connolly. "Besides the obvious paper qualifications, Williams & Connolly wants to hire associates (and summer associates) who have thought extensively about what they are looking for in a law firm," reports a senior associate. "Applicants who say they want to work here because it is highly ranked tend to do less well than those who have studied up on the firm and are able to thoughtfully explain why they want to work here."

In short, the firm doesn't just want it all, they want it all and then some. "You have to be at the top of your class with a plus," which can include a clerkship or prior work experience. "Applicants need top grades, an interesting resume and an excellent interview," notes another source. "It's extremely competitive," observes a lawyer. "Applicants need more than just good grades—they really need an X-factor that sets them apart." "I think once you get in the door for an interview, the most important thing is to seem genuinely interested in the firm and to have a compelling personality," says a contact.

OUR SURVEY SAYS

Big boy work

Everyone seems to love it at Williams & Connolly. "I have had a terrific experience at Williams & Connolly," gushes one insider. "If you take the initiative to seek out interesting work and good mentors, it's hard to imagine a better law firm experience." "I

Visit the Vault Law Channel, the complete online resource for law careers, featuring firm profiles, message boards, the Vault Law Job Board and more. www.vault.com/law

VAULT CAREER LIBRARY   203

can't imagine being happier at another firm," agrees a junior associate. "The work is consistently engaging and intellectually rewarding, the people are friendly and interesting, and the firm's commitment to excellence inspires you to do your best work." Everyone gets along, too. "I am fortunate to work with incredibly bright people who are all professionals that treat their colleagues with respect," states an attorney. That source is never bored by her work, which helps. "I am also fortunate to have a real diversity of cases, many of which are smaller, and many of which have a political or otherwise high-profile aspect. Nearly all of my cases are genuinely interesting."

Perhaps the best part of the Williams & Connolly experience: "New associates are given lots of responsibility immediately. There is no training period at the start of work. You learn how to write motions and briefs as you are doing them, which is the best way to learn. In team meetings, everyone's view matters, from senior partners to the greenest associates." Indeed, all agree that junior associates are given substantive work much earlier than peers at other firms. "I took three depositions and argued a motion in federal court alone before my ninth month here!" exclaims one second-year. "The firm cares about the development of its associates and gives them a lot of responsibility early on," says another junior associate. "In fact, I get to do depositions, consult with experts, and meet with clients as a second-year associate, which is almost unheard of at most firms of Williams & Connolly's size and stature."

Meet me in the cafeteria

Williams & Connolly associates enjoy a "highly collegial" culture, the highlight of which is "mutual respect across the board." The firm has a "very collegial, congenial atmosphere" and is "generally not at all competitive." Like high school, the social life seems to revolve around the lunch room. "The attorneys at Williams & Connolly are all very nice and very collegial," reports an insider. "Overall, people are surprisingly laid-back for a bunch of litigators. The attorney dining room, where every attorney can eat lunch for free, helps quite a bit, giving the attorneys a more casual outlet to get to know one another." It also gets four stars. "The attorney dining room provides a great place to socialize—and, by the way, the food is spectacular," says a junior associate. "The attorney dining room also goes a long way toward fostering camaraderie amongst partners and associates, as do the attorney retreat/dinner dance and the Christmas party," notes another young associate. "There are exceptions, but most people here are not your typical socially-challenged lawyers—they are funny, outgoing and not competitive with each other," concludes that source. "Lawyers here tend to be 'sporty,' both personally and professionally," notes a litigator. "There's a definite aura of team-mindedness and a sense that our clients are in the right."

No bonuses

Surprise: bonuses aren't a given at BigLaw. "Williams & Connolly has never offered a bonus, but the trade-off has been a higher base salary without a hard-line hours requirement," says a contact. While Williams & Connolly associates accept that, there are rumblings that the firm isn't keeping up its end of the bargain. "Williams & Connolly has always been conservative about pay," notes a lawyer. The revolt is spreading. "We obviously are paid well in comparison with most other jobs," concedes a senior associate, "but Williams & Connolly is always behind the curve in terms of pay ... Our base salaries may seem high, but we have no bonus."

Done? Go home

The lack of bonus does have its benefits: no scrambling to make hours. Of course, that doesn't mean Williams & Connolly is a picnic. "Billing is irrelevant in that there is no bonus for billing a lot of hours," says a junior associate. "There is plenty of work to go around, so getting out the door at night is more a function of getting the work done well in a timely manner than hitting a bonus target." Williams & Connolly litigators seem to be similarly situated to litigators at other firms. "The hours can at times be demanding, but no more so than hours typically expected of an attorney involved in significant litigation matters," reports a source. At least they can be treated like adults. "Professionals come to work here because they are treated like professionals," says a midlevel associate. "We work as much as we need to do our work at the highest standards. That takes time, no doubt; but it is great to be treated like a grown-up."

You're on your own

Some firms are sink-or-swim. Williams & Connolly throws new associates into the middle of the ocean and expects them to start writing memos. Most seem to prefer it that way. The firm is "very much a 'watch one, do one, teach one' environment," according to insiders. "Orientation lasts less than a day," notes a source. "You get assignments on your first day of work and start learning how to do your job by doing your job. This is a good thing." The firm isn't completely devoid of assistance to young associates. "There is very little formal training, though the firm holds monthly meetings with new associates to provide information in a particular area and to give us an opportunity to meet with senior partners," reports one lawyer. "Other than that, they pretty much throw you into the fire and expect that you'll be fine." What training the firm does supply seems to be getting better. "We have monthly in-house training programs that are very good and getting better," says a senior associate. "But the firm generally believes in hands-on training in real cases, which is better."

"A very welcoming environment"

"The firm needs to take a more active approach to recruiting and retaining women and minorities," observes an attorney. Williams & Connolly "does not have a lot of structure, which has many, many benefits. However, the unstructured environment has caused the firm to lag behind its peers in creating programs to recruit and retain women and minorities," says a source. "Any attorney (associate or partner) can use a part-time schedule, and female part-time associates have made partner—but there's always more that can be done," warns a contact. When it comes to minority associates, "There's always more that any firm can do, but I think Williams & Connolly does a fantastic job of this. We are fortunate to be able to choose from the very best law students—including the very best minority students—the very best law schools. And I detect no bias, and no racism, whether implicit or explicit." "There are openly gay associates and partners," notes a lawyer. "And we have domestic partner benefits. I believe the firm to be a very welcoming environment."

Visit the Vault Law Channel, the complete online resource for law careers, featuring firm profiles, message boards, the Vault Law Job Board and more. **www.vault.com/law**

VAULT CAREER LIBRARY

205

Sidley Austin LLP

One South Dearborn
Chicago, IL 60603
Phone: (312) 853-7000

787 Seventh Avenue
New York, NY 10019
Phone: (212) 839-5300
www.sidley.com

LOCATIONS

Chicago, IL • Dallas, TX • Los Angeles, CA • New York, NY
• San Francisco, CA • Washington, DC • Beijing • Brussels
• Frankfurt • Geneva • Hong Kong • London • Shanghai •
Singapore • Sydney • Tokyo

MAJOR DEPARTMENTS & PRACTICES

Antitrust/Competition • Bankruptcy • Business & Financial
Transactions • Capital Markets • Corporate & Securities •
Employee Benefits • Employment & Labor • Environmental •
Insurance • Intellectual Property • International Trade &
Dispute Resolution • Investment Products • Litigation •
Pharma/Life Sciences • Product Liability • Real Estate •
Regulatory • Tax

THE STATS

No. of attorneys: 1,700
No. of offices: 16
Summer associate offers: 171 out of 179 (2006)
Executive Committee Chair: Thomas A. Cole
Management Committee Chair: Charles W. Douglas
Hiring Partners:
Chicago, IL: Holly A. Harrison & Anthony J. Aiello
New York, NY: Robert P. Hardy & John J. Kuster

BASE SALARY (2007)

All offices
1st year: $160,000
Summer associate: $3,100/week

UPPERS

• "We are paid really well"
• Collegial atmosphere
• "Reasonable work expectations of (most) partners"

DOWNERS

• "The quality of work varies greatly by practice group"
• "Formal training is a bit lacking"
• Large firm bureaucracy

NOTABLE PERKS

• Friday happy hours, Thursday lunches
• MoMA membership (NYC)
• Subsidized emergency child care nearby (for LA, CHI, NYC, DC, SF)
• $42 per month toward public transportation (CHI, DC, NYC, SF)

THE BUZZ
WHAT ATTORNEYS AT OTHER FIRMS ARE SAYING ABOUT THIS FIRM

• "What all megafirms should be"
• "Want you to work Christmas day!"
• "More humane than others at top"
• "A bit dry"

© 2007 Vault Inc.

RANKING RECAP

Best in Region
#2 - Chicago
#10 - Washington, DC
#16 - New York

Best in Practice
#3 - International Law

Partner Prestige Rankings
#22 - Overall Prestige

EMPLOYMENT CONTACTS

Chicago
Ms. Jennifer L. Connelly
National Recruiting Manager
Phone: (312) 853-7495
Fax: (312) 853-7036
E-mail: jlconnelly@sidley.com

New York
Lauryn Bronstein
Legal Recruiting Manager
Phone: (212) 839-5407
Fax: (212) 839-5599
E-mail: lbronstein@sidley.com

Washington, DC
Kathy Steadman
Legal Recruiting Manager
Phone: (202) 736-8087
Fax: (202) 736-8711
E-mail: ksteadman@sidley.com

Los Angeles
Susan McGrady
Phone: (213) 896-6855
Fax: (213) 896-6600
E-mail: smcgrady@sidley.com

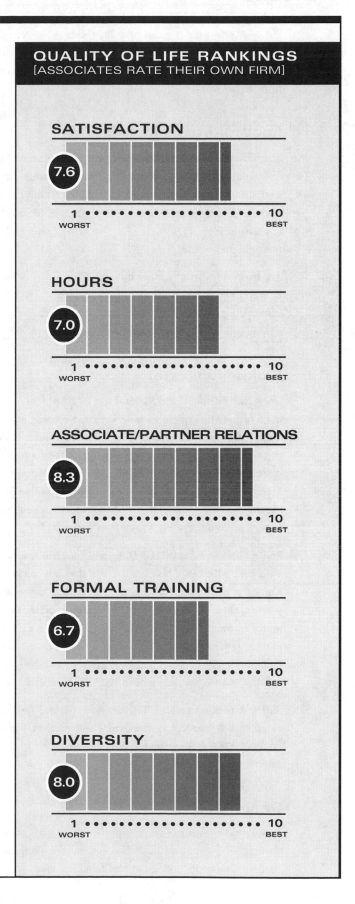

QUALITY OF LIFE RANKINGS
[ASSOCIATES RATE THEIR OWN FIRM]

SATISFACTION
7.6
1 WORST — 10 BEST

HOURS
7.0
1 WORST — 10 BEST

ASSOCIATE/PARTNER RELATIONS
8.3
1 WORST — 10 BEST

FORMAL TRAINING
6.7
1 WORST — 10 BEST

DIVERSITY
8.0
1 WORST — 10 BEST

Visit the Vault Law Channel, the complete online resource for law careers, featuring firm profiles, message boards, the Vault Law Job Board and more. www.vault.com/law

VAULT CAREER LIBRARY   207

THE SCOOP

Sidley Austin—the product of a 2001 merger between Chicago's Sidley & Austin and New York-based Brown & Wood—has over 1,700 attorneys in 16 offices around the world. The combined firm was initially known as Sidley Austin Brown & Wood, but shortened its name in 2006. The name may be truncated, but Sidley Austin is still one of the top corporate, tax and litigation firms in the world.

East meets (Mid)west

The Sidley Austin story starts way back in 1866, when the firm that would be known as Sidley & Austin was founded in Chicago. Sidley & Austin rose to prominence by representing corporate clients in litigation, transaction and regulatory matters. The firm went through a growth spurt in the late 20th century, adding lawyers through merger and opening outposts in Los Angeles, New York and Washington, D.C., as well as several overseas offices. The other half of the current Sidley Austin, Brown & Wood, was founded in New York in 1914. The firm quickly built a Wall Street reputation by representing investment banks and other financial institutions.

The two firms came together in May 2001. Sidley & Austin and Brown & Wood consolidated their New York offices in Brown & Wood's facilities at the World Trade Center. The office was destroyed in the September 11 terror attacks (one of the firm's employees perished in the attack) and the firm was forced to scramble to negotiate a new lease where Sidley & Austin maintained a small office. The firm later moved to a larger New York office in July 2002.

Sidley superstar

Good luck beating Carter G. Phillips in a courtroom. Phillips, the managing partner of Sidley Austin's Washington, D.C., office, has a resume that might as well be cast in bronze. After clerking for a court of appeals judge and Supreme Court Chief Justice Warren Burger, Phillips served as assistant solicitor general and argued nine cases in front of the Supreme Court. Moving to private practice hasn't kept Phillips out of the courthouse on First Street either. Since joining Sidley Austin, he has argued a whopping 45 cases in front of the high court—including six in the 2005-2006 term alone. For example, he argued on behalf of Mohawk Industries in a case involving the definition of a RICO enterprise. He also successfully argued on behalf of eBay that the standard for issuing injunctions in patent cases should be the same as in other cases, a decision cited by numerous patent law experts as among the most important in the field.

Phillips also represented IBP (formerly known as Iowa Beef Processors, Inc.) in an important labor law case. The Supreme Court awarded Phillips (and his client) a partial victory in that case, finding that employers do not have to pay employees for time spent waiting to put on protective gear, but the time spent putting on the gear and walking to and from the job site wearing the gear is compensable. Phillips' frequent appearances before the Supreme Court led the *National Law Journal* to name him as a runner-up for its annual lawyer of the year award. In a case in front of the plain old Second Circuit Court of Appeals in New York, Phillips represented Fox Television in a challenge to the Federal Communications Commission's tighter obscenity standards. Fox and other television networks claimed that the FCC's shifting standards on obscenity are too vague for networks to avoid liability and violate the First Amendment. The case was argued in late 2006, and a decision is expected sometime in 2007.

Sidley Austin client OSI Systems was thankful for the firm's representation in mid-2006. OSI sued L-3 Communications, claiming L-3 reneged on an agreement to purchase Perkin Elmer Security Detection Systems together in 2002. A jury ruled in favor of OSI, finding that L-3 breached its fiduciary duty and committed fraud. The jury awarded OSI $33 million in compensatory damages and $92 million in punitive damages.

Dealmaking

Among Sidley Austin's recent significant corporate engagements in 2006 is a debt offering by Deutsche Bank. The firm advised the banking giant on a €1.2 billion commercial mortgage-backed securities deal. Sidley Austin also advised Washington Mutual Bank in a groundbreaking covered bond issuance involving the export of U.K. technology to the U.S., which was named "deal

© 2007 Vault Inc.

of the year" by a number of publications. It also advised Agile Property Holdings when the China-based property development company issued $400 million in bonds on the Hong Kong stock exchange. Sidley Austin advised Merrill Lynch's Singapore unit in a $279 million leveraged buyout of an Indonesian coal company. Sidley Austin also counseled JPMorgan and UBS in a $400 million bond offering by Greentown China Holdings in Hong Kong.

Sidley Austin handled several major mergers and acquisitions in 2006-2007, representing Equity Office Properties Trust in its $39 billion acquisition by The Blackstone Group (the largest leveraged buyout transaction ever); representing CNL Hotels & Resorts, the nation's second largest hotel real estate investment trust, in its $6.6 billion acquisition by Morgan Stanley Real Estate; representing First Data Corp. in its agreement to be taken private by Kohlberg Kravis Roberts in a transaction valued at approximately $29 billion (the second largest leveraged buyout ever); and representing Tribune Company in a plan proposed by Samuel Zell to take the company private at a cost of $8.2 billion. In addition, Sidley Austin represented the underwriters in Fortress Investment Group's $634 million initial public offering, the first IPO of a hedge fund/private equity fund in the United States.

Welcome to Sidley

Sidley Austin boosted several of its key practices with some lateral hires. In October 2006, the firm announced that Georg Rützel would join its Frankfurt office as a partner. Rützel, an M&A expert, had been at the Frankfurt office of Clifford Chance. The firm also lured intellectual property partner Sandra A. Bresnick from Weil Gotshal & Manges that October; Bresnick will practice out of the firm's New York office. Sidley Austin New York also welcomed Chiu-Ti Jansen as a partner in November. Jansen, an insurance law expert, had been a partner at LeBoeuf, Lamb, Greene & MacRae. The firm has also beefed up its London insurance practice with the addition of Dorothy Cory-Wright. More recently in May 2007, the firm opened a Sydney office with the addition of Bob Meyers of Pillsbury Winthrop Shaw Pittman.

On an interesting political note, Illinois Senator (and early frontrunner for the 2008 Democratic presidential nomination) Barack Obama summered at Sidley & Austin in the late 1980s.

GETTING HIRED

The "Usual Suspects" ... and some new faces too

No, not Keyser Söze. Though Sidley certainly "draws the majority of new associates from top-10 law schools," the usual suspects don't necessarily mean Harvard or Yale either. A windy city old-timer, Sidley takes care of its neighbors: "they love the University of Chicago," hiring there in quantity for the home office. The New York office is meanwhile "Fordham-friendly." Your law school not down the road from a Sidley branch? No problem. The firm "also cherry-picks truly outstanding students from other schools."

Now we know the where, but what about the who? A candidate's GPA should be high, though associates differ on whether there are actual cutoffs. A good rule of thumb: "[Sidley] tends to look for top 25 to 30 percent (B+ or higher) from top-10 schools and top 10 percent from other top tier schools." Yeah, yeah, says a real estate associate, "Of course grades matter, but experiences, sense of humor and personality are also important." The firm "want[s] well-rounded people who can have fun and contribute more than just billable hours." When it comes time to meet the parents, "Modest, friendly, communicative and likeable people do the best at these interviews." This is the place for the unusual suspects to shine—"Exceptional achievement elsewhere or relevant skills/experience and professional demeanor go a long way." The story of an associate from Duke exemplifies the meritocratic power of a good interview. "I certainly was not a star in law school. A partner alumnus went to bat for me because he liked me during OCI."

Visit the Vault Law Channel, the complete online resource for law careers, featuring firm profiles, message boards, the Vault Law Job Board and more. www.vault.com/law

VAULT CAREER LIBRARY   209

OUR SURVEY SAYS

The people in our neighborhood

When they're good, they're good. Most partners are "very respectful," "foster a positive working environment" and "deal with associates as colleagues rather than as underlings." These lawyers must have done well in kindergarten—associates make note of their impeccable manners: "All partners in our group say 'please' and 'thank you' in all correspondence, whether it be in person or in an e-mail" and "apologize when last-minute assignments require a late night or weekend."

When they're not good ... well, a San Francisco associate warns the firm's partners that their "difficult personalities ... are the basis for retention issues." Others are less dire in their assessments. "We have some random bad people, but doesn't every firm?" Maybe Sidley associates are just more willing to call a spade a spade. The majority are also quick to qualify that while "there's one jerk I sometimes work with, *everyone else* I work with is really very pleasant." When the "bad seeds" or those with a "passive-aggressive streak" darken their doorsteps, associates know they are "the exception, not the rule."

Communication of management decisions mostly occurs during semiannual "associate town meetings," during which "associates are apprised of policy changes or other important events or discussions going on among the partnership," and management "fields anonymous questions (posed by e-mail in advance through the associate relations committee) about changes to firm policies" and other concerns. It's a serviceable system, by which associates neither feel left out nor vital to the process. "On a firmwide basis, management certainly appears to value the associates' input, although I can't say how much our thoughts are actually acted upon rather than just heard."

Bringing rivalry to the bank

When it comes to compensating lawyers, it's always something. Sidley associates did get their STB-inspired raises, and admit (however paradoxically) that the firm is "a salary market leader" which "will follow any moves of its peers." Base salary is not the problem. Well, only insofar as "We're on the New York-gets-more program." Ouch. Californians complain about the discrepancy that their bonuses are "almost half of what the associates in the New York office get," and they have to bill more hours to get them (2,000 on the West Coast vs. 1,800 in New York). Bonuses are a grumbling point in Chicago as well. Associates also want the firm to stop bean-counting bonus hours. 2,001 hours get $20K. Not 1,950, not 1,982. Thus, "Message: 2,000 hours or bust."

Maybe it is unfair to harp on the naysayers. Plenty of associates rate compensation a 10, and one even chides his colleagues with "any other answer is ridiculous." Because Sidley matches so quickly, "there is no internal griping" and "it is basically a nonissue."

Getting it done

Confucius say, herein a great truth of BigLaw: "You're not getting paid this amount of money to work 9 to 5." At Sidley, associates knew what they were getting into and say they have it pretty good, all things considered. "Sometimes I'd like to spend a little less time here, but I don't feel like I'm killing myself working too hard," says a litigator. The prevailing attitude is "do your work", not "be seen at work"—associates report "the firm is not into face time. As long as you get the work done and people can find you, no one bothers you about the hours you keep in the office." A corporate associate spells it out: "it is OK to take work home." When crunch time requires extended in-office hours, associates don't mind that much. "I do have to pull, on average, one all-nighter every month, but my hours are SO flexible now that I do not care at all." Be assured, when you're working late, it's for a good reason. "The hours are dictated more by case demands than pressure to meet a billable hours target," though a New Yorker tells us "no one has a problem" reaching those 2,000 hours.

Vacations, maternity and paternity leaves are all well utilized and flexible. "I just returned from a three-week vacation and got no grief about it," raves a Washington, D.C., associate. Flex-time is, for the most part, seen as a viable option, and we hear from

© 2007 Vault Inc.

associates who are successfully working 60 to 80 percent hours schedules. The only Sidley-specific hours complaint is that the "firm makes us account for at least 7.5 hours every day" … which can be "inconvenient and annoying."

Quantity aside, the quality of Sidley associates' work varies with department, level and even time of the month. A first year gushes forth about "interesting work, minimal document review, and a great deal of client and partner face time." A colleague said his "first nine months were like hell" (but have since gotten much better). One corporate financier claims partners give "challenging and exciting work" (thus "show[ing] a lot a faith in their associates"). In contrast, another corporate finance associate complains about the group's dependence on large transactions for Fortune 500 companies, which "leads to spending a majority of one's time handling administrative matters on deals." Tax practice, too, can make for "a lot of high-volume repetitive work." But after less than half a year at Sidley, a D.C. litigator has "second-chaired at least four depositions in the last month."

"Mentors abound"

Partner mentor? You got it. Associate mentor? That too. Practice group mentor? Of course. Diversity? Women's mentoring circle? Informal? No problem. Maybe that's why associates say "you don't need to look very far to find a mentor." No kidding … and thus it's no wonder that "more so than formal training, the informal training is where we tend to learn the most." Partners and senior associates are not only "good and willing teachers" but also "genuinely want associates to become better trained." One simple thing Sidley partners do that goes a long way toward producing high-quality associates is check their work. "It is very common for a partner to revise a draft and send a redline [copy] back to me so that I can see what the changes were and ask about them." It's rare that we hear about partners giving such concrete feedback on written pieces.

Comments on informal training are not uniformly positive, however. It's not concentrated in any one practice or office, but a few think (as far as partner mentoring) that "some don't have the time and others don't have an interest" or that "the firm could do a lot more, formally and informally, to help associates learn how to practice."

Needs a little something

As for formal training, yeah, they've got that, too … though no one is nearly excited to talk about it as their mentoring experiences. "The formal training program could use work—while it's not terrible, it seems like something of an afterthought." Those who did find it helpful refer to their departmental training, not the firmwide ones. The firmwide programs have trouble engaging associates for a variety of reasons. For one, the emphasis on the "mock trial" is "ceremonial" and not practically applied day-to-day. (Plus, this approach is only relevant to litigators. A real estate source scoffs, "What would we do, have a mock closing?") At the start of their careers, first-years go to training sessions "almost weekly." Afterwards, there is a dearth of more specified training for midlevels (although they are free to keep attending the introductory trainings if they wish). Improvements in training are rumored to be under development. Until they come out though, it's likely most Sidley associates will continue to see that "formal training's value is taking care of CLEs."

Brave New World

Last year, in what one associate calls "one of its rare acts of generosity," Sidley officially did away with the 60-hour cap on pro bono, and now all are counted toward billables (previously, 60 hours counted automatically, and getting approval for more was a mere formality). Though a midlevel says, "I'd never heard of a legitimate pro bono project not getting approved," associates now take advantage of the reduced red tape to pile it on. "I had over 200 hours of pro bono work that counted as billables, for purposes of my bonus," brags a litigator. Indeed, "Sidley has become much more focused on pro bono work in the last few years," and also recently hired a pro bono coordinator, an omen of the pro-pro bono future to come.

Visit the Vault Law Channel, the complete online resource for law careers, featuring firm profiles, message boards, the Vault Law Job Board and more. **www.vault.com/law**

VAULT CAREER LIBRARY   211

Gibson, Dunn & Crutcher LLP

333 South Grand Avenue
Los Angeles, CA 90071-3197
Phone: (213) 229-7000
www.gibsondunn.com

LOCATIONS

Century City, CA • Dallas, TX • Denver, CO • Irvine, CA •
Los Angeles, CA • New York, NY • Palo Alto, CA • San
Francisco, CA • Washington, DC • Brussels • London •
Munich • Paris

MAJOR DEPARTMENTS & PRACTICES

Administrative Law • Antitrust & Trade Regulation •
Appellate & Constitutional Law • Business Crimes &
Investigations • Business Restructuring & Reorganization •
Capital Markets • Consumer Class Action • Corporate
Transactions • Crisis Management • Emerging
Technologies • Energy & Infrastructure • Environment &
Natural Resources • Executive Compensation & Employee
Benefits • Financial Institutions • Global Finance •
Government & Commercial Contracts • Health Care & Life
Sciences • Insurance & Reinsurance • Intellectual Property •
International Trade Regulation & Compliance • Labor &
Employment • Latin America • Legal Malpractice Defense •
Litigation • Media & Entertainment • Private Equity • Public
Policy • Real Estate • Securities Litigation • Tax

THE STATS

No. of attorneys: 864
No. of offices: 13
Summer associate offers: 110 out of 116 (2006)
Managing Partner: Kenneth M. Doran
Hiring Partner: Steven E. Sletten

BASE SALARY (2007)

Firmwide
1st year: $160,000
2nd year: $170,000
3rd year: $185,000
4th year: $210,000
5th year: $230,000
6th year: $250,000
7th year: $265,000
Summer associate: $3,080/week

UPPERS

• "Real" work, and early on
• Flexible hours—no "face time" requirement
• Respectful partners

DOWNERS

• Some associates can get lost in free market system
• "Document review"
• Typical BigLaw hours

NOTABLE PERKS

• "Great retreats"
• "Free coffee and free parking"
• $1,000 client development budget
• $12,000 bar study stipend

THE BUZZ
WHAT ATTORNEYS AT OTHER FIRMS ARE SAYING ABOUT THIS FIRM

• "Appellate powerhouse"
• "Conservative gurus, unite!"
• "Powerful. Scary"
• "Premium shop"

© 2007 Vault Inc.

RANKING RECAP

Best in Region
#5 - Southern California
#6 - Northern California
#7 - Texas
#9 - Washington, DC

Best in Practice
#8 - Antitrust

Partner Prestige Rankings
#16 - Overall Prestige

Quality of Life
#9 - Selectivity

EMPLOYMENT CONTACT

Ms. Leslie Ripley
Director, Legal Recruiting & Diversity
Phone: (213) 229-7273
E-mail: lripley@gibsondunn.com

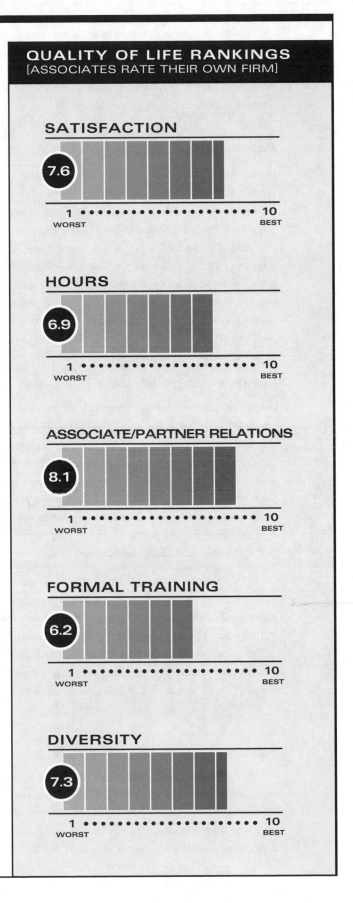

QUALITY OF LIFE RANKINGS
[ASSOCIATES RATE THEIR OWN FIRM]

SATISFACTION
7.6
1 WORST .... 10 BEST

HOURS
6.9
1 WORST .... 10 BEST

ASSOCIATE/PARTNER RELATIONS
8.1
1 WORST .... 10 BEST

FORMAL TRAINING
6.2
1 WORST .... 10 BEST

DIVERSITY
7.3
1 WORST .... 10 BEST

Visit the Vault Law Channel, the complete online resource for law careers, featuring firm profiles, message boards, the Vault Law Job Board and more. www.vault.com/law

VAULT CAREER LIBRARY   213

THE SCOOP

While Gibson Dunn is well known for its bet-the-company litigation and high-end corporate work, the firm made *The American Lawyer*'s prestigious A-List ranking for the first time in 2006, making significant improvement in diversity and pro bono. Last year, Gibson Dunn increased its annual number of pro bono hours by 81 percent, to 64,949 donated attorney hours, meeting the Pro Bono Institute's Pro Bono Challenge, which asks law firms to donate 60 hours per attorney to pro bono work, in the first full year since the firm signed the Challenge.

Born supremacy

Gibson Dunn is perhaps best known for appellate and constitutional law. In recent years the firm counseled then-Governor George W. Bush in litigation related to the Florida recount of 2000—and regardless of where one falls on the political compass, the firm's victory in the vote count case stands as one of the most important Supreme Court cases in U.S. history. During U.S. Supreme Court's 2005 term, Gibson Dunn argued and won four cases, including two argued on the same day (both of which the firm won 9-0)—a rare occurrence for even a top Supreme Court practice. Most recently, the firm argued three cases in the Supreme Court's 2006 term, winning (in April 2007) on behalf of Microsoft, Microsoft v. AT&T, a patent law case with far-reaching implications for worldwide software and tech industries. Still pending is Leegin Creative Leather Products v. PSKS, a potentially landmark antitrust case in which the Supreme Court will reconsider its nearly century-old holding that agreements between a manufacturer and its retailers establishing minimum retail prices constitute a per se violation of the Sherman Act, and Waston v. Philip Morris, in which the Supreme Court will consider the scope of the federal officer removal statute.

Long, strange lawsuit it's been

Gibson Dunn's entertainment practice recently shot to fame, taking on such high-profile matters as representing rock icons the Grateful Dead, Carlos Santana and Led Zeppelin in a lawsuit alleging illegal sales of concert memorabilia and merchandise from web site wolfgangsvault.com. The firm is also representing Jay Leno, Rita Rudner and other comedians in a federal lawsuit against writer Judy Brown and several book publishers for reproducing thousands of their jokes in several book compilations. Taking a star turn, the firm also defended Jennifer Lopez, UPN and CBS in a copyright claim relating to the television show *South Beach*, pursued a case for Mariah Carey's production company against a concert promoter and represents Bob Dylan in his litigation matters, including a recent dispute with the producers of the film *Factory Girl*—in addition to generally handling high-profile and cutting-edge cases for the leading entertainment companies in the country, including HBO, Sony Pictures, Warner Music Group, Fox, Viacom and CBS.

On the transactional side, the firm's clients include major film studios, where it routinely advises such clients as Universal Pictures, 20th Century Fox and New Line Cinema on film financings and promotional, licensing and distribution matters, and major music companies in licensing, joint ventures and acquisitions, including CBS and Universal Pictures in a recent multi-picture financing and distribution deal with Alejandro Inarittu, Guillermo del Toro and Alfonso Cuarón and a 2006 representation of Rhino Entertainment in a landmark license agreement with Grateful Dead Productions. Other recent transactions of note involve representing a private equity fund in its purchase of a television station, representation of a Spanish language media company in the sale of five radio stations, representation of Technicolor in connection with its rollout of digital cinema in the Unites States and Europe.

Setting antitrust standards

The firm's antitrust group has been retained by Intel Corporation as lead trial counsel to defend against a lawsuit brought by Advanced Micro Devices alleging that Intel has violated Section 2 of the Sherman Act by unlawfully maintaining an alleged monopoly of a worldwide market for x86 microprocessors, the "brains" of most computers. AMD's counsel has characterized the case as one of "largest antitrust cases in history." In September 2006, Intel obtained dismissal of AMD's foreign conduct allegations, which form a significant part of the case. The case is set for trial in April 2009. On another note, the firm is currently

© 2007 Vault Inc.

representing Sony BMG in 35 antitrust class action complaints now consolidated into a single multidistrict litigation alleging a conspiracy by the major record labels to fix the price of downloaded music.

Big time in the big apple

Gibson Dunn New York has gained local attention for its willingness to tangle with the City. Indeed, *The New York Times* recently touted partner Randy Mastro as "one of the biggest legal thorns in the side of the Bloomberg administration, challenging and winning contract disputes." Through litigation and a successful lobbying strategy, the firm helped Cablevision defeat the controversial West Side Stadium project, which arguably became the most contentious public policy issue in New York City in 2005. Later that year, the firm won a victory against the Bloomberg administration over its plan, when Manhattan's notorious Fulton Fish Market moved to the Bronx, to leave behind the only new business that the Giuliani administration earlier put into that market to unload fish in order to thwart organized crime. In a high-profile trial covered extensively by local TV and press, the case then settled with Gibson Dunn's client, Laro, remaining when the Fulton Fish Market moved to the Bronx as its exclusive unloading firm for the next three years. More recently, the firm in 2006 represented Hunts Point Terminal Produce Cooperative Association, in its attempt to annul an award by the city and its Economic Development Corporation of a long-term lease opportunity to a competitor.

It's a Wally, Wally World

Winning a unanimous opinion from the Arkansas Supreme Court in April 2007, Gibson Dunn secured a complete victory for Wal-Mart in its appeal of the Benton County Circuit Court's dismissal of Wal-Mart's complaint against Thomas Coughlin, the former No. 2 executive, when the Arkansas high court unanimously reversed and remanded the circuit court's ruling that Wal-Mart had released all of its claims against Coughlin seeking to void his multi-million-dollar retirement package on grounds of fraudulent inducement and breach of fiduciary duty. In a significant decision regarding the duties of good faith, honesty and fair dealing imposed on corporate officers and directors, the Arkansas Supreme Court held that corporate officers and directors have a fiduciary duty to disclose material facts concerning their own wrongdoing before they can enter into a retirement package or other self-dealing contract with the corporation, that Wal-Mart had adequately pled that Coughlin breached this fiduciary duty to disclose, that Wal-Mart had also alleged with adequate particularity affirmative misrepresentations made by Coughlin over the course of several years that induced Wal-Mart to enter into the retirement package and release with him, and that, if Wal-Mart's allegations are ultimately proven, the retirement agreement and release would be null and void ab initio.

I brake for Gibson Dunn litigators

Gibson Dunn acted as both trial and national coordinating counsel for DaimlerChrysler in a series of class actions filed across the United States alleging safety defects, false advertising and breach of warranty, in connection with the braking system of certain 1999-2004 Jeep Grand Cherokee vehicles. While dispositive and class motions were pending in most of the actions, Gibson Dunn negotiated a complicated settlement of all claims on a nationwide basis, involving over 1.4 million vehicles and 2.8 million consumers. A court in New Jersey approved, over several objections, a nationwide class settlement that the class plaintiffs valued at approximately $14.5 million. The court awarded slightly more than $2 million in attorneys' fees, about $1 million less than what was requested, with all attorneys' fees deducted from a $12 million dollar maximum payout fund (the additional value the plaintiffs assigned to the settlement referred to coupons under which owners of Jeep Grand Cherokees could obtain inspections and brake repairs under warranty in certain circumstances). According to Gibson Dunn's L.A. office, the settlement was "a fair resolution for all concerned," and ended litigation filed in New York, New Jersey, Florida, Ohio, Kansas, Missouri and California.

From Russia with love

Not just a litigation shop, Gibson Dunn showed its corporate chops when its New York and London offices advised RUSAL Limited, the world's third-largest aluminum producer and its shareholder in its estimated $25 billion merger with domestic rival SUAL International Limited and Swiss group Glencore International AG, creating the world's largest aluminum corporation.

Visit the Vault Law Channel, the complete online resource for law careers, featuring firm profiles, message boards, the Vault Law Job Board and more. **www.vault.com/law**

VAULT CAREER LIBRARY   **215**

Other major deals include counseling Itron in its $1.7 billion purchase of Actaris Metering Systems, a designer and manufacturer of meters and associated systems for the electricity, gas, water and heat markets, Saxon Capital, Inc., a Virginia mortgage REIT, in its $856 million acquisition by Morgan Stanley, Intel in connection with its $600 million investment in Clearwire, Leonard Green its $1.3 billion acquisition of The Sports Authority. On the financial advisor side, the firm represented Lazard Freres as financial advisor to Supervalu as part of a consortium to acquire grocery chain Albertson's for $17 billion and UBS as financial advisor to Univision Communications in its $13 billion acquisition by an investor group.

Those in glass houses ...

In an episode that highlights the growing influence of GCs in shaping firms' diversity efforts, a 2005 *American Lawyer* piece that focused on Gibson Dunn's imbalanced diversity statistics earned the firm some lecturing from aforementioned client Wal-Mart, whose legal department has taken to championing diversity in its outside firms. In 2006 Chairman Kenneth Doran says Gibson Dunn's diversity initiatives are "an active, ongoing effort that will continue," and that the firm is "aware of the initiatives of Wal-Mart … and are we working with them? Absolutely." The firm now updates Wal-Mart on its diversity campaign and has partnered with it on various diversity initiatives. As mentioned above, the firm made the AmLaw A-List last year, in part for its improvement in diversity. The firm recently announced that it gained five minority partners, four through lateral hiring and one through promotion.

Everybody deserves a home sweet home

In July 2006, Gibson Dunn was honored for its work in expediting the adoption process for thousands of children. The North American Council on Adoptable Children (NACAC), a national nonprofit organization dedicated to helping foster children find permanent families, lauded the firm for its pro bono efforts for the cause. In 1998, Gibson Dunn spearheaded the Adoption Saturday project, which brings volunteer attorneys and judges together to finalize the adoptions of thousands of children living in foster care. Since the program was created, Gibson Dunn attorneys and staff have personally handled more than 2,000 adoptions.

GETTING HIRED

A high bar

"Gibson is snobby when it comes to grades, and there are specific GPA cutoffs that range from school to school," as an L.A. litigator reports. A New Yorker describes an extremely stringent hiring process: "It is very difficult to get hired at Gibson. Candidates must meet a very high bar before the firm will even consider interviewing them. And success at a top school is no guarantee of an offer. I have a friend who graduated Order of the Coif at a top-five school and, despite his affable nature and my endorsement, he wasn't made an offer. Gibson looks for both good grades and a cultural match. They would rather bring in associates from other offices to help an office that is getting slammed than hire what they view as subpar associates."

But don't think that you can sneak in a weak GPA by transferring in as a lateral, associates report. "There's no question that the firm looks for (and gets) the best and the brightest— the G.P.A. cutoff is taken very seriously, even for laterals." And not just for associates: "The firm has a strict GPA cutoff—even for very senior lateral partners with millions of dollars worth of portable business!" The firm responds that while it is proud of the quality and academic achievements of its lawyers, it is not nearly as rigid as the comments suggest. It does not have a narrow focus strictly on grades but is looking for a compelling, diverse group of leaders interested in practicing law at the highest level.

A litigation associate elaborates on the personality type the firm is seeking: "Gibson Dunn was competitive when I was a law student, and this has not changed. We are looking for people who want to work hard, have demonstrated some commitment beyond simply getting good grades, and whose personality is conducive to a 'free market' system. In other words, no jerks. I'm

© 2007 Vault Inc.

sure a few firms have more difficult grade cutoffs and call-back requirements, but I am always amazed at the number of wonderful people I interview each fall who never receive an offer."

OUR SURVEY SAYS

Friendly culture

Associates call Gibson Dunn a "friendly," "social," "professional," and "very collegial" "meritocracy." A junior L.A. attorney reports, "I have made great friends at the firm since I started working here, people I enjoy seeing even beyond the office environment. And it seems like everyone here easily finds colleagues with whom they like to socialize." A second-year Los Angeleno says, "People are friendly and respectful at all levels. People do socialize with one another, and it is easy to work with my colleagues." A real estate specialist adds, "The firm's culture is very friendly and everyone tends to get along both socially and professionally. The younger associates socialize together at either firm sponsored happy hours or social events, and outside of work as well." That said, a number of associates gripe about the absent, or forced, camaraderie. "To be honest, it's somewhat lame," complains an L.A. attorney. "Certain departments are more fun than others and there is certainly a vibe that some feel more 'holy' than others."

How about the work?

As for the work itself, Gibson Dunn's associates express a wide array of opinions—no one attitude predominates. It's easy, for example, to find associates who proclaim they wouldn't work anywhere else. An L.A. litigator professes, "We have a wide variety of deals, partners who care about teaching us and clients who are generally pleasant to work with. For a big firm, I don't think it gets any better." Another L.A. associate adds, "I am learning a lot and unlike many of my peers at other firms, have not simply been stuck on endless document reviews." On the other hand, it's also easy to find associates who espouse the completely opposite opinion. As one young insider puts it, "I dislike my work. I don't dislike being a lawyer, but I dislike the work I've done here so far." A colleague adds, "As a first-year litigation associate, most of my work is document review, which is not particularly fulfilling. I have had the opportunity to work on a pro bono case that has given me good opportunities to write legal documents, which is great, but much of the great experience of legal argument is counteracted by the lousy experience of getting absolutely no positive feedback from the partners working on the case."

A friendly free market

However, associates generally credit the firm's free-market system for fostering strong associate/partner relations. As one junior litigator puts it, "Our free-market system creates strong incentives for managing attorneys to be respectful and flexible with associates." A senior associate adds, "The partners tend to be great on an individual level. They work associates way too hard, but we knew that going in, and they tend to be very respectful and civil." On the other hand, a number of associates complain that individual partners can be overbearing and the partnership as a whole fails to include the associates in firmwide decisions in any meaningful way. "While this used to be one of the firm's stronger points, the pressure to deliver for clients and bring in new cases has resulted in associates being treated with less respect," warns a senior L.A. attorney. A junior L.A. associate reports, "On a whole, I don't get the sense that the partnership cares a whole lot about the associates. There is an associates' committee that participates in firm decisions, but it is made up entirely of associates who are going for partner and that seems to hamper their ability to zealously advocate for the rest of us."

Seek out your own training

Associates describe the firm's formal training program as "typical." Here's one associates positive spin on the offerings: "Keeping in line with the firm's entrepreneurial spirit, associates must for the most part seek out their own training." A corporate attorney advises that training "varies greatly depending on office. The L.A. office has formal training programs. Not as much

Visit the Vault Law Channel, the complete online resource for law careers, featuring firm profiles, message boards, the Vault Law Job Board and more. **www.vault.com/law**

VAULT CAREER LIBRARY

217

at other offices." A midlevel litigator adds, "The firm has a generous CLE reimbursement—it is basically unlimited. But it is hard to make time for CLE and there are no formal firm training programs."

Informal training at Gibson Dunn is a roll of the dice, associates say. Nearly every associate describes the availability of meaningful mentoring in the same way: It depends on the partner. "This is hit-or-miss just like at other firms—if you are able to find a partner interested in teaching, you are in great shape. Otherwise, you are on your own," says one insider. Another insider reports, "Informal training and mentoring entirely depends on the partner for whom you work." A third associate makes it unanimous: "Mentoring is on an ad hoc basis, so it depends on the partners or senior associates with whom you are working." The firm responds that it cares deeply about the professional development and success of its lawyers. It also recognizes the importance of mentoring to overall success, recently adopting a formalized mentoring program across its offices. In Los Angeles, this has involved the creation of mentoring groups, consisting of a partner and three associates, who meet collectively and individually in informal settings to discuss career development and associate issues.

Top of the market

Gibson Dunn's compensation plan may be at the top of the market, but is nonetheless a sore subject among associates. One supporter says, "You work long hours and you are paid well to do it." But the complainers are much more numerous. "The biggest issue of late has been the slow trigger finger on associate's salaries," according to an L.A. associate. "While other firms have moved first-year salaries to $160,000 and others quickly followed, it seemingly took some time to get first-year salaries up to match." A senior L.A. associate complains, "The firm always matches what it considers 'market' compensation, but the firm selects what it considers peer firms to determine what it considers 'market' compensation." Another insider adds, "Partners are paid at the top of the market. Associates are not."

No billing just to bill

The firm's hours expectations also inspire a wide array of opinions, though the consensus appears to be that the firm is flexible and doesn't obsess over "face time." "There is no pressure to bill hours for the sake of billing hours," says a senior L.A. litigator. A junior corporate attorney advises, "Most people I know work about 2,050 hours. The office generally is empty on weekends." A junior litigator says, "The firm expects as many hours as any other big firm, but they don't necessarily expect you to work all of those hours in the office. I've certainly spent whole days working at home, and I very rarely miss out on getting home in time for dinner. When it comes right down to it, as long as you're getting your hours in, the firm doesn't seem to care where you're doing them." And a senior L.A. attorney adds, "Everyone wants to work less, right? The hours can be long, but I think that people are as accommodating as they can be about your schedule. We all try to help each other out when someone is too busy, and, in my experience, it's not a problem to find someone to cover for you if you have another engagement or a vacation." Some associates praise the firm's focus on pro bono work. A junior litigator crows, "All pro bono hours count towards billable, one to one, meaning you don't have to make the billable target to make your pro bono hours count. This is one of the best things about the firm."

© 2007 Vault Inc.

"We have a wide variety of deals, people who care about teaching us, and clients who are generally pleasant to work with."

—*Gibson, Dunn & Crutcher associate*

Visit the Vault Law Channel, the complete online resource for law careers, featuring firm profiles, message boards, the Vault Law Job Board and more. **www.vault.com/law**

VAULT CAREER LIBRARY   219

O'Melveny & Myers LLP

400 South Hope Street
Los Angeles, CA 90071
Phone: (213) 430-6000
www.omm.com

LOCATIONS

Century City, CA • Los Angeles, CA • Menlo Park, CA •
New York, NY • Newport Beach, CA • San Francisco, CA •
Washington, DC • Beijing • Brussels • Hong Kong • London
• Shanghai • Tokyo

MAJOR DEPARTMENTS & PRACTICES

Adversarial Department

Antitrust/Competition • Appellate • Class Action, Mass
Torts, & Aggregated Litigation • Electronic Discovery •
General Trial & Litigation • Global Enforcement & Criminal
Defense • Intellectual Property & Technology • International
(Trade & Arbitration) • Labor & Employment • Securities
Enforcement & Regulatory Counseling • Securities
Litigation • Strategic Counseling

Transactions Department

Asia • Capital Markets • Corporate • Entertainment & Media
Mergers & Acquisitions • Private Equity • Project
Development & Real Estate • Restructuring • Tax • Venture
Capital

Industry Practices

Aviation • Energy • Environmental • Fund and Investment
Management • Health Care & Life Sciences • Insurance

THE STATS

No. of attorneys: 1,012
No. of offices: 13
Summer associate offers: 145 out of 152 (2006)
Chairman: A.B. Culvahouse
Hiring Partner: Brian Brooks

THE BUZZ
WHAT ATTORNEYS AT OTHER FIRMS ARE SAYING ABOUT THIS FIRM

- "Collegial, top notch"
- "Good lawyers, painful environment"
- "Excellent litigators"
- "Dorsal fins under their suits"

BASE SALARY (2007)

1st year: $160,000
Summer associate: $3,100/week

UPPERS

- Sophisticated clients and deals
- Individuality appreciated: "not a cookie-cutter firm"
- Pro bono encouraged

DOWNERS

- Demanding cases and clients = long hours
- "Staffing is sometimes top-heavy"
- "Mentoring could be improved"

NOTABLE PERKS

- First-year "O'Melveny University," midlevel and counsel retreats
- Affinity Groups with budgets
- $10,000 Bar stipend
- "Just about all the free Starbucks you can handle"

© 2007 Vault Inc.

RANKING RECAP

Best in Region
#3 - Southern California
#5 - Northern California
#11 - Washington, DC

Best in Practice
#8 - Labor & Employment

Partner Prestige Rankings
#19 - Overall Prestige

EMPLOYMENT CONTACT

Paige Drewelow
Director of Attorney Recruiting—Firmwide
Phone: (415) 984-8700
Fax: (415) 984-8701
E-mail: pdrewelow@omm.com

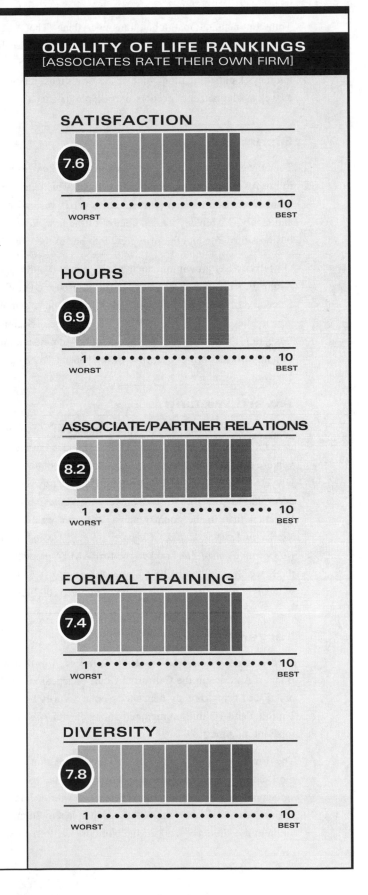

QUALITY OF LIFE RANKINGS
[ASSOCIATES RATE THEIR OWN FIRM]

SATISFACTION
7.6
1 WORST ·········· 10 BEST

HOURS
6.9
1 WORST ·········· 10 BEST

ASSOCIATE/PARTNER RELATIONS
8.2
1 WORST ·········· 10 BEST

FORMAL TRAINING
7.4
1 WORST ·········· 10 BEST

DIVERSITY
7.8
1 WORST ·········· 10 BEST

Visit the Vault Law Channel, the complete online resource for law careers, featuring firm profiles, message boards, the Vault Law Job Board and more. **www.vault.com/law**

VAULT CAREER LIBRARY   221

THE SCOOP

Transcontinental, trans-global, trans-everything. That's the story of O'Melveny & Myers. The firm was founded in Los Angeles and has four other California offices. O'Melveny also has two East Coast offices (in New York and D.C.), as well as six international offices (four in Asia and two in Europe)—a total of 13 offices that employ more than 1,000 lawyers. Those attorneys handle litigation—one of the firm's most renowned practice areas, which O'Melveny calls its "adversarial practice"—as well as all manner of corporate work, plus tax, labor and employment, government relations and white-collar criminal defense.

Bipartisan spirit

The O'Melveny story starts way back in 1885, when 26-year-old Henry W. O'Melveny and Jackson Graves founded a partnership in Los Angeles. The partnership agreement (which the firm has on its web site) allowed for a 60/40 split of expenses and profits, with Graves as the senior partner. However, it was under O'Melveny's stewardship that the firm grew in the early 20th century, and Henry O'Melveny passed control of the firm down to his son, John O'Melveny, after World War II. John kept the family business thriving, and the firm grew into one of the world's largest by the time he retired in 1974.

O'Melveny has grown into such a legal power it attracts legal heavyweights of all political persuasions. The firm's chairman, Arthur B. Culvahouse Jr., served as White House counsel to President Ronald Reagan. Over to the left is Warren Christopher, Secretary of State to President Bill Clinton and a senior partner in the firm's Century City office. Other notable former government lawyers include Bill Colman, former Secretary of Transportation and chair of the NAACP Legal Defense and Education Fund; Walter Dellinger, Clinton Administration Solicitor General; Alejandro Mayorkas, former U.S. Attorney; and Timothy Muris, former chairman of the Federal Trade Commission.

Award winning

Fifty-four O'Melveny lawyers appear in the 2007 *Chambers USA Guide to Leading Business Lawyers* and *Chambers UK* guide gave O'Melveny its "top ranking." Four London lawyers are among the U.K.'s best in private equity investment funds, buyouts, venture capital investment and tax. A fifth is recognized in the area of high-value corporate finance. In addition, 42 O'Melveny lawyers were singled out for praise by *The Best Lawyers in America*. The firm also ranked among the top-10 U.S. defense firms according to *Corporate Counsel* magazine. *Securities Law 360* ranked O'Melveny as the fourth most frequently hired securities litigation firm in the country and O'Melveny was described as "the 'go-to' law firm for financial services companies" by *American Lawyer Media*. *Corporate Board Member* chose the firm as the "Top Corporate Firm in Los Angeles" last year. *Corporate Control Alert* ranked the firm's M&A practice No. 5 for deals valued at $100 million or more that were announced in the first half of 2006. In 2006 alone, clients entrusted O'Melveny with approximately 150 mergers and acquisitions transactions with an aggregate transaction value of almost $100 billion.

Larger than life litigation

O'Melveny's "adversarial" practice is, indeed, a formidable adversary. Evidence: in 2006, O'Melveny prevailed on behalf of Bank of America in the California Court of appeal in Miller v. Bank of America, a class action about the legality of the bank's practice of using directly deposited Social Security benefits to pay overdrafts and overdraft fees. The class numbered between 1 million and 1.3 million members; according to *The Recorder*, the judgment could have led to "almost unfathomable" liability for Bank of America

The firm also secured a significant victory for longtime client Apple Computer in a landmark trademark suit filed by Apple Corps, the Beatles' holding company in which Apple Corps sued Apple Computer contending that Apple Computer violated a 1991 agreement by using its marks in connection with the iTunes Music Store. The firm also represented Sutter Health in a lawsuit against a national labor union, that resulted in a multimillion-dollar jury award (one of the highest ever awarded against a labor union in the United States) for the Northern California healthcare provider.

© 2007 Vault Inc.

Global transactions powerhouse

Among the firm's recent high-profile transactions: the London office represented the private equity arm of the government of Singapore as a consortium member in the $19.89 billion takeover of BAA plc, the world's leading airport company. The firm also represented Warner Bros. Entertainment in its joint venture with CBS Corporation to form a new television network, The CW, that launched in the fall of 2006. And 2007 got off to a bang with the firm's representation of CCMP Capital Advisors and Goldman Sachs Capital Partners in their $6.4 billion acquisition of Triad Hospitals, Inc.

The firm barely had time to stop and take stock of its achievements before it found itself representing the NYSE's board of directors in the merger of the NYSE and Archipelago Holdings in a deal that transformed the 213-year-old Big Board into a for-profit company, the NYSE Group, Inc. In a subsequent transaction, O'Melveny advised the NYSE Group in its merger with Euronext, the first cross-border exchange organization in Europe.

Doing it for free

Those cases and deals pay the bills, but O'Melveny is equally proud of its pro bono work. In 2006, the firm contributed more than 68,000 hours to pro bono, a whopping 35 percent increase from the year before, in addition to representing former FBI Special Agent Denise Woo (which was prominently featured in *The American Lawyer* article "The Deception of Denise Woo"), the firm also prepared an amicus brief on behalf of the National Women's Law Center and the National Partnership for Women & Families in the recent Supreme Court case challenging the use of race as a factor in public school admissions. The firm's entertainment practice came in handy in securing an arrangement with Participant Productions, producer of such films such as *Syriana* and *An Inconvenient Truth*. Participant currently has 10 films in production. Around the release of each film, Participant plans to "launch significant social action campaigns focused on the issues raised in the films." Among other activities, the firm will represent the various nonprofits around the United States that are asked to work (with Participant) in their communities to advance the causes depicted in the films.

GETTING HIRED

And other entrancing metaphors

To get a callback at OMM, you'll have to get your foot in the door first. A top-third finish at an Ivy League school is the easiest way (no revelation there, such a standing will get any firm's attention). A high GPA is a "threshold" to the interviewing process. cutoffs are on a sliding scale based on school, and they are enforced, but not myopically so. Other factors that could tip the scales in your favor for that preliminary look include "impressive professional experience" (especially for laterals), or "IP or entrepreneurial backgrounds" (in Silicon Valley). The N.Y. and L.A. offices, at least, recruit regionally as well as from the traditional powerhouses, and a New Yorker says, "While we have our share of lawyers from top-five schools, some of the most impressive are from Fordham and Brooklyn Law Schools."

You've made the grade? Excellent! So did hundreds of others. "Credentials get you an interview but personality gets you hired," sources tell us. "From here on out, OMM wants "the total package—top grades and academic profile, a compelling background, variety of interests and bright personality." And, "Outside life experience is very important."

This business associate paints a picture of an ideal (and extremely well-rounded) firm candidate: "OMM is about smart, witty, hardworking people who know how to be leaders, play the game with integrity, and have excellent conversations about 16th century European history, 1980s Supreme Court decisions and the latest episode of your favorite reality TV show. It's about that fine balance of funny, collegial and team player mentality that not everyone has, but those that do succeed." First stop, OMM. Next stop: *Jeopardy Tournament of Champions*.

Visit the Vault Law Channel, the complete online resource for law careers, featuring firm profiles, message boards, the Vault Law Job Board and more. **www.vault.com/law**

VAULT CAREER LIBRARY   **223**

OUR SURVEY SAYS

They could be resting on their laurels. At the oldest law firm in L.A., O'Melveny & Myers lawyers have the perks of working at a firm with "Ansel Adams art and a sense of history." Instead, improvement has been the name of the game at OMM these past few years. The firm has "tried hard" to enact institutional change across many different platforms, from formal training to mentoring to pro bono. Have they succeeded in their reforms? Read on to find out.

A class act

Bleeding hearts, take heart! There are firms out there trying valiantly to restore the public's faith in a maligned industry. O'Melveny maintains "a classy attitude to the practice of law." A litigation associate notes, "Ethics are really important to the firm, and that is reflected in the culture." No cutthroat competition here, only "great, quirky, smart, idiosyncratic people." In fact, "the people … make the rigors of this job as easy to handle as possible." As in any large firm, the amount of socialization varies. But "while the people here are quite professional and work hard, they are always up for a meal or a drink." And many associates gave shout-outs to their co-worker BFFs. "Sometimes it feels as though I am doing some of the biggest deals in the city with a group of friends, who just also happen to be extremely talented." How's that for bonhomie?

OMM goes to great lengths to make sure lawyers of all shapes and sizes feel welcome. "The firm has made a special effort to reach out to so-called affinity groups (gays, women, etc.) and basically subsidize social gatherings among them. That is a nice touch, and it actually works," says a labor associate. Although, some find these groups (and those that naturally form along practice lines) "bordering on cliquey." In New York, there are signs of a rivalry between the litigation and transactions divisions. They "rarely interact, and their cultures could not be more different." Mr. Culvahouse, tear down this wall!

It's not about the zeroes

When you get right down to it though, no matter how great the culture, no lawyer joins a BigLaw firm to socialize—she joins for the work. OMM associates say they are logging those long hours doing "intellectually challenging and interesting work." See also, in corollary, "great clients in exciting industries." And this counts for first-years too. An IP associate explains, "I am getting terrific training and experience; each time I clear a performance 'bar' I am given better work and more responsibility, including client contact, deposition work and drafting." Here's the report from Newport Beach: "I have more responsibility than I ever imagined, contrary to the rumors that you only do document review for the first two years." Of course, some amount of paper-pushing cannot be avoided, but "document review is actually not bad considering how interesting much of what we review is." Document review…'interesting'!? We had to read that twice too. Maybe simple pleasures are the key to a happy life. Laterals seem happy with their projects as well. "Having lateraled over from a very prestigious NY firm, I found O'Melveny's practice to be as engaging as my former employer, and although the deal value doesn't always have as many zeros, the work is still top of the market," says a very satisfied M&A associate. "It's easy to get challenging work—you just have to ask. Sometimes you don't have to ask!"

You get what you pay for

Not to be outdone by the Joneses, OMM was one of the first firms to match Simpson Thacher's new salary standards this past January, with pay scales starting at $160,000 for first-years in New York. They were also one of the first West Coast firms to raise first-year salaries in their California and D.C. offices to $160,000 in May 2007. Associates noticed and definitely appreciated their firm's quick response. "They are throwing money at us with a shovel," says an L.A. associate.

© 2007 Vault Inc.

Some stubs snubbed—some stubs loved

Even though the salaries are now equal across the board, Californian first-years report getting the short end of the stick this year as far as total compensation. While New Yorkers took home prorated bonuses as usual, L.A. "eliminated stub bonuses altogether," a move which has the Class of 2006 bewildered. "As first-years, we are probably the group most in need of cash infusion, and the least amount of cash would have made us happy. It would have been a nice gesture!" says an L.A. newbie. For next year, however, these associates can look forward to a very humane bonus system. Like many other firms, OMM bonuses are tied to billable hours, but "it is not a rigid tie-in. The firm also considers your citizenship to the firm and community. If you're a few hours short of the requirement, it doesn't necessarily mean you won't get the bonus."

O'Melveny 'n Me

The OMM firmwide P.A. system is up and running: the powers that be are good at communicating management decisions to the masses. Whether the associates had any real influence regarding that decision is less obvious. There is an active associates' and counsel committee, which meets once a month to bring concerns before the partners, and the management committees do "ask for [their] input." Some have high regard for this process, but many feel "associate committees are kept up mostly for the sake of appearances."

Associates find their partners much more receptive once they're separated from the herd. Immediate practice group supervisors earn the most respect: "OMM does not have a rigid hierarchy—juniors' ideas on the case, thoughts about the precedent, the facts, the concerns, etc., are all part of the team's strategy. The partners stay late with us when we have to work late, and we all get [the work] done faster (and better) for it. As we all work together, we learn so much," explains a litigator. A real estate associate agrees; good feedback abounds. "My partner and senior associates are great. They tell me when I screwed up and they tell me when I've done a good job. They also take the time to explain the transaction as a whole so I am never left working on some small component with no idea where or how it fits into the larger picture. As anyone who has ever worked in a large firm will attest, this is critical to your overall satisfaction." When they're good, they're good, but "Some partners are amazing, others are decidedly less than amazing." Or in other words, "Most of the partners are great. But there always has been and always will be a few jerks." No screamers, but a few "dump-and-dash" offenders, who come bearing last-minute assignments, only to disappear back from whence they came.

"A Herculean effort"

Fresh for '07, the house that Henry and Jack(son) built has unrolled all new mentoring programs. It may be too early to tell if the new formalized approach will have all the effects the firm intended, but so far associates say it's been "very exciting" and "very successful." Good start. Under the new program, "the mentor-mentee selection process is mutual (i.e., not randomly assigned)." An M&A lawyer tells us, "This is a huge advantage because this means that mentors and mentees usually have had some interaction, either socially or through work assignments, and thus have some preexisting rapport." The new mentoring scheme is a step in the right direction, not a fix-all. One New Yorker warns, "They make lots of tools available, but if you don't make use of them, you're not going to be coddled and handheld the whole time."

And then there are those who differentiate between informal training and mentoring … and say that while the former is good, the latter is lacking. "'Mentoring' would be a stretch, but there are plenty of opportunities for informal training, asking questions, and learning in that manner." Formal training has also received the firm's special attention these past couple of years, as OMM "has become very dedicated to formalized training." Their efforts have paid off. There are "lots of training opportunities, most of which are very good … most presentations are made by associates and counsel, so it keeps attorneys intellectually engaged." The most extensive training does remain geared toward first-years and other younger associates, leaving midlevels occasionally bored with the material.

Visit the Vault Law Channel, the complete online resource for law careers, featuring firm profiles, message boards, the Vault Law Job Board and more. **www.vault.com/law**

VAULT CAREER LIBRARY   225

A chicken on every table, a pro bono coordinator in every office

Ok, bean counters. I'm an OMM associate: How many pro bono hours can I count? "As many as you can bill." Really? "I billed over 300 hours to pro bono last year and no one blinked an eye," says a New Yorker. Of course, some find it difficult to find time for such an intense commitment. More realistically, the firm "strives for at least 50 hours per attorney. Attorneys billing 75 hours or more are placed on the pro bono 'honor roll' for the year, and some candidates are singled out for special awards based on their efforts." In any case, the new pro bono structure, with a network of local and firmwide coordinators, means everyone can find a project that appeals to their particular interests and talents.

© 2007 Vault Inc.

"Sometimes it feels as though I am doing some of the biggest deals in the city with a group of friends, who just also happen to be extremely talented."

—*O'Melveny & Myers associate*

Visit the Vault Law Channel, the complete online resource for law careers, featuring firm profiles, message boards, the Vault Law Job Board and more. **www.vault.com/law**

VAULT CAREER LIBRARY

227

White & Case LLP

1155 Avenue of the Americas
New York, NY 10036
Phone: (212) 819-8200
www.whitecase.com

LOCATIONS

Los Angeles, CA • Miami, FL • New York, NY • Palo Alto,
CA • Washington, DC • Almaty • Ankara • Bangkok •
Beijing • Berlin • Bratislava • Brussels • Budapest •
Dresden • Düsseldorf • Frankfurt • Hamburg • Helsinki •
Hong Kong • Istanbul • Johannesburg • London • Mexico
City • Milan • Moscow • Munich • Paris • Prague • Riyadh •
São Paolo • Shanghai • Singapore • Stockholm • Tokyo •
Warsaw

MAJOR DEPARTMENTS & PRACTICES

Antitrust • Asset Finance • Bank Advisory • Bank Finance •
Banking • Capital Markets/Securities • Construction &
Engineering • Corporate • Corporate Defense & Special
Litigation • Energy, Infrastructure & Project Finance •
Environmental • European Union • Executive Compensation
& Employee Benefits • Financial Restructuring &
Insolvency • Global Equity Based Compensation • India •
Insurance • Intellectual Property • International Arbitration •
International Trade • Labor, Employment & Immigration •
Latin America • Legislative/Law Reform • Litigation •
Mergers & Acquisitions • Privacy • Private Clients •
Privatization • Public Finance • Public International Law •
Real Estate • Securitization • Sovereign • Tax • Technology
• Telecommunications, Media & Technology • Trade &
Commodity Finance

THE STATS

No. of attorneys: 2,000+
No. of offices: 35
Summer associate offers (2006):
     U.S. offices: 111 out of 111
Managing Partner: Duane D. Wall
Hiring Partner: Arthur A. Scavone

THE BUZZ
WHAT ATTORNEYS AT OTHER FIRMS ARE SAYING ABOUT THIS FIRM

• "Fabulous securities lawyers"
• "Surviving on old reputation"
• "Extremely nice people"
• "Uninspired"

BASE SALARY (2007)

New York, NY
1st year: $160,000
2nd year: $170,000
3rd year: $185,000
4th year: $210,000
5th year: $230,000
6th year: $250,000
7th year: $265,000
Summer associate: $3,077/week

UPPERS

• "Responsibility afforded associates on major client
  matters"
• "Hours not slavish"
• International network

DOWNERS

• Unpredictable workflow
• "Technology is not cutting edge"
• Spotty mentoring

NOTABLE PERKS

• On-site gym (New York)
• Paternity leave
• Subsidized skiing trip (London)
• "Really strong health and wellness program"

© 2007 Vault Inc.

RANKING RECAP

Best in Region
#1 - Miami
#13 - New York City

Best in Practice
#1 - International Law

Partner Prestige Rankings
#24 - Overall Prestige

EMPLOYMENT CONTACT

Ms. Jane P. Stein
Assistant Director, Attorney Recruiting
Phone: (212) 819-8271
Fax: (212) 354-8113
E-mail: recruit@whitecase.com

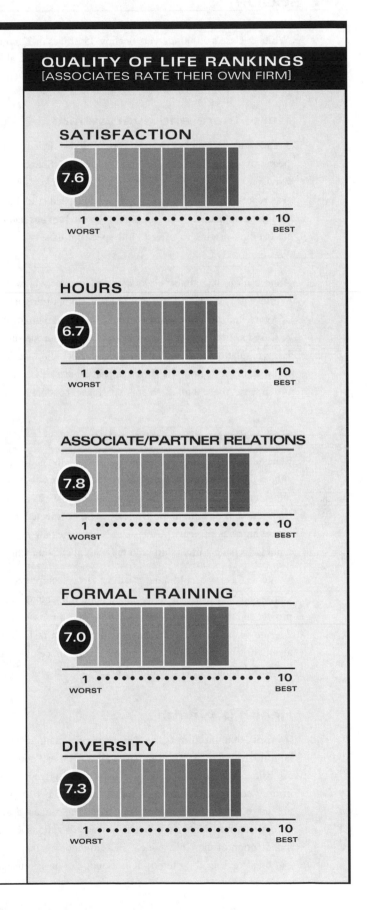

QUALITY OF LIFE RANKINGS
[ASSOCIATES RATE THEIR OWN FIRM]

SATISFACTION
7.6
1 WORST — 10 BEST

HOURS
6.7
1 WORST — 10 BEST

ASSOCIATE/PARTNER RELATIONS
7.8
1 WORST — 10 BEST

FORMAL TRAINING
7.0
1 WORST — 10 BEST

DIVERSITY
7.3
1 WORST — 10 BEST

Visit the Vault Law Channel, the complete online resource for law careers, featuring firm profiles, message boards, the Vault Law Job Board and more. www.vault.com/law

VAULT CAREER LIBRARY   229

THE SCOOP

White & Case's 2,000 lawyers occupy 35 offices in 23 countries, managing a broad spectrum of matters from antitrust litigation to Islamic finance. The firm prides itself on offering local and global capabilities in both well-established and emerging markets, and in virtually every area of law. In 2006, Chambers Global named the firm its "Client Service Firm of the Year."

Here, there and everywhere

J. DuPratt White and George B. Case founded their firm in 1901, in a two-room office in downtown New York City. The firm began by serving the surrounding banking and finance community; among its early clients was J.P. Morgan financier Henry P. Davison, who hired the firm to organize the Banker's Trust Corporation, a predecessor to Deutsche Bank. Soon White & Case was representing the nation's leading banks, and still counts more than 100 banks and financial institutions among its clients—including old pal J.P. Morgan, for which the firm has handled many overseas deals. Over the years, the firm has expanded from its banking origins to offer a full spectrum of services, and added domestic offices in Los Angeles, Miami, Palo Alto and Washington, D.C.

As a result of its extensive work writing contracts between American suppliers and the British and French governments during World War I, White & Case would open its first European office in Paris in the 1920s. A London practice was established over 35 years ago, and in recent years the firm joined with local firms to bolster its capabilities in Belgium, Germany and Italy. White & Case has been active in Central and Eastern Europe since 1990, helping governments develop the necessary post-privatization laws, regulations and capital markets, and participating in various M&A, project finance and capital markets transactions. For its work in the region, the firm is a past winner of Chambers Global Awards' "Eastern Europe Law Firm of the Year." In Asia, the firm has more than 25 years experience, conducting engagements throughout the continent from seven Asian offices.

For whom the road tolls

Stateside, the firm has been busy advising on the nation's largest highway privatization, the $3.8 billion Indiana tollway. In the July 2006 deal, White & Case counseled ITR Concession Company and Macquarie Infrastructure Group, who will lease, operate and maintain the tollway in exchange for a fixed payment. The tollway project, the largest transportation infrastructure transaction of its kind in the United States, is expected to revitalize Indiana's construction industry as well as provide income for future highway projects. Cintra and Macquarie had previously joined together for the $1.83 billion Chicago Skyway Toll Road, a public-private partnership credited with alleviating Chicago's budget deficit.

White & Case is an old hand at advising on such projects in the U.S., Europe and South America. In addition to representing Cintra and Macquarie in the wrapped bond refinancing of the Chicago Skyway, the firm advised on the Autopista del Maipo road project and the Costanera Norte toll road in Chile, as well as the €750 million MS Motorway in Hungary. In 2005, *Infrastructure Journal* named the firm "Transportation and Infrastructure Legal Advisor of the Year," while *Project Finance International* awarded it "Global Law Firm of the Year." Since 2003, the firm has closed more than 100 project finance transactions for a combined value of more than $40 billion.

Health is wealth

In April 2006, the firm helped drug company Sandoz clear itself of claims that it caused $21 million in damages to one of its largest customers. California-based HMO Kaiser Foundation had sued both Abbot Pharmaceuticals and Geneva (now Sandoz, a subsidiary of Novartis), alleging that a secret agreement between the companies resulted in Kaiser overpaying some $7 million in drug costs. Kaiser claimed that following the 1998 agreement, Geneva delayed marketing its generic version of Abbott's popular blood pressure medication, Hytrin, in exchange for Abbot paying the firm $4.5 million a month. Since the late 1990s, several pharma giants have faced antitrust allegations associated with delays in the launches of generics; the deals have earned the attention of the FTC, which filed litigation against several companies, including the makers of heart medication Cardizem and breast cancer drug tamoxifen. Sandoz's win is unusual in that it has been relatively rare for drug companies to take such

© 2007 Vault Inc.

cases to trial; Sandoz had in fact settled Hytrin-related claims with other class action plaintiffs, and had been close to a settlement with Kaiser until talks broke down.

Minting Euros in Europe

White & Case was one of the lucky law firms to win an advisory role in two of the largest acquisition financings in the European market. In March 2006, the firm counseled Commerzbank, Deutsche Bank, Dresdner Kleinwort Wasserstein, Morgan Stanley and the Royal Bank of Scotland in the £8.2 billion financing of Linde's acquisition of BOC. U.K.-based BOC is one of the world's leading industrial gases companies, employing 30,000 people and serving customers across 50 countries. Employing 41,000 and reporting 2004 sales of $12.8 billion, Linde runs a forklift truck and warehouse equipment-making division in addition to its industrial gases business. The Linde/BOC merger will create the world's largest industrial gas group.

In an acquisition that will create the world's largest steel company, in June 2006 the firm's London office represented lead arrangers Goldman Sachs, Citibank and Société Générale in the financing of Mittal Steel's €26.9 billion acquisition of rival Arcelor. Mittal has operations in 16 countries, a workforce of 164,000 and reported revenues of $31.2 billion in 2004. In 2005, Arcelor employed 96,000 employees across 60 countries, and reported turnover of $32.6 billion.

Destination Kazakhstan

Borat notwithstanding, there's no holding back progress in Kazakhstan. In November 2006, White & Case represented JSC Kazkommertsbank in a LSE offering of global depository receipts (GDRs); the offering raised $845 million and is the first significant equity offering by a bank from a former Soviet state. The deal is just one of several that the firm has had in the country. In October 2006, the firm advised JSC KazMunaiGas, a subsidiary of the Kazahk state oil and gas company, on its $2 billion IPO. The IPO is the largest in Kazakhstan's history, almost twice the size of the second-largest deal, the $1.16 million flotation of copper company Kazakhmys.

Tied up in Thailand

Thailand's bloodless coup, in which prime minister Thaksin Shinawatra was thrown out of office while attending a U.N. convention in New York in September 2006, has thrown a kink in some ongoing litigation. White & Case had been representing the Thai government in its arbitration talks with bankrupt construction company Walter Bau, which alleges that the Thai government owes it some $100 million in unpaid construction fees. Walter Bau is a shareholder in the Don Muang Tollway, which won a 25-year contract to build and manage a tolled motorway in Bangkok. Despite the displacement of the Thai government, the arbitration is still progressing, with all parties continuing with previous representation. Following U.N. International Trade Law rules, arbitration is being conducted in Geneva by an international tribunal. International arbitration lawyers are watching the case closely, as the outcome will signify Thailand's stability to investors.

Multi-faceted and multicultural

Because the firm has more than 30 years experience in the structuring and implementation of Islamic law compliant financing, in March 2006 White & Case officially launched its Islamic finance unit. The new group comprises 25 lawyers from the New York, London, Paris, Riyadh and Washington, D.C. offices, culled from its asset finance, banking, capital markets, corporate and project finance groups. Recent projects for the firm include advising on the largest Islamic project financing to date—the refinery and integrated petrochemical complex in Rabigh, Saudi Arabia. The firm counseled Saudi Aramco during the $9.9 billion joint venture with Sumitomo Chemicals; the project, one of the world's largest of its kind, was the first project financing undertaken by Saudi Aramco and the largest project financing to date in Saudi Arabia. The Rabigh deal follows the firm's work on the $2.12 billion Q-Chem2 project in Qatar and on the $2.4 billion Sohar smelter in Oman.

Visit the Vault Law Channel, the complete online resource for law careers, featuring firm profiles, message boards, the Vault Law Job Board and more. **www.vault.com/law**

VAULT CAREER LIBRARY   231

Comings and goings

In the last year, the firm has seen the departure of several high-flyers—as well as welcomed some new hands on board. In October 2006, the firm's New York office suffered the loss of four litigation partners and 12 associates to rival Linklaters. Well, you lose some, you win some: in September 2006, the Berlin office augmented its ranks with three corporate lawyers from Clifford Chance's Düsseldorf digs (the scoop comes seven months after the Berlin office lost a team of four to Mayer Brown). The London office ramped up its European funds practice by welcoming aboard another Clifford Chance partner in December 2006; the hire brings the global investment funds' headcount to 25, 11 of whom are in Europe. And in November 2006, White & Case raided Dewey Ballantine's D.C. office, nabbing two prominent energy lawyers noted for their work in electricity law. The firm describes the coup as "especially timely with the increased M&A and consolidation activity within the U.S. energy sector." Over the past year, White & Case expanded its high yield practice through the addition of a partner from Latham & Watkins, and a five-partner and four-associate team from Mayer Brown.

GETTING HIRED

"Um, I'm looking to get paid handsomely to travel the world?"

In the U.S., White & Case looks for the "top 10 percent from most schools, probably top third if coming from a prestigious school such as Harvard, Yale, Penn, Columbia or NYU," guesstimates one senior level in New York. A second-year corporate associate thinks the firm will take "B+ or better students," and believes that while "certain schools are targeted, if you do well at a lesser-known school, you will still be considered." Declares one hire, "The firm needs a lot of associates, and thus chances of an offer are good if you meet requirements." As for grades, these are "very crucial at the on-campus phase, but less so once called back." A banking associate in New York observes that since "most people that get an interview are 'booksmart' enough to be here, what matters most at that point is 1) whether the person has enough common sense to know how to apply his/her intelligence to a real life situation, and 2) whether s/he is somebody who would enjoy working at the firm and would be enjoyable to work with."

Take note: "If you want to get hired here, you're going to have to come up with something better than 'I want to work at a 'global' law firm', or 'I want to do international arbitration'. For many of us, this transparently translates into 'I'm looking to get paid handsomely to travel the world.' Also, [recruiters] look very carefully at writing samples. You do not necessarily have to be law review, but if your sample isn't carefully bluebooked, you'll fall out of consideration, no matter how well-qualified you otherwise are."

OUR SURVEY SAYS

Group dynamics

"The firm offers cutting-edge work in a very collegial atmosphere," declares one contented camper. An associate in Los Angeles seconds this assessment: "Intellectually extremely satisfying, very good atmosphere, nice team." States a New York third-year approvingly, "There is a nice degree of socializing—available if one wants, but not forced." "Many associates are friends," observes one associate, but "at the same time, one can work with people every day in the same office and never actually meet them in person, nor express any desire to do so." As for the international offices, a first-year in London was pleased to discover "lots of socializing (regular drinks, ski trip, Christmas party and general 'who wants to go out for a drink?' rounds) within the banking group and across the firm." A Hamburg associate says that "social culture among associates and local partners is good," while Stockholm checks in with "we socialize a lot and the atmosphere is really good at the office." Some respondents report that the firm's Asian offices are a bit more stand offish: "The culture is fairly conservative and not very conducive to lawyers socializing together. In particular, it is rare to see Japanese lawyers socializing with non-Japanese lawyers."

© 2007 Vault Inc.

Countdown 'til 2000

As one associate sees it, "For a big New York firm, the hours expectations really aren't that bad. It's just that if you deviate slightly downward, you lose your bonus." Clarifies a London colleague, "Although the target is 2,000 hours, no one is punished for not meeting the target." A sixth-year in Los Angeles thinks it over: "Overall I am satisfied with the firm's policies regarding hours. I wish I were more efficient and could meet my billable requirements more quickly, but I think it is the nature of the business. I need to be at work 10 to 12 hours to have eight billable." Reports one first-year, "We're expected to always be on call and to work wherever and whenever we are needed. On the flip side, if we aren't working on a busy case, we can leave the office to run errands or take time off (as long as we check our BlackBerries while out)." Adds a junior associate in Los Angeles, "Although the hours are demanding, there is not a lot of face time. If you're done with your work, you can leave." And "provided you look after your clients and put in a reasonable number of hours, this office takes a fairly flexible attitude to how you work. There is no [requirement] to simply be in the office late to show commitment," offers one source in Asia. An M&A associate in New York feels lucky that "you manage to take your vacations and don't have to work on weekends unless really necessary." On the plus side, associates applaud the firm's current efforts to improve flex-time options: "The firm did roll out a new flexible work policy last fall (2005), and it'll be interesting to see how this works out. The firm released this policy with much internal fanfare, so I think it's genuine on the partners' part. Whether it's actually feasible for an associate to work part-time at a law firm is another story." Still, shrugs a first-year in New York, "The firm has a ton of work, and this requires putting in the time."

The middle road

"W&C always matches the market; you never have to sweat it out," reassures a senior associate in New York. Notes one source, "Salary is good for first-year associates, but the bonus system is very unclear. 'Life is like a big box of chocolates, you never know what you're gonna get.'" There are two schools of thought here. You can quote a movie … or you can quote the bonus memo itself, as did one New Yorker: "The bonus awarded to an associate in the New York office for a given year is a function of a number of different factors, including the firm's financial results, an associate's overall performance and the market for bonuses among other top New York firms ... Given all of the different factors that go into determining the range of bonuses paid in a year and an individual associate's bonus in that year, we simply cannot say 'if you do X, you will receive a bonus of Y.'"

Domestic offices are generally happier with their take than their counterparts abroad (though there are some who think the firm could do better). "We get a very good salary but understand that our U.S. colleagues get much better bonuses. I think it should be uniform," reasons a London associate. Insiders also evince some resentment regarding the disparity in compensation between geographic regions, particularly in comparison to the New York office. As a midlevel in Los Angeles notes, "The salaries in our offices do not match. NYC associates are paid more above the fourth year. This means that I make less than a New York associate a year behind me, despite the fact that we may be working on the same matter and I will probably have more responsibility."

R-E-S-P-E-C-T

"This varies from partner to partner, but overall, partners and associates have a great deal of mutual respect," offers a senior level in Washington. Concurs one midlevel, "On the whole, partners in my department treat associates with great respect, although occasionally they can be insensitive and unreasonable." It is really luck of the partner draw: "Some partners are incredibly busy and difficult to approach. Others have more of an 'open door' policy and are friendlier and more receptive. It depends entirely on who you work for." A senior corporate associate has only "experienced very good relations with the partners. I've heard other experiences have varied, however." Regarding participation in firm management, "associates are encouraged to serve on committees, and my feeling is that their ideas are taken seriously," but "most major decisions that affect associates are kept under wraps until they are announced."

Back to school

"In the last three to four years, the firm has improved dramatically on formal training opportunities for associates in litigation and other departments," notes one approving source. "First-year associates are required to attend monthly training," reports a

Visit the Vault Law Channel, the complete online resource for law careers, featuring firm profiles, message boards, the Vault Law Job Board and more. www.vault.com/law

 VAULT CAREER LIBRARY 233

Los Angeles litigator, and "there are also formal training programs throughout the year for practical training, such as deposition, motion practice, trial, etc." A Washington midlevel agrees that the firm has "a fair number of training programs, including a three-day 'mini-MBA' course that was quite good." An associate in Miami believes that W&C provides "a ton of mandatory and non-mandatory training opportunities. The firm definitely offers extensive training on a variety of topics. Being in a satellite office, however, means that we are on videoconference for most of the training, which can be a little boring." Overseas, a Londoner finds that "the firm puts great effort in putting on seminars and training programs. They are generally helpful and well attended," while a source in Tokyo thinks W&C is "getting better at this, but is still in the initial stages of providing a formal regional training programme in Asia."

Let it snow, let it snow, let it snow ... 'cause that means pizza

Yawns one New Yorker, W&C's perks are "nothing that every other large firm in New York doesn't do. The firm stays with the pack here and is neither ahead nor behind." This equates to "car rides, great dinner allowance, in-house gym, free admission to area museums, subsidized health insurance, paid BlackBerries and BlackBerry service." In Washington, "the firm has offered weekly yoga classes. Also, monthly happy hours are a mainstay. Pizza for lunch is provided on snowy days." To offset that pepperoni, the office also has "a really strong health and wellness program, such as health screenings and reasonably priced, on-site massage." Miami gets free parking, while in Los Angeles it's "moving expenses," a "fancy weekend summer retreat" and "access to tickets for events, sports, concerts, etc." In Paris, there is an "open bar every month, some cocktails from time to time, a Christmas party and a weekend with significant others." London gets excited about "fresh baked cookies for meetings," "departmental ski trips instead of department Christmas party!" and the fact that "we do not have to start early."

© 2007 Vault Inc.

"W&C always matches the market [salaries]. You never have to sweat it out."

—*White & Case associate*

Visit the Vault Law Channel, the complete online resource for law careers, featuring firm profiles, message boards, the Vault Law Job Board and more. **www.vault.com/law**

VAULT CAREER LIBRARY   **235**

21

Arnold & Porter LLP

555 Twelfth Street, NW
Washington, DC 20004-1206
Phone: (202) 942-5000
www.arnoldporter.com

LOCATIONS

Washington, DC (HQ)
Denver, CO
Los Angeles, CA
McLean, VA
New York, NY
San Francisco, CA
Brussels
London

MAJOR DEPARTMENTS & PRACTICES

Antitrust • Bankruptcy • Consumer Product & Safety •
Corporate & Securities • Employee Benefits • Environmental
• European Cosmetics Regulation & Product Liability •
Financial Services • Government Contracts • Health Care •
Intellectual Property • International Trade • Life Sciences •
Litigation • National Security • Pharmaceuticals & Medical
Technology • Privacy • Product Liability • Project Finance •
Public Policy & Legislation • Real Estate • Regulatory •
Securities Litigation & Enforcement • Tax & Estates •
Telecommunications • White Collar Crime

THE STATS

No. of attorneys: 625+
No. of offices: 8
Summer associate offers: 72 out of 73 (2006)
Chairman: Thomas H. Milch
Hiring Partners: Elissa Preheim, Justin Antonipillai

BASE SALARY (2007)

All U.S. offices
1st year: $160,000
Summer associate: $3,080/week

UPPERS

• High compensation
• "People are proud to work here"
• Great pro bono practice

DOWNERS

• "Long, long hours"
• "So large it's easy to get lost in the shuffle"
• "The firm's technology is not up to par"

NOTABLE PERKS

• "Six weeks paid paternity leave" (and 12 weeks paid
  maternity leave)
• "'Garden room' open bar every night"
• "On-site child care" (in Washington)
• "Free lunch for new associates and their mentors for
  life"

THE BUZZ
WHAT ATTORNEYS AT OTHER FIRMS ARE SAYING ABOUT THIS FIRM

• "Family-friendly"
• "Very political"
• "A DC institution"
• "Holy smokes!"

© 2007 Vault Inc.

RANKING RECAP

Best in Region
#4 - Washington, DC

Best in Practice
#1 - Antitrust

Partner Prestige Rankings
#2 - Antitrust
#18 - Overall Prestige

Quality of Life
#13 - Pro Bono
#16 - Office Space

Best in Diversity
#19 - Overall Diversity

EMPLOYMENT CONTACT

Ms. Andrea Glosser
Manager of Legal Recruitment
Phone: (202) 942-5000
E-mail: Andrea.Glosser@aporter.com

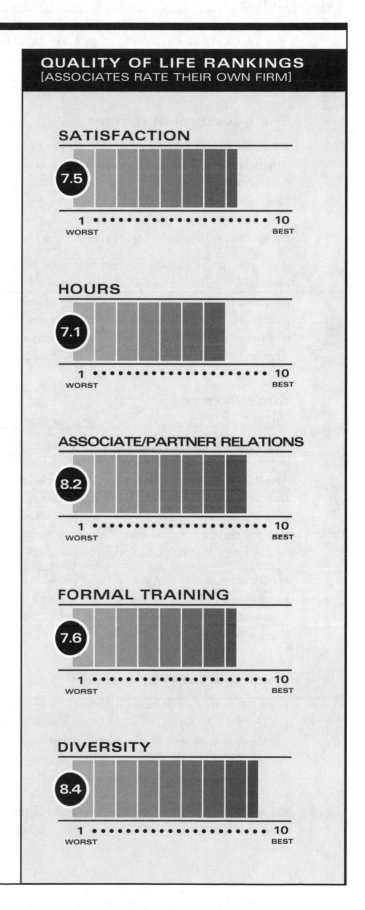

Visit the Vault Law Channel, the complete online resource for law careers, featuring firm profiles, message boards, the Vault Law Job Board and more. www.vault.com/law

VAULT CAREER LIBRARY   237

THE SCOOP

Trust them, they're antitrustworthy. Arnold & Porter is top of the pile when it comes to antitrust work, as evidenced by the firm's recent success facilitating AT&T's domination daydreams. Also commendable are the firm's litigation, transactional and regulatory practices, and its long record of pro bono activism.

The government game

D.C.-based Arnold & Porter plays the government game well—and no wonder, given its antecedents. Shortly after World War II, three New Deal veterans founded a law firm then known as Arnold, Fortas & Porter. Thurman Arnold was a former law school professor and dean, assistant attorney general and U.S. Court of Appeals judge. Abe Fortas, who would later serve as a Supreme Court justice, was a past undersecretary of the interior. "Quintessential Washington lawyer" Paul Porter was a former chairman of the FCC and administrator of the wartime Office of Price Administration. In successive years, firm attorneys have held senior positions in the Departments of State, Justice and Treasury, the Federal Reserve, FTC, FCC, CIA and SEC.

Among the firm's top achievements is its 1963 victory in Gideon v. Wainwright, the landmark Supreme Court case that established a criminal defendant's right to counsel. During the McCarthy era, the firm was a staunch defender of academics and government officials accused of disloyalty. In 1999, Arnold & Porter lawyers secured from President Clinton the first posthumous presidential pardon in American history. The recipient was Lt. Henry Ossian Flipper, the first African-American graduate of West Point and the first African-American commissioned officer in the U.S. Army. Flipper was dismissed from the Army in 1882 after a court martial that has been long regarded as racially motivated.

Super-size me

A huge victory for Arnold & Porter's antitrust department came in December 2006, when the Federal Communications Commission at last approved a $86 billion merger between Arnold & Porter client AT&T and BellSouth. The federal thumbs-up ended a partisan standoff between Democratic commission members and their Republican counterparts. Earlier in the year, the AT&T and BellSouth deal had easily won approval from the antitrust division of the Department of Justice, riling the FCC's two Democratic commissioners, who had expected some conditions to be placed on the merger. The FCC factions eventually came to agreement. The merger will create a super-sized AT&T, set to become the nation's dominant phone company, with control of over half the telephone and internet access lines in the United States. The deal follows the firm's major telecom merger work for SBC, including SBC's 2005 acquisition of AT&T Corp.

In other antitrust activity, Arnold & Porter continues its representation of Wyeth Pharmaceuticals in antitrust claims related to its menopause drug Premarin. Past successes for the division include representing Hoffmann-LaRoche and Roche Vitamins in the resolution of the largest price-fixing case in U.S. history, and achieving dismissal of a U.S. government case against General Electric for purportedly fixing the price of industrial diamonds.

Paint the town lead

In June 2006, the firm suffered a setback in its representation of several major paint manufacturers, including Atlantic Richfield, Conagra and E.I. Du Pont, all facing litigation related to lead-based paints. The California Supreme Court refused to reconsider a ruling that would force the paint manufacturers to pay for the removal and cleanup of lead-based paint in 12 Bay Area counties. Though a Superior Court judge had initially thrown the case out in summary judgment in 2003, a court of appeals reinstated the claims in March 2006. The hospitals, schools and public buildings in question were all built prior to 1978, the year the federal government banned lead paint for residential use. In March 2000, government entities sued the paint manufacturers on behalf of the public, claiming public nuisance, negligence and fraud. Scientific studies delineating the effects of lead-based paints were released in 1998, from which point a three-year statute of limitations on liability claims began.

© 2007 Vault Inc.

Smoke and mirrors

In 2006, the firm continued its five-decade-long representation of tobacco conglomerate Philip Morris. In November 2006, firm attorneys won a stay in proceedings when a federal appeals court agreed to review a lower court ruling that allowed a $200 billion lawsuit filed by light cigarette smokers to proceed as a class action. In September 2006, a federal judge had certified class-action status in McLaughlin v. Philip Morris, a suit filed in 2004. But the court took its time doing so, admitting that adjudging the thought processes and rationales of light cigarette smokers was problematic. Though plaintiffs cited a study showing that 90 percent of light cigarette smokers were drawn by the perceived health benefits, the court pointed out that consumers could have believed that assertion to various degrees, or even known that such claims were false, but been willing to "pay for the illusion" that they were true. In August 2006, a racketeering suit brought by the U.S. Justice Department resulted in a ruling that tobacco companies had in fact defrauded consumers through the false marketing of light cigarettes as less harmful. After the DOJ verdict, the court had asked both parties in McLaughlin v. Philip Morris to consider the issue of collateral estoppel.

Are you ready for some football? No, not that kind.

Arnold & Porter won an advisory role in billionaire Randy Lerner's August 2006, £62.6 million takeover of England's Aston Villa Football Club. The firm is the main advisor to the U.S.-based Lerner family. Lerner, who owns the Cleveland Browns, conducted the offer through the new company, Reform Acquisitions, which was specifically created to launch his bid. The Arnold & Porter team was led by the London corporate department, with the firm's Washington office advising on international tax issues.

He wrote, she wrote

The London office's IP team won a much-publicized victory for defendant Random House, publisher of the international bestseller *The Da Vinci Code*, in a suit accusing the publishing giant of copyright infringement. The case centered on a claim that *Da Vinci* author Dan Brown had stolen the central theme of the plaintiff's book, *The Holy Blood and the Holy Grail*. In April 2006, the High Court of London cleared Random House of copyright infringement. In dismissing the claim, the court noted that while Brown did rely on *The Holy Blood and the Holy Grail* in writing a section of *The Da Vinci Code*, plaintiffs had failed to prove what the central theme of their book was (a charge that could be leveled at many a modern novelist) and thus failed to prove that Brown had stolen it. The ruling's bearing on copyright matters is expected to stretch far beyond the publishing realm.

Forewarned is forearmed

In 2006, Arnold & Porter was instrumental in the passing of the International Marriage Broker Regulation Act, which addresses domestic abuse of mail-order brides. Among other protections, the new legislation prohibits international marriage brokers from marketing women under 18; requires agencies to provide women information relating to clients' violent histories; and ensures that prior to entry in the U.S., a consular officer will inform women about their rights and resources should they become victims of domestic violence. The 2006 legislation was spurred by the firm's work representing a mail-order bride from the Ukraine who was abused by her American husband; Arnold & Porter won the woman $400,000 in damages from marriage broker Encounters International.

Mr. Nice Guy

Once again in 2006, Arnold & Porter places high on workplace satisfaction lists. For the fifth year in a row, *Fortune* named the firm one of its "100 Best Companies to Work For." *Colorado Parent* magazine gave it the "Best Companies for Working Families" award, and for the seventh year, *Working Mother* named it one of the "100 Best Companies for Working Mothers." The Human Rights Campaign's Corporate Equality Index listed Arnold & Porter as one of only 12 law firms in the country with a 100-percent rating in providing gay, lesbian, bisexual and transgender benefits and protections for employees.

Visit the Vault Law Channel, the complete online resource for law careers, featuring firm profiles, message boards, the Vault Law Job Board and more. www.vault.com/law

VAULT CAREER LIBRARY   239

GETTING HIRED

Two out of three ain't bad

Arnold & Porter focuses on top-tier schools, but not religiously, associates report. "The firm tends to hire mainly from top-25 schools," reports a D.C. antitrust expert. "But I think the firm is also good about reaching outside the top 25 for excellent students." As a government regulations attorney puts it, "The firm wants what every other firm of its caliber wants—top schools, top grades, law review, etc. However, I think you can get away with not having one of the three, especially if you're at a top school." A D.C.-based litigator adds, "I am under the impression that the hiring standards are growing increasingly competitive, with a focus on the top graduates of top-tier firms." Not all insiders think that the firm's hiring and recruiting trends are for the better: "The firm is trying to attract more competitive students, but that means that the firm has fewer summers. I don't think that they realize that sometimes, the superstar students at a lower-ranked school can be better than the midlevel students from a great school."

The branch offices seem to have even stricter standards than the D.C. headquarters, focusing their recruiting efforts primarily on local students from top schools. A junior Manhattan associate reports, "The New York office is fairly small, and it used to be that you had to come from a top-five law school. With the recent expansion, however, that doesn't seem to be the case. Nonetheless, in my class, 75 percent of the people graduated with honors from a top-five school." A Los Angeles litigator advises, "Our office sticks to top-tier schools, and I think we exclude some very good talent at 'lesser' schools. We have also been burned by out-of-market students in the past, so there's a bit more focus on commitment to being in Los Angeles."

OUR SURVEY SAYS

Satisfaction virtually guaranteed

The majority of Arnold & Porter's associates rate their job satisfaction somewhere between average and stellar. As one products liability expert (succinctly) puts it, "I have good work, and get paid well." A junior litigator reports, "The work is challenging and stimulating. I am constantly given new projects and opportunities to develop as a lawyer." One D.C. associate says, "For a big firm, A&P is a good place. I get daily calls asking me to go elsewhere, but I can't imagine finding another big firm I would like better." A second-year Washingtonian reveals, "Overall, I'm very happy here ... I've liked the partners I've worked with, and the work I've received, especially of late, has been interesting ... I feel as though I'm learning a lot and beginning to really develop a practice." She adds, "The firm has shown a strong commitment to professional development, which makes me more aware of needing to develop as an attorney, and gives me opportunities to take my career in the direction I want." That said, there are at least a few associates with their eyes on the door that wouldn't mind calls from recruiters. "Most days are boring, relieved only by occasional periods of stress that result from poor management at the senior associate and partner level," gripes a young litigator.

Associates call Arnold & Porter "friendly," "laid-back," "inclusive" and moderately social. "There is a decent amount of socialization and a collegial, friendly and informal atmosphere," affirms a bankruptcy associate. An IP attorney says, "The firm is considerate of personal needs and desires, including workouts and time with family. The staff is kept happy so that there is a very pleasant atmosphere." A senior associate adds, "There is a very relaxed atmosphere and my colleagues are very easy to work with on the whole. There are many firm-sponsored opportunities for socializing and many lawyers and staff socialize together outside of the office. I've taken vacations with colleagues and attended numerous parties held by both partners and associates."

Looped associates

Associates give the firm's partners rave reviews, and even suggest that, as an institution, A&P generally keeps its associates in the loop. "It varies [from] partner to partner, of course, but I feel like most partners, especially those in smaller groups, genuinely

© 2007 Vault Inc.

make an effort to treat associates fairly and with respect. In one instance, a partner sent a follow-up e-mail specifically to thank me (for a very minor piece of work) and to apologize for not thanking me previously," says a junior associate. "I've never been treated disrespectfully by a partner," reports a D.C. midlevel. "Some of them have better 'bedside manners' than others, but I have yet to be yelled at or berated by anyone. I think the associates and partners generally get along well." He adds, "Management does try to keep associates involved in major decisions, or at least ask for our input. There is a committee of associates, elected by the associates, that interacts with management for that purpose." That said, another D.C. insider complains, "I don't think associates are kept that well informed, [though] the firm does reach out on decisions that affect associates and seeks our input."

Opportunities abound

The firm's formal training opportunities are good and only getting better, associates claim. "The formal training program has been improved greatly over the past several years," discloses one insider. "There is a considerable emphasis on training for new associates, and there are ongoing training opportunities for more senior associates, too." A D.C. litigator reports, "Training for litigators is improving, and the thoughtful litigation partners view associate training as an important objective." However, a junior D.C. attorney warns, "Training opportunities abound, but at times are not as useful as they could be. This tends to happen when the partners get too involved in the training rather than leaving it to the professional development [people] or senior associates."

"I'm in a small group with few associates, and so I have had great training and mentoring from the partners," says a midlevel associate about the mentoring culture at Arnold & Porter. "I've heard similar things from other associates in small groups, but I think that the experience varies pretty widely among associates in the bigger groups, such as in the litigation group. I think it tends to be more 'luck of the draw' in those situations." As another midlevel summarizes, "Informal training and mentoring is dependent on the partner you work for. Some are good about providing feedback and helping you improve, others are not." Yet another midlevel adds, "My experience with informal training has been exceptional, but I know that my experience is not shared by my peers."

Better late than never

A&P's associates have virtually no complaints about their salary. "The pay matches the market, as do the bonus amounts. But, the bonus structure is better than average because it's a structure that was developed by the associates through surveys and the committee of associates," boasts a D.C. attorney. A midlevel reports, "The firm keeps up with market rates. Sometimes it takes management a few days longer than the other firms to get around to matching pay raises, but they're always retroactive and it's only a few days, so I don't think it really matters at all." A D.C. banking specialist reports, "I thought it was good until Dechert came out with their unequal pay scale—which I approve. But given the more relaxed atmosphere at A&P, I'd rather take the pay cut and have my sanity than drive myself crazy at Dechert."

Generous and flexible

Associates report that the firm's hours requirements are typical of big law firms, though A&P's partners are reportedly reasonable, flexible and unconcerned about face time. A midlevel D.C. associate reveals, "Of course I'd rather spend fewer hours in the office, but the firm is good about being flexible. If you need to come in late or leave early some days, that's not a problem, so long as you get your work done. The new bonus system has increased the focus on hours, however, but it's what we asked for. Maternity and paternity leave is generous." Another midlevel agrees, saying, "Like most big firms, you work a lot of hours. The firm does have good policies in allowing part-time work. And the parental leave of six weeks for dads and 12 weeks for moms is great. And you feel like you can come in or leave when you want, so long as the work gets done and you bill enough hours." An insider from D.C. adds, "The firm was extremely generous with leave time when my significant other was ill—the particularly generous part is that since we don't live together, he did not meet the definition of a 'domestic partner,' but the firm was still very flexible about the time I spent away from the office and let me take the time as family leave rather than vacation."

Visit the Vault Law Channel, the complete online resource for law careers, featuring firm profiles, message boards, the Vault Law Job Board and more. **www.vault.com/law**

VAULT CAREER LIBRARY 241

I've been workin' on pro bono, all the live-long day

Associates declare A&P's pro bono policy one of its strongest suits. "This is—hands down—the best firm to come to if you are interested in pro bono work," says a junior litigator. "I'm currently working on three pro bono projects. I spend hours each day on these, and I don't know anyone in this office who doesn't do pro bono work on a regular basis." Specifically, according to a D.C. associate, "All work is counted toward billable hours. You may use pro bono hours to account for 15 percent of a bonus qualifier. So, for the 2,400-hour bonus, 360 hours can be pro bono." That said, another D.C.-based associate cautions, "The scale slides depending on the size of the bonus. Unfortunately, [those] who work a great deal of pro bono hours hurt their chances to earn a bonus, even if such work was encouraged or required."

© 2007 Vault Inc.

"I've taken vacations with colleagues, and attended numerous parties held by both partners and associates."

—*Arnold & Porter associate*

Visit the Vault Law Channel, the complete online resource for law careers, featuring firm profiles, message boards, the Vault Law Job Board and more. **www.vault.com/law**

VAULT CAREER LIBRARY

243

22

PRESTIGE
RANKING

Jones Day

51 Louisiana Avenue, NW
Washington, DC 20001-2113
Phone: (202) 879-3939
www.jonesday.com

LOCATIONS

Atlanta, GA • Chicago, IL • Cleveland, OH • Columbus,
OH • Dallas, TX • Houston, TX • Irvine, CA • Los Angeles,
CA • New York, NY • Pittsburgh, PA • San Diego, CA •
San Francisco, CA • Silicon Valley, CA • Washington, DC •
Beijing • Brussels • Frankfurt • Hong Kong • London •
Madrid • Milan • Moscow • Munich • New Delhi (associate
firm) • Paris • Shanghai • Singapore • Sydney • Taipei •
Tokyo

MAJOR DEPARTMENTS & PRACTICES

Antitrust & Competition Law • Banking & Finance •
Business Restructuring & Reorganization • Capital Markets •
Corporate Criminal Investigations • Employee Benefits &
Executive Compensation • Energy Delivery & Power •
Environmental, Health & Safety • Government Regulation •
Health Care • Intellectual Property • International Litigation
& Arbitration • Issues & Appeals • Labor & Employment •
M&A • Oil & Gas • Private Equity • Product Liability & Tort
Litigation • Real Estate • Securities and Shareholder
Litigation & SEC Enforcement • Tax • Trial Practice

THE STATS

No. of attorneys: 2,220+
No. of offices: 30
Summer associate offers: 190 out of 200 (2006)
Managing Partner: Stephen J. Brogan
Firm Hiring Partner: Gregory M. Shumaker

BASE SALARY (2007)

Atlanta, Cleveland, Columbus and Pittsburgh
1st year: $135,000
Summer associate: $2,596.15/week

Chicago
1st year: $160,000
Summer associate: $2,788.46/week

**Irvine, Los Angeles, New York, San Diego, San
Francisco, Silicon Valley and Washington, DC**
1st year: $160,000
Summer associate: $3,076.92/week

Dallas and Houston, TX
1st year: $150,000
Summer associate: $2,884.62/week

UPPERS

• "Quality of clients, cases, colleagues"
• "Partners take pride in mentoring the junior lawyers"
• Collegial atmosphere

DOWNERS

• Hours are long and unpredictable
• "Information does not trickle down to associates"
• Some juniors get stuck on document review

NOTABLE PERKS

• Weekly happy hours
• Discounted cultural tickets
• 4 weeks paid paternity leave
• Emergency day care 20 days/year

THE BUZZ
WHAT ATTORNEYS AT OTHER FIRMS ARE SAYING ABOUT THIS FIRM

• "Glamorous appellate group"
• "Too big and lacks identity"
• "M&A leader"
• "They always wear suits"

© 2007 Vault Inc.

RANKING RECAP

Best in Region

#1 - Midwest

#3 - Atlanta

#3 - Pennsylvania/Mid-Atlantic

#5 - Texas

#8 - Chicago

#12 - Washington, DC

Best in Practice

#5 - Antitrust

#6 - Intellectual Property

#7 - Labor & Employment

#9 - Bankruptcy/Creditors' Rights

Partner Prestige Rankings

#1 - Antitrust

#4 - Intellectual Property

Quality of Life

#9 - Office Space

#16 - Formal Training

EMPLOYMENT CONTACT

Ms. Jolie A. Blanchard

Firm Director of Recruiting

Phone: (202) 879-3788

E-mail: jablanchard@jonesday.com

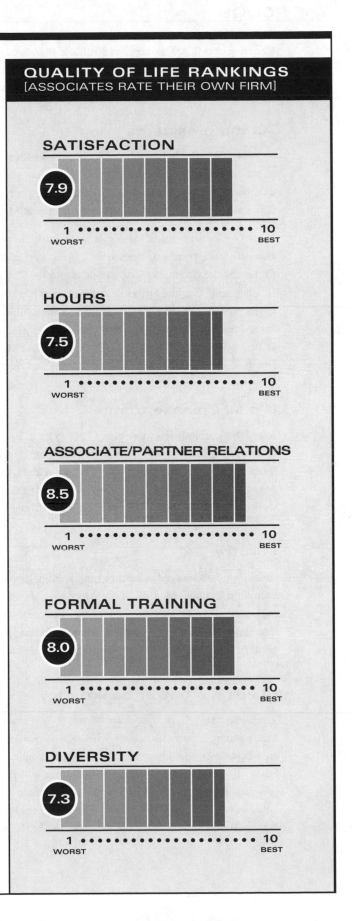

QUALITY OF LIFE RANKINGS
[ASSOCIATES RATE THEIR OWN FIRM]

SATISFACTION

7.9

1 WORST · · · · · · · · · · · · · · · · · · 10 BEST

HOURS

7.5

1 WORST · · · · · · · · · · · · · · · · · · 10 BEST

ASSOCIATE/PARTNER RELATIONS

8.5

1 WORST · · · · · · · · · · · · · · · · · · 10 BEST

FORMAL TRAINING

8.0

1 WORST · · · · · · · · · · · · · · · · · · 10 BEST

DIVERSITY

7.3

1 WORST · · · · · · · · · · · · · · · · · · 10 BEST

Visit the Vault Law Channel, the complete online resource for law careers, featuring firm profiles, message boards, the Vault Law Job Board and more. **www.vault.com/law**

VAULT CAREER LIBRARY   245

THE SCOOP

Counting over 2,200 lawyers and 30 offices from San Diego to Sydney, Jones Day is America's third-largest law firm, and among the largest law firms in the world. Jones Day boasts a globally recognized M&A practice and a burgeoning presence in Asia. The firm also fields top practices in antitrust, bankruptcy, IP and employment.

All the presidents' men

In 1893, Judge Erwin Blandin and William Lowe Rice started their Cleveland practice by representing Midwestern manufacturers and transportation companies. Appointing its first managing partner in 1913, the firm was one of the first in the nation to adopt a corporate management structure. In 1946, the partnership opened a satellite office in Washington, D.C., ushering in an era of national expansion. A 1986 merger with Surrey & Morse added offices in New York, Paris, London and Riyadh.

Jones Day's distinguished history includes a share of presidential entanglements and associations. In 1952, the firm faced down Harry Truman, protesting the seizure of U.S. steel mills during the Korean War. 1980 saw the firm simultaneously sue Jimmy Carter and defend Ronald Reagan, and during the Watergate investigation of 1974, Richard Nixon sought out Jones Day litigator H. Chapman "Chappie" Rose. (Chappie turned Nixon down, insisting that representing Tricky Dick without being able to listen to the presidential tapes would hinder him from fulfilling his duties.) As for famous alum, the firm can count Supreme Court Justice Antonin Scalia; former U.S. Solicitor General and Harvard Law School Dean Erwin Griswold; Nextel founder Morgan O'Brien; U.S. Congresswoman Jane Harman; and McKinsey & Company founder Marvin Bower. In 1969, Jones Day alum David Morse accepted the Nobel Peace Prize on behalf of his association, the International Labour Organization.

It's all Chinese to me

Jones Day currently has more than 120 lawyers in Beijing, Shanghai, Hong Kong and Taipei, and expanding the China practice remains a top priority. In March 2006, beefing up its capabilities in corporate finance, M&A and joint ventures, the firm snagged the head of Heller Ehrman's China practice; in 2005, the firm infused new blood to its Asian IP practice via several lateral hires. Jones Day also continues adding to its ranks of full-time Chinese legal consultants. At Jones Day, roughly half of lawyers working in the Chinese offices were trained in Chinese schools.

Eurotrip

Jones Day has succeeded in becoming a major European presence, with over 400 lawyers based in eight offices (Brussels, Frankfurt, London, Madrid, Milan, Moscow, Munich and Paris). The firm intends these offices to "function as an integrated organization" with matters staffed by a balance of U.S. and European lawyers. The firm regularly advises on U.S. and international law, the laws of the European Union, and also those of many European countries. Although they have yet to establish an office in the region, Jones Day has also been active for decades in a wide variety of Latin America projects.

Building a better bankruptcy

The Jones Day bankruptcy department is structuring a novel reorganization for building material manufacturer USG, incorporating a landmark settlement of asbestos personal injury liabilities with the company's Chapter 11 filings. USG will fund an asbestos personal injury trust holding approximately $900 million, if asbestos national trust fund legislation passes, or $3.95 billion if such legislation fails; the settlement will resolve some 150,000 claims, as well as any future demands. Under the proposed reorganization, creditors will be fully paid in cash and shareholders will retain all equity interests, the current market value of which is nearly $5 billion. The settlement is partly funded by a $1.8 billion rights offering to existing shareholders by Warren Buffet's Berkshire Hathaway, and will be the largest rights offering of its kind in a Chapter 11 case.

© 2007 Vault Inc.

Guilty until proven innocent?

In a case that some say echoed the Dreyfus affair and raises the issue of government accountability regarding media leaks, in June 2006 Jones Day obtained a massive settlement on behalf of a Los Alamos National Labs scientist falsely accused of espionage. Nuclear physicist Dr. Wen Ho Lee had waged a six-year battle with the U.S. government, seeking remuneration for leaks to the press during an investigation of security lapses at the Los Alamos labs in the 1990s. In his suit, Lee accused the government of violating privacy laws by disclosing his employment and travel history, finances and polygraph results to several news organizations. In the course of litigation, the news organizations and reporters had faced federal sanctions for refusing to release the names of their sources. Under terms of the $1,645,000 settlement, ABC, The Associated Press, *The Los Angeles Times*, *The New York Times* and *The Washington Post* will contribute $750,000, with the U.S. government paying the remainder.

Painted into a corner

Jones Day is one of several law firms representing some of the nation's largest paint manufacturers in litigation pertaining to lead-based paints. In June 2006, the California Supreme Court refused to review an appellate court ruling that ordered the companies to pay for the removal of lead-based paints used on public buildings in 12 Bay Area counties. The buildings were all painted before 1978, the year the government banned such paints for residential use. In 1998, a study that delineated the negative effects of such paints was released, and within the three-year statute of limitations for filing claims, government agencies filed suit against the manufacturers, alleging public nuisance, negligence and fraud. The firm's Silicon Valley office is representing Sherwin-Williams.

Cigarette manufacturer breathes easy

For the time being, Jones Day client R.J. Reynolds Tobacco Co. can breathe a bit easier: in November 2006, a federal appeals court agreed to review a lower court ruling allowing a $200 billion lawsuit filed by "light" cigarette smokers to proceed as a class action. In September 2006, a federal judge in Brooklyn granted the plaintiffs class-action status, allowing the suit to go forward on behalf of smokers of "light" cigarettes. Plaintiffs contend that for decades tobacco companies defrauded smokers into thinking light cigarettes were safer than regular cigarettes, and that "lights" brought tobacco companies hundreds of billions of dollars in extra sales. Lawyers for the defense maintain that there is no way to determine how many people relied on the word "light" when choosing cigarettes, and thus the smokers cannot be grouped together as a class action.

The "light" class-action case is one of several in the firm's ongoing representation of R.J. Reynolds. In May 2006, the firm won a defense verdict for the tobacco company in a suit brought by the widower of a smoker who died of lung cancer after smoking Reynolds' cigarettes for 26 years. The plaintiff had sought $10.5 million in damages. And in August 2006, the firm's antitrust department obtained an appellate win for RJR, successfully defending it against antitrust claims filed by cigarette chain Cigarettes Cheaper. The retail chain filed antitrust counterclaims after RJR sued Cigarettes Cheaper for trademark infringement.

Watch your mouth

In 2006, Jones Day appeared as amicus curiae before the California Supreme Court in a case concerning the limits of employer liability for sexual harassment by nonemployees—e.g., vendors, clients or patients. In the case, a woman working as a nurse in a Barstow veteran's home sued the California Department of Veteran Affairs after an 84-year-old tenant repeatedly sexually harassed her (among the plaintiff's complaints is that the tenant chased her down nursing home hallways on his motorized scooter). A verdict for the plaintiff initially awarded her $185,000 in damages, but was overturned on an appeal. When the case hit the California Supreme Court, however, justices affirmed that the original intent of California harassment legislation was to hold employers liable for harassment from both internal and external sources, and reinstated the verdict. Jones Day had filed amicus briefs for the defendant, a result of their work defending a similar case in 2000, where a teacher at Palisades High School sued the Los Angeles Unified School District for failing to stop students from publishing an underground paper that characterized her as a porn actress. The teacher won a $4.35 million jury verdict.

Visit the Vault Law Channel, the complete online resource for law careers, featuring firm profiles, message boards, the Vault Law Job Board and more. www.vault.com/law

VAULT CAREER LIBRARY   247

Tax adPfizer

Jones Day's tax department has long served Pfizer, the world's largest pharmaceutical company, advising on such deals as Pfizer's $120 billion acquisition of Warner-Lambert in 2000 and the company's $50 billion acquisition of Pharmacia in 2003. In June 2006, the firm advised Pfizer on tax aspects related to the $16.6 billion announced sale of its health care business to Johnson & Johnson. The Pfizer portfolio includes such global brands as Listerine, Benadryl, Lubriderm and Rogaine; in 2005, Pfizer Healthcare reported revenue of $3.9 billion. The complicated, multi-jurisdictional sale entailed the handover of operating assets and subsidiaries in over 50 countries, and involved the firm's New York, Washington, Frankfurt, London, Milan, Madrid, Paris and Tokyo offices.

Let the evidence reflect

In 2006, Jones Day won a new trial for an inmate who had spent 17 years on death row. In 1989, the inmate was convicted of murder and sentenced to death, but in March 2006 an Ohio court accepted the firm's argument, agreeing that evidence that could have aided the defense—i.e., the existence of another suspect with a motive to kill the victim—was wrongfully withheld during the initial trial. In other pro bono activism, Jones Day joined several blue-chip firms in writing amici curiae briefs supporting Salim Hamdam, Guantánamo detainee and alleged chauffeur to Osama Bin Laden. Among other points, the briefs question the legality of the military tribunals that sentenced Hamdan and others.

Pro bono of the north

The Alaska Legal Services Corporation awarded Jones Day a "Certificate of Merit" in recognition of the firm's hundreds of pro bono hours spent on a case involving Alaska's treatment of Native American children in the state's foster care system. Jones Day lawyers won an interlocutory appeal before the Alaska Supreme Court in State of Alaska et al. v. Native Village of Curyung, as co-counsel with Alaska Legal Services Corporation. The tribes allege that when tribal children are placed in state custody, it is very common for the state to send them far from home and from relatives, to place them in emergency shelters rather than home-like settings, and repeatedly move them from placement to placement, all of which would be tremendously harmful to the children and their communities, and violates rights granted by a number of statutes. After the defendants moved to dismiss on numerous grounds, Jones Day led the largely successful effort to oppose the motions.

GETTING HIRED

No ego, no cry

"Jones Day is very competitive, but not the most competitive that I've seen," adjudges one fair-minded associate. "The firm does not arbitrarily limit its hiring based on grades or school attended. It considers a broad variety of talents and attributes, and looks for candidates committed to practicing law on the highest levels, regardless of background," concurs a source in the D.C. office. Reports another, "Jones Day has specific guidelines for each school, so I cannot say there is a specific GPA cutoff across the board. But you should be in the top 10 to 15 percent." An upper-level in Cleveland observes that "being a 'second-tier' city, they take elite school applicants seriously, but are skeptical if you don't have a local connection." For any Jones Day office, however, it "helps significantly to have geographic connections."

An M&A dealmaker in New York notes that "if you are at the top of your class at a lower-level school, not only will you get an interview, in many cases, you will get an offer. You just need the grades to get in the door. Once inside, it is really a personality issue." A San Francisco associate seconds this: "We are even more selective about whether someone will be a 'good fit' with our office culture. We don't make offers to someone just because they go to a top-10 school. There has to be some personality and substance that comes with it." The ideal candidate? "Normal, down-to-earth, able to communicate with people. This office is made up of regular people who hang out, get along and are genuinely friends. Do not come here with an ego, an attitude or an expectation that you deserve anything. Do not be a prima donna."

© 2007 Vault Inc.

OUR SURVEY SAYS

Humble Midwestern pie

When asked what she most appreciates about her firm, a Jones Day attorney easily lists: "cutting-edge work, talented attorneys at all ranks, opportunities for challenge." Affirms one Ohioan, "The work is interesting, varied and important. I am given a significant amount of responsibility and feel a genuine stake in the work and case." A colleague adds, "Overall, I'm fairly satisfied. I've been given a lot of responsibility and opportunities (sometimes too much!) and could not imagine wanting to practice in a large law firm anywhere else." And where misgivings do exist, one insider puts it this way: "It's always tough to separate out satisfaction with my job from satisfaction with my career choice. Certainly most of [the] negative feelings I have [are] because of the latter, not the former."

One Manhattan associate classes the firm as "socially reserved; politically well balanced between left and right, professionally humble. The firm touts its Midwest values, which even in New York ring true." An associate in Columbus feels that the firm "promotes a team atmosphere designed to give the best service to the client. It is not an 'eat what you kill' firm, but treats everyone as part of the same team working toward the same goal. This atmosphere prevents some of the internal politics and dissension [of] other firms." Across offices, the "atmosphere is cordial and relaxed. People chat in the hallways, go to lunch together, organize happy hours, throw birthday parties. It's a friendly place to work." In Silicon Valley, "Most of the attorneys have families, and so do not really socialize together outside of work. That said, everyone is very friendly, sociable and works well together." A source in Atlanta classes the firm as "professional and friendly. We socialize at work to some extent, but rarely outside of work." In the Chicago office, "Lawyers work hard, and then go home. They tend to have a few good friends at work who they see socially, and participation in firmwide social events is very high." One associate describes Jones Day lawyers as "low-key and friendly. Most lawyers here would pass the 'would I mind being stuck on a three-hour plane ride with this person' test with flying colors." In Los Angeles, "The people are wonderful. While they have extremely divergent viewpoints politically and professionally, overall they are a gregarious group." And "sports is always a hot topic."

Remote control

Due to Jones Day's relative flexibility with hours and their ability to work remotely, most associates are accepting of their hours. "We are expected to bill at least 2,000 hours," reports one source, but "the firm is very flexible" and "good about allowing attorneys to work from home when needed." Well, qualifies one Houston source, "The firm as a whole is very flexible with leave, flex-time and part-time, but it is the associate's job to mitigate and remind senior associates and partners of this, which I can imagine would be a little awkward and difficult to navigate."

It's not so important where you are working, as "the most important thing is that you bill at the level that you are supposed to bill." And thankfully "remote-access software," beams one associate, "allows me to access everything I could at my desk." "face time is not an issue," affirms one member of the firm's bankruptcy group. "Most hours in the office are spent working on something of reasonable importance (even if non-billable). Working from home from time to time is not problematic. [The] firm is also very accommodating for illness (whether personal or in family) or other personal matters." An Atlanta source feels that "I have been extremely fortunate and have not worked the crazy hours that most expect from large law firms. The firm also offers part-time schedules under certain circumstances." An associate in the same office notes that "vacation and taking time off is not a problem. I feel as though I can really control my hours most of the time. But I am expected to be, and will be, at the office for long periods of time if my help is needed. I am totally fine with that because I otherwise have a lot of flexibility."

Singing the bonus blues

Across regions, associates do feel that "base pay is good." Affirms one source, "The base salary at Jones Day is very competitive, and I feel like my yearly salary is fair." In Manhattan, the firm met the New York salary increases (though, associates mutter, not as promptly as it could have). However, while rookies were celebrating, a midlevel in Atlanta reports that "midlevel associates were, for the most part, not given raises to keep up with the market. Before the last two years, I always felt I was well

Visit the Vault Law Channel, the complete online resource for law careers, featuring firm profiles, message boards, the Vault Law Job Board and more. www.vault.com/law

VAULT CAREER LIBRARY

249

paid. Now I feel like I could go to most firms here and get paid more. It is frustrating when a first-year gets a $15,000 raise and I got a much, much smaller raise." And while an associate in Ohio acknowledges that "compensation can't be beat in Cleveland for senior associates (and now for junior associates, now that recent raises have occurred)," he feels that these numbers are less impressive "in comparison to billing rates. Partners still are making a killing on senior associate hours." But according to a Los Angeles litigator, "considering that my workload is manageable, that my work schedule is flexible and that I'm rarely obligated to work later than I want or on the weekends, I think I am very well compensated."

But it's not really the salary—the real issue with compensation is bonuses. "We get paid a ridiculous amount of money, so there is really no reason to complain! But we do not receive bonuses, and even if so, certainly not based on hours." "Bonuses are not typically given, even for billing 2,300 hours," an IP associate in Atlanta concurs. One associate writes that the firm's lack of bonuses is not just a disappointment to hardworking associates, but "is an embarrassment, and shows a lack of respect for the associates who generate huge revenue for the firm." A source in Houston feels the polar opposite: "I truly appreciate the compensation system—each person's compensation is determined individually and not shared with others. This takes a lot of the pressure off. Not having a bonus structure also provides for less competition."

49 lovely people, and that one guy

"The partners generally treat associates very well. But as with all places, there is usually one person to avoid," says a source in Cleveland, presumably rolling his eyes. A New York source feels that "associates are treated very well by partners. There is an open door policy and partners are very willing to train and talk to associates. There is a good deal of respect for people's time outside of work as well." Gushes one New Yorker, "I have yet to meet a partner who was not helpful and instructive." In Houston, "The firm seems to understand that associates help the place run and, therefore, they keep us informed and allow us to play a part in important committees, etc." An antitrust attorney thinks that while it "largely depends on the partner, the majority of partners have a teamwork approach and respect each member's contribution to the team." "My only gripe is associates are not kept well informed about firm decisions," contributes one midlevel. A litigator in San Francisco reports that his office is taking steps to address this: "Our office is considering implementing a 360 review process. How partners treat associates is extremely important. We have a 'no asshole' rule."

Helping hands

"There are extensive opportunities to attend training, both internal as well as with the National Institute of Trial Advocacy," offers one insider. "The NITA instructors are incredible, and partners fly in from all over the country to assist." Additionally, "the firm pays for CLE courses" and "new associates are assigned mentors," though "the mentors are usually second- to fourth-year associates. I haven't received any feedback or mentoring from partners," ruminates a rookie in Los Angeles. Lucky me, gloats one associate: "I happen to work for a partner who is exceptional at training her associates. I do know that most of the partners here, however, are not of the same mindset. Indeed, many partners in our general litigation practice do not permit associates to do any of the good work (depositions, etc.) because they keep those opportunities for themselves." An associate in the New York office concurs that "at present, mentoring is not very prevalent," but reports that "the firm is aware this is a weak point and has been very responsive to criticism in this area. They are rolling out a new program soon."

© 2007 Vault Inc.

"The firm does not arbitrarily limit its hiring based on grades or school attended. It considers a broad variety of talents and attributes."

—*Jones Day associate*

Visit the Vault Law Channel, the complete online resource for law careers, featuring firm profiles, message boards, the Vault Law Job Board and more. www.vault.com/law

VAULT CAREER LIBRARY   251

23
PRESTIGE RANKING

Morrison & Foerster LLP

425 Market Street
San Francisco, CA 94105-2482
Phone: (415) 268-7000
www.mofo.com

LOCATIONS

San Francisco, CA (HQ)

Denver, CO • Los Angeles, CA • New York, NY • Northern Virginia • Orange County, CA • Palo Alto, CA • Sacramento, CA • San Diego, CA • Walnut Creek, CA • Washington, DC • Beijing • Brussels • Hong Kong • London • Shanghai • Singapore • Tokyo

MAJOR DEPARTMENTS & PRACTICES

Antitrust & Competition Law • Bankruptcy & Restructuring • Capital Markets • Communications & Media • Corporate (Emerging Companies & Venture Capital, Joint Ventures and Strategic Alliances, Mergers & Acquisitions, Private Equity Funds, Public Companies & Corporate Governance, REITs) • Energy • Entertainment • Environmental • Financial Services • Intellectual Property • International • Investment Management • Labor & Employment • Land Use & Natural Resources • Life Sciences • Litigation • Privacy • Project Finance & Development • Real Estate • Securities & White Collar Defense • Sourcing • Tax • Technology Transactions

THE STATS

No. of attorneys: 1,087
No. of offices: 18
Summer associate offers: 90 of 97 (2006)
Managing Partner: Keith C. Wetmore
Hiring Partner: Pamela J. Reed

BASE SALARY (2007)

All US offices and for US practice attorneys in international offices

1st year: $160,000
2nd year: $170,000
3rd year: $185,000
4th year: $210,000
5th year: $230,000
6th year: $250,000
7th year: $265,000
8th year: $280,000
Summer associate: $3,080/week

UPPERS

• Arguably the most diverse firm ever
• Super-collegial culture
• Early responsibility

DOWNERS

• Some complaints about support staff
• Could be more mentoring
• The hours

NOTABLE PERKS

• Free BlackBerry and cell phone
• Bagels and fruit on Friday morning
• Free soda fountain (LA)
• Bar exam and moving expenses

THE BUZZ
WHAT ATTORNEYS AT OTHER FIRMS ARE SAYING ABOUT THIS FIRM

• "MoFo is fun!"
• "Used to be great. Now it's a factory"
• "Diverse, pro-gay"
• "Self-consciously 'cool'"

© 2007 Vault Inc.

RANKING RECAP

Best in Region

#2 - Northern California

#7 - Southern California

Best in Practice

#2 - Technology

#4 - Intellectual Property

Quality of Life

#6 - Best Firms to Work For

#11 (tie) - Overall Satisfaction

#12 - Associate/Partner Relations

#12 - Informal Training/Mentoring

#15 - Pro Bono

#20 - Pay

Best in Diversity

#5 - Diversity with Respect to Minorities

#5 - Diversity with Respect to GLBT

#6 - Overall Diversity

#20 - Diversity with Respect to Women

EMPLOYMENT CONTACT

Mr. Anand David

Director of Recruiting

Phone: (212) 468-8039

E-mail: Adavid@mofo.com

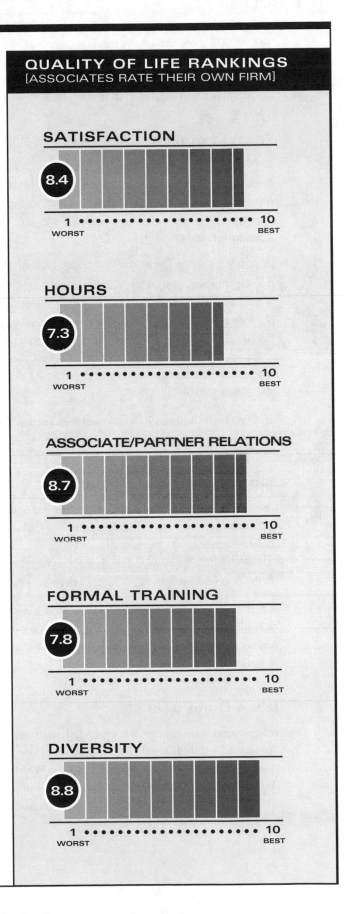

QUALITY OF LIFE RANKINGS
[ASSOCIATES RATE THEIR OWN FIRM]

SATISFACTION

8.4

1 WORST .... 10 BEST

HOURS

7.3

1 WORST .... 10 BEST

ASSOCIATE/PARTNER RELATIONS

8.7

1 WORST .... 10 BEST

FORMAL TRAINING

7.8

1 WORST .... 10 BEST

DIVERSITY

8.8

1 WORST .... 10 BEST

Visit the Vault Law Channel, the complete online resource for law careers, featuring firm profiles, message boards, the Vault Law Job Board and more. www.vault.com/law

VAULT CAREER LIBRARY   253

THE SCOOP

Yes, in 1973 those hep cats in San Fran approved "MoFo" as Morrison & Foerster's official nickname, accentuating the firm's unconventional modus operandi. Still, the firm is distinguished by much more than its rebel epithet. MoFo complements its expertise in finance, life sciences, technology, IP and litigation with a long reach across the Pacific Rim. And, as one might expect from a firm with its roots in a city with flowers in its hair, the firm's pro bono commitment is deep-rooted.

Fastest guns in the West

124 years and 14 name changes ago, Alexander Morrison and Thomas V. O'Brien founded the firm that became today's Morrison & Foerster. Due to the philanthropic work of Morrison's widow, the firm's name is woven through the fabric of Bay Area community life. May Treat Morrison's early 20th century bequests, augmented by her late husband's law firm, are responsible for libraries, lecture series, endowed chairs at U.C. Berkeley and Stanford, scholarships and a planetarium at the California Academy of Sciences.

Despite the firm's Northern California prominence, it wasn't until the early 1960s that the firm ventured south, hopping on for the ride when one of its major San Francisco clients, Crocker National Bank, decided to open an L.A. office. In the second half of the 1980s the firm grew swiftly, sprouting offices across the Bay Area, and in 1987 merged with New York firm Parker Auspitz Neesemann & Delehanty. That same year, MoFo became one of the first American law firms to practice in Japan, unveiling a Tokyo office; a 2001 joint enterprise with Japanese firm Ito & Mitomi made Morrison & Foerster the largest international firm in Tokyo. The firm was also one of the first into China. Morrison & Foerster now numbers over a thousand lawyers in 18 offices around the world, and counts on its client list such companies as Apple, Bank of America, Hershey, Lucasfilm, Oracle, Sprint Nextel and Yahoo!.

In 2006 MoFo Chairman Keith Wetmore relocated to New York. Wetmore's move underscores the firm's commitment to nabbing weightier corporate transactions, as well as the increasing importance of the New York office, now 170 attorneys strong.

Big in Japan and China

The firm has over 140 corporate, technology and litigation lawyers in Japan and China and a household names client base, including Astellas, Fujitsu, Hitachi, Kirin, Matsushita, Minolta, Nikon, SOFTBANK, Toshiba in Japan and Carlyle, Goldman Sachs, Netease, and Warburg Pincus in China. In June 2006, Morrison & Foerster/Ito & Mitomi took honors for the "IT/Telecommunications Deal of the Year" at the Asian Legal Business Awards. The group served as counsel to the underwriters on the Japanese law aspects of Jupiter Telecommunication's global IPO, listed on the Jasdaq Securities Exchange.

Activities in China include representing China Resources Power Holdings during its August 2006 HK$555 million acquisition of holding stakes in two PRC power plants. CR Power is one of the largest public power generation companies in mainland China. The firm also continues as outside international counsel for the organizing committee of the 2008 Olympic Games in Beijing.

It's a Dunn deal

In September 2006, the firm's white-knight, white-collar team galloped in to defend ex-Hewlett Packard chairman Patricia Dunn. Dunn, who resigned from HP's board in September 2006, was invited to testify before Congress following the company's ill-fated attempts to discover the source of a boardroom leak. In search of the boardroom bigmouth, HP investigators "misrepresented" themselves to phone companies in order to gain access to confidential call logs. Dunn had come under scrutiny for ordering the probe. Representing Dunn is litigator James Brosnahan, whose high-profile clients have included John Walker Lindh, the so-called "American Taliban."

© 2007 Vault Inc.

Piggybacking on the piggybank trend

Home Depot, America's favorite purveyor of detachable shower nozzles and aluminum siding, has a new gig: banking. The home renovation giant chose MoFo's Washington office to represent it as it seeks federal approval for a proposed acquisition of Salt Lake City's EnerBank. The company faces strong opposition to its application, ranging from the National Association of Realtors to the Fed's Ben Bernanke and his predecessor, Alan Greenspan. Opponents fear that the entry of home-retailer giants such as Home Depot and Wal-Mart to the banking arena could pose a special risk, even though industrial-loan companies are FDIC insured banks and thus are subject to essentially the same stringent banking laws and regulations as traditional banks. Others are worried that if an industrial-loan bank owned by such a massive company fails, Federal Deposit Insurance might not be able to cover the losses. Home Depot (and MoFo) contend that it is clear under federal law that such deposit insurance only applies to the bank itself, and not to the parent company, and that no ILC owned by such a large commercial company has ever failed. Home Depot has further argued that ILCs are still subject to the same examination standards of the FDIC as all other federally insured banks, and that it does not plan to open EnerBank branch offices or issue credit cards; EnerBank would make loans to homeowners, via builders and contactors, for home improvement projects.

Point & click = bricks & mortar?

MoFo class-action specialists represent Target in a suit brought by disability rights advocates seeking to force the retail giant to make its online store more accessible to the blind. Arguing that a virtual store is no different from one contained in a building, the plaintiffs filed suit under the American with Disabilities Act (ADA), the California Unruh Civil Rights Act, and the California Blind and Disabled Persons Act. The plaintiffs allege that Target does not use alt.text as an alternative to pictures, making it difficult for the screen-reading software to read the Target screen. To date, no court has ever held that any of these three statutes have anything to do with access to the internet. The judge in this case has already dismissed those claims. The plaintiffs are now litigating a claim that denying someone access to the internet in fact denies them access to the physical store. Plaintiff groups, which include the National Federation of the Blind, will seek class certification, which would allow them to seek damages for class members resident in California. Federal disability statutes only allow for injunctive measures.

Green is gold

Sustainability is no longer a movement—it now represents a major market opportunity. Hot on the heels of the latest scientific studies, many firms are reshuffling their IP, corporate and environmental teams in anticipation of regulations related to climate change and significant natural resource constraints (such as energy and water). At Morrison & Foerster, a new cross-discipline "Green" Cleantech group has been formed to address the needs of multiple players and industries focusing on the strategies and technologies evolving in light of the regulatory and technology revolution in the U.S. and internationally around climate change, energy and other resource conservation and clean technologies, including advising venture capital and private equity firms interested in investing in alternative technologies. The firm also anticipates more work from alternative fuel, solar, carbon and other greentech companies, as well as the Fortune 500, which are investing billions in sustainability initiatives. All of these companies will need project finance, corporate, IP/patent, regulatory, land use and environmental services. Competitor firms presently honing their green game include Davis Wright Tremaine, Holland & Hart, Hunton & Williams and Latham & Watkins.

A vindication of the rights of man

In July 2002, the firm lived up to its reputation as defender of human rights by winning a $54.6 million judgment against two former El Salvadoran ministers of defense, now living in Florida. This victory, affirmed by the Eleventh Circuit Court of Appeals in January 2006, was achieved on behalf of three torture victims, émigrés to the U.S. after El Salvador's civil war, who were persecuted during the early 1980s by that country's military. Plaintiffs have successfully recovered more than $300,000 of this judgment from defendants. Also in January 2006, the firm won the Supreme Court's unanimous affirmation that Congress does indeed have the power under the 14th Amendment to allow prisoners with disabilities to recover damages from states for violations of the Americans with Disabilities Act. The case centered on the injury allegations of a Georgia prisoner, who claimed

Visit the Vault Law Channel, the complete online resource for law careers, featuring firm profiles, message boards, the Vault Law Job Board and more. www.vault.com/law

VAULT CAREER LIBRARY   255

that his treatment at the hands of the Georgia Department of Corrections violated the constitutional prohibition against cruel and unusual punishment as well as the Act's prohibition on discrimination.

In 1986, The Morrison & Foerster Foundation was established to assist the firm's partners in making the best use of their charitable resources. Since its founding, firm partners have donated a percentage of the firm's annual net income to the Foundation which, in turn, makes charitable donations in its principal giving areas, including Children & Youth, Legal Aid, Scholarships & Fellowships, Food & Shelter, and Health and the Arts. Over the years, the Foundation has donated close to $20 million to nonprofit organizations at the local and national levels.

GETTING HIRED

Why you? Well, why them?

"To be hired, you have to have outstanding academic credentials and you have to fit in," says a senior associate who defines fitting in as having "an easygoing, get-along-well manner." "They definitely look at only the top candidates academically, but once a candidate has gotten an interview, personality and an interesting background are extremely important," reports a New York associate. The firm is "more interested in well-rounded individuals than bookworms" and "likes to hire interesting and unique candidates, but in addition to being interesting and unique, you have to have demonstrated that you're a really good student and a hard worker as well." Morrison & Foerster has no specific grade cutoff, "but C's aren't very well received."

Interviewers expect you "to know why you want to be at MoFo and that particular office, and articulate that during interviews." "Candidates should be able to answer the 'Why MoFo?' question," agrees a source—but don't worry, "the answer doesn't have to be too deep." On the other hand, "If you can't figure out the basic answer, I wouldn't bother to apply," advises that insider. Naturally, "law review or moot court" are positives, and the "firm also likes to hire former law clerks." Things get a little tougher for would-be IP lawyers. For that practice area, "attending a good law school with good grades and having a desired technical background and even some prior patent law experience" are desirable.

OUR SURVEY SAYS

You're gonna love it at MoFo

Oh, how they gush at Morrison & Foerster. "I could not be happier at MoFo," says one happy lawyer. "My abilities and knowledge are stretched and challenged every day and my efforts are properly rewarded." "As far as a big law firm goes, I can't imagine myself working elsewhere," notes a San Francisco attorney. "The quality of the work and attorneys is excellent. It is still a business, which means you work hard and long hours." A senior associate praises MoFo's "superb quality of work and attorneys" as well as the "consistent opportunities to do cutting-edge legal work" and "great access to partners and work from across the firm." Some gripes get mixed in. "I love my job—the work that I get, the people that I work with," says a source. "My only issue is the unpredictability of the hours."

"I find my work interesting and challenging, and I enjoy working with the smart and inspirational people in my firm," reports an IP lawyer. "The positive firm culture is also a key factor in my high level of job satisfaction." Associates love solving their clients' problems. "MoFo is a 'big case' firm," states one senior associate. "The matters it handles are generally of the highest importance to the clients and are often found in the headlines. It is enormously satisfying to know that when a client is really in trouble, they turn to you to solve their problem." "Most of the time, I really like the work I am doing," reports another insider. "Sometimes [we] have to staff projects that are less than entirely engaging; however, we also get to pursue our passions via our pro bono work, which is really great." Some are less impressed with the firm's pro bono system. "While this firm is known for its support of pro bono, I have not found the partners very supportive of such work. Each time I attempt to take a pro bono project I must struggle to get approval," gripes a junior associate.

© 2007 Vault Inc.

The lefty firm?

Associates call Morrison & Foerster a liberal, collegial firm. "Politically, MoFo is definitely left of center, but most chose to be here because of that leaning," says one insider. Even those who don't share that outlook feel welcome. "Although the firm has a reputation for being very liberal (I decided it would be a good idea to take the gun rack and the 'Reagan Country' bumper sticker off my car when I started here), seriously speaking, I have found the political and social culture here to be very diverse," reports a senior associate. "My firm has a friendly and welcoming culture," notes a contact. "There is a strong level of support and camaraderie, especially among associates." "I am fortunate to work with the best and brightest in many fields—most are very savvy yet practical in their practices," observes a source. The firm seems—to some—to be abandoning its West Coast roots. "Although MoFo seems to be moving more toward a 'New York' attitude, overall the people who work here are extremely progressive, liberal and interesting," states one San Francisco lawyer. Still, things are pretty good right now. "Across the board, the associates at MoFo tend to be a pretty cool bunch," gushes an awestruck associate.

Humane targets

MoFo associates have it pretty good when it comes to hours. "The hours here are very reasonable for a law firm, and there is no face time required," notes a lawyer in the firm's D.C. office. "That said, I wouldn't mind more time with the family." The firm has a reasonable billing target, but some feel a little pressure to go beyond. "While the firm's billing requirement is 1,950, there is a great deal of pressure to work far more hours," reports a source. "MoFo is no different than any other elite law firm when it comes to billable hours," says a senior associate. "Associates are expected to work hard because that is what drives the profitability of all firms. But the hours are extremely reasonable. 2,100 hours is viewed as a good target. There is no expectation of 2,400-hour years." "I would love to have more free time for the same pay—who wouldn't?" asks a lawyer. "But, along with the high pay at MoFo comes an expectation that you work hard and make yourself available when needed. Partners encourage and respect vacation time, though." "I would like to work fewer hours, but I am not willing to give it up at this point because the quality of work and the people I work with is very high, and the compensation is very good," says a litigator. "A major factor in wanting to work less is really the desire to have a less 'on-call' schedule because it is very hard to plan vacations and weekends off."

At the market

Compensation at Morrison & Foerster is the same story told at firms the world over. "The firm is not a leader, but they don't drag their feet once the market has been set, and pay the market salaries and bonuses without [an] hours requirement," says one junior associate. Hard work is recognized, as is good work. A source says there is "one bonus for hitting 1,950, another for hitting 2,100 and another for hitting 2,300. There was also a merit component thrown in." Despite all those bonuses, the firm does have its compensation issues, including the complaint that "benefits are very poor," specifically the cost of "health care coverage for families, though changes will be made for 2008." "In terms of law firms, we pay at the top of the pay scale with any major California presence," reports a contact. "And our New York office pays commensurate salaries with their elite New York peers."

MoFo U

There's plenty of learning going on at Morrison & Foerster. "The firm is very strong on offering frequent training and CLE programs," reports one source. "There is a very good formal training program that typically includes video teleconference presentations from a number of different firm offices," according to a second-year. "The litigation department has developed a very good training program over the past few years, including deposition clinics and mock trials," observes a lawyer. If there's an issue, it might be that there's too much of a good thing. "There are great training opportunities here. The greatest challenge is finding the time to attend them all," says a harried lawyer.

Visit the Vault Law Channel, the complete online resource for law careers, featuring firm profiles, message boards, the Vault Law Job Board and more. www.vault.com/law

VAULT CAREER LIBRARY

257

The firm for everyone

Diversity at Morrison & Foerster is "better than any large firm, I'm sure," boasts an insider. For example, "It is no secret that MoFo makes a point of hiring, mentoring and promoting women. This is not window dressing." "Our firm seems active in hiring women," observes another. "It provides good maternity leave benefits, with three months' paid maternity leave and three months' unpaid leave (though the firm is flexible in allowing the individual attorney to extend the period of unpaid leave). The firm actively facilitates attorneys' ability to work remotely in order to balance work and home life." Additionally, "The firm makes a significant effort to improve diversity through its recruiting practices," according to a source. How does the firm handle gay associates? Well, MoFo is "a San Francisco-based firm with an openly gay managing partner," as one insider states. "Gay and lesbian attorneys are warmly welcomed in our firm, and several senior partners in our firm are openly gay."

© 2007 Vault Inc.

"It is enormously satisfying to know that when a client is really in trouble they turn to you to solve their problem."

—*Morrison & Foerster associate*

Visit the Vault Law Channel, the complete online resource for law careers, featuring firm profiles, message boards, the Vault Law Job Board and more. www.vault.com/law

VAULT CAREER LIBRARY   259

Milbank, Tweed, Hadley & McCloy LLP

One Chase Manhattan Plaza
New York, NY 10005
www.milbank.com

LOCATIONS

New York, NY (HQ)
Los Angeles, CA
Washington, DC
Beijing
Frankfurt
Hong Kong
London
Munich
Singapore
Tokyo

MAJOR DEPARTMENTS & PRACTICES

Banking & Institutional Investments
Corporate Finance
Financial Restructuring
Intellectual Property
Litigation
M&A
Project Finance
Real Estate
Structured Finance
Tax
Transportation Finance
Trusts & Estates

THE STATS

No. of attorneys: 500+
No. of offices: 10
Summer associate offers: 74 out of 75 (2006)
Managing Partner: Mel M. Immergut
Hiring Partners: Daniel D. Bartfeld, Jay D. Grushkin and
Alexander M. Kaye

BASE SALARY (2007)

New York
1st year: $160,000
Summer associate: $3,077/week

UPPERS

• Top-notch pay
• High prestige
• "Lots of responsibility at junior levels"

DOWNERS

• "Very, very few people make partner"
• "They are cheap"
• "It's all about the money (and maybe the ego too, but mainly the money)"

NOTABLE PERKS

• Subsidized cafeteria
• Free breakfast every Friday morning
• "Associate happy hour every month or so"
• Pro bono internship

THE BUZZ
WHAT ATTORNEYS AT OTHER FIRMS ARE SAYING ABOUT THIS FIRM

• "Generally nice to work with"
• "Old school; resting on laurels"
• "Bankruptcy experts"
• "Doing better, but don't have a clue outside of NYC"

© 2007 Vault Inc.

RANKING RECAP

Best in Region
#17 - New York City

Best in Practice
#5 - Bankruptcy/Creditors' Rights

Partner Prestige Rankings
#20 - Overall Prestige

EMPLOYMENT CONTACT

Ms. Joanne Dezego
Manager of Legal Recruiting
Phone: (212) 530-5966
E-mail: jdezego@milbank.com

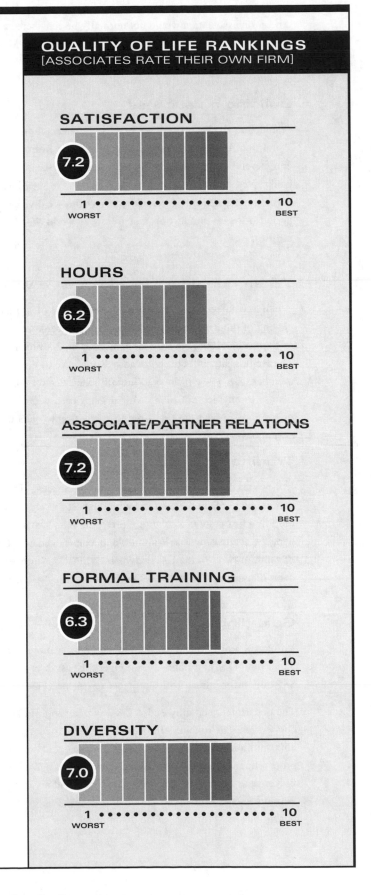

QUALITY OF LIFE RANKINGS
[ASSOCIATES RATE THEIR OWN FIRM]

SATISFACTION
7.2
1 WORST — 10 BEST

HOURS
6.2
1 WORST — 10 BEST

ASSOCIATE/PARTNER RELATIONS
7.2
1 WORST — 10 BEST

FORMAL TRAINING
6.3
1 WORST — 10 BEST

DIVERSITY
7.0
1 WORST — 10 BEST

Visit the Vault Law Channel, the complete online resource for law careers, featuring firm profiles, message boards, the Vault Law Job Board and more. www.vault.com/law

VAULT CAREER LIBRARY   261

THE SCOOP

An Enron association would not normally be considered a good thing—unless you are one of the law firms racking up hours by helping unravel the mess. Milbank, Tweed, Hadley & McCloy, which boasts one of the world's preeminent restructuring teams, figured prominently in the Enron cleanup; the firm's other special strengths include securities law, project finance and litigation.

Building on success

Founded in the heart of New York City's financial district in 1866, Milbank's strongest practices have deep roots. Post World War I, the firm would resolve disputes arising from commodities shortages and bank loans, as well as structure financing for commercial endeavors both domestic and overseas. The financial collapse of the 1920s resulted in the ascent of the firm's bankruptcy and reorganization sector; later, the securities disputes and regulatory reforms of the 1930s fed the growth of its corporate department. Milbank's project finance division dates back to the development of America's first railroads, and in the period of heavy production that followed World War II, the firm developed expertise in the growth and expansion of public utilities.

When one door closes, open a window

When key defections in 2006 (most notably that of IP head James Pooley, who crossed over to Morrison & Foerster) led to the closing of the firm's Silicon Valley office, Milbank mapped a quick escape, refocusing its energies by digging its way to China. In September 2006, the firm launched a Beijing office to complement its existing offices in Hong Kong, Tokyo and Singapore. The Beijing site will house Anthony Root, head of the firm's Asia corporate practice, as well as a Hong Kong partner and a 10-member team. The office had initially been slated to open in March, but was postponed due to delays in processing the firm's license to practice in China. Milbank has been well established in Hong Kong for 30 years and, with the creation of a Tokyo office in 1977, was the first American law firm to plant its flag in Tokyo soil.

Trading spaces

In Europe, the firm's new game is Trading Spaces. The London practice took up new digs—at 30,000 square feet, some 50 percent bigger than the old (and with the cost of London real estate, testimony to Milbank's profit column). Not to be outshone, the Frankfurt crew is also sitting pretty in more spacious quarters. Milbank first opened shop in London almost three decades ago, and set up offices in Frankfurt and Munich in early 2001 and 2004. The firm's expansion of office space highlights a period of rapid growth; in the last two years, Milbank's European presence has doubled, with the firm now counting 21 partners and over 70 associates in its three European offices.

Gold diggers

Milbank's project finance department comprises more than 100 attorneys worldwide, including 17 partners, and is fully qualified under both U.S. and English law. Over the past three years, the firm closed more than 140 project financings, raising more than $85 billion for infrastructure projects across the globe.

The department certainly ended 2006 with a bang. In December, Milbank closed a $1 billion financing for Equinox Minerals' copper mine in Zambia, estimated to be one of the largest copper projects in the world. In November 2006, the firm secured the $300 million financing for the Cerro Corona gold and copper mine in Peru, sponsored by South Africa's Gold Fields. Other project finance involvement for the year includes a $2 billion semiconductor chip plant in China; the Kwale mineral sands project in Kenya; a mining project in Mozambique; and an aluminum refinery in Brazil. For deals of this size, in 2006 Chambers and Partners named Milbank its "Global Project & Energy Law Firm of the Year," while *International Financial Law Review* hailed the firm as its "Project Finance Team of the Year" for Europe, the Middle East and Africa.

© 2007 Vault Inc.

The difference between right and En-wrong

Milbank's financial restructuring practice, which occupies eight partners and more than 30 associates and senior attorneys in the New York and Los Angeles offices, ranks among the nation's most prestigious. Most notable in recent years was the firm's omnipresence during the Enron meltdown. Throughout the mess, the firm played all the angles, first as counsel to Enron, then to the company's i-banks, and later to its unsecured creditors; a judgment addressing these creditors' claims awarded Milbank fees tallying a cool $61,354,093. The Enron association did come with its share of finger pointing: in 2004 the firm was sued for aiding and abetting fraud by the Regents of the University of California, but dismissed as a defendant by a federal judge in December 2005. In June 2006, Milbank again represented Enron during the $2.1 billion sale of its subsidiary Prisma to Ashmore Energy. Prisma holds Enron's energy assets in Latin America, Turkey, Poland and the Phillipines.

Post-Enron, the firm led the fourth-largest bankruptcy filing of 2006, that of Mexican satellite operator Satelites Mexicanos, which had $925.3 million in assets. The bankruptcy was especially noteworthy in that proceedings were aligned to fit both Mexican and U.S. bankruptcy statutes.

You gotta have connections

During Aussie bank Macquarie's audacious bid for the London Stock Exchange in early 2006, Milbank Tweed represented Goldman Sachs, Macquarie's financial advisor. Though Macquarie dropped out after LSE shareholders played hardball, the firm's work on the LSE offer was enough to earn it a mandate advising on another Macquarie venture, the June 2006 £263.6 million acquisition of bus service provider Stagecoach London. The failed LSE bid also led to Milbank's role as advisor to Dresdner, Macquarie's lender on the LSE offer, for loan financing work arising out of an unsuccessful offer for U.K. airports operator BAA.

Shake your moneymaker

In May 2006 Milbank acted as advisor on the £3.16 billion IPO of Reliance Petroleum—India's largest-ever IPO. Reliance was formed to set up a petroleum refinery and polypropylene plant in the state of Gujarat, and will be part of the world's largest oil refinery complex.

In private equity deals, in March 2006 the London office secured a lead role advising Apax Partners, The Blackstone Group and Goldman Sachs in a leveraged recapitalization of media company ITV. Under the proposed deal, the first ever of its kind in the UK, the consortium will shell out £1.3 billion in return for a 48 percent stake, with existing shareholders receiving a cash payout of $3.6 billion; ITV would remain public, with private equity and incumbent shareholders reaping future benefits of the restructuring.

Patent infringement is not fun and games

In late December 2006, Milbank won a second trial for world's largest toy maker Mattel's subsidiary Fisher Price. In the second trial, a jury awarded the company an additional $1.3 million in damages, finding rival company Safety 1st guilty of willful patent infringement in violation of a 2003 injunction. The award follows the firm's win in the initial trial, in which Fisher Price was awarded $1.9 million (later reduced to $1 million) for Safety 1st's infringement of patents related to portable infant bassinets and bouncers. With treble damage considerations, total damages and attorney fees in the second trial could run as high as $10 million.

And Salomon Smith Barney has Milbank litigators to thank for the dismissal of a class-action lawsuit related to alleged mutual fund mismanagement; in dismissing the claims with prejudice, a federal judge insisted that plaintiffs had failed to prove loss causation. Investors had accused the investment house of offering undisclosed incentives to brokers and financial advisors, and encouraging its funds to invest in companies with poor performance records solely because of their status as Smith Barney clients. The plaintiffs filed suit in the wake of mutual fund investigations first initiated in 2003 by New York Attorney General Eliot Spitzer.

Visit the Vault Law Channel, the complete online resource for law careers, featuring firm profiles, message boards, the Vault Law Job Board and more. www.vault.com/law

VAULT CAREER LIBRARY   263

The iPod or the stick

In 2006, Milbank gave iPods to 190 attorneys who had tallied 20 hours of pro bono. The iPod carrot may have been an effective strategy: the firm jumped to 33rd on the AmLaw pro bono rankings—a huge leap from the firm's previous 74th place ranking.

Among pro bono activities for the year, in April 2006 the firm won a federal court's affirmation that poor, disabled New Yorkers have the right to access their benefits (food stamps, public assistance and Medicaid) from offices near their homes. Previously, such recipients were only allowed to collect benefits from three disabled-only welfare centers, located in Manhattan, the Bronx and Brooklyn. Disabled individuals in Queens or Staten Island had to endure the expense and pain of lengthy travel in order to receive help, conditions that proved prohibitive to many.

GETTING HIRED

Top schools, plus a few "diamonds in the rough"

The firm cares about grades and schools, grades and schools, associates report. A first-year advises, "They're looking for top schools with above-average grades or almost-top schools with stellar grades—a good variety of schools are represented, but there are a lot of people from NYU and Columbia." A New Yorker adds, "Getting in is easy, provided you come from a top-20 school with a 3.5 or better GPA and law review." As for specific cutoffs, another associate says, "It really depends upon the school you went to. My office seems to fall all over candidates from NYU, Columbia and the like, regardless of GPA. However, I went to a lower-ranked school and my firm only interviewed candidates from my school who were in the top 5 percent of class." Another New Yorker reports, "Milbank is in the market for candidates from all the top tier schools, like all the other big New York firms. But the firm also likes to cherry-pick the over-achievers from less prestigious local schools. Recently, the firm has been hiring more Canadians and Australians." Underscoring this point, a finance associate notes, "It gets tougher and tougher. Milbank has always like diamonds in the rough, though, so if you've done well at a non-Ivy law school, you have a chance of getting hired."

Grades and pedigree are only the beginning: "I think the firm looks for folks that will fit in to the culture here—hardworking and modest people seem to succeed," an insider reports. A corporate attorney adds, "The firm is looking to hire people who take their work seriously, but not themselves seriously. Having the best grades is not enough; the person has to 'fit' in the culture. Which is not that hard considering everyone is pretty easygoing socially."

OUR SURVEY SAYS

New York gets a smiley face!

Milbank's New York associates seem rather satisfied with their jobs, though the news from the Left Coast is strikingly different. "Given that I am working at a large New York City firm, I couldn't ask for a better situation to be in," says a typical New Yorker. "The quality of work and guidance that I have received in the time I've been here is phenomenal." Another New York associate reports, "Milbank is a fantastic firm. I work with extremely bright, motivated professionals, and the environment is friendly and supportive." Yet another Big Apple attorney adds, "There are aspects of practicing at a large New York law firm that I do not like, which are not specific to the firm, but in general I think Milbank is a pleasant place to practice law, and in recent years the firm has made a noticeable effort to improve associate life in a number of areas."

The L.A. attorneys paint a very different picture. A Los Angeleno says that he is "completely unsatisfied," and that the "office is falling apart and the managing partner and everyone else seem oblivious." A senior L.A. attorney adds, "Partners do not encourage marketing or other career development. It feels like a temporary employment agency where no one takes an interest in your career, because they know it's unlikely you'll be here for very long." A SoCal colleague piles on, "Associates are treated as dispensable commodities—where the only reward for a job well done is more work and without any correlation to an improvement in the quality of assignments received."

© 2007 Vault Inc.

Kudos for culture

Milbank associates, especially in New York, are generally upbeat about the firm's culture. As one voluble, though not unrepresentative, junior associate puts it, "This is not a high-pressure environment, even when something high pressure is happening. People are relaxed but with high expectations— they're not going to yell at you, but they expect you to turn out high-quality work. This firm attracts people who are intelligent but somewhat laid-back, not at all high-maintenance or intense. In terms of socializing, people in my group are incredibly collegial and always willing to give advice or answer silly questions, with a very obvious and welcoming open door policy, even with partners." A New Yorker adds, "Associates are generally cool, smart and personable and tend to bond through shared misery." A corporate finance expert puts in his two cents: "The department I work in is very collegial. We all work as a team and are very supportive of one another. We socialize at the office and outside of the office."

An Angeleno offers this taxonomy of the L.A. office: "Milbank's L.A. office has three major groups: litigation, corporate and project finance. Each of these groups tends to have a separate culture. The corporate group is very collegial and very friendly. With few exceptions, associates and partners in the group tend to have open doors and make themselves available to others for advice, information, etc. Associates regularly eat lunch together (occasionally with partners), but (with some exceptions) tend not to spend a lot of time together after work hours."

Depends on the partner

While the culture and satisfaction levels vary largely office by office, the associate/partner relationships seem to vary largely from partner to partner. As one New Yorker puts it, "Some make a genuine effort to mentor young associates; some fail to even learn our names." Or, as an L.A. litigator reports, "We have some partners whom I absolutely adore and could not imagine a better working situation with. There are some that are okay and occasionally treat associates poorly. And then there are a few that I cringe at the prospect of working for." Another New Yorker optimistically adds, "Some are obviously better than others on an individual level. Across the firm, I think the respect for associates is not bad, but associates are not particularly well informed about firmwide decisions, nor is there any means to participate in issues that affect the firm."

Mixed reviews: training

The firm's formal training receives mixed reviews. A New York midlevel advises, "At the junior level, the training is decent, though not great. At the senior level, it is nonexistent (useless seminars on 'how great it is to be a Milbank partner, wouldn't you like to be one too?' count)." A skeptic says, "The firm aims to have some formal training and does have some off-site programs, but most of it is only marginally helpful." And an optimist adds, "The firm appears to be making efforts to increase the training opportunities."

As for informal training and mentoring, one insider tells us, "Senior associates are great mentors. Partners not so much." A New Yorker agrees: "Informal training by partners simply does not exist here. It does with some senior associates." That said, some associates offer more upbeat insights, with an important qualification: "Partners in my group are great at training and mentoring—once they take an interest in you (and after you have demonstrated good work and willingness to work hard)," a corporate finance specialist says. An L.A. first-year reports, "Both opportunities are available, but associates must be self-motivated to seek them out." Still, this L.A. colleague is less sanguine and calls mentoring "almost non-existent."

Bonuses: both automatic and standard

The firm's compensation plan is the one issue that garners essentially no complaints. A corporate associate reports, "Milbank was the third firm to match the latest salary increase. Bonuses are automatic and not based on target hours, which is sweet." A senior associate adds, "The firm's compensation is in line with the other big New York City firms. As with many other firms, it is not structured to reward hard work, skill and initiative. Bonuses are awarded to everyone, regardless of hours or value to the firm." Or, as a well paid attorney in L.A. puts it, "The money and the bonus structure are great."

Visit the Vault Law Channel, the complete online resource for law careers, featuring firm profiles, message boards, the Vault Law Job Board and more. **www.vault.com/law**

VAULT CAREER LIBRARY   265

Long, but no so bad, hours

Associates say that Milbank's hours are long, but not as bad as you might fear. As one associate describes it, "Let's be realistic: this is a law firm, and you are receiving a six-figure salary—I expect to have long days pretty frequently. Weekend work depends on how efficient you are during the week and whether something comes up, but I don't think it's the norm until you get to be a more senior associate. My firm is very sensitive to vacations and tries its best to let you enjoy them." There are those who put a less rosy spin on the issue, however. "It's a big firm in New York—the hours are going to be brutal, especially at the more senior levels," says a seventh-year. "What grates, however, is that aside from a little lip service, these hours are thankless."

© 2007 Vault Inc.

"Milbank was the third firm to match the latest salary increase. Bonuses are automatic and not based on target hours, which is sweet."

—*Milbank, Tweed, Hadley & McCloy associate*

Visit the Vault Law Channel, the complete online resource for law careers, featuring firm profiles, message boards, the Vault Law Job Board and more. **www.vault.com/law**

VAULT CAREER LIBRARY   **267**

Clifford Chance LLP

31 West 52nd Street
New York, NY 10019
Phone: (212) 878-8000
www.cliffordchance.com

LOCATIONS

New York, NY • Washington, DC • Amsterdam • Bangkok • Barcelona • Beijing • Brussels • Bucharest* • Budapest • Dubai • Düsseldorf • Frankfurt • Hong Kong • London • Luxembourg • Madrid • Milan • Moscow • Munich • Paris • Prague • Rome • São Paulo • Shanghai • Singapore • Tokyo • Warsaw

*Associated office

MAJOR DEPARTMENTS & PRACTICES

Antitrust/Competition • Asset Management • Banking & Finance • Capital Markets • Commercial • Construction • Employment, Employee Benefits & Pension • Environment • Financial Institutions & Markets • Insurance • Intellectual Property • Litigation • M&A/Corporate • Private Equity • Private Funds • Projects • Public Policy • Real Estate • Restructuring/Insolvency • Tax

THE STATS

No. of attorneys: 3,300
No. of offices: 27
Summer associate offers: 36 out of 36 (2006)
Global Managing Partner: David Childs
Regional Managing Partner: Craig S. Medwick
Hiring Partner: Karl A. Roessner

BASE SALARY (2007)

New York, NY
1st year: $160,000
2nd year: $170,000
3rd year: $185,000
4th year: $210,000
5th year: $230,000
6th year: $250,000
7th year: $265,000
8th year: $280,000
Summer associate: $3,077/week

UPPERS

• People-friendly culture
• Great pay and great perks
• Tons of training

DOWNERS

• Occasional quirky partners
• The typical BigLaw hours pressure
• Dearth of junior associates in some offices

NOTABLE PERKS

• Free dinner (up to $400) if you work more than 250 hours in a month
• Bar and moving expenses
• Free admission to MoMA
• Use of firm-owned Florida condos for vacations

THE BUZZ
WHAT ATTORNEYS AT OTHER FIRMS ARE SAYING ABOUT THIS FIRM

• "Magic Circle! Squash courts!"
• "Biggest isn't always best"
• "Best UK firm"
• "Reputation varies widely by office worldwide"

© 2007 Vault Inc.

RANKING RECAP

Best in Practice

#6 (tie) - International Law
#8 (tie) - Mergers & Acquisitions
#10 - Securities
#10 - Corporate

Quality of Life

#4 - Formal Training
#9 - Pay
#13 - Best Firms to Work For
#19 - Overall Satisfaction

EMPLOYMENT CONTACT

Ms. Madeleine Conlon
Manager of Legal Recruiting
Phone: (212) 878-8252
Fax: (212) 878-3375
E-mail: madeleine.conlon@cliffordchance.com

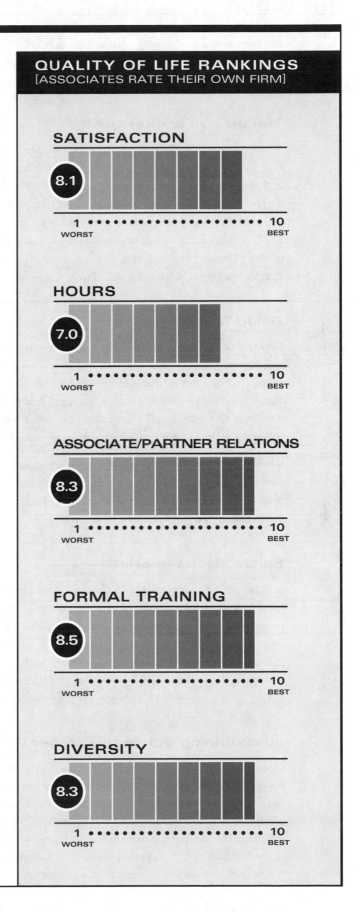

QUALITY OF LIFE RANKINGS
[ASSOCIATES RATE THEIR OWN FIRM]

SATISFACTION
8.1
1 WORST   10 BEST

HOURS
7.0
1 WORST   10 BEST

ASSOCIATE/PARTNER RELATIONS
8.3
1 WORST   10 BEST

FORMAL TRAINING
8.5
1 WORST   10 BEST

DIVERSITY
8.3
1 WORST   10 BEST

Visit the Vault Law Channel, the complete online resource for law careers, featuring firm profiles, message boards, the Vault Law Job Board and more. **www.vault.com/law**

VAULT CAREER LIBRARY   269

THE SCOOP

Clifford Chance has been regarded as a bit more colorful than its Magic Circle peers, thanks to past commotion both inside and outside the office. In 2007, the firm gathered its strengths and left the drama behind, focusing on its growing Asian ventures and its sturdy corporate and dispute resolution practices.

The empire strikes back

A 1987 merger between U.K. firms Coward Chance and Clifford Turner led to today's Clifford Chance. In 2000, a ménage-à-trois with U.S.-based firm Rogers & Wells and Germany's Punder Volhard Weber & Axster resulted in the creation of what may be the world's largest law firm (though Baker & McKenzie would probably beg to differ). In a series of partnerships and buyouts, the new firm blazed its way around the globe, creating an empire of 3,300 attorneys and 29 offices in 20 countries. In December 2005, the firm voted to reform its compensation plan, agreeing to raise the top level of its U.S. compensation to $2.5 million. The U.S. partnership will determine which partners will be paid at the top level. In 2006, the firm posted revenue of $2.039 billion. The firm's reputation is growing and the firm is hard at work nabbing new talent; in September 2006 the firm scored King & Spalding's M&A head, and other recent hires hail from Paul Hastings, Chadbourne & Parke and Winston & Strawn.

Asian fusion

For the time being, the firm has refocused its expansionist hopes on Asia. In September 2006 Clifford Chance announced a plan to link arms with a Chinese law firm—as soon as the Chinese government allows it, that is. In anticipation, the firm poached a China corporate partner from Morrison & Foerster, who moved to Clifford's Beijing office. In January 2007, the firm hired four associates to staff its Shanghai office, hoping to double its Chinese presence in the next five years to more than 100 lawyers, and will target native Chinese lawyers educated or with work experience abroad. Clifford Chance is just one of several foreign firms chomping at the bit, waiting for their chance to expand in the highly protected Chinese market.

In other Asian endeavors, anticipating the deregulation of India's legal market, in 2006 the firm hired its first Indian team. In November 2006, Clifford Chance partners traveled to New Delhi to recruit qualified lawyers, interviewing some 25 candidates from Indian law schools and extending offers to half. Once permitted to practice in India, eligible lawyers will be able to take the Qualified Lawyers Transfer Test in the U.K.

Salsa-lacious gossip

In 2006, the firm represented two champion dance instructors in a suit filed by one of Hong Kong's richest women. In 2004, Mimi Monica Wong, shipping heiress and head of HSBC's Asian private banking business (she advises clients on how to invest their money wisely), entered into a contract with two Latin dance instructors, agreeing to pay the equivalent of $15.4 million for eight years of lessons. But the tango came to a grinding halt during Wong's performance at a Hong Kong restaurant, when one instructor offered constructive criticism that included the phrase "lazy cow." Lessons ceased and the three ended up in court, with Wong demanding her money back and the instructors countersuing for the remainder of the payment. In September 2006, a Hong Kong judge sided with Wong, ordering that her money be returned.

Just running out to the corner Delhi

Due to confidentiality concerns, law firms have traditionally resisted outsourcing billing and client documents; subcontracting is generally relegated to travel arrangements or record storage. While all client work remains at home, that doesn't mean firms can't boost their bottom lines by relocating auxiliary services. Clifford Chance announced in October 2006 that some of its administrative work will now take place in India. The changeover is the latest in a string of cost-cutting measures instituted by Chairman David Childs; it will also be the biggest off-shoring ever undertaken in the legal profession, and is expected to yield more than $18 million in annual savings. A service center in Delhi is due to open in spring 2007, employing 300 workers handling IT, accounts and other business support matters.

© 2007 Vault Inc.

The name is bonds, Islamic bonds

Clifford Chance's Islamic finance unit has been steadily growing, completing approximately $15 billion in Islamic finance transactions in 2006. In December the Dubai and London offices advised Dubai World and Nakheel on a $3.52 billion sukuk-al-ijara issue, the largest sukuk (Islamic bond) issue in the world to date. Nakheel, a subsidiary of Dubai World, is responsible for real estate developments throughout Dubai, such as manmade islands The Palm and The World. The sukuk certificates will be listed on the Dubai International Financial Exchange, and proceeds will go to financing Nakheel's future projects. In October, the firm scored a lead role in the London Stock Exchange flotation of a $225 million sukuk. The five-year bond was issued by the Sharjah Islamic Bank, and was only the second bond to have been floated on the LSE. In 2006, Clifford Chance also advised on Saudi Aramco's $9.9 billion Rabigh petrochemical complex.

Magic Circle, magic touch

The M&A upsurge of the last years has been a global phenomenon. Three of the top-five deals occurred not in the developed U.S. market but within Europe, and for the first time since 2000, U.K. Magic Circle firms led the world rankings. Clifford Chance, second to only Freshfields in deals, handled the largest transaction of the period, representing Spanish power provider Endesa during its $56.6 billion hostile bid by German utility company E.ON. With $350.1 billion in deal value, Clifford Chance jumped nine slots from its previous year's ranking. Other M&A involvement for the firm includes the $34.5 billion merger between Caisses d'Epargne and Banques Populaires that created new entity Natixis; the merger of Spain-based Abertis Infraestructuras with Autostrade; representation of Siemens during the £8.5 billion merger of their communications service provider business with Nokia; and American Power Conversion's $6.1 billion merger with Schneider Electric. Additionally, Clifford Chance is representing SL Green Realty Corporation in connection with its $4 billion acquisition of Reckson Associates Realty Corporation. Clifford Chance has been ranked number one legal adviser in the Global and European M&A league tables for the first quarter of 2007, according to the latest published results from Bloomberg.

GETTING HIRED

Hard, but not impossible

Clifford Chance associates say the firm is looking for "interesting, dynamic candidates" with "high GPAs." It clearly helps to come from a top school, but that's not a deal-breaker. "The firm takes a very hard look before hiring people who didn't attend the top schools, but if you can show them that you've got drive and something to contribute, you can get an offer even if you aren't from a top-tier school," says an associate who himself didn't attend a "top-tier school." "As a tier-two grad with a very high GPA, it was hard but not impossible to get a job at Clifford Chance," reports an associate whose school does not have an exalted place on the *US News* rankings. "The hardest part was getting the on-campus interview. Then, once I got to meet attorneys and really click with them, it was easy. Personality was definitely taken into account."

"School doesn't matter as much as grades/past experience do, although there is a current focus on top schools in the area," observes a D.C. associate who finds that Penn, Georgetown and UVA are among the best-represented schools at that location. "There is a sense that there will be much more of a focus on lateral recruitment in the D.C. office and less emphasis on the summer program." The lateral hiring process isn't grueling. "I was hired as a lateral and interviewed twice before being offered a job," notes a contact.

Visit the Vault Law Channel, the complete online resource for law careers, featuring firm profiles, message boards, the Vault Law Job Board and more. www.vault.com/law

VAULT CAREER LIBRARY   271

OUR SURVEY SAYS

We heart CC

For some associates, work at Clifford Chance is a love-in. "Not only do I find the work to be challenging and interesting, but I truly enjoy the people I work with, both at the firm and our clients," says an insider. "I am in love with Clifford Chance," gushes another attorney. Even those with a more tempered emotional attachment to the firm are generally pleased with their experience, with some reservations. "I am fairly satisfied with the deals I am currently getting and the people with whom I work, but the proper systems are not in place to ensure that mentoring and quality/quantity of work are distributed well across all levels," gripes a source. "The result is that junior associates are not consistently well trained, that seniors are forced to work longer than necessary." Others say that "work/life balance needs to be addressed more aggressively" and that "hours and billing time are big negatives."

"I like working here very much," says a senior associate. "Whatever I don't like has much more to do with the job itself than working at Clifford Chance." If you like good work, you'll probably like it at Clifford Chance. "The work is very high-level, and the firm tends to be engaged in very innovative deals," says a happy insider. "I get a broad range of excellent M&A work, including public and private matters, domestic and international matters, and hostile and negotiated matters," says a well-rounded corporate attorney.

There are things other than law?

"The firm has a great culture," states a source. "Culturally diverse (at least in the associate ranks) and I've had several opportunities to socialize both with partners and associates. I'm quite pleased." "The culture can be best described as one of people with a general commonality of interests," says a midlevel associate. "Civility in the treatment of others is remarkably high. People socialize regularly together." Better have a funny bone. "You can joke around with people, yet respect goes without saying," says a first-year. "For me, this is important to maintain a healthy balance between professional and personable—sometimes polar opposites elsewhere." "There is a lot of joking and laughter around, particularly when people are busy," says an M&A lawyer. If you have other interests besides the law (as if such a thing is possible!), you'll find kindred spirits at Clifford Chance. "Luckily the attorneys here are able to talk about things other than the law," notes a contact. "I regularly socialize with my firm friends outside of the office—i.e., during the evenings and weekends. The fun people here are what make the long hours tolerable."

It's partnership, not deification

Clifford Chance associates' opinions of the firm's partnership run the gamut. "There are one or two partners who forget that it can be very difficult to be an associate and who sometimes have less patience than they need, but generally partners are very respectful and go out of their way to acknowledge the work you've done and the time you've put into an assignment," says one source. The partners understand the limits of young attorneys. "As a first-year, I've felt that the partners have been nothing but welcoming," notes a lawyer. "They understand the (low) skill level of a first-year, are forgiving and spend time to make sure you understand everything—the business background of a case, the basics of the law, etc." Unfortunately, other partners have a bit of a God complex. "There are some individual partners that think they have been chosen to replace God and are too important to be human," exclaims a non-worshipping lawyer. On the whole, however, most insiders agree that the environment is one of mutual respect: "Associates are treated with lots of respect. The partners usually give us a heads-up before major decisions are taken," reports one corporate associate. There is also an internal communications program with monthly e-mails from the managing partner as well as quarterly associate and business services' meetings with management. Some insiders even profess to understand the underlying reasons for the partners' demands: "I have never worked or heard of anyone who worked with a partner who didn't treat the associates with respect. At times, partners can be demanding, but usually it's because the client is being demanding."

Welcome to a new tax bracket

Clifford Chance "always matches Sullivan, Cravath and Simpson types"—and those firms are in a pay-raising mood. "The firm was quick to match the recent salary increase," reports a midlevel. "Associates get paid the same as the 'white-shoe' firms but work somewhat [fewer] hours, meaning we're probably paid more on an hourly basis." Even in D.C., the "salary is highest in town and tied to New York," and "bonuses are not tied to hours worked and it is not difficult to get the full bonus." "I still can't believe they pay me this much to do something that gives me so much pleasure," says a lawyer who loves M&A work. "My only complaint is that the firm does not match 401(k) contributions," gripes a first-year. That sting is mitigated somewhat by the firm's "small incentives," including "free dinner with a $400 limit" for associates who "work more than 250 hours in a month."

Bang for their buck

Big firm cash means big firm hours. "It is life in a big law firm in New York City; hours are expectedly long," notes a source. "The hours are manageable most of the time," says an M&A attorney. "Other times, they are not, but it very rarely is because of someone here being unreasonable. They try to be humane about hours and making sure you are not overburdened." "The firm is very understanding about working long hours," agrees another insider. "If there isn't a lot of working going on they don't expect you to put in face time. But if there is work to be done, they expect associates to help out, which is completely understandable."

It's best to try and go above and beyond. "Clifford Chance has the stated, reasonable expectation of approximately 2,000 billable hours per year," reports a source. "Generally, associates should strive more toward 2,200 to avoid scrutiny." That can lead to some late nights (and early mornings) in the office. "In my group, working long hours late into the night is the norm," says an associate in one of the firm's international offices. "More junior associates are required to handle the more menial aspects of transactions and better upper management is necessary to allocate work flow and manage client expectations."

You've got a lot to learn

No one gets thrown in the deep end—or any end—at Clifford Chance. "The firm places a strong emphasis on training and helping you develop the skills necessary to advance your career up the law firm ladder," reports one insider. The training is "more extensive than I have heard about anywhere else," asserts one senior associate, and lawyers who have experience elsewhere agree. "I lateralled in, and the midlevel training in terms of teaching you to deal with clients and business issues is unlike anything I have ever heard of," gushes an awestruck attorney. The firm's curriculum includes "both legal training (motions practice, deposition training by NITA) and business skills development (presentations, etc.)."

The melting pot

"This must be the most diverse firm on the planet," says one enthusiastic Clifford Chance lawyer. While that might be an overstatement, associates say that the firm tries to follow through on its commitment to diversity. "There are a large number of women working here, with a significant percentage of female partners," observes a contact. "The firm is very supportive of women in the workplace and is making great efforts to create an atmosphere that encourages them to stay," notes another source. The efforts don't always work, of course. "It seems more difficult to retain women for partnership," according to a senior associate. "Because the firm is so international, minorities of all kinds are not only welcome, but they are sought after," brags an attorney. However, another contact finds that there are "certainly not enough minorities employed as attorneys—especially for an international firm."

Visit the Vault Law Channel, the complete online resource for law careers, featuring firm profiles, message boards, the Vault Law Job Board and more. **www.vault.com/law**

VAULT CAREER LIBRARY   273

Cadwalader, Wickersham & Taft LLP

One World Financial Center
New York, NY 10281
Phone: (212) 504-6000
www.cadwalader.com

LOCATIONS

New York, NY (HQ)
Charlotte, NC
Washington, DC
Beijing
London

MAJOR DEPARTMENTS & PRACTICES

Antitrust
Business Fraud
Capital Markets
Corporate/Mergers & Acquisitions
Financial Restructuring
Funds, Regulation, Enforcement & Equity Derivatives
Global Finance
Health Care/Not-for-Profit
Insurance & Reinsurance
Litigation
Private Client
Real Estate
Tax

THE STATS

No. of attorneys: 635
No. of offices: 5
Summer associate offers: 87 out of 87 (2006)
Chairman & Managing Partner: Robert O. Link Jr.
Hiring Partners:
New York, NY: Paul W. Mourning
Charlotte, NC: Henry A. LaBrun
Washington, DC: Michael E. Horowitz

BASE SALARY (2007)

1st year: $160,000
2nd year: $170,000
3rd year: $185,000
4th year: $210,000
5th year: $230,000
6th year: $250,000
7th year: $265,000
Summer associate: $3,075/week

UPPERS

- Challenging work, even for juniors
- Compensation leader
- Relatively easy to work from home

DOWNERS

- Serious, occasionally "brutal," hours
- Some "grumpy" partners
- "Top-down communication issues"

NOTABLE PERKS

- Monthly lunch with associate mentor
- Month-long sabbatical after five years
- "Great" in-house gym
- Generous referral bonus

THE BUZZ
WHAT ATTORNEYS AT OTHER FIRMS ARE SAYING ABOUT THIS FIRM

- "Prestigious, intense"
- "Indentured servitude"
- "Securitization king"
- "Glengarry Glen Ross"

© 2007 Vault Inc.

RANKING RECAP

Best in Region
#19 - New York

Best in Practice
#5 - Real Estate
#7 - Bankruptcy/Creditors' Rights

Partner Prestige Rankings
#4 - Bankruptcy/Creditors' Rights
#25 - Overall Prestige

Quality of Life
#6 - Pay

EMPLOYMENT CONTACTS

New York, NY
Ms. Monica R. Brenner
Manager of Legal Recruitment
Phone: (212) 504-6044
E-mail: monica.brenner@cwt.com

Charlotte, NC
Ms. Emily M. Thomas
Manager of Associate Development & Recruitment
Phone: (704) 348-5238
E-mail: emily.thomas@cwt.com

Washington, DC
Ms. Dyana Pinkerton Barninger
Manager of Associate Development & Recruitment
Phone: (202) 862-2240
E-mail: dyana.barninger@cwt.com

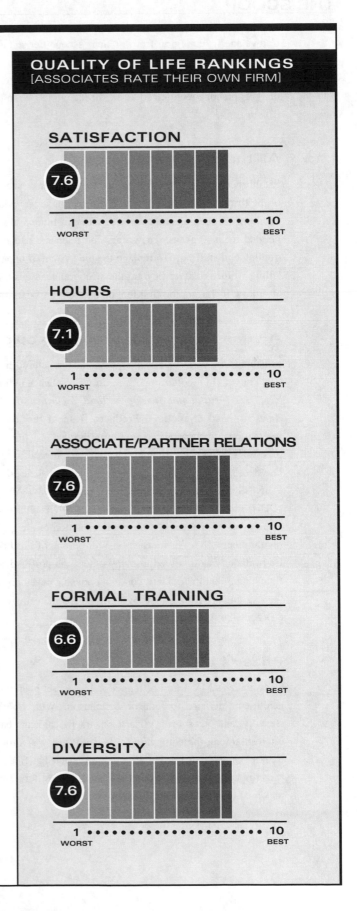

QUALITY OF LIFE RANKINGS
[ASSOCIATES RATE THEIR OWN FIRM]

SATISFACTION
7.6
1 WORST   10 BEST

HOURS
7.1
1 WORST   10 BEST

ASSOCIATE/PARTNER RELATIONS
7.6
1 WORST   10 BEST

FORMAL TRAINING
6.6
1 WORST   10 BEST

DIVERSITY
7.6
1 WORST   10 BEST

Visit the Vault Law Channel, the complete online resource for law careers, featuring firm
profiles, message boards, the Vault Law Job Board and more. www.vault.com/law

VAULT CAREER LIBRARY   275

THE SCOOP

Cadwalader is emerging from its once second-tier status to become one of the nation's most profitable law firms: in 2006, the firm recorded per-partner profits of over $2.5 million, just behind outfits like Wachtell and Cravath. That healthy figure is attributable to more than the firm's top-class real estate, bankruptcy, corporate, litigation and tax divisions, as well as a capital markets practice recognized as one of the world's strongest. Analysts attribute the firm's sharp rise in profitability to Chairman Robert Link.

All the president's men

Established over 200 years ago, Cadwalader, Wickersham & Taft LLP is the oldest Wall Street firm still in existence. At the time of the firm's founding, folks were still sealing letters with wax and writing with feathers, but we just might have Cadwalader to thank for all the bells and whistles that constitute a modern law firm. In the late 19th century, the firm introduced such new-fangled technology as typewriters and telephones to its offices. Cadwalader was similarly revolutionary in its approach to training and staffing. To replace the old system of unpaid law clerkships, the firm established the role of the associate. As for letting women venture beyond the stenographer's desk, the outbreak of World War II saw Cadwalader add a handful of female attorneys, including the first female partner of a Wall Street firm in 1942.

A yuan by any other name would smell as sweet

Engaging in a variety of securitization and structured finance transactions, Cadwalader's capital markets practice is perhaps its best known. In recognition of the firm's excellence in this area, in 2007 alone, Cadwalader's team was named "Law Firm of the Year" by *Institutional Investor's Total Securitization*, "Securitization and Structured Finance Team of the Year" by *IFLR Americas*, and "Structured Products Team of the Year" by *IFLR Europe*. The firm has extensive experience in complex international securitizations and cross-border structures in Europe, Asia and Latin America, and is frequently called upon by investment banks and financial institutions in need of new products and structures. In September 2006 lead arranger Lehman Brothers recommended Cadwalader to handle all legal aspects of a transaction involving Hua An Fund Management, one of China's largest asset management companies. Hua An is the first fund to be granted Qualified Domestic Institutional Investor (QDII) status by the Chinese government; QDII status enables domestic funds to convert renminbi yuan to other denominations, to be invested overseas. The implementation of the QDII plan is widely regarded as a key market reform for China, and the revolutionary Hua An transaction will be one of the first instances of Chinese integration into foreign markets. In addition, Cadwalader was involved in many other high-profile deals, including the whole-business securitization of Dunkin' Donuts, the financing of landmark New York City housing developments Stuyvesant Town and Peter Cooper Village for future securitization, the ongoing securitization program with RBS Greenwich Capital and Goldman Sachs, and the first-ever commercial real estate CDO for the European market.

Pfizer's advisor

Cadwalader's M&A group stepped in to counsel pharma giant Pfizer in June 2006 during the $16.6 billion sale of its consumer health care division to Johnson & Johnson. With a portfolio of well-known global brands like Listerine, Nicorette, Sudafed, Benadryl and Neosporin, Pfizer Consumer Healthcare had $3.9 billion in revenue in 2005. The sale engendered high levels of interest: among the competitor bids that Pfizer was sifting through were offers from GlaxoSmithKline, Colgate-Palmolive and Reckit Benkiser. Lazard and Bear Stearns acted as financial advisors to Pfizer on the transaction. Cadwalader also represented Pfizer in most of its recent acquisitions and divestitures, including the drug company's 2003 $60 billion acquisition of Pharmacia, maker of the popular arthritis drug Celebrex.

© 2007 Vault Inc.

Come fly with me

Cadwalader is lead counsel for Northwest Airlines in its Chapter 11 proceedings, helping Northwest accomplish in six months what took United Airlines two years, according to a March 2006 *New York Times* report. Northwest achieved the major goals of its restructuring by reducing $2.4 billion in annual costs from its business, including labor savings and aircraft fleet costs. To ensure that Northwest had an efficient and effective fleet, Cadwalader helped to reaffirm purchase agreements with Airbus, Boeing, GE Aircraft Engines, and Pratt and Whitney, which allowed the continued modernization of its long-range fleet with A330 and 787 aircraft. Northwest now has one of the youngest transatlantic fleets in the industry. Cadwalader also helped to negotiate additional purchase agreements with Bombardier and Embraer for new dual-class regional jetliners. With Cadwalader's assistance, Northwest completed an unprecedented $1.225 billion debtor-in-possession financing which, subject to certain conditions, converts to a five-year revolving credit facility upon emergence from Chapter 11. Cadwalader has also been successful in other activities including the resolution of disputes with the Pension Benefit Guaranty Corporation and pension reform legislation. Throughout this process, Cadwalader has helped with the defense and prosecution of various litigations.

Oil slick

In a leading case regarding overseas bribery laws, Cadwalader represented Vetco International Limited, an oil field services company, in connection with a settlement with the Criminal Division, Fraud Section of the U.S. Department of Justice. The matter related to Vetco's voluntary disclosure that certain of its foreign and U.S. subsidiaries had authorized a third party to make corrupt payments to Nigerian customs officials. A settlement resulted in the payment of criminal fines totaling $26 million by three subsidiaries. The settlement facilitated the impending sale of the Vetco Gray entities to General Electric for $1.9 billion.

Knavery and thievery

Cadwalader's "superstar" system and emphasis on mega-earners, as well as stringent pro capita revenue expectations, has led to some comings and goings. Critics claim that such emphasis on rainmakers is risky and that a practice can be left vulnerable if a superstar goes. In January 2007, Skadden walked away with the D.C. office's head of antitrust, Steven Sunshine, as well as two partners. However, the firm acted quickly to bring in noted antitrust practitioner and former assistant attorney general in charge of the antitrust division, Rick Rule. In February 2006, the firm lost its sole London projects partner, who left to set up his own consultancy, a departure that signaled the end of Cadwalader's London project practice. In June 2006, Orrick stole two structured finance partners from the firm, including James Croke, who had been head of Cadwalader's structured finance department in London from 1999 to 2004. Undaunted, in July 2006 Cadwalader fattened its capital markets and securities practice by nicking a CDO specialist from A&O as well as a Norton Rose partner. Former Davis Polk partner, Steven Lofchie, a leader in broker-dealer regulatory affairs, joined the firm in October 2006, while Deryck Palmer, John Rapisardi, George Davis and Andrew Troop joined Cadwalader as partners in the financial restructuring department in March 2007. Formerly partners at Weil Gotshal, the four brought significant restructuring experience with them, as well as a team of lawyers.

Go forth and advertise

Law firms have avoided using television as an advertising outlet, considering it the domain of the personal injury attorney, but legal marketing experts suggest that the stigma is fading, and that more firms will turn to the medium as the fastest way to build and strengthen their brand. In the vanguard is Cadwalader: in December 2006 the firm ran 60-second TV ads on cable channel MSNBC. According to *The Wall Street Journal*'s law blog, the firm was approached by an organization that offered to handle the ad's production and placement, and though Cadwalader's marketing director, Claudia Freeman, acknowledges that the firm had not previously considered this route, "The cost was very reasonable." The clip ran for a week, but is not slated to run again.

C'mon-a my house

In July 2006, Cadwalader attorneys were instrumental in striking down a 201-year-old North Carolina statute that made it illegal for unmarried couples to cohabitate. On a pro bono basis, the firm stepped in to handle the case of an unmarried woman who

Visit the Vault Law Channel, the complete online resource for law careers, featuring firm profiles, message boards, the Vault Law Job Board and more. **www.vault.com/law**

VAULT CAREER LIBRARY

277

lost her job as a 911 operator for the Pender County Sheriff's Department because she was living with her boyfriend. In 2004, shortly after starting the job, the woman was informed that she would have to either marry her partner, move out or lose her job. In deeming that the law violated civil rights and privacy laws, a North Carolina Superior Court judge cited Lawrence v. Texas, a 2003 Supreme Court decision that struck down a Texas sodomy law.

GETTING HIRED

Help wanted

Cadwalader has plenty of work, so it needs plenty of people who want to work hard. "They always need fresh meat for the grill," states a senior associate. "The firm really wants doers," agrees another insider. "Spoiled kids who feel entitled to a great salary, but are unwilling to do commensurate work that it requires won't be a match." What the firm doesn't care about—at least not as much as many firms—is where you went to school. "Unlike many top firms that only care about what school you went to and your GPA, Cadwalader gives a lot of credit to people who have had real work experience and who have a demonstrated interest in the area of law they seek to work in," observes a contact. "Grades are still important, but the firm does a great job at looking at the full package." A colleague elaborates, "What I love about CWT is that they are willing to look at good candidates from schools that are not in the Ivies or the top 15 law schools. I would rather be working with a top student at Rutgers or St. John's that has a strong finance background than someone who finished in the bottom of their class at U Penn or Columbia. Our practice looks more at things like undergraduate background and previous work experience to determine whether candidates have a strong finance background as opposed to focusing on rank of law school. This is probably why all the first-years get along. We don't have too many of the egos that other firms struggle with."

The firm has a typical recruiting process, and after an on-campus interview "applicants who are invited to our offices for call-back interviews participate in a hospitality suite with junior associates as well as four interviews with associates and partners in their indicated areas of interest. Applicants who are extended an offer to participate in our summer program are invited to participate in additional, informal meetings with associates to answer any additional questions they may have about the firm."

OUR SURVEY SAYS

Like a challenge? You'll love Cadwalader

"The work was challenging from the first day I started," says one young lawyer. "You have a chance to see deals from start to finish which is very fulfilling. Even as a first-year I interact with clients at the highest levels of investment banks on a daily basis." "Cases and clients are very high profile, but sometimes they are so large that is difficult to get meaningful experiences," notes a senior associate. "The firm is very encouraging of pro bono work and associates are usually lead counsel on their pro bono matters." All that "challenge" can be, well, a challenge. "The work is challenging and interesting, but also overwhelming in volume," reports a Charlotte associate. "As a result, there is little training and frequent turnover, which results in additional stress for the remaining associates. Partners in the office have indicated that they intend to redress this beyond salary increases." At least the partners are feeling the pinch, too. "Attorneys here work hard, and that includes the partners," says a lawyer. "I have had a great experience so far," reports a contact. "I have found the work challenging and the partners are very accessible to work through any issues that may come up or answer any questions I may have."

The firm tries to ease its new attorneys into the mix. "Cadwalader is making a genuine, concerted effort to ease first-years into the junior associate routine," says an insider. After that, you're on your own. "It's a pretty gruff place to work," reports a midlevel. "There are great resources and there's a lot of work to be done, so it's possible to grow your skills. However, you're pretty much left to do it on your own. There isn't a lot of friendly interaction between partners, which trickles down to the associate interaction."

© 2007 Vault Inc.

The mixed cultural bag

Associates at Cadwalader describe a hard-driving culture. "'Working hard to serve clients' needs is the priority here, which should be the ultimate goal of any law firm," says a source. "An attorney is not fooled into thinking otherwise at Cadwalader." Others gripe about partners run amok. "The firm made a value judgment when it hired in some of its major partners—profits over culture," grumbles a lawyer. "For example, one of the firm's most dominant partners is known for yelling [at] associates. However, he's a big profit generator, so he's untouchable." Though the firm has in the past been compared unfavorably to a "shark tank," a real estate lawyer says, "I find nothing unusual about the culture and that lawyers and support staff are quite cordial."

Since 2005, New York attorneys work in a high-tech new office space that includes a conference center with 55 meeting rooms and state-of-the-art audio and video capabilities, as well as "incredible views" of the harbor and the Statue of Liberty. Despite the luxury, some feel the firm's new digs in New York hurt the culture. "The new building is very isolating and you can go months without seeing other lawyers in your department, even ones you work with," notes an associate. Cadwalader is trying to combat the isolation. "The monthly mixers are a great idea, to bring together lawyers of all levels, and staff as well," says an attorney. The mixers are based around a different theme each month and are complemented by other programs offered by the firm to help foster a collegial culture. These include monthly dinners for attorneys working late, a mentor program with a generous budget, departmental get-togethers and team gatherings, and intramural sports teams. "The firm is somewhat [of] a meritocracy," states one insider. "Because there's so much work to do, it's just a matter of who can do it. There isn't a lot of attention paid to class year, pedigree or seniority here."

No foot dragging

Cadwalader is a pay leader, say its associates. The firm "follows the New York market, and does not drag its feet. When the last raise was set by Simpson Thacher, Cadwalader matched the next day." The firm is "always at market," agrees one source. "Last year, just about everyone received full bonuses, even if they did not meet [the] firm's billable hour requirement." Indeed, coming close to the requirements seems to be enough to get you a bonus. "Bonuses are given out to every associate that bills 1,900 hours and to all associates who have positive reviews but fail to reach the 1,900," reports a lawyer. "I know of at least five associates in the real estate group who billed less than 1,850 hours and still got full bonuses." Still, there are some complaints. "Given partner profits, however, salaries at upper levels should be higher," gripes a senior associate. "They pay market, so I can't complain. However, I can complain about the fact that they think that paying market absolves them of all other responsibility when it comes to associate satisfaction," fumes another insider. In the end, there's plenty of cash being thrown around. "The firm is obscenely profitable, and they take pains to make sure the associates get top of the market pay/bonus," says a source.

Wall Street hours

Know what you're getting into. "A Wall Street practice will inevitably keep Wall Street hours," says a source. "While all-night work sessions come with the territory, learning to take advantage of and appreciate the down time between deals is critical to maintaining sanity." The day doesn't always end when you leave the office. "The hours are long, but the partners in my office do not have strict face time requirements, and are very understanding about associates' lives outside the office," notes a contact. "That being said, the expectation is that the work will get done, so working from home is a must." Cadwalader "has [an] excellent remote computer access system which gives attorneys full access to their computer desktop, allowing work to be done at home and not in the office," according to a junior associate. A supervisor can really shape an associate's quality of life: "Some allow you to catch your breath and others do not," according to one M&A attorney.

Getting more bang for your training buck

"Cadwalader provides regular professional training sessions for entry-level associates and I find them very useful," reports a corporate lawyer. "These programs allow associates to stay current on the latest practices, policies and developments in their areas as well as to fulfill their New York CLE requirements." Associates want more than just CLE credits, though. "The firm has made improvements to make the training more than just what is needed to keep us in compliance with the CLE requirements,"

Visit the Vault Law Channel, the complete online resource for law careers, featuring firm
profiles, message boards, the Vault Law Job Board and more. **www.vault.com/law**

VAULT CAREER LIBRARY   **279**

says a lawyer. It works for some departments. "In addition to the initial week of training provided by the firm when first-year associates arrive, my department holds a monthly class which reviews different sections of the Bankruptcy Code and the latest developments in bankruptcy law," notes a lawyer from that department. Complaints tend to concern the training for brand-new associates: "The 'Cadwalader Academy' is too general an overview to have substantive value to new associates," complains a source. "There are no sessions which guide an associate through the types of tasks that he/she is expected to complete in their first few months and no helpful practice tips in terms of dealing with our day-to-day tasks." According to the firm, "Every new associate is assigned a mentor to help them acclimate to the firm, and for their first six months at the firm, first-year associates attend monthly training luncheons on topics such as bar admission requirements, marketing and time management. The bi-annual Path to Partnership program provides mid-to-senior level associates with professional development advice as well as strategies for achieving career goals. All associates benefit from training programs specific to their department as well as firmwide ethics programs."

© 2007 Vault Inc.

"You have a chance to see deals from start to finish, which is very fulfilling. Even as a first-year, I interact with clients at the highest levels of investment banks on a daily basis."

—Cadwalader, Wickersham & Taft associate

Visit the Vault Law Channel, the complete online resource for law careers, featuring firm profiles, message boards, the Vault Law Job Board and more. **www.vault.com/law**

VAULT CAREER LIBRARY   281

27

Hogan & Hartson LLP

555 Thirteenth Street, NW
Washington, DC 20004-1109
Phone: (202) 637-5600
www.hhlaw.com

LOCATIONS

Baltimore, MD • Boulder, CO • Colorado Springs, CO •
Denver, CO • Houston, TX • Los Angeles, CA • McLean,
VA • Miami, FL • New York, NY • Philadelphia, PA •
Washington, DC • White Plains, NY • Beijing • Berlin •
Brussels • Caracas • Geneva • Hong Kong • London •
Moscow • Munich • Paris • Shanghai • Tokyo • Warsaw

MAJOR DEPARTMENTS & PRACTICES

Antitrust, Competition & Consumer Protection • Appellate
Litigation • Aviation & Surface Transportation • Bankruptcy
& Creditors' Rights • Capital Markets • Class Action
Litigation • Climate Change • Corporate & Securities •
Corporate Governance • Education • Employee Benefits &
Executive Compensation • Energy • Environmental • Estate
Planning & Administration • Financial Services • Food, Drug,
Medical Device & Agriculture • Government Contracts •
Government Investigations • Health • Immigration •
Intellectual Property • International Arbitration & Litigation •
International Business Transactions • International Trade •
Labor & Employment • Latin America • Legislative • Lending
Litigation • Medical Devices • Mergers & Acquisitions •
Pharmaceutical & Biotechnology • Privacy • Private Equity •
Pro Bono • Project & International Finance • Public Finance
Real Estate • REITs • Tax • Telecommunications, Media &
Entertainment • White Collar Litigation

THE STATS

No. of attorneys: 1,000+
No. of offices: 22
Summer associate offers: 96 out of 96 (2006)
Chairman: J. Warren Gorrell Jr.
Hiring Chairs:
  Chair: Robert J. Waldman
  Co-chair/New York: Peter W. Smith

THE BUZZ

WHAT ATTORNEYS AT OTHER FIRMS ARE SAYING ABOUT THIS FIRM

- "Great FCC practice"
- "Smarty pants"
- "Chief Justice Roberts"
- "People get lost in the shuffle"

BASE SALARY (2007)

Washington, DC, and most other US offices
1st year: $160,000
2nd year: $170,000
3rd year: $185,000
4th year: $210,000
5th year: $230,000
6th year: $250,000
7th year: $265,000
8th year: $280,000
Summer associate: $3,080/week

UPPERS

- Flexible, two-tier hours system
- Friendly culture
- Superb training at H&H Academy

DOWNERS

- Sub-par top-end bonuses
- Is growth straining the culture?
- A few "problem partners"

NOTABLE PERKS

- Free BlackBerry and $2,000 for a new laptop
- Free parking (some offices)
- Marketing budget
- Bar and moving expenses

© 2007 Vault Inc.

RANKING RECAP

Best in Region

#5 - Miami

#7 - Washington, DC

#10 - Pennsylvania/Mid-Atlantic

Best in Practice

#8 - Technology

#9 - Antitrust

EMPLOYMENT CONTACT

Ms. Irena McGrath

Chief Associate Recruitment Officer

Phone: (202) 637-8601

E-mail: imcgrath@hhlaw.com

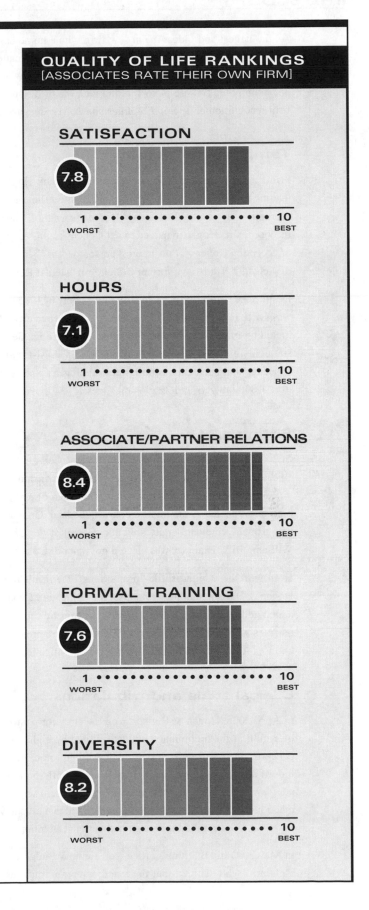

QUALITY OF LIFE RANKINGS
[ASSOCIATES RATE THEIR OWN FIRM]

SATISFACTION

7.8

1 WORST — 10 BEST

HOURS

7.1

1 WORST — 10 BEST

ASSOCIATE/PARTNER RELATIONS

8.4

1 WORST — 10 BEST

FORMAL TRAINING

7.6

1 WORST — 10 BEST

DIVERSITY

8.2

1 WORST — 10 BEST

Visit the Vault Law Channel, the complete online resource for law careers, featuring firm profiles, message boards, the Vault Law Job Board and more. **www.vault.com/law**

VAULT CAREER LIBRARY   283

THE SCOOP

As the largest and oldest major law firm with a home base in Washington, D.C., Hogan & Hartson's special strengths include complex litigation, business and finance, regulatory matters and intellectual property. Since 2000, the firm has seen revenue growth of a whopping 167 percent, with revenue per lawyer up 73 percent—all while making good on its vow to up its per capita pro bono hours. These factors, along with the firm's strong record on diversity and levels of associate satisfaction, brought the firm recognition as one of *The American Lawyer* magazine's "A-List" of Top 20 U.S. Law Firms in 2006.

Tempest in a teapot

Firm founder and Teddy Roosevelt intimate Frank Hogan began his solo practice in 1904, rising to fame as one of America's leading trial lawyers. Among his many high-profile cases, Hogan defended oil magnate Edward L. Doheny against bribery and corruption charges in the "Teapot Dome" scandal of the late 1920s, which involved leasing rights to government-held oil fields in Wisconsin. Hogan managed to get Doheny acquitted, despite the fact that Secretary of the Interior Albert Fall was found guilty of accepting Doheny's "no-interest personal loans." In 1925, Hogan's litigation practice was augmented by the corporate practice of Nelson T. Hartson, a former Solicitor of Internal Revenue.

Despite the firm's 100-year history, it was only in 1985 that Hogan & Hartson first branched out from its D.C. roots. Expansion was swift: in the following decades, the firm opened eight domestic offices and 13 throughout Europe, Asia and South America—including offices in Munich, Shanghai, Hong Kong, Geneva and Caracas in the last several years. In 2004, the firm formed a strategic alliance with Saudi Arabian firm Salah Al-Hejailan. Next up could be an outpost in San Francisco, though firm brass concedes that such expansion hinges on Hogan's ability to lure away top-string laterals. Hogan & Hartson now numbers just over 1,000 lawyers and 22 global offices.

Sitting pretty

In 2005, former Hogan partner John Glover Roberts Jr. became the 17th chief justice of the United States, replacing Chief Justice William H. Rehnquist. Roberts joined Hogan's Washington office in 1986, and from 1993 until 2003 presided over its appellate practice before leaving to serve on the U.S. Court of Appeals for the District of Columbia. In September 2005, another prominent partner graduated to the highest court in the land: Gregory Garre, who took over from Roberts as head of the appellate practice, was named principal deputy solicitor general of the United States. And in November 2006, Denver litigation partner August William "Bill" Ritter Jr. was elected governor of Colorado.

Even with these high-profile "promotions," the firm's litigation practice continues to flourish. *The American Lawyer* included Hogan & Hartson among its finalists for "Litigation Department of the Year" for the second time in a row in 2006. And the firm added additional breadth and depth to its litigation group in the past year with the additions of three Houston-based litigation partners who serve as principal U.S. counsel for a prominent European aircraft manufacturer, and of four litigators in New York and Los Angeles who handle substantial U.S. litigation for European auto manufacturers.

Clinical trials and tribulations

In April 2006, Hogan & Hartson won a victory for pharmaceutical company Amgen, when an appeals court affirmed the denial of a motion for preliminary injunction filed by eight participants in a clinical trial of Parkinson's drug GDNF. Citing safety concerns and the drug's lack of demonstrable value, Amgen cancelled its study, distressing plaintiffs who felt that GDNF was indeed alleviating their symptoms. The plaintiffs brought claims against the pharmaceutical company for breach of contract, alleging that Amgen had promised to provide them with GDNF indefinitely. A district court disagreed, finding that Amgen had made no such contract with the plaintiffs, and that all study documentation maintained Amgen's authority to cancel the study at any time. The emotional case gained national attention as the subject of a *60 Minutes* segment in September 2005.

In May 2006 the Baltimore office won summary judgment on behalf of drug giant Bristol-Myers Squibb in an action brought by a plaintiff who claimed that the manufacturer's drug warnings were inadequate and the drug itself defective. A U.S. District

© 2007 Vault Inc.

Court in Maryland awarded summary judgment based upon Maryland's "learned intermediary" doctrine, which states that a manufacturer is not obligated to warn the consumer of possible drug risks if the prescribing doctor has already received adequate notice of those risks.

Home Depot, police thyself

Stock-option backdating, the "It-girl" of corporate fraud, ain't too bad for business. In June 2006, with an SEC examination of its stock-option procedures looming, blue-chip retailer Home Depot called in Hogan & Hartson's white collar litigation group to provide independent outside counsel as the company's board of directors conducted an internal review. In December 2006 Home Depot reported its findings, admitting that there was "some backdating" on annual option grants and certain quarterly option grants from 1981 through November 2000, amounting to $200 million in unrecorded expenses, excluding related tax consequences, over the past 26 years it has operated as a public company.

Auto industry steeled for regulatory relief

In a decision that earned coverage in publications such as *The Wall Street Journal*, in December 2006 the firm's litigation and international trade groups combined to win six of the world's largest auto producers—DaimlerChrysler, Ford, General Motors, Honda, Nissan and Toyota a major victory before the International Trade Commission. The successful suit involved the removal of antidumping and countervailing duties on corrosion-resistant carbon steel; the ITC voted to remove duties on four of the six countries subject to these duties, covering most import shipments.

The firm's historically strong government regulatory and legislative practices were bolstered further as a result of key partner acquisitions in 2006 and early 2007. Energy lawyer Daniel Stenger came to the firm with over 25 years of experience representing electric utilities and others in matters before the U.S. Nuclear Regulatory Commission, the Federal Energy Regulatory Commission and the Department of Energy. Former partner Tom Leary rejoined the firm after serving six years as a commissioner of the Federal Trade Commission. And the firm's legislative practice recently welcomed to the fold former Democratic staff director and chief counsel of the House of Representatives Committee on Energy and Commerce, Reid Stuntz, who will both handle legislative matters and serve as co-chair with a white collar litigation partner of the newly-created working group on governmental oversight and investigations matters.

In another example of inter-departmental cooperation, the firm's regulatory and intellectual property groups both advised Symbol Technologies on international antitrust and IP issues relating to the company's $3.9 billion acquisition by Motorola in 2006. The deal created one of the largest sellers of hand-held scanners, mobile computers, and wireless local area network infrastructure, with the potential to tap a huge corporate market spanning much of North America, the EU, South Africa and Asia.

"Intellectual" property?

In January 2006 the firm defended Disney's creative honor in a suit filed by two screenwriters who claimed that Disney subsidiary Miramax Publishing stole ideas from a script treatment they submitted to the motion picture studio in 1995. It might have been a case of "he said, she said," were it not for the plaintiffs' impressive lack of research. The purported 1995 script submission contained extensive references to a "PalmPilot" handheld device—a term that the Palm company did not coin until 1997. In his verdict, a New York judge harshly chastised the plaintiffs for fabricating evidence, and ordered them to pay the defendant's attorney fees. Considering Disney's deep pockets, it won't be a pretty bill.

Turning to more serious matters, the IP department also helped the American Red Cross enter into an outsourcing agreement with Verizon, in the wake of Hurricane Katrina and before the 2006 hurricane season, to make emergency call-center services available in the event of natural, and non-natural, mass-impact catastrophes. And Hogan IP lawyers have long worked with energy drink pioneer Red Bull, to protect it against trademark and trade dress infringement and unfair competition by the makers of the numerous energy drink manufacturers that are trying to take advantage of its leadership in the market. The firm obtained the latest injunction in 2006 against Matador Concepts, which sought to promote its drink with identical colors and bull-related indicia.

Visit the Vault Law Channel, the complete online resource for law careers, featuring firm profiles, message boards, the Vault Law Job Board and more. www.vault.com/law

VAULT CAREER LIBRARY   285

Pulling their pro bono weight

Hogan established a community services department, headed by a full-time partner, in 1970. From the onset, pro bono was serious business: the first lawyer to head the department would later hold the firm's top post, administrative partner. In 2004, Chairman J. Warren Gorrell Jr. emphasized his expectation that everyone, rainmakers included, pull their pro bono weight. Thanks to Gorrell's push, the firm jumped from No. 26 to No. 4 in the AmLaw pro bono rankings—a jump that also helped the firm break into the AmLaw "A-list." The community services department now claims a full-time staff of five lawyers, and has designated liaisons in each of Hogan's 22 offices. Pro bono issues also make the agenda at partner and practice group meetings. In 2006, Hogan & Hartson earned the NAACP's "Civil Rights Champion Award," the District of Columbia Bar's large firm "Pro Bono Law Firm of the Year Award" and an "Outstanding Legal Services Award" from the National Coalition to Abolish the Death Penalty.

Among the firm's recent high-profile civil rights achievements is a case that took place in Tulia, Texas, where nearly 10 percent of the African-American population was arrested in a 1999 drug sting. By exposing the racist views and dishonesty of a white undercover officer whose account led to the arrests, Hogan & Hartson lawyers were able to win release for all arrestees, as well as full pardons for those convicted. In November 2006, lawyers in the firm's Miami office won some $2.5 million in damages for a man who suffered disability-related discrimination at the hands of the Department of Homeland Security.

GETTING HIRED

Personality, grades, pedigree—you need it all

Good luck getting a job at Hogan & Hartson. "It ain't easy," observes one insider. "My sense—especially as of late—is that Hogan & Hartson focuses its recruitment efforts at the historical top-10 law schools and, on top of that, only the top 25 percent of the student body at those schools. You've certainly got a shot if you didn't attend a top-10 school, but it's harder to get an offer." "Hogan & Hartson is very pedigree-oriented," notes another contact. "We hire a lot of court clerks and associates from well-known law schools." Brush up on your writing skills while in law school. The firm "seems to hire from a variety of schools, though most come from top-tier schools," advises a Washingtonian. "While I am not aware of a GPA cutoff per se, grades are very important. In addition, participation on a journal is important."

Even if you have the right pedigree, it's still important to ... well, not be a jerk. "We have started concentrating on higher-tier schools, but other than that we are very picky about personality," warns a source. "It's not that we're snobby, we just don't want to work with jerks." It also helps to have done something with your life (other than stand out at law school). "The firm seems to value pre-law school experience quite highly," observes a contact. "They look for independent people who can be productive immediately." "The partners are often looking for the perfect fit and often turn away qualified candidates," states a midlevel.

OUR SURVEY SAYS

Nice, for a law firm

No one loves life at a big law firm, but Hogan & Hartson associates are as happy as can be. "Aside from conditions endemic to law firm life—unpredictable and sometimes long hours, for example—I find work at the firm rewarding," says one insider. "In terms of the quality of the work and the quality of my colleagues, I cannot ask for more." "Overall, Hogan & Hartson is a great place to work," agrees a contact. "I do spend long days in the office, which I dislike, but this certainly is not unique to Hogan & Hartson and, rather, is pretty much a hallmark of any law firm job."

Getting good work is a huge factor in associate satisfaction. "I have had the opportunity to work on a broad range of issues and on truly cutting-edge issues," brags a young D.C. associate. "I have also had an unusually high volume of direct client contact for someone of my tenure. However, like every other large law firm, the sheer volume of the work and the expectation to be on

© 2007 Vault Inc.

call 24-hours a day can be overwhelming." "I enjoy the cases I work on," adds a senior associate. "The cases are interesting and the partners I work with are smart and nice." "My work is consistently interesting, intellectually engaging and challenging," brags another satisfied Hogan & Hartson contact.

Friendly culture, but will it stay that way?

What's not to love about the culture at Hogan? Nothing, according to this guy: "I love the culture of Hogan & Hartson. We have a very collegial environment and socialize together quite a lot." Then it's a good thing that "Hogan seems filled with friendly, well-rounded individuals." A midlevel agrees, saying that the firm sports a "very collegial and friendly culture. Everyone has the common goal of producing top-caliber work and I have sensed no back-biting or competitiveness in my office." While one's experience varies by location and practice, the firm manages to maintain a one-firm feel. "Hogan & Hartson is a big firm made up of small teams," says a lawyer on the M&A team. "The camaraderie is excellent within these groups, yet there is a cohesive culture that runs across the whole firm."

One senior associate thinks that, with growth, "Hogan & Hartson has become a very bottom-line firm." "The chairman is a number cruncher and that is reflected in most aspects of the current culture." But others are more optimistic. "Despite growing in numbers and developing into more of a New York-style firm generally, the firm has maintained its distinctive culture, which is epitomized by pleasant lawyers and staff, all of whom have and value priorities aside from billing hours," reports a D.C.-based associate.

Finally, a voice

Associates are generally pleased with how they're treated by their bosses. "In my experience, partners treat associates with respect," says a D.C. lawyer. "Screamers are not tolerated in the firm culture." "Although there are a few partners who do not treat associates with respect, most of the partners are good to work with," states another source. "Most of the partners here treat associates with respect and as valued members of the team," agrees a third lawyer. "However, there are a few bad apples who treat associates like commodities."

Associates now have a chance to voice their concerns, however. "In terms of firmwide decisions, the partnership is getting better," notes a contact. "We now have an associates committee, which helps. Firm management seems to be acknowledging and responding to our opinions a lot more." "The firm management is actively working to ensure that associate needs and concerns are addressed," agrees a junior associate. Of course, the best way to get a say in firm management is from the inside: 27 lawyers were advanced into the partnership in January 2007, more than half of whom were women.

What are bonuses made of?

"The firm pays market rates for base compensation, but the bonuses and additional compensation continue to be an issue," gripes a midlevel. A colleague elaborates, "The firm has recently stepped up its efforts to become more competitive in terms of its basic pay scale. We currently are on par with our key D.C. competitors (Wilmer, Covington and A&P)." "Hogan's attitude towards compensation seems to be that 'we pay them what the market says we have to,'" notes another lawyer. "Although this is quite certainly the case, the firm would do better from a PR standpoint to be less transparent in this regard. I do commend Hogan for stepping up immediately in this most recent round of raises—they were the first D.C. firm to raise salaries."

Well, there's a feather in the firm's cap. As for bonuses, the reviews are far less glowing. "Hogan's D.C. associate bonuses are low compared to its peers," complains a lawyer from that office. "It is not lock-step and is not tied to billable hours. No one really seems to know how bonuses are determined. There is a consensus among the associates that it does not pay to be a senior associate or to have huge hours. Generally, senior associates who billed more than 2,100 hours received smaller bonuses than those received by midlevel associates at other peer firms." "It is disappointing to talk to friends at other major law firms, including several that are considered less 'prestigious' in D.C., only to learn that they are receiving bonuses that are double the amount earned by associates who are performing at the top of their class at H&H."

Visit the Vault Law Channel, the complete online resource for law careers, featuring firm profiles, message boards, the Vault Law Job Board and more. www.vault.com/law

VAULT CAREER LIBRARY   287

Pick your poison

Don't want to be chained to your desk? You can choose to take it easy (well, easier) at Hogan & Hartson. The firm allows associates to choose from a two-tier system with target billable goals of 1,800 or 1,950 hours per year. "The two-tiered track for billable hours at Hogan gives an associate a lot of flexibility in deciding the best balance between work and life outside of work," states one source. Better news: the firm actually sticks to its targets. "I am on the firm's 1,800-hour track and there is no stigma for billing only that amount, although the compensation is significantly less than if you billed 1,950," says a source. "Compared to other law firms, Hogan is extremely reasonable when it comes to hours," agrees a D.C. lawyer. We have a two-track system which allows associates to choose to work fewer hours for less money and still be full-time and on the partner track." It's not perfect, though. "Hogan's reputation as a lifestyle firm is only accurate for certain departments—corporate attorneys can expect to have every last hour squeezed out of them," says one fresh-squeezed corporate lawyer.

Thank the Academy

Hogan & Hartson is the place to learn. "There are many training opportunities, both in-house and outside the firm," notes a source. "The firm's training program—H&H Academy—has an array of interesting and topical programs, from public speaking, time management and legal writing programs of general interest, to programs developing skills sets necessary in specific practice groups." "Training at Hogan is excellent," agrees a contact. "Apart from our regular in-house training and professional development programs, we are encouraged to attend outside events as well." Don't worry about out-of-pocket expenses. "There is plenty of training available both online and through seminars," states a lawyer. "The firm has also partnered up with outside sources to provide additional training at no cost to the associates."

© 2007 Vault Inc.

"Hogan & Hartson is a big firm made up of small teams. The camaraderie is excellent within these groups, yet there is a cohesive culture that runs across the whole firm."

—*Hogan & Hartson associate*

Visit the Vault Law Channel, the complete online resource for law careers, featuring firm profiles, message boards, the Vault Law Job Board and more. **www.vault.com/law**

V∧ULT CAREER LIBRARY

289

28

Mayer, Brown, Rowe & Maw LLP

71 South Wacker Drive
Chicago, IL 60606
Phone: (312) 782-0600
www.mayerbrown.com

LOCATIONS

Charlotte, NC • Chicago, IL • Houston, TX • Los Angeles, CA • New York, NY • Palo Alto, CA • Washington, DC • Berlin • Brussels • Cologne • Frankfurt • Hong Kong • London • Paris

The firm also has a representative office in Beijing and alliances with three firms that have offices in Mexico City, Madrid, Italy and Eastern Europe.

MAJOR PRACTICES

Banking & Finance • Bankruptcy • Corporate & Securities • Derivatives • Environmental • ERISA/Compensation • Government/Global Trade • Intellectual Property • Litigation/Dispute Resolution • Real Estate • Tax Controversy • Tax Transactions • Wealth Management

THE STATS

No. of attorneys: 1500+
No. of offices: 14
Summer associate offers: 88 out of 90 (2006)
Chairman: James D. Holzhauer
Vice chairmen: Kenneth S. Geller & Paul Maher
  Charlotte: Rodney Alexander
  Chicago: J. Thomas Mullen
  Houston: Harry "Hap" Weitzel
  Los Angeles: Michael F. Kerr
  New York: Edward Davis
  Palo Alto: Ward Johnson
  Washington, DC: Miriam R. Nemetz

BASE SALARY (2007)

Chicago; LA; New York; Palo Alto; Washington, DC
1st year: $160,000
2nd year: $170,000
3rd year: $185,000
4th year: $210,000
5th year: $230,000
6th year: $250,000
7th year: $265,000
Summer associate: $3,077/week

Charlotte, NC
1st year: $145,000
2nd year: $155,000
3rd year: $170,000
4th year: $190,000
5th year: $210,000
6th year: $225,000
7th year: $240,000
Summer associate: $2,500/week

Houston, TX
1st year: $135,000 (5K bonus)
2nd year: $145,000
3rd year: $150,000
4th year: $160,000
5th year: $170,000
6th year: $180,000
7th year: $185,000
Summer associate: $2,700/week

UPPERS

• "Working directly with talented partners"
• Collegial atmosphere
• High pay

DOWNERS

• Recent partner departures
• Alas, great pay = long hours
• "Growing pains"

THE BUZZ
WHAT ATTORNEYS AT OTHER FIRMS ARE SAYING ABOUT THIS FIRM

• "Top appellate shop"
• "Used to be better"
• "Great private equity"
• "De-equitize, demoralize"

NOTABLE PERKS

• Aeron chairs
• Free Starbucks coffee
• Ballgame/event tickets
• "All the usual big-firm stuff, plus subsidized parking, which is a big deal in NYC"

© 2007 Vault Inc.

RANKING RECAP

Best in Region
#4 - Chicago
#13 - Washington, DC

Best in Practice
#6 - Technology
#9 - Real Estate

Partner Prestige Rankings
#4 (tie) - Tax

EMPLOYMENT CONTACTS

Please see the firm's web site,
www.mayerbrownrowe.com/careeropportunities, for full
contact information.

Charlotte
Alison Rogers, Marketing & Recruiting Coordinator
E-mail: arogers@mayerbrownrowe.com

Chicago
Laura Kanter, Attorney Recruitment Manager
E-mail: RecruitingDepartment-CHGO@mayerbrown.com

Houston
Amy Carrington, Legal Recruitment Manager
E-mail: acarrington@mayerbrownrowe.com

Los Angeles
Casey Quigley, Attorney Recruitment Manager
E-mail: cquigley@mayerbrown.com

New York
Frances Vaughn, Associate Recruitment Manager
E-mail: fvaughn@mayerbrown.com

Palo Alto
Clint Kennedy, Director of Administration
E-mail: ckennedy@mayerbrownrowe.com

Washington, DC
Suzanne Alderete, Attorney Development & Recruitment
   Manager
E-mail: salderete@mayerbrown.com

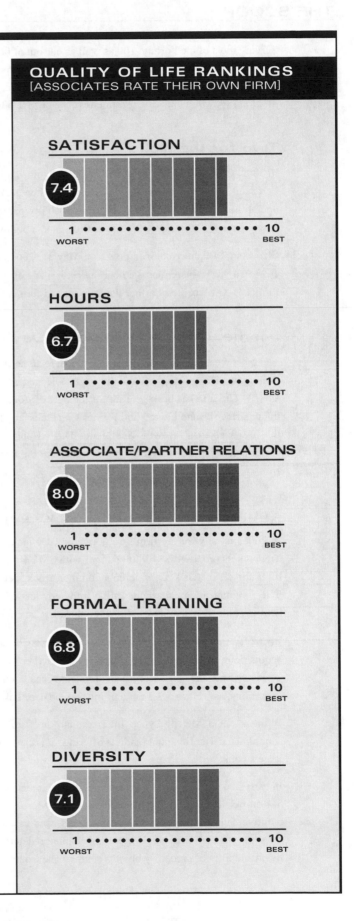

QUALITY OF LIFE RANKINGS
[ASSOCIATES RATE THEIR OWN FIRM]

SATISFACTION
7.4
1 WORST — 10 BEST

HOURS
6.7
1 WORST — 10 BEST

ASSOCIATE/PARTNER RELATIONS
8.0
1 WORST — 10 BEST

FORMAL TRAINING
6.8
1 WORST — 10 BEST

DIVERSITY
7.1
1 WORST — 10 BEST

Visit the Vault Law Channel, the complete online resource for law careers, featuring firm
profiles, message boards, the Vault Law Job Board and more. **www.vault.com/law**

VAULT CAREER LIBRARY   291

THE SCOOP

Serving most of the Fortune 100 as well as one out of three U.S. banks, Mayer, Brown, Rowe & Maw is renowned for top-flight corporate and finance work. By recruiting attorneys from the Solicitor General's office in the early 1980s, the firm was also one of the first in the nation to devise a specialized U.S. Supreme Court practice. 2006 numbers show the firm continuing a pattern of strong growth, tabulating top-line revenue of $1.1 billion, an 11 percent increase over 2005.

Two for the globe

In 2002, Chicago-based Mayer, Brown & Platt joined up with the U.K.'s Rowe & Maw; the pairing strengthened Mayer Brown's U.K. and European practices, while Rowe & Maw gained greater U.S. visibility and a larger global platform. Today, the firm operates as a combination of two limited liability partnerships, counting 1,500+ lawyers and 14 offices. The firm also has a strong German operation with three offices, and a highly rated Paris office—all the result of mergers.

Chairman Ty Fahner stepped down on May 31, 2007, and a new leadership team took over. The three-partner "office of the chairman," who share management duties, is made up of Chairman and former GC James Holzhauer, plus two vice chairmen— former U.K. Managing Partner Paul Maher and former D.C. office head Kenneth Geller.

I came, I saw, I stole Jones Day's guy

The most recent addition to the firm's global roster is Hong Kong. Though Mayer Brown already had a representative office in Beijing, the Hong Kong office will be a full-fledged entity, focusing on corporate and banking transactions, as well as real estate and IP. The firm has been gearing for the opening for a while now, beefing up its China expertise with such hires as D.C.-based trade partner Duane Layton and former Chinese affairs foreign affairs ministry official Connie Wang. And in November 2006, the firm walked away with rival Jones Day's Hong Kong finance partner Jeffrey H. Chen. Until now, the firm's Chinese consultancies have focused on global trade, and the firm intends to leverage these clients and generate mandates for the Hong Kong team.

You've got the brawn, we've got the brains, let's make lots of money

In 2006, activity for the firm's corporate practice included advising CBOT Holdings, parent company of the Chicago Board of Trade, in its proposed $8 billion merger with CME Holdings; representing Illinois Tool Works in its September 2006 cash tender offer for all of Click Commerce's common stock; counseling Andrew Corporation during its May 2006 merger with ADC Telecommunication; and representing Infor, provider of "extended enterprise solutions and services," in an agreement to acquire SSA Global. The deal makes Infor the third-largest enterprise software provider in the industry.

In 2007, a multidisciplinary team of Mayer Brown Chicago- and New York-based lawyers advised Nestlé S.A. on its $5.5 billion acquisition of Gerber Products Company and Gerber Life Insurance Company from seller Novartis AG. And in December 2006, Mayer Brown advised energy provider TransCanada on its $3.4 billion acquisition of ANR's natural gas pipeline and storage operations, as well as a 3.5 percent interest in Great Lakes Gas Transmission, from the El Paso Corporation.

With its client Merrill Lynch International, the firm recently structured a high-profile deal in Africa—the first-of-its-kind subordinated Tier II capital markets offering for issuance of $175 million in debt for the First Bank of Nigeria PLC, the country's largest bank.

In early 2007, the firm made two successful arguments for major clients in the U.S. Supreme Court. In one case, the Court ruled 5-4 on behalf of Philip Morris USA in Philip Morris USA v. Williams, a ruling expected to impose new curbs on the use of punitive damages across the country. The second case, Weyerhaeuser Co. v. Ross-Simmons Hardwood Lumber Co., held that the same standard that the Court articulated for predatory pricing cases applies in cases alleging predatory buying, vastly limiting the availability of predatory buying claims. The Court ruled unanimously in favor of the firm's client, Weyerhaeuser.

© 2007 Vault Inc.

Here's to not playing with fire

The tragic 2003 fire in The Station nightclub in Rhode Island resulted in claims filed by more than 300 people against Pactiv Corporation, a company that manufactures polyethylene foam. However, Pactiv did not manufacture the foam installed at the nightclub, which ignited during a heavy metal band's performance with pyrotechnics. Mayer Brown, with help from various retained experts, worked hard to convince the plaintiffs' counsel that the foam involved was not made by Pactiv. Plaintiffs filed a stipulation conceding that Pactiv's motion for summary judgment should be granted and the Federal District Court entered judgment in favor of Pactiv on all claims. Aggregated damages would have exceeded $1 billion.

All together now

Ohmygod the Beatles are BACK … in court. In August 2006, a federal judge in Manhattan ruled that a suit filed by the remaining Beatles and Beatles' heirs against Mayer Brown clients Capitol and EMI Records will be allowed to go forward. The Beatles' complaint alleges that Capitol and affiliate EMI hid sales of the Beatles' recordings, pocketing millions in royalties. The Beatles are joined in the action by their recording label Apple Records; the plaintiffs seek $25 million in damages and lost royalties. The case was actually only the latest round in a series of royalty and accounting disputes between the Fab Four and their record company going back more than three decades.

Howdy ex-pardner

In March 2007, Mayer Brown made the front pages of legal tabloids with the announcement that it was shedding 45 equity partners, approximately 10 percent of its worldwide total. In a statement issued in response to inquiries, the firm confirmed that the partners were asked to either leave the firm or accept other positions. The firm stressed that the cuts were not related to past profitability, but rather its desire to be "properly staffed" to efficiently meet client needs. The firm praised those affected as "fine lawyers," and promised to provide "ample transition and placement support." According to *The American Lawyer*, 2006 profits per equity partner exceeded $1 million.

In 2006, the firm had added 39 new partners worldwide, with the London office tallying nine—a sharp increase for London on the 2005 total of two. According to the firm, "The U.K. promotions highlight the significant economic growth that Europe has undergone in the last years, and underscore the firm's optimism regarding the region. In 2005, the U.K. branch adopted a merit-based system of compensation, with partners reporting an average of £480,000 in 2006. The firm is adopting a new system globally, which is both a management and compensation system based on goal-setting."

New web site coming

The firm's web team is completely revamping its public web site, www.mayerbrown.com, during 2007. According to the firm, "By the end of the year, most of the content will be rewritten for more consistency and better expression of the firm's capabilities. One of the changes will be eliminating the many 'mini-sites' that have been featured on the site. Content is being updated gradually and the new visual design will be implemented by the end of the year."

A brighter side of Yale

Two of the firm's noted Supreme Court practitioners have joined the faculty of the newly created Yale Law School Supreme Court Advocacy Clinic (YLSCA), which combines classroom instruction about the court—its history, rules, etc.—with hands-on involvement in litigation projects. Students will draft petitions for writs of certiorari, write merits briefs in granted cases and represent amici curiae. Andrew J. Pincus and Charles Rothfeld are members of the firm's appellate advocacy practice, as well as former assistants to the solicitor general; each has been involved in more than 100 cases before the court. Of note: five former Mayer Brown summer associates will be SCOTUS clerks in 2008.

Visit the Vault Law Channel, the complete online resource for law careers, featuring firm profiles, message boards, the Vault Law Job Board and more. **www.vault.com/law**

VAULT CAREER LIBRARY   293

GETTING HIRED

Clerkships! Clerkships! Clerkships!

Mayer Brown's associates in the D.C. office say that the office's narrow focus on the top two or three law schools is easing, but that it still remains passionately devoted to clerkships and, of course, impressive transcripts. A D.C. litigator reports, "It used to be that we only focused on Chicago, Harvard and Yale, but we have recently expanded our search to include other top national schools as well as local D.C. and Virginia law schools. As always, law review, good grades and interesting backgrounds are desired, and a judicial clerkship is almost a prerequisite if you want to litigate." An antitrust expert adds, "We have a history of being intellectual snobs. We have a premier appellate practice, so the emphasis is on grades, prestigious law schools, law review and clerkships, clerkships, clerkships!" A Chicago associate summarizes, "Top schools for recruiting are Harvard, Chicago, Northwestern and Michigan." Offices typically try to recruit from local schools; for example, the Chicago office "has had good success at Loyola, DePaul and Valparaiso in recent years."

What exactly does "fit" constitute at Mayer Brown? According to one midlevel, "The firm is looking for people who have done well in school, who have an interesting background and who can articulate his or her interest in working at Mayer Brown." Another midlevel associate advises, "We look for someone who is bright and puts themselves together well." That said, still another midlevel adds, "You get hired if you are smart. Unless you are a complete jerk in interviews, we don't care about personality."

OUR SURVEY SAYS

Somewhere between deeply satisfied and deeply in love

The majority of Mayer Brown's associates report that they are quite satisfied with their jobs, careers and firm. "This is probably very odd, but I love my work," says a junior corporate finance specialist. "It is interesting and challenging and since day one has defied all of my expectations in the best ways. I learn something new every day and that makes me really happy with what I do." A New York litigator crows, "I think the firm strikes a nice balance by providing opportunity for junior and midlevel associates to get front-line experience without making associates sacrifice a life outside the office." Another litigator adds, "I can't really think of much to complain about other than the hours, but that's what I signed up for. My practice is varied and interesting, I have a lot of responsibility on my cases, no one hangs over me and watches my every move and I don't have to work for any partners whom I dislike. And I get paid a lot." Okay, here's one last glowing review: "I find working here to be quite enjoyable, but I also work with some of the best partners," says a D.C. trial attorney. "If you can find yourself a good mentor—of which there are quite a few—you can have a very rewarding and fulfilling career here."

Professional? Yes. Pompous? No

Associates call the vibe at Mayer Brown "collegial," "social," "professional," "very friendly" and "not pompous at all." A young real estate attorney says, "People have a lot of personality, and impressively, a bit of an edge to them—a certain sarcasm and swagger that I really like. I socialize all the time, from firm happy hours to drinks out, often sponsored by the firm but often not." Describing her office's culture, a Chicago litigator says, "I find that most of my colleagues (including me) prefer to go home to our families after work, although I have socialized with other lawyers on occasion and enjoyed it more than I thought I would. There is a lot of informal socialization within the office— impromptu discussions, lunches, office visits and so on."

Partners all great (except that one guy)

Mayer Brown's associates are positively effusive about their firm's partners, both as individuals and as a whole. "The partners are very professional and respectful with associates," says a junior New York litigator. "We constantly have meetings updating us on the status of the firm and any internal changes that are happening." An L.A. litigator reports, "We just brought in a new head of the litigation department who goes out of his way to treat associates well and keep them informed. Our new office managing partner is very approachable." However, another New Yorker warns, "There were some troubling breakdowns in communication this year regarding strategic decisions made by the firm, although the firm is making an effort to rebound from these lapses by getting associate input on new initiatives." And another Big Apple associate adds, "Aside from one partner, overall, the partners in my group treat the associates with great respect, at least that has been my experience. They respect our individual lives and take great care to commend our efforts, explain the transactions, explain our mistakes (versus yelling and degrading) and generally treat us as peers instead of subordinates."

Formal training varies

Associates say that Mayer Brown's formal training varies office by office and by practice, so don't read too much into what that real estate lawyer from L.A. told you (unless you're considering a job in the firm's L.A. real estate practice). As one T&E specialist from Chicago puts it, "This varies greatly by group, but my group is particularly active in ongoing legal education and associate training." A D.C. associate reports, "Unlike the New York and Chicago offices, there is an absence of on-site training programs in the D.C. office, especially for transactional associates. Most of the programs offered are 'teleconferences' with the other offices." And a D.C. litigator adds, "Last year, the firm implemented a litigation training workshop that was extremely well received, and followed that up with a NITA-run deposition workshop in the fall. A recent lunch series on securities law has been similarly successful."

Likewise, informal training

Associates give the firm generally good, though mixed, reviews for its mentoring and formal training, but mostly agree that things vary from partner to partner. As one junior L.A. associate puts it, "Mentoring is hit-or-miss, but I think that's true everywhere. I happen to have had very good experiences finding mentors here." A corporate finance specialist reports, "I can't say enough for informal training at this firm. Almost universally, every single person that I have worked with, from partner, to counsel, to senior and midlevel associates, has taken the time to fully explain the relevant transaction structures, provided useful written materials for further inquiry and patiently answered all questions. The people in this group have not, so far, been selfish with their knowledge at all." However, a junior Chicago associate warns, "The mentoring program is not supported within the firm. Informal training must be diligently sought out."

The pay at Mayer Brown is so high that it makes some leery. As one insider reports, "We are very well paid. In fact, I fear the recent pay increases will lead to higher billing minimums and billing rates. It just does not seem to be a sustainable system in the long run." As one junior associate in New York's corporate department sees it, "It's difficult to complain about the salary here. We received a raise before we started working and a second raise after only four months of work." A New York litigator adds, "Top of the market and recent salary and bonus bumps have made the expense of living in New York much more palatable."

Long, flexible and exactly as advertised

The firm's hours are long, perhaps even staggering, associates report, but oddly flexible, and exactly what they expected. "I do not mind the hours at this stage in my life and career, but I do not know how feasible it would be to combine my job with having children," says a fourth-year. "The firm as a whole talks up the concept of part-time schedules, but it has never happened in my (admittedly small) group, and rumor has it that there would be a push against it if one were to pursue it." A first-year adds, "It's hard to be happy with the hours that we work; but to be fair, we all knew what we were getting into when we signed up for a job in finance in New York." As one Mayer Brown insider puts it, "The firm is very flexible. In fact, there are several policies and programs in place with regard to part-time work and leave, and the firm tries to ensure that employees will not be held back by what they may see as a possible effect of switching to a part-time type of employment."

Visit the Vault Law Channel, the complete online resource for law careers, featuring firm profiles, message boards, the Vault Law Job Board and more. **www.vault.com/law**

VAULT CAREER LIBRARY   295

29

PRESTIGE RANKING

Fried, Frank, Harris, Shriver & Jacobson LLP

One New York Plaza
New York, NY 10004
Phone: (212) 859-8000
www.friedfrank.com

LOCATIONS

New York, NY (HQ)
Washington, DC
Frankfurt
Hong Kong
London
Paris

MAJOR DEPARTMENTS & PRACTICES

Antitrust • Bankruptcy & Restructuring • Benefits & Compensation • Corporate (Asset Management, Capital Markets, Corporate Governance, Financings, M&A, Private Equity) • Corporate Real Estate • Financial Institutions • Government Investigations & Regulatory Counseling • Intellectual Property & Technology • International Trade • Litigation • Real Estate • Securities Regulation & Enforcement • Tax • Trusts & Estates

THE STATS

No. of attorneys: 628
No. of offices: 6
Summer associate offers: 88 out of 90 (2006)
Chairperson: Valerie Ford Jacob
Managing Partner: Justin Spendlove
Hiring Partners:
New York: David Hennes & Steven Steinman
Washington: Vasiliki Tsaganos & Michael Waldman

BASE SALARY (2007)

New York, NY; Washington, DC
1st year: $160,000
Summer associate: $3,100/week

UPPERS

• "Great clients, complex deals"
• Casual atmosphere
• "Excellent" pay, lock-step bonus

DOWNERS

• "Same as any elite firm—the hours"
• Opaque partnership process
• Uneven work distribution

NOTABLE PERKS

• Friday evening cocktail parties
• Paternity leave
• Moving expenses
• Subsidized health club membership

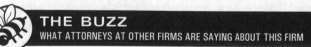

THE BUZZ
WHAT ATTORNEYS AT OTHER FIRMS ARE SAYING ABOUT THIS FIRM

• "The best real estate firm"
• "Vanilla"
• "Pro bono-minded"
• "Overworked"

© 2007 Vault Inc.

RANKING RECAP

Best in Region
#15 - Washington, DC
#18 - New York City

Best in Practice
#2 - Real Estate

Partner Prestige Rankings
#21 - Overall Prestige
#3 (tie) - Real Estate

Quality of Life
#17 - Pay

EMPLOYMENT CONTACTS

New York, NY
Robert O. Edwards, Esq.
Director of Legal Recruitment
Phone: (212) 859-8671
E-mail: robert.edwards@friedfrank.com

Washington, DC
Niki Kopsidas
Director of Legal Recruitment
Phone: (202)639-7286
Fax: (202) 639-7008
E-mail: niki.kopsidas@friedfrank.com

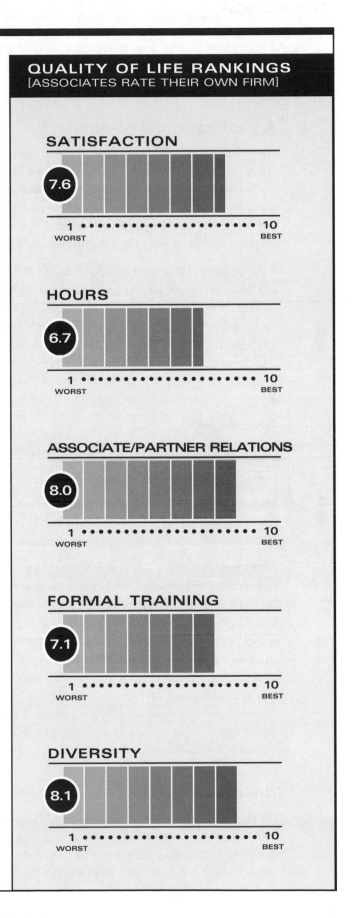

QUALITY OF LIFE RANKINGS
[ASSOCIATES RATE THEIR OWN FIRM]

SATISFACTION
7.6
1 WORST — 10 BEST

HOURS
6.7
1 WORST — 10 BEST

ASSOCIATE/PARTNER RELATIONS
8.0
1 WORST — 10 BEST

FORMAL TRAINING
7.1
1 WORST — 10 BEST

DIVERSITY
8.1
1 WORST — 10 BEST

Visit the Vault Law Channel, the complete online resource for law careers, featuring firm profiles, message boards, the Vault Law Job Board and more. **www.vault.com/law**

VAULT CAREER LIBRARY   297

THE SCOOP

The firm with the long name and the international footprint, Fried Frank continues to impose its will on the legal world. With only 628 lawyers, Fried Frank is smallish by some measures, but remains an international legal power that excels in corporate, tax, litigation and—especially—real estate work.

A century in the making

Fried Frank traces its history to the early 1900s firm of Riegelman & Bach; that firm became Riegelman Hess & Strasser, which eventually became Strasser Spiegelberg Fried and Frank. The firm opened its second office in Washington, D.C., in 1949 and took on its current name in 1971, one that includes Sam Harris, who had worked for the Securities and Exchange Commission during its start in the New Deal era of the 1930s and who also helped the United States prosecute war criminals in the Nuremberg trials in the 1940s and Sargent Shriver, a former U.S. ambassador to France who is also well known for directing the Peace Corps when it started in the early 1960s during President John F. Kennedy's administration.

With several periods of rapid growth, by the late 1990s Fried Frank represented nearly all of the major investment banking firms and broker/dealers, major accounting firms and major insurance companies in securities regulation, compliance and corporate governance matters and was involved in nearly every high-profile securities enforcement matter. The firm had also gained a reputation for having a significant transactional (M&A) business. International expansion has also been a key component of the firm's growth. Today Fried Frank has offices in each of the world's key strategic financial centers—New York, Washington, D.C., London, Paris and Frankfurt. In December 2006, the firm opened its Hong Kong office in association with Huen Wong & Co.

Cap-à-pied

All around the globe, Fried Frank keeps the corporate world spinning. On the M&A front, the firm has advised on some of the biggest and most newsworthy transactions including 2006's largest, the $89 billion merger of AT&T and Fried Frank client, BellSouth; as counsel to Mittal Steel Company NV in its $33 billion acquisition of Arcelor SA; as counsel to Merrill Lynch, the financial advisor to the consortium, in the $33 billion private equity acquisition of HCA Inc., announced in July 2006; and as counsel to NTL Incorporated (now Virgin Media) in the financing arrangements in connection with the $8.8 billion merger of NTL Incorporated and the Telewest group of companies.

Fried Frank also helped two private equity clients raise record-breaking funds, advising European-based private equity firm Permira when it launched its €11 billion investment fund, Permira IV, the largest ever raised by a European private equity fund, and Goldman Sachs Capital Partners in the formation of its $20 billion private equity fund, Goldman Sachs Capital Partners VI. Both funds continue to knock on Fried Frank's doors for transactional advice including Permira in the $17.6 billion leveraged buyout of Freescale Semiconductor, Inc. and Goldman Sachs Capital Partners in the $44 billion TXU leveraged buyout by a consortium of investors that included KKR, TPG and Goldman Sachs Capital Partners. The firm has been very active in the high-yield debt and equity/IPO markets for blue chip companies, leading private equity firms and investment banks. For example, the firm has done billions of dollars in financing for Procter & Gamble and its investment banks. And on the other end of the corporate spectrum, Fried Frank helped persuade a French bankruptcy court to accept a restructuring plan on behalf of Silver Point Capital, which set up a French subsidiary that acquired all of the assets of automotive parts maker CF Gomma Barre Thomas in a plan approved in July 2006.

The house that Fried Frank built

The House that Ruth built will give way to the House Built with Financing Arranged by Fried Frank. The firm represented the New York Yankees in the development and financing of a new Yankee stadium. The new park, which will sit right next door to the current Yankee Stadium, will be built with approximately $960 million in bonds arranged with Fried Frank's help. The deal was announced in August 2006; the new ballpark is scheduled to see its first pitch in 2009. The firm is also representing Forest

© 2007 Vault Inc.

City Ratner Cos. in its quest to bring the New Jersey Nets—and an eight-million-square-foot real estate project including retail space, office buildings and residences—to Brooklyn. The $4 billion deal was approved by the necessary state agencies in December 2006 and initial work has begun. The firm also is representing a venture consisting of Related Companies and Vornado in its Moynihan Station Project, which contemplates moving Madison Square Garden to the site of the current Farley Post Office in Midtown Manhattan and replacing it with a new Penn Station and some six million square feet of office, retail and residential space.

In other huge New York real estate news, Fried Frank represented Tishman Speyer Properties and private equity firm BlackRock Inc. in their purchase of Stuyvesant Town and Peter Cooper Village in Manhattan's Lower East Side. The two building complexes take up 80 acres near the East River and have approximately 11,000 apartments. Tishman Speyer and BlackRock bought the buildings for $5.4 billion in October 2006.

Court dates

Fried Frank lawyers also spend plenty of time in the courtroom. Fried Frank serves as counsel to the special litigation committee (SLC) of the board of directors of Computer Associates International, Inc., one of the country's leading software makers. The SLC was formed in February 2005 to investigate allegations made in federal and state derivative suits against certain of the company's current and former directors, officers and employees. The accusations relate to accounting fraud that occurred at the company from at least 1998 through 2002 which, to date, has resulted in the criminal convictions of eight of the company's senior executives. The SLC was also charged with investigating certain decisions of the board to settle previously filed securities and derivative lawsuits relating to the company's accounting practices. Following an intensive investigation led by a team of Fried Frank litigation partners, the SLC issued a 390-page report in April 2007, which was the subject of a front page article in *The Wall Street Journal.*

Also in April 2007, the U.S. Supreme Court handed down a unanimous decision in favor of Fried Frank client KSR International in KSR International Co. v. Teleflex Inc. The KSR decision overruled a longstanding Federal Circuit precedent interpreting the "non-obvious subject matter" condition for patentability, and has been called "the furthest reaching patent case in decades." Fried Frank litigation partner James Dabney handled the case from its inception, and argued it before the Supreme Court. The KSR argument was Dabney's second trip to the high court; he was also successful in a 2002 case.

Fried Frank also successfully represented Delta and Pine Land Company, a national agricultural-biotechnology company, in a variety of large litigation matters, from a multibillion-dollar claim for breach of a merger agreement, to antitrust and intellectual property disputes. In 2006, Fried Frank litigators, working in conjunction with the firm's antitrust and corporate practices, counseled DPL in its $1.5 billion acquisition by Monsanto Company, which also resolved significant litigation between the companies.

GETTING HIRED

The populist circle

Fried Frank "has lawyers from the elite schools and the not so elite. If you didn't attend a top law school, as long as you are in the top of your class and show that you have the work ethic and ability, you'll be able to do well. Many of the top lawyers in corporate aren't from the top law schools." Many report that "graduates from the top law schools are easily hired"—but as one Harvard grad muses, "My firm spent a long time trying to decide whether to hire me. I didn't feel like the firm was in any rush, even though I have decent credentials." One New York-based litigator offers, "The firm likes all the New York City schools and Boston schools, also Boalt." Unsurprisingly, in Washington, "The firm seems to recruit heavily at the D.C. law schools." Still, observes one midlevel, "Second-tier schools get recruited lightly, and your grades must be great, along with journal (preferably law review)." An antitrust lawyer in D.C. claims that "there is no specific GPA cutoff, but there are some on the recruiting committee that are very grade conscious. However, great work experience and great writing skills are definite pluses." With regard to the firm's international offices, a source in Frankfurt stresses that "good marks are important, but only as a starting

Visit the Vault Law Channel, the complete online resource for law careers, featuring firm profiles, message boards, the Vault Law Job Board and more. www.vault.com/law

VAULT CAREER LIBRARY   299

point. Almost all of the associates working here wrote a doctoral thesis and/or studied abroad (LLM degree)." One New York litigator assures you that "accomplishment/personality can make the difference, even if you didn't go to a 'name' school. The firm is not snobby in that way—it just wants good attorneys."

OUR SURVEY SAYS

No unpleasant surprises

"I feel very lucky to work at Fried Frank," one associate makes clear. "Despite the occasional long and unpredictable hours, the people I work with are consistently professional and courteous, and do the little things to show they appreciate and reward my hard work. Hearing 'thank you' and 'great job' makes all the difference to me." A first-year in New York is relieved that "there haven't been any unpleasant surprises," no screamers and no hours beyond the BigLaw usual. A colleague feels "lucky to be at such a friendly and hardworking firm. [There is] lots of work but a great bunch of people to work with," while a junior associate checks in with, "I become more satisfied the more experience I get." A source in the corporate department describes "days filled working alongside partners on cutting-edge deals," and insists that "the separation between partners and associates is perception, not reality (and thankfully so)." A corporate attorney in New York tries to see the whole picture, admitting that he "wish[es] we were better at setting up boundaries for clients, but it's great that we are so responsive."

We're gonna rock down to Eclectic Avenue

"The firm does not impose any culture of its own, other than 'be a good lawyer and treat each other with professional respect,'" asserts one source in the New York office. Associates rate the firm as surprisingly low key, "unstructured and laid-back. People socialize with one another and generally get along, but it is not forced." Some think the firm is "a bit clique-y by department," with certain practice groups being tighter than others; however, a Washington insider feels that while "the kids may socialize, the firm is clearly a study in [separation] between partners [and] everyone else." A litigator in New York notices that "most attorneys are independent and individualism is respected." A Washington source definitely agrees: "Despite being politically diverse, attorneys respect each other and enjoy each other's differences. This is not a cookie-cutter firm. There are a lot of different personalities and that makes it fun." Reminisces one lateral: "Upon settling in here, I was pleasantly surprised to discover that this Wall Street law firm was full of lively, approachable and rather colorful personalities. This is definitely not an environment where you have to check your individuality at the door. It's the eclectic mix of people, both at the partner and associate level, that makes this office a great place to work."

Just get the job done

"The one downside of a very dynamic, cutting-edge practice is that clients expect quick turnaround. There is no sense of hours here for the sake of hours, but the quantity of business and the fast-paced nature of the deals result in a large time commitment," explains one Fried Frank insider. A source in the corporate group acknowledges that "long and sometimes crazy hours are just part of the territory. Generally though, people don't care what hours you keep as long as you get the job done." "I would certainly like to spend fewer hours in the office," sighs one tax attorney, "but I doubt that any other comparable firm is much better in that department." For one Washington midlevel, "There are some weeks where I am not busy at all, followed by weeks where I am so busy that I can barely breathe." According to one New Yorker: "Firm policies seem pretty accommodating in general—but in practice, it seems to depend on department/practice group and the specific people you work with." Delineates one midlevel, "It's the difference between saying they are flexible and actually acting like they are, or that they care."

As far as planning a Paris rendezvous: "We work hard, but in five years I've not once had to cancel/alter vacation plans. I take all four weeks each year," says one source in the corporate group. Agrees a colleague, "People generally bend over backward to make sure that doesn't happen." In the experience of a D.C. associate, "Partners have allowed me to take vacation, attend family functions, go to doctor's appointments. I just have to make it known that I need to do those things and they respect my plans."

On the other hand, says a lower-level, "Every weekend that I want to go away has been a struggle, with partners never wanting to commit. Everything seems to be a last-minute decision."

Match point

One insider sleeps easy knowing that "Fried Frank always matches. No issues. You will always make the market salary, bonus and raises. Also, almost all associates get full bonuses, even the ones who bill 1,800 or sometimes even less." Co-workers agree, "The firm is careful and conscientious about maintaining competitive compensation levels." Even better, says one D.C. source, "Associates in the D.C. office make the same base salary as in our New York office." As for those in London, there is a "cost of living adjustment," which U.K. associates say "works out quite nicely." Don't forget, reminds a corporate attorney in New York, "The firm also should be credited for counting pro bono and certain other types of work that benefit the firm (e.g., helping establish a document database to help a particular practice group) as billable hours." "We make a lot of money. We had better, seeing as the nature of the beast is that we are at the beck and call of clients who can be very demanding seven days a week," points out one M&A specialist.

Regarding the lock-step bonuses, there are those who approve and those who feel somewhat cheated. One third-year writes, a bit naïvely, "The firm abides by a lock-step approach to compensation, which everyone seems to be comfortable with." Not so fast, mister, says an associate in the corporate practice—"Bonuses go to everyone in the firm. This sucks for people who normally bill more than anyone else." Still, he does concede that "you can't complain making this much money."

Great guys ... except for their secret cabal

"On an individual level, the vast majority of partners are great to work for and seem to appreciate the hard work that we do," reports one associate. A tax attorney in New York feels that "partners are generally quite nice and approachable, although there are certainly exceptions to every rule. There are some partners that I would genuinely consider to be my friends, which I think is rare among law firms." The firm does have its share of partners who "under stress and time pressure, do not show associates as much respect as they should," and "who feel that it is acceptable to demand that work be done on a timetable that is unrealistic." But what most bothers one insider is that "the partnership as a whole is very secretive about its decision-making processes."

Jacks and Jills

Even though "the chairperson of the firm is female," associates tell us that Fried Frank still "needs more women at partnership level." However, "sexual orientation is a nonissue here. The firm actively seeks to attract qualified openly gay/lesbian attorneys and is heavily involved in civil rights pro bono." Jokes one source, "Tim Hardaway wouldn't be welcome here."

Visit the Vault Law Channel, the complete online resource for law careers, featuring firm profiles, message boards, the Vault Law Job Board and more. **www.vault.com/law**

VAULT CAREER LIBRARY   301

30

PRESTIGE
RANKING

Ropes & Gray LLP

One International Place
Boston, MA 02110
Phone: (617) 951-7000
www.ropesgray.com

LOCATIONS

Boston, MA
New York, NY
Palo Alto, CA
San Francisco, CA
Washington, DC

MAJOR DEPARTMENTS & PRACTICES

Antitrust • Bankruptcy & Business Restructuring •
Corporate • Fish & Neave Intellectual Property Group •
Government Relations & Regulatory • Health Care •
International • Labor & Employment • Investment
Management • Litigation • Private Client Group • Private
Equity • Tax & Benefits

THE STATS

No. of attorneys: 750+
No. of offices: 5
Summer associate offers: 131 out of 131 (2006)
Chairman: R. Bradford Malt
Managing Partner: John T. Montgomery
Hiring Partner: Susan M. Galli

BASE SALARY (2007)

All offices
1st year: $160,000
Summer associate: $3,100/week

UPPERS

• Excellent training
• Culture that doesn't tolerate "screamers"
• Diversity efforts showing results

DOWNERS

• Increasing pressure to bill, bill, bill
• "Challenging" part-time track
• Uncertain culture after mergers, lateral hires

NOTABLE PERKS

• Investment fund for junior associates
• Generous technology budget
• On-site cafeteria (some offices)
• Bar and moving expenses

THE BUZZ
WHAT ATTORNEYS AT OTHER FIRMS ARE SAYING ABOUT THIS FIRM

• "Boston powerhouse"
• "Bluebloods"
• "Elite, humane"
• "Pompous"

© 2007 Vault Inc.

RANKING RECAP

Best in Region
#1 - Boston

Best in Practice
#9 - Intellectual Property

Quality of Life
#3 - Formal Training
#5 - Pay
#15 - Selectivity
#20 - Best Firms to Work For

EMPLOYMENT CONTACT

Ms. Katharine von Mehren
Director of Legal Recruiting
Phone: (617) 951-7660
Fax: (617) 235 7690
E-mail: katharine.vonmehren@ropesgray.com

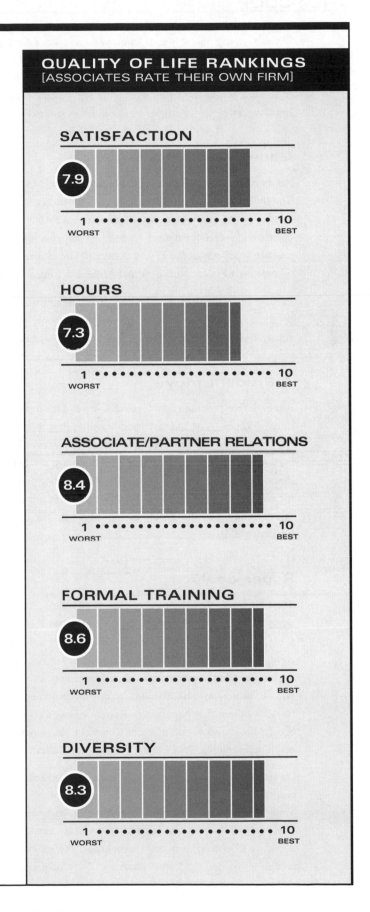

QUALITY OF LIFE RANKINGS
[ASSOCIATES RATE THEIR OWN FIRM]

SATISFACTION
7.9
1 WORST — 10 BEST

HOURS
7.3
1 WORST — 10 BEST

ASSOCIATE/PARTNER RELATIONS
8.4
1 WORST — 10 BEST

FORMAL TRAINING
8.6
1 WORST — 10 BEST

DIVERSITY
8.3
1 WORST — 10 BEST

Visit the Vault Law Channel, the complete online resource for law careers, featuring firm profiles, message boards, the Vault Law Job Board and more. **www.vault.com/law**

VAULT CAREER LIBRARY

303

THE SCOOP

If you're doing business in Boston, you know Ropes & Gray LLP. The firm is a Boston institution that's been serving Boston-area business since 1865 and is especially known for its corporate work, though a recent merger has made it an intellectual property power, too. All told, Ropes & Gray has about 800 lawyers in five offices around the country, plus a "conference center" in London where the firm meets with international clients. The firm is planning on opening an office in Tokyo in fall 2007, initially staffed with partners and associates from existing firm offices.

Gone fishin'

Ropes & Gray is no Johnny-come-lately to the legal scene, but the firm has only recently stepped up into the national limelight. The old-name firm relied on a 21st century merger to raise its profile. In January 2005, after a long courtship, Ropes & Gray merged with New York-based IP powerhouse Fish & Neave, which counted Thomas Edison and the Wright Brothers as early clients. The combined firm operates as Ropes & Gray ("Gray Fish" would have been cooler), but the intellectual property practice is known as the Fish & Neave IP Group (catchy). Despite some early bumps (including an unsuccessful lawsuit filed by departing Fish & Neave partners), the new Ropes & Gray appears to have integrated Fish & Neave well.

In early 2007, the firm consolidated all redundant offices in New York, making Ropes & Gray a leaner IP-law machine. The new combined office covers six floors and 250,000 square feet at 1211 Avenue of the Americas, with an option to take another 150,000 square feet in the same building, should the firm further expand.

A Prudent move

Ropes & Gray announced its intended lease of the top floors of Prudential Tower, to begin fall of 2010. It will certainly be a big move—Ropes is the fourth-largest tenant in Boston, and their share of the "Pru'" (as it is affectionately known) will amount to more than 400,000 square feet (just barely under seven football fields). Only a handful of potential tenants are looking for spaces even a quarter of this size, and some Boston real estate mavens suspect that Prudential Tower is cutting Ropes an excellent deal in order to attract their business. The new location is in notoriously expensive Back Bay, where commercial rent can easily go for $60 to $75 a square foot. Though the Pru' is not without its own bragging rights—it was the recipient of the 2006 BOMA "Best Building of the Year" Award. But until the deal and the Pru' is ready, Ropes will remain in the financial district at International Place.

Ropes deals

The new Ropes & Gray machine keeps on rolling, and bringing new engagements along with it. In November 2006, the firm advised Audax Group on its acquisition of TriMark USA, a food services equipment supplier, for an undisclosed amount. That same month, the firm also advised MassMutual Capital Partners LLC and Cerberus Capital Management when the two private equity firms purchased a stake in Scottish Re Group. MassMutual and Cerberus ponied up $300 million each for their stake in the insurer. On the other side of the private equity coin, Ropes & Gray advised three private equity firms—Bain Capital, Thomas H. Lee Partners, and Blackstone Group—which owned publishing house Houghton Mifflin in its sale to Irish publisher Riverdeep for $3.4 billion that November. Ropes & Gray also is representing Thomas H. Lee Partners and Bain Capital Partners in the $26.7 billion acquisition of Clear Channel Communications, the nation's largest radio company with more than 1,100 stations, and is representing Bain Capital Partners and Catterton Partners in their $3.2 billion acquisition of OSI Restaurant Partners.

On the litigation side, Ropes & Gray represented several U.K.- and European-based insurance companies in a lawsuit filed by real estate developer Larry Silverstein regarding the September 11 terrorist attacks. Silverstein, who held the lease on the World Trade Center, claimed that the destruction of the complex was two separate incidents, which would entitle him to two payments. The insurers claimed that the attack should be considered a single incident for insurance purposes, and a trial court agreed in 2004. A federal appeals court upheld that verdict in October 2006, and the firm is now litigating the same issue against the complex's owner, the Port Authority of New York and New Jersey. A month later, in November, Ropes & Gray won a court

© 2007 Vault Inc.

victory for client Massachusetts Eye and Ear Infirmary (MEEI), which claimed that Canadian pharmaceutical company QLT was unjustly enriched and committed unfair business practices in connection with its use of work by MEEI researchers to develop a treatment for macular degeneration. A federal jury sitting in Boston awarded MEEI three percent of worldwide sales of the drug Visudyne®, which amounted to $2.2 billion at the time of the November verdict. The jury also awarded MEEI attorney's fees.

Ropes & Gray is currently representing The TJX Companies (operator of well-known off-price store chains T.J. Maxx, Marshalls, HomeGoods and A.J. Wright) in litigations and regulatory investigations stemming from the much-publicized criminal intrusions into, and thefts of customer transaction data from TJX's computer system. As of May 2007, the litigations included upwards of 20 class actions filed in the U.S. and Canada on behalf of customers and credit card issuers claiming to have suffered injuries by reason of the intrusions, and the regulatory investigations encompassed proceedings initiated in the U.S. by the Federal Trade Commission and 36 separate state attorneys generals as well as proceedings initiated by a variety of regulatory authorities in Canada, the United Kingdom and the Republic of Ireland.

The firm also is currently representing the audit committee of Forrester Research, Inc. in connection with an internal investigation into the granting of stock options, principally during the period 1997 through 2003. The investigation is ongoing.

Welcome to Ropes & Gray

The firm is taking steps to strengthen some key practices. In June 2006, former Jones Day partner Jesse Witten joined Ropes & Gray and will act as a litigation partner specializing in health care. The firm also welcomed Geoffrey Leonard and Scott Elliott to its San Francisco office. Leonard and Elliott, who had been at Orrick, Herrington & Sutcliffe, joined Ropes & Gray's corporate practice in June 2006. That same month, Daniel Hirsch joined Ropes & Gray's investment management group as a partner in the Washington, D.C., office and Michael McGovern joined as a partner in the firm's litigation practice in New York. Hirsch had been at Deutsche Asset Management, and had previously spent 16 years at the SEC. McGovern had previously spent seven years in the U.S. attorney's office for the Southern District of New York. In July 2006, William Kim joined Ropes & Gray's New York office as a partner in the firm's international group.

In February and March 2007, three former K&L Gates partners joined Ropes & Gray in New York: Richard Marshall joined the investment management and securities litigation groups; Robert Borzone joined the investment management group; and Eva Carman joined the securities litigation and government enforcement groups. In April 2007, former Heller Ehrman partner Harry Rubin joined Ropes & Gray as a partner in the Fish & Neave Intellectual Property Group in New York, with a focus on transactional matters. In June 2007, former Chadbourne & Parke partner Jerome Katz joined Ropes & Gray's New York office as a partner in the commercial and business litigation group.

GETTING HIRED

Be on your best behavior

"Ropes & Gray looks for candidates who are intelligent, curious and engaging. I think it says a lot about our culture that the firm places importance on whether a candidate is socially engaging, as well as intellectual," reports an insider. "To my knowledge, the firm has no specific [GPA] cutoffs and we are currently looking to expand the schools at which we concentrate our recruiting efforts," adds a colleague. "More than anything, the firm looks for motivated, interesting and interested people who can bring a lot of energy, curiosity and drive to their job." A source reports that "typical candidates getting offers are on a journal, have grades in the top 10 to 15 percent of [their] class, and had a strong undergrad record." Grades don't lessen much in importance for lateral hires. "The firm remains focused on your GPA and transcript even as you move up in years," warns a source.

It's vital to impress everyone you meet, and "candidates should not slack off at lunch or with a junior associate." That's because the firm has a "lengthy and extensive one-day interview process with lawyers [of] all levels interviewing candidates, so the decision to hire the candidate is really a firm decision." "Ropes & Gray really cares about both grades and fit, so they will scrutinize your transcript and have you meet with what feels like a million people before they give you an offer," says a lawyer.

Visit the Vault Law Channel, the complete online resource for law careers, featuring firm profiles, message boards, the Vault Law Job Board and more. www.vault.com/law

VAULT CAREER LIBRARY   305

"The firm makes you interview with a huge number of lawyers to ensure you're a good personality fit—arrogant or obnoxious folks need not apply," cautions an insider.

OUR SURVEY SAYS

Ropes is the place

With a few caveats, associates say Ropes & Gray is the place in Boston to practice law—and it's pretty good elsewhere, too. "High-quality work, capable and friendly colleagues, and interesting legal issues make Ropes & Gray stand out," says a senior associate. "The people are great—exactly the people you'd want to spend long hours with if you had to (and in New York, you have to)," shares a Big Apple lawyer. "I never thought I'd say this, but I am really loving my job," says a D.C. lawyer who swears "I'm pretty sure I didn't drink the Kool-Aid." That insider continues, "I just enjoy the kind of work that I'm doing and the core group of people that I work with. Associates are also paid an obscene amount of money and despite working long hours, they're not nearly as long as big New York-firm hours." "I love my job," gushes a lawyer from the main Boston office. "My assignments are varied and challenging. There is some amount of typical first-year grunt work, like closing documents, but also high-level analysis. When partners ask you to do research, they truly care about and value your opinion."

A few gripes pop up. "The schedule is a bit unpredictable for my taste," says a second-year. "I have partners calling me and reserving my time, which means I'm not busy but I will be. It's very unnerving." "I feel that I am always treated with respect, but that I have very little ability to direct the course of my career in terms of emphasizing the skills I want to develop," complains a litigator. Some feel increased hours pressure. "On the whole, Ropes is pretty good as far as big firms go," states an insider. "But they are putting a lot more pressure on hours (including sending out detailed monthly reports and projections) than they did in the past, which increases the general sense of angst and stress among associates." "I'm not always thrilled with the way work assignments are handed out," says a junior associate who gripes that "the centralized system doesn't always work as it should."

No screamers allowed

Thankfully, Ropes & Gray is "not an 'eat-what-you-kill' business model, so the lawyers work together well and have a 'we're-all-in-this-together' attitude which makes for a better work environment." "This is not a firm filled with screamers," says a source. "There is no yelling in the hallways or behind closed doors." Everyone is in on the love-fest. "People are respectful to each other, no matter what you are, lawyers, secretaries, or support staff," observes a lawyer. "This is a very nice firm where you are appreciated for the work you do and treated like a human being." "Although people work hard, it does get acknowledged and people say 'thank you' and tell you when you do a good job," notes a senior associate. "On the flip side, some lawyers can be a bit passive-aggressive." Ropes & Gray associates don't know how good they have it. Let this Boston lawyer tell you. "From my experience dealing with peer firms, it strikes me that the atmosphere here is much better than at other firms—people actually crack jokes here and feel they can have a sense of humor while still producing top-notch work product," reports that contact. Another attorney describes the firm as "respectful, if somewhat staid. You will always be treated as a human being." Some insiders sense that change is in the air. "I would say that the firm's culture is evolving somewhat as it grows with many recent lateral hires and mergers, which is not consistent with prior history," says a worried lawyer. "It is unclear the extent to which Ropes & Gray will be able to maintain its collegial work atmosphere and academic feeling as it integrates firms recently acquired and lateral partner hires."

Side-by-side

Things are getting hectic at Ropes & Gray. "They work you hard. They work you New York hard," says a Boston lawyer. "The hours are long—especially recently, as the firm's clients have been especially busy," notes a lawyer. But at least that source isn't working alone. "The interesting thing on deals I've been on is that partners will often be working side-by-side with associates late at night." Some feel the bottom line is looming larger than ever: "There has definitely been an increased emphasis on billable hours in the past few years, particularly in light of the billable rate increases," reports an insider. Currently, "1,900 billable (client

© 2007 Vault Inc.

or pro bono) hours" are the hours target. "That requires somewhere in the neighborhood of 2,300 hours at work, just to satisfy … That is a lot." Virtually no one is happy about the new system. "Increased pressure on hours this year has caused general grumbling," observes a contact. "They have instituted a 'target' for the first time ever, which has really changed the culture around hours and how people think about staffing." The firm is applying pressure subtly, which doesn't cushion the blow. "With the increase in associate pay in 2007 came the first ever monthly e-mail indicating hours worked" by the individual associate (not a firmwide posting; individual attorneys are only informed of their own hours, not their peers' hours), which "could open the door to becoming like the model of the New York law firm" where "posting hours so every associate knows their status only generates unnecessary competition and pressure."

Meet the market

Some associates are pretty pleased with their compensation. "We meet the New York market," says a lawyer from that office. "Bonus is the market on average but you may be paid significantly more based on your performance review and billables." "Base compensation is the same as other large New York firms," reports another New Yorker, who adds that, "Bonuses historically have been generous as well." Bonuses can be a source of complaint. "Everyone gets a bonus [and] you get more if you bill more," says a senior associate. "However, you will not get more even if your work is very good unless you are also billing a lot. It's really the hours that are determinative rather than merit." Ropes & Gray does make up for it in other ways. An attorney reports, "The firm provides a [benefit] in which $10,000 is invested by the firm each year on behalf of each associate," in a firm-sponsored investment partnership created to invest and co-invest with the firm's clients.

An abundance of training

You won't lack for training at Ropes & Gray. "The firm is almost obsessed with training, and there are opportunities all over the place," reports a source. "The training opportunities here are amazing, both in terms of formal training and the informal training we receive on a daily basis from the partners we work with," gushes a first-year. "Our pro bono policies allow on-the-job training," observes another junior associate. "I am lead counsel on several pro bono matters." It's not just litigators who get lucky. "The firm has excellent formal training programs for every type of law and specialty practiced at the firm," says a contact. "There is ongoing training not just for the junior associates, but also for midlevel and senior associates."

Making strides

Sources say Ropes & Gray "seems to be great on hiring and promotion" of female associates. "Like a lot of large firms, we don't seem able to retain many of the great women. The maternity leave policy is generous and they have on-site backup day care if your regular day care falls through. Still, the firm is losing too many good women associates and partners." The firm's efforts include "a Women's Forum, which discusses female issues, a part-time committee, and a rather generous six-month maternity leave policy." The best thing might be the one-on-one between partners and associates. "I work primarily with young female partners. They have been great mentors to me," reports a female lawyer. "Ropes & Gray is welcoming to minorities, but it is nonetheless a rather homogenous place," observes a source. "However, the firm is getting more diverse among the younger associates." Another insider agrees, stating that "it seems the firm has done a good job in recent years of hiring more minorities at the firm."

Visit the Vault Law Channel, the complete online resource for law careers, featuring firm profiles, message boards, the Vault Law Job Board and more. www.vault.com/law

VAULT CAREER LIBRARY   307

Paul, Hastings, Janofsky & Walker LLP

Park Avenue Tower
75 E. 55th Street
First Floor
New York, NY 10022
Phone: (212) 318-6000
Fax: (212) 319-4090
www.paulhastings.com

LOCATIONS

Atlanta, GA • Chicago, IL • Los Angeles, CA • New York,
NY • Orange County, CA, Palo Alto, CA • San Diego, CA •
San Francisco, CA • Stamford, CT • Washington, DC •
Beijing • Brussels • Hong Kong • London • Milan • Paris •
Shanghai • Tokyo

MAJOR DEPARTMENTS & PRACTICES

Capital Markets/Securities • Employment Law • ERISA •
FARGO (Finance and Restructuring Group) • Global Projects
• Intellectual Property • Internal Investigations •
International Arbitration & Dispute Resolution • Investment
Management • Mergers & Acquisitions • Private Equity •
Product Liability & Toxic Tort • Real Estate • Securities
Litigation • Tax • White Collar

THE STATS

No. of attorneys: 1,200
No. of offices: 18
Summer associate offers: 118 out of 121 (2006)
Firm Chair: Seth Zachary
Managing Partner: Greg M. Nitzkowski
Hiring Partner: Leigh Ryan

BASE SALARY (2007)

**Orange County, Los Angeles, Palo Alto, San Francisco,
San Diego, CA; Chicago, IL; Stamford, CT; New York,
NY; Washington, DC**
1st year: $160,000
Summer associate: $3,070/week

Atlanta, GA
1st year: $130,000
Summer associate: $2,500/week

UPPERS

• "Terrific client contact"
• "Great partners"
• "Work is cutting edge"

DOWNERS

• "Path to partnership is lengthy and unclear"
• "You are always aware of your billable hours"
• "Poor administrative support"

NOTABLE PERKS

• Subsidized gym memberships
• Cappuccinos and latte bar
• Attorney referral bonus
• Free parking

THE BUZZ
WHAT ATTORNEYS AT OTHER FIRMS ARE SAYING ABOUT THIS FIRM

• "Excellent reputation, huge bonuses"
• "One-trick pony"
• "Great pro bono"
• "You'll never see daylight"

© 2007 Vault Inc.

RANKING RECAP

Best in Region

#6 - Atlanta

#10 - Southern California

Best in Practice

#3 - Labor & Employment

#6 - Real Estate

Partner Prestige Rankings

#1 - Labor & Employment

#2 - Real Estate

Quality of Life

#7 - Informal Training/Mentoring

#11 (tie) - Overall Satisfaction

#19 - Best Firms to Work For

EMPLOYMENT CONTACT

Mr. Demetrius Greer

Director of Attorney Recruiting

Phone: (213) 683-6000

E-mail: recruit@paulhastings.com

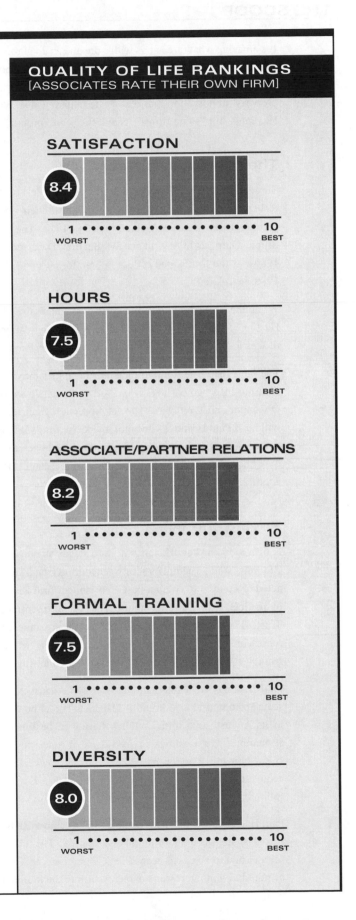

QUALITY OF LIFE RANKINGS
[ASSOCIATES RATE THEIR OWN FIRM]

SATISFACTION

8.4

1 WORST — 10 BEST

HOURS

7.5

1 WORST — 10 BEST

ASSOCIATE/PARTNER RELATIONS

8.2

1 WORST — 10 BEST

FORMAL TRAINING

7.5

1 WORST — 10 BEST

DIVERSITY

8.0

1 WORST — 10 BEST

Visit the Vault Law Channel, the complete online resource for law careers, featuring firm profiles, message boards, the Vault Law Job Board and more. www.vault.com/law

VAULT CAREER LIBRARY   309

THE SCOOP

It's amazing what three guys with a dream can do. From a three-man partnership founded in Los Angeles in 1951, Paul, Hastings, Janofsky & Walker LLP is now an international legal powerhouse, with 1,100 attorneys in 18 offices around the world. Though renowned for its employment practice, Paul Hastings is a full-service law firm featuring corporate, litigation, intellectual property, immigration and real estate departments. While that might be enough for some firms to rest on their laurels, Paul Hastings isn't "some firms." New offices are sprouting up at Paul Hastings, and existing ones are growing at a furious rate.

The three law-kateers

Three Harvard Law School graduates gathered in Los Angeles with a vision—or, at least, a partnership agreement. Lee Paul, Robert Hastings and Leonard Janofsky began their small practice in November 1951, and watched it grow. The fourth name partner, tax law Charles Walker, joined in 1962. The firm ventured outside of Los Angeles in 1974, opening an Orange County office. Outposts in Atlanta and Washington, D.C., soon followed (in 1980). More East Coast expansion came about in the early 1980s, as the firm added offices in Stamford, Conn., (1983), and New York (1986). The first international office popped up in 1988, in Tokyo.

While the firm's growth in the 1980s was impressive, the early part of the turn of the millennium has dwarfed that spree. Paul Hastings merged with Chinese law shop Koo and Partners in 2002, adding offices in Hong Kong and Beijing. The firm opened offices in San Diego and Shanghai the next year, Paris and Brussels in 2004, and Palo Alto and Milan in 2005.

The most recent addition to the Paul Hastings family is the Chicago office, opened in November 2006. To staff this office, the firm poached two partners from Midwest giant Jones Day: Steve Catlett (who clerked for Supreme Court Justice Sandra Day O'Connor and Whitewater special prosecutor Kenneth Starr when Starr was on the Court of Appeals) and Rick Chesley (who will head Paul Hastings Chicago) joined the firm's Windy City outpost at its founding. Paul Hastings expects the Chicago office to boost the firm's bankruptcy practice and hopes to grow to 50 lawyers. The firm reportedly has plans for Europe, too. Chairman Seth Zachary told *The Lawyer* that Paul Hastings intends to boost its presence in London, where the firm now has approximately 40 lawyers, to 100 within two years.

Paying the bills

A firm as big as Paul Hastings needs a steady stream of deals to keep up the growth. In July 2006, the firm represented Applied Biosystems in its acquisition of Agencourt Personal Genomics. The deal was worth $120 million. Also that July, Paul Hastings acted as counsel to Atlanta-based investment firm River Capital in its purchase of Signature Designs International, an importer of artificial flower arrangements. The firm also represented Lexington Corporate Properties Trust in its sale to Newkirk Realty Trust. The $4.6 billion union of real estate investment trusts closed that July. Staying in the real estate market, Paul Hastings represented New York hedge fund Marathon Asset Management in its $2.1 billion purchase of Reckson Associates Realty Corp. from SL Green Realty Corp. That deal closed in August 2006.

Paul Hastings went international later that August, representing the U.S. and U.K. divisions of First Title Insurance in a debt securitization deal in Germany. The cross-border transaction was worth €5.2 billion. The firm represented Crystal River Capital in its August 2006 initial public offering. The financial services firm raised $162 million with Paul Hastings' help. That September, Paul Hastings advised Bank of America on its role in arranging for $1.75 billion in credit and debt financing for a U.K. company. London-based Paul Hastings lawyers represented Addax Petroleum Corp. in financing issues related to Addax's acquisition of certain subsidiaries of Pan-Ocean Energy Corp. The deal, worth $1.6 billion, closed in September 2006. The following October, the firm advised Softbank Corp. when the Japanese tech company completed a $625 million bond offering.

Paul Hastings kept the deals coming. In December 2006, the firm represented international investment bank UBS and Indonesian bank Danareksa on a $1 billion bond offering. The firm also advised Bear Stearns when the bank raised $265 million in financing for a casino to be based near Philadelphia. Later that month, the firm represented Tokyo Electric Power Co. when the company acquired a joint interest in an energy firm in the Philippines. That deal was worth $3.4 billion.

© 2007 Vault Inc.

Employable on employment

Paul Hastings' internationally-acclaimed employment law department again was named "Global Labour & Employment Law Firm of the Year" by *Who's Who of Business Lawyers* in 2007 and is filled with top names in the practice whose work and writings have shaped the law. During the past two years alone, the department has defended more than 150 multi-plaintiff employment claims. The team has represented the world's largest employers in financial services, technology, telecommunications and nearly every industry. In Chand v. Target Corp., the firm blocked class certification in a case involving more than 3,000 Target Executive Team Leaders throughout the State of California. The employees had alleged that they had been misclassified as exempt and denied required overtime compensation, meal periods and rest breaks, and other compensation. While a prior law firm was defending a case against Remedy, one of the largest temporary help employers, the court certified a class of 200,000 and denied summary judgment in a case involving the compensability of prehire training time. Paul Hastings persuaded the court to allow a new summary judgment motion and won total summary judgment. In a major appellate victory, Paul Hastings won a reversal on appeal of a $13 million retaliation judgment against Storage Technology Corporation, a subsidiary of Sun Microsystems. Paul Hastings wrote amicus briefs for the United States Chamber of Commerce articulating the winning theories in Ledbetter v. Goodyear Tire and Rubber, and AARP v. EEOC, Supreme Court and appellate victories for employers.

Court dates

The firm's litigation department has scored a few big wins for clients recently. In a landmark securities litigation case, the U.S. Supreme Court ruled in favor of the firm's client Dura Pharmaceuticals—a decision that marked a significant legal victory for publicly held companies. Paul Hastings successfully argued that a securities fraud claim must specifically include allegations of a direct link between a fall in the company's stock price and the alleged fraud or misrepresentation. The suit was dismissed on two previous occasions in California federal district court. The Ninth Circuit Court of Appeal reversed, setting the stage for the Supreme Court arguments a subsequent ruling.

Ride the wave

Paul Hastings scored a victory for another of its clients, pharmaceutical company Eisai Co., in November 2006. Rival Teva Pharmaceuticals USA filed a suit claiming Eisai is infringing on Teva's patents. A federal judge dismissed Teva's summary judgment motion in November, winning temporary reprieve for Eisai. The suit is still pending. The firm won another battle on behalf of PrediWave Corp. that November. Sanctions were dismissed against PrediWave and its CEO in a lawsuit filed by Chinese corporation New World Group, which claimed that PrediWave failed to deliver certain video-on-demand technology as promised by contract. PrediWave admitted it did breach the contract, but disputed New World's claims that it was part of an effort to defraud the company. A California judge agreed, dismissing a claim for sanctions against PrediWave. Hearings on issues of compensatory damages for the breach are pending.

GETTING HIRED

Offers? Neither often nor easy

Paul Hastings does not hand out offers freely. As one midlevel litigator describes the firm's hiring program, "We have become increasingly demanding while maintaining our priorities." Or, as a senior corporate attorney puts it, "The firm has pretty high standards and hires some great kids out of school." One insider calls hiring "very competitive." She adds, "[We] are extremely selective when giving call-back offers."

So what exactly is Paul Hastings looking for? A senior labor lawyer advises, "The firm likes candidates from top-tier law schools. A junior litigator says, "The first step is tough because the standards are high. The next step is tough because it's a close-knit group and 'fit' matters." As for specific cutoffs, one insider reports, "Each school has a different GPA cutoff. They

Visit the Vault Law Channel, the complete online resource for law careers, featuring firm profiles, message boards, the Vault Law Job Board and more. www.vault.com/law

VAULT CAREER LIBRARY   311

more or less match the *US News* rankings. Top-five schools, we'll take the top half of the class, six to 15 we'll take the top third. For 15 to 50, you'd better be in the top-10 percent. If you're below that, you'd better be top five in your class." As for personality and "fit" characteristics, a New York tax attorney suggests that it "depends on need and department, but general thresholds apply—school pedigree, grades, personality, eagerness to work hard, maturity, professionalism, good attitude."

OUR SURVEY SAYS

Super-satisfied associates

Paul Hastings associates say that they wouldn't work anywhere else. "I am very pleased with the quality and quantity of substantive work given to junior associates," reports a junior New York litigator. "First- and second-year associates are not simply relegated to document review. We are also very strongly encouraged to do pro bono work for which we are given full billable credit. Thus, the firm truly puts its money where its mouth is." A D.C. litigator commends the "great opportunities for training and professional growth." A junior environmental specialist advises, "Within weeks of starting, I found myself in court, responding to clients directly and even coordinating team efforts for a large, ongoing compliance project. Moreover, my experience has not been unique. Very early on, several of my peers worked directly with clients." And a midlevel litigator makes it near-unanimous, adding, "The questions I am asked to resolve are more often than not very interesting."

Friendly from N.Y. to S.F. to D.C.

As far as firm culture, associates find it "friendly," "respectful" and "very laid-back." A D.C. associate reports, "There is a strong feeling of camaraderie among the associates. The firm sponsors a lot of events for associates only, which is great. The partners in the corporate department are excellent, with informal socializing as well as professional mentoring." A real estate specialist says, "Associates in my group socialize together all the time—e.g., going to lunch and drinks after work. It's a very collegial environment." Another Big Apple attorney says, "People are generally cooperative and friendly. Partners and senior associates are surprisingly respectful, amicable and engaging, considering the pressure everyone is under to perform." And a San Francisco litigator adds, "Some people go out, and some don't. There's fun to be had if you want it, but no one is pushing."

Three cheers for the bosses?

Paul Hastings's associates call the individual attorneys "fantastic," though they voice many of the usual concerns vis-à-vis feeling left out of firmwide decision making. "There are good relations between associates and partners," says a young associate. "However, despite involvement of associates in firm committees, my perception is that associates have little role in shaping firmwide decisions." On the other hand, another insider reports, "Partners are very respectful of associates and the firm has an unprecedented level of disclosure to associates about firm finances. Associates at all levels work directly with partners in a collegial manner." A litigator says, "Some are aloof while others are friendly. All are busy, so there's not a lot of interaction. However, seeking out a partner in your area of interest, for work or advice, is always well received." Another litigator adds, "Big firm decisions (such as opening a new office) definitely happen at the upper level, but associate-related decisions (like retreat planning) are oftentimes discussed with associates."

Fairly fantastic formal training

The firm's formal training offerings far outclass those of the typical major law firm, according to Paul Hastings's associates. "The firm has outstanding formal training that includes a weeklong orientation usually held in California for all first-year associate worldwide," says a junior litigator. "It is a great introduction to the firm, provides practical advice and allows first-years from all the Paul Hastings offices, whether in the United States, Europe or Asia, to meet and establish important relationships." A senior litigator appreciates the "excellent training programs that combine both in-house as well as external programs. Trial lawyers are exposed to the NITA programs for motion practice, depositions and trial advocacy at appropriate levels in their careers, which are great opportunities." A second-year adds, "We seem to have all the standard programs of a big

© 2007 Vault Inc.

law firm—new-hire training, midlevel associate training, etc. We're working on a new mentoring and orientation program that spreads this training out over several weeks rather than cramming it into just a few days. This program shows a lot of promise. The firm also seems to be very supportive of attorneys who want to attend outside training as well." One less-impressed midlevel litigator calls the training "fairly standard." He adds, "We do as well as any other firm."

Ripe for the plucking

Associates say that a good mentor won't magically appear at your desk at Paul Hastings, but that one can be found with a little footwork. As one litigator reports, "Informal training is on a case-by-case basis depending on how much the associate seeks out a mentor or group of mentors. If you are proactive, you'll receive all the mentoring you want." A real estate expert advises, "Except in the busiest of times, informal training is common. We have a formalized 'buddy' system for first-year associates to help their transition to full-time work in a law firm." An S.F. litigator adds, "Everyone—and I mean everyone—is helpful and collegial. You may prefer being trained by associates, but the partners are there if you need them." Another S.F. trial attorney adds, "Every associate is assigned a mentor, which mostly consists of taking associates to lunch or dinner from time to time and providing an opportunity to seek advice or air grievances. Beyond that, informal training and mentoring is very organic."

Complaint-free compensation

The firm gets very high marks for its compensation plan (though there is more than a little confusion about how the bonus system works). Says one typical associate, "The firm pays market rates plus generous merit-based bonuses, which brings our total compensation well above market. Our bonuses are not simply based on billable hours, but also reflect the quality of our legal work, our pro bono efforts, recruiting efforts, community involvement and other contributions we may make to the firm." A midlevel attorney adds, "We meet 'market' salaries and the bonuses are on par with peer law firms. Nice thing about bonuses is that even though you need to be close to the budgeted 2,000 hours, hours are stressed to not be the driving force behind bonus allocations." However, another insider reports the opposite scenario "Base salary is astronomical. From what I understand, the bonus system fails to differentiate those who go above and beyond from those who just meet requirements. I have no economic complaints, but this incentive system seems to be off," he says. The closest you'll hear to a bona fide complaint about pay Paul Hastings sounds something like this: "Compensation is pretty static across big firms, and we're neither a trendsetter nor below the average."

Even the hours score all A's

Associates call the firm's hours-requirements extremely reasonable—see, for example, the firm's "unlimited-vacation" plan. "The firm is very flexible—we have unlimited vacation days and can work from home. You just need to get your work done and meet your hours," is how one first year explains it. A midlevel litigator reports, "Face time is not an issue here. Everyone knows the minimum billable requirement—how and when you achieve that is up to you." And a real estate specialist adds, "The hours are pretty good—the 'budget' is 2,000 hours per year. So long as you meet your budget, you may take as much vacation as you'd like. Also, the firm has its first part-time partner this past year."

Visit the Vault Law Channel, the complete online resource for law careers, featuring firm profiles, message boards, the Vault Law Job Board and more. **www.vault.com/law**

VAULT CAREER LIBRARY

313

32
PRESTIGE RANKING

Willkie Farr & Gallagher LLP

787 Seventh Avenue
New York, NY 10019
Phone: (212) 728-8000
www.willkie.com

LOCATIONS

New York, NY (HQ)
Washington, DC
Brussels
Frankfurt
London
Milan
Paris
Rome

MAJOR DEPARTMENTS & PRACTICES

Asset Management • Business Reorganization &
Restructuring • Corporate & Financial Services •
Environmental • Executive Compensation & Employee
Benefits • Government Relations • Intellectual
Property/Patent Litigation • Litigation • Private Clients • Real
Estate • Tax • Telecommunications

THE STATS

No. of attorneys: 600
No. of offices: 8
Summer associate offers: 47 out of 47 (2006)
Hiring Partners:
　New York, NY: David Boston, John Longmire, Rosalind
　　Kruse, Loretta Ippolito, Terence McLaughlin
　Washington, DC: Robert Meyer

BASE SALARY (2007)

New York, NY
1st year: $160,000
2nd year: $170,000
3rd year: $185,000
4th year: $210,000
5th year: $230,000
6th year: $250,000
7th year: $265,000
8th year: $280,000
Summer associate: $3,080/week

UPPERS

• A true no-minimum billables policy
• Collegial culture
• Early responsibility

DOWNERS

• Uneven assignment system
• Occasional tough hours
• Support services haven't kept up with firm growth

NOTABLE PERKS

• $1,000 client entertainment budget
• Free gym
• Bar and moving expenses
• Attorney lounge (featuring bagels, cookies)

THE BUZZ
WHAT ATTORNEYS AT OTHER FIRMS ARE SAYING ABOUT THIS FIRM

• "Good firm and great work environment"
• "Overlawyering"
• "Excellent real estate, prestige IP"
• "Fratty"

© 2007 Vault Inc.

RANKING RECAPS

Best in Region
#15 - New York City

Best in Practice
#10 - Bankruptcy/Creditors' Rights

Partner Prestige Rankings
#3 (tie) - Real Estate

Quality of Life
#12 - Pay

EMPLOYMENT CONTACTS

New York, NY
Ms. Bonnie Hurry
Chief Legal Personnel Officer
Phone: (212) 728-8495
E-mail: bhurry@willkie.com

Washington, DC
Ms. Gail P. McGinley
Manager, Legal Personnel and Recruiting
Phone: (202) 303-1305
Fax: (202) 303-2000
E-mail: gmcginley@willkie.com

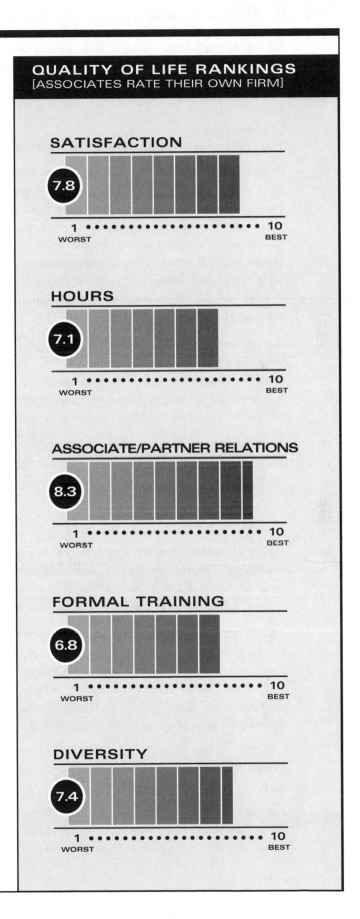

QUALITY OF LIFE RANKINGS
[ASSOCIATES RATE THEIR OWN FIRM]

SATISFACTION
7.8
1 WORST — 10 BEST

HOURS
7.1
1 WORST — 10 BEST

ASSOCIATE/PARTNER RELATIONS
8.3
1 WORST — 10 BEST

FORMAL TRAINING
6.8
1 WORST — 10 BEST

DIVERSITY
7.4
1 WORST — 10 BEST

Visit the Vault Law Channel, the complete online resource for law careers, featuring firm profiles, message boards, the Vault Law Job Board and more. **www.vault.com/law**

VAULT CAREER LIBRARY   **315**

THE SCOOP

Willkie Farr & Gallagher has all the history you could ask for, and then some. The firm's clients have included former presidents (or at least their brokerage firms), inventors and industrial titans. Willkie's attorneys have included presidential candidates, Supreme Court justices and governors. The firm has approximately 600 lawyers in eight offices—two in the United States, six in Europe. Willkie is a full-service firm, advising clients on corporate, litigation, intellectual property, real estate and tax matters.

Hurry up and change that name

Willkie's oldest ancestor is Hornblower & Byrne, a firm founded in New York with four attorneys in 1888. The founding partner, William Hornblower, was a political ally of Grover Cleveland. In 1893, Cleveland, starting his second term as president, nominated Hornblower to the Supreme Court. Hornblower's candidacy was rejected—not due to any deficiency of his, but due to a dispute between President Cleveland and an influential senator who was able to derail the nomination. Hornblower would have to settle for arguing cases before the high court, which he did until his appointment to New York's highest court in 1914. Unfortunately, Hornblower passed away soon after, leaving behind a firm that had gone through several name changes and represented such clients as New York Life Insurance, Grant & Ward (a brokerage firm partly owned by former President Ulysses S. Grant) and Thomas Edison. The firm also added as associates Charles Evans Hughes and Felix Frankfurter, both of whom eventually became Supreme Court justices.

After Hornblower's death, the firm he left behind kept charging on, adding Lindley Garrison, former Secretary of War under President Woodrow Wilson, as a partner in 1916. But the firm's second great leader, Wendell L. Willkie, joined up in 1940 after losing the presidential election. Willkie's name shot to the top of the masthead, and he soon earned his keep, representing the movie industry in a congressional investigation into communist infiltration into the business. The firm also picked up new sports law clients such as baseball's National League and the National Football League.

Willkie took on its current moniker in 1968, and began expanding overseas in 1971, opening an office in Paris. A Washington, D.C., outpost came in 1971, London in 1988, and Milan, Rome and Frankfurt offices opened in 2000 with Brussels following in 2002.

RICO suave

Willkie's litigation department was recently victorious in an industrywide insurance antitrust and RICO case for longtime client Marsh & McClennan. On April 15, 2007, the U.S. District Court for the District of New Jersey dismissed all claims against insurance broker and insurance carrier defendants, including Marsh, the world's largest insurance broker, in the Multidistrict Class Action Litigation arising out of the New York Attorney General's investigation of the insurance industry.

Un Rico más: The firm represented the Puerto Rico Aqueduct and Sewer Authority (PRASA) against civil charges brought by the Environmental Protection Agency, which sought $200 million in penalties. Willkie negotiated that sum down to a comparatively paltry $1 million, though PRASA did commit to spending $1.7 billion to upgrading sewage facilities all over Puerto Rico. The settlement was announced in June 2006. The firm also represented Third Point LLC in a settlement of a proxy contest with one of its investments, Nabi Biopharmaceuticals. As part of the agreement, reached that November, two-thirds of the board members proposed by Third Point were approved and the board agreed to seek alternatives to Nabi's current strategies.

Men behaving not as badly as was previously thought

Wal-Mart is also pleased with Willkie's recent work. In August 2006, the firm won dismissal of racketeering claims in a civil suit filed by undocumented workers. The plaintiffs claimed that Wal-Mart, who employed cleaners through independent contractors, violated immigration, money-laundering and involuntary servitude laws. However, a federal judge dismissed those claims, though others remain in the pending suit.

© 2007 Vault Inc.

Willkie's litigation group includes a thriving white collar practice. Willkie attorney Benito Romano, former United States attorney for the Southern District of New York., is currently keeping a team of Willkie lawyers busy defending criminal charges against Peter Atkinson, the former vice president and general counsel of Hollinger International, who is being tried with Conrad Black for allegedly defrauding the company.

Dealing with Willkie

Allied World Assurance Co. is flush with cash thanks, in part, to Willkie. Allied, a Bermuda-based insurance company, turned to Willkie for legal advice when it completed a $500 million debt offering and a $300 million stock offering in the summer of 2006. The firm also advised GateHouse Media when the newspaper company completed a public stock offering in July. That deal raised $200 million. That August, the firm advised private equity shop Insight Venture Partners when it purchased a stake in eCommerce Industries, a business software developer. Willkie also advised Warburg Pincus when the private equity firm was one of several that participated in a leveraged buyout of Aramark Corp. for $8.3 billion, also in August 2006.

In other acquisition news, Willkie advised Monsanto Company on its purchase of Delta and Pine Land, which produces cotton seed. The deal, worth $1.5 billion, was announced in August 2006. The firm's Paris office advised Compagnie Generale de Geophysique in the French company's acquisition of Veritas DGC for $3.1 billion that September. Later that month, Willkie advised Ventas, Inc., on a deal to acquire 67 health care and senior-living properties from a family-owned business in Canada in a deal worth $649 million.

Hey, sports fans

Willkie advised a special transaction committee appointed by Cablevision's board of directors to examine a proposal by the Dolan family to take the company private. The Dolans are part-owners of Cablevision, as well as the New York Knicks and New York Rangers. In October 2006, they proposed a $19.2 billion leveraged buyout of the corporation. Willkie is advising the special committee, which will determine whether the deal is fair to Cablevision's shareholders. In addition, the firm is presenting The Topps Company, Inc., the iconic maker of baseball cards, its is sale to a group led by Michael Eisner's The Tornante Company LLC. Finally, the firm advised Macklowe Properties when it submitted a $4.6 billion bid (along with co-investor Carl Icahn) to purchase Reckson Associates Realty Corp., a New York-based commercial real estate developer.

GETTING HIRED

Got it all? Willkie wants you

There's a pretty simple road map to getting hired at Willkie. "Be smart. Be industrious. Be nice. Be hired," says one insider. The firm can afford to want it all in candidates. "We see tons of resumes every year, and we have to turn down some really outstanding candidates," reports a junior associate. So what exactly does the firm want? "Willkie looks for smart lawyers with personalities who are willing to work hard," states a contact. "To work at Willkie, you need to have a great resume and some personality [and] outside interests (which are often times not compatible traits)," notes a New Yorker. "The firm seems to prefer the down-to-earth all-arounder with street smarts and a strong work ethic to the entitled trust-funder with contacts at the club," offers a source.

"Grade expectations are high, but even people with straight As will get rejected if their personality seems like a bad fit," observes a senior associate. "Willkie is a social firm and looks for social people," notes another attorney. "Wallflowers and people who are going to hide in their office all day need not apply." Bombing one exam isn't going to kill your chances. "Hiring is always competitive and you have to have good grades, but we look for good people, so amazing personality and potential may overcome that one bad grade," says a contact. An insider says that "while grades/school are important factors, one's personality and a willingness to work hard and well with others is equally, if not more, important in hiring decisions." Don't give up if you didn't do your 2L summer at Willkie—reportedly the firm is "open to hiring 3Ls who didn't summer here."

Visit the Vault Law Channel, the complete online resource for law careers, featuring firm profiles, message boards, the Vault Law Job Board and more. **www.vault.com/law**

VΛULT CAREER LIBRARY   **317**

OUR SURVEY SAYS

Willkie's great, but ...

For the most part, Willkie's associates can't stop singing the firm's praises. "I think this is a great place to work," says one junior associate who finds that the firm offers "great partners to work for, great associates to work with." Less effusive associates at least concede that things at Willkie are as good as it's ever going to get at a law firm. "The life of an associate is going to suck wherever one might be," muses one first-year. "I like to think, however, that we at Willkie have it somewhat better than those at other firms. No minimum billables requirement hanging over our heads, and a friendly group of people means happier associates (but still associates)." "Although first-year associate work can be tedious at times (regardless of which firm you work for), I am happy with the law firm choice I made and with the career I am pursuing here," agrees a New York associate. "I am convinced that no large firm would provide me with greater job satisfaction than Willkie," states an attorney. "At the same time, corporate litigation is inherently boring, no matter how high profile the work. Sadly, a high-paying job cannot be entirely fulfilling. That's why it pays so well."

Getting the work you want seems to be the key to enjoying the Willkie experience. "I have been provided with a broad array of assignments in various fields that have given me the opportunity to learn about all aspects of litigation," reports one source. "The partners and associates with whom I work are very interested in teaching and working closely with those around them." "The work is incredibly stimulating, and Willkie is always willing to give you as much responsibility as you can handle," notes a junior associate. Not all agree. "Much of the work can be classified as 'grunt work,' especially at the junior levels," complains a midlevel. "Assignments and opportunities tend to be handed out very unevenly," complains another insider. "Too much depends on which partner happens to like you."

The mellow firm

Don't expect a pressure cooker. "I find Willkie to be a casual, welcoming and mellow place to work," reveals one attorney. Willkie's professional culture is exceptional," brags another source. "We are presented with opportunities to do top-notch work throughout the United States and the rest of the world. Individuals at all levels, from the most senior partner to the most junior associate, work together as a team and create a very open and friendly atmosphere in which to learn and develop skills." Willkie's hiring policies go a long way toward developing the culture. "The firm facilitates friendships by emphasizing social events and through a policy of hiring 'normal' people," reports a first-year. The result is that "the firm's culture is one of its best qualities," according to D.C. lawyer. "The firm has a very pleasant, collegial culture," agrees a New York attorney. "People are remarkably polite to one another." And the firm is trying to get even better. "We are developing a new mentoring program to enhance the associate experience by providing confidential, regular meetings between partners and junior associates, which has been a great success," states a contact. "The firm seems very committed to the professional growth and happiness of its associates."

No floor at Willkie

Among law firms, Willkie is unique. "I never believe any firm when they say there is no minimum requirement or that they don't judge you by your hours, but both statements are actually true of Willkie," exclaims a source. "There is no minimum billable hours requirement at the firm, but attorneys on all levels still work hard," notes a senior associate. "Our inventory is, in a sense, time, so the hours are never going to be great." "The hours are much more flexible than other big firms," says one junior associate. All told, the firm's system keeps hours manageable. "Naturally, people gunning for partner work harder than the rest of us," concedes a lawyer. "There are no billable hours requirements, and the assigning system is such that you ask for more work when you have time available, but there is little pressure to ask for more work outside of your own conscience." Things are sometimes unpredictable, but again, the firm does its best to help out. "The ebb and flow of work are hard to predict, making personal planning a challenge," says a contact. "The leave policy is generous, and we are encouraged to use our vacation time. In addition, with the use of laptops and BlackBerries, it can be relatively easy to work from home when necessary."

© 2007 Vault Inc.

Market rates; how long can the market last?

Law firms are just throwing cash at associates, and Willkie is tossing greenbacks as fast as all the others. "Our compensation matches the market, no more, no less. 'Twas always thus and thus 'twill always be." OK, Shakespeare. One (less poetic) associate says the compensation is "as good as everyone else, not a penny more, not a penny less." Associates can put their pay in perspective. "When I'm a second-year associate who'll make more this year than the Chief Justice of the U.S. Supreme Court, I can't complain," says a source. D.C. associates get a windfall of sorts. "A major plus of working at Willkie's D.C. office, compared with other D.C. firms, is that the firm pays the same salaries and bonuses for New York and D.C. associates," reports a lawyer from that office. Another plus: "bonuses are never tied to billable hours, which is what makes the 'no minimum billable requirement' a real policy," says a source. There are those who wonder how long the manna from heaven can last. "I am delighted with my salary, but sometimes I worry about how long the big firms can sustain the billing rates necessary to paying high associate salaries," frets a midlevel. "I've already seen some smaller clients blanch or swallow hard when they hear the estimated cost of a particular set of legal services."

Getting better at making you better

What once was a weakness is now turning into a strength at Willkie. Though associates once thought the firm thin in training, sources now say that the firm has "greatly improved in recent years with the addition of a director of professional development that came from the senior associate ranks." Willkie now has "excellent in-house training seminars and access to external training as well." "The formal program has improved substantially over the past 18 months," concurs a lawyer. "I think there are a lot more opportunities for formal training now than there has been in the past," states a source. "The firm is now making a more concerted effort to inform associates of these opportunities within and outside the firm, which is a good development." There's still room for improvement, though. "[We] could definitely use more formal training, especially when it comes to learning things in a highly specialized field of law, like telecom," notes a lawyer who practices in that area. "We've got some great partners who know a lot of stuff—it would be great if we could formalize the knowledge transfer, so to speak." Some partners seems to be stepping up to the plate. "The mentoring program is good and partners tend to act as informal mentors," says an associate.

Doing its best

It's a familiar refrain at today's BigLaw: Willkie tries to attract and retain a diverse associate pool, but stumbles on occasion. The firm "has tried to be welcoming to minorities and provide support through mentoring and other programs, but has not been that effective in promotion of minorities," according to one attorney. Luckily, Willkie "recognizes the issue is important in recruiting and retention, and has a committee (with large associate representation) to work on the issue." Willkie does have some retention issues for female lawyers. "The firm has a good number of female attorneys at the junior level. Those numbers diminish markedly in the partnership ranks," reports a source. "The firm is actively working to improve in this area." One recent initiative is "a Women's Professional Development Committee devoted to women's issues." In addition, 25 percent of the partners made in the firm's headquarters this year were women.

Visit the Vault Law Channel, the complete online resource for law careers, featuring firm profiles, message boards, the Vault Law Job Board and more. **www.vault.com/law**

VAULT CAREER LIBRARY   319

Akin Gump Strauss Hauer & Feld LLP

Robert S. Strauss Building
1333 New Hampshire Avenue, NW
Washington, DC 20036-1564
Phone: (202) 887-4000
www.akingump.com

LOCATIONS

Austin, TX • Dallas, TX • Houston, TX • Los Angeles, CA •
New York, NY • Philadelphia, PA • San Antonio, TX • San
Francisco, CA • Silicon Valley, CA • Washington, DC •
Beijing • Dubai • London • Moscow • Taipei

MAJOR DEPARTMENTS & PRACTICES

Antitrust • Communications & Information Technology •
Corporate & Securities • Corporate Governance • ERISA •
Energy Transactions • Environment & Land Use • Financial
Restructuring • Global Projects • Government Contracts •
Health Industry • Intellectual Property • International Trade •
Investment Funds/Private Equity • Labor & Employment •
Litigation • Policy & Regulation • Real Estate & Finance •
Russia/CIS • Tax

THE STATS

No. of attorneys: 950
No. of offices: 15
Summer associate offers: 76 out of 81 (2006)
Chairman: R. Bruce McLean
Firmwide Hiring Partner: Dennis M. Race

BASE SALARY (2007)

New York, NY; Washington, DC; all California offices
1st year: $160,000
2nd year: $170,000
3rd year: $185,000
4th year: $210,000
5th year: $230,000
6th year: $250,000
7th year: $265,000
8th year: $280,000
Summer associate: $3,077/week

UPPERS

• "Real" work for junior associates
• "Reasonable" hours (relatively)
• "Top-of-the-market" pay

DOWNERS

• Typically tough BigLaw hours
• Lack of integration/communication between practice
  groups and different offices
• "A few bad apple partners"

NOTABLE PERKS

• Wellness program
• Weekly open bar happy hour
• "There is always free food—always"
• "Great New York office (with a new one to come!)"

THE BUZZ
WHAT ATTORNEYS AT OTHER FIRMS ARE SAYING ABOUT THIS FIRM

• "Great appellate team; great international practice"
• "Strong in market but not great national reach"
• "Lifestyle-oriented; great for associates"
• "Overrated"

© 2007 Vault Inc.

RANKING RECAP

Best in Region

#6 - Texas

#14 - Washington, DC

Best in Practice

#4 - Bankruptcy/Creditors' Rights

#9 - Labor & Employment

EMPLOYMENT CONTACT

Ms. Marybeth W. Jarrard

Director of Attorney Recruiting

Phone: (202) 887-4000

Fax: (202) 887-4288

E-mail: mjarrard@akingump.com

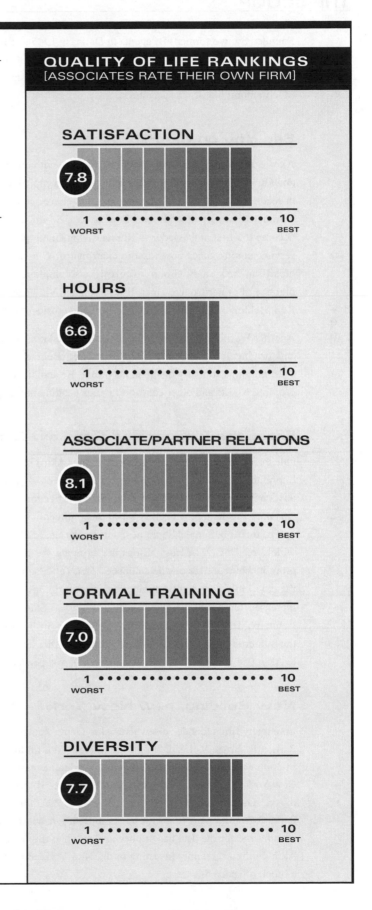

QUALITY OF LIFE RANKINGS
[ASSOCIATES RATE THEIR OWN FIRM]

SATISFACTION

7.8

1 WORST — 10 BEST

HOURS

6.6

1 WORST — 10 BEST

ASSOCIATE/PARTNER RELATIONS

8.1

1 WORST — 10 BEST

FORMAL TRAINING

7.0

1 WORST — 10 BEST

DIVERSITY

7.7

1 WORST — 10 BEST

Visit the Vault Law Channel, the complete online resource for law careers, featuring firm profiles, message boards, the Vault Law Job Board and more. **www.vault.com/law**

VAULT CAREER LIBRARY   **321**

THE SCOOP

Founded by two former FBI agents in Dallas in 1945, the firm now known as Akin Gump Strauss Hauer & Feld quickly became one of the first major postwar, international law firms. Coming in 25th on the NLJ 250 with 939 lawyers, Akin Gump is not just big in size, it is also big in practice—with energy, investment funds/private equity, bankruptcy, white collar criminal defense and M&A among the firm's specialties.

See You on the Hill

Akin Gump offers a general corporate practice, with outposts that now extend from Houston and Washington, D.C., to Moscow and Dubai. With its largest office in the nation's capital, the firm has found itself well represented in the halls of political power in recent years as senior Akin Gump partners have served presidents from both sides of the aisle. President George H. W. Bush nominated name-partner Robert Strauss as U.S. ambassador to the Soviet Union and then, after its collapse, selected him to become the first ambassador to Russia. Akin Gump partner Vernon Jordan counseled (and golfed with) President Bill Clinton, serving among other posts as the chairman of Clinton's transition team and more recently as a member of James Baker's bipartisan Iraq Study Group. The firm also employs many people making the transition from government office to private practice. Former Congressmen Bill Paxon and Vic Fazio, House Speaker Tom Foley, Senator Lauch Faircloth, RNC Chairman Ken Mehlman and HHS Secretary (and GOP presidential hopeful) Tommy Thompson all hang their hats at Akin Gump.

Another Washington insider gracing the halls of Akin Gump is Sandy Kress, former senior adviser to the second President Bush, and driving force behind the No Child Left Behind initiatives. Kress now works out of Akin Gump's Austin office, but Washington is still very much on his mind. He and his team lave been lobbying on behalf of the U.S. Chamber of Commerce to promote NCLB and other education issues pending in Congress.

Enter the Blogger and Con Law Guru

One major new attorney score this year helped Akin Gump improved its cred in two very different venues: the staid, time-honored Supreme Court and that hip, irreverent interweb. Thomas Goldstein, who "rocked the rarified world of Supreme Court advocacy," decided to leave his three-man practice to work from "a bigger platform" and promptly was named by *National Law Journal* in its list of the country's 100 most influential lawyers. What was he doing previously? Arguing 17 cases (and winning half of them) before the Supreme Court by the age of 35, certainly, but what Goldstein is most famous for is having launched the widely read *SCOTUSblog*. Blogs are bringing the power back to the people by providing a cheap way to disseminate and promote content over a wide audience. *SCOTUSblog* in particular covers any and everything Supreme Court related. Gone are the days Goldstein spent combing lower court rulings for split decisions in order to drum up clients; his impact on the field has increased tenfold as he landed teaching gigs at Stanford and Harvard law schools, and his case credits include Georgia v. Randolph, IBP Inc. v. Alvarez and the infamous Bush v. Gore. No longer the little guy in a big courtroom, Goldstein now heads the Supreme Court practice at Akin Gump, a smaller division of the appellate and litigation departments. Goldstein was followed to Akin Gump by his longtime mentor, con law superstar Larry Tribe from Harvard, who serves as a consultant to the firm.

New Building, new New York

Like many firms founded elsewhere, Akin Gump wants very much to be relevant in New York because, in the words of Managing Partner R. Bruce McLean, "Firms are in New York for the same reason John Dillinger robbed banks: that's where the money is." In 2006 we reported that Akin Gump planned to increase its New York lawyer count by at least 10 percent. As of June 2007, the New York office now houses 168, up 11 percent. If this sort of growth becomes a trend, Akin Gump will be ready to make the move. The firm recently leased six floors and 203,000 square feet in the new Bank of America Tower going up at One Bryant Park. When it opens (the firm hopes in 2008), it will be New York's most environmentally advanced office tower. While the bottom line for the deal has not been released, asking rents in the building are reported to be in excess of $100 per square foot. Akin Gump is certainly investing in the New York branch; according to the Co-Star Group, that's the highest rent ever paid for a block of space this large.

© 2007 Vault Inc.

Beijing's the thing

Akin Gump celebrated the New Year by going overseas. A brand new Beijing office just opened its doors in December 2006, joining the Taipei office (established in 2005) in representing the firm's interests on the Pacific Rim. Akin Gump has already had success in the Far East even without a permanent presence. Bob Strauss negotiated America's first trade agreement with China in 1977, when he was President Carter's special trade representative, and he escorted Deng Xiaoping on the Chinese leader's tour of the United States. Thirty years later, China has huge potential for enterprising international practices in areas from finance and trade to energy—and who knows energy better than Texas? Eliot Cutler, a partner whose practices include public law and policy and energy, heads the Beijing office.

Many middle-market mergers

Financially, Akin Gump has a top-notch command of the middle market. For 2006, the firm completed 46 middle-market M&A transactions, demonstrating an impressive success rate in aggressively closing deals which led to its recognition as "Law Firm of the Year" by *The M&A Advisor*. Akin Gump recently added 15 experienced attorneys to the group, which counts among its notable deals advising Clear Channel in its $19 billion buyout by a private equity consortium and Anadarko Petroleum in its twin $23.5 billion acquisitions of Kerr-McGee and Western Gas. Akin Gump's financial restructuring practice also continues to soar. The group was involved in four of the ten largest bankruptcy filings and three of the five-largest emergences in 2006, including Delta Air Lines' restructuring; the airline emerged from bankruptcy in April 2007.

C'mon, Share the Wealth

The litigation practice scored big with a $153 million win for Hexion Specialty Chemicals in a case involving theft of trade secrets (the jury verdict was among the 10-largest defense wins of the year) and a patent litigation win for Samsung involving DRAM technology. The firm's negotiation of the $468 million settlement in the Spartanburg v. Hillenbrand class-action lawsuit was notable not just because it was one of the largest antitrust settlements in history, but because Akin Gump shared its enormous attorney's fee with every employee of the firm.

Going pro

As far as the wider community goes, Akin Gump has always encouraged associates and partners alike to volunteer their services. Their official commitment has only deepened with the addition of Steven H. Schulman, who joined the firm in 2006 as its very first full-time pro bono partner. Schulman was previously in charge of pro bono at Latham & Watkins, and was instrumental in developing that firm's program into the largest pro bono practice in the world. Notable recognitions for Akin Gump include the Frank W. Newton Award (given to the firm by the State Bar of Texas for its assistance in providing legal advice to victims of Hurricanes Katrina and Rita); two NLADA awards: the 2007 Beacon of Justice Award and the 2006 Exemplar Award (for litigation partner Mark MacDougall's pro bono trial representation of indigent defendants facing the death penalty); and the 2005 Law Firm of the Year Award (presented by the Dallas Volunteer Attorney Program).

In autumn of 2006, Akin Gump won an important victory in an ongoing pro bono case on behalf of Steven Dewitt, who was released in 2004 after more than 13 years in prison, having been wrongly convicted of murder. His exoneration was the first under D.C.'s 2001 Innocence Protection Act. In October, a district judge ruled that Dewitt may proceed with a lawsuit against the District of Columbia and five former D.C. Metropolitan Police detectives. This will be the first time a case brought under the 26-year-old Unjust Imprisonment Act will move past the "motion to dismiss" stage.

Visit the Vault Law Channel, the complete online resource for law careers, featuring firm profiles, message boards, the Vault Law Job Board and more. **www.vault.com/law**

VAULT CAREER LIBRARY   **323**

GETTING HIRED

Good grades, great schools

Akin Gump's hiring attorneys look for candidates with good grades from great law schools, according to associates. New York sources tell us the office recruits from "a handful of schools"—Harvard, New York University, Columbia, Virginia, Michigan, Georgetown, Penn, UVA, Boalt Hall, Stanford, UT and Fordham. "From Harvard, Columbia or NYU you need an A-/B+ average, but you can have one or two B's (a B- will probably knock you out). From other top schools, you need A/A- grades and law review." As a New York tax attorney puts it, "They seem to be putting more emphasis on grades and schools, but I was an average student at a top-five school and had no problem getting hired." According to Akin Gump, the firm "looks at law school grades but also looks at other indicia of excellence as well as diversity."

Another New Yorker adds, "This firm loves the Ivies, but hires others as well." In California, "It can be tough because the L.A. office can be snooty. As a lateral, you need to come from a good firm and good law school. I don't think there is a GPA cutoff. The schools we focus on for recruiting are NYU, Columbia, Boalt, UCLA, USC and Loyola," reports one leftcoaster.

Of course, Akin Gump also emphasizes fit. As one associate describes it, "I think the firm is looking for a really smart candidate, one who is willing to work hard, but one that will also 'fit' into the culture of the firm, meaning the person has to be a team player." Or, as a midlevel adds, "The firm tends to focus on GPA for initial interviews, but once a summer associate is hired the most important factors for receiving an offer are to possess rudimentary social skills, and to be able to write well." A colleague notes, "Once you're in the summer program, though, the permanent offer is only yours to lose."

OUR SURVEY SAYS

Most associates can get satisfaction

Akin Gump associates generally rate their job satisfaction quite highly. One of the biggest reasons, they report, is the quality of the work. "Good work and good people," crows a first-year. "I'm learning a lot." A junior litigator reveals, "Akin Gump's New York litigation practice is a wonderful place to work. The cases are interesting, the responsibilities are high even at junior levels, and the people are fantastic." A first-year adds, "The experience you are given matches your ability, not an artificial hierarchy based on when you graduated law school. Akin Gump provides its young attorneys with amazing experience, far beyond that provided at other firms, and the training needed to succeed in these experiences. First-years aren't stuck doing document review 24/7; document review goes to staff attorneys and leaves associates largely free to take more active roles in their cases."

Associates call the vibe at Akin Gump "friendly," "social," "collegial" and "anti-stodgy." A junior tax attorney reports that support trickles down from the top. "We have a very collegial atmosphere in our department and attorneys frequently visit one another's offices to solicit advice," she says. "As a first-year, I have found my senior colleagues to be approachable and encouraging. The other important aspect of our firm's culture, in the New York office at least, is an entrepreneurial sentiment that I believe comes from having so many young partners—I think of it as the anti-stodgy element." A New York litigator advises, "The lawyers are friendly—many people have gone out of their way to mentor me and just to check in to see how I am doing. Also, Akin recently held a conference in D.C. for all female attorneys worldwide. I like that the women leaders in the firm are willing to take time out to mentor junior associates." Another junior litigator adds, "Associates are friendly and routinely socialize outside of the office." Or, as a midlevel New Yorker puts it, "The firm, and especially the New York litigation section, is very collegial. It is a tight-knit group, in which everyone has a stake in everyone else's practice. The partners very obviously care about the associates. The group tends to attract sociable people—it is not a great place for the less social, or people with high opinions of themselves. Gunners need not apply."

© 2007 Vault Inc.

"Firmwide" decisions means associates too

One of Akin Gump's greatest strengths, its associates profess, is its associate/partner relations. As one first-year puts it, "I have found the partners to be very supportive. Many have gone out of their way to mentor me and teach me. Several partners in litigation are great to work with because they work with you and teach you at the same time. People care that you get a variety of experiences (white collar, criminal, depositions, client time, etc.), and will definitely offer tips and advice freely." A junior litigator says that the firm even includes associates in its firmwide decisions, a true rarity at major law firms. "Partners treat associates very well-giving associates a large amount of responsibility and allowing associates to be part of the firm's decision making at all levels," she attests. That said, at least one litigator sorta-complains, "Some partners are a little too cool for school, but most are down-to-earth, friendly and very approachable."

Formal training, shmormal training

Akin associates report that the firm has decent formal training if you're into that kind of thing. "There are many training classes offered to cover every imaginable topic," reports a junior litigator. "The firm also gets PLI memberships for all of its attorneys." Another litigator adds, "The advocacy training program for litigation, bankruptcy and labor associates is fantastic." However, other priorities often take precedence at Akin Gump. As one associate puts it, "A lot of training is offered—there is just not always time to take advantage of it." Another associate complains, "We have a lot of useless seminars in conference rooms regarding depositions, etc., and very little realistic experience to work through the abstract ideas."

Associates give the firm's informal training stellar grades. "The partners and other associates have gone out of their way to informally mentor me," says a junior attorney. "This ranges from discussions at social events to formal feedback and includes people stopping by my office to chat. I feel comfortable stopping by others' offices with random questions." A litigator adds, "I have been extremely impressed with the mentoring in my department. The partners are making an investment in our first-year class and have really dedicated time to encourage our development." And this final review makes it unanimous: "Informal training is fantastic from most partners—they take time to explain things and follow through on projects."

Not so crazy

Associates say that, while Akin Gump is still a top-notch firm, the hours really aren't as crazy as you might think. "The hours for litigation seem to be an ebb and flow," says a junior New Yorker. "If you are going to trial, you work a lot; if you are not, you work less. People are flexible about personal commitments, community activities and other similar activities." A Big Apple litigator reports that Akin Gump "is flexible with hours, and the firm gives merit bonuses (on top of market bonuses) to those whose work product and workload is high." Another litigator adds, "I work a lot—all attorneys do, but I do not need to do my work in the office. I often work at home and get to work later in the day or whenever I feel like it. No pressure for face time here."

Visit the Vault Law Channel, the complete online resource for law careers, featuring firm profiles, message boards, the Vault Law Job Board and more. **www.vault.com/law**

VAULT CAREER LIBRARY

325

34

Winston & Strawn LLP

35 West Wacker Drive
Chicago, IL 60601
Phone: (312) 558-5600
www.winston.com

LOCATIONS

Chicago, IL (HQ)
Los Angeles, CA
New York, NY
San Francisco, CA
Washington, DC
Geneva
London
Moscow
Paris

MAJOR DEPARTMENTS & PRACTICES

Appellate & Critical Motions • Corporate & Financial •
Employee Benefits & Executive Compensation • Energy •
Environmental • Government Regulations & Regulatory
Affairs • Health Care • Inellectual Property • International
Arbitration • Labor & Employmen • Litigation • Maritime &
Admirality • Real Estate • Restructuring & Insolvency • Tax
• Trusts & Estates

THE STATS

No. of attorneys: 985
No. of offices: 9
Summer associate offers: 68 out of 68 (2006)
Managing Partner: Thomas P. Fitzgerald
Hiring Partners: Julie A. Bauer & Stephen V. D'Amore

BASE SALARY (2007)

1st year: $160,000
Summer associate: Based on first-year salary

UPPERS

• Famously associate-friendly culture
• Abundance of training
• Humane hours

DOWNERS

• "Firm is cheap"
• Opaque bonus system
• Increasing emphasis on billables

NOTABLE PERKS

• Free Starbucks coffee
• Attorney dining room (Chicago)
• Firm-sponsored Friday happy hours
• Moving expenses

THE BUZZ
WHAT ATTORNEYS AT OTHER FIRMS ARE SAYING ABOUT THIS FIRM

• "Prestigious and a decent work culture"
• "George Ryan trial was a drain"
• "Quality of life is wonderful"
• "Very conservative"

© 2007 Vault Inc.

RANKING RECAP

Best in Region
#5 - Chicago

Best in Practice
#10 - Labor & Employment

Quality of Life
#3 - Office Space

EMPLOYMENT CONTACTS

Julie A. Bauer, Esq.
Hiring Committee Co-Chair
E-mail: jbauer@winston.com

Stephen V. D'Amore
Hiring Committee Co-Chair
E-mail: sdamore@winston.com

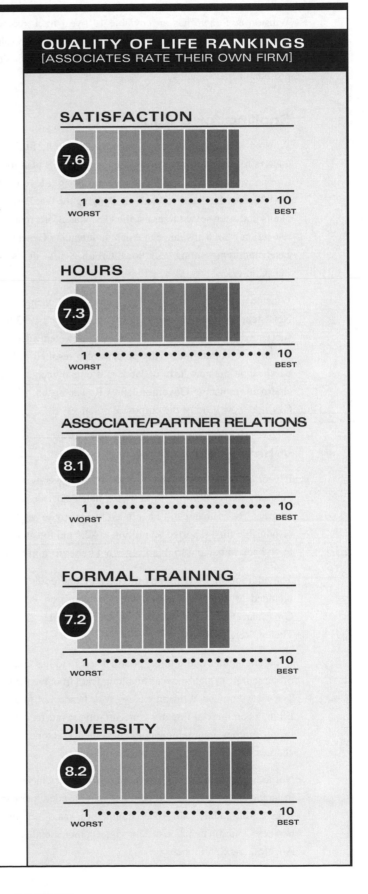

QUALITY OF LIFE RANKINGS
[ASSOCIATES RATE THEIR OWN FIRM]

SATISFACTION
7.6
1 WORST — 10 BEST

HOURS
7.3
1 WORST — 10 BEST

ASSOCIATE/PARTNER RELATIONS
8.1
1 WORST — 10 BEST

FORMAL TRAINING
7.2
1 WORST — 10 BEST

DIVERSITY
8.2
1 WORST — 10 BEST

Visit the Vault Law Channel, the complete online resource for law careers, featuring firm profiles, message boards, the Vault Law Job Board and more. **www.vault.com/law**

VAULT CAREER LIBRARY   327

THE SCOOP

Winston & Strawn has an enviable 150-year track record in litigation and transactional work. A series of mergers, office openings, and lateral hires in the last two decades has resulted in a global law firm spanning nine offices across the United States and Europe, serving such deep-pocket clients as McDonald's, Philip Morris and Verizon. Also noteworthy are the firm's varied pro bono achievements.

Spoiling for a fight

Winston & Strawn has its origins in a Chicago outfit founded by Harvard grad Fredrick Hampden Winston in 1853. Historic matters for the firm include devising an air rights plan for Chicago & North Western Railroad to sell space to Marshall Field & Company on the Chicago River without losing title to the land, resulting in the construction of the largest building in the world in 1930, the Merchandise Mart; challenging the War Powers Act in 1944 on behalf of department store Montgomery Ward, whose plants had been seized to assist the U.S. war effort; representing the Braves baseball franchise in 1966 in litigation related to its relocation from Milwaukee to Atlanta; defending General Electric in 1994 in its much-publicized industrial diamond price-fixing case; and representing Luxottica Group S.p.A. in its $1.6 billion hostile takeover of U.S. Shoe Corporation, owner of LensCrafters.

Winston's more recent history includes several changes in firm management positions. In August 2006, managing partner Jim Neis stepped down after serving in this role since 1993 to open the leadership ranks of the firm to younger attorneys Neis was succeeded by Tom Fitzgerald, who was selected after an extensive application and review process conducted by the firm's governance committee. This process also resulted in the selection of Tom Frederick as the new head of litigation and Rex Sessions as the new head of labor and employment. In September 2006, the firm elected superstar litigator Dan Webb as its chairman, replacing Governor James R. Thompson, who stepped down after 12 years in this role. Winston also named Steve Gavin its new head of the corporate practice.

What a catch

It's certainly not unusual for entire teams to cross over to rival firms, but the defection of a managing partner is noteworthy. In February 2007, Winston & Strawn's San Francisco office scored Nossaman Guthner Knox & Elliot managing partner Scott Devries. Nossaman can't have been too happy to see him go: trial lawyer DeVries had been Nossaman's No. 2 moneymaker, responsible for a reported $2 million to $2.5 million annually. As DeVries said of his new firm to *The Recorder*: "If you're going to go back to being a trial lawyer, what better firm in the country to be at than Winston & Strawn."

The addition of DeVries was the exclamation point on a string of recent Winston litigation hires on the West Coast that has included Martin Sabelli from the San Francisco Public Defender's Office, Devan Beck and Kristina Diaz from Alschuler Grossman, Steven Atlee from Latham & Watkins, David Bloch from McDermott Will & Emery, and Becky Troutman from Thelen, Reid & Priest.

In other comings and goings, poor Thelen Reid has taken a bit of a beating. In February 2007 Winston & Strawn's New York office scored an eight-lawyer litigation team from the firm, and walked off a month later with four more former Thelen associates. The hires bumped Winston's New York headcount to approximately 155. Included in the haul was star practitioner Michael Elkin, a commercial litigator concentrating in music, entertainment and technology copyright disputes, as well as IP litigation in the technology, entertainment and new media sectors. Elkin also headed New York City's suit against gun manufacturers, which charges them with creating a public nuisance.

Not to be outdone by the two coasts, Winston's Chicago office landed a team of prominent bankruptcy and corporate attorneys in January 2007 from Jenner & Block that included four partners, one of counsel and two associates. This team brings experience representing public and private companies, senior secured lenders, syndicated loan agents and official committees in complex business and financial restructurings, complementing Winston's existing bankruptcy practice in Chicago, New York, Los Angeles, and San Francisco.

© 2007 Vault Inc.

Supreme specialization

In 2005 Winston & Strawn created a formal appellate and critical motions practice group via the hire of Gene Schaerr from Sidley Austin and Linda Coberly from Mayer Brown. Since then, the firm has seen its court time increase dramatically. In the current term alone, the group has argued or submitted briefs or petitions in more than a dozen cases before the U.S. Supreme Court. Last term, the firm filed an amicus brief and presented oral argument on behalf of several states, securing a decision declining, at least temporarily, to apply the full requirements of the Americans with Disabilities Act to state prisons. In Holmes v. South Carolina, another recent case before the Supreme Court, Winston represented 18 states as amici in briefing and oral argument in defense of a challenge to a rule concerning exclusion of third-party-guilt evidence, resulting in a ruling clarifying the validity of the amici states' rules.

Where there's smoke there's money

Cigarette manufacturer Philip Morris is putting a generation of lawyers' kids through college (and paying for their iPods, tuba lessons and psychotherapy). Winston & Strawn is one many firms defending the ciggie biggie in a series of billion-dollar class-action lawsuits alleging that the company deliberately withheld information on the health risks of smoking. In December 2005, the firm brought home a major appellate trophy, when the Illinois Supreme Court threw out a $10 billion award against the company for the alleged mismarketing of light cigarettes. In July 2006, the Florida Supreme Court vacated a $145 billion damages award in Engle v. Philip Morris, and ordered decertification of the class. And in August 2006, though a D.C. federal judge ruling in United States v. Philip Morris USA found the defendants liable for violations of federal racketeering laws, the ruling included no monetary damages and no court monitors.

McLawsuits and McLiability

In 2003, *Fortune* magazine predicted that lawsuits against the fast food industry would be the next Big Tobacco litigation. Pelman v. McDonald's sought to hold the world's largest fat ... um, fast-food chain accountable for obesity and other health problems suffered by children who ate the company's products. McDonald's turned to Winston & Strawn, which has obtained dismissal of two class-action complaints, settled another claim brought under California's consumer protection statute, and is currently defending the company in New York and Illinois against consumer protection claims.

Calling Vonage out

Winston & Strawn's IP litigators had reason to celebrate in March 2007, when they won telecom giant Verizon a $58 million jury verdict against rival Vonage. A Virginia federal court jury found that Vonage had infringed on three Verizon patents related to the transmission of telephone calls over the internet. The jury further determined that if Vonage is not prohibited from continued infringement of Verizon's patents, it will be required to pay a 5.5 percent royalty on all future sales. Lead Winston trial lawyer Dan Webb immediately moved for a permanent injunction to prevent any further infringement of Verizon patents.

Gimme an M, gimme an A, gimme an IPO

Deal lawyers at Winston have been making news as well, handling several significant corporate and private equity transactions. In January 2007, the firm represented telecom giant Motorola in its $3.9 billion acquisition of Symbol Technologies, maker of of bar-code scanner and other devices. In another billion-dollar-plus tech industry M&A deal, Winston assisted Nasdaq-listed IT services provider Kanbay International with its $1.3 billion sale to French consulting firm Capgemini. The firm's corporate attorneys also were tapped by IPG Photonics and InnerWorkings to serve as counsel for these companies' recent IPOs. On the private equity side Winston has been particularly active in the leveraged buyout arena, most recently representing Arbor Private Investment Company in its purchase of an 80 percent stake in Sam's Wines & Spirits.

Visit the Vault Law Channel, the complete online resource for law careers, featuring firm profiles, message boards, the Vault Law Job Board and more. **www.vault.com/law**

VAULT CAREER LIBRARY   329

Once upon a time, on a continent far away ...

Winston & Strawn continued the expansion of its Paris office with the June 2006 addition of an eight-lawyer group nicked from France's largest law firm, FIDAL, that includes a corporate partner and a pair of tax partners. Established in 1995, the Paris office now has more than 50 attorneys with plans to increase its numbers to over 60. Recent activities in Winston's French outpost include the representation of Soitec S.A., maker of silicon wafers for the microchip industry, in its €204.7 million initial public offering listed on the Euronext Stock Exchange. Paris office litigators scored a high profile victory for La Française des Jeux, the French State lottery, when the Criminal Court of Paris ruled against the French cinema industry in a case involving claims of illegal downloading against Winston's client and several other plaintiffs.

Keeping the lights on

In July 2006, Winston nabbed a prominent group from White & Case to establish a West Coast presence for the firm's well known energy practice. Led by Jerry Bloom, this group has consistently been rated as a top-tier energy practice in California by Chambers since inception of its United States ratings. Recently, Bloom accompanied California Governor Arnold Schwarzenegger on his trade mission to China to promote the integration of alternative energy into China's resource plans for meeting its rapidly expanding demands for energy.

Closer to home, this group has been involved in the development of policies such as the historic Global Warming Solutions Act that support and encourage the development and operation of renewable power projects in California. On the transactional side, Winston & Strawn had a hand in the largest wind energy supply contract ever signed by a U.S. utility. Representing Oak Creek Energy Systems and Alta Windpower Development, the firm drew up contracts that provide for the development of wind projects in California's Tehachapi wind region, and for the sale of the resulting energy to Southern California Edison Company.

Discovering e-discovery

In February 2007, Winston declared the formation of a new electronic discovery practice group consisting of 13 attorneys who provide counsel on such issues as document retention, discovery in litigation or regulatory matters, and motions practice with regard to electronically stored information. Notes litigation chair Tom Frederick, "New federal e-discovery rules require our clients to understand their electronic data on a more comprehensive level and with greater speed than ever before. This group will help our clients respond more fully and with greater alacrity to government requests or when a lawsuit is filed."

Project protect the innocent

Winston's commitment to pro bono and public service runs deep. It was the first large firm in the country to adopt a written pro bono policy, has a full-time director of public interest law, and requests that its attorneys devote a minimum of 35 pro bono hours a year. Protecting the innocent continues to be a cause that is near and dear to Winston's heart. Most recently, a Winston team won the post-conviction release of an inmate by challenging the only physical evidence linking him to the crime: a set of "lip prints" that police had removed from duct tape found at the crime scene. He was released from prison in March 2006 after serving almost nine years of a 45-year murder sentence. The firm also continues to provide pro bono support to The Innocence Project, a database of 172 defendants who have been exonerated by the use of DNA evidence.

GETTING HIRED

Credentials-plus

Winston is looking for people with everything. "To its credit, Winston seems interested in hiring both the credentials superstars and those without the federal clerkship-type resumes, if they have demonstrated competency, involvement, and dedication inside and outside of class," says one insider. "You can get hired here without a 3.7 and law review if you have a record that shows you are an active, capable and successful person." "Winston generally looks for well-rounded candidates in the top 10 to 20

© 2007 Vault Inc.

percent of their class, but there is no specific GPA cutoff," notes a lawyer. "I think the firm is looking for people who are well rounded, smart and not jerks," reports another source. "A bad attitude or excessive arrogance can easily cost you an offer from Winston."

Also key: make sure you let everyone know you want Winston. "You need to make sure your interviewers know you want to work here—if you seem iffy, we'll write you off," warns an attorney. "Make sure to display your personality and have fun, especially with junior associate interviews/lunches." If you get past that hurdle, "have the good sense not to do anything inappropriate as a summer or an interviewee." "You must come across as a competent person who is responsible and dedicated to the job but also fitting into our culture of teamwork," observes another contact.

OUR SURVEY SAYS

Are the rumors true?

Winston has a reputation in the BigLaw community—rumor has it the firm is one of the best places to work in the industry. How do associates feel about that? "It's been gratifying to have Winston's reputation for high associate satisfaction born out in my personal experience," gushes an insider. "You never know, until you get to a firm, how you'll fit in and whether you'll be happy there—but I do think you can improve your odds by doing your homework and choosing carefully. I chose Winston and have been, for the most part, one happy camper." Other campers are just as happy. "I truly enjoy working here, something that initially came as a surprise because I never saw myself as a big-firm lawyer," reports a senior associate. "I get great work from great people and have never found Winston to be anything but supportive and fair. This is a business run by human beings who haven't forgotten the need to treat people well and fairly." It's not perfect, of course. "On the whole, Winston associates are probably more satisfied than typical big law firm associates, but it's not the nirvana that people have heard about," warns a contact.

So what are some of the negatives? "The only ... concern is that there is absolutely no satisfactory mentorship provided to junior and midlevel associates," warns an insider. "It is a sink or swim type of environment where each of the associates is on their own to develop." Of note, Winston rolled out a revamped formal mentoring program for all associates in mid-2007. "There are several problems [demonstrating] a lack of leadership, including transparency of bonus system, equitable distribution of assignments, and some mistreatment of associates that should not be allowed to persist," gripes an associate. Still, Winston seems to be living up to the hype. "Winston & Strawn routinely goes out of its way to make sure that associates have a great experience," shares a typical insider.

Right, left, center; they're all at Winston

Associates have much praise for Winston & Strawn's culture. "Winston has a unique culture among large law firms," says a source. "We're all bright individuals with great social skills." Well somebody doesn't have a self-esteem problem. Still, the firm does have a friendly culture. "I find Winston to be a very social place," reports another insider. "I met some of my best friends working at Winston." "If you are open and outgoing, this is a great group of people," says a senior associate. "The firm culture is a collegial, relaxed atmosphere," notes another contact. "There is a high level of professionalism in existence at the firm and this is definitely something to be proud of." Politicos of all stripes are welcome at Winston. "Politically, the firm is known as being very conservative, and many of our senior partners are well known Republicans," reports a lawyer. "However, I've found that there are also plenty of Democrats around, despite our reputation. And aside from the occasional light humor, the Republican partners are very respectful of divergent political views even among associates." The bottom line is what you bring to the firm. "Quality of work trumps everything. If you do bad work, you won't be yelled at, but you also won't be here next year," warns a New York associate.

Visit the Vault Law Channel, the complete online resource for law careers, featuring firm profiles, message boards, the Vault Law Job Board and more. **www.vault.com/law**

VAULT CAREER LIBRARY   331

Reasonable billables

Winston associates aren't swamped, relatively speaking. "Given the economics of law practice, the firm does well by its associates," observes a senior associate. "The billable hour requirement is not artificial." That insider adds, "One of the best features is the firm's pro bono policy. It is widely understood that even large amounts of pro bono work will be fully compensated. This is a tremendous opportunity for associates to get experience, and many of us take advantage of it." The hours can vary somewhat by department. "Litigation and corporate associates probably work 2,200 to 2,400 per year, while smaller departments (labor, real estate, environmental, etc.) bill [closer] to the 1,950 minimum," says a source. No one looks over your shoulder, which is nice. "Winston, in my experience, is tremendously flexible in terms of how and where you choose to get your work done," says a contact. "For the most part, no one watches when you come and when you go. As long as the work gets done everyone is happy." There's less happiness when a sudden deadline pops up. "A drawback is that there is a certain 'drop everything' attitude when work comes in, so it's not terribly unusual to have to cancel plans and, less frequently, trips because of unexpected work," reports a source. "The mentality ends up being 'We want you to have a life outside of the office ... that you are prepared to drop at a given moment if we tell you to.'"

Low-balled

The big gripe about Winston: the firm is "cheap, cheap, cheap." To wit: "One associate a few years back legendarily billed nearly 3,000 hours and got a bonus less than $30,000." That's not all. "They also nickel-and-dime you other ways," says a source. "For example, associates are forced to pay for their own bar fees. No better way to welcome an associate to your firm than forcing the associate to spend nearly a grand on bar fees and get laughed at by their peers." The firm's penny-pinching ways are affecting morale. "I'm happy with the salary, but the bonuses are on the low end for this tier of firm," says a real estate lawyer. "They need to do something about that or people will jump ship." "The base salary is on par with other firms in the market," says a Chicago lawyer. "Bonuses tend to be much lower. This may have flown when hour requirements were not so high, but it's become much more common for associates who work a lot to leave to go other big firms because of this situation." Lack of transparency is an issue. "The firm's bonus structure is a little frustrating, since it is never fully explained and nobody ever knows how they calculate the bonuses," gripes an attorney.

Learn the ropes

Training at Winston has its ups and downs. "The firm provides quite a bit of formal training throughout the years and encourages independent training as well," says a contact. "Winston has an extensive first-year training program," notes a junior associate. "I generally felt I learned something useful at the training sessions, though often the main benefit I received was basic familiarity with a topic that would enable me to know what to do when a situation arose later." The training is mandatory for junior associates. "First-year associates have to attend weekly litigation or transactional training sessions," reports a source. There's some interdepartmental strife. A corporate lawyer grumbles that there is "lots of training for litigation associates, but corporate associates don't get the same level of attention." A litigator seems to back up that assessment, noting that "in the litigation department, initial training is fairly extensive" including "weekly sessions over the course of several months. After the initial training there is yearly practice specific training with NITA programs."

Room at the top

Winston & Strawn is trying—and to some extent, succeeding—to develop a diverse workplace. "Winston makes some good efforts about women's issues," says one female associate. "There is a group specifically for women, though I wish it would meet a bit more often." "The firm even sponsored a women's event where it brought together all the women in the firm for a two-day conference in Chicago," says a source. That event won rave reviews. "The Women 2 Women program is a wonderful formal program," and associates add that "the female partners are also wonderful resources and supporters." "The firm is dedicated to diversity with respect to minorities," reports a contact. "However, there needs to be a more concerted effort to recruit minority associates to the firm, and to retain them." Others echo that sentiment. "The summer classes demonstrate a real interest in making the firm more diverse," observes a lawyer. "However, the firm appears to be insufficiently committed to attracting

© 2007 Vault Inc.

minority partners." GLBT attorneys have nothing to fear. "Gays and lesbians are welcomed in the partnership and management ranks of the firm," notes a source.

Visit the Vault Law Channel, the complete online resource for law careers, featuring firm profiles, message boards, the Vault Law Job Board and more. **www.vault.com/law**

VAULT CAREER LIBRARY   333

Dewey Ballantine LLP

1301 Avenue of the Americas
New York, NY 10019
Phone: (212) 259-8000
www.deweyballantine.com

LOCATIONS

New York, NY (HQ)

Austin, TX • East Palo Alto, CA • Los Angeles, CA •
Washington, DC • Charlotte, NC • Beijing • Frankfurt •
London • Milan • Rome • Warsaw

MAJOR DEPARTMENTS & PRACTICES

Antitrust & Trade Regulation • Arbitration & Alternative
Dispute Resolution • Bank & Institutional Finance • Bank &
Financial Institutions Litigation • Bankruptcy Litigation •
Compensation & Benefits • Corporate Finance • Corporate
Reorganization & Bankruptcy • Derivatives • Emerging
Markets • Employment Law • Energy • Entertainment Law •
Insurance • Insurance/Reinsurance Litigation & Arbitration •
Intellectual Property Litigation • Intellectual Property
Transactions & Technology • International Arbitration &
Alternative Dispute Resolution • International Litigation •
International Trade • Latin America • Leasing & Tax-
Advantaged Financing • Life Sciences & Health Care •
Litigation • Mergers & Acquisitions • Private Clients •
Private Equity • Project Finance • Public Policy: Legislative
& Executive Branch • Real Estate • Securities, M&A &
Corporate Governance • Sports Law Litigation • Structured
Finance • Tax • White Collar Crime & Government
Investigations

THE STATS

No. of attorneys: 550+
No. of offices: 12
Summer associate offers: 62 out of 63 (2006)
Co-chairs: Morton A. Pierce, Gordon E. Warnke
Hiring Partner: Henry J. Ricardo

THE BUZZ
WHAT ATTORNEYS AT OTHER FIRMS ARE SAYING ABOUT THIS FIRM

- "Top tier"
- "Should have merged"
- "Top-market pay"
- "Way to kill that merger, guys"

BASE SALARY (2007)

All US offices

1st year: $160,000
2nd year: $170,000
3rd year: $185,000
4th year: $210,000
5th year: $230,000
6th year: $250,000
7th year: $265,000
8th year: $280,000
Summer associate: $3,077/week

UPPERS

- "High compensation and high-caliber clients"
- Recruiting hours and pro bono hours count toward bonuses
- "People are generally friendly and the partners are not yellers."

DOWNERS

- "As with all big NY firms—the hours"
- "System of distributing work is not well organized"
- "Disruptive aborted merger"

NOTABLE PERKS

- "Great" cafeteria with a Starbucks
- Global Firm Forum
- $50 Amex gift card as birthday gift (Birthday gifts vary by office location)
- "The mentor program—you get to go out to eat or do an 'event' every month"

© 2007 Vault Inc.

RANKING RECAP

Quality of Life
#4 - Office Space
#15 - Pay
#20 - Formal Training

EMPLOYMENT CONTACT

Ms. Nicole Gunn
Manager of Legal Recruitment
Phone: (212) 259-7050
Fax: (212) 259-6333
E-mail: db.recruitment@deweyballantine.com

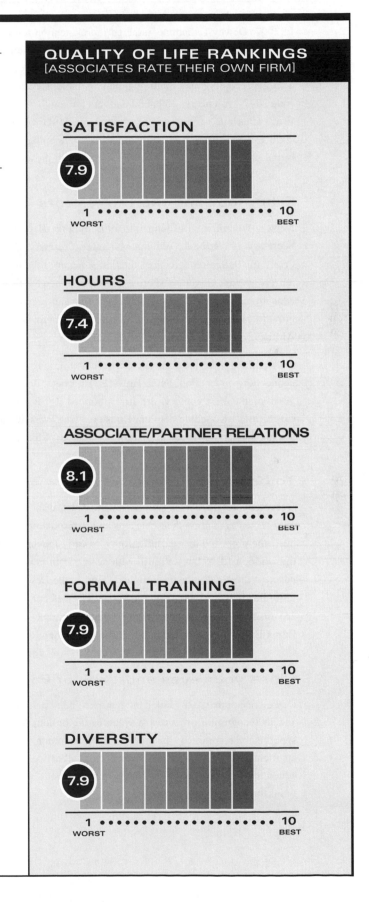

QUALITY OF LIFE RANKINGS
[ASSOCIATES RATE THEIR OWN FIRM]

SATISFACTION
7.9
1 WORST — 10 BEST

HOURS
7.4
1 WORST — 10 BEST

ASSOCIATE/PARTNER RELATIONS
8.1
1 WORST — 10 BEST

FORMAL TRAINING
7.9
1 WORST — 10 BEST

DIVERSITY
7.9
1 WORST — 10 BEST

Visit the Vault Law Channel, the complete online resource for law careers, featuring firm profiles, message boards, the Vault Law Job Board and more. **www.vault.com/law**

VAULT CAREER LIBRARY   335

THE SCOOP

In 2007, Dewey Ballantine garnered more attention for what it didn't do: finalize that much-talked-about merger with Orrick. Despite the abrupt navigational shift, Dewey sailed on, turning its focus overseas and to individual and small group lateral partner acquisitions, while continuing to grow revenue by concentrating on its core strengths: M&A, corporate and securities work, tax advisory, project finance and litigation. All told, Dewey has grown its headcount by 10 percent from the period of June 2006 to June 2007, with nearly 25 lateral partners joining the firm between March and June 2007. Highlights include the opening of the firm's Charlotte office, and the addition of a 20-lawyer group in Milan from the prestigious Galgano firm in Italy. Fiscal year 2006 was the firm's best on record with PPP topping $1.4 million and revenue reaching $408 million, and with its aggressive hiring, its clear that the firm has its sights set on growth for 2007.

Elihu Root and the firm's roots

Dewey Ballantine was founded in 1909 by three Harvard Law grads, one of whom was Elihu Root Jr., son of Elihu Root, the Secretary of War under William McKinley, Secretary of State under Theodore Roosevelt, and winner of the 1912 Nobel Peace Prize. In 1919, after serving as the first solicitor of the Internal Revenue, Arthur A. Ballantine came aboard. In the 1950s, three-term New York Governor Thomas E. Dewey joined the firm; as governor, Dewey is best remembered for cutting taxes, increasing educational funds and passing the state's first anti-racial discrimination employment legislation. In the ensuing decades, the firm grew to fame by cultivating such clients as General Motors, Morgan Stanley, Martin Marietta, Phillips Petroleum and United Airlines.

During the 1980s, the firm opened offices in Los Angeles and Washington, D.C.; by 1996, Dewey had offices or established connections in London, Paris, Brussels, Budapest, Prague and Warsaw, as well as an outpost in Hong Kong. During the early years of the 21st century, the firm plumped its IP practice with offices in Palo Alto and Austin, and energized its energy capabilities by opening doors in Houston. The Warsaw bureau is now one the largest law firms in Poland, while the last years saw the launch of offices in Charlotte, Frankfurt, Milan, Rome and Beijing.

To be or not to be?

Definitely not to be. Though Dewey and California-based Orrick basked in the attention for months, announcing their engagement, counting their chickens and rhapsodizing about expanded capabilities, and even going so far as to unveil a planned logo, the proposed merger fell through in early January 2007. The union would have resulted in one of the largest law firms in the world, a 1,200 lawyer outfit with nearly $1 billion in revenue. Since the deal collapsed, speculation as to what went wrong has kept the legal industry intrigued—and as the Dewey integration was Orrick's fifth failed merger attempt, engendered a fair bit of head-shaking and "We told you so's." Defections at Dewey (since the announcement, the firm lost 13 partners and added 25), disagreements about the firm's future governance and the $5 million in yearly compensation demanded by Orrick Chairman Ralph Baxter are regarded as the major stumbling blocks.

Close your eyes and think of England

Dewey responded to the failed merger by rolling up its sleeves and looking to Europe. In response to London partner defections, and in recognition of Europe's value to the bottom line, the firm embarked on a management revamp and launched a new supervisory committee. In order to foster communication between partners, Dewey's five-member European committee was augmented to 13, comprising partners from all offices and all regional managing partners. Four European partners will also be added to the firmwide executive committee. Over a third of Dewey's 550 lawyers are based in five offices in London, Warsaw, Frankfurt, Milan and Rome.

© 2007 Vault Inc.

Gambling men

In 2003 Dewey picked over three law firms and an I-bank to launch its Italian practice, with offices in Milan and Rome. In March, the firm announced a collaboration agreement with the prestigious Galgano firm, which resulted in the addition of 20 lawyers to Dewey's Milan office. With the Milan practice already quadrupled in size to 14 partners and over 50 fee-earners, Italy has proven to be dolce indeed—with the firm now counting one of the largest Italian operations of any U.S. firm. Recent deals for the Italian contingent include advising Weather Investments on its $12.2 billion acquisition of Italian telecom company Wind—Europe's largest-ever leveraged buyout. And in a deal that drew upon the Milan, London and New York offices, Dewey advised Italy's Lottomatica in its $4.5 million purchase of Rhode Island-based GTech, the world's largest lottery systems operator, in August 2006. Lottomatica, a subsidiary of the De Agostini Group, is license holder for the Italian National Lottery, while GTech manages state lotteries in the United States as well as local and national lotteries in Europe, Australia, Latin America, the Caribbean and Asia. The transaction created one of the world's largest online lottery technology providers, and will control over 50 percent of the online lottery business worldwide. The Lottomatica deal was the largest-ever acquisition of a U.S. company by an Italian company.

Dr. Deals

M&A has always been the core of Dewey's business; in 2006, *MergerMarket* ranked Dewey No. 10 in North America for cumulative deal value, 12 slots up from its 2005 position. Among the deals that kept the firm flying high was its work as counsel to Eli Lilly in its $2.1 billion acquisition of ICOS in January 2007. The drug companies had previously partnered in a 1998 joint venture involving erectile dysfunction drug Cialis.

Dewey Ballantine's Corporate Department has seen a surge in high-profile matters recently. One of those transactions, the IPO of 3SBio Inc., was the first U.S. IPO by a China-based biotech company. Amidst the well-publicized subprime lending market crisis, the firm also represented Accredited Home Lenders in connection with its proposed $400 million acquisition by Lone Star Funds. On recent M&A matters, Dewey Ballantine is currently representing MedImmune, Inc. in its agreement to be acquired for $15.2 billion by AstraZeneca PLC in an all-cash transaction.

It's all Ελληνικα to me

Let the tourists idle on the isles—when it comes to Greece, Dewey's all business. The firm has found a niche advising on a series of major Greek capital markets and M&A transactions, e.g., representing Greek telecom company Cosmote on its acquisition of Cyprus-based competitor Germanos, as well as portfolio management company DEKA and the Greek Ministry of Finance on a purchase of over 2.3 million shares of Emporiki Bank. In August 2006 the firm represented the Greek state-owned mortgage lender in connection with the securitization of mortgage-backed receivables; the $950 million transaction is one of the largest-ever securitizations out of Greece.

I'll have what he's having

Simpson & Thatcher set the salary bar, but Dewey nudged it higher: in late January 2007 Dewey not only matched Simpson's $160,000 first year pay hike, but was the first firm to apply the pay hike to all its offices, London included. Senior associates can now earn $370,000 (inclusive of a maximum bonus of $80,000), and London associates are protected against slumps in the U.S. dollar by a hedge rate, set at around $1.82 per £1.

Putting out fires

Among its varied pro bono activities, the firm assists the Citizens Commission to Protect the Truth—a committee that includes such health officials as former U.S. Secretaries of Health, Surgeon Generals and directors for the Center for Disease Control—in filing amici curiae briefs that argue that the funding of youth smoking prevention campaigns is an effective and appropriate remedy for tobacco companies found guilty of perpetrating fraudulent information on the hazards of smoking. The firm also

Visit the Vault Law Channel, the complete online resource for law careers, featuring firm profiles, message boards, the Vault Law Job Board and more. www.vault.com/law

VAULT CAREER LIBRARY

337

partners with the National Center for Missing and Exploited Children to represent parents in federal court proceedings related to international child abductions.

GETTING HIRED

If you've got personality ...

Of course grades and schools matter, but associates say that Dewey Ballantine places an unusual degree of emphasis on personality. As a third year from New York puts it, "If you are from a top-five school with above a 3.0, you will get your foot in the door for an interview, but there's still no chance of coming back if you have the wrong personality. If you are the slightest bit arrogant or take yourself too seriously, you should look elsewhere." A junior New Yorker advises, "Once you get past the first interview on campus, Dewey's focus is on finding candidates that are 'normal,' down-to-earth and just plain nice people—people that everyone here would enjoy working with." A midlevel adds, "Really socially awkward people don't do well here."

As for specific assets, the firm looks for "top-third or higher grades from well-regarded law schools, but exceptions are made at times. Prior relevant job or educational experience and demonstrated interest in a particular area of the law are helpful. Many hires in the D.C. office are from Georgetown, Harvard, Northwestern, George Washington, UVA," according to a senior corporate associate. A D.C. litigator adds, "It's hard to get through the door for an interview unless you're in IP or you have a high GPA. Journal experience and clerkships are a plus, but not required. We recruit from multiple schools, but we hire mostly from top-50 or tier-two schools."

OUR SURVEY SAYS

A plethora of positives

Dewey Ballantine's satisfied associates have a plethora of reasons for their contentment. "The work I receive is consistently challenging and interesting while at the same time, I've found that the partners and associates I work with are really nice and down-to-earth," boasts a first-year. A midlevel associate reports, "Although I work hard, I feel that the partners and the firm appreciate my contributions and take my comments and input seriously." A corporate associate appreciates the "interesting work," the "good people to work with" and having "plenty of responsibility." And another corporate attorney adds, "I couldn't be happier: the experience that I received as a first-year was outstanding; I got to work closely with partners and with senior associates; I dealt directly with clients and was able to take the lead on calls with opposing counsel; the atmosphere in my group is very informal and laid-back; there is no 'face time' required; people do respect your free time."

A cornucopia of compliments for the culture

Dewey-centric adjectives associates use to describe the firm's culture are "laid-back," "collegial," social," "friendly" and "nice. A junior associate in Manhattan reports, "Dewey's culture can best be described as laid-back, informal and fun. Lawyers do socialize together, but more importantly, most people really are very nice—and everyone generally does get along!" Another junior New York associate advises, "People are generally laid-back, not too competitive and value their time outside of work. There is a lot of after-hours socializing if that's what you're looking for." As a tax attorney from the Big Apple puts it, "The firm offers plenty of opportunities for lawyers to socialize together, which most associates, and to a lesser degree, partners, take advantage of. Biweekly tax dinners as well as monthly tax lunches are often well-attended. Practically on a daily basis I eat lunch with my colleagues." However, a [excluded?] litigator warns, "It is a social place, which is nice, but it is hyper-political ... Lawyers do tend to socialize together, which is good, however it can become exclusionary of others."

© 2007 Vault Inc.

Typical top-down

A Washington associate sums up the consensus about the firm's management: "The partners I've worked with have been stellar," he says. Or, as one corporate attorney puts it, "Partners here are very approachable and do respect your life outside of Dewey. I have never been spoken down to, or yelled out, and I have never seen anyone else treated that way either. It is truly a team atmosphere (at least in my group, I cannot speak to other areas here, but have heard similar comments)." That said, a number of associates complain about "institutional issues." An M&A associate, for example, reports, "The partnership definitely keeps associates informed of firmwide decisions on a very timely basis, but associates are not included in the decision-making process." And a midlevel litigator adds, "The individual partners are respectful of associates and generally maintain good working relations. The firm as a whole has a 'top down' mentality from the partnership to the associates, but I think that's typical of large law firms."

Gimme a D! Gimme a B! Gimme a U!

Rarely do associates give their firm's formal training program higher scores than do Dewey's. As one junior litigator puts it, "They take training very seriously. There are constant opportunities to learn as a junior associate." A midlevel associate says, "Dewey makes a real effort to bring all of its attorneys to New York for centralized, focused training. There are also frequent CLEs on useful topics sponsored by the different sections." An M&A associate reports, "Well-prepared and helpful department-wide training sessions are scheduled monthly, and officewide less often." A corporate expert adds, "Dewey now has Dewey Ballantine University (a/k/a DBU) with mandatory training for certain class years and certain groups. There is so much training available that it sometimes seems too much! My group itself has monthly CLE lunches on various topics within private equity and/or real estate."

Line by line

The firm's informal training and mentoring receive equally rave reviews. "Each first year is given an associate mentor and a partner mentor," says a New Yorker. "My associate mentor is great. My partner-mentor has introduced himself and says 'Hi' in the halls. Depends on who you get." A midlevel litigator recalls, "Senior associates and partners have always been willing to take the time to explain the reasoning behind their decisions, as well as to offer impromptu tutoring sessions (on deposition taking, or oral argument, etc.). After I took my first deposition, I had a senior partner sit down with me and go through it line by line, offering pointers and constructive criticism." A tax attorney from New York adds, "I enjoy my relationship with both my partner mentor and my associate mentor, both of whom have taken time to take me out for lunches and have been a great source of support and help during first few months at Dewey. They are both awesome 'fellas' too!" However, a D.C. corporate attorney suggests, "There is a formal mentoring program, but best mentoring and training comes from informal relationships between partners and associates."

Rewarding the strivers

Dewey's associates have few or no complaints about their compensation. A midlevel associate advises, "Dewey compensates its attorneys very well, using the same pay scale for its associates in every office. I don't mind working until 10:30 on a Saturday night because I feel that the firm pays me for my time." A New York litigator reports, "I love that Dewey provides a 'super' bonus to associates who demonstrate a higher 'quantity and quality' in their work. I've received it for several years now, and I appreciate that the firm does reward associates when they strive to excel. I find it so strange that other firms discourage meritocracy by providing the same bonus to all associates who reach their minimum hour requirements." Here are the closest things you'll find to gripes concerning compensation at Dewey: As a midlevel New Yorker says, "Dewey is a firm that follows the other firms' leads. So we all get paid the same as all other associates at big firms in New York. Same with bonuses," and an M&A expert adds, "Bonus is based solely on hours and 'accountable hours.'"

Visit the Vault Law Channel, the complete online resource for law careers, featuring firm profiles, message boards, the Vault Law Job Board and more. www.vault.com/law

V**A**ULT CAREER LIBRARY   **339**

Long hours, sure, but you were expecting otherwise?

The hours at Dewey can be long, of course—really long, in fact—but the partners are generally thoughtful and reasonable, associates report. As one IP expert sees it, "The firm is fairly flexible—it largely depends on the discretion of the partners you're working with. Hours and leave can be fairly flexible as long as the partners have reasonable notice." A midlevel litigator advises, "I put in 10- to 12-hour days during the weekday, and work the weekends when necessary, but I don't think the hours are that bad. When I can get away early, I do, and no one at the firm has a problem with it. No one monitors my schedule as long as I'm getting my work done and meeting my hours goals." And a New York corporate attorney adds, "On the whole my hours are very manageable. Of course, there have been weeks that I have billed 100 hours, but there are many, many more weeks where I billed only about 40."

© 2007 Vault Inc.

"I enjoy my relationship with both my partner mentor and my associate mentor ... they are both awesome 'fellas' too!"

— *Dewey Ballantine associate*

Visit the Vault Law Channel, the complete online resource for law careers, featuring firm profiles, message boards, the Vault Law Job Board and more. www.vault.com/law

VAULT CAREER LIBRARY

341

Wilson Sonsini Goodrich & Rosati

650 Page Mill Road
Palo Alto, CA 94304-1050
Phone: (650) 493-9300
www.wsgr.com

LOCATIONS

Palo Alto, CA (HQ)

Austin, TX • New York, NY • Salt Lake City, UT • San
Diego, CA • San Francisco, CA • Seattle, WA •
Washington, DC • Shanghai

MAJOR DEPARTMENTS & PRACTICES

Antitrust • Clean Technology & Renewable Energy •
Corporate Finance • Corporate Law & Governance •
Employee Benefits & Compensation • Employment Law •
Export Controls • Fund Services • Intellectual Property
(Counseling & Patents, Litigation, Outsourcing & IT
Procurement, Technology Transactions, Trademarks,
Copyrights & Advertising) • Life Sciences • Litigation
(Antitrust, Appellate, Complex Commercial, Consumer,
Intellectual Property, Corporate Governance and M&A) •
Mergers & Acquisitions • Project Finance • Real Estate &
Environmental • Retail, Consumer & Advertising • Securities
Litigation • Tax • Venture Capital • Wealth Management •
White Collar Crime & Investigations

THE STATS

No. of attorneys: 650
No. of offices: 9
Summer associate offers: 71 out of 71 (2006)
Chair, Executive Management Committee: Larry W. Sonsini
Hiring Partners: Kathleen Rothman, John Slafsky, Rodney
Strickland, James Otteson, Steven Guggenheim, Robert
Day

BASE SALARY (2007)*

1st year: $160,000
2nd year: $170,000
3rd year: $185,000
4th year: $210,000
5th year: $230,000
6th year: $250,000
7th year: $265,000
Summer associate: $3,077 per week

Certain locations

UPPERS

• Great tech and startup clients
• Relatively high level of autonomy
• Colleagues and support staff

DOWNERS

• "Being in Palo Alto!"
• Not much mentoring/guidance
• Unpredictable hours

NOTABLE PERKS

• Opportunity to invest in clients via company fund
• "Really cool gadgets"
• "Great discounts from tech clients"
• Firm pays for all cell phones (including long distance)

THE BUZZ

WHAT ATTORNEYS AT OTHER FIRMS ARE SAYING ABOUT THIS FIRM

• "Highest of high tech"
• "Heyday has passed"
• "Great for IPOs"
• "Still recovering from dot-com burst"

© 2007 Vault Inc.

RANKING RECAP

Best in Region

#10 - Texas

Best in Practice

#1 - Technology

EMPLOYMENT CONTACT

Ms. Carol A. Timm

Director, Attorney Recruiting & Retention

Phone: (650) 493-9300

E-mail: attorneyrecruiting@wsgr.com

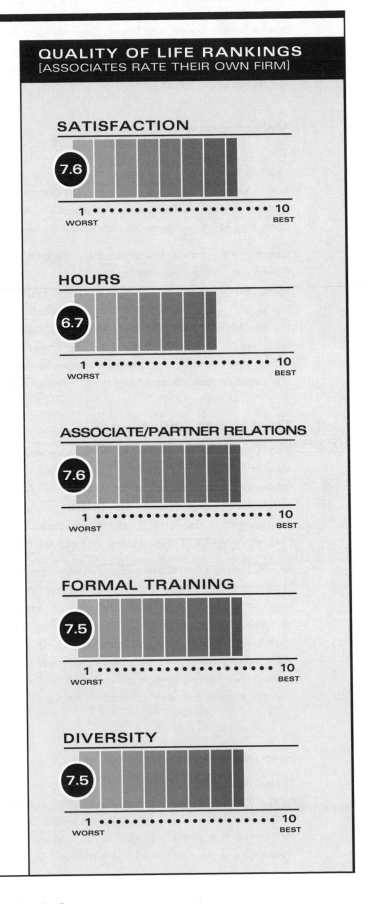

QUALITY OF LIFE RANKINGS
[ASSOCIATES RATE THEIR OWN FIRM]

SATISFACTION

7.6

1 WORST · · · · · · · · · · · · · · · · · 10 BEST

HOURS

6.7

1 WORST · · · · · · · · · · · · · · · · · 10 BEST

ASSOCIATE/PARTNER RELATIONS

7.6

1 WORST · · · · · · · · · · · · · · · · · 10 BEST

FORMAL TRAINING

7.5

1 WORST · · · · · · · · · · · · · · · · · 10 BEST

DIVERSITY

7.5

1 WORST · · · · · · · · · · · · · · · · · 10 BEST

Visit the Vault Law Channel, the complete online resource for law careers, featuring firm profiles, message boards, the Vault Law Job Board and more. www.vault.com/law

VAULT CAREER LIBRARY   343

THE SCOOP

Wilson Sonsini Goodrich & Rosati is internationally recognized as a premier provider of legal services to the technology, life sciences, and growth enterprises, as well as to the investment banks and venture capital firms pumping the industries' lifeblood. The firm is known for deep roots throughout the tech sector, and for its role in the historic IPOs, mergers and litigation that shook and shaped a new economy.

Valleyspeak

The Valleyspeak that made Wilson Sonsini's name wasn't the "like, totally!" variety. Rather, it was the firm's thorough comprehension of its clients' businesses, its capacity to talk the talk of burgeoning tech and bioscience industries spreading across Silicon Valley. As these industries gathered shape, the firm began representing companies in all phases of growth. Since its founding in 1961, Wilson Sonsini has advised on more IPOs, completed more tech licensing transactions, advised on more technology M&A, and defended more securities class actions than any other U.S. law firm.

Historic matters for the firm include the 1980s IPOs of Apple and Sun Microsystems; Hewlett-Packard's late 1990s spinoff of Agilent and 2002 merger with Compaq; the $82.5 million Netflix IPO; and Google's $1.7 billion stock offering in 2004, and its subsequent follow-ons valued at more than $6 billion. Internationally, the firm advised India's Infosys in its $70.4 million Nasdaq IPO, as well as three secondary ADS offerings valued at $294 million, $938 million and $1.65 billion. More recently, the firm advised LSI Logic in its $4.1 billion acquisition of Agere Systems; The McClatchy Company in its $6.5 billion acquisition of Knight Ridder and subsequent divestiture of 12 Knight Ridder papers with an aggregate value of more than $2 billion; YouTube in its $1.65 billion acquisition by Google, and Dolby Laboratories' in its $495 million IPO. In 2006, the firm is advised Freescale Semiconductor in its $17.6 billion sale to a private equity consortium—the tech sector's largest buyout ever.

Take me to your leader

It was Larry Sonsini who carved the firm's path, visualizing its IT future and cultivating its base. Described by one private equity client to *Fortune* magazine as "the Larry Bird of Silicon Valley," "the go-to guy … the ice-in-his-veins, blue-collar, scramble-for-the-ball, great-teammate, no-ego, championship-caliber guy," Sonsini enjoys great loyalty from clients, many of whom represent the biggest names in West Coast technology. In 2001 Sonsini joined the NYSE's board of directors, as the resident expert on tech issues. It was Sonsini who led Pixar's $7.4 billion acquisition by Disney in 2006, as well as the trifling matter of Google's 2004 IPO. Though Sonsini stepped down from a CEO role in 2005, he continues as the firm's chairman.

In 2006 Sonsini's considerable achievements were overshadowed by, in Lemony Snicket terms, a series of unfortunate events. In autumn 2006 longtime client Hewlett-Packard stood accused of misrepresenting itself to phone companies in order to gain access to confidential call logs, in an effort to find a boardroom leak. As general counsel to HP, Sonsini came under scrutiny for his alleged role in the "pretexting" scandal. Some—including a congressional committee—questioned the depth of Sonsini's involvement and culpability. In September 2006 HP's board let its longtime lawyer go, while emphasizing that "Hewlett-Packard and Wilson Sonsini continue to enjoy a strong relationship." In November 2006, *Fortune* reported that the most serious criticisms of Sonsini's involvement were unfounded: the pretexting operation had been approved by a small outside law firm, and that it was only after the operation's completion that Sonsini was asked to weigh in, and then only for advice on what to do about the leak.

Securities blanket

The bad press didn't end with HP. When the feds showed an interest in stock option backdating, Wilson Sonsini found itself in the eye of an SEC storm. In the early part of the investigation, of the 42 Silicon Valley companies facing review, some 40 percent were Wilson Sonsini clients. As the probe widened to include more than 140 companies—many of them outside the Valley—the focus on WSGR lessened significantly. Though law firms that drew up stock option plans would generally have had little involvement in the administration of these plans, Sonsini himself came under scrutiny for sitting on the board of several client

© 2007 Vault Inc.

companies facing investigation. One such company, Brocade Communications, was the first company unlucky enough to earn a criminal indictment in the sting. But when life tosses you federal investigations, make lemonade, eh? Thanks in part to the focus on backdating, in 2006 Wilson Sonsini beat out Skadden as the defense leader in securities litigation—a development that, not so surprisingly, has had a ripple effect on the firm's white-collar defense practice.

Totally YouTubular

Given that both YouTube and Google are longstanding Wilson Sonsini clients, when Google decided to purchase the video sharing web site in October 2006, there was some question as to which side the firm would choose to represent. This time, Wilson Sonsini went with the little guy and represented YouTube in the $1.65 billion sale. The choice could be explained by, to paraphrase one Sonsini associate, Larry Sonsini's belief that while there are several firms that can adequately represent financiers, there are very few firms that can counsel the companies the big boys want to back, and thus the firm's highest use in such cases is to go with the underserved. Simpson Thacher & Bartlett represented Google in the deal.

Biotechnically speaking

While many Valley firms put all their eggs in the dot-com basket, Wilson Sonsini never abandoned its interest in biotech. And since we all know what happened next, the firm's biotech practice has taken on a new importance, and is generating "an increasingly larger piece" of the firm's bottom line. Although the industry has cooled somewhat as an investment opportunity for the general market, strategic partnerships and acquisitions have been on the rise. As the cash-cow patents on older drugs edge closer to their expiration dates, Big Pharma is increasingly anxious to find the next Viagra or Lipitor, to acquire up-and-coming drugs with vast market potential. One such Big Pharma acquisition was Pfizer's April 2006 purchase of Wilson Sonsini client Rinat Neuroscience, a developer of drugs for pain, Alzheimer's and neurological disorders.

Sue happy

In the last year, though the majority of IP teams have seen a drop-off in patent litigation, Wilson Sonsini is among the rare firms bucking the slowdown trend. In 2006 the firm was one of the few to actually see an increase in the number of cases it is litigating. At present the firm is representing tech manufacturer Palm in a case brought by Compression Labs and alleging patent infringement on JPEG technology, and Taiwanese device maker Laser Dynamics in litigation relating to a patent for optical disk drive recognition.

We're all entitled to our e-pinions

In 2006, Wilson Sonsini relocated its Reston, Va., office to D.C., to be closer to regulatory institutions such as the SEC and the International Trade Commission. In 2005, the firm fortified its New York office with the hire of two Akin Gump antitrust experts; the steal gained the firm such clients as Coca-Cola, American Express and Nielson Media Research. The antitrust practice was further expanded with the addition of the former director of the Bureau of Competition of the Federal Trade Commission, the former legal advisor to bureau directors in the FTC's Bureau of Competition, the former chief of the Networks and Technology Enforcement Section of the Department of Justice's Antitrust Division, and the former assistant director of the Mergers IV Division of the FTC. In fact, Wilson Sonsini Goodrich & Rosati now has an accomplished team of 20 focusing on antitrust matters.

Nouveau chic

The firm also has expanded a few additional practices over the past year. In April 2007, the firm announced that two partners were joining its San Francisco and Seattle offices respectively, bringing to the firm a nationally-recognized practice representing developers and financing sources involved in renewable energy and biofuel projects in the U.S. and abroad. Shortly after, the firm announced the addition of two partners to the D.C. office to help build the firm's export controls and economic sanctions practice and strengthen the existing internal investigations capabilities by adding an export controls dimension.

Visit the Vault Law Channel, the complete online resource for law careers, featuring firm profiles, message boards, the Vault Law Job Board and more. www.vault.com/law

VAULT CAREER LIBRARY

345

When longtime firm client Google bought YouTube in 2006, they didn't know that the ink would be barely dry on the M&A files before the litigation department stepped in. Viacom sued Google for (insert Doctor Evil impression here) $1 billion on the grounds of massive copyright infringement in YouTube video posting form. Google and Wilson Sonsini maintain that YouTube is protected under the Digital Millennium Copyright Act, but all signs indicate a long road ahead, with many interested parties watching their computers in anticipation.

Techheads, warmhearts

In the past 15 years, the firm's WSGR Foundation has donated nearly $6 million to local legal groups, and sponsored fellowships at both Stanford Law School and Berkeley's Boalt School of Law. Pro bono activity for the firm includes representation of asylum seekers from around the world who are fleeing abusive personal or political situations, and regular involvement with legal aid societies such as the AIDS Legal Referral Panel and the Lawyers' Committee for Civil Rights. In March 2005, the Eleventh Circuit Court of Appeals affirmed the $4 million verdict the firm had previously won for family members of a victim of a 1973 Chilean death squad.

GETTING HIRED

Local law grads make good

Bay Area-based Wilson Sonsini "will hire almost anyone from Boalt or Stanford," assures one California midlevel. Adds a Silicon Valley source, "If you go to Harvard, Yale, Stanford, it's very easy. If you go to schools further down the chain, the standards become incredibly stringent, particularly for schools in this region." Due to the firm's IT/IP focus, "people with tech backgrounds have a bit of a headstart, [but it's] by no means a requirement." A source in the Washington office thinks that, regarding grades, there are "no firm cutoffs, but to have a realistic shot at a callback, you need to be at least top half at a top-10 school, though top three is the more likely standard. Cutoffs are higher (i.e., top 10) at remaining top-25 schools, and much higher at regional schools. That said, allowances are made for associates that are well matched to our corporate or speciality groups, typically with extensive experience in industry or technology. Also, the firm targets entrepreneurs who are comfortable interfacing with and counseling clients, and assuming early responsibility." A Bay Area source notes that "once you have your foot in the door, the most important factor might simply be how well you mesh with the people in the group (and this really varies by group)." While the firm is "prestige-focused," "on the other hand, they also care about personality—people who seem like they would get along with clients, people who are willing to take initiative, people with a sense of humor." And in the observation of a Menlo Park source, "They hire all their summer associates, unless there are glaring problems (one or two per summer don't get offers)."

OUR SURVEY SAYS

U of Wilson

In the Palo Alto headquarters, the firm operates "like a small college, with a campus, many classes, many committees and lots of energetic bright attorneys." Comments one California-based associate, "I'm learning so much here, and there are interesting things every day. Sometimes it's tedious, but that's to be expected at a junior associate level." Adds a colleague, "The firm has generally happy people and a great legal support apparatus." A litigator in Silicon Valley remembers feeling a bit surprised that the firm, though "very friendly," is also "a bit formal." A colleague views his fellow associates "cordial but competitive." A rookie to the corporate group finds that people are "occasionally friendly, and always willing to work together to get the job done. I have made a few friends I socialize with outside of work, but only a few groups frequently socialize." On the East Coast, D.C is "an office where most people do their work and then head home to their families. There is very little socializing." In Manhattan, "no one expects you to (socialize), but the opportunities are there." A distinct plus, remarks a midlevel in the Valley,

© 2007 Vault Inc.

is that Wilson Sonsini Goodrich & Rosati on the whole is "very accepting. We have great diversity, not just ethnically but politically and in styles and values." And "there are very little politics. People are generally committed to the success of the firm."

The client sets the clock

"I think the flexibility with hours is very individual, depending on your practice group and specific partners. This can be good or bad," muses one California associate. "I didn't get a lot of pressure to keep ridiculously high hours, but we are of course expected to be responsive to clients, which can mean weekends or late nights." Offers one associate in the corporate group, "The firm doesn't micromanage hours. Individual groups must contribute on an economic basis to the firm and have targets that they must hit. Groups manage these numbers in different ways. My group is pretty humane about it." Adds a colleague, "Hours are flexible and based on the amount of work to be done, but people generally try to be in the office during the normal workday in order to best work together. Part time is available (but it's understood that you must 'pay your dues' first and then have a 'good reason,' such as children), but it makes partner track ridiculously long." On the plus side, says one New York source, "Face time simply does not exist." A Silicon Valley associate complains that "the worst part for me is the unpredictability. It's hard not to be able to tell by 5 p.m. whether I can commit to dinner plans." A Washingtonian notes that added responsibility is the real culprit: "I have complete flexibility over my schedule, but when working on major deals, hours often grow long—proving that added levels of client contact and responsibility function as a double-edged sword." A source in the Palo Alto office is grateful that "I can set my own hours—arrive early and leave by 5 p.m. without worrying who is looking at where I am. As long as the work is done and is good, no one complains." A colleague in the same office reports that "One real advantage of this office is that most people tend not to work late nights or weekends except when deal flow is especially heavy." Clarifies another source, "The firm is divided into groups run by rainmakers, so it is difficult to get help from one's immediate group when the group is short-staffed. It is not unusual to see groups where people are billing in the mid 2,000s, while other groups bill less than 2,000."

Price wars

"I would like to make the same as the New York salaries" says one California associate, "But I am still generally satisfied with what I make." That associate must be even more satisfied now—since Vault's survey was conducted, the firm matched New York rates in Silicon Valley and certain other offices. A third-year reports, "We match other big firms in California, but we'll never be a leader and the bonuses are not as large." On that topic, a colleague shakes his head, "We kept hearing how great the firm was doing, so the actual bonuses we received seemed low this year." In fact, a colleague in the corporate department does the math, and goes so far as to say the "bonus is submarket." A long-termer feels that "the firm's stance on compensation has gotten more and more depressing. During the heydays this firm was a market leader. Now they wait until they absolutely have to (i.e., after all the other California firms have announced) to announce pay raises. More offensive than this are the bonuses. Class of 2002 at a max of $27,500 at the end of one of the biggest years in the firm's history? Not only do we trail other Northern California firms (Orrick and MoFo) but they also avoid any discussion of this."

Still, there are others who wouldn't trade the West Coast workload for the East Coast paycheck. Worries one newbie in Menlo Park, "I am a little concerned that as compensation goes up, there is a risk that even more will be expected of associates, and that hours will become more of an obsession, especially in certain groups. I would rather the firm retain more of its lifestyle aspects and leave the moneygrubbing to Northeast firms!" Agrees a litigator, "More money would likely mean more pressure to bill outrageous hours, so I'm happy we are not at the very top."

That giant sucking sound ...

"Most of the stress, drama, sucking up, etc., is associate-driven, not partner-driven," tattles one midlevel. "Partners are nice, very receptive to feedback, generally pretty young. In fact, they expect us to disagree, challenge them." Concurs a colleague, "Partners are not usually disrespectful to associates and are usually understanding, even friendly, but I've heard of some notable exceptions in other groups." Reports another, "On an individual basis, I feel like the partners I work with respect me. I get a lot of direct contact with the clients, which would not happen if the partners did not trust/respect me." If there are screamers or

Visit the Vault Law Channel, the complete online resource for law careers, featuring firm profiles, message boards, the Vault Law Job Board and more. **www.vault.com/law**

VAULT CAREER LIBRARY   **347**

yellers, most associates do not see it: "The partners in our group are great ... I don't find much different in terms of my more limited experience with other partners." Sources report that "firm management has been making a concerted effort to listen to associates and allow them to participate in decisions, which has been beneficial," but note that "decision making by partners is too opaque and does not seem to include associate input."

A little something something

Perks at Wilson Sonsini Goodrich & Rosati range from "free dinners after 7, car after 8," "subsidized lunches in the café, free coffee, tea, hot chocolate and soup in each pod's kitchen," "free parking" and "emergency backup child care." The firm also pays moving and bar expenses, and provides a "$12,000 bonus for third year summer." And of course the firm's techcentricism results in some "really cool gadgets, including absolute top of the line laptops and wireless devices. Plus free long distance anywhere in the world," reports one midlevel. The electronic goody-bag also includes "great discounts from our tech clients (e.g., Apple, HP, Dell)," "IBM laptops, Motorola Razor cell phones, BlackBerry/Treo/Cingular 8100 e-mail devices." Additionally, there is the chance for "equity participation in the fund that invests in client companies." As one associate notes, "the opportunity to invest in clients is huge, but that costs money."

© 2007 Vault Inc.

"[We get] really cool gadgets, including absolute top-of-the-line laptops and wireless devices."

— Wilson Sonsini Goodrich & Rosati associate

Visit the Vault Law Channel, the complete online resource for law careers, featuring firm profiles, message boards, the Vault Law Job Board and more. **www.vault.com/law**

VAULT CAREER LIBRARY   **349**

Linklaters

One Silk Street
London, EC2Y 8HQ
United Kingdom
Phone: +011 44 20 7456 2000

1345 Avenue of the Americas
New York, NY 10105
Phone: (212) 903-9000
www.linklaters.com

LOCATIONS

New York, NY • Amsterdam • Antwerp • Bangkok • Beijing
• Berlin • Bratislava • Brussels • Bucharest • Budapest •
Cologne • Dubai • Frankfurt • Hong Kong • Lisbon • London
• Luxembourg • Madrid • Milan • Moscow • Munich • Paris
• Prague • Rome • São Paulo • Shanghai • Singapore •
Stockholm • Tokyo • Warsaw

MAJOR DEPARTMENTS & PRACTICES

Banking* • Capital Markets* • Competition/Antitrust* •
Corporate/M&A* • Employee Incentives • Employment •
Environment & Planning • Financial Markets • Insurance •
Intellectual Property • Investment Management* • Litigation
& Arbitration* • Pensions • Private Equity* • Projects* •
Real Estate & Construction • Restructuring & Insolvency* •
Structured Finance & Derivatives* • Tax* • Technology,
Media & Telecommunications

Practice areas covered by US practice

THE STATS

No. of attorneys:
    Firmwide: 2,000+
    New York: 135
No. of offices: 30
Summer associate offers: 20 out of 20 (2006)
Senior Partner: David Cheyne
Managing Partner: Simon Davies
US Managing Partner: R. Paul Wickes
Hiring Partners: Mary Warren & Andrew Mackie (New York)

THE BUZZ
WHAT ATTORNEYS AT OTHER FIRMS ARE SAYING ABOUT THIS FIRM

• "Sophisticated, international savvy"
• "Struggling with their US identity"
• "Great management. Truly global"
• "They may be good on their home turf"

BASE SALARY (2007)

New York, NY
1st year: $160,000
2nd year: $170,000
3rd year: $185,000
4th year: $210,000
5th year: $230,000
6th year: $250,000
7th year: $265,000
8th year: $280,000
Summer associate: $3,077/week

UPPERS

• "The work is intellectually stimulating and challenging"
• "A lot of communication between all levels of lawyers"
• "We are paid market, but are treated much better"

DOWNERS

• "The hours can be quite long—but that's to be expected"
• "Very strict nanny internet patrol"
• "International travel can get very tiring"

NOTABLE PERKS

• Retreats in Europe
• Friday afternoon drinks trolley
• "Terrific" cafeteria
• "Deloitte & Touche does my taxes"

© 2007 Vault Inc.

RANKING RECAP

Best in Practice
#10 - Antitrust

Quality of Life
#14 - Pay
#14 - Formal Training

EMPLOYMENT CONTACT

Ms. Anne Mahoney
Legal Recruitment Manager
Phone: (212) 830-9603
Fax: (212) 903-9100
E-mail: anne.mahoney@linklaters.com

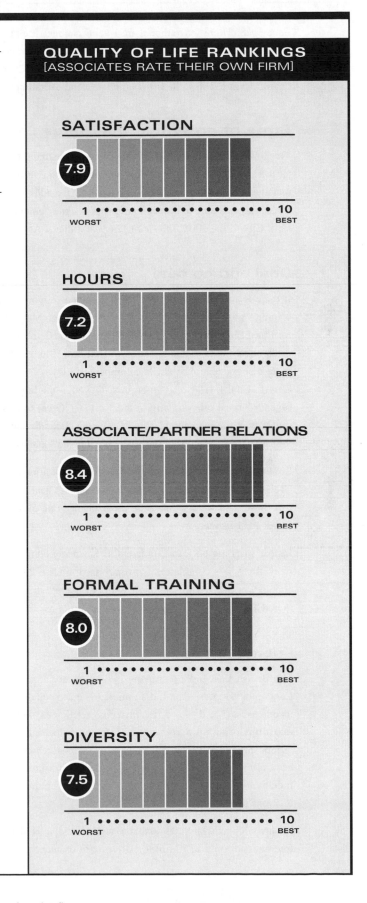

QUALITY OF LIFE RANKINGS
[ASSOCIATES RATE THEIR OWN FIRM]

SATISFACTION
7.9
1 WORST • • • • • • • • • • • • • • • • • • 10 BEST

HOURS
7.2
1 WORST • • • • • • • • • • • • • • • • • • 10 BEST

ASSOCIATE/PARTNER RELATIONS
8.4
1 WORST • • • • • • • • • • • • • • • • • • 10 BEST

FORMAL TRAINING
8.0
1 WORST • • • • • • • • • • • • • • • • • • 10 BEST

DIVERSITY
7.5
1 WORST • • • • • • • • • • • • • • • • • • 10 BEST

Visit the Vault Law Channel, the complete online resource for law careers, featuring firm profiles, message boards, the Vault Law Job Board and more. **www.vault.com/law**

VAULT CAREER LIBRARY   351

THE SCOOP

Fancy a morning tea rather than a venti caramel frappe? U.K.-based Linklaters brings British sensibility to legal work and business transactions the world over. Its success, however, is anything but reserved. In 2006, Linklaters posted record profits, with average profit per equity partner increasing by 26 percent to $1.06 million. According to Thomson Financial's fourth-quarter league tables, the firm came in second overall in M&A productivity, closing 313 deals worth $394.7 billion total in 2006.

State of growth in the States

The New York office has been undergoing some major expansion recently—four prominent NYC litigators were brought over as partners in October 2006, with an of counsel and a team of 12 new associates. During that same month, the office's investment management practice was also enhanced by the addition of one new partner and two new associates. Maybe part of the reason Linklaters was able to attract so many was some good press the year before: the firm was named the No. 2 place to work in New York City in the 2005 *American Lawyer* Midlevel Associates' Survey.

Deal and no deal

If there is a major international deal going down, you can bet Linklaters is lurking behind the scenes. The firm was named the leading legal adviser on European, U.K. and Asian M&A deals in 2006. Linklaters also came in second place on the league tables for European transactions as well, behind Magic Circle rival Freshfields Bruckhaus Deringer. Though Linklaters scored 15 more deals, Freshfields pulled ahead in overall deal value. Who has Linklaters to thank for working its M&A in 2006? Many of the more recognizable Anglophone companies: Lloyds TSB (for its acquisition of Scottish Widows), Citibank (for its acquisition of KorAm Bank), BP (for its merger with TNK—the largest investment ever by a western company in Russia, which created the seventh-largest oil company in the world), L'Oréal (on its takeover of The Body Shop), British staples Sainsbury's and Argos (outsourcing agreements), Allied Breweries, Bacardi and telecommunications giants BT, Vodafone and T-Mobile. On the table for 2007 are roles in both the AWG bid and the Thames Water sale, among many others.

Linklaters' M&A is dominant, not infallible. Traditional client Royal Bank of Scotland passed the firm by in favor of competitor CMS Cameron McKenna, who snagged a sweet deal advising the bank on its plan to jettison £1 billion worth of Marriott hotels (for those who were wondering, the exchange rate of Marriotts to pounds is 47/£1 billion). The slated buyer is Israeli investor Delek Real Estate.

Instead of going back to Linklaters, U.K. energy company Centrica decided to give Addleshaw Goddard its trademark portfolio work for 2007. Linklaters isn't surprised; after a 2006 IP review, the firm eviscerated its trademark and portfolio practice, concluding that it "no longer fit with our overall strategy." The head of the former trademark department, Roland Mallinson, joined Taylor Wessing, and several other senior associates had already left before the dissolution was announced.

Friends 4 eva

The British East India Company is long gone, but you can't blame the notoriously protective subcontinent for being wary of London interlopers. The Indian market is much sought after by international law firms, and Linklaters has found a way to crack its defenses. The deal is a "best friends" relationship between Linklaters and Mumbai-based Thawar Thakore & Associates. The two firms drew up a contract to refer work to each other, each increasing its access to business from abroad. While this "friendship" does not violate Indian regulations, which prohibit outside firms to directly enter the market, some say it could set back efforts to liberalize India's attitude toward global firms. Negotiations are underway by other parties to try to convince Indian officials to allow mergers and joint ventures, but for now, Linklaters and Thawar Thakore are happy with their relationship.

Meanwhile, Linklaters is also having success next door in Pakistan. In October 2006, the firm acted for Merrill Lynch International on a $150 million offering of ordinary shares, in the form of 8.6 million Global Depositary Receipts (GDRs), by

© 2007 Vault Inc.

MCB Bank Limited. It was the first ever Pakistani bank offering of GDRs, and the first Pakistani/international private sector equity deal in 10 years.

Breaking another decade-long record, Linklaters also advised Merrill Lynch International on the purchase of shares (in the form of GDRs) at the IPO of INA-Industrija Nafte. The privatization of this Croatian state-owned oil and gas company turned out to be that country's largest IPO in the last decade. Noteworthy forays like these are what earned Linklaters the distinction of being "Global Law Firm of the Year" at the Chambers Global Awards 2006.

Green tea and crumpets

Also at the Chambers Global Awards, the firm won the "Asian Law Firm of the Year" award for the second year running. For Asia (excluding Japan), Linklaters ended 2006 as the leading firm for completed M&A deals, providing legal advice on 47 deals valued at $16.8 billion in total. Particularly impressive was its representation of Vodafone on the telecommunications company's ¥1.8 trillion sale of its Japanese subsidiary to SoftBank—Asia's largest-ever leveraged buyout. Back on the mainland, Linklaters advised Citigroup on the $3.06 billion consortium acquisition of Guangdong Development Bank—the first time a major international financial services company, leading a consortium of co-investors, has been permitted to assume significant influence over the management of a Chinese commercial bank.

Increasingly, China is becoming the name of the game in Asia. In 2006, the region took off as many of the world's leading firms battled it out for control of this potentially enormous market. Firm managers are calling China one of the "fastest-growing" markets, which makes the country "impossible to ignore." There is a potential roadblock to success in the People's Republic, however. Foreigners looking to buy corporate assets in the country will find that, as of January 2007, overseas acquisitions of large Chinese companies must undergo an antimonopoly probe before they will be allowed to proceed. Linklaters is taking the cautiously optimistic route, saying that the increased regulation "could fuel foreign interest in Chinese companies," but a lot depends on how it is implemented—will the central government abuse its power over local brand names in the interest of national economic security?

Room at the top

No monarchy this; senior management at Linklaters is elected by vote, and holds expiring terms. And the firm is in the middle of a power shift. In 2006, David Cheyne, former global head of the firm's corporate department (the most politically significant intra-firm position) was elected senior partner. Spring 2007 saw Simon Davies, former managing partner for Asia, elected as managing partner. He will start his five-year term in September 2007.

No "eat what you kill"

Among Magic Circle firms, only Slaughter and May and Freshfields hold onto a one-ladder-for-all compensation system. Linklaters, like Clifford Chance, modified its lock-step regionally—after it underwent eight separate mergers with firms with different profit levels. Linklaters U.S. Managing Partner Paul Wickes has observed that lock-step—even his firm's modified version—often works to the firm's advantage in recruiting. "We have found the lock-step system brings a collegial culture that is appealing to many partners coming from typical U.S. merit-based systems. The effect of lock-step is that everybody works as part of a team, rather than advancing their self-interests," Wickes told *Legal Week* in March 2005.

GETTING HIRED

No cookie-cutter lawyers

"The schools at which Linklaters recruits are currently fairly limited, and the firm will not really look at other candidates unless they are among the top students of their class," advises one young associate. "However, grades are not everything. The interview

Visit the Vault Law Channel, the complete online resource for law careers, featuring firm profiles, message boards, the Vault Law Job Board and more. **www.vault.com/law**

VAULT CAREER LIBRARY   353

process involves passing through many offices and speaking to a lot of attorneys, so character can be evaluated. Language skills are very important, and so are skills that are outside the purely legal sphere (e.g., a business degree, etc.)." In addition to the usual "very good grades from very good schools," associates report that an international background is a boon to getting hired at Linklaters. One young associate advises, "We are especially interested in candidates who have international backgrounds, or who bring something interesting to the table. You need to be the right fit to get hired, particularly as a lateral." (However, one insider laments, "In the old days, the firm only hired people with international backgrounds, but it seems like that's over now. Too bad.") Another insider adds, "The firm tends to look for individuals, not cookie-cutter lawyers. Most of the hires tend to have an international background or demonstrated interest." Or, as one young New York litigator puts it, "Linklaters is extremely selective. The focus is not only on law school performance and depth of resume, but also social skills and commercial awareness." Finally, be outgoing, but keep your voice down: "I've noticed that most of the people here are well rounded and nice to be around, no screamers or hermits," one insider cautions.

OUR SURVEY SAYS

Mostly love

Associates give Linklaters nearly universal off-the-chart rave reviews. Some of the testimonials sound like love letters. "It's a great firm to work at," boasts a junior investment management expert from New York. "You always feel like your work is valued." A banking specialist praises the firm's "great work and career advancement opportunities." A senior corporate finance associate credits his happiness to the "superb working environment, the truly international work and colleagues and the opportunity to work on large-scale, multi-jurisdictional transactions." And a midlevel litigator adds, "I could not imagine working at another firm." There are, as at any firm, at least a few complainers, but they sound ambivalent at worst. A New York banking associate says, "The work is interesting and the people are collegial, but the hours can be difficult and unpredictable." Another junior associate takes an "it's all relative" attitude: "Being a New York corporate lawyer is very unsatisfying in general, but there are far worse places I could be doing it." But a few firm associates are simply bored; one corporate finance expert from the New York office sighs, "I feel pigeonholed and largely do the same work over and over again."

Who knew that multi-jurisdictional transactional work was so much fun!

Linklaters associates describe the vibe at their firm as so inviting that it's surprising that people from other firms don't just come over after hours to unwind. "There is a very pleasant social culture at the firm," reports a midlevel associate. "There are frequent social events planned at various group levels and numerous occasions for spontaneous social get-togethers." A London associate reports that her branch is "unbelievably social." She says, "A drinks trolley weekly at 4:45 says something, doesn't it? And that is sandwiched in between all the other drinking and social activities." But don't think the firm is one big kegger. As a senior New York litigator reports, Linklaters attorneys are "very social, but no party animals." That said, he adds that his office provides "weekly drinks, and the support staff is invited."

Associates heart partners

The love-fest continues when the associates' conversation turns to the firm's partners, both individually and institutionally. "With very few exceptions, partners are very pleasant to work with," reports a junior New York attorney. "Interpersonal skills are very highly valued, and it is sometimes surprising how well partners and associates get along. There is also a lot of communication between all levels of lawyers, so formal barriers cannot be felt a lot in everyday life." A midlevel litigator adds, "The firm is exceptionally open on the business of running a large law firm, and provides us with a great deal of inside information on how the firm works." A white-collar crime expert adds, "There is a mutual respect between partners and associates. Associates have real opportunities to voice any concerns and effectuate change." That said, the associates do not just blindly praise the entire partnership. One young litigator advises, "I feel that most of the partners treat me very well. We've had some new partners join the firm that are less aware of junior associates."

© 2007 Vault Inc.

When it comes to training, Linklaters schools

Even formal training—the nearly universal subject of young-associate ire—scores major points at Linklaters. One Big Apple litigator praises the "excellent mix of in-house training based on real experience and outsourced training, e.g., oral argument skills." Another insider advises, "For first-year associates, the firm has an extensive induction program. However, what is most helpful is the baseline training that the firm does throughout the year in the different departments. These help to build your foundational knowledge in your practice area. The firm also provides training in useful skills, such as understanding financial documents." A senior associate adds, "This is the first firm I've worked at in New York (and there have been a few) that seems interested in developing their associates into excellent attorneys and don't just view them as billing machines."

If you're looking for the flaw at Linklaters, it's not in the informal training and mentoring, associates report. "I can go to a partner or a senior associate [at] any time of the day, any day of the week, and unless they are working against a tight deadline, I will get as much time as I need to understand new concepts," crows a New York attorney. A corporate associate reports, "The firm doesn't have any 'official' mentoring program, but in my experience, I've felt really comfortable talking with senior associates and partners about concerns and my career." Another New Yorker adds, "The partners and counsel are always free to discuss practice tips and areas of law that are challenging or new to associates." However, one senior New York associate warns, "Informal training and mentoring occur by virtue of the cases on which you work and whether a partner above you takes a liking to you. You take what you can get."

How's the weather up there at the top of the market?

Associates call the firm's compensation plan top of the market. A senior New York associate reports that the "firm matches market in both base salary and bonus," and that there is "no hours requirement to receive a bonus." As an international law specialist puts it, "We are paid market, but are treated much better than in an average New York firm." An associate assigned to the firm's London office reports, "Linklaters seems to be committed to sticking with the New York market, which is good. As an employee in a foreign office, they also provide a decent cost-of-living adjustment and exchange benefits." And an antitrust expert adds, "Linklaters always meets the market. Sometimes it takes them a week or two longer than other firms to meet the salary increases, but they always match and they always pay retroactively."

For a major international law firm, Linklaters demands surprisingly reasonable hours from its attorneys, associates say. "This is not the usual New York sweatshop," says a New Yorker. "Hours can get bad, as they can get in any other law firm, but on average they are much, much better. Where else will the firm be satisfied with an average of eight billable hours per day?" A corporate attorney adds, "Work hours can be unpredictable, which is the worst part of it. But when there isn't a lot of work to do, there's no particular pressure to put in 'face time' and that is a great thing." As a Manhattan litigator reports, "The demands of the job directly track the hours. There is no pressure to bill if you don't have any work to do. As a result, morale is higher even when people are working a ton of hours because the emphasis is on the work, not the clock."

Visit the Vault Law Channel, the complete online resource for law careers, featuring firm profiles, message boards, the Vault Law Job Board and more. **www.vault.com/law**

VAULT CAREER LIBRARY 355

Orrick Herrington & Sutcliffe LLP

666 Fifth Avenue
New York, NY 10103-001
Phone: (212) 506-5000

The Orrick Building
405 Howard Street
San Francisco, CA 94105
Phone: (415) 773-5700
www.orrick.com

LOCATIONS

Irvine, CA • Los Angeles, CA • Menlo Park, CA • New York,
NY • Portland, OR • Sacramento, CA • San Francisco, CA •
Seattle, WA • Washington, DC • Beijing • Hong Kong •
London • Milan • Moscow • Paris • Rome • Shanghai •
Taipei • Tokyo

MAJOR DEPARTMENTS & PRACTICES

Bankruptcy & Restructuring • Compensation & Benefits •
Corporate • Employment • Global Finance • Intellectual
Property • International Arbitration & Dispute Resolution •
Life Sciences • Litigation • Public Finance • Real Estate •
Securities Litigation & White-Collar Crime • Structured
Finance • Tax • Venture/Emerging Companies

THE STATS

No. of attorneys firmwide: 980
No. of offices: 18
Summer associate offers: 75 out of 78 (2006)
Chairman and CEO: Ralph H. Baxter Jr.
West Coast Hiring Partner: James Kramer
East Coast Hiring Partner: Lauren Elliot

BASE SALARY (2007)

California offices
1st year: $160,000
2nd year: $170,000
3rd year: $185,000
4th year: $210,000
5th year: $230,000
6th year: $250,000
7th year: $265,000
8th year: $280,000
Summer associate: $3,100/week

New York, NY; Washington, DC
1st year: $160,000
Summer associate: $3,100/week

Pacific Northwest; Sacramento, CA
1st year: $145,000
Summer associate: $2,800/week

UPPERS

• "Casual atmosphere of mutual respect"
• Sophisticated clients and transactions
• "Everyone's vacation time is sacred"

DOWNERS

• "Occasionally brutal hours"
• "Too much expansion. *Slow down!*"
• "Rigid tying of bonus to reaching minimum hour
  requirement"

NOTABLE PERKS

• Well-stocked kitchens
• Backup day care
• Generous recruiting/summer associate/mentoring
  entertainment budget.
• Subsidized cafe "with beautiful views of the city" (San
  Francisco)

THE BUZZ
WHAT ATTORNEYS AT OTHER FIRMS ARE SAYING ABOUT THIS FIRM

• "Seeking global domination"
• "They all worship their leader"
• "Better than Dewey"
• "Always the bridegroom"

© 2007 Vault Inc.

RANKING RECAP

Best in Region

#4 - Northern California

EMPLOYMENT CONTACTS

Ms. Karen Massa
Firmwide Attorney Recruiting Manager
Phone: (415) 773-5588
Fax: (415) 415-773-5759
E-mail: kmassa@orrick.com

Ms. Liz Cha
San Francisco Recruiting Manager
Phone: (415) 773-5458
E-mail: echa@orrick.com

Ms. Rebecca Whittall
Silicon Valley Recruiting Manager
Phone: (650) 614-7352
E-mail: rwhittall@orrick.com

Ms. Camille Rubino
Los Angeles Recruiting Manager
Phone: (213) 629-2495
E-mail: crubino@orrick.com

Ms. Linda Partmann
Sacramento Recruiting Coordinator
Phone: (916) 447-7936
E-mail: lpartmann@orrick.com

Ms. Mary Lou Buntz
Pacific Northwest Recruiting Coordinator
Phone: (206) 839-4330
E-mail: mbuntz@orrick.com

Ms. Jennifer Youngquist
New York Recruiting Manager
Phone: (212) 506-3553
E-mail: jyoungquist@orrick.com

Ms. Francesca Runge
New York Lateral Recruiting Manager
Phone: (212) 506-3556
E-mail: frunge@orrick.com

Ginny Comly
Washington, DC Recruiting Manager
Phone: (202) 339-8446
E-mail: gcomly@orrick.com

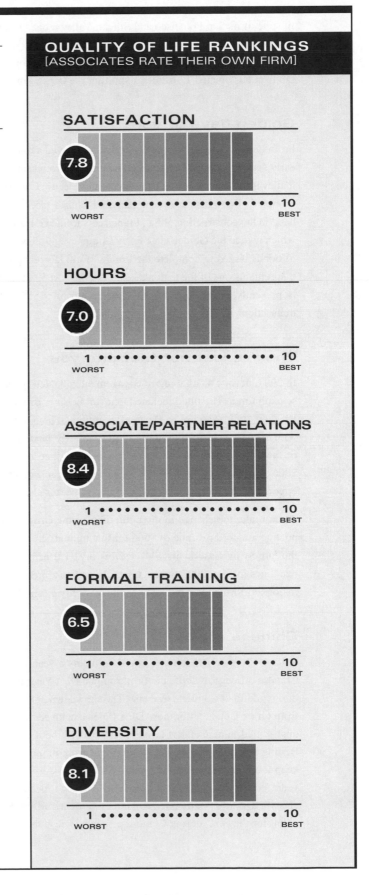

QUALITY OF LIFE RANKINGS
[ASSOCIATES RATE THEIR OWN FIRM]

SATISFACTION
7.8
1 WORST — 10 BEST

HOURS
7.0
1 WORST — 10 BEST

ASSOCIATE/PARTNER RELATIONS
8.4
1 WORST — 10 BEST

FORMAL TRAINING
6.5
1 WORST — 10 BEST

DIVERSITY
8.1
1 WORST — 10 BEST

Visit the Vault Law Channel, the complete online resource for law careers, featuring firm profiles, message boards, the Vault Law Job Board and more. www.vault.com/law

VAULT CAREER LIBRARY

357

THE SCOOP

In spite of its San Francisco and Silicon Valley roots, Orrick more than weathered the dot-com implosion. Strong corporate and restructuring practices, top-caliber intellectual property and litigation departments, and world-class capabilities in structured, public and project finance ensured that Orrick made money in the hard times as it had in the good—and even more. Since 1995, the firm has opened 13 offices, exporting the Orrick brand far beyond the Golden State.

Golden days of yore

From its founding days in 1885, Orrick has played a role in Northern California finance. Founder John J. Jarboe was among the early settlers aiding San Francisco's transition from campsite to commercial center. The firm helped incorporate the companies that eventually became the Pacific Gas and Electric Company (PG&E), and in 1906 was instrumental in the reorganization of the Fireman's Fund Insurance Company, which had faced collapse due to an overload of earthquake claims. The firm even had a hand in the construction of San Francisco's iconic Golden Gate Bridge, which was completed in 1937. Southern Pacific Railroad, which owned the Golden Gate Ferry Company and stood to lose heavily if the bridge was constructed, had challenged the legality of bonds issued to complete the bridge. Firm lawyers presented a successful rebuttal, and the case engendered a bond practice that remains one of the nation's best. For the past 50 years, Orrick has served as lead bond counsel to the state of California, and is presently overseeing the implementation of a $15 million deficit bond program—one of the largest municipal finance transactions in U.S. history.

They're just not that into you

In 2007, despite an announced engagement with New York's Dewey Ballantine, Orrick once again failed to tie the knot—for the seventh time. The jilted include Donovan Leisure, Bird & Bird, Cooley Godward, Venture Law Group, Swidler Berlin, Coudert Brothers (twice) and now, Dewey Ballantine. Though the firms' proposed merger would have resulted in a 1,500-lawyer team, with an estimated $1 billion in revenue, in early January 2007 talks came to a halt. Analysts attribute the breakup to a number of factors, including a sudden onslaught of partner losses at Dewey and disagreement as to the future entity's governance. A 2006 *Wall Street Journal* article analyzing organizational strategies classed Orrick Managing Partner Ralph Baxter as "the epitome of the 21st century lawyer" in part because he no longer practices, but serves instead as the firm's full-time manager.

At any rate, the change in direction didn't slow Orrick down. Rather, the firm basked in its 17th consecutive year of growth, posting a record revenue of $666 (gasp!) million. In recognition of a successful year, the firm expanded its partner class by 16, the largest increase in its 144-year history. Partners are not the only ones benefiting from the big bux influx. Orrick made headlines in May 2007, when it set a West Coast precedent by upping its first-year associate compensation to $160,000. Other major California players like O'Melveny & Myers and Morrison & Foerster quickly followed suit.

Chinese stakeout

After waiting on its Chinese orders for nearly a year, in September 2006 Orrick at long last won operating licenses for its two Chinese offices. In 2005, the firm trumped DLA Piper Rudnick in the battle for the Beijing, Hong Kong and Shanghai practices of now-defunct Coudert Brothers. The showdown got a bit ugly—i.e., Orrick found itself slapped with an unfair termination suit from an ex-Coudert, and now DLA Piper employee, which impeded resolution to the ongoing licensing case. By the time the dust settled, nine Coudert lawyers had crossed the divide, with Orrick paying the defunct firm an estimated $1 million for the Beijing and Shanghai leases, fixtures and work in progress. But that was the easy part; convincing the Chinese government to keep the mainland offices running was another story. Local regulations require law firms to operate in one location for three years before applying for a license in a second location; to sidestep this, Orrick had petitioned to have the Chinese offices classified as an asset transfer, and not as new enterprises. Even California's second-term-inator, Governor Schwarzenegger, went to bat for the firm, urging Chinese officials to push the process along.

© 2007 Vault Inc.

In other Asia activity, Orrick cosponsored a patent litigation conference at Seoul National University in June 2006. Hmm, could be a sign of offices to come—South Korea is home to a fast-growing IT industry, and looks poised to open its legal market in the next years.

Manifest destiny

To oversee its international growth, Orrick reconfigured its European management structures in March 2006, creating managerial roles for each of the firm's main practice areas. The roles were created to manage the firm's rapid growth; David Syed, European managing partner, tells *The Lawyer*, "Three years ago we had 40 lawyers across Europe, and now we have close to 200. We used to be very finance-focused, but now we have a good balance across our key areas of finance, corporate and litigation." In January 2006, the firm opened shop in Paris via a merger with Rambaud Martel, and has now set its sights on Germany. U.S. operations, which comprise 650 lawyers and eight offices, will be now be run by San Francisco Partner Joseph Malkin, with Peter Bicks serving as partner-in-charge of the New York office.

The DLA Piper rivalry that was set off in China has spilled over to Italy. In June 2006 DLA scooped a six-member public law team from Orrick's Milan office. In an attempt to take advantage of the corporate resurgence in Italy, that month Orrick launched a corporate practice in Rome by nabbing boutique firm Tantalo & Associati. Lead partner Pietro Tantalo is well known in the Roman corporate and private equity market; he is presently working on the privatization of the state broadcasting company RAI and will cart the project with him to Orrick.

In the U.K., an 18-month strategy to grow the London office from 60 to approximate 130 lawyers is underway; in 2005 the London office more than doubled in size. In anticipation of a full house, the firm is looking to double the size of its London office space to approximately 45,000 square feet. One promising client for the U.K. team: in March 2006, French bank Société Générale added Orrick to its global legal panel. Though, in a bit of bad news, the London office lost its head of European M&A to Winston Strawn in July 2006.

Barbarians at the gate

In August 2006 Orrick's crafty M&A team stepped in to help Onyx Software thwart a takeover attempt by CDC Corporation, a Hong Kong-based software corporation. The firm helped Onyx, manufacturer of customer management software, arrange its eventual $92 million white knight acquisition by Made2Manage Systems. Since December 2005, CDC had made three unsolicited proposals to acquire Onyx; all were rejected by Onyx's board due to concerns over shareholder value. The Orrick team consisted of three offices and several legal disciplines, including M&A, tax, compensation and securities litigation.

Recent M&A transactions include representing Laserscope, provider of medical lasers, on its $715 million acquisition by medical device supplier American Medical Systems Holdings in June 2006. A few months later, in November, Orrick advised Tokyo-based financial services group Nomura on its purchase of Instinet, provider of electronic trading services for institutional investors. The acquisition will enable Nomura to offer its clients Instinet's products, particularly in Asia and Europe. Instinet was sold at auction by private equity firm Silver Lake Partners.

In Asia, the firm's Hong Kong office won the Asian-Council M&A deal of the year for a transaction involving an Argentinean conglomerate, a Philippine power complex, U.S. and Japanese investors, and Hong Kong bankers. The Hong Kong team also won *Asian Legal Business*' "Real Estate and Construction Deal of the Year" for work on the Shanghai Square Project, a 38-story, 80,000-square-meter office and retail project. Orrick advised lender Credit Suisse First Boston in the deal.

Playing the distinguished dozens

In January 2006, *The American Lawyer* named the firm one of its "Distinguished Dozen" litigation departments of the year. Highlighted were several major Orrick wins, including the acquittal of McKesson Corporation's former CFO on securities and criminal conspiracy charges; the defeat of a $40 million patent infringement claim; a win in a securities class action; and a defense verdict in a Texas asbestos liability case, which involved more than $5 billion in potential damages. Other Orrick

Visit the Vault Law Channel, the complete online resource for law careers, featuring firm profiles, message boards, the Vault Law Job Board and more. **www.vault.com/law**

VAULT CAREER LIBRARY   359

triumphs include a successful Daubert challenge in a case involving childhood vaccines, and the procurement of a $325 million settlement for client EMC—the result of aggressive counterclaims that effectively turned the tables on plaintiff Hewlett-Packard. Recent high-profile cases include representing CNET general counsel Sharon Le Duy in a stock option backdating probe and handling French media company Vivendi's long-running suit against Deutsche Telekom, the parent of T-Mobile. The latter case alleges that the German telecom giant colluded with a Polish investor to filch Vivendi's shares in a Polish cellular company.

Gambling on tribal law

As Native American tribes gain stature economically, they are increasingly turning to big ticket law firms to help them negotiate federal, state and local laws. Catering to this specialized clientele, several big-scale firms have organized Indian law practice groups; Orrick (along with Holland & Knight, Akin Gump, Dorsey & Whitney and Pillsbury Winthrop) is one of the few firms in the country to field a specialized practice in Indian law. Orrick's tribal finance group was formalized in 2003 and now includes 18 lawyers. The group typically deals with several sets of laws, advising tribes and underwriters like JP Morgan Chase on financing deals across California, Arizona and New Mexico. Many of these tribes, like the Pojoaque Pueblo, turn to bond financing, trickier for tribes to achieve as it requires solid credit history, which many tribes don't yet have.

In 2006, the firm advised the Pojoaque Pueblo in New Mexico on a $245 million financing for casino, resort and infrastructure development. Hilton Hotels and the Pueblo of Pojoaque will embark on 390-room hotel and casino project, the Buffalo Thunder Resort. The complex will be owned entirely by the Pueblo, but managed by Hilton Hotels.

Semester abroad

Ah, junior year abroad—sleeping bags in train stations, disco, libidinous Scandinavians ... well, if you missed all that, Orrick gives you a second chance. In an effort to better integrate the firm's overseas operations, in 2006 the firm announced a new program in which associates in the global structured finance group will be able to swap jobs with colleagues in a foreign office for six months. If the program proves successful, it will be rolled out to encompass other practice groups. More than 25 percent of Orrick lawyers are now based outside the United States.

Reporting on Katrina

In August 2006, Orrick and eight participating law firms released a 100-page report titled "A Continuing Storm," which analyzed the efficacy of Hurricane Katrina relief efforts and detailed best practices for the future. Eighteen Orrick lawyers, 12 associates and staff spent over 3,000 hours examining how host cities Atlanta, Baton Rouge, Birmingham, Houston and San Antonio cared for the estimated 700,000 evacuees. The report was commissioned by Appleseed, a nonprofit network of public interest law centers.

GETTING HIRED

No square pegs in round O

Yes, Orrick looks at grades. Yes, "If you did well at a top-five law school or are on law review at a top-20 school you will probably get [an interview]." Yes, "your resume should stand out." All of these are mere formalities compared to the firm's first-, second-, and third-most important requirements: Fit, fit and (no really, we're not kidding) *fit*!

"The hardest part a candidate will face interviewing here is whether we like you and [you] fit in with our culture," says a Los Angeles associate. Orrick takes great pride in its reputation, and isn't willing to risk that fun, cooperative atmosphere for a few extra GPA tenths—"esprit de corps over on-paper credentials." "We get enough qualified candidates that we can afford to take only those we think have dynamic, sociable personalities that are easy to work with," says a San Francisco associate. So don't mess up the call-back interview. The process is "very extensive, with the goal that each candidate meet as many people as possible." Everyone shares in the decision-making process, and "the firm is very cautious about hiring anyone who receives even one negative comment." Associates agree; an attitude that might go over well elsewhere is a deadly faux pas at Orrick, and that is arrogance. "The arrogant need not apply" … because "arrogance doesn't get hired here."

A senior associate who is quite involved in recruiting confirms everything: "Orrick is unusually committed to hiring non-jerks … [the firm will] consistently turn down candidates if any one person (associate or partner) in the review process indicates that the candidate was either arrogant or nasty or somehow gave off a bad vibe. There have been many candidates who were stars on paper, but duds in person." The Washington-hopeful should also take note: In D.C., they want "people who enjoy and want to be lawyers—political wannabes, lobbyists, etc., should look elsewhere."

OUR SURVEY SAYS

Culture club (culture cult?)

Read their lips: it's not lip service. Keeping a laid-back culture is serious business. "At Orrick, we take 'firm culture' seriously. Seriously." "Orrick's core values are more than just a cute saying or a plaque on the wall." The firm's zealous commitment to hiring only the best personalities (the "no assholes policy") extends into and affects daily life as well. "Everyone is treated with respect, [and] everyone has a voice," says a happy corporate lawyer.

No matter where you go, Orrick associates describe the culture around a common theme. It's "open and friendly" in San Francisco, "a casual and comfortable bunch" (Sacramento), "supportive and collaborative" (Menlo Park), "relaxed" and "meritocratic" (Silicon Valley), "low key but highly professional" (New York) and even "warm and fuzzy" in Tokyo. There is "no 'club' atmosphere" and even the D.C. office "is refreshingly free of political overtones." D.C. associates go on to call the atmosphere "laid-back and easygoing—an oasis of San Francisco culture." Somewhere Ralph Baxter is smiling.

Like, it's chill, dude

Perhaps because Orrick attorneys feel the love from 9 to 5, they don't have an urgent need to reaffirm their camaraderie after hours. Everyone agrees that "hanging out is very low key and not mandatory." Some offices, like the smaller Sacramento outpost, report frequent associate socialization. Others prefer to go home to their families or significant others. Accordingly, associates describe the firm as an "open and accepting" place, with a decent amount of lifestyle diversity. "I like the fact that a lot of different types of people work here: young singles, parents of small kids, gay, straight, liberal, conservative." "Idiosyncrasies are fondly tolerated," which means there's "room for the quirkier among us in the legal profession." Just how quirky, no one specified. One assumes the truly weird have been vetted at the door.

Or the take-it-or-leave-it social life could be by necessity: "Because of billable hours, most people are pretty nose-to-the-grindstone, get-work-done types and often eat lunch in their offices" (as one labor associate observes anyway).

Talk to Ralph

The late merger discussions with Dewey Ballantine proved a true test of partnership receptiveness and transparency. Instead of rumors and unrest, Orrick associates got town meetings and webcasts. Firm management "actively solicited and responded to feedback from associates" and several survey respondents feel that associate reservations about the differences in culture between Orrick and Dewey contributed to the firm's decision not to merge (though, "it certainly did not make or break the merger"). This openness was not a one-off either. According to a D.C. associate, even when it's business as usual, "we drown in knowledge of the partnership's finances."

If "senior management really cares about associate happiness," then local management definitely has some big shoes to fill. A representative opinion, from a New York litigator (with bonus vocabulary builder!): "Associates really feel like they are respected and valued here, and are not simply fungible items." Some more adjectives to associate with Orrick partners:

Visit the Vault Law Channel, the complete online resource for law careers, featuring firm profiles, message boards, the Vault Law Job Board and more. **www.vault.com/law**

VAULT CAREER LIBRARY

361

"supportive and encouraging," "first class," and a less traditional "groovy." For all of Orrick's careful hiring, there are still some spoilers. "A few (a *very* few) are very hierarchical in their thinking." "We do have a few unpleasant types who are inconsiderate of weekends and nighttime."

In Paris, associate/partner relations are on the Yoda system: "We don't have the relationship of a boss vs. an employee but [one] of a master and a trainee." Elsewhere, the relationship trends toward "friends." A Tokyo associate explains, "one partner dropped by my office to chat about global warming and frogs last week." Can't beat that ... or can you? A New York corporate lawyer claims "The partner I work for helped me move apartments." We recommend you call your law school buddies instead.

Teach me, Seymour

Might as well face it now—as a baby associate, you're going to screw up. So it might be best to do it somewhere "Partners look at mistakes as opportunities to teach, not opportunities to scream." Not that you won't be asked to put in some serious effort. "The learning curve is very steep. Help is there, but you must ask for it." Some partners simply "are extremely busy and do not have the bandwidth to really mentor associates" on a formal level but both partners and senior associates are "more than willing to provide advice." Also, a system of "mentor families" makes it "more likely that you will find someone you really get along with."

Of course, there is plenty to learn, but Orrick associates would rather learn it from a partner than a lecture. Formal training received low, though not abysmal marks. The prevailing complaint seems to be boredom, either from "too many PowerPoint presentations," noninteractive telecasts and lectures, or "redundant" classes (which either teach topics that aren't particularly relevant to their specific practice, or that were already covered in the same training as a first-year). This litigator goes on to explain that "they want to train me on a broad range of substantive topics, but what I really need to know is the procedure for filing a brief." On the positive side, CLE credits are easy to come by, and "they say they are in the process of revamping the training program."

"The only associate in the room"

At Orrick, the question is not "will I have a good level of responsibility?" but "how much can you take?" "On big, multiparty cases," a litigator says, "I am often the only associate in the room, where other law firms send partners." "I have been able to take on writing and research projects, had contact with clients and helped interview witnesses, all within my first six months" reveals another. In some offices, understaffing has caused a crunch. An associate in Washington tells a much different story: "I do the work that a paralegal should do. Orrick should have a more robust litigation support department ... We are left fighting over the same four paralegals." Counterparts elsewhere find that lean staffing leads to good work, but "brutal work schedules leading up to deadlines." At least, when you're not busiest, schedules are "extraordinarily flexible" and no one's doing bed-checks. Associates note that a healthy number of their peers work flex-time, which is a viable option.

Comp- and con-

Controversy abounds concerning how the firm defines its compensation competitors. Should Orrick compare itself to other top-tier (and high PPP) California firms, national second-tier firms also based in California, or "the New York firms down the street" with whom it competes for clients and recruits? Some accuse the management of having a purposely narrow vision, "selectively defining 'market' to include firms that pay what it pays." Despite this, complaints about base salary itself are few and far between (and now that the firm has raised California salaries to the New York standard, we imagine there will be not a peep). Instead, associates condemn the bonuses. Any way you slice it, bonuses are below market across the board. And, associates note, based on a prohibitive tier system. The tiers are at "2,000, 2,100, 2,200, and 2,300 billable hours" respectively, with "$10K awarded at each level" (the California standard—New York and D.C. earn different amounts) and a "discretionary" component (which is not as "mythical" as at least one associate believes. "I was also paid a discretionary bonus for my work on the office diversity committee," confirms a San Francisco lawyer).

© 2007 Vault Inc.

Pro bono—what's your pleasure?

Like any good culture firm, Orrick does not shirk the pro bono. Your mileage may vary (some departments report partners that are less enthusiastic than the firmwide norm) but the firm policy is that all pro bono hours count toward billables and bonuses.

Those feeling civic-minded have only to check their inbox: "We get almost daily e-mails of new pro bono projects we can work on." If none of these appeals to you, the office pro bono coordinator will help you find one that does. In San Francisco, for instance, firm lawyers coach a high school mock trial team, a very popular and successful project. Associates estimate a minimum standard of 25 hours, and a "target" of 150, but "associates have, in unusual circumstances, billed over 300 hours and the firm counted every last one." One litigator even told us that this year, thanks to a series of trials, he will count over 600 pro bono hours! Now there's someone who will likely be in contention for the firm's yearly awards given to "standout associates" for their dedication to pro bono matters.

Visit the Vault Law Channel, the complete online resource for law careers, featuring firm profiles, message boards, the Vault Law Job Board and more. **www.vault.com/law**

VAULT CAREER LIBRARY   363

Freshfields Bruckhaus Deringer

520 Madison Avenue, 34th Floor
New York, NY 10022
Phone: (212) 277-4000

701 Pennsylvania Avenue NW
Suite 600
Washington, DC 20004
Phone: (202) 777-4500

65 Fleet Street
London EC4Y 1HS
United Kingdom
Phone: +44 20-7936-4000
www.freshfields.com

LOCATIONS

London (HQ)

New York, NY • Washington, DC • Amsterdam • Barcelona
• Beijing • Berlin • Bratislava • Brussels • Budapest •
Cologne • Dubai • Düsseldorf • Frankfurt • Hamburg •
Hanoi • Ho Chi Minh City • Hong Kong • Madrid • Milan •
Moscow • Munich • Paris • Rome • Shanghai • Tokyo •
Vienna

MAJOR DEPARTMENTS & PRACTICES

Antitrust, Competition & Trade • Banking • Corporate •
Dispute Resolution (including International Arbitration) •
Employment • Finance • Intellectual Property • Mergers &
Acquisitions • Real Estate • Tax

THE STATS

No. of attorneys: 2,400+
No. of offices: 27
Summer associate offers (US): 7 out of 7 (2006)
CEO: Ted Burke
US Managing Partner: Brian Rance

BASE SALARY (2007)

1st year: $160,000
2nd year: $170,000
3rd year: $185,000
4th year: $210,000
5th year: $230,000
6th year: $250,000
7th year: $265,000
Summer associate: $3,077/week

UPPERS

• "Sophisticated, professional" atmosphere
• Interesting, international work
• Generous vacation and leave policies

DOWNERS

• "Some very demanding partners"
• "The corporate practice is still fledgling" (NYC)
• Small office + huge matters = very long hours

NOTABLE PERKS

• Fresh fruit in the morning
• Free gym membership
• Opportunity for six-month secondment to any office in
  the world (if you speak the language)
• Training and associate development in Europe

THE BUZZ
WHAT ATTORNEYS AT OTHER FIRMS ARE SAYING ABOUT THIS FIRM

• "London powerhouse"
• "Very wide variation in quality"
• "Top international firm"
• "Ego and name bigger than work product"

© 2007 Vault Inc.

RANKING RECAP

Best in Practice
#2 - International Law
#4 (tie) - Antitrust
#10 - Mergers & Acquisitions

Best in Diversity
#3 - Diversity with Respect to GLBT
#2 (tie) - Overall Diversity
#4 - Diversity with Respect to Women
#11 - Diversity with Respect to Minorities

EMPLOYMENT CONTACT

Ms. Margaux Gillman
US Legal Recruiting Manager
Phone: (212) 284-4999
Fax: (212) 277-4001
E-mail: margaux.gillman@freshfields.com

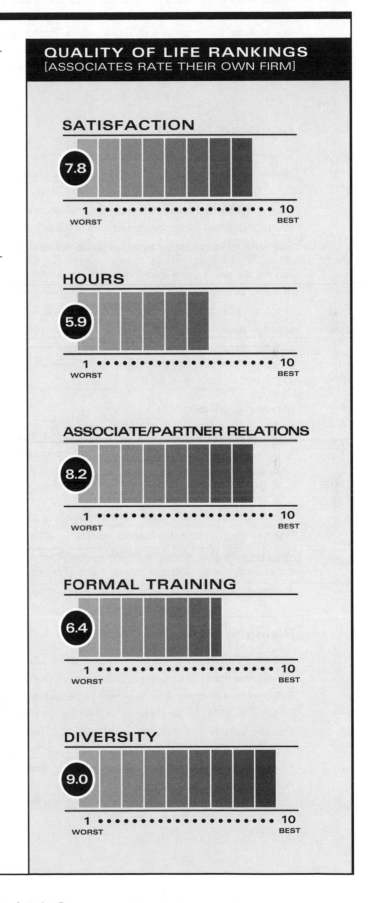

QUALITY OF LIFE RANKINGS
[ASSOCIATES RATE THEIR OWN FIRM]

SATISFACTION
7.8
1 WORST ... 10 BEST

HOURS
5.9
1 WORST ... 10 BEST

ASSOCIATE/PARTNER RELATIONS
8.2
1 WORST ... 10 BEST

FORMAL TRAINING
6.4
1 WORST ... 10 BEST

DIVERSITY
9.0
1 WORST ... 10 BEST

Visit the Vault Law Channel, the complete online resource for law careers, featuring firm profiles, message boards, the Vault Law Job Board and more. **www.vault.com/law**

VAULT CAREER LIBRARY   **365**

THE SCOOP

Due to successful mergers with German firms, Freshfields Bruckhaus Deringer now reigns as the Magic Circle's most European law firm. A multifaceted practice encompasses antitrust, international corporate work, finance, dispute resolution, real estate, tax, intellectual property and governmental organization. And extra credit for the logo—a spear-wielding angel. Now that's moral certitude.

Continental drift

Established in 1743 (50 years before America's title holder, Cadawalader Wickersham & Taft) Freshfields just might be the oldest international law firm in the world. In the 18th century, the Freshfields family served as solicitors to the Bank of England, while the Industrial Revolution engendered a formidable corporate practice. Though pedigreed, prestigious and profitable, until the last decade Freshfields remained a relatively small outfit whose growth had followed a predictable pattern. All that changed in 2000, due to integration with two of Germany's top houses, Bruckhaus Westrick Heller Löber, and Deringer Tessin Herrmann & Sedemund. The result was a pan-European behemoth, numbering 2,400 lawyers and 27 locations.

Among the post-merger transformations was a major shift in structure, with senior roles split between English and German partners. In early 2006, Freshfields announced successors to its management thrones: former U.S. Managing Partner Ted Burke now serves as chief executive, while U.K.-based financial services head Guy Morton and Frankfurt-based corporate and tax expert Konstantin Mettenheimer share duties as co-senior partners. Despite the Continental shift and the division of power, the firm has managed to maintain its U.K. prominence, posting the highest profit margins of all its charmed circle rivals. In 2006 Freshfields was named *PLC* magazine's "International Law Firm of the Year."

American pie

Freshfields is one of the few U.K. firms to maintain two U.S. offices (New York and Washington, D.C.) In the last years, the firm has expanded its American operations; approximately 70 lawyers work out of the U.S. offices, and 100 American lawyers work abroad in the firm's global offices. And while Freshfields' European brot und butter is M&A, stateside the game is finance and antitrust.

Significantly, in January 2006 Morton revealed his aims for a U.S. merger, admitting that to achieve this he is prepared to look beyond New York as well as unlock the firm's traditional lock-step compensation plan. Freshfields is also the only Magic Circle firm operating as an all-equity partnership, a structure that could hinder its U.S. merger plans. In 2000, the firm briefly explored the idea of a joint securities practice with Debevoise & Plimpton, while in July 2006 *The Lawyer* reported that Freshfields declined merger overtures from Magic Circle compatriot Allen & Overy.

Rising in the east

Many U.S. firms are only discovering the Asian market in the last decade, but Freshfields is, to recycle a phrase from the Empire, "an old Asia hand." The firm has been active in Vietnam and China for over 25 years, sustaining offices in six Asian cities. The Asian practice covers public & private M&A, international securities, structured and project finance, litigation and intellectual property. In 2006, the firm was named "International Law Firm of the Year" at the Asian Legal Business Awards. In the Middle East, Freshfields' involvement in MTN's $5.53 billion acquisition of Investcom, the first public offer in Dubai; Dubai International Capital's $1.32 billion acquisition of Doncasters; the acquisition of Inchcape shipping services by Istithmar; and the $5.7 billion acquisition of ports operator P&O by Dubai Ports World landed the firm "M&A Team of the Year" in *International Financial Law Review*'s Middle East Awards 2006.

© 2007 Vault Inc.

Winning combinations

Undoubtedly, Freshfields is one of Europe's leading M&A firms. In 2006 deal value soared nearly 400 percent to $283.3 billion, a figure that punted Freshfields from No. 15 on Bloomberg's 2005 M&A rankings to the very top spot. In final tables for 2006, Bloomberg ranked the firm No. 1 in European M&A; Freshfields advised on 251 deals worth $352.2 billion, and maintained a No. 3 position in the global rankings (just behind Skadden Arps and Sullivan & Cromwell) with deals totaling $369.1 billion. Bloomberg also ranked the firm its No. 1 M&A adviser for Hong Kong, China and Japan. Major M&A deals include representing Hutchison Telecom in the divestiture of its stake in Hutchison Essar, India's fourth-largest mobile phone operator, to Vodafone for $11.1 billion. Hutchison Essar is valued at approximately $18.8 billion, making the sale India's largest foreign investment transaction and one of its largest-ever M&A transactions. Deals in Germany include representation of Siemens during its €4.2 billion purchase of Bayer's diagnostics division in July 2006.

In February 2007 Freshfields, partnered with Cravath Swain & Moore, succeeded in helping the London Stock Exchange fend off a second hostile takeover attempt by U.S. exchange Nasdaq. Nasdaq's £2.7 billion bid expired on February 10, after Nasdaq (represented by Skadden Arps and Allen & Overy) failed to win over LSE investors. Nasdaq still holds a 29 percent stake in the LSE. Sharing the mandate with rival Lovells, Freshfields also advised independent broadcaster ITV during a takeover attempt by a private equity consortium that included Goldman Sachs and Apax. Other work for ITV includes managing its acquisition of community web site Friends Reunited and ITV's delisting from the NYSE.

And though Freshfields was slow to jump on the private equity wagon, recent transactions suggest that it's making up for lost time. In 2005 Freshfields advised BC Partners and Cinven on the €4.3 billion buyout of travel bookings company Amadeus, the largest Spanish LBO to date. In 2006, mandates for KKR, Apax and Permira earned the firm the "Private Equity Team of the Year" award from *Legal Business*.

Banking on the Bank of China

Freshfields' capital markets group also enjoyed a strong year, taking first place on the issuer tables with a rousing IPO practice. London's managing partner of corporate attributes the firm's strong showing to the increase in non-U.K. companies listing on the LSE. In June 2006 the firm handled Bank of China's IPO, the largest ever Chinese IPO, and the world's largest IPO in six years. Total proceeds from the IPO hit $9.7 billion, and could exceed $11.2 billion should the 15 percent over-allotment option be exercised in full. Bank of China is the second-largest bank in China by assets, and the second of the major formerly state-owned banks to go public. It is the largest Asian IPO since 1998, the world's largest IPO in six years, and currently the sixth-largest IPO globally.

Marketing "the Market"

In August 2006, the firm figured in the $420 million sale of U.K. tourist icon Covent Garden. Freshfields advised investment groups and longstanding clients Scottish Widows and Henderson Global on the sale of a 31-property portfolio in the central piazza. Buyer Capital & Counties inherits a portfolio that includes Covent Garden Market, the London Transport Museum and Jubilee Hall. The transaction is the jewel in the crown for Freshfields' real estate team, which turned over $51 million in 2005 and 2006.

That was dope, man

In June 2006 Freshfields' litigators successfully defended the International Olympic Committee in an anti-doping appeal spearheaded by a Russian cyclist and the Russian Olympic Committee. The plaintiffs sought to annul a 2004 IOC decision that U.S. cyclist Tyler Hamilton would not face further sanctions related to non-conclusive results of an anti-doping test held after he won a time-trial event at the 2004 Olympic Games in Athens. Plaintiffs requested that Hamilton be disqualified and that the gold medal be awarded to the second-place finisher, Russian cyclist Viatcheslav Ekimov. The appeal was supported by Australian cyclist and fourth-place finisher Michael Rogers, as well as the Australian Olympic Committee. The appeal was dismissed by a Court of Arbitration.

Visit the Vault Law Channel, the complete online resource for law careers, featuring firm profiles, message boards, the Vault Law Job Board and more. www.vault.com/law

VAULT CAREER LIBRARY   367

In other ongoing litigation, the firm is representing longstanding client MFI furniture group in a $10 million legal malpractice suit against Magic Circle rival Clifford Chance. The retailer claims that advice CC gave in 1999 and 2000 was negligent, and led to a £50 million increase in their pension deficit.

Putting partners out to pasture

In early November 2006 Freshfields radically revamped its unfunded pension plan, offering an early retirement option to partners over the age of 50. Eligible partners had until the end of October 2006 to lock in their entitlement under the firm's old pension plan; 30 partners, one-third of those eligible, decided to take the money and run. Retiring partners were also given the option to work as consultants for up to two years; they can continue to draw a salary, but will not receive pension payments until their employment with the firm ceases. Under the pension plan overhaul, partners who did not bite at the early retirement option can expect to receive some 65 percent of their previous pension entitlement. In 2006, the firm's average per partner profit leapt 19 percent from £700,000 to £830,000, with the full range of the partner take-home pay ranging from £390,000 to £980,000.

GETTING HIRED

No automatons

Freshfields is "competitive in a healthy way. We want people who will get on in our environment and think along similar lines, but not automatons. It's not just based on grades." Still, associates rate the firm "surprisingly selective" and note that it is a bit name-school "snobby." As one midlevel sees it, "In general the firm likes people who have gone to well known schools, who have an international background or bent, and who are well rounded." Adds another, "U.S. hires are typically from top law schools and have impressive academic and business credentials."

Considering the firm's U.K. base, "international experience is a plus"—according to one source, "We tend to hire people with some sort of international background (whether traveling, living or working abroad, studying international fields)." And social dynamics are important; a New Yorker points out that "given that this is a small office, to maintain the familiar and friendly atmosphere, the people that are employed here all tend to be fairly social, with a similar attitude to working and an international outlook on life." Observes one source, "Recruiting puts a high premium on hiring people who are interesting and fun to work with."

OUR SURVEY SAYS

Early bird gets the worm

"Life at Freshfields is far better than life at other large law firms," insists one Manhattan midlevel. "The New York office has a 'small firm feel' backed by a behemoth global network." And one of the benefits of this small size, associates report, is that there is ample opportunity for even junior associates to take on early responsibility and weighty cases. "I think generally the quality of work that you undertake at Freshfields is better than at many of the larger firms as there are fewer people to share the work with," reports one source. "Excellent matters and excellent work. Lean staffing means you will be assigned very high levels of responsibility," agrees another. While partners who are "willing to entrust projects to associates with relatively light supervision" can certainly be a plus, one midlevel feels that when "fairly junior associates are responsible for complex deals, I think the partners should review the associates' work more carefully."

We the people

"One of the main reasons I enjoy working here (and stay working here) is that this is the best group of colleagues I've worked with," enthuses a source in the New York office. "The office is small (70 lawyers), but a close bunch and definitely 'on the same

© 2007 Vault Inc.

wavelength,' as regards how we interrelate." One D.C. insider adds, "There is almost always a welcome lunch or going away happy hour going on, because foreign lawyers pass through the office fairly often." Notes another D.C. colleague, "The firm's strong international culture carries over into its U.S. offices. There is an emphasis on our global network, and frequent secondments and conferences facilitate interaction with foreign colleagues." Associates tell us that their colleagues are "friendly, professional and collegial," and that "post-work events/happy hours are frequent." As one source describes it, "People feel comfortable enough to go to their colleagues' offices and chat, and it is not rare for groups of associates to go out for lunch together." "But [there's] no pressure to hang out," another points out. And as for political leanings, "Politics are a topic of bemusement, not something people delve into at work." Well, we are not bemused.

Is everybody decent?

An associate in the New York office gets a bit defensive: "The hours are long enough, although no longer than they would be at any other 'decent' firm. And the partners and other associates are all working hard as well, so it's not like it's just me." Insiders agree that the firm does try to be flexible, but "when there is lots of work to do, flexibility means less. There are only so many hours in the week." Nevertheless, "There is absolutely no face time here. People are encouraged to leave if they are not busy. While partners expect that people will need to work on weekends and public holidays, they do try to warn you in advance and express their appreciation for the effort people are making when working extra-long hours."

A bullish market has, of course, had an impact on hours. Sighs one first-year, "The past year has been busier than I would wish, though my perception is that this is true at all similar firms in this market." Another tired associate confides, "Hours have been getting ridiculous recently. This was definitely not what I had signed up for when I first started at Freshfields. We are very stretched at the associate level and there aren't enough lawyers to cover all the work that is flowing in. I would be resentful if I were the only one that was getting killed, but it's busy for everyone—including the partners, so I guess it's just the economy. The people are, however, fairly good at accommodating special plans, if they were given advance notice." A colleague confirms that the firm is "very demanding, but at the same time very accommodating and understanding whenever associates have personal crises necessitating leave. Vacation can be difficult to take, but when you are able to get away it seems that people can do so for several weeks at a time." Additionally, "associates with young families are able to negotiate for special work hours" and "a significant amount of vacation time can be planned in advance because the firm has chosen to acknowledge a good number of public holidays." Though one insider gloats that his "weekends are always free!" another cautions that "to view this firm as a 'lifestyle' firm is incorrect." But as one associate sees it, "If you don't feel that your time and skills are being wasted, longer hours matter less."

Crossing the pay divide

According to one satisfied source, "The firm pays full New York salary and bonuses in all U.S. offices, covers full medical and is generous—reimburses all bar expenses, flies all associates to worldwide practice group conferences, etc." Adds another, "We have 26 days of vacation per year. Benefits are very good and they cover 100 percent health insurance costs for associates and family." The benefit package ("one of the best among all the law firms in NYC") is a big plus: "For a lawyer with a family, that equals a $6,000 pay advantage over most firms in D.C." Still, wonders one associate, "I don't understand why, when matching the salary increase, Freshfields New York again did not make the increase retroactive, and did not explain to us the reasoning. Seems petty." Gripes a fellow associate, "Freshfields advertises as paying 'market,' but never gives raises retroactively." Sulks another, "Even more disappointing was that there was no 'thank you' in the memo about the raise." And from a correspondent in D.C.: "The divide between U.S. and U.K./E.U. pay needs to be addressed. The latter is considerably lower and yet the charge out rate for E.U./U.K. lawyers is higher than in the U.S."

It's all good

"Associate/partner 'interaction' is the wrong word. I have a working, collegial relationship with the partners here," corrects one lower-level. Yup, adds another, "Partners and associates at the office have a very relaxed attitude with each other. The partners are very friendly and always available to answer questions." As one associate sees it, "'Open-door offices' is not just a policy, and associates are not afraid to stop by and talk to partners." It's clear who's running the ship, says one rookie, "but there is no unpleasant hierarchy." Partners are generally good about feedback, and they "do carve out time for informal discussions and meetings. Great guidance is given when working on client/matters" and they "are quite approachable on work-related/personal problems. [They] take time out to seek out young associates to ensure that they are doing well in the work environment." Another positive trend is that "associates are becoming increasingly involved in issues such as recruitment, business development and financial reporting."

So you say it's your birthday?

"Homemade birthday cakes" tops one associate's list of favorite perks. Other freebies high on the appreciation list include "espresso, soda, popcorn, rides home, dinner and moving expenses." For the healthy crowd, there is "fresh fruit in the morning," as well as "free gym membership (although you need to get a card from reception, which is annoying)." For rookies, "The startup bonus is a great perk!" And travel prospects are popular: associates happily report that "training always takes place in Europe about once a year" and that there is "opportunity for secondment to any office in the world for six months (provided you speak the language)." Freshfields also offers "more vacation time than most firms—more than five weeks," gloats one associate, "which you are actually expected to use!" Additionally, there is a "more liberal paternity/maternity leave policy than most firms." And let's not forget that fully-paid health insurance, which earns the firm consistent raves.

© 2007 Vault Inc.

"One of the main reasons I enjoy working here (and staying here) is that this is the best group of colleagues I've worked with."

— *Freshfields Bruckhaus Deringer associate*

Visit the Vault Law Channel, the complete online resource for law careers, featuring firm profiles, message boards, the Vault Law Job Board and more. www.vault.com/law

VAULT CAREER LIBRARY

371

Proskauer Rose LLP

1585 Broadway
New York, NY 10036
Phone: (212) 969-3000
www.proskauer.com

LOCATIONS

New York, NY (HQ)
Boca Raton, FL
Boston, MA
Los Angeles, CA
New Orleans, LA
Newark, NJ
Washington, DC
Paris

MAJOR DEPARTMENTS & PRACTICES

Capital Markets
Financial Services
Health Care
Intellectual Property
Labor & Employment
Litigation
Media & Entertainment
Mergers & Acquisitions
Personal Planning
Private Equity
Real Estate
Sports
Taxation
White Collar Crime

THE STATS

No. of attorneys: 713
No. of offices: 8
Summer associate offers: 69 out of 70 (2006)
Chairman: Allen I. Fagin
Hiring Partner: Julie M. Allen

THE BUZZ
WHAT ATTORNEYS AT OTHER FIRMS ARE SAYING ABOUT THIS FIRM

- "Cool clients"
- "Aggressive"
- "Great firm, great people"
- "Proskauer Rose: we never close"

BASE SALARY (2007)

New York, NY; Boston, MA; Los Angeles, CA
1st year: $160,000
Summer associate: $3,077/week

Washington, DC
1st year: $145,000
Summer associate: $2,788/week

Newark, NJ; Boca Raton, FL
1st year: $130,000
Summer associate: $2,500/week

New Orleans, LA
1st year: $97,500
Summer associate: $1,875/week

UPPERS

- High compensation
- "Significant responsibility and working directly with partners"
- "The firm's culture is more relaxed than other big city firms"

DOWNERS

- Tough hours
- "Very limited promotional opportunities"
- "The New York office ignores the other offices"

NOTABLE PERKS

- "Great cookies"
- Massages for litigators each week
- Free Starbucks coffee on every floor
- Backup day care

© 2007 Vault Inc.

RANKING RECAP

Best in Practice
#6 - Labor & Employment

Partner Prestige Rankings
#5 - Labor & Employment

EMPLOYMENT CONTACT

Ms. Diane M. Kolnik
Manager of Legal Recruiting
Phone: (212) 969-5071
E-mail: dkolnik@proskauer.com

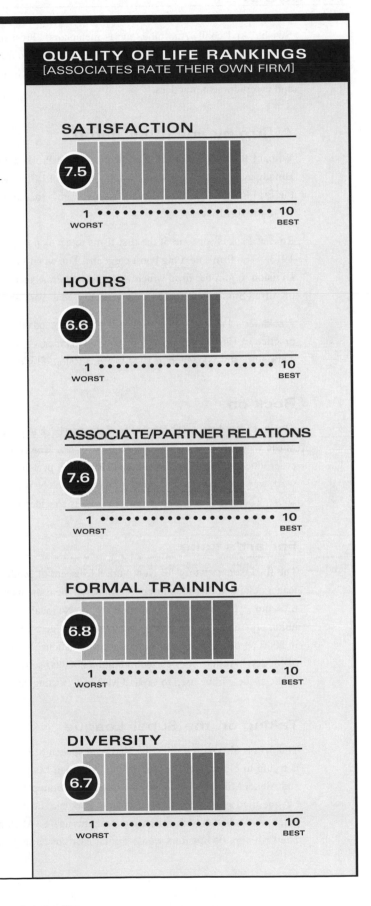

QUALITY OF LIFE RANKINGS
[ASSOCIATES RATE THEIR OWN FIRM]

SATISFACTION
7.5
1 WORST — 10 BEST

HOURS
6.6
1 WORST — 10 BEST

ASSOCIATE/PARTNER RELATIONS
7.6
1 WORST — 10 BEST

FORMAL TRAINING
6.8
1 WORST — 10 BEST

DIVERSITY
6.7
1 WORST — 10 BEST

Visit the Vault Law Channel, the complete online resource for law careers, featuring firm profiles, message boards, the Vault Law Job Board and more. www.vault.com/law

VAULT CAREER LIBRARY   373

THE SCOOP

Swish! And goal! And other sports metaphors! Proskauer Rose LLP is practically synonymous with "sports law" (clients include Major League Baseball, the NFL, the NHL and the NBA.). However, this reputation shortchanges the rest of the firm's incredibly diversified practice, which features top-notch corporate, litigation, labor and employment, real estate, tax, health care and entertainment practices.

A firm by any other name

William R. Rose wrote the first chapter of the Proskauer Rose story when, at just 21 years of age, he opened a law firm on Broadway in Downtown Manhattan in 1875. In 1907, Rose promoted associate Benjamin Paskus to the partnership and renamed the firm Rose & Paskus. Alfred Rose, William's son, joined the firm in 1911 and became a partner in 1920 (taking time out to serve in World War I).

Rose & Paskus was one of the first firms to develop a specialized tax practice after the passage of the Sixteenth Amendment in 1913. The firm's next big boost came in 1930, when Judge Joseph M. Proskauer resigned his position on New York's Appellate Division to join the firm, which was renamed Proskauer, Rose & Paskus. Judge Proskauer was a close friend and political ally of Alfred Smith, who served as governor of New York and lost the 1928 presidential election to Herbert Hoover.

Proskauer's labor law practice—still a strength today—was established in 1939, and the firm began building its sports law practice in 1963, when it welcomed a new partner, George Gallantz, along with his client, the NBA. The firm's first non-New York outpost was opened in 1977 in Boca Raton, Florida.

Rock on

Thanks to Proskauer, The White Stripes can go back to pretending to be brother and sister, or divorced, or whatever—and making music without someone swiping their royalties. The firm defended the Detroit-bred musical duo in a copyright suit filed by a co-producer of their first two albums. Proskauer persuaded a federal jury sitting in Michigan to find that the producer's technical work was not protected by copyright law, and that he was thus not eligible for any royalties. The jury returned its verdict in June 2006. The case was widely publicized and is considered an important landmark in the protection of recording artists' rights.

For art's sake

The firm won a victory for New York's Museum of Modern Art in August 2006 in an employee relations case. Several union leaders claimed that the museum terminated them prematurely in 2002, just before a planned renovation that closed down the museum. The employees complained to the National Labor Relations Board (NLRB), saying the layoffs were in retaliation for union organizing activity. An administrative judge agreed with them in December 2004, but the NLRB overturned the decision in 2006. Proskauer also represented the international real estate firm Hines in its acquisition of a parcel of land from the Museum of Modern Art that will be used to build a 200,000-square-foot mixed-use structure bordering the museum's main building. Part of the space will be used to expand MoMA's existing galleries.

Taking on the Super League

The firm is also representing the NHL and several of its clubs in a dispute with the Russian Super League. The Russian league is trying to block three Russian players—Evgeni Malkin of the Pittsburgh Penguins, Andrei Taratukhin of the Calgary Flames and Alexei Mikhnov of the Edmonton Oilers—from playing in the NHL, claiming they are under contract in Russia. The Super League filed suit in federal court in New York and the Proskauer team came away victorious, most recently convincing a federal judge in Manhattan to dismiss the complaints against Malkin and the Penguins, clearing the way for Malkin to play in the NHL. The firm's sports litigators won a similar case concerning Russian star Alexander Ovechin in 2005.

© 2007 Vault Inc.

The corporate Rose

Corporate clients need Proskauer's help, too. So much so that in December 2006, The Legal U.S. 500's annual ranking of the top law firms for corporate work singled out Proskauer in several categories, including private equity (for advising on both buyouts and fund formation), international M&A, high-yield debt and hedge fund formation.

The firm's high rating was likely the result of its participation in many high-profile deals. For example, the firm's M&A Group teamed with lawyers from the private equity, tax, securities and other corporate practices to represent Merrill Lynch Global Private Equity in what at the time was the largest leveraged buyout in history, the $33 billion acquisition of HCA, the largest for-profit health care provider in the United States. In summer 2006, the firm advised Citigroup for its role in a $547 million public bond offering that will be used to finance a new stadium for the New York Mets. (No word on whether the deal includes a provision requiring Mets players to swing instead of looking at a called third strike in the bottom of the ninth inning in game seven.) In November 2006, the firm counseled Celgene Corp. when the international pharmaceuticals company completed a $1 billion stock offering. A month later, Proskauer advised Corporacion UBC Internacional when the Panama-based financial services company sold its Grupo Cuscatlan subsidiary to Citigroup. The $1.51 billion deal closed in December 2006.

Pro bono help, too

In between paying gigs, Proskauer has fulfilled its pro bono commitments. In the summer of 2006, Proskauer lawyers, summer associates and staff built a house in New Orleans for Habitat for Humanity. The firm's attorneys also partnered with the Lawyers' Committee for Human Rights to assist voters in Ohio during the 2006 election. Proskauer attorneys staffed the Lawyers' Committee's Election Protection hotline, which allowed voters to call in to get advice on election law and procedures. Also that year, the firm launched a new pro bono initiative, led by senior counsel Scott Harshbarger, former Massachusetts attorney general that encourages all lawyers to spend at least 50 hours a year on pro bono work.

Going great guns outside NY

Proskauer is well known in New York, but the firm's non-New York offices are its fastest growing. The Boston office, which features a strong corporate group led by one of the world's leading private equity practices and well-developed finance, securities and M&A practices, complemented by a top-tier patent litigation and counseling practice, is on a tear. Launched just a few short years ago, the office has been named by the *Boston Business Journal* for two years running as the fastest-growing law office in the city. In L.A., the firm continues to build its corporate transactional practices, along with its real estate, tax, corporate defense and entertainment teams. The D.C. office added a quartet of top patent lawyers last year and looks to continue its expansion; and in Paris, the firm continues a growth path that was accelerated with the addition of a large group from one of Paris's elite firms, Rambaud Martel.

GETTING HIRED

Top tier or bust

Proskauer Rose fancies students from fancy law schools, indeed perhaps to the point of being—for better or for worse—flexible about their grades and skills, associates report. A New York corporate attorney says, "The firm seems to be a bit relaxed on GPAs from Ivy League schools, but a bit tougher on second- and third-tier schools. I think it is not an unusual thing at law firms. The firm recruits heavily at Cornell, Harvard and Columbia." A first-year adds, "Proskauer only looks at people from certain schools and is very selective, but I'm living proof that your personality matters just as much as your GPA and that there is no GPA cutoff." But as a junior New York litigator sees it, the firm does itself a disservice in that "a very dynamic and intelligent student from a lower-tier school will get rejected out of hand unless he or she is in the top-five percent or so." One New Yorker summarizes: "You must be intelligent, well-spoken and hard-working to receive an offer from Proskauer. We are not the typical white shoe

Visit the Vault Law Channel, the complete online resource for law careers, featuring firm profiles, message boards, the Vault Law Job Board and more. www.vault.com/law

VAULT CAREER LIBRARY   375

firm—qualified candidates from second- and third-tier law schools can and do receive offers from Proskauer ... however, if you are at one of those schools, make sure that you are at the top of your class!"

As for specific personality traits that might service you well, a New York litigator advises that the firm is "looking for good people who are enjoyable to work with, and really clever attorneys." A junior L.A. associate adds, "the firm is interested in recruiting interesting, enthusiastic people. The interviews are what matter the most."

OUR SURVEY SAYS

A satisfied majority

Proskauer's associates are (mostly) truly happy campers. A litigator who recently joined the firm's New York office reports, "The firm is awesome. Little things, like replacing the old nasty coffee with Starbucks on each floor, go a long way. Also, the litigation partners are geniuses—and nice!" A Los Angeles labor specialist says, "The partners and senior counsel treat us with respect. The compensation is terrific and the offices are very nice. I have a view of the Pacific from my window." A junior litigator adds, "I feel that I get diverse assignments and a good amount of responsibility. On most of my matters, I work directly with partners. On some matters, I am the only associate, which is often very beneficial." That said, there is also a small minority of dissatisfied associates. As one senior New Yorker reports, "Many of my colleagues are very fine lawyers and good people and I have worked on many interesting cases, but I have often been dissatisfied with the level of responsibility I am allowed or the particular work I am given on cases. There are hierarchical limitations and also a substantial focus on hours, the more one bills the more worth they have, which is not necessarily a correct formula." A midlevel adds, "I enjoy the work I do and the people I work with, but I am unsatisfied with the lack of balance and the very heavy volume of work. I would be much more satisfied if I felt more control over my workload."

Goldilocks says, this amount of socializing is just right ...

Associates say that the firm is "amicable," "open," "congenial," "friendly" and "supportive," and that it strikes a healthy balance between work and socializing. "Lots of lunches—team lunches, client lunches and lunches just to get away for a little brunch," says a New York litigator. "Plus, happy hours are on the rise—we had one upstairs with a full bar, White Castle hamburgers and Proskauer T-shirts just a couple weeks ago, just so everyone could take a break and relax." Another New Yorker adds, "We have work events and they are well attended. People really get along here, for the most part, and attorneys do socialize outside of work (for example, if there is a deal-closing dinner), but I would not say there is socializing apart from work related events." An L.A. litigator advises, "The younger associates in the litigation department get along very well and spend some time socializing outside of work. Overall, it does not feel as though there is a strict 'hierarchy.' Doors are always open, and a first-year associate generally feels comfortable going to speak with the office's managing partner, or any other partner for that matter."

A few exceptions apparently prove the rule

Proskauer associates praise the partners, though they admit that a few duds persist. "There are some jerks, but the tenor is more-or-less good," reports a New Yorker. "I think if you make a commitment to the firm, partners make it a point to mentor you." A junior litigator says, "I have yet to hear of a partner treating an associate with anything less than the utmost respect. Management seems to keep us informed and take our feedback into account—after years of associates' complaining about the house coffee, we just switched over to Starbucks, which will be available and complimentary at all times." A corporate attorney adds, "Most partners I know are very courteous, polite, personable. Management is excellent. Very well run ship." That said, a number of complaints resemble this one from a senior Los Angeleno: "Most people are cordial, except [individual partner] can be very intimidating and demanding to associates, especially those he perceives to be 'weak.'"

© 2007 Vault Inc.

Good—maybe great—but not always an option

Proskauer's associates say that there is "formal training galore," but that they prefer to learn on the beat. As one litigator puts it, "Most of my training comes informally through the matters I am working on." As for specific offerings, another litigator reports, "We had a week of training at the start of our first year and then a one day writing workshop later." A corporate attorney adds, "I love the corporate training we have. We meet at least once a week for a CLE training on something very useful to our practice. Associates and partners come to speak with us about how to format documents, what they expect of us in a deal or how private-equity markets work. It is invaluable." However, a senior associate warns, "It's much better at the junior level than later years." And a midlevel adds, "Because of client demands, it's often difficult to find time to attend training."

Informal training (e.g., mentoring) gets mixed reviews at Proskauer, though most associates seem to agree that it's there for the taking. As one junior associate reports, "All the partners I work with want me to succeed, and generally express their approval when I have done good work. I feel I can speak freely about concerns and seek professional advice. There is a 'formal' mentoring program, but I find the couple of partners I work with most often (and choose to work with) are the ones I seek out for mentoring as well." Another junior associate adds, "I don't get a whole lot of training from partners, but the senior associates do a very good job of showing us how to handle assignments." However, a New York litigator says, "Informal training goes on in every matter you handle. Mentoring is basically nonexistent or, at best, an intermittent forced activity."

Complaint-free compensation

What Proskauer associates don't complain about (or at least not very much) is their pay. Associates have various ways of expressing their praise and thankfulness. "More is always better, but the amount of money we get is ridiculous," says a first year. "Proskauer always keep pace and is generous with covering our costs," reports another first year. A senior associate—repeating a theme—adds, "We get paid a lot of money, more than I would have ever imagined that I would make at this point in my life while in college. Having said that, I could always use a little more."

Proskauer is flexible about hours, associates report, at least to the degree that one can be flexible about working all the time. As one insider puts it, "The firm is very flexible about time. As long as you get the work done, you can keep odd hours. But there is a lot of work to do." Another insider adds, "It's a lot of hours, but it's hard to argue with it considering the amount of money we make."

Visit the Vault Law Channel, the complete online resource for law careers, featuring firm profiles, message boards, the Vault Law Job Board and more. **www.vault.com/law**

VAULT CAREER LIBRARY   377

41
PRESTIGE RANKING

King & Spalding LLP

1180 Peachtree Street, NE
Atlanta, GA 30309
Phone: (404) 572-4600
www.kslaw.com

LOCATIONS

Atlanta, GA (HQ)
Houston, TX
New York, NY
Washington, DC
Dubai
London

MAJOR DEPARTMENTS & PRACTICES

Corporate/Transactional
Finance & Restructuring
Government & Regulatory
Intellectual Property
International Arbitration
Tort & Commercial Litigation

THE STATS

No. of attorneys: 800+
No. of offices: 6
Summer associate offers: 89 out of 96 (2006)
Chairman: Robert D. Hays
Hiring Partners:
    Atlanta: Carolyn Z. Alford
    Houston: Tracie J. Renfroe
    New York: Stephen M. Wiseman
    Washington, DC: Peter M. Todaro

BASE SALARY (2007)

Atlanta, GA
1st year: $130,000
Summer associate: $2,500/week

Houston, TX
1st year: $140,000
Summer associate: $2,700/week

New York, NY
1st year: $160,000
Summer associate: $3,077/week

Washington, DC
1st year: $145,000
Summer associate: $2,800/week

UPPERS

• Quality work
• Quality reputation
• "No yellers"

DOWNERS

• Opaque bonus system
• Business formal attire
• Few perks

NOTABLE PERKS

• Free Coke products
• Subsidized parking
• Tickets to sporting events and other entertainment
• Attorney lounge with foosball and pool table

THE BUZZ
WHAT ATTORNEYS AT OTHER FIRMS ARE SAYING ABOUT THIS FIRM

• "Vibrant, growing"
• "Stodgy"
• "Southeast's finest"
• "Very tough atmosphere"

© 2007 Vault Inc.

RANKING RECAP

Best in Region
#1 - Atlanta

Quality of Life
#12 - Office Space

EMPLOYMENT CONTACTS

Atlanta
Ms. Amy Miele
Recruiting Manager
Phone: (404) 572-4990
Fax: (404) 572-5100
E-mail: amiele@kslaw.com

Houston
Ms. Cheyanne Powers
Recruiting Manager
Phone: (713) 751-3200
Fax: (713) 751-3290
E-mail: cpowers@kslaw.com

New York
Ms. Ana Lesce
Recruiting Manager
Phone: (212) 556-2200
Fax: (212) 556-2222
E-mail: alesce@kslaw.com

Washington, DC
Ms. Rebecca B. Grady
Recruiting Manager
Phone: (202) 626 2387
Fax: (202) 626-3737
E-mail: rgrady@kslaw.com

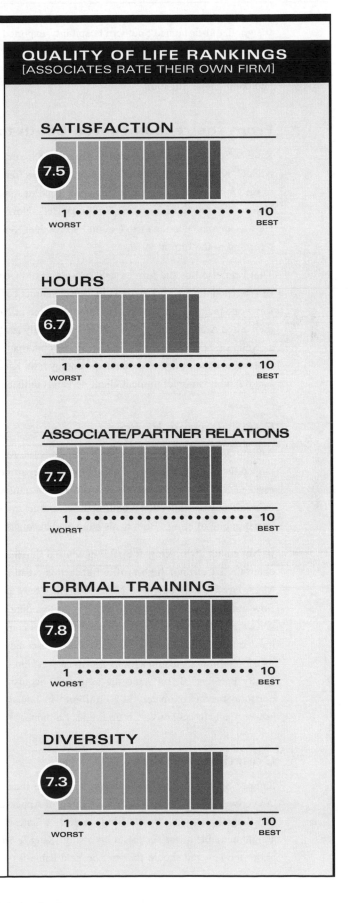

QUALITY OF LIFE RANKINGS
[ASSOCIATES RATE THEIR OWN FIRM]

SATISFACTION
7.5
1 WORST .... 10 BEST

HOURS
6.7
1 WORST .... 10 BEST

ASSOCIATE/PARTNER RELATIONS
7.7
1 WORST .... 10 BEST

FORMAL TRAINING
7.8
1 WORST .... 10 BEST

DIVERSITY
7.3
1 WORST .... 10 BEST

Visit the Vault Law Channel, the complete online resource for law careers, featuring firm profiles, message boards, the Vault Law Job Board and more. www.vault.com/law

VAULT CAREER LIBRARY   379

THE SCOOP

It's good, old-fashioned Southern hospitality, exported around the country—and around the world. King & Spalding got its start in Atlanta, and now has offices in Washington, D.C., New York, Houston, London and Dubai. King & Spalding is full service, handling corporate and transactional work, government relations, intellectual property, bankruptcy, international arbitration, tort and commercial litigation.

From the reconstructed South to Dubai

King & Spalding was founded in Atlanta in 1885, just one score after the Civil War ended. The "King" in King & Spalding is Alex C. King, one of the firm's founding partners (the other being Jack J. Spalding). King would later serve as solicitor general of the United States and as a judge on the Court of Appeals for the Fifth Circuit (which, at that time, included Georgia). The firm also counts among its members Griffin B. Bell. Now senior counsel at the firm, Bell at one time served as its managing partner. He was appointed to the Fifth Circuit by President Kennedy in 1961 and served as attorney general under President Carter before returning to the firm in 1979.

That year also saw the firm expand outside its old Georgia home, as King & Spalding opened a Washington, D.C., office. The firm opened a New York outpost in 1990 to attract corporate work; a Houston office followed in 1995. King & Spalding's first foray outside the United States (to London) came in 2003. In January 2007, King & Spalding opened an office in Dubai, part of the United Arab Emirates. The office was initially staffed with lawyers relocated from Atlanta, London, New York and Houston, as well as associates from the Dubai office of international firm Baker Botts. King & Spalding Dubai will concentrate on Islamic finance, private equity, real estate and energy law. King & Spalding has also established an affiliation with a law firm in Riyadh, Saudi Arabia, in order to meet client demands in that region.

Earning their keep

Among King & Spalding's recent big deals is the August 2006 work it did for Belk, Inc. The private department store giant tapped the firm when it agreed to purchase 38 department stores from Saks Inc. The deal was worth $285 million. The firm also assisted SunTrust Banks in setting up two credit transactions. SunTrust agreed to provide Bristow Group Inc. with $125 million in credit and also extended credit facilities to Buckeye GP Holdings L.P. at the same time the oil and gas company completed an initial public offering. Both deals happened in August 2006.

In November 2006, King & Spalding advised Caremark Rx, Inc. when the health care company agreed to merge with drugstore chain CVS Corp in a high-profile transaction creating the nation's premier integrated pharmacy services provider. The firm's M&A lawyers kept busy that November when they advised Per Se Technologies on its purchase by McKesson Corp. The deal flow continued into December, as King & Spalding acted as counsel to John H. Harland Co. when Harland, which provides software and print products to financial services companies, agreed to be acquired by M&F Worldwide Corp in a $1.7 billion transaction. The firm switched sides and represented an acquirer in January 2007. King & Spalding advised GE Real Estate on its $2.2 billion acquisition by merger of a portfolio of 147 assets from Crow Holdings' third real estate fund, Crow Holdings Realty Partners III, L.P., and the associated acquisition by affiliates of Kimco Realty Corporation of 19 retail assets in the portfolio for approximately $920 million. In January 2007, the firm advised energy company Mirant Corp. when it sold six power plants to LS Power Group for $1.4 billion.

Courting success

King & Spalding saved client National Service Industries (NSI) from millions of dollars in liabilities thanks to some skilled lawyering before the Second Circuit Court of Appeals. NSI purchased the assets of Serv-All Uniform Rental Corp.; Serv-All had illegally dumped dry cleaning waste at a Staten Island landfill in 1978. The state of New York sued NSI, arguing that it should be liable as the successor company. King & Spalding successfully argued to a federal judge that NSI wasn't a successor under the law and should thus not be held liable for the clean-up of Serv-All's pollution. The appeals court agreed in August

© 2007 Vault Inc.

2006, upholding the lower court's dismissal of the claims against NSI. In that same month, the firm also won an arbitration victory for client Azurix in a dispute with the Argentinean government. In 1999 Azurix agreed to a contract to provide water services for the province of Buenos Aires. But the deal was abruptly terminated in 2002 after Azurix claimed the government was not allowing it to charge tariffs, as provided for in the agreement. The International Centre for the Settlement of Investment Disputes sided with Azurix, awarding the company $185 million.

In another international dispute, King & Spalding successfully persuaded Mexico's Ministry of the Economy to revoke an anti-dumping order that prevented rice imports from U.S. companies. Mexico had slapped anti-dumping duties on rice imports in violation of trade law and World Trade Organization decisions; with King & Spalding's help, U.S. rice exporters convinced Mexico to revoke the order in September 2006. King & Spalding won a patent victory for client Internet Security Systems, Inc. (ISS) that October. SRI International accused ISS of infringing on four patents relating to network intrusion and detection technology. A federal judge in Delaware granted summary judgment for ISS and a co-defendant, finding that all the patents-in-suit were invalid. The firm also secured a victory for a group of welding rod manufacturers in a trial in Texas. The plaintiff in that case alleged injury from fumes while using the defendants' products, but a jury rejected those claims in November 2006. (This was the second victory for these clients in Texas, and the firm represents them in similar claims in a pending suit in Georgia.)

GETTING HIRED

Schools, grades & clerkships, schools grades & clerkships, schools, grades ...

Associates suggest that landing a job at King & Spalding requires either good grades from an Ivy League school or great grades from a top local school. Also, a clerkship would be nice. "It's tough to get hired here. If you're from an Ivy or a top-10 ranked school, your grades can be a little more compromised. Otherwise, K&S is the primary target for students from Georgia, Emory, Mercer and Georgia State, and most associates from those schools graduate in the top tier of their class," advises an Atlanta litigator. "It's surprising how many people have clerkships as well; the firm seems to really put a premium on hiring clerks."

The firm also places an emphasis on that mysterious, intangible quality known as "fit," associates say. And what constitutes "fit" at K&S? "Driven, committed, articulate, mature, good writer, intelligent and socially intelligent," advises one young associate. A banking associate adds, "I think getting hired here is extremely difficult [without] top grades from a top law school, but there is something to be said for a candidate with a great personality, strong abilities and good networking skills." That said, another insider warns that if you're not at least in the top half of your class, all the fit in the world might not help. "Persons under the median (even at great schools) have a hard time getting callbacks, even if their personality is great," says a junior associate. "We look to hire dynamic people who we would want to work with."

OUR SURVEY SAYS

"Relatively satisfying"

One fairly typical King & Spalding associate reports, "The firm is a good place to practice law. It keeps up with the market compensation, it provides young associates with opportunities to do advanced level work and you can see the fruits of your labor in high-profile matters." A New York IP associate says, "I feel like I'm receiving a great salary for reasonable hours, and I am learning new things all the time." A real-estate attorney advises, "I am generally happy with the work that I do and the people I work with, most of whom are really nice and good lawyers. Sometimes I wish we had more high-profile work." But a lot of attorneys sound like this midlevel: "My particular practice area and my colleagues make my work relatively satisfying."

Visit the Vault Law Channel, the complete online resource for law careers, featuring firm profiles, message boards, the Vault Law Job Board and more. www.vault.com/law

VAULT CAREER LIBRARY   381

After you've gone

It seems that King & Spalding's culture makes a long-lasting impression. One Atlanta litigator reports, "The firm culture is professional, but not cold by any means ... I have kept in touch with people who have left to go in-house. They tell me that what they miss about King & Spalding is the relationships and social life they were able to have here." It's fun times in Washington as well: "The firm definitely socializes together. I have had friends go to other firms and say the people there are fine to work with, but this firm is where you make friends you want to see outside the office." As another litigator puts it, "Lawyers socialize together from time to time. There are certainly efforts to do so, especially among the young associates, but time constraints often thwart those plans."

Individually, yea; institutionally, nay

Individual partners treat associates with respect, but the firm overall fails to include them in important decisions, associates report. A junior attorney from Atlanta finds, "In my brief experience the partners have been very respectful. I am aware that the partners don't regularly let the associates participate in firmwide decisions, but I am not sure that would make sense given the somewhat divergent incentives and situations of the two groups." Another junior adds, "Associates are treated very well, but aren't kept in the loop on firmwide decisions, let alone allowed to participate." On the other hand, "The partnership makes efforts to be more transparent. In my short time here, I have attended several meetings presenting how the partners make money and how they measure profitability for each associate. They have formed a new associates committee composed of associates spanning different groups and levels of experience. The partners seem to be aware of what's going on with the associates, especially those younger, non-equity partners. In general, there are obviously universal ideas about seniority that require that partners receive respect, but for the most part, they have tried to earn it."

Formal training aplenty—if you're into that sort of thing

Associates praise the firm's formal training program, calling it "not too overbearing, but always there if you want it." One associate from the firm's New York office offers, "Generally, the firm has a number of relevant and helpful training programs. The week-long training in the firm's Atlanta office was particularly helpful, and it was great to meet people from all the different offices." A banking lawyer adds, "The training is very intensive and can seem overwhelming at times, but is very helpful in associate development." However, one litigator warns, "There are CLEs here and there, but it's basically learn as you go, which is the only way to actually learn how to be a lawyer, it seems. The CLEs are marginally useful, but the real way to learn is to actually write a motion or attend a hearing."

Great unless angered

Associates say that the firm's informal training opportunities vary partner to partner. "I've received phenomenal mentoring from no less than five partners," crows one junior associate. A junior Atlanta litigator adds, "I have had very positive experiences with midlevel associates, younger partners and more senior partners all taking an interest in my development as a lawyer. They tend to be accommodating and try to make the time, if you ask for it, to provide feedback." One third-year in New York says, "I have been most impressed with the opportunities for informal training. The partners I have worked for have been very good about taking the time to improve my skills as a lawyer." On the other hand, a junior associate reports, "Lack of mentoring is an issue." And a midlevel associate warns, "You only learn something from partners when they are angrily explaining to you what you screwed up."

Top of the market

K&S's compensation may be at the top of the market ("The recent raises in the market in general, and at King & Spalding specifically, have certainly increased associate satisfaction in this respect."), but, like BigLaw associates everywhere, K&S lawyers still have a number of gripes about their pay. "The firm likes to think of itself as a leader in Atlanta, but only raises salaries if other firms have already moved in order to keep up and fails to pay competitive bonuses for those actually getting work

© 2007 Vault Inc.

done," complains a midlevel associate. Another insider adds, "We're constantly reminded that K&S is the best law firm in the South, and are expected to work accordingly. But we don't raise salaries until Alston does, and even then only to match Alston precisely." As for how the bonuses are calculated, some associates are puzzled: "The bonuses are sort of a black box," shares one typical insider. However, a New Yorker reports, "Our bonus system used to be the biggest issue I and other people at the firm had. We are now compensated at market level and have received market bonuses, which is very much appreciated."

Crazy hours—but isn't that the norm?

Associates say that they work long, often ridiculous hours, but that the firm is flexible and they don't think that they'd be any better off anywhere else. "I think the firm is flexible with policies regarding part-time and taking vacation days, but the nature of the work is that it is hours-intensive," says a first-year. "I have been here for six months and several emergency matters fit the stereotype of first-year associate work: all-nighter sessions from Sunday noon until Monday 6 p.m., rooms filled with documents, and it seems ... billing 200-plus hours in a month is completely average." As a litigation associate from Atlanta puts it, "As long as I get my work done, I am allowed to maintain a schedule that fits with my life (within reason, of course)." A New Yorker adds, "There is no face time in the litigation department of the New York office. Partners, many of whom commute, are fine with associates working from home on the occasional day or leaving if there is no more work for the day. I have never had a problem with taking vacation time." But apparently, with flexible hours comes a fluctuating workload. According to one Houston associate, "It's feast or famine around here. Two weeks ago, I worked late every night, this week I'm struggling to bill five hours a day."

Visit the Vault Law Channel, the complete online resource for law careers, featuring firm profiles, message boards, the Vault Law Job Board and more. **www.vault.com/law**

VAULT CAREER LIBRARY

383

Morgan, Lewis & Bockius LLP

1701 Market Street
Philadelphia, PA 19103
Phone: (215) 963-5000

LOCATIONS

Boston, MA • Chicago, IL • Dallas, TX • Harrisburg, PA •
Houston, TX • Irvine, TX • Los Angeles, CA • Miami, FL •
Minneapolis, MN • New York, NY • Palo Alto, CA •
Philadelphia, PA • Pittsburgh, PA • Princeton, NJ • San
Francisco, CA • Washington, DC • Beijing • Brussels •
Frankfurt • London • Paris • Tokyo

MAJOR DEPARTMENTS & PRACTICES

Antitrust • Business & Finance • Business Transactions •
Corporate Investigations & White Collar • Emerging
Growth • Employee Benefits/Executive Compensation •
Energy • Environmental • FDA/Healthcare Regulation •
Finance • Immigration • Intellectual Property •
International • Internet & E-Commerce • Investment
Management • Labor & Employment • Litigation • Mergers
& Acquisitions • Private Equity • Real Estate •
Restructuring • Securities • Tax

THE STATS

No. of attorneys: 1,342
No. of office: 22
Summer associate offers: 95 out of 95 (2006)
Chairman: Francis M. Milone
Hiring Partners: Firmwide: Eric Kraeutler
    Chicago, IL: Barry A. Hartstein
    Los Angeles and Irvine, CA: Douglas C. Rawles and
      Allison N. Shue
    New York, NY: Michele A. Coffey and Christopher T.
      Jensen
    Palo Alto, CA: Rahul Kapoor
    Philadelphia: Glen R. Stuart
    Washington, DC and Dallas, TX: Tara Reinhart
    Pittsburgh, PA: Kimberly A. Taylor
    Princeton, NJ: Frank C. Testa
    San Francisco, CA: Howard Holderness
    Washington, DC and Houston, TX: John F. Ring

THE BUZZ
WHAT ATTORNEYS AT OTHER FIRMS ARE SAYING ABOUT THIS FIRM

- "Great firm—breadth and depth"
- "Growth crazy"
- "Famous labor group"
- "Uneven"

BASE SALARY (2007)

Philadelphia, PA; Pittsburgh, PA; and Princeton, NJ
1st year: $145,000
Summer associate: $30,800/summer

Chicago, IL; Irvine, CA; Los Angeles, CA; Palo Alto, CA; San Francisco, CA; and Washington, DC
1st year: $160,000
Summer associate: $30,800/summer

New York, NY
1st year: $160,000
Summer associate: $34,100/summer

Miami, FL
1st Year: $135,000
Summer associate: $27,560/summer

Dallas and Houston, TX
1st Year: $135,000
Summer Associate: $28,600/summer

UPPERS

- "People are friendly, smart, social and professional"
- "Clients and cases are of the highest caliber"
- Increasing training opportunities

DOWNERS

- Disparity in pay for senior associates
- Big firm hours pressure
- "Satellite offices feel distant"

NOTABLE PERKS

- Weekly happy hours
- Subsidized gym membership/free on-site gym
- Free snacks and beverages
- Bar and moving expenses

© 2007 Vault Inc.

RANKING RECAP

Best in Region
#1 - Pennsylvania/Mid-Atlantic
#6 - Miami

Best in Practice
#1 - Labor & Employment

Partner Prestige Rankings
#2 - Labor & Employment

Quality of Life
#6 - Pro Bono

EMPLOYMENT CONTACTS

Chicago
Ms. Emily Faistenhammer
Legal Recruiting Manager
Phone: (312) 324-1714
E-mail: efaistenhammer@morganlewis.com

Los Angeles
Ms. Victoria Gamble
Legal Recruiting Manager
Phone: (213) 612-7248
E-mail: vgamble@morganlewis.com

New York
Ms. Susan Reonegro
Legal Recruiting Manager
Phone: (212) 309-6933
E-mail: nyresumes@morganlewis.com

Philadelphia/Dallas/Princeton
Ms. Lindsay A. Callantine
Legal Recruiting Manager
Phone: (215) 963-5105
E-mail: lcallantine@morganlewis.com

Pittsburgh
Ms. Loreen A. Lubin
Legal Recruiting Manager
Phone: (412) 560-3345
E-mail: llubin@morganlewis.com

San Francisco/Palo Alto
Ms. Caryn Schreiber
Legal Recruiting Manager
Phone: (415) 442-1187
E-mail: cschreiber@morganlewis.com

Washington, DC/Houston
Ms. Jennifer R. Kraemer
Legal Recruiting Manager
Phone: (202) 739-5503
E-mail: WALegalRecruiting@morganlewis.com

QUALITY OF LIFE RANKINGS
[ASSOCIATES RATE THEIR OWN FIRM]

SATISFACTION

7.8

1 WORST .... 10 BEST

HOURS

7.1

1 WORST .... 10 BEST

ASSOCIATE/PARTNER RELATIONS

8.2

1 WORST .... 10 BEST

FORMAL TRAINING

7.5

1 WORST .... 10 BEST

DIVERSITY

7.9

1 WORST .... 10 BEST

Visit the Vault Law Channel, the complete online resource for law careers, featuring firm profiles, message boards, the Vault Law Job Board and more. www.vault.com/law

VAULT CAREER LIBRARY

385

THE SCOOP

The Morgan Lewis empire has been a long, long time in the making. Morgan, Lewis & Bockius LLP got its start in Philadelphia in 1873 when Civil War veteran Charles Eldridge Morgan, Jr., and Francis Draper Lewis started a law practice. Their firm quickly became one of the most important in the Eastern United States, representing railroads, newspapers, banks and other Philadelphia institutions. Modern-day Morgan Lewis is hardly a Philly firm anymore—it has large offices (with approximately 250 attorneys) in both New York and Washington, D.C., part of its 22-office, 1,300-lawyer global legal empire.

Winter in Minneapolis

In NeoNetworks, Inc. v. Cisco Systems, Inc., the firm obtained a rare mid-trial dismissal for Cisco Systems, Inc. The $450 million case was brought in Hennepin County (Minneapolis) District Court by a former employer of the founders of NuSpeed Internet Systems, Inc., a startup company acquired by Cisco. It alleged usurpation/misappropriation of corporate opportunity, unjust enrichment, interference, and breaches of contract and fiduciary duty. Morgan Lewis was brought into the case in January 2006, after the court denied Cisco's summary judgment motion. The Morgan Lewis trial team quickly got up to speed and after two months of trial, the court granted Cisco's motion to dismiss after the close of the plaintiff's case.

Victory for LG.Philips

After a five-week trial, on November 21, 2006, a federal jury in Los Angeles awarded damages of $53.5 million to Morgan Lewis client, LG.Philips, in a lawsuit over its LCD—liquid crystal display—technology patents. LG. Philips is the world's leading innovator of thin-film transistor liquid crystal display (TFT-LCD) technology. The Seoul, Korea-based company sued multiple defendants, including Chunghwa Picture Tubes (CPT) and Tatung Co., for infringement of patents relating to the structure and manufacture of TFT-LCD panels. The jury verdict marked the end of a four-year-long patent dispute between LG.Philips LCD and the defendants. (Because the jury found that the defendants willfully infringed LG.Philips' patents, U.S. District Court Judge Consuelo Marshall may increase the damages at her discretion up to three times the jury's $53.5 million award.)

On guard for Vanguard

Among the firm's recent triumphs is its successful defense of the Philadelphia-based investment management giant The Vanguard Group in a major employment-discrimination action. Plaintiff Mary Pat Russell, a former IT project manager at Vanguard, challenged the company's decision to fire her for alleged insubordination and poor job performance. In a retaliation action filed in the U.S. District Court for the Eastern District of Pennsylvania, Russell, who is black, alleged that she was fired for making internal complaints about racial and gender discrimination and for filing two EEOC charges against prior Vanguard managers. In March 2007, following a seven-day trial, a jury rendered a unanimous verdict in favor of Vanguard, finding that Russell did not have a reasonable, good faith belief in her claims of discrimination.

In defense of East Chicago

In another wrongful-firing matter, Morgan Lewis has also been hired to defend the city of East Chicago in nearly three dozen lawsuits filed against it. Apparently, the firm has been succeeding: of the 33 municipal and school employees who sued after being laid off in early 2005, 10 have withdrawn their cases, with a total of zero liability to the city. Local press reports referred to the firm as the "international legal powerhouse Morgan, Lewis & Bockius," and stated that the city has already dropped upwards of $1.5 million in legal fees on the matter.

Transactional glory

Obviously, Morgan Lewis does more than litigate labor and employment cases. In early 2007, the firm also represented the private-equity company Apollo Management in its $3.1 billion buyout of costume-jewelry retailer Claire's Stores Inc., the mall-centric bangles monopoly. The sale marked the end of a long era in which the world of costume jewelry was dominated by a

© 2007 Vault Inc.

single family (seriously). Founded by entrepreneur Rowland Schaefer in the 1970s, the 3,000-store retailer so loved by precious young tweens for 30 years has been run by his daughters, Bonnie and Marla, for more than a decade. "The decision to sell the company that our father founded was reached after an enormous amount of soul-searching over time, and brings our strategic review to a successful conclusion," the Schaefer sisters announced at the time of the sale. The $3.1 billion made that decision a little easier, to be sure.

Transactional glory (part II)

In April 2007, the firm acted as both financial and legal adviser to the nation's No. 2 steelmaker, U.S. Steel, in its purchase of Lone Star, a leading manufacturer of welded oilfield pipes and tubes in a cash deal valued at about $2.1 billion. Second in size only to Mittal Steel USA, U.S. Steel paid for its little impulse purchase via a combination of cash and financing obtained from, among other sources, its receivables-purchase program. In a sign of the company that Morgan Lewis keeps, Goldman Sachs and Weil, Gotshal & Manges advised Lone Star. (Initial post-purchase reports appeared positive for both companies: Shares of Lone Star rocketed up by more than 37 percent and shares of U.S. Steel climbed 3.4 percent.)

Pro bono triumph

Not everything is about the bottom line at Morgan Lewis. The firm has impressive, quantifiable pro bono bona fides as well. In 2006, the firm's attorneys spent over 76,000 hours on pro bono work, among the tops in the nation. The firm employs a full-time pro bono counsel and promises to work toward dedicating the equivalent of at least 3 percent of its billable hours to pro bono cases. Perhaps the firm's most famous public advocacy victory involves Louisiana inmate John Thompson, whom Morgan Lewis partners Michael Banks and J. Gordon Cooney Jr. represented for more than 14 years. The attorneys first won Thompson, who had been convicted of murder and sentenced to death, a new trial. Then they won an acquittal, which freed him after 18 years in Louisiana's notorious Angola prison. In February 2007, a federal jury awarded Thompson a $14 million verdict in his lawsuit against state prosecutors, who were found to have withheld crucial evidence of his innocence.

With great victories come great awards

The firm's recent successes have earned it a seemingly endless stream of awards and accolades. Here's a small sample of some of the more impressive ones. Among collective honors, the firm ranked as the No. 1 law firm in *Corporate Counsel*'s 2006 listings of "Who Represents America's Biggest Companies?" Morgan Lewis' labor and employment law practice was named *The American Lawyer*'s "2006 Litigation Department of the Year" for its work in this area. The firm was also named No. 1 in the prestigious publication's 2005 "Corporate Scorecard" ranking of the nation's leading counsel for mutual funds (based on number of new issues). *Corporate Board Member* named Morgan Lewis the top corporate law firm in Philadelphia, as well as one of the top 20 nationwide in 2006.

As for individual honors, over 100 Morgan Lewis lawyers (well, 102 to be exact) were included in the 2006 edition of *Chambers USA: America's Leading Business Lawyers*, and 18 lawyers and 10 practice groups were included in *Chambers Global: The World's Leading Lawyers*. Over 100 lawyers were listed in the 13th edition of *The Best Lawyers in America* (okay, 130) and two Morgan Lewis partners were recent recipients of the prestigious "California Lawyer Attorney of the Year" award. Seven firm partners have been named Fellows of the College of Employee Benefits Counsel, nine have been named Fellows of the American College of Trial Lawyers and 13 have been named Fellows of the College of Labor and Employment Lawyers.

GETTING HIRED

Join the team

What Morgan Lewis craves more than anything in its applicants is the demonstrated ability to fit in with the team. "I think there are two types of top law firms when it comes to hiring: (1) strictly on grades and (2) grades are important, but maybe more

Visit the Vault Law Channel, the complete online resource for law careers, featuring firm profiles, message boards, the Vault Law Job Board and more. **www.vault.com/law**

VAULT CAREER LIBRARY

387

important is personality fit," says a lawyer who notes that Morgan Lewis definitely fits into the latter category. "I am involved in recruiting and I will say this: Morgan Lewis does not hire people who they feel are not going to be team players," states a litigator. "I fully believe that the firm is committed to hiring good people, who will fit in [with the] professional collegial environment." "Once you get the interview, you must be friendly, not overly competitive with your fellow associates, poised, mature, and with a sense of humor," warns a junior associate.

Getting hired at Morgan Lewis is no walk in the park. "I'm surprised at how tough our interviewing process is. We'll conduct 10 interviews for lateral candidates from peer firms and not take any," notes a contact. Those seeking employment at Morgan Lewis' Philly office should be on notice: "Students should show a connection to Philadelphia and a passion for the law and remember that you are competing to be at the top of the food chain in the Philadelphia legal market," states an attorney from that office. That insider warns law students who are in demand: "Do not try to use Morgan as a backup to other markets."

OUR SURVEY SAYS

All this and chocolate, too

"As far as big firms go, I think Morgan Lewis is top-notch," reports one source. "I couldn't ask for anything more," raves a junior associate who lists "great work, great partners, great associates, great pay" as the perks of working at Morgan Lewis. "I enjoy the level of work and the type of work that I get to do at Morgan Lewis," shares another source. "Also, the mentoring and attention to associate development is amazing." "The job provides really interesting work, opportunities to learn from the best, a collegial atmosphere and the opportunity to wear jeans to work, and the freedom and encouragement to do significant pro bono work ... oh, and there is chocolate, too!" exclaims a sweet-toothed Silicon Valley lawyer.

Of course, your mileage may vary. "Morgan Lewis is a good firm, but it all really depends on which office you work in," reports an attorney from a satellite office. "If you work at the mothership (Philly) or in D.C., New York or one of the California offices, life is good—tons of work, good pay and the firm cares about what's going on. However, working in a small satellite office like Dallas [can be] a different experience altogether. Associates in the smaller offices feel like we are not on the firm's radar, we are seldom able to have our questions answered, and every little request needs to be cleared by the mothership. This makes it a very frustrating experience." Morgan Lewis responded by acknowledging that one of the most challenging aspects of its geographic and practice area breadth and depth is "keeping everyone connected," but stated that it remains committed to ensuring that all of its attorneys and staff are well integrated into the firm and their practice group. Not that things are perfect in the "main" offices. "I have not been given much work since I started six months ago," reports a New York lawyer. "It's frustrating, given that I've been begging for work." Also, a San Francisco lawyer says, "As an associate, you are expected to take ownership of your career. That is great but a little more guidance and help with that process would make my satisfaction greater."

Work buddies

"The firm's culture is professional, but not stiflingly so—everyone is pretty laid-back but gets their work done," reports one source. Getting your work done, of course, is vital: "The firm culture is lighthearted and respectful while focused on giving clients good legal advice," says a Palo Alto attorney. The firm's culture is helped by the friendliness of its partners. "The partners for whom I work share their hobbies with me, making recommendations and sharing bottles of especially good wine," reports a happy first-year. "They also dine with me and my fiancée informally." "Morgan Lewis has a pretty friendly, social environment," reports a New Yorker. "Partners are almost always approachable, and most of them are very friendly and caring." To some extent, your practice area defines the culture in which you work. "The firm is organized in practice group silos," says an associate from the labor and employment silo. "There is little interaction between associates in different practice groups." Still, if you're in the right silo, the culture can be one of the best things about Morgan Lewis. "My colleagues are one of the firm's best assets," says a senior associate. "You have to like the people you work with and I truly do—they are the reason I have stayed here so long."

© 2007 Vault Inc.

Everyone gets paid

No one goes hungry at Morgan Lewis. "The firm matches the salary structure in the New York market," says a Big Apple lawyer. "The baseline bonus for each year is below market, but associates can earn extra money by reaching certain incentives." Those "incentives" can be a little difficult to decipher. "There is little structure to the bonus structure," complains a source. "For example, the partners I spent the most time working for last year were not even present when the firm was reviewing my end of the year performance and setting my bonus level." At least the firm has a reasonable target for bonus. One insider reports that "1,975 is the billable hours target and generally bonuses are given to those who meet at least that target." More good news: the firm listens to associate complaints. "After much griping last year, our bonuses were much better this year," reports a lawyer. "We've also received raises the last two years in a row." Yet senior associates want more. "Over the past couple of years, the firm made a real effort to match the market and was doing well until the latest round of salary increases was announced in early 2007," says one senior associate. "Here, although firm management publicly declared that it was matching the market increases, in reality, the firm only matched salary increases through the eighth-year associate level." (Wait: only?) In any event, the firm does seem to be trying. "The firm just provided significant raises for mid- and senior-level associates, which many associates understood as a tacit admission that senior associates were underpaid for the last few years," reports one contact.

Hours: tough, but fair

No one said BigLaw would be easy. "If you choose to work at a big firm, you choose a certain life," says a source, sounding a little like an extra from *The Sopranos*. "That being said, Morgan Lewis is fair about workload and life outside the office." "Work hours are very big here," notes a lawyer. "They are monitored regularly, and you can expect a lecture if you don't meet your hours in a given month." That's generally not a problem for litigators. "We have a target of 1,975 billables. I would say that the majority of attorneys in the litigation group come in above that number," says an attorney from that department. "I have not billed over 2,100 hours in my time here." Associates do enjoy a measure of control over their schedule. "With the understanding that the hours at a big law firm are demanding, I feel that I am able to control the hours I spend in the office," notes a source. "I think the firm is flexible with regards to hours, as long as you get your work done," says another lawyer.

Training for some

There's a before and after effect at Morgan Lewis. "The firm had no formal training program until about two years ago," reports a senior associate. "There is now a partner in charge of this firmwide, and great strides have been made." Reviews are mixed. "The firm has implemented a number of training programs over the last two years, but it still does not offer enough training and CLE opportunities to the associates," grumbles one lawyer. Litigators are learning a lot. "The firm now holds an Annual Trial Academy which provides senior associates with the opportunity to conduct a trial from start to finish," says a contact. "The program is lead by the firm's most experienced trial attorneys and takes place over a week each year. Many who've attended call it the most rewarding training they've received in their career." Others aren't so lucky. "Given how specialized patent work it, the lack of formal patent-related training in all of the formal training programs is somewhat disappointing," tsk-tsks a lawyer from that department.

Need better numbers, better policies

"Morgan Lewis needs to rethink its policies with respect to woman," states one lawyer. "Although the firm excels in hiring women, it has problems with retention, which stem from deficiencies with its part-time policy." However, some associates see some improvement. "The firm has many women in the partnership with significant responsibility," observes a contact. "In the corporate practice, the firm could improve its track record. The firm is working hard to increase the numbers of women attorneys in corporate and securities practice."

Visit the Vault Law Channel, the complete online resource for law careers, featuring firm profiles, message boards, the Vault Law Job Board and more. www.vault.com/law

VAULT CAREER LIBRARY   389

Quinn Emanuel Urquhart Oliver & Hedges LLP

865 S. Figueroa Street, 10th Floor
Los Angeles, CA 90017
Phone: (213) 443-3000
www.quinnemanuel.com

LOCATIONS

Los Angeles, CA (HQ)
New York, NY
San Francisco, CA
Sillicon Valley, CA

MAJOR PRACTICE AREAS

Antitrust & Trade Regulation
Appellate Practice
Banking & Financial Institutions
Bankruptcy Litigation
Construction
Domestic and International Arbitration & Mediation
Employment
Entertainment
Government Contracts
Health Care
Intellectual Property
Internet Litigation
Media
Real Estate
Securities
White Collar Crime

THE STATS

No. of attorneys firmwide: 350
No. of offices: 4
Summer associate offers firmwide: 54 out of 55 (2006)
Managing Partner: John B. Quinn
Hiring Partner: A. William Urquhart

BASE SALARY (2007)

Firmwide
1st year: $160,000
2nd year: $170,000
3rd year: $185,000
4th year: $210,000
5th year: $230,000
6th year: $250,000
Summer associate: $2,600/week

UPPERS

• Lack of bureaucracy
• Intellectual freedom and flexibility
• Friendly, approachable associates

DOWNERS

• Long hours
• Communication gap between partners and associates
• "Stingy with office expenses"

PERKS

• Summer backpacking trip
• Annual office outings (skiing in NorCal, Rose Bowl party in LA, golf in NYC)
• $1,000 personal laptop subsidy
• Full-service coffee bar (in LA)

THE BUZZ
WHAT ATTORNEYS AT OTHER FIRMS ARE SAYING ABOUT THIS FIRM

• "Becoming the preeminent litigation shop in the country"
• "'Fun' image but 'BigLaw' reality"
• "Flip-flops to work … enough said"
• "Myocardial infarction"

© 2007 Vault Inc.

RANKING RECAP

Best in Region
#9 - Southern California

Best in Practice
#8 - Litigation

EMPLOYMENT CONTACT

Ms. Selene Dogan
National Director of Recruiting
Phone: (213) 443-3000
Fax: (213) 443-3100
E-mail: selenedogan@quinnemanuel.com

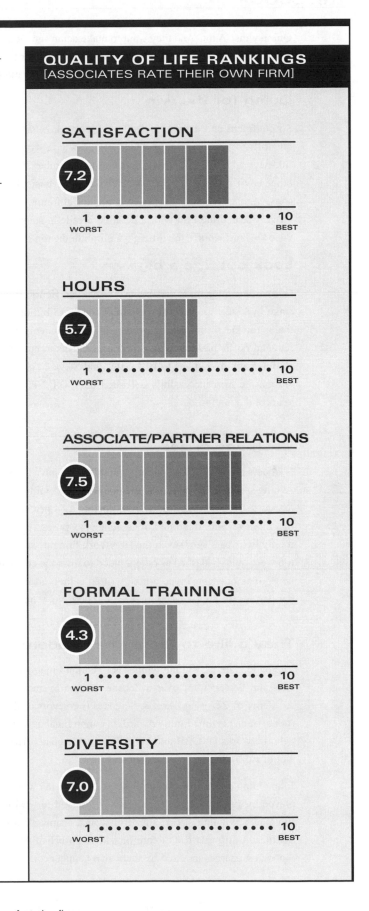

QUALITY OF LIFE RANKINGS
[ASSOCIATES RATE THEIR OWN FIRM]

SATISFACTION
7.2
1 WORST — 10 BEST

HOURS
5.7
1 WORST — 10 BEST

ASSOCIATE/PARTNER RELATIONS
7.5
1 WORST — 10 BEST

FORMAL TRAINING
4.3
1 WORST — 10 BEST

DIVERSITY
7.0
1 WORST — 10 BEST

Visit the Vault Law Channel, the complete online resource for law careers, featuring firm profiles, message boards, the Vault Law Job Board and more. **www.vault.com/law**

VAULT CAREER LIBRARY   391

THE SCOOP

Quinn wins. A lot. And they want to make damn sure you know it. It's only been 21 years since Quinn Emanuel Urquhart Oliver & Hedges (well, Quinn and Emanuel anyway, the other three were later additions) set up a shop in Los Angeles, and the firm has already rocketed into the stratosphere of boutique litigation.

Quinn for the win

So confident and assured is Quinn of its record that the firm can afford to tout its success with some exceedingly unusual quantification. For example, "Our attorneys have won 1,066 of 1,160 cases, or an astounding 92 percent." The firm took out a full-page ad in *The Wall Street Journal* in September 2005, informing readers that it has "won more nine-figure verdicts than any other law firm in America." At that point, the business and legal world started to take notice of the bold Quinn Emanuel as something more than a plucky little niche California firm where the partners show up to the office in flip-flops. *The American Lawyer* sealed the deal with a detailed profile in summer 2006, touting Quinn as American business' dream equation: unique vision + hard work = the little guys climb to the top of the heap. The rest, as they say, is history (albeit recent history).

Look out, it's a big win

German media giant Bertelsmann AG has Jan Henric Buettner and Andreas von Blottnitz to thank for the 2000 sale of half its stake in AOL Europe to Time Warner for $6.75 billion. And as of 2004, the two internet rainmakers have Quinn Emanuel to thank for the record-setting verdict of approximately $250 million in recompensed equity. Bertelsmann was found to have reneged on its oral and contractual agreements to cut Muettner and Blottnitz a piece of the pie. After all, they did introduce Bertelsmann executives to Bill Gates and Steve Case ... that's gotta be worth something. The year 2003 was a good one for Quinn: the firm successfully defended Shell Oil, Nike and IBM in respective patent cases. IBM has been a firm client for 12 years and counting.

Cash and prizes

Numbers don't lie. "The mighty Quinn" might have been flying under the public's radar, but there's no fooling the accountants. Average partner compensation in 2005 was $1.65 million, making it the most lucrative firm outside of New York. In 2006, Quinn leaped to 78th on the AmLaw 100, posting a 54 percent increase in gross revenue to $298,000,000. What did they do with all that money? Set off a round of associate pay raises. Base pay for first-year associates got bumped to $135,000, back when (was it only two years ago?) even the New York firm rate started at $125,000. Of course, Bill Urquhart's dreams of being alone at the top were quickly dashed as others raced to meet the challenge. Apparently, matching the latest round of raises (and breaking the news to associates with an e-mail written entirely in lowercase) hasn't had the slightest effect on the bottom line either. Profits per partner for 2006 cashed in at $2,430,000, No. 9 on the AmLaw 100.

They'd like to thank the Academy

The ballots are in, and the winner is ... Quinn Emanuel! The firm has been general counsel to the Academy of Motion Picture Arts and Sciences for over a decade. These overachievers work in other mediums, too. Clients also include the National Academy of Recording Arts & Sciences (purveyors of the Grammy Awards) and the Academy of Television Arts and Sciences (home of prime time Emmy Awards). Quinn Emanuel's entertainment practice represents clients from every walk of Hollywood, from networks (WGBH and WNET) to cable giants (HBO) to actors (Leonard Nimoy and William Shatner), yet firm lawyers would still rather win a case than an Oscar.

John Quinn and Bill Urquhart are something in the way of litigation celebrities themselves, but neither can claim to have been played by Julia Roberts. That honor is reserved for real-life whistleblower Erin Brockovich. Not even she could break Quinn Emanuel's winning streak: the firm won a dismissal in the first of nearly 30 qui tam lawsuits Brockovich has filed against Southern California health care providers on behalf of Medicare (claiming these various hospitals and providers had double-dipped on charges incurred by their own negligence).

© 2007 Vault Inc.

A not-so-arbitrary win

Litigators don't necessarily have to go to trial to bring home a win. In February 2007, Quinn Emanuel secured one of the largest damages ever awarded by an arbitration panel: $76 million to a limited partnership hedge fund from its general partner and his sister, who was a stockbroker to the fund. The two had engaged in post-trade allocation, taking the most lucrative trades for themselves after the fact, at the expense of the rest of the partnership. Quinn boasts that it was their hard-hitting cross examinations of the accused that led to such a favorable decision. The $76 million breaks down roughly into $16 million in compensatory damages, $16 million in punitive damages, $36 million in disgorgement of all compensation paid to the general partner, $4 million in brokerage commissions, and another $4 million in attorneys' fees and expenses.

Internationally, the firm recently won a complex arbitration on behalf of a Japanese engine manufacturer who had spent significant time and money developing a new engine for a Minnesota company—who refused to pay for the development on the grounds that the service was already covered in a pre-existing supply agreement. Thanks to Quinn's cross-oceanic tightrope act, the Japanese company is now free to take its multi-million dollar damage claim to federal court.

Biggest loser—Apple?

It took Quinn Emanuel and corporate investigations partner John Potter three months to review Apple's extensive finance and trading records back in the spring of '06. When they were done (after reading 650,000 e-mails and conducting interviews with more than 40 people), what they had found was evidence tying at least two former executives to stock options backdating. Backdating gives employees higher profits by letting them buy shares at past lower prices. So far CEO Steve Jobs has been spared any charges, or even serious accusations.

Portia, meet Shylock

The restaurant business is a gamble, even in the best of times. After 9/11, thousands of eateries were struggling to stay afloat. They turned to Rewards Network (formerly iDine), who paid floundering restaurants millions of dollars in "advances" on their credit rewards program—basically frequent flier miles for your favorite bistro. The catch? A 100 percent interest rate. Representing a class-action lawsuit from 3,000 restaurant owners, Quinn argued usury, and won a partial summary judgment in 2006. No longer could Rewards Network claim their high-interest loans were mere advances. Eager to avoid what was an all-but-certainly unfavorable damages trial, Rewards Network settled for a package valued at approximately $64 million—cash, airline miles, debt forgiveness ... the works.

Quinns just wanna have fun

Cleary may be known for its swanky affairs, but Quinn definitely takes the cake when it comes to a good old-fashioned day out. Bonding and leisure events abound, from baseball games to boat cruises. Not to mention the bigger, bolder yearly blowouts.

You don't have to be a USC linebacker to party in Pasadena style. Quinn Emanuel's annual Rose Bowl party takes place on the actual football field, and the firm pulls out all the stops: rides, games, food, a live band, prizes for the kids, psychics and an open bar for the adults ... even a game of touch for the "how cool would it be to play football at the Rose Bowl!?" crowd.

Another famous Quinn tradition is the annual firm hike, during which lawyers and summer associates must use all of their litigation and camping skills in order to avoid being eaten by bears. No slacking off, either—these hikes are personally led by Managing Partner (cum triathlete) John Quinn. This year, 65 attorneys (including 25 unsuspecting summer associates) from three offices spent threes days hiking 30 miles in Durango, Colorado.

Visit the Vault Law Channel, the complete online resource for law careers, featuring firm profiles, message boards, the Vault Law Job Board and more. **www.vault.com/law**

VAULT CAREER LIBRARY   393

GETTING HIRED

"Only true litigators need apply"

They do one thing, and one thing well—litigation. So should you. Candidates "have to have an intensity and passion for litigation," as exemplified by "a lot of clerkships, a lot of law review or at least journal, and a lot of moot court experience." Laterals have it even tougher. "You are expected to have substantial litigation experience, have written motions, argued motions, handled entire cases, taken depositions, etc." In any stage of your career, it's important to exhibit that certain Litigators' Character on top of your impeccable resume. There is "equal emphasis on finding candidates whom the partners feel comfortable putting in front of a judge." "The kind of people you'd want to meet at a party," says one associate, "Almost everyone [here] has an interesting background beyond the law ... intelligent, personable, and easy to work with." The firm seeks out these sorts of traits as signs of "those who will make good advocates in the courtroom."

You won't find a sweet sugar-coating on Quinn's hiring expectations. They "want only the top [students] from the top schools" and you bet they're "strict ... and getting stricter" about the school-snobbery. "Don't bother applying if you're not from a top-10 school" sniffs a Harvard grad. OK, they might consider you if you're "first in your class" somewhere else. Top-tiers like Harvard and Stanford remain the golden ticket.

OUR SURVEY SAYS

Raise the roof

Careful—don't give the Quinn Emanuel compensation committee a map, lest they figure out what coast they're on. Back in the winter of '07 salary wars, Quinn was the only California-based firm "matching New York [salaries] nationwide." Associates noticed. "They treat us well. Damn well." How well? "The pay at QE borders on obscene." And what qualifies as "obscene compensation?" "I've had three raises since I signed on to join the firm after my clerkship," says a first-year litigator. Given the highest salaries around, Quinn associates aspire to nothing less than the stratosphere: "Though it would be nice to get paid like we're at Wachtell, I'm perfectly happy not working their hours."

Associates will admit to one fly in the ointment, regarding the bonus system. It's not the bonuses themselves, but the hours required to level up. "Everyone gets a bonus," yes, and the first bump is at an industry-typical 2,000 billable hours. However, associates are hard-pressed to make the second threshold, which is 2,500! And only the most hard-core billers can even dream of making the next, at 3,000. Apparently even some partners say it's "not worth it" to make the 500-hour jumps.

"The billables and the Benjamins, baby"

That's what it's all about. Business is indeed booming, and "there aren't enough people to do it." To put it bluntly, "People generally work too much here." There's plenty of corroborating evidence to back that statement up. "I haven't seen my fiancé or family in months. I've worked every weekend since December (excluding Christmas)," moans a New York associate. At least such suffering is not uniform. Another New Yorker says, "I have most weekends free, and was able to take all of my vacation last year." "If things are slow, you're free to go on vacation or take a long weekend somewhere." If. Opinions differ on whether it's necessary to put in those hours physically at the office. "[I] do a lot of work from home, which I prefer," says one lawyer, "No one seems really to care as long as you're reachable during normal business hours." According to a Silicon Valley associate, on the other hand, "There is very little flexibility on working from home, or remotely. They like to see us in the office." (Paradoxically, he prefaces this with "there is no face time really required.") Flex-time is like a mythical beast ... no one is really sure if it exists. One brave senior associate is going to find out, having forced the flex-time issue and set up "a temporary part-time arrangement" to begin shortly. The firm is "understandably not delighted" but to its credit has been "supportive" and "more than willing to accommodate."

© 2007 Vault Inc.

Sharks in sandals

Litigators: the rock stars of the legal profession. They live to work on their feet, in front of an audience. So at Quinn Emanuel, an enclave of elite litigators, if you want court time, you better be willing to fight for it. The work assignment system is "free-market" and in Quinn's market, the competition is brutal. Ability to beat the other sharks to the choice morsels really affects job satisfaction. Some come out on top: "The opportunities are truly amazing. I came to this firm because I wanted to litigate tough cases and get responsibility early on. They've delivered in spades." And some are left behind: "[I have a] low level of responsibility; [I] haven't stepped foot in court," laments a second-year. A senior associate warns, "Many midlevel 'litigation' associates have never even taken a deposition."

Welcome to the Hotel California

Fame changes people—and firms. Some old hands have noticed a change in the atmosphere as Quinn proceeds through its meteoric ascent. They are concerned that their firm has "lost its roots." The California Culture, however, remains alive and well. "The firm's culture is very relaxed and informal," from associate relations down through the dress code ("We wear jeans, flip-flops and t-shirts"). Most offices report that they are "very social," mostly in an informal kind of way which matches the overall culture. Spontaneous outings are preferred over planned functions (though "in New York, we have a weekly poker game"). Associates may spend much more time working than playing, but thanks to firm camaraderie, "the hours go by relatively quickly."

This "meritocracy" is also very egalitarian. "When recruiters said that 'work is all that matters' at QE, they weren't just spouting a line"—that is to say, "there is little concern about other superficial issues here like what you wear, what you look like, what color skin you have, what religion you are, your sexual preference, etc." Quinn has "all types" and a "'come as you are' philosophy" which accepts those who don't quite fit the standard deviation. "There are some wacky people here, but I like that," says a San Franciscan. Wacky? One litigator tells us, "I carry a football everywhere I go." Because it's Quinn we're talking about here, we have to assume the football signifies "quirky" free-spiritedness and not a Dilbertesque team-building exercise.

California egalitarianism does not here extend so far as associate participation in firm management. Munger, Tolles & Olson, this ain't. "I often refer to the partnership decision-making process as a black box: who knows what goes in and what goes on inside? We just see the results." One could assume policy is made "by fiat of [John] Quinn;" it's as plausible a theory as any other.

A spelling lesson with Ms. Franklin: R-E-S-P-E-C-T

Throw away that org chart—Quinn Emanuel definitely does not subscribe to multi-layered management. "I regularly work under the direct supervision of partners. I have rarely worked through a senior associate." It might even approach an anti-hierarchy. Associates "work *with* the partners, not just for them," creating "less of a division between partners and associates," which our respondents "appreciate a lot." A close working relationship combines with an open-door culture to "encourage first-years to be open and candid about questions, concerns and ideas." This may even make up for a lack of mentoring, as mentoring efforts are "tempered by the busy schedules of all the partners" and the senior associates as well. "I find I learn a lot more that way," says an associate about this system, "and it's also just more pleasant to talk through problems together, rather than just get instructions, then edits." Those looking for a little something more in the mentorship area will find it is "up to you" to form the individual relationship necessary.

A second-year tells us, "The partners I've worked with have all been great and communicative, and have given me good work, but I know that this isn't always the case." Unluckier colleagues speak of certain partners who "wouldn't hesitate to throw you under the bus." Someone went so far as to name one partner who "should not be permitted to interact with associates." We assume the partners associates "try to avoid" are not the ones who "are always willing to grab a drink. Especially on the weekend or Sunday afternoon after putting in a full day's work."

Visit the Vault Law Channel, the complete online resource for law careers, featuring firm profiles, message boards, the Vault Law Job Board and more. **www.vault.com/law**

VAULT CAREER LIBRARY   **395**

Goin' swimmin'

"Few things are formal at Quinn"—why should the training be any different? "The thing is, the firm has built its reputation on its informal aspect, and that is exactly how they handle training." When asked, one litigator said, "[I'm] not sure we have 'formal training.' Not sure I'd want to ..." To clear things up, both for this second-year and our readers, yes, Quinn does have a variety of training programs throughout the year, all in-house and hands-on, which "all new associates are invited to attend. Partners teach associates about issues like service of process, taking depositions, etc."

There is also an annual "one-week trial advocacy program given to young associates" and an annual deposition training workshop. Small potatoes, perhaps, but no one seems to care. "Our trial advocacy program is going to a real trial," reports one insider. According to the firm, Quinn is so committed to getting every associate into a trial by the end of their second year that "the firm assigns a junior associate to every trial at no cost to the client. In fact, the firm's goal is that over 90 percent of associates experience a trial by the end of their second year."

"Jumping in feet first ... can be somewhat harrowing at first," but for this second-year, "it's a style that has quickly made me into an actual litigator and not just some doc reviewer with a six-figure salary." In sum: If it ain't broke ... and other clichés ("sink or swim," "trial by fire," etc.). At least as far as trial skills go. A practical young litigator points out that the lack of "administrative training" is a more pressing problem: "I didn't know how to effectively search through the firm database because we were not instructed on its operations until five months after my start date."

© 2007 Vault Inc.

"I came to this firm because I wanted to litigate tough cases and get responsibility early on. They've delivered in spades."

— *Quinn Emanuel associate*

Visit the Vault Law Channel, the complete online resource for law careers, featuring firm profiles, message boards, the Vault Law Job Board and more. **www.vault.com/law**

VAULT CAREER LIBRARY   **397**

44

PRESTIGE
RANKING

Baker & McKenzie

One Prudential Plaza
130 East Randolph Drive, Suite 2500
Chicago, IL 60601
Phone: (312) 861-8000
www.bakernet.com

LOCATIONS

Chicago, IL • Dallas, TX • Houston, TX • Miami, FL • New
York, NY • Palo Alto, CA • San Diego, CA • San Francisco,
CA • Washington, DC

+ 60 other offices worldwide

MAJOR DEPARTMENTS & PRACTICES

Antitrust/Competition & Trade • Banking & Finance •
Commercial • Employment • Energy, Chemicals, Mining &
Infrastructure • Intellectual Property • IT/Communications •
Litigation & Dispute Resolution • M&A • Pharmaceuticals &
Healthcare • Private Equity • Real Estate • Securities • Tax

THE STATS

No. of attorneys: 3,500
No. of offices: 70
Summer associate offers: 54 out of 60 (2006)
Chairman of Executive Committee: John J. Conroy Jr.
Hiring Partners:

Chicago: Paul E. Schick
Dallas: Kimberly F. Rich
Houston: Jonathan B. Newton
Miami: Lee Stapleton
New York: Scott L. Brandman
San Diego: Katherine A. Bacal
San Francisco/Palo Alto, CA: Peter J. Engstrom
Washington: Richard L. Slowinski

THE BUZZ
WHAT ATTORNEYS AT OTHER FIRMS ARE SAYING ABOUT THIS FIRM

- "Internationally renowned"
- "Office-by-office culture"
- "The tax guys ... and gals"
- "Unwieldy"

BASE SALARY (2007)

Chicago, IL
1st year: $145,000   2nd year: $155,000
Summer associate: $2,788/week

Miami, FL
1st year: $135,000   2nd year: $145,000

New York, NY
1st year: $160,000   2nd year: $170,000
Summer associate: $3,076.92/week

San Diego, CA
1st year: $160,000   2nd year: $170,000
Summer associate: $3,077/week

San Francisco/Palo Alto, CA
1st year: $145,000   2nd year: $155,000
Summer associate: $2,788/week

Texas offices
1st year: $140,000   2nd year: $145,000
Summer associate: $2,600/week

Washington, DC
1st year: $145,000   2nd year: $155,000
Summer associate: $2,788.46/week

UPPERS

- Collegial and respectful partners
- Worldwide resources
- "Great professional development opportunities"

DOWNERS

- "The bureaucracy can sometimes be a bit overwhelming"
- Opacity of partnership prospects
- Practice groups not well integrated

NOTABLE PERKS

- Annual practice group meetings in different cities
- Pizza and beer nights
- Free parking
- Free pirozhki (sweet pies) on Fridays (Moscow)

© 2007 Vault Inc.

RANKING RECAP

Best in Region
#10 - Chicago

Best in Practice
#6 (tie) - International Law
#6 - Tax Law

Partner Prestige Rankings
#3 (tie) - International

EMPLOYMENT CONTACTS

Chicago
Ms. Eleonora Nikol
Phone: (312) 861-8924
E-mail: eleonora.nikol@bakernet.com

Dallas
Ms. Kimberly Rich
Phone: (214) 978-3000
E-mail: kimberly.f.rich@bakernet.com

Houston
Ms. Jana J. Roper
Phone: (713) 427-5041
E-mail: jana.j.roper@bakernet.com

Miami
Ms. Lee Stapleton
Phone: (305) 789-8900
E-mail: lee.stapleton.milford@bakernet.com

New York
Ms. Tami J. Bregman
Phone: (212) 626-4280
E-mail: tami.j.bregman@bakernet.com

San Diego
Ms. Katherine A. Bacal
Phone: (619) 236-1441
E-mail: katherine.a.bacal@bakernet.com

San Francisco/Palo Alto
Ms. Naomi Smith
Phone: (415) 576-3000
E-mail: naomi.j.smith@bakernet.com

Washington, DC
Richard L. Slowinski
Phone: (202) 452-7000
E-mail: richard.l.slowinski@bakernet.com

QUALITY OF LIFE RANKINGS
[ASSOCIATES RATE THEIR OWN FIRM]

SATISFACTION
7.7
1 WORST — 10 BEST

HOURS
6.6
1 WORST — 10 BEST

ASSOCIATE/PARTNER RELATIONS
7.8
1 WORST — 10 BEST

FORMAL TRAINING
7.0
1 WORST — 10 BEST

DIVERSITY
7.5
1 WORST — 10 BEST

Visit the Vault Law Channel, the complete online resource for law careers, featuring firm profiles, message boards, the Vault Law Job Board and more. **www.vault.com/law**

VAULT CAREER LIBRARY

399

THE SCOOP

The sun never sets on the Baker & McKenzie empire. The firm, with its 3,500+ attorneys, 250 jurisdictions, 75 languages and 70 offices in 38 countries, is by many measures the largest law firm in the world (and employs roughly 200 more lawyers than its nearest competitor, DLA Piper).

Best in translation

Baker & McKenzie has long been among the largest law firms in terms of lawyers and global footprint, and shows no signs of slowing down—it has opened 29 offices since 1990, the latest in Cancún, Mexico in 2006. Recent case locations read like an atlas, representing major markets like China, England, Saudi Arabia, Spain and Mexico, but also more off-the-beaten-path places like Vietnam and the Ukraine.

B&M has been developing foreign offices for nearly its whole existence, and has often established a foothold in places long before the legal gold rush. But as firms like DLA Piper merge into legal behemoths and push into new foreign markets, will B&M still be able to retain its edge? There's no denying that this is the age of global community and global business, but as far as how law firms respond to intercontinental demand, there are two schools of internationalism. First, and more commonly, there are firms that do extensive deals overseas without a glut of exotic locations. Second, there is B&M, which sticks to a philosophy of "go where the work is," developing local talent to provide more specialized, efficient representation. It remains to be seen if megafirms will cut into Baker & McKenzie's profits, but so far the firm's international revenue continues to weigh in at over $1.5 billion a year. Not too shabby.

Looking at overseas markets? B&M publishes a series of guides for businesses who want to learn more about investing or operating abroad. Next time you're on the firm's web site, increase your international know-how with a PDF or two ... we recommend "Doing Business in Azerbaijan."

Where you at?

Russell Baker and John McKenzie shared a Chicago cab in 1948. By 1949, they shared a Chicago legal practice. McKenzie took over the litigation so that Baker could focus on going international. Baker's practice was in Chicago, but his heart was in the Southwest. Since his teenage years in New Mexico, Baker retained strong ties to the Hispanic population. The first international office opened in Venezuela in 1955—way ahead of the global expansion curve. Today, the firm retains a strong Central and South American presence (16 offices), which is unusual for BigLaw. B&M is also the largest law firm in Mexico.

Other firms may soon very well be rushing to establish offices where Baker & McKenzie reigns supreme. According to government estimates, by 2014 the Central American Free Trade Agreement should spur an additional $2.5 billion in annual sales in California alone. The 2005 agreement between the United States, the Dominican Republic and five Central American countries, creates the 10th-largest U.S. export market—and where there is business, firms inevitably profit.

The legal market on the opposite hemisphere is opening up as well. In July 2006, the firm had its hand in Russia's first public residential mortgages securitization. Taking advantage of the changing business climate in the former Soviet republic, Baker & McKenzie created $88 million in notes in cooperation with JSC Vneshtorgbank, the second-largest bank in Russia. Deprivatization has been slow going (the government still owns 99.9 percent of JSC Vneshtorgbank), but you can bet B&M will be taking more opportunities like these in the future.

Now we're talkin' chicken

After over nine months of effort—including a tender offer and proxy solicitation—No. 3 chicken producer Gold Kist Inc. agreed to the unsolicited buyout proposal by rival Pilgrim's Pride Corporation. The sale went through at $21 per share. The final price was a 20 percent increase from the original offer (which was in the neighborhood of $17.50/share), up from a total value of $1.05 billion to $1.24 billion. The combination of Pilgrim's Pride and Gold Kist created the world's largest chicken company by market

© 2007 Vault Inc.

share, surpassing Tyson Foods Inc. Baker & McKenzie partner Alan G. Harvey of Dallas was lead counsel to Pittsburg, Texas-based Pilgrim's Pride.

Protective Cup

Long before the first soccer fan donned his favorite jersey to watch his team play the 2006 World Cup, B&M took steps to ensure he would be watching in the pub—not on the internet. Its client, Infront Sports & Media AG, owns the exclusive broadcast rights to the World Cup games, and the firm's IP lawyers were determined to block any interlopers. About 4,500 letters were sent to web sites and internet service providers in 24 countries, warning them of the perils of unauthorized downloading. But the aggressive move backfired when *Boing Boing*, a high-tech blog with 1.75 million daily visitors, posted—and proceeded to trash—the letter. Many companies receiving the letter thought it in poor taste. B&M stands by its preemptive strike, saying it wanted to get ahead of the fast-moving internet media.

Combining two increasingly litigious aspects of the media, B&M recently won a case before The California 2nd District Court of Appeal concerning video game giant Sega's right to create a character who shared some traits with Kieren Kirby (former lead singer of defunct funk band Deee-Lite). "Ulala," a 25th-century reporter in the game *Space Channel 5*, has pink hair and wears a short skirt with platform boots, similar to Kirby. Not similar enough, however. The case is the first in California to apply First Amendment rules to right-of-publicity.

Pimp my Prius

Green is the new black for Baker & McKenzie, which was the first firm to open a separate practice on global climate change, clean energy and emissions trading, and continues to work on global environmental issues. The Kyoto Treaty has proven a key battleground for Baker & McKenzie environmental lawyers, and their efforts are well recognized. Awards include the "2006 Best Law Firm for EU Emissions Trading" and the "2006 Best Law Firm for Kyoto Project Credits," by *Environmental Finance* magazine.

In the United States, increased concern about emissions and oil prices abroad has led to expansion in energy alternatives at home. New York is soon to get its first alternative fuel plant, thanks in part to B&M. The firm represented Jefferies & Company, Inc., and Goldman, Sachs & Co. in connection with the equity and debt financing of the Northeast Biofuels project, a 100-million-gallon-per-year ethanol facility. It will be the largest plant of its type on the East Coast—most ethanol production takes place in the Plains states, where corn, which is the basis of the process, grows.

GETTING HIRED

All over the map

Due to Baker & McKenzie's international breadth, it's hard to generalize about hiring standards. As a rule of thumb, "The firm will generally look for someone with international training, prior experience and top 10 percent of his/her class." As a Washington insider adds, "It is much easier to get hired from a top-tier school, but there are people from lower-ranked schools as well." On the West Coast, compares a Southern Californian, "I believe the Palo Alto office is more competitive than the San Diego office, but both are relatively competitive. In Palo Alto they focus on top tier law schools only—Boalt, Stanford, Yale, Harvard, NYU, Georgetown, etc." Such stringency annoys one New Yorker: "For some reason, they are ridiculously picky. It is somewhat unjustified and hampers our recruiting efforts. I think it is a holdover from the days when this was a much smaller office." A Chicagoan feels similarly: "Sometimes I think we are more demanding than we can afford to be. On the plus side, everyone here is really smart. It's very hard to get an offer here—they want junior associates with perfect name schools and good work experience. They like Northwestern here. That said, any top school is welcome, but transcripts are always required." A Melbourne insider feels that "while there aren't GPA equivalent cutoffs, it is difficult to get in, mainly as we don't take as many as other firms. However, the attraction to overseas work has left the domestic market a candidate's dream." A São Paolo source

Visit the Vault Law Channel, the complete online resource for law careers, featuring firm profiles, message boards, the Vault Law Job Board and more. www.vault.com/law

VAULT CAREER LIBRARY   401

thinks "there are usually lots of requirements (specific schools, fluency in English)." A Bangkok insider believes he's worked out the formula: "The firm looks for lawyers with high academic records, good command of English, commitment and maturity."

OUR SURVEY SAYS

"Sharing a pint"

A Chicago upper-level adjudges his co-workers as "nice … for lawyers." A less cynical source finds his fellow associates "very professional and intelligent, but at the same time cordial and relatively laid-back." A newbie in Sydney is pleased that "although I have not been here for very long the firm has been very welcoming and my practice group has done its best to involve me in interesting work." A tax associate enjoys "the international work I do and working on projects with our colleagues all over the world." As for office chit chat, remarks one New Yorker, it "depends on the group. But we tend to lean towards less socializing outside work." In Manhattan, "younger associates do socialize more than the seniors," but both lower and senior levels decompress with "wine and cheese socials in the library every Friday evening." A Dallas insider thinks that the firm "can be a little political, as all firms can," but differences are pushed aside over "weekly happy hours/pizza nights in and out of the office." A Tokyo source calls his office "fairly relaxed, even during periods of intense time pressures. We often catch a pint after work." A London associate deems his group a "collegiate, inclusive, progressive meritocracy," while Bogotá is "laid-back without being a frat party." In Monterrey, "We are like a small family."

The firm is flexible, but the work is not

"Work hours, especially for a first-year, vary. If the project is picking up speed, approaching closing, etc., obviously you'll spend the legendary 'New York associate' hours. But at other times the hours are reasonable. In sum, the crazy hours tend to balance out the lax times. It's not always full speed ahead all the time," reports one B&M associate. A Dallas midlevel thinks that "for a big firm, the hours are very reasonable. Partners actually tell associates to go home even when the partner will be up at the office late." In the Windy City, "it goes up and down, a couple of 50 or 55 hour workweeks, followed by a 35-hour week or two. 200-plus-hour months are unusual among associates." A Moscow litigator puts in his two cents: "I often have to work late hours, and on weekends, in light of deadlines. Between deadlines I may be very relaxed, and even seeking some billable work from other PGs." A source in Tokyo guesses his "average day is only about 10 hours in the office." Rationalizes one insider, "Basically, you know when you start working for an international law firm it will effect your life and personal time management. It's part of the job. In busy periods the days can be long (12 or more hours in the office). In calmer periods, I try to leave earlier. The policy is just stay till the work is done." On the plus side, there is "no face time" and "you do not have to stay in the office if there is no work left to do." Stresses one associate, "We work hard, but that's the nature of the business. It's not a sweatshop." As a source in Mexico City points out, "The firm is flexible, but the work is not."

Better late than never

"Due to its bureaucracy, the firm does not handle compensation changes well," claims a litigator in New York. "They attempted to match the recent associate raises, but did so slowly (months after the first firms)." Outside of the New York jungle, B&M salary gets a better reception; a senior level in the Golden State thinks that "we are in line with the California pay scale for first tier firms," while in Chicago, "base compensation is great." As one source sees it, "I think we get paid really well in light of our hours. The really big money only comes with the really big hours." On the international front, a London source writes: "I personally think it's very good as a package, in terms of hours/pressure vs. pay. Basic pay in my view is right up there with the large U.K. firms (that seems to be the benchmark—we do not get U.S. salaries here)." Not quite, says an officemate, "Compensation is good compared to a similarly-sized office of a U.K. firm, but below our competitors in the market (e.g., Magic Circle, top-10 U.K. and large U.S. firms)." According to a source in Moscow, "The salary the firm pays in the local market is lower than that of many other international law firms. Baker & McKenzie has the biggest office in Russia and arguably could offer the same salaries that are offered by much smaller U.S. law firms."

© 2007 Vault Inc.

The topic of bonuses does get B&M associates grumpy. A New Yorker outlines the grievance: "They said they were going to match bonuses, and then paid about a third of what the other firms paid, relying on the small print of their bonus policy. Basically, they said that if you meet the billable hours target, you are 'eligible' for the full bonus. In actuality, however, they only give you a 'minimum' bonus and the full bonus is based on a bunch of discretionary factors (which was basically news to everyone)."

On the outside looking in

At B&M, "Partners generally treat associates in a civil manner." An East Coast source feels that "by and large, my relationships with the partners I have worked with have been excellent." Nope, "Haven't encountered any screamers," adds another. Still, says one West Coaster, he's a little tired of the "frequent complaints from some partners about associates being 'whiny' or 'greedy' or always costing money." And a New York source would like to make clear that, while he finds the majority of partners to be pleasant, "The few partners that are disrespectful to associates are so disrespectful as to cause me to lower my overall score for the firm in this respect."

As one midlevel sees it, partner relations aren't the real issue: "The partners are easy to get along with. However, sometimes it seems as though associates are on the outside, very far on the outside, looking in at firm decisions." Colleagues concur, noting that "communication to associates from management is moderate" and that "firmwide decisions generally rest with the management committee, and input from junior associates is not usually solicited."

I saw you eat that third pirozhki

Clarifies one Chicago source, "Associates are generally perk-less. None of the examples given are offered firmwide, only if a particular partner/group will cover." In Dallas, that means "free parking, pizza and wine every Wednesday, bagels and doughnuts every Friday, jeans every Friday." New Yorkers have a fairly standard Big Apple package, "car rides home and free dinners after eight, moving expenses," while in Madrid, there are "specific programs to learn English." Chilly Chicagoans can warm up with a "free soup lunch almost every day," and "monthly First Friday happy hours." The Moscow office gets "payment for field rent for our soccer team" and "pirozhki (sweet pies) on Friday morning in every kitchen. Two per person."

Visit the Vault Law Channel, the complete online resource for law careers, featuring firm profiles, message boards, the Vault Law Job Board and more. www.vault.com/law

VAULT CAREER LIBRARY   403

Baker Botts LLP

One Shell Plaza
910 Louisiana
Houston, TX 77002-4995
Phone: (713) 229-1234
www.bakerbotts.com

LOCATIONS

Austin, TX
Dallas, TX
Houston, TX
New York, NY
Washington, DC
Beijing
Dubai
Hong Kong
London
Moscow
Riyadh

MAJOR DEPARTMENTS & PRACTICES

Corporate
Environmental
Global Projects
Intellectual Property
Litigation
Tax

THE STATS

No. of attorneys: 750
No. of offices: 11
Summer associate offers: 97 out of 100 (2006)
Managing Partner: Walter J. Smith
Hiring Partners:
 Austin: Joe Knight
 Dallas: Van Beckwith
 Houston: John Anaipakos
 New York: Jonathon Gordon
 Washington, DC: Casey Cooper

THE BUZZ
WHAT ATTORNEYS AT OTHER FIRMS ARE SAYING ABOUT THIS FIRM

- "Great appellate team"
- "Old School"
- "Texas powerhouse"
- "Oil Barons"

BASE SALARY (2007)

Texas offices
1st year: $140,000
2nd year: $140,000
3rd year: $145,000
4th year: $150,000
5th year: $160,000
6th year: $170,000
7th year: $180,000
8th year: $185,000
Summer associate: $2,700/week

New York, NY
1st year: $160,000
Summer associate: $3,077/week

Washington, DC
1st year: $145,000
Summer associate: $2,700/week

UPPERS

- Friendly atmosphere
- "Interesting mix of work and clients"
- Strong mentoring and associate development

DOWNERS

- "No real part-time policy"
- Failure to match recent major-market pay raises
- Complaints about support staff

NOTABLE PERKS

- Bonuses for recruiting
- Free parking
- "Free M&Ms on Fridays"
- "Free Treos with unlimited minutes for your office and personal use"

© 2007 Vault Inc.

RANKING RECAP

Best in Region
#1 - Texas

EMPLOYMENT CONTACT

Ms. Melissa O. Moss
Manager of Attorney Employment
Phone: (713) 229-2056
Fax: (713) 229-7856
E-mail: melissa.moss@bakerbotts.com

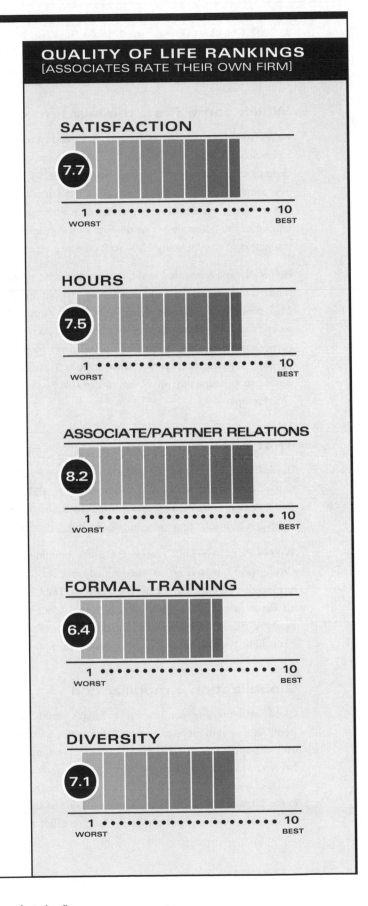

QUALITY OF LIFE RANKINGS
[ASSOCIATES RATE THEIR OWN FIRM]

SATISFACTION
7.7
1 WORST .... 10 BEST

HOURS
7.5
1 WORST .... 10 BEST

ASSOCIATE/PARTNER RELATIONS
8.2
1 WORST .... 10 BEST

FORMAL TRAINING
6.4
1 WORST .... 10 BEST

DIVERSITY
7.1
1 WORST .... 10 BEST

Visit the Vault Law Channel, the complete online resource for law careers, featuring firm profiles, message boards, the Vault Law Job Board and more. www.vault.com/law

VAULT CAREER LIBRARY   405

THE SCOOP

In 2007, Chambers Global named Bakers Botts No. 1 for oil and gas transactions—unsurprising, due to the firm's Texan roots, century of service to the oil industry, and close connections to the Republican administrations of the last 25 years. Sturdy teams in technology, complex litigation, white collar defense and appellate advocacy helped rank Baker Botts as Vault's Best in Texas.

Which came first, the law firm or the oil well?

Baker Botts was launched in Houston in 1840, just three years after the formation of the city itself. The firm had early success representing agricultural interests, primarily sugar, cotton and timber, and later with such clients as the Southern Pacific and Union Pacific Railroads. The hurricane of 1900, which devastated the city of Galveston and established Houston as the state's new commercial center, was also integral in the firm's ascension. In the early 20th century, a much-publicized murder case made Baker Botts a household name, when an investigation spearheaded by Captain James Baker (son of the original name-partner) uncovered the homicide of one the firm's most prominent clients, cotton king William Marsh Rice. (The butler did it, upon the instigation of an unsavoury New York probate lawyer).

Homicides and hurricanes aside, the firm found its calling when oil was discovered in the region in 1901. Since its early days, Baker Botts has had a nose for black gold, shepherding the companies that eventually evolved into Exxon, Chevron and Texaco. 2007 sees the firm homesteading in the oil frontiers of Russia, Saudi Arabia and the United Arab Emirates, where it was the second major U.S. firm to set up shop, following Akin Gump. These days, it has its eyes on what will soon be the world's largest energy market—in 2005, the firm opened doors in Hong Kong, and promptly joined the law firms queuing up for a Beijing license. Longstanding energy clients include Shell, Amoco and Reliant, and an obscure energy contractor called Halliburton. Among its partners, the firm counts former U.S. Secretary of State James A. Baker and former Texas Supreme Court Chief Justice Tom Phillips.

That hand that feeds

Baker Botts has had long, strong ties to the Bush administration, in all its incarnations. In 1967, a 15-year-old George W. did his tour of duty in the firm's mail room; James A. Baker III, a direct descendant of the original Baker, has served under four Republican presidents, two of them named Bush. During the Florida recount of 2000, Baker would serve as Bush/Cheney campaign counsel, vigorously defending Bush's right to the throne.

With such pals in high places, the firm's prominence in the energy sector must be viewed through Bush-tinted glasses. Government ties have scored the firm engagements with the Saudi royal family and contractor-du-jour Halliburton, and Baker has faced open criticism for his connection to The Carlyle Group, his role in the creation of an oil pipeline in Afghanistan, and his Enron ties. Some contend that the firm's recent entry to hot energy markets has been "eased" by its powerful connections; James A. Baker IV, when asked if his father's connections had anything to do with the firm's emergence in Russia, affirmed that it would be "disingenuous to say it hasn't been an asset."

Globalization = mobilization

Globalization means mobilization, and that's exactly what Baker Botts has been up to. In 2007, Baker Botts won permission from Chinese authorities to open its Beijing office, joining a league of Texas firms now resident in the country. The firm's other overseas operations are also faring well. In London, the energy group has acted on North Sea acquisitions and gas sales from Nigeria, while the corporate group has kept busy advising a bidder for BP subsidiary Innovene Chemical. A London arbitration business is also taking off, fueled by new mandates (read: power-grabs) from the Russian market. In August 2006, client demand in the London office led to the transfer of one of the firm's Houston energy litigation and arbitration specialists. The move bolsters the number of partners in the London office to seven.

© 2007 Vault Inc.

The go-to guys

In November 2006, *IP Law & Business* named Baker Botts top of the list for IP litigation, while a September 2006 survey of Fortune 250 general counsel, "Who Represents America's Biggest Companies?", placed Baker Botts No. 1 in intellectual property. The firm also placed second in the patent prosecution category. Baker Botts employs over 120 patent attorneys in five cities, with most holding at least one engineering or science degree, and maintaining membership in the patent bar. The firm presently represents several university-based research institutes and biotech companies in protecting and developing pharmaceuticals, procedures and methods for disposal of hazardous wastes. In 2007, the firm expanded its New York IP department with the hire of two additional partners.

Safe and securities

In March 2007, Baker Botts successfully defended Thomas W. Jones, former chief executive of Citigroup's asset management division, when the SEC accused him of cheating mutual fund investors out of tens of millions of dollars. The SEC maintained that when Jones and co-defendant Lewis E. Daidone, the former vice president of Smith Barney Management, renegotiated a contract with First Data Investment Management, they kept the discount for themselves rather than passing the savings onto investors. The SEC estimates that over the last five years, the misappropriated funds earned Citigroup some $100 million in profits. In dismissing the suit, a federal district court in New York ruled that the SEC had waited too long to sue, and lacked evidence to support its bid to recover the gains. Jones was represented by James R. Doty, a former SEC general counsel and current partner at Baker Botts.

In March 2006, Baker Botts securities litigators won a dismissal for client Administaff in a lawsuit filed by the company's shareholders. The suit claimed that Administaff had repeatedly made misleading statements concerning its projected costs and earnings; in dismissing the claim, the court held that Administaff had fairly identified its projections as "forward looking," cloaked them in cautionary language, and referred readers to its SEC filings for information on other risk factors—all in accordance with the Safe Harbor Provision of the Private Securities Litigation Reform Act of 1995.

An answer to the $65,000,000 question

In February 2007, the firm received good news in its appeal of Cailloux vs. Baker Botts, an estate planning malpractice suit which resulted in a plaintiff's award of $65.5 million in 2005. In awarding the original judgment, a court found that the firm had breached its fiduciary duty by failing to inform the heirs of Floyd Cailloux, founder of the Keystone valve company, of all options concerning the inheritance they received after Cailloux's death in 1997. Baker Botts attorneys had advised Cailloux's widow to cede 90 percent of her entitlement, some $60 million, to a charitable foundation in order to avoid a weighty tax bill; plaintiffs also maintained that the decision to donate to the foundation was influenced by a biased party. Two years later, a Texas court reversed the judgment, finding that Baker and co-defendant Wells Fargo owed nothing, and ruling that the Cailloux heirs had failed to prove loss causation.

Now that's a hootenanny

Law firm client appreciation parties can be staid, "everybody on your best behavior" affairs. But Texas is not about subtle (especially Dallas), and all about hospitality, so Baker Botts parties are something of an art. In fact, clients have RSVPed so enthusiastically that the firm was once forced to rescind invitations to some of its lowest-level associates, in order to stay within fire code ordinances. With five bars, three chocolate fountains and musical performers like Willie Nelson and the B-52s, Baker Botts' fêtes are high-energy events where clients, attorneys and Willie Nelson can really let down their hair.

Visit the Vault Law Channel, the complete online resource for law careers, featuring firm profiles, message boards, the Vault Law Job Board and more. **www.vault.com/law**

VAULT CAREER LIBRARY   **407**

GETTING HIRED

Grades are a threshold; personality gets you hired

Hiring standards at Baker Botts may be high, but not outlandishly so, and increasingly flexible. One midlevel corporate attorney reports that the firm's hiring attorneys require "pretty good grades from lower-tier schools and whatever from the top 10." A junior litigation associate advises, "Grades, work experience and law school involvement are very important. Grades are more of a threshold; experience and involvement get you an interview, but personality, interest and ambition get you hired." As for specifics, a junior associate reports that the firm requires a "3.2-plus GPA generally from top-tier law schools." A Dallas litigator says the firm maintains a "top 10 percent cutoff" and that it "focuses on top-25 schools." A senior associate adds, "The firm focuses on top-25 law schools and has cutoff GPAs for each. There is some GPA flexibility when the candidate has specific skills (language, scientific background for IP, etc.)." One Texan sets forth some essentials about the process: "Extremely competitive to get hired, particularly in the Austin office. They really only interview in the top 25 percent, although there are sometimes exceptions. Looking for smart, good communication skills and someone that we would enjoy working with. We do a LOT of recruiting from UT, but [the firm has] tried to branch out so that we can have a more diverse summer class."

A tax attorney says the firm's failure to stay at the top of the market for compensation may work in favor of borderline candidates. "With the recent lack of raises for Texas offices, perhaps the firm will become a little less competitive for top talent, making it a bit easier for those who are somewhat lower in their law school classes to be hired on here," he suggests.

OUR SURVEY SAYS

"The sky's the limit at this firm"

For the most part, Baker Botts associates give the firm rave reviews. A Houston litigator expounds at length about the virtues thereof. "I am very satisfied with my job," he says. "The sky is the limit at this firm. An aspiring associate seeking to learn and grow as a lawyer can take on as much work, of as much complexity and depth, as he is capable of handling. The firm is happy to see young associates rise in skill and responsibility, and the partners and senior associates not only share work willingly, but also actively mentor to make sure that young associates are not merely left out to sea, but rather are actively guided even as they are challenged." Another Houston litigator reports, "The work, particularly in the trial department, is very interesting and rewarding. There is no lack of cases to get involved with and the mentoring and levels of responsibility both defy the traditional stereotype of large-firm practice. Associates are given a lot of responsibility at a young age/low experience level, once they prove that they are capable." Yet another Houstonian adds, "I couldn't be happier. I learn new things every day, and the work is more interesting than I could have imagined. We work with the top clients, but the hours are (generally) manageable enough to maintain an active life outside the office. The salary and bonus structure is very generous."

Friendly, but not "let's-go-get-a-beer" friendly

Associates call Baker Botts "friendly," "laid-back," "professional," "family-oriented" and kind of, but not really, "social." Here's how one Houston litigator describes his office's vibe: "The lawyers are friendly, but not social ... That is, interactions in the office are cordial, but not chatty. And little socializing occurs outside the office. It is evident that most of the folks here have lives outside the office that they value highly. While they take their work seriously and bring a sincere devotion to it, they see no reason to linger at the office or otherwise prolong their time away from those lives any more than they have to." Another Houston lawyer adds, "From my perspective, lawyers do not spend a lot of time together as most attorneys have families and children. Happy hours are very rare. While this is the case, the office is very friendly and your peers are very helpful."

Associates say that there are methods for measuring associate/partner relations at Baker Botts, which result in two very different answers—personally, and institutionally. "On a personal level, partners treat associates very well. However, on a firmwide basis, management has made it clear that increasing profit per partner is the most important goal, and associates get the message that they should be grateful for their job and bill more with less support and resources," is how one Houston associate puts it. A Washington, D.C., litigator adds, "Individual associate/partner relationships are good in the D.C. office but firmwide partnership communication with associates is poor, with very little input by associates on firmwide decisions." On the other hand, an IP expert counters, "The partners exhibit a mentoring attitude and truly want us to do good work while growing as lawyers. Associate opinions are seriously considered, even if another choice is taken."

"Not sure what 'formal training' is"

Formal training at Baker Botts is a low institutional priority, associates say. "There are some CLEs, [but] not nearly enough training for younger associates," complains a junior associate. "Associates are not even encouraged to attend CLEs in their practice area if the CLE location would require travel/time out of the office." As a junior attorney puts it, "'Training' for first-year associates is limited to three days of introduction to the computer and phone systems." A nonplussed labor specialist in Houston adds that he's "not sure what formal training is."

"It is what you make of it here"

Informal training—i.e., mentoring—varies from partner to partner. So you'll hear a lot of comments like this: "Informal mentoring is excellent. One must be proactive; mentorship will not be foisted upon you. But if you seek it out, almost anyone here will take the time to sincerely help you understand how things work and why." Or this: "It is what you make of it here. If you seek out partners and their advice, they will happily give it to you and you learn a lot. If you are a shy, retiring type and don't seek out your own mentoring relationship, you won't get one." But on the other hand, a few comments sound like this: "There's not nearly enough. I suppose this is a problem at most law firms." Or, as another Houstonian puts it, "It's sink or swim. The firm has a 'mentoring' program, but no one knows what that means. New associates generally look to a few generous partners and to senior associates for training and mentoring."

Top-notch pay, but ...

Associates seem to agree that they were well paid, at least until the firm failed to match—or even acknowledge—the recent salary jumps elsewhere in the country. These remarks from a tax attorney typify the consensus: "Compensation is all right, but relative to other national markets it was disappointing to not receive even a small bump in pay when most other markets did receive raises." That said, an appreciative Houston litigator professes, "My compensation is excellent. As highly as I think of myself, I think you'd have to be pretty arrogant to think that you're really worth what we're being paid around here." And a Houston corporate attorney adds, "Bonuses are not on par with the rest of the country, but the starting salary makes up for the lack in bonus because of the low cost of living and no state income tax."

Long + Flexible = Not So Crazy Hours

Associates say that they are pleasantly surprised by the reasonableness of the work demands at Baker Botts. "One of the things I love most about Baker Botts is the complete control you have over your schedule," says a young Houston litigator. "Nobody ever knows or cares where you are at any given moment. If your work slips or you aren't there when you are needed, that is of course a problem." Another junior Houston litigator adds, "No one pays attention to when I leave, which is often early, so I can eat dinner with my family." There are, of course, a few naysayers. Says a sarcastic midlevel: "'Quality of life' is excellent, if your life consists of serving clients and billing."

Visit the Vault Law Channel, the complete online resource for law careers, featuring firm profiles, message boards, the Vault Law Job Board and more. www.vault.com/law

VAULT CAREER LIBRARY   409

Boies, Schiller & Flexner LLP

575 Lexington Avenue, 7th Floor
New York, NY 10022
Phone: (212) 446-2300
www.bsfllp.com

LOCATIONS

Albany, NY • Armonk, NY • Fort Lauderdale, FL • Hanover, NH • Las Vegas, NV • Miami, FL • New York, NY • Oakland, CA • Orlando, FL • Short Hills, NJ • Washington, DC

MAJOR DEPARTMENTS & PRACTICES

Antitrust • Appellate • Business Crimes • Class Actions • Corporate • Constitutional Law/First Amendment • Employment Labor • Environmental • False Claims Act • Healthcare • Intellectual Property • Internal Investigation/Corporate Governance • International Arbitration • Product Liability • Reorganization/Work-outs • Securities Litigation • SEC Enforcement • Sports & Media • Tax

THE STATS

No. of attorneys: 211
No. of offices: 11
Summer associate offers: 22 out of 23 (2006)
Managing Partners: David Boies, Donald L. Flexner & Jonathan D. Schiller
Hiring Partners:
  Albany: George Carpinello
  Armonk: Robin A. Henry
  New York: Jack G. Stern, Magda M. Jimenez
  Washington, DC: Amy J. Mauser, Hamish Hume
  Miami: Mark J. Heise
  Orlando: Gary Harris
  Fort Lauderdale: Stuart Singer
  Oakland: Ken Rossman
  Las Vegas: Richard J. Pocker
  New Jersey: David Stone
  New Hampshire: Richard Drubel
  Corporate: Christopher Boies

THE BUZZ
WHAT ATTORNEYS AT OTHER FIRMS ARE SAYING ABOUT THIS FIRM

- "Everyone knows who HE is"
- "Great litigators"
- "Trial Studs"
- "Jumped the shark"

BASE SALARY (2007)

All offices
1st year: $160,000
Summer associate: $3,075/week

UPPERS

- "Unparalleled" cases
- "Real" work from the get-go
- Unpretentious, low-key environment

DOWNERS

- "Do you want to sleep or win?" attitude
- Opaque, discretionary bonus system
- "Training? Huh?"

NOTABLE PERKS

- Annual firm retreat to the Caribbean
- Free soda and snacks in the office
- "Actually obtainable tickets to box at MSG and sporting events"
- All associates have their own offices

© 2007 Vault Inc.

RANKING RECAP

Partner Prestige Rankings

#5 (tie) - Antitrust

EMPLOYMENT CONTACTS

Armonk

Legal Recruiting Coordinator

Phone: (914) 749-8200

Fax: (914) 749-8300

New York

Legal Recruiting Coordinator

Phone: (212) 446-2300

Fax: (212) 446-2350

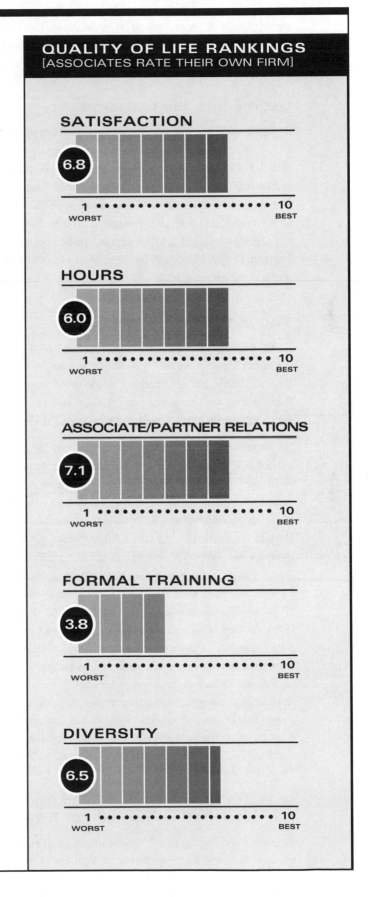

QUALITY OF LIFE RANKINGS

[ASSOCIATES RATE THEIR OWN FIRM]

SATISFACTION

6.8

1 WORST — 10 BEST

HOURS

6.0

1 WORST — 10 BEST

ASSOCIATE/PARTNER RELATIONS

7.1

1 WORST — 10 BEST

FORMAL TRAINING

3.8

1 WORST — 10 BEST

DIVERSITY

6.5

1 WORST — 10 BEST

Visit the Vault Law Channel, the complete online resource for law careers, featuring firm profiles, message boards, the Vault Law Job Board and more. www.vault.com/law

VAULT CAREER LIBRARY   411

THE SCOOP

Boies, Schiller & Flexner is scarcely a decade old, but already boasts 210 lawyers in 11 far-flung offices across the country, from Armonk to Oakland. As one of the nation's premier litigation shops, Boies is no stranger to heavy-hitter clients—when Microsoft got too big for its britches, no less than the U.S. Department of Justice came calling.

Let me into the ballgame

It was David Boies' independent streak, or perhaps sheer cussedness, that led to his walking out on Cravath, Swaine & Moore in 1997. Star litigator Boies had spent 30 years under the Cravath awning (where he was notorious for running a "firm within a firm"), but knocked heads with firm brass when he decided to take on representation of Yankees owner George Steinbrenner in a lawsuit against Major League Baseball. Boies' representation of Steinbrenner posed a purported conflict of interest for Cravath, whose longtime client, Time Warner, also owned the Atlanta Braves. In a story that made the front page of *The New York Times*, 48 hours after receiving an ultimatum to drop the Steinbrenner case, Boies hung up his Cravath hat. Within a matter of months he persuaded Jonathan Schiller, a litigation and international arbitration specialist and partner in the D.C. office of Kaye, Scholer, Fierman, Hays & Handler, to join him; at the end of 1998, Donald Flexner, a partner in D.C.-based Crowell and Moring's antitrust group, came onboard.

You gotta have a Plan B

Boies' Plan B—a humble "10-lawyer firm that would take on interesting and difficult cases"—was thrown rudely off-kilter when the Justice Department came knocking. Between the Steinbrenner case and the little Microsoft matter, Boies required manpower. To achieve this, he brought aboard some talent from his old firm, and absorbed the 20-lawyer Barrett Gravante Carpinello & Stern, themselves Cravath ex-pats. Though Boies took the Microsoft antitrust case at $40 an hour, a slight concession from his then $550 hourly rate, the publicity surrounding the issue was beyond price.

No longer hemmed by conflicts of interest, and keeping costs low by locating offices outside of major centers (one outpost is located in Hanover, New Hampshire, population 11,000), the new firm was free to take on riskier, high-stakes plaintiffs' work. In its early years, the firm scored big in two separate price-fixing class-action cases, one against major manufacturers of bulk vitamins, in which the firm won a $1.1 billion settlement in 2000, and the other against auction houses Christie's and Sotheby's, in which the firm nailed a $512 million settlement. By 2000, Boies was serving as lead counsel for former Vice President Al Gore in litigation relating to the Florida election vote count. And when Napster found itself in hot water, it sought out David Boies. Other firm successes include obtaining a jury defense verdict on behalf of Lloyds of London and other insurers in the World Trade Center trial, a hugely favorable arbitral award in a case for the Yankees Entertainment Sports Network against Cablevision; freeing the New York Yankees from MSG Network's long-term contract for the local broadcast and cable rights to all Yankees games; successfully defending NASCAR from a $1 billion antitrust challenge to its method of choosing venues for its Nextel Cup races; bailing insurance gain Zurich Financial Services out of a bankruptcy judge's determination that it was liable for $750 million in debts of a bankrupt nursing home chain; and obtaining a $74 million award in a complex insurance coverage arbitration. Other high-profile engagements include representing Maurice "Hank" Greenberg and two companies he is associated with in multibillion-dollar lawsuits between those companies and AIG, representing the New York Jets in a suit claiming that Cablevision monopolized the New York City cable television market by preventing development of a new sports stadium and convention center, and representing Miramax founders Harvey and Robert Weinstein in successfully negotiating their separation from the Walt Disney Company. Over the years the firm's clients have included American Express, Ernst & Young, Georgia Pacific, Goldman Sachs, Monsanto, Northwest Airlines, Philip Morris, USA, SBC Communications (now AT&T), Siemens, Trizec Properties, Tyco and Unisys.

It's not whether you win or lose ...

Such are the cases that Boies Schiller litigates that even when it tastes defeat, the firm is lauded for having gotten in the ring in the first place, and for the caliber of its argument. The Gore and Napster losses are cases in point, and in 2005, the firm also lost its challenge to the state of New York's decision not to allow cameras in the courtroom. The ban results from a 1952 law that specifically prohibits televising New York's courtrooms; though 43 states now permit the practice, New York has held firm. Representing Court TV, the firm argued that categorically banning televising courtroom proceedings was an impediment to free speech, and therefore unconstitutional. A New York court of appeals didn't buy it, and affirmed lower court findings that the question of cameras in the courtroom did not actually compromise any state or federal constitutional rights.

Out from the shadow?

Of late, the firm has seen some departures of its younger partners, those who had trailed Boies from Cravath. Two of the first partners recruited, Steven R. Neuwirth and Andrew W. Hayes, left the firm in early 2006; Neuwirth crossed over to New York's all-litigation Quinn Emanuel, while Hayes will head a nonprofit. In February 2006, Quinn Emanuel scored another Boies partner, Phillip Z. Selendy. Critics of Boies Schiller suggest that under the shadow of such star litigators, younger partners cannot shine, which raises questions about the firm's longevity. It must be noted that, according to the firm, "almost all of the original partners remain at the firm, which continues to groom and promote outstanding partners from its talented associate ranks, and recently added two prominent IP litigators to its Washington office." As a result, Schiller brushes off such doubts, telling *The New York Law Journal* that "people have been saying this about us since we started."

Lerach out, Boies Schiller in

In February 2007, Boies Schiller scooped a fresh client from class-action specialist Lerach Coughlin's lap. A U.S. District Judge in Dallas granted a request from the Archdiocese of Milwaukee Supporting Fund to part ways with its Lerach lawyers as it pursues shareholder litigation against oil giant Halliburton. The Supporting Fund claims that its relationship with Lerach worsened in part due to William Lerach's past association with Milberg Weiss; in May 2006, the U.S. government indicted Milberg for allegedly paying kickbacks to class-action clients. The Archdiocese of Milwaukee Supporting Fund is currently refuting a shareholder settlement offer made by Halliburton, which it claims is inadequate. Damages experts for the fund estimate that Halliburton's deceptive accounting practices cost its investors between $799 million and $4 billion.

A breakdown in communications

In 2007, the firm resolved a skirmish with cable television company and ex-client Adelphia Communications. Adelphia, which the firm began representing during its 2002 bankruptcy proceedings (and for which the firm recovered hundreds of millions of dollars looted by the family that founded the company), delayed paying the remainder of the $30 million fee that it owed the firm. Adelphia initially claimed that Boies Schiller had an obligation to tell the cable company that the litigation support companies it was using were indirectly part-owned by firm lawyers, including children of David Boies. Adelphi asked Boies Schiller to resign as its special litigation counsel in August 2005. In February 2006, a judge presiding over Adelphia's Chapter 11 proceedings denied the company's request to have a special examiner look into the charges. In fact, the judge stated that Boies Schiller had done an outstanding job for Adelphia. Recently, Adelphia agreed that the firm did nothing deliberately wrong and the firm agreed to reduce its outstanding bill.

GETTING HIRED

The best of the best of the best

One of the nation's most prestigious law firms, Boies Schiller is accustomed to getting its pick of the litter. As one of the firm's young associates puts it, "If you go to a top law school, and are towards the top of the class, they will hire you. If not, I hope you're related to someone here." A midlevel corporate attorney advises, "Top grades from a top law school is a requirement. That alone doesn't cut it, as we look hard at personality and whether the individual will fit in." And a senior litigator adds, "The firm rarely hires from outside top-five law schools. Even candidates from those schools must have top grades. Candidates from

Visit the Vault Law Channel, the complete online resource for law careers, featuring firm profiles, message boards, the Vault Law Job Board and more. **www.vault.com/law**

VAULT CAREER LIBRARY   413

law firms outside the top five must have been at the very top of their class or have had very unique and impressive work experience."

As for personal qualities, one litigator suggests that the firm is "generally looking for self-starters who won't expect much formal training and who will fit into the firm's relaxed environment." According to the firm itself, Boies Schiller "doesn't lead associates by the hand, but teaches them how to litigate by involving associates in meaningful roles where they can work directly with and learn from experienced partners who treat the associates as colleagues, not cannon fodder, and who are confident enough to allow the associates to interact with clients, take and defend depositions, and appear in court." In addition, the firm reports that it has instituted monthly training sessions where the firm's senior partners make presentations on topics such as taking and defending depositions, working with experts and preparing for trial. Another litigator says, "The firm looks for smarts, drive and spark. This is not a place for people who are not self-starters and we weed for that in the interviews." A junior corporate associate adds, "Out of the many people qualified to do the work, we try to find the ones that fit the best with our existing attorneys, the ones that will help us perpetuate the unique culture we have already developed."

OUR SURVEY SAYS

Not for the faint of heart

Both Boies Schiller and its associates pride themselves on the firm's off-and-running attitude: There's real work from the beginning, and lots of it. "Associates in the corporate group feel vested in both the development and growth of the group as well as in each and every deal that we work on," offers one young attorney. "This adds to the level of fulfillment, as you feel that you are actually contributing to the success of the group." A Manhattan litigator adds, "I've worked very hard but I've done a lot of great work, including writing several summary judgment motions, taking and defending depositions and sitting in on most meetings and conferences with client and partners." Or, as a litigator from the Westchester HQ puts it, "While not for the faint of heart, where else will a first-year associate be immediately thrown into the thick of trials, filings and client contact?"

A colleague adds, "The firm is definitely trial by fire. I have been here, off a clerkship, for five months and have taken five depositions. Nobody wastes your time and there is no rigid hierarchy. It's certainly not for everyone, but if you are self-driven and happy to jump in the deep end, there's more opportunity here." That said, a few associates want a hotter fire, or a deeper end, or something: "The cases are interesting, but the firm does not do a good job of giving enough responsibility to associates and making them feel as though they are part of a case," complains a midlevel. "For instance, I have not had the opportunity to attend any of the hearings for which I have prepared partners (and there have been many), have only attended one deposition and have not attended a single client meeting." Other associates have argued in federal appellate court for and handled numerous court hearings and arguments on their own. The firm points out that "although it always wants to be a place where personal drive and determination are rewarded, it has also undertaken systematic efforts to make sure all associates receive opportunities to do exciting work early in their careers."

You say "tuh-may-toe," I say "tuh-mah-toe"

Associates offer up a wide variety of views about the culture at Boies Schiller. A Washington litigator enthuses, "It's a vibrant, informed, politically conscious and social group." A New Yorker says his office boasts a "very collegial atmosphere." He adds that it is "nonhierarchical," and that "all the partners are easily accessible and take a very hands-on approach to associate development. We work together and play together." However, one litigator complains, "The firm's culture is one of work, bill, and then work some more. Lawyers do not socialize together at all." A California contact says, "The culture is open and friendly ... We enjoy each other's company and socialize together some, but for the most part we focus on work." Another New York litigator warns, "The gap in ages between the associate body and the partners (at least in the New York City and Armonk offices) has led to serious communication problems. Associates have overall been left in the dark about all important matters, including the most recent salary changes in the market."

© 2007 Vault Inc.

For the most part, the partners are great. For the most part ...

Associates feel that the firm's partners emphasize respect and inclusion, though definitely not without exception. "We are treated with great respect and the partners really care about our job satisfaction," boasts a midlevel litigator. A Manhattan corporate attorney adds, "Partners really care about associate development. They take the time to get to know each associate personally so you're not just another cog." That said, it's not uncommon to find associates who sound more like this Armonk attorney. "It's a mixed bag," she says. "There is not really a firm division between partners and associates and, for most projects, there's truly a team feel. However, given the high stress levels at times, some partners have been known to be unreasonable to staff or junior attorneys. There is little flow of information on firm decisions at all, let alone participation of associates in decisions, though the firm does sincerely and immediately try to respond to associate complaints."

Training? Huh?

How's the formal training at Boies Schiller? Um, funny you should ask. According to the firm's associates, there's no such thing as "formal training," per se. "There isn't really formal training," says a second-year. "There are lunches every month where we are dictated something by speakerphone, but not hands-on formal training." As a Big Apple attorney puts it, "As in any New York corporate firm, training is more hands-on than 'classroom.' We do, however, have monthly training sessions that cover a wide variety of relevant and useful topics." As one litigator spins it, "There is minimal training, but I generally see that as a positive because it means you learn on the job by playing a meaningful role."

"Hit-or-miss"

Associates generally consider the informal training at Boies Schiller to be "hit-or-miss." A junior litigator reports, "Some partners develop close mentoring relationships with associates, others are more hands off. Luckily there are plenty of cases to go around, and enough flexibility to request work with different individuals. The firm is definitely designed for self-starters, as the mentoring and resources are out there, but you have to be assertive to take advantage of them." Or, as one midlevel litigator puts it, "Partners and senior associates want to help but they are at times too busy to be able to do so." A senior litigator echoes those sentiments, adding, "People at this firm, including partners, are very eager to help each other and provide training. That said, people are also extremely busy with their case loads. But by and large, there is an open-door policy and associates can get help and consultation with more senior lawyers when they need it."

Top o' the market?

Associates say that the firm's hours may rank among the profession's longest, but that the firm is flexible and compensates well for the time. As one associate puts it, "It's much easier to work the 'N.Y. corporate' hours when you like the people you work with. Plus, the way compensation works here, the more hours you work, the more you get paid."

One New Yorker reports that the firm "pays well above market. The firm pays you 30 percent of all revenue you bring to the firm as salary plus bonus as well as some credit for pro bono. As a result, it's not uncommon for junior associates here to make $40 to $50K more than their peers at other big New York firms." However, in light of the recent BigLaw salary wars, some worry the firm is conceding its place as a market leader: "The firm, though previously above-market in pay, has not yet (to our knowledge) upped associate pay to either the same level as Simpson Thatcher, Cravath, etc.—or above them, where the firm's compensation used to be." Boies Schiller, however, points out that its associate base salaries "remain at or above market despite the recent salary wars, as many of the firms mentioned above simply increased base salaries to the level Boies Schiller already occupied."

To the extent there are any associate compensation-related complaints, they focus on the bonus system: "Salary is competitive and on the higher side I think, but the bonus system can be a negative if you work substantially on contingency cases (that ultimately are not as successful as anticipated), therefore there is more risk that you will not get a bonus. You end up working a ridiculous amount of hours on billable matters in order to see any kind of bonus," says a New York litigator. "Of course, if the contingency case pans out, then you have opportunity to receive a windfall." Another litigator adds, "The salary received by

Visit the Vault Law Channel, the complete online resource for law careers, featuring firm profiles, message boards, the Vault Law Job Board and more. www.vault.com/law

VAULT CAREER LIBRARY   415

associates is equal to that offered by most New York firms. The bonus system, however, needs to be changed. I work in a branch office in which the two partners do not bring in billable clients. As a result, at bonus time, I am punished because of the type of cases I work on. I obviously have very little control over my docket and cannot demand billable cases." One huge fan of the firm's policy is having none of this grousing: "It always amazes me that more people don't know about our unique compensation system. It incentivizes associates in all the right ways."

© 2007 Vault Inc.

"Partners really care about associate development. They take the time to get to know each associate personally, so you're not just another cog."

— *Boies, Schiller & Flexner associate*

Visit the Vault Law Channel, the complete online resource for law careers, featuring firm
profiles, message boards, the Vault Law Job Board and more. www.vault.com/law

VAULT CAREER LIBRARY   417

47

PRESTIGE
RANKING

Munger, Tolles & Olson LLP

355 South Grand Avenue, 35th Floor
Los Angeles, CA 90071-1560
Phone: (213) 683-9100
www.mto.com

LOCATIONS

Los Angeles, CA (HQ)
San Francisco, CA

MAJOR DEPARTMENTS & PRACTICES

Bankruptcy
Corporate
Environmental
Intellectual Property
Labor
Litigation
Real Estate
Tax

THE STATS

No. of attorneys: 185
No. of offices: 2
Summer associate offers: 22 out of 27 (2006)
Co-Managing Partners: Mark B. Helm & Bart H. Williams
Recruiting Committee Co-Chairs: Mary Ann Todd & Paul
   J. Watford

BASE SALARY (2007)

Both offices
1st year: $160,000
2nd year: $170,000
3rd year: $185,000
4th year: $210,000
5th year: $230,000
6th year: $250,000
7th year: $265,000
Summer associate: $3,080/week

UPPERS

- "Very smart lawyers who are passionate about doing a good job"
- High responsibility, freedom and autonomy
- "The support and security of a large firm structure with the intimacy of a small group"

DOWNERS

- Hours and tasks can be unpredictable
- Not as much international work
- "Lack of a meaningful in-house training program"

NOTABLE PERKS

- Friday in-house happy hour—"the Sherry Sip"
- Annual weekend retreat for attorneys and their families
- In-house lunches served three days per week with frequent prominent guest speakers
- Generous clerkship bonuses

THE BUZZ
WHAT ATTORNEYS AT OTHER FIRMS ARE SAYING ABOUT THIS FIRM

- "The Wachtell of the West Coast"
- "Intellectual snobbery"
- "As avant-garde as law firms get"
- "Some of the most pretentious people from law school went here"

© 2007 Vault Inc.

RANKING RECAP

Best in Region
#4 - Southern California

Quality of Life
#2 - Selectivity
#4 - Associate/Partner Relations
#16 - Overall Satisfaction

EMPLOYMENT CONTACT

Ms. Kevinn C. Villard
Director of Legal Recruiting
Phone: (213) 683-9242
Fax: (213) 683-5142
E-mail: kevinn.villard@mto.com

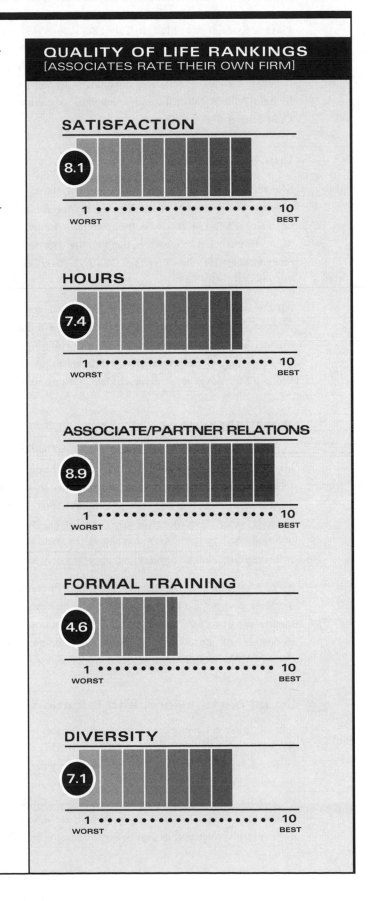

QUALITY OF LIFE RANKINGS
[ASSOCIATES RATE THEIR OWN FIRM]

SATISFACTION
8.1
1 WORST — 10 BEST

HOURS
7.4
1 WORST — 10 BEST

ASSOCIATE/PARTNER RELATIONS
8.9
1 WORST — 10 BEST

FORMAL TRAINING
4.6
1 WORST — 10 BEST

DIVERSITY
7.1
1 WORST — 10 BEST

Visit the Vault Law Channel, the complete online resource for law careers, featuring firm profiles, message boards, the Vault Law Job Board and more. **www.vault.com/law**

VAULT CAREER LIBRARY   419

THE SCOOP

Playing six degrees of Munger, Tolles & Olson is easy if you're trying to connect the firm to big-name players in law, business and entertainment. Here's a few to get you started: Charlie Munger is also business partner to none other than Warren Buffett, second-richest person in the world (the two of them head Berkshire Hathaway). On the entertainment side, the firm handles copyright claims for the estates of Buddy Holly and Jimi Hendrix. Add to this numerous connections to the bench: over 125 of Munger Tolles & Olson attorneys served as law clerks to federal judges and almost two dozen were law clerks to justices of the United States Supreme Court.

Who's who

Munger's commitment to hiring litigation dynamos was one factor in the firm's finalist ranking in *The American Lawyer*'s "Litigation Department of the Year" contest in January 2006. Also significant was the firm's representation of high-profile clientele—Phillip Morris, Abbott Laboratories, former Disney CEO Michael Ovitz and Boeing all among the most prominent on Munger's client list. Nowadays, the litigation department continues to garner both accolades (in 2007, two Munger partners were recognized as "Bet-the-Company" lawyers by *Best Lawyers in America*) and noteworthy clientele, including Apple, Verizon, and Twentieth Century Fox.

All litigation all the time could be dull, and Munger is a well-rounded firm with a corporate practice as deep as its litigation practice. For example, Berkshire Hathaway, the founders of Google and the management of DreamWorks have all turned to Munger for legal counsel regarding securities offerings. Other corporate clients include KB Home, Southern California Edison, Countrywide and Oaktree Capital Management, as well as a cadre of prominent entertainment industry clients such as The William Morris Agency, Universal Music Group and International Creative Management (ICM).

An apple a day ...

The firm known as the "Wachtell of the West" holds weighty and honorable associations within the legal community. For litigators, this is the place to be. MTO's reputation precedes itself in 11 different litigation subdivisions, including entertainment, securities and white-collar crime. Several cases that combine securities and white-collar crime have certainly made for some good entertainment this past year. We begin at Apple, where MTO defended ex-CFO Fred Anderson, who (along with ex-General Counsel Nancy Heinen) was accused of falsifying stock-option paperwork to increase profitability. In May 2007, with the aid of Munger's Jerry Roth, Anderson negotiated a deal. He admits no wrongdoing, and can still serve an office or as a director, but will pay a $150,000 fine and refund approximately $3.5 million in option gains.

As of May 2007, 140 companies were under investigation for such backdating—retroactively granting employees or board members company stock options dated to a time when the price was lower. Munger is also representing Henry Nichols, co-founder of Broadcom, with regard to a stock-options backdating scandal. Nichols and Henry Samueli founded the Irvine, Ca., chipmaker and are both under investigation for questionable stock options grants issued between 1998 and 2003. Partner Gregory Weingart, former head fraud prosecutor for L.A.'s U.S. attorney's office, heads the case for the defense.

Equal parts silicon and litigation

Rambus, pioneer developers of a veritable alphabet soup of memory interfaces in the DRAM series (RDRAM, SDRAM, 2006's XDR DRAM, and the forthcoming XDR2 DRAM) is something of a Silicon Valley darling. From 1996 to 2002, the company even had an exclusive contract with Intel. Simply put, if you've used a computer made in this millennium, you've used Rambus-designed chips. Because Rambus researches and licenses memory systems to manufacturers, and does not produce any chips itself, patent protection is crucial to its business. So in 2000, it started filing patent infringement suits against other memory chip producers. Munger Tolles' Gregory Stone is at the helm of this high-profile litigation, and the firm most recently won a $306.9 million jury verdict against Hynix Semiconductor Inc. Beginning with Samsung back in 2002, seven chipmakers have chosen

© 2007 Vault Inc.

to settle, but the courtroom battles continue. Rambus also has its own defense to worry about, including an FTC antitrust action (dismissed in 2004 but overturned in 2006) and—noticed a theme yet?—an SEC investigation for backdating.

Let's clean up this town

It's a clash of the art titans: in this corner, the J. Paul Getty Trust and Museum (famous resting place for an impressive amount of art); and in this corner, the sovereign nation of Italy (famous producer of an even more impressive amount of art). Italy accuses the Getty Trust and its former antiques curator of obtaining dozens of pieces of ancient art from illegitimate dealers and demands the return of the disputed items to their rightful national owner. Of the original 42 pieces in question, only 21 remain disputed, the most impressive of which is a seven-and-a-half-foot tall limestone and marble statue of Aphrodite. There have been antiquities ownership disputes before, but what makes this case different is that MTO is negotiating on the trust's behalf. In the past, Italian authorities have hammered out deals with the directors of Boston's MFA and New York's Met for the return of disputed objects, in exchange for loans from Italy's collection. Unless MTO's team can negotiate an agreement, the Getty is facing the threat of cultural embargo: no excavations, no exhibitions—and certainly no more Apollos or Aphrodites—until Italy is appeased.

The Italian job is not the Getty's only challenge. It's also been plagued with a rash of management scandals. When the board suspected highly improper expenditures on the part of CEO Barry Munitz, they called in Munger Tolles to do some serious investigating. They even went so far as to secretly copy Munitz's hard drive—with the chairman's blessing of course. The evidence was damning. Munitz resigned in February 2006 after Ron Olson, omnipresent "corporate troubleshooter," and his team delivered its findings to the Getty's board. The former chief executive agreed to forgo $2 million of severance pay, and return $250,000 to settle outstanding claims with the Getty. And then there came the problem of former chairman David Gardner's aborted book deal—yet another MTO investigation concluded that the canceled coffee-table book on the history of the Getty violated tax laws prohibiting excess compensation and self-dealing. Gardner returned nearly $100,000 to the institution in August 2006. The $6 million in fees Munger has received as reward for its work on these cases indicates that the Getty is serious about cleaning up its act, no matter the cost.

Gimme shelter

Charlie Munger met Warren Buffet in 1959, founded Munger Tolles & Olson in 1962, and as of 2007 he is worth over $1.6 billion. He might have gotten there a little faster if not for his philanthropic streak—in 2004, he donated $43.5 million to his wife's alma mater Stanford for graduate housing. It was quite possibly the largest gift ever given to a U.S. law school. Meanwhile, Munger's law firm continues to follow his example with numerous pro bono measures. MTO was a charter signatory of the ABA's pro bono challenge, and has since devoted more than 3 percent of its total time to nonprofit work. Areas in which firm lawyers have committed their time include adoptions, inmates' rights, political asylum, handicapped accessibility and civil rights.

As amicus counsel, Munger has also filed briefs before the Supreme Court on pro bono matters, including oppositions to two hot-button topics: the exclusion of gays from the Boy Scouts and challenges to the constitutionality of affirmative action programs in university admissions. The firm also represents Senate and House sponsors of the McCain-Feingold campaign finance reform act against challenges to its constitutionality.

In 2007, the San Francisco office received top honors for its contributions to the Food from the Bar annual food drive for the second consecutive year. Other recognition includes the "ABA Pro Bono Publico Award" and the State Bar of California law firm pro bono award. The firm is also proud of its accolades in other quality-of-life areas, having ranked fifth nationally in *The American Lawyer*'s most recent midlevel associate satisfaction survey.

Visit the Vault Law Channel, the complete online resource for law careers, featuring firm profiles, message boards, the Vault Law Job Board and more. **www.vault.com/law**

VAULT CAREER LIBRARY   421

GETTING HIRED

Everyone gets a say—and (almost) no one gets hired

Munger handles things a little differently than most law firms. Rather than having a focused hiring committee, "The whole firm participates in the decision whether to accept a certain candidate." "Because all decisions are by firmwide consensus, the scrutiny is intense," says a second-year. "All attorneys at the firm get a vote on new hires." And scrutiny it is. "Getting hired here has become impossible," reports one Los Angeles associate. "I've seen people knocked because of their college grades—even though those grades were good enough to get into Harvard Law School." "It's crazy selective here," exclaims another insider. "I've been astounded at some of the people we've turned away—Harvard, Yale and Stanford grads, law review, amazing grades, clerkships. Firm lore has it that a Supreme Court clerk was once turned away after failing to impress lawyers during the interview process."

So if clerking for the highest court in the land doesn't guarantee a job at Munger, what does? "The firm looks for people with very high grades and really emphasizes clerkship experience," stresses a first-year. "The firm also appreciates public interest background." "There is no explicit GPA cutoff, but we tend to more seriously consider candidates with top grades from first-tier law schools," notes another contact. "Journal/law review, moot court and clerkship experience are major pluses." According to a senior associate, Munger "generally looks to top-10 or -20 schools in the country and for people in the top 10 percent there." and "prefers law review and people with outside interests and other achievements."

OUR SURVEY SAYS

Not your typical big firm

According to associates, Munger tries to be the un-firm firm. "Munger really tries to avoid the pathologies of big law firms—and I've seen that borne out in my time here thus far," says one first-year. "Most cases are leanly staffed. Associates are given much responsibility, and aren't segmented into categories of: 'This is second-year associate task.' People here are happier than other friends at other firms I've spoken to." Many think the firm is as good as it gets for BigLaw. "It is a private, corporate law firm, so how fulfilling could it possibly be to work here?" asks a Los Angeles lawyer (rhetorically). "That said, there are interesting opportunities to be had here, and some excellent senior attorneys to learn from. But the firm's trend is to take larger, more lucrative, big document cases, so the luster of the firm's early years is now wearing thin for associates." "As far as corporate firms go, it is hard to imagine how it could be better," agrees a litigator. "But it is still a corporate firm, with all of the well-documented drawbacks of corporate attorney life."

That sad fact isn't dragging everybody down. "I feel quite happy here, and I feel very lucky to have found a firm that is a good fit for me," gushes a first-year. "Munger is a great place to work," reports a junior associate. "Associates are given a lot of responsibility very early on in their careers. I don't think you could find another law firm with more, sheer candle power than the lawyers here possess. People here are wicked smart!" Wicked? Either way, associates are lucky to get good work early on. "I am doing much more meaningful work than my friends stuck in thankless doc review at other, so-called 'prestigious' firms," sniffs a first-year.

Egghead culture (in a good way)

Munger's super-selectiveness has had an impact on the firm's culture. "Munger is, if anything, eclectic—which is to say, hard to categorize. But if pushed, I'd say we are progressive," reports an insider. "The culture is nonhierarchical," says a first-year. "People refer to each other as 'colleagues,' not as 'partners' or 'associates.' That's what we were told to do when starting." "The firm's culture is based on mutual respect amongst colleagues, regardless of seniority level," agrees another contact. "The people at the firm are very friendly and personable, if a bit quirky," discloses an insider. "But that's what you get with people this smart." Munger is full of "a bunch of badass, top-of-their-class nerds who love working together, and who socialize well at work, but who generally respect each other's privacy," according to one nerd, on whom the oxymoronic irony of "badass nerds" is apparently lost. "I have formed several good friendships with other attorneys here," says a friendly attorney. "The firm really respects your personal life. Even from the very senior attorneys at the firm, there is a strong encouragement to do other fulfilling activities during the weekend and to leave at a reasonable hour during the week."

Market Munger

As for pay, "The firm does not lead the pack but it doesn't stray too far behind either," reports a second-year. It might be behind New York firms, though. "[Munger] moved along with other L.A. firms recently to the higher rate of compensation, although stayed behind the New York firms that other shops in the area bumped to," says a source. "The raise was much appreciated." There are some complaints, though. "Munger is not a market leader in terms of compensation, but the firm definitely keeps pace with most of its competition," notes an attorney. "And there's no question that we're compensated handsomely." But? "I have to say, though, that the health care costs are unacceptably high," he continues. "The costs of a standard PPO plan are prohibitively expensive, given the outrageously high premiums and deductibles." "I have been happy with my bonuses—happy, but not over the moon," mutters a senior associate. "Others have felt they are too low. One problem is publishing the range of bonuses but not the median, which leads many to think they are in the bottom portion of their class when in fact they are average or even above average."

No minimums!

Munger has one rather unique feature. The firm has "no billable requirements here, but that is probably because it is filled with overachieving Type As that are going to work themselves into the ground without any external pressure to do so," reports a contact. That doesn't mean you can slack off. "There is no minimum billing requirement, but if your hours drop below 1,800 a year you get a visit to make sure you have work," warns a senior associate. "And, of course, those who don't bill 2,200 or more during their last years before partnership aren't taken seriously." Even at the relatively relaxed Munger, the hours can take their toll. "BigLaw hours are grueling. There's no getting around it," sighs a lawyer. "That said, however, I think Munger compares quite favorably hours-wise to its peer firms. Partners here aren't looking to milk every last billable minute out of their associates and seem genuinely concerned about lawyers not burning themselves out." Others agree that the firm has serious, but not ludicrous, expectations. "While there may be particularly onerous weeks (and the occasional weekend work), my colleagues are very respectful of my other commitments and have proven to be flexible in most situations," notes a contact.

Swim meet

A firm that prides itself on recruiting the best doesn't always take the time to train those superstars. "It's a learn-as-you go culture," says a source. "Formal training?" laughs another, who says Munger is "sink-or-swim, baby, with great informal training [and] a few conferences on the side." "Formal training is minimal, but the firm's model is that we learn not by being trained, but by doing it," says a first-year. "For that reason, I never saw a model for a motion to compel until I was assigned to such a motion and found a model myself. This firm is for proactive people who don't need to take baby steps." The firm won't let anyone drown, though. "Sink-or-swim is how I'd describe our approach to training, with the caveat that—to extend the metaphor—we don't put people in situations where they won't be able to swim," observes an insider. The firm is trying to formalize some of its swimming lessons. "[Munger] has adopted an in-house training program, albeit a very modest one, so most people still get trained on the job—which potentially is more effective anyway," notes a Los Angeles attorney. "That said, there is a generous policy supporting associate efforts to get training on the outside. Many here have participated in the L.A. city attorney trial training program, and other trial advocacy and pretrial skills programs."

Visit the Vault Law Channel, the complete online resource for law careers, featuring firm profiles, message boards, the Vault Law Job Board and more. **www.vault.com/law**

VAULT CAREER LIBRARY

423

Dechert LLP

30 Rockefeller Plaza
New York, NY 10112
Phone: (212) 698-3500

Cira Centre
2929 Arch Street
Philadelphia, PA 19104-2808
Phone: (215) 994-4000

1775 I Street, N.W.
Washington, DC 20006
Phone: (202) 261-3300
www.dechert.com

LOCATIONS

Austin, TX • Boston, MA • Charlotte, NC • Hartford, CT •
Newport Beach, CA • New York, NY • Philadelphia, PA •
Princeton, NJ • San Francisco, CA • Silicon Valley, CA •
Washington, DC • Brussels • Frankfurt • London •
Luxembourg • Munich • Paris

MAJOR DEPARTMENTS & PRACTICES

Corporate & Securities • Finance & Real Estate • Financial
Services • Intellectual Property • Litigation • Tax

THE STATS

No. of attorneys: 900+
No. of offices: 17
Summer associate offers: 62 out of 65 (2006)
Chairman & CEO: Barton J. Winokur
Hiring Partners:

Boston, MA: Timothy C. Blank
Charlotte, NC: Timothy J. Boyce
Hartford, CT: Laura G. Ciabarra
New York, NY: Daniel C. Malone
Newport Beach, CA: Douglas Dick
Palo Alto, CA: Frederick G. Herold
Philadelphia, PA: Carolyn H. Feeney, R. Craig Smith
Princeton, NJ: David A. Kotler
San Francisco, CA: Joseph B. Heil
Washington, DC: Catherine Botticelli

THE BUZZ
WHAT ATTORNEYS AT OTHER FIRMS ARE SAYING ABOUT THIS FIRM

- "Major leagues, huge bucks"
- "Aggressive in recruiting associates"
- "Hip, proactive, IT-friendly"
- "High growth—is it sustainable?"

BASE SALARY (2007)

New York, NY
1st year: $160,000
Summer associate: $3,100/week

Philadelphia, PA
1st year: $145,000
Summer associate: $2,800/week

Washington, DC
1st year: $160,000
Summer associate: $2,800/week

UPPERS

- "Prestigious partners and big-name clients"
- "Face time not critical"
- "Honestly, the salary is ridiculous"

DOWNERS

- "It is not clear how bonuses are calculated"
- Poor firmwide communication
- Weak mentoring

NOTABLE PERKS

- "Thank God it's Thursday" dinners
- Annual pig roast
- Summer associate trip to London
- Domestic partner benefits

© 2007 Vault Inc.

RANKING RECAP

Best in Region
#2 - Pennsylvania/Mid-Atlantic

Best in Practice
#10 (tie) - Real Estate

EMPLOYMENT CONTACT

Ms. Susie E. Elitzky
Director of Recruiting, US
Phone: (212) 698-3523
Fax: (212) 698-3599
E-mail: legal.recruiting@dechert.com

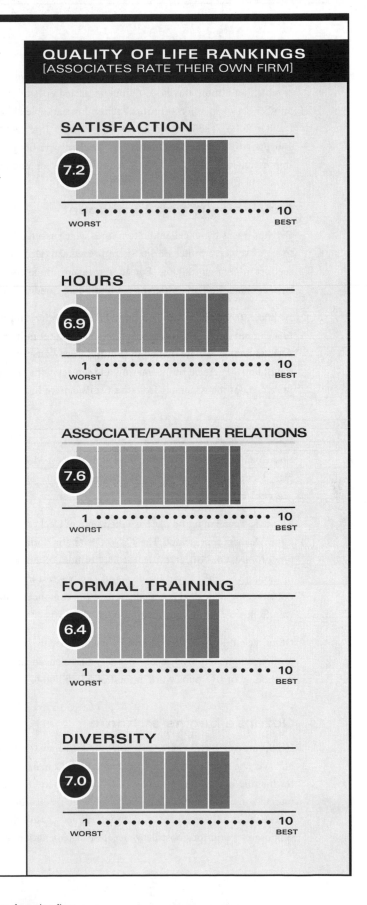

QUALITY OF LIFE RANKINGS
[ASSOCIATES RATE THEIR OWN FIRM]

SATISFACTION

7.2

1 WORST .... 10 BEST

HOURS

6.9

1 WORST .... 10 BEST

ASSOCIATE/PARTNER RELATIONS

7.6

1 WORST .... 10 BEST

FORMAL TRAINING

6.4

1 WORST .... 10 BEST

DIVERSITY

7.0

1 WORST .... 10 BEST

Visit the Vault Law Channel, the complete online resource for law careers, featuring firm profiles, message boards, the Vault Law Job Board and more. **www.vault.com/law**

VAULT CAREER LIBRARY

425

THE SCOOP

In the money

Rolling in at 21st on the 2006 NLJ 250, Dechert was six lawyers shy of four digits. It has since broken one thousand with no trouble, but c'mon, this is 2007: one thousand doesn't even put you in the top 20. What's really impressive about Dechert is another set of numbers—profits. After a remarkable showing in 2005, Dechert's finances continued their impressive upward trend in 2006. The firm's gross revenue is up 26.1 percent to $728 million, and revenue per lawyer rose 6.5 percent to $816,000. But the really impressive statistic is Dechert's profits per partner (PPP): $1.985 million, up 27 percent again after the same impressive jump the year before. Only 15 firms topping the AmLaw 100 had a higher PPP in 2006.

Now, about that headcount

Perhaps it was the excellent bottom lines which assured Dechert in 2005 that it could afford to take on 57 lawyers from the soon-to-be-dissolved Swidler Berlin Shereff Friedman (Dechert got the New York office, Bingham McCutchen finalized a merger for the rest in February 2006). For good measure, at the end of the same year, the firm effectively quadrupled its French presence by absorbing the Paris office of the imploding Coudert Brothers.

At home, the swelling rolls prompted Dechert to look for a larger New York office, with great motivation. The firm has agreed to an ambitious long-term lease for almost a quarter million square feet on six floors in the former Verizon building at 1095 Sixth Avenue, which is now owned by EquityOffice. One minor snag—they have to wait until the developers are done gutting and rebuilding 80 percent of the interior, and replacing the entire marble façade with an energy-efficient glass curtain wall. The move to Avenue of the Americas from the firm's current home at Rockefeller Plaza should be complete by January 2008.

Dealer's advantage

Someone, somewhere, is making a list of the best M&A law firms. How much do you want to bet Dechert is on it? The firm's prized department has regularly graced the rolls of such publications as *Mergerstat*, *Bloomberg*, *Thomson Financial* and *MergerMarket*.

The U.K. scene in particular has taken note of Dechert's ability to move a lot of dough—pounds and pounds of it. Try to follow now: Dechert represented The Crown Estate in forming The Gibraltar Limited Partnership with The Hercules Unit Trust (a property trust out of Jersey, worth £3.4 billion). Said partnership incorporates three retail park properties in a deal worth £680 million, gives The Crown Estate significant interest in those locations and gives British Land (advisor to the HUT) 36.6 percent holder status. The deal is actually way more complicated than that, but it just goes to show that not just anyone can blunder their way to the top of the corporate transactions charts.

Other recent deals for Dechert attorneys include advising Edmond de Rothschild Investment Partners on an investment in a €50 million fundraising by French specialty pharmaceutical company, Novexel, and Gourmet Holdings and other private investors on the sale of five pubs worth a total of £7 million to U.K. brewer Fuller Smith & Turner.

Defense begins at home

It's been a rough two years for former Dick Cheney Chief of Staff I. Lewis "Scooter" Libby. Maybe even rough enough to make him wish he hadn't left his job as Dechert's D.C. managing partner to join the W bandwagon back in 2001. Long under scrutiny for his role in the alleged leak of CIA agent Valerie Plame's identity to *The New York Times* reporter Judith Miller, Libby was indicted in 2005 and found guilty in March 2007 of perjury, obstructing justice and making false statements to federal investigators. Bizarrely, no underlying crime—wasn't there supposed to be a leak or something?—in connection with Libby's supposedly perjurious/obstructionist/false statements was ever even alleged. Libby's civilian life did avail him of some excellent

© 2007 Vault Inc.

connections. In the various proceedings, he has been represented by Dechert partner and white-collar litigator Joseph Tate, litigator Ted Wells of Paul Weiss and litigator William Jeffress from Baker Botts.

When it hurts so bad

Fifteen down … 28,000 to go. Partners Hope S. Freiwald and Diane Sullivan (and the rest of Dechert's pharmaceuticals mass-tort litigation team) have been representing Merck in its defense of its former prescription pain medication, Vioxx. With 12 more trials scheduled in 2007 (the 28,000 is an estimate of potential individual suits), no doubt Dechert will be devoting many more years to this high-profile case before it is completely settled.

After a September 2004 study linked the drug to an increased risk of heart attacks and strokes, Merck voluntarily withdrew Vioxx from the market. The litigation floodgates opened immediately. Since the first trial in the summer of 2005, Merck has won 10 and lost five, with each losing verdict costing in the tens to hundreds of millions of dollars. Legal fees meanwhile are estimated to have cost the pharmaceutical company $785 million, or roughly $1 million a day. Merck is more than willing to pay Dechert and other firms such high rates, however, in the hopes of avoiding what Wall Street analysts conjecture could be "a $30 billion verdict." So far, so good. Dechert secured the very first win for Merck, a defense verdict featured in *The National Law Journal*'s "Top 10 Defense Wins in 2005."

The Ponz(i)

Shame on (Ba)you. Bayou Management was a Connecticut hedge fund firm producing excellent returns … until it collapsed and its founders pleaded guilty to federal criminal-fraud charges in September 2005. Dechert represented them in their bankruptcy filing, securing a very important ruling regarding Ponzi schemes (Bayou's modus operandi having been a modified version of this famous scam, in which lucrative returns are "paid" not from actual profits, but the constant influx of new investor money). The Southern District of New York judge held that "overpaid redemptions to Ponzi scheme investors are inherently fraudulent, and subsequently can be recovered in bankruptcy," explains partner H. Jeffrey Schwartz, Dechert's head counsel on the matter. Good news for those who got hosed by the scheme and are looking to recover their losses, bad news for those who got their money "out" soon enough to enjoy a tidy profit—Bayou now has carte blanche to sue for the dividends' return.

Sheikh sheikh sheikh …

Islamic finance partners Michael McMillen, Andreas Junius and Abradat Kamalpour have developed a prominent and well-recognized practice, which is currently working on a number of financial, real estate and other projects, including laying the groundwork for the issuance of sukuk (corporate bonds). According to *Euromoney*, Dechert is the "Best Global Islamic Finance Legal Advisor for the Year 2006-2007," and The International Islamic Finance Forum previously awarded the firm the "Sheikh Mohammad Bin Rashid Al-Makhtoum Award for Special Recognition in Islamic Finance."

GETTING HIRED

Increasingly selective

Dechert has grown increasingly selective in recent years, according to firm insiders. "The firm has gotten very selective and I've seen many candidates with 3.3 GPAs from top schools not make the cut. My impression is that the firm is very forgiving when it comes to certain Ivies though." Underscoring this point, a senior litigator advises, "The thicker the Ivy, the better your chances." According to a products liability specialist, "The firm has recently implemented strict hiring guidelines based on law school and grades. Many of our (best) current associates wouldn't be hired if the guidelines had been implemented when they were in law school." An IP expert adds, "First-year grades are most important, top 10 to15 percent at lower first-tier schools. High-ranking schools are also important. Dechert is extremely selective in its hiring, almost snobby, even with regard to lateral candidates." A colleague elaborates on the specific guidelines: "From top-tier schools, Dechert generally will take top 25 percent;

Visit the Vault Law Channel, the complete online resource for law careers, featuring firm profiles, message boards, the Vault Law Job Board and more. www.vault.com/law

VAULT CAREER LIBRARY   427

from second-tier schools, top 5 percent; law review or moot court mandatory; all others generally need not apply, except that a crush of lit work has resulted in a spate of staff attorney hirings." A midlevel associate warns, "There is a complicated set of hiring standards that vary from law school to law school. Exceptions to this policy are rarely, if ever, granted." As for school preferences, one Philadelphia associate reports, "Dechert seems to recruit a lot of people from the local schools: Penn, Temple and Villanova. There is also, however, an unusually large number from Georgetown."

OUR SURVEY SAYS

"I couldn't be happier with the people I work with"

Dechert's associates call the firm's culture "laid-back," "relaxed," "professional," "academic," "social" and "great." A midlevel from Philadelphia advises, "I would say it is a social firm, in the sense that there are frequent firm-sponsored or practice-group-sponsored functions. It does, of course, depend on your practice group. Some groups are definitely less active at making sure everyone gets to know one another." A junior business attorney from San Francisco reports, "The hierarchy among the lawyers seems to vanish once we leave the office, and each person is treated equally. I like that. The firm has some outings for the entire office about quarterly, so we don't get sick of each other. Everyone is very accepting." Another Philadelphian adds, "I couldn't be happier with the people I work with. While I often work late, I take comfort knowing that I am working late with people I enjoy spending time with."

For some insiders, however, the firm is more of a mixed bag. "It goes from pretty good to 'Get me outta here!' ... depending on the availability of work," reports a midlevel associate. "The firm is very practice-group oriented and it can be difficult to work on varied matters. The biggest plus is that people here are unusually cordial for a large law firm office and the older partners seem to genuinely care that this place remain a good place to work. There are opportunities to receive mentoring from partners, but it's incumbent upon the associate to seek those opportunities out." On the plus side, an IP expert boasts, "The partners are incredibly friendly and eager to help me further my career." A New Yorker adds that she handles "generally very interesting work" and maintains "good relationships with other associates and partners." On the other hand, a junior Philly attorney complains, "The two biggest problems for me are that I sometimes find myself without enough work and I don't feel that I am getting enough writing experience."

Partners vary, partner by partner

Associates report that Dechert partners range from "terrible" to "excellent," with the majority landing, thankfully, far closer to the latter. Institutionally, however, the firm has a few shortcomings. "Ninety percent of the time, on a one-on-one basis, the partners here are incredible," advises a senior financial services specialist. "As a group to a group, the communications are not quite so wonderful." As another junior associate puts it, "My encounters with partners have been nothing but positive and my observation is that they treat other associates well also. There could be improved communication with salary issues, etc. That is not handled well at times." A junior litigator says, "I have found the partnership to be very attentive to associates and their concerns." A Philly attorney adds, "So far, every partner that I have interacted with has been respectful and easy to work with." However, one particularly disgruntled associate warns, "The partners are generally cordial to associates, but are all part of the system designed solely for the tippy top of the partner pyramid—thus, junior partners feel incredible pressure to produce and senior partners are out of touch with reality. Probably similar to many overly-profitable firms."

Average formal training (which is actually pretty good)

Associates call the firm's formal training program fairly average, which in comparison to most other top firms, is actually quite a compliment. As one Philly corporate attorney describes the offerings, "They do a good job with the formal training, providing useful workshops on relevant topics and issues." A junior litigator adds, "First-years receive one week of intensive training, which is followed up by other training programs throughout the year, including mock depositions." There are, however, a few people who find the offerings lacking. "Unfortunately, the training opportunities are scattershot, and the information provided

© 2007 Vault Inc.

is redundant, at best," complains a Philly trial attorney. Another Philly source adds, "The firm does have formal training programs, which range from very useful to complete wastes of time. But the firm deserves points for trying." As a business and finance expert puts it, "There are too many formal mandatory training sessions in which little practical or applicable information is learned."

Informal training? Better off with the formal stuff ...

With all the other work there is to do, Dechert associates lament that informal training can get lost in the shuffle. As one midlevel puts it, "Informal training is falling by the wayside as everyone is forced to become busier and busier." Meanwhile, a litigator finds the lack of lateral mentoring frustrating, saying, "You're not part of a 'class' because you're a lateral, so you have no idea whom to go to for questions about how the firm works." Not everyone feels "left on an island," however. A fourth-year advises, "If an associate seeks out advice, partners are glad to give it. You have to be outgoing though. Partners are too busy to seek you out and find out how you're doing. You might have to knock on a few doors a few times before you get the mentoring you're looking for, but it's there if you look hard enough." Here's one senior associate who's looking out for his mentees: "Some partners dedicate significant attention to informal training during the course of a transaction or project, while others tend to allow associates to flounder until the day before closing. As a senior associate, I try to give context to whatever work I assign to a junior, but I don't overdo it by requiring that the junior understand every element of deal."

The compensation is high, but ...

Associates generally agree that the compensation is "great," but some complain anyway. "Our compensation is top notch for Philadelphia, and really nothing to complain about in general," reports one satisfied associate. This insider notes, "The firm isn't a market leader, but it will follow the market in due time." On the other hand, "Dechert matches the market, but is the pay adequate reparation for taking a part of your life (and soul) away?" asks one melodramatic attorney. As for bonuses, these comments from a Philly associate echo a common refrain: "I understand the rationale for hours-based bonuses, but I don't think it is fair. There are many people willing to work the hours required for bonus, but do not have the opportunity due to availability of work."

Hours may be long, but at least they're flexible

Associates recommend bracing yourself for big-time hours, but say that the firm's flexibility cushions the blow. A senior associate advises, "We work a lot here, but there are no face time requirements. You can avoid working weekends, for the most part." A Philly litigator adds, "I'm very happy with my hours. But then again, if you don't have any work to do, you will of course have low hours. While this may be great from a personal life point of view, it certainly isn't helpful to your career overall." On the other hand, a corporate attorney warns, "New York-style hours are firmwide now—consider it working a double shift."

Visit the Vault Law Channel, the complete online resource for law careers, featuring firm profiles, message boards, the Vault Law Job Board and more. **www.vault.com/law**

VAULT CAREER LIBRARY   **429**

Irell & Manella LLP

1800 Avenue of the Stars, Suite 900
Los Angeles, CA 90067
Phone: (310) 277-1010
Fax: (310) 203-7199
www.irell.com

LOCATIONS

Los Angeles, CA (HQ)
Newport Beach, CA

MAJOR DEPARTMENTS & PRACTICES

ADR & Arbitration • Antitrust • Appellate • Art • Aviation • Class Action Defense • Creditors' Rights & Insolvency • Debt Finance • Employee Benefits & Executive Compensation • Entertainment Litigation • Entertainment Transactions • Insurance • IP Litigation • IP Transactions • Labor & Employment • Land Use & Environmental • Litigation • Mergers & Acquisitions • Patent, Copyright & Trademark • Personal Planning • Private Equity & Venture Capital • Professional Liability Defense • Public Offerings & Private Placements • Real Estate • Securities Law & Corporate Governance • Securities Litigation • Tax • White Collar Defense

THE STATS

No. of attorneys firmwide: 218
No. of offices: 2
Summer associate offers: 30 out of 30 (2006)
Managing Partner: David Siegel
Hiring Partner: Laura Seigle

BASE SALARY (2007)

Los Angeles, CA
1st year: $160,000
2nd year: $170,000
3rd year: $185,000
4th year: $210,000
5th year: $230,000
6th year: $250,000
7th year: $265,000
8th year: $280,000
Summer associate: $3,080/week

UPPERS

• Being "among the best of the best"
• Early responsibility
• "Individualistic and flexible" environment

DOWNERS

• Difficult partnership track
• "Can be a very stressful environment"
• Buy your own BlackBerry

NOTABLE PERKS

• $500 office decorating budget
• $500 technology budget
• Free parking (LA)
• Dinners with potential recruits

THE BUZZ
WHAT ATTORNEYS AT OTHER FIRMS ARE SAYING ABOUT THIS FIRM

• "Great California firm; interesting IP work"
• "Conceited"
• "Extremely impressive"
• "High maintenance lawyers"

© 2007 Vault Inc.

RANKING RECAP

Best in Region
#6 - Southern California

Partner Prestige Rankings
#5 - Intellectual Property

Quality of Life
#5 - Selectivity

Best in Diversity
#2 - Diversity with Respect to GLBT

EMPLOYMENT CONTACT

Ms. Robyn Steele
Recruiting Administrator
Phone: (310) 277-1010
Fax: (310) 203-7199
E-mail: rsteele@irell.com

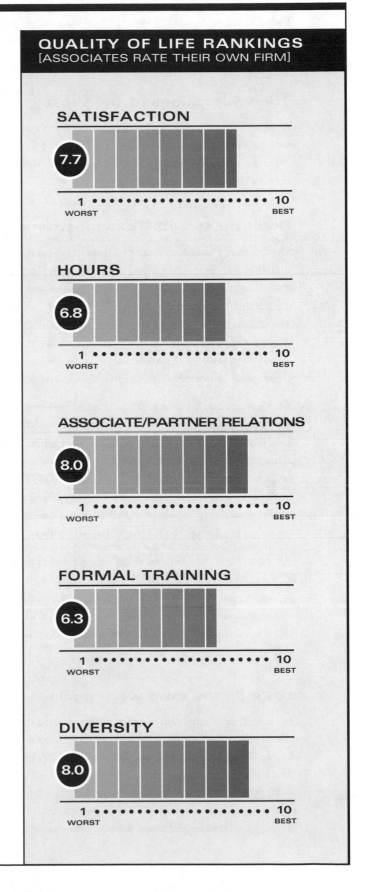

QUALITY OF LIFE RANKINGS
[ASSOCIATES RATE THEIR OWN FIRM]

SATISFACTION

7.7

1 WORST   10 BEST

HOURS

6.8

1 WORST   10 BEST

ASSOCIATE/PARTNER RELATIONS

8.0

1 WORST   10 BEST

FORMAL TRAINING

6.3

1 WORST   10 BEST

DIVERSITY

8.0

1 WORST   10 BEST

Visit the Vault Law Channel, the complete online resource for law careers, featuring firm profiles, message boards, the Vault Law Job Board and more. www.vault.com/law

VAULT CAREER LIBRARY   431

THE SCOOP

Founded in Los Angeles in 1941, Irell & Manella positions itself as a smaller, West Coast version of the New York powerhouse firms. With its two offices located in Southern California, the firm nonetheless pays East Coast salaries, hires lots of Ivy Leaguers and handles high-profile, big-stakes cases.

The white shoes of the West

As proof of the firm's burgeoning national presence and reputation, when Enron Task Force Chief John C. Hueston (who gained national fame for his searing cross-examination of Kenneth Lay) cashed in on his newfound prominence and chose the firm over countless other well-heeled suitors in November 2006, he proclaimed, "Pound for pound, Irell & Manella is undoubtedly one of the best law firms in the nation."

Don't mess with Texas Instruments

The firm has handled a number of recent high-profile cases, many in one of its core strengths: general business litigation, IP litigation and entertainment litigation. Recently, Irell & Manella represented AAC Acoustic Technologies, the defendant in a trade secrets case filed in the United States District Court in Chicago. After two months of expedited discovery, including depositions in China and all across the U.S., the case was tried for three weeks in February and March 2007; AAC prevailed. The United States District Court Judge who presided over the trial remarked on Irell & Manella having two associates handle major witnesses: "I was especially gratified to see that younger counsel were permitted to participate in the trial ... I think too often young lawyers are consigned to the chairs and not allowed to participate. I think it's a good thing after all if our bar is going to develop, we have got to give the younger people an opportunity."

Also in early 2007, the firm defeated a $94 million federal patent-infringement claimed filed by Microprocessor Enhancement Corporation (a subsidiary of Acacia Research) against the firm's client, Texas Instruments Incorporated. The chief judge of the U.S. District Court for the Central District of California granted summary judgment that Dallas-based Texas Instruments did not infringe any claim of MEC's patent, and that each claim of MEC's patent is invalid. The patent related to the architecture of high-performance processors and, in addition to the $94 million, MEC was seeking a permanent injunction against TI's C6000 line of digital signal processors. In a February 2007 decision, Chief Judge Alicemarie H. Stotler granted TI's motion for summary judgment of noninfringement on two separate grounds, and also ruled that the claims of MEC's patent are invalid on two separate grounds. In addition, the judge ordered MEC to pay TI's litigation costs.

As more Americans became obsessed with the evils of "trans fats," one of the nation's most popular fast food restaurants, Kentucky Fried Chicken (KFC), found itself faced with a lawsuit in the Southern District of California accusing KFC of not telling its customers that some of its food contained trans fats. Irell & Manella represented KFC. Despite the plaintiff's repeated attempts to allege various causes of action against KFC, including violations of state and federal FDA regulations, Irell moved twice to dismiss the complaint in its entirety. Both times, the court dismissed the complaint— the second time, with prejudice and without leave to amend.

Let's do the time warp again

In an extremely important case for the burgeoning digital-video recorder industry, in 2006 the firm scored a victory for DVR manufacturer TiVo. Last year, a Texas jury awarded TiVo $74 million for its patent infringement claim against EchoStar, best known for its Dish Network satellite television service. The jury found that EchoStar willfully infringed on TiVo's patent for its "time-warp" technology. Although the trial stretched out for more than two weeks, the jurors deliberated for less than three hours before they came to their unanimous verdict. In a separate bench trial, TiVo also prevailed on all of EchoStar's alleged equitable defenses. The court granted TiVo's injunction request, and increased the damages award to approximately $94 million based on prejudgment interest and supplemental damages. EchoStar's appeal is pending in the Federal Circuit.

© 2007 Vault Inc.

The firm's transactions group had a busy year in 2006 as well, handling deals totaling more than $4 billion in value. Perhaps the most publicized transaction overseen by the firm was the negotiation of the sale of Gustav Klimt's portrait of Adele Bloch Bauer (by heirs of Ms. Bloch Bauer) for a reported $135 million, then the highest price ever paid for a single painting. In 2006, the firm's art law practice negotiated or consulted on the sale, consignment and purchase of art and collectibles valued at over $575 million, and also set several world records for their sale and auction. The portrait of Ms. Bloch Bauer, along with four other oil paintings by Klimt, had been seized by the Nazis during World War II and only recently returned to Ms. Bloch Bauer's family.

And a transactional accomplishment for an icon of the 90s

Irell's other major deals in 2006 included overseeing the sale by a private equity-sector fund of energy-software provider SPL Worldgroup to software giant Oracle Corp. The firm also handled the sale of Genscape, a provider of real-time energy generation and transmission data, as well as the sale of electric utilities software and hardware specialist Cannon Technologies. The firm advised the Las Vegas gaming company Pinnacle Entertainment on numerous deals in 2006, including its acquisition of the Sands Hotel and Casino in Atlantic City (from entities affiliated with financier Carl Icahn), as well as various Louisiana assets from Harrah's Entertainment and the concurrent sale of a casino site in Biloxi, Mississippi. In 2006, the firm also advised ultra light jet manufacturer Eclipse Aviation—a developer of low-cost, high-performance jet aircrafts—regarding private placements of convertible debt and preferred stock to institutional investors in deals valued at over $250 million.

We are so honored ...

Of course, such accomplishments lead to frequent and notable commendations. The individual and collective awards the firm won over the last year include "Entertainment Lawyer of the Year" by the Century City Bar Association for partner Henry Shields (whose cases last year included successfully defending NBC in three separate major lawsuits). Thirty-nine of the firm's attorneys (an impressive 20 percent) were named to the 2007 edition of the *Best Lawyers in America*. Partners Tina Byrd and Laura W. Brill were listed among "California's Top 75 Women Litigators" by the *Daily Journal* in 2007 and 2006 respectively, and partner Morgan Chu was ranked in the top-tier of intellectual property attorneys in the inaugural Chambers Awards for Excellence.

It's not all about business at this top business firm. Irell & Manella ranked first among all Los Angeles-based firms for total pro bono work in *The American Lawyer*'s annual review of the nation's top law firms. Irell allows associates to count pro bono hours toward their billing goals, and last year's efforts included a number of notable cases. The firm represented both environmental-conservation and animal-welfare advocates in their fight to limit the U.S. Navy's use of high-intensity, mid-frequency sonar (which, among other problems, are harmful to both whales and dolphins) during its war games in the ocean off Hawaii. The firm also stopped the L.A. suburb of Santa Ana from shutting down a Catholic Worker House homeless shelter and represented two high school students in their fight against the Orange (County) Unified School District regarding the creation of a gay-straight alliance club. In the widely cited case, a federal court ruled that the Equal Access Act created a federally protected right to meet for the students. Recently, Irell assisted the Thai Community Development Center with an investigation of alleged illegal human trafficking of Thai national workers. Each year, many Irell attorneys represent needy children and families in dozens of adoption proceedings, specializing in Spanish-language clients—each summer, Irell summer associates have the opportunity to handle one of these adoption cases.

GETTING HIRED

High grades or the highway

"The firm is one of the most selective in the country." No exaggeration there. Irell has staked out a spot at the top of our selectivity rankings and has no plans to budge any time soon. A first-year litigator tells us that "the firm's hiring standards are excruciating to the point of being capricious." What all this fancy verbiage boils down to is "the firm only hires from select schools and then only the absolute top students. Generally, a top 10 percent cutoff is strictly enforced." Some firms will let such cutoffs slide if they see an Ivy League logo on the top of your transcript but Irell plays no such games. The firm has the "highest

Visit the Vault Law Channel, the complete online resource for law careers, featuring firm profiles, message boards, the Vault Law Job Board and more. www.vault.com/law

VAULT CAREER LIBRARY

433

standards and no funny business." With such a highly selective bent, associates aren't just being snooty when they say "Be brilliant or don't bother."

It may be impossible to stress academic success enough, but there are other things Irell looks for besides grades—namely, "people who are smart and willing to work enough hours to do a good job." Pretty standard there. "Also, we try to get people who are interesting, ethical and have a sense of self," says one self-actualized litigator.

OUR SURVEY SAYS

Silly putty and Romanian gymnasts

Category: things that are flexible. Throw Irell's hours in there, too. The firm is "extremely flexible with creative schedules," beginning with "no face time and no micromanagement of associates' hours." Vacations and personal time are respected, and "when it comes to time off to deal with personal crises, [the firm] has no peer." Meanwhile, part-time appears to be a good compromise between time and money, or so say several part-timers who responded to our survey. Others, however, find flex-time policies "ill-defined."

Noticeably absent from associates' responses about their office time is any mention of billable hours. Irell is "results-oriented," which is a nice way of saying "you just have to get your work done to the best of your ability." When the hours are long, it's because there's plenty to do, and "the lawyers here want to do a good job." Don't mistake this for some kind of resort firm— "Irell is known for long hours, at least by L.A. standards." It's just that "if things slow down, no one cares that you are not in the office." Stick around after dark and you might just hear associates singing the timeless BigLaw blues. "Of course I would like to spend fewer hours in the office, but that is the nature of the beast and I feel I have nothing to complain about," says a litigator. "When it is good, it is very, very good. When it is bad ...."

Professionally nerdy

Much of the Irell culture is a direct result of the work ethic, which is focused on "professionalism and [client] loyalty." The goal is to "produce the best work product possible," not to have the most fun or outdo your peers. (In this vein, lock-step salaries and bonuses actually "contribute to a more collegial environment in the firm" by "eliminating competition among associates and reduces pressure to bill outlandish hours.") Irell lawyers are "intellectual and hardworking" or "cerebral and cooperative," but "not social butterflies." "Lawyers are here because they like the law for the law's sake"—the kind of folks you meet at the library, not the downstairs bar. Politics is a subject for friendly debate, not serious proselytizing. It's not all *Revenge of the Nerds* though; many associates are "good friends" and those with similar interests find time to take part together. "There are groups that play basketball and poker. There are other groups that have children and hence have family activities together," says an IP associate. Door open or door closed, "nobody minds" their colleagues' different preferences. A midlevel offers this reasoned explanation: "Like any group filled with professional overachievers ... the lawyers are brilliant and perceptive, but socializing is not high on their list of priorities."

Another important aspect of Irell culture is its "exceptionally great" acceptance of GLBT lawyers. Openly gay partners and associates are well represented, and Irell routinely tops the Vault "GLBT Diversity" rankings. Associates agree that "Irell is very accepting of alternate lifestyles." A third-year tells us it's so good, in fact, "I have heard it said that attorneys come to Irell to come out." Irell similarly scores high on other diversity rankings, such as coming in sixth on the *Minority Law Journal*'s list of firms with the highest percentage of minority partners.

Light on "existential enlightenment"

Love is in the air. As in "I love this place" and "I love my job." Yes, these associates are serious, though the lovebug has yet to become a full-fledged plague. Most are more reserved in their satisfaction, but bring up similar plusses. For example, "Lawyers are incredibly smart, the expectations are very high, the partners look for (and find) meaningful opportunities to bring even first-

© 2007 Vault Inc.

year associates in on the action." A "low partner-to-associate ratio" and "lean structure" give "associates plenty of early responsibility, which can be both exhilarating and stressful." First-years sound more susceptible to Irell fever: "I can't believe they pay me to do this, let alone this amount." This midlevel has perhaps lost that wide-eyed wonder in favor of a pragmatist's contentment (expecting and receiving no "existential enlightenment"): "Understanding that one works at a large law firm not for personal happiness, but in order to make money, achieve status or live up to some sort of social expectations, I have found working at this firm to be totally fulfilling for my purposes."

Remember to check under any bridges

That low associate/partner ratio makes for "lots of interaction" and "a two-way exchange of ideas." Partners "treat associates as colleagues, not employees," and this rapport makes it easy to let your boss know you want to kick it up a notch. "Associates are encouraged to ask for additional responsibility (depositions, oral arguments, trial time) when they think they are ready." Working closely doesn't always mean working well, and Irell insiders describe their partnership relations as "a mix." "Some partners are very difficult to work with and drive associates from the firm. Other partners are great and take the time to mentor you," reports this source. "Socially, some partners are very easy to work with; others are awkward like law professors," observes another. When partners are disliked, it's "not so much yelling/berating as failure to respect time and appreciate effort," though an L.A. associate has "heard there are one or two ogres around here."

Individually, partners are mentors and colleagues. But when their powers combine, they become Management, a "removed," "impersonal" and "reserved" alter ego. The partnership doesn't have the "same inclusive attitude as it used to maybe four or five years ago." A senior associate, who has been on staff long enough to witness the change, says, "Over the years it has become a more traditional firm, more focused on running a business than forming and keeping relationships with associates." As the culture stands now, associates are "generally informed" on financial matters and other management decisions, and "encouraged to participate" in the process. Don't be fooled, though—"Associates are not calling the shots." They do, however, have "significant roles on the hiring and summer committees."

Formal training as a tourism metaphor

Formal training is to Irell associates as the Statue of Liberty is to New Yorkers. They know it's there, and they might have gone once or even twice, but it's really not that big a deal. Over the last two years, "Irell has been instituting more formal training," and now "there is a fair amount of training for new lawyers, and regular MCLE presentations." With the exception of "an extremely useful deposition training seminar," associates find such formalities "less than useful." As at any leanly staffed firm, "the most valuable training is on the job." A first-year brags, "'Early responsibility' means you may have done the 'real' thing before the 'training.'"

No need for a classroom when associates can get training on the clock. Associates are "pushed to see what [they] can accomplish" and "firm culture rewards being proactive—i.e., if you need to know something, ask." It is very important to "take the initiative" because of the "time issue—everyone is so busy." Quick questions are no problem, but long-term mentoring "depends on the individual partner." Some associates report having "a lot of encouragement" from the firm "to grow as a lawyer and become known in the local legal community." When looking for that special relationship, a litigator reminds us that "junior partners can be valuable mentors for junior associates."

Bucket loads

It's tough at the top. Irell has "first-tier compensation" and "prides itself on keeping par with top N.Y. firms": in May 2007, the firm matched the "Simpson" scale of $160,000 to start. In all, the Irell partners "work hard to get research on the compensation levels at other firms to ensure that we are the highest paid associates on average." And if they're not … well, a bonus will take care of that. "Our bonuses are so superior," gushes one associate, and "designed to put us over or near the top of the scale." Some would rather have the salary "more evenly distributed throughout the year than in a lump sum"—a minor complaint, as

Visit the Vault Law Channel, the complete online resource for law careers, featuring firm profiles, message boards, the Vault Law Job Board and more. www.vault.com/law

VAULT CAREER LIBRARY

435

"when all is said and done, the firm *always* does right by its associates in setting comp at the highest end of market." Translation (courtesy of a midlevel): "I'm making bucket loads of money."

© 2007 Vault Inc.

"Lawyers are incredibly smart, the expectations are very high, the partners look for (and find) meaningful opportunities to bring even first-year associates in on the action."

— *Irell & Manella associate*

Visit the Vault Law Channel, the complete online resource for law careers, featuring firm profiles, message boards, the Vault Law Job Board and more. **www.vault.com/law**

V/\ULT CAREER LIBRARY   **437**

VAULT TOP 100

50
PRESTIGE RANKING

McDermott Will & Emery

227 W. Monroe Street
Suite 4400
Chicago, IL 60606
Phone: (312) 372-2000
www.mwe.com

LOCATIONS

Boston, MA • Chicago, IL • Irvine, CA • Los Angeles, CA •
Miami, FL • New York, NY • Palo Alto, CA • San Diego, CA
• Washington, DC • Brussels • Düsseldorf • London •
Munich • Rome • Shanghai (Strategic Alliance with MWE
China Law Offices)

MAJOR DEPARTMENTS & PRACTICES

Antitrust & Competition • Bankruptcy/Troubled
Transactions • Corporate • Energy • Environmental •
Executive Compensation • Finance & Banking • Government
Strategies • Health • Hedge Funds • Insurance • Intellectual
Property, Media & Technology • International • Labor &
Employment • Mergers & Acquisitions • Private Client • Real
Estate • Securities • Tax • Trial

THE STATS

No. of attorneys: 1,100
No. of offices: 14
Summer associate offers: 79 out of 83 (2006)
Chairman: Harvey W. Freishtat
Hiring Partner: Lydia R.B. Kelley & David E. Rogers

BASE SALARY (2007)

Miami
1st year: $135,000
Summer associate: $2,596/week

All Other Offices
1st year: $160,000
Summer associate: $3,076/week

UPPERS

• Generous and transparent compensation system
• Reasonable and flexible hours
• Respected and respectful partners

DOWNERS

• "The firm is cheap"
• "The hours"
• "Lots of doc review for young litigators"

NOTABLE PERKS

• Free parking (certain offices)
• Subsidized gym membership
• Profit-sharing program
• Bagels on Fridays (certain offices)

THE BUZZ
WHAT ATTORNEYS AT OTHER FIRMS ARE SAYING ABOUT THIS FIRM

• "Excellent quality"
• "Health care wizards"
• "Inconsistent"
• "Ho hum"

© 2007 Vault Inc.

RANKING RECAP

Best in Region
#9 - Chicago

Best in Practice
#10 - Tax Law

Partner Prestige Rankings
#5 (tie) - Tax Law

EMPLOYMENT CONTACT

Ms. Nancy Berry
Director, Legal Recruiting
Phone: (312) 984-3377
Fax: (312) 984-7700
E-mail: nberry@mwe.com

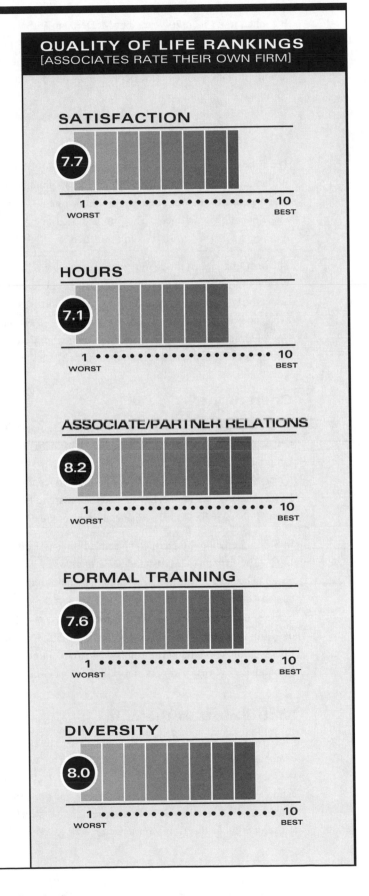

QUALITY OF LIFE RANKINGS
[ASSOCIATES RATE THEIR OWN FIRM]

SATISFACTION
7.7
1 WORST — 10 BEST

HOURS
7.1
1 WORST — 10 BEST

ASSOCIATE/PARTNER RELATIONS
8.2
1 WORST — 10 BEST

FORMAL TRAINING
7.6
1 WORST — 10 BEST

DIVERSITY
8.0
1 WORST — 10 BEST

Visit the Vault Law Channel, the complete online resource for law careers, featuring firm profiles, message boards, the Vault Law Job Board and more. www.vault.com/law

VAULT CAREER LIBRARY

439

THE SCOOP

It's taken more than 70 years, but McDermott Will & Emery has evolved from a small Chicago practice into an international superstar. The Chicago-based firm has 1,100 lawyers practicing in 14 offices in the United States and Europe and a strategic alliance with MWE China Law Offices (Shanghai). The firm excels at corporate and tax work (one of its first practices) and also handles litigation matters (McDermott calls that department its "trial" practice), real estate, bankruptcy, intellectual property and antitrust.

70 years, 1,100 lawyers

The firm got its start in 1934 when Edward H. McDermott set up a Chicago law practice specializing in tax advice along with William M. Emery. The firm added a corporate practice—and a name partner—in 1941 when Howard A. Will came aboard. That year also saw the arrival of Richard J. Frankenstein Jr., who established McDermott Will & Emery's (as the firm was now known) estate planning department. The firm launched an employee benefits department in 1954 and signed on super-litigator Theodore A. Groenke in 1961 to start its trial practice.

The firm first passed the century mark (in number of lawyers) in 1974. Three years later, McDermott began expanding from the Windy City when it opened a Miami office. Locations in Washington, D.C., and Boston soon followed (in 1978 and 1981, respectively). The firm opened two California offices in 1987 and a New York outpost in 1988. The late 1990s saw another expansion as it moved into Silicon Valley (in 1997) and London (1998). McDermott moved into Germany in 2002 with Düsseldorf and Munich; Rome and San Diego followed in 2003. Brussels, the newest office, opened in 2004. In February 2007, the firm established a strategic alliance with MWE China Law Offices (Shanghai).

Cash money

McDermott's status as an international player requires its having a hand in a bevy of huge deals. In June 2006, the firm's U.K. practice advised British underwriter C.E. Unterberg, Towbin LLC in its role in the £12 million U.S. stock offering of Leadcom Integrated Solutions. The London office also advised British internet gaming company 32Red plc when it purchased Bet Direct, which provides telephone and online betting services. The deal, completed in June 2006, was worth approximately £18.5 million. Later that same month, McDermott advised Carlyle Europe Technology Partners when it acquired a share in German marketing giant Global Media GmbH. Financial terms of the deal were not disclosed.

In September 2006, McDermott counseled NationsHealth, Inc., when it sold its discount prescription drug card unit to HealthTran LLC. The firm also advised Arden Partners when it acted as underwriter to Hat Pin plc, the British human resources services group that sold £5.5 million in stock in September 2006. Mercantile traders celebrated as only merc traders can when McDermott helped Chicago Board of Trade (CBOT) in its merger with the Chicago Mercantile Exchange. The firm advised the CBOT's board of directors in the historic merger, which created an exchange trading approximately $4.2 trillion in commodities contracts daily. In October 2006, McDermott advised Click Commerce, Inc., a supply chain management company, when it merged with Illinois Tool Works Inc. The firm's deal flow continued into November 2006, with The Stationery Office Holdings Limited on its purchase by Apax Partners and Williams Lea Group Limited.

McDermott in the court

McDermott's 45-year-old trial practice is going strong. In June 2006, the Republican National Committee (RNC), a firm client, celebrated a Supreme Court victory that came about with McDermott's help. The firm filed an amicus brief on behalf of the RNC with the high court. The RNC interceded in a challenge to Vermont's stringent campaign finance laws. Vermont law limited candidate expenditures in statewide contests and put strict restrictions on the amount of money individuals and political parties could contribute in elections. The Supreme Court struck down the law, finding it an unconstitutional restriction of free speech. In August 2006, the firm won a victory for its client Robert Manza, former controller at computer retailer Gateway. The

© 2007 Vault Inc.

Securities and Exchange Commission filed a civil suit against Manza, charging him with improperly recording seven transactions in 2000. A federal judge dismissed five of the seven claims in 2006.

McDermott is serving as North American M&A counsel to Tyco International in its split into three publicly traded companies—Tyco Healthcare, Tyco Electronics, and the combination of Tyco Fire & Security and Engineered Products and Services. Tyco intends to accomplish the separation through a complex internal corporate restructuring, followed by tax-free stock dividends of the stock of Tyco Healthcare and Tyco Electronics to Tyco shareholders. Among the largest and most significant deals of its kind in history, this enormously complex transaction is being conducted under much public scrutiny.

The firm managed to score a victory outside the courtroom in August 2006. Firm client Creative Technology settled an ongoing legal dispute with Apple, which agreed to pay Creative Technology $100 million to use patents for audio technology in computers. McDermott also represented Europackaging when its Malaysian operations were hauled before the European Commission and charged with illegally dumping plastic bags on the European market in violation of trade laws. The European Commission found for Europackaging, stating that no illegal dumping had taken place. In a December 2006 patent decision, McDermott secured a victory for Tercica, which licensed patents from Genentech for drugs that produced growth hormones. Tercica and Genentech alleged that Insmed Inc. and a subsidiary violated those patents. In December 2006, a jury found for Tercica and Genentech, and awarded them $7.5 million—plus a portion of the sales on the infringing drugs.

Pro bono heroes

Sometimes, good deeds are their own rewards. And sometimes, pro bono work is recognized with awards. McDermott has experienced both recently. In August 2006, the California state bar awarded McDermott's Silicon Valley office its 2006 "President's Pro Bono Service Award." The Silicon Valley office donated approximately 1,500 hours in pro bono service in 2005. The firm's other offices get into the philanthropic act, too. The firm also worked, on a pro bono basis, for Duke University grad student Blue Macellari. Macellari filed suit against R2C2, Inc., which operates web sites that post term papers; she claimed the site used a paper she wrote as an undergrad without her permission. The parties settled in January 2006.

GETTING HIRED

Top tier or top grades

"If you did not graduate from a top-tier school, you must be top of your class, and even then they will not consider people from the lowest-tier schools," one health law expert cautions. Another junior associate agrees, "You must have attended a top-tier law school to be considered, or be at the top of your class at a second-tier school. Third- and fourth-tier schools are not even considered." A regulatory attorney from D.C. adds, "The hiring committee definitely focuses on bringing in lawyers from top-25 law schools. I've presented a few candidates that I considered excellent who weren't even brought in for interviews because of the schools they went to. I don't think GPA is considered to nearly to the same extent." Not everyone thinks the firm's pedigree criteria are so stringent: "I think we are more open to candidates from schools that other big firms are not, although I think the GPA requirement is much higher at lower-ranked schools. They seem to focus more on personality than on grades—we have a 'no jerk' policy, which I feel is strongly applied."

Speaking of personality, a D.C. litigator says that the firm's priorities include "proven leaders, both academically and socially, work ethic, commitment to promoting diversity, participating in pro bono and supporting community efforts." A Chicagoan elaborates, "We are looking for smart people with personality. Grades are important, but if you're boring or have no personality, you will not be hired. The flip side is that the firm will sometimes make an exception for a candidate with OK grades but a dynamic personality who interviews very well." Another D.C. associate adds, "During call-back interviews, one 'no' vote can ding a qualified candidate. Successful applicants have achieved and are presentable and personable. The firm is looking for industrious individuals that will pursue issues to the end."

Visit the Vault Law Channel, the complete online resource for law careers, featuring firm profiles, message boards, the Vault Law Job Board and more. www.vault.com/law

VAULT CAREER LIBRARY   441

OUR SURVEY SAYS

High praise (though long hours)

McDermott's associates generally offer up different versions of the same sentiment: There's no place they'd rather work, they'd just like to work there a little less often. As one midlevel corporate attorney puts it, "Generally this is a great place to work. Currently, staffing levels are not appropriate and the firm needs to be more committed to hiring lateral associates." A midlevel litigator adds, "I love the work I do (it's challenging, interesting, etc.), and I really enjoy the people I work with. The hours and stress are more than I would like, though." Another litigator says, "At this point in my career, there is no other firm where I would rather be. I am receiving significant responsibility in important cases, while working with some of the brightest—yet nicest—attorneys in our nation's capital." An energy and derivatives associate says that she has a lot to be thankful for, including "very stimulating work; top-rate, sophisticated clients, including mostly top investment banks and hedge funds; a lot of freedom to take on responsibility, be a leader in the group and firm, take on clients, write articles, etc."

Whether in L.A. or N.Y., Chicago or New York, the song remains the same

Associates call McDermott "more laid-back than typical New York firms" and "small enough to make meaningful relationships with partners and associates, yet big enough to get a wide variety of experience." A Boston litigator boasts, "We have a fun, quirky, laid-back trial department in my office that I thoroughly enjoy. I am good friends with a number of other associates, though this isn't the sort of place where associates socialize after work every evening." A Los Angeles litigator describes his office as "very professional, and the expectation is that people will have separate social lives away from the firm. Lawyers do not tend to socialize together." A D.C. attorney shares, "The firm's culture is one of its best attributes. From partners to associates, everyone is friendly, open and willing to help each other when needed. There are frequent social events that people attend, but most people have lives outside the firm as well." And a corporate attorney from Chicago adds, "The firm has a great culture. The atmosphere is very professional with the right amount of socializing."

Perhaps the exceptions prove the rule?

McDermott associates rate partners among the firm's strengths, though they feel obliged to point out that there are, alas, a few very notable exceptions. "By and large, the partners are likeable people and more respectful of associates than one might expect to find at a large firm," says a young litigator. "However, at least a handful prove that there are true and enduring exceptions made to the firm's 'no jerks' policy." A corporate finance expert reports, "I get along with all my partners. They are very good at providing me with challenging assignments and allowing me to develop an approach to tackling each project. People are available for questions and you are encouraged to participate in phone calls with clients." A New York litigator says that, aside from "a few bad apples," McDermott's partners are "a pleasure to work with and for, and where an associate does good work, he or she is rewarded with more responsibility and involvement in decision making." As one associate succinctly sums things up, "Associate/partner relations vary a lot depending on which partners you work with."

Apparently, there can be too much of a good thing

Even formal training gets good grades from McDermott's associates. As one midlevel New York attorney puts it, "McDermott has training every week and it is always useful to me." A corporate finance associate reports, "Each practice group has weekly training sessions that address topics of interest and general information to associates." An environmental expert adds, "The firm has increased its offering of training programs tenfold since I started in 2000; it encourages formal training sessions, partners lead these sessions, they are well prepared, the materials are helpful and always useful." However, sometimes enough's enough. "Sometimes there is too much training and too much pressure on associates to attend every single training session," complains a midlevel. "We are professionals; we can determine on our own which sessions we need to attend and how we need to prioritize our time."

© 2007 Vault Inc.

If you want it, you got it

You've got to make the effort, associates advise, but mentoring is there for the taking at McDermott. "The firm has a very good mentoring program," reports one insider. "It is important for the associate to seek out the resources and assistance provided by this program, but so far, it has been an excellent experience." A midlevel D.C. attorney says that the firm's informal training offerings are "very good, but you have to be proactive. If you care about your work, take ownership of projects and in your career and ask questions: There are always partners and other attorneys very willing to help you reach your goals." And an antitrust expert adds, "The firm makes sure you have a formal mentor. Many people also have informal mentors, as the atmosphere is pretty collegial."

Generous and transparent

Associates appreciate both the size of their paychecks and the clarity of the compensation system overall. "The firm pays market and makes a big effort to keep up with any market developments with regard to salaries and bonuses," reports a first-year. "The firm openly shares its policies and levels of compensation (including bonuses) with all associates, so it is pretty easy to figure out where you stand." Another D.C. attorney boasts, "Bonuses have been very good. They are based not only on hours, but also quality. I have always received very competitive bonuses." Another insider adds, "Bonuses tend to be tied to billable hours. But the firm no longer says that you must bill 2,000 hours to get a bonus. However, the link between hours and bonuses seems pretty clear when comparing notes."

Long but flexible

Associates say that the firm demands long hours, but that the partners are relatively reasonable, flexible and considerate about outside demands. "The firm has been exceptionally supportive and accommodating with unforeseen circumstances, special needs and flexibility regarding hours. Certainly, when presence in the office is necessary, then it's important to be in the office, but if the work can be done outside of the office, the firm is supportive of such possibilities," says a senior Boston associate. A D.C. litigator reports, "McDermott is not a 'face time' firm. As long as you work during normal business hours, complete your assignments on time and make your hours, no one will question you about working from home outside normal business hours (i.e., at night or on the weekend). For example, I never eat dinner at the firm because I am out of the office by dinnertime." Another D.C. litigator adds, "The firm has a very good part-time associate policy. The practical effect of the policy depends on the nature of one's practice. In any event, my experience is that the firm is not a 'face time' firm, and I have been able to telecommute when necessary to deal with family or other issues."

Visit the Vault Law Channel, the complete online resource for law careers, featuring firm profiles, message boards, the Vault Law Job Board and more. **www.vault.com/law**

VAULT CAREER LIBRARY

443

VAULT
THE MOST TRUSTED NAME IN CAREER INFORMATION

"Fun reads, edgy details"
— FORBES MAGAZINE

Vault guides and employer profiles have been published since 1997 and are the premier source of insider information on careers.

Each year, Vault surveys and interviews thousands of employees to give readers the inside scoop on industries and specific employers to help them get the jobs they want.

"To get the un-varnished scoop, check out Vault"
— SMARTMONEY MAGAZINE

VAULT

THE VAULT 100:
FIRMS 51-100

Jenner & Block LLP

330 N. Wabash Avenue
Chicago, IL 60611-7603
Phone: (312) 222-9350
www.jenner.com

LOCATIONS

Chicago, IL (HQ)

Dallas, TX • New York, NY • Washington, DC

MAJOR DEPARTMENTS & PRACTICES

Antitrust & Trade Regulation • Appellate & Supreme Court Practice • Arbitration: Domestic & International • Association Practice • Bankruptcy, Workout & Corporate Reorganization • Business Litigation • Class Action Litigation • Climate & Clean Technology Law • Commercial Law & Uniform Commercial Code • Construction Law • Corporate • Corporate Finance • Defense & Aerospace • Employee Benefits & Executive Compensation • Entertainment & New Media • Environmental, Energy & Natural Resources Law • ERISA Litigation • Family Law • Government Contracts • Health Care Law • Insurance Litigation & Counseling • Intellectual Property • Labor & Employment • Litigation Department • Media & First Amendment Practice • Mergers & Acquisitions • Pharmaceutical, Biotech & Medical Devices • Private Client Practice • Private Equity/Investment Management • Products Liability & Mass Tort Defense • Professional Liability Litigation • Public Policy • Real Estate • Real Estate Securities Practice • Reinsurance Practice • Securities • Securities Litigation • Tax Controversy Practice • Tax Practice • Telecommunications • Trade Secrets & Unfair Competition • White Collar Criminal Defense & Counseling

THE STATS

No. of attorneys: 474
No. of offices: 4
Summer associate offers: 65 out of 66 (2006)
Chairman: Jerold S. Solovy
Managing Partner: Gregory S. Gallopoulos
Hiring Co-chairs: Katherine A. Fallow, Reginald J. Hill,
              Charlotte L. Wager

THE BUZZ
WHAT ATTORNEYS AT OTHER FIRMS ARE SAYING ABOUT THIS FIRM

- "The classic American litigation firm"
- "Best days gone"
- "Strong diversity and pro bono tradition"
- "Reality doesn't live up to the hype"

RANKING RECAP

Best in Region
#7 - Chicago

Quality of Life
#15 - Best Firms to Work For
#15 - Overall Satisfaction
#17 - Formal Training
#11 - Pro Bono

Diversity
#1 - Diversity with Respect to GLBT
#5 - Overall Diversity
#13 - Diversity with Respect to Minorities
#18 - Diversity with Respect to Women

NOTABLE PERKS

- "Three different PDAs to choose from. Two laptop choices"
- Bar and moving expenses
- Friday happy hours
- "Gold-level frequent flyer status"

EMPLOYMENT CONTACT

Christine J. Carlson
Senior Manager of Legal Recruiting
Phone: (312) 840-7803
Fax: (312) 840-7616
E-mail: ccarlson@jenner.com

BASE SALARY (2007)

Chicago, IL; Dallas, TX; New York, NY; Washington, DC

1st year: $160,000
Summer associate: $2,788/week (Chicago and DC)

© 2007 Vault Inc.

THE SCOOP

Chicago-based Jenner & Block is best known for its world-class litigators—beneficiaries of the firm's services range from industry giants like General Motors and MGM Studios, to society's destitute and marginalized. In January 2006, *The American Lawyer* ranked Jenner & Block among the nation's top-five litigation shops, citing its "astonishing" victories, "hard-fought" settlements and "extraordinary efforts" in providing pro bono services to the needy. The firm played a leading role in negotiating what is believed to be the largest copyright infringement settlement in history in coordination with the Recording Industry Association of America (RIAA), the International Federation of Phonographic Industries (IFPI), and counsel on three continents on behalf of the world's major recording companies. The settlement is a worldwide deal that resolved the long-running copyright infringement litigation against Kazaa, then one of the world's most popular peer-to-peer file-trading networks. The agreement resulted in a settlement of $115 million for the record companies, and Kazaa has also introduced "filtering technologies" to ensure that its users cannot distribute copyright-infringing files in the future. In November 2006, Jenner & Block was back on familiar territory, defending the First Amendment freedoms of America's video game manufacturers. The firm successfully convinced a Louisiana court that a recently enacted state law seeking to criminalize the sale of violent video games to minors and subject violators to fines of up to $2,000 constituted a violation of video game manufacturers' and retailers' freedom of speech. The firm's corporate practice continues to grow. In 2007, for instance, it represented Sam Zell in his offer to buy the Tribune Company and is representing GM and General Dynamics in high-stakes transactions.

GETTING HIRED

According to many insiders, your chances at Jenner & Block were greatly influenced the day you took your LSAT. "Recruiting efforts are focused on the Ivies and certain regional schools, but the firm recruits candidates from all over the country," reports another insider. The firm does seek candidates with more than just a stellar name on the transcript, though "transcripts from Harvard and Yale help." What else helps? "A solid Jenner candidate is a smart and ambitious law student who has not lost his or her sense of humor," states a second-year. "Expect a couple of rounds of interviewing," warns a contact. "Top grades [are] a must; clerkship helps, of course." "The firm looks for people with outside interests, social skills and pride in their work ethic," observes another insider.

OUR SURVEY SAYS

Working at Jenner & Block has its advantages. "Obviously, not every day is entirely fulfilling, but I can say with sincerity that most days, I'm very satisfied with my work," says one insider. Not exactly a ringing endorsement, but among law firms, that ain't bad. Others are more effusive, even if they can see some flaws. "Perhaps my favorite part about working here is the people," gushes a source. "The partners I have worked with have been exceptionally nice, willing to mentor and respectful of associates. The senior and midlevel associates have also been really helpful in offering advice and feedback." So what could be wrong with a firm so friendly? "As is probably the case with every big firm, unpredictability of hours and finding good quality work are my biggest complaints." Associates do love the firm's commitment to pro bono work. "The culture of encouraging pro bono at all levels means that as a junior associate, I get a high level of responsibility and experience, and more senior associates and partners, can use their expertise to give back to the community," reports a lawyer. "At the end of the day, I feel good about the experience I am getting and the firm I work for." "I feel there are fewer barriers between partners and associates than those I sense at other firms," notes a midlevel associate. Jenner & Block is family-friendly as well. "The firm culture is also quite supportive of attorneys with young families, so the face time demands are minimal," says a senior associate. "The focus is on doing the work, and doing it well." All told, the firm's culture is a bright spot. "Colleagues are not just colleagues—they're friends as well," states one contact. Jenner & Block insiders enjoy a firm where "the environment is friendly and collegial." "Lawyers tend to be awkward socially, but I have found Jenner & Block lawyers to be remarkably interesting and engaging on a social, professional and political level. Jenner & Block lawyers are pretty darned dynamic," exclaims an attorney who lateralled into the firm, and thus has some basis for comparison.

Visit the Vault Law Channel, the complete online resource for law careers, featuring firm profiles, message boards, the Vault Law Job Board and more. www.vault.com/law

VAULT CAREER LIBRARY   447

52
PRESTIGE
RANKING

LeBoeuf, Lamb, Greene & MacRae LLP

125 West 55th Street
New York, NY 10019
Phone: (212) 424-8000
Fax: (212) 424-8500
www.llgm.com

LOCATIONS

New York, NY (HQ)

Albany, NY • Boston, MA • Chicago, IL • Hartford, CT •
Houston, TX • Jacksonville, FL • Los Angeles, CA • San
Francisco, CA • Washington, DC • Almaty • Beijing •
Brussels • Hong Kong • Johannesburg • London • Moscow
• Paris • Riyadh

MAJOR DEPARTMENTS & PRACTICES

Bankruptcy & Debt Restructuring • Corporate & Finance •
Energy & Utilities • Entertainment, Media & Sports •
Environmental, Health & Safety • Executive Compensation,
Employee Benefits & ERISA • Insurance Regulatory •
Legislation & Public Policy • Litigation & Dispute Resolution
• Public International Law • Real Estate • Tax • Technology,
Intellectual Property & Media • Trusts & Estates

THE STATS

No. of attorneys firmwide: 741
No. of offices: 19
Summer associate offers firmwide: 50 out of 50 (2006)
Managing Partner: Steven H. Davis
Hiring Partner: Ellen M. Dunn & Robert S. Rachofsky

RANKING RECAP

Quality of Life
#7 - Pay

Best in Diversity
#20 - Diversity with Respect to GLBT

NOTABLE PERKS

• Subsidized gym memberships
• Monthly mentoring budgets
• Subsidized cafeteria

EMPLOYMENT CONTACT

Ms. Lauren Rasmus
Director of Legal Recruiting
Phone: (212) 424-8000
Fax: (212) 424-8500
E-mail: llgmrecruiting@llgm.com

BASE SALARY (2007)

**New York, NY; Los Angeles, CA; San Francisco, CA;
Hartford, CT; Houston, TX**
1st year: $160,000
2nd year: $170,000
3rd year: $185,000
4th year: $210,000
5th year: $230,000
6th year: $250,000
7th year: $265,000
8th year: $280,000
Summer associate: $3,077/week

THE BUZZ
WHAT ATTORNEYS AT OTHER FIRMS ARE SAYING ABOUT THIS FIRM

• "Smart folks"
• "Spread too far too thinly"
• "Good project and energy practices"
• "Insurance is where it's at"

© 2007 Vault Inc.

THE SCOOP

There are few international law firms more, well, international than LeBoeuf, Lamb, Greene & MacRae. The New York-based LeBoeuf maintains offices in many of the world's financial capitals, from Johannesburg to Moscow, from Almaty to Riyadh. A quick survey of its cases suggests that LeBoeuf's strengths are both a cause and product of its worldwide presence. In 2006, the firm successfully represented the U.S. software company Telcordia Technologies in a landmark case against Telkom, the South African telecommunications goliath, before South Africa's highest court, the Supreme Court of Appeal. The SCA overturned a High Court decision that stated that Telkom need not abide by an international arbitration that found that Telcordia should recover damages for Telkom's breach of an agreement between them. The SCA ruling could result in a payment of more than $200 million for Telcordia. LeBoeuf also advised Vneshtorgbank and Goldman Sachs regarding a $328 million loan that reportedly constituted the first leveraged buyout in the history of Kazakhstan. (Capitalism is *niiiiiice!*) The money will be used by the private equity fund Baring Vostok Capital Partners and financier Vyacheslav Kim to, among other things, acquire 94 percent of Bank Caspian, one of the nation's largest banks. One sign of how international the deal (and the firm) truly are: The closing took place in eight different locations, truly spanning the globe—London, Moscow, Almaty, Astana, Amsterdam, Guernsey, Washington, D.C., and the Cayman Islands.

GETTING HIRED

LeBoeuf insiders report that the firm "is definitely changing its hiring criteria—more students from the elite schools, and more of a focus on grades." A New Yorker reports, "I think there is more of an effort now to focus on recruiting from top law schools. At the same time, the firm is willing to hire associates from local New York schools (Cardozo, Brooklyn, etc.)." Not everyone at LeBoeuf thinks the hiring trends are positive: "I think that the firm is heading in the wrong direction in terms of hiring. They want to confine themselves only to the cream of the Ivy Leagues and Ivy League-equivalent schools. But the partners I work with and nearly all of the best associates I've worked with haven't fit that mold." Of course, not every well-credentialed body passes muster. One attorney notes that "grades and school reputation aren't dispositive. I've seen people having both of those traits not get hired for personality reasons." This New York attorney also observes that LeBoeuf "associates are hired from just about every school in the city." Another insider elaborates, "They are looking for associates with strong academic credentials, international experience and unique work/academic experiences outside of the law firm environment."

OUR SURVEY SAYS

At LeBoeuf, salaries bring smiles. "I signed up for this gig at $125,000," recounts a LeBoeuf associate. "Less than six months in, I've gotten two raises, up to $160,000. Hard not to like." Another attorney exclaims, "They're paying me $160K! WTF!" If there is a common compensation related complaint among LeBoeuf associates, it is that "we still have a 2,000 billable requirement for bonus, which this year was strictly enforced and left many associates very unhappy." As for the hours, "When projects demand the time, the hours can be strenuous, but overall the hours are manageable," says one attorney. In particular, "Many litigators go home to their families at a reasonable hour," notes one such litigator. Another attorney says: "If you are working with reasonable and considerate people as you are at LeBoeuf, it is much easier to put in long days. I have never been expected to stay late just to get in 'face time.'" Insiders disagree on the availability of part-time schedules. "There is no viable part-time alternative," one attorney complains, but another insists that "there are a number of part-time lawyers." As for the firm's training program, one associate comments, "It's OK, if mostly ad hoc as partners take an individual interest. They tend to farm it out to NITA, which is pretty good." Another attorney points out: "The firm has recently made an effort to increase training of corporate and first-year associates. There are also regular litigation training sessions. This is not the case in the specialized departments." Culturally, LeBoeuf "is not a social club, but almost everyone gets along fairly well. There is an active associates committee that is working to add some more social activities to firm life." A Washington associate says, "I feel completely comfortable and welcomed no matter whose office I walk into." The firm's culture really consists of various cultures, according to the associate who argues that "LeBoeuf has been taking in a lot of laterals, so there really is no definitive firm culture anymore. It's best to look at each department individually. The corporate attorneys are dandies, the IP attorneys are geeks, and the litigation attorneys are reasonably normal." (No points for guessing which department that survey respondent works in.)

Visit the Vault Law Channel, the complete online resource for law careers, featuring firm profiles, message boards, the Vault Law Job Board and more. **www.vault.com/law**

VAULT CAREER LIBRARY   449

Allen & Overy

1221 Avenue of the Americas
New York, NY 10020
Phone: (212) 610-6300
Fax: (212) 610-639
www.allenovery.com

LOCATIONS

New York, NY • Amsterdam • Antwerp • Bangkok • Beijing
• Bratislava • Brussels • Budapest • Dubai • Frankfurt •
Hamburg • Hong Kong • London • Luxembourg • Madrid •
Milan • Moscow • Paris • Prague • Rome • Shanghai •
Singapore • Tokyo • Warsaw

MAJOR DEPARTMENTS & PRACTICES

Asset Finance & Leasing • Antitrust • Banking •
Corporate/M&A • Debt Capital Markets • Derivatives •
Employee Benefits & Executive Compensation •
Environmental • Equity Capital Markets • Global Loans •
International Capital Markets • Litigation & Arbitration •
Project Finance • Real Estate • Regulatory • Repackagings &
Structured Finance • Restructuring & Insolvency •
Securitization • Tax

THE STATS

No. of attorneys firmwide: 2,200
No. of offices: 24
Summer associate offers: 26 out of 26 (2006)
Managing Partners: Michael Feldberg & Ian Shrank
Hiring Partners: Michael Gilligan, David Lewis, John
Williams

RANKING RECAP

Best in Practice
#5 - International Law

NOTABLE PERKS

- In-house gym (London)
- "International secondment program"
- "Regular off-sites in cool places (Paris, Amsterdam,
  Dubai, London)"

EMPLOYMENT CONTACT

Ms. Elizabeth Fuchs
Senior Manager, Legal Recruitment & Associate
   Development
Phone: (212) 610-6300
E-mail: Elizabeth.Fuchs@allenovery.com

BASE SALARY (2007)

New York, NY
1st year: $160,000
2nd year: $170,000
3rd year: $185,000
4th year: $210,000
5th year: $230,000
6th year: $250,000
7th year: $265,000
8th year: $280,000
Summer associate: $3,076.92/week

THE BUZZ
WHAT ATTORNEYS AT OTHER FIRMS ARE SAYING ABOUT THIS FIRM

- "Top Magic Circle firm"
- "Stick to England, lovey"
- "Finance giant"
- "British grades snobs"

© 2007 Vault Inc.

THE SCOOP

London-based Allen & Overy is the epitome of a global law firm. Its 24 offices are spread out fairly evenly throughout the world—from Madrid to Bratislava, from Shanghai to Dubai. The firm's sole U.S. outpost is in New York. The New York office, less than a decade old, already employs over 140 attorneys. The Big Apple branch specializes in cross-border transactions. For example, in May 2006, Allen & Overy represented the Export-Import Bank of the United States in its $100 million financing of a wireless network in Saudi Arabia. In September 2006, the firm advised Sinopec International Petroleum Exploration and Production Corporation of China (SIPC) on its acquisition of Texas-based Omimex Resources. The deal was a joint venture with Indian concern ONGC Videsh Limited and worth $850 million. In June 2005, the firm counseled several U.S. banks in an $81.8 billion global debt offering—the largest international capital markets transaction ever. Back home, Allen & Overy advised JER Partners in its $371 million purchase of Jameson Inns, Inc. The deal closed in July 2006. In November 2005, the firm helped negotiate an agreement for the settlement of credit derivatives trades involving Delphi Corp., a bankrupt auto supplies company. Allen & Overy also represented the U.S.-based Export-Import Bank and the Japan Bank for International Cooperation in what is known as the "Qatargas 3" project. Working with a team of A&O attorneys from London, the New York office advised the Export-Import Bank and JBIC as they provided a loan guarantee of $403.5 million to support the export of American equipment and services to the Qatar Liquefied Gas Company 3 Ltd. (hence, "Qatargas 3") for the construction of a natural gas liquefaction plant and related facilities in Qatar.

GETTING HIRED

The expansion of Allen & Overy's New York outpost means that the firm is hungry for new recruits and is relaxing its standards, associates say. "We are growing and have too much work, so we are really looking to hire new people (mostly junior attorneys out of law school)," reports a third-year. A midlevel agrees, adding, "In the past we were considered to be a bit of a grade snob, but we are growing so it looks like we are opening up the pool a bit." As for specifics, "We want international candidates, and usually students who did not go straight through to law school from college," advises a junior banking specialist. A litigation associate adds, "Although A&O has interviewed at only a few schools in the past, the firm is beginning to branch out. The firm looks for a candidate with international experience, or a discernible international interest. Languages are a big plus."

OUR SURVEY SAYS

The vast majority of Allen & Overy's associates say they wouldn't want to work anywhere else. As one junior associate puts it, "I am happy here, and would never switch to another New York firm. A junior litigator says, "I really like the people I work with, which makes even tedious tasks seem better. It also helps that more senior associates and partners express their appreciation for your work." Another New Yorker adds, "Would I like more responsibility, better mentorship and fewer hours? Sure. But I enjoy far more responsibility than friends at other firms and better access to senior people than I would almost anywhere else." Associates agree the firm's "relaxed," "friendly" and "professional" culture is its strongest asset. "A&O is very laid-back," advises a junior environmental associate. "There is almost no hierarchy. People are very friendly. Our group has a nice dinner together once every few months." A midlevel litigator calls the firm "extremely collegial." She adds, "There is a noticeable lack of hierarchy between staff, associates and partners. In the litigation department, there are monthly social events to which everyone is invited. Generally speaking, people really enjoy each other here." Another litigator adds, "The atmosphere is very pleasant and civil. My impression is that some younger associates socialize together outside of work, but most people have their own family life, friends, etc." A&O's junior attorneys report the firm's training is another strong suit. A New York litigator advises, "There are constant trainings offered both in house and off site. All first-year U.S. associates (in New York, London and Hong Kong) attend a five-day training session; lectures include substantive basics in all practice areas, marketing, interacting with clients and how the firm is operated as a business." The compensation is top of the market, associates report. Says one insider, "Although not a market leader, A&O matches whatever the New York market is." While associates find it "truly marvelous" that they are "paid at the same levels as the top Wall Street firms." Some insiders are green with envy at their friendly neighborhood I-banker's paycheck, but one logical lawyer is thankful for what he has at A&O: "I work hard, but I work a lot less than my friends for the same pay and bonus."

Visit the Vault Law Channel, the complete online resource for law careers, featuring firm profiles, message boards, the Vault Law Job Board and more. **www.vault.com/law**

VAULT CAREER LIBRARY   451

DLA Piper

1251 Avenue of the Americas
27th Floor
New York, NY 10020-1104
Phone: (212) 335-4500
www.dlapiper.com

LOCATIONS

Atlanta, GA • Austin, TX • Baltimore, MD • Boston, MA • Chicago, IL • Dallas, TX • Easton, MD • Edison, NJ • La Jolla, CA • Las Vegas, NV • Los Angeles, CA • Minneapolis, MN • New York, NY • Philadelphia, PA • Phoenix, AZ • Raleigh, NC • Reston, VA • Sacramento, CA • San Diego, CA • San Francisco, CA • Seattle, WA • Silicon Valley, CA • Tampa, FL • Washington, DC • Amsterdam • Antwerp • Bangkok • Beijing • Bergen • Birmingham • Bratislava • Brussels • Budapest • Cologne • Dubai • Edinburgh • Frankfurt • Glasgow • Hamburg • Hong Kong • Kiev • Leeds • Liverpool • London • Madrid • Manchester • Milan • Moscow • Oslo • Paris • Prague • Rome • Salzburg • Sarajevo • Shanghai • Sheffield • Singapore • St. Petersburg • Sofia • Tbilisi • Tokyo • Vienna • Zagreb

MAJOR DEPARTMENTS & PRACTICES

Commercial Contracts • Corporate • Employment, Pensions, & Benefits • Finance • Intellectual Property • Litigation & Arbitration • Projects & Infrastructure • Real Estate • Regulatory & Government Affairs • Restructuring • Tax • Technology & Media

THE STATS

No. of attorneys: 3,400+
No. of offices: 63
Summer associate offers: 102 out of 108 (2006)
Global Chairman: George Mitchell
Joint CEOs: Francis B. Burch Jr., Nigel Knowles, Lee I. Miller
US Managing Partner: Terry O'Malley
National Hiring Partner: Benjamin S. Boyd

THE BUZZ
WHAT ATTORNEYS AT OTHER FIRMS ARE SAYING ABOUT THIS FIRM

• "Something for everyone"
• "Way overgrown"
• "Money machine"
• "Some interesting pieces, but will they fit?"

RANKING RECAP

Best in Practice
#1 - Real Estate

Partner Prestige Rankings
#1 - Real Estate

NOTABLE PERKS

• Emergency child care
• Six free massages a year
• "Amazing" parental leave policy
• Hybrid car benefit

EMPLOYMENT CONTACTS

East Coast
Ms. Diane Ross
Director of Legal Recruiting
Phone: (202) 689-7948
E-mail: diane.ross@dlapiper.com

West Coast
Ms. Leslie Colvin
Director of Legal Recruiting
Phone: (650) 833-2133
E-mail: leslie.colvin@dlapiper.com

BASE SALARY (2007)

California offices (other than Sacramento); Boston, MA; Chicago, IL: New York, NY; Reston, VA; Washington, DC
1st year: $160,000
Summer associate: $3,076/week effective on June 1, 2007

Austin, TX; Baltimore, MD; Dallas, TX; Raleigh, NC; Sacramento, CA; Seattle, WA
1st year: $145,000
Summer associate: $2,800/week

Atlanta, GA; Philadelphia, PA; Tampa, FL
1st year: $135,000
Summer associate: $2,600/week

© 2007 Vault Inc.

THE SCOOP

Lawyers and clients around the globe breathed a collective sigh of relief in September 2006, when DLA Piper Rudnick Gray Cary—with its 3,400 lawyers in 63 offices across 24 countries—announced that its name would officially be shortened to a more modest DLA Piper. A mere sampling of the deals and cases DLA Piper is working on worldwide includes advising YO! Sushi in a £17.5 million deal with Barclays Bank, which will fund a release of capital to all of YO! Sushi's shareholders; representation of Indochina Capital Vietnam Holdings Limited as U.S. counsel in its $500 million initial public offering (the largest public offering ever by a Vietnam-based company); representation of Taurus Investment Holdings, LLC and its affiliates in real estate activities to include the structuring and closing of two Luxembourg funds established to acquire approximately €600 million in properties in Europe; counseling Dublin investment group Sorrento Structuring in its acquisition of the U.S.-based hospitality group BridgeStreet Worldwide; and advising Donald Trump on a condominium project planned for downtown Chicago. DLA Piper also recently became the exclusive pro bono service provider for the French Red Cross. DLA Piper is not afraid to take its international business into some very contentious arenas. Just recently, the firm closed a decade-long case on behalf of victims of the 1996 Khobar Towers bombing. A truck bomb blasted apart this military housing area in Saudi Arabia, killing 19. The resulting lawsuit required delicate navigation considering that it would inevitably be pointing fingers in a very sensitive region. In January 2006, a federal judge ordered the Iranian government to pay $254 million to families of 17 Americans who died in the bombing. The ruling found that the bombing, conducted by a militant Saudi wing of the Islamist terrorist group Hezbollah, was financed and directed by Iranian government agencies and senior ministers.

GETTING HIRED

DLA Piper recruiters approach their hires with the same careful analysis that they approach a case. They even use some of the same lingo. "Due diligence for potential candidates is thorough." It starts with credentials, of course. DLA Piper "prefers top-25 schools." Prefers, not requires. Regional offices in less traditional cities report more spaces given to graduates from local law schools, "but they have to be at the very top of their class." According to the firm, DLA Piper's "development of an interview training program based on core competencies suggests the firm is taking a more holistic approach to recruiting and hiring candidates." A member of the recruiting committee weighs in: "We don't want just smart bookworms who will churn out briefs all day. We want real people, who are well rounded, smart and interesting." The firm reports that the 2007 summer class is "45 percent diverse."

OUR SURVEY SAYS

Whether they show it by going out for drinks or just grabbing lunch together, DLA Piper lawyers generally report that they "actually really like each other" and nearly every office has some kind of socialization. "My wife comments on 'how cool' the people I work with are," confides a litigator. It is a "diverse culture" and those with "various and unique backgrounds get along very well together." Vertical collegiality also contributes to job satisfaction as (for the most part) "partners take a personal interest" in making sure associates have "significant responsibility and client interaction." Though, it can be tough out there for a JD—some report feeling like "a cog in a wheel of some mega-case." A realistic San Francisco associate, talking about associates' relations with their superiors, says, "In a firm this size, it varies by partner." Drastically. On the positive side, we received comments like "truly A+," and "Everyone treats the associates with much respect and tries to keep them busy with meaningful work." In opposition, there are partners who are "set in their ways" creating "a standoff, subservient relationship with their associates." First, the good news: the "firm is very committed to meeting market demands" and many are enjoying their salary increase. The bad news, though, is that not everyone got bumped, which has "hurt morale." For example, "less expensive" cities and those who didn't make 2,000 billables created a nebulous "three-tier" system. The firm quickly responded to the market changes in spring 2007, adjusting the compensation structure in several markets and assured associates that the increases would not impact the bonus structure, hours expectations or billing rates. Formal training opportunities "abound" and include CLEs, NITA, mock trials, litigation retreats, teleconferences, webcasts and the firm's own Marbury Institute.

Visit the Vault Law Channel, the complete online resource for law careers, featuring firm profiles, message boards, the Vault Law Job Board and more. **www.vault.com/law**

VAULT CAREER LIBRARY   453

55
PRESTIGE RANKING

Cahill Gordon & Reindel LLP

80 Pine Street
New York, NY 10005
Phone: (212) 701-3000
Fax: (212) 269-5420
www.cahill.com

LOCATIONS

New York, NY (HQ)
Washington, DC
London

MAJOR DEPARTMENTS & PRACTICES

Antitrust & Trade Regulation • Bankruptcy & Restructuring •
Corporate • Corporate Governance & Internal Investigations
• Crisis Advisory & Management • Employee Benefits &
Executive Compensation • Environmental • Insurance •
Intellectual Property • Litigation • Media • Pro Bono • Real
Estate • Taxation • Trusts & Estates

THE STATS

No. of attorneys firmwide: 250
No. of offices: 3
Summer associate offers: 48 out of 48 (2006):
Managing Partner: William Hartnett
Hiring Partner: Noah Newitz

RANKING RECAP

Partner Prestige Rankings
#23 - Overall Prestige

NOTABLE PERKS

• Technology stipend
• Discounted gym membership
• Dental coverage
• Twice daily cookie trays

EMPLOYMENT CONTACT

Legal Hiring Office
Cahill Gordon & Reindel LLP
Phone: (212) 701-3944
Fax: (212) 269-5420
E-mail: recruiting@cahill.com

BASE SALARY (2007)

New York, NY
1st year: $160,000
2nd year: $170,000
3rd year: $185,000
4th year: $210,000
5th year: $230,000
6th year: $250,000
7th year: $265,000
8th year: $280,000
Summer associate: $3,075/week

THE BUZZ
WHAT ATTORNEYS AT OTHER FIRMS ARE SAYING ABOUT THIS FIRM

• "Corporate powerhouse"
• "Profit hungry"
• "Never underestimate them"
• "Eat what you kill"

© 2007 Vault Inc.

THE SCOOP

Leveraged buyouts and high-yield bonds have been Cahill's mainstay from the RJR Nabisco days to the present. Cahill has represented the financing sources in 13 of the 20 largest buyouts in history, including in such widely publicized megadeals as the $44 billion buyout of TXU Corp., the $33 billion buyout of hospital operator HCA, $12 billion buyout of Dutch media giant VNU, N.V. (the parent company of ACNielsen and *Billboard* magazine), the $26.7 billion buyout of Clear Channel Communications, the $27.8 billion buyout of Harrah's Entertainment, the $10.9 billion buyout of Biomet and the $8.3 billion buyout of food-service provider Aramark. The firm also advised Nasdaq regarding its purchase of an equity stake in The London Stock Exchange and oversaw Boston Scientific's acquisition of Guidant Corporation. Cahill has a reputation as the firm of choice for companies and individuals faced with "bet the company" disputes that require innovative, aggressive and tailored litigation strategies. Recently, Cahill represented Deutsche Bank in one of the most significant litigations to arise out of the September 11 terrorist attacks, resulting in a substantial settlement for its clients and the 130 Liberty Street building being deconstructed and bagged for hazardous waste removal. Among the notable historic cases successfully litigated by the firm are National Broadcasting Co. v. United States, which played a role in the establishment of the Federal Communications Commission; and Times Picayune v. United States, which established a leading precedent in antitrust law.

GETTING HIRED

The composition of a Cahill summer class is reportedly made up of "about half people from top-five schools (particularly NYU and Columbia) and about half top students from other local schools (e.g., St. John's, Brooklyn, Seton Hall). I think [the] top half of the class from NYU or Columbia would be enough to get hired. From other local schools, top grades are necessary," an insider reports. Now might be a good time to knock on the firm's door, as "Cahill is looking to expand the firm." And what personal qualities is the firm looking for? "We don't hire just anyone," advises a Cahill attorney. "We look for people who are bright, mature and capable of working on their own without supervision. We need people who can take on lots of responsibility early in their careers." A New Yorker cautions, "Good grades and a good personality will get you hired—but don't try and be something you are not on an interview. This is not a white shoe place—be yourself, be natural, and you will be fine."

OUR SURVEY SAYS

What are the hours like at Cahill Gordon? One attorney sums it up nicely: "Ton of hours, but no face time required." Another attorney elaborates: "Our workload is in our own hands and very flexible. If we are busy, there is no problem at all with turning down more work [...] If I don't need to be in the office, I will work from home." Cahill attorneys, predictably, seem generally pleased that they are not chained to their desks. "The firm is flexible in that if you get your work done, there is a huge amount of personal autonomy to come and go as you please. As a first-year, I appreciate the respect. No need for face time; no need to keep your office door open." Also of note, "Cahill just adopted very generous maternity leave and flex-time policies." Cahill attorneys also seem happy with their compensation. "Cahill will always pay the top of the market, and bonuses are not tied to hours in any way," notes an insider. The benefits also bring smiles: "In the past year [Cahill has] also introduced a technology stipend, dental insurance and other secondary forms of comp." That said, there are a few grumbles. "I think we don't adequately reward associates who bill the most," complains one associate. Explains another, "The nature of the system provides ability for associates to fly under the radar or do minimal work. This is not the problem—the problem is those associates that do extra work are not properly compensated for the extra effort." Cahill has recently revamped its formal training offerings, with noteworthy results. "The firm is making great strides in improving the formal training program, and has been extremely receptive to past comments of associates," raves an insider. "The training is becoming more hands on and practical." Although not everyone is blown away by the offerings, any deficiency in formal training "is more than made up for with informal training/mentoring," according to one attorney. In general, Cahill attorneys seem pleased with their workplace. "The firm culture is the best thing about Cahill," beams one lawyer. "Just about everyone in the firm is friendly and willing to help out." Notes another, "Everyone is friendly and respects each other, and there is no such thing as a screamer. Because of Cahill's free-market system, the mean people are weeded out. If someone yells, people will start turning down projects for that person."

Visit the Vault Law Channel, the complete online resource for law careers, featuring firm profiles, message boards, the Vault Law Job Board and more. www.vault.com/law

VAULT CAREER LIBRARY   455

56
PRESTIGE RANKING

Fish & Richardson P.C.

225 Franklin Street
Boston, MA 02110
Phone: (617) 542-5070
Fax: (617) 542-8906
www.fr.com

LOCATIONS

Atlanta, GA
Austin, TX
Boston, MA
Dallas, TX
Minneapolis, MN
New York, NY
San Diego, CA
Silicon Valley, CA
Washington, DC
Wilmington, DE

MAJOR DEPARTMENTS

Intellectual Property
Litigation & Dispute Resolution
Patent Prosecution & Strategic Counseling
Corporate & Securities
Licensing
Regulatory & Government Affairs
Trademarks, Copyrights, Media & Entertainment

THE STATS

No. of attorneys firmwide: 400+
No. of offices: 10
Summer associate offers (2006): 49 out of 51
President: Peter J. Devlin
Firmwide Hiring Principal: John F. Hayden

RANKING RECAP

Best in Region
#6 - Boston

Best in Practice
#1 - Intellectual Property
#5 - Technology

Partner Prestige Rankings
#2- Intellectual Property

Quality of Life
#1 - Overall Satisfaction
#2 - Hours
#2 - Pay
#3 - Associate/Partner Relations
#4 - Best Firms to Work For
#10 - Informal Training/Mentoring
#13 - Selectivity

Best in Diversity
#12 - Overall Diversity
#10 - Diversity with Respect to Minorities
#19 - Diversity with Respect to Women

NOTABLE PERKS

- $500/year technology stipend
- Discounts on Bose products
- Backup child care

EMPLOYMENT CONTACT

Ms. Kelly Mixon
Director of Attorney Hiring
Phone: (888) 314-8886
Fax: (512) 320-8935
E-mail: work@fr.com

BASE SALARY (2007)

All offices
1st year: $160,000
Summer associate: $2,600/week

THE BUZZ
WHAT ATTORNEYS AT OTHER FIRMS ARE SAYING ABOUT THIS FIRM

- "Gold-standard IP"
- "One-trick pony"
- "Very generous"
- "Only if you like patents"

© 2007 Vault Inc.

THE SCOOP

The firm now known as Fish & Richardson ranks as one of the largest and most esteemed intellectual property firms in the country. F&R's other major practices include litigation and corporate law. According to a recent study by *IP Law & Business*, it handles more patent litigation cases than any other law firm—way more. With 75 new cases in 2006, it easily outpaced its nearest competitor, Jones Day, which had only 53. Founded in 1878, F&R's historical client roster contains almost all of the nation's most revered inventors, including Thomas Edison, Alexander Graham Bell and the Wright Brothers. The firm obtained or defended patents for such seminal inventions as the telephone, the radio, the automobile and the steam turbine. These days, of course, the firm's work focuses more on computers and information technology. For example, the firm represented Microsoft in a variety of patent infringement cases. Arendi and Hyperphrase Technologies are two companies that filed suits claiming that the SmartTag feature of Microsoft Office, which allows one-click information retrieval, infringed on their patents. In both cases, Microsoft prevailed. Fish & Richardson has also represented Microsoft in patent cases relating to ergonomic keyboards, video game systems, graphical user interfaces and audio processing.

GETTING HIRED

Insiders seem to agree: it's tough to get an offer at Fish & Richardson. Successful candidates will be "at least top 10 percent," reports one insider. In addition to scores, experience and background appear to be important. "We like ee and cs degrees in particular," (and those who don't know what those initials stand for are already in trouble). "IP practices want hard science degrees and corporate wants people with prior experience," says another insider. But credentials aren't everything. "The firm tries to look beyond grades and screen out jerks," one attorney warns. The greedy should also beware: "Because the firm pays young associates at extremely high salaries, there is a constant effort to avoid candidates who are seeking employment only for the money." As is typical in BigLaw, students and laterals face a different hurdles: "The hiring criteria for each office is different, but in terms of summer associates and first-year associates, great grades and good work experience are musts. For laterals, its all about the personality and whether they fit into our office," according to a representative insider.

OUR SURVEY SAYS

Hours can be flexible at Fish & Richardson. "There's no face time requirement," explains one insider, "I can work from home or from the train." This same attorney also notes that "the firm has a 1,900-hour requirement, which is not too onerous, and most people you ask say '1,900 is 1,900'—there's no hidden requirement to work more." (Another attorney points out, "However, the firm is simply way too busy right now for associates to honestly think that they're going to only bill 1,900 hours a year.") As for taking time off, "The firm's leave policies are very generous, but its policies for part time or flex time are nonexistent." All in all, "the firm does not enter the upper stratosphere of the larger NYC firms in terms of hours," a Big Apple associate explains. But Fish & Richardson does reach toward the stratosphere in one regard: salary. As a Boston attorney says, the firm has "matched the pay scale of the largest New York law firms." Big bonuses, however, are not taken for granted. "They have great base salaries," another attorney says, "but they really make you earn your bonus through their guaranteed, hours-based bonus system. The discretionary bonuses are pretty small." As for training opportunities at Fish & Richardson, they are apparently on the increase. "The firm seems to be focusing increasingly on better formalized training," says one attorney. Another insider explains, "We provide excellent formal patent prosecution training, and formal litigation training is improving. Enrollment in NITA courses is readily approved." One associate comments, "I have received wonderful informal training from the more senior lawyers." And how do Fish & Richardson partners treat associates? "Partners treat associates well. This comes from the top." And according to some insiders: "Fish is very good at communication and transparency. The standards may be high, but at least the associates know what the standards are." Overall, the atmosphere here is "healthy—great daily workday interactions, with some moderate socializing on the side." A midlevel provides a detailed analysis: "Many of the attorneys started their professional lives as engineers. The fundamental pragmatism of engineering balances the adversarial nature of the practice of law to make the firm culture very relaxed and pragmatic." In short: "Fun, smart, creative geeks—a good atmosphere."

Visit the Vault Law Channel, the complete online resource for law careers, featuring firm profiles, message boards, the Vault Law Job Board and more. www.vault.com/law

VAULT CAREER LIBRARY   457

Fulbright & Jaworski L.L.P.

1301 McKinney, Suite 5100
Houston, TX 77010-3095
Phone: (713) 651-5151
Fax: (713) 651-5246
www.fulbright.com

LOCATIONS

Houston, TX (HQ)

Austin, TX • Dallas, TX • Denver, CO • Los Angeles, CA •
Minneapolis, MN • New York, NY • San Antonio, TX • St.
Louis, MO • Washington, DC • Beijing • Dubai • Hong Kong
• London • Munich • Riyadh*

* Associated office

MAJOR DEPARTMENTS & PRACTICES

Bankruptcy, Reorganization & Creditor's Rights
Corporate, Banking & Business
Energy & Real Property
Environmental Law
Health Law—Federal Practice & Reimbursement
Health Law—Finance & Business Organization
Health Law—Litigation & Administration
Intellectual Property & Technology
International
Labor & Employment Law
Litigation
Public Finance & Administration
Tax, Trusts, Estates & Employee Benefits

THE STATS

No. of attorneys firmwide: 950+
No. of offices: 16
Summer associate offers firmwide: 113 out of 137 (2006)
Managing Partner: Steven B. Pfeiffer
Hiring Partner: Gerry Lowry (Firmwide)

RANKING RECAP

Best in Region
#4 - Texas

NOTABLE PERKS

• Weekly lunches
• Backup child care
• "Free parking" (LA)
• Monthly happy hours

EMPLOYMENT CONTACT

Ms. Leslie Rice
Director of Attorney Recruiting
Phone: (713) 651-5518
Fax: (713) 651-5246
E-mail: lrice@fulbright.com

BASE SALARY (2007)

Texas offices
1st year: $140,000
Summer associate: $2,700/week

Los Angeles, CA; Washington, DC
1st year: $145,000
Summer associate: $2,800/week

Minneapolis, MN
1st year: $130,000
Summer associate: $2,400/week

New York, NY
1st year: $160,000
Summer associate: $3,077/week

THE BUZZ
WHAT ATTORNEYS AT OTHER FIRMS ARE SAYING ABOUT THIS FIRM

• "Excellent litigation"
• "Behind the times"
• "Best Texas firm"
• "Recent recruiting faux pas"

© 2007 Vault Inc.

THE SCOOP

Founded by railway regulation expert R.C. Fulbright in Houston in 1919, the firm now known as Fulbright & Jaworski has expanded from its deep Texas roots and now represents major corporations worldwide. The firm specializes in corporate finance and litigation, with a lot of its clients, such as ExxonMobil, coming from the oil and gas industry. In fact, the firm maintains offices in oil-rich Riyadh and Dubai (where the firm was among the first American law firms to set up shop, in December 2005). Fulbright has also been building up its already substantial practice in the health care industry. Among other recent victories, the firm won dismissal of a class-action lawsuit against clients Baptist Health System and American Hospital Association in which the plaintiffs alleged that BHS charged unfair rates for treatment of uninsured patients. A senior Fulbright associate grabbed a few headlines in 2006 when she successfully defended the skateboard company 360Skate LLC in an important internet rights case. SkateboardDirectory.com, a web site dedicated to skateboards and skateboarding, initiated a complaint before the National Arbitration Forum, alleging among other claims that 360Skate's use of "skatedirectory" was confusingly similar to "skateboarddirectory.com' and "skateboarddirectory." Fulbright successfully contended that the plaintiff could not have exclusive rights on its alleged "service marks," as they were generic descriptors of the company's services.

GETTING HIRED

"Our firm can be a bit of a 'school snob,' but not overly so," confesses a Dallas-based associate. "Still, if you're in the middle of your class at a mid-tier law school, it's safe to say you won't be hired here. The GPA cutoff is pretty strict." A D.C. insider elaborates: "We are looking for smart people with whom we also would enjoy working ... personality matters. Good writing helps. GPA cutoffs vary by school. Georgetown, Harvard, UVA and Duke are focus schools." In Los Angeles, the firm seeks "outgoing, hardworking, intelligent, fun candidates who have a lot to offer. We recruit at UCLA, USC, Hastings, Boalt, Stanford, Loyola." Notwithstanding the locale, the L.A. office "doesn't look for the superstars ... but instead looks for what it perceives to be 'workhorses' who will stick around." And L.A. summer associates should not slack off: "The summer associate classes are very small and the summer associate program is definitely a 'working' summer, so no one's a shoo-in just because they have a summer job."

OUR SURVEY SAYS

"Compared to people at other firms, I believe my hours are very reasonable," shares an attorney in Fulbright's Washington office. "It's not a sweatshop at all," seconds an L.A. insider. "As long as your work gets done, and you're appropriately available, nobody hassles you about being in the office." A Dallas attorney can boast, "I am home for dinner nearly every night, I rarely work weekends, and if I do it's usually by choice and not for longer than a few hours." And in Houston, "The firm is also pretty flexible on face time. Some attorneys with young children are at the office from 9 to 6, and then work from home after the kids go to sleep if necessary." Considering their hours, several Fulbright attorneys feel they can't complain about compensation. An L.A. attorney sums up: "I think we are a little below market, but no big deal. I'd rather work somewhere where I'm treated well than someplace that makes me suffer for the extra money." Among the complainers, a New Yorker notes that "the bonuses are way off market ... Not worth the time needed to earn it." A Washington associate adds that non-billable work such as "pro bono work, firm committees, mandatory firm training and meetings, and employment clerkship time should count more than it does [toward bonuses]." If you're a litigator in need of training, take heart: Fulbright provides an "excellent training program for litigators that begins with weekly sessions at the home office and culminates with a 10-day intensive trial advocacy program in Houston." However, "On the transactional front, like most firms, I think [training is] a bit lacking." Another little gripe: the training "is more suited to the Texas offices than the D.C. office." Overall, Fulbright culture is "collegial," but no frat house. A Dallas insider explains: "The firm is very client-focused and sensitive to anything that might tarnish the firm's reputation. Some lawyers socialize together, and some prefer to keep their work and social lives separate." A New Yorker reports: "Very professional and collegial. Not much socialization outside of the office. A trace of southern gentility even here in the N.Y. office. No yellers that I have encountered."

Visit the Vault Law Channel, the complete online resource for law careers, featuring firm profiles, message boards, the Vault Law Job Board and more. www.vault.com/law

VAULT CAREER LIBRARY

459

Pillsbury Winthrop Shaw Pittman LLP

1540 Broadway
New York, NY 10036
Phone: (212) 858-1000

50 Fremont Street
San Francisco, CA 94105
Phone: (415) 983-1000

2300 N Street, NW
Washington, DC 20037
Phone: (202) 663-8000
www.pillsburylaw.com

LOCATIONS

Costa Mesa, CA • Houston, TX • Los Angeles, CA • McLean,
VA • New York, NY • Palo Alto, CA • Sacramento, CA • San
Diego, CA • San Diego-North Country, CA • San Francisco,
CA • Washington, DC • London • Shanghai • Tokyo

MAJOR DEPARTMENTS & PRACTICES

Aviation • Bankruptcy (Insolvency & Restructuring) • Climate
Change & Sustainability • Communications • Corporate &
Securities (including Emerging Growth & Technology, M&A,
Private Equity & VC funding) • Employment & Labor • Energy
• Environment, Land Use & Natural Resources • Estates,
Trusts & Tax Planning • Executive Compensation & Benefits •
Finance • Global Sourcing • Government Contracts & Disputes
• Health Care • Intellectual Property • International Practices
(China, Europe, India & Asia, Israel, Japan) • International
Trade • Litigation (including Antitrust, Appellate, Arbitration &
White-Collar Defense) • Nonprofit Organizations • Public Policy
& Political Law • Real Estate • Tax • Wine Beer & Spirits Law

THE STATS

No. of attorneys: 827
No. of offices: 14
Summer associate offers: 84 out of 102 (2006)
Firm Chair: James M. Rishwain Jr.
Hiring Partners:
   San Francisco: Michael J. Kass
   New York: Vipul Nishawala
   Washington, DC: Thomas C. Hill
   Los Angeles: Roger Wise
   Virginia: David Houston

THE BUZZ
WHAT ATTORNEYS AT OTHER FIRMS ARE SAYING ABOUT THIS FIRM

• "Progressive"
• "In flux"
• "Pleasant atmosphere"
• "Lacking direction"

RANKING RECAP

Best in Practice
#7 (tie) - Technology

Best in Diversity
#7 - Overall Diversity
#9 - Diversity with Respect to Women
#18 - Diversity with Respect to GLBT
#19 - Diversity with Respect to Minorities

NOTABLE PERKS

• On-site chef and cafeteria (NY, DC, LA)
• Keg in the cafeteria twice a month (Tyson's Corner)
• Public transportation subsidies and/or free parking
• Discount movie and entertainment tickets

EMPLOYMENT CONTACTS

New York, NY
Angela Eliane
Phone: (212) 858-1000
Fax: (212) 858-1500
E-mail: Recruit_NY@pillsburylaw.com

San Francisco, CA
Stephanie D. Persi
Phone: (415) 983-1320
Fax: (415) 983-1200
E-mail: Recruit_SF@pillsburylaw.com

Washington, DC
Kenia Garner
Phone: (202) 663-8144
Fax: (202) 663-8007
E-mail: Recruit_DC@pillsburylaw.com

Los Angeles, CA
Melissa L. Eurtron
Phone: (213) 488-7592
Fax: (213) 629-1033
E-mail: Recruit_LA@pillsburylaw.com

BASE SALARY (2007)

New York, DC, Virginia and California offices
1st year: $160,000
Summer associate: $2,788/week (CA), $3,076/week (NY)

© 2007 Vault Inc.

THE SCOOP

Two years after its last merger, national law firm Pillsbury Winthrop Shaw Pittman is still finding its footing. The 2005 integration created one of the nation's larger firms, a 900 lawyer enterprise with practices bridging the spectrum, real estate to IP, life sciences to telecom, corporate to regulatory. In January 2006, after seven years at the firm's helm, visionary Chair Mary Cranston announced that she would not seek re-election. Cranston was the first female chair of a megafirm, and the mastermind behind the 2001 and 2005 mergers, the latter of which added $200 million to the bottom line, bumping total revenue to $600 million. Pillsbury consequently reworked its management team, electing real estate partner James Rishwain as its new chair. In 2006, Pillsbury scored big in its representation of a communications company, which spent $600 million on a carve-out acquisition of Intel's chip unit. The firm also stepped up for private equity owners of PETCO, in their $1.8 billion bid to go private; and the firm's New York office led Varig Airlines, one of the largest airlines in Latin America, through the first-ever bankruptcy filed in Brazil. Pillsbury convinced the airline's creditors to approve a restructuring plan that included a $24 million sale. Also in 2006, the firm's litigators successfully defended Sinclair Broadcast group in litigation filed by cable company Mediacom, which asserted that Sinclair violated antitrust laws by linking major and minor network stations together. The past year has seen no shortage of honors for Pillsbury. Chambers USA ranked 34 of Pillsbury's practices and 64 of its lawyers as the best in their field. In further acknowledgement of its practices, the 2007 *Corporate Counsel* survey featured 10 Fortune 500 companies that named Pillsbury a "Go-To Firm" in the areas of corporate transactions, litigation, IP litigation, IP patent counseling, and labor and employment. *Working Mother* and *Minority Law Journal* ranked Pillsbury as one of the "Best Companies for Families" and among the top-20 firms for diversity, respectively. And finally, *American Lawyer* magazine's Summer Associate Survey ranked Pillsbury 10th in satisfaction.

GETTING HIRED

A Pillsbury associate says that the firm "usually has a 3.3 cutoff, but it can be less for candidates outstanding in other areas." As a San Francisco technology expert puts it, "With mid-range associates in such short supply, [there] is less law school snobbery." A junior litigator adds, "Not as cutthroat competitive as it was nine years ago, but VERY hard. You better be bright and energetic. Prior work experience before law school helps." Pillsbury associates also report that the firm genuinely emphasizes personality and fit. A New York associate says, "Candidate needs to be more than just a good student—the firm looks for energetic team players, with friendly dispositions." A junior litigator advises, "While the firm looks for top-quality law students from the top-20 law schools, it is not grade-focused. Personality is most important." So, what personality characteristics are favored? A senior San Francisco attorney suggests a couple that *aren't*: "Obnoxious jerks and total wallflowers won't get hired."

OUR SURVEY SAYS

As one fairly typically satisfied Pillsbury associate reports, "I love the work I do. I just do more of it than I would like." A first-year litigator says, "I love my job—from a high-profile pro-bono case to a case on national security in the same day. I've even appeared in court already. I'm very fortunate to be here." A number of somewhat more ambivalent associates sound a bit more like this midlevel: "If I have to be at a firm," she says, "this isn't a bad place to be." Associates call their firm "collegial" and "friendly," but not particularly social. A junior San Franciscan reports, "There are few young unmarried attorneys, many fewer than New York. It is less likely that attorneys will socialize together here." A midlevel associate says, "People are polite and respectful of one another, but not especially personal." On the other hand, a Washington associate says "Within my practice group it is very much like a family." The firm scores unusually high grades for its formal training offerings. "The firm has an excellent loaner program to the San Francisco public defender's office and the Alameda County D.A.'s office," says a senior associate. "These are great training for litigation and are actively supported by the firm. Lawyers get to try criminal cases at their full firm salaries." A New York insider adds, "First-year training is extensive. Training opportunities for all other associates abound … The variety and breadth of the training programs [are] great."

Visit the Vault Law Channel, the complete online resource for law careers, featuring firm profiles, message boards, the Vault Law Job Board and more. **www.vault.com/law**

VAULT CAREER LIBRARY   461

59

PRESTIGE RANKING

Goodwin Procter LLP

Exchange Place
53 State Street
Boston, MA 02109
Phone: (617) 570-1000
www.goodwinprocter.com

LOCATIONS

Boston, MA (HQ)
Los Angeles, CA (Downtown LA)
Los Angeles, CA (Century City)
New York, NY
Palo Alto, CA
San Diego, CA
San Francisco, CA
Washington, DC

MAJOR DEPARTMENTS & PRACTICES

Corporate
Energy
Financial Services
Intellectual Property
Litigation
Private Equity
Products Liability & Mass Torts
Real Estate
REITs & Real Estate Capital Markets
Tech Companies & Life Sciences

THE STATS

No. of attorneys: 750
No. of offices: 7
Summer associate offers: 43 out of 43 (2006)
Chairman & Managing Partner: Regina M. Pisa
Hiring Partner: Michael J. Kendall

THE BUZZ
WHAT ATTORNEYS AT OTHER FIRMS ARE SAYING ABOUT THIS FIRM

- "Great Boston firm"
- "Dull culture"
- "Excellent quality of life"
- "Growing too fast"

RANKING RECAP

Best in Region
#4 - Boston

Partner Prestige Rankings
#4 (tie) - Real Estate

NOTABLE PERKS

- "The best suite in the Banknorth Garden"
- A biannual ski or beach outing
- Pizza and beer every other Friday
- A "really nice gym" in the building in DC

EMPLOYMENT CONTACTS

Boston/West Coast offices
Ms. Maureen Shea
Director of Legal Recruitment
Phone: (617) 570-1288
E-mail: mshea@goodwinprocter.com

New York
Ms. Susan Rose
Legal Recruitment Manager
Phone: (212) 813-8800
E-mail: srose@goodwinprocter.com

Washington
Ms. Cindy Jahr Evans
Legal Recruitment Manager
Phone: (202) 346-4171
E-mail: cevans@goodwinprocter.com

BASE SALARY (2007)

All offices:
1st year: $160,000
2nd year: $170,000
3rd year: $185,000
4th year: $210,000
5th year: $230,000
6th year: $250,000
7th year: $265,000
8th year: $280,000
Summer associate: $3,077/week

© 2007 Vault Inc.

THE SCOOP

Based in Boston, Goodwin Procter is more than a Beantown firm. The firm was founded in Boston in 1912. It now has approximately 750 lawyers in seven offices around the country. The firm's West Coast presence is a fairly recent development—its Los Angeles and San Francisco offices were both opened in 2006, with a second L.A. office and a San Diego office opening in 2007. Goodwin Procter handles litigation, intellectual property, real estate, products liability, technology and corporate matters. The corporate practice, in fact, is the firm's largest. The firm is keeping with its Boston roots and helping to clean up (figuratively) one of the city's biggest messes. In March 2007, Massachusetts Attorney General Martha Coakley named Goodwin Procter Partner Paul F. Ware Jr. to head the probe into a recent accident at the Big Dig, a massive public works project designed to move Interstate 93 underground. The project was plagued by cost overruns, delays and scandal before its completion in January 2006. A ceiling collapse in September 2006 killed a motorist; Ware, chair of the firm's litigation department, is tasked with investigating contractors to determine if any laws were broken. The firm's other recent engagements include the dismissal of a class-action lawsuit filed by shareholders in Arbinet-thexchange, Inc. in February 2007, and advising Locus Pharmaceuticals in raising $30 million in venture capital that same month. Goodwin Procter also assisted internet TV company Brightcove on $59.5 million in venture capital financing in January 2007.

GETTING HIRED

Insiders report a selective hiring process at Goodwin Procter. "Top quarter of class is strongly preferred," reports one associate, "and several rounds of interviews are necessary to receive an offer." Recruits should possess the right mix of attributes: "The firm is looking for smart associates that are also social and have a go-getter personality without being stuck-up. It's not an easy combination, and I have seen a lot of very smart and successful associates and summer candidates not get offers because they did not have the type of personality that would mesh here." Another attorney puts things more simply: "The firm prefers individuals with actual personalities." One Goodwin Procter source reports possible regional differences in selectivity. "Boston is very competitive, but I have heard NYC is less selective," says this Boston associate. A Washington-based attorney says, "There is no GPA cutoff that I am aware of, but the D.C. office concentrates on the top schools and top of the class from local schools." Finally, laterals can take heart: "I came in as a lateral," reports a Boston insider, "and it was relatively easy." In a 2007 survey conducted by the legal recruitment firm Major, Lindsay and Africa, which sought to identify which large national law firms met expectations and satisfied their lateral partners the most, Goodwin Procter placed second.

OUR SURVEY SAYS

At Goodwin Procter, "[h]ours can be long at times, but they are better than most firms of comparable size," according to an attorney in the Washington office. A Boston attorney confesses, "I don't think [the hours are] atypical of other large law firms ... though I had to make a bed under my desk one weekend!" On the bright side: "The firm is more and more flexible with accommodating associates as they begin to build families. A number of female associates work four days a week in the office and one day from home." Additionally: "Pro bono counts toward billable hours, which means associates can do pro bono work without worrying about making up lost time. Also, the firm is very good about associates' vacations." And how well are associates compensated for all the hours they work? "Wow, I can't believe how much they pay me," exclaims a corporate associate. Others are less easily impressed. "They claim to be market leaders ... but they still have not yet matched Ropes salaries in senior ranges," notes a vigilant first-year. Also, "The firm does not disclose to associates the amount of bonuses granted and on what basis." The firm's formal training offerings have been called "excellent." "We have so much training that it is ridiculous at times," says a first-year, "though I am very thankful for it." A litigator expands: "The firm has a deposition training series for first- and second-year associates, and trial training for fourth-years. The firm goes to great expense and effort, but I found that the deposition training suffered from the same problems of any simulated program." And a corporate associate notes, "Formal training pretty much stops after the fourth year," adding, "This is kind of a silly question. Anything worth learning in corporate finance is learned on deals."

Visit the Vault Law Channel, the complete online resource for law careers, featuring firm profiles, message boards, the Vault Law Job Board and more. **www.vault.com/law**

VAULT CAREER LIBRARY   **463**

Cooley Godward Kronish LLP

60
PRESTIGE
RANKING

Five Palo Alto Square
3000 El Camino Real
Palo Alto, CA 94306-2155
Phone: (650) 843-5000
Fax: (650) 857-0663
www.cooley.com

LOCATIONS

Palo Alto, CA (HQ)
Broomfield, CO
New York, NY
Reston, VA
San Diego, CA
San Francisco, CA
Washington, DC

MAJOR DEPARTMENTS & PRACTICES

Corporate Law
Information Technology
Intellectual Property Litigation & Prosecution
International
Investments
Life Sciences
Litigation
Mergers & Acquisitions
Securities
Technology
Venture Capital/Private Equity

THE STATS

No. of attorneys firmwide: 570
No. of offices: 7
Summer associate offers firmwide: 46 out of 50 (2006):
Managing Partner: Stephen C. Neal
Hiring Partner: Matthew B. Hemington

RANKING RECAP

Best in Practice
#3 - Technology

Quality of Life
#9 - Formal Training

NOTABLE PERKS

- Gym reimbursement
- Free fountain soda (Reston)
- Wednesday "all attorney" lunches (San Francisco)
- Free backup child care (Palo Alto, San Francisco, Reston, Washington DC, San Diego)

EMPLOYMENT CONTACT

Jo Anne Larson
Phone: (650) 843-5000
Fax: (650) 849-7400
E mail: larsonja@cooley.com

BASE SALARY (2007)

1st year: $160,000
2nd year: $170,000
3rd year: $185,000
4th year: $210,000
5th year: $230,000
6th year: $250,000
7th year: $265,000
8th year: $280,000
Summer associate: $3,077/week

THE BUZZ
WHAT ATTORNEYS AT OTHER FIRMS ARE SAYING ABOUT THIS FIRM

- "Great reputation on the West Coast"
- "Also ran"
- "Killer IP"
- "Seems in flux"

© 2007 Vault Inc.

THE SCOOP

For Silicon Valley's Cooley Godward, it wasn't enough to be "the iconic firm of the dot-com boom" (in the words of *The New York Law Journal*). In October 2006, the 425-attorney technology leader finally attained the broader recognition it wanted in a merger with 110-attorney Manhattan bankruptcy, tax and commercial/white collar litigation firm of Kronish Lieb Weiner & Hellman. The newly merged firm—now known as Cooley Godward Kronish LLP—will officially maintain its headquarters at the firm's largest office, in Palo Alto. Although Cooley was much larger than Kronish, the two share common ground in the converging areas of technology, finance and high-stakes litigation. With the merger, Cooley gained its long-sought-after substantial New York presence; Kronish gained the reputation of one of the leading, iconic firms of the dot-com era. Indeed, for the New York office, the deal means an instant eminence in all of the emerging technology capitals of the United States, including Palo Alto and San Francisco. And as one of the top firms of the original internet boom, Cooley oversaw more than 200 IPOs in the 1990s, raising more than $25 billion. In recent years, Cooley has represented just under one-third of the companies on the Nasdaq Biotechnology and BioCentury 100 Indices, as well as more than one-half of those on the AMEX Biotech Index. The firm's current client list includes such IT bigwigs as Bluetooth, Adobe, Nvidia, Monolithic Power Systems and a frisky little startup you may have heard by the name of eBay.

GETTING HIRED

"Cooley is big on interviewing and fit," according to insiders. Highly credentialed applicants should not count on getting an offer from the firm, unless their personalities mesh with Cooley's "relaxed, respectful and friendly culture." As one source in the San Francisco office explains, "I don't think Cooley is a place where you can walk into an interview and coast on your experience or resume—you need to be very likeable as well." Likeability is only the final test an applicant has to pass to earn an offer from Cooley. To get invited for an interview in the first place, a candidate's credentials must pass muster. Graduates from less than stellar institutions should be the cream of the crop— "top 10 percent is the cutoff," according to an insider. One attorney insists that candidates from outside the top-20 schools should be among "the top-10 or so students in the class (top-10 students, not top 10 percent)."

OUR SURVEY SAYS

"The firm culture is incredible," says an attorney in Cooley's Northern Virginia office. "Partners thank associates for their hard work and encourage taking vacation. This firm is a breath of fresh air after working at a sweatshop." Although there are dissenters who insist "Cooley Culture" is "a thing of the past," one San Franciscan maintains that Cooley is "probably as collaborative and friendly as a law firm can get. There are no 'gunners' here." As far as hours are concerned, "the seeming minimal hourly billing requirements" are only part of the story. "The reality on the ground is there is a lot of pressure to bill far more [than the stated minimum]," says an insider. But others disagree: "As an associate I do not feel obligated or pressured to bill in significant excess of the firm's stated billable minimum in order to receive a bonus." There is some consensus on the firm's approach to face time. "There is no real 'face time' required and one can work from home if needed." Also, the "firm has generous flex-time and part-time work schedules." A working mother in the San Diego office elaborates: "I work on an hourly basis due to my two small children and the firm is very accommodating of my home life and is a wonderful place to work for someone who wants to have a legal career and still spend a lot of time with family." Newcomers to Cooley are treated to "Cooley College," "an excellent weeklong training program," according to a San Francisco associate. A Silicon Valley colleague calls Cooley College "useful" but "way too front loaded. It becomes information overload. By the end of the week, everyone was begging for it to be over." After Cooley College, attorneys get regular training offerings, which at least one finds "somewhat lacking." Associates at Cooley "are well paid and salaries were just raised," asserts an insider. And "the bonuses are very generous," some agree. All and all it's "on par with California firms" but there is a dark cloud in this silver lining. "I'm not sure I'd be comfortable being paid any more than I currently am because it would make it really hard to push back on requests to do more at work" worries a corporate associate.

Visit the Vault Law Channel, the complete online resource for law careers, featuring firm profiles, message boards, the Vault Law Job Board and more. www.vault.com/law

VAULT CAREER LIBRARY   465

Alston & Bird LLP

One Atlantic Center
1201 West Peachtree Street
Atlanta, GA 30309-3424
Phone: (404) 881-7000
Fax: (404) 881-7777
www.alston.com

LOCATIONS

Atlanta, GA • Charlotte, NC • New York, NY • Raleigh, NC
• Washington, DC

MAJOR DEPARTMENTS & PRACTICES

Antitrust • Bankruptcy, Workouts & Reorganization •
Corporate Governance & Compliance • Construction &
Government Contracts • Debt Finance & Products •
Employee Benefits & Executive Compensation • Energy •
Environmental & Land Use • Entertainment & New Media •
ERISA Litigation • Exempt Organizations • Financial Services
& Products • Health Care • Intellectual Property (Litigation,
Patents/Biotechnology, Patents/Chemical & Pharmaceutical,
Patents/Electronics & Computer Technology,
Patents/Mechanical, Trademarks & Copyrights,
Transactional) • International Litigation • International Trade
& Regulatory • Labor & Employment • Legislative & Public
Policy • Life Sciences • Mergers & Acquisitions • Products
Liability • Public Finance • Real Estate • Securities •
Securities Litigation • Tax - Federal Income • Tax—
International • Tax—State & Local • Technology •
Telecommunications • Trial & Appellate • Wealth Planning •
White Collar Crime

THE STATS

No. of attorneys: 736
No. of offices: 5
Summer associate offers firmwide: 112 out of 115 (2006)
Managing Partner: Ben F. Johnson III
Hiring Partner: Jonathan W. Lowe

THE BUZZ
WHAT ATTORNEYS AT OTHER FIRMS ARE SAYING ABOUT THIS FIRM

• "BigLaw South"
• "Nice place to work but wouldn't want to live there"
• "Fantastic perks"
• "Stodgy"

RANKING RECAP

Best in Region
#2 - Atlanta

Best in Diversity
#16 - Diversity with Respect to GLBT

NOTABLE PERKS

• Subsidized dining room with "really good food" (Atlanta only)
• Friday bar
• Near-site day care (Atlanta only)
• Infertility benefit up to $25,000

EMPLOYMENT CONTACT

Ms. Emily Leeson
Director of Attorney Hiring & Development
Phone: (404) 881-7014
Fax: (404) 253-8334
E-mail: emily.leeson@alston.com

BASE SALARY (2007)

Atlanta, GA
1st year: $130,000
Summer associate: $2,500/week

Charlotte, NC
1st year: $145,000
Summer associate: $2,750/week

New York, NY
1st year: $160,000
Summer associate: $3,075/week

Raleigh, NC
1st year: $145,000
Summer associate: $2,750/week

Washington, DC
1st year: $145,000
Summer associate: $2,800/week

© 2007 Vault Inc.

THE SCOOP

Alston & Bird has added some big political names to its roster in recent years. Former Senate Democratic Leader Thomas Daschle joined the firm in 2005. Daschle—not an attorney—serves as a policy advisor to the firm. He joins former Senator Robert J. Dole and Thomas A. Scully, former administrator for Centers for Medicare & Medicaid Services, among the firm's political heavyweights. Health care and government aren't the firm's only expanding practice areas. J. Bradford Anwyll, a prominent tax litigator, is a recent addition to the firm's already substantial tax practice in Washington, D.C. With close to 740 attorneys, Atlanta-based Alston & Bird now ranks as the 40th-largest law firm in the United States, according to *The National Law Journal*. The firm counts as clients such business giants as UPS, CNN, Delta Air Lines, Goldman, Sachs & Co., NASCAR and the University of North Carolina at Charlotte. In 2006 Alston & Bird was named a "Best Place to Work in Greater Washington, D.C." by the *Washington Business Journal*. The firm had 118 lawyers named in *The Best Lawyers in America* 2007 edition. *The National Law Journal* listed the firm as having won the largest verdict in the U.S. in 2006—an $850 million verdict in a complex fraudulent transfer suit. The firm itself was ranked the 13th most active legal advisor (based on number of deals handled) by the M&A publication *MergerWatch*.

GETTING HIRED

The degree of difficulty for getting hired at Alston & Bird "depends on the practice group," according to an insider. Says another attorney, "Everyone has great grades and comes from great schools. We really try to recruit people we are going to want to be around." What is such a person like? "Personable but not cocky. Very intelligent on paper and in person. Communicate in a very relaxed and engaging way." A member of the hiring committee elaborates: "Although grades are important we look for well-rounded people that can show some life experiences aside from just getting into a good college and law school." But be warned: the name of your law school does matter. In fact, "with the current hiring partner, where you go to law school makes a *huge* difference," cautions one insider. "The firm is looking for superstars with an Atlanta connection and impeccable credentials." Another Alston attorney agrees, adding, "They are kind of tough on where you went to law school—luckily I went to Emory, but I heard that they were rough on others who interviewed for this position that went to lower-ranked schools." One Atlanta attorney summarizes: "Not easy, but not impossible. Looking to hire law journal, moot court, 3.5+ unless you are talking about a top-10 law school. Firm also seems to heavily recruit from UVA, Vanderbilt, Emory, UNC and to some extent, UGA."

OUR SURVEY SAYS

In general, Alston & Bird attorneys rave about their firm's culture: "The firm's culture is excellent. Associates often socialize and some of the partners socialize with the associates, as well. Partners are very willing to mentor and help associates and I have found the firm to be very open and above board about their policies," says one Atlanta insider. An associate in D.C. echoes these sentiments: "Very friendly, open and welcoming culture. Associates are treated as equals with partners and feel valued." On the other hand, some associates see some negative trends, "Because of the exponential growth, due to the hiring of many lateral partners and associates in the past few years, the culture has considerably changed and not for the better. Colder. Somewhat more cutthroat, but still not as bad as some of the sweatshop firms." Whether attorneys socialize after work depends on whom you ask. "Our firm culture is great at the office," says an Atlanta associate. "However, not many attorneys tend to socialize outside of the office together." A Charlotte-based lawyer reports, "Some attorneys socialize and others do not, but there does not appear to be any negative impact associated with belonging to either category." By contrast, a New York attorney calls Alston "a very social firm." Most attorneys at Alston & Bird seem relatively satisfied with their hours. This assessment comes from the New York office: "Dissatisfaction is not with the firm per se, but with the profession in general, which demands long hours." Adds an Atlanta-based associate, "The hours are reflective of the big law firm practice. They are what they are." With regard to flex-time, an attorney in the labor and employment division reports, happily, "My group is terrific about flex-time and telecommuting—really supportive of alternative work schedules."

Visit the Vault Law Channel, the complete online resource for law careers, featuring firm profiles, message boards, the Vault Law Job Board and more. www.vault.com/law

VAULT CAREER LIBRARY

467

62

Heller Ehrman LLP

Although Heller Ehrman is a global firm without any one particular office serving as headquarters, for ease of communications, correspondence can be sent to:

333 Bush Street
San Francisco, CA 94104-2878
Phone: (415) 772-6000
Fax: (415) 772-6268
www.hellerehrman.com

LOCATIONS

Anchorage, AK • Los Angeles, CA • Madison, WI • New York, NY • San Diego, CA • San Francisco, CA • Silicon Valley, CA • Seattle, WA • Washington, DC • Beijing • Hong Kong • London • Singapore

MAJOR DEPARTMENTS & PRACTICES

Antitrust & Trade Regulation • Appeals & Strategy • Asia Capital Markets • Compensation & Benefits • Consumer Litigation • Corporate Governance • Corporate Securities • Debt Finance • Energy • Energy & Clean Technologies • Environmental Litigation & Counseling • FDA • Hospitality • Information Technology • Insurance Recovery • Intellectual Property Litigation • Intellectual Property Transactions • International • International Arbitration & ADR • Labor & Employment • Life Sciences • Mergers & Acquisitions • Patents & Trademarks • Private Equity & Fund Formation • Product Liability • Project Finance • Real Estate & Finance • Restructuring & Insolvency • Securities Litigation • Structured Finance • Tax • Venture Law Group/Emerging Companies • Wealth Management • White Collar Criminal Defense

THE STATS

No. of attorneys firmwide: Approximately 700
No. of offices: 13
Summer associate offers firmwide: 76 out of 78 (2006)
Chairman: Matthew L. Larrabee
Director of Attorney Recruiting: Michael R. Gotham

THE BUZZ
WHAT ATTORNEYS AT OTHER FIRMS ARE SAYING ABOUT THIS FIRM

- "Progressive, liberal firm"
- "Wants to be harder-core than it is"
- "Brainy Bay-area kids"
- "Overly 'wacky'"

RANKING RECAP

Best in Region
#1 - Pacific Northwest
#9 - Northern California

NOTABLE PERKS

- "Totally free public transportation"
- "Very liberal parental leave policy"
- Regular associate/partner lunches

EMPLOYMENT CONTACT

Mr. Michael R. Gotham
Director of Attorney Recruiting
Phone: (415) 772-6003
Fax: (415) 772-6268
E-mail: michael.gotham@hellerehrman.com

BASE SALARY (2007)

Los Angeles, CA; Madison, WI; New York, NY; San Diego, CA; San Francisco, CA; Silicon Valley, CA; Washington, DC
1st year: $160,000
2nd year: $170,000
3rd year: $185,000
4th year: $210,000
5th year: $230,000
6th year: $250,000
7th year: $265,000

Seattle, WA
1st year: $145,000
2nd year: $150,000
3rd year: $160,000
4th year: $180,000
5th year: $190,000
6th year: $210,000
7th year: $225,000

© 2007 Vault Inc.

THE SCOOP

Founded in 1890, Heller Ehrman now maintains 13 offices that span both the United States and the globe. The firm's domestic offices stretch from Alaska to New York. In early 2007, the firm opened a London office, marking its entrance into the European market. Additionally, the firm maintains offices in three of the largest financial capitals of Asia—Beijing, Hong Kong and Singapore. With approximately 700 attorneys, Heller Ehrman ranks among the nation's top-50 law firms. Heller Ehrman may be best known for its litigation practice and its work with technology and science-related companies. Among Heller's bigger clients are QUALCOMM, Yahoo! Inc., Fairmont Hotels & Resorts, Pacific Gas & Electric, Sony Electronics, Washington Mutual, Microsoft, Genentech, and VISA U.S.A. The firm's trophy case overfloweth, considering the impressive roster of awards it has won over the last few years. From *The American Lawyer*: No. 5 on the 2006 "A-List" of U.S. firms, top five for intellectual property litigation and ninth overall for pro bono work. That same year, *The National Law Journal* also recognized Heller as one of four firms nationally to receive its Pro Bono Award. Heller snagged nods for diversity both from The Human Rights Campaign ("Best Places to Work for GLBT Equality") and *Multicultural Law Magazine* ("Top 100 Law Firms for Diversity"). And then there are the corporate rankings to consider: Fourteenth in U.S. M&A transactions for the first quarter of 2007 (Thomson Financial), and sixth as issuer legal advisor for global IPOs by U.S. issuers in 2006 by the same. Plus top-10 finishes in rankings published by Venture Capital Analyst/Dow Jones VentureOne, PrivateRaise.com and IPO Vital Signs.

GETTING HIRED

"We want people who are open-minded, fun, intelligent and good sports," reports a Heller Ehrman insider. Another says the "firm looks for [the] candidate who doesn't take [him or her] self too seriously, is friendly, not overbearing, verbally intelligent." The firm "is particularly interested in candidates that fit well into the particular practice groups based on interest and experience." Credentials are important at Heller Ehrman. One brutally frank associate says, "If you aren't from an excellent school, the chances of getting in are slim. Harvard, Boalt, Stanford, USC, Georgetown, GW, UCLA are where most everyone is from. We do seem to take one of the top students from the best school at each office location, though, e.g., University of San Diego, UC Hastings, etc." And Texans take heart: the "firm recently expanded recruiting to UT-Austin." As for GPA cutoffs, they seem to follow a predictable sliding scale: "The GPA cutoffs are inversely proportional to the law school's ranking. The higher ranked the school, the lower the cutoff, and vice versa."

OUR SURVEY SAYS

"About 70 percent [of] the time, the hours are completely manageable," says a Heller Ehrman associate in the Washington office. "The rest of the time, things just have to get done and there is too much to do, so the days are very long and the weekends nonexistent." A San Francisco source says there is "more work than average for San Francisco, but ... about a third of time is done remotely. Mandatory face time is nonexistent." An L.A. attorney adds, "I really like that I can work from home or from anywhere I choose. Also, I am very rarely asked to work on the weekends or over holidays." And reporting from the Seattle office, an insider notes, "there's definitely weekend and evening work expected, but with a recognition and appreciation that it is a sacrifice of your personal and family time." Formal training is "comprehensive in the first few years," according to one Heller contact. Another agrees, "Heller's intake training is excellent," but adds that "The firm needs to develop ... ongoing training and integration of new associates." Another source warns "The firm has a good first-year training program in certain practice groups, such as litigation," but training is "nonexistent in others (mostly correlates with practice group size)." As for the Heller Ehrman culture, "the firm is extremely laid-back," according to a Washington-based attorney. "People socialize together but they tend to do so in small groups—not in large, forced outings." A San Franciscan says the firm vibe is "collegial, although lawyers do not tend to do much socializing after work hours (although more at the junior levels)." Another San Francisco associate says, "Lawyers are friendly and noncompetitive with one another, at least outwardly. Lawyers are not frat-boyish, but rather intellectual and sometimes nerdy. A lot of self-deprecation and ironic humor."

Visit the Vault Law Channel, the complete online resource for law careers, featuring firm profiles, message boards, the Vault Law Job Board and more. www.vault.com/law

VAULT CAREER LIBRARY   469

63

PRESTIGE RANKING

Vinson & Elkins, L.L.P.

1001 Fannin Street, Suite 2300
Houston, TX 77002-6760
Phone: (800) 833-1594
Fax: (713) 615-5245
www.velaw.com

LOCATIONS

Houston, TX (HQ)
Austin, TX
Dallas, TX
New York, NY
Washington, DC
Beijing
Dubai
Hong Kong
London
Moscow
Shanghai
Tokyo

MAJOR DEPARTMENTS & PRACTICES

Capital Markets
Energy
Environmental
Insolvency & Reorganization
Intellectual Property
International
Litigation
Public Finance
Securities
Tax & Employment Benefits
Transactional

THE STATS

No. of attorneys firmwide: 700+
No. of offices: 12
Summer associate offers firmwide: 92 out of 99 (2006)
Managing Partner: Joseph C. Dilg
Hiring Partner: Thomas S. Leatherbury

THE BUZZ
WHAT ATTORNEYS AT OTHER FIRMS ARE SAYING ABOUT THIS FIRM

- "Tough litigation competitors"
- "Still recovering"
- "Actively seeking diversity"
- "Big Oil"

RANKING RECAP

Best in Region
#3 - Texas

Quality of Life
#17 - Office Space

NOTABLE PERKS

- Free health club
- Free parking
- In-house, subsidized Starbucks

EMPLOYMENT CONTACT

Ms. Patty Harris
Director of Attorney Employment & Development
Phone: (713) 758-4544
Fax: (713) 615-5245
E-mail: pharris@velaw.com

BASE SALARY (2007)

Houston, TX
1st year: $135,000
Summer associate: $2,700/week

© 2007 Vault Inc.

THE SCOOP

Founded in Houston in 1917, Vinson & Elkins grew up during the "wildcatter" era of pre-World War II Texas. (For those not from Texas, a "wildcatter" is "a person who drills oil wells in areas that are not in advance known to be oil fields.") Though the firm still prides itself on its old-time oil roots, V&E has developed into a large, diverse general practice firm. On top of that, it's also apparently a great place to work. In 2006, for the second consecutive year, V&E's Houston headquarters was named the second-best large company in the *Houston Business Journal*'s survey rankings of the city's Best Places to Work. A couple of the firm's success stories from 2006 illustrate the types of cases and transactions potential V&E associates can expect to handle. In December, a team from the firm's international trade group won a decision before the U.S. International Trade Commission. In a "sunset review" of antidumping and other orders on "cut-to-length carbon steel" (CTL), the ITC voted to revoke all such orders. The decision allows CTL to be imported duty-free from a host of foreign countries. V&E represented Mexico and Brazil, and served as lead counsel for the petitioners. In November, the firm advised the North Sea-centered energy company Endeavour International in its $400 million acquisition of Talisman Expro Limited. Endeavour acquired interests in eight oil and gas fields in the Central North Sea section of the U.K. Continental Shelf. There's no doubt Vinson & Elkins is big in Texas—on the Texas tables for Chambers USA's 2007 guide to *America's Leading Lawyers for Business*, V&E received top rankings in 15 practice areas, more than any other firm listed in the state. But the firm also did well nationally, earning high honors in 12 practice areas and top rankings in two of its specialties: Energy: Oil & Gas and Transportation: Energy. *The American Lawyer*'s Corporate Scorecard reminds us that Vinson & Elkins is also quite good on the corporate end, having handled the most IPOs of any firm in the nation for two years running, as well as the largest IPO of 2005.

GETTING HIRED

A V&E insider reports, "There are specific GPA cutoffs for each school. The higher-ranked the school, the lower the GPA cutoff will be. The firm concentrates heavily on hiring from the Ivies, UT and UVA, although they do recruit at top-20 schools and local schools. Personality, however, is a strong factor in the interview." One Texan believes Vinson & Elkins is "the most competitive [law firm] in the region. To find more competitive law firms, you have to go to the East and West Coasts, and even then, there are few firms more competitive." The firm is attracted to Ivy, up to a point: "If you come from an elite school (like Harvard, Yale, etc.), it can help but by no means guarantee an offer." And in true Texas style, the firm is also fond of extroverts: "In addition to high grades, clerkships, and the like, the firm seems to attract outgoing individuals with strong leadership credentials." Vinson & Elkins is also drawn to "very smart, well-rounded attorneys who are excited to work for V&E in the respective city."

OUR SURVEY SAYS

"A bit of Texas chivalry is a nice influence on even the non-Texas offices," reports a D.C. associate. "The atmosphere is very collegial, but not chummy," observes another. There is no overwhelming pressure to socialize: "Lawyers that actually want to socialize with one another do so, but there are no ramifications—professionally or socially—for a lawyer that would rather head home for dinner with his spouse or a walk with the dog." In keeping with its locale, the firm tends toward red, but being blue won't hurt you: "Politically, the firm leans right, but even in Texas we have partners who are active in Democratic politics." Office clowns and wiseacres be warned: "The partners frown upon anything that might suggest that you are not a 'serious lawyer.' I make sure that, when I walk down the hall, I have a very serious look on my face. It's silly." At Vinson & Elkins, "The hours are sometimes intense but not over the top." An insider explains, "I have never found the need for any face time at the office. People here care that you get your work done and it is done very well, not where you did it." Also, "The firm has been supportive of taking vacations." Some of the happiest V&E associates are in the New York office: "The New York office is the best of all worlds. Texas culture and hours with New York pay. Most law students just haven't figured that out yet. But laterals coming from Cravath, Skadden and S&C *totally* get it." Also, "The firm has an excellent training program." However: "Firm training falls off significantly after the second year. I joined the firm in the middle of my second year and was not included in the majority of the training that may have been helpful to help me get to know the firm."

Visit the Vault Law Channel, the complete online resource for law careers, featuring firm profiles, message boards, the Vault Law Job Board and more. www.vault.com/law

VAULT CAREER LIBRARY   471

Bingham McCutchen LLP

150 Federal Street
Boston, MA 02110
Phone: (617) 951-8000
Fax: (617) 951-8736
www.bingham.com

LOCATIONS

Boston, MA
Hartford, CT
Los Angeles, CA
New York, NY
Orange County, CA
San Francisco, CA
Santa Monica, CA
Silicon Valley, CA
Walnut Creek, CA
Washington, DC
Hong Kong
London
Tokyo

MAJOR DEPARTMENTS & PRACTICES

Corporate
Financial Institutions
Litigation
Securities

THE STATS

No. of attorneys firmwide: 973
No. of offices: 13
Summer associate offers: 60 out of 60 (2006)
Managing Partner: Jay Zimmerman
National Hiring Partner: Mary Gail Gearns

RANKING RECAP

Best in Region
#5 - Boston

NOTABLE PERKS

- Backup emergency child care
- Generous maternity/paternity leave
- "Wellness programs" and gym membership subsidies
- Tickets to Major League baseball games (Red Sox, Yankees, Giants, Nationals)

EMPLOYMENT CONTACT

Fiona Trevelyan
National Director of Legal Recruiting
Phone: (617) 951-8556
Fax: (617) 951-8736
E-mail: legalrecruit@bingham.com

BASE SALARY (2007)

Boston, MA
1st year: $160,000
2nd year: $170,000
3rd year: $185,000
4th year: $210,000
5th year: $230,000
6th year: $250,000
Summer associate: $3,100/week

THE BUZZ
WHAT ATTORNEYS AT OTHER FIRMS ARE SAYING ABOUT THIS FIRM

- "Balance, quality"
- "Lack of real presence in certain markets"
- "Progressive, cutting edge"
- "Too big, too quickly"

© 2007 Vault Inc.

THE SCOOP

Over the last decade, Boston-based Bingham McCutchen has resembled Pac-Man, running around and gobbling up all the little firms in its path. Since 1995, Bingham McCutchen has grown by nearly 500 percent to more than 950 attorneys by merging with a wide range of firms throughout the United States as well as in Japan and the U.K. The firm's two most recent mergers took place in January 2007, when Bingham McCutchen joined forces with Sakai & Mimura, a 22-lawyer Tokyo-based firm specializing in financial restructuring and mergers and acquisitions, and on May 1, 2007, when Bingham combined with Alschuler Grossman, a high-stakes litigation firm in Los Angeles. The firm has also led the legal trend of branching off into other industries, establishing subsidiary businesses, running three such companies: Bingham Consulting Group (business/government relations strategies), Bingham Sports Consulting ("services to identify growth opportunities and maximize franchise performance"), and Bingham Strategic Advisors (advice on mergers and acquisitions, joint ventures and business restructurings). The firm's rapid growth notwithstanding, it's still reputed to be a great place to work: In 2007, for the third year in a row, *Fortune* named it one of the "100 Best Companies to Work For" in the country, making it one of only five law firms on the list.

GETTING HIRED

Reports a source in M&A, "I am not aware of a GPA cutoff, but decent grades are required. Bingham does a great job recruiting beyond school names and GPAs, as we attempt to hire diverse individuals with interesting backgrounds who have a sense of humor." Or, as a junior litigator puts it, "We look for well-rounded people we would enjoy working with and [who] would contribute positively to the firm. Candidates usually have very strong GPAs, extracurricular activities and come from top-tier schools." Speaking of top-tier schools, one Bostonian offers this observation: "There has been a recent push it seems to hire more from the top schools like Harvard and Yale, which is ironic given that many of our greatest partners went to "second tier" schools (e.g. Fordham, Villanova, etc.). They would be smart to stick with hiring great people regardless of the name of the school they attended."

OUR SURVEY SAYS

One satisfied senior associate says, "I get to do interesting and challenging work with a variety of individuals. My job is rarely boring and I am constantly learning." A happy colleague reports that the firm is "very collegial at all ranks from partners to staff. One of the things I like the most about the firm is that the staff are regarded as critical parts of the team and treated accordingly." But another senior associate complains, "Great for a junior associate, but there are fewer opportunities to develop as you get more senior." A junior litigator sums it up as, "Bingham McCutchen is like any other big firm. Associates are expected to bill a lot of hours and a lot of those hours are spent reviewing documents." Associates call the culture at Bingham "laid-back," "supportive" and "very friendly." Whether or not it may be deemed "social" remains up for debate. One sixth-year associate reports, "The firm makes a great effort of socially integrating lawyers especially those who work in the same practice group." A litigator says, "Some lawyers socialize together; but firm culture depends on which group you are in. Litigation is congenial and the hours are reasonable." Another senior associate adds, "In spite of its tremendous growth during my tenure at the firm, Bingham has maintained a highly professional but extremely collegial environment. Attorneys in the firm are some of my closest friends." Associates call the firm's formal training offerings both plentiful and useful. "As first-years, we have training at least twice a week," says one insider. A senior litigator adds, "The firm has excellent and intensive training for all levels of associates including deposition, negotiation, arbitration and trial training." "Top of the market" is where Bingham's salaries are at. One associate who works hard for the money claims "if anything, we get paid too much. I would take a pay cut for an hour cut!" The major complaint is that pro bono hours don't necessarily count one for one, and their application toward bonuses is (according to the firm) "done on a case-by-case basis." And of course, "you have to meet the annual hour requirement first to trigger the bonus (2,000 hours)."

Visit the Vault Law Channel, the complete online resource for law careers, featuring firm profiles, message boards, the Vault Law Job Board and more. www.vault.com/law

VAULT CAREER LIBRARY   473

65
PRESTIGE RANKING

Sonnenschein Nath & Rosenthal LLP

7800 Sears Tower
233 S. Wacker Drive
Chicago, IL 60606
Phone: (312) 876-8000
www.sonnenschein.com

LOCATIONS

Charlotte, NC • Chicago, IL • Dallas, TX • Kansas City, MO
• Los Angeles, CA • Menlo Park, CA • New York, NY •
Phoenix, AZ • St. Louis, MO • San Francisco, CA • Short
Hills, NJ • Washington, DC • West Palm Beach, FL •
Brussels

MAJOR DEPARTMENTS & PRACTICES

Antitrust • Bankruptcy & Restructuring • Climate Change •
Congressional Investigations • Corporate • Employee
Benefits & Executive Compensation • Energy •
Environmental • Financial Institutions & Lending •
Government Contracts • Health Care • Insurance •
Insurance Regulatory • Intellectual Property & Technology •
Labor & Employment • Litigation • Patent Litigation • Real
Estate • Taxation • Telecommunications • Trusts & Estates
• Venture Technology & Emerging Growth Companies

THE STATS

No. of attorneys: 700
No. of office: 14
Summer associate offers: 34 out of 37 (2005)
Chairman: Elliott I. Portnoy
Hiring Partner: Kara Baysinger

RANKING RECAP

Best in Region
#6 - Midwest

Best in Diversity
#8 - Diversity with Respect to Women
#16 - Overall Diversity

NOTABLE PERKS

• "Very reduced gym memberships"
• "Backup child care"
• "We only stay at five-star hotels"
• "Great" maternity leave policy

EMPLOYMENT CONTACT

Ms. Karalyn Powell
Attorney Recruitment Manager
Phone: (202) 408-3940
E-mail: kpowell@sonnenschein.com

BASE SALARY (2007)

**Chicago, IL; Los Angeles, CA; New York, NY; San
Francisco, CA; Silicon Valley, CA; Washington, DC**
1st year: $160,000

THE BUZZ
WHAT ATTORNEYS AT OTHER FIRMS ARE SAYING ABOUT THIS FIRM

• "Quality, innovative, amiable"
• "Pigeonholes associates"
• "Wonderful people, interesting work"
• "HP what?"

© 2007 Vault Inc.

THE SCOOP

Here's to the next century. Sonnenschein Nath & Rosenthal LLP celebrated its centennial in 2006, and hopes to reach 2106 even bigger and better than it is today. The firm has approximately 650 attorneys in 14 offices, including brand-new offices in Silicon Valley (Menlo Park, Ca.), Dallas and Charlotte. Sonnenschein is also on a lateral hiring kick, adding 150 lateral partners in the last decade, according to *The American Lawyer*. Sonnenschein's plan, according to AmLaw, is to double its revenue through its aggressive recruitment of lateral partners in key areas. Recent key hires include, in Dallas, Matthew D. Orwig, former U.S. attorney for the Eastern District of Texas, and in Washington, D.C., John R. Russell IV and Gilberto S. Ocañas, who joined the firm's lobbying and government relations group. Russell had served as deputy chief of staff to former House Speaker Dennis Hastert, while Ocañas was a lobbyist for Hispanic causes and active in the Democratic Party. Working pro bono cases is one thing, but in 2005 Sonnenschein went where no law firm has gone before, opening the Legacy Charter School in North Lawndale, a disadvantaged neighborhood west of downtown Chicago. At first, Legacy had only four grades, prekindergarten through second. The plan is to add another grade every year, drawing on Sonnenschein's support of office equipment, professional services, and $1 million annually. Real estate and securities partner Errol Stone cut the original deal for Legacy to share space with Mason Elementary, and remains at the helm of the charter school project.

GETTING HIRED

Sonnenschein's associates describe a relaxed and flexible recruitment program. As for grades, a senior litigator reports, "The firm has a suggested GPA cutoff; however, it can deviate from that if it is warranted. The firm is looking for bright individuals whose personality would be a good fit." A senior corporate attorney adds, "They generally don't want to see a C on the transcript and want to see at least one A. Big firm experience is a plus." Another insider suggests that standards may be stiffer for transfers. "They are demanding grade-wise, and for laterals your work experience really matters," she says. A senior litigator from the firm's Chicago office advises, "We recruit in all the Chicago schools, with a particular interest in Northwestern and the University of Chicago. We also recruit at Harvard and other schools out of state." A real estate specialist cautions prospective applicants that the hiring process is a tough one: "I am always shocked at the number of qualified candidates I recommend who don't get offers."

OUR SURVEY SAYS

Associates say that they enjoy their work for Sonnenschein, but are concerned about the firm's growth and direction. One Chicago litigator reports, "Overall, SNR remains a terrific place to practice law. However, given its current growth plans, aspects that make it a terrific place are rapidly changing, so the verdict is out for the future." A second Chicago litigator says, "Overall, I am happy with my level of responsibility and the quality of work. However, I'm seeing a shift away from smaller- or medium-sized cases, where associates get their best experience, to large, complex litigation." Another (more optimistic) insider advises, "I am extremely happy to be working at Sonnenschein. Although we have been through, and continue to go through, 'strategic' changes, I am confident that Sonnenschein will retain its image as a humane and rewarding place to work." Similarly, associates express fondness for the firm's current culture and some concern about its future. "Professionally, most of my co-workers are great," says a junior Chicago associate. "The partners overall will take the time to explain assignments and provide constructive feedback. While the atmosphere is civil and friendly, there are decreasing opportunities to interact socially because of billing pressures." A San Francisco associate adds, "The firm is currently going through a strategic overhaul in an attempt to make the AmLaw Top-25. Because of this, there is some apprehension regarding the direction of the firm, which has taken its toll on the firm's otherwise stellar culture. However, in general, the San Francisco office culture is friendly, social and absolutely not a sweat shop." "There are some formal training programs for junior associates, which is helpful, and in-house ethics programs—in order to get the CLE credits!" reports one insider. However, Sonnenschein associates are nearly unanimous in stressing the primacy of the informal over the formal varieties of training. As one typical associate says, "Training is less formal and more individualized, and is tailored for specific projects or situations. I feel this is a benefit." Echoing this theme, a Chicago litigator shares, "Most of the training at Sonnenschein is hands-on."

Visit the Vault Law Channel, the complete online resource for law careers, featuring firm profiles, message boards, the Vault Law Job Board and more. www.vault.com/law

VAULT CAREER LIBRARY   475

Greenberg Traurig, LLP

Greenberg Traurig is an international law firm with no principal or headquarter office. Founding office:

1221 Brickell Avenue
Miami, Florida 33131
Phone: (305) 579-0500
Fax: (305) 579-0717
www.gtlaw.com

LOCATIONS*

Albany, NY • Atlanta, GA • Boca Raton, FL • Boston, MA • Chicago, IL • Dallas, TX • Denver, CO • Florham Park, NJ • Fort Lauderdale, FL • Houston, TX • Las Vegas, NV • Los Angeles, CA • Miami, FL • New York, NY • Orange County, CA • Orlando, FL • Philadelphia, PA • Phoenix, AZ • Sacramento, CA • Silicon Valley, CA • Tallahassee, FL • Tampa, FL • Tysons Corner, VA • Washington, DC • West Palm Beach, FL • Wilmington, DE • Amsterdam • Tokyo • Zurich

*Additionally, the firm has strategic alliances with the following independent law firms in Europe: Olswang, London and Brussels; Studio Santa Maria, Milan and Rome; and in Asia: Hayabusa Asuka Law Offices in Tokyo.

MAJOR DEPARTMENTS & PRACTICES

ADA, Accessibility, Building & Life Safety Codes • Antitrust & Trade Regulation • Appellate • Automotive Dealerships • Aviation & Aircraft Finance • Business Immigration & Compliance • Business Reorganization & Bankruptcy • Class Action Litigation • Corporate & Securities • eDiscovery & eRetention • Energy & Natural Resources • Entertainment • Environmental • Export Controls • Federal Marketing • Financial Institutions • Franchising • Global • Global Benefits & Compensation • Global Trade • Globalization & Commercialization • Government Contracts • Governmental Affairs • Health Business • Hotel, Resort & Club • Insurance Recovery & Advisory • Intellectual Property • International Dispute Resolution • Labor & Employment • Land Development • Life Sciences • Litigation • Products Liability & Mass Torts Litigation • Project & Infrastructure Finance • Public Finance • Public Infrastructure • Public Utility • Real Estate • Real Estate Investment Trusts (REIT) • Real Estate Operations (REOPS) • Retail Industry • Securities & Shareholder Litigations • Sports Facilities & Entertainment Venues • Structured Finance & Derivatives • Tax • Technology, Media & Telecommunications • Transportation • Trusts & Estates • Wealth Management • White Collar Criminal Defense

THE BUZZ
WHAT ATTORNEYS AT OTHER FIRMS ARE SAYING ABOUT THIS FIRM

- "Great firm"
- "Sharks"
- "Run like a business, which is where the legal field is going"
- "Unimpressive"

THE STATS

No. of attorneys firmwide: 1,685*
No. of offices: 29
Summer associate offers firmwide: 57 out of 66 (2006)
Chief Executive Officer: Cesar L. Alvarez

*includes governmental professionals

RANKING RECAP

Best in Region
#3 - Miami

Best in Practice
#4 - Real Estate

NOTABLE PERKS

- Marketing budgets for all levels of associates
- Very good maternity leave policy
- Profit sharing

EMPLOYMENT CONTACTS

"Greenberg Traurig is actively hiring for summer 2008 for 24 offices. Please see www.gtlaw.com for hiring contacts."

BASE SALARY

1st year salary range: $76,000–$160,000 ("market rates in all locations")
Summer associate salary range:
$1,300/week–$3,076/week ("market rates in all locations")

© 2007 Vault Inc.

THE SCOOP

Greenberg Traurig was founded in Miami in 1967. However, its New York outpost is now the firm's largest office. In total, the 1,685-attorney firm ranks as the seventh-largest law firm in the United States, according to the 2006 AmLaw 100 survey. Indeed, Greenberg Traurig has experienced enormous growth in the last decade, expanding more than eightfold over the last 10 years and increasing annual revenue from $91 million in 1996 to just north of $1 billion in 2006. A general practice corporate firm, Greenberg Traurig counts among its clients some of the biggest names in information technology, energy, entertainment, telecommunications and health care. The firm represented MetLife in connection with the $5.4 billion sale of New York's Peter Cooper Village and Stuyvesant Town Complex to a joint venture between Tishman Speyer Properties and BlackRock Investments. The 11,000+ unit apartment complex is the largest in Manhattan and its sale is widely considered to be the largest real estate transaction in U.S. history. Greenberg Traurig served as counsel to Restco Iberoamericana Limited in its agreement to acquire the business and assets of McDonald's Corporation's Latin American operations. The firm also represented The Seminole Tribe of Florida and its subsidiary, Seminole Hard Rock Entertainment, Inc., in the $1 billion acquisition of Hard Rock International, Inc. and $1.7 billion of related financing transactions. Greenberg Traurig grabbed headlines in April 2007 with two major, associate-friendly changes. First, it became Florida's market leader by raising first-year salaries in Miami (and Fort Lauderdale) to $135,000. Next, the firm reversed its notoriously stingy pro bono policy, deciding that attorneys may now count hours of such work toward their billing requirements each year. Perhaps this new policy will be enough to stem the tide following a 15 percent drop in pro bono hours in 2006.

GETTING HIRED

"I couldn't get hired here if I tried today," one Greenberg associate confesses. Another explains: "The firm is trying with mixed results to get first-years from top-10 schools, but it's really growing through laterals from prestigious firms, coming from a diverse group of law schools." One insider insists that skills, not polished resumes, are the trump card: "We consistently favor people with outstanding practical skills—like writing ability, client relations skills and oral advocacy—[in addition to] candidates with those skills plus glistening resumes." A corporate lawyer adds, "The firm looks for mature candidates who have accomplishments/interests outside the law." And according to a Miami associate, "Our firm is looking for a business savvy, entrepreneurial candidate." As for the interview, it "was unlike previous interviews I've been on," says one who made the cut. "Candidates are interviewed by the partner they'll ultimately be working for, and that partner appears to have the final say in hiring decisions, with the approval of the managing partner."

OUR SURVEY SAYS

A Greenberg Traurig insider offers this overview on the firm's culture: "GT is a very young firm, and there is good interaction between associates and partners and even support staff. At the end of the day, it is still a big firm with the typical dynamic you will find in most large office settings, but overall, I believe there is a better relationship amongst the people in the office than you would find at most other firms." Another associate says: "Greenberg Traurig subscribes to an 'adults only' mentality—meaning that partners here treat associates like adults. Unlike other law firms, partners will not require 'face time' in the office, nor will they—in many instances—offer favorable work to only the more senior associates." Others say the firm is "very flexible" about hours: "As a parent, I've been told more than once that I may work from home when needed. Technologically, this firm allows us to do absolutely everything from home easily. I am in the office during working hours, but have gotten no pressure to stay late." "However," another attorney points out, "because of the nature of the work we do, it can be difficult to hit the target hours without putting in very long days." A Dallas associate reports: "I am very happy with my hours. I typically work from 8:30 to 7 and around two weekends of every month. If you have an appointment you can simply leave and no one will question you." Formal training reportedly "depends on the department." A litigator says that "this area is getting better with the firm's litigation training academy but most of the training still happens one-on-one by watching partners." A corporate attorney observes: "They adopted a corporate boot camp and I appreciated the effort. Like most firms the training is on the job."

Visit the Vault Law Channel, the complete online resource for law careers, featuring firm profiles, message boards, the Vault Law Job Board and more. www.vault.com/law

VAULT CAREER LIBRARY

477

Kaye Scholer LLP

425 Park Avenue
New York, NY 10022
Phone: (212) 836-8000
www.kayescholer.com

LOCATIONS

New York, NY (HQ)
Chicago, IL
Los Angeles, CA
Washington, DC
West Palm Beach, FL
Frankfurt
London
Shanghai

MAJOR DEPARTMENTS & PRACTICES

Antitrust
Bankruptcy & Reorganization
Corporate, Securities & Finance
Entertainment, Media & Communications
Intellectual Property
International
Labor
Legislative & Regulatory
Litigation
Product Liability
Real Estate
Tax
Technology & E-commerce
Trusts & Estates
White Collar Crime

THE STATS

No. of attorneys: 540
No. of offices: 8
Summer associate offers: 45 out of 46 (2006)
Managing Partner: Barry Willner
Hiring Partners: Jeanette Bionda, Jeffrey A. Fuisz, Mark
  Kingsley

THE BUZZ
WHAT ATTORNEYS AT OTHER FIRMS ARE SAYING ABOUT THIS FIRM

- "Litigationally brilliant"
- "More sweatshop than you'd think"
- "Nice people"
- "Bad karma"

NOTABLE PERKS

- Free dinners if working until 8 p.m.
- Mentor lunches
- "Wine downs"
- Occasional sporting events tickets

EMPLOYMENT CONTACT

Ms. Melissa Huffman
Legal Personnel Administrator
Phone: (212) 836-8893
Fax: (212) 836-7153
E-mail: mhuffman@kayescholer.com

BASE SALARY (2007)

1st year: $160,000
2nd year: $170,000
3rd year: $185,000
4th year: $210,000
5th year: $230,000
6th year: $265,000
7th year: $280,000
Summer associate: $3,080/week

© 2007 Vault Inc.

THE SCOOP

Got a problem? Try your luck with Kaye Scholer LLP. The 500-lawyer firm is known for its litigation expertise—*The National Law Journal* and *The American Lawyer* have both recently honored Kaye Scholer as one of the top litigation firms (*The National Law Journal* recognized it as among the top-10 defense firms in 2005 and 2006, and *The American Lawyer* named it the top products liability firm of 2006). The firm's other areas of expertise include bankruptcy, corporate, real estate and intellectual property. Kaye Scholer's 500 attorneys practice in eight offices around the world. Recently Kaye Scholer helped Harrah's Entertainment hit the jackpot in connection with its representation of the Special Committee of Independent Directors in the proposed $27.8 billion sale of Harrah's to prive equity giants Texas Pacific Group and Apollo Management. Kaye Scholer's real estate department has also built a name for itself over the years and is often involved in the nation's largest transactions. In December of 2006, the firm represented RBS Greenwich Capital and Lehman Brothers in providing mortgage and mezzanine financing to Broadway Real Estate Partners L.L.C. for their $3.3 billion acquisition by merger of Becon Capital Strategic Partners L.L.C's building office portfolio. The transaction, at approximately seven million square feet of space, is one of the largest real estate transactions ever between private investors, and included high-profile properties such as the John Hancock Tower (Boston), the Citigroup Center (downtown L.A.), and eight other buildings in Boston, L.A., Washington, D.C., and Denver.

GETTING HIRED

A succinct Kaye Scholer insider summarizes the firm's recruiting process: "Typical on-campus and in-office interview system for summer associates and students; in-office interviews for laterals. Top schools sought after; midrank school graduates often hired." Another insider explains, "We are small, which makes us stingy with offers. That being said, anyone reasonably articulate from a top school should have little trouble." A colleague echoes that sentiment: "If you're from a top school and don't act like a jerk, you'll get an offer." One happy camper offers a happy view: "My impression of the firm is that as a rule, the firm seeks eager, bright and personable law students who are committed to becoming eager, bright and personable lawyers." A more specific peer names some names: "Columbia, U Penn, NYU, Fordham, Cornell, St. Johns are all well represented here and firm appears to recruit highly from the New York area. For the interview process, because the firm is so social, it is *essential* to be yourself and show a personality."

OUR SURVEY SAYS

Kaye Scholer is "much less buttoned up than other NYC law firms I've been at," according to a lateral hire. "Lawyers socialize together all of the time," says another associate—in fact, it's "a little too social," according to this New York lawyer. One litigator breaks things down: "There is a group of lawyers that can be consistently found closing down the open bar events/cocktail parties, or taking the party to a neighboring bar. There is also the former Clifford Chance group that hangs together." By contrast, the California contingent seems less chummy than the New York crowd. "Very few people socialize together after work," states a relatively understated Los Angeles associate. What are the hours like at Kaye Scholer? "My hours are very good for a big firm associate," says one insider. "I often have very busy weeks, but when I have a slower week I have no reservations about leaving at 6:30." Another agrees: "The hours are very manageable. Associates are not expected to be at their desks even if they do not have work to do." However, one attorney reports: "'face time' in [the] real estate group." Notably, "the firm is very flexible about working from home as needed," according to one associate. Also of interest: "The firm is notoriously bad about having clear policies on things like paternity leave (even maternity leave policy isn't very clear), but in general they seem to be fair." Kaye Scholer gets mixed reviews on its training programs. "The firm's training program consists only of occasional CLE programs," says a Washington lawyer. And an LA attorney confesses, "To date, we have not really had a truly organized and formalized training program." But a New Yorker insists that "litigation training is solid." In fact, "maybe there's a little too much training here," according to another. And a Chicago-based associate asserts, "The training program is comprehensive and addresses pertinent information." Regardless of the training program's quality, the pay is solid, according to associates. "I'm getting paid NYC market rates," says one attorney, "which I feel are starting to border on unseemly."

Visit the Vault Law Channel, the complete online resource for law careers, featuring firm profiles, message boards, the Vault Law Job Board and more. **www.vault.com/law**

VAULT CAREER LIBRARY   479

Holland & Knight LLP

195 Broadway, 24th Floor
New York, NY 10007
Phone: (212) 513-3200
www.hklaw.com

LOCATIONS

Atlanta, GA • Bethesda, MD • Boston, MA • Chicago, IL •
Fort Lauderdale, FL • Jacksonville, FL • Los Angeles, CA •
McLean, VA • Miami, FL • New York, NY • Orlando, FL •
Portland, OR • San Francisco, CA • Tallahassee, FL •
Tampa, FL • Washington, DC • West Palm Beach, FL •
Beijing • Caracas* • Helsinki* • Mexico City • Tel Aviv* •
Tokyo

Representative office

MAJOR DEPARTMENTS & PRACTICES

Business • Government • Litigation • Real Estate

THE STATS

No. of attorneys firmwide: 1150
No. of offices: 23
Summer associate offers firmwide: 60 out of 64 (2006)
Managing Partner: Howell W. Melton
Firmwide Professional Development & Recruiting Partner:
    Adolfo E. Jimenez

RANKING RECAP

Best in Region
#7 - Miami

Best in Practice
#8 - Real Estate

Partner Prestige Rankings
#5 (tie) - Real Estate

NOTABLE PERKS

- Free parking
- "Great rates on hotels you can use for personal travel"
- Backup child care

THE BUZZ
WHAT ATTORNEYS AT OTHER FIRMS ARE SAYING ABOUT THIS FIRM

- "Sophisticated work; family-friendly"
- "Ginormous"
- "Florida's finest"
- "Tries to be what it isn't"

EMPLOYMENT CONTACT

Ms. Carrie Weintraub
Chief Professional Development and Recruiting Officer
Phone: (813) 769-4314
E-mail: carrie.weintraub@hklaw.com

BASE SALARY (2007)

Atlanta, GA
1st year: $125,000
Summer associate: $2,500/week

Boston, MA
1st year: $145,000
Summer associate: $2,600/week

Chicago, IL
1st year: $145,000
Summer associate: $2,788/week

Jacksonville, FL; Orlando, FL; Tampa, FL
1st year: $105,000
Summer associate: $1,900/week

Los Angles, CA; San Francisco, CA
1st year: $145,000
Summer associate: $2,788/week

Mid-Atlantic (Washington, DC; McLean, VA; Bethesda, MD)
1st year: $145,000
Summer associate: $2,600/week

New York, NY
1st year: $160,000
Summer associate: $3,076/week

Portland, OR
1st year: $93,000

South Florida (Miami, Fort Lauderdale, West Palm Beach)
1st year: $125,000
Summer associate: $2,400/week

Tallahassee, FL
1st year: $90,000

© 2007 Vault Inc.

THE SCOOP

In the 1990s, Holland & Knight began an expansion spree. Most of its existing offices were enlarged, and new locations were opened across the country and around the world, raising the total from nine offices in 1990 to 23 today (including three representative offices located in Caracas, Helsinki and Tel Aviv). Most of the expansion came through mergers, bringing the firm's head count to about 1,150. While the firm claims that no one office serves as its headquarters, its roots are deep in Florida, where it is the state's largest law firm. The firm is organized into four practice groups: business, government, litigation and real estate. In 2005, Kos Pharmaceuticals relied on Holland & Knight to guide them through the $104 million acquisition of six cardiovascular medications from Biovail. In October of the same year, the firm represented Bunim/Murray Productions as neighbors tried to shut down production of the popular reality show *The Real World* in Key West. The judge ruled that noise and lights complaints were unfounded. A distressed employee figures in a bizarre case that occupied the firm during 2006. Holland & Knight won a dismissal for McDonald's Corp. in a lawsuit brought by a female employee of one of its franchises, alleging the company was liable when, on the telephoned instructions of someone pretending to be an authority, another employee conducted a body cavity search and imprisoned her on the restaurant's premises.

GETTING HIRED

A Chicago associate reports: "Our office hires very few associates directly from law school, so this makes it more competitive than it otherwise would be. The office concentrates on Chicago and Midwestern schools (Northwestern, University of Illinois, Michigan, DePaul, Loyola)." The firm looks for various characteristics, says another insider: "People should have a 3.5 or better GPA (top 15 percent), law review or moot court experience, some school or community involvement, a great writing sample, and be outgoing and articulate in the screening interviews." A Florida attorney says: "Candidates must generally be in the top 10 percent. This office focuses its recruiting efforts on the University of Florida, Florida State University and several top Southeastern universities (Vanderbilt, University of Virginia)." And a Washingtonian reports: "If you are already at a large law firm, it is probably easier to get hired here. If not, then it is quite competitive since your GPA has to be over a 3.0." According to a New Yorker, the firm "does not only look at grades. It also looks at who you are as a person, interesting things you have done in your life, and your enthusiasm and willingness to work."

OUR SURVEY SAYS

Many Holland & Knight associates are sanguine about their firm's culture: "The Miami office has an exceptional culture. The attorneys are friendly, polite and professional. All political views and sexual orientations are welcome." Shares a Chicago lawyer: "The associates and partners interact professionally, and the partners treat the associates with a great deal of respect. You really feel like you are a valuable member of the team." But these upbeat views aren't unanimous: "We are definitely moving away from the values touted on the firm web site and becoming a firm that is ruled by the bottom line," laments a Washington-based associate. The firm "has become more like the typical big law firm focusing primarily on the billable hour and numbers," seconds an Orlando attorney. Hours seem manageable: "The firm is fairly relaxed about associate hours. As long as you are billing enough to be profitable and stay on pace with the scheduled minimum, people give you flexibility to come and go as you need to." Another insider boasts, "I am in the office typically no more than eight to nine hours a day. My colleagues have had no complaints about me working from home when necessary." Also, "The firm has excellent leave policies and several attorneys are on flex-time and part-time schedules." (Although one attorney disagrees, saying: "Even if such policies are on paper, they are not supported by management.") Associates are divided about how open the communication channels are with management. According to some, "The partnership keeps associates very informed regarding firmwide decisions." But others say: "The partners are easy to get along with, however, sometimes it seems as though associates are on the outside, very far on the outside, looking in at firm decisions." Either way, trends may be positive: "The firm is getting much better about keeping associates informed about what's going on within the firm," according to one New Yorker.

Visit the Vault Law Channel, the complete online resource for law careers, featuring firm profiles, message boards, the Vault Law Job Board and more. **www.vault.com/law**

VAULT CAREER LIBRARY   481

Steptoe & Johnson LLP

1330 Connecticut Avenue, N.W.
Washington, DC 20036
Phone: (202) 429-3000
Fax: (202) 429-3902
www.steptoe.com

LOCATIONS

Washington, DC (HQ)
Century City, CA • Chicago, IL • Los Angeles, CA • New York, NY • Phoenix, AZ • Brussels • London

THE STATS

No. of attorneys: 454
No. of offices: 8
Summer associate offers firmwide: 21 out of 22 (2006)
Chairman, Executive Committee: Roger E. Warin
Co-Chairs, Associates Hiring Committee: Edmund W. Burke, Daryl A. (Sandy) Chamblee

NOTABLE PERKS

- Skybox tickets at Verizon Center
- "Subsidized backup emergency day care across the street"
- Free after-hours Dupont Circle parking
- Complimentary exercise facility on site

EMPLOYMENT CONTACT

Ms. Rosemary Kelly Morgan
Director of Attorney Services & Legal Recruiting
Phone: (202) 429-8036
Fax: (202) 429-3902
E-mail: Legal_Recruiting@steptoe.com

BASE SALARY

Washington, DC (2007)
1st year: $145,000
Summer associate: $2,600/week

THE BUZZ
WHAT ATTORNEYS AT OTHER FIRMS ARE SAYING ABOUT THIS FIRM

- "Very thoughtful, intelligent"
- "Laid-back but work is not interesting"
- "Great white-collar practice"
- "Reid Weingarten, then what?"

MAJOR DEPARTMENTS & PRACTICES

Alternative Dispute Resolution • Anti-Boycott • Anti-Money Laundering • Antitrust & Competition • Appellate & Supreme Court • Asset Finance • Aviation • Bad Faith • CALEA/Wiretap • Capital Markets/Securities • Chemical Regulatory • Class Action • Commercial Litigation Insolvency & Creditors' Rights • Complex Litigation • Consumer Products/Products Liability • Copyright • Corporate Compliance, Investigations & Responsibility • Corporate Governance • Corporate Tax Transactions • Corporate, Securities & Finance • Cross-Border Litigation • Customs • E-Commerce/Internet • Economic Sanctions • E-Discovery & Document Retention • Electric Power • Employee Benefits/ERISA & Executive Compensation • Employment Advice & Litigation • Encryption • Energy • Energy Transactions • Entertainment • Environment & Natural Resources • ERISA, Labor & Employment • ERISA/Employee Benefits/Litigation/Executive Compensation • EU Environmental • EU Law • EU Regulatory Compliance • Exempt Organizations • Export Controls • FCPA/Anti-Corruption • Financial Restructuring & Insolvency • Food & Dietary Supplements • Foreign Investment Reviews • Government Affairs & Public Policy • Government Contracts • Government Relations • Hospitality, Hotels & Resorts • Immigration • Industrial Security • Infrastructure & Project Finance • Insurance & Reinsurance • Insurance Tax • Intellectual Property • International IP Policy • International Regulation & Compliance • International Tax • International Trade • International Trade Litigation • International Trade Policy & Strategy • IP Government Contracts • IP Litigation • IRS Controversy & Tax Litigation • Labor/Management Relations • Lease Finance • Legislative & Administrative, Congress & Treasury • Licensing • Litigation • Mass Tort • Media Law • Mergers & Acquisitions • Multilateral Agency Financing • Native American Indian Affairs • Partnerships/LLCs/S Corporations • Patent • Pesticides & Antimicrobials • Pipeline • Privacy & Data Security • Private Equity/Venture Capital • Professional Liability • Property • Public International Law • Rail Transportation • Reinsurance Litigation & Counseling • Section 337/ITC Litigation • Securities & Directors/Officers Litigation • State & Local Tax • Strategic Alliances/Joint Ventures • Surface Transportation • Tax • Telecom, Internet & Media • Telecommunications Law • Toxic Tort • Trade Secrets • Trademark • Transportation • Transportation & Infrastructure Policy • US/EU Environmental Life Sciences • White-Collar Criminal Defense • World Trade Organization • Worldwide Arbitration & Dispute Resolution

© 2007 Vault Inc.

THE SCOOP

In more than 60 years of practice, Steptoe has garnered a reputation as an international powerhouse for its vigorous defense of clients. The firm's Washington office now houses nearly 300 attorneys. The past year has been filled with significant growth for both the Washington office and the firm as a whole, highlighted by the launch of two new domestic offices: in Century City, Calif., and Chicago, Ill. The firm augmented its public policy practice with the addition of eight accomplished attorneys and professionals based in Washington, D.C. The members of the Scott Group have extensive Congressional experience and a balanced, bipartisan and broadly-based government affairs practice. Both domestically and internationally, Steptoe is routinely ranked among the top firms in international trade, insurance and reinsurance, tax, intellectual property, energy and white-collar defense litigation. Reid Weingarten, a partner in Steptoe's litigation department, is a major player in the world of white-collar criminal defense. During his illustrious career, he has represented several high-profile individuals including Enron Corporation's chief accounting officer, Richard Causey; Tyco's general counsel, Mark Belnick; WorldCom's chief executive, Bernard Ebbers; Secretary of Commerce Ronald H. Brown; Secretary of Agriculture Michael Espy; and former Teamsters President Ron Carey. Firm alumni are regularly kept abreast of developments within the firm through a quarterly electronic alumni newsletter developed as part of Steptoe's newly-launched alumni network. The network will be expanded during 2007 to utilize an online portal that will include a searchable alumni database, news items and information about attorney-focused events.

GETTING HIRED

According to a Steptoe insider: "The firm looks to hire the top of the top. Often appears to recruit heavily at Harvard, Yale, Penn, Georgetown and UVA. If you are not at an Ivy League school, then usually you will not be considered unless you are on law review." Another attorney warns, "The firm will not even interview people with certain GPAs from local schools like Georgetown and GW, which I think is ridiculous." Law school pedigree may be less important for laterals: "More senior lawyers from 'lesser' schools are considered as lateral hires, but they must have superior grades and experience (a clerkship is helpful)." Personality is also important: "I know some top caliber folks that didn't get hired here. But I think it's because the firm hires a lot on the basis of personality. While people are smart and driven here, the uptight, OCD types won't fit in." At the same time, the interview is low pressure, according to one associate: "Once you are in the door, you have a good chance of getting an offer—the interview process itself is not difficult."

OUR SURVEY SAYS

"Steptoe is generally great about treating associates like professionals. As long as I get my work done, the partners I work for are very flexible about me making my own hours or working from home or elsewhere. Face time is not an issue here," reports one D.C. insider. Moreover, "the firm has a very flexible part-time policy for people who are interested." However, some Steptoers feel that the firm's hours culture is changing—and not for the better: "Steptoe historically was a firm that valued quality of life," says one litigator, but "in the last several years the firm culture has morphed into an hours-based culture that is burning out associates." Treating attorneys "like professionals" seems to inform Steptoe's culture: "Attorneys at Steptoe tend to be respectful and independent. Although associates occasionally socialize, many lawyers at the firm in fact seem to have lives outside the office. It is not a place that tolerates many jerks." Another attorney explains: "Partners treat associates very respectfully (for the most part), and associates are all friendly with one another. It's not the type of firm where everyone hangs out together on the weekends or after work, though." One associate says, "There are a fair number of firm get-togethers and departmental breakfasts, but the place is designed to avoid watercooler chitchat." Overall, "Steptoe is best described as open and democratic—everyone has a say, and everyone is heard. The partnership clearly listens to associates and associate concerns, and has shown that on a repeated basis throughout my tenure here." The compensation at Steptoe is "comparable to other firms for the lower level associates, a bit lower than market for more senior associates." One attorney complains that "the fact that Steptoe makes receiving full salary contingent on billing 1,950 hours is ridiculous, as all other D.C. firms did away with this a long time ago." A second-year notes, "The firm is behind the curve when it comes to compensation. Some would say this is because we are asked to work less."

Visit the Vault Law Channel, the complete online resource for law careers, featuring firm profiles, message boards, the Vault Law Job Board and more. www.vault.com/law

VAULT CAREER LIBRARY   483

Foley & Lardner LLP

777 E. Wisconsin Avenue
Milwaukee, WI 53202-5306
Phone: (414) 271-2400
Fax: (414) 297-4900
www.foley.com
www.foleyrecruiting.com

LOCATIONS

Milwaukee, WI (HQ)

Boston, MA • Chicago, IL • Detroit, MI • Jacksonville, FL •
Los Angeles, CA • Madison, WI • New York, NY • Orlando,
FL • Sacramento, CA • San Diego, CA (2 offices) • San
Francisco, CA • Silicon Valley, CA • Tallahassee, FL •
Tampa, FL • Washington, DC • Brussels • Tokyo

MAJOR DEPARTMENTS & PRACTICES

Business Law
Government & Public Affairs
Health
Intellectual Property
Litigation
Tax & Individual Planning

THE STATS

No. of attorneys (2006): 1,000+
No. of offices: 19
Summer associate offers:
    94% of 2Ls received new associate offers (2006)
Managing Partner: Stanley S. Jaspan
Hiring Partners: James N. Bierman, Lisa S. Neubauer

RANKING RECAP

Best in Region
#4 - Midwest

NOTABLE PERKS

• "All the fountain cherry Coke you can drink"
• Free parking (some locations)
• "Preferred rates and terms on a home mortgage"
  (Wisconsin, Illinois, Michigan & Florida)
• Free Wednesday night dinners

EMPLOYMENT CONTACT

Ms. Kara E. Nelson
Director, Legal Recruiting & Development
Phone: (414) 297-5587
E-mail: kenelson@foley.com

BASE SALARY (2007)

**Boston, MA; California offices; Chicago, IL;
Washington, DC**
1st year: $145,000
Summer Associate: $2,800/week

Detroit, MI; Milwaukee, WI
1st year: $135,000/$145,000 (IP)
Summer Associate: $2,400/week

Florida offices
1st year: $110,000/$145,000 (IP)
Summer Associate: $2,100/week

Madison, WI
1st year: $125,000/$145,000 (IP)
Summer Associate: $2,400/week

New York, NY
1st year: $160,000
Summer Associate: $3,100/week

THE BUZZ
WHAT ATTORNEYS AT OTHER FIRMS ARE SAYING ABOUT THIS FIRM

• "Great securities group"
• "Demanding of associates"
• "Good rep for quality of life, good lawyers"
• "Everything driven by Milwaukee main office"

© 2007 Vault Inc.

THE SCOOP

Foley & Lardner ranks as a leader in the Midwestern market, particularly since its 2001 merger with the historic firm Hopkins & Sutter. But the firm's 1,000 legal eagles are actually spread among 19 offices, including three (New York, Silicon Valley and Boston) set up in the past two years as part of its life sciences push. The firm services clients ranging from Coors Brewing Company to Harley Davidson to Hewlett-Packard. What's more, Chambers USA was sufficiently wowed by the firm's health care know-how to deem it the No. 1 practice in the country. In 2006, the BTI Consulting Group named Foley just one of four "market trailblazers," alongside such larger and better-known majors as DLA Piper, Jones Day and Skadden Arps. Foley & Lardner recently scored a victory for its client Kymsta Corp., a Los Angeles-based women's clothing manufacturer, in a copyright action against the surf-wear giant Quiksilver. The United States Court of Appeals for the Ninth Circuit concluded that a Los Angeles trial judge wrongfully held in his 2004 decision that Quiksilver's extremely successful "Roxy" trademark had superior trademark rights to Kymsta's "Roxywear." The case was remanded to the trial court for a new jury trial.

GETTING HIRED

Foley & Lardner "concentrates on hiring from top-tier schools, though we have great attorneys (associates and partners) from top-tier schools, third-tier schools, and everywhere in between." One San Diego-based associate describes successful candidates as "Well rounded individuals, who are not only book smart, but are presentable to clients and treat all, including staff, with dignity. No amount of intelligence is enough to overcome a poor personality." The question of whether there is a GPA cutoff gets varying responses. "There is no longer a GPA floor," says one insider. But another associate claims, "General GPA requirement is 3.3, but is on a sliding scale depending on school," adding, "Moot court and law review preferred." One prolix insider offers a handy summary of the firm's criteria: "An excellent law school and undergraduate record. Most candidates considered are in the top of their respective classes and are involved in many extracurricular activities, including law reviews, moot court and clinics. The firm certainly recruits heavily at the top law schools, but also frequently hires top performers at less established law schools."

OUR SURVEY SAYS

Politically, Foley & Lardner bends neither left nor right, according to insiders. "The firm has an interesting mix of political views, from staunch conservatives to staunch liberals." And Foley & Lardner associates are particularly fond of the adjective "collegial" when describing the firm's culture: "Foley is an extraordinarily collegial firm, while still respecting its attorneys' desire to go home and be with family. Lawyers do socialize together, but I would not use the euphemism 'we work hard and play hard' (which ordinarily means, 'we work too hard and then get drunk together to cope with working too hard') to describe the firm." One Foley & Lardner happy camper reports on the topic of training: "I am happy with the training; however, I do notice that training varies among departments and practice groups and some are definitely better than others." And training can come at a cost: "Firm training opportunities are quite good. However, the 'cost' of attending such training, which is usually out of office or out of state (i.e. two to three days) is less time in the office to bill. Thus, the training sessions in effect are an associate's 'vacation time.'" At Foley & Lardner, "The firm is fairly flexible with hours. However, associates in my practice group (regulatory) often find it a challenge to have enough hours. Because Foley punishes associates who do not make their hours by not advancing them to the next comp class, this is a very demoralizing problem." And how many hours are expected? "Working 1,850 hours per year is expected, 1,950 is preferred and rewarded with 'deferred compensation.'" The firm seems willing to provide flex-time for those with family demands: "The firm has a paper 'flex-time' policy, however, it is only available to attorneys with children and/or elder care issues." One Foley associate succinctly sums up the compensation picture at Foley & Lardner: "We are not the highest paid, but we also aren't required to bill as much as other firms. I will take that trade-off." The "not-out-of-this-world" bonuses are structured as follows: "Deferred compensation is paid for reaching 1,950 billable hours. Bonuses are received at 2,050 and 2,150 hours." One pleased associate shares, "I am happy with my compensation as it matches that of top Chicago firms, and I'm in Milwaukee."

Visit the Vault Law Channel, the complete online resource for law careers, featuring firm profiles, message boards, the Vault Law Job Board and more. www.vault.com/law

VAULT CAREER LIBRARY   485

Kirkpatrick & Lockhart Preston Gates Ellis, LLP

Henry W. Oliver building
535 Smithfield Street
Pittsburgh, PA 15222-2312
Phone: (412) 355-6500
Fax: (412) 355-6501
www.klgates.com

LOCATIONS

Anchorage, AK • Boston, MA • Coeur D'Alene, ID • Dallas, TX • Harrisburg, PA • Irvine, Ca • Los Angeles, CA • Miami, FL • New York, NY • Newark, NJ • Palo Alto, CA • Pittsburgh, PA • Portland, OR • San Francisco, CA (x2) • Seattle, WA • Spokane, WA • Washington, DC (x2) • Beijing • Berlin • Hong Kong • London • Taipei

MAJOR DEPARTMENTS & PRACTICES

Antitrust Law & Trade Regulation • Appellate • Constitutional & Gov't Litigation • Arbitration • Asia • Bankruptcy/Insolvency • Benefits/ Exec Comp • Broker-Dealer • Class Action Defense • Commercial Litigation • Commercial Technology Contracts & Outsourcing • Construction • Corp • M&A • Securities • Corporate/Transactional • Depository Institutions • E-DATG • Energy & Utilities • Environmental • Land Use & Nat. Resources • FDA • Finance • Financial Services • Gov't Contracts & Procurement • Health Care • Insurance Coverage • Intellectual Property • Investment Management • IP Corporate • IP Litigation • Labor & Employment • Licensing & E-merging Commerce • Litigation & Dispute Resolution • Mortgage Banking • Policy & Regulatory • Private Clients • Public Finance • Public Policy & Law • Real Estate • School Districts • Securities Enforcement • Tax • Tax-Exempt Organizations • Telecom • Media & Technology • Toxic Tort/Product Liability • Transportation • White Collar

THE STATS

No. of attorneys firmwide: Approximately 1,400
No. of offices: 22
Summer associate offers firmwide: 72 out of 98 (2006)
Chairman and Global Managing Partner: Peter J. Kalis

THE BUZZ
WHAT ATTORNEYS AT OTHER FIRMS ARE SAYING ABOUT THIS FIRM

- "Emerging power"
- "Does the merger work?"
- "Genial attorneys, impressive deals"
- "Losing identity"

RANKING RECAP

Best in Region
#3 - Pacific Northwest

NOTABLE PERKS

- Subsidized gym membership
- Healthy snacks
- Moving expenses
- "In-office yoga"

EMPLOYMENT CONTACT

Roslyn M. Pitts
Director of Legal Recruitment and Professional
    Development (U.S.)
Phone: (412) 355-6500
E-mail: roz.pitts@klgates.com

BASE SALARY

Boston, MA; Los Angeles, CA; Orange County, CA; Palo Alto, CA; San Francisco, CA; Washington, DC
1st year: $145,000
Summer Associate: $2,800/week

Dallas, TX
1st year: $120,000
Summer Associate: $2,310/week

Harrisburg, PA
1st year: $105,000
Summer Associate: $2,020/week

Miami, FL; Seattle, WA
1st year: $115,000
Summer Associate: $2,210/week

New York, NY
1st year: $160,000
Summer Associate: $3080/week

Newark, NJ
1st year: $122,000
Summer associate: $2350/week

Pittsburgh, PA
1st year: $130,000
Summer associate: $2,500/week

Portland, OR
1st year: $105,000
Summer Associate: $1900/week

Seattle, WA
1st year: $115,000
Summer Associate: $2050/week

© 2007 Vault Inc.

THE SCOOP

You can be forgiven if you have trouble remembering the history and etymology of K&L Gates. Here's a quick primer: On January 1, 2007, the combination of Kirkpatrick & Lockhart Nicholson Graham and Preston Gates & Ellis became official. Kirkpatrick had been the product of a 2005 union of Pittsburgh-born Kirkpatrick & Lockhart and London's Nicholson Graham— indeed one of the largest U.S.-U.K. legal combinations in history. (The American half was founded in 1981, and had established a major East Coast presence; the firm's British half dated back to the early 1900s.) Pre-combination Preston Gates was considered a top West Coast firm. Thanks to the firm's location and lineage (the "Gates" in "Preston Gates" is William H. Gates Sr., father of Microsoft founder Bill Gates), the firm was best known for technology law, as well as complex transactions, strategic litigation, public law and policy, intellectual property and lobbying. The newly combined firm's full name is Kirkpatrick & Lockhart Preston Gates Ellis LLP, but branded as "K&L Gates." K&L Gates immediately ranks as one of the largest law firms in the world, with more than 1,400 lawyers, 22 offices around the globe, and annual revenue approaching approximately $750 million. K&L Gates' two predecessor firms ranked 10th and 13th, respectively, out of 105 firms nationally in a recent Harvard Law School Women's Law Association survey that measured the treatment of women in law firms. The firm's progressive policies were also recognized by DuPont, which bestowed its "Meeting the Challenge" award onto the firm for its creation of the K&L Gates Balanced Hours Program. In August 2007, the American Bar Association will inaugurate its second president from K&L Gates, William H. Neukom, chair of Preston Gates Ellis.

GETTING HIRED

A K&L Gates associate draws from personal experience to give the lowdown on getting in the door: "While our firm focuses on Ivy League and tiers one and two, we also recruit heavily at local law schools, as well as other schools around the country (myself being an example). If a student is not from a top school, however, the GPA must be high and the resume impressive (I, personally, had high grades, an MBA and fluency in a foreign language)." A colleague elaborates, "We do pay attention to the personality … if you are a 4.0 student but have a 'flat' personality, you probably won't get an offer." Another attorney adds: "If you are from a third- or fourth-tier school you need to be in a single-digit rank to even get a first interview." Summer associates might be well advised to keep on their toes. A Boston insider warns, "Several immature and unprofessional summer associates did not end up getting offers."

OUR SURVEY SAYS

From the Portland side of the K&L Gates family comes this appraisal: "Given the firm's very recent merger, the 'culture' of the firm appears to be in flux. The Preston Gates side of the firm was, speaking very generally, socially and politically progressive … For example, we have a relatively large number of gay and lesbian attorneys, including some in management positions like office managing partner. I am much less familiar with the 'culture' of the K&L side of the firm, except to say that it appears to be a more traditional East Coast model." In a similar vein, one Pittsburgh associate reports that the firm has a traditional sense of decorum: "five men and one woman are waiting for an elevator, when it arrives none of the men will get onto the elevator until the woman has." A D.C. associate sums up the training opportunities: "There are a decent amount of training options, but most is on the job." And from Harrisburg comes this appraisal of the firm's hours: "The firm is extremely flexible with hours— typically make your own hours as long as you get the work done. Bonuses are given out for those billing 1,950 per year." And how's the pay? In Pittsburgh, "Overall, the compensation is good, but the firm tells us we are leaders in our market. This is not true when you calculate in bonuses." Associates are far from unanimous about bonuses: One San Franciscan, reports, "firm matches market for first-year associates and then falls behind every year." By contrast, a New Yorker claims that "bonuses are very high." And in Washington, D.C., "Bonus packages are sizeable and fair."

Visit the Vault Law Channel, the complete online resource for law careers, featuring firm profiles, message boards, the Vault Law Job Board and more. www.vault.com/law

VAULT CAREER LIBRARY   487

72

PRESTIGE
RANKING

Chadbourne & Parke LLP

30 Rockefeller Plaza
New York, NY 10112
Phone: (212) 408-5338
www.chadbourne.com

LOCATIONS

New York, NY (HQ)
Houston, TX
Los Angeles, CA
Washington, DC
Almaty
Beijing
Dubai
Kyiv
London
Moscow
St. Petersburg
Warsaw

MAJOR DEPARTMENTS & PRACTICES

Corporate
CIS
Bankruptcy & Restructuring
Insurance/Reinsurance
Intellectual Property
Latin America
Litigation/Product Liability
Project Finance
Real Estate
Tax
Renewable Energy
Trusts & Estates

THE STATS

No. of attorneys firmwide: 432
No. of offices: 12
Summer associate offers firmwide: 23 out of 23 (2006)
Managing Partner: Charles K. O'Neill
Hiring Attorney: Scott D. Berson

THE BUZZ
WHAT ATTORNEYS AT OTHER FIRMS ARE SAYING ABOUT THIS FIRM

- "Mr. Project Finance"
- "Inconsistent"
- "Great international work"
- "Past its prime"

NOTABLE PERKS

- "A percentage of whatever new business one brings in regardless of level"
- Starbucks coffee, apple pie at Thanksgiving, pumpkins at Halloween
- $200 entertainment coupons to reward high billing periods
- $950 annually toward gym membership

EMPLOYMENT CONTACT

Ms. Lisa Featherson
Legal Recruiting Manager
Phone: (212) 408-5538
E-mail: recruiting@chadbourne.com

BASE SALARY (2007)

New York, NY; Washington, DC; Los Angeles, CA
1st year: $160,000
2nd year: $170,000
3rd year: $185,000
4th year: $210,000
5th year: $230,000
6th year: $250,000
7th year: $265,000
8th year: $280,000
Summer associate: $3,077/week

© 2007 Vault Inc.

THE SCOOP

In early 2007, Chadbourne bolstered its "green team" in the renewable energy and project finance sector. George E. Pataki, the former governor of New York, and his chief of staff, John P. Cahill, joined the New York office to focus on energy, environmental and corporate matters, and in L.A., Edward Zaelke, Adam Umanoff and Thomas Dupuis joined to concentrate and collaborate with Chadbourne's formidable team on wind power and other renewable energy projects. Chadbourne represented Energias de Portugal SA in the $2.5 billion acquisition of Horizon Wind Energy LLC of Houston, Texas, the biggest acquisition of a U.S. wind power company to date. Attorneys from Chadbourne's London and Almaty offices recently helped to facilitate the sale of an interest in the Shymkent Refinery to Kazakhstan's government-run oil and gas enterprise. (Yes, Chadbourne keeps an office in Almaty, the one-time capital of Kazakhstan—the real Kazakhstan, which produces 1.2 million barrels of oil per day, not the fictional backwater of the movie *Borat*.) The firm also represented Polish artist Ludwika Ogorzelec when a New York gallery owner, unable to sell her sculptures, refused to return them. Handling the case pro bono, Chadbourne sued the gallery owner, weathered one or more somewhat outlandish counterclaims, and recovered most of Ms. Ogorzelec's work. Thomas Chadbourne might have been proud. Clients are happy with the firm as well. In May 2007, BTI Consulting Group named Chadbourne among the 20 "Power Elite" for superior client service and satisfaction.

GETTING HIRED

One Chadbourne insider in D.C. describes the hiring process as "quite competitive. Very thorough interview process. Talented hiring partner who takes the job seriously." A senior colleague advises, "The firm has a specific GPA cutoff for each school at which it recruits." A corporate associate from the New York office reports, "There seems to be a new shift in hiring to recruit heavily from top schools like Harvard and Columbia, whereas in the past the firm focused on finding strong individual candidates. Chadbourne has even expanded its summer program to hire first-year law students as a way to hook competitive recruits early on." And a midlevel litigator adds, "Getting a job here is not easy, and although the firm prefers top law school graduates, it considers students from other schools who demonstrate their ability to perform." Of course, personality factors in: "C&P is looking for top grades from top schools, law review, etc., but they'll also look at the person individually to see if they think you'll fit in. Of course, if you're the former governor of New York, you're in."

OUR SURVEY SAYS

"Chadbourne is a great place to work. The firm has a collegial atmosphere, a diverse and interesting client base and provides associates with the opportunity to get high-level, extensive experience earlier than most other firms," says one litigator on the happier side of the scale. "The other associates, both junior and senior, are very helpful, take time to answer questions, and make themselves easily accessible." A colleague adds, "The work at Chadbourne challenges my intellect rather than my ability to churn. This is very satisfying." However, a handful of associates sound somewhat disgruntled. One litigator complains, "Sometimes associates are swamped while others are extremely slow, and there is some favoritism by partners for associates. Mentoring is an issue, as is training and development." Associates call the firm's culture "collegial," if not necessarily social. As one IP associate reports, "Everyone is friendly, respectful of each other and willing to help, but there doesn't seem to be much socializing outside the office." A senior bankruptcy associate agrees. She says, "Chadbourne is pretty friendly. The partners have been more open with the firm's finances in the last few years, and are taking steps to make associates happy to work here. I think their efforts are definitely working." One thing Chadbourne definitely seems to get right is compensation, particularly the pay-per-hour-worked ratio. A midlevel New Yorker boasts, "I would bet this is one of the best firms in the world in terms of how much you make per hour." A first-year adds, "Chadbourne matched the latest salary increases and bonuses are market. They give prorated bonuses to first-year associates." As for the required hours, one corporate associate reports, "1,900 billable, 2,100 overall. This is not a hard rule though. The firm is good at acknowledging that you have a personal life and that stuff can happen during the course of the year that prevents you from hitting the targets."

Visit the Vault Law Channel, the complete online resource for law careers, featuring firm profiles, message boards, the Vault Law Job Board and more. **www.vault.com/law**

VAULT CAREER LIBRARY 489

73

PRESTIGE
RANKING

Hunton & Williams

Riverfront Plaza, East Tower
951 East Byrd Street
Richmond, VA 23219-4074
Phone: (804) 788-8200
Fax: (804) 788-8218
www.hunton.com

LOCATIONS

Atlanta, GA • Austin, TX • Charlotte, VA • Dallas, TX •
Houston, TX • Knoxville, VA • Los Angeles, CA • McLean,
VA • Miami, FL • New York, NY • Norfolk, VA • Raleigh,
VA • Richmond, VA • Washington, DC • Bangkok • Beijing
• Brussels • London • Singapore

MAJOR DEPARTMENTS & PRACTICES

Bankruptcy & Creditors Rights • Commercial Litigation •
Competition • Corporate transactions & Securities Law •
Intellectual Property • International & Government Relations
• Regulatory Law • Products Liability • Privacy &
Information Management.

THE STATS

No. of attorneys firmwide: 975+
No. of offices: 19
Summer associate offers firmwide: 56 out of 64 (2006)
Managing Partner: Walfrido J. Martinez
Hiring Partners: William A. Walsh Jr., Jo Anne E. Sirgado

RANKING RECAP

Best in Region
#4 - Miami
#8 - Atlanta

NOTABLE PERKS

• Free premium beer on Fridays
• Emergency baby-sitting
• "Gym allowance"
• Free parking

EMPLOYMENT CONTACT

Amee R. McKim
Legal Recruiting Director
Phone: (804) 788-7395
E-mail: amckim@hunton.com

BASE SALARY (2007)

New York, NY
1st year: $160,000
Summer associate: $3,080/week

All other offices
1st year: $145,000
Summer associate: $2,800/week

THE BUZZ
WHAT ATTORNEYS AT OTHER FIRMS ARE SAYING ABOUT THIS FIRM

• "Awesome place to work!"
• "Old South"
• "Well-connected"
• "Snooty"

© 2007 Vault Inc.

THE SCOOP

Hunton & Williams was founded in Virginia over a century ago, and has been expanding its national and international reach ever since. In 2006, the firm made a bold move westward, acquiring Los Angeles litigation outfit O'Donnell & Mortimer to form a new California office. Hunton & Williams also scored a major coup in capturing client Alcoa away from LeBoeuf, Lamb, Greene, & MacRae. Alcoa, a major Pittsburgh-rooted aluminum producer, had been with LeBoeuf since 1993, paying that firm a fixed-fee retainer rather than an hourly fee. But the company grew tired of the agreement when LeBoeuf didn't meet Alcoa's "desire for flexibility" and failed to "focus on results," according to an Alcoa spokesperson. Presumably, Hunton & Williams can better fill both of these needs. To handle the new account, Hunton & Williams might open a new Pittsburgh office of its own. (The firm may even hire from among the 30 LeBoeuf attorneys left without a home base, when the lost account caused their office to close its doors.) A steel city move is still up in the air, however, as much of Alcoa's litigation is apparently global rather than Pittsburgh-based. In addition to the proposed LeBoeuf move, Hunton &Williams took nearly 100 Texas lawyers left homeless with the closing of the IRS-troubled Jenkens & Gilchrist under its wing in April 2007. The influx has tripled the size of Hunton's Dallas office. In 2007, *The Minority Law Journal* ranked Hunton & Williams among the top 16 percent of the 209 largest national law firms on its "Diversity Scorecard" for having a high percentage of minority partners. The firm also made headlines when it elected Wally Martinez as its firmwide managing partner. He is among the few Hispanic Americans to lead a major, U.S.-based law firm with international offices.

GETTING HIRED

At Hunton & Williams, the "emphasis is on well-rounded individuals. Jerks are not hired. Associate views are respected—candidates must impress all on the interview schedule (partners and associates alike) or they may not receive an offer." Another attorney adds, "Big egos and screamers will not be tolerated here. Neither will whiners or geeks. Normal, smart, hardworking and interactive are key attributes." There is "no specific GPA cutoff, but the firm is attempting to raise its profile, particularly among the good regional law schools (UVA, UNC-Chapel Hill, Georgetown, George Washington)," says a Richmond-based associate. An Atlanta attorney adds, "I get the distinct impression that the firm has gotten more picky over the past couple of years." Overall, says one insider, the "most important piece is that the firm is looking for people who want to commit to the firm. They are not looking for people that are looking to stay for two years and leave."

OUR SURVEY SAYS

Hunton & Williams associates describe their compensation favorably, but with caveats. "General compensation is great," says one attorney, "however, the firm does not provide many other incentives, such as matching 401(k) or pension benefits." Another says, "Although I think our base salary compensation is very good and, certainly, at market, our bonus system seems to substantially lag behind most firms our size." Another attorney notes, "Recent raises have made Hunton & Williams competitive in New York, D.C. and Richmond, and a leader in other U.S. cities. In general, "the firm is conservative with compensation and slow to adapt, but is fair when compensation adjustments are made." And how fair are the hours? "The hourly requirement is 2,000 per year, but the firm is generally flexible with our schedules, client work permitting," says one associate. And with regard to alternative work arrangements, Hunton & Williams "is definitely trying to accommodate flex-time and part-time work schedules. It would be nice if these schedules were given to attorneys without children, but so far these schedules have been used to accommodate parents." Another attorney explains, "Although we have a part-time option, associates must provide a justification for moving to part time, and doing so has the practical effect of ending movement toward partnership." Hunton & Williams' training offerings get middling reviews. "There were trainings on firm policy but little formal training [on] substantive aspects of the law," says one attorney. "Nonetheless, the orientation program that the firm has was very helpful, enjoyable and well organized." Generally, insiders report a friendly, though not overly social, culture. "Everyone in the firm gets along and it is generally a fun place to work," says one source, adding, "The lawyers do not socialize often outside the office." Generally, insiders report a friendly and not overly social culture. "Everyone in the firm gets along and it is a generally friendly and fun place to work," says one source, adding, "The lawyers do not socialize often outside of the office."

Visit the Vault Law Channel, the complete online resource for law careers, featuring firm profiles, message boards, the Vault Law Job Board and more. www.vault.com/law

VAULT CAREER LIBRARY

491

Nixon Peabody LLP

437 Madison Avenue
New York, NY 10022
Phone: (212) 940-3000
Fax: (212) 940-3111
www.nixonpeabody.com

LOCATIONS

Albany, NY • Boston, MA • Buffalo, NY • Chicago, IL •
Hartford, CT • Long Island, NY • Los Angeles, CA •
Manchester, NH • New York, NY • Palm Beach Gardens, FL
• Philadelphia, PA • Providence, RI • Rochester, NY • San
Francisco, CA • Silicon Valley, CA • Washington, DC

MAJOR DEPARTMENTS & PRACTICES

Affordable Housing • Antitrust • Class Actions • Corporate
Governance & Regulatory • Corporate Trust • Energy &
Environmental • Equipment Finance • Financial Restructuring
& Bankruptcy • Financial Services • Franchise Distribution •
Global Finance • Government Contracts • Government
Investigations & White Collar Defense • Health Services •
Immigration • Insurance & Reinsurance • Intellectual
Property • International • International Arbitration • Labor &
Employment • Life Sciences • Litigation & Dispute
Resolution • Private Clients • Private Equity • Products
Liability, Mass & Complex Tort • Project Finance • Public
Finance • Real Estate • Securities • Syndication • Tax •
Technology

THE STATS

No. of attorneys firmwide: 750+
No. of offices: 16
Summer associate offers firmwide: 38 out of 41 (2006)
Chairman and Managing Partner: Harry P. Trueheart III
Chair, Recruiting Committee: Melissa B. Tearney

NOTABLE PERKS

• Free on-site gym in DC
• MoMA membership in NY
• On-site chef in Boston
• Local sports tickets

EMPLOYMENT CONTACT

Ms. Julie Zammuto
National Lateral Attorney Recruiting Manager
Phone: (617) 345-1161
E-mail: jzammuto@nixonpeabody.com

BASE SALARY (2007)

New York, NY
1st year: $160,000
Summer associate: $3,100/week

THE BUZZ
WHAT ATTORNEYS AT OTHER FIRMS ARE SAYING ABOUT THIS FIRM

• "Up-and-coming in private equity"
• "Nothing special"
• "Cutting edge IP"
• "Muni bond are not sexy"

© 2007 Vault Inc.

THE SCOOP

Nixon Peabody's evolution started with the 1999 merger of two firms: Rochester, N.Y.'s Nixon, Hargrave, Devans & Doyle and Boston's Peabody & Brown. Since then the firm has added offices and attorneys from Massachusets to Virginia to Chicago to California. Neither a specialty shop nor a general practice firm, Nixon Peabody is best known for its corporate work, particularly public finance. Nixon Peabody was recognized by *Fortune* magazine as one of the "100 Best Companies To Work For" in 2006 and 2007. The firm handles a wide range of high-profile clients and cases. For example, when everybody's favorite startup airline, JetBlue Airways, initiated its fifth public offering in 2005, it selected Nixon Peabody to handle the $250 million deal. The firm's New York office—which oversaw all four of the previous offerings—took on the deal, which (for the securities wonks out there) entailed 3.75 percent convertible debentures due in 2035. Nixon Peabody demonstrates a strong commitment to pro bono in its communities. Recent highlights include the firm's submission of an amicus curiae brief to the U.S. Supreme Court, supporting the Jefferson County, Ky,. and Seattle, Wash., school districts' use of voluntary school desegregation plans in K-12 public schools. Nixon won asylum on behalf of a woman from Zambia, a man from Kenya, and a man from Tibet, all of whom were persecuted in their home countries because of their political beliefs. In addition, the firm won custody on behalf of an Italian mother, whose son was kidnapped by the child's father and brought to Rochester, New York. This was a complex matter asserted under the Hague Convention. In the end, the mother and son were reunited and returned together to Italy.

GETTING HIRED

How hard is it to get a job at Nixon Peabody? According to one associate: "It depends on the department. It is quite competitive in the boutique practices such as white collar, affordable housing, TIP group, but is much easier in litigation and corporate." A Rochester-based attorney reports: "In this office, you have to be from a respected law school and be at the top of your class. They look at journal experience and employment history as well." A Bostonian further explains: "We recruit nationally and place a lot of emphasis on the interview and probably less on the hard numbers. There is no set GPA cutoff and while we tend to get a lot of graduates from the Boston schools, we look for the best candidates nationally." Generally, the firm is looking for lawyers who are: "Well rounded and personable—an Ivy League pedigree is impressive, but even that is not automatic. We actually (recently) refused to extend an offer to one Ivy League summer associate because that person just didn't seem to have the social skills to be here yet."

OUR SURVEY SAYS

"The best thing about Nixon Peabody is the people you work with. Really nice and friendly and understanding," shares an attorney in the firm's New York office. An associate from Long Island effuses: "I count among my closest friends the 10 attorneys with whom I most frequently work. We go out to lunch together every day; play poker together once a month; and attend each other's weddings, baptisms, kid's bar mitzvahs, etc." A conflicting view comes from the Rochester office: "The firm is becoming increasing less collegial as it grows. Lawyers are more likely to just work their hours and head home to their families." And how about the hours? A pleased Rochester associate says, "My whole department is typically gone by 6:30 p.m." Another insider explains that Nixon Peabody is "very flexible with hours, I set my schedule as I see fit, even as a young associate." The firm delivers when it comes to training its attorneys, according to several insiders. "The firm should get kudos for its formal training programs—they are frequent and valuable, especially as a litigator!" one insider crows. A colleague chimes in: "The training at this firm is excellent. There are both formal and informal training programs and I feel that the firm is committed to my professional success." A real estate associate is less fulsome: "I understand that litigation is more formalized and regular. My practice group's training is more sporadic." According to the firm, Nixon Peabody is "focused on expanding the transactional programs. A full-time transactional curriculum specialist has been hired in 2007 to help accomplish this goal." With regard to compensation, one associate provides a nice overview: "Salary wise, we are certainly paid 10 percent to 15 percent less than our peer firms in our peer markets, however the hours/life-style trade-off is well worth it … The firm, however, pays terrible bonuses. Again, it is a trade-off, I am willing to make." By contrast, a Manchester associate claims that pay does not lag behind other local firms. Instead, the associate says, "My salary far exceeds those of my peers in my geographic region."

Visit the Vault Law Channel, the complete online resource for law careers, featuring firm profiles, message boards, the Vault Law Job Board and more. www.vault.com/law

 VAULT CAREER LIBRARY   493

Thacher Proffitt & Wood LLP

Two World Financial Center
New York, NY 10281
Phone: (212) 912-7400
www.tpw.com

LOCATIONS

New York, NY (HQ)
Summit, NJ
Washington, DC
White Plains, NY
Mexico City

MAJOR DEPARTMENTS & PRACTICES

Banking
Bankruptcy
Compensation & Benefits
Corporate & Securities
International
Litigation & Dispute Resolution
Maritime
Real Estate
Structured Finance
Tax
Technology & Intellectual Property
Trusts & Estates

THE STATS

No. of attorneys firmwide: 315
No. of offices: 5
Summer associate offers firmwide: 37 out of 37 (2006)
Managing Partner: Paul Tvetenstrand
Hiring Partner: Kathryn Cruze

RANKING RECAP

Quality of Life
#5 - Office Space

NOTABLE PERKS

- On-site gym
- "Pizza Fridays"
- Baseball & basketball tickets
- Discounted movie tickets

EMPLOYMENT CONTACT

Ms. Sarah Cannady
Director of Legal Personnel
Phone: (212) 912-7859
Fax: (212) 912-7751
E-mail: scannady@tpw.com

BASE SALARY (2007)

New York, NY
1st year: $160,000
Summer associate: $3076.92/week

THE BUZZ
WHAT ATTORNEYS AT OTHER FIRMS ARE SAYING ABOUT THIS FIRM

- "Excellent in secured transactions"
- "Inflexible"
- "Rapidly rising"
- "Cookie-cutter work"

© 2007 Vault Inc.

THE SCOOP

Thacher Proffitt & Wood traces its roots all the way back to 1848, when a New York lawyer named Benjamin Franklin Butler started a law firm called Butler & Butler. Butler had apprenticed with future-President Martin Van Buren, but like Forrest Gump, the firm would not be content to cross paths with just one American president—it would go on to advise an Illinois lawyer named Abraham Lincoln. More recently, Thacher Proffitt ranked as the No. 1 issuers' counsel for asset-backed securities, according to both *The American Lawyer*'s "2006 Corporate Scorecard" as well as the *New York Law Journal*'s "2006 Book of Lists." In a deal representative of the plus-size transactions associates can expect to work on at Thacher, the firm's structured finance and corporate groups joined forces to represent Citigroup in providing a comprehensive $1 billion refinancing package to Opteum, Inc., a publicly traded real estate investment trust specializing in mortgage finance. In 2006, the firm found itself representing a man more accustomed to issuing legal decisions than seeking legal counsel. Thacher Proffitt's client is Acting Supreme Court Justice William Wetzel, the subject of an investigation by the New York State Commission on Judicial Conduct into whether Wetzel consulted with another justice who issued a decision finding fault with Manhattan District Attorney Robert Morgenthau, a rival to Wetzel's alleged favorite in the district attorney election. *The New York Law Journal* quoted Justice Wetzel as saying the investigation "has nothing to do about judicial misconduct, and everything about judicial independence."

GETTING HIRED

"The firm seeks candidates with excellent legal education from top tier law schools. It also actively seeks lateral candidates who may not have attended a top tier law school, but have excellent compatible practical experience," one D.C.-based Thacher Proffitt associate says. According to another insider, Thacher Proffitt's rapid growth has created opportunities for applicants: "The firm is growing fast so I think that if you come from a good law school or have a decent GPA, your chances of getting hired are strong." A New York-based colleague tells us that the firm "recruits at top tier school and N.Y. schools. Students at lower-tier schools have to be ranked very high in their class."

OUR SURVEY SAYS

Thacher Proffitt is a "very friendly" law firm. "No one yells or screams and everyone respects each other." Thacher Proffitt is "a big firm, with a medium-sized firm feel," remarks another attorney. One associate points out that "socializing among lawyers is very common and encouraged by firm partners and management through the sponsorship of many firm social events." The culture within the firm can vary from department to department, according to insiders. Although the perception is that "structured finance is definitely the group you want to be in if you are at TPW," the firm itself points out "there is an enormous focus on the expansion of the CFI and litigation departments. A perfect example of this are recent later partner hires in both departments from Paul Weiss, Shearman & Sterling, DLA Piper and Cravath, just to name a few. The firm remains actively shopping the lateral partner market to further grow these departments." The hours, of course, "are long" at Thacher Proffitt. "However, when your work is completed at 7, you can leave and people are happy for you that you get out early." An insider explains: "With the firm getting bigger, everyone's been a lot busier so the hours have definitely gotten longer. However, no one's vacations get cut and everyone's pretty flexible as long as you give them advance notice." As another attorney puts it: "Although I work many, many hours, no one is watching my comings and goings." And how well does Thacher Proffitt train its associates? "Firmwide formal training is presented, but there needs to be more training specifically tailored to associates by department," says one lawyer. Reports another: "There is training for first-year associates, but the ongoing training seems to be a little light. There have been some efforts of late to improve this in certain groups." According to insiders, compensation at Thacher Proffitt matches the market, at least until "after the fifth year." According to the firm, "there is a slight difference in the senior associate salaries, but TPW makes a three-percent contribution to all associate 401(k) plans, which can more than make up this difference, and is a rare benefit at most law firms." This deviation is justified, according to one lawyer: "Senior associates get less than at other firms, but given the real chances for partnership, it's not a bad trade-off."

Visit the Vault Law Channel, the complete online resource for law careers, featuring firm profiles, message boards, the Vault Law Job Board and more. **www.vault.com/law**

VAULT CAREER LIBRARY

495

76
PRESTIGE RANKING

Bryan Cave LLP

One Metropolitan Square
211 North Broadway, Suite 3600
St. Louis, MO 63102
Phone: (314) 259-2000
www.bryancave.com

LOCATIONS

Chicago, IL • Irvine, CA • Kansas City, MO • Los Angeles, CA • New York, NY • Phoenix, AZ • St. Louis, MO • Washington, DC • Hamburg • Hong Kong • Kuwait City • London • Milan • Shanghai

MAJOR DEPARTMENTS & PRACTICES

Agribusiness, Ag Biotechnology & Food Processing • Antitrust/U.S. Trade • Appellate • Audit Committee Counseling • Banking, Business & Public Finance • Bankruptcy, Restructuring & Creditors' Rights • Class & Derivative Actions • Commercial Litigation • Commercial Practice Rapid Response Team • Corporate Compliance & Defense • Corporate Finance & Securities • Employee Benefits • Entertainment & Media • Environmental • Financial Institutions • Financial Institutions Regulatory • Franchise & Distributor Law • Government Contracts • Health Care • Hedge Fund • Information Technology • Intellectual Property • International Trade • Labor & Employment • Land Use • Latin American • Outsourcing • Private Client • Product Liability • Real Estate • Regulatory Affairs, Public Policy & Legislation • Risk Management • Securities Enforcement, Compliance & Litigation • Tax Advice & Controversy • Technology, Entrepreneurial & Commercial Practice • Transactions

THE STATS

No. of attorneys firmwide: 798
No. of offices: 14 (as of August 1)
Summer associate offers firmwide: 53 out of 56 (2006)
Chairman: Don G. Lents
Hiring Attorneys:
    Chicago: Brian A. Sher
    Los Angeles: David G. Andersen
    New York: Kira P. Watson
    St. Louis: Robert J. Endicott
    Washington: John C. Peirce

THE BUZZ
WHAT ATTORNEYS AT OTHER FIRMS ARE SAYING ABOUT THIS FIRM

• "Best St. Louis firm, growing nationally"
• "Subpar salary structure"
• "Juggernaut"
• "Provincial"

RANKING RECAP

Best in Region
#5 - Midwest

NOTABLE PERKS

• Biannual firm retreats
• New Lawyer Lunch program
• "Good business development budget"
• Generous parking/commuting allowance

EMPLOYMENT CONTACT

Ms. Jennifer Guirl
Recruiting Coordinator
Phone: (314) 259-2615
Fax: (314) 552-8615
E-mail: jguirl@bryancave.com

BASE SALARY (2007)

Chicago, IL; Irvine, CA; Los Angeles, CA; Washington, DC
1st year: $145,000
Summer associate: $2,600/week

New York, NY
1st year: $160,000
Summer associate: $3,077/week

St. Louis, MO
1st year: $110,000
Summer associate: $1,825/week

© 2007 Vault Inc.

THE SCOOP

Bryan Cave opened its doors over 130 years ago, in St. Louis. Today, it has grown far beyond its regional roots, with growth highlights including a 2002 merger with New York firm Robinson Silverman Pearce Aronsohn & Berman and the upcoming Milan office (to open August 1st, under the leadership of Paolo Barozzi and Fulvio Pastore-Alinante, currently partners in the Milan office of Willkie Farr & Gallagher). The firm is just as good at acquiring real estate for others as it is for itself. 2007 continued the successful trend in the real estate market when the firm, as reported by *The New York Times*, closed four of the 10 largest deals in the country: $1.2 billion for 1290 Avenue of the Americas (NYC), and $1.05 billion for the Bank Of America Center (SF), as well as deals running into the hundreds of millions of dollars for the State Street Financial Center in Boston and the Citadel Center in Chicago. While real estate was dealing in buildings, the M&A group was busy merging client HR/payroll services provider TALX with Equifax, a $1.4 billion acquisition for the credit reporting giant. Shea it ain't so … Bryan Cave attorneys negotiated with the New York Mets to stamp Citigroup Global Consumer Group's name on the ballpark soon to replace Shea Stadium. In what might be, according to Bryan Cave, "the most expensive naming rights deal in sports history," the Mets will spend at least two decades playing in "Citi Field."

GETTING HIRED

One Bryan Cave insider reports, "I don't know of a specific GPA cutoff, but the biggest barrier to entry is not only top grades, but personality. Because we have a good mix of personalities that get along well, we look for people we really think we'd like to work with both on a professional level and as individuals." A Bryan Cave associate from St. Louis reports, "Candidates from top national schools can usually get an offer pretty easily in the St. Louis office, simply because there are not as many big school candidates looking at St. Louis; the firm tends to be much more competitive for local schools—even local national schools in recent years." An attorney from the New York office adds, "If you are from a good school, have respectable grades and are personable, you'll probably get an offer. They like to hire from the Ivies, but also take good students from New York City regional schools and other good law schools." A midlevel associate adds, "Coming in as a lateral it seemed that emphasis was primarily on a good match between my qualifications and my compatibility with the firm's 'core values.'"

OUR SURVEY SAYS

While Bryan Cave's associates may for the most part report that they enjoy their jobs, they don't sound like the kind of workers who would keep on showing up for work even after, say, winning the lottery. As one typical corporate attorney puts it, "I like the people and variety of assignments, and the ratio of pay to hours is very good. But it's still working for The Man—it's not like I get up every day thinking, 'Yes! I'm going to work!'" A midlevel in St. Louis reports, "The work is great, the people are great. The hours can be brutal and compensation is behind most other cities." Associates call Bryan Cave "supportive," "collegial" and somewhere in the range of "fairly social" and "somewhat social." A real estate expert reports, "The firm's culture is friendly, but hardworking. People expect to excel, but not to make others miserable in the pursuit. The attorneys socialize frequently, especially in the summer." A co-worker in the office's environmental department says, "Lawyers are quite friendly, primarily within practice groups. The newer associates socialize, but older attorneys tend to focus more on family." For the most part, associates give good marks to the firm's formal training program. A litigator says that there is "lots of formal training for litigation associates, including a trial training program, deposition training program, writing seminars, client development seminars and a new associate development program." That said, a number of comments by associates in the firm's smaller offices sound a lot like this first-year's: "We're small, so it's not a considerable amount, but they do make an effort." St. Louis associates call their compensation "top of the market," but some feel that's not necessarily the proper yardstick. As one senior associate says, "While we are tops in the area, the general feeling is that we are underpaid compared to peers across the country and for the type of work we do." A colleague summarizes, "Bryan Cave sets the compensation market in St. Louis, and the firm tries to make starting salaries comparable to those in other Midwest cities (adjusted downward for cost of living and billing rates). Whether the starting salary here is too low when compared to, say, Chicago, is an open question."

Visit the Vault Law Channel, the complete online resource for law careers, featuring firm profiles, message boards, the Vault Law Job Board and more. www.vault.com/law

VAULT CAREER LIBRARY 497

Schulte Roth & Zabel LLP

919 Third Avenue
New York, NY 10022
Phone: (212) 756-2000
Fax: (212) 593-5955
www.srz.com

LOCATIONS

New York, NY (HQ)
London

MAJOR DEPARTMENTS & PRACTICES

Bank Regulatory
Business Reorganization
Business Transactions
Employment & Employee Benefits
Environmental
Finance
Individual Client Services
Intellectual Property
Investment Management
Litigation
Real Estate
Structured Finance & Derivatives
Tax

THE STATS

No. of attorneys: 427
No. of offices: 2
Summer associate offers firmwide: 52 out of 52 (2006)
Executive Director: Gary Fiebert
Hiring Attorneys: Stephanie R. Breslow & Kurt F. Rosell

NOTABLE PERKS

- Monthly lunches with "associate buddies"
- Equinox gym membership with pool at discounted rate
- Technology discounts on Microsoft products & Dell computers

EMPLOYMENT CONTACT

Alissa K. Golden
Manager of Legal Recruiting
Phone: (212) 610-7185
Fax: (212) 593-5955
E-mail: alissa.golden@srz.com

BASE SALARY (2007)

New York, NY
1st year: $160,000
2nd year: $170,000
3rd year: $185,000
4th year: $210,000
5th year: $230,000
6th year: $250,000
7th year: $265,000
8th year: $280,000
Summer associate: $3,077/week

THE BUZZ
WHAT ATTORNEYS AT OTHER FIRMS ARE SAYING ABOUT THIS FIRM

- "Best hedge fund practice"
- "Hedge Funds and that's it"
- "Good people getting things done"
- "Hard on associates"

© 2007 Vault Inc.

THE SCOOP

When it comes to hedge funds, nobody does it better. Both the 38-year-old New York headquarters and the brand new London office have been recognized for their investment management practices. This success has paid dividends in the surge of its M&A practice. Cerberus (a major private equity firm) has been a client since 1990. In spring 2007, Cerberus agreed to acquire roughly 80 percent ownership of Chrysler, an immense and complex deal which employed SRZ attorneys from virtually every practice group. In addition, last year's GMAC acquisition earned Marc Weingarten a "Dealmaker of the Year" nod from *The American Lawyer*. The firm also had its hands in deli meat. Specifically, the firm represented Eric Bischoff, great-grandson of Frank Brunckhorst, the Brooklyn meat seller whose operation grew into Boar's Head Provisions, and whose familiar emblem can be seen in many delis today. As the *New York Law Journal* recounted, Boar's Head meats are distributed by a company called Frank Brunckhorst Co. Bischoff, a 20 percent shareholder in Frank Brunckhorst Co., contends that the company's profits have been improperly diverted. Bischoff called on Schulte Roth & Zabel to represent him. The firm secured a ruling from a Manhattan federal judge that Bischoff, as a shareholder, had the right to file suit derivatively on behalf of Frank Brunckhorst Co., a limited liability company. Although such a right is not explicitly delineated in New York statutes, the court found that the right was available under common law. In 2006, Schulte Roth & Zabel continued its pro bono representation of New Orleans citizens displaced by Hurricane Katrina, who fought to prevent FEMA from evicting them from temporary residences.

GETTING HIRED

One SRZ insider puts it, "Unlike many close-minded firms, SRZ is open-minded about taking smart senior people with good related experience and molding them into what they need with good training and patience." This insight comes from this Manhattan real estate specialist: "the difficulty of getting a job here depends on the group. Litigation and T&E have very high standards; corporate is somewhat more relaxed." As for specific credentials, another corporate attorney advises that there is "no GPA cutoff. SRZ seems to focus on New York-area law schools, but also goes to other states. It looks for people with an interest in the firm." A Big Apple colleague elaborates, "Schulte looks for well-rounded individuals with personality as well as brains. The firm concentrates its efforts on schools in the N.Y. area (Columbia, NYU, Fordham) and a few other schools for which it recruits on campus." Schulte notes that it "recruits are more than 25 schools." Two thoughts on laterals: "Getting in through the summer program is fairly rigorous, but lateraling is much easier" and "the firm is looking for laterals that have the experience they need rather than just a great GPA or attendance at an impressive law school."

OUR SURVEY SAYS

SRZ's associates offer up a wide range of opinions about their firm. One crew say things like, "There's good work and plenty of it," or "There's a fair amount of drafting from forms, however there is also enough original drafting to keep things interesting. Low-level associates are given responsibility very early, which has its problems and benefits." However, the dissatisfied contingent is vocal. "In the corporate department there is not enough work for all of the first-year associates," says a New Yorker. Conversely, another junior attorney advises, "Hours are brutal; the expectation is that no real estate associate will bill under 2,300 hours." Associates call their firm "social," "casual," "professional" and "a good mix." As one investment management specialist puts it, "The culture is friendly and mature. Associates are treated as adults—not babies with a law degree." An M&A attorney adds, "This is a firm where you come, do your work and go home. It's not that we don't like each other, but relationships don't go beyond the doors of the office." The firm's formal training program is "useful" and "practical," associates report. A senior corporate associate reports, "Formal in-house training has improved significantly over the past year. We now have numerous CLE programs and can view many of them from our computers. A huge improvement!" And a labor lawyer adds, "Employment group associates are invited to training lunches held by the litigation group and our group also does some formal training at some of our monthly department meetings."

Visit the Vault Law Channel, the complete online resource for law careers, featuring firm profiles, message boards, the Vault Law Job Board and more. www.vault.com/law

VAULT CAREER LIBRARY   499

Perkins Coie LLP

1201 Third Avenue, Suite 4800
Seattle, WA 98101-3099
Phone: (206) 359-8000
Fax: (206) 359-9000
www.perkinscoie.com

LOCATIONS

Seattle, WA (HQ)

Anchorage, AK • Bellevue, WA • Boise, ID • Chicago, IL •
Denver, CO • Los Angeles, CA • Menlo Park, CA • Olympia,
WA • Phoenix, AZ • Portland, OR • San Francisco, CA •
Seattle, WA • Washington, DC • Beijing • Shanghai

MAJOR DEPARTMENTS & PRACTICES

Business Law
Environment & Natural Resources
Estate Planning & Trust Services
Finance
Intellectual Property
Labor & Employment
Litigation
Product Liability
Real Estate & Land Use
Regulatory & Government Affairs
Tax

THE STATS

No. of attorneys firmwide: 600+
No. of offices: 13
Summer associate offers firmwide: 43 out of 46 (2006)
Managing Partner: Robert Giles
Hiring Attorney: Georges Yates

THE BUZZ
WHAT ATTORNEYS AT OTHER FIRMS ARE SAYING ABOUT THIS FIRM

- "Seattle's best"
- "Provincial"
- "Happy campers"
- "Mixed bag"

RANKING RECAP

Best in Region
#2 - Pacific Northwest

NOTABLE PERKS

- Subsidized mass transit
- "Take a new associate or partner to lunch, eat for free"
- Paid sabbaticals
- "The beer refrigerator"

EMPLOYMENT CONTACTS

Ms. Laura Kader
Legal Recruiting Manager—Seattle
Phone: (206) 359-3174
Fax: (206) 359-4174
E-mail: lawstudenthiringSEA@perkinscoie.com

Ms. Heidi Thomas
Legal Recruiting Manager
Phone: (206) 359-3170
Fax: (206) 359-4170
E-mail: lawyerhiringSEA@perkinscoie.com

BASE SALARY (2007)

Washington, DC (1,850 hours minimum)

1st year: $130,000   2nd year: $137,000
Summer associate: $2,400/week

Seattle, WA; Bellevue, WA (1,850 hours minimum)

1st year: $120,000   2nd year: $125,000
Summer associate: $2,300/week

Portland, OR (1,850 hours minimum)

1st year: $110,000 (includes $5,000 guaranteed bonus)
2nd year: $112,500–$117,500
Summer associate: $2,000/week

Menlo Park, San Francisco & Los Angeles, CA (1,950 hours minimum)

1st year: $160,000   2nd year: $170,000
Summer associate: $2,800/week

Phoenix, AZ (1,850 hours minimum)

1st year: $115,000   2nd year: $120,000
Summer associate: 2Ls: $2,200/week, 1Ls: $2,100/week

Chicago, IL (2,000 hours minimum)

1st year: $145,000   2nd year: $155,000
Summer associate: $2,800/week

© 2007 Vault Inc.

THE SCOOP

A few years ago, Georgetown Law Professor Neal Katyal and JAG Lawyer and Navy Lt. Commander Charles Swift, working on behalf of Guantánamo detainee Salim Ahmed Hamdan, settled on Seattle as their venue of choice to file a lawsuit against the government. One of Katyal's former students happened to work at Seattle-based Perkins Coie, and this fortuitous connection led to Perkins Coie devoting substantial resources toward the detainee's case. The law firm helped secure Hamdan's 2006 victory in the Supreme Court case Hamdan v. Rumsfeld, in which President Bush's use of military commissions to try terrorism suspects was ruled unconstitutional. The dramatic rebuke to executive overreaching was one of Perkins Coie's notable victories in 2006. The year also marked the debut of the law firm's Shanghai office, located in a part of the city known as Zhangjiang Hi-Tech Park, a/k/a/ China's Silicon Valley. The two attorneys who will staff the office can plan to focus on intellectual property and other issues facing high-tech companies and pharmaceutical industry clients in the area. But the Shanghai office is not the firm's first foray into China. Perkins Coie already has a branch in Beijing, in addition to domestic offices in a number of Western states and the District of Columbia.

GETTING HIRED

"Perkins seeks those candidates who have diverse backgrounds, aren't timid, and are eager to develop their practice," says one Perkins Coie insider. Another elaborates: "The firm doesn't just interview top-ranked candidates from top-ranked schools. We want to hire interesting people. Many of us had careers prior to going to law school and bring those connections with us to the firm." An associate in the firm's Seattle office summarizes: "Applicants from Pacific Northwest schools have to be at the top of their class." Candidates that took a couple years off before law school are especially liked. Commitment to the region is important, too (often shown through a secondary reason to live in the area, such as family ties)." A Chicagoan reports, "We are particular about pedigree of school, and fairly particular about grades—usually require a 3.5. We focus recruiting (for this office only) on Northwestern, University of Chicago, and Michigan." Insiders also suggest that potential summers should be both competent and nice: "Once hired for the summer, antisocial or rude people are just as likely not to get hired as the ones who don't do good work."

OUR SURVEY SAYS

How to describe the culture at Perkins Coie? "Socially accepting. Politically liberal. Professionally encouraging." It is also "very supportive of pro bono work, including large, politically important cases. The lawyers get along, and are generally even fun to be around. But it's also possible not to see anyone, because people put in their hours and get home to their families." Happily for younger associates, "seniority takes a backseat to talent and ability. Everyone in the firm is required to do both the grunt work, discovery responses and document review, and the more interesting work, depositions, court appearances, etc." As for the partners, they "epitomize professionalism. Everyone is courteous, friendly, disciplined and principled." "The culture is relaxed (we have a minimum billable of 1,850 and our managing partner stressed that he does not want us to bill over 2,000 hours)." Furthermore, "This firm treats attorneys as the professionals they are. You have to take responsibility for billing your hours and being available to the clients, but there is no need for face time at the firm." The implications of going part-time are unfortunately a mystery: "There's a great deal of gossip as to what part time means for partnership, but it's pretty much unclear." The firm gets generally high marks for women's issues: "no one bats an eye at extended maternity leave, and usually no one particularly cares if fathers take paternity leave for a couple weeks. Women's support infrastructure is the most active among diversity-oriented efforts, and include retreats and various social events." However, future daddies should know, "For a firm that brags about its benefits and overall workplace happiness, it is shocking that there is ZERO paid paternity leave." As for the money, Perkins Coie's "screwy multitiered and personalized compensation system" is "set about right for the market" in Seattle, is "tops in the Phoenix area," and is "quite generous for Portland." However, "bonus system is not (yet) transparent" and "health benefits could be much better."

Visit the Vault Law Channel, the complete online resource for law careers, featuring firm profiles, message boards, the Vault Law Job Board and more. www.vault.com/law

VAULT CAREER LIBRARY   501

Stroock & Stroock & Lavan LLP

180 Maiden Lane
New York, NY 10038-4982
Phone: (212) 806-5400
www.stroock.com

LOCATIONS

New York, NY (HQ)
Los Angeles, CA
Miami, FL

MAJOR DEPARTMENTS & PRACTICES

Corporate
Derivatives & Commodities
Employee Benefits & Executive Compensation
Employment Law
Energy & Project Finance
Entertainment
Financial Restructuring
Financial Services Litigation
Insurance
Intellectual Property
Investment Management
Litigation
Personal Client Services
Real Estate
Structured Finance
Tax

THE STATS

No. of attorneys firmwide: 345
No. of offices: 3
Summer associate offers: 27 out of 27 (2006)
Co-Managing Partners: Stuart Coleman & Alan Klinger
Hiring Partners: Claude Szyfer & Patricia Perez

NOTABLE PERKS

- "Profit sharing if you bring in clients"
- Moving expenses
- New laptops
- Free health club memberships

EMPLOYMENT CONTACT

Ms. Bernadette L. Miles
Director of Legal Personnel & Recruiting
Phone: (212) 806-7070
E-mail: bmiles@stroock.com

BASE SALARY (2007)

New York, NY
1st year: $160,000
2nd year: $170,000
3rd year: $185,000
4th year: $210,000
5th year: $230,000
6th year: $250,000
7th year: $265,000
8th year: $280,000
Summer associate: $3,076.92/week

THE BUZZ
WHAT ATTORNEYS AT OTHER FIRMS ARE SAYING ABOUT THIS FIRM

- "Real estate powerhouse"
- "Slick marketing"
- "Friendly"
- "Middle of the road"

© 2007 Vault Inc.

THE SCOOP

Stroock & Stroock & Lavan's noteworthy corporate clients include HSBC, UBS, Merrill Lynch, and Washington Mutual. Overall, almost 400 investment companies (with combined assets exceeding $300 billion) rely on the firm for legal representation. Stroock's real estate department, meanwhile, has been busy with several construction projects that will certainly be making a big impact on their respective skylines. For example, Bearn Stearns, American Express and the United Federation of Teachers all built their world headquarters with Stroock's help. In addition, sports fans will soon be looking at two Flushing Meadows icons differently—the United States Tennis Association and the New York Mets are (respectively) slated to build a new tennis center and baseball stadium. Stroock recently celebrated the ascension of another of its own to the federal bench. In May 2006, Brian M. Cogan, a litigation partner in the New York office, was confirmed by the Senate for a seat in the U.S. District Court in Brooklyn. The prestigious judgeship by no means represents the firm's only newsworthy event that year. Also hitting the papers was the matter of Stroock client Alan Hevesi, formerly New York's state comptroller. Hevesi, represented by partner Joel Cohen, was under fire for providing his ailing wife with a chauffeur paid for by the state of New York. The decision cost taxpayers upwards of $80,000 and was the subject of an investigation by the New York attorney general's office. The scandal forced Hevesi's guilty plea and resignation in December 2006.

GETTING HIRED

Stroock reportedly "wants solid academic candidates, from top schools, but will hire from a wide range of schools. [The firm] seems to like mature candidates with some work experience prior to law school." One Stroock insider breaks things down: "Despite associate efforts to steer the firm away from an emphasis on grades/law review, Stroock usually shoots for people with top grades and/or law review at midtier law schools, or those with passable grades at top-tier schools. We recruit heavily at New York schools—Columbia, NYU, Fordham—as well as at Georgetown, BU, BC, UVA, Michigan, Chicago, Penn." An L.A. Stroockie reports that the firm, "hires at UCLA, USC, Loyola in L.A. … Most hires are top 15 to 20 percent of class. [We] are willing to take risks on student that does not meet grade cutoffs." Finally, according to one insider, "Stroock is very interested in the "fit" of a particular person with the personality of the firm—that approach seems to have weeded out a lot of the crazies that are attracted to large N.Y. firms!"

OUR SURVEY SAYS

"Compared with the vast majority of major New York City law firms, Stroock actually may have a claim of being a lifestyle firm," marvels an insider. Another associate explains, "Even though my department is very busy, the people I work with are good about letting me make time for outside interests. Although face time is (regrettably) important, if you make your outside interests known to others, they are generally understanding and supportive." "'Face time' requirements vary among departments," says another attorney, who also mentions a "big technology upgrade to facilitate working from places other than the office." "For the limited hours, pay is good," one insider tells us. "Stroock was quick to match the market when the firms started raising salaries this year. Both associates and the firm itself were quick to point out that "the firm has no minimum hours thresholds for bonus determination." Which is not to say that hours are irrelevant—one litigator advises, "It is not officially a requirement, but 2,000 seems to be expected" if you want to find more than the minimum bonus on your desk come year's end. Stroock "has done a nice job keeping up" with salaries, but the bonus structure remains "too opaque." As for the firm's culture, Stroock is reportedly a "pretty social, laid-back place. Very family-friendly, meaning that you see photos of kids and family everywhere, and in my department [business and finance], people do try to get home at a decent time to see the family and then work later from home." A bankruptcy attorney says: "Lawyers are friendly within our group but as a firm do not socialize much together." Litigators seem fairly social: "At least the litigation department, is very collegial. Attorneys socialize together and the atmosphere is generally very pleasant." Another litigator says, "There is a group of young attorneys who hang out. There are always social dinners with members of the practice group I work in."

Visit the Vault Law Channel, the complete online resource for law careers, featuring firm profiles, message boards, the Vault Law Job Board and more. www.vault.com/law

VAULT CAREER LIBRARY   **503**

Patton Boggs LLP

2550 M Street, NW
Washington, DC 20037
Phone: (202) 457-6000
www.pattonboggs.com

LOCATIONS

Washington, DC (HQ)

Anchorage, AK • Dallas, TX • Denver, CO • McLean, VA •
Newark, NJ • New York, NY • Doha

MAJOR DEPARTMENTS & PRACTICES

Administrative & Regulatory • Antitrust • Appropriations •
Bankruptcy & Restructuring • Business • Construction
Projects, Infrastructure & Finance • Corporate Finance •
Employee Benefits & ERISA • Employment Law • Energy •
Environmental Law • Estate Planning & Wealth Preservation
• Federal Marketing • Food & Drug • Government Contracts
• Health & Safety Law—OSHA/MSHA/NIOSH • Health Care
• Homeland Security, Defense & Technology Transfer •
Housing • Immigration • Intellectual Property • International
Trade & Transactions • Litigation & Dispute Resolution •
Mergers & Acquisitions • Middle East Practice • Municipal
Representation • Native American Affairs • Political Law •
Postal Regulation • Public Policy & Lobbying • Real Estate •
Securities • Tax • Telecommunications & Technology •
Transportation & Infrastructure

THE STATS

No. of attorneys firmwide: 488
No. of offices: 7
Summer associate offers firmwide: 22 out of 24 (2006)
Managing Partner: Stuart Pape
Hiring Attorney: Philip G. Feigen

RANKING RECAP

Quality of Life
#4 (tie) - Pro Bono
#8 - Best Firms to Work For
#8 - Overall Satisfaction
#10 - Hours
#15 - Formal Training
#18 - Associate/Partner Relations

Best in Diversity
#6 - Diversity with Respect to Women

NOTABLE PERKS

• Subsidized gym membership
• Free beverages
• "On-site cafeteria"
• "Great health benefits"

EMPLOYMENT CONTACT

Ms. Kara P. Reidy
Director, Professional Recruitment
Phone: (202) 457-6342
Fax: (202) 457-6315
E-mail: kreidy@pattonboggs.com

BASE SALARY (2007)

Washington, DC
1st year: $145,000
2nd year: $150,000
3rd year: $165,000
4th year: $185,000
5th year: $195,000
6th year: $210,000
7th year: $220,000
8th year: $225,000
Summer associate: $2,780.00/week

THE BUZZ
WHAT ATTORNEYS AT OTHER FIRMS ARE SAYING ABOUT THIS FIRM

• "Still the K Street Kings"
• "Lobbyists, not lawyers"
• "Interesting policy work"
• "Too D.C."

© 2007 Vault Inc.

THE SCOOP

Washington, D.C. power player Patton Boggs opened its pocketbook wide for political candidates in the run-up to 2006. As reported in *Legal Times*, lawyers at the firm and its PAC gave $770,498 in political contributions from 2005 to August 2006. Only one big D.C. firm gave more. And Patton Boggs gave most of that money—over $526,000 of it—to Democratic campaigns, party committees and PACs. (However, the firm's own PAC aimed for even-handed contributions.) The firm's political donations may have presaged the 2006 upheaval in Congress, but 2006 was also a year of upheaval for Patton Boggs; the firm saw some significant defections, and substantially reorganized its management structure. The firm also participated in a number of notable legal battles. Partner Robert Luskin successfully completed his representation of Karl Rove in the Valerie Plame leak investigation. And Patton Boggs signed on to lobby for a group calling itself Airline Pilots Against Age Discrimination. As the name suggests, the group is pushing for a change in federal regulations that currently require pilots to hang up their uniforms at age 60. *USA Today* recently made Patton Boggs' job a little easier, calling the rule "unfair and out of step with the rest of the world."

GETTING HIRED

An insider summarizes the hiring philosophy at Patton Boggs thusly: "Just like all other firms, Patton Boggs trolls the top law schools for candidates. But I have also noticed that PB values individuals with real experience, be it government, military, industry or in house. Some of our best lawyers did not go to top law schools and did not even start out practicing law. In most cases, particularly with lateral hires, they look at the individual more than the pedigree, and this has benefited the firm. I do not think you would find this creative, eclectic bunch at most national law firms." Another attorney adds that the firm is "also looking for 'go-getters' who will be willing to seek work out and forge their own paths (as associates are not assigned to any particular practice group as first-years). The firm wants people who are outgoing and independent thinkers." Candidates should be nice to everyone on their interview schedules, because "even the most junior attorneys have a say in who gets hired." And students at far-flung schools take note: "The firm is looking to expand the schools it recruits from—more nationwide."

OUR SURVEY SAYS

At Patton Boggs, "The firm culture is both politically and professionally diverse and members often socialize with each other, which makes [the firm] a great place to work." One woman warns of an "old boy network," although a colleague notes that "Women's Forum is good support for female associates and partners and events are very well attended." A Denver associate marvels, "For a firm of this size, it is amazing that the culture is as unstuffy and nonhierarchical as it is here." Another insider notes, "Because of the large lobbying practice, the firm is extremely politically active, but there is no pressure on associates to become involved." With regard to hours, one Patton Boggs insider observes, "The firm is on a big push to increase associate hours. [The] yearly billable goal is 1,900 plus 100 pro bono, but not all associates meet this goal and the firm is trying to change that." "Face time is not really an issue," another attorney advises, "so you can come in late or leave early as long as you get your work done on time and well. There are, of course, nights and weekends every once in a while, but that's pretty standard fare." This attorney also boasts, "Our firm is about as flexible as possible on alternative work schedules, part-time attorneys, etc. For example, we have a reduced 1,650-hour track that associates can elect after their second year." (But another associate warns that part-time attorneys can wind up taking "a lot of work home during hours you're technically supposed to be 'off.'") Formal training is apparently on the upswing. "The firm has put a lot of effort in recent years into revamping the training program, offering more in-house and outside opportunities for training, and creating 'training ladders' for associates to use to track their own progress and needs. Training ladders and opportunities are more clear for litigators and business attorneys than for regulatory/policy attorneys, but the firm's trying to address that. Still a work in progress, but heading in a positive direction." As for compensation, "Salaries are market for entry level, but there is a significant amount of compression beginning in the second year," relates one attorney. Another says that "bonuses will now be split between a billable hours bonus and a discretionary bonus."

Visit the Vault Law Channel, the complete online resource for law careers, featuring firm profiles, message boards, the Vault Law Job Board and more. www.vault.com/law

VAULT CAREER LIBRARY   505

81

PRESTIGE RANKING

Howrey LLP

1299 Pennsylvania Avenue, NW
Washington, DC 20004
Phone: (202) 783-0800
www.howrey.com

LOCATIONS

Washington, DC (HQ)
Chicago, IL
East Palo Alto, CA
Falls Church, VA
Houston, TX
Irvine, CA
Los Angeles, CA
New York, NY
Salt Lake City, UT
San Francisco, CA
Amsterdam
Brussels
London
Munich
Paris
Taipei

MAJOR DEPARTMENTS & PRACTICES

Antitrust
Global Litigation
Intellectual Property

THE STATS

No. of attorneys firmwide: 650
No. of offices: 16
Chairman and CEO: Robert Ruyak
Hiring Attorney: Laura Shores

RANKING RECAP

Best in Practice
#3 - Antitrust
#8 - Intellectual Property

Partner Prestige Rankings
#3 - Antitrust

Quality of Life
#17 (tie) - Pro Bono

NOTABLE PERKS

• Free parking (LA)
• Late evening dinners & cab rides
• Great continental breakfast every Monday (SF)
• Moving expenses

EMPLOYMENT CONTACT

Ms. Janet Brown
Manager, Associate Programs
Phone: (202) 783-0800
E-mail: BrownJanet@howrey.com

BASE SALARY (2007)

Washington, DC
1st year: $145,000
2nd year: $155,000
3rd year: $170,000
4th year: $190,000
5th year: $200,000
6th year: $215,000
7th year: $230,000
8th year: $245,000
Summer associate: $2,788/week

THE BUZZ
WHAT ATTORNEYS AT OTHER FIRMS ARE SAYING ABOUT THIS FIRM

• "THE patent guys"
• "Bootcamp?"
• "Trial specialists"
• "Scorched earth"

© 2007 Vault Inc.

THE SCOOP

Start spreading the news. Washington, D.C.-based intellectual property and general practice firm Howrey LLP is making a break for the Big Apple. In November 2006, the firm announced the opening of its first New York City branch, an office that the firm has started the old fashioned way: by acquiring it. Specifically, Howrey took over Engel McCarney & Kenney, a small New York-based litigation outfit. Mr. Engle and Mr. McCarney and a band of a half dozen lawyers will now be sailing under the Howrey banner. (The third name partner, John Kenney, decided not to come onboard.) With Michael Armstrong, Bill Purcell and Paul Rooney—three senior established NY lawyers who joined in January 2007—this group will form the core of what Howrey hopes will soon grow into a New York operation of more than 30 attorneys. And the expansion couldn't come a moment too soon—as of the announced opening, Howrey already had 35 cases pending in New York. Howrey strives to excel in select areas, rather than serve as a jack-of-all-trades; and the focused approach—including its unique in-house consulting affiliate, The CapAnalysis Group LLC—has lent itself to success. *IP Law & Business'* 2006 "Who Protects IP America" survey lists Howrey as the second-most mentioned firm for IP work by Fortune 250 companies, and *Managing Intellectual Property* ranks it the No. 1 U.S. IP firm. On the antitrust front, *The Financial Times* describes Howrey as "The Most Prominent Competition Firm," and *Global Competition Review*'s GCR 100 survey routinely recognizes the firm as the world leader, in revenue and size. *Competition Law360* says Howrey "continues to bask in its firmly established position as king of the competition mountain in Washington, D.C." Howrey also has been among the top-ranked firms for the last five years in *National Law Journal*'s surveys entitled "Who Defends Corporate America?/Who Represents Corporate America?" and made the publication's 2005 "Defense Hot List."

GETTING HIRED

The magic word at Howrey, apparently, is "litigation." "If you're not a hardcore litigation person, you won't get hired. Simple as that," says one Washington associate. Referring to potential laterals, a D.C. insider explains, "I think if you have serious litigation experience or other niche antitrust or intellectual property experience, you have a strong chance of being hired at Howrey." Yet another Washington associate gives a more detailed picture of what Howrey is looking for. "Apart from getting good grades, the firm seems to also value candidates who demonstrate advocacy skills (moot court participation is almost a prerequisite) and adequate people skills. Personality is a must. As a first-year, approximately half of my class consists of candidates from top-15 law schools, while the remaining half consists of candidates from regional Washington, D.C., schools (such as Georgetown, George Washington, American and Howard)." A Houston associate summarizes that the firm is "looking for candidates in the top 10 percent of their class with good technical backgrounds and the ability to work well with others."

OUR SURVEY SAYS

Happily, "Partners are very considerate about the associates' hours, and it is not unusual for a partner to tell you not to stay too late or, if it is a Friday night and 8 p.m., to stop working and go home." Also: "No face time! You can work as hard as you want. I know plenty of people who just barely made their minimum billables. However, if you seek out responsibility, be prepared to put in more hours." Finally, "Part-time and leave programs appear to be limited to people who have recently become parents." On the other hand, "The firm has been pretty slow in terms of keeping up with market salary raises," complains a Howrey associate. Another says that "bonuses are well below market." One attorney reports, "The N.Y. office is not at market level and recruiting at that office is going to suffer. D.C. is not at market from years four and on." And an associate based in Houston explains: "It used to be that this was a firm where if you stayed for seven to eight years you would make partner, so you were willing to make a little bit less money while working as an associate. Now, however, there is no guarantee that if you stay for eight or nine years, that you will make partner ... so many associates are not as willing to tolerate lower compensation." As for training, "Howrey has LOTS of formal training available [...] and associates are encouraged to attend the extensive training." Another insider agrees: "Howrey is all about training. If you want training, come to Howrey—from in-house seminars to associate 'academies,' you will get your fill of training and then some."

Visit the Vault Law Channel, the complete online resource for law careers, featuring firm profiles, message boards, the Vault Law Job Board and more. www.vault.com/law

VAULT CAREER LIBRARY   507

82

PRESTIGE RANKING

Reed Smith

435 Sixth Avenue
Pittsburgh, PA 15219
Phone: (412) 288-3131
Fax: (412) 288-3063
www.reedsmith.com

LOCATIONS

Century City, CA • Chicago, IL • Falls Church, VA • Leesburg, VA • Los Angeles, CA • New York, NY • Oakland, CA • Philadelphia, PA • Pittsburgh, PA • Princeton, NJ • Richmond, VA • San Francisco, CA • Washington, DC • Wilmington, DE • Abu Dhabi • Birmingham • Dubai • Greece • London • Munich • Paris

MAJOR DEPARTMENTS & PRACTICES

Advertising Media & Technology • Appellate • Commercial Litigation • Commercial Restructuring & Bankruptcy • Construction Industry • Corporate & Securities • Energy, Trade & Commodities • Environmental • Europe & Middle East Corporate • Financial Services • Health Care • Insurance Recovery • Intellectual Property • Investment Management • Labor/Employment • Private Equity • Product Liability • Real Estate • Regulatory Litigation • Securities Litigation • Shipping • Tax/Benefits & Wealth Planning

THE STATS

No. of attorneys firmwide: 1,500
No. of offices: 21
Summer associate offers firmwide: 49 out of 52 (2006)
Managing Partner: Gregory B. Jordan
Hiring Partner: Kirsten R. Rydstrom

RANKING RECAP

Best in Region
#5 - Pennsylvania/Mid-Atlantic

NOTABLE PERKS

• Tickets to Sixers games (Philadelphia)
• Profit sharing once you hit 1,950 hours
• Elective three-month secondment in the London office
• "Great infant care leave program for dads"

EMPLOYMENT CONTACT

Dana B. Levin
US Director of Legal Recruiting
Phone: (215) 851-1406
E-mail: dlevin@reedsmith.com

BASE SALARY (2007)

Century City, Los Angeles, Oakland and San Francisco, CA; Chicago, IL; Washington, DC
1st year: $160,000
Summer associate: $3,076/week

Falls Church, VA
1st year: $135,000
Summer associate: $2,596/week

Philadelphia, PA; Wilmington, DE
1st year: $145,000
Summer associate: $2,788/week

Pittsburgh, PA; Princeton, NJ
1st year: $130,000
Summer associate: $2,500/week

Richmond, VA
1st year: $120,000
Summer associate: $2,307/week

THE BUZZ
WHAT ATTORNEYS AT OTHER FIRMS ARE SAYING ABOUT THIS FIRM

• "Excellent diversity"
• "Oversized"
• "Good appellate work"
• "Unremarkable"

© 2007 Vault Inc.

THE SCOOP

Reed Smith's approximately 1,500 lawyers practice from 14 locations in the United States, two in the United Kingdom, two in the United Arab Emirates, and single offices in France, Germany and Greece. Firm clients include a majority of the Fortune 500, 28 of the top-30 U.S. banks, and nine of the 10 leading global pharmaceutical companies. 2006 was a year of mergers for Pittsburgh-founded firm. The firm completed two significant strategic growth transactions in early 2007. On January 1st, the firm merged with top-30 London firm Richards Butler. And on March 1st, Reed Smith combined with 130-lawyer, Chicago-based Sachnoff & Weaver, Ltd. Even as the firm binges on mergers, it has shed one U.S. office: The Newark office is no more after having faced recruitment difficulties, due in part to its location, according to partner Steven Picco, who was quoted in *New Jersey Law Journal*. In Picco's view, Newark faces a perception problem: it can't hold a candle to New York as an urban ideal, nor to Princeton for suburban comforts. Accordingly, the Newark office's work has now been collapsed into the Princeton and New York offices. In another urban locale, Reed Smith saw considerable courtroom drama recently. A state court jury in Philadelphia, deliberating a hormone therapy case involving pharmaceutical company Wyeth, a Reed Smith client, had one member ejected for wielding a table leg to threaten a fellow juror, and another member who failed to disclose a criminal history.

GETTING HIRED

The competitiveness of Reed Smith's hiring process depends on not only the office you apply to, but also the department you want to work for, associates report. "Hiring is done office by office and group by group," says a midlevel litigator. Another litigator advises, "The candidate has to fit in with the personality of the firm. I've seen the hiring committee pass on people with great qualifications because they didn't necessarily fit the personality of the firm (i.e., they were too high strung, etc.). Good grades help and/or coming from a good school will definitely help, but they're not essential." One midlevel in L.A.—who ought to be on the recruiting committee if she's not—offers this summary: "Being hired entails a very competitive process. The firm looks at many qualities before hiring an attorney. The overall person (which includes GPA, level and type of experience for lateral hires, personality, ambition) must be the right match for Reed Smith. Looking at many factors in selecting a candidate (rather than strictly GPA and law school) allows for the greatest talent to enter the firm, and Reed Smith should be commended for this approach."

OUR SURVEY SAYS

Most associates are positive about their experiences at Reed Smith. "I have the opportunity to work on a wide variety of matters—from complex cases with large teams of lawyers to much smaller matters. And I've been able to take on increasing levels of responsibility," says a midlevel litigator. Of course, the praise is qualified: "management and coordination on many large cases is very poor." Another litigator reports, "I am satisfied with my work and the level of responsibility I have. I wish the partnership process was more transparent." As one senior associate succinctly sums things up, "The work is good and the firm is doing very well." As with the firm's hiring process, don't expect to experience a uniform culture from one Reed Smith office to another. As one Pittsburgh attorney puts it, "Reed Smith has grown into a megafirm through mergers, and its culture is now a hodgepodge. Attitudes and hours vary widely from one office or group to another." In Philadelphia, that translates to an office that is "relatively laid-back," where "screamers are not tolerated" and "people may socialize outside of work." In San Francisco, "We regularly have impromptu lunches, happy hours and even weekend snowboarding trips with colleagues." Another associate advises, "Pittsburgh doesn't have very many young single people. Those that are single, tend to socialize together, but there aren't that many of them." Associates call the firm's formal training program a true asset. A junior litigator boasts, "The firm encourages training on a diverse range of topics. There is actually a 'university' set up that hooks up all the offices via video conference to take 'classes.'" Reed Smith associates say that there is room for improvement regarding pay and hours requirement. As one insider puts it, "our salaries are lower than other firms of our size and perceived level, but that our bonus structure is so terrific that it makes up for it. However, the fact of the matter is that the most significant bonus is generally unattainable for associates and the firm can 'take into account' that we qualified for one bonus when considering others. So the only bonus you can assure yourself of is to work at least 150 billable hours more than required."

Visit the Vault Law Channel, the complete online resource for law careers, featuring firm profiles, message boards, the Vault Law Job Board and more. www.vault.com/law

VAULT CAREER LIBRARY   509

Crowell & Moring LLP

1001 Pennsylvania Avenue, N.W.
Washington, DC 20004
Phone: (202) 624-2500
www.crowell.com

LOCATIONS

Washington, DC (HQ)

Irvine, CA • New York, NY • Brussels • London

MAJOR DEPARTMENTS & PRACTICES

Antitrust • Aviation • Bankruptcy • C&M Capitolink • C&M
International • Construction • Corporate/Securities •
E-Discovery • Energy • Environment & Natural Resources •
European Practice • Government Contracts • Health Care •
Insurance/Reinsurance • Intellectual Property • International
Dispute Resolution • International Trade • Labor &
Employment • Litigation/Arbitration • Plaintiff's Recovery
Practice • Privacy & Data Protection • Products & Torts •
Tax • Victims of Terrorism • White Collar & Securities
Litigation

THE STATS

No. of attorneys firmwide: 361
No. of offices: 5
Summer associate offers firmwide: 21 out of 21 (2006)
Chairman: Kent A. Gardiner
Hiring Attorney: Beth Nolan

RANKING RECAP

Best in Diversity
#19 - Diversity with Respect to GLBT

NOTABLE PERKS

- "Subsidized full-time child care center"
- "Cheap booze" Thursday happy hours
- "Library allowance"
- "Yoga lessons in the office"

EMPLOYMENT CONTACT

Ms. Torey P. Phillips
Senior Manager of Legal Recruiting
Phone: (202) 624-2771
E-mail: tphillips@crowell.com

BASE SALARY (2007)

Washington, DC
1st year: $145,000
2nd year: $155,000
Summer associate: $2,790/week

THE BUZZ
WHAT ATTORNEYS AT OTHER FIRMS ARE SAYING ABOUT THIS FIRM

- "Excellent quality of life"
- "Rubber ducks"
- "Diverse and well regarded"
- "Middle of the road"

© 2007 Vault Inc.

THE SCOOP

In 1979, a group of attorneys left a large law firm to establish Crowell & Moring LLP, and the firm has been growing steadily ever since. In 1995, the firm passed a milestone for diversity when it became the first big-name Washington law firm to vote in a woman as chair. Two months after opening a New York office in the fall of 2006, Crowell & Moring pumped up its litigation bench when the lawyers from a 20-person health care and labor litigation boutique came onboard. In that same time, they lured four prestigious hires to its environment and natural resources group, including Ann R. Klee, general counsel of the EPA, and Chet M. Thompson, deputy general counsel of the EPA. The white collar and securities litigation group has seen a recent bump as well with four new additions, including Philip T. Inglima, whose client work has involved representing executives from Enron, AOL, Reliant Energy, KPMG, Fannie Mae and Freddie Mac. Crowell & Moring is serving as lead counsel for a major aviation client in a global antitrust investigation that has been brought against every international carrier in the world alleging an international cartel to fix the surcharges for air transport. The firm's government contracts group represented a major defense company in defeating a $299 million government defective pricing claim. As the firm continues to increase its focus on intellectual property litigation, it represented a large multinational company in a series of patent infringement actions on a groundbreaking technology used in the oil refining industry. Representing a client that has filed a claim against the Republic of Turkey, Crowell & Moring's international arbitration group is leading the way in the largest claim ever filed at the World Bank's arbitration center.

GETTING HIRED

Get your applications in fast, because Crowell & Moring's "standards are rapidly rising as [the firm] continues to set its sights on competing with larger national firms." The name of a candidate's law school can reportedly make a difference: "If you went to a top-10 school, you will get an offer, no matter what." Another insider narrows the field even further: "Crowell's hiring is extremely slanted towards Harvard and Yale." With regard to nonacademic attributes, one attorney says, "The hiring committee always appears willing to consider candidates with nontraditional backgrounds or less-than-stellar grades who bring something else of value to the table." But be warned: "If you are a freak, even if supersmart, you won't be hired. This is not a beauty contest, but social skills are a must and prima donnas will not be tolerated." The UVA grad who provides this warning adds: "UVA grads fit C&M like a glove." Finally, laterals take note: "Crowell has a very rigorous lateral interview process—much more so than many other firms in the D.C. market."

OUR SURVEY SAYS

"C&M is very relaxed for its size and the level of work it does," insiders report. "It's very collegial and social (particularly among associates)." And "lawyers frequently socialize together." Politically, "while the majority of the lawyers here lean left, the firm features both liberal and conservative attorneys." In sum: "Great people who know how to balance work and life." But the culture may be changing. A couple of insiders take note of the firm's "growing pains." According to one attorney, Crowell's "desire to be a 'top firm' and grow rapidly through lateral hires" means that the firm "closely resembles the firms that it tries to distance itself from." This culture clash appears to play out in the hours requirements. One attorney explains: "While the hours expectation is equal to that of any other big D.C. firm, C&M management still claims that it is a 'lifestyle' firm. That being said, the minimum (to be eligible for a bonus) is a reasonable 1,900 and as a first-year associate I retain a fair amount of control over how hard and when I work." Attorneys may keep "flexible hours as long as you get the work done." But the demands of work can be erratic: "It's feast-or-famine," says one insider, "and I prefer regular meals." As far as part-time work is concerned, "the firm is supposedly amenable to part time, but most part-timers are counsel, rather than associates." However, "they did recently promote a part-time counsel to partner, which I think was a first here." With regard to its formal training offerings, Crowell gets mixed reviews. "Formal training at the firm is somewhat lacking" summarizes one source. "However, the firm is very willing to allow you to attend outside training." And some don't mind staying at home: "[Formal training] has gotten better in the recent past. I give the firm credit for its efforts to think a bit 'out of the box' when it comes to training sessions," says a fourth-year.

Visit the Vault Law Channel, the complete online resource for law careers, featuring firm profiles, message boards, the Vault Law Job Board and more. www.vault.com/law

VAULT CAREER LIBRARY   511

84

McGuireWoods LLP

901 East Cary Street
Richmond, VA 23219
Phone: (804) 775-1000
Fax: (804) 775-1061
www.mcguirewoods.com

LOCATIONS

Atlanta, GA
Baltimore, MD
Charlotte, NC
Charlottesville, VA
Chicago, IL
Jacksonville, FL
Los Angeles, CA
New York, NY
Norfolk, VA
Pittsburgh, PA
Richmond, VA
Tysons Corner, VA
Washington, DC
Almaty
Brussels

MAJOR DEPARTMENTS & PRACTICES

Commercial Litigation
Complex Products Liability & Mass Tort Litigation
Corporate Services
Financial Services
Health Care
International
Labor & Employment
Real Estate & Environmental
Taxation & Employee Benefits
Technology & Business

THE STATS

No. of attorneys firmwide: 750
No. of offices: 15
Summer associate offers: 45 out of 47 (2005)
Chairman: Robert L. Burrus Jr.
Hiring Partner: Jacqueline Stone

THE BUZZ
WHAT ATTORNEYS AT OTHER FIRMS ARE SAYING ABOUT THIS FIRM

- "Getting better and better"
- "Lackluster"
- "Stock on the rise"
- "Archaic"

NOTABLE PERKS

- $100 stipend for cell phone/BlackBerry
- Tickets to football & baseball games
- Breakfast is delivered every Friday morning
- Annual retreats

EMPLOYMENT CONTACT

Ms. Ann McGhee
Firmwide Manager of Attorney Recruiting
901 East Cary Street
Richmond, Virginia 23219
Fax: (804) 775-1061

© 2007 Vault Inc.

THE SCOOP

McGuireWoods is frequently called on by leading publicly traded and privately held companies as counsel for both litigation and corporate transactions. Among those corporate giants are the Ford Motor Company, Verizon Communications, International Paper Co. and E.I. du Pont de Nemours & Co. In March 2007, the firm won a major victory for client Verizon Communications, Inc. over internet phone provider Vonage Holdings Corp. A U.S. District Court jury found that Vonage had infringed upon three Verizon patents, and awarded Verizon $58 million. Verizon's motion to permanently enjoin Vonage from using the patented technology was granted. McGuireWoods has been in steady, far-flung expansion since in the firm was established 1834 in Charlottesville. Think you're feeling remote in Richmond? Try Central Asia. Most people never heard of it before *Borat* came along, but McGuire certainly did. And contrary to the 15 minutes of sociological hype, McGuire's interests are fiscally visionary. The firm established an office in Almaty, Kazakhstan, back in 1994, just after the country's 1991 emergence. Now that it has market economy status, and stands to become a very significant energy exporter, the modest eight-attorney practice is in a niche that could pay off big time. Initially working with government agencies, the firm now represents companies seeking to do business there and the 2006 U.S. government white paper, *Doing Business in Kazakhstan* advises others looking to get in on the Great Game's free market chapter.

GETTING HIRED

When McGuireWoods has to choose between a good school and good grades, associates generally agree that it usually favors the former. "The firm focuses primarily on recruiting top candidates from top-15 schools," says an IP expert. "Grades are important, but matter less the higher up your school is in the *U.S. News & World Reports* pecking order." As for personality types, one firm insider reminds us there is no "I" in team: "The best candidates will be those who give the impression that they will work well as part of a team. This is not a place where those with a "superstar" mentality will thrive. Sure it's great to *be* a superstar, but what will impress people most is your ability to get along with your co-workers and contribute to team goals. The uptight attorney who just focuses on billing and impressing the partners will not fit in here."

OUR SURVEY SAYS

One typically positive firm insider shares, "While every job has good and bad elements, I can honestly say that I enjoy my assignments and the individuals with whom I work." An associate from the Richmond headquarters adds "My job is both challenging and rewarding. As a senior associate, I have been given managerial responsibilities over our team of legal assistants, argue at critical hearings and defend expert depositions in 'bet the company' cases." That said, McGuire has at least its share of malcontents. One dissatisfied associate reports, "Junior associates get very little to no training or guidance." The consensus among associates is that McGuireWoods is a particularly social firm, especially in Richmond. One products liability expert reports, "My firm encourages interaction between its lawyers on both a social and professional level. The lawyers socialize outside of the work setting a great deal." Another Richmond attorney adds, "Most folks are cordial and I have a few friends from work. We'll chat during the day about nonwork things, have the occasional lunch, but there isn't much socializing outside work except among the newest classes." McGuireWoods associates have some complaints about the firm's formal training offerings. Although "All new associates participate in a legal skills program that culminates in a mock jury trial," a senior litigator gripes, "Training for litigators should mean actually going to events such as mediations, motion hearings—not hearing about them on a teleconference." The firm's compensation plan receives mixed reviews at best. One satisfied associate says, "I think that associates are well paid. McGuireWoods does not pay market or pay as much as firms like Mayer or Kirkland, but I believe that salaries are just under market—the trade-off maybe being that our hours are lower." But it's very easy to find associates that sound more like one Richmond first-year. "The firm has not responded to recent market shifts in associate salaries and is currently paying $15,000 to $30,000 less per year than other firms its size nationally," she says. "The firm has failed to communicate with associates about changes in the market."

Visit the Vault Law Channel, the complete online resource for law careers, featuring firm profiles, message boards, the Vault Law Job Board and more. **www.vault.com/law**

VAULT CAREER LIBRARY   513

Hughes Hubbard & Reed LLP

One Battery Park Plaza
New York, NY 10004
Phone: (212) 837-6000
Fax: (212) 422-4726
www.hugheshubbard.com

LOCATIONS

New York, NY (HQ)
Jersey City, NJ
Los Angeles, CA
Miami, FL
Washington, DC
Paris
Tokyo

MAJOR DEPARTMENTS & PRACTICES

Antitrust • Arbitration • Corporate Reorganization • Cross-border Transactions • IP • Labor • Litigation • Mergers & Acquisitions • Product Liability • Public Offerings • Real Estate • Securities • Tax

THE STATS

No. of attorneys firmwide: 336
No. of offices: 7
Summer associate offers: 31 out of 32 (2006)
Chairman: Candace K. Beinecke
Hiring Partner: George A. Tsougarakis (NY)

RANKING RECAP

Quality of Life
#2 - Pro Bono
#3 - Best Firms to Work For
#3 - Overall Satisfaction
#6 - Formal Training
#16 - Associate/Partner Relations

Best in Diversity
#2 (tie) - Overall Diversity
#3 - Diversity with Respect to Women
#3 - Diversity with Respect to Minorities
#15 - Diversity with Respect to GLBT

 ## THE BUZZ
WHAT ATTORNEYS AT OTHER FIRMS ARE SAYING ABOUT THIS FIRM

- "Fun, quirky"
- "Very sociable"
- "Past its prime"
- "Routine work"

NOTABLE PERKS

- "Lots of team dinners at nice restaurants"
- "Thursday pizza night for all lawyers and staff, cocktail parties once a month"
- "You will get reimbursed for anything you spend that is related to work, no questions asked"
- "HHR was the ONLY law firm to have a tent set up across from the Jacob Javits Center providing box lunches, drinks and quiet snacks on the days of the bar exam!"

EMPLOYMENT CONTACTS

New York, NY
Mr. Adrian Cockerill
Director of Legal Employment
Phone: (212) 837-6131
E-mail: cockeril@hugheshubbard.com

Washington, DC
Ms. Maria Marchioni
Phone: (202) 721-4601
E-mail: marchion@hugheshubbard.com

Los Angeles, CA
Mr. Noah Graff
Phone: (213) 613-2878
E-mail: graff@hugheshubbard.com

Miami, FL
Ms. Bonnie Sterling
Phone: (305) 379-7235
E-mail: sterling@hugheshubbard.com

BASE SALARY (2007)

1st year: $160,000
2nd year: $170,000
3rd year: $185,000
4th year: $210,000
5th year: $230,000
6th year: $240,000
7th year: $250,000
8th year: $265,000
Summer associate: 3,077/week

© 2007 Vault Inc.

THE SCOOP

Hughes Hubbard's history dates back to 1888 when it counted among its partners former New York governor and U.S. Supreme Court Chief Justice Charles Evans Hughes. Hughes nudged the firm towards a litigation practice, at a time when most Wall Street firms were immersed in transactional work. The firm now has an illustrious track record of litigation in product liability and niche practices, such as a credit card practice and art law, in which the firm represents some of the most prominent artists and institutions in the world. It filed a friend-of-the-court brief with the United States Supreme Court on behalf of a group of 20 artists, successfully challenging the constitutionality of the Communications Decency Act of 1996 under the First Amendment. Hughes Hubbard was recently ranked 14th among *American Lawyer*'s picks of the 20-best firms in the July 2006 "A-List" issue. At the same time, it was ranked the nation's No. 1 law firm in diversity by *Multicultural Law Magazine*, and has the highest percentage of female partners among the AmLaw 200. The firm has also received the 2006 New York State Bar Association's President's Pro Bono Service Award, in the large law firm category. One major recent victory was on behalf of client Christie's auction house, for whom the firm won a dismissal of a federal suit blocking the sale of Picasso's *The Absinthe Drinker*. Hughes Hubbard argued successfully that the plaintiff's claim (which proved groundless) that the painting had originally been sold under duress to Nazi interests but had been willed to the plaintiff's ancestor was further barred by laches because no legal action was taken in the years prior to the 2006 auction.

GETTING HIRED

Hughes Hubbard's associates say the firm places extraordinary emphasis on fit. "The firm looks for bright, confident, personable people who can carry on an interesting conversation," reports a junior litigator. "They look for candidates with diverse backgrounds and experience. Most of all they look for candidates who they think are positive, intelligent and would be a joy to work with." Another litigator says, "Grades and journal are essential, but the firm is looking to hire people with personality and substance—people you wouldn't mind working with late if you had to. You will stand out if you are engaging and can demonstrate in what is not a very long interview that you are interesting and personable." And a corporate attorney adds, "Having good grades and doing well in school is a given. Above and beyond that, the firm is looking for people who can carry on a conversation, care about work product and are upbeat and positive."

OUR SURVEY SAYS

Hughes Hubbard associates' reviews are nearly off the charts. Here's how they describe their satisfaction level. A first-year litigator says, "Despite my being a young associate, I feel involved in all aspects of the life of the firm: recruiting, meeting clients, representing the firm at seminars. I am also impressed by the quality of work I get: while some assignments may be considered tedious, most are interesting." Another first year reports, "I have the opportunity to do a broad variety of interesting work. The people I work with are intelligent, caring and very supportive of junior associates. I am often given the opportunity to do things that junior associates at other firms would never be allowed to do, and the feedback I get from partners and senior associates is invaluable." A midlevel adds, "I get high-quality work and am given good responsibility." Associates say that the firm's culture is the primary reason to seek out a position there. As one representative insider puts it, "The culture is one of the best aspects of the firm. The communion among staff, associates and partners is very harmonious and that translates into a very pleasant and collegial work environment. While a hierarchy exists as is the case in every firm, it is in many ways invisible in everyday life." A products liability specialist adds, "HHR is very laid-back. People are social, but it's not required. Everyone here is easy to work with and not uptight." Even formal training—after billable hours requirements, perhaps the most common subject of complaint among associates at other firms—scores rave reviews at Hughes Hubbard. Here's how one litigator describes the firm's training offerings: "Especially when you first start as an associate, the firm inundates you with training sessions nearly every day. If you are in litigation (as I am), there are also very involved training programs on trial advocacy and motion practice. Almost the entire partnership and many midlevel and senior associates get involved. The firm makes it very clear that they care about our career development." Another litigator adds, "Formal training is extensive, transparent and dynamic. If there is a demand for new or different types of training, the firm leadership is very receptive to any and all ideas."

Visit the Vault Law Channel, the complete online resource for law careers, featuring firm profiles, message boards, the Vault Law Job Board and more. **www.vault.com/law**

VAULT CAREER LIBRARY   515

Arent Fox LLP

1050 Connecticut Avenue, NW
Washington, DC 20036-5339
Phone: (202) 857-6000
Fax: (202) 857-6395

1675 Broadway
New York, NY 10019-5820
Phone: (212) 484-3900
Fax: (212) 484-3990

445 S. Figueroa Street
Suite 3750
Los Angeles, CA 90071
Phone: (213) 629-7400
Fax: (213) 629-7401
www.arentfox.com

LOCATIONS

Los Angeles, CA • New York, NY • Washington, DC

MAJOR DEPARTMENTS & PRACTICES

Antitrust & Competition • Automotive • Bankruptcy &
Financial Restructuring • Consumer Product Safety •
Contests, Sweepstakes, Loyalty Programs & Gaming •
Corporate • Energy & Environmental • ERISA • Finance •
Food & Drug • Government Contracts • Government
Relations • Health Care • Higher Education • Hospitality •
Intellectual Property • International Business • International
Trade • Labor & Employment • Life Sciences • Litigation •
Long Term Care & Senior Living • Media, Sports &
Entertainment • Nonprofit • OSHA • Real Estate • Tax &
Estate Planning • Telecommunications

THE STATS

No. of attorneys: 300
No. of offices: 3
Summer associate offers firmwide: 20 out of 22 (2006)
Chairman: Marc L. Fleischaker
Hiring Partners:
   Washington DC: Dan Renberg
   New York, NY: David Dubrow
   Los Angeles, CA: Robert O'Brien

THE BUZZ
WHAT ATTORNEYS AT OTHER FIRMS ARE SAYING ABOUT THIS FIRM

- "Great firm culture"
- "Needs to find direction"
- "Smart and diverse"
- "Middle-of-the-pack DC firm"

RANKING RECAP

Quality of Life
#20 - Pro Bono

Best in Diversity
#12 - Diversity with Respect to GLBT

NOTABLE PERKS

- Full-time career coach (with confidential counseling sessions)
- Catered happy hours every Thursday
- Verizon Center suite tickets
- Attorney lounge, complete with 60-inch plasma TV

EMPLOYMENT CONTACTS

New York, NY
Ms. Lisa Visconti (laterals & law students)
Attorney Recruitment Manager
Fax: (212) 484-3990
E-mail: NYAttorneyRecruit@arentfox.com

Washington, DC
Ms. Karyn J. Thomas (laterals)
Attorney Recruitment Manager
Fax: (202) 857-6395
E-mail: DCAttorneyRecruit@arentfox.com

Ms. Jessica Salvaterra (law students & judicial clerks)
Senior Attorney Recruitment Coordinator
Fax: (202) 857-6224
E-mail: salvaterra.jessica@arentfox.com

BASE SALARY (2007)

Washington DC; Los Angeles, CA
1st year: $145,000
2nd year: $155,000
Summer Associate: $2,700/week

New York, NY
1st year: $160,000
2nd year: $170,000
Summer Associate: $3,000/week

© 2007 Vault Inc.

THE SCOOP

It took five decades to open a second office, but Arent Fox is slowly but surely pursuing a growth campaign—it opened its New York office in 1991 with nine lawyers and is currently halfway to its goal of expanding the office to 100 lawyers, with recent recruits coming in as laterals from other firms, as well as from the U.S. Department of Homeland Security. There's also a brand-new L.A. office to consider. Opened for New Year's 2007, it houses 12 lawyers working in the entertainment, software and licensing industries. In August 2006, the firm represented RLJ Development LLC in the acquisition of 24 hotels from White Lodging Services Corp. This is just one of the many deals in which the firm has assisted Robert L. Johnson, the founder of Black Entertainment Television, and his development company in its acquisitions. Sadly, founding partner Al Arent passed away in 2006, but his legacy of committed pro bono practice continues, in deed as well as in name. The firm's internal Albert E. Arent Award for outstanding pro bono work is bestowed annually and, on average, an impressive three-quarters of Arent Fox attorneys log pro bono hours. Current projects include a class-action suit against the USDA for discriminating against women farmers in loaning practices. Additionally, 30 D.C. associates participate in the donation of one day of service per month at the Legal Aid Society of D.C., assisting low-income families with legal issues. Arent Fox was chosen as one of the "50 Best Places to Work in Greater Washington" by the *Washington Business Journal* in both 2005 and 2006.

GETTING HIRED

Arent's hiring process is flexible enough to appeal to those looking for something different than the stereotypical BigLaw mentality, while still being serious enough to "keep out the riff-raff." "Arent Fox is open to smart, talented young lawyers who may not fit the 'typical lawyer' mold," reports a Washington-based insider, who continues: "I see this [firm] as a good fit for outstanding and unique individuals who may not want your run-of-the-mill big law firm." As for a successful applicant's personal characteristics, one associate advises, "Arent Fox really looks for people who not only are academic achievers, but who can get along with others well. It seems like this would go without saying for any law firm, but even now, after having been a lawyer for [X] years, I'm shocked at the behavior of some of my colleagues who work at other firms. You just need to respect those who work with you (and for you). If you have a lot of emotional issues that revolve around your sense of self worth, please don't apply."

OUR SURVEY SAYS

Arent Fox "is unusually open, tolerant and thoughtful—both in its treatment of women, racial minorities, gays and lesbians, etc., and in its general flexibility toward different personal styles and priorities," asserts a New York-based lawyer. A Washingtonian concurs: "Arent Fox is still one of the more liberal law firms in town, with a diverse, friendly group of lawyers. This is also a good firm to be gay or lesbian, with [domestic] partners welcome at the firm retreat. The firm is also supportive of new mothers and fathers." Excepting firm events, after-work socializing appears to be limited: "A group of us tend to go to happy hour downstairs at Morton's at least once a week," reports a Washington IP lawyer. Another Washingtonian says: "There is not much of a social life among associates outside of work." Regarding hours, "the firm is excellent about part-time schedules—at least one partner I know was recently promoted to partner after having been a part-time associate for several years. Face time is not required." A New York attorney adds that "the hours tend to be better than larger firms in NYC." But be warned: "The firm is actively trying to shed its reputation as a 'lifestyle firm,' and the average number of annual hours for associates has increased." The firm's compensation, which some attorneys note is behind par, "has recently been revised and is currently at market." However, Arent Fox "lags behind other comparable firms in the benefits it offers to associates, such as contributions to 401(k) plans and health care insurance." A New York-based lawyer says: "I came to Arent Fox expecting to be paid a little less than friends at top-10 firms. Still, I was very pleasantly surprised that the firm kept up with market in New York. However, bonuses and annual raises are not competitive with top New York firms." Although one associate insists that formal training "is where Arent Fox really stands out," the firm's training efforts generally get middling reviews. "There are plenty of CLEs and department lectures, but no 'useful' skill training programs," says one insider. Another says, "With a few exceptions, [the] firm's in-house training is generally not on par with outside CLE courses."

Visit the Vault Law Channel, the complete online resource for law careers, featuring firm profiles, message boards, the Vault Law Job Board and more. **www.vault.com/law**

VAULT CAREER LIBRARY   **517**

Katten Muchin Rosenman LLP

525 West Monroe Street
Chicago, IL 60661
Phone: (312) 902-5200
www.kattenlaw.com

LOCATIONS

Chicago, IL (HQ)
Charlotte, NC
Los Angeles, CA
New York, NY
Washington, DC
London

MAJOR DEPARTMENTS & PRACTICES

Bankruptcy • Commercial Finance • Corporate • Employee
Benefits & Executive Compensation • Environmental •
Financial Services • Healthcare • International Trade •
Intellectual Property • Labor • Litigation • Media,
Entertainment & Internet • Private Equity • Public Finance •
Real Estate • Tax • Trusts & Estates

THE STATS

No. of offices: 6
No. of attorneys: 650
Summer associate offers: 54 out of 55 (2006)
Managing Partner: Vincent A.F. Sergi
Hiring Partners:
  Chicago: Michael Jacobson & Pamela Smith
  New York: Jill Block
  Los Angeles: David Halberstadter & Samantha Freedman
  Washingon, DC: Brian Corcoran & Catherine Wood

NOTABLE PERKS

• $10,000 referral bonus
• Two weeks paid paternity leave
• One-month sabbatical after five years service
• LA House of Blues "VIP membership"

EMPLOYMENT CONTACT

Ms. Elaine F. Miller
Attorney Recruiting & Development Manager
Phone: (312) 902-5338
Fax: (312) 577-4556
E-mail: elaine.miller@kattenlaw.com

BASE SALARY (2007)

Chicago, IL
1st year: $160,000
2nd year: $170,000
3rd year: $185,000
4th year: $210,000
5th year: $230,000
6th year: $250,000
7th year: $265,000
Summer associate: $2,788/week

New York, NY
1st year: $160,000
2nd year: $170,000
3rd year: $185,000
4th year: $210,000
5th year: $230,000
6th year: $250,000
7th year: $265,000
Summer associate: $3,077/week

THE BUZZ
WHAT ATTORNEYS AT OTHER FIRMS ARE SAYING ABOUT THIS FIRM

• "Highly regarded capital markets group"
• "Average"
• "Realistic re: work/life balance"
• "Thinks it's a player"

© 2007 Vault Inc.

THE SCOOP

Katten's identity is strongly Chicago-centric, but that stands to change, according to an October 2006 *National Law Journal* article claiming that "for firms with a major presence in Chicago, there's a recent urge to expand in the nation's financial capital—New York. Katten Muchin Rosenman "is among the firms that expect their New York offices to approximately double in attorneys over the next two to three years." From its humble beginning as a 24-attorney practice in Chicago established in 1974, Katten Muchin and Rosenman has grown to a nationwide practice with over 650 lawyers, placing 60th in the 2007 AmLaw 100, with nearly $400 million in gross revenue. The firm also recently made it to the top five Chicago firms in *Corporate Board Member*'s CEO survey, and 13 partners were named in 2006 among Lawdragon's top 3,000 lawyers in the country. In 2002, the firm grafted onto some older roots, as they merged with NYC's Rosenman and Colin, a player in the city since 1912. R&C represented one of the world's premier broadcast networks in the 1920s, and a legacy of entertainment and music law continues, with Katten continuing to have a thriving entertainment law division, negotiating EMI's distribution on iTunes, and assisting in many of the revolutionary changes the internet has brought to radio and music distribution. The firm also has a strong tradition of pro bono arts work, winning an award for distinguished service in 2005 from Lawyers for the Creative Arts, and advising such clients as the Joffrey Ballet. In addition, Katten's Women's Leadership Forum sponsored the sixth annual "24 Hour Plays on Broadway" in October 2006.

GETTING HIRED

There are quite a few Katten associates who feel the firm really knows what its doing when it comes to recruiting and hiring: "I think this firm does a great job of evaluating the person and what that person's ability is to contribute to the department that that person is interviewing for. Grades and schools matter, but are not in themselves conclusive." Insiders report that the firm is looking to hire "smart, hardworking, creative, sociable" candidates. Although the firm doesn't focus solely on the Ivies ("we also concentrate on regional schools"), it does use school-by-school "GPA cutoffs." That said, associates say that the firm is more concerned about fit and talent than traditionally impressive resumes or transcripts. "Generally speaking, an 'A' average is preferred," advises a midlevel Chicago litigator. "Obviously, there is a focus on 'top-ranked' schools, but the firm is open to candidates from other schools and nontraditional credentials that are interesting or otherwise unique."

OUR SURVEY SAYS

Katten Muchin's associates report that they are remarkably satisfied with their jobs and their firm. "The level of work that I perform exceeds the expectations of the sort of assignments I thought I would receive as a first-year," gushes a Chicago associate. Another Chitown first-year says, "The firm is professional without being stuffy, and has high standards without being unreasonable." A junior associate adds, "Although I was unsure if I would enjoy the work at a large firm, I have found it to be very challenging and fulfilling." Associates characterize the firm's culture as "collegial," "young," "laid-back" and "hardworking." "The departments are very interactive and cross-functional," reports a real estate associate. "My department is exceptionally social. Working hard [has] made that much easier when you truly enjoy the company of your cohorts." A litigator adds, "Many of the lawyers socialize together, but it is not a firm where it is important to be 'in' with any particular crowd." Associates also give the firm's individual partners a big collective thumbs-up, though they do report that, institutionally, the firm could improve its communication skills. As one senior associate puts it, "Associates do not participate in firmwide decisions. Otherwise, associate/partner relations are not bad, perhaps because most of our partners are relatively young." Associates find the firm's hours reasonable and flexible. "I work a reduced hours schedule and have achieved a pretty good balance between my personal and professional life," says a midlevel associate. "Even before going to a reduced schedule, I was able to maintain a decent balance. Of course, it ebbs and flows, but that is the nature of the business."

Visit the Vault Law Channel, the complete online resource for law careers, featuring firm profiles, message boards, the Vault Law Job Board and more. www.vault.com/law

VAULT CAREER LIBRARY   519

88
PRESTIGE
RANKING

Finnegan, Henderson, Farabow, Garrett & Dunner, L.L.P.

901 New York Avenue, N.W.
Washington, DC 20001-4413
Phone: (202) 408-4000
Fax: (202) 408-4400
www.finnegan.com

LOCATIONS

Washington, DC (HQ)
Atlanta, GA
Cambridge, MA
Palo Alto, CA
Reston, VA
Brussels
Taipei
Tokyo

MAJOR PRACTICE

Intellectual Property

THE STATS

No. of attorneys firmwide: 300
No. of offices: 8
Summer associate offers (2006): 16 out of 16
Managing Partner: Richard Racine
Hiring Partner: Les Bookoff

RANKING RECAP

Best in Practice
#2 - Intellectual Property

Partner Prestige Rankings
#1- Intellectual Property

Quality of Life
#6 - Informal Training/Mentoring
#6 - Office Space
#9 - Best Firms to Work For
#10 - Overall Satisfaction
#12 - Formal Training
#16 - Selectivity
#18 - Pay

Best in Diversity
#7 - Diversity with Respect to Minorities
#14 - Overall Diversity

NOTABLE PERKS

- "Cheap backup child care"
- "Subsidized dining room with good food"
- "Incredible moving benefits"

EMPLOYMENT CONTACT

Mr. Paul Sevanich
Attorney Recruitment Manager
Phone: (202) 408-4000
Fax: (202) 408-4400
E-mail: attyrecruit-DC@finnegan.com

BASE SALARY (2007)

All Offices
1st year: $160,000
Summer associate: $3,000/week

THE BUZZ
WHAT ATTORNEYS AT OTHER FIRMS ARE SAYING ABOUT THIS FIRM

- "Simply the best of class in IP"
- "Unwarranted stuffiness"
- "Intelligent and quirky"
- "Not as good as hype"

© 2007 Vault Inc.

THE SCOOP

Founded in 1965, the Washington, D.C.-based firm of Finnegan, Henderson, Farabow, Garrett & Dunner ranks as one of the nation's premier intellectual property firms—though with over 800 employees, including 300 attorneys and a 500-member support staff of research and technology specialists, the firm has long since shed the "boutique" label. The firm handles IP and only IP, but its work extends to all aspects of the field, including patents, trademarks, copyrights and trade secret law. The firm has argued more cases before the U.S. Court of Appeals for the Federal Circuit than any other firm; in 2006, both *The American Lawyer* and *IP Law & Business* named Finnegan Henderson as the No.1 IP litigation firm. Perhaps the most telling (and remarkable) statistic about the firm is its retention rate: Since its founding 42 years ago, only six partners—total—have left the firm. Ever. In recent months, the firm has filed a trademark infringement action on behalf of Bridgestone/Firestone North American Tire against GPX International Tire Corporation, which claims that GPX "engaged in a systematic pattern of unlawful conduct by knocking-off a series of Firestone trademarks." The firm also successfully defended the drug company Amgen Inc. in a patent dispute over its arthritis drug Enbrel initiated by the Israel Bio-Engineering Project.

GETTING HIRED

Insiders generally concur that getting hired at Finnegan Henderson is competitive. What qualities get candidates through the door? Those who hope to get hired at this firm must do well in law school, but a sharp-looking law school record alone won't do the trick. Candidates will ideally also have spent quality time in the technical world. "Generally, good grades at a top-tier law school and at least a bachelor-level degree in a technical field is required," says one insider. Another says: "Either strong technical training or strong legal training, or, most of [the] time, both." And a third insider reports: "Technical backgrounds are required for patent positions." But when it comes to more specific hiring criteria, what is in force today might not be operable tomorrow: "Our needs change frequently, and therefore, our hiring practices seem to change frequently."

OUR SURVEY SAYS

"Hours are often long," according to one Finnegan Henderson attorney, "and there are projects requiring very short turnaround times, but our schedules are very flexible on the other hand … Many attorneys at the firm, including myself, are able to design schedules that allow for time during the day to take care of personal activities. The firm also allows for attorneys to work from home when that is most efficient." Just how long are the "long" hours? One efficient attorney reports, "I work from 7:30 or 8:00 a.m. to 6:30 p.m. That is more than enough time in the office to get the required 2,000 billable hours and still do non-billable work." Attorneys here apparently aren't asked to cancel their cruises, since "vacations are encouraged." Also of note: "Many more people are converting to 'part time.'" However, one associate complains, "Requiring a woman to bill 2,000 hours the year prior to her pregnancy to make her eligible to go part time can be unrealistic given the challenges of dealing with work and being pregnant (i.e., doctor's appointments, illness, etc)." According to firm insiders, among the firm's strong points is its collegiality: "The collegiality of the lawyers in the firm is one of its best attributes. Everyone works together as a team. Partners generally recognize that the younger attorneys and the law student employees at the firm have important technical contributions to make to our projects." Another attorney says: "The firm's culture is why I joined Finnegan. The camaraderie at this firm is unparalleled. Everyone gets along and is willing to help each other out." And do the lawyers socialize outside of work? "Yes, we often do happy hours after work, and several people play on various sports teams—soccer/kickball/etc." With regard to training, Finnegan provides "lots of training up front as first-years. We have roundtables for patent prosecution every month that are helpful. Several lunch meetings provide incredible training on updates in patent law, new cases coming down, various aspects of the practice, etc." Also, "the firm has an excellent litigation mentoring program." Finnegan Henderson is reportedly no slouch in the compensation department. "The firm remains incredibly competitive and on the cutting edge of compensation," says one associate. A colleague states: "Finnegan is at the top of the associate pay scale and has a very generous bonus structure that equates up to 40 percent of an associate's salary."

Visit the Vault Law Channel, the complete online resource for law careers, featuring firm profiles, message boards, the Vault Law Job Board and more. www.vault.com/law

VAULT CAREER LIBRARY   521

Dorsey & Whitney LLP

50 South Sixth Street, Suite 1500
Minneapolis, MN 55402-1498
Phone: (612) 340-2600
www.dorsey.com

LOCATIONS

Minneapolis, MN (HQ)
Anchorage, AK
Wilmington, DE
Denver, CO
Des Moines, IA
Fargo, ND
Great Falls, MT
Missoula, MT
New York, NY
Palo Alto, CA
Salt Lake City, UT
Seattle, WA
Irvine, CA
Washington, DC
Hong Kong
London
Shanghai
Toronto
Vancouver

MAJOR DEPARTMENTS & PRACTICES

Advocacy
Transactions

THE STATS

No. of attorneys firmwide: 631
No. of offices: 19
Summer associate offers firmwide: 53 out of 56 (2006)
Managing Partner: Marianne Short
Hiring Attorney: Kim Severson

RANKING RECAP

Quality of Life
#13 - Office Space
#13 - Associate/Partner Relations
#17 - Informal Training/Mentoring
#19 - Formal Training

NOTABLE PERKS

- Good parental leave policy
- Domestic partner benefits
- "Luxury box seats for concerts"
- Moving expenses

EMPLOYMENT CONTACT

Ms. Kelsey Shuff
Director of Lawyer Recruiting
Phone: (612) 429-5181
E-mail: shuff.kelsey@dorsey.com

BASE SALARY (2007)

Minneapolis, MN
1st year: $120,000
Summer associate: $2,300/week

THE BUZZ
WHAT ATTORNEYS AT OTHER FIRMS ARE SAYING ABOUT THIS FIRM

- "Intellectual and diverse"
- "Homogeneous"
- "Great IP practice"
- "Middle of the road"

© 2007 Vault Inc.

THE SCOOP

Northern hospitality is in full swing at Minnesota's largest law firm. Firstly, Dorsey & Whitney welcomed Marianne D. Short as its newly elected managing partner in January 2007. The firm also accepted former Iowa governor Tom Vilsack to the rolls, their second former presidential candidate. Though Vilsack's bid for the White House was short-lived, Dorsey's Minneapolis office is home to Walter Mondale, who was vice president under Carter but lost the presidential race to Reagan in 1984. Unfortunately, in addition to the big-name gain, the firm also lost 10 intellectual property attorneys from the San Francisco and Palo Alto offices. After a merger with a Palo Alto litigation boutique in 2005, Dorsey decided to consolidate its NoCal operations and close the San Francisco office. Dorsey has completed more mergers and acquisitions in the last 10 years than any other law firm, according to *Mergers and Acquisitions: The Dealmakers Journal*. Thomson Financial continues to find it hard to kick its Dorsey habit, ranking the firm in the top three among U.S. law firms for numbers of domestic M&A deals every year since the list's inception in 1994. Another long-running tradition for Dorsey is the Law Firm Pro Bono Challenge, of which it was a charter signatory in 1993. For the last 14 years, the firm has met its goal of devoting 3 percent of its billable hours to pro bono work.

GETTING HIRED

Dorsey & Whitney insiders warn that it is tough to make the cut at this firm. A couple of Minnesota insiders cited the firm's top-notch local reputation as the reason it is "extremely difficult" to get in. One Twin Cities attorney noted that most recruits "come from the top schools in the Midwest, but a few come from the elite top-five schools—usually very interesting people with Minnesota roots who chose to pass up the New York/L.A. career path." Another Dorsey attorney insists it is "a bit easier [to get hired] if you attended school in a different state." The firm looks for balanced candidates. In particular, they seek "driven, hardworking people who work well in teams, who care deeply about their professional development, and who care deeply about things other than work." Kindness also counts: "We're looking for nice, well-rounded people who treat everyone—from partners to cleaning ladies—with respect."

OUR SURVEY SAYS

A number of Dorsey & Whitney attorneys report being relatively satisfied with their hours. "I work just the right amount," boasts one Denver associate. A Minneapolis attorney crows, "Dorsey allows associates to balance stimulating work with families, friends and healthy lifestyles." However, another adds a somewhat sobering note: "While the work is rewarding, sometimes the hours are quite long." Hours *can* be flexible at Dorsey & Whitney. A litigator says, "The firm has an awesome hours policy. It is extremely flexible with respect to work schedule arrangements. Also, it counts pro bono hours toward the hourly requirement." A Minneapolis-based attorney agrees: "The firm has very good reduced- and flex-time options," but warns that "Some partners still hold reduced-time schedules against associates … perceiving it as a sign that the associate is not committed." Some Dorsey & Whitney attorneys note that the compensation level is not jaw-dropping, but is fair for the amount of work required. "I am very pleased with the compensation, especially considering the reasonable hours requirement," says a Seattle attorney. "Bonuses are underwhelming, but that's not why people are here," notes a New Yorker. Another adds, "I would rather have my weekends free than the bonus check." Formal training is a "real strength at Dorsey," according to an insider. Another explains, "The firm has training sessions on a weekly basis (too many to attend) and attorneys dedicated to the training process." A Seattle lawyer spoke of "two trips to Minneapolis for training," as well as "a 10-week estate and gift tax class for associates new to the practice area." Overall, attorneys here describe a culture that is "open and friendly." "The firm culture at Dorsey goes hand in hand with the saying 'Minnesota Nice,'" says one source. Another adds, "The culture is collaborative and friendly," and "I feel like I am a part of a community." As far as socializing goes, "The firm is relatively social, although less so than other local firms," according to a Minnesota contact. The social scene, predictably, seems to break down according to age: "Younger lawyers tend to socialize together, but cross-generational social opportunities are fewer and farther between." Another Dorsey attorney seconds the notion of a social divide: "Lawyers socialize together, but there is a social divide between partners and associates." This same attorney cryptically warns: "The overall culture and policies as stated are progressive; the reality is sometimes less progressive."

Visit the Vault Law Channel, the complete online resource for law careers, featuring firm profiles, message boards, the Vault Law Job Board and more. **www.vault.com/law**

VAULT CAREER LIBRARY   **523**

Thelen Reid Brown Raysman & Steiner LLP

875 Third Avenue
New York, NY 10022-6225
Phone: (212) 603-2000
Fax: (212) 603-2001

101 Second Street, 18th Floor
San Francisco, CA 94105-3606
Phone: (415) 371-1200
Fax: (415) 371-1211
www.thelen.com

LOCATIONS

New York, NY (HQ1)
San Francisco, CA (HQ2)
Florham Park, NJ • Hartford, CT • Los Angeles, CA • Palo Alto, CA • San Jose, CA • Washington, DC • Shanghai • London

MAJOR DEPARTMENTS & PRACTICES

Commercial Litigation • Construction • Corporate, Securities, Private Equity and Mergers & Acquisitions • Energy • Intellectual Property • Labor & Employment • Project Finance • Real Estate Finance • Tax, Benefits, Trusts & Estates • Technology

THE STATS

No. of attorneys firmwide: 600
No. of offices: 9
Managing Partners: Stephen V. O'Neal, Julian S. Millstein, Thomas E. Hill
Hiring Partners:
New York, NY: Walter Godlewski & Jeffrey Rosenstein
San Francisco, CA: Anthony Barron

NOTABLE PERKS

• Associate ski trips
• "Higher interest rate bank accounts"
• "Pizza lunches when the weather is really bad"
• Generous bar and moving expenses

EMPLOYMENT CONTACT

Ms. Sela Seleska
National Attorney Recruiting Manager
Phone: (415) 369-7636
E mail: sseleska@thelen.com

THE BUZZ
WHAT ATTORNEYS AT OTHER FIRMS ARE SAYING ABOUT THIS FIRM

• "Construction litigation pros"
• "Hit-or-miss"
• "Lovely people"
• "Problems post merger"

© 2007 Vault Inc.

THE SCOOP

Thelen Reid Brown Raysman & Steiner LLP was created in 2006 through a merger between San Francisco's Thelen Reid & Priest LLP and New York-based Brown Raysman Millstein Felder & Steiner LLP. Although the firm has yet to name an official headquarters, its two biggest offices are in San Francisco and New York. (Indeed, as of this writing the firm has two offices in New York, as well as in L.A.—a common post-merger dilemma.) With their combined specialties, the firm now boasts a client roster featuring some of the biggest names in real estate, private equity, energy, infrastructure, technology, media, communications and intellectual property. Founded in San Francisco in 1924, the pre-merger Thelen Reid was an AmLaw 100 firm and was among the top names in construction law, energy and project finance. Brown Raysman, which was established in New York in 1979, is best known for technology law, as well as for running one of the country's premier real estate finance practices. With 630 attorneys spread out over eight offices, the combined firm jumped right into *The American Lawyer*'s top-50 firms. And according to the British magazine *The Lawyer*, the new firm would have ranked 66th on its 2006 Global 100 list.

GETTING HIRED

One firm insider speaks for many of her colleagues when she tells us "I'm not sure what the policy is post merger. Pre-merger, it was fairly competitive to get a job here as a junior associate. My understanding that to land a summer associate position, you either had to come from a top tier law school or be in top 10 percent or near of second-tier school." Others have a less-speculative take: "[The firm] is looking for a hardworking candidate who understands the importance of being well rounded. GPA is not the be all and end all, although it must get you in the interview. Thelen looks for people who will fit well with the firm culture, and generally people who the partners and associates would enjoy working with." As for specific criteria that the firm favors, associates suggest that personality plays a key part. "We look for bright individuals that are hard workers and team players," reports a senior litigator. Another San Jose-based litigator adds, "Some partners here are looking for a tech background, so a tech background is a plus. Personality is really the clincher—there are a lot of people in the office with young families, so a single partygoer probably wouldn't be the best fit."

OUR SURVEY SAYS

Associates call their job satisfaction level at Thelen high, if not necessarily stratospheric. "The assignments are diverse in areas of the law, including trademark and copyright law, MDL class actions, trusts and estates law, international arbitration and much more," says one insider. A colleague reports, "What I like the most is the sense of autonomy and a lack of micromanagement." A litigator adds, "I really enjoy the people that I work with, the environment and culture within the firm, and the substantive projects I have been able to work on since arriving at Thelen." However, some associates warn that the firm's culture has taken a turn for the worse. "My satisfaction has dropped off enormously post-merger," says a senior associate from the pre-merger Brown Raysman. "While the furniture is better in the merged firm than it was at Brown Raysman, there is little else positive that I can see." Associates call the firm "friendly," "mellow" and "fairly social." As one junior associate reports, "Generally a respectful culture, not a lot of screamers. There is some socializing, but people very much have their own lives." A New Yorker adds, "The firm sponsors plenty of mixers. There is some socializing outside of work, but it depends largely on the department." The firm gets generally high marks for its formal training offerings: "The firm provides associates with a partner advisor who works with the associate to achieve goals that the associate sets for technical, personal and career advancement," advises a New York litigator. A San Francisco litigator adds, "Thelen's training program is top notch. We typically have at least one training a week for first-years ranging from issues such as pretrial discovery to business development." New Yorkers have few complaints about their salaries; associates from other offices complain about New York. As one (non-New Yorker) says, "Needless to say, the New York salaries don't translate to all the other offices." Many associates agree that the reasonable hours compensate for the below-market compensation. A senior associate says, "Although there are certainly other firms that are paying higher associate salaries, when you factor in Thelen's lower billable requirements, I feel the pay is extremely competitive."

Visit the Vault Law Channel, the complete online resource for law careers, featuring firm profiles, message boards, the Vault Law Job Board and more. www.vault.com/law

VAULT CAREER LIBRARY   525

91
**PRESTIGE
RANKING**

Baker & Hostetler LLP

3200 National City Center
1900 East 9th Street
Cleveland, OH 44114-3485
Phone: (216) 621-0200
Fax: (216) 696-0740
www.bakerlaw.com

LOCATIONS

Cleveland, OH (HQ)

Cincinnati, OH • Columbus, OH • Costa Mesa, CA •
Denver, CA • Houston, TX • Los Angeles, CA • New York,
NY • Orlando, FL • Washington, DC

International affiliates:
Juarez • São Paulo

MAJOR DEPARTMENTS & PRACTICES

Automotive • Business • Employee Benefits • Employment •
Energy • Global Practices • Healthcare • Hospitality •
Intellectual Property • International Trade • Legislative &
Regulatory • Litigation • Media • Private Wealth • Real
Estate • Sports & Entertainment • Tax

THE STATS

No. of attorneys: 620
No. of offices: 10
Summer associate offers: 47 out of 59 (2006)
Managing Partners: R. Steven Kestner, Alec Wightman
Hiring Partner: Ron Stepanovic

RANKING RECAP

Best in Region
#3 - Midwest

NOTABLE PERKS

- Six months maternity leave
- Donuts and bagels on Fridays
- Biannual practice group retreats held at "a very nice resort"

EMPLOYMENT CONTACT

Ms. Moushumi Brody
Recruiting Coordinator
Phone: (216) 861-7479
Fax: (216) 696-0740
E-mail: mbrody@bakerlaw.com

BASE SALARY (2007)

Cleveland, OH
1st year: $115,000
Summer associate: $2,100/week

THE BUZZ
WHAT ATTORNEYS AT OTHER FIRMS ARE SAYING ABOUT THIS FIRM

- "Cleveland's best"
- "Nothing special"
- "Really great people who like working there"
- "Unnecessarily competitive"

© 2007 Vault Inc.

THE SCOOP

Baker Hostetler must be one of the best $1,500 investments ever made. Established in Cleveland in 1916 when the firm's founding partners each deposited $500 into a joint account, the firm now ranks as the 58th-largest law firm in the country. Sporting the firm motto "Baker Hostetler is Counsel to Market Leaders," the firm now has 10 offices and more than 600 attorneys, ranking among the 100 top-grossing law firms in the world, according to *The American Lawyer*. Baker Hostetler has respected practices in such areas as tax, litigation, business and employment law. The firm's client roster includes 10 of the Fortune 25, as well as such corporate bigwigs as Boeing, IBM, ABC Inc., Morgan Stanley and Major League Baseball. Among the firm's achievements early in its history was the representation of the defendants in the Village of Euclid v. Ambler Realty, a landmark zoning case that paved the way for widespread zoning nationally. More recently, Baker Hostetler has helped international baseball superstars immigrate to the United States, led a successful legislative effort to ban internet gambling on professional sports (on behalf of MLB), and worked with both houses of Congress to develop legislation to regulate the use of steroids by professional athletes.

GETTING HIRED

"We look for excellent legal minds and the best cultural fit. Intelligence is required but not sufficient. No one gets through the door unless he or she is interesting, unpretentious and preferably possesses a sense of humor," advises one D.C.-based insider. A colleague in the Cleveland office reports, "The firm mostly hires from the 'national' schools (top 15-ish), but top students from Ohio State and Case Western are also well represented. I am sure that there is a GPA cutoff, though I don't know precisely what it is. I am certain that the 'cutoff' is somewhat 'flexible,' depending on the law school pedigree and the personality of the candidate." As for specific criteria, a Cleveland-based midlevel advises, "Grades below a B+ are unlikely to earn a callback. Above that, the firm looks for personable candidates. Ohio State has the strongest representation within the firm." A Houston litigator adds, "This is one firm that judges you by your skills and abilities and not just by the name of law school you attended." However, a few grumblers agree with this Cleveland senior associate: "The firm needs to be much more selective in its hiring. We are bringing in far too many people every year, many of whom are lackluster at best."

OUR SURVEY SAYS

Associates generally praise the work at Baker & Hostetler. As one typical associate puts it, "The quality of work is generally high level, and there is very little 'grunt work,' even for junior and midlevel associates. Compensation could be better, however." A senior litigator reports, "I have been extremely fulfilled with the substance of the work that I receive on a regular basis. I am constantly challenged." A tax attorney adds, "The complex level of work and ability to have client interaction early on is invaluable." Baker & Hostetler's environment is "collegial" and "social," according to those in the know. A junior Cleveland litigator says, "The firm is mindful that its attorneys have a life outside of work. They offer various activities for lawyers to socialize, including monthly wine tasting parties, monthly lunches and an annual golf outing." As another junior Cleveland attorney reports, "There is as much or as little socializing as you would like." An M&A expert adds, "I am friends with many of my colleagues and we socialize together outside of work on a regular basis. I thoroughly enjoy the people with whom I work." Formal training earns mixed reviews. As one representative insider describes it, "The formal training is as good as could be expected, although formal training is, by its nature, of limited utility in law." A senior litigator adds, "The firm will invest in sending litigation associates to NITA and has been good about doing occasional training seminars within the firm or at retreats. The firm also pays for all CLEs. Most training, though, is on the job." Most associates say the pay is below market rates, though not egregiously. A senior litigator advises, "The firm pays slightly below market, but not so low that you'd leave because of it." A junior Cleveland associate warns that "not all associates receive an annual increase." He complains that "compensation is very dependent on spotty 'formal' reviews," and that the "process is not transparent." Of course, the trade-off for the lower pay is a reduced-hours expectation. As one insider puts it, "I work hard when I am in the office, but am not at the office all day and all night just for face time. Management genuinely encourages a balance between work and life. This is something I like most about the firm."

Visit the Vault Law Channel, the complete online resource for law careers, featuring firm profiles, message boards, the Vault Law Job Board and more. **www.vault.com/law**

VAULT CAREER LIBRARY

527

92

PRESTIGE RANKING

Kramer Levin Naftalis & Frankel LLP

1177 Avenue of the Americas
New York, NY 10036
Phone: (212) 715-9100
Fax: (212) 715-8000
www.kramerlevin.com

LOCATIONS

New York, NY (HQ)
Paris

MAJOR DEPARTMENTS & PRACTICES

Antitrust • Banking and Finance • Business Immigration •
Corporate • Corporate Restructuring & Bankruptcy •
Employee Benefits & Executive Compensation • Employment
Law • Environmental • False Advertising • Financial Services
Individual Clients • Insurance • Intellectual Property • Land
Use • Litigation • Outsourcing & Technology Transactions •
Pro Bono & Community Service • Real Estate • Tax • White
Collar Defense

THE STATS

No. of attorneys firmwide: 373
No. of offices: 2
Summer associate offers: 23 out of 23 (2006)
Managing Partner: Paul Pearlman
Hiring Partners: James Grayer & Kerri Ann Law

RANKING RECAP

Quality of Life
#7 - Pro Bono
#18 - Office Space

NOTABLE PERKS

• Backup child care
• "Associates get a percentage of business they bring in"
• Free legal services for real estate closings and will
  preparation
• "Swanky" attorney lounge with flat-screen TV and
  cappuccino machine

EMPLOYMENT CONTACT

Ms. Jennifer Cullert
Director of Legal Recruiting
New York, NY 10036
Phone: (212) 715-9213
E-mail: legalrecruiting@kramerlevin.com

BASE SALARY (2007)

New York, NY
1st year: $160,000
Summer associate: $3,077/week

THE BUZZ
WHAT ATTORNEYS AT OTHER FIRMS ARE SAYING ABOUT THIS FIRM

• "Hard working smart attorneys"
• "Arrogant"
• "Donald Trump's firm"
• "Top litigation, especially white collar"

© 2007 Vault Inc.

THE SCOOP

Founded by 14 attorneys in 1968, Kramer Levin Naftalis & Frankel maintains offices in New York and Paris. With the addition of nearly 300 attorneys over the last few decades, the firm's specialties now include litigation, corporate, bankruptcy, employment, tax, intellectual property, land use, real estate and immigration. In a recent high-profile pro bono case, Hernandez v. Robles, Kramer Levin argued on behalf of its client that New York City violated the state constitution by refusing to issue marriage licenses to same-sex couples. Supreme Court Justice Doris Ling-Cohan agreed and ordered the city to allow gay marriage. In August 2006, the Court of Appeals reversed that decision, reinstating the ban. In another pro bono case, the firm currently serves as co-counsel in a First Amendment lawsuit challenging certain new restrictions on voter registration in Florida. Specifically, the federal lawsuit challenges the constitutionality of a law that imposes an initial fine of $250 on individuals who register voters with third-party groups if their forms are not delivered to election officials within a 10-day period. Kramer Levin also has plenty of high-profile work outside the pro bono realm. It represented Michael Eisner, former chairman of Disney, in the landmark Delaware case In re The Walt Disney Company Derivative Litigation, and represented Fortune 500 company Liz Claiborne in its acquisition of many other fashion industry companies, including Kate Spade, Jack Spade, and Juicy Couture.

GETTING HIRED

Associates call Kramer Levin competitive, but maybe not as competitive some of the biggest of BigLaw firms. As one IP expert puts it, "We tend to recruit at top-10 schools and high GPAs at non-top 10 schools." A senior litigator says, "Kramer Levin can be surprisingly competitive. We focus on the top-20 schools, and tend to do better among the ones in New York City, which makes it more competitive for students from those schools." A midlevel corporate associate adds, "Kramer is pretty tough on grades, and generally likes to see membership on a journal." That said, at least one corporate attorney thinks all this talk of competitiveness and grades and such may be overstated: "[We] really need corporate associates." Associates hoping to transfer in will be well served by scoring a clerkship first, associates advise. As a number of associates report, "Lateral hiring, especially in litigation, is very competitive, and the firm strongly favors former clerks."

OUR SURVEY SAYS

"I have a wide range of clients and types of work—from representing restaurants to large public companies to participating in SEC inquiries to small fashion companies," reports a senior corporate attorney, who speaks for the many Kramer Levin's associates who rate their job satisfaction highly. "I like the juniors and midlevels I work with, and the partners. Not everyone is perfect and the hours can be long, but overall it is very stimulating and I am never bored." Striking a similar note, a junior tax says, "My work is very diverse and keeps me interested and challenged every day. The partners I work for are interested in my development as an attorney, not just in how many hours I can bill. Unlike my previous firm, I can see myself staying at Kramer Levin for the rest of my career." A midlevel associate adds, "I've had a good amount of responsibility and opportunities, however, the hours have been high." Associates call Kramer Levin's vibe "collegial," "social" and "friendly." A senior associate puts it this way: "People tend to be pretty sociable at the firm, but for the most part they want to do their work and go home (at least I do), so people aren't going out to party after work. But plenty of people go to each other's weddings and other special events." Another senior associate calls his officemates "respectful, approachable and great groups. He adds, "There is less socialization than at other firms, but that's partly because many people have families, and everyone respects that commitment." Kramer Levin's formal training is "fine," associates report. As one insider puts it, "It's not as good as what I imagine a huge firm would be like, but there are lots of opportunities for training." A more positive associate adds, "We have mandatory CLEs, and the firm is always throwing training opportunities at us, and paying for all costs. It's great." Associates call the firm's compensation generous, particularly relative to the hours. "Compensation is good except I think most associates would prefer a bonus system where those who work 2,000 hours per year get market, or one without any hours threshold," suggests a midlevel. A newbie adds, "The bonus might be a little low, but considering the hours, it is very good." It must be noted that, for bonus purposes, pro bono work and a variety of business development and recruiting activities count toward that 2,000-hour threshold.

Visit the Vault Law Channel, the complete online resource for law careers, featuring firm profiles, message boards, the Vault Law Job Board and more. www.vault.com/law

VAULT CAREER LIBRARY

529

Venable LLP

575 7th Street, NW
Washington, DC 20004
Phone: (202) 344-4000
Fax: (202) 344-8300
www.venable.com

LOCATIONS

Washington, DC (HQ)
Baltimore, MD
Los Angeles, CA
New York, NY
Rockville, MD
Tysons Corner, VA
Towson, MD

MAJOR DEPARTMENTS & PRACTICES

Corporate Law & Business Transactions
Government & Regulatory Affairs
Litigation
Technology & Intellectual Property

THE STATS

No. of attorneys firmwide: 540+
No. of offices: 7
Summer associate offers: 30 out of 34 (2006)
Managing Partner: Karl A. Racine
Hiring Partners: Robert Bolger, Sharon Kroupa (co-chairs)

RANKING RECAP

Quality of Life
#13 - Hours

NOTABLE PERKS

- Gym in DC office
- Baseball tickets
- Summer bocce tournament with "great prizes"

EMPLOYMENT CONTACT

Ms. Grace Cunningham
Director of Professional Development & Recruiting
Phone: (202) 344-4875
Fax: (202) 344-8300
E-mail: ggcunningham@venable.com

BASE SALARY (2007)

Washington, DC
1st year: $145,000
Summer associate: $2,600/week

THE BUZZ
WHAT ATTORNEYS AT OTHER FIRMS ARE SAYING ABOUT THIS FIRM

- "The BEST local counsel for Maryland"
- "Points off for lame name"
- "Some of the friendliest people I interviewed with"
- "Wannabes"

© 2007 Vault Inc.

THE SCOOP

Venerable Venable maintains seven offices, six of which are in the Washington-New York corridor. The firm's 500-plus attorneys landed it just one spot outside of the top 100 in the *National Law Journal*'s 2006 rankings, and the D.C. office has scored a number of noteworthy victories in recent months. A team of Venable litigators won a case in October 2006 before the U.S. Court of Appeals for the Federal Circuit on behalf of its client Gemmy Industries Corporation, maker of "seasonal décor, animated gifts and unique novelty items" (according to Gemmy's web site). The legal fight centered on a patent for inflatable pumpkins and snowmen. A lower court invalidated the patent, holding that the product had been on sale more than one year before the filing of the patent application. Venable was hired for the appeal, and won the reversal. On the transactional side, in May 2006, a Venable team completed a $45 million offering on behalf of Columbia Union Revolving Fund, a religious nonprofit corporation that raises money by selling interest-bearing notes. That same month the firm closed an $82 million IPO for Harbor Acquisition Corporation, a so-called "blank check" company formed for acquiring an "operating business in the consumer or industrial products sectors," as the American Stock Exchange description vaguely notes.

GETTING HIRED

"There are GPA guidelines depending on the law school, but the guidelines are not hard and fast. It definitely is easier to be hired through the on-campus recruiting process than as a 'walk-in.' Venable looks for candidates who were superstars in their undergraduate career, and who have the potential to stay with the firm for many years. We steer clear of egotistical candidates and search out those who are friendly and easy conversationalists," summarizes one insider." Observes one real estate expert: "[the firm] is not particularly snotty about grades or school." As for specific traits, a midlevel litigator suggests that the firm favors "academic, outgoing, friendly and articulate" candidates. A junior banking associate from D.C. says that his office has "no GPA cutoff" and that the hiring partners "look for well-rounded people who are both smart and personable. Venable recruits at many schools near Maryland, D.C. and Virginia." Finally, some say the firm might not be for those afraid of a strict learning curve, as the firm is "looking for people who can step up and do the work."

OUR SURVEY SAYS

Associates recommend accepting that offer from Venable. "Venable is a great place to work," a senior D.C. associate reports. "There is a great deal of interesting work and the people are great to work with." A Baltimore tax attorney says, "The work itself is challenging, and the partners are not shy about giving associates meaningful responsibility and client contact once you prove yourself. They are extremely flexible with scheduling, quantity of work and deadlines. The partners are exceptionally smart, very approachable, make associates feel as though they are part of the team." An environmental law specialist adds, "The work I receive is challenging. I am also not pigeonholed into any one type of assignment." Associates call Venable's vibe "cooperative," "collegial" and "very friendly." A junior real estate associate says, "People are very friendly and supportive. Associates can approach partners easily and usually work directly with partners. There is a great deal of respect for personal and family time." An IP associate adds, "Lawyers socialize together and are very helpful both on a personal and professional basis." Venable's young attorneys say the firm's formal training offerings are meager, but perhaps on the rise. "There's formal training for some groups, but needs to be more for others," advises a first-year. "The firm has just implemented a more formal training program for associates of all levels." A real estate attorney jokes, "They are getting better, but keep in mind that during the invention of the wheel, an octagon was considered progress." Venable associates generally agree that there is a trade-off between compensation and hours at the firm. "Venable is considerably below market value, but there is more flexibility with making your hours," says one insider. "I don't know anyone who was dismissed for failure to make the 1,900—and there are plenty of people who bill below that." Others consider the firm's pay more than generous. As a Maryland attorney puts it, "$145,000 for first-year associates in Baltimore? Sounds good to me. A bonus at 1,950 hours? Sign me up." As for hours, associates agree that they're entirely civilized. A midlevel associate advises, "Venable's hours are very sane. There is no expectation to regularly work late, on weekends or be on beck and call. Venable has a terrific flex- and part-time reduced schedule."

Visit the Vault Law Channel, the complete online resource for law careers, featuring firm profiles, message boards, the Vault Law Job Board and more. www.vault.com/law

V∧ULT CAREER LIBRARY   531

Squire, Sanders & Dempsey L.L.P.

Administration Center
1500 West Third Street, Suite 450
Cleveland, OH 44113-1408
Phone: (800) 743-1773
Fax: (216) 687-3401
www.ssd.com

LOCATIONS

Cincinnati, OH • Cleveland, OH • Columbus, OH • Houston,
TX • Los Angeles, CA • Miami, FL • New York, NY • Palo
Alto, CA • Phoenix, AZ • San Francisco, CA • Tallahassee,
FL • Tampa, FL • Tysons Corner, VA • Washington, DC •
West Palm Beach, FL • Beijing • Bratislava • Brussels •
Bucharest • Budapest • Buenos Aires • Caracas • Dublin •
Frankfurt • Hong Kong • Kyiv • London • Milan • Moscow •
Prague • Rio de Janeiro • Riyadh • Santiago • Santo
Domingo • Shanghai • Tokyo • Warsaw

MAJOR DEPARTMENTS & PRACTICES

Business
Advocacy
Regulated Industries
Capital Markets

THE STATS

No. of attorneys firmwide: 808
No. of offices: 30
Summer associate offers firmwide: 36 out of 39 (2007)
Chairman: R. Thomas Stanton
Hiring Partner: Timothy J. Sheeran

RANKING RECAP

Best in Region
#2 - Midwest
#8 - Miami

NOTABLE PERKS

• Free parking
• "We have a rec room in the office stocked with TV,
  etc."
• Moving expenses

EMPLOYMENT CONTACT

Ms. Crystal L. Arnold
Firmwide Recruiting Coordinator
Phone: (216) 687-3465
Fax: (216) 687-3401
E-mail: carnold@ssd.com

BASE SALARY (2007)

Arizona and Ohio offices
1st year: $120,000
Summer associate: $2,307.69/week

Florida offices
1st year: $130,000
Summer associate: $2,500/week

California offices
1st year: $145,000
Summer associate: $2,596.15/week

THE BUZZ
WHAT ATTORNEYS AT OTHER FIRMS ARE SAYING ABOUT THIS FIRM

• "Stand-up lawyers"
• "Needs laterals"
• "Explosive growth"
• "Cleveland only"

© 2007 Vault Inc.

THE SCOOP

Since 1890, when Squire Sanders started to address the needs of the local industrializing economy, the big dog from Cleveland has become a global force, sniffing out emerging opportunities, such as diving into the newly opened markets of Eastern Europe in the 1990s. It is now one of the largest international firms in the world, with thirty global offices and strong practices in corporate transactions and project finance. *The Bond Buyer* chose Squire Sander's deal with Citizen's Property Insurance Corporation in a $750 million taxable security issue to assist funding in inevitable and mounting hurricane disaster relief claims in Florida as its 2005 "Deal of the Year." In 2006, the magazine chose the firm again for bond issue by the City School District of the City of Rensselaer, N.Y. In another recent major deal, Squire Sanders negotiated a multibillion-dollar deal for Abbott Laboratories in its acquisition of Kos Pharmaceuticals. Squire Sanders also does a lot of IP and copyright work, rooting out publishing and knockoff-label pirates worldwide, as well as within corporations: working in partnership with the Copyright Clearance Center, they have formed a licensing agreement to address the problems of employees distributing material over corporate networks.

GETTING HIRED

What is Squire Sanders looking for? A Phoenix associate reports that "Top third required, top 25 percent preferred. Well-rounded people with diverse interests, foreign language/international interests preferred." A junior Cleveland associate advises, "Grades are important, but SSD is very proud of how its people work together. The most important thing is to show that you're onboard with being part of a team." Echoing this sentiment is this insider from Miami, "There are academic standards that determine whether someone gets in the door, but once we have a pool of candidates we are looking for someone who would be easy to work with and who can support others." Another Ohioan says the ideal candidate is "Independent and self motivated. Personality counts." "Recently, the firm seems to be more interested in applying the warm-body theory than in actually bringing in the top candidates (perhaps this is a function of necessity, but the firm shouldn't drop its standards)," complains a corporate attorney from the Cleveland headquarters. As a Miami attorney puts it, "Hires have gone from top 50 percent first-tier schools to third- and fourth-tier schools." Another Miami source adds, "If you went to a top law school they will fall all over themselves to hire you."

OUR SURVEY SAYS

Associate satisfaction at Squire Sanders falls all over the spectrum. One content associate appreciates the "high-level work" she is assigned and the "great team-focused approach." Another boasts, "My work is always challenging and interesting. I get a lot of responsibility and client contact, and have since the day I started working here." There are a number of grumblers, however, particularly in the firm's Miami outpost. "The administration, both locally and nationally is extremely layered, disconnected, very slow to act and frustrating to deal with," complains a litigator working there. A department-mate adds, "Litigation is not all its cracked up to be, especially at a large firm. Many assignments are document review. However, after an initial 'proving' period, associates who demonstrate an ability to work independently will be placed on fewer document reviews." Associates call Squire Sanders "social," but "professional" and "family-oriented." A Cleveland litigator reports, "Younger lawyers do tend to socialize together, and so might older lawyers. Right now, I'm in the middle group of lawyers who have young children. I don't socialize too often, except to occasionally grab lunch with someone." An officemate adds, "No one is too busy to be polite, but it is also perfectly acceptable to close your door when you really need to knuckle down on an assignment." The firm's formal training offerings are hit-or-miss, associates seem to agree. "We have a firmwide training program that seems to come and go depending on how busy everyone is," according to a midlevel litigator. "But the firm encourages associates to seek out and take outside training opportunities." Another midlevel lawyer adds, "I would say the formal training is just average. The most helpful training comes from mentoring."

Visit the Vault Law Channel, the complete online resource for law careers, featuring firm profiles, message boards, the Vault Law Job Board and more. www.vault.com/law

VAULT CAREER LIBRARY

533

Kelley Drye & Warren LLP

101 Park Avenue
New York, NY 10178
Phone: (212) 808-7800
Fax: (212) 808-7897
www.kelleydrye.com

LOCATIONS

New York, NY (HQ)
Chicago, IL
Parsippany, NJ
Stamford, CT
Washington, DC
Brussels

MAJOR DEPARTMENTS & PRACTICES

Advertising Law • Antitrust/Trade Regulation • Aviation Law
• Bankruptcy & Restructuring • Broker-Dealer • Consumer
Financial & Merchant Services • Consumer Product Safety •
Corporate • Corporate Finance & Securities • Economic
Consulting & Data Securities • Employee Benefits &
Executive Compensation • Environmental Law • Financial
Institutions • Food & Drug Laws • Government Contracts •
Government Relations & Public Policy • Homeland Security •
Insurance Recovery • Intellectual Property & Technology •
International • India • Labor & Employment • Litigation •
Mergers & Acquisitions • Occupational Safety & Health •
Outsourcing • Private Clients • Private Equity • Products
Liability • Project Finance • Real Estate • Real Estate
Finance • Site Selection • Tax • Telecommunications •
Trade Associations • White Collar Crime/Internal
Investigations

THE STATS

No. of attorneys: 350+
No. of offices: 6
Summer associate offers: 26 out of 27 (2006)
Managing Partner: James J. Kirk
Hiring Partner: Karyn E. Fulton

THE BUZZ
WHAT ATTORNEYS AT OTHER FIRMS ARE SAYING ABOUT THIS FIRM

• "Nice, friendly"
• "Stagnant"
• "Well-rounded"
• "Small fish"

NOTABLE PERKS

• Emergency child care
• "Gym in the building"
• "Friday happy hours"
• "Car rides home after 8 p.m."

EMPLOYMENT CONTACT

Tina Metis, Esq.
Manager of Legal Recruiting
Phone: (212) 808-7728
Fax: (212) 808-7897
E-mail: tmetis@kelleydrye.com

BASE SALARY (2007)

New York, NY
1st year: $160,000
Summer associate: $3,077/week

© 2007 Vault Inc.

THE SCOOP

The New York-based, general-practice firm of Kelley Drye & Warren LLP maintains 26 practice areas, but its primary strengths include advertising, bankruptcy, intellectual property, labor and employment, litigation, real estate and tax law. The 170-year-old firm has managed to put together a rather contemporary client roster, including the likes of Yahoo!, the Dow Chemical Company and, JPMorgan Chase, Bear Stearns and Morgan Stanley. In a 2006 *American Lawyer* survey of summer associate satisfaction, the firm's New York office ranked fourth-highest in the city. Of the 170 firms ranked nationally, Kelley Drye came in 12th overall. The firm's major 2006 transactions included representing India's i-flex solutions in its $122.6 million acquisition of Mantas, Inc., a Virginia-based provider of anti-money laundering and compliance software. The firm also represented Access Integrated Technologies, Inc. in its private placement of $22 million in senior unsecured notes. AccessIT, a leader in providing software and services to the motion picture industry, will use the proceeds to expand its international digital cinema rollout. Kelley Drye's real estate group also represented JPMorgan Chase in connection with the $410,000,000 financing of Prudential Plaza in Chicago and the $363,000,000 financing of the Bank of America Plaza in Atlanta in 2006. Kelley Drye litigators scored a victory in November 2006 when a U.S. District judge denied Canon, Inc.'s motion for summary judgment in an intellectual property case filed by Kelley Drye on behalf of Nano-Proprietary, Inc. (NPI). The suit claims that the Canon/Toshiba joint venture known as SED, Inc., is not covered by a 1999 patent license that NPI granted Canon. The decision dismissing the motion begins poetically: "Dead fish don't swim, dead dogs don't hunt, and Canon's dead voting rights don't give it a majority of the shares entitled to vote' in SED."

GETTING HIRED

Personality is important at Kelley Drye. "The firm seems to like very affable candidates," says one insider. Another adds, "the call-back interview is all about personality." According to one D.C.-based insider, "The firm looks at smart, outgoing people who are interested in life outside the office. There is no specific GPA cutoff that I know of, but as best I can recall, I've never interviewed anyone with a GPA lower than a 3.0. The firm concentrates on D.C.-area schools ('the Georges,' as I call them): George Washington, Georgetown, George Mason. It also likes to get students from UVA." Another insider reports, the "firm looks for congenial leaders who can work as part of a team and also lead; not as focused on GPAs as rivals." A New York associate agrees: "They are looking for good GPAs, but not amazing … They seem to like all the New York schools." And a final thought: "We have attorneys from many schools," according to one insider, and the firm itself points out that "we recruit from 29 schools on campus."

OUR SURVEY SAYS

"Hours are not so bad," reports one Kelley Drye associate. Another says, "I have weeks in which I'm incredibly busy, but for the most part I feel like my hours are great. I work some weekends and late nights but that is definitely not the norm." One junior associate comments, "Even as a first-year, I've felt very little pressure for face time—and several other junior associates at the firm have noted the same thing." Flex-time is a work in progress: "The firm only recently formalized its flex-time policy (ridiculously late in the game) so we have yet to see if this will work out better than the adhoc flex-time policy that used to exist." The manageable hours at Kelley Drye seem to go hand in hand with a congenial culture: "Lawyers generally get along very well here, and the merger last year did not change that. I know associates often socialize together, especially in the summer, when there are more happy hours and softball games." Another attorney reports, "communication between firm management and associates is less than stellar, but overall everyone has a healthy respect for one another, which leads to a productive work environment." Training, however, "is an area that Kelley Drye could really improve on." One associate explains: "Not a whole lot of formal training. There is a mentoring system, and they provide useful strategic guidance (how to handle situations), but very little in the way of formal training focuses on enhancing legal skills." What the firm does have by way of training is "many if not all of the CLE services" and one antitrust associate found "the Lexis and Westlaw research sessions were very useful."

Visit the Vault Law Channel, the complete online resource for law careers, featuring firm profiles, message boards, the Vault Law Job Board and more. **www.vault.com/law**

VAULT CAREER LIBRARY 535

Dickstein Shapiro LLP

1825 I Street, NW
Washington, DC 20006
Phone: (202) 420-2200
www.dicksteinshapiro.com

LOCATIONS

Washington, DC (HQ)
Los Angeles, CA
New York, NY

MAJOR DEPARTMENTS & PRACTICES

Antitrust & Dispute Resolution
Business & Securities Law
Corporate & Finance
Energy
Government Law & Strategy
Insurance Coverage
Intellectual Property

THE STATS

No. of attorneys: 400
No. of offices: 3
Summer associate offers: 16 out of 16 (2006)
Chairman: Michael E. Nannes
Hiring Partner: Patrick W. Lynch

RANKING RECAP

Quality of Life
#8 - Informal Training/Mentoring
#9 - Pro Bono
#10 - Best Firms to Work For
#14 - Overall Satisfaction
#14 - Associate/Partner Relations
#14 - Office Space
#16 - Hours

Best in Diversity
#1 - Diversity with Respect to Minorities
#1 - Overall Diversity
#2 - Diversity with Respect to Women
#6 - Diversity with Respect to GLBT

NOTABLE PERKS

- Free in-building gym (DC), subsidized gym (NY)
- Cafeteria with "Starbucks kiosk" (DC)
- Extracurricular classes, including yoga and foreign languages
- "Firm-sponsored happy hours"

EMPLOYMENT CONTACT

Ms. Julie B. Miles
Manager of Attorney Recruiting
Phone: (202) 420-4875
Fax: (202) 420-2201
E-mail: MilesJ@dicksteinshapiro.com

BASE SALARY (2007)

All Offices
1st year: $160,000
Summer associate: $3,100/week

THE BUZZ
WHAT ATTORNEYS AT OTHER FIRMS ARE SAYING ABOUT THIS FIRM

- "Up-and-coming"
- "NY culture firm"
- "Happy associates"
- "Litigation heavy"

© 2007 Vault Inc.

THE SCOOP

For over 50 years, since 1953, Dickstein Shapiro went about its business in Washington, known for its insurance, energy, IP and litigation work it does for such clients as Fox Entertainment Group, KeySpan, and Hitachi. Then in 2003, PPP soared above $1 million thanks to a very sweet settlement in an antitrust case against vitamin manufacturers accused of price fixing. Four years hence, Dickstein is still using the windfall to invest in its own growth. After bringing onboard the entirety of L.A. insurance practice Pasich and Kornfeld in 2005, Dickstein Shapiro went on a lateral recruiting spree. Recent acquisitions include Arnold Gulkowitz and Brian E. Goldberg from Orrick, Herrington & Sutcliffe, hired with the intent of launching a New York bankruptcy practice for the firm. The firm has also brought in former FEC Chairman Scott Thomas to head and develop its political law practice, and two former members of the Oversight and Investigations Subcommittee for the U.S. House Committee on Energy & Commerce, Mark Paoletta and Andrew Snowdon, to expand the congressional investigations practice. The firm is also looking to impress recent grads with its sweet digs. Dickstein Shapiro D.C. put the finishing touches on a major renovation in time for New Year's 2007, coming only months after they moved to their new headquarters on I street. For its 30 years at L street, the firm didn't have a cafeteria. Now, the Fireside Café is the highlight of the office, with its contemporary design, glass-enclosed fireplace, armchairs and banquettes. The goal was to create a space "where people feel more at home."

GETTING HIRED

The prevailing adjective for Dickstein Shapiro's hiring process is "competitive." The longer you wait to apply, the harder it may get—a popular qualifier for that "competitive" is "and getting more[so]." Although some worry that the firm "is getting too selective and missing out on quality associates because of a combination of grades/schools," "the firm does hire people with excellent grades from local law schools." Associates warn that, while Dickstein is not as difficult a gig as some other places, "underperformers need not apply." Statistical qualifications aside, "personality and demeanor is key," says a corporate lawyer. When we asked associates to define the type of candidate the firm prefers to hire, the discussion was less about GPA and percentages, and more about listing positive personality traits. For example: "respectfulness and initiative," "organized and energetic," "upbeat and articulate." Overall, be "interesting." ("No boring, long-winded candidates need apply.") And don't forget the practical: "good judgment, strong research and writing skills … and demonstrated leadership ability."

OUR SURVEY SAYS

It must be something in the air. Dickstein associates keep referring to their "great environment!" and "relaxed atmosphere." Basically, "I enjoy the work I'm doing, [and] the people I work with," as a Washington associate puts it. With a few exceptions (associates whose interests don't match their assignments) the work is "fulfilling [and] challenging." A first-year commented that, out of five months on the job, he has "spent fewer than two weeks doing doc review." The people are fittingly "professional, considerate and courteous" … and social, though mainly along "floor assignment, case and class year" lines. Plus, the new café allows for lunch congregations. Teamwork and respect characterize associate/partner relations. Partners "seem to understand that keeping associates happy is in their best interests too" and "senior lawyers … genuinely want associates to succeed." Beware also that you might run into one of the few partners with an excellent business reputation but poor associate management skills. The firm "makes all the right efforts" to encourage mentoring relationships and even if "individual partners don't always live up to the firm's goals," most of them do. "There's no 'hiding the ball' about skills, information, or knowledge" and a first-year finds "it has been a pleasure to receive positive and constructive feedback and telephone calls and e-mails with appreciation for hard work and jobs well done." Management keeps associates well informed through presentations and associate reps, but a skeptical senior associate notes, "The news is always positive …" Dickstein associates are happy (and in some cases "surprised") to note that the firm has matched market salaries, in every market. Instead, it's the bonus structure that concerns them. All three Dickstein offices recently changed to "what appears to be a traditional lock-step" system, though transparency in this area is somewhat lacking. Merit awards do exist, but are "reserved only for a few," causing jealousy toward perceived partner favorites. You won't get too sweaty earning that "sweat bonus" though: as far as hours, "My firm is extremely flexible and willing to accommodate different lifestyles."

Visit the Vault Law Channel, the complete online resource for law careers, featuring firm profiles, message boards, the Vault Law Job Board and more. www.vault.com/law

VAULT CAREER LIBRARY

537

97

Fenwick & West LLP

Silicon Valley Center
801 California Street
Mountain View, CA 94041
Phone: (650) 988-8500
Fax: (650) 938-5200
www.fenwick.com

LOCATIONS

Mountain View, CA (HQ)
Boise, ID
San Francisco, CA

MAJOR DEPARTMENTS & PRACTICES

Antitrust • China Practice • Copyright • Copyright Litigation
• Corporate • Electronic Information Management •
Employment Practices • Executive Compensation &
Employee Benefits • Intellectual Property • Litigation •
Mergers & Acquisitions • Patent • Patent Litigation •
Privacy & Data Security • Private Equity • Securities •
Securities Litigation • Start-ups & VC • Tax • Tax Litigation
• Technology Transactions • Trade Secret • Trade Secret
Litigation • Trademark • Trademark Litigation

THE STATS

No. of attorneys firmwide: 244
No. of offices: 3
Summer associate offers firmwide: 22 out of 25 (2006)
Managing Partner: Kathryn J. Fritz
Hiring Partners: Rajiv Patel & Jedediah Wakefield

RANKING RECAP

Best in Practice
#4 - Technology

Quality of Life
#19 - Office Space

Best in Diversity
#18 - Diversity with Respect to Minorities

NOTABLE PERKS

• Firm condos in Hawaii
• "Pet insurance"
• Treos and "standard-issue dual monitors"
• Free late evening dinners Monday through Thursday

EMPLOYMENT CONTACTS

Ms. Julieta Wiley
Manager of Attorney Recruiting & Diversity
Phone: (650) 335-4949
Fax: (650) 938-5200
E-mail: recruit@fenwick.com

BASE SALARY (2007)

Mountain View, CA
1st year: $160,000
Summer associate: $2,800/week

THE BUZZ
WHAT ATTORNEYS AT OTHER FIRMS ARE SAYING ABOUT THIS FIRM

• "Excellent emerging company practice"
• "Always the stepchild"
• "Cutting edge; great environment"
• "Nerdy"

© 2007 Vault Inc.

THE SCOOP

Established by four techie attorneys in the center of the Silicon Valley in 1972, the boutique of Fenwick & West has played about as big of a role in technology law as any firm in the country: the firm, for example, incorporated Apple Computer in 1976 and helped take Oracle public in 1986. In the ensuing decades, Fenwick has been the go-to firm for Silicon Valley IPOs and M&As, including both the largest-ever internet merger (VeriSign's $21 billion acquisition of Network Solutions) and the largest-ever software merger (Symantec's $13 billion purchase of VERITAS). The firm's IP practice pioneered numerous technologies and practices that are now considered industry standards, including the use of "shrinkwrap" license agreements in the 1970s and the creation of software development "clean rooms" in the 1980s. Fenwick is now the second-largest law firm in Silicon Valley, the second most profitable in the Bay Area and the 15th-largest in California. The many notable technology lawsuits handled by the firm's litigators include its successful defense of Amazon.com's "1-Click" patent (just in time, incidentally, for the 1999 holiday shopping season); its defense of Napster against the RIAA; and representation of Macromedia against arch rival Adobe Systems over the copyrights and patents covering software interfaces. More recently, the firm's corporate attorneys represented Macromedia in its acquisition by Adobe; the enterprise wireless handheld computing software and services company Good Technology in its acquisition by Motorola; and Cisco in its acquisition of WebEx.

GETTING HIRED

What do the hiring attorneys at Fenwick look for? According to one junior associate, "Everyone who does recruiting at Fenwick puts a strong emphasis on choosing people who 'fit' with our culture. Of course, strong grades are essential, but people who are social, well adjusted, outgoing and genuinely enthusiastic have the best shot." Fenwick's criteria are in fact too stringent, according to one insider who opines: "Our numerical standards are too high. We cut really good candidates because they don't fit the Mold." Numerical standards aside, a sense of motivation catches Fenwick's eye. The hiring committee is "looking for dynamic self-starters," notes one Fenwick attorney. Another insider agrees. "The firm looks for people that are motivated, self-sufficient, and that will be a good fit within a practice group," explains a Silicon Valley associate, who also says, "The firm mostly looks for graduates from particular schools and with certain GPAs, however, there are many associates from lower 'tiered' schools as well." One school has special appeal: "The firm loves Boalt students," says an insider.

OUR SURVEY SAYS

A San Francisco attorney raves about the Fenwick culture: "The firm leadership takes active steps to maintain our culture of being kind, caring people who treat each other well, even when things are stressful. I have made many close friends at the firm, and people definitely socialize outside of work." Others describe a "flat hierarchy" and call the firm "quirky cool," noting that "people are encouraged to remain individuals—diversity is celebrated." On a slightly more sober note, a Silicon Valley lawyer says, "It's definitely not as closely-knit socially as it used to be, but I think it's getting better," and a San Francisco attorney laments: "Culture is changing; seems a bit harsher and a little more formal." Attorneys give the firm's formal training offerings varying appraisals. One midlevel explains: "Our firm has the standard boot camps for junior and entry-level associates, but as you move up, there is almost no training. If you want it, you have to almost demand it." A midlevel associate offers solid praise: "There are tons of training programs, and the firm is good about letting people go to off-site trainings." Although Fenwick attorneys report relative satisfaction with their hours, one attorney complains that "the hours can be horrible at Fenwick." Mitigating this, another attorney explains, is the fact that "the firm does not care whether you do [your work] from your office or at home or at Starbucks." The flexibility is gratifying for one working father, who says: "The firm is really good about understanding when I need to take off to take care of my daughter so long as I get all my work done. Face time really isn't a huge factor here. We're treated like professionals in that the partners just trust us to take care of the clients' needs. But, this place is definitely not a lifestyle firm." Another associate comments: "We have a number of attorneys, both male and female, working part time here." And how well are associates compensated for the hours they work? "Salary is fine," one Fenwick attorney observes, but "bonuses are not worth billing the extra hours." Another complains that "[b]onuses this year were meager compared to a lot of other firms, and we're always 'last' to bump salaries."

Visit the Vault Law Channel, the complete online resource for law careers, featuring firm profiles, message boards, the Vault Law Job Board and more. www.vault.com/law

V∧ULT CAREER LIBRARY

539

98

Kilpatrick Stockton LLP

1100 Peachtree Street
Suite 2800
Atlanta, GA 30309-4530
Phone: (404) 815-6500
Fax: (404) 815-6555
www.ksrecruits.com

LOCATIONS

Atlanta, GA (HQ)
Augusta, GA
Charlotte, NC
New York, NY
Raleigh, NC
Washington, DC
Winston-Salem, NC
London
Stockholm

MAJOR DEPARTMENTS & PRACTICES

Administrative • Antitrust • Aviation • Banking • Bankruptcy
• Charitable Foundations • Construction Law • Copyright •
Corporations • Creditors' Rights • Employee Benefits •
Entertainment • Equal Opportunity • Environmental • Estate
Planning • Dispute Resolution • Franchising • Government
Contracts • Health Care Law • Insurance • Intellectual
Property • International • Labor • Legislative Affairs •
Litigation • Medical Malpractice Defense • Municipal Finance
Native American Law • Oil & Gas • Patent • Probate •
Products Liability Litigation • Public Utility • Real Estate •
Securities • Taxation • Trademark • Trust & Unfair
Competition

THE STATS

No. of attorneys firmwide: 503
No. of offices: 9
Summer associate offers firmwide: 48 out of 48 (2006)
Managing Partner: William E. Dorris & Diane L. Prucino
Hiring Partner: Elizabeth G. Wren

THE BUZZ
WHAT ATTORNEYS AT OTHER FIRMS ARE SAYING ABOUT THIS FIRM

• "Pays well; treats people well"
• "Fading"
• "Regional powerhouse"
• "Nothing special"

RANKING RECAP

Best in Region
#5 - Atlanta

Quality of Life
#12 - Pro Bono

NOTABLE PERKS

• Subsidized health club memberships
• Associate retreats
• 401(k) matching
• "Tons of free meals"

EMPLOYMENT CONTACT

Ms. Naomi Horvath
Recruiting Coordinator
Phone: (404) 541-6675
Fax: (404) 815-6555
E-mail: nhorvath@kilpatrickstockton.com

BASE SALARY (2007)

Atlanta, GA
1st year: $130,000
Summer associate: $2,500/week

© 2007 Vault Inc.

THE SCOOP

Kilpatrick Stockton was established in 1997 as a product of the merger of Kilpatrick & Cody (founded in 1874 in Atlanta) and Petree Stockton (founded in 1918 in Winston-Salem). The combined firm now employs over 500 attorneys and represents clients from Latin America to Asia from seven domestic offices, located mostly in the South, as well as London and Stockholm. The firm ranks as the 78th-largest in the United States, according to the 2005 *National Law Journal* survey. Kilpatrick Stockton's roster of clients include such well known brand names as Aaron Rents, Blue Cross and Blue Shield of North Carolina, Delta Air Lines, Inc., Harley-Davidson Motor Company and the Krispy Kreme Doughnut Corporation. Among Kilpatrick Stockton's recent IP victories include winning summary judgment on behalf of firm client Texas Tech University in a landmark trademark case before the United States District Court for the Northern District of Texas. By holding the defendant, John Spiegelberg, owner of Lubbock's "Red Raider Outfitter" liable for willful and intentional trademark infringement, unfair competition and dilution, the decision bolstered the ability of universities to protect their brands against unlawful use. Spiegelberg may no longer produce items with Texas Tech's trademarked phrases, "Tech," "Raiderland" and "Wreck 'Em Tech." The firm also serves as the preferred counsel on intellectual property matters for food giant Sara Lee, the Cartoon Network and Hewlett-Packard.

GETTING HIRED

Kilpatrick's hiring attorneys look for all of the usual qualities: good grades, good schools and, of course, that mystical quality known as "fit." As one senior associate reports, "Excellent law school grades are a must; diligence and hard work is needed to flourish here and we look for those qualities in the interview process." As for the specifics, a junior corporate attorney advises that the firm requires a "GPA of 3.7 or better, law review, top-25-law-schools-only for new hires and preferably for laterals." A first-year adds that the firm seeks out "top-third grades with journal or moot court/mock trial experience," and holds a strong preference for standouts from Emory, the University of Virginia and the University of Georgia. One junior associate recommends holding out hope to those who weren't successful during OCI. "All I know is I got the job," he says. "I could not get an interview here while I was in law school, but I was able to lateral over fairly easily."

OUR SURVEY SAYS

Associates have a lot of love for their jobs at Kilpatrick Stockton. "From the first day I started at the firm, I have been given challenging and interesting work with a high level of client interaction," reports a midlevel associate. "I believe that I have more courtroom, deposition and mediation experience than most associates at large law firms of my same level." Another midlevel Atlantan says, "I feel that I have received solid training at the firm and that I have had ample opportunities to take on additional responsibilities. My work has afforded me plenty of opportunities to learn more about particular issues in my practice area as well." Alas, not everyone is happy: "The hours are great. The work is mediocre (at best), the expectations are minimal, the partners are indifferent," shares a midlevel. Associates call Kilpatrick's culture both "very social" and "family-oriented." As one second-year puts it, "This firm has a great social culture. My co-workers and I enjoy each other's company at work as well as at social events. We frequently meet up outside of work." An Atlanta IP specialist says, "Everyone in my group is friendly and approachable. People get along outside of work and go out socially on weekends." An associate in the firm's corporate finance department adds, "There's a tight-knit group of associates in my practice group who often socialize together outside of the office." Kilpatrick's associates generally agree that the firm's formal training is unusually strong. "The firm provides boot camps during your first two years to drill practice-specific and firm-specific best practices," reports an insider. "In addition, practice groups have a formal training program that normally has roughly two to three sessions per month. We also have a coaching and mentoring program." A labor specialist advises, "Each practice group in the firm establishes an annual budget for CLEs. Generally, associates attend one to two extensive CLE courses a year and are encouraged to attend other bar-related CLE courses during the year." Compensation receives a major thumbs-up as well. "The firm pays top of the market, with a premium on IP work," reports a first-year. A corporate finance specialist adds, "We recently received a market bump-up. The base compensation we have is solid. My only complaint may be the bonus structure, as with my practice group it is pretty hard to hit the bonus levels."

Visit the Vault Law Channel, the complete online resource for law careers, featuring firm profiles, message boards, the Vault Law Job Board and more. **www.vault.com/law**

VAULT CAREER LIBRARY   **541**

Mintz Levin Cohn Ferris Glovsky and Popeo PC

One Financial Center
Boston, MA 02111
Phone: (617) 542-6000
Fax: (617) 542-2241
www.mintz.com

LOCATIONS

Boston, MA (HQ)
Los Angeles, CA
Palo Alto, CA
New York, NY
San Diego, CA
Stamford, CT
Washington, DC
London

MAJOR DEPARTMENTS & PRACTICES

Antitrust & Federal Regulation • Bankruptcy, Workout • Business & Finance • Communications & IT • Consulting Services • Employment, Labor, Benefits • Environmental • Health • Immigration • Intellectual Property • Israel Business • Litigation • Public Finance • Real Estate • Tax • Trusts & Estates

THE STATS

No. of attorneys firmwide: 468
No. of offices: 8
Summer associate offers firmwide: 19 out of 19 (2006)
Managing Partners: Steven Rosenthal & Andrew Urban
Hiring Attorneys:
    Boston, MA: Thomas R. Burton III, Deborah Daccord
    New York, NY: Ivan Wool
    Washington, DC: Karen Lovitch
    San Diego: Carl Kukkonen

RANKING RECAP

Best in Region
#9 - Boston

Quality of Life
#14 - Hours

NOTABLE PERKS

- Thursday ice cream
- Free soda
- Flexible work arrangements
- Weekly cocktail parties

EMPLOYMENT CONTACT

Ms. Kerry Oliver
Entry Level Associate Recruiting Manager
Phone: (617) 348-4414
Fax: (617) 542-2214
E-mail: koliver@mintz.com

BASE SALARY (2007)

Boston, MA
1st year: $160,000
2nd year: $170,000
3rd year: $185,000
4th year: $210,000
5th year: $230,000
6th year: $250,000
7th year: $265,000
Summer associate: $2,788/week

THE BUZZ
WHAT ATTORNEYS AT OTHER FIRMS ARE SAYING ABOUT THIS FIRM

- "A good place to work"
- "Obsessed with the bottom line"
- "Supportive, friendly, nurturing"
- "Aggressive"

© 2007 Vault Inc.

THE SCOOP

With nearly 500 attorneys working in eight offices, Mintz Levin is an international firm with such brand-name clients as Gillette, Mobil, General Electric and Fidelity Mutual Funds. In 2006 the firm closed more than $13 billion in corporate transactions. In 2006, Mintz Levin made a bold foray into the land of sunshine and surfboards, by launching offices in two California cities. The firm acquired the attorneys of Reed Intellectual Property Law Group to form the basis of its Palo Alto operation; and then lured a dozen Fish & Richardson attorneys to build its San Diego outpost. The San Diego office has already tripled in size, recently adding partners from Greenberg Traurig and the General Counsel of Hollis-Eden Pharmaceuticals. Mintz is also growing it Clean Tech and Energy practice and recently took EnerNoc public. Mintz Levin was one of the first law firms to offer consulting services with the addition of ML Strategies nearly 15 years ago. MLS has offices in Boston and Washington and focuses on state and federal government relations. Its Washington office has been steadily growing with former staffers from the offices of Rep. Lois Capps and Sen. James Jeffords who join former staffers of John Kerry and Sen. John McCain. ML Financial Advisors oversee $1 billion in client assets and is consistently ranked by Bloomberg as one of the top wealth management firms in the country. Particularly noteworthy is Mintz Levin's extensive Israel-focused practice. In addition to representing numerous Israeli Nasdaq companies in deals with U.S. businesses, the firm also sponsors and curates events, panels, and workshops designed to open the U.S.-Israeli marketplace. Perhaps most notably, the firm-sponsored U.S./Israel Venture Summit in February 2006 featured dozens of Israeli entrepreneurs networking with U.S. venture capitalists and investors.

GETTING HIRED

A Boston associate states, "The firm is open to recruiting at schools of all levels of prestige," while a New Yorker reports, "Typically, the New York office only hires from first-tier schools (though I am unaware of any GPA cutoff)." But regardless of law school pedigree, personality is crucial: "Mintz looks for well-rounded individuals and not just Ivy grads." Another attorney explains: "Almost as important as legal ability and 'statistics' is whether a prospective hire 'fits' with the firm's and the local office's culture. We also stress ability and willingness to work well with attorneys from other specialties and to actively market and cross sell the firm in the community." One insider chimes in: "Of course, grades, experience, ability, and motivation are very important. But I'd say personality is also key because nobody here wants to work with a robot. So be yourself!" Desirable non-robotic qualities include "entrepreneurial spirit and hard work."

OUR SURVEY SAYS

An insider summarizes the compensation picture at Mintz: "The firm's salary is competitive. The bonus structure is not quite as competitive as other big firms but that is because billable hours are significantly lower than at those firms. If you ask me, the trade off is well worth it." With regard to those bonuses, "The firm has just instituted a new bonus policy that is much more heavily biased towards hours rather than merit." The work schedule at Mintz Levin can be flexible. One attorney boasts: "I'm full time but have never had to miss a vacation, child's school event, or medical appointment. The firm respects outside commitments. The firm was also wonderful to me while I was out for four months on maternity leave—completely respected my time at home with a new baby." Others agree that "the firm is fantastic with respect to accommodating flex-time and part-time schedules." But not all Mintz Levin associates share this view: "The ebb and flow at Mintz is more extreme than at other firms. It is truly feast or famine and this makes it extremely difficult to manage family obligations." Another attorney says, "I'd like to work less, but it's not awful. I definitely work nights and weekends from time to time, but it's not overwhelming." And what about formal training? "There has been significant improvement in the amount and quality of formal training over the past few years," reports one insider. And as for the social atmosphere, "Lawyers socialize together on an in-firm basis (i.e., lunch) and occasionally get together outside of the office. People are friendly and there is an open-door policy at the firm." Another says, "[I've] made some great friends while here. Ice cream socials and firm-sponsored happy hours are a plus. Political views are well represented, recently saw fund-raisers for both left- and right-wing causes."

Visit the Vault Law Channel, the complete online resource for law careers, featuring firm profiles, message boards, the Vault Law Job Board and more. **www.vault.com/law**

VAULT CAREER LIBRARY   **543**

Manatt, Phelps & Phillips, LLP

11355 W. Olympic Boulevard
Los Angeles, CA 90064-1614
Phone: (310) 312-4000
Fax: (310) 312-4224
www.manatt.com

LOCATIONS

Los Angeles, CA (HQ)
Albany, NY
New York, NY
Orange County, CA
Palo Alto, CA
Sacramento, CA
San Francisco, CA
Washington, DC

MAJOR DEPARTMENTS & PRACTICES

Advertising • Antitrust • Appellate • Banking & Specialty
Finance • Bankruptcy & Financial Restructuring • Corporate
& Finance • Criminal Defense & Investigations •
Employment & Labor • Energy, Environment & Natural
Resources • Entertainment • Financial Services •
Government & Regulatory • Healthcare • Insurance •
Intellectual Property • International Policy • Internet & E-
Commerce • Litigation • Media • Not-for-Profit Organizations
• Real Estate & Land Use • Tax, Employee Benefits &
Global Compensation • Technology • Unfair Competition
Litigation • Venture Capital

THE STATS

No. of attorneys firmwide: 325
No. of offices: 8
Summer associate offers: 8 out of 8 (2006)
Managing Partner: William T. Quicksilver
Chief Recruiting Officer: Diana N. Iketani

RANKING RECAP

Quality of Life
#3 - Pro Bono
#11 - Hours
#12 - Overall Satisfaction
#17 - Best Firms to Work For
#20 - Informal Training/Mentoring

Best in Diversity
#8 - Overall Diversity
#9 - Diversity with Respect to Minorities
#13 - Diversity with Respect to Women

NOTABLE PERKS

- Pizza night every Wednesday
- Friday morning breakfast
- "Incredible opportunities to get tickets to concerts and events"
- Moving expenses

EMPLOYMENT CONTACT

Ms. Diana Iketani
Chief Recruiting Officer
Phone: (310) 312-4356
Fax: (310) 996-6957
E-mail: diketani@manatt.com

BASE SALARY (2007)

Los Angeles, CA
1st year: $145,000
2nd year: $155,000
3rd year: $170,000
4th year: $190,000
5th year: $210,000
6th year: $225,000
7th year: $240,000
Summer associate: $2,788/week

Los Angeles, CA (2008)
1st year: $160,000
2nd year: $170,000
3rd year: $185,000
4th year: $210,000
5th year: $230,000
6th year: $250,000
7th year: $265,000

© 2007 Vault Inc.

THE SCOOP

And though its offices stretch from its L.A. headquarters to an Albany outpost, Manatt has a distinctively Hollywood bent, with numerous clients in the entertainment industry, as well as institutional corporate clients. Founded in 1965, the firm's clients range from such blue chips as the city of Los Angeles, Coca-Cola, DreamWorks, MasterCard, Tommy Hilfiger, Wal-Mart, British Petroleum, Time Warner to sexagenarian songbirds Cher and Barbara Streisand and, of course, the unstoppable Dr. Phil. Clearly, the home office's proximity to Tinseltown has allowed the firm to become a major player in "The Industry": its star-studded clientele also includes Michael Douglas, The Rolling Stones, R. Kelly and Neil Young. Outside of the entertainment world, the litigation division is one of the hallmarks of this firm, the largest on the Westside of Los Angeles, with litigators comprising approximately 50 percent of the firm's professionals. In addition, Manatt is committed to pro bono work, having signed on to the pro bono initiative stating that its attorneys pledge to dedicate 3 percent of billable hours to pro bono work each year. And pro bono hours count towards yearly billable minimums. Manatt also represents more than 3,000 former National Football League players, including Hall of Fame defensive back Herbert A. Adderley, in a class action filed in federal court in San Francisco against Players Inc., the players' union's licensing and marketing subsidiary. The players claim they are owed tens of millions of dollars for payments that have been withheld since 1994. Specifically, they allege that 90 percent of the league's retired players have never received a payment from the $750 million company and that all of the players "have been cheated since the day [it] was formed."

GETTING HIRED

The hiring standards at Manatt Phelps resemble what you might expect from an elite, smallish, boutique-ish firm. "Because of the size they don't hire people willy-nilly," advises one insider. "They want to make sure there is a real need." An L.A. litigator says, "There are always exceptions, but the general rule of thumb is top of the class from a nationally recognized law school." As for specific qualities that may sway the decision-makers, an L.A. entertainment attorney suggests, "I think we are looking for leaders and self motivated individuals." A corporate finance expert says, "My experience both interviewing and as an interviewer is that we look at a lot of candidates and are selective for people who would be a long-term fit—principally because the firm does not hire huge classes of associates." A litigator adds, "We have become extremely picky and competitive in our hiring. Great grades from a top law school is not enough, you must have a great personality and bring something different to the table."

OUR SURVEY SAYS

Manatt Phelps's associates profess to be among the happiest in the business. As a senior IP specialist describes things, "Manatt is generally a very good place to work. It has competitive pay and challenging work with a relatively relaxed but professional atmosphere." An L.A. litigator reports, "I am given interesting and challenging assignments and a wide range of case management responsibilities, which allows me to grow as an attorney." And an L.A. entertainment attorney adds, "I have had good opportunities to work closely with firm clients and on interesting matters. I have had the opportunity to take on significant responsibility, but I have also had support from partners and senior associates when I needed it. This is a fun and challenging place to practice law." Associates characterize the vibe at Manatt Phelps "professional," yet "collegial" and "fun." As one L.A. insider reports, "While everyone is friendly, the lawyers tend to focus on getting the work done and there is no socialization, either during or after work." Another Los Angeleno says that the firm is "socially friendly and informal, but still committed to high professional standards." The otherwise-satisfied associates call formal training one of the rare aspects of the firm that could use a little bit more TLC. An L.A. litigator reports, "It is primarily a 'learn-as-you-go' experience." Associates praise their salaries, but gripe a bit about their bonuses. As one representative L.A. associate advises, "Manatt has very competitive associate base compensation. It has a weaker bonus system." Another L.A. attorney complains, "The firm's bonus structure has much to be desired. It is entirely discretionary no matter how many hours are billed in a given year."

Visit the Vault Law Channel, the complete online resource for law careers, featuring firm profiles, message boards, the Vault Law Job Board and more. **www.vault.com/law**

VAULT CAREER LIBRARY   545

GO FOR THE GOLD!

GET VAULT GOLD MEMBERSHIP
AND GET ACCESS TO ALL OF VAULT'S
AWARD-WINNING LAW CAREER INFORMATION

◆ Access to **500+ extended insider law firm profiles**

◆ Access to **regional snapshots** for major non-HQ offices of major firms

◆ Complete access to **Vault's exclusive law firm rankings**, including quality of life rankings, diversity rankings, practice area rankings, and rankings by law firm partners

◆ Access to **Vault's Law Salary Central**, with salary information for 100s of top firms

◆ Receive **Vault's Law Job Alerts** of top law jobs posted on the Vault Law Job Board

◆ Access to complete **Vault message board archives**

◆ **15% off** all Vault Guide and Vault Career Services purchases

For more information go to
www.vault.com/law

V▲ULT
> the most trusted name in career information™

THE BEST OF THE REST

Adams and Reese LLP

One Shell Square
701 Poydras Street, Suite 4500
New Orleans, LA 70139
Phone: (504) 581-3234
www.adamsandreese.com

LOCATIONS

New Orleans, LA (HQ)

Baton Rouge, LA • Birmingham, AL • Houston, TX •
Jackson, MS • Memphis, TN • Mobile, AL • Nashville, TN •
Nashville/Music Row • Washington, DC

MAJOR DEPARTMENTS & PRACTICES

Agricultural Chemicals • Antitrust & Unfair Competition •
Appellate Advocacy • Arbitration & Alternative Dispute
Resolution • Asbestos • Banking & Finance • Casualty &
Coverage • Class Action & Complex Litigation • Commercial
Dispute Resolution • Commercial Restructuring &
Bankruptcy • Construction & Real Estate • Corporate /
Securities / M&A • D&O and Professional Liability •
Economic Development • Education & Public Entity • Energy
• Entertainment & New Media • Environmental & Toxic Tort
• ERISA & Employee Benefits • Forestry • Governmental
Relations • Health Care • Intellectual Property & Technology
• Labor & Employment • Maritime & Offshore • Oil & Gas •
Pharmaceutical & Medical Device • Product Liability • Public
Finance • Real Estate • Tax • Technology & Telecom

THE STATS

No. of attorneys: 300
No. of offices: 10
Summer associate offers: 14 out of 37 (2006)
Chairman of Executive Committee: M. Ann Huckstep
Managing Partner: Charles P. Adams, Jr.
Hiring Partner: Janis van Meerveld

NOTABLE PERKS

• Free parking
• Thursday cocktail hour
• Tickets to sporting events
• Free firmwide lunch on Fridays

EMPLOYMENT CONTACT

Ms. Kristen Koppel
Legal Recruiting Manager
Phone: (504) 585-0462
Fax: (504) 566-0210
E-mail: Kristen.koppel@arlaw.com

BASE SALARY (2007)

Baton Rouge, LA; New Orleans; LA, Jackson, MS
1st year: $90,000
Summer associate: $1,250/week

Birmingham, AL
1st year: $95,000
Summer associate: $1,250/week

Houston, TX
1st year: $120,000
Summer associate: $$2000/week

Mobile, AL
1st year: $85,000
Summer associate: $1,100/week

Memphis, TN
1st Year: $90,000
Summer Associate: $1,450/week

Nashville, TN
1st Year: $100,000
Summer Associate: $1,450/week

THE BUZZ
WHAT ATTORNEYS AT OTHER FIRMS ARE SAYING ABOUT THIS FIRM

• "Prestigious in New Orleans"
• "Insurance defense"
• "Excellent practitioners that are well-entrenched in
  their markets"
• "High turn-over"

© 2007 Vault Inc.

Allen Matkins Leck Gamble Mallory & Natsis LLP

515 South Figueroa Street, 7th Floor
Los Angeles, CA 90071
Phone: (213) 622-5555
www.allenmatkins.com

LOCATIONS

Los Angeles, CA (HQ)
Century City, CA
Del Mar Heights, CA
Irvine, CA
San Diego, CA
San Francisco, CA
Walnut Creek, CA

MAJOR DEPARTMENTS & PRACTICES

Bankruptcy & Creditors' Rights • Construction • Corporate & Securities • Emerging Company & Venture Capital • Employee Benefits • Finance & Capital Markets • Government Advocacy • Hotels & Resorts • Labor & Employment • Land Use, Environmental & Natural Resources • Litigation • Mergers & Acquisitions • Real Estate • Tax • Technology & Intellectual Property • Water Rights & Resources

THE STATS

No. of attorneys: 200+
No. of offices: 7
Summer associate offers: 7 out of 7 (2006)
Managing Partner: Brian C. Leck
Firmwide Recruiting Partner: John C. Gamble

RANKING RECAP

Best in Practice
#7 - Real Estate

Partner Prestige Rankings
#3 (tie) - Real Estate

Quality of Life
#3 - Hours

NOTABLE PERKS

- Free parking
- Tickets to sporting events
- "Outstanding" health benefits
- Annual firm retreat for all attorneys

EMPLOYMENT CONTACT

Ms. Lorraine R. Connally
Director of Legal Recruiting
Phone: (213) 622-5555
Fax: (213) 620-8816
E-mail: lconnally@allenmatkins.com

BASE SALARY (2007)

All offices
1st year: $145,000
2nd year: $155,000
3rd year: $170,000
4th year: $185,000
5th year: $200,000
6th year: $210,000
7th year: $220,000
8th year: $225,000
Summer associate: $2,700/week

THE BUZZ
WHAT ATTORNEYS AT OTHER FIRMS ARE SAYING ABOUT THIS FIRM

"Strong real estate practice"
"Moving up on the West Coast"
"Past its prime"
"Lifestyle firm"

Visit the Vault Law Channel, the complete online resource for law careers, featuring firm profiles, message boards, the Vault Law Job Board, and more. www.vault.com/law

VAULT CAREER LIBRARY   549

Andrews Kurth LLP

600 Travis, Suite 4200
Houston, TX 77002
Phone: (713) 220-4200
www.andrewskurth.com

LOCATIONS

Houston, TX (HQ)
Austin, TX
Dallas, TX
Los Angeles, CA
New York, NY
Washington, DC
The Woodlands, TX
Beijing
London

MAJOR DEPARTMENTS & PRACTICES

Antitrust • Appellate • Arbitration & Mediation • Banking &
Finance • Bankruptcy & Restructuring • Corporate
Compliance, Investigations and Defense • Corporate &
Securities • Energy • Environmental • ERISA, Employee
Benefits & Executive Compensation • Health Care •
Intellectual Property • International • Labor & Employment •
Litigation • Mass Tort Litigation • Mergers & Acquisitions •
Personal Tax Planning • Project Finance • Public Law • Real
Estate • Securitization • South Asia • Tax

THE STATS

No. of attorneys: 424
No. of offices: 9
Managing Partner: Howard T. Ayers
Hiring Partners: Alex Gomez, Martha "Marty" Smith

RANKING RECAP

Best in Region
#8 - Texas

NOTABLE PERKS

• Free dinners, charity events and paid retreats
• Bar and moving expenses
• 401(k) match
• Free parking in most Texas offices

EMPLOYMENT CONTACT

Ms. Hope Young
Manager of Firm Development
Phone: (713) 220-4200
Fax: (713) 220-4815
E-mail: hopeyoung@andrewskurth.com

BASE SALARY (2007)

Austin, Dallas, Houston, TX
1st year: $135,000
Summer associate: $2,700/week

The Woodlands, TX
1st year: $110,000
Summer associate: $2,100/week

Los Angeles, CA
1st year: $120,000
Summer associate: $2,100/week

New York, NY
1st year: $137,500
Summer associate: $2,400/week

Washington, DC
1st year: $120,000
Summer associate: $2,300/week

THE BUZZ

WHAT ATTORNEYS AT OTHER FIRMS ARE SAYING ABOUT THIS FIRM

• "Good oil and gas attorneys"
• "Great corporate; good regional firm"
• "Party firm"
• "Behind the curve"

© 2007 Vault Inc.

The Vault Guide to the Top 100 Law Firms • 2008 Edition
....
The Best of the Rest

Baker & Daniels LLP

300 North Meridian Street, Suite 2700
Indianapolis, IN 46204
Phone: (317) 237-0300
www.bakerdaniels.com

LOCATIONS

Indianapolis, IN (2 offices) • Elkhart, IN • Fort Wayne, IN •
South Bend, IN • Washington, DC • Beijing • Qingdao

MAJOR DEPARTMENTS & PRACTICES

Antitrust • Appellate Practice • Arbitration & Mediation •
Aviation • Banking & Commercial Finance • Bankruptcy &
Business Restructuring • Benefits & Executive Compensation •
Business Litigation • Certified Business Enterprises & Supplier
Delivery • China • Commercial, Financial & Bankruptcy •
Communications & Public Affairs • Construction • Corporate
Finance • E-Discovery & Record Retention • Education Law •
Emerging Companies • Employee Benefits • Energy & Public
Utilities • Environmental • Government Affairs • Health Care •
Health & Life Sciences • Immigration • Individual/Family •
Insurance Coverage • Insurance & Financial Service •
Intellectual Property • International • Labor & Employment •
Life Sciences • Litigation • Media Law • Medical Devices &
Pharmaceuticals • Mergers & Acquisitions • Nonprofit •
Northern Business • Private Capital, Venture Capital &
Investment Management • Product Liability • Public Finance •
Public Sector • Real Estate • Real Property Litigation • RV
Focus • Securities & Shareholders Litigation • Sports &
Entertainment • Tax • Transportation • Trusts & Estates •
White Collar Criminal Defense, Corporate Compliance & Internal
Investigations

THE STATS

No. of attorneys: 310
No. of offices: 8
Summer associate offers: 29 out of 33 (2006)
Chair & Chief Executive Officer: Brian K. Burke
Hiring Partner: Scott M. Kosnoff

NOTABLE PERKS

- Free or subsidized health club membership
- Tickets to sporting and entertainment events
- Free legal assistance for employees
- Free BlackBerry and laptop

 THE BUZZ
WHAT ATTORNEYS AT OTHER FIRMS ARE SAYING ABOUT THIS FIRM

- "Nice regional firm"
- "Arrogant partners"
- "Good for Indianapolis; nice lifestyle"
- "Friendly, very good attorneys"

RANKING RECAP

Best in Region
#9 - Midwest

Quality of Life
#3 - Informal Training/Mentoring
#4 - Hours
#5 - Overall Satisfaction
#6 - Associate/Partner Relations
#7 - Best Firms to Work For

Best in Diversity
#15 - Diversity with Respect to Women

EMPLOYMENT CONTACT

Indianapolis
Ms. Alisha Couch
Manager of New Lawyer Hiring
Phone: (317) 237-0300
Fax: (317) 237-1000
E-mail: alisha.couch@bakerd.com

Fort Wayne
Mrs. Julie Kyler
Legal Recruiting Coordinator
Phone: (260) 424-8000
Fax: (260) 460-1700
E-mail: julie.kyler@bakerd.com

Elkhart & South Bend
Ms. Beckie Mills
Recruiting Coordinator
Phone: (574) 234-4149
Fax: (574) 472-4584
E-mail: beckie.mills@bakerd.com

Washington, DC
Ms. Carol Torrico
Operations Coordinator
Phone: (202) 312-7440
Fax: (202) 312-7460
E-mail: carol.torrico@bakerd.com

BASE SALARY (2007)

Indiana offices
1st year: $100,000
Summer associate: $1,825/week

Washington, DC
1st year: $139,750
Summer associate: $2,200/week

Visit the Vault Law Channel, the complete online resource for law careers, featuring firm
profiles, message boards, the Vault Law Job Board, and more. www.vault.com/law

VAULT CAREER LIBRARY   551

Ballard Spahr Andrews & Ingersoll, LLP

1735 Market Street, 51st Floor
Philadelphia, PA 19103-7599
Phone: (215) 665-8500
www.ballardspahr.com

LOCATIONS

Philadelphia, PA (HQ)

Baltimore, MD • Bethesda, MD • Denver, CO • Las Vegas,
NV • Phoenix, AZ • Salt Lake City, UT • Voorhees, NJ •
Washington, DC • Wilmington, DE

MAJOR DEPARTMENTS & PRACTICES

Bankruptcy, Reorganization & Capital Recovery • Business
& Finance • Business Litigation • Construction • Consumer
Financial Services • Eminent Domain & Valuation •
Employee Benefits & Executive Compensation • Energy &
Project Finance • Environmental • Family Wealth
Management • Franchise & Distribution • Health Care •
Housing • Insurance • Intellectual Property • International •
Investment Management • Labor, Employment &
Immigration • Life Sciences/Technology • Litigation •
Mergers & Acquisitions • Planned Communities &
Condominiums • Product Liability & Mass Tort • Public
Finance • Public-Private Partnerships—P3 Practice • Real
Estate • Real Estate Development • Real Estate Finance •
Real Estate Leasing • Resort & Hotel • Securities •
Securitization • Tax • Technology & Emerging Companies •
Telecommunications • Transactional Finance • White Collar
Litigation • Zoning & Land Use

THE STATS

No. of attorneys: 500
No. of offices: 10
Summer associate offers: 21 out of 25 (2006)
Managing Partner: Lynn E. Rzonca (Philadelphia)
Hiring Partner: David S. Fryman (Philadelphia)

RANKING RECAP

Best in Region
#8 - Pennsylvania/Mid-Atlantic

Best in Diversity
#17 - Diversity with Respect to Women

NOTABLE PERKS

• Profit-sharing plan
• Domestic partner benefits
• Business development budget
• Paid child care leave

EMPLOYMENT CONTACT

Kimberly A. Short, Esq.
Manager of Attorney Recruitment
Phone: (215) 864-8727
Fax: (215) 864-9079
E-mail: short@ballardspahr.com

BASE SALARY (2007)

Philadelphia, PA; Wilmington, DE
1st year: $135,000
Summer associate: $2,600/week

Baltimore, MD; Bethesda, MD; Voorhees, NJ
1st year: $130,000
Summer associate: $2,500/week

Denver, CO; Las Vegas, NV; Phoenix, AZ; Salt Lake City, UT
1st year: $123,000
Summer associate: $2,400/week

Washington, DC
1st year: $142,500
Summer associate: $2,700/week

THE BUZZ
WHAT ATTORNEYS AT OTHER FIRMS ARE SAYING ABOUT THIS FIRM

• "Prestigious, but very local to Philadelphia"
• "Political powerhouse"
• "Long hours"
• "Snooty"

© 2007 Vault Inc.

Barnes & Thornburg LLP

11 South Meridian Street
Indianapolis, IN 46204-3556
Phone: (317) 236-1313
www.btlaw.com

LOCATIONS

Chicago, IL
Elkhart, IN
Fort Wayne, IN
Grand Rapids, MI
Indianapolis, IN
South Bend, IN
Washington, DC

MAJOR DEPARTMENTS & PRACTICES

Antitrust • Appeals • Associations & Foundations • Aviation
• Construction • Creditors Rights • Energy/Telecom/Utilities
• Environmental • Entrepreneurial Services • Estate Planning
• Government Services • Healthcare • Human Resources
Consulting • Immigration • Intellectual Property • Labor &
Employment • Life Sciences • Litigation • Media • Pensions
& Benefits • Product Liability • Real Estate • School Law •
Sports & Entertainment • Tax • Technology •
Transportation • White Collar Crime

THE STATS

No. of attorneys: 420
No. of offices: 7
Summer associate offers: 29 out of 33 (2006)
Managing Partner: Alan A. Levin
Hiring Partners:
  Chicago: Jonathan P. Froemel
  Elkhart: Brian J. Clark
  Fort Wayne: Matthew M. Hohman
  Grand Rapids: Robert W. Sikkel
  Indianapolis: Charles P. Edwards
  South Bend: Laurence A. McHugh
  Washington, DC: Karen A. McGee

RANKING RECAP

Best in Region
#7 - Midwest

Quality of Life
#15 - Informal Training/Mentoring
#15 - Office Space
#19 - Hours

NOTABLE PERKS

• $2,000 CLE budget
• On-site fitness facility
• Free soda
• $5,000 stipend for bar study

EMPLOYMENT CONTACT

Ms. Deborah A. Snyder
Director of Recruiting
Phone: (317) 231-7289
Fax: (317) 231-7433
E-mail: dsnyder@btlaw.com

BASE SALARY (2007)

Indiana offices; Grand Rapids, MI
1st year: $100,000
Summer associate: $1,700/week

Chicago, IL; Washington, DC
1st year: $110,000
Summer associate: $1,900/week

THE BUZZ
WHAT ATTORNEYS AT OTHER FIRMS ARE SAYING ABOUT THIS FIRM

• "Excellent regional firm"
• "Not very impressed"
• "Stuffy"
• "Good clients, good work"

Visit the Vault Law Channel, the complete online resource for law careers, featuring firm profiles, message boards, the Vault Law Job Board, and more. www.vault.com/law

 VAULT CAREER LIBRARY   553

Blackwell Sanders LLP

4801 Main Street, Suite 1000
Kansas City, MO 64112
Phone: (816) 983-8000
www.blackwellsanders.com

LOCATIONS

Kansas City, MO • Belleville, IL • Lincoln, NE • Omaha, NE
• Overland Park, KS • Springfield, MO • St. Louis, MO •
Washington, DC • London

MAJOR DEPARTMENTS & PRACTICES

Advertising & Marketing • Alternative Dispute Resolution •
Antitrust & Unfair Competition • Appellate Litigation • Aviation
• Bankruptcy, Restructuring & Creditors' Rights • Business &
Commercial Litigation • Class Actions • Closely Held Business
• Commercial Transactions • Construction & Design •
Copyright • Customs & Trade • Digital Discovery & Records
Management • Education • Employee Benefits & Executive
Compensation • Energy & Public Utility • Entertainment &
Media • Environment, Natural Resources & Water •
ERISA/Employee Benefits Litigation • Estate Planning, Trusts &
Estates • Finance & Lending • Food Law • Franchising &
Distribution • Government Compliance, Investigations &
Litigation • Governmental Affairs • Health Care • Hospitality •
Immigration • Insurance Litigation • Intellectual Property •
Intellectual Property Litigation • International • Investment
Management • Labor & Employment • Mergers & Acquisitions
• Municipal • Patents • Private Equity & Closed-End Funds •
Products Liabilty • Public Finance • Real Estate • Safety &
Health • Securities Industry Regulation & Litigation •
Securities/ Captial Markets • Tax Exempt Organizations •
Taxation • Technology & E-Commerce • Telecommunications
Regulatory Practice • Trademarks • Transportation • Venture
Capital/Private Equity Financing

THE STATS

No. of attorneys: 331
No. of offices: 9
Chairman: David A. Fenley
Hiring Partner: Wade Kerrigan

THE BUZZ
WHAT ATTORNEYS AT OTHER FIRMS ARE SAYING ABOUT THIS FIRM

- "Good Midwestern firm"
- "Stuffy, old school"
- "Some of the best lawyers around"
- "Wannabe BigLaw"

NOTABLE PERKS

- Subsidized health club membership
- Tickets to sporting events
- Domestic partner plan
- Free parking

EMPLOYMENT CONTACT

Ms. Stacie L. Cronberg
Manager of Legal Recruiting
Phone: (816) 983-8782
Fax: (816) 983-8080
E-mail: scronberg@blackwellsanders.com

BASE SALARY (2007)

Kansas City, MO
1st year: $105,000
Summer associate: $1,750/week

Omaha, NE
1st year: $90,000
Summer associate: $1,500/week

Springfield, MO
1st year: $85,000
Summer associate: $1,400/week

St. Louis, MO; Washington, DC
1st year: $110,000
Summer associate: $1,750/week

© 2007 Vault Inc.

Blank Rome LLP

One Logan Square
130 North 18th Street
Philadelphia, PA 19103-6998
Phone: (215) 569-5500
www.blankrome.com

LOCATIONS

Philadelphia, PA (HQ)
Boca Raton, FL
Cherry Hill, NJ
Cincinnati, OH
New York, NY
Trenton, NJ
Washington, DC
Wilmington, DE
Hong Kong

MAJOR DEPARTMENTS & PRACTICES

Antitrust Litigation • Business Restructuring & Bankruptcy •
Corporate Governance • Employment • Energy •
Environmental • Financial Institutions • Financial Services •
Government Contracts • Government Relations • Health
Care • Intellectual Property • International Trade • IP
Litigation • Leasing • Litigation • Maritime • Matrimonial •
Mergers & Acquisitions • Product Liability • Public Finance •
Real Estate • Securities • Tax • Trusts & Estates • White
Collar, Internal and Government Investigations

THE STATS

No. of attorneys: 500+
No. of offices: 9
Managing Partner & CEO: Charles M. Buchholz
Hiring Partner: Gregg W. Winter

RANKING RECAP

Best in Region
#7 - Pennsylvania/Mid-Atlantic

NOTABLE PERKS

- Subsidized cafeteria
- Cab rides home after dark
- On-site or subsidized gym in many offices
- Business generation bonus

EMPLOYMENT CONTACT

Ms. Donna M. Branca
Director of Attorney Relations
Phone: (215) 569-5751
Fax: (215) 569-5555
E-mail: branca@blankrome.com

BASE SALARY (2007)

Philadelphia, PA
1st year: $125,000
Summer associate: $2,400/week

New York, NY; Washington, DC
1st year: $135,000
Summer associate: $2,596/week

THE BUZZ
WHAT ATTORNEYS AT OTHER FIRMS ARE SAYING ABOUT THIS FIRM

- "Good Philly firm"
- "Big, white shoe, prestigious"
- "Stuffy and conservative"
- "Understaffed"

Visit the Vault Law Channel, the complete online resource for law careers, featuring firm
profiles, message boards, the Vault Law Job Board, and more. www.vault.com/law

VAULT CAREER LIBRARY   555

Bracewell & Giuliani LLP

711 Louisiana Street, Suite 2300
Houston, TX 77002
Phone: (713) 223-2300
www.bgllp.com

LOCATIONS

Houston, TX (HQ)

Austin, TX • Dallas, TX • Hartford, CT • New York, NY •
San Antonio, TX • Washington, DC • Almaty, Kazakhstan •
Astana, Kazakhstan • Dubai • London

MAJOR DEPARTMENTS & PRACTICES

Bankruptcy • Banks & Financial Institutions • Broker-Dealer
& Market Regulation • Corporate & Securities • Educational
Institutions • Employee Benefits • Energy • Environmental
Strategies • Finance • Financial Restructuring • Government
• Indian Law • Intellectual Property • Internal Investigations
• International Practice • Labor & Employment • Private
Investment Funds • Real Estate and Projects • Strategic
Communication • Tax • Trial • White Collar Criminal
Defense

THE STATS

No. of attorneys: 400
No. of offices: 11
Summer associate offers: 42 out of 48 (2006)
Managing Partner: Patrick C. Oxford
Hiring Partner: Andrew M. Edison

RANKING RECAP

Best in Region
#9 - Texas

NOTABLE PERKS

- $1,200 annual client development budget
- Subsidized parking
- Bar and moving expenses
- BlackBerries

EMPLOYMENT CONTACT

Ms. Jean P. Lenzner
Director of Attorney Employment
Phone: (713) 221-1296
Fax: (713) 221-1212
E-mail: jean.lezner@bgllp.com

BASE SALARY (2007)

Austin, Dallas, Houston, TX
1st year: $160,000
Summer associate: $2,700/week

San Antonio, TX
1st year: up to $160,000
Summer associate: $2,300/week

New York, NY
1st year: $160,000
Summer associate: $3,076/week

Washington, DC
1st year: $160,000
Summer associate: $2,788.47/week

THE BUZZ
WHAT ATTORNEYS AT OTHER FIRMS ARE SAYING ABOUT THIS FIRM

- "Best firm to work at in Houston"
- "Snobbish"
- "Good lawyers"
- "The Rudy Show"

© 2007 Vault Inc.

Brown Rudnick Berlack Israels LLP

One Financial Center
Boston, MA 02111
Phone: (617) 856-8200
www.brownrudnick.com

LOCATIONS

Boston, MA (HQ)
Hartford, CT
New York, NY
Providence, RI
Washington, DC
Dublin
London

MAJOR DEPARTMENTS & PRACTICES

Aviation & Transportation • Bankruptcy and Corporate Restructuring • Biotechnology • Commercial Finance • Corporate • Distressed Debt • Education • Employee Benefits & Compensation • Employment & Labor • Energy & Utilities • Environmental • Estates • Finance • Gaming • Government Law & Strategies • Health Care • Housing • Information Technology • Intellectual Property • Leasing • Life Sciences • Litigation • Media & Publishing • Medical Devices • Mergers & Acquisitions • Military & Defense • Pharmaceuticals • Precious Metals • Private Equity • Real Estate • Restaurants & Hospitality • Retail & Shopping Centers • Securities & Corporate Governance • Semiconductors • Software • Structured Finance • Tax • Telecommunications • Venture Capital

THE STATS

No. of attorneys: 200
No. of offices: 7
Summer associate offers: 19 out of 19 (2006)
Chief Executive Officer: Joseph F. Ryan
Hiring Partner: Michael R. Dolan

RANKING RECAP

Quality of Life
#4 - Pay
#7 - Office Space
#19 - Informal Training/Mentoring

NOTABLE PERKS

• Bar and moving expenses
• BlackBerry reimbursement
• Great Times Square views
• Box seats at sporting events

EMPLOYMENT CONTACT

Ms. Carolyn M. Manning
Director of Professional Recruiting
Phone: (617) 856-8140
Fax: (617) 856-8201
E-mail: cmanning@brownrudnick.com

BASE SALARY (2007)

Boston, MA
1st year: $160,000
Summer associate: $3,077/week

New York, NY
1st year: $160,000
Summer associate: $3,077/week

THE BUZZ
WHAT ATTORNEYS AT OTHER FIRMS ARE SAYING ABOUT THIS FIRM

• "Aggressive"
• "Cutting edge"
• "Progressive firm culture"
• "How many times can a firm merge?"

Visit the Vault Law Channel, the complete online resource for law careers, featuring firm profiles, message boards, the Vault Law Job Board, and more. www.vault.com/law

VAULT CAREER LIBRARY

557

Buchanan Ingersoll & Rooney PC

One Oxford Centre
301 Grant Street, 20th Floor
Pittsburgh, PA 15219-1410
Phone: (412) 562-8800
www.buchananingersoll.com

LOCATIONS

Pittsburgh, PA (HQ)

Alexandria, VA • Aventura, FL • Buffalo, NY • Cleveland,
OH • Harrisburg, PA (two offices) • Miami, FL • Newark, NJ
• New York, NY • Philadelphia, PA • Princeton, NJ •
Redwood Shores, CA • San Diego, CA • Tampa, FL •
Washington, DC • Wilmington, DE

MAJOR DEPARTMENTS & PRACTICES

Antitrust • Appellate • Bankruptcy • Biotech • Corporate
Finance & Technology • Environmental Law • Federal
Procurement • Financial Services • Food & Drug •
Government Contracts • Government Relations • Health
Care • Immigration • Insurance & Reinsurance • Intellectual
Property • Labor & Employment Law • Litigation • National
Defense & Homeland Security • Non-Traditional Couples •
Public Finance • Real Estate • Securities Litigation • Tax •
Technology Transactions

THE STATS

No. of attorneys: 550+
No. of offices: 15
Summer associate offers: 30 out of 32 (2006)
Chief Executive Officer: Thomas L. VanKirk
Hiring Partners: James D. Newell and Gina Ameci

NOTABLE PERKS

• Cab rides and meals if working late
• Happy hours
• Bar expenses
• Concert and sporting event tickets

THE BUZZ
WHAT ATTORNEYS AT OTHER FIRMS ARE SAYING ABOUT THIS FIRM

• "Nice firm for which to work"
• "Past its prime"
• "Good government relations"
• "Stuffy"

EMPLOYMENT CONTACT

Ms. Laurie S. Lenigan
Director, Legal Recruiting
Phone: (412) 562-1470
Fax: (412) 562-1041
E-mail: laurie.lenigan@bipc.com

BASE SALARY (2007)

Pittsburgh, PA
1st year: $120,000
Summer associate: $2,200/week

Harrisburg, PA
1st year: $105,000
Summer associate: $1,800/week

Philadelphia, PA
1st year: $135,000
Summer associate: $2,400/week

Miami, FL
1st year: $120,000
Summer associate: $2,100/week

New York, NY
1st year: $140,000
Summer associate: $2,400/week

San Diego, CA
1st year: $140,000
Summer associate: $2,600/week

Tampa, FL
1st year: $105,000
Summer associate: $1,800/week

Alexandria, VA
1st year: $TBD
Summer associate: $2,200/week

Washington, DC
1st year: $140,000
Summer associate: NA

Princeton, NJ
1st year: $120,000
Summer Associate: $2,300/week

Wilmington, DE
1st year: $135,000
Summer associate: $2,400/week

© 2007 Vault Inc.

Carlton Fields, P.A.

Corporate Center Three at International Plaza
4221 West Boy Scout Boulevard, Suite 1000
Tampa, FL 33607
Phone: (813) 223-7000
www.carltonfields.com

LOCATIONS

Atlanta, GA • Miami, FL • Orlando, FL • St. Petersburg, FL
• Tallahassee, FL • Tampa, FL • West Palm Beach, FL

MAJOR DEPARTMENTS & PRACTICES

Affordable Housing • Antitrust & Trade Regulation •
Appellate & Trial Support • Aviation • Bankruptcy &
Creditors' Rights • Business Litigation & Trade Regulation •
Business Transactions • Class Actions • Community and
Condominium Development • Construction & Design •
Corporate, Securities & Tax • Disaster Preparedness,
Response & Recovery • Distressed Assets & Workouts •
Eminent Domain • Energy & Utility • Environmental • ERISA
• Estate & Trust Planning, Administration & Litigation •
Family Law • Financial Services • Gaming • Government
Law & Consulting • Health Care & Life Sciences • Insurance
Litigation & Regulation • Intellectual Property & Technology
• International Trade & Transactions • Labor & Employment
• Land Use & Zoning • Leasing & Management • Medical
Malpractice • Mergers & Acquisitions • Mold Management
& Litigation • Pharmaceutical & Medical Device • Private
Equity & Venture Capital • Products & Toxic Tort Liability •
Real Estate & Finance • Real Property Litigation • Resort
Development • Securities & Derivative Litigation • Sports •
Taxation • Telecommunications & Technology • Title
Insurance & Examination • White Collar Crime &
Government Investigations

THE STATS

No. of attorneys: 249
No. of offices: 7
Summer associate offers: 8 out of 9 (2006)
President & CEO: Gary L. Sasso
Hiring Partners: John A. Camp and Lannie D. Hough, Jr.

THE BUZZ
WHAT ATTORNEYS AT OTHER FIRMS ARE SAYING ABOUT THIS FIRM

- "Nurturing"
- "Up and coming"
- "Old school Florida"
- "Great lifestyle firm"

RANKING RECAP

Best in Region
#10 - Miami

Quality of Life
#5 - Informal Training/Mentoring
#8 - Pro Bono
#10 - Associate/Partner Relations
#13 - Overall Satisfaction
#18 - Best Firms to Work For

Best in Diversity
#1 - Diversity with Respect to Women
#2 - Diversity with Respect to Minorities
#3 - Overall Diversity

NOTABLE PERKS

- Free parking
- Generous funding for client development
- Firm happy hours
- Free health insurance

EMPLOYMENT CONTACT

Ms. Shannon Williams
Director of Attorney Recruitment
Phone: (813) 229-4172
Fax: (813) 229-4133
E-mail: recruiting@carltonfields.com

BASE SALARY (2007)

Atlanta, GA
1st year: $130,000
Summer associate: $2,200/week

Miami, West Palm Beach, FL
1st year: $120,000
Summer associate: $2,100/week

Orlando, St. Petersburg, Tampa, FL
1st year: $100,000
Summer associate: $1,800/week

Tallahassee, FL
1st year: $90,000
Summer associate: $1,550/week

Visit the Vault Law Channel, the complete online resource for law careers, featuring firm
profiles, message boards, the Vault Law Job Board, and more. www.vault.com/law

VAULT CAREER LIBRARY   559

Choate Hall & Stewart LLP

Two International Place
Boston MA 02110
Phone: (617) 248-5000
www.choate.com

LOCATION

Boston, MA

MAJOR DEPARTMENTS & PRACTICES

Antitrust • Business & Technology • Class Action Defense •
Creditors' Rights & Bankruptcy • Energy & Utilities •
Fiduciary & Investment Services • General Corporate &
Securities • Government Enforcement & Compliance •
Health Care • Intellectual Property • Land Use &
Environmental • Litigation • Mergers & Acquisitions •
Private Equity • Specialty Finance • Tax • Technology
Licensing • Transactional Real Estate • Wealth Management

THE STATS

No. of attorneys: 200+
No. of offices: 1
Summer associate offers: 25 out of 28 (2006)
Managing Partners: William P. Gelnaw Jr., John A. Nadas
Hiring Partners: John F. Ventola, Diana K. Lloyd

RANKING RECAP

Best in Region
#8 - Boston

NOTABLE PERKS

• Annual lawyers outing
• Bar and moving expenses
• Thursday Pizza Nights
• Emergency day care

EMPLOYMENT CONTACT

Ms. Robin C. Ketterer
Director of Recruiting
Phone: (617) 248-4926
Fax: (617) 248-4000
E-mail: rketterer@choate.com

BASE SALARY (2007)

Boston, MA
1st year: $160,000
Summer associate (2007) $3100/week

THE BUZZ
WHAT ATTORNEYS AT OTHER FIRMS ARE SAYING ABOUT THIS FIRM

• "Very good regional firm"
• "Academic, stuffy"
• "Preppy"
• "Blue blood"

© 2007 Vault Inc.

Cozen O'Connor

1900 Market Street, The Atrium
Philadelphia, PA 19103
Phone: (215) 665-2000
www.cozen.com

LOCATIONS

Philadelphia, PA (HQ)

Atlanta, GA • Charlotte, NC • Cherry Hill, NJ • Chicago, IL
• Dallas, TX • Denver, CO • Houston, TX • Los Angeles,
CA • Miami, FL • New York, NY (2 offices) • Newark, NJ •
San Diego, CA • San Francisco, CA • Santa Fe, NM •
Seattle, WA • Trenton, NJ • Washington, DC • West
Conshohocken, PA • Wilmington, DE • London • Toronto

MAJOR DEPARTMENTS & PRACTICES

Bankruptcy, Insolvency & Restructuring • Complex Torts &
Products Liability • Corporate Governance & Compliance •
Corporate Law, Emerging Business & Venture Capital •
Employee Benefits & Executive Compensation • Energy,
Environmental & Public Utilities • English Law Practice •
Enterprise Risks • Family Business Services • Family Law •
General Litigation • Government Relations • Health Law •
Insurance Corporate & Regulatory • Insurance Coverage
Claims/Litigation • Intellectual Property • International
Markets • Labor & Employment • Professional Liability •
Public & Project Finance • Real Estate • Securities &
Financial Services Litigation • Securities Offering &
Regulation • Subrogation & Recovery • Tax • Trust &
Estates • White Collar & Complex Criminal Defense

THE STATS

No. of attorneys: 515
No. of offices: 23
Summer associate offers: 8 out of 11 (2006)
Chairman: Stephen A. Cozen
President & CEO: Patrick J. O'Connor
Hiring Partner: Sarah E. Davies

THE BUZZ
WHAT ATTORNEYS AT OTHER FIRMS ARE SAYING ABOUT THIS FIRM

- "Very good in New Jersey and Philly"
- "Unsophisticated"
- "Well respected"
- "Insurance defense firm"

NOTABLE PERKS

- Paid parking
- Frequent free lunches
- Firm credit card for marketing and networking
- Bar expenses

EMPLOYMENT CONTACT

Lori C. Rosenberg, Esq.
Director of Legal Recruiting
Phone: (215) 665-4178
Fax: (215) 665-2013
E-mail: lrosenberg@cozen.com

BASE SALARY (2007)

Philadelphia, PA
1st year: $125,000
Summer associate: $2,400/week

Visit the Vault Law Channel, the complete online resource for law careers, featuring firm
profiles, message boards, the Vault Law Job Board, and more. www.vault.com/law

VAULT CAREER LIBRARY   561

Davis Wright Tremaine LLP

2600 Century Square
1501 Fourth Avenue
Seattle, WA 98101-1688
Phone: (206) 622-3150
www.dwt.com

LOCATIONS

Seattle, WA (HQ)

Anchorage, AK • Bellevue, WA • Los Angeles, CA • New York, NY • Portland, OR • San Francisco, CA • Washington, DC (two offices) • Shanghai

MAJOR DEPARTMENTS & PRACTICES

Admiralty & Maritime • Advertising & Marketing Law • Aircraft Industry • Antitrust • Appellate • Business & Corporate • Broadcast • Cable • China Practice • Climate Change • Construction • Corporate Diversity Counseling • Corporate Finance • Credit Recovery & Bankruptcy • Education • Emerging Business & Technology • Employment Related Services • Energy • Entertainment • Environmental • Estate Planning • Finance & Commercial Law • Financial Services • Food & Agriculture • Government Contracts • Government Investigations & Criminal Defense • Government Relations • Health Care • Hospitality • Immigration • Information Technology • Intellectual Property • International • Internet & E-Commerce • Life Sciences • Legislation • Litigation • Media • M&A • Municipal Finance • Nonprofit • Patent • Privacy & Security • Real Estate & Land Use • Retail & Restaurant • Securities • Tax • Tax-Exempt Organizations • Technology • Telecommunications • Trusts & Estates

THE STATS

No. of attorneys: 400+
No. of offices: 10
Managing Partner: Richard Ellingsen
Hiring Partner: Craig Miller

THE BUZZ
WHAT ATTORNEYS AT OTHER FIRMS ARE SAYING ABOUT THIS FIRM

- "Quality attorneys"
- "Family friendly, great people"
- "OK for Seattle"
- "Great atmosphere, low pay"

RANKING RECAP

Best in Region
#4 - Pacific Northwest

NOTABLE PERKS

- Company retreats
- Bar and moving expenses
- Lots of free food
- Generous business development budget

EMPLOYMENT CONTACT

Ms. Carol Yuly
Recruiting Administrator
Phone: (206) 628-3529
Fax: (206) 628-7699
E-mail: carolyuly@dwt.com

BASE SALARY (2007)

Seattle, WA; Bellevue, WA
1st year: $100,000
Summer associate: $2,000/week

Anchorage, AK
1st year: $85,000
Summer associate: $1,500/week

Los Angeles, CA
1st year: $116,000
Summer associate: $2,115/week

Portland, OR
1st year: $90,000
Summer associate: $1,600/week

San Francisco, CA
1st year: $122,000
Summer associate: $2,346/week

© 2007 Vault Inc.

Drinker Biddle & Reath LLP

One Logan Square
18th and Cherry Streets
Philadelphia, PA 19103-6996
Phone: (215) 988-2700
www.drinkerbiddle.com

LOCATIONS

Philadelphia, PA (HQ)

Albany, NY • Berwyn, PA • Chicago, IL • Florham Park, NJ
• Los Angeles, CA • Milwaukee, WI • New York, NY •
Princeton, NJ • San Francisco, CA • Washington, DC •
Wilmington, DE

MAJOR PRACTICES

Antitrust and Securities Matters • Commercial Litigation •
Communications Litigation • Complex Class-Action Defense
• Corporate Governance • Corporate Restructuring •
Corporate Securities • Environmental • Government &
Regulatory Affairs • Health Law • Human Resources Law •
Insurance • Intellectual Property • Investment Management
• Life Sciences • Mergers & Acquisitions • Products Liability
& Mass Tort • Private Client Representations • Real Estate •
Tax • Venture Capital & Private Equity • White Collar Crime
& Corporate Investigations

THE STATS

No. of attorneys: 630
No. of offices: 12
Summer associate offers: 43 out of 45 (2006)
Chairman: Alfred W. Putnam, Jr.
Hiring Partner: Audrey C. Talley

RANKING RECAP

Best in Region
#4 - Pennsylvania/Mid-Atlantic

NOTABLE PERKS

• $10,000 stipend plus bar-related expenses
• Moving cost reimbursement
• $10,000 federal judicial clerk bonus
• Complimentary on-site gym

EMPLOYMENT CONTACT

Ms. Maryellen Altieri
Director of Professional Recruitment
Phone: (215) 988-2663
Fax: (215) 988-2757
E-mail: maryellen.altieri@dbr.com

BASE SALARY (2007)

All offices
1st year: $ 145,000
Summer associate: $ 2,600/week

THE BUZZ
WHAT ATTORNEYS AT OTHER FIRMS ARE SAYING ABOUT THIS FIRM

• "Good Philly firm"
• "Nice people"
• "Unimpressive"
• "Old school"

Visit the Vault Law Channel, the complete online resource for law careers, featuring firm
profiles, message boards, the Vault Law Job Board, and more. www.vault.com/law

 VAULT CAREER LIBRARY

563

Duane Morris LLP

30 S.17th St. United Plaza Bldg.
Philadelphia, PA 19103-7396
Phone: (215) 979-1000
www.duanemorris.com

LOCATIONS

Philadelphia, PA (HQ)

Atlanta, GA • Baltimore, MD • Boston, MA • Chicago, IL • Houston, TX • Lake Tahoe, NV • Las Vegas, NV • Los Angeles, CA • Miami, FL • New York, NY • Newark, NJ • Pittsburgh, PA • Princeton, NJ • San Diego, CA • San Francisco, CA • Washington, DC • Wilmington, DE • London • Singapore

MAJOR DEPARTMENTS & PRACTICES

Business Reorganization & Financial Restructuring • Capital Markets • Corporate • Employment, Benefits & Immigration • Energy & Resources • Environmental • Estates & Asset Planning • Health Law • Insurance & Financial Products • Intellectual Property • International • Real Estate • Sports & Recreation • Tax • Technology • Trial

THE STATS

No. of attorneys: 646
No. of offices: 20
Summer associate offers: 11 out of 12 (2006)
Chairman and CEO: Sheldon M. Bonovitz
Hiring Partner: Matthew C. Jones

RANKING RECAP

Best in Region
#9 - Pennsylvania/Mid-Atlantic

NOTABLE PERKS

• Matching 401(k)
• Cab and dinner when working late
• Weekly wine and cheese reception

EMPLOYMENT CONTACT

Ms. Peggy Simoncini Pasquay
Manager of Attorney Recruitment & Relations
Phone: (215) 979-1161
Fax: (215) 979-1020
E-mail: recruiting@duanemorris.com

BASE SALARY (2007)

Philadelphia, PA
1st year: $135,000
Summer associate: $2,600/week

THE BUZZ

WHAT ATTORNEYS AT OTHER FIRMS ARE SAYING ABOUT THIS FIRM

• "Better than reputation"
• "Great in Philly, good in other offices"
• "Growth for growth's sake"
• "Not impressive"

© 2007 Vault Inc.

The Vault Guide to the Top 100 Law Firms • 2008 Edition
....
The Best of the Rest

Dykema Gossett PLLC

400 Renaissance Center
Detroit, MI 48243
Phone: (313) 568-6800
www.dykema.com

LOCATIONS

Ann Arbor, MI • Bloomfield Hills, MI • Chicago, IL • Detroit, MI • Grand Rapids, MI • Joliet, IL • Lansing, MI • Lisle, IL • Los Angeles, CA • Washington, DC

MAJOR DEPARTMENTS & PRACTICES

Administrative Law & Regulation • Antitrust • Appellate • Automotive • Bank Regulatory • Bankruptcy & Restructuring • Biotechnology & Life Sciences • Casino Gaming Law • China Law • Class Action Defense • Commercial Finance • Commercial Litigation • Construction Law • Consumer Financial Services • Corporate Finance • Corporate Governance • E-Commerce & Technology • Economic Development & Tax Incentives • Elections & Campaign Finance Compliance • Employee Benefits • Employment • Energy, Telecommunications & Public Utilities • Environmental • Estate Planning & Administration • Family Law • Financial Services • Franchise Law • Government Contracts • Government Policy & Lobbying • Health Care • HIPAA • Immigration Law • Indian Law • Insurance Law • Intellectual Property • Intellectual Property Litigation • International Law & Trade Regulation • Investment Management • Litigation • Medical Malpractice • Mergers & Acquisitions • Nonprofit Organizations • Pharmaceutical & Medical Products • Private Company & Corporate Counseling • Product Liability Litigation • Product Safety • Public Finance • Real Estate • Securities • Securities Litigation • Structured Finance & Securitizations • Syndication • Taxation & Estates • Trade & Professional Associations • Venture Capital & Private Equity

THE STATS

No. of attorneys: 360
No. of offices: 10
Summer associate offers: 23 out of 28 (2006)
Chairman & CEO: Rex E. Schlaybaugh Jr.
Hiring Partner: Brendan J. Cahill

THE BUZZ
WHAT ATTORNEYS AT OTHER FIRMS ARE SAYING ABOUT THIS FIRM

- "Well regarded in Midwest"
- "Rust belt regional"
- "Solid firm ... Good people"
- "Arrogant"

RANKING RECAP

Best in Region
#12 - Midwest

NOTABLE PERKS

- Free parking
- Bar review
- Free Starbucks coffee and sodas

EMPLOYMENT CONTACT

Ms. Sarah K. Staup
Professional Personnel Specialist
Phone: (313) 568-6831
Fax: (313) 568-6691
E-mail: sstaup@dykema.com

BASE SALARY (2007)

Michigan offices
1st year: $105,000
Summer associate: $1,900/week

Washington, DC
1st year: $125,000
Summer associate: $2,400/week

Chicago, IL
1st year: $125,000
Summer associate: $2,400/week

Visit the Vault Law Channel, the complete online resource for law careers, featuring firm profiles, message boards, the Vault Law Job Board, and more. www.vault.com/law

VAULT CAREER LIBRARY   565

Edwards Angell Palmer & Dodge LLP

111 Huntington Ave.
Boston, MA 02199
Phone: (617) 239-0100
Fax: (617) 227-4420
www.eapdlaw.com

LOCATIONS

Boston, MA
Fort Lauderdale, FL
Hartford, CT
New York, NY
Providence, RI
Short Hills, NJ
Stamford, CT
West Palm Beach, FL
Wilmington, DE
London

MAJOR DEPARTMENTS & PRACTICES

Antitrust • Bankruptcy & Creditors' Rights • Class Action &
Mass Litigation • Corporate • Debt Finance & Capital
Markets • Environmental • Gaming • Government
Enforcement • Insurance & Reinsurance • Intellectual
Property • International • Labor & Employment • Litigation •
Life Sciences • Mergers & Acquisitions • Private Client •
Private Equity • Public Finance • Real Estate • Securities &
Public Companies • Tax • Technology • Venture Capital

THE STATS

No. of attorneys: 536
No. of offices: 10
Summer associate offers: 22 out of 22 (2006)
Managing Partners: Charles E. Dewitt Jr., Terrence M. Finn
Hiring Partner: Charles E. Dewitt Jr.

NOTABLE PERKS

• Domestic partner benefits
• Bar and moving expenses
• 401(k) plan available immediately
• Three months paid maternity and paternity leave

EMPLOYMENT CONTACT

Ms. Elizabeth Armour
Director of Legal Recruiting
2800 Financial Plaza
Providence, RI 02903
Phone: (401) 455-7665
E-mail: earmour@eapdlaw.com

BASE SALARY (2007)

Boston, MA; New York, NY; Wilmington, DE
1st year: $145,000
Summer associate: $2,800/week

Providence, RI; Hartford, Stamford, CT
1st year: $130,000
Summer associate: $2,500/week

Short Hills, NJ; Ft. Lauderdale, W. Palm Beach,FL
1st year: $125,000
Summer associate: $2,430/week

THE BUZZ
WHAT ATTORNEYS AT OTHER FIRMS ARE SAYING ABOUT THIS FIRM

• "Knowledgeable, above board"
• "Pride of Providence"
• "Great insurance work"
• "Losing identity after merger"

© 2007 Vault Inc.

Epstein Becker & Green, P.C.

250 Park Avenue
New York, NY 10177
Phone: (212) 351-4500
www.ebglaw.com

LOCATIONS

Atlanta, GA
Chicago, IL
Dallas, TX
Houston, TX
Los Angeles, CA
Miami, FL
Newark, NJ
New York, NY
San Francisco, CA
Stamford, CT
Washington, DC

MAJOR DEPARTMENTS & PRACTICES

Business Law
Healthcare & Life Sciences
Labor and Employment
Litigation
Real Estate

THE STATS

No. of attorneys: 389
No. of offices: 11
Managing Partner: George P. Sape
Hiring Partners:
New York: Evan J. Spelfogel
Washington, DC: Carrie Valiant

NOTABLE PERKS

- One bar expense covered plus additional if required
- Domestic partner benefits
- One Bar exam and one Bar Review course covered
- On-going training and development for attorneys

EMPLOYMENT CONTACT

Ms. Zeynep Ersin
Manager of Legal Recruitment & Professional Development
Phone: (212) 351-4500
Fax: (212) 661-0989
E-mail: zersin@ebglaw.com

Washington, DC
Ms. Amy L. Simmons
Marketing & Recruitment Manager
1227 25th St., NW, Suite 700
Washington, D.C. 20037
Phone: (202) 861-1811
Fax: (202) 861-3511
E-mail: asimmons@ebglaw.com

BASE SALARY (2007)

New York, NY
1st year: $110,000 - $130,000
(depending on practice area)
Summer associate: $2,019/week

Washington, DC
1st year: $130,000
Summer associate: $2,600/week

THE BUZZ
WHAT ATTORNEYS AT OTHER FIRMS ARE SAYING ABOUT THIS FIRM

- "Healthcare gurus"
- "Declining"
- "Strong employment law practice"
- "Underpaid for the hours"

Visit the Vault Law Channel, the complete online resource for law careers, featuring firm profiles, message boards, the Vault Law Job Board, and more. www.vault.com/law

VAULT CAREER LIBRARY   567

Faegre & Benson LLP

2200 Wells Fargo Center
90 South Seventh Street
Minneapolis, MN 55402-3901
Phone: (612) 766-7000
www.faegre.com

LOCATIONS

Minneapolis, MN (HQ)
Boulder, CO
Denver, CO
Des Moines, IA
Frankfurt
London
Shanghai

MAJOR DEPARTMENTS & PRACTICES

Advertising • Alternative Dispute Resolution • Appellate •
Bankruptcy & Insolvency • Computer & Internet • Copyright
Protection • Corporate Finance & Securities • Emerging
Companies • Employee Benefits & Executive Compensation
• Environmental • Government Relations • Food Safety •
Health • HIPAA Privacy • Housing Development •
Immigration • Insurance Coverage Compliance •
International Arbitration • Investment Management • Labor
& Employment • Litigation • M&A • Mold Defense • Natural
Resources • Nonprofit Organizations • Oil & Gas
Transactional Experience • Patent Litigation Results •
Product Liability • Real Estate • Sports • Tax • Trusts &
Estates • White Collar Criminal Defense

THE STATS

No. of attorneys: 500
No. of offices: 7
Summer associate offers: 24 out of 25 (2006)
Chairman: Thomas G. Morgan
Hiring Partner: James R. Steffen

THE BUZZ
WHAT ATTORNEYS AT OTHER FIRMS ARE SAYING ABOUT THIS FIRM

- "Best in Minnesota"
- "Good quality of life"
- "Very friendly, competent lawyers"
- "Smart, a bit of a sweatshop"

RANKING RECAP

Quality of Life
#9 - Overall Satisfaction
#9 - Hours
#9 - Informal Training/Mentoring
#11 - Associate/Partner Relations
#11 - Best Firms to Work For

NOTABLE PERKS

- Generous marketing and mentoring budgets
- Liberal parental leave/part-time policies
- Annual canoe trip
- Taxi and dinner when working late

EMPLOYMENT CONTACT

Minneapolis/Des Moines
Ms. Dana Gray
Manager of Legal Personnel Services
Phone: (612) 766-7000
Fax: (612) 766-1600
E-mail: dgray@faegre.com

Colorado
Ms. Amy Schneider
Colorado Legal Personnel Manager
Phone: (303) 607-3500
Fax: (303) 607-3600
E-mail: aschneider@faegre.com

BASE SALARY (2007)

Minneapolis, MN; Boulder, CO; Denver, CO
1st year: $120,000
Summer associate: $2,050/week (2006)

Des Moines, IA
1st year: $100,000
Summer associate: $1,650/week

© 2007 Vault Inc.

Fitzpatrick, Cella, Harper & Scinto

30 Rockefeller Plaza
New York, New York 10012-3800
Phone: (212) 218-2100
www.fchs.com

LOCATIONS

New York, NY (HQ)
Costa Mesa, CA
Washington, DC

MAJOR DEPARTMENTS & PRACTICES

Biotechnology
e-Commerce & New Media
Electronics & Computers
Interferences
Nanotechnology
Pharmaceuticals & Chemicals

THE STATS

No. of attorneys: 150
No. of offices: 3
Summer associate offers: 21 out of 24 (2006)
Managing Partner: Dominick A. Conde
Hiring Attorney: Michael Sandonato

RANKING RECAP

Best in Practice
#10 - Intellectual Property

NOTABLE PERKS

- Annual dinner at the Four Seasons
- Free soda
- Tickets to Rockefeller Center tree lighting
- Car rides, dinner after 8:00 p.m.

EMPLOYMENT CONTACT

Ms. Kristen Ramos
Director of Recruiting & Professional Development
Phone: (212) 218-2274
Fax: (212) 218-2200
E-mail: kramos@fchs.com

BASE SALARY (2007)

New York, NY
1st year: $160,000
Summer associate: $3,076/week

Costa Mesa, CA; Washington, D.C.
1st year: $160,000
Summer associate: $3,076/week

THE BUZZ
WHAT ATTORNEYS AT OTHER FIRMS ARE SAYING ABOUT THIS FIRM

- "Specialized, but strong at what it does"
- "IP boutique"
- "Lost some of its prime-time players"
- "Sweatshop"

Visit the Vault Law Channel, the complete online resource for law careers, featuring firm profiles, message boards, the Vault Law Job Board, and more. www.vault.com/law

 VAULT CAREER LIBRARY   569

Foley Hoag LLP

Seaport World Trade Center West
155 Seaport Boulevard
Boston, MA 02210-2600
Phone: (617) 832-1000
www.foleyhoag.com

LOCATIONS

Boston, MA (HQ)
Washington, DC

MAJOR DEPARTMENTS & PRACTICES

Accountants Professional Liability • Administrative •
Alternative Dispute Resolution • Banking • Bankruptcy
Reorganization & Workout Practice • Business • Business
Crimes & Government Investigation • Business Litigation •
Construction & Development Disputes • Corporate
Finance/Securities • Corporate Social Responsibility •
Education • Energy & Regulated Industries • Environmental
• Government Strategies • Health Care • Immigration •
Infrastructure & Transportation • Insurance • Insurance
Litigation • Intellectual Property • International • Investment
Management • Labor & Employment • Land Use &
Development • Life Sciences • Litigation • M&A • Patent •
Real Estate • Securities & Corporate Disputes • Taxation •
Technology Transfer & Licensing • Telecommunications •
Trade Regulation • Trademark • Trusts & Estates • Venture
Capital/Emerging Companies

THE STATS

No. of attorneys: 240
No. of offices: 2
Managing Partners: Robby Sanoff, Michele Whitham
Summer associate offers: 22 out of 22 (2006)
Hiring Partner: Kenneth Leonetti

RANKING RECAP

Best in Region
#7 - Boston

Quality of Life
#17 (tie) - Pro Bono

Best in Diversity
#10 - Diversity with Respect to GLBT
#18 - Overall Diversity

NOTABLE PERKS

• Technology subsidy
• Bar and moving expenses
• Concierge services
• Subsidized cafeteria, billiards and TV rooms

EMPLOYMENT CONTACT

Ms. Dina M. Wreede
Dir. Legal Recruiting & Professional Development
Phone: (617) 832-7060
Fax: (617) 832-7000
E-mail: dwreede@foleyhoag.com

BASE SALARY (2007)

Boston, MA; Washington, DC
1st year: $160,000
Summer associate: $2,788/week

THE BUZZ
WHAT ATTORNEYS AT OTHER FIRMS ARE SAYING ABOUT THIS FIRM

• "Smart attorneys, family friendly"
• "Overly pompous"
• "Premier Boston firm"
• "Very academic"

© 2007 Vault Inc.

Frost Brown Todd LLC

2200 PNC Center
201 East Fifth Street
Cincinnati, Ohio 45202-4182
Phone: (513) 651-6800
www.frostbrowntodd.com

LOCATIONS

Cincinnati, OH
Columbus, OH
Lexington, KY
Louisville, KY
Middletown, OH
Nashville, TN
New Albany, IN

MAJOR DEPARTMENTS & PRACTICES

Alternative Dispute Resolution • Appellate • Banking •
Bankruptcy • Business/Commercial Litigation • Commercial
& Real Estate • Corporate & Securities • E-Business •
Environmental Law • First Amendment, Media & Advertising
• Food & Restaurant • Franchise & Distribution •
Government Relations • Health Law • Immigration •
Insurance • Intellectual Property • International • Labor and
Employment • Litigation • Mass Tort • M&A • Products
Liability • Real Estate • Securities • Trademark/Copyright •
Tax & Estate Planning • White Collar Crime

THE STATS

No. of attorneys: 350
No. of offices: 7
Summer associate offers: 17 out of 22 (2006)
Co-Managing Partners: Richard J. Erickson, C. Edward
   Glasscock
Hiring Partner: Theresa A. Canaday

RANKING RECAP

Best in Region
#10 - Midwest

NOTABLE PERKS

- Profit-sharing plan
- Free BlackBerry service
- Client development/entertainment opportunities
- Bar study stipend

EMPLOYMENT CONTACT

Ms. Karen Laymance
Director of Attorney Recruitment & Development
Phone: (513) 651-6800
Fax: (513) 651-6981
E-mail: klaymance@fbtlaw.com

BASE SALARY (2007)

Cincinnati, Middletown, OH
1st year: $95,000 (2006)
Summer associate: $1,750/week

Columbus, OH
1st year: $100,000 (2006)
Summer associate: $1,900/week

Lexington, Louisville, KY; New Albany, IN
1st year: $88,000 (2006)
Summer associate: $1,600/week

Nashville, TN
1st year: $95,000 (2006)
Summer associate: $1,750/week

THE BUZZ
WHAT ATTORNEYS AT OTHER FIRMS ARE SAYING ABOUT THIS FIRM

- "They do great work"
- "Underwhelming"
- "Best firm in Cincinnati"
- "Nice, down to earth people"

Visit the Vault Law Channel, the complete online resource for law careers, featuring firm
profiles, message boards, the Vault Law Job Board, and more. www.vault.com/law

VAULT CAREER LIBRARY   571

Gardere Wynne Sewell LLP

1601 Elm Street, Suite 3000
Dallas, TX 75201
Phone: (214) 999-3000
www.gardere.com

LOCATIONS

Dallas, TX (HQ)
Austin, TX
Houston, TX
Mexico City

MAJOR DEPARTMENTS & PRACTICES

Antitrust • Appellate • Arbitration/ADR • Banking •
Bankruptcy • Biotechnology • Chemical Industry & Refining
Team • Class Action Defense • Corporate Governance •
Corporate Securities • Employee Benefits • Energy •
Entertainment • Environmental • ERISA/Employee Benefits •
ESOP • Family Law • Food & Beverage • Government
Contracts • Health Care • Immigration • Insurance Coverage
• Intellectual Property • Labor • Latin America • Litigation •
M&A • Maritime Finance • Oil & Gas • Patent, Copyright &
Trademark • Products Liability • Professional Malpractice •
Real Estate • Securities • Tax • Trusts & Estates • Water
Law • White Collar Crime & Compliance

THE STATS

No. of attorneys: 300
No. of offices: 4
Summer associate offers: 17 out of 19 (2006)
Managing Partner: Stephen D. Good
Hiring Partners:
  Dallas: Randy Gordon John G. Caverlee
  Houston: Stephen D. Elison

NOTABLE PERKS

• Subsidized parking
• Annual associate-only retreat
• Recruiting dinners at upscale restaurants
• Extensive Attorney Development and Training
  Program

EMPLOYMENT CONTACTS

Dallas
Ms. Tammy Patterson
Director of Recruiting and Professional Development
Phone: (214) 999-4177
Fax: (214) 999-3177
E-mail: tpatterson@gardere.com

Houston
Ms. Jill C. Buja
Recruiting Manager
1000 Louisiana, Suite 3400
Houston, TX 77002
Phone: (713) 276-5217
E-mail: jbuja@gardere.com

BASE SALARY (2007)

Dallas, Houston, TX
1st year: $140,000
Summer associate: $2,600/week

THE BUZZ

WHAT ATTORNEYS AT OTHER FIRMS ARE SAYING ABOUT THIS FIRM

• "Good for Texas"
• "Not where they used to be"
• "Very friendly"
• "Lower tier of the 'Big Tex'"

© 2007 Vault Inc.

Goulston & Storrs

400 Atlantic Avenue
Boston, MA 02110-3333
Phone: (617) 482-1776
www.goulstonstorrs.com

LOCATIONS

Boston, MA (HQ)
New York, NY
Washington, DC
London

MAJOR DEPARTMENTS & PRACTICES

Capital Markets • Commercial Law • Corporate •
Employment & Labor Law • Environmental Law • Healthcare
• Hospitality & Recreation • Intellectual Property •
International Litigation • Philanthropic Advisors • Private
Client & Trust • Public Law & Policy • Real Estate • Tax •
Technology • Transportation

THE STATS

No. of Attorneys: 190
No. of offices: 4
Summer associate offers: 11 out of 12 (2006)
Co-Managing Directors: Kitt Sawitsky and Douglas M.
 Husid
Hiring Attorney: James Wallack

RANKING RECAP

Best in Region
#10 - Boston

Best in Practice
#10 (tie)- Real Estate

Partner Prestige Rankings
#3 (tie) - Real Estate

NOTABLE PERKS

• Great health care and dental benefits
• Summer BBQs on deck overlooking Atlantic Ocean
• In-house professional chef and kitchen
• Weekly social activities

EMPLOYMENT CONTACT

All Partner Inquiries (firmwide)
Nancy Needle
Director of Legal Recruitment
Phone: (617) 574-6447
E-mail: nneedle@goulstonstorrs.com

Lateral Associate Inquiries (firmwide)
Jill Nussbaum
Lateral Recruitment Specialist
Phone: (617) 574-4004
E-mail: jnussbaum@goulstonstorrs.com

**Entry-level Attorney and Paralegal Inquiries
(firmwide)**
Ms. Jennifer Smith
Entry-level Recruitment Manager
Phone: (617) 574-4072
E-mail: jsmith@goulstonstorrs.com

BASE SALARY (2007)

1st year: $145,000
Summer associate: $2,600/week

THE BUZZ
WHAT ATTORNEYS AT OTHER FIRMS ARE SAYING ABOUT THIS FIRM

• "Family-friendly and top notch"
• "Small, but high quality"
• "Stuffy and pretentious"
• "Cutting-edge real estate department"

Visit the Vault Law Channel, the complete online resource for law careers, featuring firm
profiles, message boards, the Vault Law Job Board, and more. www.vault.com/law

VAULT CAREER LIBRARY   573

Haynes and Boone, LLP

901 Main Street, Suite 3100
Dallas, TX 75202
Phone: (214) 651-5000
www.haynesboone.com

LOCATIONS

Austin, TX • Dallas, TX • Fort Worth, TX • Houston, TX •
New York, NY • Richardson, TX • San Antonio, TX •
Washington, DC • Mexico City • Moscow

MAJOR DEPARTMENTS & PRACTICES

Antitrust • Appellate • Aviation • BioScience & Medical
Technology • Business Litigation • Business Reorganization/
Bankruptcy • Corporate/Securities • Employee Benefits/
Executive Compensation • Energy/Power • Environmental •
ERISA Litigation • Finance • Franchise & Distribution •
Government Contracts • Health Care • HIPPA • Privacy &
Security • Immigration • Insurance Coverage • Intellectual
Property • Intellectual Property Litigation • International •
Investment Funds • Iraq Transactions & Claims • Labor &
Employment • Media Law • Mergers & Acquisitions •
Outsourcing • Projects Practice • Real Estate • Restaurant &
Foodservice • Sarbanes-Oxley/Corporate Governance •
Securities Litigation • Tax, Business & Estate Planning •
Technology Contracts • Venture Capital • White Collar
Criminal Defense

THE STATS

No. of attorneys: 439
No. of offices: 10
Summer associate offers: 50 out of 62 (2006)
Managing Partner: Robert E. Wilson
Hiring Partner: Kathleen M. Beasley

RANKING RECAP

Quality of Life
#15 - Associate/Partner Relations
#16 - Informal Training/Mentoring

Best in Diversity
#15 - Diversity with Respect to Minorities
#16 - Diversity with Respect to Women

NOTABLE PERKS

- 401(k)/Profit sharing
- Frequent happy hours
- Bar and moving expenses
- Discounts on gym memberships

EMPLOYMENT CONTACT

Ms. Amanda Knocke
Recruiting Coordinator
Phone: (214) 651-5176
Fax: (214) 200-0859
E-mail: amanda.knocke@haynesboone.com

BASE SALARY (2007)

All offices
1st year: $135,000
Summer associate: $2,700/week

THE BUZZ
WHAT ATTORNEYS AT OTHER FIRMS ARE SAYING ABOUT THIS FIRM

- "Very Texas, but very good"
- "Regional player"
- "High hours"
- "Highly regarded in Texas, unknown nationally"

© 2007 Vault Inc.

Hinshaw & Culbertson LLP

222 N. LaSalle Street, Suite 300
Chicago, IL 60601
Phone: (312) 704-3000
www.hinshawlaw.com

LOCATIONS

Chicago, IL (HQ)

Appleton, WI • Belleville, IL • Boston, MA • Champaign, IL
• Crystal Lake, IL • Edwardsville, IL • Ft. Lauderdale, FL •
Jacksonville, FL • Joliet, IL • Lisle, IL • Los Angeles, CA •
Miami, FL • Milwaukee, WI • Minneapolis, MN • New York,
NY • Peoria, IL • Phoenix, AZ • Portland, OR • Providence,
RI • Rockford, IL • San Francisco, CA • Schererville, IN •
Springfield, IL • St. Louis, MO • Tampa, FL • Waukegan, IL

MAJOR DEPARTMENTS & PRACTICES

Construction • Corporate & Business Law • Environmental •
Government • Health Care • Insurance Services • Labor &
Employment • Litigation • Professional Liability • School
Law

THE STATS

No. of attorneys: 450
No. of offices: 27
Summer associate offers: 14 out of 17 (2006)
Chairman: Donald L. Mrozek
Managing Partner: J. William Roberts
Hiring Partner: David R. Creagh

RANKING RECAP

Best in Region
#14 - Midwest

NOTABLE PERKS

• Bonuses for bringing in new clients
• Happy hours and lunches
• Annual attorney weekend
• Free dinner after 7 p.m.

EMPLOYMENT CONTACT

Miss Paula A. Dixton
Legal Recruitment & Development Manager
Phone: (312) 704-3000
Fax: (312) 704-3001
E-mail: pdixton@hinshawlaw.com

BASE SALARY (2007)

Chicago, IL
1st year: $95,000

THE BUZZ

WHAT ATTORNEYS AT OTHER FIRMS ARE SAYING ABOUT THIS FIRM

• "Good shop, need to expand"
• "Past its prime"
• "Great work environment, good training"
• "Overworked"

Visit the Vault Law Channel, the complete online resource for law careers, featuring firm
profiles, message boards, the Vault Law Job Board, and more. www.vault.com/law

VAULT CAREER LIBRARY   575

Holland & Hart LLP

555 17th Street, Suite 3200
Denver, CO 80202
Phone: (303) 295-8000
www.hollandhart.com

LOCATIONS

Denver, CO (HQ)
Aspen, CO
Billings, MT
Boise, ID
Boulder, CO
Cheyenne, WY
Colorado Springs, CO
Greenwood Village, CO
Jackson, WY
Las Vegas, NV
Salt Lake City, UT
Santa Fe, NM
Washington, DC

MAJOR DEPARTMENTS & PRACTICES

Corporate • Litigation • Intellectual Property •Natural
Resources • Technology Law • Health Care • Employment
Law • Real Estate • Securities Litigation • Tax

THE STATS

No. of attorneys: 360
No. of offices: 13
Summer associate offers: 13 out of 13 (2006)
Managing Partner: Lawrence J. Wolfe
Hiring Partner: Katherine LeVoy

RANKING RECAP

Quality of Life
#8 - Office Space
#21 - Associate/Partner Relations

NOTABLE PERKS

• Access to firm condos in Aspen and Steamboat
  Springs
• Regular sabbaticals for partners
• Fee-splitting arrangements
• Comprehensive professional development
  programs for summer clerks through partner level
  attorneys

EMPLOYMENT CONTACT

Ms. Miriam Connor
Manager of Recruitment
Phone: (303) 295-8509
E-mail: meconnor@hollandhart.com

BASE SALARY (2007)

Denver, CO
1st year: $110,000
Summer associate: $2,115/week

Colorado Springs, CO; Salt Lake City, UT
1st year: $110,000
Summer associate: $2,115/week

Boise, ID
1st year: $86,000
Summer associate: $1,653/week

Cheyenne, WY
1st year: $90,500
Summer associate: $1,740/week

THE BUZZ
WHAT ATTORNEYS AT OTHER FIRMS ARE SAYING ABOUT THIS FIRM

• "Good, solid firm"
• "Too big for its britches"
• "Good Western regional litigation firm"
• "Lifestyle over money"

© 2007 Vault Inc.

Jackson Lewis LLP

One North Broadway, 15th Floor
White Plains, NY 10601-2305
Phone: (914) 328-0404
www.jacksonlewis.com

LOCATIONS

Atlanta, GA • Boston, MA • Chicago, IL • Cleveland, OH •
Dallas, TX • Denver, CO • Greenville, SC • Hartford, CT •
Houston, TX • Long Island, NY • Los Angeles, CA • Miami,
FL • Minneapolis, MN • Morristown, NJ • New York, NY •
Orlando, FL • Pittsburgh, PA • Portland, OR • Providence, RI
• Raleigh-Durham, VA • Richmond, VA • Sacramento, CA •
San Francisco, CA • Seattle, WA • Stamford, CT • White
Plains, NY • Vienna, VA

MAJOR DEPARTMENTS & PRACTICES

Affirmative Action • Alternative Dispute Resolution • Class
Action Litigation • Disability Leave & Health Management •
Drug Testing • Employee Benefits Counseling, Benefits
Litigation & Private Practice Group • Immigration Law •
International Employment Issues • Labor Relations, including
Preventative Practices • Litigation • Management Training •
Public Sector • Reduction in Force • Trade Secrets, Non-
Competes, & Workplace Technology • Wage & Hour •
Workplace Safety

THE STATS

No. of attorneys: 410
No. of offices: 28
Managing Partner: Patrick L. Vaccaro
Hiring Partner: Thomas Walsh

RANKING RECAP

Best in Practice
#4 - Labor & Employment

NOTABLE PERKS

• Budget for client development or recruiting
  activities
• Frequent happy hours
• Firm retreat for attorneys and spouses
• 401(k) contribution

EMPLOYMENT CONTACT

Susan Bridges
Director of Human Resources
Phone: (914) 328-0404
Fax: (914) 328-1882
E-mail: bridgess@jacksonlewis.com

 THE BUZZ
WHAT ATTORNEYS AT OTHER FIRMS ARE SAYING ABOUT THIS FIRM

• "Good labor and employment"
• "Great people"
• "Too regional"
• "The best L&E boutique but no match for big firm
  lawyers"

Visit the Vault Law Channel, the complete online resource for law careers, featuring firm
profiles, message boards, the Vault Law Job Board, and more. www.vault.com/law

VAULT CAREER LIBRARY   577

Jackson Walker L.L.P.

901 Main Street, Suite 6000
Dallas, TX 75202
Phone: (214) 953-6000
www.jw.com

LOCATIONS

Dallas, TX (HQ)

Austin, TX • Fort Worth, TX • Houston, TX • San Angelo,
TX • San Antonio, TX

MAJOR DEPARTMENTS & PRACTICES

Agriculture • Antitrust • Appellate • Aviation • Bankruptcy •
Business Transactions • Construction • Corporate &
Securities E-Discovery • Eminent Domain • Energy •
Entertainment & Sports • Environmental • ERISA • Financial
Services • Health Care • Immigration • Insurance •
Intellectual Property • IP Litigation • International •
Internet/E-Commerce • Labor & Employment Land Use • Life
Sciences/Medical Technology • Litigation • Media • Medical
Malpractice • Municipal Law Private Equity/Hedge Funds •
Public Finance • Real Estate • Regulatory & Legislative •
Special Investigations • Tax • Technology •
Telecommunications • Toxic Tort • Wealth Planning &
Transfer

THE STATS

No. of attorneys: 325
No. of offices: 6
Summer associate offers: 18 out of 23 (2006)
Managing Partner: T. Michael Wilson
Hiring Partner: James S. Ryan III

NOTABLE PERKS

- Signing bonus, summer stipend and approved
  relocation expenses
- Home loan program
- Bar expenses
- 401(k)

EMPLOYMENT CONTACT

Ms. Kimberly DiLallo
Director of Attorney Recruiting & Professional
  Development
Phone: (214) 953-6160
Fax: (214) 661-6852
E-mail: kdilallo@jw.com

BASE SALARY (2007)

All offices
1st year: $135,000, plus guaranteed $5,000 bonus
Summer associate: $2,600/week

THE BUZZ
WHAT ATTORNEYS AT OTHER FIRMS ARE SAYING ABOUT THIS FIRM

- "Great place to work, good people"
- "Tough litigators"
- "Reputable"
- "Needs to improve compensation"

© 2007 Vault Inc.

Kasowitz, Benson, Torres & Friedman LLP

1633 Broadway
New York, New York 10019
Phone: (212) 506-1700
www.kasowitz.com

LOCATIONS

New York, NY (HQ)
Atlanta, GA
Houston, TX
San Francisco, CA
Newark, NJ

MAJOR DEPARTMENTS & PRACTICES

Antitrust • Appeals • Arbitration/ADR • Complex
Commercial Litigation • Corporate • Creditors' Rights &
Bankruptcy • Employment Practices • Environmental •
Insurance Coverage • Intellectual Property • Mass Tort &
Product Liability • Matrimonial & Family Law • Plaintiff's
Representation • Real Estate • Securities • White Collar
Crime

THE STATS

No. of attorneys: 200+
No. of offices: 5
Summer associate offers: 8 out of 8 (2006)
Chairman: Marc E. Kasowitz
Hiring Attorney: Aaron H. Marks

NOTABLE PERKS

• Annual golf and tennis outing
• Monthly birthday celebrations
• Great summer events
• Discounts at Brooks Brothers, Tiffany's, New York
  Sports Club

EMPLOYMENT CONTACTS

New York
Ms. Mindy J. Lindenman
Director of Legal Recruiting
Phone: (212) 506-1918
Fax: (212) 506-1800
E-mail: mlindenman@kasowitz.com

Houston
Ms. Karen Holcombe
Recruiting Coordinator
Phone: (713) 220-8869
Fax: (713) 222-0843
E-mail: kholcombe@kasowitz.com

BASE SALARY (2007)

New York, NY
1st year: $160,000
Summer associate: $3,077.00/week

THE BUZZ
WHAT ATTORNEYS AT OTHER FIRMS ARE SAYING ABOUT THIS FIRM

• "Growing fast; good lawyers"
• "Aggressive, smart"
• "Quality boutique"
• "Snappy"

Visit the Vault Law Channel, the complete online resource for law careers, featuring firm
profiles, message boards, the Vault Law Job Board, and more. www.vault.com/law

VAULT CAREER LIBRARY   579

Kenyon & Kenyon LLP

One Broadway
New York, NY 10004
Phone: (212) 425-7200
www.kenyon.com

LOCATIONS

New York, NY (HQ)
San Jose, CA
Washington, DC

MAJOR DEPARTMENTS & PRACTICES

Asian Practice • Copyrights • Counseling Practice •
Licensing & Transactions • European Practice • Intellectual
Property Litigation • International Experience • Life Sciences
• Patents • Trademarks • Trade Secrets • Unfair
Competition & Trade Practices

THE STATS

No. of attorneys: 173
No. of offices: 3
Summer associate offers: 25 out of 28 (2006)
Managing Partner: Richard S. Gresalfi
Hiring Partner: Patrick J. Birde

RANKING RECAP

Best in Practice
#5 - Intellectual Property

NOTABLE PERKS

• Frequent firm events
• Great Yankees seats
• Incredible views of the Statue of Liberty

EMPLOYMENT CONTACT

Ms. Kathleen Lynn
Director of Legal Recruiting
Phone: (212) 908-6177
Fax: (212) 425-5288
E-mail: klynn@kenyon.com

BASE SALARY (2007)

New York, NY
1st year: $160,000
2nd year: $170,000
3rd year: $185,000
4th year: $210,000
5th year: $230,000
6th year: $240,000
7th year: $250,000
8th year: $255,000
Summer associate: $3,077/week

THE BUZZ
WHAT ATTORNEYS AT OTHER FIRMS ARE SAYING ABOUT THIS FIRM

• "Great IP firm"
• "IP boutique"
• "Struggling"
• "Past its prime"

© 2007 Vault Inc.

Kutak Rock LLP

1650 Farnam Street
Omaha, NE 68102-2186
Phone: (402) 346-6000
www.kutakrock.com

LOCATIONS

Omaha, NE (HQ)
Atlanta, GA • Chicago, IL • Denver, CO • Des Moines, IA •
Fayetteville, IN • Irvine, CA • Kansas City, MO • Little
Rock, AR • Los Angeles, CA • Oklahoma City, OK •
Richmond, VA • Scottsdale, AZ • Washington, DC •
Wichita, KS

MAJOR DEPARTMENTS & PRACTICES

Antitrust • Appellate • Arbitrage Rebate Compliance •
Banking & Commercial Lending • Bankruptcy • Blue Sky •
Construction • Corporate • Corporate Finance • Emerging
Companies • Employee Benefits • Environmental • Federal
Practice & National Security • Government Contracts •
Government Relations • Health Care • Insurance •
Intellectual Property & Technology • Labor & Employment •
Litigation • Public Finance • Real Estate & Commercial
Practice • Securities • Securities Litigation, Arbitration &
Regulatory • Structured Finance • Tax • Tax Credits •
Workouts & Surveillance

THE STATS

No. of attorneys: 375
No. of offices: 15
Chair of Executive Committee: David A. Jacobson
Hiring Partner: John L. Petr

NOTABLE PERKS

• Gym facility in Omaha office
• Firm-paid commuting costs
• Free soda and Starbucks coffee (Denver)
• Domestic partner benefits

EMPLOYMENT CONTACT

Ms. Jeanne G. Salerno
Director of Professional Development
Phone: (402) 346-6000
Fax: (402) 346-1148
E-mail: jeanne.salerno@kutakrock.com

BASE SALARY (2007)

Omaha, NE
1st year: $78,000
Summer associate: $1,400/week

Denver, CO
1st year: $100,000

THE BUZZ
WHAT ATTORNEYS AT OTHER FIRMS ARE SAYING ABOUT THIS FIRM

• "Family-friendly, laid back culture"
• "Minor league, but pretty good"
• "Great people to work with"
• "Very average"

Visit the Vault Law Channel, the complete online resource for law careers, featuring firm
profiles, message boards, the Vault Law Job Board, and more. www.vault.com/law

VAULT CAREER LIBRARY   581

Littler Mendelson P.C.

650 California Street
San Francisco, CA 94108-2693
Phone: (415) 433-1940
www.littler.com

LOCATIONS

San Francisco, CA (HQ)
Atlanta, GA • Boston, MA • Charlotte, NC • Chicago, IL • Cleveland, OH • Columbia, SC • Columbus, OH • Dallas, TX • Denver, CO • Fresno, CA • Houston, TX • Indianapolis, IN • Kansas City, MO • Las Vegas, NV • Long Island, NY • Los Angeles, CA • Miami, FL • Minneapolis, MN • Mobile, AL • New Haven, CT • New York, NY • Newark, NJ • Northwest, AR • Orange County, CA • Orlando, FL • Philadelphia, PA • Phoenix, AZ (two offices)* • Pittsburgh, PA • Portland, OR • Providence, RI • Reno, NV • Sacramento, CA • San Diego, CA • San Jose, CA • Santa Maria, CA • Seattle, WA • Stamford, CT • Stockton, CA • Tysons Corner, VA • Walnut Creek, CA • Washington, DC • Shanghai*

Littler Global

MAJOR DEPARTMENT & PRACTICE

Employment & Labor Law

THE STATS

No. of attorneys: 600+
No. of offices: 43
Summer associate offers: 10 out of 16 (2006)
Managing Director & President: Mr. Marko J. Mrkonich
Hiring Attorney: Mr. Robert Hulteng

RANKING RECAP

Best in Practice
#2 - Labor & Employment

Partner Prestige Rankings
#4 - Labor & Employment

Quality of Life
#18 - Formal Training

Best in Diversity
#4 (tie) - Overall Diversity
#8 - Diversity with Respect to GLBT
#4 - Diversity with Respect to Minorities
#11 - Diversity with Respect to Women

NOTABLE PERKS

- Extensive professional associate training
- Part time associate policy
- Free Blackberry
- Back-up day care

EMPLOYMENT CONTACT

Ms. Michele Lotta
National Recruitment Coordinator
Phone: (415) 433-1940
Fax: (415) 399-8490
E-mail: lawrecruit@littler.com

BASE SALARY (2007)

San Francisco, Los Angeles, Orange County CA; New York, NY
1st year: $130,000

Chicago, IL; San Jose, Walnut Creek, CA
1st year: $125,000

Philadelphia, PA; Houston, TX; Long Island, NY; Newark, NJ; Tysons Corner, VA; Washington, DC
1st year: $120,000

San Diego, CA; Atlanta, GA
1st year: $115,000

Miami, Orlando FL; Mobile, AL
1st year: $105,000

THE BUZZ
WHAT ATTORNEYS AT OTHER FIRMS ARE SAYING ABOUT THIS FIRM

- "Best employment boutique"
- "Diverse, friendly"
- "Not quite with the big boys"
- "Mid-size salary for full-size work schedule"

© 2007 Vault Inc.

Locke Liddell & Sapp LLP

2200 Ross Avenue, Suite 2200
Dallas, TX 75201-6676
Phone: (214) 740-8000
www.lockeliddell.com

LOCATIONS

Austin, TX • Dallas, TX • Houston, TX • New Orleans, LA •
Washington, DC

MAJOR DEPARTMENTS & PRACTICES

Administrative/Regulatory • Admiralty & Maritime •
Affordable Housing • Antitrust • Appellate • Aviation •
Bankruptcy & Creditors' Rights • Construction • Corporate
& Securities • Employee Benefits & ERISA • Energy •
Environmental • Financial Services • Franchise &
Distribution • Health Care • Insurance • Intellectual Property
• Internal & Government Investigations • International •
Labor & Employment • Litigation • Media • Oil, Gas &
Energy • Public Law • Real Estate • REITS • Tax •
Technology • Transportation • Trusts & Estates • White
Collar Defense

THE STATS

No. of attorneys: 400
No. of offices: 5
Summer associate offers: 41 out of 52 (2006)
Managing Partner: Jerry Clements
Hiring Partners:
  Austin: L. Jeffrey Hubenak
  Dallas: Clint Schumacher and Karin Torgerson
  Houston: Hanna Norvell and Charlie Baumann

RANKING RECAP

Quality of Life
#2 - Informal Training/Mentoring
#7 - Associate/Partner Relations
#18 - Overall Satisfaction

NOTABLE PERKS

• Free or subsidized parking (depending on office)
• Generous client development budget
• Easy access to sports tickets
• Cake day and doughnut day

EMPLOYMENT CONTACTS

Austin
Ms. Amanda Jensen
Phone: (512) 305-4778
Fax: (512) 391-4778
E-mail: ajensen@lockeliddell.com

Dallas
Mrs. Holly Lawrence
Phone: (214) 740-8824
Fax: (214) 756-8824
E-mail: hlawrence@lockeliddell.com

Houston
Ms. Brandee Houston
Phone: (713) 226 1246
Fax: (713) 223-3717
E-mail: bhouston@lockeliddell.com

New Orleans
Mr. Rob Mouton
Phone: (504) 558-5113
Fax: (504) 558-5200
E-mail: rmouton@lockeliddell.com

Washington, DC
Ms. Holly Lawrence
Phone: (214) 740-8824
Fax: 214-756-8824
Email: hlawrence@lockeliddell.com

All Laterals
Ms. Erin Johnston, Esq.
Phone: 214-740-8175
Fax: 214-756-8175
Email: ejohnston@lockeliddell.com

THE BUZZ
WHAT ATTORNEYS AT OTHER FIRMS ARE SAYING ABOUT THIS FIRM

• "Solid"
• "Syriana-style energy clients"
• "Reputable"
• "High pressure"

BASE SALARY (2007)

All offices
1st year: $140,000
Summer associate salary: $2,700/week

Visit the Vault Law Channel, the complete online resource for law careers, featuring firm
profiles, message boards, the Vault Law Job Board, and more. www.vault.com/law

VAULT CAREER LIBRARY   583

Lord, Bissell & Brook LLP

111 South Wacker Drive
Chicago, IL 60606
Phone: (312) 443-0700
www.lordbissell.com

LOCATIONS

Chicago, IL (HQ)
Atlanta, GA
Los Angeles, CA
New York, NY
Sacramento, CA
Washington, DC
London

MAJOR DEPARTMENTS & PRACTICES

Antitrust & Competition • Appellate • Aviation • Bankruptcy
& Restructuring • Business Litigation & Arbitration •
Business Technology • Capital Investments • Class Action •
Construction • Corporate • Corporate Compliance •
Directors & Officers • Employee Benefits & Executive
Compensation • Entertainment & Media • Environmental •
Financial Services • Health Care • Insurance • Intellectual
Property • Investment Management • Investment
Transactions • Labor & Employment • Nonprofit
Organizations • Private Companies • Product Liability • Real
Estate • Reinsurance

THE STATS

No. of attorneys: 285
No. of offices: 7
Summer associate offers: 24 out of 28 (2006)
Managing Partner: Lawrence A. Gray
Hiring Partner: John F. Kloecker

RANKING RECAP

Quality of Life
#2 - Office Space

NOTABLE PERKS

• Business generation bonus (50 percent of firm profit)
• Unlimited funding for business development
• Subsidized health club
• BlackBerry devices and monthly data fees

EMPLOYMENT CONTACT

Ms. Kerry B. Jahnsen
Legal Recruiting Coordinator
Phone: (312) 443-0455
Fax: (312) 896-6455
E-mail: kjahnsen@lordbissell.com

BASE SALARY (2007)

Chicago, IL; Los Angeles, CA; New York, NY
1st year: $145,000
Summer associate: $2,788/week

Atlanta, GA
1st year: $130,000
Summer associate: $2,500/week

THE BUZZ
WHAT ATTORNEYS AT OTHER FIRMS ARE SAYING ABOUT THIS FIRM

• "Good Chicago firm"
• "Highly respected and professional"
• "Decent middle market Chi-town firm"
• "Not quite top tier"

© 2007 Vault Inc.

Lovells LLP

Atlantic House
Holborn Viaduct
London, EC1A 2FG
Phone: +44 (0) 20-7296-2000

One IBM Plaza
330 North Wabash Avenue, Suite 1900
Chicago, IL 60611
Phone (312) 832-4400

590 Madison Avenue
New York, NY 10022
Phone: (212) 909-0600
www.lovells.com

LOCATIONS

Chicago, IL • New York, NY • Alicante • Amsterdam •
Beijing • Brussels • Budapest* • Dubai • Düsseldorf •
Frankfurt • Hamburg • Ho Chi Minh City • Hong Kong •
London • Madrid • Milan • Moscow • Munich • Paris •
Prague • Rome • Shanghai • Singapore • Tokyo • Warsaw •
Zagreb*

*Associated offices

MAJOR DEPARTMENTS & PRACTICES

Competition & EU Law • Corporate • Dispute Resolution •
Employment & Employee Share Incentives • Energy, Power
& Utilities • Engineering & Construction • Finance •
Intellectual Property • Pensions • Real Estate • Tax •
Technology, Media & Telecommunications

THE STATS

No. of attorneys: 1,600+
No. of offices: 26
U.S. Summer associate offers: 5 out of 7 (2006)
Managing Partner & CEO: David Harris
Hiring Partners:
  Chicago: David C. Linder
  New York: David Alberts

THE BUZZ
WHAT ATTORNEYS AT OTHER FIRMS ARE SAYING ABOUT THIS FIRM

- "A diverse group of highly skilled international litigators"
- "Good outside the US"
- "Very big and impersonal"
- "Lovely people"

NOTABLE PERKS

- Karaoke nights
- Abundance of sodas and snacks
- Overseas travel
- Gym membership subsidy

EMPLOYMENT CONTACTS

New York, NY
Elizabeth A. Kaye, Esq.
Legal Recruiting Manager
Phone: (212) 909-0600
Fax: (212) 909-0666
E-mail: Elizabeth.Kaye@Lovells.com

Chicago, IL
Kelly Koster
Legal Recruiting Manager
Phone: (312) 832-4487
Fax: (312) 832-4444
E-mail: Kelly.Koster@Lovells.com

BASE SALARY (2007)

New York, NY
1st year: $160,000
Summer associate: $3,070/week

Chicago, IL;
1st year: $145,000
Summer associate: $2,780/week

Visit the Vault Law Channel, the complete online resource for law careers, featuring firm profiles, message boards, the Vault Law Job Board, and more. www.vault.com/law

VAULT CAREER LIBRARY   585

Lowenstein Sandler PC

65 Livingston Avenue
Roseland, NJ 07068-1791
Phone: (973) 597-2500
www.lowenstein.com

LOCATIONS

Roseland, NJ (HQ)
New York, NY
Somerville, NJ

MAJOR DEPARTMENTS & PRACTICES

Bankruptcy • Corporate (Corporate Finance, Intellectual
Property & Patents, Investment Management, M&A,
Mortgage Finance, Specialty Finance, Technology, Venture
Capital & Angel Investments) • Labor & Employment
(Business Immigration, Employment Law & Litigation,
Executive Compensation & Benefits) • Litigation (Antitrust &
Trade Regulation, Class-Actions, Commercial Litigation,
Construction, Environmental, Fiduciary Litigation, Insurance,
Product Liability & Toxic Tort, Securities Litigation, White
Collar Crime) • Real Estate • Tax • Trusts & Estate
(Planning & Administration)

THE STATS

No. of attorneys: 275
No. of offices: 3
Summer associate offers: 16 out of 16 (2007)
Managing Director: Michael L. Rodburg
Hiring Partner: Raymond P. Thek

NOTABLE PERKS

• Back-up child care
• Cafeteria on-site, coffee bar
• Fitness center and park setting with Wi-Fi
• Free real estate closings and discounted estate
  planning

EMPLOYMENT CONTACT

Ms. Jane E. Thieberger
Director of Legal Personnel
Phone: (973) 597-2500
Fax: (973) 597-6117
E-mail: jthieberger@lowenstein.com

BASE SALARY (2007)

All Offices
1st year: $140,000
Summer associate: $2,700/week

THE BUZZ

WHAT ATTORNEYS AT OTHER FIRMS ARE SAYING ABOUT THIS FIRM

• "Top New Jersey firm"
• "Growing"
• "Fun & social place"
• "Overworked"

© 2007 Vault Inc.

McCarter & English, LLP

Four Gateway Center
100 Mulberry Street
Newark, New Jersey 07102
Phone: (973) 622-4444
www.mccarter.com

LOCATIONS

Newark, NJ (HQ)
Baltimore, MD
Boston, MA
Hartford, CT
New York, NY
Philadelphia, PA
Stamford, CT
Wilmington, DE

MAJOR DEPARTMENTS & PRACTICES

Business Litigation • Commercial Litigation - Debtor/Creditor • Construction • Corporate Securities & Financial Institutions • Environmental • Financial Services Litigation • Franchising & Distribution Law • Government Contracts • Health Care • Immigration • Insurance Coverage • Intellectual Property/Information Technology • Investment Management • Labor & Employment Law • Private Clients • Product Liability • Public Finance • Public Strategy • Real Estate • Redevelopment • Securities Litigation, Government & White Collar Crime • Tax & Benefits

THE STATS

No. of attorneys: 400+
No. of offices: 8
Summer associate offers: 12 out of 12 (2006)
Chairman: Andrew T. Berry
Firmwide Managing Partners: Lois M. Van Deusen, Richard Eittreim

EMPLOYMENT CONTACT

Christine A. Lydon, Esq.
Director of Professional Personnel
Phone: (973) 622-4444
Fax: (973) 848 0541
E-mail: recruiting@mccarter.com

BASE SALARY (2007)

1st year: $125,000
Summer associate: $2,100/week

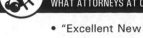
THE BUZZ
WHAT ATTORNEYS AT OTHER FIRMS ARE SAYING ABOUT THIS FIRM

- "Excellent New Jersey firm"
- "Not yet impressed"
- "Solid reputation"
- "Indistinguishable"

Visit the Vault Law Channel, the complete online resource for law careers, featuring firm profiles, message boards, the Vault Law Job Board, and more. www.vault.com/law

 VAULT CAREER LIBRARY   587

McKee Nelson LLP

One Battery Park Plaza, 34th Floor
New York, NY 10004
Phone: (917) 777-4200

1919 M Street NW, Suite 200
Washington, DC 20036
Phone: (202) 775-1880
www.mckeenelson.com

LOCATIONS

New York, NY
Washington, DC

MAJOR DEPARTMENTS & PRACTICES

Business Litigation
Corporate
International Tax
Securities
Structured Finance
Tax Litigation
Tax Planning
White Collar/Investigations

THE STATS

No. of attorneys: 193
No. of offices: 2
Summer associate offers: 25 out of 25 (2006)
Managing Partner & CEO: William F. Nelson
Hiring Partners:
  New York: Thomas J. Amico
  Washington, DC: Raj Madan, Scott Faga

THE BUZZ
WHAT ATTORNEYS AT OTHER FIRMS ARE SAYING ABOUT THIS FIRM

• "Strong, structured finance practice"
• "Tax experts, very knowledgeable"
• "Competitive atmosphere"
• "Great perks, but you never leave the office"

RANKING RECAP

Best in Practice
#7 - Tax

Partner Prestige Rankings
#5 (tie) - Tax

Quality of Life
#1 - Associate/Partner Relations
#1 - Best Firms to Work For
#2 - Overall Satisfaction
#3 - Pay
#4 - Informal Training/Mentoring

Best in Diversity
#4 (tie) - Overall Diversity
#6 - Diversity with Respect to Minorities
#4 - Diversity with Respect to GLBT
#14 - Diversity with Respect to Women

NOTABLE PERKS

• Weekly attorney lunches and breakfasts
• Free soda, water, Gatorade
• Emergency child care
• 401(k) matching

EMPLOYMENT CONTACTS

New York
Ms. Carrie Marker
Director of Legal Recruiting & Professional
  Development
Phone: (917) 777-4556
Fax: (917) 777-4299
E-mail: cmarker@mckeenelson.com

Washington, DC
Ms. Carter Patteson
Legal Recruiting & Professional Development
  Coordinator
Phone: (202) 775-8707
Fax: (202) 327-2121
E-mail: cpatteson@mckeenelson.com

BASE SALARY (2007)

All offices
1st year: $160,000
Summer associate: $3,076/week

© 2007 Vault Inc.

McKenna Long & Aldridge LLP

303 Peachtree Street, NE, Suite 5300
Atlanta, GA 30308
Phone: (404) 527-4000
www.mckennalong.com

LOCATIONS

Albany, NY • Atlanta, GA • Denver, CO • Los Angeles, CA
• New York, NY • Philadelphia, PA • Sacramento, CA • San
Diego, CA • San Francisco, CA • Washington, DC •
Brussels

MAJOR DEPARTMENTS & PRACTICES

Appellate • Bankruptcy • Construction • Corporate Finance
& Securities • Domestic Relations • Employee Benefits •
Energy • Environmental • Government Contracts • Health
Care • Intellectual Property • International • Litigation •
Mergers & Acquisitions • Nonprofit • Public Finance •
Securities • Sports & Entertainment • Tax • Technology •
Trusts & Estates • Venture Capital & Private Equity • White
Collar Crime

THE STATS

No. of attorneys: 400+
No. of offices: 11
Summer associate offers: 39 out of 43 (2006)
Chairperson: Jeffrey K. Haidet
Managing Partner: T. Mark Flanagan Jr.
Hiring Partners:
  James Levine (Atlanta)
  Jean-Paul Menard (Los Angeles)
  Ross Hyslop (San Diego)
  Meak Meagher (Denver)
  Lora Brzezynski (Washington, DC)

RANKING RECAP

Best in Region
#10 - Atlanta

NOTABLE PERKS

- Free BlackBerry service
- Bar and moving expenses
- Breakfast on Mondays and fresh-baked cookies daily
- Monthly attorney lunches

EMPLOYMENT CONTACT

Ms. Jennifer S. Queen
Director of Legal Recruitment & Professional
Development
Phone: (404) 527-4139
Fax: (404) 527-4198
E-Mail: jqueen@mckennalong.com

BASE SALARY (2007)

Los Angeles, San Diego, CA; Washington, DC
1st year: $145,000
Summer associate: $2,600/week

Atlanta, GA
1st year: $130,000
Summer associate: $2,100/week

Denver, CO
1st year: $130,000
Summer associate: $2,100/week

THE BUZZ
WHAT ATTORNEYS AT OTHER FIRMS ARE SAYING ABOUT THIS FIRM

- "Effective, organized, professional"
- "Small potatoes"
- "Great government contracts practice"
- "Conservative"

Visit the Vault Law Channel, the complete online resource for law careers, featuring firm
profiles, message boards, the Vault Law Job Board, and more. www.vault.com/law

VAULT CAREER LIBRARY   589

Moore & Van Allen

Bank of America Corporate Center
100 North Tryon Street, Suite 4700
Charlotte, North Carolina 28202-4003
Phone: (704) 331-1000
www.mvalaw.com

LOCATIONS

Charlotte, NC (HQ) (Two offices)
Research Triangle, NC
Charleston, SC

MAJOR DEPARTMENTS & PRACTICES

Bankruptcy & Restructuring • Business • Commercial Real
Estate • Construction & Safety • Employee Benefits •
Employment • Energy & Project Finance • Environmental
Law • Financial Services • Government & Regulatory Affairs
• Government Contracts • Health Care • Immigration • IT &
E-Commerce • Intellectual Property • International •
Litigation • Maritime • Patent • Public Policy • Taxation •
Trusts & Estates

THE STATS

No. of attorneys: 254
No. of offices: 4
Summer associate offers: 13 out of 19 (2007)
Executive Director: Matthew F. Gillespie
Hiring Attorney: David L. Eades

RANKING RECAP

Quality of Life
#8 - Hours
#10 - Office Space
#17 - Associate/Partner Relations
#19 - Selectivity

NOTABLE PERKS

• Back-up day care
• 100% paid health insurance (for individual
  coverage)
• Subsidized parking
• Subsidized gym membership

EMPLOYMENT CONTACT

Ms. Taylor Grayson
Recruiting Coordinator
Phone: (704) 331-2406
Fax: (704) 339-5863
E-mail: taylorgrayson@mvalaw.com

BASE SALARY (2007)

Charleston, SC
1st year: $95,000
Summer associate: $1,300/week

Charlotte, NC
1st year: $145,000
Summer associate: $2,200/week

Research Triangle, NC
1st year: $130,000 - $145,000
Summer associate: $2,000/week

THE BUZZ
WHAT ATTORNEYS AT OTHER FIRMS ARE SAYING ABOUT THIS FIRM

• "Solid firm. Top associates"
• "Old boys network"
• "Excellent attorneys, collegial atmosphere"
• "Work hard, then work harder"

© 2007 Vault Inc.

Morgan & Finnegan, L.L.P.

3 World Financial Center
New York, New York 10281
Phone: (212) 415-8700
Fax: (212) 415-8701
www.morganfinnegan.com

LOCATIONS

New York, NY (HQ)
San Francisco, CA
Stamford, CT
Washington, DC
Shanghai

MAJOR DEPARTMENTS & PRACTICES

Alternative Dispute Resolution • Antitrust & Related Matters
• Appeals • Damage Awards • Patent Litigation •
International Trade Commission • Trademark & Unfair
Competition

THE STATS

No. of attorneys: 93
No. of offices: 5
Summer associate offers: 9 out of 12 (2006)
Managing Partner: by Executive Committee
Hiring Attorney: Gerard A. Haddad

RANKING RECAP

Quality of Life
#7 - Hours

NOTABLE PERKS

• Firm happy hours
• Paid bar association membership fees
• Moving expenses
• Free BlackBerries

EMPLOYMENT CONTACT

Ms. Kristan Lassiter
Legal Recruitment Manager
Phone: (212) 415-8590
Fax: (212) 415-8701
E-mail: klassiter@morganfinnegan.com

BASE SALARY (2007)

All offices:
1st year: $160,000
2nd year: $170,000
3rd year: $185,000
4th year: $210,000
5th year: $230,000
6th year: case-by-case
7th year: case-by-case
Summer associate: $3,100/week

 THE BUZZ
WHAT ATTORNEYS AT OTHER FIRMS ARE SAYING ABOUT THIS FIRM

• "Decent"
• "Quality work, reasonably happy people"
• "Past its prime"
• "Middle of the pack"

Visit the Vault Law Channel, the complete online resource for law careers, featuring firm
profiles, message boards, the Vault Law Job Board, and more. www.vault.com/law

VAULT CAREER LIBRARY   591

Patterson Belknap Webb & Tyler LLP

1133 Avenue of the Americas
New York, NY 10036
Phone: (212) 336-2000
www.pbwt.com

LOCATION

New York, NY

MAJOR DEPARTMENTS & PRACTICES

Alternate Dispute Resolution • Antitrust • Appellate • Art &
Museum Law • Complex Commercial Actions • Corporate •
Cross-Border Transactions • Debtor-Creditor • Employee
Benefits & Executive Compensation • Employment Law •
Intellectual Property • Law Firm Defense • Litigation •
Media & Entertainment • Mergers & Acquisitions • Personal
Planning • Private Equity, Venture Capital & Investment
Funds • Products Liability • Real Estate • Securities &
Commodities Litigation • Tax • Tax-Exempt Organizations •
White Collar Crime & Internal Investigations

THE STATS

No. of attorneys: 200
No. of offices: 1
Summer associate offers: 9 out of 9 (2006)
Executive Director: Marvin J. Brittman
Hiring Partner: Robert W. Lehrburger

RANKING RECAP

Quality of Life
#1 - Hours
#1 - Pro Bono
#2 - Best Firms to Work For
#2 - Associate/Partner Relations
#6 - Overall Satisfaction
#18 - Informal Training/Mentoring

Best in Diversity
#9 - Diversity with Respect to GLBT
#11 - Overall Diversity
#20 - Diversity with Respect to Minorities

NOTABLE PERKS

- $750 annual technology allowance
- Popular firm "teas"
- Extensive training and CLE programs
- Frequent attorney lunches

EMPLOYMENT CONTACT

Ms. Robin L. Klum
Director of Professional Development
Phone: (212) 336-2733
Fax: (212) 336-2222
E-mail: rlklum@pbwt.com

BASE SALARY (2007)

New York, NY
1st year: $160,000
Summer associate: $3,076/week

THE BUZZ
WHAT ATTORNEYS AT OTHER FIRMS ARE SAYING ABOUT THIS FIRM

- "Nice place to practice law"
- "Family friendly, diverse"
- "Snobby"
- "Prestigious, mid-size firm"

© 2007 Vault Inc.

Pepper Hamilton LLP

3000 Two Logan Square
Eighteenth and Arch Streets
Philadelphia, PA 19103-2799
Phone: (215) 981-4000
www.pepperlaw.com

LOCATIONS

Philadelphia, PA (HQ)

Berwyn, PA • Boston, MA • Detroit, MI • Harrisburg, PA •
New York, NY • Orange County, CA • Pittsburgh, PA •
Princeton, NJ • Washington, DC • Wilmington, DE

MAJOR DEPARTMENTS & PRACTICES

Antitrust • Appellate Practice • Bankruptcy &
Reorganization • Construction Law • Corporate & Securities
• Corporate Governance • Energy Practice • Environmental
Law • ERISA & Employee Benefits • Executive
Compensation • Family Business •Financial Services &
Banking • Franchising • Government Regulation • Insurance
& Reinsurance • Intellectual Property • International • Health
Care Services • Labor & Employment • Litigation • Natural
Resources • Real Estate • Retail Industry • Sports Practice •
Tax • Technology • Toxic Tort Litigation • Transportation •
Trust & Estates • Venture Capital • White Collar Criminal
Defense

THE STATS

No. of attorneys: 450
No. of offices: 11
Summer associate offers: 32 out of 34 (2006)
Managing Partner: Robert E. Heideck
Hiring Partner: Christopher W. Wasson

RANKING RECAP

Best in Region
#6 - Pennsylvania/Mid-Atlantic

NOTABLE PERKS

• Frequent happy hours and cocktail parties
• On-site gym open 24/7
• In-house cafeteria

EMPLOYMENT CONTACT

Ms. Meg Urbanski Cranford
Director of Professional Recruiting
Phone: (215) 981-4991
Fax: (215) 981-4750
E-mail: cranfordm@pepperlaw.com

BASE SALARY (2007)

Berwyn, Philadelphia, Pittsburgh, PA; Princeton, NJ; Wilmington, DE
1st year: $145,000
Summer associate: $2,400/week

Detroit, MI; Harrisburg, PA
1st year: $125,000
Summer associate: $2,200/week

THE BUZZ
WHAT ATTORNEYS AT OTHER FIRMS ARE SAYING ABOUT THIS FIRM

• "Great place to work"
• "Growing in prestige"
• "Strong, mid-level firm"
• "Well managed, but regional"

Visit the Vault Law Channel, the complete online resource for law careers, featuring firm
profiles, message boards, the Vault Law Job Board, and more. www.vault.com/law

VAULT CAREER LIBRARY   593

Powell Goldstein LLP

One Atlantic Center, 14th Floor
1201 West Peachtree Street, NW
Atlanta, GA 30309-3488
Phone: (404) 572-6600
www.pogolaw.com

LOCATIONS

Atlanta, GA
Dallas, TX
Washington, DC

MAJOR DEPARTMENTS & PRACTICES

Advocacy & Government Relations • Antitrust & Trade
Regulations • Bankruptcy & Financial Restructuring •
Biotechnology & Life Sciences • Business & Finance •
Business Litigation & Arbitration • Commercial Lending •
Corporate Compliance, Governance & Securities • Employee
Benefits & Executive Compensation • Energy •
Environmental • Financial Institutions • Government &
Construction Contracts • Health Care • Homeland Security •
Immigration • Information Security & Privacy • Intellectual
Property • International • Labor & Employment • Litigation •
Public Finance • Real Estate Capital Markets • Real Estate
Finance & Development • Securities, Corporate & Fiduciary
Litigation • Special Matters & Investigations • State & Local
Government • Tax • Tort Litigation • White Collar Crime

THE STATS

No. of attorneys: 300
No. of offices: 3
Summer associate offers: 15 out of 17 (2006)
Chairman: James J. McAlpin Jr.
Hiring Partners:
  Atlanta: Nicole J. Wade
  Washington, DC: Donna Marie Rodney

RANKING RECAP

Best in Region
#9 - Atlanta

Quality of Life
#11 - Office Space

NOTABLE PERKS

- Friday happy hours
- Attorney dining room (Atlanta)
- BlackBerries and laptops
- 401(k) match, Professional Development Fund

EMPLOYMENT CONTACTS

Atlanta, GA; Dallas, TX
Ms. Leah N. Fisher
Recruiting Manager
Phone: (404) 572-6968
Fax: (404) 572.6999
E-mail: lfisher@pogolaw.com

Washington, DC
Ms. Lynn Ann Herron
Recruiting Manager
Phone: (202) 624-7348
Fax: (202) 624-7222
E-mail: lherron@pogolaw.com

BASE SALARY (2007)

Atlanta, GA
1st year: $130,000
Summer associate: $1,900/week

Washington, DC
1st year: $145,000
Summer associate: $2,600/week

THE BUZZ

WHAT ATTORNEYS AT OTHER FIRMS ARE SAYING ABOUT THIS FIRM

- "Good Southern firm"
- "Declining"
- "Well regarded locally"
- "Good place, good people"

© 2007 Vault Inc.

Quarles & Brady LLP

411 East Wisconsin Avenue
Milwaukee, WI 53202-4497
Phone: (414) 277-5000
www.quarles.com

LOCATIONS

Chicago, IL • Madison, WI • Milwaukee, WI • Naples, FL •
Phoenix, AZ • Tucson, AZ

MAJOR DEPARTMENTS & PRACTICES

Antitrust & Trade Regulation Litigation • Antitrust, Trade Regulation
& Franchising • Bankruptcy & Creditors' Rights • Commercial
Financial Services • Commercial Transactions Litigation •
Commercial Transactions & Real Estate Financing on Indian Lands •
Community Associations & Country Clubs • Construction •
Construction Litigation • Corporate Finance/Securities • Corporate
Services • Employee Benefits • Energy • Environmental •
Environmental and Natural Resources for the Indian Community •
Family & Domestic Relations • Financial Institutions • Financial
Institutions Litigation • Government Relations • Health •
Immigration • Insurance Regulation • Indian Law • Insurance
Coverage Litigation • Insurance Regulation • Intellectual Property •
Intellectual Property & Technology Litigation • Intellectual Property
Issues for Indian Tribes • International Business • Labor &
Employment • Mergers & Acquisitions • Private Equity/Venture
Capital • Privately Held Business Group • Product Liability, Toxic
Tort & Personal Injury Litigation • Product Marketing & Distribution
• Professional Liability • Project Finance Services • Public Finance •
Real Estate • Real Estate, Land Use & Condemnation Litigation •
School • Securities Litigation • Tax • Tax-Exempt Organizations •
Technology Law • Telecommunications • Trade Secrets & Unfair
Competition Litigation • Tribal Economic Development Projects •
Trust & Estates • White Collar Criminal & Governmental
Investigations

THE STATS

No. of attorneys: 441
No. of offices: 6
Summer associate offers: 33 out of 39 (2006)
Managing Partner: Patrick M. Ryan
Hiring Partner: Sarah E. Coyne

THE BUZZ
WHAT ATTORNEYS AT OTHER FIRMS ARE SAYING ABOUT THIS FIRM

- "Great smaller firm"
- "Identity crisis"
- "Good practice, nice people"
- "Family friendly, great benefits"

RANKING RECAP

Best in Region
#11 - Midwest

Quality of Life
#1 - Informal Training/Mentoring
#4 - Overall Satisfaction
#5 - Best Firms to Work For
#5 - Pro Bono
#5 - Hours
#8 - Associate/Partner Relations

Best in Diversity
#10 - Diversity with Respect to Women
#17 - Overall Diversity

NOTABLE PERKS

- Paid medical, maternity and parental leave
- Profit-sharing and 401(k) with firm contribution
- Health club membership reimbursement (up to $200)
- Free snacks (nuts, trail mix, M&Ms, Cheezits)

EMPLOYMENT CONTACTS

Chicago and Naples offices
Ms. Marguerite Durston
Administrator, Attorney Recruitment
Phone: (312) 715-5025
Fax: (312) 632-1716
E-mail: mdurston@quarles.com

Madison and Milwaukee offices
Ms. Michelle Bigler, Manager, Attorney Recruiting
Phone: (414) 277-5290
Fax: (414) 978-8860
E-mail: mbigler@quarles.com

Phoenix and Tucson offices
Ms. Lynda Anderson, Manager, Attorney Recruiting
Phone: (602) 229-5314
Fax: (602) 420-5068
E-mail: llanders@quarles.com

BASE SALARY (2007)

Naples, FL; Madison, Milwaukee, WI; Phoenix, Tucson, AZ
1st year: $115,000
Summer associate: $2,215/week

Chicago, IL
1st year: $135,000
Summer associate: $2,600/week

Visit the Vault Law Channel, the complete online resource for law careers, featuring firm profiles, message boards, the Vault Law Job Board, and more. www.vault.com/law

VAULT CAREER LIBRARY   595

Robins, Kaplan, Miller & Ciresi LLP

2800 LaSalle Plaza
800 LaSalle Avenue
Minneapolis, MN 55402
Phone: (612) 349-8500
www.rkmc.com

LOCATIONS

Minneapolis, MN (HQ)
Atlanta, GA
Boston, MA
Los Angeles, CA
Naples, FL
Washington, DC

MAJOR DEPARTMENTS & PRACTICES

Antitrust & Trade Regulation • Bankruptcy & Insolvency •
Base Closure & Privatization • Business Trial & Litigation •
Corporate Criminal & Regulatory Defense • Corporate
Finance & Securities • Distributorships & Dealerships /
Franchising • Employment • Estate Planning, Trust &
Succession Planning & Administration • Financial Litigation •
Government Relations / Regulatory Law • Health Care
Litigation • Insurance Litigation • Intellectual Property
Litigation • Licensing & Protection of Intellectual Property •
Mass Tort • Medical Malpractice • Mergers & Acquisitions •
Nursing Home Neglect & Nursing Home Malpractice •
Personal Injury • Project Finance & Real Estate Development
• Surety, Fidelity & Construction • Tax & Executive
Compensation

THE STATS

No. of attorneys: 271
No. of offices: 6
Summer associate offers: 19 out of 20 (2006)
Managing Partner: Steven A. Schumeister
Hiring Partner: Munir R. Meghjee

NOTABLE PERKS

• Moving expenses and bar-study stipend
• 401(k) profit sharing
• Backup child care
• Free and unlimited soda

EMPLOYMENT CONTACT

Ms. Martha G. Capper
Recruiting Administrator
Phone: (612) 349-8500
Fax: (612) 339-4181
E-mail: mgcapper@rkmc.com

BASE SALARY (2007)

Minneapolis, MN
1st year: $120,000
Summer associate: $2,000/week

Atlanta, GA; Boston, MA; Los Angeles, CA
1st year: TBD
Summer associate: $2,000/week

Washington, DC
1st year: TBD
Summer associate: $2,500/week

THE BUZZ
WHAT ATTORNEYS AT OTHER FIRMS ARE SAYING ABOUT THIS FIRM

• "One hit wonders"
• "Nice IP litigation practice"
• "Churn 'um"
• "Excellent work, great place to work"

© 2007 Vault Inc.

Saul Ewing LLP

Centre Square West
1500 Market Street, 38th Floor
Philadelphia, PA 19102-2186
Phone: (215) 972-7777
www.saul.com

LOCATIONS

Baltimore, MD
Chesterbrook, PA
Harrisburg, PA
Newark, NJ
Philadelphia, PA
Princeton, NJ
Washington, DC
Wilmington, DE

MAJOR DEPARTMENTS & PRACTICES

Bankruptcy & Reorganization • Business • Construction •
Corporate Governance • Environmental • Financial Services
• Health Law • Insurance • Intellectual Property &
Technology • Labor, Employment and Employee Benefits •
Life Sciences • Litigation • Owner Managed Businesses •
Personal Wealth Trusts & Estates • Public Finance • Real
Estate • Securities • Tax • Utility • Venture Capital • White
Collar & Government Enforcement

THE STATS

No. of attorneys: 275 +
No. of offices: 8
Summer associate offers: 15 out of 16 (2006)
Managing Partner: David S. Antzis
Hiring Partner: Cathleen M. Devlin

RANKING RECAP

Quality of Life
#11 - Informal Training/Mentoring
#19 - Pro Bono

NOTABLE PERKS

• Merit based bonuses
• Hours based bonus
• Technology stipend ($500 every two years)
• $100/month connectivity stipend (for internet/cell phone)

EMPLOYMENT CONTACT

Naomi A. Mukalian
Director of Attorney Recruiting
Phone: (215) 972 7980
E mail: nmukalian@saul.com

BASE SALARY (2007)

All offices except Harrisburg
1st year: $135,000 (effective 9/1/07)
Summer associate: $2,403/week

Harrisburg, PA
1st year: $125,000 (effective 9/1/07)
Summer associate: $2,211/week

THE BUZZ
WHAT ATTORNEYS AT OTHER FIRMS ARE SAYING ABOUT THIS FIRM

• "Top shelf in Philadelphia"
• "Down to Earth partners"
• "Big fish, small pond"
• "Indistinguishable"

Visit the Vault Law Channel, the complete online resource for law careers, featuring firm profiles, message boards, the Vault Law Job Board, and more. www.vault.com/law

VAULT CAREER LIBRARY   597

Schiff Hardin LLP

6600 Sears Tower
Chicago, IL 60606-6473
Phone: (312) 258-5500
www.schiffhardin.com

LOCATIONS

Chicago, IL (HQ)
Atlanta, GA
Lake Forrest, IL
New York, NY
San Francisco, CA
Washington, DC

MAJOR DEPARTMENTS & PRACTICES

Antitrust & Trade Regulations • Bankruptcy, Workouts &
Creditors Rights • Class Action Litigation • Construction •
Corporate & Securities • Employee Benefits & Executive
Compensation • Energy & Communications • Environmental
• Private Clients, Trusts & Estates • Finance • Financial
Institutions • Government Contracts • Insurance •
Intellectual Property • International • Labor & Employment •
Litigation • Private Equity & Venture Capital • Public Law &
Finance • Real Estate • Securities • Sports & Entertainment
• Taxation • White Collar Defense & Corporate Compliance

THE STATS

No. of attorneys: 400
No. of offices: 6
Summer associate offers: 19 out of 20 (2006)
Managing Partner: Ronald S. Safer
Hiring Partner: Antony S. Burt

NOTABLE PERKS

• Public interest law initiative summer stipend
• Glitzy, black-tie, firmwide party
• Paid bar and moving expenses
• Cab and dinner when working late

EMPLOYMENT CONTACT

Mrs. Lilly Tuller
Law Student Recruitment Coordinator
Phone: (312) 258-5500
Fax: (312) 258-5600
E-mail: ltuller@schiffhardin.com

BASE SALARY (2007)

All offices
1st year: $145,000
Summer associate: $2,800/week

THE BUZZ
WHAT ATTORNEYS AT OTHER FIRMS ARE SAYING ABOUT THIS FIRM

• "Old school"
• "Smart. Hardworking"
• "Solid Chicago firm"
• "Stodgy"

© 2007 Vault Inc.

Sedgwick, Detert, Moran & Arnold LLP

One Market Plaza
Steuart Tower, 8th Floor
San Francisco, CA 94105
Phone: (415) 781-7900
Fax: (415) 781-2635
www.sdma.com

LOCATIONS

San Francisco, CA (HQ)
Austin, TX
Chicago, IL
Dallas, TX
Irvine, CA
Houston, TX
Los Angeles, CA
Newark, NJ
New York, NY
Bermuda (associated office)
London
Paris
Zurich

MAJOR DEPARTMENTS & PRACTICES

Antitrust • Appellate • Bankruptcy & Creditors' Rights •
Business Litigation • Construction • Employment & Labor •
Environmental & Toxic Tort • Healthcare • Insurance
Practices • Intellectual Property • Mass Tort & Complex
Litigation • Professional Liability • Real Estate &
Transactions

THE STATS

No. of attorneys: 350
No. of offices: 13
Firm Chairman: Kevin J. Dunne
Hiring Partner: Stephanie A. Sheridan

THE BUZZ
WHAT ATTORNEYS AT OTHER FIRMS ARE SAYING ABOUT THIS FIRM

- "Diverse, family-friendly"
- "Creative, smart"
- "Needs revitalization"
- "Nothing special"

RANKING RECAP

Quality of Life
#11 - Formal Training
#17 - Hours

NOTABLE PERKS

- Lifestyle-friendly vacation policy and benefits
- Free or subsidized parking
- "Trial Academy"—NITA-style training
- Great office space and location

EMPLOYMENT CONTACT

Ms. Vicky Berry
Director of Attorney Recruiting
Phone: (949) 852-8200
Fax: (949) 852-8282
E-mail: vicky.berry@sdma.com

BASE SALARY (2007)

All US offices
1st year: $115,000
Summer associate: $2,211/week

Visit the Vault Law Channel, the complete online resource for law careers, featuring firm
profiles, message boards, the Vault Law Job Board, and more. www.vault.com/law

VAULT CAREER LIBRARY   599

Seyfarth Shaw LLP

131 South Dearborn Street, Suite 2400
Chicago, Illinois 60603-5577
Phone: (312) 460-5000
www.seyfarth.com

LOCATIONS

Chicago, IL (HQ)

Atlanta, GA • Boston, MA • Houston, TX • Los Angles, CA
• New York, NY • Sacramento, CA • San Francisco, CA •
Washington, D.C. • Brussels

MAJOR DEPARTMENTS & PRACTICES

Advertising, Promotions & Sweepstakes • Alternative
Dispute Resolution • Antitrust/Trade Regulation •
Bankruptcy • Business Torts • Commercial Litigation •
Construction • Copyright • Corporate • Employee Benefits &
Executive Compensation • Environmental • Franchise •
Government Contracts • Health Care • Insurance •
Intellectual Property • International • Internet & Privacy •
Investment Management • Labor & Employment • M&A •
Patent • Private Equity/Venture Capital • Product Liability •
Real Estate • Securities • Tax • Technology • Toxic Tort •
Trusts & Estates

THE STATS

No. of Attorneys: 700+
No. of offices: 10
Summer associate offers: 29 out of 31 (2006)
Managing Partner: J. Stephen Poor
Hiring Attorneys: Brian Gannon (Atlanta), Brigitte Duffy
(Boston), Gerald Pauling & Adam Greetis (Chicago),
David Waddell (Houston), Laura Shelby & Geoff Long
(Los Angeles), Dov Kesselman & Charles Modlin (New
York), Samuel McAdam (Sacramento), Kari Levine
(San Francisco), David Blake (Washington, DC)

THE BUZZ
WHAT ATTORNEYS AT OTHER FIRMS ARE SAYING ABOUT THIS FIRM

• "Good employment lawyers"
• "Doesn't pay market"
• "Fun group of people with good work"
• "Conservative"

RANKING RECAP

Best in Practice
#5 - Labor & Employment

Partner Prestige Rankings
#3 - Labor & Employment

NOTABLE PERKS

• Free breakfast on Fridays
• Free parking
• Paternity leave
• On-site exercise classes

EMPLOYMENT CONTACT

Ms. Linda Maremont
Director of Legal Recruiting
Phone: (312) 460-6643
Fax: (312) 460-7000
E-mail: chi-legal@seyfarth.com

BASE SALARY (2007)

Chicago, IL; Boston, MA; Los Angeles, CA; San Francisco, CA; Washington, DC
1st year: $145,000
Summer associate: $ 2,788/week

Atlanta, GA
1st year: $130,000
Summer associate: $2,500/week

Houston, TX
1st year: $135,000
Summer associate: N/A

New York, NY
1st year: $160,000
Summer associate: $3,077

Sacramento, CA
1st year: $135,000
Summer associate: N/A

© 2007 Vault Inc.

Sheppard, Mullin, Richter & Hampton LLP

333 South Hope Street, 48th Floor
Los Angeles, CA 90071
Phone: (213) 620-1780
www.sheppardmullin.com

LOCATIONS

Los Angeles, CA (HQ)
Century City, CA
Costa Mesa, CA
Del Mar Heights, CA
New York, NY
San Diego, CA
San Francisco, CA
Santa Barbara, CA
Washington, DC
Shanghai

MAJOR DEPARTMENTS & PRACTICES

Antitrust • Appellate • Corporate • Entertainment & Media •
Environmental • Finance & Bankruptcy • Global Climate
Change • Government Contracts • Health Care • Intellectual
Property • Labor & Employment • Land Use & Natural
Resources • Life Sciences • Litigation • Real Estate &
Construction • Tax • White Collar Defense

THE STATS

No. of attorneys: 480
No. of offices: 10
Summer associate offers: 48 out of 50 (2006)
Executive Committee Chairman: Guy N. Halgren
Hiring Partner: Robert E. Williams

NOTABLE PERKS

• Free parking
• Free high-speed home internet access
• Free health insurance
• Sports and concert tickets

EMPLOYMENT CONTACT

Ms. Sally C. Bucklin
Manager of Attorney Hiring
Phone: (213) 617-4101
Fax: (213) 620-1398
E-mail: sbucklin@sheppardmullin.com

BASE SALARY (2007)

All Offices
1st year: $160,000
Summer associate: $3,080/week

THE BUZZ
WHAT ATTORNEYS AT OTHER FIRMS ARE SAYING ABOUT THIS FIRM

• "Excellent firm with some truly exceptional lawyers"
• "Tons of hours, not a lot of associate appreciation"
• "On the rise"
• "Pleasant place to work"

Visit the Vault Law Channel, the complete online resource for law careers, featuring firm
profiles, message boards, the Vault Law Job Board, and more. www.vault.com/law

601

Shook, Hardy & Bacon L.L.P.

2555 Grand Boulevard
Kansas City, MO 64108
Phone: (816) 474-6550
www.shb.com

LOCATIONS

Kansas City, MO (HQ)
Houston, TX
Miami, FL
Orange County, CA
San Francisco, CA
Tampa, FL
Washington, DC
Geneva
London

MAJOR DEPARTMENTS & PRACTICES

Agribusiness & Food Systems • Antitrust & Trade
Regulation • Appellate • Arbitration • Banking & Financial
Services • Bankruptcy & Creditors' Rights • Business
Litigation - Class Actions • Commercial/UCC • Consumer
Financial Services • Corporate • Design & Construction • E-
Discovery • Employee Benefits • Employment Litigation and
Policy • Environmental • ERISA Litigation • Estate Planning
• Franchising & Distribution • Government Enforcement &
Compliance • Health • Insurance • Intellectual Property •
Litigation Support • Non Profit and Tax-Exempt •
Pharmaceutical & Medical Device • Product Liability
Litigation • Public Policy • Real Estate • Securities •
Strategic Issues Management • Tax • Tort • Toxic Tort

THE STATS

No. of attorneys: 502
No. of offices: 9
Summer associate offers: 19 out of 22 (2006)
Chairman: John F. Murphy
Hiring Partner: Terrence J. Sexton

THE BUZZ
WHAT ATTORNEYS AT OTHER FIRMS ARE SAYING ABOUT THIS FIRM

- "Great Midwest firm"
- "Tobacco clients"
- "Stuffy, rigid"
- "Associates get great experience"

RANKING RECAP

Best in Region
#9 - Miami

Quality of Life
#7 - Formal Training
#14 - Informal Training/Mentoring

NOTABLE PERKS

- Sabbatical program
- "Fantastic" money purchase pension plan
- Cabs and dinner when working late
- Subsidized parking

EMPLOYMENT CONTACT

Ms. Colleen Liesmann
Director of Legal Recruiting
Phone: (816) 474-6550
Fax: (816) 421-5547
E-mail: cliesmann@shb.com

BASE SALARY (2007)

Kansas City, MO; Tampa, FL
1st year: $95,000
Summer associate: $1,800 /week

Houston, TX; Irvine, CA; San Francisco, CA
1st year: $130,000
Summer associate: $2,500/week

Miami, FL
1st year: $110,000
Summer associate: $ 2,200/week

Washington, DC
1st year: $135,000
Summer associate: $2,600 /week

© 2007 Vault Inc.

Stoel Rives LLP

900 SW Fifth Avenue, Suite 2600
Portland, OR 97204
Phone: (503) 224-3380
www.stoel.com

LOCATIONS

Portland, OR (HQ)

Boise, ID • Sacramento, CA • Salt Lake City, UT • San Diego, CA • San Francisco, CA • Seattle, WA • Tahoe City, CA • Vancouver, WA • Minneapolis, MN

MAJOR DEPARTMENTS & PRACTICES

Air Quality • Alternative Dispute Resolution • Antitrust & Trade Regulation • Appellate • Business Finance & Insolvency • Construction & Design Law • Contaminated Land • Copyrights • Corporate • Employee Benefits • Employment Law & Labor Relations • Endangered Species Act • Energy Law • Environmental & Natural Resources • Ethics & Professional Responsibility • Exempt Organizations • Franchising • Insurance • Intellectual Property • International Business • Land Use • Litigation • Mergers & Acquisitions • Municipal Law & Finance • Occupational Safety & Health • Patents • Private Businesses • Product Liability & Toxic Torts • Publicly Held Companies • Real Estate Law • Securities Litigation • Taxation • Technology Ventures Group • Telecommunications Law • Trademarks • Tribal Law • Water Quality • Water Rights • Wealth Management • White Collar Criminal Law

THE STATS

No. of attorneys: 353
No. of offices: 10
Summer associate offers: 16 out of 16 (2006)
Managing Partner: Beth A. Ugoretz
Hiring Attorney: Margaret B. Kushner (chair of Portland office's recruiting committee) and Lourdes Fuentes (Director of Lawyer Recruiting and Diversity)

THE BUZZ
WHAT ATTORNEYS AT OTHER FIRMS ARE SAYING ABOUT THIS FIRM

- "Friendly, respectful attorneys"
- "Environmental lawyers"
- "Associate mill"
- "Great work, great people"

RANKING RECAP

Best in Region
#5 - Pacific Northwest

NOTABLE PERKS

- Firm and practice-group retreats
- Annual $5,000 prorated 401(k) contribution
- Firmwide coaching and mentoring program
- Associates only lunch program

EMPLOYMENT CONTACT

Ms. Michelle Baird-Johnson
Lawyer Recruiting Manager
Phone: (503) 224-3380
Fax: (503) 220-2480
E-mail: mbjohnson@stoel.com

BASE SALARY (2007)

Portland, OR; Salt Lake City, UT
1st year: $105,000
Summer associate: $1,700/week

Boise, ID
1st year: $85,000
Summer associate: $1,350/week

San Francisco, CA
1st year: $120,000
Summer associate: $2,100/week

Seattle, WA
1st year: $110,000
Summer associate: $1,850/week

Sacramento, CA
1st year: $110,000
Summer associate: $2,100/week

Visit the Vault Law Channel, the complete online resource for law careers, featuring firm profiles, message boards, the Vault Law Job Board, and more. www.vault.com/law

VAULT CAREER LIBRARY   603

Sutherland Asbill & Brennan LLP

999 Peachtree Street, NE
Atlanta, GA 30309-3996
Phone: (404) 853-8000

1275 Pennsylvania Avenue, NW
Washington, DC 20004-2415
Phone: (202) 383-0100
www.sablaw.com

LOCATIONS

Atlanta, GA
Austin, TX
Houston, TX
New York, NY
Tallahassee, FL
Washington, DC

MAJOR DEPARTMENTS & PRACTICES

Aerospace, Defense & Homeland Security • Biotechnology
& Life Sciences • Broker-Dealer & Securities Litigation •
Business Reconstructing & Bankruptcy • Construction •
Corporate • Employee Benefits & Executive Compensation •
Energy • Environmental • Estate Planning • Financial
Services • Intellectual Property • International • Litigation •
Outsourcing Real Estate • Securities & Corporate
Governance • Securities Regulatory, Enforcement & White
Collar • Tax • Technology • Telecommunications • Timber
& Forest Products • Trade Regulation White Collar Crime

THE STATS

No. of attorneys: 450
No. of offices: 6
Summer associate offers: 40 out of 41(2006)
Managing Partner: Mark D. Wasserman
Hiring Partners:
  Atlanta: Matthew W. Nichols
  Washington: Richard G. Murphy Jr.

RANKING RECAP

Best in Region
#4 - Atlanta

Partner Prestige Rankings
#4 (tie) - Tax

Quality of Life
#2 - Formal Training
#10 - Pro Bono
#12 - Best Firms to Work For
#13 - Informal Training/Mentoring
#15 - Hours
#20 - Overall Satisfaction
#20 - Associate/Partner Relations

NOTABLE PERKS

• Tickets to concerts and sporting events
• Free snacks, soda and Friday breakfasts
• Subsidized in-house massages (certain offices)
• Free BlackBerries

EMPLOYMENT CONTACTS

Atlanta, GA; Austin, TX; Tallahassee, FL
Ms. Kimberly M. Hensarling
Attorney Recruiting Manager
Phone: (404) 853-8000
Fax: (404) 853-8806
E-mail: atlantalawyerrecruiting@sablaw.com

Washington, DC; Houston, TX; New York, NY
Ms. Melissa C. Wilson
Director of Legal Recruiting
Phone: (202) 383-0100
Fax: (202) 637-3593
E-mail: washingtonlawyerrecruiting@sablaw.com

THE BUZZ
WHAT ATTORNEYS AT OTHER FIRMS ARE SAYING ABOUT THIS FIRM

• "Highly regarded"
• "Great culture,
• "Pays below market"
• "Southeast sweatshop"

BASE SALARY (2007)

Atlanta, GA
1st year: $130,000
Summer associate: $2,100/week

Washington, DC
1st year: $145,000
Summer associate: $2,400/week

© 2007 Vault Inc.

Thompson & Knight LLP

1700 Pacific Avenue, Suite 3300
Dallas, TX 75201
Phone: (214) 969-1700
www.tklaw.com

LOCATIONS

Dallas, TX (HQ)
Austin, TX • Fort Worth, TX • Houston, TX • New York, NY •
Algiers* • London • Mexico City • Monterrey • Paris* • Rio de
Janeiro* • Vitória*

*Associated Office

MAJOR DEPARTMENTS & PRACTICES

Antitrust • Appellate •Aviation • Chemicals • China •
Computer Hardware & Software • Construction • Consumer
Products • Corporate and Securities • Corporate
Reorganization & Creditors' Rights • Employee Benefits
(ERISA) • Energy • Environmental • Estate Planning &
Individual Wealth Management • Executive Compensation •
Finance • Financial Institutions • Food & Beverage •
Franchise • Global Projects & Infrastructure • Government •
Health Law • Hospitality • Immigration • Insurance •
Information Management & E- Discovery Solutions •
Insurance • Intellectual Property • International Energy •
Investment & Hedge Funds • Labor & Employment • Latin
America • LNG • Manufacturing • Non-Profit Organizations •
Oil & Gas • Pharmaceuticals & Medical Devices • Pipelines •
Railroad • Real Estate & Real Estate Finance • Regulatory •
Restaurants • Retail • School Law • Semiconductors •
Sports, Entertainment, & Media Law • Tax • Technology •
Telecommunications • Transportation • Trial

THE STATS

No. of attorneys: 427
Summer associate offers firmwide: 28 out of 33 (2006)
Managing Partner: Peter J. Riley
Hiring Partners: J. Holt Foster III (Dallas), Victor Alcorta III
(Austin), Jennifer B. Henry (Fort Worth), Vivienne (Lie) R.
Schiffer (Houston)

RANKING RECAP

Quality of Life
#18 - Hours

Best in Diversity
#8 - Diversity with Respect to Minorities

NOTABLE PERKS

- Free parking (in many offices)
- Free BlackBerry and notebook computers
- Signing and graduation bonus
- Entertainment venues (suites) in Dallas and
  Houston

EMPLOYMENT CONTACTS

Dallas, Austin, Fort Worth, New York
Ms. Meg Munson
Recruiting Coordinator
Phone: (214) 969-1180
Fax: (214) 969-1751
E-mail: Meg.Munson@tklaw.com

Houston
Ms. Elizabeth Hudson
Houston Recruiting Coordinator
Phone: (713) 217-2829
Fax: (832) 397-8153
E-mail: Elizabeth.Hudson@tklaw.com

BASE SALARY (2007)

Texas offices (2007)
1st year: $135,000**
Summer associate: $2,700/week***

**Plus first-year $5,000 signing bonus and $5,000
graduation bonus; $35,000 bonus and partnership
track credit for certain judicial clerkships.*
***Plus $2,500 first half bonus.*

THE BUZZ
WHAT ATTORNEYS AT OTHER FIRMS ARE SAYING ABOUT THIS FIRM

- "Highly regarded and friendly"
- "Family-friendly"

Visit the Vault Law Channel, the complete online resource for law careers, featuring firm
profiles, message boards, the Vault Law Job Board, and more. www.vault.com/law

VAULT CAREER LIBRARY   **605**

Thompson Coburn LLP

One US Bank Plaza
St. Louis, Missouri 63101-1611
Phone: (314) 552-6000
www.thompsoncoburn.com

LOCATIONS

St. Louis, MO (HQ)
Belleville, IL
Washington, D.C.

MAJOR DEPARTMENTS & PRACTICES

Admiralty • Appellate • Banking & Commercial Finance •
Business Bankruptcy, Restructuring & Creditors' Rights •
Business Immigration • Business Litigation • Class Action •
Complex & Mass Litigation • Construction & Real Estate
Litigation • Corporate & Securities • Corporate Compliance,
Investigation & Defense • Employee Benefits •
Environmental • ERISA • Financial Services • Government
Contracts • Health Care • International Commerce •
Intellectual Property • Labor & Employment • Maritime •
Media, Communications & Internet • Non-Profit
Organizations • Postal • Private Client • Product Liability •
Public Finance & Public Law • Railroad Litigation • Real
Estate • Tax • Tobacco Litigation • Toxic Tort •
Transportation • Utilities

THE STATS

No. of attorneys: 300
No. of offices: 3
Chairman: Thomas J. Minogue
Hiring Attorney: Linda Shapiro

RANKING RECAP

Best in Region
#13 - Midwest

NOTABLE PERKS

• Free lunch on Fridays
• Subsidized parking
• Free cell phone, BlackBerry service
• Firm covers 50% of cost of home computer

EMPLOYMENT CONTACT

Ms. Nichole Clasquin
Recruiting Manager
Phone: (314) 552-6234
Fax: (314) 552-7234
E-mail: nclasquin@thompsoncoburn.com

BASE SALARY (2007)

1st year: $100,000
Summer associate: $1,700/week

THE BUZZ
WHAT ATTORNEYS AT OTHER FIRMS ARE SAYING ABOUT THIS FIRM

• "Friendly, growing"
• "Big shots in St. Louis, little player everywhere
  else"
• "Above average"
• "Local"

© 2007 Vault Inc.

Thompson Hine LLP

3900 Key Center
127 Public Square
Cleveland, OH 44114-1216
Phone: (216) 566-5500
www.thompsonhine.com

LOCATIONS

Atlanta, GA
Cincinnati, OH
Cleveland, OH
Columbus, OH
Dayton, OH
New York, NY
Washington, DC
Brussels

MAJOR DEPARTMENTS & PRACTICES

Admiralty & Maritime • Banking & Insurance • Bankruptcy •
Business Litigation • Commercial and Public Finance •
Competition, Antitrust & White Collar Crime • Construction
• Corporate Transactions & Securities • eBusiness &
Emerging Technologies • Employee Benefits & Executive
Compensation • Energy • Environmental • Health Care •
Intellectual Property • International Trade & Customs •
Labor & Employment • Product Liability Litigation • Real
Estate • Taxation • Telecommunications • Transportation •
Worker's Compensation

THE STATS

No. of attorneys: 374
No. of offices: 8
Managing Partner: David J. Hooker
Hiring Partner: Robert F. Ware

THE BUZZ
WHAT ATTORNEYS AT OTHER FIRMS ARE SAYING ABOUT THIS FIRM

- "Good litigators"
- "Amateurish"
- "Friendly, get lots of experience"
- "Think too much of themselves"

RANKING RECAP

Best in Region
#8 - Midwest

Quality of Life
#12 - Hours

Best in Diversity
#7 - Diversity with Respect to Women

NOTABLE PERKS

- Car rides and dinner when working late
- Great social events: poker night, skit night, mini golf, etc.
- Tickets to sporting events
- Moving expenses

EMPLOYMENT CONTACT

Ms. Jennifer J. Irwin
Associate Director Lawyer Recruiting &
    Development
Phone: (216) 566-5558
Fax: (216) 566-5800
E-mail: Jennifer.Irwin@thompsonhine.com

BASE SALARY (2007)

Atlanta, GA; Cleveland, OH
1st year: $110,000
Summer associate: $2,115/week

Cincinnati, Columbus, Dayton, OH
1st year: $100,000
Summer associate: $1,924/week

New York, NY; Washington, DC
1st year: $125,000
Summer associate: $2,404/week

Visit the Vault Law Channel, the complete online resource for law careers, featuring firm
profiles, message boards, the Vault Law Job Board, and more. www.vault.com/law

VAULT CAREER LIBRARY   607

Torys LLP

Suite 3000
79 Wellington Street West
Box 270, TD Centre
Toronto, Ontario
M5K 1N2 Canada
Phone: (416) 865-0040

237 Park Avenue
New York, NY 10017
Phone: (212) 880-6000
www.torys.com

LOCATIONS

New York, NY
Toronto

MAJOR DEPARTMENTS & PRACTICES

Antitrust & Competition • Arbitration • Commercial
Litigation • Communications • Construction • Corporate •
Criminal • Employment • Energy • Environmental • Food &
Drug • Government Relations • Health Care • Intellectual
Property • Labor & Employment • Life Sciences • Litigation
& Dispute Resolution • Media & Defamation • Private Equity
• Products Liability • Real Estate • Restructuring &
Insolvency • Securities • Tax • Technology • Trusts &
Estates

THE STATS

No. of attorneys: 330
No. of offices: 2
Summer associate offers: 4 out of 5 (2006)
Managing Partner: Les Viner

NOTABLE PERKS

• Firm retreat and many parties
• Subsidized gym membership
• Lunch and dinner daily
• Bar expenses

EMPLOYMENT CONTACT

New York
Arna Berke-Schlessel
Manager, Legal Recruitment & Professional
   Development
Phone: (212) 880-6365
E-mail: aberke-schlessel@torys.com

BASE SALARY (2007)

New York, NY
1st year: $160,000
Summer associate: $3,076.92/week

THE BUZZ
WHAT ATTORNEYS AT OTHER FIRMS ARE SAYING ABOUT THIS FIRM

• "Wonderful lawyers"
• "Small, but good"
• "Great in Toronto, no profile in New York"
• "Not that prestigious, but very friendly"

© 2007 Vault Inc.

Troutman Sanders LLP

600 Peachtree Street, NE
Atlanta, GA 30308-2216
Phone: (404) 885-3000
www.troutmansanders.com

LOCATIONS

Atlanta, GA (HQ)
Newark, New Jersey
New York, NY
Norfolk, VA
Raleigh, NC
Richmond, VA (2 offices)
Tysons Corner, VA
Virginia Beach, VA
Washington, DC
Hong Kong
London
Shanghai

MAJOR DEPARTMENTS & PRACTICES

Antitrust • Bankruptcy • Compensation & Employee Benefits
• Construction • Energy • Environmental • Financial
Institutions • Government • Health • Intellectual Property •
International Trade • Labor & Employment • Lending &
Structured Finance • Litigation • Media & Entertainment •
Mergers, Acquisitions & Business Ventures • Multi-Family
Housing • Real Estate • Securities & Corporate Governance
• Tax • Technology & Telecommunications • Transportation
• Trusts & Estates

THE STATS

No. of attorneys: 600+
No. of offices: 13
Summer associate offers: 54 out of 57 (2006)
Chairman and Managing Partner: Robert W. Webb Jr.
Hiring Partner: Andrea M. Farley

THE BUZZ
WHAT ATTORNEYS AT OTHER FIRMS ARE SAYING ABOUT THIS FIRM

- "Firm of the future"
- "Solid regional firm, happy lawyers"
- "Good firm, but turmoil"
- "Having growing pains"

RANKING RECAP

Best in Region
#7 - Atlanta

NOTABLE PERK

- Free candy
- Gym membership (varies with office)
- Annual retreat and frequent happy hours
- Tickets to sporting events

EMPLOYMENT CONTACT

Ms. Clare Roath
Director of Recruiting
Phone: (404) 885-3800
Fax: (404) 962-6572
E-mail: clare.roath@troutmansanders.com

BASE SALARY (2007)

Atlanta, GA
1st year: $130,000
Summer associate: $2,500/week

McLean, VA; Washington, DC
1st year: $145,000
Summer associate: $2,700/week

Richmond, VA
1st year: $130,000
Summer associate: $2,500/week

Virginia Beach, VA
1st year: $105,000
Summer Associate: $2,200/week

Raleigh, NC
1st year: $130,000
Summer associate: $2,500/week

New York, NY
1st year: $160,000
Summer associate: $3,000/week

Visit the Vault Law Channel, the complete online resource for law careers, featuring firm profiles, message boards, the Vault Law Job Board, and more. www.vault.com/law

VAULT CAREER LIBRARY   609

Wildman, Harrold, Allen & Dixon LLP

225 West Wacker Drive, Suite 3000
Chicago, IL 60606
Phone: (312) 201-2000
www.wildman.com

LOCATIONS

Chicago, IL

MAJOR DEPARTMENTS & PRACTICES

Advertising, Marketing & Promotions • Antitrust • Class
Actions • Commercial Litigation • Compensation & Benefits
• Copyrights • Corporate • Corporate Governance • Data
Security • Electronic Transactions • Employment & Labor •
Environmental • Government Affairs • Healthcare •
Intellectual Property • Investigations • M&A • Patents •
Privacy & Data Security • Private Equity • Product Liability •
Real Estate • Restructuring & Insolvency • Securities • Tax
• Technology • Toxic Tort • Trade Secrets • Trademarks •
Wealth Management • White Collar Crime

THE STATS

No. of attorneys: 192
No. of offices: 1
Summer associate offers: 12 out of 14 (2006)
Managing Partner: Robert L. Shuftan
Hiring Attorney: John E. Frey

EMPLOYMENT CONTACT

Ms. Susan A. Cicero
Recruiting Coordinator
Phone: (312) 201-2574
E-mail: Cicero@wildman.com

BASE SALARY (2007)

1st year: $135,000
Summer associate: $2,400/week

THE BUZZ
WHAT ATTORNEYS AT OTHER FIRMS ARE SAYING ABOUT THIS FIRM

- "Strong Chicago litigation firm"
- "Declining"
- "Solid firm with decent lawyers"
- "Regional player in Chicago"

© 2007 Vault Inc.

Wiley Rein LLP

1776 K Street NW
Washington, DC 20006
Phone: 202.719.7000
www.wileyrein.com

LOCATIONS

Washington, DC
McLean, VA

MAJOR DEPARTMENTS & PRACTICES

Advertising • Antitrust • Appellate • Aviation • Bankruptcy
& Financial Restructuring • Business & Finance • Chemicals,
Safety & Environment • Communications • Election Law &
Government Ethics • Employment & Labor • Food & Drug
and Product Safety • Franchise • Government Affairs •
Government Contracts • Health Care • Insurance •
Intellectual Property • International Trade • Litigation •
Postal • Privacy • Tax • White Collar Defense

THE STATS

No. of attorneys: 268
No. of offices: 2
Summer associate offers: 21 out of 21 (2006)
Managing Partner: Richard E. Wiley
Hiring Partner: Scott M. McCaleb

RANKING RECAP

Quality of Life
#20 - Hours

NOTABLE PERKS

• Annual technology budget
• 401(k) contribution
• Matching charitable donations
• Monthly wine and cheese gatherings

EMPLOYMENT CONTACT

Ms. Jill Bartelt
Director of Attorney Recruitment
Phone: (202) 719-7548
Fax: (202) 719-7049
E-mail: jbartelt@wileyrein.com

BASE SALARY (2007)

Washington, DC
1st year:
    $145,000 (1,950 billable hours)
    $125,000 (1,800 billable hours)
Summer associate: $2,800/week

THE BUZZ
WHAT ATTORNEYS AT OTHER FIRMS ARE SAYING ABOUT THIS FIRM

• "Great DC firm"
• "No. 1 in telecom"
• "Great work environment"
• "Conservative, Republican"

Visit the Vault Law Channel, the complete online resource for law careers, featuring firm
profiles, message boards, the Vault Law Job Board, and more. www.vault.com/law

VAULT CAREER LIBRARY   611

Winstead PC

5400 Renaissance Tower
1201 Elm Street
Dallas, TX 75270-2199
Phone: (214) 745-5400
www.winstead.com

LOCATIONS

Dallas, TX (HQ)
Austin, TX
Fort Worth, TX
Houston, TX
San Antonio, TX
The Woodlands, TX
Washington, DC

MAJOR DEPARTMENTS & PRACTICES

Appellate • Aviation • Banking & Credit Transactions •
Bankruptcy • Biotechnology • Business Restructuring •
Condominium • Construction • Corporate/Securities •
Energy • Environmental • ERISA/Employee Benefits •
Financial Institutions • Government Relations/Public Policy •
Immigration • Insurance • Intellectual Property •
International • Labor & Employment • Litigation/Dispute
Resolution • Nanotechnology • Public Finance • Real Estate
• Securities Litigation & Enforcement • Sports &
Entertainment • Tax • Technology • Telecommunications •
Transportation • Turnaround & Workout • Wealth
Preservation • Zoning & Land Use

THE STATS

No. of attorneys: 302
No. of offices: 7
Summer associate offers: 20 out of 26 (2006)
Chairman & CEO: Denis Clive Braham
Hiring Partner: Richard C. Leucht, II

RANKING RECAP

Quality of Life
#6 - Hours

NOTABLE PERKS

- Attorney retreat (with spouses/significant others)
- Group health insurance offered to domestic partners
- 401(k) matching and profit-sharing plans
- Free downtown parking and laptop computers

EMPLOYMENT CONTACT

Ms. Dominique Anderson
Director of Attorney Recruitment
Phone: (214) 745-5306
Fax: (214) 745-5769
E-mail: danderson@winstead.com

BASE SALARY (2007)

All offices
1st year: $135,000
Summer associate: $2,600/week

THE BUZZ
WHAT ATTORNEYS AT OTHER FIRMS ARE SAYING ABOUT THIS FIRM

- "Family-friendly, nice folks, great real estate work"
- "Decent, but not top"
- "Past its prime"
- "Outstanding"

© 2007 Vault Inc.

Wolf, Block, Schorr and Solis-Cohen LLP

1650 Arch Street, 22nd Floor
Philadelphia, PA 19103-2097
Phone: (215) 977-2362
www.wolfblock.com

LOCATIONS

Philadelphia, PA (HQ)
Boston, MA
Boston, MA*
Cherry Hill, NJ
Harrisburg, PA
Harrisburg, PA*
New York, NY
Norristown, PA
Philadelphia, PA
Roseland, NJ
Washington, DC*
Wilmington, DE

Wolf Block Government Relations office

MAJOR DEPARTMENTS & PRACTICES

Bankruptcy • Business Litigation • Communications •
Complex Fidelity/Liability • Corporate/Securities • Employee
Benefits • Employment Services • Environmental • Family
Law • Government-Assisted & Affordable Housing • Health
Law • Intellectual Property & Information Technology •
Private Client Services • Real Estate • Securitization • Tax •
Utility Regulation

THE STATS

No. of attorneys: 304
No. of offices: 11
Managing Partner: Mark L. Alderman
Hiring Partner: Jay A. Dubow

NOTABLE PERKS

- Monthly associate lunches
- Free dinners, taxis and parking after 7 p.m.
- Emergency child care
- 401(k) plan

EMPLOYMENT CONTACT

Ms. Eileen M. McMahon
Director, Legal Personnel & Recruitment
Phone: (215) 977-2362
Fax: (215) 405-3962
E-mail: emcmahon@wolfblock.com

BASE SALARY (2007)

Philadelphia, PA
1st year: $125,000
Summer associate: $2,400/week

THE BUZZ
WHAT ATTORNEYS AT OTHER FIRMS ARE SAYING ABOUT THIS FIRM

- "Great work for associates"
- "Past its prime"
- "Good Philly firm"
- "Struggling to keep up with large firms"

Visit the Vault Law Channel, the complete online resource for law careers, featuring firm profiles, message boards, the Vault Law Job Board, and more. www.vault.com/law

VAULT CAREER LIBRARY   613

Womble Carlyle Sandridge & Rice, PLLC

One West Fourth Street
Winston-Salem, NC 27101
Phone: (366) 721-3600
www.wcsr.com

LOCATIONS

Atlanta, GA
Charlotte, NC
Greensboro, NC
Greenville, SC
Linthicum, MD
Raleigh, NC
Research Triangle Park, NC
Tysons Corner, VA
Washington, DC
Wilmington, DE
Winston-Salem, NC

MAJOR DEPARTMENTS & PRACTICES

Alternative Dispute Resolution • Antitrust, Distribution &
Franchise Law • Appellate • Bankruptcy & Creditors' Rights
• Business Litigation • Capital Markets Business Group •
Construction Law • Corporate & Securities • Economic
Development • Employee Benefits • Federal & State
Government Affairs • Gaming Law • Government Contracts
• Health Care • Intellectual Property • International Trade •
Labor & Employment • Patent • Product Liability Litigation •
Public Finance • Real Estate • Tax • Telecommunications,
Cable & Broadcast • Toxic Tort & Environmental Litigation •
Trusts & Estates

THE STATS

No. of attorneys: 518
No. of offices: 11
Managing Partner: Keith W. Vaughan
Hiring Partner: Ellen M. Gregg

NOTABLE PERKS

• Profit-sharing program
• Free parking (certain offices)
• Happy hours and free lunches
• $2,500 toward CLE expenses

EMPLOYMENT CONTACT

Ms. Cynthia K. Pruitt
Professional Development & Recruiting Manager
Phone: (336) 721-3680
Fax: (336) 733-8403
E-mail: cpruitt@wcsr.com

BASE SALARY (2007)

**Charlotte, Greensboro, Raleigh, Winston-Salem,
NC, Greenville, SC**
1st year: $115,000
Summer associate: $1,800/week

Atlanta, GA
1st year: $115,000
Summer associate: $1,850/week

Tysons Corner, VA; Washington, DC
1st year: $125,000
Summer associate: $2,200/week

THE BUZZ
WHAT ATTORNEYS AT OTHER FIRMS ARE SAYING ABOUT THIS FIRM

• "Professional and diverse"
• "Treats associates with respect"
• "Strong player in the South"
• "Advertisers, trying too hard"

© 2007 Vault Inc.

FEATURED
LAW FIRMS

Vault's Featured Law Firms section features information from Vault law firm sponsors.

VAULT CAREER LIBRARY
© 2006 Vault Inc.

Bilzin Sumberg Baena Price & Axelrod LLP

200 South Biscayne Boulevard
Suite 2500
Miami, FL 33131
Phone: (305) 374-7580
Fax: (305) 374-7593

THE STATS

Number of Attorneys Firmwide: 95
Summer Associate Hires Firmwide: 6 (2005); 12 (2006)
Full-Time First-Year Hires Firmwide: 6 (2005)
Full-Time Lateral Hires Firmwide: 26 (2005)
Summer Associate Salary (Weekly): $2,140
First-Year Associate Salary (Base): $111,300
Firm Leadership: John C. Sumberg, Managing Partner
Hiring Partner: Alvin D. Lodish

MAJOR DEPARTMENTS & PRACTICES

Corporate & Securities • Litigation • Real Estate • Land
Use & Government Relations • Restructuring &
Bankruptcy • Technology & Telecommunications •
Environmental Law • Commercial Finance • Tax • Trusts
& Estates

LAW SCHOOLS FIRM RECRUITS FROM

- Columbia
- Florida
- Georgetown
- Harvard
- Miami
- NYU
- Pennsylvania
- Duke
- Miami
- Off-campus Job Fair
- Southeastern Minority Job Fair
- Lavender Law Career Fair

EMPLOYMENT CONTACT

Jessica L. Buchsbaum
Director of Recruiting & Professional
Development
Phone: (305) 374-7580
Fax: (305) 374-7593
jbuchsbaum@bilzin.com

FIRM DESCRIPTION

Bilzin Sumberg is a full-service commercial law
firm with nearly 100 attorneys emanating from a
variety of high-profile practices and backgrounds.
Our attorneys handle complex, sophisticated
transactions in an intimate, collegial environment.
Our attorneys are recognized as leaders in their
fields by publications such as Chambers USA,
Best Lawyers in America, Florida Trend and
others. We combine legal expertise with business
insight and innovative solutions to assist clients in
achieving their objectives - whether in the court
room or in the board room, we shoulder every
client's problem as if it were our own.

RECENT TRANSACTIONS

Some of the firm's recent transactions include the
$3.8 billion sale of LNR Property Corporation to
Cerberus Capital Management, L.P.; the
representation of Eller & Co. in the widely
publicized case to prevent an entity owned by the
government of Dubai from acquiring the Port of
Miami; and assisting with many of the luxury
development and redevelopment projects taking
place throughout South Florida.

Vault's Featured Law Firms section features information from Vault law firm sponsors. For
information on listing your firm in the directory, contact corporatesales@vault.com

VAULT CAREER LIBRARY   617

Bromberg & Sunstein LLP

125 Summer Street
Boston, MA 02110 -1618
Phone: (617) 443-9292
Fax: (617) 443-0004
www.bromsun.com

THE STATS

Number of Attorneys Firmwide: 39
Summer Associate Hires Firmwide: 4 (2004)
Full-Time First-Year Hires Firmwide: 3 (2004)
Full-Time Lateral Hires Firmwide: 1 (2004)
Summer Associate Salary (Weekly): $2,403
Chairman: Lee Carl Bromberg
Managing Partner: Robert L. Kann
Hiring Attorney: Joel R. Leeman

MAJOR DEPARTMENTS & PRACTICES

Business Transactions • Copyright • Litigation • Patent
Litigation & Prosecutions • Trademark

LAW SCHOOLS FIRM RECRUITS FROM

- Boston College
- Boston University
- Cornell
- Harvard
- AIPLA Job Fair
- Cornell Job Fair in Boston
- Patent Law Interview Program

EMPLOYMENT CONTACT

Roberta O'Brien
Firm Administrator
Phone: (617) 443-9292

FIRM DESCRIPTION

All attorneys at Bromberg & Sunstein LLP are immersed in the challenging and fast-paced world of intellectual property law. We represent nationally prominent clients in a wide range of industries. Our attorneys are comfortable working in the most sophisticated and advanced areas of science and technology. Our work environment emphasizes collegiality and the sharing of specialized knowledge and expertise across disciplines both to deliver outstanding services to our clients and to foster professional growth of our attorneys.

© 2005 Vault Inc.

Goulston & Storrs, PC

400 Atlantic Avenue
Boston, MA 02110
Phone: (617) 482-1776
Fax: (617) 574-4112
www.goulstonstorrs.com

OTHER OFFICE LOCATIONS

- New York, NY
- Washington, DC
- London

THE STATS

Number of Attorneys Firm wide: 185
Number of Attorneys in this office: 170
Summer Associate Hires in this office: 12 (2006)
Full-time First-Year Hires in this Office: 7 (2006)
Lateral Hires in this Office: 25 (2005 & 2006)
Summer Associate Salary (weekly): $2,600
First-Year Associate Salary (base): $135,000

MAJOR DEPARTMENTS & PRACTICES

Banking & Finance • Business Law & Corporate •
Litigation • Private Client & Trust Group • International •
Real Estate • Environmental • Tax • Technology

LAW SCHOOLS FIRM RECRUITS FROM

- Boston College
- Boston University
- Columbia
- Cornell
- Georgetown
- Harvard
- Howard University
- Michigan
- NYU
- Northeastern
- Pennsylvania
- Suffolk

EMPLOYMENT CONTACT

Nancy Needle
Director of Legal Recruitment
Phone: (617) 574-6447
Fax: (617) 574-4112
E-mail: nneedle@goulstonstorrs.com

FIRM DESCRIPTION

Goulston & Storrs works hard to provide associates with the opportunities and support they need to be successful. Our steadfast commitment has not gone unnoticed. For the past eight years, Goulston & Storrs has been voted one of the top firms in the United States at which to practice law in the American Lawyer magazine's satisfaction survey of summer and mid-level associates. Based on recommendations of Placement Directors at the top national law schools, the firm was selected for inclusion in Kimm Walton's book, America's Greatest Places to Work with a Law Degree.

As a firm of 185 attorneys, we offer the expertise and resources of a large firm, and the personal attention of a smaller one. Founded more than a century ago, Goulston & Storrs has an international practice. Our associates are encouraged to assume significant responsibilities early on, but always have a place to turn for information, feedback and guidance. In addition to learning from lawyers with whom they are working, each associate is assigned an associate "sibling" and a partner "mentor" on whom he or she can rely for guidance. Learning is continuous, and much of this education comes from in-house seminars and Continuing Legal Education opportunities. For more information, please visit our website at www.goulstonstorrs.com.

Vault's Featured Law Firms section features information from Vault law firm sponsors. For information on listing your firm in the directory, contact corporatesales@vault.com

VAULT CAREER LIBRARY   619

Kasowitz, Benson, Torres & Friedman LLP

1633 Broadway
New York, NY 10019
Phone: (212) 506-1700
Fax: (212) 506-1800
www.kasowitz.com

OTHER OFFICE LOCATIONS

- Houston, TX
- Atlanta, GA
- San Francisco, CA
- Newark, NJ

THE STATS

Number of Attorneys Firmwide: 185
Number of Attorneys in this Office: 156
Summer Associate Hires in this Office: 8 (2006)
Full-Time First-Year Hires in this Office: 10 (2005)
Lateral Hires in this Office: 16 (2005)
Summer Associate Salary (Weekly): $2,790 (2006)
First-Year Associate Salary (Base): $145,000 (2006)
Managing Partner: Marc E. Kasowitz
Hiring Partner: Aaron H. Marks

MAJOR DEPARTMENTS & PRACTICES

Litigation • Bankruptcy • Employment • Intellectual
Property • Matrimonial

LAW SCHOOLS FIRM RECRUITS FROM

- Cardozo
- Columbia
- Cornel
- Fordham – in office
- Georgetown
- Harvard
- NYU
- University of Pennsylvania
- University of Virginia
- BLSA Job Fair.

EMPLOYMENT CONTACT

Mindy J. Lindenman
Director of Legal Recruiting
Phone: (212) 506-1918
Fax: (212) 506-1800
E-mail: mlindenman@kasowitz.com

FIRM DESCRIPTION

KBT&F has built a highly sophisticated, national practice specializing in complex civil litigation. The firm was founded in 1993 by leading lawyers from prominent law firms who sought to build an entrepreneurial firm where highly-talented lawyers are committed to pursuing creative, aggressive and winning approaches to our clients' most challenging legal matters. Our principal areas of practice are rapidly growing and intensely active.

© 2006 Vault Inc.

Miles & Stockbridge P.C.

10 Light Street
Baltimore, MD 21202
Phone: (410) 727-6464
Fax: (410) 385-3700
www.milesstockbridge.com

OTHER OFFICE LOCATIONS

Cambridge, MD
Columbia, MD
Easton, MD
Frederick, MD
Rockville, MD
Towson, MD
McLean, VA

THE STATS

Number of Attorneys Firmwide: 210
Number of Attorneys in this Office: 123
Summer Associate Hires in this Office: 8 (2005)
Full-Time First-Year Hires in this Office: 7 (2003)
First Year Salaries: $115,000
Summer Associate Salary (Weekly): $2,000
Firm Leadership: John B. Frisch, Chairman; John H.
Murray, President; Suzzanne W. Deker, Recruitment
Committee Chair

MAJOR DEPARTMENTS & PRACTICES

Business & Commercial Litigation • Labor and
Employment Law • Products Liability • Mass Torts •
Professional Malpractice • Insurance Regulation and
Litigation • Commercial Real Estate and Finance • General
Corporate • Mergers & Acquisitions • Securities •
Immigration • International Child Abduction • ERISA and
Benefits • Tax • Public and Corporate Finance

LAW SCHOOLS FIRM RECRUITS FROM

Boston College • Catholic • Duke • Emory • Georgetown
• George Washington • Harvard • Howard University •
University of Baltimore • University of Maryland •
University of Pennsylvania • University of Virginia •
Washington & Lee • Washington University in St. Louis •
William & Mary

EMPLOYMENT CONTACT

Randi S. Lewis, Esq.
Director of Diversity and Professional
Development
Phone: (410) 385-3563
Fax: (410) 385-3700
E-mail: rlewis@milesstockbridge.com

FIRM DESCRIPTION

Miles & Stockbridge has a long tradition of
sophisticated legal practice in an informal,
friendly atmosphere. The high morale and
unusual degree of personal satisfaction
experienced by our lawyers arises from our client-
centered approach to lawyering that teaches
personal responsibility for clients. Enthusiasm
and a spirit of camaraderie pervade the firm. Our
unique culture, which has been recognized in
nationally published surveys of associates and
summer associates, promotes a non-hierarchical,
open door environment that welcomes and
supports people of diverse backgrounds. Miles &
Stockbridge has adopted a Diversity Action Plan
that embodies a serious commitment to
recruiting, mentoring, developing and promoting
minorities and women.

Vault's Featured Law Firms section features information from Vault law firm sponsors. For
information on listing your firm in the directory, contact corporatesales@vault.com

VAULT CAREER LIBRARY

621

Atlanta
Beijing
Brussels
Chicago
Hong Kong
London
Los Angeles
Milan
New York
Orange County
Palo Alto
Paris
San Diego
San Francisco
Shanghai
Stamford
Tokyo
Washington, DC

1,200 *diverse perspectives,*

1 *clear vision.*

Our team of **1,200 lawyers** is the force behind a global practice that shares a singular belief: **diversity drives business.** We see no better path to success, both for our people and our clients.

Paul *Hastings*

18 Offices Worldwide | Paul, Hastings, Janofsky & Walker LLP | www.paulhastings.com

LEGAL
EMPLOYER
DIRECTORY

ARIZONA

Bryan Cave LLP

One Renaissance Square
Two North Central Ave., Suite 2200
Phoenix, AZ 85004-4406
Phone: 602/364-7000
Fax: 602/364-7070
www.bryancave.com

Lynne Traverse
Recruiting and Professional Development
Manager - Phoenix
Phone: (602) 364-7000
Fax: (602) 716-7400
lltraverse@bryancave.com

CALIFORNIA

Manatt, Phelps & Phillips, LLP

11355 W. Olympic Blvd.
Los Angeles, CA 90064
Phone: (310) 312-4000
Fax: (310) 312-4224
www.manatt.com

Diana Iketani
Chief Recruiting Officer
Phone: (310) 312-4356
Fax: (310) 312-4224
E-mail: diketani@manatt.com

Number of Attorneys Firmwide: 320

Practice Areas: Advertising, Marketing & Media; Antitrust; Appellate; Banking & Financial Services; Bankruptcy & Financial Restrucuring; Climate Change; Corporate Finance; Criminal Defense & Investigations; Employment & Labor; Entertainment; Energy, Environment & Resources; Food & Drug Administration ("FDA"); Healthcare; Insurance; Intellectual Property & Internet; Real Estate & Land Use; Sports; Tax, Employee Benefits & Global Compensation; Unfair Competition; Venture Capital & Technology

Law Schools Firm Recruits From: Boalt, Brooklyn, Columbia, Emory, George Washington, Georgetown, Harvard, Loyola-Los Angeles, Northwestern, NYU, Stanford, UC-Davis, UC-Hastings, UC-LA, University of Chicago, University of Michigan, USC, Yale

Firm leadership: William T. Quicksilver, Chief Executive & Managing Partner

Firm Description: Manatt, Phelps & Phillips, LLP is a full-service fully integrated firm, focusing on a group of core industries. Manatt clients are among the world's most prestigious enterprises from industries including consumer goods and services, energy and natural resources, entertainment, advertising, marketing and media, financial services, healthcare, real estate and land use, venture capital and technology. Manatt also possesses a powerhouse litigation capability, with more than half of its professionals involved in dispute resolution for major national and international clients.

This Vault Legal Employer Directory is a special advertising section in the Vault Guide to the Top 100 Law Firms. For information on listing your firm in the directory, contact corporatesales@vault.com

VAULT CAREER LIBRARY

625

McKenna Long & Aldridge LLP

444 South Flower Street, Suite 800
Los Angeles, CA 90071
Phone: (213) 688-1000
Fax: (213) 243-6330
www.mckennalong.com

Julie T. Inouye
Senior Legal Recruitment Manager
Phone: (213) 243-6148
Fax: (213) 243-6330
E-mail: jinouye@mckennalong.com

Number of Attorneys Firmwide: 430
Number of Attorneys in this Office: 60
Summer Associate Hires in this Office: 4 (2007)
Full-Time First-Year Hires in this Office: 2 (2007)

Lateral Hires in this Office: 4 (2007)
Summer Associate Salary (Weekly): $2,600 (2007)
First-Year Associate Salary (Base): $145,000 (2007)

Practice Areas: Corporate; Government Contracts; Environmental & Regulatory, Intellectual Property; Litigation; Public Policy & International, Real Estate & Finance

Law Schools Firm Recruits From: Loyola of Los Angeles; Pepperdine; Southwestern, UCLA, USC, Western Regional, BLSA Job Fair

Firm Leadership: Jeff Haidet (Chairman); Mark Flanagan (Managing Partner); Board of Directors

Office Managing Partners: Phil Bradley (Atlanta); Claudio Mereu (Brussels); Tom Papson (DC); Mark Meagher (Denver); Michael Kavanaugh (Los Angeles); Robert Brewer, Jr. (San Diego); Christian Volz (San Francisco)

Firm Description: McKenna Long & Aldridge LLP ("MLA") is an international law firm comprised of approximately 430 lawyers and public policy advisors in 10 offices including Albany, Atlanta, Brussels, Denver, Los Angeles, New York, Philadelphia, San Diego, San Francisco and Washington, DC. The firms is divided into seven large departments: Corporate, Government Contracts, Environmental & Regulatory, Intellectual Property, Litigation, Public Policy & International, and Real Estate & Finance. Each department is comprised of smaller practice groups that provide a broad array of legal services to our clients.

The quality and commitment of our lawyers is the foundation of McKenna Long & Aldridge. We are looking for individuals who share our commitment to the profession, to our clients and to our firm. We believe that associates will be successful at MLA and realize their potential by working in an environment that provides an appropriate balance between oversight and independence. The firm places a strong emphasis on academic and professional excellence. We are looking for people who are committed to becoming excellent lawyers, who are able to inspire confidence among colleagues and clients and how thrive in a team approach to problem solving. Our associates have a strong desire for signification responsibility early in their career, while possessing the corresponding judgment to know when to ask for help. We believe that the best lawyers are well-rounded people who have interest outside of work and who are active in their community.

We Invite you to review our webpage @ www.mckennalong.com for more in-depth information.

Quinn Emanuel Urquhart Oliver & Hedges LLP

865 S. Figueroa Street, 10th Floor
Los Angeles, CA 90017
Phone: (213) 443-3000
Fax: (213) 443-3100
www.quinnemanuel.com

Ms. Selene Dogan
National Director of Recruiting
Phone: (213) 443-3000
Fax: (213) 443-3100
E-mail: selenedogan@quinnemanuel.com

Number of Attorneys Firmwide: 350
Number of Attorneys in this Office: 298
Summer Associate Hires in this Office: 65 (2006)
Full-Time First-Year Hires in this Office: 33 (2006)

Lateral Hires in this Office: 63 (2006)
Summer Associate Salary (Weekly): $2,600
First-Year Associate Salary (Base): $160,000 (2007)

Practice Areas: All areas of business litigation

Law Schools Firm Recruits From: Columbia University Law School; Duke University School of Law; Fordham University School of Law; Georgetown University Law Center; Harvard Law School; New York University School of Law; Stanford Law School; UCLA School of Law; University of California at Berkeley, Boalt Hall School of Law; University of Chicago Law School; University of Michigan Law School; University of Pennsylvania Law School; University of Texas School of Law; University of Virginia School of Law; Yale Law School

Firm Leadership: John B. Quinn (Managing Partner)

Firm Description: Quinn Emanuel Urquhart Oliver & Hedges is a 250+ lawyer litigation firm with offices in Los Angeles, New York, San Francisco, Silicon Valley and San Diego. Our lawyers have tried over 1073 cases and won 988 or 92% of them. When representing plaintiffs, our lawyers have garnered over $3.3 billion in judgments and settlements. Quinn Emanuel is the only law firm in America to receive three 9-figure jury verdicts in the last 4 years.

© 2007 Vault Inc.

Skadden, Arps, Slate, Meagher & Flom LLP

300 South Grand Avenue
Suite 3400
Los Angeles, CA 90071
Phone: (213) 687-5000
Fax: (213) 687-5600
www.skadden.com

Kelly Nystrom
Attorney Recruiting Supervisor
Phone: (213) 687-5000
E-mail: knystrom@skadden.com

Number of Attorneys Firmwide: 1,790
Number of Attorneys in This Office: 144
Summer Associate Hires in This Office: 20 (2006); 41 (2007)

Full-Time First-Year Hires in This Office: 16 (2007)
Summer Associate Salary (Weekly): $3,100 (2007)
First-Year Associate Salary (Base): $160,000 (2007)

Practice Areas: Banking & Institutional Investing; Corporate; Corporate Compliance; Corporate Restructuring; Litigation; Labor; Real Estate; Tax; ERISA

Law Schools Firm Recruits From: Boalt Hall; Chicago; Columbia; Georgetown; Harvard; Hastings; Loyola - Los Angeles; Michigan; NYU; Northwestern; Stanford; Texas; UCLA; USC

Firm Leadership: Robert Sheehan, Executive Partner; Howard Ellin, Global Hiring Partner

Firm Description: Since its opening in 1983, Skadden, Arps' Los Angeles office has become a dominant force in California. Our prominence is noted in publications and our attorneys are recognized among the local legal community as a formidable, indigenous law firm. Unlike most local offices of national firms, virtually all of our work is generated by attorneys in L.A. We provide a structured series of training programs and send new associates for one week of training to New York. Summer associates participate in depositions, trial advocacy, writing and research, and corporate seminars.

Skadden, Arps, Slate, Meagher & Flom LLP

525 University Avenue
Suite 1100
Palo Alto, CA 94301

4 Embarcadero Center, Suite 3800
San Francisco, CA 94111-5974

Matthew Lai
Attorney Recruiting Manager
Phone: (650) 470-3193
E-mail: malai@skadden.com

Number of Attorneys Firmwide: 1,790
Number of Attorneys in this Office: 50 (Palo Alto); 23 (SF)
Summer Associate Hires in Palo Alto: 9 (2006); 14 (2007)
Summer Associate Hires in SF: 9 (2006); 5 (2007)

Full-Time First-Year Hires in This Office: 11 (Palo Alto, 2007); 2 (SF 2007)
Summer Associate Salary (Weekly): $3,100 (2007)
First-Year Associate Salary (Base): $160,000 (2007)

Practice Areas: Alternative Dispute Resolutions; Antitrust; Banking and Institutional Investing; Communications; Corporate Compliance Programs; Corporate Finance; Corporate Restructuring; Energy - Project Finance; Energy - Regulatory; Environmental; Government Enforcement; Litigation; Health Care; Intellectual Property and Technology; International Trade; Investment Management; Labor and Employment Law; Mass Torts/Insurance Litigation; M&A; Political Law; Privatizations; Products Liability; Real Estate; Structured Finance; Tax; Trusts and Estates; White Collar Crime

Law Schools Firm Recruits From: Boalt Hall; Chicago; Columbia; Harvard; Hastings; NYU; Northwestern; Santa Clara; Stanford; UCLA

Firm Leadership: Robert Sheehan, Executive Partner; Howard Ellin, Global Hiring Partner

Firm Description: The Palo Alto office of Skadden, Arps was opened in 1998. This office represents clients in a wide range of corporate and securities transactions, intellectual property and technology matters, litigation, labor and employee benefits and antitrust matters. The different practice areas regularly collaborate on matters, so there is frequent interaction amongst the various practice groups within the office. The San Francisco office was opened in 1987 and represents clients in various corporate and securities transactions, complex mass tort and insurance litigation matters, and environmental law matters. Our litigators handle all types of litigated corporate, commercial and securities disputes. Due to the relatively small size of the office, opportunities for development and meaningful responsibility for associates are plentiful. Attorneys in both offices handle a number of pro bono matters.

This Vault Legal Employer Directory is a special advertising section in the Vault Guide to the Top 100 Law Firms. For information on listing your firm in the directory, contact corporatesales@vault.com

VAULT CAREER LIBRARY

627

Bryan Cave LLP

120 Broadway, Suite 300

Los Angeles, CA 90401-2386

Phone: (310) 576-2100

Fax: (310) 576-2200

www.bryancave.com

Sheryl A. Jones

Manager of Legal Recruiting and

Professional Development - Los Angeles

Phone: (310) 576-2303

Fax: (310) 576-2200

sajones@bryancave.com

Bryan Cave LLP

1900 Main Street, Suite 700

Irvine, CA 92614-7328

Phone: (949) 223-7000

Fax: (949) 223-7100

www.bryancave.com

Esther Villa

Recruiting Coordinator

Phone: (949) 223-7374

Fax: (949) 223-7100

etvilla@bryancave.com

Chadbourne & Parke LLP

350 South Grand Avenue

Suite 3300

Los Angeles, CA 90071

Phone: (213) 892-1000

Fax: (213) 622-9865

www.chadbourne.com

Jay R. Henneberry

Hiring Partner

Phone: (213) 892-1000

Fax: (213) 622-9865

E-mail: jhenneberry@chadbourne.com

Cooley Godward Kronish LLP

Five Palo Alto Square

3000 El Camino Real

Palo Alto, CA 94306-2155

Phone: (650) 843-5000

Fax: (650) 857-0663

www.cooley.com

Jo Anne Larson

Phone: (650) 843-5000

Fax: (650) 849-7400

E mail: larsonja@cooley.com

Fenwick & West LLP

Silicon Valley Center

801 California Street

Mountain View, CA 94041

Phone: (650) 988-8500

Fax: (650) 938-5200

www.fenwick.com

Ms. Julieta Wiley

Manager of Attorney Recruiting & Diversity

Phone: (650) 335-4949

Fax: (650) 938-5200

E-mail: recruit@fenwick.com

Gibson, Dunn & Crutcher LLP

333 South Grand Avenue

Los Angeles, CA 90071-3197

Phone: (213) 229-7000

www.gibsondunn.com

Ms. Leslie Ripley

Director, Legal Recruiting & Diversity

Phone: (213) 229-7273

E-mail: lripley@gibsondunn.com

Heller Ehrman LLP

333 Bush Street

San Francisco, CA 94104-2878

Phone: (415) 772-6000

Fax: (415) 772-6268

www.hellerehrman.com

Mr. Michael R. Gotham

Director of Attorney Recruiting

Phone: (415) 772-6003

Fax: (415) 772-6268

E-mail: michael.gotham@hellerehrman.com

Irell & Manella LLP

1800 Avenue of the Stars, Suite 900

Los Angeles, CA 90067

Phone: (310) 277-1010

Fax: (310) 203-7199

www.irell.com

Ms. Robyn Steele

Recruiting Administrator

Phone: (310) 277-1010

Fax: (310) 203-7199

E-mail: rsteele@irell.com

Latham & Watkins LLP

633 West Fifth Street, Suite 4000

Los Angeles, CA 90071

Phone: (213) 485-1234

www.lw.com

Ms. Debra Perry Clarkson

Director of Global Recruiting

Phone: (858) 523-5400

Fax: (858) 523-5450

E-mail: debra.clarkson@lw.com

Manatt, Phelps & Phillips, LLP

Park Tower

695 Town Center Drive

4th Floor

Costa Mesa, CA 92626

Phone: (714) 371-2500

Fax: (714) 371-2550

www.manatt.com

Shirley Hands

Office Administrator

Phone: (714) 371-2500

Fax: (714) 371-2550

shands@manatt.com

Manatt, Phelps & Phillips, LLP

1001 Page Mill Road, Building 2

Palo Alto, CA 94304

Phone: (650) 812-1300

Fax: (650) 213-0260

www.manatt.com

Joanna Bartlett

Marketing & Recruiting Coordinator

Phone: (650) 812-1300

Fax: (650) 213-0260

jbartlett@manatt.com

Manatt, Phelps & Phillips, LLP

1215 K Street, Suite 1900

Sacramento, CA 95814

Phone: (916) 552-2300

Fax: (916) 552-2323

www.manatt.com

Joanna Bartlett

Marketing & Recruiting Coordinator

Phone: (650) 812-1300

Fax: (650) 213-0260

jbartlett@manatt.com

Morrison & Foerster LLP

425 Market Street

San Francisco, CA 94105-2482

Phone: (415) 268-7000

www.mofo.com

Mr. Anand David

Director of Recruiting

Phone: (212) 468-8039

E-mail: Adavid@mofo.com

© 2007 Vault Inc.

Munger, Tolles & Olson LLP

355 South Grand Avenue, 35th Floor
Los Angeles, CA 90071-1560
Phone: (213) 683-9100
www.mto.com

Ms. Kevinn C. Villard
Director of Legal Recruiting
Phone: (213) 683-9242
Fax: (213) 683-5142
E-mail: kevinn.villard@mto.com

O'Melveny & Myers LLP

400 South Hope Street
Los Angeles, CA 90071
Phone: (213) 430-6000
www.omm.com

Paige Drewelow
Director of Attorney Recruiting-Firmwide
Phone: (415) 984-8700
Fax: (415) 984-8701
E-mail: pdrewelow@omm.com

Quinn Emanuel Urquhart Oliver & Hedges LLP

50 California St., 22nd Floor
San Francisco, CA 94104
Phone: (415) 875-6600
Fax: (415) 875-6700
www.quinnemanuel.com

Alice McKinley
Recruiting Coordinator
Phone: (415) 875-6600
Fax: (415) 875-6700
E-mail: alicemckinley@quinnemanuel.com

Quinn Emanuel Urquhart Oliver & Hedges LLP

555 Twin Dolphin Drive, Suite 560
Redwood Shores, CA 94065
Phone: (650) 801-5000
Fax: (650) 801-5100
www.quinnemanuel.com

Maryann Curtis
Recruiting Coordinator
Phone: (650) 620-4500
Fax: (650) 620-4555
E-mail: maryanncurtis@quinnemanuel.com

Wilson Sonsini Goodrich & Rosati

650 Page Mill Road
Palo Alto, CA 94304-1050
Phone: (650) 493-9300
www.wsgr.com

Ms. Carol A. Timm
Director, Attorney Recruiting & Retention
Phone: (650) 493-9300
E-mail: attorneyrecruiting@wsgr.com

DISTRICT OF COLUMBIA

McKenna Long & Aldridge LLP

1900 K Street, NW
Washington, DC 20006
Phone: (202) 496-7500
Fax: (202) 496-7756
www.mckennalong.com

Number of Attorneys Firmwide: 430
Number of Attorneys in this Office: 135
Summer Associate Hires in this Office: 9 (2007)
Full-Time First Year Hires in this Office: 7 (2007)

Mr. Daniel J. Conway
Senior Legal Recruitment Manager
Phone: (202) 496-7512
Fax: (202) 496-7756
E-mail: dconway@mckennalong.com

Lateral Hires in this Office: 14 (2007)
Summer Associate Salary (Weekly): $2,600 (2007)
First-Year Associate Salary (Base): $145,000 (2007)

Practice Areas: Litigation, Government Contracts, Intellectual Property, Public Policy & International, Environmental and Regulatory, Corporate, and Real Estate & Finance

Law Schools Firm Recruits From: George Washington; Georgetown; Duke; Havard; Howard; UVA

Firm Leadership: Jeff Haidet (Chairman); Mark Flanagan (Managing Partner); Board of Directors

Office Managing Partners: Phil Bradley (Atlanta); Claudio Mereu (Brussels); Tom Papson (DC); Mark Meagher (Denver); Michael Kavanaugh (Los Angeles); Robert Brewer, Jr. (San Diego); Christian Volz (San Francisco)

Firm Description: McKenna Long & Aldridge LLP ("MLA") is an international law firm comprised of approximately 430 lawyers and public policy advisors in 10 offices including Albany, Atlanta, Brussels, Denver, Los Angeles, New York, Philadelphia, San Diego, San Francisco and Washington, DC. The firms is divided into seven large departments: Corporate, Government Contracts, Environmental & Regulatory, Intellectual Property, Litigation, Public Policy & International, and Real Estate & Finance. Each department is comprised of smaller practice groups that provide a broad array of legal services to our clients.

The quality and commitment of our lawyers is the foundation of McKenna Long & Aldridge. We are looking for individuals who share our commitment to the profession, to our clients and to our firm. We believe that associates will be successful at MLA and realize their potential by working in an environment that provides an appropriate balance between oversight and independence. The firm places a strong emphasis on academic and professional excellence. We are looking for people who are committed to becoming excellent lawyers, who are able to inspire confidence among colleagues and clients and how thrive in a team approach to problem solving. Our associates have a strong desire for signification responsibility early in their career, while possessing the corresponding judgment to know when to ask for help. We believe that the best lawyers are well-rounded people who have interest outside of work and who are active in their community.

We invite you to review our webpage @ www.mckennalong.com for more in-depth information.

This Vault Legal Employer Directory is a special advertising section in the Vault Guide to the Top 100 Law Firms. For information on listing your firm in the directory, contact corporatesales@vault.com

VAULT CAREER LIBRARY   629

Skadden, Arps, Slate, Meagher & Flom LLP

1440 New York Avenue, NW
Washington, DC 20005
Phone: (202) 371-7000
Fax: (202) 393-5760
www.skadden.com

Lauren Yost
Attorney Recruiting Coordinator
Phone: (202) 371-7732

Number of Attorneys Firmwide: 1,790
Number of Attorneys in This Office: 257
Summer Associate Hires in This Office: 20 (2006);
  34 (2007)

Full-Time First-Year Hires in This Office: 29 (2007)
Summer Associate Salary (Weekly): $3,100 (2007)
First-Year Associate Salary (Base): $160,000 (2007)

Practice Areas: Antitrust; Banking/Regulatory; Communications; Corporate/Securities; Energy; Environmental; Intellectual Property; International Trade; Litigation; Political Law; Tax

Law Schools Firm Recruits From: American; Chicago; Columbia; Duke; George Washington; Georgetown; Harvard; Harvard BLSA Job Fair; Howard; Michigan; NYU; Penn; Stanford; UVA; Yale

Firm Leadership: Robert Sheehan, Executive Partner; Howard Ellin, Global Hiring Partner

Firm Description: Skadden, Arps has a full-service practice unmatched by any other law firm in DC, because it combines both a transactional DC and a national practice. The Firm has developed a traditional DC practice in such diverse fields as communications, energy, environmental, international trade, legislation, litigation and political law. At the same time, attorneys interested in antitrust, banking and institutional investing, general corporate, corporate finance, corporate restructurings, domestic and international project finance, M&A and tax have the opportunity to engage in the kind of transactional work that is ordinarily associated only with a New York practice.

Akin Gump Strauss Hauer & Feld LLP

Robert S. Strauss Building
1333 New Hampshire Avenue, NW
Washington, DC 20036-1564
Phone: (202) 887-4000
www.akingump.com

Ms. Marybeth W. Jarrard
Director of Attorney Recruiting
Phone: (202) 887-4000
Fax: (202) 887-4288
E-mail: mjarrard@akingump.com

Arent Fox LLP

1050 Connecticut Avenue, NW
Washington, DC 20036-5339
Phone: (202) 857-6000
Fax: (202) 857-6395
www.arentfox.com

Ms. Karyn J. Thomas (laterals)
Attorney Recruitment Manager
Fax: (202) 857-6395
E-mail: DCAttorneyRecruit@arentfox.com

Ms. Jessica Salvaterra (law students & judicial clerks)
Senior Attorney Recruitment Coordinator
Fax: (202) 857-6224
E-mail: salvaterra.jessica@arentfox.com

Arnold & Porter LLP

555 Twelfth Street, NW
Washington, DC 20004-1206
Phone: (202) 942-5000
www.arnoldporter.com

Ms. Andrea Glosser
Manager of Legal Recruitment
Phone: (202) 942-5000
E-mail: Andrea.Glosser@aporter.com

Bryan Cave LLP

700 Thirteenth Street N.W.
Washington, DC 20005-3960
Phone: (202) 508-6000
Fax: (202) 508-6200
www.bryancave.com

Meaghan Gibbs
Recruiting and Professional Development
Manager - Washington
Phone: (202) 508-6050
Fax: (202) 508-6200
meaghan.gibbs@bryancave.com

Cadwalader, Wickersham & Taft LLP

1201 F Street, N.W.
Suite 100
Washington, DC 20004
Phone: (202) 862-2200
Fax: (202) 862-2400
www.cadwalader.com

Dyana Barninger
Manager of Associate Development and Recruitment
Phone: (202) 862-2200
Fax: (202) 862-2400
E-mail: dyana.barninger@cwt.com

Chadbourne & Parke LLP

1200 New Hampshire Avenue, N.W.
Washington, DC 20036
Phone: (202) 974-5600
Fax: (202) 974-5602
www.chadbourne.com

Kenneth W. Hansen
Hiring Partner
Phone: (202) 974-5600
Fax: (202) 974-5602
E-mail: khansen@chadbourne.com

© 2007 Vault Inc.

Covington & Burling LLP

1201 Pennsylvania Avenue, NW

Washington, DC 20004-2401

Phone: (202) 662-6000

www.cov.com

Ms. Ellen Purvance

Director, Legal Personnel Recruiting

Phone: (202) 662-6200

Fax: (202) 662-6291

E-mail: legal.recruiting@cov.com

Crowell & Moring LLP

1001 Pennsylvania Avenue, N.W.

Washington, DC 20004

Phone: (202) 624-2500

www.crowell.com

Ms. Torey P. Phillips

Senior Manager of Legal Recruiting

Phone: (202) 624-2771

E-mail: tphillips@crowell.com

Dickstein Shapiro LLP

1825 I Street, NW

Washington, DC 20006

Phone: (202) 420-2200

www.dicksteinshapiro.com

Ms. Julie B. Miles

Manager of Attorney Recruiting

Phone: (202) 420-4875

Fax: (202) 420-2201

E-mail: MilesJ@dicksteinshapiro.com

Finnegan, Henderson, Farabow, Garrett & Dunner, L.L.P.

901 New York Avenue, N.W.

Washington, DC 20001-4413

Phone: (202) 408-4000

Fax: (202) 408-4400

www.finnegan.com

Mr. Paul Sevanich

Attorney Recruitment Manager

Phone: (202) 408-4000

Fax: (202) 408-4400

E-mail: attyrecruit-DC@finnegan.com

Hogan & Hartson LLP

555 Thirteenth Street, NW

Washington, DC 20004-1109

Phone: (202) 637-5600

www.hhlaw.com

Ms. Irena McGrath

Chief Associate Recruitment Officer

Phone: (202) 637-8601

E-mail: imcgrath@hhlaw.com

Howrey LLP

1299 Pennsylvania Avenue, NW

Washington, DC 20004

Phone: (202) 783-0800

www.howrey.com

Ms. Janet Brown

Manager, Associate Programs

Phone: (202) 783-0800

E-mail: BrownJanet@howrey.com

Jones Day

51 Louisiana Avenue, NW

Washington, DC 20001-2113

Phone: (202) 879-3939

www.jonesday.com

Ms. Jolie A. Blanchard

Firm Director of Recruiting

Phone: (202) 879-3788

E-mail: jablanchard@jonesday.com

Manatt, Phelps & Phillips, LLP

1501 M Street NW, Suite 700

Washington, D.C. 20005

Phone: (202) 463-4300

Fax: (202) 463-4394

www.manatt.com

Delores Butler

Office Administrator

Phone: (202) 585-6500

Fax: (202) 585-6600

dbutler@manatt.com

Patton Boggs LLP

2550 M Street, NW

Washington, DC 20037

Phone: (202) 457-6000

www.pattonboggs.com

Ms. Kara P. Reidy

Director, Professional Recruitment

Phone: (202) 457-6342

Fax: (202) 457-6315

E-mail: kreidy@pattonboggs.com

Steptoe & Johnson LLP

1330 Connecticut Avenue, N.W.

Washington, DC 20036

Phone: (202) 429-3000

Fax: (202) 429-3902

www.steptoe.com

Ms. Rosemary Kelly Morgan

Director of Attorney Services & Legal Recruiting

Phone: (202) 429-8036

Fax: (202) 429-3902

E-mail: Legal_Recruiting@steptoe.com

Venable LLP

575 7th Street, NW

Washington, DC 20004

Phone: (202) 344-4000

Fax: (202) 344-8300

www.venable.com

Ms. Grace Cunningham

Director of Professional Development & Recruiting

Phone: (202) 344-4875

Fax: (202) 344-8300

E-mail: ggcunningham@venable.com

Williams & Connolly LLP

The Edward Bennett Williams Building

725 Twelfth Street, N.W.

Washington, DC 20005

Phone: (202) 434-5000

www.wc.com

Ms. Donna M. Downing

Attorney Recruiting Manager

Phone: (202) 434-5605

Fax: (202) 434-5029

E-mail: ddowning@wc.com

This Vault Legal Employer Directory is a special advertising section in the Vault Guide to the Top 100 Law Firms. For information on listing your firm in the directory, contact corporatesales@vault.com

VAULT CAREER LIBRARY

631

FLORIDA

Bilzin Sumberg Baena Price & Axelrod LLP

200 South Biscayne Boulevard, Suite 2500
Miami, FL 33131
Phone: (305) 374-7580
Fax: (305) 374-7593
www.bilzin.com

Jessica L. Buchsbaum
Director of Legal Recruiting
Phone: (305) 374-7580
Fax: (305) 374-7593
jbuchsbaum@bilzin.com

Number of Attorneys Firmwide: 93
Summer Associate Hires: 12 (2006)
Full-Time First Year Hires: 6 (2006)

Lateral Hires: 6 (2006)
Summer Associate Salary (Weekly): $2,308
First year Associate Salary (base): $120,000

Practice Areas: Bankruptcy, Reorganization, Creditors Rights • Capital Markets • Corporate, Securities • Environmental, Government, Land Use • Litigation • Real Estate • Tax, Trusts, Estate • Technology • Telecommunications

Firm Leadership: John C. Sumberg, Managing Partner; Alvin D. Lodish, Hiring Partner

Law Schools Firm Recruits From: Columbia University Law School • Duke University School of Law • Georgetown University Law Center • Harvard Law School • New York University School of Law • University of Florida Levin College of Law • University of Miami School of Law • University of Pennsylvania Law School

Firm Description: Bilzin Sumberg is a full-service commercial law firm with more than 90 attorneys emanating from a variety of high-profile practices and backgrounds. With offices in Miami and Tallahassee, our attorneys handle complex, sophisticated transactions in an intimate, collegial environment. We combine legal expertise with business insight and innovative solutions to assist clients in achieving their objectives - whether in the court room or in the board room, we shoulder every client's problem as if it were our own.

Greenberg Traurig, LLP

1221 Brickell Avenue
Miami, Florida 33131
Phone: (305) 579-0500
Fax: (305) 579-0717
www.gtlaw.com

Please see www.gtlaw.com for hiring contacts.

© 2007 Vault Inc.

GEORGIA

Ford & Harrison LLP

1275 Peachtree St., NE, Suite 600
Atlanta, GA 30309
Phone: (404) 888-3800
Fax: (404) 888-3863
www.fordharrison.com

FORD & HARRISON LLP

Courtney E. Dyar
Attorney Recruiting Coordinator
Phone: (404) 888-3800
Fax: (404) 888-3863
E-mail: cdyar@fordharrison.com

Number of Attorneys Firmwide: 190
Number of Attorneys in this Office 44

Summer Associate Salary (Weekly): $1,700 (2006)

Practice Areas: Labor & Employment (Defense); Employee Benefits; Business Immigration

Law Schools Firm Recruits From: University of Georgia; Georgia State; Wake Forest; University of North Carolina; North Carolina Central University; University of Florida; University of South Carolina; Emory; University of Virginia; W&L; Florida State; Georgetown; Stetson; Vanderbilt; University of Memphis; University of Arizona; University of Miami; Arizona State; Ole Miss; University of Tennessee; University of Minnesota

Firm Leadership: C. Lash Harrison, Managing Partner

Firm Description: Ford & Harrison is a national labor and employment law firm with close to 200 lawyers in 18 offices: Asheville (NC), Birmingham, Chicago, Dallas, Denver, Jacksonville, Los Angeles, Melbourne (FL), Memphis, Miami, Minneapolis, New York, Orlando, Phoenix, Spartanburg, Tampa, and Washington, DC. The firm represents employers in labor, employment, immigration, and employee benefits matters, including litigation, in issues involving national and internal jurisdictions. Please visit our website to learn more - www.fordharrison.com."

McKenna Long & Aldridge LLP

303 Peachtree Street, N.E., Suite 5300
Atlanta, GA 30308
Phone: (404) 527-4000
Fax: (404) 527-4198
www.mckennalong.com

Jennifer S. Queen
Director of Hiring & Professional Development
Phone: (404) 527-4139
Fax: (404) 527-4198
E-mail: jqueen@mckennalong.com

Number of Attorneys Firmwide: 430
Number of Attorneys in this Office: 152
Summer Associate Hires in this Office: 20 (2006)
Full-Time First Year Hires in this Office: 7 (2006)

Lateral Hires in this Office: 39 (2006)
Summer Associate Salary (Weekly): $2,100 (2007)
First-Year Associate Salary (Base): $130,000 (2007)

Practice Areas: Real Estate, Corporate Securities, Environmental & Regulatory, Financial Restructuring, Litigation, Mergers & Acquisitions, Public Policy & International, Tax, Employee Benefit, Trusts & Estates

Law Schools Firm Recruits From: Duke, Emory, Georgetown, Georgia, Georgia State, Harvard, Howard, Mercer, Michigan, North Carolina, Virginia, Vanderbilt

Firm Leadership: Jeff Haidet (Chairman); Mark Flanagan (Managing Partner); Board of Directors

Office Managing Partners: Phil Bradley (Atlanta); Claudio Mereu (Brussels); Tom Papson (DC); Mark Meagher (Denver); Michael Kavanaugh (Los Angeles); Robert Brewer, Jr. (San Diego); Christian Volz (San Francisco)

Firm Description: McKenna Long & Aldridge LLP ("MLA") is an international law firm comprised of approximately 430 lawyers and public policy advisors in 10 offices including Albany, Atlanta, Brussels, Denver, Los Angeles, New York, Philadelphia, San Diego, San Francisco and Washington, DC. The firms is divided into seven large departments: Corporate, Government Contracts, Environmental & Regulatory, Intellectual Property & Technology, Litigation, Public Policy & International, and Real Estate & Finance. Each department is comprised of smaller practice groups that provide a broad array of legal services to our clients.

The quality and commitment of our lawyers is the foundation of McKenna Long & Aldridge. We are looking for individuals who share our commitment to the profession, to our clients and to our firm. We believe that associates will be successful at MLA and realize their potential by working in an environment that provides an appropriate balance between oversight and independence. The firm places a strong emphasis on academic and professional excellence. We are looking for people who are committed to becoming excellent lawyers, who are able to inspire confidence among colleagues and clients and how thrive in a team approach to problem solving. Our associates have a strong desire for signification responsibility early in their career, while possessing the corresponding judgment to know when to ask for help. We believe that the best lawyers are well-rounded people who have interest outside of work and who are active in their community.

We Invite you to review our webpage @ www.mckennalong.com for more in-depth information.

This Vault Legal Employer Directory is a special advertising section in the Vault Guide to the Top 100 Law Firms. For information on listing your firm in the directory, contact corporatesales@vault.com

 VAULT CAREER LIBRARY

633

Alston & Bird LLP

One Atlantic Center
1201 West Peachtree Street
Atlanta, GA 30309-3424
Phone: (404) 881-7000
Fax: (404) 881-7777
www.alston.com

Ms. Emily Leeson
Director of Attorney Hiring & Development
Phone: (404) 881-7014
Fax: (404) 253-8334
E-mail: emily.leeson@alston.com

Kilpatrick Stockton LLP

1100 Peachtree Street
Suite 2800
Atlanta, GA 30309-4530
Phone: (404) 815-6500
Fax: (404) 815-6555
www.ksrecruits.com

Ms. Naomi Horvath
Recruiting Coordinator
Phone: (404) 541-6675
Fax: (404) 815-6555
E-mail: nhorvath@kilpatrickstockton.com

King & Spalding LLP

1180 Peachtree Street, NE
Atlanta, GA 30309
Phone: (404) 572-4600
www.kslaw.com

Ms. Amy Miele
Recruiting Manager
Phone: (404) 572-4990
Fax: (404) 572-5100
E-mail: amiele@kslaw.com

ILLINOIS

Skadden, Arps, Slate, Meagher & Flom

333 West Wacker Drive
Chicago, IL 60606
Phone: (312) 407-0700
Fax: (312) 407-8361
www.skadden.com

Number of Attorneys Firmwide: 1,790
Number of Attorneys in This Office: 174
Summer Associate Hires in This Office: 30 (2006);
  37 (2007)

Kate Arnold
Attorney Recruiting Manager
Phone: (312) 407-0909
Fax: (312) 407-0851
E-mail: karnold@skadden.com

Full-Time First-Year Hires in this office: 25 (2007)
Summer Associate Salary (Weekly): $3,100 (2007)
First-Year Associate Salary (Base): $160,000 (2007)

Practice Areas: Banking; Communications; Corporate; Corporate Restructuring; Litigation; Mass Torts/Insurance Litigation; Real Estate; Tax

Law Schools: Chicago; Chicago-Kent; Columbia; Cornell; DePaul; Duke; Georgetown; Harvard; Howard; Illinois; Iowa; Loyola-Chicago; Michigan; Minnesota; North Carolina; Northwestern; Notre Dame; NYU; Stanford; Washington University; Wisconsin; Yale

Firm Leadership: Robert Sheehan, Executive Partner; Howard Ellin, Global Hiring Partner

Firm Description: The Chicago office offers a diversified practice. Major areas of activity include negotiated acquisitions and leveraged buyouts; contested takeovers; corporate restructuring; federal income tax work; and litigation, among others. Opportunities for development and expansion of responsibility for associates early in their careers have been, and are expected to continue to be plentiful. The goal of the summer program is to provide a practical approach toward understanding what it is like to be an attorney at Skadden, Arps. Our firm is committed to the professional development and continued legal education of our attorneys.

Baker & McKenzie

One Prudential Plaza
130 East Randolph Drive, Suite 2500
Chicago, IL 60601
Phone: (312) 861-8000
www.bakernet.com

Ms. Eleonora Nikol
Phone: (312) 861-8924
E-mail: eleonora.nikol@bakernet.com

Jenner & Block LLP

330 N. Wabash Avenue
Chicago, IL 60611-7603
Phone: (312) 222-9350
www.jenner.com

Christine J. Carlson
Senior Manager of Legal Recruiting
Phone: (312) 840-7803
Fax: (312) 840-7616
E-mail: ccarlson@jenner.com

Katten Muchin Rosenman LLP

525 West Monroe Street
Chicago, IL 60661
Phone: (312) 902-5200
www.kattenlaw.com

Ms. Elaine F. Miller
Attorney Recruiting & Development Manager
Phone: (312) 902-5338
Fax: (312) 577-4556
E-mail: elaine.miller@kattenlaw.com

© 2007 Vault Inc.

Kirkland & Ellis LLP

Aon Center
200 East Randolph Drive
Chicago, IL 60601
Phone: (312) 861-2000
www.kirkland.com

Ms. Betsy Zukley
Attorney Recruiting Manager
Phone: (312) 861-2054
Fax: (312) 861-2200
E-mail: attorney_recruiting@kirkland.com

Mayer, Brown, Rowe & Maw LLP

71 South Wacker Drive
Chicago, IL 60606
Phone: (312) 782-0600
www.mayerbrown.com

Laura Kanter, Attorney Recruitment Manager
E-mail: RecruitingDepartment-CHGO@mayerbrown.com

McDermott Will & Emery

227 W. Monroe Street
Suite 4400
Chicago, IL 60606
Phone: (312) 372-2000
www.mwe.com

Ms. Nancy Berry
Director, Legal Recruiting
Phone: (312) 984-3377
Fax: (312) 984-7700
E-mail: nberry@mwe.com

Sidley Austin LLP

One South Dearborn
Chicago, IL 60603
Phone: (312) 853-7000
www.sidley.com

Ms. Jennifer L. Connelly
National Recruiting Manager
Phone: (312) 853-7495
Fax: (312) 853-7036
E-mail: jlconnelly@sidley.com

Sonnenschein Nath & Rosenthal LLP

7800 Sears Tower
233 S. Wacker Drive
Chicago, IL 60606
Phone: (312) 876-8000
www.sonnenschein.com

Ms. Karalyn Powell
Attorney Recruitment Manager
Phone: (202) 408-3940
E-mail: kpowell@sonnenschein.com

Winston & Strawn LLP

35 West Wacker Drive
Chicago, IL 60601
Phone: (312) 558-5600
www.winston.com

Julie A. Bauer, Esq.
Hiring Committee Co-Chair
E-mail: jbauer@winston.com
Stephen V. D'Amore
Hiring Committee Co-Chair
E-mail: sdamore@winston.com

MARYLAND

Miles & Stockbridge P.C.

10 Light Street
Baltimore, MD 21202
www.milesstockbridge.com
Phone: (410) 727-6464
Fax: (410) 385-3700

Randi S. Lewis, Esq.
Director of Diversity and Professional Development
Phone: (410) 385-3563
Fax: (410) 385-3700
E-mail: rlewis@milesstockbridge.com

Number of Attorneys Firmwide: 204
Number of Attorneys in this Office: 119
Summer Associate Hires in this Office: 8 (2006)
Full-Time First-Year Hires in this Office: 8 (2006)

Lateral Hires in this Office: 15 (2006)
First year salaries: $125,000 (2007)
Summer Associate Salary (Weekly): $2,250

Practice Areas: Business & Commercial Litigation, Labor and Employment Law, Products Liability, Mass Torts, Professional Malpractice, Insurance Regulation and Litigation, Commercial Real Estate and Finance, General Corporate, Mergers & Acquisitions, Securities, Immigration, International Child Abduction, ERISA and Benefits, Tax, Public and Corporate Finance

Law Schools Firm Recruits From: Catholic University of America, Columbus School of Law; George Washington University Law School; Georgetown University Law Center; Howard University School of Law; University of Baltimore School of Law; University of Maryland School of Law; University of Virginia School of Law; Washington and Lee University School of Law; William & Mary School of Law

Firm Leadership: John B. Frisch, Chairman; John H. Murray, President; Suzzanne W. Deker, Recruitment Committee Chair

Firm Description: Miles & Stockbridge has a long tradition of sophisticated legal practice in an informal, friendly atmosphere. The high morale and unusual degree of personal satisfaction experienced by our lawyers arises from our client-centered approach to lawyering that teaches personal responsibility for clients. Enthusiasm and a spirit of camaraderie pervade the firm. Our unique culture, which has been recognized in nationally published surveys of associates and summer associates, promotes a non-hierarchical, open door environment that welcomes and supports people of diverse backgrounds. Miles & Stockbridge has adopted a Diversity Action Plan that embodies a serious commitment to recruiting, mentoring, developing and promoting minorities and women.

This Vault Legal Employer Directory is a special advertising section in the Vault Guide to the Top 100 Law Firms. For information on listing your firm in the directory, contact corporatesales@vault.com

VAULT CAREER LIBRARY

635

MASSACHUSETTS

Bromberg & Sunstein LLP

125 Summer Street
11th Floor
Boston, MA 02110 -1618
Phone: (617) 443-9292
Fax: (617) 443-0004
www.bromsun.com

Joel R. Leeman
Hiring Partner
Phone: (617) 443-9292
Fax: (617) 443-0004
employment@bromsun.com

Number of Attorneys: 46
Number of Offices: 1
Summer Associate Hires in this Office: 4 (2007)
Full-Time 1st-Year Hires in this Office: 5 (2007)
Lateral Hires in this Office: 3 (2007)

Summer Associate Salary (Weekly): $2,600 (2007)
First-Year Associate Salary (Base): $135,000 (2007)
Chairman: Lee Carl Bromberg
Hiring Attorney: Joel R. Leeman

Firm Description: Bromberg & Sunstein attorneys have an outstanding record of important wins for our technology and life sciences clients through litigation, patent prosecution, IP portfolio development and business transactions. We represent internationally prominent clients in a wide range of industries. Our attorneys work in the most sophisticated and advanced areas of science and technology. Our work environment emphasizes collegiality and the sharing of specialized knowledge and expertise across disciplines both to deliver outstanding services to our clients and to foster professional growth to our attorneys. Bromberg & Sunstein was named One of the Best Places to Work in a 2007 *Boston Business Journal* poll.

Goulston & Storrs, PC

400 Atlantic Avenue
Boston, MA 02110
Phone: (617) 482-1776
Fax: (617) 574-4112
www.goulstonstorrs.com

Jennifer Smith
Entry-Level Recruitment Manager
Phone: (617) 574-4072
Fax: (617) 574-4112
E-mail: jsmith@goulstonstorrs.com

Jill Nussbaum
Lateral Recruitment Specialist
Phone: (617) 574-4004
E-mail: jnussbaum@goulstonstorrs.com

Number of Attorneys Firmwide: 195
Number of Attorneys in this Office: 175
Summer Associate Hires in this Office: 12 (2007)
Full-Time First Year Hires in this Office: 8 (2007)

Lateral Hires in this Office: 20 (2007)
Summer Associate Salary (Weekly): $2,800 (2007)
First-Year Associate Salary (Base): $160,000 (2007)

Practice Areas: Banking & Finance; Bankruptcy; Business Law & Corporate; Litigation; Private Client & Trust Group; International; Real Estate; Environmental; Tax; Technology

Law Schools Firm Recruits From: Boston College; Boston University; Columbia; Cornell Georgetown; Harvard; Howard University; Michigan; NYU; Northeastern; Pennsylvania; Suffolk

Firm Leadership: Co-Managing Directors: Douglas M. Husid; Kitt Sawitsky

Firm Description: Goulston & Storrs works hard to provide associates with the opportunities and support they need to be successful. Our steadfast commitment has not gone unnoticed. For the past 10 years, Goulston & Storrs has been voted on of the top firms in the United States at which to practice law in the *American Lawyer* magazine's satisfaction survey of summer and mid-level associates. Based on recommendations of placement directors at top national law schools, the firm was selected for inclusion in Kimm Walton's book, *America's Greatest Places to Work with a Law Degree*. For more information on our firm, please visit our web site at www.goulstonstorrs.com.

As a firm of 190 attorneys, we offer the expertise and resources of a large firm, and the personal attention of a smaller one. Founded more than a century ago, Goulston & Storrs has an international practice. Our associates are encouraged to assume significant responsibilities early on, but always have a place to turn for information, feedback and guidance. In addition to learning from lawyers with whom they are working, each associate is assigned an associate "sibling" and a partner "mentor" on whom he or she can rely for guidance. Learning is continuous, and much of this education comes from in-house seminars and Continuing Legal Education opportunities. For more information, please visit our website at www.goulstonstorrs.com.

© 2007 Vault Inc.

Bingham McCutchen LLP
150 Federal Street
Boston, MA 02110
Phone: (617) 951-8000
Fax: (617) 951-8736
www.bingham.com

Fiona Trevelyan
National Director of Legal Recruiting
Phone: (617) 951-8556
Fax: (617) 951-8736
E-mail: legalrecruit@bingham.com

Fish & Richardson P.C.
225 Franklin Street
Boston, MA 02110
Phone: (617) 542-5070
Fax: (617) 542-8906
www.fr.com

Ms. Kelly Mixon
Director of Attorney Hiring
Phone: (888) 314-8886
Fax: (512) 320-8935
E-mail: work@fr.com

Goodwin Procter LLP
Exchange Place
53 State Street
Boston, MA 02109
Phone: (617) 570-1000
www.goodwinprocter.com

Ms. Maureen Shea
Director of Legal Recruitment
Phone: (617) 570-1288
E-mail: mshea@goodwinprocter.com

Mintz Levin Cohn Ferris Glovsky and Popeo PC
One Financial Center
Boston, MA 02111
Phone: (617) 542-6000
Fax: (617) 542-2241
www.mintz.com

Ms. Kerry Oliver
Entry Level Associate Recruiting Manager
Phone: (617) 348-4414
Fax: (617) 542-2214
E-mail: koliver@mintz.com

Ropes & Gray LLP
One International Place
Boston, MA 02110
Phone: (617) 951-7000
www.ropesgray.com

Ms. Katharine von Mehren
Director of Legal Recruiting
Phone: (617) 951-7660
Fax: (617) 235 7690
E-mail:
katharine.vonmehren@ropesgray.com

Wilmer Cutler Pickering Hale and Dorr LLP
60 State Street
Boston, MA 02109
Phone: (617) 526-6000
www.wilmerhale.com

Ms. Karen Rameika
Legal Recruitment Manager
Phone: (617) 526-5565
E-mail:
boston.legalrecruiting@wilmerhale.com

MINNESOTA

Dorsey & Whitney LLP
50 South Sixth Street, Suite 1500
Minneapolis, MN 55402-1498
Phone: (612) 340-2600
www.dorsey.com

Ms. Kelsey Shuff
Director of Lawyer Recruiting
Phone: (612) 429-5181
E-mail: shuff.kelsey@dorsey.com

MISSOURI

Bryan Cave LLP
One Metropolitan Square
211 North Broadway, Suite 3600
St. Louis, MO
Phone: (314) 259-2000
www.bryancave.com

Ms. Jennifer Guirl
Recruiting Coordinator
Phone: (314) 259-2615
Fax: (314) 552-8615
E-mail: jguirl@bryancave.com

Bryan Cave LLP
One Kansas City Place
1200 Main Street, Suite 3500
Kansas City, MO 64105-2100
Phone: 816/374-3200
Fax: 816/374-3300
www.bryancave.com

Cristy M. Johnson
Recruiting and Professional Development
Manager - Kansas City
Phone: (816) 374-3362
Fax: (816) 374-3300
cmjohnson@bryancave.com

This Vault Legal Employer Directory is a special advertising section in the Vault Guide to the Top 100 Law Firms. For information on listing your firm in the directory, contact corporatesales@vault.com

NEW JERSEY

Lowenstein Sandler PC

Attorneys at Law
65 Livingston Avenue
Roseland, NJ 07068
Phone: (973) 597-2500
Fax: (973) 597-2400
www.lowenstein.com

Jane Thieberger
Director of Legal Personnel
Phone: (973) 597-2500
Fax: (973) 597-6117
E-mail: jthieberger@lowenstein.com

Number of Attorneys Firmwide: 273
Number of Attorneys in this Office: 240
Summer Associate Hires in this Office: 16 (2007)
Full-Time First-Year Hires in this Office: 25 (2007)

Lateral Hires in this Office: 45 (2006)
Summer Associate Salary (Weekly): $2,700 (2008)
First-Year Associate Salary (Base): $140,000 (2008)

Practice Areas: Bankruptcy, Corporate (M&A/Corporate Finance, Intellectual Property, Investment Management, Mortgage Finance, Real Estate, Technology, Venture Capital & Angel Investments), Employment (Employment Law & Litigation, Compensation & Benefits), Environmental, Litigation (Antitrust, Class-Actions, Commercial Litigation, Construction, Insurance, Securities Litigation, White Collar Crime), Tax (Corporate Tax, Estates & Trusts)

Law Schools Firm Recruits From:

Boston College, Boston University, Cardozo, Columbia, Cornell, Duke, Emory, Fordham, George Washington, Georgetown, Harvard, New York University, Rutgers-Newark, Seton Hall, UNC Law, Notre Dame, University of Pennsylvania, University of Virginia, Massachusetts Law School Consortium, NJ Law Firm Group Job Fair, Northeast BLSA Job Fair; Washington and Lee/William and Mary Job Fair.

Firm Leadership: Michael L. Rodburg, Managing Partner

Firm Description: Lowenstein Sandler's corporate department was ranked as the No. 1 corporate department in New Jersey in Chamber USA - America's Leading Lawyers for Business. The litigation department has won national acclaim from The National Law Journal. AmLaw's tech survey recently ranked it first among New Jersey law firms, and fourth nationally, in the use of technology. The firm has received both local and national awards for its pro bono activities. Lowenstein Sandler's headquarters are about 25 minutes from midtown Manhattan. The firm is the second largest law firm in New Jersey with over 270 attorneys. It is also recognized in the AmLaw 200 and The American Lawyer A-List.

© 2007 Vault Inc.

NEW YORK

Dorsey & Whitney LLP

250 Park Avenue
New York, NY 10177
Phone: (212) 415-9200
Fax: (212) 953-7201
www.dorsey.com

Number of Attorneys Firmwide: 631
Number of Attorneys in this Office: 70
Summer Associate Hires in this Office: 5 (2006)
Full-Time First-Year Hires in this Office: 4 (2006)

Shell Zambardi
Manager of Lawyer Recruiting
Phone: (212) 415-9200
Fax: (212) 953-7201
zambardi.shell@dorsey.com

Lateral Hires in this Office: 11 (2006)
Summer Associate Salary (Weekly): $2,400
First-Year Associate Salary (Base): $125,000

Practice Areas: Our NY attorneys specialize in a full range of practice areas, including corporate law (e.g., M&A, securities, hedge funds, commodities and derivatives, commercial finance, project finance, securitization and tax), litigation and alternative dispute resolution (e.g., securities, banking, insurance, white collar defense, international arbitration, and labor and employment) and intellectual property (e.g., trademark, copyright and patent litigation and counseling).

Law Schools Firm Recruits From: Dorsey accepts applications from students attending any law school. For a list of schools we visit for fall OCI, log onto our website at www.dorsey.com. Dorsey is looking for students who have achieved academic excellence and possess superior writing and analytical skills, as well as having demonstrated leadership, responsibility and creativity as participants in their Universities and communities.

Firm Leadership: Marianne Short, Managing Partner

Firm Description: Dorsey is one of the largest U.S. based international law firms. Our 600 lawyers are based in offices around the globe, but operate as one firm rather than as a collection of individual offices. Our NY office is at the center of the Firm's international practice and provides the best of all worlds: the resources of a large sophisticated global firm, the challenges of cutting-edge practice and a collegial atmosphere of a mid-size NYC firm dedicated to attorney development and world-class service for its US and foreign clients.

Kasowitz, Benson, Torres & Friedman LLP

1633 Broadway
New York, NY 10019
Phone: (212) 506-1700
Fax: (212) 506-1800
www.kasowitz.com

Number of Attorneys Firmwide: 234
Number of Attorneys in this Office: 197
Summer Associate Hires in this Office: 11 (2007)

Mindy J. Lindenman
Director of Legal Recruiting
Phone: (212) 506-1918
Fax: (212) 506-1800
E-mail: mlindenman@kasowitz.com

Lateral Hires: 47 (2007)
Summer Associate Salary (Weekly): $3,077 (2007)
First-Year Associate Salary (Base): $160,000 (2007)

Practice Areas: Antitrust; Appeals; Arbitration/ADR; Complex Commercial Litigation; Corporate; Creditors' Rights & Bankruptcy; Employment Practices; Environmental; Insurance Coverage; Intellectual Property; Mass Tort & Product Liability; Matrimonial & Family Law; Plaintiff's Representation; Real Estate; Securities; White Collar Crime

Law Schools Firm Recruits From: Cardoza; Columbia; Cornell; Emory University; Fordham; Georgetown; Harvard; Notre Dame; University of Michigan; University of Pennsylvania; University of Virginia; Northeast BLSA Job Fair.

Firm Leadership: Marc E. Kasowitz, Managing Partner; Aaron H. Marks, Hiring Partner

Firm Description: KBT&F has built a highly sophisticated, national practice specializing in complex civil litigation. The firm was founded in 1993 by leading lawyers from prominent law firms who sought to build an entrepreneurial firm where highly-talented lawyers are committed to pursuing creative, aggressive and winning approaches to our clients' most challenging legal matters. Our principal areas of practice are rapidly growing and intensely active.

This Vault Legal Employer Directory is a special advertising section in the Vault Guide to the Top 100 Law Firms. For information on listing your firm in the directory, contact corporatesales@vault.com

VAULT CAREER LIBRARY

639

Skadden, Arps, Slate, Meagher & Flom LLP

Four Times Square
New York, NY 10036
www.skadden.com

Ms. Carol Lee H. Sprague
Director, Associate/Alumni Relations & Attorney Recruiting
Phone: (212) 735-2076
E-mail: csprague@skadden.com

Number of Attorneys Firmwide: 1,790
Number of Attorneys in This Office: 707
Summer Associate Hires in This Office: 98 (2006);
  160 (2007)

Full-Time First-Year Hires in This Office: 93 (2007)
Summer Associate Salary (Weekly): $3,100 (2007)
First-Year Associate Salary (Base): $160,000 (2007)

Practice Areas: Antitrust; Corporate Restructuring; Banking; Corporate Finance; M&A; Litigation; Mass Torts; Real Estate; Tax; Intellectual Property; Project Finance; Investment Management; Structured Finance

Law Schools Firm Recruits From: Brooklyn, Boston College, Columbia, Cornell, Duke, Georgetown, Harvard, Michigan, New York University, Northwestern, Stanford, UCLA, Virginia, Yale, Boalt Hall, Texas, Chicago

Firm Leadership: Robert Sheehan, Executive Partner; Howard Ellin, Global Hiring Partner

Firm Description: The New York office of SASM&F is based in a state-of-the-art building at Four Times Square. This office is the headquarters of the Firm's national and international practices. Our clients are a substantial and diverse group which includes many "Fortune 500" companies. We are engaged in more than 40 practice areas as well as active in pro bono work. Our Summer Associates generally work 8-12 weeks; their work assignments are substantially the same as the work assignments for first-year associates. Our Firm is committed to the professional development and continued legal education of our attorneys. We have established a Committee on Diversity and Retention, and participate in numerous minority sponsored job fairs and conferences, as well as the Tulane Minority Clerkship Program.

Allen & Overy

1221 Avenue of the Americas
New York, NY 10020
Phone: (212) 610-6300
Fax: (212) 610-639
www.allenovery.com

Ms. Elizabeth Fuchs
Senior Manager, Legal Recruitment &
Associate Development
Phone: (212) 610-6300
E-mail: Elizabeth.Fuchs@allenovery.com

Boies, Schiller & Flexner LLP

575 Lexington Avenue, 7th Floor
New York, NY 10022
Phone: (212) 446-2300
www.bsfllp.com

Legal Recruiting Coordinator
Phone: (212) 446-2300
Fax: (212) 446-2350

Bryan Cave LLP

1290 Avenue of the Americas
New York, NY 10104-3300
Phone: (212) 541-2000
Fax: (212) 541-4630
www.bryancave.com

Nicole White
Recruiting and Professional Development
Manager - New York
Phone: (212) 541-3150
Fax: (212) 541-1450
nicole.white@bryancave.com

Cadwalader, Wickersham & Taft LLP

One World Financial Center
New York, NY 10281
Phone: (212) 504-6000
www.cadwalader.com

Ms. Monica R. Brenner
Manager of Legal Recruitment
Phone: (212) 504-6044
E-mail: monica.brenner@cwt.com

Cahill Gordon & Reindel LLP

80 Pine Street
New York, NY 10005
Phone: (212) 701-3000
Fax: (212) 269-5420
www.cahill.com

Legal Hiring Office
Cahill Gordon & Reindel LLP
Phone: (212) 701-3944
Fax: (212) 269-5420
E-mail: recruiting@cahill.com

Chadbourne & Parke LLP

30 Rockefeller Plaza
New York, NY 10112
Phone: (212) 408-5338
www.chadbourne.com

Ms. Lisa Featherson
Legal Recruiting Manager
Phone: (212) 408-5538
E-mail: recruiting@chadbourne.com

© 2007 Vault Inc.

A Few of Our Many Hats

At Chadbourne, our diverse array of practices means we wear a lot of different hats, from special investigations and litigation to intellectual property, project finance, renewable energy and a full range of corporate work. And we're committed to strategic growth in all practice areas. In fact, we've expanded our practices in all of these areas over the past year. Chadbourne offers attorneys the opportunity to develop their practices with the support of more than 400 lawyers in 12 U.S. and overseas offices. So before you throw your hat in the ring, try one of ours.

For more information, contact Sandra Bang, Director of Legal Personnel, (212) 408-5338.

CHADBOURNE
& PARKE LLP

www.chadbourne.com
New York Washington Los Angeles Houston
London (a multinational partnership) Moscow St. Petersburg
Warsaw (a Polish partnership) Kyiv Almaty Dubai Beijing

Cleary Gottlieb Steen & Hamilton LLP

One Liberty Plaza
New York, NY 10006
Phone: (212) 225-2000
www.cgsh.com

Ms. Norma F. Cirincione
Director of Legal Personnel
Phone: (212) 225-3150
Fax: (212) 225-3159
E-mail: nyrecruit@cgsh.com

Clifford Chance LLP

31 West 52nd Street
New York, NY 10019
Phone: (212) 878-8000
www.cliffordchance.com

Ms. Madeleine Conlon
Manager of Legal Recruiting
Phone: (212) 878-8252
Fax: (212) 878-8375
E-mail:
madeleine.conlon@cliffordchance.com

Cravath, Swaine & Moore LLP

Worldwide Plaza
825 Eighth Avenue
New York, NY 10019-7475
Phone: (212) 474-1000
www.cravath.com

Ms. Lisa A. Kalen
Associate Director of Legal Personnel &
Recruiting
Phone: (212) 474-3215
Fax: (212) 474-3225
E-mail: lkalen@cravath.com

Davis Polk & Wardwell

450 Lexington Avenue
New York, NY 10017
Phone: (212) 450-4000
www.dpw.com

Ms. Sharon L. Crane
Director of Legal Recruiting
Phone: (212) 450-4143
Fax: (212) 450-3143
E-mail: sharon.crane@dpw.com

Debevoise & Plimpton LLP

919 Third Avenue
New York, NY 10022
Phone: (212) 909-6000
www.debevoise.com

Ms. Sandra E. Herbst
Director of Legal Recruiting
Phone: (212) 909-6657
E-mail: recruit@debevoise.com

Dechert LLP

30 Rockefeller Plaza
New York, NY 10112
Phone: (212) 698-3500
www.dechert.com

Ms. Susie E. Elitzky
Director of Recruiting, US
Phone: (212) 698-3523
Fax: (212) 698-3599
E-mail: legal.recruiting@dechert.com

Dewey Ballantine LLP

1301 Avenue of the Americas
New York, NY 10019
Phone: (212) 259-8000
www.deweyballantine.com

Ms. Nicole Gunn
Manager of Legal Recruitment
Phone: (212) 259-7050
Fax: (212) 259-6333
E-mail:
db.recruitment@deweyballantine.com

DLA Piper

1251 Avenue of the Americas
27th Floor
New York, NY 10020-1104
Phone: (212) 335-4500
www.dlapiper.com

Ms. Diane Ross
Director of Legal Recruiting
Phone: (202) 689-7948
E-mail: diane.ross@dlapiper.com

Freshfields Bruckhaus Deringer

520 Madison Avenue, 34th Floor
New York, NY 10022
Phone: (212) 277-4000
www.freshfields.com

Ms. Margaux Gillman
US Legal Recruiting Manager
Phone: (212) 284-4999
Fax: (212) 277-4001
E-mail: margaux.gillman@freshfields.com

Fried, Frank, Harris, Shriver & Jacobson LLP

One New York Plaza
New York, NY 10004
Phone: (212) 859-8000
www.friedfrank.com

Robert O. Edwards, Esq.
Director of Legal Recruitment
Phone: (212) 859-8671
E-mail: robert.edwards@friedfrank.com

Holland & Knight LLP

195 Broadway, 24th Floor
New York, NY 10007
Phone: (212) 513-3200
www.hklaw.com

Ms. Carrie Weintraub
Chief Professional Development and
Recruiting Officer
Phone: (813) 769-4314
E-mail: carrie.weintraub@hklaw.com

Hughes Hubbard & Reed LLP

One Battery Park Plaza
New York, NY 10004
Phone: (212) 837-6000
Fax: (212) 422-4726
www.hugheshubbard.com

Mr. Adrian Cockerill
Director of Legal Employment
Phone: (212) 837-6131
E-mail: cockeril@hugheshubbard.com

KayeScholer LLP

425 Park Avenue
New York, NY 10022
Phone: (212) 836-8000
www.kayescholer.com

Ms. Melissa Huffman
Legal Personnel Administrator
Phone: (212) 836-8893
Fax: (212) 836-7153
E-mail: mhuffman@kayescholer.com

Kelley Drye & Warren LLP

101 Park Avenue
New York, NY 10178
Phone: (212) 808-7800
Fax: (212) 808-7897
www.kelleydrye.com

Tina Metis, Esq.
Manager of Legal Recruiting
Phone: (212) 808-7728
Fax: (212) 808-7897
E-mail: tmetis@kelleydrye.com

Kramer Levin Naftalis & Frankel LLP

1177 Avenue of the Americas
New York, NY 10036
Phone: (212) 715-9100
Fax: (212) 715-8000
www.kramerlevin.com

Ms. Jennifer Cullert
Director of Legal Recruiting
New York, NY 10036
Phone: (212) 715-9213
E-mail: legalrecruiting@kramerlevin.com

© 2007 Vault Inc.

LeBoeuf, Lamb, Greene & MacRae LLP

125 West 55th Street
New York, NY 10019
Phone: (212) 424-8000
Fax: (212) 424-8500
www.llgm.com

Ms. Lauren Rasmus
Director of Legal Recruiting
Phone: (212) 424-8000
Fax: (212) 424-8500
E-mail: llgmrecruiting@llgm.com

Linklaters

1345 Avenue of the Americas
New York, NY 10105
Phone: (212) 903-9000
www.linklaters.com

Ms. Anne Mahoney
Legal Recruitment Manager
Phone: (212) 830-9603
Fax: (212) 903-9100
E-mail: anne.mahoney@linklaters.com

Manatt, Phelps & Phillips, LLP

30 S. Pearl Street, 12th Floor
Albany, NY 12207
Phone: (518) 431-6700
Fax: (518) 431-6767
www.manatt.com

Patricia Sanjuan
Recruiting Coordinator
Phone: (212) 830-7185
Fax: (212) 536-1839
psanjuan@manatt.com

Manatt, Pelps & Phillips, LLP

7 Times Square
New York, NY 10036
Phone: (212) 790-4500
Fax: (212) 790-4545

Patricia Sanjuan
Recruiting Coordinator
Phone: (212) 830-7185
Fax: (212) 536-1839
psanjuan@manatt.com

Milbank, Tweed, Hadley & McCloy LLP

One Chase Manhattan Plaza
New York, NY 10005
www.milbank.com

Ms. Joanne Dezego
Manager of Legal Recruiting
Phone: (212) 530-5966
E-mail: jdezego@milbank.com

Nixon Peabody LLP

437 Madison Avenue
New York, NY 10022
Phone: (212) 940-3000
Fax: (212) 940-3111
www.nixonpeabody.com

Ms. Julie Zammuto
National Lateral Attorney Recruiting
Manager
Phone: (617) 345-1161
E-mail: jzammuto@nixonpeabody.com

Orrick Herrington & Sutcliffe LLP

666 Fifth Avenue
New York, NY 10103-001
Phone: (212) 506-5000
www.orrick.com

Ms. Karen Massa
Firmwide Attorney Recruiting Manager
Phone: (415) 773-5588
Fax: (415) 415-773-5759
E-mail: kmassa@orrick.com

Paul, Hastings, Janofsky & Walker LLP

Park Avenue Tower
75 E. 55th Street
First Floor
New York, NY 10022
Phone: (212) 318-6000
Fax: (212) 319-4090
www.paulhastings.com

Mr. Demetrius Greer
Director of Attorney Recruiting
Phone: (213) 683-6000
E-mail: recruit@paulhastings.com

Paul, Weiss, Rifkind, Wharton & Garrison LLP

1285 Avenue of the Americas
New York, NY 10019
Phone: (212) 373-3000
www.paulweiss.com

Pamela H. Nelson
Legal Recruitment Director
Phone: (212) 373-2548
Fax: (212) 373-2205
E-mail: pnelson@paulweiss.com

Pillsbury Winthrop Shaw Pittman LLP

1540 Broadway
New York, NY 10036
Phone: (212) 858-1000
www.pillsburylaw.com

Angela Eliane
Phone: (212) 858-1000
Fax: (212) 858-1500
E-mail: Recruit_NY@pillsburylaw.com

Proskauer Rose LLP

1585 Broadway
New York, NY 10036
Phone: (212) 969-3000
www.proskauer.com

Ms. Diane M. Kolnik
Manager of Legal Recruiting
Phone: (212) 969-5071
E-mail: dkolnik@proskauer.com

Quinn Emanuel Urquhart Oliver & Hedges LLP

51 Madison Ave., 22nd Floor
New York, NY 10010
Phone: (212) 849-7000
Fax: (212) 849-7100
www.quinnemanuel.com

Zoe Ehrlich
East Coast Director of Recruiting
Phone: (212) 702-8100
Fax: (212) 849-7100
E-mail: zoeehrlich@quinnemanuel.com

Schulte Roth & Zabel LLP

919 Third Avenue
New York, NY 10022
Phone: (212) 756-2000
Fax: (212) 593-5955
www.srz.com

Alissa K. Golden
Manager of Legal Recruiting
Phone: (212) 610-7185
Fax: (212) 593-5955
E-mail: alissa.golden@srz.com

Shearman & Sterling LLP

599 Lexington Avenue
New York, NY 10022
Phone: (212) 848-4000
www.shearman.com

Ms. Trisha Weiss
Professional Recruiting
Phone: (212) 848-8977
E-mail: trisha.weiss@shearman.com

This Vault Legal Employer Directory is a special advertising section in the Vault Guide to the Top 100
Law Firms. For information on listing your firm in the directory, contact corporatesales@vault.com

VAULT CAREER LIBRARY   643

Simpson Thacher & Bartlett LLP

425 Lexington Avenue
New York, NY 10017
Phone: (212) 455-2000
www.simpsonthacher.com

Ms. Dee Pifer
Director Legal Employment
Phone: (212) 455-2698
Fax: (212) 455-2502
E-mail: dpifer@stblaw.com

Stroock & Stroock & Lavan LLP

180 Maiden Lane
New York, NY 10038-4982
Phone: (212) 806-5400
www.stroock.com

Ms. Bernadette L. Miles
Director of Legal Personnel & Recruiting
Phone: (212) 806-7070
E-mail: bmiles@stroock.com

Sullivan & Cromwell LLP

125 Broad Street
New York, NY 10004
Phone: (212) 558-4000
www.sullcrom.com

Ms. Patricia J. Morrissy
Phone: (212) 558-3518
Fax: (212) 558-3588
E-mail: morrissyp@sullcrom.com

Thacher Proffitt & Wood LLP

Two World Financial Center
New York, NY 10281
Phone: (212) 912-7400
www.tpw.com

Ms. Sarah Cannady
Director of Legal Personnel
Phone: (212) 912-7859
Fax: (212) 912-7751
E-mail: scannady@tpw.com

Thelen Reid Brown Raysman & Steiner LLP

875 Third Avenue
New York, NY 10022-6225
Phone: (212) 603-2000
Fax: (212) 603-2001
www.thelen.com

Ms. Sela Seleska
National Attorney Recruiting Manager
Phone: (415) 369-7636
E mail: sseleska@thelen.com

Wachtell, Lipton, Rosen & Katz

51 West 52nd Street
New York, NY 10019-6150
Phone: (212) 403-1000
www.wlrk.com

Ms. Elizabeth F. Breslow
Director of Recruiting & Legal Personnel
Phone: (212) 403-1334
Fax: (212) 403-2000

E-mail: efbreslow@wlrk.com

Weil, Gotshal & Manges LLP

767 Fifth Avenue
New York, NY 10153
(212) 310-8000
www.weil.com

Ms. Petal Modeste
Director, Legal Recruiting
Phone: (212) 833-3669
Fax: (212) 310-8007
E-mail: recruit@weil.com

White & Case LLP

1155 Avenue of the Americas
New York, NY 10036
Phone: (212) 819-8200
www.whitecase.com

Ms. Jane P. Stein
Assistant Director, Attorney Recruiting
Phone: (212) 819-8271
Fax: (212) 354-8113
E-mail: recruit@whitecase.com

Willkie Farr & Gallagher LLP

787 Seventh Avenue
New York, NY 10019
Phone: (212) 728-8000
www.willkie.com

Ms. Bonnie Hurry
Chief Legal Personnel Officer
Phone: (212) 728-8495
E-mail: bhurry@willkie.com

NORTH CAROLINA

Cadwalader, Wickersham & Taft LLP

227 West Trade Street, 24th Floor
Charlotte, NC 28202
Phone: (704) 348-5100
Fax: (704) 348-5200
www.cadwalader.com

Lauren E. Marsh
Legal Recruitment Coordinator
Phone: (704) 348-5126
Fax: (704) 331-3052
E-mail: lauren.marsh@cwt.com

© 2007 Vault Inc.

OHIO

Baker & Hostetler LLP
3200 National City Center
1900 East 9th Street
Cleveland, OH 44114-3485
Phone: (216) 621-0200
Fax: (216) 696-0740
www.bakerlaw.com

Ms. Moushumi Brody
Recruiting Coordinator
Phone: (216) 861-7479
Fax: (216) 696-0740
E-mail: mbrody@bakerlaw.com

**Squire, Sanders & Dempsey
L.L.P.**
Administration Center
1500 West Third Street, Suite 450
Cleveland, OH 44113-1408
Phone: (800) 743-1773
Fax: (216) 687-3401
www.ssd.com

Ms. Crystal L. Arnold
Firmwide Recruiting Coordinator
Phone: (216) 687-3465
Fax: (216) 687-3401
E-mail: carnold@ssd.com

PENNSYLVANIA

**Kirkpatrick & Lockhart Preston
Gates Ellis, LLP**
Henry W. Oliver building
535 Smithfield Street
Pittsburgh, PA 15222-2312
Phone: (412) 355-6500
Fax: (412) 355-6501
www.klgates.com

Roslyn M. Pitts
Director of Legal Recruitment and
Professional Development (U.S.)
Phone: (412) 355-6500
E-mail: roz.pitts@klgates.com

Morgan, Lewis & Bockius LLP
1701 Market Street
Philadelphia, PA 19103
Phone: (215) 963-5000
www.morganlewis.com

Ms. Lindsay A. Callantine
Legal Recruiting Manager
Phone: (215) 963-5105
E-mail: lcallantine@morganlewis.com

Reed Smith
435 Sixth Avenue
Pittsburgh, PA 15219
Phone: (412) 288-3131
Fax: (412) 288-3063
www.reedsmith.com

Dana B. Levin
US Director of Legal Recruiting
Phone: (215) 851-1406
E-mail: dlevin@reedsmith.com

TEXAS

Baker Botts LLP
One Shell Plaza
910 Louisiana
Houston, TX 77002 4995
Phone: (713) 229-1234
www.bakerbotts.com

Ms. Melissa O. Moss
Manager of Attorney Employment
Phone: (713) 229-2056
Fax: (713) 229-7856
E-mail: melissa.moss@bakerbotts.com

Chadbourne & Parke LLP
1100 Louisiana
Suite 3500
Houston, TX 77002
Phone: (713) 571-5900
Fax: (713) 571-5970
www.chadbourne.com

David Schumacher
Managing Partner
(713) 571-5900
dschumacher@chadbourne.com

Fulbright & Jaworski L.L.P.
1301 McKinney, Suite 5100
Houston, TX 77010-3095
Phone: (713) 651-5151
Fax: (713) 651-5246
www.fulbright.com

Ms. Leslie Rice
Director of Attorney Recruiting
Phone: (713) 651-5518
Fax: (713) 651-5246
E-mail: lrice@fulbright.com

Vinson & Elkins, L.L.P.
1001 Fannin Street, Suite 2300
Houston, TX 77002-6760
Phone: (800) 833-1594
Fax: (713) 615-5245
www.velaw.com

Ms. Patty Harris
Director of Attorney Employment &
Development
Phone: (713) 758-4544
Fax: (713) 615-5245

E-mail: pharris@velaw.com

This Vault Legal Employer Directory is a special advertising section in the Vault Guide to the Top 100
Law Firms. For information on listing your firm in the directory, contact corporatesales@vault.com

VAULT CAREER LIBRARY   645

VIRGINIA

Hunton & Williams
Riverfront Plaza, East Tower
951 East Byrd Street
Richmond, VA 23219-4074
Phone: (804) 788-8200
Fax: (804) 788-8218
www.hunton.com

Amee R. McKim
Legal Recruiting Director
Phone: (804) 788-7395
E-mail: amckim@hunton.com

McGuireWoods LLP
901 East Cary Street
Richmond, VA 23219
Phone: (804) 775-1000
Fax: (804) 775-1061
www.mcguirewoods.com

Ms. Ann McGhee
Firmwide Manager of Attorney Recruiting
901 East Cary Street
Richmond, Virginia 23219
Fax: (804) 775-1061

WASHINGTON

Perkins Coie LLP
1201 Third Avenue, Suite 4800
Seattle, WA 98101-3099
Phone: (206) 359-8000
Fax: (206) 359-9000
www.perkinscoie.com

Ms. Laura Kader
Legal Recruiting Manager-SEA
Phone: (206) 359-3174
Fax: (206) 359-4174
E-mail:
lawstudenthiringSEA@perkinscoie.com

WISCONSIN

Foley & Lardner LLP
777 E. Wisconsin Avenue
Milwaukee, WI 53202-5306
Phone: (414) 271-2400
Fax: (414) 297-4900
www.foley.com
www.foleyrecruiting.com

Ms. Kara E. Nelson
Director, Legal Recruiting & Development
Phone: (414) 297-5587
E-mail: kenelson@foley.com

© 2007 Vault Inc.

LEGAL
RECRUITING
FIRM DIRECTORY

Arizona

Phyllis Hawkins & Associates, Inc.

105 East Northern Avenue
Phoenix, AZ 85020
Phone: (602) 263-0248
Fax: (602) 678-1564
www.azlawsearch.com

Phyllis Hawkins
President
Phone: (602) 263-0248
Fax: (602) 678-1564
phassoc@qwest.net

Looking for a legal position? Need a change of venue?

Find your dream career opportunity on the Vault Law Job Board. Featuring hundreds of top positions throughout the U.S. and Canada.

Positions for all positions, including:

- Associate
- Partner
- Paralegal
- In-house Counsel

Positions in all practice areas, including

- Corporate
- Intellectual Property
- Labor/Employment
- Litigation
- Real Estate
- Tax
- Trusts & Estates

Go to www.vault.com/law

California

ABA Search Staffing

33 New Montgomery Street
Suite 800
San Francisco, CA 94105
Phone: (415) 434-4222
Fax: (415) 434-3958
www.abastaff.com

Since 1986, ABA has been bringing together uniquely skilled legal professionals with high caliber law firms and corporate legal departments. Our placements range from attorneys and general counsels (managed nationwide by our Search division) to paralegals, litigation support teams, contract administrators, legal secretaries, and case clerks (facilitated in the SF Bay Area by our Staffing team).

ABA has built its business by gathering more and better information from clients and candidates and then using that knowledge to create high quality employment matches. By taking a personal interest in the needs of our clients and candidates, spending the time to ask comprehensive, detailed questions, and consistently listening more than we speak, ABA achieves results that exceed the expectations of the individuals we serve. Thats what makes us "the name to know in legal recruiting."

Garb Jaffe & Associates Legal Placement, LLC

12100 Wilshire Boulevard, Mezzanine Level, Suite 90
Los Angeles, CA 90025
Phone: (310) 207-0727 | Fax: (310) 207-0470
www.garbjaffe.com

Eve Jaffe, Esq., President
Phone: (310) 998-3388
evejaffe@garbjaffe.com

Garb Jaffe & Associates Legal Placement LLC was founded in 1992 and specializes in placing both partners and associates within law firms and corporations in Southern California. We work with virtually every law firm in Southern California that utilizes the services of legal recruiters. All of our active recruiters are attorneys that graduated from top law schools and practiced law in Southern California.
One reason clients come to Garb Jaffe & Associates, and also provide frequent referrals, is due to our commitment to excellence and ethics. We have offices in the Los Angeles and Orange County/San Diego areas.
Member of NALSC. We abide by the NALSC Code of Ethics.

© 2007 Vault Inc.

JM Associates

Client-Centered Marketing Programs
Consulting " Retreats "Training

2222 Martin
Suite 255
Irvine, CA 92612
Phone: (949) 260-9200 | **Fax:** (949) 260-0940
www.jmassociates.com

Emily Friedman, Esq., Director of Recruiting
Phone: (949) 260-0945
efriedman@jmassociates.com

Since 1988, JM Associates has assisted attorneys with full time placement to achieve career success and satisfaction beyond their expectations. More than 98% of our placements have withstood the test of time because we listen, communicate, and work tirelessly to create the perfect match. As a member of the National Association of Legal Search Consultants (NALSC), we subscribe to a stringent code of ethics that guarantees our candidates strict confidentiality, dignity and respect.

Looking for a legal position? Need a change of venue?

Find your dream career opportunity on the Vault Law Job Board. Featuring hundreds of top positions throughout the U.S. and Canada.

Positions for all positions, including:

* Associate
* Partner
* Paralegal
* In-house Counsel

Positions in all practice areas, including

* Corporate
* Intellectual Property
* Labor/Employment
* Litigation
* Real Estate
* Tax
* Trusts & Estates

Go to www.vault.com/law

Katharine C. Patterson Consulting, Inc.

235 Montgomery Street
Suite 1850
San Francisco, CA 94104
Phone: (415) 398-2622 / (800) 248-6556 (U.S. Toll Free)
Fax: (415) 391-2826

Katharine C. Patterson, President
Phone: (415) 398-2622
gneisserperson@msn.com

Reece Legal Search, Inc.

555 W. Fifth Street
Suite 3100
Los Angeles, CA 90013
Phone: (213) 996-8585
Fax: (213) 996-8579
www.reecelegalsearch.com

reece
legal
search

ATTORNEY SEARCH CONSULTANTS

Carl D. Reece
info@reecelegalsearch.com

Number of Recruiters/Consultants: 3
Domestic office locations: Los Angeles
Date founded: 1999
Percentage of Business Devoted to Placing Attorneys: 100%
% of Placements Law Firm vs. Corporate Legal Departments:
80% Law Firm and 20% In-House

Carl D. Reece, the firm's founder and principal, has been a legal recruiter since 1987. He has placed associates and partners at premier national and boutique law firms and Fortune 500 companies globally. His clients have expertise in a wide array of practice specialties, including banking, bankruptcy, corporate securities entertainment, finance, intellectual property and real estate law.

Before establishing RLS in 1999, Mr. Reece was a senior attorney search consultant with a nationally recognized recruiting firm based in Los Angeles. He has been a contributing panelist and seminar moderator at numerous industry conferences. Most recently, he was a guest lecturer at the University of Southern California School of Law. He is currently Co-President of the National Association of Legal Search Consultants (NALSC).

The Vault Legal Recruiter Directory is a special advertising section in the *Vault Guide to the Top 100 Law Firms*.
For information on listing your firm in the directory, contact H.S. Hamadeh, Esq. at hshamadeh@staff.vault.com.

Rifkin Consulting, Inc.

PMB 423
30251 Golden Lantern
Suite E
Laguna Niguel, CA 92677
Phone: 949-218-1925
Fax: 949-218-0374
www.rifkinconsulting.com

info@rifkinconsulting.com

Rifkin Consulting, Inc. focuses on attorney placement of associates and partners with law firms and corporations, including group mergers and acquisitions, in all practice areas. Our geographic market is primarily California, with both national and international affiliates. Rifkin Consulting also provides career and interview counseling, compensation analysis, business development skills, compensation negotiation and resume building services to clients and candidates. Personalized service and uncompromised integrity are the standards upon which we base our reputation.

Rifkin Consulting, Inc. is a member of NALSC and abides by its Code of Ethics. All inquiries are treated with the utmost confidentiality.

Russo & Fondell, Inc.

RUSSO & FONDELL, INC.
ATTORNEY SEARCH CONSULTANTS

190 N. Canon Dr., Suite 300
Beverly Hills, CA 90210
Phone: (310) 277-1717 | **Fax:** (310) 277-3777
www.russofondell.com

Joan Fondell or Mary Jo Russo, Principals
info@russofondell.com

In a survey of top law firms in California, Russo & Fondell. Inc. received highest praise, recognized as Headhunters Extraordinaire and was rated one of California's top legal recruiting firms. Russo & Fondell is considered a leader in the placement of Associates, Partners and Counsel in law firms and corporations. The firm strictly adheres to NALSC's Code of Ethics.
The two principals, Mary Jo Russo and Joan Fondell, have a combined 43 years of legal recruiting experience. They have extensive contacts throughout California and nationwide and have developed outstanding relationships with law firms and corporations. Their professionalism is measured by the trust and respect of their clients and candidates.

Seltzer Fontaine Beckwith

2999 Overland Avenue, Suite 120
Los Angeles, CA 90064
Phone: (310) 839-6000
Fax: (310) 829-4408

www.sfbsearch.com
Madeleine Seltzer or Valerie Fontaine
Partners
Phone: (310) 839-6000
info@sfbsearch.com

The Vault Legal Recruiter Directory

is a special advertising section in the *Vault Guide to the Top 100 Law Firms*. For information on listing your firm in next year's directory, or our legal recruiting directories in other Vault law guides, contact H.S. Hamadeh, Esq. at hshamadeh@staff.vault.com.

Vault Law Career Guides include:

• Vault Guide to Top 100 Law Firms
• Vault Regional Law Firm Guides (New York, Washington, DC, Boston, Chicago, Texas, etc.)
• Vault Practice Area Guides (Corporate, Litigation, Labor & Employment, Bankruptcy, etc.)

© 2007 Vault Inc.

District of Columbia

GroupMagellan Attorney Placement

1050 17th Steet N.W.
Suite 600
Washington, DC 20036
Phone: (202) 625-0606 | **Fax:** (202) 625-0315
www.groupmagellan.com

Tom Goldstein, Esquire, President, Career Counselor
tom@groupmagellan.com

Professional and experienced career counseling for positions at the partner, of counsel, and associate levels. Call or email us for confidential career counseling and job placement. We place candidates in top law firms and companies in the Washington, D.C. metro and Boston, Massachusetts metro areas. Questions about trends in the job market, and non-profit or Capitol Hill careers are also welcome. Staffed by attorneys, and founded by Yale law school graduate and former Skadden Arps associate.

The Vault Legal Recruiter Directory

is a special advertising section in the *Vault Guide to the Top 100 Law Firms*. For information on listing your firm in next year's directory, or our legal recruiting directories in other Vault law guides, contact H.S. Hamadeh, Esq. at hshamadeh@staff.vault.com.

Vault Law Career Guides include:

- Vault Guide to Top 100 Law Firms
- Vault Regional Law Firm Guides (New York, Washington, DC, Boston, Chicago, Texas, etc.)
- Vault Practice Area Guides (Corporate, Litigation, Labor & Employment, Bankruptcy, etc.)

Legal Placements Inc.

LEGAL PLACEMENTS INCORPORATED
We put the pros in place™

901 15th St., NW
Suite 1050
Washington, DC 20005
Phone: (703) 917-1829
Fax: (703) 917-1841
www.legalplacements.com

Amy Savage, Executive Attorney Recruiter
Phone: (703) 917-1829 x224
Amy.savage@legalplacements.com

Legal Placements, Inc (LPI) is a leading provider of professionals to the legal industry. Since 1996, LPI has been providing a large array of these individuals for temporary and permanent positions within law firms and corporate legal departments. Collectively, the professionals at LPI bring over 80 years of high-quality staffing experience to the clients we serve.

LPI is comprised of three divisions; Legal Placements, IT Placements and Proven Placements. Each division has a unique focus to recruit specific individuals with expertise in a specialized field. These three divisions combined work with a variety of attorneys, paralegals, law clerks, legal secretaries, technical professionals, administrative personnel as well as other legal professionals.

At LPI, we carefully screen all candidates through a precise interviewing process, which includes extensive resume review, meeting each candidate in person, portfolio and project review, salary history review, complete references, degree verification, bar status and criminal background checks. Upon the client's request, we also conduct drug screening of our candidates. All of this collected data is shared directly with clients so that everyone is well informed about each candidate.

We realize that not all businesses operate under traditional business hours. Therefore, the staff of LPI is available 24-hours a day, 7-days a week through a contemporary paging system. Leaving a voice-mail in a LPI employee's voice mailbox activates their pager.

The Vault Legal Recruiter Directory is a special advertising section in the *Vault Guide to the Top 100 Law Firms*.
For information on listing your firm in the directory, contact H.S. Hamadeh, Esq. at hshamadeh@staff.vault.com.

VAULT CAREER LIBRARY   651

Florida

AMERICAN Legal Search, LLC

Where Lawyers Look for Lawyers®

Founded in 2001, AMERICAN Legal Search, LLC has continued its rapid growth and has established itself with eight regional offices serving lawyers, law firms and corporations throughout the United States and abroad.

With a team comprised of the premier legal recruiters in the industry, AMERICAN Legal Search is the country's best resource for legal talent.

AMERICAN Legal Search operates three core business divisions:

- Permanent Attorney Search and Placement
- Contract Attorneys
- Law Firm Mergers, Expansions, and Practice Group Acquisitions

For information on specialized attorney search services, please visit www.AmericanLegalSearch.com or contact your Regional Office at:

Atlanta, GA	(404) 745-9050
Birmingham	(205) 397-9500
Houston	(713) 864-4222
Los Angeles	(310) 914-0011
Louisville	(502) 935-2929
Miami	(305) 466-4619
Nashville	(615) 251-9600
New York	(212) 984-1086
Or Toll Free:	(888) 220-9111

Please visit www.AmericanSearchCompanies.com for other professional placement services.

Illinois

McCormack Schreiber Legal Search Inc.

303 West Madison Street, Suite 2150
Chicago, IL 60606
Phone: 312.377.2000 / **Toll Free:**
866.819.4091
Fax: 312.377.2001
www.thelawrecruiters.com

Amy L. McCormack and Gay R. Schreiber, Principals
info@thelawrecruiters.com

McCormack Schreiber Legal Search Inc. is the largest all attorney search firm in Chicago. At McCormack Schreiber, we place associates and partners at large, midsize and boutique law firms, and in-house counsel of all levels at regional, national and international corporations. McCormack Schreiber also participates in acquisitions and transfers of practice groups, and in law firm mergers. The principals and recruiters at McCormack Schreiber have over 70 years of combined experience as practicing attorneys and as legal recruiters. McCormack Schreiber is a member of the NALSC, and Amy McCormack is on its Board of Directors. We welcome the opportunity to assist you, in confidence, with your search and placement needs.

www.thelawrecruiters.com

© 2007 Vault Inc.

Where Lawyers Look for Lawyers®

AMERICAN Legal Search, LLC is one of the nation's fastest growing legal search firms, and we've built a team of the premier legal recruiters in the industry.

So if you think you've exhausted all possibilities, we're prepared to take it one step further.

2006 Honoree

(888) 220-9111

www.AmericanLegalSearch.com

Atlanta • Birmingham • Houston • Los Angeles
Louisville • Miami • Nashville • New York

Use the Internet's
MOST TARGETED
job search tools.

Vault Job Board

Target your search by industry, function, and experience level, and find the job openings that you want.

VaultMatch Resume Database

Vault takes match-making to the next level: post your resume and customize your search by industry, function, experience and more. We'll match job listings with your interests and criteria and e-mail them directly to your in-box.

> the most trusted name in career information™

New Jersey

E M Messick Legal Recruiting & Consulting

E·M·MESSICK
LEGAL RECRUITING & CONSULTING

444 Washington Blvd.
Suite 2331
Jersey City, NJ 07310
Phone: (201) 386-9484 • **Fax:** (253) 660-2326
www.emmcjob.com

Edna Messick, President
info@emmcjob.com

E M Messick Legal Recruiting & Consulting, Legal search and consulting firm, places corporate counsel, partners and junior/senior-level associates in major corporations and international law firms worldwide. The firm specializes in the placement of diverse candidates in the areas of Banking, Bankruptcy, Corporate, Corporate Securities, Mergers and Acquisitions, International Finance, Structured Finance, Project Finance, Intellectual Property, Tax, ERISA, Real Estate, Litigation and Labor and Employment. Consulting services are also available for firms contemplating mergers and practice group acquisitions.

The Vault Legal Recruiter Directory

is a special advertising section in the *Vault Guide to the Top 100 Law Firms*. For information on listing your firm in next year's directory, or our legal recruiting directories in other Vault law guides, contact H.S. Hamadeh, Esq. at hshamadeh@staff.vault.com.

Vault Law Career Guides include:

• Vault Guide to Top 100 Law Firms
• Vault Regional Law Firm Guides (New York, Washington, DC, Boston, Chicago, Texas, etc.)
• Vault Practice Area Guides (Corporate, Litigation, Labor & Employment, Bankruptcy, etc.)

Oliveras & Company, Inc.

1605 John Street
Suite 119
Fort Lee, NJ 07024
Phone: (201) 947-6662
Fax: (201) 947-5934
www.oliverascoinc.com

Wendy Oliveras, MS, President & CEO
Phone: (201) 947-6662
wo@oliverascoinc.com

Oliveras & Company, Inc. ("OC") is a full service professional attorney search firm specializing in the recruitment of intellectual property attorneys, partners, practice groups, and IP and general firm mergers and acquisitions. Recruitment services are also provided for all legal and administrative support staff, including all Human Resources positions. OC's clientele includes law firms, in-house legal departments, and corporations, most of whom have domestic and international presence. OC is unique in that it brings over 22 years of hands-on experience in the legal, intellectual property and recruitment industries. Other specialized services include Career Planning and Development Services.

Looking for a legal position? Need a change of venue?

Find your dream career opportunity on the Vault Law Job Board. Featuring hundreds of top positions throughout the U.S. and Canada.

Positions for all positions, including:

• Associate
• Partner
• Paralegal
• In-house Counsel

Positions in all practice areas, including

• Corporate
• Intellectual Property
• Labor/Employment
• Litigation
• Real Estate
• Tax
• Trusts & Estates

Go to www.vault.com/law

The Vault Legal Recruiter Directory is a special advertising section in the *Vault Guide to the Top 100 Law Firms*.
For information on listing your firm in the directory, contact H.S. Hamadeh, Esq. at hshamadeh@staff.vault.com.

VAULT CAREER LIBRARY   655

New York

Ann Israel & Associates, Inc.

ANN ISRAEL & ASSOCIATES
CONSULTANTS TO THE LEGAL COMMUNITY

The Crown Building
730 Fifth Avenue, Suite 900
New York, NY 10019
Phone: (212) 659-7730 | **Fax:** (212) 659-7731
www.attorneysearch.com

Ann Israel, President
aisrael@annisrael.com

Ann Israel & Associates dedicates itself to serving the search and consulting needs of the global legal community. With a large and diverse network of contacts, along with one of the most sophisticated and extensive databases known in the legal search profession, we offer a broad range of recruiting and consulting services.

Ann Israel is the immediate Past President of the National Association of Legal Search Consultants (NALSC) and served on the Board of Directors for over 12 years. Ann writes a weekly advice column called, "Advice for the Lawlorn." Please visit the column through the link at www.attorneysearch.com, or at www.nylawyer.com, or at www.law.com; we encourage you to submit questions.

Gardiner Simpson Legal Search, Inc.

10 Park Avenue
New York, NY 10016
Phone: (212) 779-1125 | **Fax:** (212) 696-4524

Donna Hurry, Managing Director
Phone: (212) 779-1125
dhurry@garsim.com

J. Smith Associates, Inc.

420 Lexington Avenue
Suite 1708
New York, NY 10170
Phone: (212) 867-9203 | **Fax:** (212) 867-9219
www.smithcounsel.com

Judith E. Smith, President
Phone: (212) 867-9203
info@smithcounsel.com

Greene-Levin-Snyder LLC

greene
levin
snyder
llc

150 E. 58th Street
16th Floor
New York, NY 10155
Phone: (212) 752-5200 | **Fax:** (212) 752-8245
www.glslsg.com

Karin L. Greene, Alisa F. Levin, Esq., Susan Kurz Snyder, Esq., Principals
search@glslsg.com

Greene-Levin-Snyder conducts exclusive and co-exclusive searches for General Counsel, partners, in-house counsel and associates of all levels in every practice area. The firm also places lawyers in business and quasi-business positions. Clients include domestic and international law firms as well as financial institutions, media and entertainment companies, and a variety of other corporations. Many of our twelve search professionals are former practicing attorneys who, combined, have over five decades of legal search expertise. Search consultants work in teams to ensure that clients receive the full benefit of our collective knowledge and experience. The firm provides permanent placement as well as long-term temporary placement, career counseling and strategic planning services. Member NALSC, WBENC.

Klein Windmiller, LLC

Klein Windmiller
Legal Search Consultants

230 Park Avenue
10th Floor
New York, NY 10017
Phone: (212) 808-3038
Fax: (212) 808-4082
www.kwrecruit.com

E-mail: mk@kwrecruit.com

Klein Windmiller, LLC is a global attorney placement firm with offices in New York and San Francisco. Our focus is a more personalized approach toward legal placement. With a staff composed of four attorney recruiters and two professional consultants, we work in teams to offer candidates the benefit of our combined knowledge and responsive service. We conduct searches for general counsel, partners, in-house counsel and associates of all levels in every practice area. Our clients include domestic and international law firms, investment banks and a variety of financial and consumer products companies.

© 2007 Vault Inc.

Lateral Link Group, LLC

LATERAL LINK

319 Lafaeyette St. #204
New York, NY 10012
USA
Phone: 866.374.5829
Fax: 866.728.3096
www.laterallink.com

Michael Allen
President
Phone: 213.785.2362 (ext. 101)
mallen@laterallink.com

Lateral Link is an exclusive network of elite attorneys and premier legal jobs. We provide a web-based platform that allows attorneys to easily find new opportunities suited to their skills and interests. Lateral Link members have obtained positions at major law firms, financial services companies, entertainment companies, hedge funds and publicly traded companies. Lateral Link members receive unique benefits including a $10,000 placement bonus for most placements and free access to the online Vault Career Guides.

Lexolution, LLC

Lexolution LLC.

295 Madison Avenue
Suite 310
New York, NY 10017
Phone: 212-370-9400 | **Fax:** 212-377-9401

1776 I Street, N.W.
Washington, DC 20006
Phone: 202-756-4874 | **Fax:** 202-756-1583
www.lexolution.net

Scott Krowitz, Nora Plesent, Dick Osman, Karen Stempel, Principals
jobs@lexolution.net

Lexolution, LLC is a leading contract legal staffing firm in the New York and Washington, DC metropolitan regions. Founded by accomplished attorneys who practiced at leading law firms, Lexolution provides top attorney and paralegal talent to law firms and corporations in all practice areas. Lexolution makes the effort to identify and recruit the very best person for every job, often providing creative solutions for difficult staffing situations. Temporary staffing can be the best way to manage personnel costs for: large document production projects; corporate and real estate due diligence projects; maternity or extended leave coverage; unique brief or other non-recurring legal writing projects; as well as for special situations requiring outside legal expertise.

Pittleman & Associates, Inc.

PITTLEMAN & ASSOCIATES

336 East 43rd Street
New York, NY 10017
Phone: (212) 370-9600
Fax: (212) 370-9608
www.pittlemanassociates.com
E-mail: attysearch@pittlemanassociates.com

For more than 20 years, we have been placing at investment banks, media companies and Fortune 500 corporations in addition to the most selective law firms. Our recruiters are graduates of NYU, Columbia and Duke law schools who practiced at HBO, United Artists, Davis Polk, Simpson Thacher, etc. Our background and experience allows us to provide unusually sophisticated counsel and our track record affords us unparalleled access to interesting opportunities.

We currently are conducting in house searches at the following areas:

- Investment management
- Private Equity
- Derivatives
- Compliance
- Capital Markets
- Banking
- Securitization
- Litigation
- Tax .

Sivin Tobin Associates, LLC

516 Fifth Avenue
14th Floor
New York, NY 10036

Phone: (212) 573-9800
Fax: (212) 573-6122
www.sivintobin.com

SIVIN TOBIN
ASSOCIATES, LLC
THE LEADERS IN LATERAL PARTNER
PLACEMENT & PRACTICE GROUP MOVES

E-mail: info@sivintobin.com

The two principals of Sivin Tobin have an aggregate of over 35 years of legal recruiting experience. Over that time frame, they have placed a myriad of lawyers at firms and companies throughout the US and internationally. Many of those attorneys have risen to senior positions in their organizations, providing Sivin Tobin with a range and breadth of contacts throughout the legal community which is second to none. The firm's leading position in partner and practice group movement also enables it to work on associate positions which other firms do not have access to, enhancing its service in that area.

The Vault Legal Recruiter Directory is a special advertising section in the *Vault Guide to the Top 100 Law Firms*.
For information on listing your firm in the directory, contact H.S. Hamadeh, Esq. at hshamadeh@staff.vault.com.

VAULT CAREER LIBRARY   657

Pennsylvania

Abelson Legal Search

1700 Market Street
Suite 2130
Philadelphia, PA 19103
Phone: (215) 561-3010 | **Fax:** (215) 561-3001
www.abelsonlegalsearch.com

Cathy Abelson, President
abelson@abelsonlegalsearch.com

Abelson Legal Search, Philadelphia's personalized search firm, is ommitted to permanent and contract/temporary attorney, paralegal and legal professional placement. We work with law firms primarily in the Greater Philadelphia area, DE, and NJ and with major, established local, national and international corporations and start-up companies. Abelson Legal Search's record of long, successful placements and many repeat clients is testimony to our effective, efficient work, based on highly individualized service and sophisticated data management, including use of the most current technologies. (Please visit www.abelsonlegalsearch.com for more information or to register in our database.) Member NALSC.

Carpenter Legal Search, Inc.

One Oxford Centre Suite, 3030
301 Grant Street
Pittsburgh, PA 15219-6401
Phone: (412) 255-3770 | **Fax:** (412) 255-3780
www.carpenterlegalsearch.com

Lori J. Carpenter, President
lcarpenter@carpenterlegalsearch.com

Carpenter Legal Search, Inc. was established to satisfy the increasing need for strategic, well defined search services in today's dynamic legal market. Our clients comprise a diverse field ranging from Fortune 500 corporations to closely held businesses and internationally recognized law firms to prominent regional law firms. Whether you are searching to join a law department or another law firm, or creating an in-house legal department, adding partners or associates, building a new practice area, or opening additional offices, CLS provides strategic consulting services to identify the foremost opportunities or candidates to meet your needs. Member, NALSC.

Tennessee

AMERICAN Legal Search, LLC

209 10th Ave South, Suite 428
Nashville, TN 37203
Phone: (615) 251-9600 | **Fax:** (415) 532-1641
www.americanlegalsearch.com

Joe Freedman, CEO
joe@americanlegalsearch.com

AMERICAN Legal Search, LLC is a full-service national legal search firm. Before launching AMERICAN, our executive management team founded and built one of the largest privately held legal search firms in North America. From law firm mergers and practice group acquisitions to permanent search and contract staffing, AMERICAN's principals have been serving the legal communities throughout the country for more than a decade.

AMERICAN operates three core business divisions:

1. Assist law firms with firm mergers, practice group acquisitions and expansions into new cities.
2. Placement of associates and partner-level lawyers with law firms and corporations on a permanent basis.
3. Placement of contract (temporary) attorneys for specific projects.

Looking for a legal position? Need a change of venue?

Find your dream career opportunity on the Vault Law Job Board. Featuring hundreds of top positions throughout the U.S. and Canada.

Positions for all positions, including:

- Associate
- Partner
- Paralegal
- In-house Counsel

Positions in all practice areas, including

- Corporate
- Intellectual Property
- Labor/Employment
- Litigation
- Real Estate
- Tax
- Trusts & Estates

Go to www.vault.com/law

Where Lawyers Look for Lawyers®

Serving the legal communities throughout North America for more than a decade.

Nationwide Legal Search
- Law Firm Mergers & Acquisitions
- Permanent Placement
- Contract (Temporary) Placement

Serving the United States from these locations:

New York, NY	212.984.1086
Los Angeles, CA	310.914.0011
Nashville, TN	615.251.9600
Birmingham, AL	205.930.9811
Memphis, TN	901.277.2563
New Orleans, LA	504.616.4166
Tampa, FL	813.239.4044

888.220.9111
www.AmericanLegalSearch.com

NEW YORK • LOS ANGELES • NASHVILLE • BIRMINGHAM • NEW ORLEANS • MEMPHIS

Canada

ZSA Legal Recruitment Limited

20 Richmond Street East
Suite 315
Toronto, Canada M5C 2R9
Phone: 416-368-2051 • **Fax:** 416-368-5699
www.zsa.ca

Christopher Sweeney, President
info@zsa.ca

ZSA Legal Recruitment is Canada's leading and only national legal recruitment firm. With offices in Vancouver, Calgary, Edmonton, Toronto, Ottawa and Montreal, we are uniquely positioned to serve the legal recruitment needs of both law firms and corporations across Canada. ZSA provides its services to a broad range of domestic and international clients including the largest law firms and global corporations to sole practitioners and start-up companies. Our unparalleled success to date is the result of both our pioneering "selection" or non-headhunting-based recruitment strategy, and our single-minded focus of meeting the demands of our clients. Our services range from recruiting partners, associates, and general counsels/assistant general counsels to paralegals/law clerks, and legal assistants. Both lawyers and support personnel can be supplied on either a permanent or a temporary basis.

Asia

Cypress Recruiting Group, Inc.

475 Park Avenue South
31st Floor
New York, New York 10016
USA
Phone: 212.979.5900
Toll Free Number: 800.459.5773
Fax: 212.979.5922
www.Cypressrecruiting.com

Dawn P. Robertson, Esq., Executive Director
info@Cypressrecruiting.com

Cypress Recruiting Group specializes in the permanent placement of US, UK and PRC trained attorneys and bengoshi in Tokyo, Hong Kong, Shanghai and Beijing. As ex-practicing attorneys, we pride ourselves on offering a personalized, professional and quality service that gets results. Having worked with most of the new and expanding foreign offices in Asia from their inception, we are well positioned within the legal community to provide professional and knowledgeable career advice and make introductions with the appropriate decision makers.

Intellectual Property

Janet Zykorie Legal Search, Inc.

INTELLECTUAL PROPERTY ATTORNEYS
Founded in 1985
P.O. Box 20709
New York, NY 10025
Phone: (212) 362-1709

Janet Zykorie, President
Phone: (212) 362-1709

JANET ZYKORIE LEGAL SEARCH, INC. specializes in the recruitment and placement of patent, trademark, and copyright attorneys nationwide. INTELLECTUAL PROPERTY ATTORNEYS, PARTNERS, IN-HOUSE COUNSEL, PARTNER GROUPS, ASSOCIATES.

AWARDED HIGHEST RATING
"The time spent in finding the proper 'marriage' of attorney and prospective firm or corporation is unusual, refreshing, and simply unparalleled," rhapsodized one candidate in Chicago. Another added, "Of about 20 head-hunters I used, Janet Zykorie was the most professional and most dedicated."
"Rating Recruiters 1989"
– The American Lawyer.

PTO Legal Search Ltd.

1200 Smith Street
Suite 1600
Houston, TX 77002
Phone: (281) 812-1103 | **Fax:** (281) 812-1198
www.ptolegal.com

David Sewell, Director
Phone: (281) 812-1103
jobs@ptolegal.com

PTO Legal Search is a national search firm specializing in the permanent placement of intellectual property attorneys, patent agents and patent paralegals. Our clients include some of the finest intellectual property law firms, general practice law firms and corporations of all sizes. PTO Legal Search was formed to answer the industry demand for expertise in the intellectual property legal market.

The firm's founding partners were practicing lawyers in major law firms and Fortune 100 companies prior to becoming legal recruiters. Their combination of experience and specialization in the IP industry enables them to truly understand the needs and aspirations of their candidates and the expectations of their clients. Whether you are a qualified candidate or looking to hire one, PTO Legal Search can assist you.

© 2007 Vault Inc.

DIVERSITY PROGRAMS
DIRECTORY

ADAMS & REESE LLP

One Shell Square
701 Poydras Street, Suite 400
New Orleans, LA 70139
www.adamsandreese.com

At Adams and Reese, our approach to the practice of law is guided by an appreciation of the rich diversity found in our own communities and throughout the global marketplace. This appreciation is served by our recognition that a corporate philosophy and culture that is fundamentally diverse in both sensibility and structure, allows us a heightened awareness that enhances the depth and quality of the services we provide.

Our Objective

Adams and Reese strives to foster a working environment of inclusion, understanding, respect and opportunity for all employees.

Our Commitment

Our primary commitment is to provide our clients with the highest quality legal service in the most prompt, cost effective and efficient manner possible. Upholding this commitment comes with an appreciation of the unique differences among people and how we benefit from the diverse backgrounds, experiences and talents of our attorneys and staff. Diversity in our workforce enhances our ability to deliver services to our clients and enrich the lives of both our employees and the communities in which we work and live.

Diversity Task Force

The Adams and Reese Diversity Task Force was developed to support and ensure the success of efforts that foster the firm's overall commitment to diversity, further establishing a corporate culture defined by understanding, respect and opportunity.

AKIN GUMP STRAUSS HAUER & FELD

1333 New Hampshire Ave, NW
Washington, DC 0036
www.akingump.com

Akin Gump has 15 offices worldwide and more than 950 attorneys from diverse backgrounds. Of these attorneys, 45 are African American, 32 are Hispanic, 74 are Asian/Pacific Islander and 6 are Native American/Alaskan Native. In total, attorneys of color comprise over 16% of our entire legal team. Akin Gump is a leader among major law firms in the number of minority partners within the partnership, with minority partners constituting 10% of the firm's total partnership. In addition, we have 312 female lawyers. Women constitute over 15 percent of our partnership, over 30 percent of our senior counsel and nearly 42 percent of our associates and counsel. The firm has 17 self-identified openly gay and lesbian attorneys firmwide.

As historical barriers to achievement in the legal profession have continued to fall, the best and brightest lawyers in their fields, and the best and brightest young lawyers emerging from law schools, come from ever more diverse backgrounds. Our success in the global market, and our success in meeting internal objectives and excellence in mentoring, supervision and professional development, depends on ensuring that we achieve and maintain a critical mass of diversity in our partnership and in our associate

VAULT CAREER LIBRARY

© 2007 Vault Inc.

ALSTON & BIRD LLP

1201 West Peachtree Street

Atlanta, GA 30309-3424

www.alston.com

Alston & Bird is committed to diversity and inclusion. Praised as one of the most open and receptive in the US, the firm ranked number 19 on FORTUNE magazine's 2007 "100 Best Companies to Work For" and has been ranked consecutively for eight years, making it the highest and most frequently ranked law firm.

We strive to develop a culture which promotes the recruitment, retention and advancement of attorneys and staff without regard to race, gender, religion, ethnicity, sexual orientation or physical disability. We have in place specific policies for affirmative action for equal employment opportunity and preventing harassment. We believe a truly diverse working team embraces the principles of collegiality, teamwork, individual satisfaction, professional development and fairness, both in spirit and in practice. Our diversity efforts can be categorized in four areas: (1) ensuring representation; (2) understanding differences; (3) managing workforce diversity and accessing top talent; and (4) strategic diversity management.

The addition of our Alternative Career Path Policy demonstrates our ongoing efforts to evaluate and add benefits to support our diverse workforce. In 2001, we added domestic partner benefits; in 2002, we constructed a stand-alone, state-of-the-art, near-site child care center in Atlanta, available to all Alston & Bird employees.

To continue developing diversity education specific to the needs of each office, we have taken our diversity management education to a higher level with training sessions focusing on skills for working through specific diversity issues. We focus on recognizing and educating our lawyers and staff about cultural differences.

ARENT FOX PLLC

1050 Connecticut Avenue, N.W.

Washington, DC 20036-5339

www.arentfox.com

Arent Fox is proud that its commitment to diversity has been recognized in recent Vault rankings. We have achieved an exciting atmosphere in which teamwork and strategic initiatives are encouraged and rewarded. A high priority for the next 12 months will be working with the very impressive talent we have attracted among our minority attorneys so as to actualize their entrepreneurial potential and enable them to envision and achieve satisfying career goals.

We continue to sponsor a number of receptions, bar association events and diversity clerkship opportunities, all of which are designed to increase our profile in the area of diversity and promote the message that we want to attract minority candidates who will share our vision of strategic growth.

The Vault Diversity Programs Directory is a special advertising section in the *Vault Guide to the Top 100 Law Firms*. For information on listing your firm in the directory, contact corporatesales@vault.com.

VAULT CAREER LIBRARY

663

ARNOLD & PORTER LLP

555 12th Street, N.W.

Washington, DC 20004

www.arnoldporter.com

Diversity is a core value at Arnold & Porter LLP. Arnold & Porter seeks through its diversity policy to promote the treatment of every person with dignity and respect, value the contribution that each person makes, enable our colleagues to be comfortable being themselves, and encourage every person to realize his or her potential. The firm believes that each individual has the right to work in a professional atmosphere that promotes equal opportunity and prohibits discriminatory practices.

Our Washington, D.C. office received the Minority Corporate Counsel Association's (MCCA) Thomas L. Sager Award five times, an award given to law firms to recognize extraordinary commitment to diversity. MCCA presented the Sager Award to the firm's New York office twice. In 2001, Arnold & Porter was named an "Employer of Choice," and is the only law firm MCCA has recognized as an Employer of Choice.

Arnold & Porter has been recognized on Fortune's 2003-2007 list of the "100 Best Companies to Work For." Arnold & Porter is one of five organizations in the country, and the only law firm, honored in 2007 with an award from the Great Place to Work Institute. The firm was recognized for its inclusive and comprehensive diversity initiatives. Our firm has appeared seven times on Working Mother magazine's list of the "100 Best Employers for Working Mothers." American Lawyer ranked Arnold & Porter on its "A-List" of law firms in four of the last five years.

BINGHAM MCCUTCHEN LLP

150 Federal Street

Boston, MA 02110

www.bingham.com

Our diversity program is a critical element of our aspiration to become and remain one of the leading international law firms. We have achieved and sustained recognition as a premier firm by recruiting women and men from diverse backgrounds, cultures and experiences; their differences have made Bingham McCutchen stronger, more energetic, dynamic and creative than we would be with a homogenous workforce. In turn, our clients are better served, more diverse across industries, and more loyal.

In furtherance of our commitment and ambition in this area, we have planned and executed a number of objectives:

- Firmwide diversity action plan developed through comprehensive diversity audits led by Novations Group and Catalyst; draft of the action plan circulated to all attorneys and staff; town hall meetings to solicit feedback; final action plan approved by senior firm management; implementation led by Ralph Martin and Julia Frost-Davies, Co-chairs of diversity committee.

- Firmwide Attorneys of Color Retreat (2004 & 2006); Firmwide LGBT Retreat (2005 & 2007).

- Our signature, Celebrating Women series; women's mentoring; pilot part-time group; parents groups.

- Participation in various minority job fairs; founding member and active supporter of both the Boston Lawyers Group (BLG) and the Lawyers Collaborative for Diversity of Connecticut (LCD); Bingham McCutchen Diversity Programming Fund and Bingham McCutchen Scholarship Fund at the University of Connecticut.

© 2007 Vault Inc.

BILZIN SUMBERG BAENA PRICE & AXELROD LLP

200 South Biscayne Boulevard

Suite 2500

Miami, FL 33131

www.bilzin.com

Bilzin Sumberg's culture is built upon the unique experience, skills, perspectives and values of each of our attorneys and staff. Our diverse backgrounds and individual differences are seen as assets that enhance the quality of life for each of us and strengthen what we can accomplish as a firm. We are committed to maintaining a diverse workforce and to increasing the awareness of and sensitivity to our cultural differences in order to create an inclusive environment.

Bilzin Sumberg is comprised of exceptionally talented attorneys from a wide array of backgrounds and cultures. We pride ourselves on our ability to handle complex, sophisticated legal work, while maintaining the intimacy afforded by a law firm of 100 attorneys. Associates work closely with partners, and attorneys from different practice groups routinely work together as a cohesive team in order to provide clients with comprehensive, effective and efficient legal counsel. This culture supports and drives a commitment to diversity and to fostering a well-balanced workforce by providing all our lawyers with the resources and opportunities to realize their full potential regardless of race, religious beliefs, ethnicity, gender or sexual orientation.

We fully appreciate that asserting an interest in diversity will not produce results. Strategic initiatives and steadfast commitment are essential to the recruitment, mentoring and retention of a diverse group of attorneys reflective of the community in which we practice law. For this reason, in 2005, Bilzin Sumberg embarked upon a structured Diversity Initiative that includes a Diversity Committee to spearhead our efforts.

BROWN RAYSMAN MILLSTEIN FELDER & STEINER, LLP

900 Third Avenue

New York, NY 10022

Phone: (212) 895-2000

Fax: (212) 895-2900

Brown Raysman Millstein Felder & Steiner LLP has long recognized that diversity is an important element in ensuring that we serve our clients with the best legal talent possible. Diversity has aided us to be recognized as a renowned general practice law firm in the new millennium. We know that it is important to take our diversity initiatives even further by ensuring that the women and minority attorneys that work in the firm are provided with essential tools to satisfy their career development goals. With the full support of the firm's Executive Committee, the Diversity Committee has put forth a solid firm-wide diversity plan that focuses on recruitment, retention and career development.

Recruitment

Enlisting the assistance of search firms that specialize in minority partner and lateral attorney hiring has been an important element in increasing the number of minority attorneys in all of our offices and departments. The Diversity Committee also has initiated an aggressive campaign to hire more women and minority law school students. We routinely contact women and minority organizations at law schools and encourage students to come to our offices and meet with partners and associates at the firm. We also fund various cultural and pro bono events that support women and minority causes at law schools.

The Vault Diversity Programs Directory is a special advertising section in the *Vault Guide to the Top 100 Law Firms*. For information on listing your firm in the directory, contact corporatesales@vault.com.

VAULT CAREER LIBRARY   665

BRYAN CAVE LLP

211 North Broadway, Suite 3600
St. Louis, MO 64102-2750
www.bryancave.com

Core Values. The heart of Bryan Cave's core values is diversity. Although diversity has many meanings to many people, to us diversity means a professional home where people of varied backgrounds and perspectives gather to reach their personal best and contribute to the success of the organization. We achieve diversity by creating an environment in which all people are treated with respect and dignity and encouraged to be their authentic selves. In a profession that is often demanding, and sometimes adversarial, we believe it is crucial to foster a workplace infused with teamwork, collegiality and, most importantly, respect for that which makes each of us distinctive.

Global Reach. We believe that our success as a Firm depends on ensuring a diverse environment. As a global law firm, our clients are located and do business throughout the world — they deserve and expect guidance from professionals with the vision, footprint and perspective as broad and global as their own. The diverse traditions and viewpoints of our attorneys enable us to work with our clients as full business partners, alert to their challenges and invested in their success.

Professional Responsibility. Most importantly, diversity at Bryan Cave is not merely a business strategy, it is a professional responsibility. We have an inherent obligation to support diversity here and in the business community. We take that obligation personally in our work, in the business we are building, and in our service to the community at large. We have been involved with many organizations, programs and events to promote diversity in the legal profession, including the Diversity Pipeline Program in Phoenix, Ariz., the Human Rights Campaign, the Women in Leadership Conference in Chicago, Ill., Charting Your Own Course, Minority Corporate Counsel Association, NAPABA, Corporate Counsel Women of Color and Lavender Law. We also support the individual efforts of Bryan Cave lawyers who are actively involved in minority bar associations.

CHADBOURNE & PARKE LLP

30 Rockefeller Plaza
New York, NY 10112
www.chadbourne.com

We at Chadbourne & Parke LLP take great pride in the Firm's commitment to building and nurturing a workplace of diverse individuals with varied backgrounds and interests. We're serious about devoting firmwide resources to enhancing diversity here. That level of commitment shows in our Diversity Committee, which includes partners, associates, Committee Chair Anthony Roncalli, Managing Partner Charles O'Neill and the Manager of Diversity Initiatives.

Partners on the committee bring distinct perspectives and life experiences to their service. They ensure that the committee considers projects that include a range of LGBT, women's and race/ethnic perspectives.

The Firm's Diversity Committee turns that strategic goal into action. The committee provides initiative, focus and direction as we:

- Pursue equity, inclusion and pluralism in our policies, practices and business relationships

- Recruit the best from a diverse candidate pool

- Sustain a fair, inclusive, non-judgmental and respectful working environment

Our Managing Partner, Charlie O'Neill speaks for the firm when he says "Diversity works. It enhances Chadbourne's ability to innovate and enriches the quality of services, which ultimately benefits our clients."

© 2007 Vault Inc.

CLIFFORD CHANCE US LLP

31 West 52nd Street

New York, NY 10019

Phone: (212) 878-8000

Fax: (212) 878-8375

www.cliffordchance.com

As a global law firm, Clifford Chance is comprised of individuals representing a significant portion of the world's cultures, races, religions and nationalities. The diversity of our community guides our efforts to recruit and retain the best lawyers, and is the foundation for producing a supportive work environment so each person can develop to their fullest potential.

Our Diversity Committee, and a number of subcommittees, work alongside firm management to ensure support for the advancement of every lawyer and for increasing diversity within the firm's partnership. We sponsor a number of diversity awareness events throughout the year, including most recently a civil rights retrospective and a forum on current Asian diversity issues.

As part of our ongoing commitment, we have implemented a number of initiatives. We are the first law firm to endow a scholarship to the An-Bryce Program, a ground-breaking diversity program at the NYU Law School and we are sponsoring faculty research at Columbia Law School on diversity and its implications within the legal community. We also continue our long-standing affiliation with the Thurgood Marshall Academy in Washington, DC, established by local lawyers and law students to provide children attending under-served public schools with a first-class education.

COVINGTON & BURLING LLP

1201 Pennsylvania Avenue, NW

Washington, DC 20004

www.cov.com

Covington lawyers bring a wide variety of backgrounds, perspectives, and life experiences to our practice. We recognize the differences among us as an asset and a source of strength.

Leaders in Diversity

Lawyers of diverse backgrounds have thrived at Covington for decades. We elected our first woman partner in 1974, first African American partner in 1975, first Hispanic partner in 1985, first openly gay partner in 1989, and first Asian American partner in 1995. We were ranked on the American Lawyer's "A-List" (which ranks firms based on pro bono work, diversity, associate satisfaction and profitability) four of the five years since the list was first published in 2003 — a mark of our continued success. In 2006, the firm and its partner David Remes received the National Ally of Justice Award from the Human Rights Campaign in recognition of the firm's work on behalf of equality for GLBT individuals.

Also in 2006, the firm was named one of the country's 100 Best Companies by Working Mother magazine and was ranked seventh nationally in the third edition of Presumed Equal: What America's Top Women Lawyers Really Think About Their Law Firms, a survey of more than 100 law firms measuring training and advancement opportunities, work/life balance policies, mentoring, diversity, and firm culture and leadership.

The Vault Diversity Programs Directory is a special advertising section in the *Vault Guide to the Top 100 Law Firms*. For information on listing your firm in the directory, contact corporatesales@vault.com.

VAULT CAREER LIBRARY   667

CRAVATH, SWAINE & MOORE LLP

Worldwide Plaza, 825 Eighth Avenue

New York, NY 10019

www.cravath.com

Cravath, Swaine & Moore LLP's overarching goal is to provide the best possible representation to our clients. We have long held the conviction that excellence and diversity go hand in hand, and that we cannot provide our clients with the highest level of representation unless we recruit and retain outstanding lawyers from diverse backgrounds, with different perspectives, experiences and insights. Just as we pride ourselves on the diversity of our practice, we are proud of our commitment to promoting the diversity of our people at all levels. As part of this commitment, we established a Diversity Committee to formulate and propose diversity goals for the Firm, develop and implement practices that promote diversity, and analyze and track the Firm's progress in achieving those goals.

In keeping with the objectives of Cravath's diversity mission statement and our commitment to fostering diversity, the Firm solicits input from summer associates, associates and alumni about diversity and inclusion at the Firm. The Firm hired a diversity manager to coordinate attorney recruitment, development and retention efforts with respect to associates of color, women associates and GLBT associates.

Cravath encourages women students, GLBT students and students of color to apply to the Firm. In 2006 and 2007, we hosted 1L receptions for women law students in the New York area, women law students at the University of Pennsylvania and students at Howard Law School. We also were a sponsor of, and had associates attend, the Lavender Law Conference and the inaugural Ms. JD Conference. Additionally, for more than a decade, Cravath has provided several pre-law students of color with internships through the Sponsors for Educational Opportunity Program.

DAVIS POLK & WARDWELL

450 Lexington Avenue

New York, NY 10017

www.dpw.com

At Davis Polk, we are strongly committed to cultivating a workplace that supports diversity. We believe that diversity in backgrounds, experiences and ideas enriches our workplace experience and enhances the quality of the work we do for our clients. Our differences translate into the ability to look at problems from multiple perspectives and to be more creative, thus strengthening the firm's collaborative approach.

Current Stats

- Our lawyers come from 47 countries and collectively speak 43 languages.

- 129 of our lawyers were born outside of the United States, including 30 partners.

- 21.5% of our lawyers are ethnic minorities, including 26% of our associates.

- The partner class of 2007 is Davis Polk's largest and most diverse: 40% of the new partners are ethnic minorities, 27% are women, and more than half of the class was born outside of the United States.

How We Rank

- Davis Polk ranked first among New York law firms in Vault's 2006 rankings of the "Top 20 Law Firms in Diversity Issues With Respect to Minorities."

- Davis Polk ranked first among New York law firms in Vault's 2006 rankings of the "Top 20 Law Firms for Women."

- Davis Polk routinely ranks among the top firms in The American Lawyer's A-List rankings of elite U.S. law firms, which measures the firm's financial performance, pro bono activity, associate satisfaction and lawyer diversity.

- In June 2003, The American Lawyer ranked Davis Polk first among the country's largest law firms based on the percentage of women partners at the firm. (This is the most recent such ranking by The American Lawyer.)

© 2007 Vault Inc.

CROWE & DUNLEVY

20 North Broadway, Suite 1800

Oklahoma City, OK 73102

www.crowedunlevy.com

Diversity Policy: We at Crowe & Dunlevy are committed to diversity as a core value. Crowe & Dunlevy recognizes that diversity is fundamental to our success, as well as the success of our clients, the communities we serve and our judicial system. Crowe & Dunlevy has and will continue to work to break down barriers to equal opportunity. We celebrate and value the perspectives and varied experiences that are common to a diverse workplace. Crowe & Dunlevy strives to create an atmosphere in which each lawyer and staff person can grow and develop to his or her fullest potential and to be a model of diversity that others will follow.

Equal Employment Opportunity Policy: Crowe & Dunlevy has long been committed to a broad policy of equal employment opportunity, from recruiting and hiring to training and promotion. Crowe & Dunlevy is an equal opportunity employer. Our firm policies require equal opportunity at all times without regard to race, color, religion, national origin, sex, disability or age through all levels of employment, including recruitment, promotion, training and partnership consideration.

Our long history of nurturing inclusion and mutual respect continues with racial and ethnic minorities. For example, in 2000, in response to Crowe & Dunlevy shareholder William G. Paul's initiative as president of the American Bar Association to promote diversity in the legal profession, Crowe & Dunlevy contributed $50,000 as a founding firm of the ABA Legal Opportunity Scholarship. Mr. Paul and his wife Barbara also made a contribution of $50,000. To date, at least 100 ABA scholars have benefited from the financial assistance afforded them by the American Bar Association.

DAVIS POLK & WARDWELL

450 Lexington Avenue

New York, NY 10017

www.dpw.com

At Davis Polk, we are strongly committed to cultivating a workplace that supports diversity. We believe that diversity in backgrounds, experiences and ideas enriches our workplace experience and enhances the quality of the work we do for our clients. Our differences translate into the ability to look at problems from multiple perspectives and to be more creative, thus strengthening the firm's collaborative approach.

Current Stats

- Our lawyers come from 47 countries and collectively speak 43 languages.

- 129 of our lawyers were born outside of the United States, including 30 partners.

- 21.5% of our lawyers are ethnic minorities, including 26% of our associates.

- The partner class of 2007 is Davis Polk's largest and most diverse: 40% of the new partners are ethnic minorities, 27% are women, and more than half of the class was born outside of the United States.

How We Rank

- Davis Polk ranked first among New York law firms in Vault's 2006 rankings of the "Top 20 Law Firms in Diversity Issues With Respect to Minorities."

- Davis Polk ranked first among New York law firms in Vault's 2006 rankings of the "Top 20 Law Firms for Women."

- Davis Polk routinely ranks among the top firms in The American Lawyer's A-List rankings of elite U.S. law firms, which measures the firm's financial performance, pro bono activity, associate satisfaction and lawyer diversity.

- In June 2003, The American Lawyer ranked Davis Polk first among the country's largest law firms based on the percentage of women partners at the firm. (This is the most recent such ranking by The American Lawyer.)

The Vault Diversity Programs Directory is a special advertising section in the *Vault Guide to the Top 100 Law Firms*. For information on listing your firm in the directory, contact corporatesales@vault.com.

VAULT CAREER LIBRARY 669

DAY, BERRY & HOWARD, LLP

City Place, 185 Asylum Street

Hartford, CT 06103

Phone: (860) 275-0100

Fax: (860) 275-0343

Day, Berry & Howard LLP is committed to developing a work force that reflects our community and our clients. We have established programs and policies to recruit and retain minority and women attorneys and staff, and to encourage community involvement. We provide equal employment opportunity at all times without regard to race, color, religion, gender, citizenship status, age, national origin, disability, veteran status, sexual orientation, or any other state or federal law protected status. This applies to recruiting, hiring, training, promoting, evaluating, terminating, compensating, benefits eligibility, working conditions and other employment issues.

We actively recruit and retain a diverse workforce which both supports our Equal Employment Opportunity Policy and furthers our ability to provide our clients excellent legal service.

Each of us at Day, Berry and Howard, working individually and together, is committed to the principle that every person at the Firm deserves to be treated with dignity and respect. We are proud of our tradition of fostering and maintaining a work environment in which the diversity of each individual is valued and celebrated. We aspire to develop and manage a strong and inclusive Day, Berry and Howard, firm-wide.

We believe that the contributions of each individual are essential to our continued growth and to our ultimate goal of providing to our clients the highest quality legal services in a timely manner at a reasonable cost. We believe that our diversity contributes to our ability to serve our clients more effectively.

DEWEY BALLANTINE LLP

1301 Avenue of the Americas

New York, NY 10019

www.deweyballantine.com

Dewey Ballantine LLP is an initial signatory to the Statement of Diversity Principles of the Association of the Bar of the City of New York and a founding contributor to the Office of Diversity of the City Bar. A firm partner serves on the City Bar's Committee to Enhance Diversity in the Profession and Committee on Recruitment and Retention. The firm has participated for a number of years in the Minority Fellowship Program sponsored by the City Bar and the Equal Justice America Fellowship Program.

The firm has established a Diversity Committee whose members include partners from our U.S. and European offices. The Diversity Committee is currently working on initiatives to increase hiring, retention and promotion of minorities and to ensure that Dewey Ballantine continues to maintain a working environment that is respectful and welcoming to all.

Members of the firm's Executive and Diversity Committees meet periodically with representatives of bar associations and minority organizations to discuss ways to develop procedures and programs to make the firm a welcoming place for all who work here. We also give financial support to bar and student groups that represent minorities. We encourage our lawyers to be active in such groups to ensure the continued flow of ideas. Some of the groups we support include the Asian American Law Fund of New York, Asian American Legal Defense and Education Fund, Asian Americans for Equality, Asian Professional Extension, Asian Pacific American Law Students Association, Black Law Students Association, Latin American Law Students Association, Metropolitan Black Bar Association, National Asian Pacific American Bar Association, the NAACP Legal Defense and Education Fund, the Thurgood Marshall Scholarship Fund, and the Lesbian and Gay Law Association Foundation of Greater New York.

© 2007 Vault Inc.

DICKSTEIN SHAPIRO LLP

1825 Eye Street, NW
Washington, DC 20006-5403
www.dicksteinshapiro.com

At Dickstein Shapiro LLP, our innovative solutions and superior client service come from the talent and diversity of our attorneys and staff. The Firm has a steadfast commitment to fostering a diverse work environment in which racial and ethnic minorities, women, disabled individuals, and people of varying sexual orientations enjoy an atmosphere of inclusion and respect. Our well-balanced workplace and diverse culture not only enrich the quality of life for Dickstein Shapiro employees, but also enhance the superior service we provide to our clients.

Dickstein Shapiro supports a variety of initiatives to ensure that diversity at the Firm is embraced and enhanced. Diversity initiatives include recruitment, retention, and mentor programs geared toward the advancement of diverse employees; a women's initiative; support for research projects focused on diversity in the legal industry; a diversity speakers series that features respected community leaders; and scholarship opportunities for minority law students. Dickstein Shapiro continues to be a leader in law firm diversity and has been recognized as superior by clients and a myriad of independent publications. Recently the Firm was awarded the Minority Corporate Counsel Association's prestigious Thomas L. Sager Award.

DLA PIPER US LLP

203 North LaSalle Street, Suite 1900
Chicago, IL 60601
www.dlapiper.com

DLA Piper is committed to providing an inclusive environment where attorneys of all ethnic backgrounds can be successful. We are committed to developing a culture where the opportunities for success are available to everyone and the processes for that success are transparent. We are creating programs and processes designed to enhance our representation of diverse lawyers and encourage and support the retention of those lawyers.

Diversity is a core value of the firm. Whenever there is any communications on the firm, diversity is a stated value and priority. It is communicated whenever our national leadership speaks and diversity is represented in all of our formal communications (newsletters, reports, etc.)

The firm has committed extraordinary resources to this effort. A full time director (opposed to manager or coordinator) functions on a strategic and management level with a presence on the hiring and associate review and compensation committees. As part of that process, the director monitors the hours and the quality of the work assigned to associates and partners. The director is also asked for input and recommendations on the partnership nominations process. She works closely with the director of training and professional development to insure that diversity is an integral part of the mentoring and professional development programs. The diversity director travels to all of the offices at least once a year to meet with partners and associates to assesstheir needs and concerns. Our regional managers (one east coast; one west coast) travel more.frequently and provide one-on-one counseling and support to the diverse attorneys in their regions.

The Vault Diversity Programs Directory is a special advertising section in the *Vault Guide to the Top 100 Law Firms*. For information on listing your firm in the directory, contact corporatesales@vault.com.

VAULT CAREER LIBRARY   671

DOW LOHNES PLLC

1200 New Hampshire Avenue, NW

Washington, DC 20036

www.dowlohnes.com

Diversity at Dow Lohnes PLLC

Dow Lohnes is committed to recruiting and retaining a diverse workforce to provide the highest level of service to our clients and our community. We actively foster an environment that welcomes and offers great opportunities to talented individuals, regardless of their race, gender, ethnicity, national origin, sexual orientation, religion, color, disability or age.

The Importance of Diversity at Dow Lohnes

While firm employees all share certain values, such as a commitment to excellence and client service, our varied backgrounds, perspectives and experiences are critical to servicing our clients effectively and enriching our work environment. Dow Lohnes' diversity efforts are overseen by a firm-wide Diversity Committee that focuses on advancing the diversity interests of the firm and the legal profession. The Committee, composed of members of the Management Committee and a diverse group of partners and associates, serves as the mainspring of our commitment to recruit, retain and develop a diverse population of attorneys. The Committee works closely with the Professional Development and Hiring Committees and often seeks input from all firm attorneys. We are determined to foster a diverse workplace and have taken a number of steps to achieve this goal.

FINNEGAN, HENDERSON, FARABOW, GARRETT & DUNNER

901 New York Avenue, N.W.

Washington, DC 20001

www.finnegan.com

Finnegan Henderson began forty-two years ago, as a full-service intellectual property law firm, with two attorneys. Today, through the efforts of a broad spectrum of personnel, the firm has grown to one of the largest intellectual property firms in the world, ranking #1 for best intellectual property practice by its clients and peers, as reported in Vault.com, the American Lawyer, and IP Law & Business. Beyond receiving acknowledgments for our skilled lawyers, Finnegan Henderson has also received recognition as one of the nation's top law firms on diversity and quality of life. In 2006, Vault.com cited Finnegan Henderson as the #2 law firm for minority diversity and the #1 firm for quality of life. Vault.com also ranked Finnegan Henderson as #6 in overall best in diversity and #6 in diversity with respect to women. This success stems from an early mission statement that remains with the firm today: "Treat everyone fairly and with respect."

Though simple in words, its repeated practice has resulted in Finnegan Henderson's present position as a premier firm for attracting and retaining attorneys of all backgrounds to practice intellectual property law. This process remains on-going, the firm continuously strives to ensure a diverse workplace and advance diversity in the legal profession, through (1) recruitment, (2) retention, (3) mentoring, (4) promotion, (5) collaborative efforts, and (6) innovative practices. We believe that the firm's collegial environment, coupled with its diverse workforce, make Finnegan Henderson a unique place to work.

© 2007 Vault Inc.

FISH & RICHARDSON P.C.

225 Franklin Street

Boston, MA 02110-2804

www.fr.com

Fish & Richardson P.C., founded in 1878, has over 400 attorneys in ten offices nationwide, representing a wide range of clients in intellectual property (IP), complex litigation and corporate matters. The firm has represented some of history's greatest innovators, including Alexander Graham Bell, Thomas Edison and the Wright Brothers. Innovation often comes from seeing things in a slightly different, or sometimes radically different, way. This is also the essential strength of diversity and why it is so meaningful to our firm and our clients.

Fish & Richardson has appointed a principal (i.e., partner) of the firm as diversity chairperson to centralize previously localized diversity efforts. The diversity chairperson and Diversity Committee work closely with the firm president and with the firm's recruiting, human resources and client services groups to set and execute the strategic direction of the firm's diversity initiatives and oversee a broad range of diversity efforts nationwide.

Minority Law Journal's 2007 Diversity Scorecard listed Fish & Richardson in the top half of more than 200 law firms. The 2005 Diversity Scorecard of the *National Law Journal* (NLJ) ranked Fish & Richardson in the top 25 percent of firms for diversity. The survey also showed that 12 percent of all the firm's principals are minorities and 10 percent of all the firm's attorneys firm-wide are minorities, while one-third are women. In April 2005, 2006, and 2007, Fish & Richardson was named as one of the Top 100 Law Firms for Diversity by *MultiCultural* Law Magazine.

FITZPATRICK, CELLA, HARPER & SCINTO

30 Rockefeller Plaza

New York, NY 10112

www.fchs.com

Diversity has long been, and continues to remain, a core Fitzpatrick value. We are proud to have been honored with the Thomas L. Sager Award for the Northeast region twice in the last four years (2002 and 2004), and prouder still of the environment that our diversity efforts have enabled us all to enjoy.

As part of our ongoing commitment, we routinely undergo a self-examination process, to track our progress in this important area. Having had done so at the close of 2004, we were disappointed to see that our percentages of minority and women attorneys had dropped a bit from the preceding year, and that in 2004 our percentages for new hires were the lowest they had been in more than five years. Eager to reverse the trend, we committed to redouble our Diversity efforts, and are pleased to report the following:

- We were successful in roughly doubling our new hire percentages from 2004 to 2005, to one-third minority and over one-half (53%) women;

- We continued the trend into 2006, in which almost one-half of our new hires were minorities (47%) and almost one-half (also 47%) were women;

- These practices allowed us to reverse the downward trend that we observed at the end of 2004, so that our overall percentages and numbers of minority and woman attorneys have increased since then, to a current 20% minority and 28% woman.

The Vault Diversity Programs Directory is a special advertising section in the *Vault Guide to the Top 100 Law Firms*. For information on listing your firm in the directory, contact corporatesales@vault.com.

VAULT CAREER LIBRARY   673

FORD & HARRISON LLP

1275 Peachtree Street Northeast

Suite 600

Atlanta, GA 30309

www.fordharrison.com

Our commitment to diversity

Ford & Harrison LLP is committed to maintaining a diverse workforce and a culture that values the unique backgrounds, beliefs, skills and attributes of all people. Our objective is to enhance the efficiency and effectiveness of delivering legal services by continuing to develop a workforce of professionals and staff that embraces diversity and appreciates the contributions to our firm by all individuals. The firm strives for a positive climate of learning, innovation, inclusion, tolerance, opportunity and growth. By doing so, Ford & Harrison as a law firm, and we as individuals, can realize the benefits of diversity as we work together in the pursuit of excellence in the practice of law.

Ford & Harrison has a Diversity Committee comprised of 10 lawyers and 3 administration professionals. The members of the committee include: Dawn Siler-Nixon, Chair (partner, Tampa office); Louis Britt (partner, Memphis office); Renee Canody (associate, Atlanta office); Lynne Donaghy (director of marketing and client service); Courtney Dyar (recruiting coordinator); Pedro Forment (partner, Miami office); Patricia Griffith (partner, Atlanta office); Meg Holman (director of professional development); Dinita James (partner, Tampa office); Ron Kimzey (partner, Atlanta office); Judith Moldover (of counsel, New York office); Kay Wolf (partner, Orlando office).

FRIED, FRANK, HARRIS, SHRIVER & JACOBSON LLP

One New York Plaza

New York, NY 10004

www.friedfrank.com

Fried Frank supports a policy of equal opportunity for all. The Diversity Committee's mandate is to provide leadership to the Firm as we strive to recruit a highly qualified, diverse group of attorneys, to improve the professional development and advancement of all our lawyers, and to enhance the Firm's working atmosphere so as to foster respect for diversity and a sense of inclusion and fairness throughout the Firm.

The Firm's Diversity Committee has been extremely active in pursuing and achieving our goals. The Firm has created working groups within our diversity committee focused on professional development, recruitment, work/life balance, and communications. Each working group comprises of partners, counsel, and associates. The Firm continues to make diversity a priority of our retention efforts by expanding mentoring programs and introducing diversity-related segments into our professional development and management training programs. The Firm has also hired Maja Hazell as the Director of Diversity and Inclusion to help further our efforts.

For the past 17 years, the Firm has been an active participant in the Sponsors for Educations (SEO) program. Each summer we hire two people of color as interns for the summer prior to their entry into law school. Often, our SEO interns return to the Firm as summer associates and associates. Four associates and one partner were SEO participants.

Fried Frank co-founded the DC Minority Attorney Networking Series in collaboration with another D.C. law firm, and recently expanded the program to New York attorneys of color in the New York metropolitan areas to network and discuss issues of professional development. Fried Frank's Attorney of Color affinity group generated the concept for the series. To date thirty-three law firms have also joined as sponsors.

© 2007 Vault Inc.

FULBRIGHT & JAWORSKI L.L.P.

Fulbright Tower, 1301 McKinney, Suite 5100

Houston, TX 77010

www.fulbright.com

Our firm is committed to the goal of strengthening our diversity through recruiting and retaining minority and women attorneys and staff personnel from all backgrounds. Our commitment is consistent with our recognition that it is the outstanding people within Fulbright & Jaworski who have always been the source of our strength. Our attorneys and staff are the firm's greatest assets. We have long embraced the principles of equal employment opportunity. We further recognize that promoting diversity is an integral component of our continuing quest for excellence as individual attorneys and as a firm. As part of the effort to advance our commitment to diversity throughout the firm, the following initiatives, among others, are being pursued:

- Improvement of the level of diversity within the firm's leadership positions, firm committees and practice development efforts;

- Development of an attorney and senior administrative manager evaluation process to review and recognize the contributions made by our attorneys and managers to advance the firm's efforts to fulfill our commitment to diversity as set forth in this message;

- Emphasis of the firm's long-standing policy that encourages reporting of any discrimination or harassment based on sex, race, national origin or other protected status;

- Participation in opportunities outside the firm to explore diversity initiatives underway with clients, bar associations and minority organizations;

- The firm has implemented the "Dignity, Courtesy & Respect" program. This program covered all of the firm's employment related policies, including the Equal Employment Opportunity Policy;

- The firm also makes affirmative efforts to recruit lawyers who are members of racial or ethnic minority groups.

GIBSON, DUNN & CRUTCHER LLP

333 South Grand Avenue

Los Angeles, CA 90071

www.gibsondunn.com

Firm Philosophy

Gibson Dunn believes that diversity among our attorneys is essential to our continued success as one of the leading law firms in the world. The top goals of our firm are threefold: (a) to expand recruitment efforts of diverse attorneys; (b) to retain a higher percentage of diverse attorneys by encouraging promotion within the firm; (c) and to expand the firm's profile in the communities in which it serves.

Diversity Committee System

Gibson Dunn maintains a two-tiered diversity committee system. The National Diversity Committee serves as a steering committee to oversee the firm's diversity efforts. Membership on the national committee includes Ken Doran, Managing Partner; partner representatives from each local office; representatives from the Management Committee; the chairs of the Hiring and Associate Committees; the Chief Legal Recruiting and Diversity Officer, and the Director of Diversity.

In addition to the National Diversity Committee, there is a diversity committee in each of our domestic offices. Our local office committees are open to all attorneys who are interested in the issue of diversity.

The Vault Diversity Programs Directory is a special advertising section in the *Vault Guide to the Top 100 Law Firms*. For information on listing your firm in the directory, contact corporatesales@vault.com.

VAULT CAREER LIBRARY   675

GODFREY & KAHN, S.C.

780 North Water Street
Milwaukee, WI 53202
www.gklaw.com

Godfrey & Kahn believes that our law firm, and the communities in which we live and work, must be committed to a professional and cultural environment of inclusion in which men and women having different backgrounds, perspectives, beliefs and cultural and ethnic heritages can thrive. Hence, Godfrey & Kahn recruits, promotes and retains attorneys and other employees of diverse backgrounds that reflect the varied backgrounds of the clients and communities we serve. Some of our diversity initiatives are described below:

Scholarships

UW Madison Law School Fellowship — In 2004, Godfrey & Kahn established a fellowship at the University of Wisconsin Law School to provide a full three-year scholarship to one student each year who enrolls as a participant in the Legal Education Opportunities (LEO) program.

Marquette University Law School Fellowship — In 2006, Godfrey & Kahn established a fellowship at the Marquette University Law School that is awarded annually to an incoming first-year law student, with selection designed to promote diversity within the law school student body. Fellowship recipients also receive mentoring from Godfrey & Kahn attorneys, as well as employment as a summer associate at the firm.

Godfrey & Kahn Diversity Scholars Program — The firm offers a $2,500 stipend to first-year law students at the University of Michigan, the University of Iowa and Northwestern University. One stipend is awarded at each school. Students who are African American, Hispanic American, Asian American, Native American or GLBT are eligible to apply.

Godfrey & Kahn Foreign Law Student Fellowship Program — Godfrey & Kahn provides an opportunity for one foreign graduate law student studying at the East Asian Legal Studies Center of the University of Wisconsin to work for the firm for a period of one month in a paid internship position.

HELLER EHRMAN LLP

333 Bush Street
San Francisco, CA 94104
www.hellerehrman.com

Since 1890, Heller Ehrman has embraced and celebrated diversity in our workforce. While the firm's founders demonstrated their commitment to diversity by assembling (uncharacteristically for the time) a group of lawyers from disparate religious backgrounds, today that commitment is manifested on many more levels. We believe that diversity enhances the quality of service we provide to clients and makes Heller Ehrman a rich and rewarding place to work, for both attorneys and professional staff.

We have set aggressive hiring and advancement goals for minority attorneys, defined as African-Americans, Asians/Pacific Islanders, Hispanics/Latinos, Native Americans and self-identified gays and lesbians. In addition, the firm supports the Heller Ehrman Lesbian/Gay/Bisexual/ Transgender Alliance (HELGA) as well as a variety of ethnic and cultural activities, including participation in World AIDS Day, celebration of Black History Month and various multicultural events within the firm and in the communities in which we live and work. We have established Diversity Committees in our major offices and we have created a firmwide Lesbian/Gay/Bisexual/Transgender Committee to help address the specific needs of the LGBT community.

© 2007 Vault Inc.

HOGAN & HARTSON LLP

555 Thirteenth Street, N.W.

Washington, DC 20004

www.hhlaw.com

Hogan & Hartson has long been committed to recruiting, retaining, and promoting attorneys with diverse backgrounds and experiences, including racial and ethnic minorities, women, and gays and lesbians. We believe that our diversity significantly enhances our ability to provide high-quality legal services to our clients. We are proud of our record on diversity, as the firm's demographics show.

We are committed to continuing to preserve and promote that diversity, through our recruitment and retention efforts, through our firm culture, and through the firm's emphasis on training and professional development of all associates. The firm's Diversity Committee has a leadership role in all these efforts.

"Hogan & Hartson has a long history of promoting diversity among its attorneys and staff. We are committed to fostering a work environment that reflects the world we live in and the clients we serve. We understand that for a global practice like ours to thrive we must be able to think and act in a diverse world."

J. Warren Gorrell, Jr.

Chairman

HOLLAND & KNIGHT LLP

195 Broadway, 24th Floor

New York, NY 10007

www.hklaw.com

Our Managing Partner has declared that not only is diversity the "right thing to do," but it positions us to deliver our very best legal work. By attracting, retaining and promoting diverse lawyers, Holland & Knight delivers superior client service. Over many years, our commitment to diversity has strengthened our team atmosphere and contributed to our broad range of talent for addressing any legal matter. We understand that the challenges of professional development vary among a diverse group of individuals. We strive to support all of our attorneys in achieving their professional goals, recognizing the value in their differences.

A Tradition of Leadership

Long before diversity programs were a business imperative, Holland & Knight leaders embraced an "inclusive" culture. More than 30 years ago, Chesterfield Smith, our firm's founding father, hired and mentored the firm's first female lawyer and later the firm's first African-American lawyer. Both women are still at Holland & Knight today and are widely recognized as leaders both within the firm and in the legal community at-large.

A Firm Foundation on Which to Grow

Along with the appointment of Paul Thomas as Diversity Partner and Chief Diversity Officer, the firm strengthened its commitment through the creation of a 13-member Diversity Council that includes the Managing Partner, the Chair of the Directors Committee and diverse partners, associates and staff. The Council oversees and supports all of Holland & Knight's diversity initiatives, programs, diversity-related charitable and community activities.

The Vault Diversity Programs Directory is a special advertising section in the *Vault Guide to the Top 100 Law Firms*. For information on listing your firm in the directory, contact corporatesales@vault.com.

VAULT CAREER LIBRARY   677

HOWREY LLP

1299 Pennsylvania Ave, N.W.
Washington, DC 20004
www.howrey.com

Diversity, among lawyers and non-lawyers alike, has proven time and again to be a pivotal element of Howrey's drive for excellence. At Howrey our commitment to diversity is one of our core values. We recognize that diversity at all levels of our workforce strengthens Howrey as a firm and provides a platform for continued excellence. We focus our commitment on seeking out and retaining qualified, talented individuals from all backgrounds and ensuring that they have the opportunities to succeed in all aspects and at all levels of the firm. Howrey strongly believes that it must actively pursue and support diversity. To that end, Howrey has established policies and practices that reflect the firm's strong commitment to diversity.

In recruiting, Howrey undertakes a number of aggressive outreach activities to attract diverse candidates and ensure a diverse summer associate class. For example, Howrey's D.C. office holds an annual diversity reception for second-year law students. Through this reception, Howrey reaches out to minority law students and introduces them to Howrey and its summer program. Howrey extends personal invitations to minority student organizations and the minority student population for each of the 1L and 2L receptions that Howrey holds during the recruiting season. Howrey also participates in regional minority job fairs to tap another source of minority candidates.

HUGHES HUBBARD & REED LLP

One Battery Park Plaza
New York, NY 10004
www.hugheshubbard.com

Diversity has been an important priority of Hughes Hubbard throughout its history. Today, Hughes Hubbard continues this tradition with an uncompromising commitment to diversity, a strong policy to articulate it and a comprehensive program to implement it. That means fostering an inclusive work environment - one free of discrimination of any kind - where individuals can flourish and do their best work. Efforts include recruiting more minorities and women. However, the Firm's commitment to furthering diversity does not end with the hiring process. To achieve meaningful and lasting progress, Hughes Hubbard has launched a strategic plan to place attorneys with varied backgrounds in positions of influence throughout the Firm, such as office and practice leaders. To further these goals, Hughes Hubbard has an active, standing committee to address issues of diversity at the Firm, as well as a diversity taskforce of associates, who assist in developing and maintaining policies to promote a diverse work force within the Firm. And Hughes Hubbard has developed a mentoring program to foster a supportive work environment for all attorneys and ensure that attorneys of diversity in particular receive interesting and challenging legal work and guidance. Such accomplishments have garnered Hughes Hubbard recognition. The National Organization of Women (NOW) honored Hughes Hubbard for its excellent record of promoting women to positions of authority with its "Women of Power and Influence Award." And in 2003, The American Lawyer reported that Hughes Hubbard had the highest percentage of female partners in the Am Law 200. In 2004, the firm ranked fourth in the Am Law 200 for overall diversity.

© 2007 Vault Inc.

HUNTON & WILLIAMS LLP

Riverfront Towers, East Tower, 951 East Byrd Street

Richmond, VA 23219

www.hunton.com

Hunton & Williams has a strong Diversity Program designed to attract and develop a workforce representative of the firm's global law practice. Hunton & Williams' diversity policy enthusiastically supports the commitments to diversity issued first in 1999 by a large group of chief legal officers of U.S. and international corporations entitled Diversity in the Workplace: A Statement of Principle and also expressed in A Call to Action-Diversity in the Legal Profession, authored in 2004 by Rick Palmore, chief legal advisor of Sara Lee. The firm also has (1) a policy on Equal Employment; (2) an Affirmative Action Plan that provides a comprehensive blueprint for implementing diversity and equal employment opportunity; and (3) a strong Policy Against Harassment that applies to sexual harassment as well as harassment based on race, national origin, disability, religion, sexual orientation and any other protected categories.

Corporate and diversity-related partnerships: Hunton & Williams is a regular sponsor of the Minority Corporate Counsel Association's Creating Pathways for Diversity Conference, the NAPABA Annual Convention, the ABA's Margaret Brent Awards and Women in Law Leadership Academy, and the Annual Leadership Academy for Women of Color Attorneys. We have partnered with Sodexho, Inc. and Duke Energy to sponsor summer internships for minority law school students, and are currently partnering with the Mecklenburg Bar Association to provide internships in our Charlotte office. We also work with our clients to ensure that their team of lawyers reflects the importance of diversity to their organizations.

JENNER & BLOCK LLP

One IBM Plaza

Chicago, IL 60611-7603

Phone: (312) 222-9350

Fax: (312) 527-0484

www.jenner.com

Jenner & Block is committed to creating the most inclusive environment possible. The Firm's dedication to diversity is reflected in our commitment of time, budget, and resources, and reinforced by the work of our Diversity Committee, which leads the efforts to implement our diversity initiatives and ensure their success.

Our success in building a diverse environment has been recognized nationally by organizations such as Human Rights Campaign and Vault 2006, which have ranked us among the top law firms in the country in diversity.

Jenner & Block has traditionally recruited from a wide range of national law schools and we have expanded our sources to include additional law schools with diverse student bodies. We have also established a Minority Scholarship Program for first-year students at several universities.

We have a number of firmwide programs that are designed to help create an inclusive environment where all of our attorneys have access to opportunities that will allow them to develop skills and progress within the firm.

As part of our efforts to strengthen retention, the Firm and its lawyers have established affinity groups that help create a community and provide opportunity for diverse lawyers to exchange resources and share ideas. These groups focus on issues such as increasing recognition of the importance of diversity in the legal profession, diversity recruiting and mentoring, and other matters of common concern.

The Vault Diversity Programs Directory is a special advertising section in the *Vault Guide to the Top 100 Law Firms*. For information on listing your firm in the directory, contact corporatesales@vault.com.

VAULT CAREER LIBRARY   679

JONES DAY

51 Louisiana Avenue, N.W.
Washington, DC 20001
www.jonesday.com

Jones Day's culture is one of teamwork and the Firm prides itself on being "One Firm Worldwide." Our lawyers, in 13 countries on four continents, work together as respected professionals and trusted colleagues to achieve our paramount goal-the advancement of the client's interests. At Jones Day we understand that a strong team is a diverse and inclusive one that permits attorneys from all backgrounds and cultures to flourish and develop their full potential.

Commitment

Jones Day is committed to recruiting, retaining, and promoting the best attorneys and law students from all backgrounds. Our Diversity Task Force supports the U.S. office and practice group leaders in entry level and lateral recruitment, development and retention of minority and female attorneys, and diversity awareness. The Task Force is composed of fifteen partners from ten domestic offices representing nine practice groups. It meets monthly to address policy and programmatic issues related to our diversity initiatives.

Recruiting

Jones Day seeks to attract diverse attorneys through participation and sponsorship of internships, fellowships, and clerkships that provide substantive legal experience to women and minority law students and through our participation and sponsorship of job fairs, recognition events, and career development programs for women and minority law school students and organizations.

KAYE SCHOLER LLP

425 Park Avenue
New York, NY 10022
www.kayescholer.com

Kaye Scholer is committed to fostering diversity in a positive and supportive work environment. We believe that a diverse group of lawyers, increases the value of our law firm, strengthens our firm's ability to attract talented individuals, and enhances our ability to retain and serve our clients. Our commitment to cultivate and maintain a diverse workforce remains at the core of our recruiting, retention and promotion efforts.

Kaye Scholer is an original signatory to the Statement of Goals of New York Law Firms and Corporate Legal Departments for Increasing Minority Hiring, Retention and Promotion, and we have surpassed the goals in each of the years of their existence. We are also an original signatory to the Statement of Goals of New York Law Firms and Corporate Legal Departments for the Retention and Promotion of Women, and we have participated in the City Bar Fellowship Program since its inception.

Kaye Scholer was the recipient of the "2006 Black Entertainment and Sports Lawyers Association Law Firm Diversity Award".

The Diversity and Recruiting Committees work together to ensure a diverse workplace. We recruit at diversity job fairs. We conduct on-campus interviews at over twenty law schools, including Howard University Law School, and we actively seek out diverse candidates at every school.

Our Diversity Consultant has conducted as assessment of the Firm. The assessment and our consultant's recommendations are enabling is to support and expand our diversity efforts.

© 2007 Vault Inc.

KELLEY DRYE & WARREN LLP

101 Park Avenue

New York, NY 10178

www.kelleydrye.com

Kelley Drye & Warren's commitment to diversity and equal opportunity in the practice of law allows us to devote significant time and resources to the recruitment and retention of the most qualified attorneys. We are able to cultivate a diverse workplace by embracing differences among employees and, in turn, promoting and implementing methods that ensure attorneys are trained, hired and promoted fairly and with attention to the goals of diversity in the practice of law. Kelley Drye has a Diversity Committee comprising representatives from the Recruiting, Associates, Executive and Training Committees. More specifically, our sustained efforts at minority recruitment and hiring include sponsorship and participation in programs that are designed to introduce the firm to minority recruits. In 1999, Kelley Drye adopted The Association of the Bar of the City of New York's Restatement and Reaffirmation of Goals for Increasing Minority Retention and Promotion. Kelley Drye has also signed the new 2003 Statement of Principles. Kelley Drye has also taken steps to increase and support diversity among its incoming summer and associate classes. The firm participates in the Association of the Bar of the City of New York's Minority Fellowship Program which allows one first-year law student an opportunity to work as a summer associate with the firm. The firm also participates in the New York City Metro Area Lesbian, Gay, Bisexual and Transgender Law Legal Career Fair which helps to promote our ongoing commitment to diversity.

KILPATRICK STOCKTON LLP

1100 Peachtree Street

Atlanta, GA 30309

www.KilpatrickStockton.com

REACH: Diversity Matters at Kilpatrick Stockton

At Kilpatrick Stockton, we are committed to fostering an environment where the self-defining differences of our diverse personnel do not divide us, but rather make us stronger. Kilpatrick Stockton established REACH to embody our Diversity Action Program because it both captures our legacy of leadership in inclusiveness and symbolizes our commitment to the future for diversity.

A Legacy of REACH

Kilpatrick Stockton has a 125-year history of creating an inclusive environment in which the best legal minds can thrive. It's one of the most important elements of our legacy, and it has contributed directly to our firm's success. Kilpatrick Stockton was one of the first large firms in the Southeast to have a female partner, and it led the major regional law firms in recruiting and hiring African-American attorneys. Other examples from our past that have helped lay the foundation for a diverse practice include:

- In the 1930's, Kilpatrick Stockton was one of the first major law firms to hire a Jewish partner, a rarity for major laws firm at the time.

- Kilpatrick Stockton was at the forefront of racial desegregation and enlightenment in the 1960's, helping Martin Luther King, Sr. when the IRS was unfairly targeting his church.

- Kilpatrick Stockton served as Pro Bono Counsel to Maynard Jackson's mayoral re-election campaign in 1989. Jackson was the first black mayor of Atlanta.

- In 1997, Kilpatrick Stockton established the James S. Dockery, Jr. Scholarship at Wake Forest Law School to support outstanding minority students.

- In 1999, Kilpatrick Stockton received Georgia's first Thomas L. Sager Award by the Minority Corporate Counsel Association for sustained commitment to improving the hiring, retention and promotion of ethnic minority attorneys.

The Vault Diversity Programs Directory is a special advertising section in the *Vault Guide to the Top 100 Law Firms*. For information on listing your firm in the directory, contact corporatesales@vault.com.

V∧ULT CAREER LIBRARY   **681**

KIRKLAND & ELLIS LLP

200 East Randolph Drive

Chicago, IL 60601

www.kirkland.com

Kirkland's commitment to diversity is reflected in the Firm's commitment of time, budget and resources, and is reinforced by the work performed by our Firmwide Diversity Committee. The committee's focus is the recruitment, retention and advancement of attorneys in a manner that promotes diversity at all levels within the Firm. The 43-member committee includes four members of Kirkland's Executive Management Committee, each of our office's recruiting chair partners, as well as associates and partners from every office of the Firm. In addition, Kirkland recently established three Diversity Subcommittees (Racial/Ethnic; Gender; and Gay, Lesbian, Bisexual, and Transgender) to improve the efficiency and effectiveness of our Firmwide Committee.

The Firmwide Diversity Committee budget supports Kirkland's diversity initiatives and permits sponsorship of a broad range of diverse organizations, events and activities. In 2006, the Kirkland & Ellis Foundation contributed $1,593,000 to the sponsorship of non-profit organizations, foundations, and programs that directly or indirectly benefit diversity-related initiatives.

In 2004, Kirkland expanded its Minority Scholarship Program, establishing the Kirkland & Ellis LLP Diversity Fellowship Program. The goal of the Diversity Fellowship is to attract more minority lawyers to Kirkland and more broadly to the practice of law. Kirkland's Diversity Fellowship awards a $15,000 stipend to students selected among candidates receiving offers to join the summer program. The Firm has established the Fellowship at fourteen leading law schools across the county and in 2006 began offering a limited number of at-large Fellowships for which applicants from any ABA accredited law school are eligible. The program has grown from nine fellowships in 2005, to eleven in 2006, to the seventeen Fellowship recipients in 2007.

KRAMER LEVIN NAFTALIS & FRANKEL LLP

1177 Avenue of the Americas

New York, NY 10036

www.kramerlevin.com

At Kramer Levin, we realize that exposure to varied perspectives, experiences and backgrounds enhances our work environment and creates a culture of acceptance and professional growth.

Our firm's mission statement is to take proactive measures to build and promote mutually beneficial relationships and to operate the Firm in an inclusive, ethical and culturally sensitive manner which represents the range of human differences. Diversity, as defined by the Firm, is an inclusive concept and encompasses, without limitation, race, color, ethnicity, gender, sexual orientation, gender identity and expression, religion, nationality, age, disability and marital and parental status.

The following are some of the of the efforts undertaken by the firm in pursuit of its commitment to diversity -

• A Diversity Speaker series that focuses on raising awareness of the various cultural heritage months. Some of our speakers have included: New Jersey Federal Judge, the honorable Judge Joseph A. Greenaway, Jr; noted author and Professor of Asian American Studies and Urban Affairs and Planning at Hunter College, Peter Kwong; and Evan Wolfson, founder and Executive Director of Freedom to Marry.

• We have a number of openly gay partners and associates and support their networking and social events.

• The firm was a sponsor in the newly organized NY Minority Attorney Networking Series for 2007.

• Partnering with clients and others to hold diversity focused seminars including "Cultural Diversity as a Business Skill" and "How to Fit your Career into your Life".

© 2007 Vault Inc.

LATHAM & WATKINS LLP

633 West Fifth Street, Suite 4000

Los Angeles, CA 90071-2007

www.lw.com

Our commitment to diversity is more than a philosophy. It's something we work at and strive for at every turn. In a recent Vault Guide to the Top 100 Law Firms, one of our associates noted that Latham "welcomes a more diverse population." A female associate recalled, "One big reason I chose Latham was the number and high profile of women partners." An openly gay associate commented on how comfortable he felt at Latham and said, "People judge you here by your work and commitment, not by your private life." And a summer associate who attended our fall Diversity Weekend for law students said, "The fact that Latham dedicated so many resources in arranging Diversity Weekend shows their commitment to recruiting a diverse summer class. With many talented minority candidates shying away from big firms, it seems that Latham has stumbled upon a very successful recruiting model: let candidates get to know the firm, and get to know each other."

We have continued our strong efforts toward maintaining and increasing diversity at Latham by forming a Diversity Committee comprised of representatives from the Recruiting, Associates, Marketing, Executive and Training Committees, among others. In addition, our internal EEO Board provides a supportive forum for addressing discrimination or harassment issues should they arise. Attorneys of diverse racial and ethnic backgrounds, sexual orientation and gender have long been represented on the firm's management committees responsible for promotions to partnership, recruiting and training, among other responsibilities.

LOEB & LOEB LLP

10100 Santa Monica Boulevard, Suite 2200

Los Angeles, CA 90067

www.loeb.com

Loeb & Loeb, along with its clients, places a high value on maintaining as diverse a workforce as possible at all levels of the firm. The firm is committed to achieving its goal of a fully diverse workplace in which all attorneys and staff feel welcome, valued and included.

The Vault Diversity Programs Directory is a special advertising section in the *Vault Guide to the Top 100 Law Firms*. For information on listing your firm in the directory, contact corporatesales@vault.com.

VAULT CAREER LIBRARY   683

LORD BISSELL & BROOK, LLP

111 South Wacker Drive

Chicago, IL 60606

www.lordbissell.com

Our Diversity Committee, Director of Diversity and firm leadership are charged with focusing on the recruitment, retention and promotion of minority and LGBT attorneys. We sponsor quarterly meetings for our minority associates. These meetings are facilitated by our outside diversity consultant and are attended by partners once per year, or if requested by the minority associates. This structure allows our associates to raise and discuss concerns freely and anonymously. Any issues are brought by our consultant to the Diversity Committee. Our Lesbian and Gay Attorney Network and Women's Initiative are strongly supported by the firm. We encourage our diverse and female attorneys to gather informally and work together from time to time for mutual support and to discuss issues of common concern. As deemed necessary, information and issues are brought to the attention of the Diversity Committee and/or firm management.

The firm makes a conscious effort to reach out to minorities in its recruitment program for summer associates. We interview students at various minority student venues and actively provide sponsorship of events organized by minority law student organizations and attend minority student job-related events at law schools.

Our diversity efforts reach beyond our office to our community. In January 2003 we held our first annual celebration of Martin Luther King Jr. Day. This event became an instant success that the firm wholeheartedly embraced, and has quickly become a widely anticipated firm tradition. In addition to firm-sponsored community activities, the firm encourages its attorneys to become involved in diverse bar and community organizations. Lord, Bissell & Brook provides funds for membership fees, seminar attendance, and event sponsorships.

LOWENSTEIN SANDLER

65 Livingston Avenue

Roseland, NJ 07068

Phone: (973) 597-2500

Fax: (973) 597-2400

Lowenstein Sandler PC has a strong commitment to a diverse workplace. The firm requires all attorneys and stall to attend diversity training. The firm also has implemented several policies and programs to encourage the recruitment, retention, and promotion of lawyers from diverse social, economic, cultural and personal backgrounds. The firm's commitment to diversity is reinforced at all levels of the firm, from senior management, throughout the partnership ranks, within the associate recruiting, training, and mentoring programs, and among the staff. As a result of these efforts, Lowenstein Sandler ranks:

- First among New Jersey's largest law firms with the greatest number of minority partners between 1995 and 2004, according to the December 6, 2004 issue of the New Jersey Law Journal.

- National recipient of the 2005 Multicultural Law magazine Diversity Initiatives Award.

- No. 20 in the 2005 "Top 100 Law Firms for Diversity" according to Multicultural Law magazine.

- Established STRIDES, a Lowenstein Sandler initiative focused on advancing the careers of women in business.

The firm's commitment to diversity is implemented primarily by three separate committees of the firm: the Diversity Initiatives Committee, the Recruiting Committee, and the Associate, Counsel & Director Committee. To solidify senior management's commitment to diversity, the firm also has integrated women and minority directors into key leadership positions in firm management such as the Board of Directors, Department Chairs, Practice Group Leaders, the New Directors Qualifications Committee, the Strategic Growth and Planning Committee, and the Recruiting Committee.

© 2007 Vault Inc.

MANATT, PHELPS & PHILLIPS, LLP

11355 W. Olympic Blvd.

Los Angeles, CA 90064

www.manatt.com

Manatt's continuing commitment to diversity mirrors the rapid growth of minority business enterprises in America. The number of minorities serving in decision-making capacities and on corporate boards has also increased dramatically. As America's boardrooms grow to look more like our diverse neighborhoods, Manatt is likewise committed to a diverse workplace that reflects the community within which our professionals and clients live and work. Diversity, therefore, is not only a business priority for our firm, but we recognize that it is essential for our success.

Manatt is committed not only to the recruitment of minority lawyers, but also to retention and professional development. Midlevel and senior partners make a concerted effort to include minority lawyers and partners in client development opportunities, challenging work and civic organizations to maximize opportunities to increase their profiles within the community.

Manatt seeks candidates who share our core values, regardless of race, color, sexual orientation, gender or religion. We seek candidates who come from a diverse background, who have a unique set of experiences and who possess a cultural awareness that will be beneficial to the firm and our clients. We are also focused on recruiting diverse partners, recognizing that increasing diversity at the highest levels of the firm is essential to creating an environment that embraces and nurtures opportunities for long-term diversity.

MAYER, BROWN, ROWE & MAW LLP

W-71 South Wacker

Chicago, IL 60606-4637

www.mayerbrownrowe.com

At Mayer, Brown, Rowe & Maw LLP, we view the attainment of diversity at all levels as crucial to, and a natural result of, building a cohesive, successful law firm. We recruit, develop and promote the highest caliber lawyers and are committed to providing our lawyers with opportunities to realize their potential regardless of race, religious beliefs, ethnicity, gender or sexual orientation.

The Firm has a Committee on Diversity and Inclusion (CDI) which is composed of 35 partners from our North American and London offices. We hired a Diversity Initiatives Manager and Coordinator to ensure every aspect of our diversity-related issues is being addressed and brought to the attention of the CDI in a timely manner.

The firm is also investing in its future with initiatives designed to better prepare and educate the next generation of diverse law students. Our "How to Succeed in Law School" panel is designed to prepare first-year diverse law students across the nation for the challenges that await them in law school. Our "Resume Workshop" and "Mock Interview Program" helps second-year diverse law students hone the skills necessary for success in today's competitive market. We sponsor and/or conduct a variety of workshops, panel discussions, and diversity-related conferences with our clients, potential clients, and through partnerships with organizations like the Minority Corporate Counsel Association (MCCA). In 2005 we became the national sponsor of the National Black Law Students Association's Frederick Douglass Moot Court Competition.

The Vault Diversity Programs Directory is a special advertising section in the *Vault Guide to the Top 100 Law Firms*. For information on listing your firm in the directory, contact corporatesales@vault.com.

VAULT CAREER LIBRARY

685

MCCARTER & ENGLISH, LLP

Four Gateway Center, 100 Mulberry Street

Newark, NJ 07102-4096

www.mccarter.com

At McCarter & English, we are committed to creating a firm that reflects the strengths and capabilities of our diverse community and profession. The embodiment of that commitment is our Diversity Committee and the initiatives we support. We seek to hire and retain attorneys who share the firm's conviction that a culturally diverse workplace is essential in combining quality of life and superior service in meeting client goals. To that end, M&E actively participates in many legal and business community organizations and programs focused on increasing diversity and awareness within our profession.

Our EEO Policy

As an Equal Opportunity employer, McCarter & English, LLP offers all candidates equal opportunity for employment and advancement based on their ability and without regard to race, religion, color, sex, sexual orientation, learning disability, age, national origin, marital status, genetic information, citizenship status or physical or mental disability or other classification or characteristics protected by federal, state or local law.

MCKENNA LONG & ALDRIDGE LLP

303 Peachtree Street, NE

Atlanta, GA 30308

www.mckennalong.com

McKenna Long & Aldridge LLP is committed to achieve the goals of diversity and inclusiveness. The following principles are the foundation of this commitment:

• To provide full access to career opportunity to everyone throughout the firm;

• To be inclusive of everyone, regardless of differences in race, color, national origin, gender, religion, age, disability, sexual orientation, culture, or lifestyle; and

• To recruit, develop, promote and retain a world-class talent base that reflects the diversity of the communities in which we live.

Our belief is that recruiting, hiring and developing a diverse work force makes MLA a stronger and more competitive firm. Therefore, MLA is committed to attracting and retaining the best and brightest employees who reflect the diversity of our society. To accomplish this, MLA has established relationships with key universities, student and professional organizations, and established an internal Diversity Committee in 2003.

Current committee members include: Tami Azorsky (Chair), Partners Michael Boucher, Donna Donlon, Hakim Hilliard, Chris Humphreys, Maggie Joslin, Mimi Lee, Mark Meagher & Tom Wardell; Associates Michael Freed, Mimi Glenn, Margaret Johnson & Rupa Singh; and Recruitment Professionals Dan Conway, Julie Inouye, Jennifer Queen & Diana Ross-Butler

© 2007 Vault Inc.

MILES & STOCKBRIDGE P.C.

10 Light Street

Baltimore, MD 21202-1487

www.milesstockbridge.com

Miles & Stockbridge P.C. is committed to recruiting, developing, retaining, and promoting intelligent and dedicated lawyers and other legal professionals from diverse cultures and backgrounds. We believe that a diverse group of talented legal professionals is critically important to the success of our firm and our clients. We define diversity broadly to encompass, without limitation, race, color, ethnicity, gender, age, sexual orientation, religion, nationality, any disability, and marital and parental status.

Since January 2003, we have appointed a diversity director, formed a Diversity Committee, hired diversity consultants and adopted a formal Diversity Action Plan. Our firm's chairman and CEO co-chairs our Diversity Committee, which includes other top leaders, principals and associates of diverse backgrounds. Our firm also supports the goals and activities of two voluntary affinity groups: The Miles Minority Network and The Women's Network, both designed not only to provide support and mentoring to each other, but also to provide outside leadership, community outreach and business development opportunities.

From January 2003 to September 2006, we have hired 13 lawyers of color. Nearly one-half of our associates are women and we are steadily increasing the number of women principals in our firm. In the summers of 2005 and 2006, four out of ten summer associates were students of color. One-third of our 2006 entry-level lawyers are lawyers of color. Miles & Stockbridge P.C. has received consistently high marks as an overall place to work in The American Lawyer Surveys of Midlevel and Summer Associates of major law firms. Our midlevel lawyers and our summer associates have given us top rankings in categories such as: training and guidance; opportunities to work with partners; confidence in the firm's leadership; collegiality; family-friendliness; and dedication to diversity. Our rankings on our efforts toward diversity have increased steadily each year. In addition, in 2005 and 2006, we ranked among the Top 100 law firms for diversity by MultiCultural Law magazine, the magazine for diversity in the legal profession.

MILLER & CHEVALIER

655 Fifteenth St. NW, Suite 900

Washington, DC 20005-5701

www.millerchevalier.com

Miller & Chevalier is committed to enhancing the diversity of its legal service team. The firm values the different individual backgrounds of all of its professionals and staff and the benefits those diverse experiences bring to the firm and its clients. Indeed, we believe that a diverse law firm environment can work to everyone's benefit. For example, a legal team composed of lawyers from diverse backgrounds and cultures can foster a more creative work environment, produce a more effective result for the client and enhance the lawyer-client relationship.

An ultimate goal of the firm is to create a workplace environment in which everyone feels encouraged to do his or her best for the client, communicates openly and honestly with colleagues, and has the opportunities needed to thrive professionally. The firm holds itself to this standard. Notably, the firm recently received the Bar Association of the District of Columbia's Constance L. Belfiore 2006 Quality of Life Award. (The firm was a finalist for this award in 2005.) The firm also received the No. 1 ranking among D.C. law firms in the 2003 American Lawyer Mid-Level Associate Survey.

Going forward, the firm knows much work remains to be done. As a result, improving our diversity is a key priority of the firm's strategic planning. In 2005, the firm's Executive Committee endorsed a comprehensive strategy to guide the firm's efforts to have a thriving, diverse attorney workforce. This effort is coordinated by the firm's Diversity Committee, which is made up of a cross-section of members and associates, plus the pro bono counsel and managers of legal recruiting and lawyer development.

The Vault Diversity Programs Directory is a special advertising section in the *Vault Guide to the Top 100 Law Firms*. For information on listing your firm in the directory, contact corporatesales@vault.com.

VAULT CAREER LIBRARY 687

MINTZ, LEVIN, COHN, FERRIS, GLOVSKY AND POPEO PC

One Financial Center
Boston, MA 02111
Phone: (617) 542-6000
Fax: (617) 542-2241

Mintz Levin Cohn Ferris Glovsky and Popeo, PC has a genuine commitment to diversity and is involved in encouraging diversity both at the firm and in the legal profession. We adhere to a strict policy of equal opportunity, both in letter and spirit, and value diversity among our employees, which we consistently work to foster. The firm is a diverse workplace defined by an open, supportive, collegial environment.

Mintz Levin's commitment to diversity is driven by its diversity mission: "To fully understand and value diversity in its employees, clients and other constituencies, and to integrate this appreciation into the Firm's values, vision, mission, culture, policies and practices." The firm has a 14-member Diversity Committee to weave this mission into the firm's strategic direction. The committee consists of 10 partners, three associates and a non-attorney professional, each representing a different constituency group. Our Diversity Committee reflects our firm's diversity and is chaired by one of the four managing partners. The committee meets every month and is charged with formulating and adopting policies that impact recruiting, retention, mentoring and promoting a diverse work force, including attorneys, other legal professionals and support staff.

In addition to the Diversity Committee, the firm actively encourages the establishment of so-called affinity groups within the firm. In late 2003, a GLBT (gay, lesbian, bisexual, transgender) Group was established, consisting of approximately 17 partners, associates and senior professionals that meet quarterly. The Minority Attorneys Group has been meeting for over a decade on a quarterly basis. These forums provide an opportunity for mutual support, sharing concerns and establishing informal mentoring.

MORGAN & FINNEGAN, L.L.P.

3 World Financial Center, 20th Floor
New York, NY 10281-2101
www.morganfinnegan.com

Morgan & Finnegan is strongly committed to fostering diversity in its workplace. We believe that encouraging and promoting a diverse professional work environment is critical to the success of the firm. This commitment and belief is demonstrated not only by these words but through our actions.

We believe that encouraging diversity increases our abilities, creativity and effectiveness, while deepening our richness as an intellectual resource for our clients. Our clients come from different parts of the United States, as well as many other countries, reflecting many different backgrounds. Fully half our work has an international component. We believe that the more our firm reflects the overall business world we serve, the better we can understand our clients' needs and concerns, and the more valuable we become as a professional resource to help them achieve their goals.

Many of our clients expect their outside service providers, including their intellectual property counsel, to actively promote diversity within their ranks. At the same time, we recognize that the record of diversity within the sphere of intellectual property law firms leaves ample room for improvement. Our commitment to our clients is not only that we will take part in the effort to promote diversity in the IP bar, but that we will take a leadership position in changing the landscape of diversity within the IP bar. We are actively taking steps that are designed not only to improve diversity in the profession today, but to foster and encourage interest in the IP profession by a more diverse group of candidates in the future.

We consider it both a moral obligation and a practical necessity to recruit, retain and promote a diverse array of candidates, and ensure that the pool of diverse candidates from which we recruit and hire grows steadily from year to year.

© 2007 Vault Inc.

MORGAN, LEWIS & BOCKIUS LLP

1701 Market Street
Philadelphia, PA 19103
www.morganlewis.com

The success of our diversity efforts at Morgan Lewis rests on the commitment of senior firm management and the successes of our people. Detailed below are just a few examples demonstrating the scope of our efforts and reports of our successes.

First, in June 2006 we hosted an extremely successful Attorneys of Color (AOC) Meeting. This meeting provided firm attorneys of color with the opportunity to:

- Network and develop relationships with other attorneys of color throughout the firm and with firm management to whom they might not otherwise have access;

- Focus on client development by maximizing the use of the natural network created through their diversity;

- Discuss the firm's diversity goals in the broader context of the firm's business strategies; and

- Gain a greater understanding of what Morgan Lewis does well and where we can improve our efforts in addressing issues that affect attorneys of color.

Conference attendees were uniformly positive about the event. For the attendees, the most meaningful "take away" from the AOC meeting was that the firm demonstrated that its' commitment to diversity is a reality. This was due in large part to the presence of the firm's chair, advisory board, practice group leaders and other senior attorneys who actively participated in the program. Participants emphasized the benefit of honest communication, interactive discussions, and the opportunity to address issues candidly in small-group settings. Finally, participants commented that the opportunity to network and build relationships with other attorneys of color was invaluable. We have scheduled another AOC meeting for April 4 and 5, 2008.

MORRISON & FOERSTER LLP

1290 Avenue of the Americas
New York, NY 10104-0050
www.mofo.com

We are a collection of individuals with different personalities, backgrounds and experiences. We share the view that our differences make a difference. We value the perspectives that the diversity of our lawyers brings to our firm. We believe that in our open-minded and collaborative environment it is easier for individuals to say what they really think, to conceptualize new solutions to problems and to embrace fresh ideas.

The firm has been recognized by The American Lawyer in its "A-List," which includes diversity as one measurement, for the past five years, by Fortune Magazine as one of the Best Companies to Work for in 2005 and 2006, and by the Minority Law Journal as sixth in diversity among U.S. law firms in 2007. The Vault Guide to the Top 100 Law Firms ranked the firm first in diversity for five years in a row and has also ranked the firm among the best with respect to minorities, women, and gays and lesbians.

The firm was honored with the Catalyst Award in 1993 for demonstrated commitment to the leadership development of female employees - one of only two law firms to have ever received the award.

Our lawyers are graduates of over 94 U.S. and 61 international law schools and are fluent in 46 foreign languages. In 2006, lawyers of color accounted for 10% of partners, 31% of associates and 45% of summer associates. Women accounted for 19% of partners, 46% of associates and 41% of summer associates.

Although the firm has made great strides in the area of diversity, we recognize that achieving our diversity goals is a work in progress, and we continue to strive to increase the diversity of our workforce realizing that much work remains to be done, for the firm and for society.

More information on diversity at Morrison & Foerster, including diversity statistics, is available at www.mofo.com.

The Vault Diversity Programs Directory is a special advertising section in the *Vault Guide to the Top 100 Law Firms*. For information on listing your firm in the directory, contact corporatesales@vault.com.

NEAL, GERBER & EISENBERG LLP

2 North LaSalle Street

Chicago, IL 60602-3801

www.ngelaw.com

Neal, Gerber & Eisenberg LLP is strongly committed to diversity. We have made great strides in recent years with respect to our diversity efforts and, yet, we recognize that the drive to diversify is a mission that is never "completed" in the true sense of the word. It is a goal that requires constant vigilance and continuous effort, and to which we are dedicated.

We Value Diversity

We recognize that diversity is a vital component of our culture, identity, strategic planning and overall well-being. It fosters equal opportunity; creates an open, positive and satisfying work environment; and promotes the highest standards and ideals of our legal system. By embracing diversity, we reflect that which is great about our community and society at large; we best serve our clients' interests; we fulfill our obligations as members of the bar; and we promote creativity, opportunity and professional development at every level.

We Look To The Future

We strive to keep our diversity efforts focused on the future - on what we can be and can accomplish. Our goal is to maximize the number of attorneys involved in our efforts, to share in the benefits of diversity and to clearly communicate the value and rewards that derive from each individual's contribution to the effort. We are driven to capitalize upon our successes and to further incentivize positive behaviors.

NGE will - as it always has - continue to respect, support, and reward individuals on the basis of personal achievement and contribution, and to build a community that recognizes the value of diversity in achieving a better work environment and a stronger firm.

ORRICK, HERRINGTON & SUTCLIFFE LLP

666 Fifth Avenue

New York, NY 10103

www.orrick.com

COMMITMENT TO INCLUSION

Orrick's commitment to global diversity and inclusion is genuine and absolute and comes from the highest levels of the firm's leadership. At Orrick, respect for individual differences is a core value, a cornerstone of the way we work.

Retention

Orrick has many policies and programs that positively impact our ability to attract, retain and develop our lawyers.

- Firmwide Diversity Committee: Since 1990, Orrick's Diversity Committee (one of the first in a major law firm) has advised management on a broad range of issues to ensure that Orrick is successful in hiring, retaining and promoting diverse lawyers. As part of our global initiative, last year the firm expanded its program to Europe and Asia.

- Affinity Groups: In 2005 we established firm wide affinity groups for Asian, Hispanic/Latino, African-American, LGBT, male and female attorneys and designated a member of its Executive Committee to serve as a "mentee" for each group. Each Affinity Group engaged in candid dialogue about their unique experiences and concerns and developed recommendations regarding the recruitment, retention and professional development of the attorneys in each group. Orrick will expand its Attorney Affinity Group initiative to its international offices this year.

- Women's Career Initiative: Orrick's Women's Career Initiative is devoted to recruiting, promoting and retaining women attorneys. It supports the professional development of our female lawyers by educating all the firm's attorneys about issues impacting women in the practice of law and in the global community; providing training and mentoring, hosting an annual women's networking event for Orrick lawyers and clients, to name just a few.

© 2007 Vault Inc.

PAUL, HASTINGS, JANOFSKY & WALKER LLP

515 S Flower Street, 25th Floor

Los Angeles, CA 90071

www.paulhastings.com

At Paul Hastings, diversity means business. And we take our business seriously.

With 1,200 attorneys in 18 offices worldwide, we are recognized as a "Firm of Choice" for diversity in law firm management and leadership. Our diversity attorneys serve as managing partners, practice group leaders and committee chairs, with more than a third holding firm leadership positions. Chambers Global, American Lawyer, Vault Inc. and others have recognized the diverse group of Paul Hastings partners as the best attorneys in the world. For 2007, we are ranked in the Top 20% of firms on the Minority Law Journal Diversity Scorecard, and we have been named one of the Top 100 Law Firms for Diversity by Multicultural Law Magazine.

Paul Hastings works closely with prominent diversity organizations and networks. Our relationships generate thousands of hours and hundreds of thousands of dollars to advance women, disabled, GLBT, and attorneys of color and others within the global legal community. We also actively recruit lawyers and law students from diverse backgrounds. For the past six years, we have continued to expand our representation of diversity in new hires around the globe.

Diversity is fundamental to our success, and we are committed to providing opportunities in a global workplace that offer equal opportunity and access without limits. Our training and development programs are designed to help our attorneys attain and maintain excellence with a particular focus on our differences and individual contributions.

We are honored that our global diversity efforts have received national and international recognition. Our people and practices reflect our diversity. It's not a buzz word. It's business to us, and diversity means business.

We reach out to diverse communities through our initiatives.

PAUL, WEISS, RIFKIND, WHARTON & GARRISON, LLP

1285 Avenue of the Americas

New York, NY 10019-6064

www.paulweiss.com

Our efforts to recruit and retain a diverse workforce have been recognized through our rankings at the top of surveys addressing the hiring and retention of lawyers of color.

• The 2007 and 2006 *Minority Law Journal*'s Diversity Scorecard survey ranked Paul, Weiss as the most diverse law firm in the United States. The survey ranks the largest firms in the country according to their percentage of racially diverse lawyers.

• The *2006 Vault Guide to the Top 100 Law Firms* named Paul, Weiss one of the top law firms in the country for diversity.

• *Multicultural Law Magazine* has consistently ranked Paul, Weiss as one of the top 100 law firms for diversity.

Our success is derived from the unique skills, talents and perspectives of our lawyers and staff - people of all backgrounds, regardless of race, ethnicity, gender, sexual orientation, religion, age, marital status or physical capability.

Paul, Weiss has undertaken numerous initiatives to fulfill our commitment to diversity:

• For more than a decade, our Diversity Committee consisting of firm partners, counsel and associates has led our efforts to design and implement recruitment and retention programs aimed at increasing diversity. The Committee meets regularly and serves as a forum for the generation of new ideas and the discussion of diversity issues throughout the firm.

• Our Women's Initiatives Committee, comprised of partners, counsel and associates, works to create an environment that develops and advances the professional lives of women at the firm through numerous programs.

The Vault Diversity Programs Directory is a special advertising section in the *Vault Guide to the Top 100 Law Firms*. For information on listing your firm in the directory, contact corporatesales@vault.com.

VAULT CAREER LIBRARY

691

PEPPER HAMILTON LLP

3000 Two Logan Square

Philadelphia, PA 19103

www.pepperlaw.com

Pepper Hamilton LLP's diversity efforts are not knee-jerk reactions to client requests and demands but part of the very fabric of our Firm. Long before "diversity" took on its present meaning, Pepper embarked on its diversity journey, electing its first woman partner nearly a half-century ago; promoting its first African-American partner (now a senior federal court judge) shortly thereafter; and choosing one of the first woman executive partners in the country.

Our journey continued in 2006, including electing a woman as Chair of the Executive Committee and by:

• Updating the assessment performed by our diversity consultant through one-on-one meetings with minority associates;

• Introducing in July 2006 "Celebrate Diversity," a Firm-wide event at the African-American Museum in Philadelphia;

• Significantly supporting Villanova Law School's Diversity Initiative, including awarding full tuition scholarships to two minority law students annually, hiring two Villanova minority 1L students annually as law clerks, sponsoring the annual King lecture, and funding the Pepper Hamilton National Summer Program for minority undergraduates, a six-week, credit-bearing program;

• Serving as an initial sponsor of Drexel University College of Law Diversity Fellowships, including providing $5,000 a year in living expenses and a six month co-op;

• Participating in the Martin Luther King Breakfast sponsored by the Barristers' Association of Philadelphia and many other minority bar association events;

• Sponsoring the ABA's Annual Conference for the Minority Lawyer;

• Sponsoring the National Asian Pacific American Bar Association's annual conference

PERKINS COIE LLP

1201 Third Avenue, 48th Floor

Seattle, WA 98101

www.perkinscoie.com

Perkins Coie is a large international law firm with a presence on the Pacific Rim. The firm values diversity as integral to the firm's culture and practice of law. The firm is committed to the growth and development of legal communities that reflect the rich diversity of our communities at large. We are proud of our history and look forward to continuous improvement in the recruitment, development and retention of a diverse workforce. We have recently created the position Director of Diversity and Professional Development.

One of the most visible ways in which the firm illustrates its commitment to diversity is through our 1L Diversity Student Fellowship. Established in the Seattle office in 1991 by an in-house Minority Hiring Task Force, the fellowship seeks applications from diverse first-year law students from around the country. The fellowship position is available in several offices and offers a summer associate job and a $7500 scholarship.

We interview at the Northwest Minority Job Fair (Host Firm 2005/2006), the Southeastern Minority Job Fair, the Oregon Minority Job Fair, the Cook County Bar Association Minority Law Student Job Fair, the Black Law Student Association's Regional Job Fairs, the Impact Disabled law student Job Fair, the Lavender Law Career Fair, the MCCA/Vault Diversity Career Fair, the ABA/CLEO Job Fair, and Howard University School of Law in Washington, D.C. We host campus outreach receptions at a number of schools. In addition, we provide a diversity contact list so that law students with questions can contact lawyers of color or other diverse backgrounds here at the firm.

© 2007 Vault Inc.

PILLSBURY WINTHROP SHAW PITTMAN LLP

50 Fremont Street

San Francisco, CA 94105

www.pillsburylaw.com

Diversity in our Firm. There is a reason we consistently rank among the top firms for diversity in the legal profession. Diversity is part of who we are, and we work hard to keep it that way. We were the first AmLaw 100 firm to elect a woman as chair. Chevron Corporation honored us with its first Law Firm Diversity Recognition Award in 2005, and again in 2006. Diversity is a key component of our strategic plan, and our chair works to ensure that inclusiveness is supported at all levels. Our goal is simple: to foster excellence in all of our people.

Diversity Committee. Pillsbury's Diversity Committee includes firm leaders recognized for their commitment. The Committee chair, Kevin Fong, currently serves on the ABA Commission on Racial and Ethnic Diversity in the Profession. The Committee sponsors networks for the firm's African-American, Asian-American, Latino, LGBT and Women Attorneys, and holds retreats, discussions and other career-building activities. We work closely with community and minority organizations, law schools, and bar associations to further our shared goals through financial support, volunteerism and pro bono activities.

Our diversity initiatives are closely aligned with our recruiting efforts. The Recruiting Committee is supported by LGBT and Minority Attorney subcommittees that actively sponsor job fairs and support local and national organizations.

Supportive Benefit Policies. Work-life balance is important to all of us. Pillsbury has been a leader in adopting generous and inclusive policies. We were one of the first to adopt a part-time program for attorneys and to extend benefits to domestic partners. Today, domestic partners are offered the same benefits as offered to spouses. Attorneys who adopt or have children through surrogacy are eligible for up to 18 weeks leave, the same as under our pregnancy leave policy.

POTTER ANDERSON & CORROON LLP

Hercules Plaza, 1313 N. Market St.

PO Box 951

Wilmington, DE 19899

www.potteranderson.com

Potter Anderson & Corroon believes that to provide "best in class" service to our clients, our lawyers and staff must reflect a broad spectrum of cultures, races and ethnicities. A leader among Delaware firms in promoting women in the legal profession since 1923, when one of the first two women admitted to the practice of law in Delaware was hired by the firm, Potter Anderson & Corroon now has the highest percentage of women partners among all large Delaware firms. Two of the firm's five Executive Committee members are women, as are the leaders of several of the firm's practice areas and the chairs of several firm committees.

The firm's commitment to diversity does not end with its unparalleled record of encouraging and promoting women to leadership positions. The firm is equally committed to recruiting and promoting lawyers of color. The firm continually seeks opportunities to attract a racially and ethnically diverse pool of candidates. For example, the firm has organized and hosted receptions for minority students at regional law schools to provide the students the opportunity to learn more about Potter Anderson & Corroon and the Delaware legal market in general. The firm has also actively participated in the Delaware Minority Job Fair for 1st and 2nd year law students since its inception in the early 1990's, and is the host of the DuPont Minority Job Fair (open to Potter Anderson & Corroon and the 37 other firms that participate in the DuPont Legal Model). In addition, the firm played a key role in the establishment of the Delaware Minority Supplemental Bar Review Course, now run by the Multicultural Judges and Lawyers Section of the Delaware State Bar Association, and has been a leader in efforts to recruit minority law students to Delaware.

The Vault Diversity Programs Directory is a special advertising section in the *Vault Guide to the Top 100 Law Firms*. For information on listing your firm in the directory, contact corporatesales@vault.com.

VAULT CAREER LIBRARY   693

QUARLES & BRADY LLP

411 East Wisconsin Avenue, Suite 2040

Milwaukee, WI 53202-4497

www.quarles.com

Quarles & Brady is committed to an aggressive agenda to promote and achieve diversity.

Diversity Committee Formed. The Executive Committee appointed a Diversity Committee in 2001 to ensure that diversity is a part of the infrastructure of our organization. Diversity Committee members represent each office, and include partners, associates and staff, and three members of the firm's Executive Committee. All attorney time spent on committee work is billable.

Diversity Consultant Retained - The "Business Case" Presented. Quarles & Brady retained a consultant to assess our diversity climate and articulate the business case. She conducted focus groups with 500 partners, associates and staff in each of our offices, developed recommendations and leads firm-specific training programs. To set the stage, representatives of seven clients spoke at two events about their diversity initiatives and expectations of outside law firms.

Tangible Examples of Our Commitment. We demonstrate our commitment to diversity with tangible actions, including:

- Leadership. Women play a pivotal role in the decision-making process at the firm. In three offices (including our largest), our managing partners are women. Additionally, women hold about 40 percent of all leadership roles, and three women serve on our 12-person Executive Committee.

- Domestic Partner Benefits. Quarles & Brady respects not only the individual differences in lawyers and staff but also in their families; thus our written policies extend domestic partner benefits to all attorneys and staff.

- Mentoring. Quarles & Brady supports a three-year mentor program at the University of Wisconsin Law School. For our own associates, we provide individual mentoring for new hires for two years and practice group mentoring for all.

ROBINS, KAPLAN, MILLER & CIRESI L.L.P.

2800 LaSalle Plaza, 800 LaSalle Avenue

Minneapolis, MN 55402-2015

www.rkmc.com

Robins, Kaplan, Miller & Ciresi L.L.P. is committed to advancing diversity through action by ensuring that fairness, respect and professional opportunity for everyone remains integral to all of our recruiting, retention and promotion initiatives. The diverse background of our people brings necessary and varied perspectives that make us more than a diverse law firm; they make us a smart one.

Leadership

Since 1999, our firm has had a Diversity Committee and in 2005 we added a Diversity Manager to assist with execution of the diversity initiatives and our strategic plan. We are committed not only to increasing the diversity of our pipeline, but also ensuring that the firm management be as diverse as our associate ranks. In 2006, of the two associates promoted to partner, both were women and one was also an attorney of color. In 2007, of the three associates promoted to partner, one was an attorney of color.

Our firm is one of the incorporating law firms for the formation of the Twin Cities Diversity in Practice whose mission is to provide resources to accelerate the efforts of its members to identify, recruit, advance and retain lawyers of color in Minnesota's legal community. We are also a member of the Boston Lawyers Group.

Training

Our Exceptional Advocate training program provides early and vigorous trial training for associates and offers an opportunity to seek advice concerning effective advocacy from experienced lawyers at our firm. The Exceptional Advocate program is a 4-year curriculum, conducted in four phases:

Phase I - Court Trial / Arbitration

Phase II - Basic Jury Trials

Phase III - Complex Jury Trials

Phase IV - Advance Jury Trial

Other training includes a motion practice seminar, a deposition skills workshop, and an evidence course, among others.

© 2007 Vault Inc.

ROPES & GRAY LLP

One International Place
Boston, MA 02110
www.ropesgray.com

Ropes & Gray has long been committed to fostering diversity in the workplace, reflecting the firm's core values of excellence, fairness, collaboration and collegiality. Accordingly, we promote the recruitment, retention and advancement of people of diverse backgrounds at all levels of the firm. At Ropes & Gray, we see our individual differences as an asset which not only enhances the quality of life for each of us, but also strengthens our accomplishments as a firm. We understand that the differences in our backgrounds mean that our lawyers bring a variety of perspectives and ideas to the problems on which we are asked to collaborate, thereby enhancing our ability to serve our clients well and run our firm effectively.

We are proud of the diversity we have achieved at Ropes & Gray. We see our work environment as one where all individuals can thrive and are motivated to do their best, strengthened by their different backgrounds, perspectives and life experiences. The firm's continuing effort to that end is led by the Diversity Committee, comprised of both lawyers and staff. With a mandate to provide guidance and recommendations to the firm on policies and programs designed to retain and enhance the firm's diverse workforce, the Diversity Committee's primary goals are to attract and retain the most talented and motivated individuals and to maintain a culture of acceptance through education and outreach.

SACHNOFF & WEAVER

30 South Wacker Dr., 29th FL.
Chicago, IL 60606
www.sachnoff.com

Overview

Sachnoff & Weaver recognizes the value of the unique contributions that attorneys of diverse backgrounds can bring to the practice of law. To achieve its diversity goals, Sachnoff & Weaver is committed to not only the recruiting of attorneys of all backgrounds, including, among others, women and attorneys of color, but also the retention and promotion of its diverse attorneys. Sachnoff & Weaver attorneys personally and professionally contribute to diversity efforts in the greater legal community. These efforts result in a supportive environment that encourages and embraces diversity.

Recruitment

Sachnoff & Weaver's Resume Writing and Interview Skills Workshops are programs unique in Chicago. These workshops especially target first-year minority law students at local law schools. Students are invited to Sachnoff & Weaver for an afternoon where attorneys in a panel discussion provide insight into the interview process and offer advice on interview skills. Students are then assigned to an attorney for one-on-one resume critique sessions. This program has been such a success that plans are underway to expand the workshops to other local and regional law schools.

Sachnoff & Weaver attorneys actively seek out qualified diverse attorneys to recruit to the firm. Sachnoff & Weaver women have participated in panel discussions sponsored by the Northwestern School of Law Women's Coalition. We support minority student organizations and participate in minority student organization events. Sachnoff & Weaver has recruited at the Cook County Bar Association Minority Job Fair since its inception, and has participated in the Mid-Atlantic BLSA Job Fair, the National BLSA Midwest Recruiting Conference and the Lavender Law Job Fair.

The Vault Diversity Programs Directory is a special advertising section in the *Vault Guide to the Top 100 Law Firms*. For information on listing your firm in the directory, contact corporatesales@vault.com.

VAULT CAREER LIBRARY

695

SCHIFF HARDIN LLP

6600 Sears Tower
Chicago, IL 60606
www.schiffhardin.com

SCHIFF HARDIN LLP'S COMMITMENT TO DIVERSITY

Diversity is our number one organizational imperative. It is reflected in the ways that we recruit new attorneys and laterals, staff matters, select management, and make partnership advancement decisions. Our Diversity Committee reports to Schiff Hardin's Executive Committee. Diversity is an agenda item at all partners' meetings, as well as at assemblies for associates and support staff. Schiff Hardin's practice group leaders are accountable for diversity within their practice group. Our Professional Personnel Committee and our practice group leaders are charged with responsibility to review associates' work and client assignments to make sure that each associate receives appropriate opportunities to develop their skills and hone their experience. In 2007 we hired a staff person to work full time on advancing the efforts of our diversity committee.

The fact is that virtually all major law firms now talk about diversity, and this is good. At Schiff Hardin the facts demonstrate that we walk the talk and that we are doing better. From 2001 to 2007 our percentage of minority associates has doubled to 20% and 38% of our 2006 summer associates are minority law students. More than 46% of the law students in our 2007 summer program were females, and women now account for 46% of our associates and 21% of our partners. We have received national recognition for these achievements from Multicultural Law and Diversity and the Bar.

Diversity is not new at Schiff Hardin, the oldest Chicago-based law firm. Schiff Hardin was among the first nine Chicago law firms to become "leadership signatories" to both of the Chicago Bar Associations' Calls to Action, aimed at recruiting, retaining and promoting women and minorities in the profession. We are a signatory to the Policy Statement Regarding the Hiring and Retention of Minority Lawyers. We were among the first law firms to convene and support a Women's Networking Group, which actively mentors and assists women attorneys to advance their careers at the firm. We have developed programs to support attorneys who desire to work reduced hours but remain on the partnership track. We were one of the city's pioneers in providing same-sex domestic partner benefits.

SEYFARTH SHAW LLP

131 S. Dearborn Street, Suite 2400
Chicago, IL 60603
www.seyfarth.com

Our vision at Seyfarth Shaw is to be recognized as a role model for diversity in the legal community. We are in the midst of a three-year plan to help us reach that goal. Our leadership team continues its commitment to developing an environment of inclusion and engagement, and our diversity efforts are a pivotal part of that strategy.

We are making strides. Leadership positions within the firm are now held by an increasing number of female and minority attorneys. We have taken some concrete action steps to better attract, retain and develop minority and female attorneys. We are developing a firm-wide network of action teams to expand our firm's outreach efforts, and we have begun partnerships with our clients to work together to improve diversity in the communities we serve.

In 2006, we concentrated on building on an integrated, national effort in three key areas. A complete diversity annual report has been developed for both our clients and the members of our Firm. Here is a summary of our progress and achievements:

Recruitment

We are focused on increasing the diversity of among our attorneys at all levels, and we are seeing some promising results from our efforts. The percentage of female associates at Seyfarth Shaw (49.0%) exceeds the national average of 44.3%, based on information from NALP, the association for legal career professionals. The percentage of minority associates at Seyfarth (19.3%) is on par with NALP average (19.6%). Among all Seyfarth partners, 18.6% are female, above the NALP average of 17.0%. We have also seen the numbers of diverse summer associates increase to a total of 31% in 2006.

© 2007 Vault Inc.

SHEARMAN & STERLING LLP

599 Lexington Avenue
New York, NY 10022
www.shearman.com

Global Diversity Initiative

Shearman & Sterling LLP's Global Diversity Initiative has four strategic goals: (1) nurture a firm culture that supports and promotes diversity; (2) facilitate diversity in all aspects of the firm; (3) increase the recruitment, retention, development and advancement of attorneys from diverse backgrounds; and (4) directly promote diversity through involvement in the global legal community, nonprofit organizations and bar associations and client relationships. The firm employs best practices in diversity and recently received the coveted Minority Corporate Counsel Association's 2006 Thomas L. Sager Award for the Northeast Region in recognition of its demonstrated and sustained commitment to improve the hiring, retention and promotion of diverse attorneys.

Diversity Committee and Innovative Practices

In 2006, the firm launched a series of formal affinity resource groups. The groups are formed voluntarily and encourage mentoring relationships and opportunities for networking. Currently, the groups consist of the Women's Initiative for Success, Excellence and Retention ("WISER") , focusing on issues of interest to female attorneys, the Black Attorneys Aligned in the Quest for Excellence ("BLAQUE") , focusing on issues of interest to black lawyers in the legal community, and Sterling Pride, focusing on the lesbian, gay, bisexual and transgender ("LGBT") community.

Shearman & Sterling's Diversity Committee, established over a decade ago, includes partners, including the firm's senior partner, and associates. The firm also has a full-time Director of Diversity. The Committee meets regularly to put into action initiatives that promote diversity within the firm and the legal community. Time spent on such matters is billed to a firm account and included in the annual partner review process.

SHEFSKY & FROELICH, LTD.

111 East Wacker Drive, Suite 2800
Chicago, IL 60601
www.shefskylaw.com

Our Commitment to Diversity is Not a Matter of Public Relations

Diversity at Shefsky & Froelich is not a program or trend. It is our commitment to each and every employee and client, and that commitment makes us a better law firm to serve our clients.

Diversity is the cornerstone of community.

Diversity means differences in all the characteristics that make one person different from another – such as personality, work style, gender, sexual orientation, age, having a disability, ethnicity, socioeconomic level, work experience, educational background and race.

We celebrate all of these differences in our workplace

To expect diversity at our Firm is more than just the right thing to do, although it is certainly that. Diversity has a clear impact on our ability to serve our clients because diversity empowers all of our employees to think more critically and imaginatively and to understand perspectives other than their own. These are the very qualities most valued at Shefsky & Froelich.

Recruitment

Our Recruitment Committee and Diversity Committee work together to promote diversity. We have come a long way, but much work needs to be done. We actively participate in the annual Cook County Bar Association Minority Job Fair. Moreover, we have initiated direct relationships with the minority law student associations at the top area law schools. Further we recruit talented minority summer associate candidates at the top law schools.

We are passionately committed to aggressive goals and innovative collaborations that will continue to provide the resources necessary to identify, attract, and retain minority attorneys.

The strength and future of our firm rests in our collective ability to make true diversity a reality at Shefsky & Froelich.

The Vault Diversity Programs Directory is a special advertising section in the *Vault Guide to the Top 100 Law Firms*. For information on listing your firm in the directory, contact corporatesales@vault.com.

VAULT CAREER LIBRARY   697

SIDLEY AUSTIN LLP

One South Dearborn
Chicago, IL 60603
www.sidley.com

Commitment to Diversity

Sidley has been one of the most prominent and progressive proponents of law firm diversity. Many of our lawyers come from diverse backgrounds, races and beliefs. Our mission is to offer our skills and talents for the betterment of the legal profession and the diverse communities in which we practice, as well as to develop, support and encourage new generations of lawyers to carry on our commitment to excellence, integrity, diversity and collegiality.

Honors and Awards

In recognition of the firm's commitment to diversity, Sidley was awarded the Minority Corporate Counsel Association's Thomas L. Sager Award in 1999 and again in 2003. The Sager Award recognizes law firms that have demonstrated a sustained commitment to improve the hiring, retention and promotion of minority attorneys.

In 2005, the firm received the Catalyst Award. The award is given annually by Catalyst, the leading research and advisory organization dedicated to expanding opportunities for women in business. The award recognizes "innovative approaches with proven results taken by companies to address the recruitment, development and advancement of women", according to Catalyst. Sidley is only the second law firm to receive this prestigious award.

SIMPSON THACHER & BARTLETT LLP

425 Lexington Avenue
New York, NY 10017
www.simpsonthacher.com

Simpson Thacher has been a pioneer in promoting diversity in the legal profession and within the firm. In 1985, our partners Cyrus Vance and Conrad Harper spearheaded the adoption by the Association of the Bar of the City of New York of its groundbreaking initial Statement of Diversity Principles. At the time, Cyrus Vance chaired the drafting committee and Conrad Harper, the firm's first Black partner, was the president of the Association. Simpson was one of the initial signatories of the Association's 2003 Statement of Diversity Principles.

The Minority Law Journal's 2007 Diversity Scorecard recently ranked Simpson Thacher as the tenth most diverse firm nationwide. Our commitment to enhancing the diversity of our attorneys continues to be one of our firm's highest priorities.

Our Diversity Committee is responsible for the oversight of policies designed to enhance our overall diversity through the hiring, retention and promotion of minority attorneys. Our Women's Committee was established in May of 2006 to focus on the retention and promotion of women leaders at all levels of the firm. The firm retained consultants in the fall of 2006 to conduct a diversity assessment of our domestic offices. In response to the assessment, the Executive Committee has appointed a Diversity Task Force to propose and implement an action plan through which Simpson Thacher can promote a work environment in which all thrive professionally regardless of race, gender, or sexual orientation.

© 2007 Vault Inc.

SKADDEN, ARPS, SLATE, MEAGHER & FLOM LLP

4 Times Square
New York, NY 10036
www.skadden.com

As part of Skadden's strong commitment to promoting diversity at all levels, many years ago the firm established its diversity committee, which now comprises partners representing our offices in the United States, Europe and Asia, as well as administrative personnel. In addition to monitoring existing policies and practices that promote diversity and inclusion, the committee implements proactive strategies to address the issues of recruiting, training, retaining and promoting our attorneys in a manner that is consistent with Skadden's core values. Our committee recently established the associates/counsel diversity council to provide a clearly designed channel through which associates and counsel may assist in shaping and advancing the firm's diversity goals and objectives.

With respect to recruitment, Skadden's overarching philosophy is to build relationships with students by working with members of the law school community to support the endeavors and development of student groups and their members, and by holding informal gatherings, hosting cultural and social events, and presenting and participating in educational seminars at which students may meet our attorneys, learn strategies for making a successful transition from law school to practice and learn more about our firm.

The availability of effective professional and skills-development opportunities is crucial to our retention efforts. For this reason, we are committed to providing all of our attorneys with access to effective mentoring relationships, ongoing skills-training curricula relevant to our various practice areas, and channels for receiving evaluations and constructive feedback.

SONNENSCHEIN NATH & ROSENTHAL LLP

7800 Sears Tower, 233 South Wacker Drive
Chicago, IL 60606
www.sonnenschein.com

Sonnenschein believes that recruiting, retaining and promoting diverse attorneys to partnership and positions of leadership in our Firm will enable us to be a better law firm to our clients.

Our diversity mission statement states that:

"Diversity at Sonnenschein means inclusion of attorneys, professionals and other staff members of different races, genders, sexual orientations, gender identities and expressions, ethnic and religious backgrounds and abilities/disabilities. The Firm's goal is that the demographics of each office reflect the community in which the office is located."

Commitment

Sonnenschein's Firmwide Diversity Plan has been recognized as one of the most aggressive diversity initiatives in the country.

- A Firmwide Diversity Committee, a fulltime Director of Diversity, who is a partner of the Firm, a Firmwide Staff Diversity Committee and local diversity committees in each office work in concert to implement the written Diversity Plan.

- We are one of the few firms to have an active diversity supplier program.

- We have an accountability ranking system in which partners' contributions to diversity are linked to their compensation.

Diverse attorneys (minorities, gay and lesbian attorneys and attorneys with disabilities) comprise approximately 17% of our attorneys, 13% of our partners and 24% of our associates. Minority attorneys comprise approximately 14% of our attorneys, 85 of our partners and 23% of our associates. Women represent approximately 36% of our attorneys, 23% of our partners and 53% of our associates.

The Vault Diversity Programs Directory is a special advertising section in the *Vault Guide to the Top 100 Law Firms*. For information on listing your firm in the directory, contact corporatesales@vault.com.

VAULT CAREER LIBRARY   699

SULLIVAN & CROMWELL LLP

125 Broad Street
New York, NY 10004
www.sullcrom.com

S&C is committed to fostering a diverse and inclusive work environment. We also believe that diversity is vital to the Firm's ability to provide our clients with the highest level of service and excellence. Accordingly, our culture and policies value the unique abilities and perspectives of every individual and support diversity in its broadest sense, including race, gender, ethnicity, sexual orientation, gender identity, gender expression, disability and religious affiliation. We maintain a number of diversity initiatives, specifically directed at improving the recruitment, retention and advancement of women and minorities. The following are some of the most notable programs and initiatives:

Women's Initiative Committee.

Director of Diversity.

Firm Leadership.

Flex-time Policy.

Forums and other Gatherings.

Speakers and Diversity Workshops.

Recruiting Initiatives.

Community Development

SUTHERLAND ASBILL & BRENNAN LLP

999 Peachtree Street, NE
Atlanta, GA 30309
www.sablaw.com

Sutherland Asbill & Brennan LLP is committed to diversity in its workplace and to enhancing diversity in the legal profession. We believe that diverse skills, knowledge, and viewpoints make us a stronger, more productive law firm. We seek to hire and promote qualified lawyers and other professionals regardless of race, color, national origin, religion, gender or sexual orientation. We are proud of the important role that diverse lawyers and others play in our firm's growth and development. Our dedication is demonstrated by our firm's actions and the leadership roles our attorneys and other professionals undertake to promote diversity in the legal profession.

Sutherland has a 27-member Diversity Committee with responsibility for supporting and enhancing our firm culture. We recruit new lawyers by participating in the Southeastern Minority Job Fair, various job fairs focused on students of color, the Lavender Law Conference and on-campus interviews at Howard University School of Law. We focus on retention and advancement by providing mentoring and training programs to help all our attorneys excel.

We believe that our diversity enhances our value to the firm's clients as it enables us to provide them with a team of professionals possessing a breadth of experiences and perspectives. We are committed to working with our clients as they pursue the common goal of a professional workplace where opportunity is available to all.

© 2007 Vault Inc.

THELEN REID & PRIEST LLP

101 Second Street, Suite 1800
San Francisco, CA 94105
Phone: (415) 371-1200
Fax: (415) 371-1211

Thelen Reid & Priest LLP (TRP) is committed to recruiting, retaining and promoting attorneys who reflect the diversity of our society. We believe that a diverse work force enhances our workplace and improves the quality of the services we provide to our clients. Therefore, we strive to create an inclusive environment in which all of our attorneys are able to develop professionally and succeed in the practice of law.

In 2002, 62 percent of the associates promoted into our partnership were women, and 37 percent were minority. This trend continued in 2003 and 2004, with the promotion of five more women, which constituted 45 percent of the promotions.

TRP recognizes that the attrition rate at law firms is higher among women and minority attorneys and therefore has undertaken efforts to combat this disparity and continue our accomplishment in retaining women and minority associates. We have created a national Diversity Committee (DC) consisting of partners, associates and professional staff from all offices. TRP has also established the Women's Forum, which addresses the specific and unique concerns of women attorneys at the firm.

TRP has ranked in the top 15 percent for the past two years in the Minority Law Journal's Diversity Scorecard, which tracks the percentage of minority attorneys at the 250 largest law firms in the United States.

THOMPSON & KNIGHT LLP

1700 Pacific Avenue, Suite 3300
Dallas, TX 75201
www.tklaw.com

Thompson & Knight creates, fosters, and maintains a substantively diverse and inclusive environment in order to recruit, retain, and promote employees. The Firm has taken crucial steps toward becoming the diversity and inclusion model for its legal communities.

In recognition of these efforts, the Firm is honored to be the recipient of the Chevron Law Firm Diversity Recognition Award, a Top 100 Law Firm for Diversity by MultiCultural Law, a "Mother-Friendly Worksite" by the Texas Department of State Health Services, and a "Best Place to Work" for four consecutive years by Dallas Business Journal. Thompson & Knight is the first Houston law firm to join the "Community of Respect" program of the Anti-Defamation League. This program provides tools and resources to help Houston-area organizations fight prejudice, bigotry, and discrimination and engender respect and appreciation for diversity.

The Firm strives to maintain an environment in which all employees have equitable access to opportunities for personal and professional growth. In support of its efforts, the Firm hired in the past year a Chief Diversity Officer and a Chief Development Officer, both of whom are female attorneys. The Chief Development Officer, a former partner with the Firm and a clinical psychologist, focuses on attorney development through structured programming, mentoring, and coaching. The Chief Diversity Officer, an ethnically diverse partner, designs, implements, and monitors initiatives that support the Firm's commitment to diversity and inclusion, and is actively involved in mentoring the Firm's diverse attorneys.

The Vault Diversity Programs Directory is a special advertising section in the *Vault Guide to the Top 100 Law Firms*. For information on listing your firm in the directory, contact corporatesales@vault.com.

VAULT CAREER LIBRARY   701

ULMER & BERNE LLP

1660 West 22nd Street, Suite 1100
Cleveland, OH 44113-1448
www.ulmer.com

At Ulmer & Berne LLP, we consider diversity to be fundamental to our success. It promotes a broader, richer work environment. It replaces tired, conventional solutions with creative ideas. It enriches individual assets and strengthens our collective value.

We believe our diverse workforce—and by "diverse," we mean a workforce made up of people of different races, religions, sexual orientations, ethnic backgrounds and genders — makes Ulmer & Berne a more resourceful, perceptive and ultimately more capable law firm.

To ensure that our commitment to a diverse workplace remains a reality, Ulmer & Berne has created a Diversity Committee. Comprised of attorneys who share the same goal of continued firm diversity. This group assists in recruiting, hiring and promoting attorneys with varied and unique backgrounds.

Ulmer & Berne actively recruits minority law students for our summer associate programs in Cleveland and Cincinnati through on-campus recruiting and participation in annual minority recruiting conferences. We're pleased to support and participate in the Cleveland Minority Clerkship Program, a competitive program designed for first year minority law students; and the Minority Access Program, a program for first year minority law students in Cincinnati.

VERRILL DANA, LLP

One Portland Square
Portland, ME 04112-0586
www.verrilldana.com

Verrill Dana, LLP has a longstanding tradition and commitment to diversity. Although our principal office is located in one of the least diverse states in the Union, we have energetically pursued a diversity initiative, believing that the goal of a diverse workplace is a challenge worthy of our serious and purposeful efforts.

As a firm, we have long been committed to diversity at a number of levels, including gender, race, ethnicity and sexual orientation, to name a few. Our commitments are formally acknowledged in strong equal opportunity and non-discrimination policies, but are also deeply rooted in the culture of the firm. We take great pride, for example, in our leadership in the integration of women in our practice. Not only did our firm welcome women to the ranks of our partners at an early stage, but we were also the first (and still the only) major Portland firm to elect a woman to serve as our managing partner, from 1992 to 1994. Women have also held a variety of leadership roles in our firm, including service on our Executive Board, as chairs of important committees, as department or practice group chairs, and as branch office leaders.

We are also committed to progressive "family-friendly" policies that help ensure that we are the employer of choice among Maine law firms, for both lawyers and members of our support staff.

© 2007 Vault Inc.

WALLER LANSDEN DORTCH & DAVIS, PLLC

511 Union Street, Suite 2100
Nashville, TN 37219
www.wallerlaw.com

Each year, Waller Lansden participates in the Southeastern Minority Job Fair and solicits the resumes of minority candidates from law schools where we do not interview on campus.

The National Association for the Advancement of Colored People Nashville Branch presented Waller Lansden with its President's Award for promoting diversity and opportunity throughout Nashville. Waller Lansden received the award at the NAACP's dinner celebrating the 50th anniversary of Brown v. Board of Education.

The Nashville Bar Association awarded Waller Lansden its Employer Recognition Award for leadership in diversity hiring.

The National Association of African Americans in Human Resources presented Waller Lansden with its Leadership Award for diversity successes.

Partner Waverly Crenshaw and Beverly Hedrick, director of business development, were speakers at the Minority Corporate Counsel Association's annual conferences held in Chicago and New York in 2005.

In 2005 the firm sponsored a statewide business summit for Hispanic, women and minority business owners in conjunction with the Tennessee Hispanic Chamber of Commerce, the Governor's Office of Diversity Business Enterprise and the U.S. Hispanic Chamber of Commerce.

Waller Lansden hosted the inaugural Middle Tennessee Diversity Forum in 2005.

WEIL, GOTSHAL & MANGES LLP

767 Fifth Avenue
New York, NY 10153
www.weil.com

Weil, Gotshal & Manges LLP has endeavored to create an environment of inclusion in which people value individual and group difference, respect the perspectives of others and communicate openly. Weil Gotshal is committed to recruiting, retaining and promoting the best attorneys from all backgrounds. The Firm's diverse workforce gives us tremendous strength, and our diversity efforts span the globe.

We were the first major law firm in New York to institute a firmwide diversity training program and a formal diversity policy in 1984. The Firm's Global Diversity Director and the Diversity Committee spearheaded the Firm's 2003-04 Cultural and Diversity Initiative. This initiative began in our U.S. and London offices, with a second firmwide diversity assessment and the development of a formal mandatory diversity and inclusion training program. By the spring of 2004 we conducted nearly 160 training classes in our U.S. and London office, with close to 100 percent participation among partners, associates and staff. As new attorneys and staff join the firm, they also participate in this training program.

In the fall of 2005, Weil commenced a culture and diversity assessment for the Continental Europe offices. These offices include: Budapest, Frankfurt, Munich, Paris, Prague and Warsaw. Based on the findings of the survey, interviews, and focus groups, we designed a training initiative for partners, associates, and staff. Pilot training programs were conducted in Warsaw and Frankfurt in Spring 2007. The full roll-out will be completed in Fall 2007.

The Vault Diversity Programs Directory is a special advertising section in the *Vault Guide to the Top 100 Law Firms*. For information on listing your firm in the directory, contact corporatesales@vault.com.

VAULT CAREER LIBRARY   703

WHITE & CASE LLP

1155 Avenue of the Americas
New York, NY 10036
www.whitecase.com

Demographics

Worldwide, our lawyers represent 86 different nationalities, speak more than 62 languages, are drawn from a wide range of schools and universities, and have a variety of backgrounds, work experiences, and personalities.

Mission

The mission of the Diversity Committee is to continue to build on our strength in diversity and create an environment where all who work here are encouraged, assisted and inspired to reach their potential, regardless of race, color, ethnicity, religion, gender, sexual orientation, national origin, age, marital status or disability.

Method

Under the leadership of an executive partner in charge of diversity, the Diversity Committee continuously communicates and reinforces our diversity principles worldwide through: mandatory diversity training, leadership training, mentoring programs, and workshops on preventing sexual harassment and discrimination.

We aim through our diversity efforts to have our lawyers represent, as much as possible, the variety of human characteristics that make up the varied global population that we serve, while recognizing that certain groups, being traditionally disadvantaged, require a more focused approach if we are to attract and support them.

The firm has sponsored many minority and women's organizations, conferences and events such as the Minority Corporate Counsel Association, the Lawyers Committee for Civil Rights under the law and LAMBDA legal. We also moderated the New York City Bar committee on Minorities in the profession panel discussion on "Finding a Voice for Women of Color at Law Firms".

WILEY REIN LLP

1776 K Street, NW
Washington, DC 20006
www.wileyrein.com

As a law firm with national and international clientele, Wiley Rein LLP is committed to a professional workforce that reflects the rich cultural and ethnic diversity of our client base. We believe our clients are enriched by working with a diverse group of exceptional attorneys who, through different perspectives and experiences, allow us to undertake more creative thinking and to produce more innovative solutions. Thus, Wiley Rein embraces diversity both as a business imperative and as a moral obligation.

As women and minority attorneys join the Firm, every effort is made to ensure they are provided with appropriate work assignments, mentoring and client networking opportunities that will allow them to succeed. Because of internal affinity group support among the Firm's minority attorneys (which includes collectively maintaining focused oversight on billable hours, work assignments and so on), problems - to the extent they might exist - are detected early and often are addressed successfully. Although the Firm is always concerned about losing good associates, (both with respect to minority and non-minority attorneys), we also recognize that many associates join the Firm in part because of its reputation as a springboard for government service, or as a proving ground for in-house counsel positions. Indeed, a number of minority and non-minority attorneys have left the Firm to assume positions of significant responsibility at government agencies (e.g., Department of Health and Human Services, Department of Justice, Securities and Exchange Commission, Federal Communications Commission) or to become in-house counsel with Firm clients. Recognizing the inevitability of attrition in today's legal market, a principal objective of the Firm is to undertake aggressive recruitment efforts that will attract a "critical mass" of minority attorneys. To this end, the Diversity Committee and others in Firm leadership have begun a campaign to provide Wiley Rein greater exposure within the minority legal community by participating in events targeted to minority lawyers and law students.

VAULT CAREER LIBRARY

© 2007 Vault Inc.

WILLKIE FARR & GALLAGHER LLP

787 Seventh Avenue
New York, NY 10019
www.willkie.com

In keeping with the belief that everyone benefits from a diverse workplace, Willkie is committed to creating and maintaining a diverse environment by recruiting and retaining people of all backgrounds and cultural experiences. To that end, Willkie established a Diversity Committee over a decade ago, through which many of our efforts in the area of diversity are coordinated. In 2003, Willkie further enhanced its efforts by appointing a Director of Diversity Initiatives, who is dedicated not only to the recruitment of minority and women attorneys but also to their retention, professional development and advancement. Additionally, Willkie recently established its Women's Professional Development Committee ("WPDC"). Its goals are similar to those of the Diversity Committee, with a particular emphasis on the training and career development of women attorneys in our firm.

Both the Diversity and WPDC are comprised of associates and partners (including executive firm management), as we recognize that the input of attorneys at all levels are necessary to our efforts to increase the number of tenure of minority, women and openly gay associates. Both committees meet monthly to address issues of concern, and to develop and implement initiatives directed at mentoring women and minority associates. Recent efforts of the Committees have been directed towards improving the partner-mentor program and assigning systems.

We also engaged a diversity consultant to assist us in a firm-wide diversity training initiative. The consultant has conducted diversity training for all attorneys and staff supervisors in the New York and D.C. offices, and conducts a diversity awareness workshop at our annual New Associates Retreat. Each of the Diversity and Women's Professional Development Committees sponsors monthly lunches and other events to encourage formal and informal discussions among our attorneys.

WILMERHALE

60 State Street
Boston, MA 02109
www.wilmerhale.com

We believe that competitive success for a global law firm in the twenty-first century requires a commitment to diversity that starts at the top and courses through the firm at every level. Our success and improvement in this area will help us to recruit and retain the very best available talent, raise our profile with an increasingly diverse and global client base, and cultivate an environment in which every person is able to do the best work possible, strengthened by our different perspectives, backgrounds and life experiences. Towards this priority, we have:

Established a diversity committee that includes representatives from the firm's leadership and subcommittees in each of our three major U.S. offices. Each committee engaged an objective outsider to identify any obstacles to the hiring, retention and promotion of minority lawyers. Based in part on the results of those projects, the committee is undertaking a variety of initiatives focused on: (i) recruitment, (ii) retention and career development, and (iii) leadership and culture. Among other steps, the firm seeks to ensure that minority lawyers:

• Receive effective support from senior lawyers in the firm, beginning before a new lawyer actually arrives;

• Form satisfying working relationships with other lawyers in the firm;

• Form connections with other minority lawyers in the firm and, if they wish, with minority bar associations and other organizations outside the firm; and

• Have full access to good assignments and effective feedback.

The Vault Diversity Programs Directory is a special advertising section in the *Vault Guide to the Top 100 Law Firms*. For information on listing your firm in the directory, contact corporatesales@vault.com.

VAULT CAREER LIBRARY   705

WOMBLE CARLYLE SANDRIDGE & RICE, PLLC

One West Fourth Street
Winston Salem, NC 27101
www.wcsr.com

Womble Carlyle is committed to being a leader in attracting, developing and retaining a diverse workforce of skilled professionals. Establishing and maintaining a firm culture that values and promotes different heritages, backgrounds and initiatives is critical to our growth and continued success as a leading, innovative provider of extraordinary legal services to our clients. To that end, the firm has a scholarship, the Womble Carlyle Scholars Program for rising second-year minority students at law schools in most of the states in which we have offices. These include North Carolina Central University, Wake Forest University, Duke University, George Washington University, Howard University, the University of North Carolina at Chapel Hill, the University of South Carolina, the University of Georgia, Emory University, and the University of Virginia. The scholarships that are offered at Howard University and North Carolina Central University are in conjunction with the Thurgood Marshall College Fund. All scholarship recipients will receive $4,000 each and a guaranteed summer associate position at the firm after their second year of law school.

We currently have two former Womble Carlyle Scholars working as full time associates in the Greenville, SC and in the Charlotte, NC offices. Two more Scholars will begin work with us this fall in the Winston Salem, NC and the Washington, D.C. offices.

In addition, the firm has adopted an active minority recruitment process which includes recruitment at law schools with large minority enrollments, participation in local and regional minority job fairs, advertising in publications which target diverse populations and utilizing search firms that are experienced with conducting searches for diverse candidates.

We participate in two minority clerkship programs - the Atlanta Bar Association Minority Clerkship Program and the North Carolina Minority Clerkship Program. Womble Carlyle has hired two first year minority students as summer associates through this program.

© 2007 Vault Inc.

PRO BONO
PROGRAMS
DIRECTORY

ADAMS & REESE LLP

701 Poydras Street, Suite 4500

New Orleans, LA 70139

Phone: (504) 581-3234

www.adamsandreese.com

Areas of pro bono work:

Adams and Reese attorneys have successfully represented pro bono clients in adoptions and custody matters, taxes and estates, bankruptcy, credit counseling contracts and employment-related issues.

In 2006, in the wake of Hurricane Katrina, Adams and Reese attorneys dedicated an extraordinary amount of time to legal issues surrounding the recovery of New Orleans and the Gulf Coast region.

Recent Pro Bono Clients:

New Orleans Pro Bono Project, Baton Rouge Bar Association Pro Bono Project, Mississippi Volunteer Lawyers Project, Memphis Area Legal Services, Alabama Bar Association—Volunteer Lawyers Program, Mobile Volunteer Lawyers Program, Young Lawyers Division of the Mississippi Bar Association—Disaster Relief Legal Services Clinic, Louisiana Disaster Recovery Foundation, Community Legal Center of Memphis, Legal Aid Society of Middle Tennessee and the Cumberlands.

Special Recognition and Awards:

While Adams and Reese has been honored in previous years for dedication and excellence to pro bono service, the firm was not recognized in 2005 or 2006.

AKIN GUMP STRAUSS HAUER & FELD LLP

1333 New Hampshire Avenue, NW

Washington, DC 20036

Phone: (202) 887-4000

www.akingump.com

Areas of pro bono work:

Litigation, corporate; international, environmental, tax; civil rights, human rights, criminal, charter schools, legal assistance to military personnel, intellectual property and public policy.

Recent Pro Bono Clients:

Texas Bar Legal Assistance to Military Personnel, KIPP Charter Schools, Human Rights First, The Legal Aid Society of New York, the Children's Law Centers of Washington, D.C., and Los Angeles, Dallas Volunteer Attorney Program, Houston Volunteer Lawyers Program, Texas C-Bar, Lawyers Committee for Civil Rights and Harvard Law School International Human Rights Clinic.

Special Recognition and Awards:

2005 National Association of Counsel for Children Inaugural Community Service Award (Los Angeles, Washington), 2005 Marine Corps Commendation for pro bono legal services (Chris Odell, associate, Houston), 2006 Texas Appleseed "Good Apple" Award (awarded with Charles Matthews of ExxonMobil,) 2006 State Bar of Texas Frank W. Newton Award, 2006 Legal Aid society of New York Pro Bono Award (John Berry, partner, New York), 2006 Rubicon Honors Award (San Francisco) 2006 Washington Council of Lawyers Pro Bono Award, 2006 NLADA Exemplar Award (Mark MacDougall, Washington)

© 2007 Vault Inc.

ALLEN & OVERY LLP

1221 Avenue of the Americas

New York, NY 10020

Phone: (212) 610-6300

www.allenovery.com

Areas of pro bono work:

International human rights, orders of protection, domestic violence and child custody, incorporation and filing for 501c(3) status for nonprofit organizations, individual asylum cases, criminal law, NYC corporation counsel programs, etc.

Recent Pro Bono Clients:

Human Rights First, New York Lawyers for Public Interest, inMotion, International Bar Association, Center for Constitutional Rights, Legal Aid Society, Lawyers Committee For Civil Rights Under Law, Lawyers Alliance for New York and Sanctuary for Families, FINCA.

Special Recognition and Awards:

The Allen & Overy Business Services team received a Highly Commended in the Team of the Year Award category at the Business in the Community, London & South East Cares Awards 2006. They were recognized for their work wtih and commitment to the Business Action on Homelessness, Ready for Work program

BAKER & DANIELS LLP

300 North Meridian

Indianapolis, IN 46204

Phone: (317) 237-0300

www.bakerdaniels.com

Areas of pro bono work:

In 2005 and 2006, Baker & Daniels performed work in the following areas: in-court advocacy on behalf of domestic violence victims; child advocacy in ad litem and CASA proceedings; criminal appeals and petitions for habeas corpus in federal appellate court; development of a state appellate pro bono project; representation of two death row defendants in South Carolina; veteran's benefits appellate representation; immigration and political asylum representation; civil rights and civil liberties education and advocacy; tax, corporate, real estate and employment representations on behalf of organizations serving the poor; intellectual property and trademark representation; gay/lesbian/bisexual/trans-gender advocacy; advocacy on behalf of disabilities community; corporate and litigation representation of income-qualified artists.

Recent Pro Bono Clients:

Protective Order Pro Bono Project; Child Advocates, Inc., Indiana Legal Services, Legal Aid Society of Indiana, Indiana Civil Liberties Union, Neighborhood Christian Legal Clinic, 7th Circuit Appellate Pro Bono program, Creative Artist Legal League, Indiana Health Advocacy Coalition and Craine House.

Special Recognition and Awards:

Baker & Daniels was not recognized for pro bono work in 2005 or 2006

The Vault Pro Bono Programs Directory is a special advertising section in the *Vault Guide to the Top 100 Law Firms.*
For information on listing your firm in the directory, contact corporatesales@vault.com.

VAULT CAREER LIBRARY   709

BINGHAM MCCUTCHEN LLP

150 Federal Street
Boston, MA 02110
Phone: (617) 951-8000
www.bingham.com

Areas of pro bono work:

Adoption, civil rights, corporate, nonprofit work, debt collection, education, environmental, estate planning, family law, health care, housing, intellectual property, political asylum, prisoners' rights, reproductive rights, uninsured motorist and unemployment compensation.

Recent Pro Bono Clients:

American Civil Liberties Union, B'nai B'rith Cuban Jewish Relief Project, New York Lawyers for the Public Interest, Lawyers Alliance of New York Lawyers, Lawyers' Committee for Civil Rights Under Law, Volunteer Lawyers for the Arts, Planned Parenthood Federation, Prison Law Office, Say Yes to Education and Telecommunications for the Deaf.

Special Recognition and Awards:

The National Legal Aid & Defender Association (NLADA) recognized Bingham McCutchen with its 2007 NLADA Beacon of Justice Award for our representation of detainees at Guantanamo Bay, Volunteer Lawyers for the Arts of Massachusetts selected Bingham to receive the 2007 Robert B. Fraser Award for Pro Bono Excellence, and Boston Bar Association awarded Bingham and 10 of our lawyers the Boston Bar Association 2007 President's Award for representing Guantanamo detainnes.

CHADBOURNE & PARKE LLP

30 Rockefeller Plaza
New York, NY 10112
Phone: (212) 408-5100
www.chadbourne.com

Areas of pro bono work:

Criminal appeals, community development (e.g., nonprofit incorporation and governance, advising microentrepreneurs, partnership with the Upper Manhattan Empowerment Zone), impact litigation, death penalty, landlord/tenant (NYC housing court cases, assistance with trial preparation, legal clinic work), political asylum, predatory lending, family justice/domestic violence, elder law (T&E), SSI disability, microfinance, IP, representation of nonprofits in D.C. (Jewish Community Center), Los Angeles, Kyiv and Moscow; court-mandated civil and criminal cases in Warsaw, and public transport bombing-related cases in London.

Recent Pro Bono Clients:

New York Lawyers for the Public Interest, The Legal Aid Society (NY & D.C.), Housing Conservation Coordinators, Human Rights First, Sanctuary for Families, Lawyers Alliance for New York, D.C. Bar Pro Bono Program, City Bar Justice Center, Advocates for Children, Asian American Legal Defense and Education Fund.

Special Recognition and Awards:

- Lawyers Allianc for New York
- Housing Conservation Coordinators
- New York Disaster Interfaith Services
- Fordam Law School

© 2007 Vault Inc.

CLEARY GOTTLIEB STEEN & HAMILTON LLP

One Liberty Plaza
New York, NY 10006-1470
Phone: (212) 225-2000
www.cgsh.com

Areas of pro bono work:

We work in almost every area of public interest law. Our work over the past two years includes immigration and asylum law, assistance to survivors of domestic violence, affordable housing development, FEMA appeals for Katrina survivors, education and children's rights, impact litigation including voters' rights and disability rights, not-for-profit and microfinance legal assistance, arts and entertainment law, assistance to small businesses, clinics at homeless shelters and housing litigation including representation of tenant organizations in bankruptcy court.

Recent Pro Bono Clients:

Center for Constitutional Rights, Human Rights First; Legal Aid Society, Lawyers Alliance for New York, Lawyers Committee on Civil Rights under the Law, MFY Legal Services, Inc, Mutual Housing Association of New York, New York Lawyers for the Public Interest, Sanctuary for Families and Volunteer Lawyers for the Arts.

Special Recognition and Awards:

- 2006Gottlieb ranked No. 8 on The American Lawyer's A-List. The firm ranked No. 19 on The American Lawyer's annual pro bono honor roll

- 2006 Judicial Conference of the District of Columbia Circuit Standing Committee on Pro Bono Legal Services 40 at 50 Honoree

- 2006 Legal Aid Society Pro Bono Awards for five Cleary Gottlieb associates

- 2006 Immigration Equality Safe Haven Awards for four Cleary Gottlieb associates

- 2006 Segal-Tweed Founders Award from Lawyers Committee for Civil Rights Under the Law for a retired Cleary Gottlieb partner

CRAVATH, SWAINE & MOORE LLP

825 Eighth Avenue
New York, NY 10019-7475
Phone: (212) 474-1000
www.cravath.com

Areas of pro bono work:

We represent indigent individuals in criminal appeals, post-conviction proceedings in death penalty cases, family law matters, civil litigation and asylum proceedings. We also represent a number of environmental advocacy groups and handle corporate, employment, tax and other matters for nonprofit clients.

Recent Pro Bono Clients:

Afro-American Police Association of Buffalo, American Civil Liberties Union, Bedford Stuyvesant Restoration Corporation, Children's Hospital at Montefiore/Morgan Stanley Children's Hospital of New York-Presbyterian, Covenant House, Human Rights First, InMotion; Lawyers' Committee for Civil Rights Under Law, The Legal Aid Society, Martha Graham Center of Contemporary Dance, Inc., and Martha Graham School of Contemporary Dance, Inc.

Special Recognition and Awards:

- Cravath was honored by the Innocence Project for our support of the organization, including work as the Innocence Project's corporate counsel and assistance in establishing the Exoneree Emergency Fund.

- The Lawyers Committee Against Domestic Violence (LCADV) recently presented Cravath with its "In The Trenches" Award in recognition of our extraordinary support of the work of the LCADV.

The Vault Pro Bono Programs Directory is a special advertising section in the *Vault Guide to the Top 100 Law Firms*.
For information on listing your firm in the directory, contact corporatesales@vault.com.

VAULT CAREER LIBRARY   711

DEBEVOISE & PLIMPTON LLP

919 Third Avenue

New York, NY 10022

www.debevoise.com

Areas of pro bono work:

Representation of asylum-seekers; voters' rights; labor/employment rights; death penalty; international human rights; prisoners' rights; First Amendment and other constitutional civil rights; indigent criminal defense; rights of gay, lesbian, bisexual and transgendered individuals; rights of individuals with mental and physical disabilities; reproductive rights; housing rights; environmental law; matrimonial law and rights of victims of domestic violence; and corporate, tax and intellectual property advice to not-for-profit organizations.

Recent Pro Bono Clients:

Brennan Center for Justice, Center for Reproductive Rights, Committee to Protect Journalists, Human Rights First, Lawyers' Committee for Civil Rights Under Law, The Legal Aid Society, New York Alliance for New Americans, New York Lawyers for the Public Interest; Inc., Robin Hood Foundation and Urban Justice Center.

Special Recognition and Awards:

Within the past two years, Debevoise has been recognized for its pro bono work by a variety of organizations. In 2006, the American Bar Association named Debevoise a recipient of its Pro Bono Publico Award, recognizing "outstanding contributions of legal services to those who cannot afford representation." Also, in 2004, 2005 and 2006, The American Lawyer's A-List ranked Debevoise the number one law firm in the United States based in part on our commitment to pro bono legal service.

DEWEY BALLANTINE

1301 Avenue of the Americas

New York, NY 10019

(212) 259-8000

www.deweyballantine.com

Areas of pro bono work:

Criminal defense, domestic violence, nonprofit board governance, insurance, child advocacy, civil rights work, special education, GLBT rights, asylum, real estate, International Law as it applies to the Hague Convention on Civil Aspects of International Child Abduction; contract law and employment.

Recent Pro Bono Clients:

Legal Aid Society (New York, Los Angeles, Washington, D.C.), The Puerto Rican Legal Defense and Education Fund, Advocates for Children, New York Lawyers for the Public Interest, New York Legal Assistance Group (NYLAG), National Center for Missing and Exploited Children, Asian American Legal Defense and Education Fund, ACLU Lesbian and Gay Rights Project.

Special Recognition and Awards:

- On November 6, 2006, The Legal Aid Society of New York presented the firm with a 2006 Pro Bono Award for the firm's participation in the Low Income Elderly Wills Project at the Brooklyn Office ranked Debevoise the number one law firm in the United States based in part on our commitment to pro bono legal service.

- On November 6, 2006, litigation associate Anna Hutchinson was honored by The Legal Aid Society of New York as a recipient of the Society's 2006 Pro Bono Awards for outstanding service to Legal Aid Society clients.

© 2007 Vault Inc.

DLA PIPER US LLP

1200 19th Street, NW

Washington, DC 20036

(202) 861-3900

www.dlapiper.com

Areas of pro bono work:

We perform pro bono work in virtually every legal area, including juvenile justice, civil rights, community economic development, poverty law, family law, international and human rights, immigration, real estate, intellectual property, legislative assistance and lobbying, rule of law and nonprofit governance.

Recent Pro Bono Clients:

Appleseed Foundation (national), Asian American Legal Services Clinic (Chicago), Bay Area Legal Services (Tampa), Community Economic Development Law Project (Chicago), Community Legal Services in East Palo Alto, D.C. Bar Pro Bono Clinic, Lawyers Alliance for New York, Public International Law & Policy Group (national), Maryland Volunteer Lawyers Service and San Diego Volunteer Lawyer Program.

Special Recognition and Awards:

- Capital Area Food Bank Dr. Martin Luther King, Jr. Keeping the Dream Alive Award (to Wiliam Minor on April 27, 2007).

- Association of Black Women Attorneys (ABWA) Award for Excellence in Corporate Diversity (to DLA Piper on March 24).

- Equal Justice Council of the Legal Aid Bureau, Inc., 2007 Champion of Justice Award (to Frank Gray)

- District of Columbia Bar Pro Bono Law Firm of the Year Award (to Washington, DC office on June 21, 2007)

DOW LOHNES PLLC

1200 New Hampshire Ave. NW

Suite 800

Washington, DC 20036

www.dowlohnes.com

Areas of pro bono work:

Asylum; intellectual property; tax; elder law.

Recent Pro Bono Clients:

Whitman-Walker Clinic; Washington Area Lawyers for the Arts; Tahirih Justice Center; Legal Counsel for the Elderly; The Legal Aid Society; Human Rights First; Archdiocesan Legal Network; International AIDS Society—USA; Washington Legal Clinic for the Homeless.

Special Recognition and Awards:

The American Heart Association has named Dow Lohnes, for the ninth consecutive year, as the Law Firm with the Biggest Heart in connection with its activities supporting Lawyers Have Heart.

The Vault Pro Bono Programs Directory is a special advertising section in the *Vault Guide to the Top 100 Law Firms.*
For information on listing your firm in the directory, contact corporatesales@vault.com.

VAULT CAREER LIBRARY

713

FENWICK & WEST LLP

801 California Street

Mountain View, CA 94041

Phone: (650) 988-8500

www.fenwick.com

Areas of pro bono work:

Child advocacy, consumer rights, predatory lending, landlord/tenant disputes, habeas corpus, civil rights, death penalty, AIDS legal services, advising start-up companies and entrepreneurs, intellectual property in the arts, tax and political asylum/immigration.

Recent Pro Bono Clients:

LACY Guardianship Panel, Pro Bono Project, AIDS Legal Referral Panel (ALRP), Women's Technology Cluster, VLSP's Low Income Tax Clinic and Landlord Tenant Clinic, Samuelson Law, Technology & Public Policy Clinic, API Legal Outreach, Ninth Circuit Court of Appeals Pro Bono Program, Federal Circuit Bar Association Pro Bono Referral Program and the Volunteer Attorney Program (VAP) of Community Legal Services in East Palo Alto.

Special Recognition and Awards:

- Public Interest Counsel Champion Award presented by Public Interest Law Firm in March 2005 for Fenwick & West's decade-plus commitment and service to pro bono work, specifically its work in a variety of impact litigations.

- Fenwick received the Partners for Justice Award for Legal Impact from Asian Pacific Islander Legal Outreach Organization for our demonstrated commitment to advancing social justice. The firm has provided our Equal Justice Works Fellow, co-sponsored by API Legal Outreach, with advice, outreach, logical and technical support as well as hosting immigration law trainings for the organization.

FOLEY & LARDNER LLP

777 E. Wisconsin Avenue

Milwaukee, WI 53203

(414) 271-2400

www.foley.com

Areas of pro bono work:

Our pro bono activities run the gamut of providing services to individuals, legal aid societies or civil rights organizations, to representing nonprofit organizations in strategic projects and litigation matters. In recent years, our firm has provided significant representation in matters referred to us by such public interest firms as the AIDS Legal Clinic, Pro Bono Advocates and Public Counsel. Foley performs work in almost every area of public interest law. A substantial portion of our work over the past two years has included immigration and asylum law as well as civil and children's rights.

Recent Pro Bono Clients:

Center for Disability and Elder Law (Chicago, Ill.), Community Legal Resources (Detroit, Mich.), Guardian Ad Litem Program (Tallahassee, Fla.), Legal Aid Society of the Orange County Bar Association (Fla.), Boys & Girls Club of Dane County, Wis., Midwest Immigrant and Human Rights Center (Chicago, Ill.), Public Counsel (Los Angeles, Calif.), Public Interest Law Initiative (Washington, D.C.), San Diego Volunteer Lawyers Association (San Diego, Calif.), and Washington Lawyers Committee for Civil Rights and Urban Affairs.

Special Recognition and Awards:

Foley's Orlando office received the Orange County Legal Aid Society's 2006 Award of Excellence on August 31.

© 2007 Vault Inc.

GOODWIN PROCTER LLP

Exchange Place
Boston, MA 02109
(617) 570-1000
www.goodwinprocter.com

Areas of pro bono work:

We work in almost every area of public interest law. A large portion of our work over the past two years has included asylum law, criminal law, real estate law, intellectual property law, corporate/nonprofit law and legal assistance to inner-city entrepreneurs.

Recent Pro Bono Clients:

The Volunteer Lawyers for the Arts, Volunteer Lawyers Project, the Lawyers Clearinghouse on Affordable Housing and Homelessness, the Political Asylum/Immigration Representation Project (PAIR), the Medical-Legal Partnership for Children, the Lawyers Alliance for New York; Lawyers Committee for Civil Rights, The Innocence Project and the D.C. Bar Clinic.

Special Recognition and Awards:

- December 2006—Lawyers Alliance for New York recognized Goodwin Procter with its Cornerstone Award;

- December 2006—Medicare Rights Center recognized Goodwin Procter;

- June 2006—The Immigrant and Refugee Rights Project of the D.C. Lawyers Committee recognized Goodwin Procter with its Outstanding Achievement Award for pro bono;

- June 2006—The Political Asylum Immigration and Representation Project recognized Goodwin Procter associates Joseph Theis and Terence Shields;

GREENBERG TRAURIG, LLP

1221 Brickell Avenue
Miami, FL 33131
Phone: (305) 579-0500
www.gtlaw.com

Areas of pro bono work:

Civil rights and affirmative action, custody and visitation, guardianship, criminal appeals, children's issues, immigration/political asylum, community economic development, domestic violence, housing and homelessness, health care, death penalty, legal problems of the elderly and international human rights.

Recent Pro Bono Clients:

Easter Seals of New York, MFY Legal Services, Georgetown Partnership, The Center for Hope, Safe Horizon, DuPage Children's Museum, Employment Justice Legal Center, Wills for Heroes, National Crime Victim Law Institute and Legal Counsel for the Elderly.

Special Recognition and Awards:

- Shareholder William Silverman received the 2006 Matthew G. Leonard Award for Pro Bono Excellence from MFY Legal Services, Inc., for his leadership of our pro bono program and his work in launching the Pro Bono Kinship Caregiver Law Project and Self-Represented Legal Services Project.

- The Florida Immigrant Advocacy Center honored Greenberg Traurig with the 2007 Sr. Maureen T. Kelleher Altruism Award, in recognition of the firm and our attorneys' pro bono work in assisting women and children detained in immigration centers in Florida.

The Vault Pro Bono Programs Directory is a special advertising section in the *Vault Guide to the Top 100 Law Firms*.
For information on listing your firm in the directory, contact corporatesales@vault.com.

VAULT CAREER LIBRARY   715

HOGAN & HARTSON LLP

555 13th Street, NW

Washington, DC 20004

Phone: (202) 637-5600

www.hhlaw.com

Areas of pro bono work:

Recent significant pro bono projects have involved civil rights and civil liberties; poverty law, housing and homeless advocacy issues (including tenants rights matters); nonprofit incorporation, taxation and transactional work; support and assistance on issues involving HIV/AIDS; legislative work; international rule of law and immigration; the environment and historic preservation; criminal law and the death penalty; and children's and health care issues.

Recent Pro Bono Clients:

Whitman-Walker Legal Clinic; Public Counsel; Washington Lawyers Committee for Civil Rights and Urban Affairs; National Parks Conservation Association; DC Appleseed Center; Friends of Karen; International Senior Lawyers Project; Lesbian, Gay, Bisexual & Transgendered Community Center; Maryland Volunteer Lawyers Service; NAACP; and NAACP LDF.

Special Recognition and Awards:

- Cristi Perez Labiosa was honored during 2006 by Sanctuary for Families for outstanding work on behalf of victims of domestic violence.

- Hogan & Hartson was honored as the D.C. Bar Pro Bono Firm of the Year (large firm) at an event in June 2006.

- The NAACP honored the firm during its National Convention in Washington, D.C., in 2006 with a Civil Rights Champion Award.

HOLLAND & KNIGHT LLP

2099 Pennsylvania Ave

Washington, DC 20006

Phone: (202) 955-3000

www.hklaw.com

Areas of pro bono work:

Holland & Knight LLP attorneys and paralegals perform pro bono work in virtually all areas of law as evidenced by our 2006 Equitas newsletter, available at www.hklaw.com/content/ newsletters/cst-equitas/equitas011807.pdf.

Recent Pro Bono Clients:

The United Nations High Commissioner for Refugees, Women's Commission for Refugee Women and Children, Southern Center for Human Rights, The Innocence Project, ACLU National Prison Project, National Center for Missing and Exploited Children, The Constitution Project, NAACP Legal Defense and Educational Fund, Immigration Equality, and The National Center for Refugee and Immigrant Children.

Special Recognition and Awards:

- 2006 Pro Bono Partner Award Presented by Corporate Pro Bono (CPBO)

- 2006 Pro Bono Service Award Presented by American Bar Association Section of Individual Rights and Responsibilities

- 2006 Safe Haven Award Presented by Immigration Equality

- 2006 Corporate Partnership Award Presented by Center for Disability and Elder Law

- 2006 Pro Bono Award Presented by The Legal Aid Society of New York to New York associate Fabian Guevara and International Law Clerk Manuel Herrero

© 2007 Vault Inc.

HUGHES HUBBARD & REED LLP

One Battery Park Plaza

New York, NY 10004

Phone: (212) 837-6000

www.hugheshubbard.com

Areas of pro bono work:

Some areas of law in which Hughes Hubbard has performed pro bono legal work include immigration and asylum matters, family law, prisoner rights, HIV/AIDS matters, housing issues, Social Security, drafting and negotiation of commercial agreements, advising small business owners and artist representation cases.

Recent Pro Bono Clients:

The Legal Aid Society; Beth Israel Hospital, Volunteer Lawyers for the Arts, New York Lawyers for the Public Interest, inMotion; Lawyers Alliance for New York, The City Bar Fund, Human Rights First, MFY Legal Services and Center for Reproductive Law and Policy.

Special Recognition and Awards:

- In 2006, Hughes Hubbard received The Legal Aid Society's 2006 Outstanding Pro Bono Publico and Public Service Law Firm Award for its "extraordinary pro bono commitment to The Legal Aid Society and its clients."

- Hughes Hubbard is the 2006 recipient of the New York State Bar Association's President's Pro Bono Service Award.

JENNER & BLOCK LLP

330 N. Wabash Avenue

Chicago, IL 60611

Phone: (312) 222-9350

www.jenner.com

Areas of pro bono work:

Asylum/immigration, criminal trials, appeals, post-conviction petitions, habeas petitions, death penalty litigation, contract, corporate, corporate governance; civil rights; disability rights, domestic/family law, elder law, environmental, housing/real estate/landlord/tenant; tax.

Recent Pro Bono Clients:

National Immigrant Justice Center, Center for Elder and Disability Law, Lawyers' Committee for Civil Rights Under Law, American Civil Liberties Union, Lambda Legal Defense and Education Fund, Southern Utah Wilderness Alliance, Chicago Volunteer Legal Services, Cabrini Green Legal Aid Clinic, Lawyers' Committee for Better Housing, and Legal Assistance Foundation of Chicago.

Special Recognition and Awards:

- The Public Interest Law Initiative honored Jenner & Block with its 2006 Pro Bono Initiative Award for the firm's "unprecedented" pro bono work in the community.

- Also in 2006, the firm received the American Bar Association's Death Penalty Representation Project's Volunteer Recognition Award for "exceptional pro bono contributions" on behalf of Death Row prisoners.

The Vault Pro Bono Programs Directory is a special advertising section in the *Vault Guide to the Top 100 Law Firms*.
For information on listing your firm in the directory, contact corporatesales@vault.com.

VAULT CAREER LIBRARY   717

JONES DAY

51 Louisiana Avenue NW

Washington, DC 20001

Phone: (202) 879-3939

www.jonesday.com

Areas of pro bono work:

Jones Day lawyers represent individuals and nonprofit organizations in both civil and criminal litigation. We also practice before a variety of courts and administrative agencies. In addition, firm lawyers in every domestic office are involved with an array of local bar and community-based services programs that address the needs of the underprivileged members of our communities.

Recent Pro Bono Clients:

Appleseed Foundation (New York, Texas, Washington, D.C.), Bet Tzedek, House of Justice (Los Angeles), Community Economic Development Law Project (Chicago), Dallas Legal Hospice, Equal Justice Foundation (Columbus), Lawyers' Committee for Civil Rights and Urban Affairs (Washington, D.C.), Legal Aid of NorthWest Texas (Dallas) and Legal Aid Society (Cleveland, Washington, D.C.), National Immigrant Justice Center (Chicago), Neighborhood Legal Services (Pittsburgh) and Public Counsel (Los Angeles).

Special Recognition and Awards:

Midwest Light of Human Rights Award; State Bar of Texas 2006 Frank J. Scurlock Award; Eighth Annual Justice Robert Benham Award for Community Service; and 2006 County of Los Angeles Commission on Human Relations' Corporate Award

KAYE SCHOLER LLP

425 Park Avenue

New York, NY 10022

Phone: (212) 836-8000

www.kayescholer.com

Areas of pro bono work:

Death penalty, asylum, civil rights and civil liberties, general litigation, landlord/tenant, criminal and court-appointed cases, intellectual property, real estate, corporate (transactional work, corporate governance advice and formation of not-for-profit corporations), tax (including obtaining 501(c)(3) status for tax exempt organizations), employment, labor issues, family law and matrimonial law.

Recent Pro Bono Clients:

The Legal Aid Society, Sanctuary for Families, The Brennan Center for Justice, Human Rights First, Washington Lawyer's Committee for Civil Rights and Urban Affairs, Lawyer's Committee on Civil Rights under Law, New York Lawyers for the Public Interest, Bet Tzedek, D.C. Bar Pro Bono Program (Community Economic Development Pro Bono Project) and Public Counsel.

Special Recognition and Awards:

New York State Bar Association 2006 President's Pro Bono Award, First Judicial District; The Legal Aid Society's 2006 Pro Bono Award; Legal Aid Society Award for Outstanding Pro Bono Service in 2005; and 2005 Scales of Justice Award presented by the MFY Legal Services, Inc.

© 2007 Vault Inc.

KENYON & KENYON

One Broadways
New York, NY 10004
Phone: (212) 425-7200
www.kenyon.com

Areas of pro bono work:

Kenyon & Kenyon provided an array of intellectual property counseling and representation for various nonprofit and hardship organizations throughout the country. We offered free legal representation, advice and education to artists and arts organizations who would otherwise not afford legal assistance. We also performed pro bono legal services in several death penalty appeals.

Recent Pro Bono Clients:

Volunteer Lawyers for the Arts, Virginia Capital Defender Office, Grameen Foundation USA, Special Olympics, League for the Hard of Hearing, Harlem Children's Zone, The New Museum of Contemporary Art, All Stars Project, Renovation House and S.D.N.Y. Pro Bono Panel.

Special Recognition and Awards:

The firm was honored with the New York County Lawyers' Association Law Related Education Committee Pro Bono Award for our longstanding dedication to community service at an event sponsored by the New York Law Journal on November 30, 2005.

KILPATRICK STOCKTON LLP

1100 Peachtree Street, Suite 2800
Atlanta, GA 30309
Phone: (404) 815-6500
www.kilpatrickstockton.com

Areas of pro bono work:

We represent low-income clients in matters including landlord/tenant, consumer, insurance and car issues; victims of domestic violence; guardian ad litem; grandparent adoption; wills and advance directives for senior citizens; civil rights and habeas death penalty. We represent over 272 nonprofit organizations in all areas, including employment; employee benefits; real estate, corporate, tax, environmental and intellectual property. We represent parents in international kidnapping cases. We represent many community groups in the legal issues facing their members.

Recent Pro Bono Clients:

Legal Aid; local pro bono and children's programs; civil rights; farmer, community revitalization and arts organizations; immigration support groups; the Appleseed Foundation; the National Center for Missing & Exploited Children and the Federal Defender Program.

Special Recognition and Awards:

- Law Firm of the Year, New Orleans Pro Bono Project

- Angels in Adoption, Congressional Coalition on Adoption Institute

- IMPACT Award, Metro Atlanta Corporate Volunteer Council

- Law Firm of the Year Award, Pro Bono Partnership

The Vault Pro Bono Programs Directory is a special advertising section in the *Vault Guide to the Top 100 Law Firms*.
For information on listing your firm in the directory, contact corporatesales@vault.com.

VAULT CAREER LIBRARY   719

KRAMER LEVIN NAFTALIS & FRANKEL LLP

1177 Avenue of the Americas

New York, NY 10036

Phone: (212) 715-9100

www.kramerlevin.com

Areas of pro bono work:

Political asylum, landlord/tenant, civil rights and civil liberties, voting rights, GLBT rights, Social Security disability, divorce and custody, elderly wills, nonprofit incorporation, real estate, IP and other transactional work for nonprofits and microentrepreneurs, aid to September 11 victims and criminal defense.

Recent Pro Bono Clients:

Lambda Legal Defense, Human Rights First, The Brennan Center, Volunteer Lawyers for the Arts, Center for Disability Advocacy Rights, South Brooklyn Legal Services, New York Legal Assistance Group, inMotion, Volunteers of Legal Services (VOLS) and the New York Lawyers for the Public Interest (NYLPI).

Special Recognition and Awards:

- In early 2007, the firm was awarded the John Minor Wisdom Public Service and Professionalism Award by the American Bar Association Section of Litigation, honoring the firm for its outstanding pro bono efforts in 2006 and its historical commitment to supporting pro bono involvement by all of the firm's lawyers. Kramer Levin is only the fifth law firm so honored in the 18 years the award has been given.

- Kramer Levin was awarded one of the National Law Journal's 2006 Pro Bono Awards for its work on the Florida voting rights case discussed above.

LATHAM & WATKINS LLP

633 West Fifth Street, Suite 4000

Los Angeles, CA 90071-2007

Phone: (213) 485-1234

www.lw.com

Areas of pro bono work:

Our pro bono accomplishments include almost every area of public interest law, including children's rights, civil rights, community economic development, consumer law, criminal trial and appellate proceedings (including death penalty litigation), disability rights, disaster relief, domestic violence advocacy and prevention, foster children adoptions, homelessness prevention, human rights and refugee issues (including immigration and asylum matters), international law, land use permitting and approvals, landlord/tenant issues, nonprofit corporation counseling and representation, public benefits and special education matters.

Recent Pro Bono Clients:

Public Counsel (Los Angeles); New York Lawyers for the Public Interest (New York); Washington Legal Clinic for the Homeless (Washington, D.C.); National Immigrant Justice Center (Chicago); Public Law Center (Orange County, CA); Lawyers Committee for Civil Rights Under Law; Human Rights First; American Civil Liberties Union; Legal Aid Foundations and Ashoka.

Special Recognition and Awards:

The San Francisco AIDS Legal Referral Panel's 2006 Firm of the Year award; Five Acres, the Boys' and Girls' Aid Society of Los Angeles County's Special Recognition Award; Legal Services for Children's Pro Bono Partner award; San Mateo Legal Aid Society's Pro Bono Honoree for April 2006.

© 2007 Vault Inc.

LEBOEUF, LAMB, GREEN & MACRAE LLP

125 West 55th Street

New York, NY 10019-5389

Phone: (212) 424-8000

www.llgm.com

Areas of pro bono work:

Asylum, bankruptcy, child custody and support, civil rights, corporate and finance (transactional work, corporate governance advice and formation of not-for-profit corporations), criminal trial and appeal, domestic violence, education, employment, entertainment and the arts, environmental, general litigation, immigration, insurance, intellectual property, landlord/tenant, legal advocacy for animal rights, real estate, tax (including obtaining 501(c)(3) status), labor issues and ERISA, and voter protection.

Recent Pro Bono Clients:

Citizens Committee for New York, Clearpool, Inc., Human Rights First, Lawyers Alliance for New York, Lawyers for Children America, Lawyers Committee for Civil Rights Under Law, Legal Aid Society (in various cities across the country), NAACP Legal Defense Fund, Rosie O'Donnell's For All Kids Foundation and South Brooklyn Legal Services.

Special Recognition and Awards:

- Covenant House 2006 Volunteer Service Award (Washington, D.C. office)

- Immigration Equality Safe Haven Award (Franklin Monsour and Ray Psonak)

- 2006 New York Bar Association Pro Bono Award (John Aerni)

- American Bar Association's 2006 Edmund S. Muskie Pro Bono Award (Larry Schiffer)

LOWENSTEIN SANDLER PC

65 Livingston Avenue

Roseland, NJ 07068

Phone: (973) 597-2500

www.lowenstein.com

Areas of pro bono work:

Asylum representation, civil rights litigation, corporate, real estate, tax, intellectual property, employment law; education law; family law and criminal law.

Recent Pro Bono Clients:

New Jersey Institute for Social Justice; Children's Rights, Inc.; Essex Newark Legal Services; New Jersey Community Development Corp.; Salvation Army, Essex County; Hyacinth Aids Foundation; Kids Corporation; Human Rights First; Centurion Ministries; and Volunteer Lawyers the for Arts—NJ.

Special Recognition and Awards:

Lowenstein Sandler has consistently been ranked as an "A" level provider of pro bono services by The New Jersey Law Journal, and in 2005 and in 2006 was ranked by The American Lawyer as the leading New Jersey-based AmLaw 200 firm with respect to pro bono initiatives.

In 2006, Lowenstein Sandler was recognized by Volunteer Lawyers for Justice—a Newark, N.J.-based agency—as its pro bono law firm of the year.

The Vault Pro Bono Programs Directory is a special advertising section in the *Vault Guide to the Top 100 Law Firms*.
For information on listing your firm in the directory, contact corporatesales@vault.com.

VAULT CAREER LIBRARY   721

MANATT, PHELPS & PHILLIPS, LLP

11355 W. Olympic Boulevard

Los Angeles, CA 90064

Phone: (310) 312-4000

www.manatt.com

Areas of pro bono work:

Specific areas of law in which the firm has performed pro bono legal work include adoption and guardianship, asylum and immigration, children's rights, civil rights, community economic development and other transactional matters, constitutional law, disaster recovery, education, entertainment and the arts, elder law, estate and probate law, Holocaust reparations, homelessness, human rights, intellectual property, poverty law, prisoners' rights, public benefits, voter protection and women's rights.

Recent Pro Bono Clients:

California Women's Law Center (all California offices), Human Rights First (firmwide), Lawyers' Committee for Civil Rights Under Law (firmwide), Legal Aid Society (Los Angeles, New York and Palo Alto), Medicare Rights Center (New York and Washington, D.C.), Mississippi Center for Justice (firmwide), National Center for Refugee & Immigrant Children (firmwide) and Public Counsel (Los Angeles).

Special Recognition and Awards:

• Wiley W. Manuel Award for Pro Bono Legal Services

• California Women's Law Center Pursuit of Justice Award

• Daily Journal Most Innovative Pro Bono Projects in California (out of 12 chosen by the newspaper, three involved Manatt's leadership)

MAYER, BROWN, ROWE & MAW LLP

71 South Wacker Drive

Chicago, IL 60606

Phone: (312) 782-0600

www.mayerbrownrowe.com

Areas of pro bono work:

Affordable housing, microfinance, nonprofit incorporation and transactional advice to not-for-profit organizations, community economic development, international rule of law development, international human rights, death penalty, indigent criminal defense, First Amendment, prisoners rights, civil liberties and civil rights, immigration and asylum, adoption, domestic violence, HIV/AIDS, landlord/tenant and public benefits.

Recent Pro Bono Clients:

The Innocence Project of the Benjamin N. Cardozo School of Law at Yeshiva University, Center for Constitutional Rights, Corporation for Supportive Housing, Cook County Circuit Court, Criminal Division (death penalty, murder and serious felony cases-Chicago), National Immigrant Justice Center (the former Midwest Immigrant & Human Rights Center-Chicago), and Charlotte-Mecklenburg Housing Partnership (Charlotte).

Special Recognition and Awards:

• The firm was honored by the NAACP with a 2006 Civil Rights Champion Award in recognition of the firm's work in support of the NAACP's fight for justice.

• The firm was honored by the U.S. District Court for the Northern District of Illinois and the Federal Bar Association for our limited appointment settlement project for pro se litigants.

© 2007 Vault Inc.

MCCARTER & ENGLISH, LLP

Four Gateway Center
100 Mulberry Street
Newark, NJ 07102
Phone: (973) 622-4444
www.mccarter.com

Areas of pro bono work:

McCarter & English performs pro bono work in a number of areas, specifically guardianship law, asylum law, death penalty appeals, missing children cases, patent law, divorce law, custody law, domestic violence cases, civil rights cases, immigration and employment law.

Recent Pro Bono Clients:

The First Occupational Center of NJ (Orange, N.J.), Habitat for Humanity, Human Rights First (New York, N.Y.), Campaign for Justice, Legal Services of NJ (New Brunswick, N.J.), NJ Institute for Social Justice (Newark, N.J.), New Jersey Crime Victims' Law Center (Sparta, N.J.), Partners for Women and Justice (Montclair, N.J.), Pro Bono Partnership (Newark, N.J.), Union County Mediation (Union, N.J.) and Volunteer Lawyers for Justice (Newark, N.J.)

Special Recognition and Awards:

- Partners for Women and Justice has selected Elise Collins as an honoree for her support of the organization's family law pro bono program. She was invited to PFWJ's annual Spring Benefit, which took place on April 27, 2006.

- Immigration Equality honored M&E and associate Jim Sheil as a Safe Haven Award recipient for his work on Haitham Noufal's asylum case. The organization's annual benefit took place at the Prince George Hotel Ballroom, 15 East 27th St., NYC.

MCGUIREWOODS LLP

McGuireWoods is a national firm with no specified main office.
www.mcguirewoods.com

Areas of pro bono work:

Immigration, legal aid referrals, criminal defense, nonprofit organization representation, domestic violence, appeals, political asylum and housing.

Recent Pro Bono Clients:

Various Legal Aid offices in multiple cities, Habitat for Humanity, community nonprofits, Boys Scouts and Girls Scouts, United Way, Legal Services Corporation and various human services charities.

Special Recognition and Awards:

- The Chicago office won recognition from the Public Interest Law Initiative as one of the top pro bono programs in the city, a city known for some of the most prodigious pro bono work in the country.

- Retired Virginia partner John Oakey won the Lewis F. Powell Jr. Award, presented by the Virginia State Bar to the most distinguished partner in service to the poor and disenfranchised.

- Melissa Bien, Lisa Clay and Gary Leung shared a $5,000 cash prize from the firm as McGuireWoods' Pro Bono Associates of the Year. They contributed a share of their winnings to the Midwest Center for Human Rights, the group that referred to them several asylum cases they effectively handled in the Seventh Circuit Court of Appeals.

The Vault Pro Bono Programs Directory is a special advertising section in the *Vault Guide to the Top 100 Law Firms*.
For information on listing your firm in the directory, contact corporatesales@vault.com.

VAULT CAREER LIBRARY   723

MCKEE NELSON LLP

1 Battery Park Plaza, 34th Floor
New York, NY 10004
Phone: (917) 777-4200
www.mckeenelson.com

Areas of pro bono work:

Securitization, immigration, corporate, tax, family law, health care and criminal defense.

Recent Pro Bono Clients:

Capital Area Immigration Rights (CAIR) Coalition, National Center for Refugee and Immigrant Children, Public Defender Service of the District of Columbia, Children's Law Center, The Community Tax Law Project, D.C. Bar Community Economic Development Project, New York City Investment Trust, inMotion, The Little Baby Face Foundation and Upper Manhattan Council for Assisting Neighbors.

Special Recognition and Awards:

McKee Nelson did not win any special recognition or awards in 2005 and 2006 for its pro bono work.

MINTZ, LEVIN, COHN, FERRIS, GLOVSKY AND POPEO, P.C.

One Financial Center
Boston, MA 02111
Phone: (617) 542-6000
www.mintz.com

Areas of pro bono work:

Domestic violence and sexual assault, political asylum and immigration, affordable housing and homelessness, human rights; prisoners' rights, nonprofit incorporation assistance, post-Katrina legal assistance, environmental protection and civil rights.

Recent Pro Bono Clients:

Political Asylum/Immigration Project, Medical-Legal Partnership for Children, Greater Boston Food Bank, Human Rights First, National Network to End Domestic Violence, Lawyers Committee for Civil Rights under the Law, Volunteer Lawyers Project, Human Rights Campaign, Women Empowered Against Violence and Mississippi Center for Justice.

Special Recognition and Awards:

- In April and again in October, Martha Koster and Noah Shaw, on behalf of the firm, received the Mississippi Center for Justice's Champions of Justice Award for advancing recovery and ensuring fairness in the wake of Hurricane Katrina. Noah Shaw has also been twice nominated by the Mississippi Center for Justice for both the 2006 Arthur von Briesen Award, given each year by the National Legal Aid and Defenders Association, and the 2006 Pro Bono Publico Award, given annually by the American Bar Association, for his work spearheading these efforts.

© 2007 Vault Inc.

MORGAN, LEWIS & BOCKIUS LLP

1701 Market Street
Philadelphia, PA 19103-2921
Phone: (215) 963-5000
www.morganlewis.com

Areas of pro bono work:

Capital punishment and other criminal work, immigration and asylum, comprehensive advice and counseling to tax-exempt nonprofit entities, homelessness, representation of artists, representation of low-income entrepreneurs, adoption, child advocacy, landlord/tenant, patent and trademark, environmental, education, international human rights, real estate, copyright, insurance recovery, guardianship, access to education, Social Security and health care advocacy.

Recent Pro Bono Clients:

Support Center for Child Advocates (Philadelphia), Sanctuary for Families (New York), Lawyers Committee for Civil Rights of the Bay Area (San Francisco, Palo Alto), Put Something Back (Miami), D.C. Bar Public Service Activities Corporation (Washington, D.C.) and Volunteer Lawyers for the Arts (New York and Philadelphia)

Special Recognition and Awards:

- Morgan Lewis' New York office received the Outstanding Volunteer Award for 2006 from Volunteer Lawyers for the Arts, New York.

- Philadelphia attorney Polly Hayes was named a Volunteer of the Year by the Campaign for Working Families for her work with the Earned Income Tax Credit clinic.

- Philadelphia attorneys Karen Pohlmann and Brian Watson received the Pennsylvania Bar Association's 2006 Pro Bono Award.

MORRISON & FOERSTER LLP

425 Market Street
San Francisco, CA 94105-2482
Phone: (415) 268-7000
www.mofo.com

Areas of pro bono work:

Education matters, children's issues, civil rights and civil liberties, criminal justice, international human rights and political asylum, disability issues, women's rights and domestic violence, sexual orientation issues, veterans' matters, animal rights, housing and homelessness, environmental matters, legal aid for the arts, nonprofit organizations and legal service clinics.

Recent Pro Bono Clients:

American Civil Liberties Union; Lawyers Committee for Civil Rights, Legal Services for Children, The Innocence Project, The Legal Aid Society, Human Rights Watch, Center For Reproductive Rights, LAMBDA Legal Defense Fund and Disability Rights Education & Defense Fund

Special Recognition and Awards:

- The Faculty of Federal Advocates Annual Award of Appreciation (2006)

- **The Law Foundation of Silicon Valley awarded the firm the Honorable Robert F. Peckham Award for outstanding public interest litigation** (2006).

- The ACLU-Los Angeles Chapter awarded the Sutton v. Riverside Police Department team a Racial Justice Award (2006).

- Resolution of the California Assembly commending the firm for "its long history of commitment to providing pro bono legal services to low-income persons and in matters of public interest both at home and abroad." (2007)

The Vault Pro Bono Programs Directory is a special advertising section in the *Vault Guide to the Top 100 Law Firms*.
For information on listing your firm in the directory, contact corporatesales@vault.com.

VAULT CAREER LIBRARY   725

NIXON PEABODY LLP

437 Madison Avenue

New York, NY 10022

Phone: (212) 940-3000

www.nixonpeabody.com

Areas of pro bono work:

We performed pro bono work in almost every area of public interest law over the past two years. A large portion of our recent work has focused on immigration and asylum law, affordable housing, not-for-profit assistance, arts and entertainment law, and housing litigation. We have also done a significant amount of legal work for victims of domestic violence, including orders of protection, custody, and divorce.

Recent Pro Bono Clients:

The Legal Aid Society, Human Rights First, The Lawyers Alliance; Volunteer Lawyers Project in Boston, The Lawyers Committee for Civil Rights, Greater Boston Legal Services, Volunteer Legal Services Project in Rochester, Public Interest Law of Rochester, Farm Worker Legal Services of New York and Habitat for Humanity.

Special Recognition and Awards:

The New York State Bar Association recognized several of our lawyers for rendering over 50 hours of pro bono work in 2006.

- Legal Services for Children Pro Bono Advocate Award, 2006

- Harlem Opera Theater has voted to award Nixon Peabody their second Corporate Leadership Award, 2006.

- The Massachusetts Licensed Site Professionals (LSPA) awarded the Nixon Peabody LLP its 2006 LSPA Sponsor Award.

O'MELVENY & MYERS LLP

400 South Hope Street

Los Angeles, CA 90071

Phone: (213) 430-6000

www.omm.com

Areas of pro bono work:

Housing, immigration, civil rights, discrimination, criminal defense, appeals, corporate governance, nonprofit tax, consumer fraud, intellectual property, adoptions and government benefits.

Recent Pro Bono Clients:

Legal Aid Foundation of Los Angeles, Public Counsel, Bet Tzedek, Alliance for Children's Rights, Lawyers Committee for Civil Rights of the San Francisco Bay Area, United States Court of Appeals for the Ninth Circuit (Pro Bono Appellate Project), Montgomery County (Md.) Public Defender's Office, Washington, D.C. Area Lawyers for the Arts and Brennan Center for Justice.

Special Recognition and Awards:

- The firm was the first ever recipient of the Los Angeles County Bar Association's Pro Bono Service Award for immigration pro bono work.

- The Constitutional Rights Foundation of Orange County chose O'Melveny as Law Firm of the Year for actively contributing to the success of the 2006-2007 Mock Trial Competition.

- The firm received the Legal Service Award from the Mexican-American Legal Defense and Education Fund.

- The firm was recognized at the Asian-American Justice Center's 10th Annual American Courage Awards in Washington, D.C.

© 2007 Vault Inc.

ORRICK, HARRINGTON & SUTCLIFFE LLP

666 Fifth Avenue

New York, NY 10103

www.orrick.com

Areas of pro bono work:

Orrick has performed pro bono legal work in the following areas: microfinance; family and matrimonial law; landlord/tenant; international human rights; immigration and asylum; employment counseling; general commercial litigation; criminal defense; civil rights and civil liberties; and general corporate, including incorporation and tax exemption, real estate and intellectual property work.

Recent Pro Bono Clients:

Bar Association of San Francisco— Volunteer Legal Services Program, D.C. Bar Pro Bono Program, Global Partnerships, Law Foundation of Silicon Valley, Lawyers Alliance for New York, Lawyers Committee for Civil Rights of the Bay Area, Legal Aid Foundation of Los Angeles, New York City Bar Public Justice Center, New York Lawyers for the Public Interest, Public International Law and Policy Group.

Special Recognition and Awards:

Pro Bono Partnerships honored Orrick with its Law Firm Volunteer of the Year Award in 2006 in recognition of the work of more than 20 attorneys who updated PBP's online employee handbook that is an invaluable resource for nonprofit executives. The firm drafted the handbook in 2002. The award honors a firm's pro bono commitment to nonprofits in Westchester, New Jersey and Connecticut.

PATTON BOGGS LLP

2550 M Street, NW

Washington, DC 20037

www.pattonboggs.com

Areas of pro bono work:

Public policy, civil rights, veterans' benefits appeals, nonprofit governance, immigration, education, environmental work, family law, appellate litigation, international human rights, IP; child welfare and adoption cases, and death penalty work.

Recent Pro Bono Clients:

Alaska Legal Services, Capital Area Immigrants Rights Coalition, Dallas Volunteer Attorney Program, Lawyers for Children America, The Legal Aid Society, the Native American Rights Fund, Texas C-Bar, the Veterans' Consortium, Washington Area Lawyers for the Arts, the Colorado and the Washington Lawyers' Committees for Civil Rights.

Special Recognition and Awards:

- Dallas Bar Association Board of Directors: for pro bono work with Dallas Volunteer Attorney Program (2006)

- Dallas Bar Association and the Dallas Volunteer Attorney Program: Silver Award for Pro Bono Services(2006)

- Women's Sports Foundation Award (2006)

The Vault Pro Bono Programs Directory is a special advertising section in the *Vault Guide to the Top 100 Law Firms*. For information on listing your firm in the directory, contact corporatesales@vault.com.

VAULT CAREER LIBRARY   727

PAUL, HASTINGS, JANOFSKY & WALKER LLP

515 South Flower Street, 25th Floor
Los Angeles, CA 90071-2228
www.paulhastings.com

Areas of pro bono work:

Paul Hastings provides pro bono legal services across legal disciplines, including: adoption and custody services, asylum and immigration cases, domestic violence and violence against women, incorporation and ongoing assistance to nonprofit organizations assisting foster children, environmental contamination, families of soldiers in Iraq and underdeveloped communities and neighborhoods, food and clothing drives, juvenile death penalty, legislative initiatives and legal reform, museum procurement, landlord/tenant disputes and estate planning for first responders.

Recent Pro Bono Clients:

Housing Development Fund, Inc., Lubavitch (U.K.) Limited, Orange County Red Cross, Tahirih Justice Center, Wall Las Memorias Project, Rainforest Alliance, Empowered Girls Circle, Children's Law Center, New York City Bar Hurricane Katrina Disaster Assistance Service Center (DASC) and Zoo Atlanta.

Special Recognition and Awards:

Paul Hastings received the University of Southern California Law School Paul Davis Memorial Award, the Fairfield County Small Business Council Leadership Recognition Award, the Paul Nicholls Memorial Foundation Award (London) and was named the Pro Bono Law Firm of the Year by Multicultural Law Magazine.

PAUL, WEISS, RIFKIND, WHARTON & GARRISON LLP

285 Avenue of the Americas
New York, NY 10019
Phone: (212) 373-3000
www.paulweiss.com

Areas of pro bono work:

Civil rights, domestic and international human rights, HIV/AIDS prevention, employment rights, reproductive rights, minority-owned small businesses, death penalty, children's rights, domestic violence, housing, not-for-profit organizations, criminal trials and appeals and intellectual property.

Recent Pro Bono Clients:

American Civil Liberties Union (ACLU), Asian American Legal Defense and Education Fund (AALDEF), Brennan Center for Justice at NYU School of Law, Business Resource & Investment Service Center (BRISC), Disability Advocates; Legal Aid Society, NAACP Legal Defense and Educational Fund, New York Lawyers for the Public Interest (NYLPI), Volunteer Lawyers for the Arts and the William J. Clinton Foundation.

Special Recognition and Awards:

- Ranked in the top 10 for the fourth year in a row in The American Lawyer's A List. The A List is compiled by measuring the performance of the Am Law 200 firms in four key areas, pro bono being one of them.

- Sanctuary for Families' Center for Battered Women's Legal Services Associates Committee honored two of our lawyers for their pro bono representation of a battered woman involved in an international custody battle in 2005.

© 2007 Vault Inc.

PERKINS COIE LLP

1201 Third Avenue, Suite 4800

Seattle, WA 98101-3099

Phone: (206) 359-8000

www.perkinscoie.com

Areas of pro bono work:

t is difficult to capture the full breadth of the areas of law covered by our pro bono program; it is truly diverse. Probably the area with the greatest number of matters has been in the area of immigration/refugee law. We also represent hundreds of nonprofit entities with respect to the establishment of their 501(c)(3) status, other formation issues, intellectual property matters, employment issues or general advice.

Recent Pro Bono Clients:

Court Appointed Special Advocate (CASA) Programs, Volunteer Advocates for Immigrant Justice, Florence Immigrant & Refugee Rights Project, King County Bar Association Housing Justice Project, Childhaven, Committee for Children, Compassion & Choices, Domestic Violence Project, Mercy Corps and American Civil Liberties Union.

Special Recognition and Awards:

Pro Bono Award from the National Law Journal, Civil Libertarian Award from the ACLU of Washington, Award of Merit from the Washington State Bar Association, Corporate Pro Bono Partner Award, Michael E. Haglund Pro Bono Award from the Multnomah Bar Association, The Japanese American Bar Association of Greater Los Angeles (JABA)'s Public Service Award, Idaho CASA Program Volunteer of the Year for 2006

SAUL EWING LLP

1500 Market Street, Centre Square West

38th floor

Philadelphia, PA 19102

Phone: (215) 972-7777

www.saul.com

Areas of pro bono work:

Bankruptcy, civil rights, constitutional law, consumer; contracts, criminal defense, domestic relations, education, environmental, estate planning, homeownership, insurance, immigration, intellectual property, labor/employment, landlord/tenant, mediation, name change, nonprofit assistance, probate, public benefits, real estate, small business/economic development, tax and veterans benefits.

Recent Pro Bono Clients:

AARP Legal Counsel for the Elderly, Community Legal Services of Philadelphia, Inc., Consumer Bankruptcy Assistance Project, Dauphin County Area Agency on the Aging, Delaware Volunteer Legal Services, Homeless Advocacy Project, Maryland Volunteer Lawyers Service and Mercer County Veterans Association.

Special Recognition and Awards:

Firm attorneys and offices have been honored with the following awards: Baltimore County Chamber of Commerce—Volunteer of the Year Award, Baltimore Mayor Martin O'Malley's Community Volunteer of the Year Award, Homeless Advocacy Project Outstanding Service Award, Judge Robert M. Bell Award for Leadership in Public Service, National Italian-American Political Action Committee National Achievement Award and Philadelphia Bar Association—Bar Medal.

The Vault Pro Bono Programs Directory is a special advertising section in the *Vault Guide to the Top 100 Law Firms*.
For information on listing your firm in the directory, contact corporatesales@vault.com.

VAULT CAREER LIBRARY   729

SHEARMAN STERLING LLP

599 Lexington Avenue

New York, NY 10022

Phone: (212) 848-4000

www.shearman.com

Areas of pro bono work:

Arts, bankruptcy, disaster relief, rule of law, criminal law and death penalty, family law, immigration, civil rights, community development, microfinance, education, nonprofit law and human rights.

Recent Pro Bono Clients:

Human Rights First; inMotion; Lawyers Committee for Civil Rights under Law; Lawyers Without Borders; Legal Aid; New York Lawyers for the Public Interest; Robin Hood Foundation; Sanctuary for Families; Volunteer Lawyers for the Arts; and Bar Associations of D.C., New York and San Francisco.

Special Recognition and Awards:

• Sanctuary for Families honored an associate for her dedicated pro bono service to immigrant women.

• The Legal Aid Society honored a partner, two counsel and a legal assistant for excellence in service.

• Immigration Equality honored an associate for his outstanding pro bono representation of GLBT refugees.

• Volunteer Lawyers for the Arts named the firm Outstanding Volunteer.

• D.C. Circuit Judicial Conference Standing Committee on Pro Bono Legal Services recognized the firm as one of the few in D.C. in which 40 percent or more lawyers dedicated at least 50 hours of pro bono in a year.

SIDLEY AUSTIN LLP

One South Dearborn Street

Chicago, IL 60603

Phone: (312) 853-7000

www.sidley.com

Areas of pro bono work:

Political asylum; state and federal criminal appeals, including substantial amounts of work in the U.S. Supreme Court; child custody; civil rights; public school education; corporate, tax and real estate work for community organizations; intellectual property; landlord/tenant; public benefits; matters involving battered women and children's rights; missing and exploited children; and habeas corpus petitions.

Recent Pro Bono Clients:

The Equal Justice Initiative (EJI), American Civil Liberties Union, Center for Disability and Elder Law, Lawyers' Committee on Civil Rights Under Law, Community Development and Economic Law Project, inMotion Justice for All Women, PILI (Public Interest Law Initiative), the Alliance for Children's Rights (Los Angeles), the National Women's Law Center and the Downtown Women's Center (Los Angeles).

Special Recognition and Awards:

In January 2007, Sidley was awarded one of The National Law Journal's 2006 Pro Bono Awards. The National Law Journal featured Sidley's work in an article entitled "Firm's Project is a Matter of Life and Death." The article highlighted the Capital Litigation Project and the work of San Francisco partner Geoffrey Ezgar, who has volunteered more than 450 hours on a case involving an Alabama inmate accused of a violent triple homicide.

© 2007 Vault Inc.

SKADDEN, ARPS, SLATE, MEAGHER & FLOM LLP

Four Times Square
New York, NY 10036-6522
Phone: (212) 735-3000
www.skadden.com

Areas of pro bono work:

Contract, merger, financing, organizational and intellectual property work for nonprofits; representing political asylum applicants; representing indigent death row inmates; will, tax and senior citizen clinics; adoptions; representing battered women in Violence Against Women Act, order of protection and divorce matters; copyright applications for artists; disability, housing termination and unemployment hearings; lawsuits challenging discrimination based on age or disability; litigation seeking re-sentencing under revisions to the Rockefeller drug laws; child custody and support matters.

Recent Pro Bono Clients:

Bet Tzedek, Human Rights First, inMotion, Lawyers Alliance for New York; Lawyers' Committee for Civil Rights Under Law, Legal Aid Societies of various cities and New York Legal Assistance Group

Special Recognition and Awards:

American Bar Association Section of Business Law's National Public Service Award, American Bar Association Death Penalty Representation Project Award for Outstanding Contributions to Pro Bono Death Penalty Work, Human Rights First's Frankel Award, Public Interest Law Initiative Award for Outstanding Pro Bono Contributions, Texas C-BAR's Community Builder Award, Western Center on Law and Poverty's Brinsley Award for Outstanding Service to the Center.

SQUIRE, SANDERS & DEMPSEY L.L.P.

4900 Key Tower, 127 Public Square
Cleveland, OH 44114-1304
Phone: (216) 479-8500
www.ssd.com

Areas of pro bono work:

From criminal appeals, including death cases, to small claims court to legal representation of nonprofit institutions and everything in between.

Special Recognition and Awards:

Court and community citations. Various from office to office, year to year.

The Vault Pro Bono Programs Directory is a special advertising section in the *Vault Guide to the Top 100 Law Firms*.
For information on listing your firm in the directory, contact corporatesales@vault.com.

VAULT CAREER LIBRARY   731

STROOCK & STROOCK & LAVAN, LLP

180 Maiden Lane

New York, NY 10038

Phone: (212) 806-5400

www.stroock.com

Areas of pro bono work:

Adoptions, amicus briefs, asylum and immigration law, civil rights, community economic development, criminal appeals, disability rights and children's advocacy, elder law, health care, nonprofit law, domestic violence and family law, September 11th and Hurricane Katrina legal relief work.

Recent Pro Bono Clients:

Association of the Bar of the City of New York, inMotion, Kings County District Attorney's Office, Lawyers Alliance for New York, Human Rights First, MFY Legal Services, New York Lawyers for the Public Interest, Pratt Area Community Council, Sanctuary for Families and The Legal Aid Society.

Special Recognition and Awards:

- Sanctuary for Families Award for Excellence in Pro Bono Advocacy (2005)

- Lawyers Alliance Cornerstone Award (2005)

- The Legal Aid Society's Community Revitalization Awards: Rehabilitation of Affordable Housing (2005)

- MFY Legal Services' 2005 Scales of Justice Award (2005)

- New York Disaster Interfaith Services Pro Bono Award (2005)

- Council on Homeless Policies and Services Honoree (2006)

SULLIVAN & CROMWELL LLP

125 Broad Street

New York, NY 10004-2498

Phone: (212) 58-4000

www.sullcrom.com

Areas of pro bono work:

Assistance to not-for-profit corporations, artists and arts groups; representation of victims of domestic violence; asylum applications; death penalty cases; prisoners rights matters; criminal matters; civil rights issues and legal assistance to AIDS patients.

Recent Pro Bono Clients:

Lawyers Alliance of New York, Human Rights First, The Legal Aid Society, inMotion, Inc., Sanctuary for Families, Volunteer Lawyers for the Arts, Volunteers of Legal Service, New York Lawyers for the Public Interest, The American Civil Liberties Union and the Lawyers' Committee for Civil Rights Under Law.

Special Recognition and Awards:

The Pro Bono Digest of New York Law Journal, published on May 6th, discussed the findings of the 15th annual pro bono survey completed by Volunteers of Legal Service (VOLS). S&C was among the firms singled out for their achievement in qualifying pro bono work. Particular mention was made of S&C's ongoing efforts in support of prisoners' rights and success in winning asylum for political activists from Africa.

© 2007 Vault Inc.

SUTHERLAND ASBILL & BRENNAN LLP

999 Peachtree St. NE
Atlanta, GA 30309
www.sablaw.com

Areas of pro bono work:

The majority of our work over the past two years includes death penalty, Guantánamo detainees, traditional poverty law, not-for-profit, traditional civil rights, claims for people with disabilities, habeas corpus, criminal appeals, immigration appeals, immigration worker litigation, affordable housing and public benefits

Recent Pro Bono Clients:

Pro Bono Partnership-Atlanta, Washington Lawyers' Committee for Civil Rights & Urban Affairs, Atlanta Legal Aid Society, D.C. Bar Pro Bono Clinic/D.C. Bar Community Economic Development Project and Georgia Legal Services Program

Special Recognition and Awards:

• On March 21, 2006, John A. Chandler received the Atlanta Bar Association Leadership Award in recognition of his long service to the Atlanta Bar and the community at large. The award is reserved for "members who inspire by their example, challenge by their deeds and remind us all of our debt to our profession and our community."

• On October 12, 2006, Sutherland was awarded the inaugural Zenith Award for Service to the Community from the Georgia Association of Black Women Attorneys (GABWA).

• In 2006, Sutherland was awarded the Georgia Civil Liberties Award by the Georgia chapter of the American Civil Liberties Union.

VENABLE LLP

575 7th Street, NW
Washington, DC 20004
Phone: (202) 344-4000
www.venable.com

Areas of pro bono work:

A wide range of poverty law issues, intellectual property, children's and women's rights, Social Security and veteran's appeals, and international human rights.

Recent Pro Bono Clients:

ABA Death Penalty Project, Bread for the City, Legal Aid of D.C. and Maryland, Maryland Volunteer Lawyers Service, Pro Bono Resource Center of Maryland, Public Interest Intellectual Property Advisors Veterans Consortium, Washington Legal Clinic for the Homeless, Wendt Center for Loss & Healing and Whitman-Walker Legal Programs.

Special Recognition and Awards:

• Brian Zemil: Maryland Volunteer Lawyers Service, Educator of the Year

• Dana Nifosi, Distinguished Volunteer Award, Whitman-Walker Clinic Legal Services

The Vault Pro Bono Programs Directory is a special advertising section in the *Vault Guide to the Top 100 Law Firms*.
For information on listing your firm in the directory, contact corporatesales@vault.com.

VAULT CAREER LIBRARY   733

VENABLE LLP

575 7th Street, NW

Washington, DC 20004

Phone: (202) 344-4000

www.venable.com

Areas of pro bono work:

A wide range of poverty law issues, intellectual property, children's and women's rights, Social Security and veteran's appeals, and international human rights.

Recent Pro Bono Clients:

ABA Death Penalty Project, Bread for the City, Legal Aid of D.C. and Maryland, Maryland Volunteer Lawyers Service, Pro Bono Resource Center of Maryland, Public Interest Intellectual Property Advisors Veterans Consortium, Washington Legal Clinic for the Homeless, Wendt Center for Loss & Healing and Whitman-Walker Legal Programs.

Special Recognition and Awards:

• Brian Zemil: Maryland Volunteer Lawyers Service, Educator of the Year

• Dana Nifosi, Distinguished Volunteer Award, Whitman-Walker Clinic Legal Services

VINSON & ELKINS LLP

1001 Fannin, Suite 2500

Houston, TX 77002

Phone: (713) 758-2222

www.velaw.com

Areas of pro bono work:

Vinson & Elkins lawyers have undertaken pro bono representation in a variety of civil, criminal and transactional matters, including: criminal defense and appeals, death penalty litigation, civil rights, political asylum, landlord/tenant disputes, environmental law, Social Security and pensions benefits, mediation, bankruptcy, mental health issues and family law.

Recent Pro Bono Clients:

Art League of Houston, Ballet Austin, Dispute Resolution Center, Hill Country Youth Ranch, Inc., KERA-TV, Leadership America, Lone Star Legal Aid, Media Law Resource Center, Texas Appleseed, Thurgood Marshall Academy Public High School.

Special Recognition and Awards:

The Thurgood Marshall Academy Public Charter High School honored Vinson & Elkins LLP by naming a classroom after Judge William Benson Bryant, chosen by the firm as a role model, in recognition of the firm's long-standing support of the school's students. V&E lawyers and employees have tutored students once a week for the past three years as part of their mandatory tutoring program in which all 11th grade students must participate. Additionally, the firm has provided monetary support to the law-related, college-preparatory school since it opened in 2001.

© 2007 Vault Inc.

WHITE & CASE LLP

1155 Avenue of the Americas

New York, NY

Phone: (212) 819-8200

www.whitecase.com

Areas of pro bono work:

Children's rights, asylum/immigration, community development, micro-entrepreneurial assistance, trust and estates, domestic violence, family law, nonprofit law, impact litigation, arts, human rights.

Recent Pro Bono Clients:

Inner City Law Center, Legal Aid Society, Lawyers Alliance for New York, inMotion, Human Rights First, Lawyers' Committee for Civil Rights Under Law, Volunteer Lawyers for the Arts, Volunteers of Legal Service, Women's World Banking, Doctors Without Borders.

Special Recognition and Awards:

- Immigration Equality awards Safe Haven awards to N.Y. W&C associates Darren Spedale, Lesley Mendoza, Eric Leibowitz, David Ernst, Jennifer Co and Andrea Chiller in recognition of the work they've done on behalf of Immigration Equality and its clients. (2006)

- Amy Robinson honored by The Legal Aid Society for her work in the Society's taxpayer clinics for the working poor. (2006)

- Los Angeles partner Daniel Woods appointed president of the Los Angeles County Bar Foundation. (2006)

- Los Angeles associate Amanda Hayes recognized by Lawyers' Committee for Civil Rights Under Law for her pro bono work on their behalf. (2006)

WILLIAMS CONNOLLY LLP

725 12th Street, NW

Washington, DC 20005

www.wc.com

Areas of pro bono work:

Criminal trial-level defense, criminal appeals, death penalty, political asylum, civil rights litigation, disability rights litigation, Section 1983 litigation, landlord/tenant litigation, representation of parolees at parole revocation hearings, veterans' benefits appeals, civil litigation and advice for nonprofit organizations and corporate and tax work for nonprofit organizations, employment litigation and administrative law.

Recent Pro Bono Clients:

Montgomery County Public Defenders' Office, Maryland Public Defender's Office, Washington Lawyers' Committee for Civil Rights and Urban Affairs, ABA Death Penalty Representation Project, D.C. Bar Pro Bono Program, Center for Science in the Public Interest and Washington Legal Clinic for the Homeless.

Special Recognition and Awards:

- Recognition by Montgomery County, Maryland's public defenders' office for the "amazing success" of the Williams & Connolly LLP partnership with the office to represent defendants in felony cases.

- Recognition by the D.C. Bar Pro Bono Program for the firm's commitment to providing pro bono legal services and for the firm's work on the program's Affordable Housing Initiative and the program's Landlord Tenant Resource Center.

- Recognition by the Veterans Consortium Pro Bono Program for the firm's handling of a veterans' benefits appeal.

The Vault Pro Bono Programs Directory is a special advertising section in the *Vault Guide to the Top 100 Law Firms*.
For information on listing your firm in the directory, contact corporatesales@vault.com.

VAULT CAREER LIBRARY   735

WILLKIE FARR & GALLAGHER LLP

787 Seventh Avenue
New York, NY 10019
Phone: (212) 728-8000
www.willkie.com

Areas of pro bono work:

Rights of noncitizen detainees; housing for disadvantaged persons; immigration rights; women's rights, including divorce, custody, support and protection matters; criminal defense; youth mentoring; artists' rights and debtor rights.

Recent Pro Bono Clients:

MFY Legal Services, inMotion (f/k/a Network for Women's Services), Habitat for Humanity, Legal Aid Society, Criminal Justice Act Panel (SDNY), Volunteer Lawyers for the Arts, Women in Need, Constitutional Education Foundation, Puerto Rican Legal Defense and Education Fund.

Special Recognition and Awards:

In the past two years, Willkie or Willkie associates have been awarded The Legal Aid Society's Pro Bono Award, several Commitment to Justice Awards from inMotion and MFY Legal Services' Scales of Justice Award. The firm won an award as "exceptional philanthropist" from two Washington educational organizations.

WOMBLE CARLYLE SANDRIDGE & RICE, PLLC

One West Fourth Street
Winston-Salem, NC 27101
Phone: (336) 721-3600
www.wcsr.com

Areas of pro bono work:

Domestic violence victim advocacy; post-conviction death penalty defense; guardian ad litem appeals; criminal defense, intellectual property, governance and contract advice for nonprofits, international children's rights (asylum, custody); homeless children's education rights; post-disaster legal relief; fair housing and community economic development.

Recent Pro Bono Clients:

Southeast Louisiana Legal Services; Atlanta Legal Aid Society; The Law Project of the Chicago Coalition for the Homeless; Legal Aid Society of Northwest North Carolina; Legal Aid of North Carolina; South Carolina Office of Indigent Defense, Appellate Division; Legal Services of Southern Piedmont; N Street Village; Thurgood Marshall Scholarship Fund and The National Center for Refugee and Immigrant Children.

Special Recognition and Awards:

The Mecklenburg County Bar Association honored Charlotte attorney Elizabeth Coss with the 2006 Legal Services for the Elderly Pro Bono Attorney of the Year Award in recognition of her extraordinary pro bono efforts on behalf of the elderly.

© 2007 Vault Inc.

APPENDIX

Use the Internet's
MOST TARGETED
job search tools.

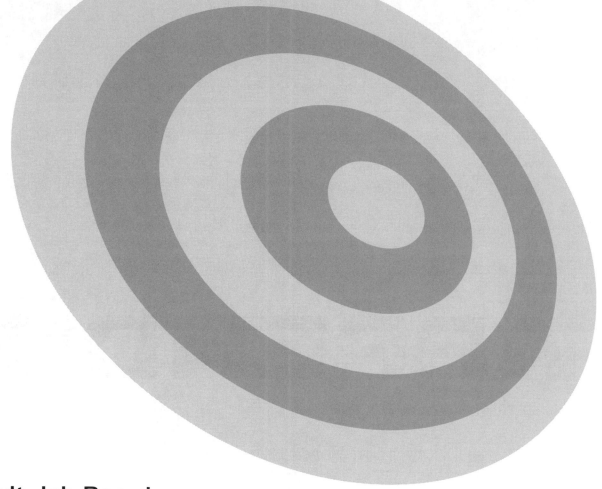

Vault Job Board

Target your search by industry, function, and experience level, and find the job openings that you want.

VaultMatch Resume Database

Vault takes match-making to the next level: post your resume and customize your search by industry, function, experience and more. We'll match job listings with your interests and criteria and e-mail them directly to your in-box.

VAULT

> the most trusted name in career information™

HR Policies

Adams & Reese LLP

1. What is your firm policy on maternity leave? Paternity leave?

Medical Leave for Associates/Special Counsel/Lobbyists - Must be employed two consecutive years before paid leave is granted. One month paid salary if employed 2-3 years, two paid months paid leave if employed 3-4 years, and three months paid leave over 4 consecutive years of employment.:

Parental Leave for Associates/Special Counsel/Lobbyists - After one year of continuous employment, a male or female may take up to 3 months paid parental leave if he or she is the primary caretaker of a child born into the family or adopted.

2. Do you offer any distinctive family-friendly options, such as adoption assistance or child care? Do you offer domestic partner benefits?

We offer dependent day-care reimbursement through our cafeteria plan (125g plan). Associates, Special Counsel and Lobbyists are available to participate. We do not offer domestic partner benefits.

3. What is your firm's vacation policy?

We do not track leave for the attorneys, so they are free to take vacations at their leisure. The firm does expect that they balance that time and still meet their annual billing goals.

4. Do you have a flex-time policy?

We do not have a flex-time policy for attorneys, but they are free to balance their work and personal time as long as they meet their billing goals.

5. Do you offer a sabbatical or leave-of-absence program? How many associates take advantage of this option on an annual basis?

We do offer leave of absences on a case-by-case basis. We may have one or two instances annually.

Akin Gump Strauss Hauer & Feld LLP

1. What is your firm policy on maternity leave? Paternity leave?

Yes, the firm provides attorneys who are absent from work as a result of childbirth twelve weeks of paid leave (8 weeks of disability and four weeks of family leave). Yes, the firm provides 4 weeks of family leave that may be taken following the birth or adoption of the attorney's child.

Visit the Vault Law Channel, the complete online resource for law careers, featuring firm profiles, message boards, the Vault Law Job Board, and more. www.vault.com/law

VAULT CAREER LIBRARY   739

2. Do you offer any distinctive family-friendly options, such as adoption assistance or child care? Do you offer domestic partner benefits?

Yes, the firm has back-up dependent care options, for every age dependent, healthy or sick, 24 hours per day, 7 days per week in every U.S. office location. In addition, our Washington, D.C. office has an on-site emergency childcare center. Yes, the firm has a Domestic Partner Benefits Policy.

3. What is your firm's vacation policy?

Attorneys may take up to twenty days of vacation during the calendar year.

4. Do you have a flex-time policy?

Yes, the firm has a reduced work schedule policy for Associates, Counsel, Senior Counsel and Partners.

5. Do you offer a sabbatical or leave-of-absence program? How many associates take advantage of this option on an annual basis?

N/A

Allen & Overy LLP

1. What is your firm policy on maternity leave? Paternity leave?

MATERNITY LEAVE: After one year of service, all regular employees are allowed up to three months or twelve weeks of paid maternity leave, for pregnancy-related disability and/or child care, following the birth or adoption of a child.

The maximum period of paid leave permitted for the purposes of child care and disability when combined shall not exceed 12 weeks. Paid maternity leave is available only if the employee has been employed by Allen & Overy for one year or more when the maternity leave begins.

In addition to the period of maternity leave described here, the employee may request additional leave without pay, subject to the approval of their department head. During maternity leave (including any approved unpaid leave), the employee shall continue to receive employee benefits previously provided and shall be eligible for salary increases and bonuses. However, if an employee requests an additional unpaid leave at the end of their maternity leave, they must make arrangements to pay their portion of their insurance premium during this portion of the leave (see Unpaid Leave section) and will not have periods of unpaid leave credited towards the relevant year when calculating bonus or vacation/paid time off accruals. Maternity leave runs concurrently with FMLA leave described above.

PATERNITY LEAVE: After one year of service, all regular employees are permitted paid leave for the purposes of paternity at the time of their child's birth or adoption. Paternity leave runs concurrently with FMLA leave. Partner and Support Staff are permitted one week paid leave. Associates and Senior Counsel are permitted four weeks paid leave.

Paternity leave for part-time staff will be pro-rata according to the time worked.

Leave should be taken within the first three months of the birth or adoption of the employee's child and approved in advance by their manager or head of department and forwarded to the HR department. This arrangement allows the father to take time off to look after their child or to make arrangements for the good of the child. Employees can apply to extend paternity leave with a period of unpaid parental leave upon the approval of their manager or supervisor.

© 2007 Vault Inc.

2. Do you offer any distinctive family-friendly options, such as adoption assistance or child care? Do you offer domestic partner benefits?

We do not offer any distinctive family-friendly options, such as adoption assistance or child care. We do offer domestic partner benefits.

3. What is your firm's vacation policy?

Regular full-time associates and counsel are eligible for four weeks vacation per year and sick and personal days as needed. Associates are required to designate personal and sick days as such in their time records and are required to notify the HR department whenever they have missed 3 or more consecutive days of work due to an illness, additionally attorneys are asked to forward copies of all absence request forms (for planned personal and vacation days, whether approved or denied) to the HR department. Employees who work on part-time schedule are eligible for this benefit on a pro-rated basis.

Vacation, personal and sick days for Regular Support Staff Employees are pooled and known as PTO (Paid Time Off). The number of PTO days for which Regular Support Staff Employees are eligible depends on length of employment, as follows:

YEARS OF SERVICE	DAYS
Less than 2	27
2-9	32
10+	35

years of service completed before May 1

4. Do you have a flex-time policy?

Yes

5. Do you offer a sabbatical or leave-of-absence program? How many associates take advantage of this option on an annual basis?

Several of our offices offer sabbatical programs. Associates have taken advantage of different types of leaves regularly.

Alston & Bird LLP

1. What is your firm policy on maternity leave? Paternity leave?

Alston & Bird offers three months paid parental leave to primary care givers and three weeks paid leave to non-primary care givers.

2. Do you offer any distinctive family-friendly options, such as adoption assistance or child care? Do you offer domestic partner benefits?

Alston & Bird's adoption policy gives up to $7000 to cover medical expenses for adoptions.

We have a near-site child care center in Atlanta as well as dedicated back-up space in Charlotte, New York and Washington, D.C. In addition, our employees have priority access to over 400 child care centers nationwide. We also offer back-up in-home child care and in-home elder care for $4/hour. There is a new mother's nursing room in each office.

We offer domestic partner benefits for opposite and same gender domestic partners.

Visit the Vault Law Channel, the complete online resource for law careers, featuring firm profiles, message boards, the Vault Law Job Board, and more. www.vault.com/law

VAULT CAREER LIBRARY   741

3. What is your firm's vacation policy?

Associates may take up to 4 weeks of vacation annually.

4. Do you have a flex-time policy?

Alston & Bird associates may utilize the Alternative Career Path policy which allows them to work reduced hours while still being considered on partnership track.

5. Do you offer a sabbatical or leave-of-absence program? How many associates take advantage of this option on an annual basis?

Partners are eligible to take a sabbatical every ten years.

AGE OF PARTNER	EXTRA VACATION TIME
30 - 40	1 month
40 - 50	2 months
50 - 60	3 months
60 - 70	4 months

Arent Fox LLP

1. What is your firm policy on maternity leave? Paternity leave?

The firm offers 4 weeks paid parental leave for the birth or adoption of a child. Women who give birth have additional 8 weeks of short-term disability leave for a total of 12 weeks paid time off.

2. Do you offer any distinctive family-friendly options, such as adoption assistance or child care? Do you offer domestic partner benefits?

We offer emergency child care and domestic partner benefits.

3. What is your firm's vacation policy?

Our associates are encouraged to take 3 weeks of vacation per year. This does not include sick leave.

4. Do you have a flex-time policy?

No.

5. Do you offer a sabbatical or leave-of-absence program? How many associates take advantage of this option on an annual basis?

No

© 2007 Vault Inc.

Arnold & Porter LLP

1. What is your firm policy on maternity leave? Paternity leave?

An attorney is entitled to six weeks of paid parental leave in connection with (i) the birth of a child, (ii) the adoption of a child, or (iii) the care of a seriously ill child. In addition, women who give birth to a child are entitled to six weeks of paid disability (maternity) leave (for a total of 12 weeks parental/maternity paid leave) and such further time as may be required for medical reasons, in accordance with the Firm's salary continuation plan.

Any attorney may take unpaid leave beyond the period of paid disability and/or parental leave described above, provided that the total period of absence from the Firm (including paid and unpaid leave) does not exceed 24 weeks within any twelve-month period.

2. Do you offer any distinctive family-friendly options, such as adoption assistance or child care? Do you offer domestic partner benefits?

For adoptions, the primary caregiver for a child that is adopted will be entitled to twelve weeks of paid leave (six weeks for the adoption and six of which are parental leave). All attorneys may also take regularly accrued vacation time in conjunction with this leave. The Firm also will pay up to $5000 (net, i.e. after taxes) toward the cost of adopting a child.

Any attorney may take unpaid leave beyond the period of paid disability and/or parental leave described above, provided that the total period of absence from the Firm (including paid and unpaidleave) does not exceed 24 weeks within any twelve-month period.

Health, vision, and dental coverage for spouses, domestic partners, and children is available.

3. What is your firm's vacation policy?

Each associate accrues four weeks of vacation each calendar year (or a pro rata portion if the associate is here less than a full year) and is encouraged to take this leave. Up to ten days of unused vacation leave may be carried over at year-end to the next calendar year.

4. Do you have a flex-time policy?

Arnold & Porter LLP is committed to offering viable part-time schedules for attorneys and we have attorneys who do work part-time.

In reviewing requests for part-time schedules, the Firm will consider the availability of work that can be handled on a part-time schedule, the needs of the Firm's clients, the general performance of the lawyer, the reason for the request, and the total number of associates on part-time schedules.

5. Do you offer a sabbatical or leave-of-absence program? How many associates take advantage of this option on an annual basis?

We do not have a sabbatical program for associates. We do have some associates who take a leave of absence, on occasion, for personal reasons. Such requests are reviewed on a case by case basis.

Visit the Vault Law Channel, the complete online resource for law careers, featuring firm profiles, message boards, the Vault Law Job Board, and more. **www.vault.com/law**

VAULT CAREER LIBRARY   743

Baker Botts LLP

1. What is your firm policy on maternity leave? Paternity leave?

We have a 12 week parental leave option for both men and women and this includes adoptions.

2. Do you offer any distinctive family-friendly options, such as adoption assistance or child care? Do you offer domestic partner benefits?

We do have domestic partner benefits.

3. What is your firm's vacation policy?

3 weeks paid for all offices except NY, they have 4 weeks of vacation

4. Do you have a flex-time policy?

We do have a reduced hours policy available for those associates that would like to take advantage of it.

5. Do you offer a sabbatical or leave-of-absence program? How many associates take advantage of this option on an annual basis?

N/A

Baker & Hostetler LLP

1. What is your firm policy on maternity leave? Paternity leave?

Female attorneys receive 12 weeks paid maternity leave. In the event the physician does not release to return to work the female attorney may be eligible for additional paid time. Male attorneys receive 4 weeks paid parental leave. Both maternity and parental leave run concurrently with FMLA. Paid vacation time may be used to extend the time of the paid leave.

2. Do you offer any distinctive family-friendly options, such as adoption assistance or child care? Do you offer domestic partner benefits?

We offer eligible dependent coverage to same-sex domestic partners under our health, dental and vision programs.

3. What is your firm's vacation policy?

Attorneys are entitled to 20 days of vacation per year to be taken anytime after the first day of credited service with the Firm. Vacation is prorated in the year of hire except for new law school graduates who are not granted vacation until the January 1 following the date of hire. Any vacation not taken during a calendar year is forfeited. Upon separation from the Firm, an attorney is paid for accrued (prorated on a monthly basis) unused vacation.

4. Do you have a flex-time policy?

No, but we do offer Alternative Work Schedules.

© 2007 Vault Inc.

5. Do you offer a sabbatical or leave-of-absence program? How many associates take advantage of this option on an annual basis?

Medical leaves of absence are offered.

Baker & McKenzie

1. What is your firm policy on maternity leave? Paternity leave?

Maternity leave for attorney staff is 12 paid weeks. Paternity leave for attorney staff is 5 paid weeks.

2. Do you offer any distinctive family-friendly options, such as adoption assistance or child care? Do you offer domestic partner benefits?

The Firm offers Adoption assistance and domestic partner benefits. Two offices (D.C. and Chicago) offer back-up (emergency) childcare

3. What is your firm's vacation policy?

An Attorney Staff employee is entitled to take time off at his or her discretion, consistent with the needs of the clients and the Firm, and so long as the employee nonetheless is able to satisfy the Firm's billable and non-billable hour and duties expectations. Attorney Staff do not accrue paid time off.

4. Do you have a flex-time policy?

We do not have a policy, but we do allow flexible schedules.

5. Do you offer a sabbatical or leave-of-absence program? How many associates take advantage of this option on an annual basis?

In addition to the required FMLA leave, Baker & McKenzie also has a policy around parental leave and general leaves. The General Leave of Absence (GLA), is unpaid and can be taken for up to four weeks. Most attorneys do not take advantage of the GLA policy; however, in 2006 we had ten associates use parental leave and fourteen use FMLA (Maternity leave).

Ballard Spahr Andrews & Ingersoll, LLP

1. What is your firm policy on maternity leave? Paternity leave?

The Firm provides to non-partner lawyers giving birth twelve weeks paid leave, consisting of eight weeks paid disability for purposes of maternity and four weeks paid Child Care Leave.The four weeks of fully-paid Child Care Leave is also available to non-partner lawyers for the birth of a newborn or placement of an adopted child. Additionally, eligible attorneys may take up to twelve weeks of unpaid leave under the Family Medical Leave Policy.

2. Do you offer any distinctive family-friendly options, such as adoption assistance or child care? Do you offer domestic partner benefits?

The Firm provides a fully-paid Child Care Leave of up to four weeks to non-partner lawyers for the birth of a newborn or placement of an adopted child.We also offer domestic partner health benefits.

Visit the Vault Law Channel, the complete online resource for law careers, featuring firm profiles, message boards, the Vault Law Job Board, and more. www.vault.com/law

VAULT CAREER LIBRARY   745

3. What is your firm's vacation policy?

The Firm offersfour weeks of annualized paid vacation time to its non-partner lawyers.

4. Do you have a flex-time policy?

The Firm addresses requests for part-time work schedules on a case-by-case basis.

5. Do you offer a sabbatical or leave-of-absence program? How many associates take advantage of this option on an annual basis?

The Firm does not offer a formal sabbatical or leave-of-absence program but is open to address such requests on a case-by-case basis.

We currently have two attorneys on non-medically related leaves-of-absence.

Barnes & Thornburg LLP

1. What is your firm policy on maternity leave? Paternity leave?

Up to 90 days paid leave of absence is allowed for female attorneys on the birth of a child and for any attorney primarily responsible for the care of an adopted child. In addition, attorneys may request a family leave without pay of not more than 12 weeks, in the event of the serious illness of a child, spouse, or parent.

2. Do you offer any distinctive family-friendly options, such as adoption assistance or child care? Do you offer domestic partner benefits?

We offer domestic partner benefits.

3. What is your firm's vacation policy?

Attorneys may take time off for vacation, with no loss of pay, consistent with the demands of their practice and the firm's billable hour goals.

4. Do you have a flex-time policy?

N/A

5. Do you offer a sabbatical or leave-of-absence program? How many associates take advantage of this option on an annual basis?

N/A

Bingham McCutchen LLP

1. What is your firm policy on maternity leave? Paternity leave?

We are very proud of what we feel is a market-leading Parental Leave policy. Birth parents, non-birth parents and adoptive parents (including same-sex domestic partners) are all eligible for Parental Leave. Our policy provides paid disability leave and

© 2007 Vault Inc.

8 weeks of paid child care leave to the birth mother (for a total of usually 14 weeks paid leave, more if disability is certified for a period longer than 6 weeks). Non-birth parents (including fathers, same-sex domestic partners and adoptive parents) are entitled to the 8 weeks paid child care leave. Leave is paid at 100% of salary. In addition, attorneys may add accrued unused vacation to extend their paid leave. Attorneys may also request up to 6 months of unpaid parental leave following the paid 8-week child care leave portion. Leave may be taken at any point in the first year after birth or adoption and must be taken in at least two-week increments.

2. Do you offer any distinctive family-friendly options, such as adoption assistance or child care? Do you offer domestic partner benefits?

We offer domestic partner benefits for both same sex and opposite sex domestic partners. In Massachusetts, where same sex couples may wed, we continue to offer domestic partner benefits. We have emergency child care available on site for most of our office locations. We have a market-leading part-time policy that we feel is a distinctive family-friendly option. More than 60 attorneys work part-time and we elected 5 partners in the past two years alone while they were on a part-time schedule.

3. What is your firm's vacation policy?

Associates accrue vacation monthly and are allowed to carry over 3 weeks of vacation time per year. Associates may take vacation as needed and merely need to coordinate the timing of vacation with the partners for whom they work. Associates may also borrow up to 1 week of vacation time against future accruals.

4. Do you have a flex-time policy?

We do not have a formal flex time policy but will consider such requests on a case-by-case basis.

5. Do you offer a sabbatical or leave-of-absence program? How many associates take advantage of this option on an annual basis?

We do not have a sabbatical policy but will consider such requests on a case-by-case basis. We do have leave programs for: FMLA (including, but not limited to, Parental Leave); bar exam study leave (3 weeks paid); military service; and jury duty. Attorneys may also request unpaid personal leaves, which are considered on a case-by-case basis. One example of such personal leave in the past is for work on a political campaign. Approximately 3-5 associates take advantage of personal leaves of a variety of durations per year.

Bryan Cave LLP

1. What is your firm policy on maternity leave? Paternity leave?

Bryan Cave has a 3-month paid maternity leave. Lawyers may take up to six weeks of paid paternity leave.

2. Do you offer any distinctive family-friendly options, such as adoption assistance or child care? Do you offer domestic partner benefits?

Bryan Cave offers six weeks of paid leave of absence in connection with adoption. The firm offers a flexible spending tax incentive plan regarding child care expenses and also offers emergency child care arrangements in some offices. We also have a "mothers room" in our offices and our Phoenix office has a maternity clothes co-op. We also have a women's affinity group. We offer domestic partner benefits.

Visit the Vault Law Channel, the complete online resource for law careers, featuring firm profiles, message boards, the Vault Law Job Board, and more. **www.vault.com/law**

VAULT CAREER LIBRARY   747

3. What is your firm's vacation policy?

Associates receive a minimum of three-four weeks paid vacation per calendar year.

4. Do you have a flex-time policy?

Yes and we also have a reduced schedule policy allowing lawyers to work a part time schedule and remain on the partnership track.

5. Do you offer a sabbatical or leave-of-absence program? How many associates take advantage of this option on an annual basis?

No, we do not have a formal sabbatical program. We consider leaves of absence on a case-by-case basis.

Cadwalader, Wickersham & Taft LLP

1. What is your firm policy on maternity leave? Paternity leave?

Parental Leave for Primary Care Givers

Associates and counsel are entitled to up to twelve weeks of paid parental leave, at full pay, by reason of the birth or adoption of a child, provided that the employee:

• is the full time primary care parent during the period of the leave; and

• has been employed by the Firm for one year or more when the employee begins any leave related to this birth or adoption.

The employee may extend this paid leave through the use of accrued but unused vacation days. Employees who took a twelve-week paid parental leave may take an unpaid personal leave following the completion of the parental leave, for up to an additional twelve weeks. Following this, further unpaid leave may be available under a federal, state or local leave law applicable to the employee, in which case, additional unpaid leave will be provided pursuant to those statutes.

Parental Leave for Secondary Care Givers

All associates and counsel who are the biological parent of a newborn or are a new adoptive parent, but who are not the full-time primary care parent, and who have been employed by the Firm for one year or more, will be entitled to a leave of absence at full salary and benefits for up to two weeks. This leave is generally to be taken immediately after the birth or adoption of the child, but may start up to one week prior to the birth or adoption. Paid vacation days may be used to extend this leave.

2. Do you offer any distinctive family-friendly options, such as adoption assistance or child care? Do you offer domestic partner benefits?

Cadwalader provides employees with access to back-up centers designed to provide child care to employees whose regular form of care is unavailable. The Firm offers benefits to same sex domestic partners.

3. What is your firm's vacation policy?

Full-time associates accrue 20 business days of vacation each calendar year. In cases where an associate cannot use all of his/her vacation days, s/he may get permission to (a) carry to the next calendar year a maximum of ten vacation days, or (b) be paid for up to five vacation days and carry over up to five remaining vacation days.

© 2007 Vault Inc.

4. Do you have a flex-time policy?

Yes. We are committed to supporting and retaining talented attorneys who have responsibilities and obligations that affect their ability to work full-time. While it is expected that most attorneys will be available on a full-time basis, in certain situations, alternative work schedules ("alternative arrangements") are available to our attorneys. Alternative arrangements are individually tailored part-time, reduced, or flexible hours arrangements designed to meet the needs of the attorney as well as the needs of the Firm and the Firm's clients.

5. Do you offer a sabbatical or leave-of-absence program? How many associates take advantage of this option on an annual basis?

Yes, the firm offers a sabbatical program that entitles full-time associates to a four-week paid leave period following five full years of service with the Firm. 16 associates took advantage of the program in 2006 and 10 in 2005.

Cahill Gordon & Reindel LLP

1. What is your firm policy on maternity leave? Paternity leave?

Our maternity leave is 12-weeks or up to 26 weeks maternity-related disability. 4 weeks paternity. Women can also return to the firm at a reduced work-load for up to 12 weeks (at a reduced salary) to ensure a smooth transition back to the firm.

2. Do you offer any distinctive family-friendly options, such as adoption assistance or child care? Do you offer domestic partner benefits?

Domestic partners are afforded all of the firm benefits that married couples are offered. Maternity and paternity leave applies to adoption. We also offer emergency child care located near the office.

3. What is your firm's vacation policy?

Attorneys are given 4 weeks vacation.

4. Do you have a flex-time policy?

We do offer flex time/alternate work schedule options

5. Do you offer a sabbatical or leave-of-absence program? How many associates take advantage of this option on an annual basis?

Leave of absence is dealt with on a case-by-case basis.

Cleary, Gottlieb, Steen & Hamilton LLP

1. What is your firm policy on maternity leave? Paternity leave?

Maternity leave - 13 weeks paid leave from date of birth/adoption. Paternity leave - 4 weeks paid leave within six months of birth/adoption.

Visit the Vault Law Channel, the complete online resource for law careers, featuring firm profiles, message boards, the Vault Law Job Board, and more. www.vault.com/law

VAULT CAREER LIBRARY   749

2. Do you offer any distinctive family-friendly options, such as adoption assistance or child care? Do you offer domestic partner benefits?

We offer "Emergency Child Care" services through Bright Horizons. We offer domestic partner benefits to same-sex couples.

3. What is your firm's vacation policy?

Four weeks (20 work days) per year, 25 days per year after four years of employment with the firm.

4. Do you have a flex-time policy?

Yes - we offer reduced schedule options on a case-by-case basis.

5. Do you offer a sabbatical or leave-of-absence program? How many associates take advantage of this option on an annual basis?

All decisions regarding leaves are made on a case-by-case basis by the firm's Associates Committee.

Clifford Chance LLP

1. What is your firm policy on maternity leave? Paternity leave?

The Firm allows associates to take a minimum of 8 weeks of paid disability leave for maternity, along with 4 weeks of paid parental leave. Male associates are entitled to 4 weeks of paid parental leave.

2. Do you offer any distinctive family-friendly options, such as adoption assistance or child care? Do you offer domestic partner benefits?

Clifford Chance provides for 4 weeks of paid parental leave for employees who adopt. In addition, the Firm adheres to the FMLA law, which allows for up to 12 weeks of leave for individuals who adopt. Clifford Chance also offers domestic partner benefits (same sex and opposite sex) and has a backup child care facility.

3. What is your firm's vacation policy?

Associates are eligible annually for 20 business days of vacation earned on an accrual basis based on date of hire. The Firm applies its associate vacation policy flexibly, taking into consideration factors such as work schedule.

4. Do you have a flex-time policy?

Yes.

5. Do you offer a sabbatical or leave-of-absence program? How many associates take advantage of this option on an annual basis?

Yes. Varies from year-to-year.

© 2007 Vault Inc.

Covington & Burling LLP

1. What is your firm policy on maternity leave? Paternity leave?

Parental leave is available to lawyers who intend to continue their employment with the firm after the conclusion of the leave period. Covington provides 90 calendar days of paid maternity leave to lawyers, and the firm also provides 90 days of leave to lawyers who are the primary caregiver of newly-adopted children. The firm recognizes the important responsibilities of the non-primary caregiver of newborn and adopted children and therefore extends 20 business days of paid leave to non-primary caregivers.

2. Do you offer any distinctive family-friendly options, such as adoption assistance or child care? Do you offer domestic partner benefits?

The firm operates a center for full-time childcare, CovingtonKids, one block from the Washington, DC office. For parents seeking less than full-time care, we have a relationship with childcare facilities located near our offices in Washington, DC, New York and San Francisco. The firm also offers an emergency back-up care program that provides in-home or center-based back-up care for children or adults in the three US cities. The firm provides domestic partner benefits, and also has a flexible spending account program to assist lawyers and others in paying for the costs of dependent care.

3. What is your firm's vacation policy?

Attorneys are encouraged to take four weeks of vacation each calendar year.

4. Do you have a flex-time policy?

The firm recognizes that some lawyers may need to work a reduced schedule because of family responsibilities or other outside obligations. Covington offers alternative work schedules so that lawyers can satisfy these personal objectives while continuing to enjoy opportunities for professional growth and career advancement. It is the firm's policy to accommodate all reasonable requests by lawyers who wish to work reduced schedules in order to care for a family member. The firm is also receptive to requests for reduced schedules for other purposes, such as teaching, community service, special projects and the like, although the firm's staffing needs will be considered in responding to such requests. Flexible scheduling arrangements not involving a reduced schedule are considered on a case-by-case basis.

5. Do you offer a sabbatical or leave-of-absence program? How many associates take advantage of this option on an annual basis?

The firm does not have a paid sabbatical program or leave-of-absence program. However, the firm recognizes that lawyers have important needs and interests outside the scope of the firm's practice, and that it is sometimes necessary or desirable for an attorney to withdraw temporarily from the firm in order to satisfy those needs or interests. It is the firm's policy to accommodate requests for leave to facilitate care of a family member. The firm will also consider requests for unpaid leaves of absence for other personal reasons, such as participation in political campaigns, under appropriate circumstances. In the last year, an associate took a leave of absence to write a book and another to work on a political campaign.

Visit the Vault Law Channel, the complete online resource for law careers, featuring firm profiles, message boards, the Vault Law Job Board, and more. www.vault.com/law

VAULT CAREER LIBRARY   751

Cravath, Swaine & Moore LLP

1. What is your firm policy on maternity leave? Paternity leave?

The Firm's maternity leave policy for associates provides for a paid leave during the period that the associate is medically disabled, both before and after the birth of a child. This is presumed not to be less than 12 weeks, and can be substantially longer if complications arise. When combined with the four-week paid child-care leave, this results in a minimum aggregate paid leave of 16 weeks for a woman upon the birth of a child.

All associates (female or male) are entitled to take up to four weeks of paid child-care leave (not charged against vacation) following the birth of a child or adoption of an infant. This leave is normally to be taken immediately following maternity leave, where applicable, or otherwise during the first three months following birth or adoption.

2. Do you offer any distinctive family-friendly options, such as adoption assistance or child care? Do you offer domestic partner benefits?

We offer on-site, back-up child care for all employees. The child care center is staffed with Cravath employees, and open during the week, as well as weekends. The center offers an extended care program that allows employees, for a nominal fee, to bring their infant/child to the center everyday for up to six months. We also offer health benefits to same sex domestic partners.

3. What is your firm's vacation policy?

All associates are entitled to 20 days of paid vacation as well as unlimited personal and sick time; Senior Attorneys are entitled to 25 days of paid vacation.

4. Do you have a flex-time policy?

Cravath seeks to support associates who have a need and desire for part-time work arrangements. We attempt to make part-time work arrangements available to allow associates to fulfill family responsibilities and in other circumstances on a case-by-case basis.

5. Do you offer a sabbatical or leave-of-absence program? How many associates take advantage of this option on an annual basis?

Unpaid leaves of absence for personal matters are available to all associates. Approximately 3-5 associates take advantage of this option annually.

Crowell & Moring LLP

1. What is your firm policy on maternity leave? Paternity leave?

10 weeks of paid maternity leave is provided to female associates. 2 weeks of paid parental leave is provided to male associates.

2. Do you offer any distinctive family-friendly options, such as adoption assistance or child care? Do you offer domestic partner benefits?

The Firm has a state-of-the-art child care and education center, back-up and emergency child care through White House Nannies and Bright Horizon's, offers domestic partner benefits as well as an EAP and Guidance Resource program.

© 2007 Vault Inc.

3. What is your firm's vacation policy?

The Firm provides 4 weeks paid vacation to its associates.

4. Do you have a flex-time policy?

There is no formal flex-time policy in place.

5. Do you offer a sabbatical or leave-of-absence program? How many associates take advantage of this option on an annual basis?

The Firm does not offer a sabbatical or formal leave-of absence program.

Davis Polk & Wardwell

1. What is your firm policy on maternity leave? Paternity leave?

Lawyer mothers are paid in full for 12 weeks of maternity leave. Lawyer fathers are paid in full for 4 weeks of paternity leave.

2. Do you offer any distinctive family-friendly options, such as adoption assistance or child care? Do you offer domestic partner benefits?

Davis Polk offers its lawyers, staff and managers access to firm-purchased slots in childcare centers. Men/women lawyers who are primary caregivers are offered up to 12 weeks of paid adoption leave. Men/women lawyers who are secondary caregivers are offered up to 4 weeks of paid adoption leave. Domestic partner benefits apply to lawyers, managers and staff.

3. What is your firm's vacation policy?

The maximum allowable vacation days in the past year for associates was 20 days for the first 5 years at the firm and 25 days after the associate completes 5 years at the firm. The maximum allowable vacation days in the past year for counsel was 25 days for the first 5 years as counsel and 30 days after the counsel completes 5 years as counsel. The maximum allowable vacation days in the past year for partners was 30 days.

4. Do you have a flex-time policy?

Davis Polk offers flex-time to lawyers, managers and staff.

5. Do you offer a sabbatical or leave-of-absence program? How many associates take advantage of this option on an annual basis?

Although Davis Polk does not have a formal sabbatical program, it has permitted associates to take unpaid leaves for reasons outside of parental or medical leave. These leaves are granted on a case-by-case basis and typically last for several months. Last year, at least two associates took non-parental, non-medical related leave.

Visit the Vault Law Channel, the complete online resource for law careers, featuring firm profiles, message boards, the Vault Law Job Board, and more. www.vault.com/law

VAULT CAREER LIBRARY   753

Debevoise & Plimpton LLP

1. What is your firm policy on maternity leave? Paternity leave?

Debevoise provides women lawyers with paid leave relating to pregnancy and childbirth. The total combined period of post-delivery disability and parental leave is presumptively 12 weeks, but the period of leave may be extended if the actual duration of the disability is longer.

All counsel or associates who become parents or co-parents (by birth or adoption) are entitled to four weeks of paid parental leave.

2. Do you offer any distinctive family-friendly options, such as adoption assistance or child care? Do you offer domestic partner benefits?

Debevoise offers benefits to lawyers' same sex domestic partners, wherever benefits are extended to lawyers' spouses.

Debevoise offers a dependent care benefit selection plan where lawyers may direct a portion of their pre-tax income into a special account from which they can be reimbursed for qualified dependent care expenses.

Debevoise provides short-term emergency care for children through Caregivers On Call, Inc., when a lawyer's child is mildly ill, when usual care arrangements fall through, or when work schedules change unexpectedly. The firm has also partnered with Bright Horizons, a childcare organization with centers located near the firm's New York City and Washington, D.C. offices, to provide back-up childcare for children from three months to 13 years old.

3. What is your firm's vacation policy?

Debevoise provides associates with four weeks of vacation a year.

4. Do you have a flex-time policy?

In 2007, Debevoise & Plimpton LLP will celebrate the 40th anniversary of its first part-time work arrangement. Consistently from that time forward Debevoise has devised progressive programs that support lawyers in balancing careers with families. Debevoise confirmed its progressive practice in 1987 with a written part-time work policy, including an explicit statement that part-time lawyers were eligible for partnership. Debevoise has promoted five part-time associates, and three associates who were part-time earlier in their careers. The number of lawyers who participate in the program is additional evidence of Debevoise's receptive attitude towards part-time work. Currently 44 counsel and associates are part-time, representing nearly 10% of the associates and counsel at the firm.

5. Do you offer a sabbatical or leave-of-absence program? How many associates take advantage of this option on an annual basis?

Debevoise does not offer a sabbatical program. Associates may request to take a leave of absence. Requests are reviewed and approved on an ad hoc basis. Associates are also eligible to take leave under the Family and Medical Leave Act.

Dickstein Shapiro LLP

1. What is your firm policy on maternity leave? Paternity leave?

A non-child bearing parent -- father, or a parent who adopts -- is entitled to a parental leave for a period of up to four weeks, and an additional eight weeks of unpaid leave for a total of 12 weeks of job protected leave under the Family Medical Leave

VAULT CAREER LIBRARY

© 2007 Vault Inc.

Act ("FMLA") Parental leave must be taken within twelve months of the birth or adoption of a child. A child-bearing mother is entitled to eight weeks of a presumptive maternity leave and to an additional four weeks leave with pay pursuant to the Firm's parental leave benefits, for a total of twelve weeks.

2. Do you offer any distinctive family-friendly options, such as adoption assistance or child care? Do you offer domestic partner benefits?

We provide both emergency back up nanny care for child care in the home, and emergency back up child care at a child care center. We offer domestic partner benefits in all categories -- health insurance, dental insurance, vision insurance, supplemental life insurance.

3. What is your firm's vacation policy?

Vacation, sick, and personal leave for all attorneys is discretionary and is taken according to the workload within the department or section.

4. Do you have a flex-time policy?

We have a long standing, extensive Alternative Work Arrangement policy. The Firm is committed to a strong policy of providing flexibility in its work arrangements, and recognizes that such a policy has allowed it to attract and retain top-quality attorneys who are committed to their professional, the Firm and its clients.

5. Do you offer a sabbatical or leave-of-absence program? How many associates take advantage of this option on an annual basis?

We offer an unpaid leave of absence for a maximum of 4 months.

DLA Piper

1. What is your firm policy on maternity leave? Paternity leave?

Maternity leave is 12 weeks of full pay and benefits.

Paternity Leave: Any qualifying lawyer, male or female, shall be entitled to take a leave of absence of up to 90 calendar days with full pay and benefits in connection with the birth or adoption of a child. (This 90-day calendar period runs concurrently with any period of short-term disability after the birth of the child. Short-term, pregnancy-related disability prior to the birth of the child will not be considered parental leave.)

In order to qualify for 90 calendar days of paid parental leave, a lawyer must: 1) have been employed by the Firm for at least one year immediately prior to taking such leave, 2) begin such leave within ten days following the birth or adoption of the child and 3) serve as the primary caregiver for the child. If a lawyer meets the first two conditions set forth in this paragraph, but not the third, he or she shall be entitled to 90 calendar days leave, of which the first 30 calendar days shall be paid leave. An associate who otherwise qualifies for paid parental leave except that he or she has been with the Firm for more than nine months but less than one year shall be entitled to be paid for that portion of the 90 calendar days (or 30 calendar days, where applicable) occurring after the first anniversary of his or her employment. Any leave beyond the terms described in this policy must be approved in advance by the Practice Group Leader and shall be unpaid.

While on paid parental leave, all benefits will remain in effect; to continue benefits during an unpaid leave of absence, a lawyer may make direct payment arrangements with the Benefits Department.

Visit the Vault Law Channel, the complete online resource for law careers, featuring firm profiles, message boards, the Vault Law Job Board, and more. **www.vault.com/law**

VAULT CAREER LIBRARY   **755**

2. Do you offer any distinctive family-friendly options, such as adoption assistance or child care? Do you offer domestic partner benefits?

Back-up child care is offered in most locations. The firm offers domestic partner benefits for medical and dental.

3. What is your firm's vacation policy?

The firm does not have a formal lawyer vacation policy. Vacation is discretionary.

4. Do you have a flex-time policy?

Alternative schedule not resulting in reduced hours. As professionals, all DLA Piper lawyers are expected to work at such times and locations, and for the duration of time necessary to provide timely and expert legal services to the firm's clients. We understand that occasionally personal needs (e.g., child care, medical appointments, family responsibilities, etc.) may arise which require a lawyer to amend his/her work schedule to attend to these issues. As long as we can continue to service our clients, we will work with any lawyer requesting such an adjustment to support a schedule that helps him/her better meet these responsibilities. However, unless otherwise specifically agreed by the Firm in writing, such an arrangement does not relieve the subject lawyer from the obligation to achieve his/her billable hours and other productivity goals. Please work with your partner to schedule your time accordingly.

5. Do you offer a sabbatical or leave-of-absence program? How many associates take advantage of this option on an annual basis?

No.

Dorsey & Whitney LLP

1. What is your firm policy on maternity leave? Paternity leave?

New mothers generally receive 6 weeks of paid leave under the firm's short-term disability policy (for a medically uncomplicated delivery) as well as an additional 6 weeks paid leave under the firm's Parental Leave Policy for Attorneys. Under the Parental Leave Policy, up to 6 months of leave is allowed for the birth or adoption of a child (for men or women), and this leave time does not affect a partner's compensation or an associate's salary increases or progression towards partnership.

2. Do you offer any distinctive family-friendly options, such as adoption assistance or child care? Do you offer domestic partner benefits?

Dorsey has an adoption assistance plan, whereby employees are reimbursed for qualified expenses incurred in the adoption of a child. Domestic partner benefits are offered to same-sex domestic partners. In addition, the firm provides 20 days of back-up child care per year per child in several offices (Minneapolis, New York, Palo Alto, Southern California and Washington, DC). Dorsey also has a comprehensive Flexible Working Arrangements policy for attorneys, under which three FWA options are available: a reduced hours hours, telecommuting, or a compressed workweek.

3. What is your firm's vacation policy?

It is recommended that attorneys take 2-4 weeks of vacation per year.

4. Do you have a flex-time policy?

Yes. See above re: family-friendly options.

© 2007 Vault Inc.

5. Do you offer a sabbatical or leave-of-absence program? How many associates take advantage of this option on an annual basis?

Dorsey has a sabbatical program that is available to partners only.

Drinker Biddle & Reath LLP

1. What is your firm policy on maternity leave? Paternity leave?

Lawyers are entitled to up to twelve weeks' leave during a twelve-month period, with pay at full salary, in connection with the birth or adoption of a child or the placement of a child for foster care with that lawyer. They are entitled to an additional 12 week period of unpaid leave, subject to extension upon approval.

2. Do you offer any distinctive family-friendly options, such as adoption assistance or child care? Do you offer domestic partner benefits?

The same leave options available to lawyers who are biological parents or adoptive parents. Lawyers are able to work part-time schedules. Back-up child care is available through our offices. Adoption support is one of the many services support by the firm's Employee Assistance Program. We offer medical, dental, vision and optional life insurance benefits for domestic partners.

3. What is your firm's vacation policy?

Four weeks annually

4. Do you have a flex-time policy?

Not formally. Special work arrangements are handled on a case by case basis

5. Do you offer a sabbatical or leave-of-absence program? How many associates take advantage of this option on an annual basis?

There is no formal sabbatical program. We have a leave-of-absence program, for medical, military or personal reasons. There are currently 7 lawyers on leave status.

Duane Morris LLP

1. What is your firm policy on maternity leave? Paternity leave?

Maternity leave is handled as a disability, with leave being authorized for the length of the disability (which must be supported by medical certification). Maternity leave is normally paid leave for the first eleven weeks of the disability. After the first eleven weeks or the period of disability, if longer, an associate may take one week of paid maternity leave, may use vacation time, and finally, may take unpaid leave or work part-time subject to the discretion and approval of the firm. For adoptions, the primary caregiver for a child that is adopted will be entitled to twelve weeks of paid leave. All male associates are eligible for one week of paid paternity leave in connection with the birth or adoption of a child. The one week of paid paternity/maternity leave does not have to be taken in consecutive work days, but the leave must be used within four months of the birth or adoption of a child and must be taken as full days.

Visit the Vault Law Channel, the complete online resource for law careers, featuring firm profiles, message boards, the Vault Law Job Board, and more. **www.vault.com/law**

VAULT CAREER LIBRARY   757

2. Do you offer any distinctive family-friendly options, such as adoption assistance or child care? Do you offer domestic partner benefits?

Yes. We have an Employee Assitance Program in place for all attorneys and provide domestic partner benefits.

3. What is your firm's vacation policy?

4 weeks paid

4. Do you have a flex-time policy?

Yes - on a case-by-case basis and at the discretion of the practice group head

5. Do you offer a sabbatical or leave-of-absence program? How many associates take advantage of this option on an annual basis?

We do not have a set program in place. Leaves of absence requests are examined on a case-by-case basis. We do not track this information.

Dykema Gossett PLLC

1. What is your firm policy on maternity leave? Paternity leave?

We offer both. Our maternity leave policy is 12 weeks fully paid. Paternity is up to 6 weeks fully paid.

2. Do you offer any distinctive family-friendly options, such as adoption assistance or child care? Do you offer domestic partner benefits?

Our adoption policy is for up to 6 weeks paid and another 6 weeks unpaid. Child care costs can be addressed via dependent care reimbursement accounts. They may set aside up to $5,000 per year on a pre-tax basis for eligible dependent care expenses. We do offer domestic partner benefits.

3. What is your firm's vacation policy?

Associates are entitled to one week if they join us before June 1st. The following January 1 they are eligible for 3 weeks. After 5 years with the firm they are eligible for 4 weeks.

4. Do you have a flex-time policy?

Yes.

5. Do you offer a sabbatical or leave-of-absence program? How many associates take advantage of this option on an annual basis?

No.

© 2007 Vault Inc.

Faegre & Benson LLP

1. What is your firm policy on maternity leave? Paternity leave?

Faegre & Benson pays associates who have been at the Firm at least one year (male for female), six weeks of paid time after the birth or adoption of a baby.

2. Do you offer any distinctive family-friendly options, such as adoption assistance or child care? Do you offer domestic partner benefits?

We offer emergency back up child care in the building. We offer benefits for same sex domestic partners.

3. What is your firm's vacation policy?

Associates receive two weeks of paid vacation in their first year at the firm and three weeks each year thereafter.

4. Do you have a flex-time policy?

Case by case.

5. Do you offer a sabbatical or leave-of-absence program? How many associates take advantage of this option on an annual basis?

We offer a sabbatical program for Partners only.

Finnegan, Henderson, Farabow, Garrett & Dunner, LLP

1. What is your firm policy on maternity leave? Paternity leave?

Female attorney -- maternity leave would be eligible for 6-8 weeks of 100% paid medical leave and then 6 weeks of 100% paid family leave. Male attorney -- paternity leave would be eligible for 6 weeks of 100% paid family leave.

2. Do you offer any distinctive family-friendly options, such as adoption assistance or child care? Do you offer domestic partner benefits?

Yes, we offer domestic partner benefits and we have on-site child care.

3. What is your firm's vacation policy?

No limit. attorneys may take as much time as they like consistent with their billing requirements.

4. Do you have a flex-time policy?

Attorneys may work from home and have no set hours, if that's what you mean. not quite sure on this one. but their schedules are VERY flexible. the firm also has an alternative work schedule policy (reduced hours options). additionally, we have lawyers who telework and telecommute.

Visit the Vault Law Channel, the complete online resource for law careers, featuring firm profiles, message boards, the Vault Law Job Board, and more. www.vault.com/law

VAULT CAREER LIBRARY   759

5. Do you offer a sabbatical or leave-of-absence program? How many associates take advantage of this option on an annual basis?

Yes, we have a leave-of-absence program not to exceed 1 year. The request would need to be approved by his/her practice group leader. i'm sorry, i do not have any data on the #s of associates who took advantage of it last year.

Fish & Richardson PC

1. What is your firm policy on maternity leave? Paternity leave?

Our parental leave policy allows for four weeks of paid time off for legal staff who have been employed by the firm for more than three months. Our maternity leave policy allows for eight weeks of paid time off for legal staff who have been employed by the firm for more than three months, and can be combined with our parental leave policy for a total of 16 weeks of paid time off.

2. Do you offer any distinctive family-friendly options, such as adoption assistance or child care? Do you offer domestic partner benefits?

Our maternity and parental leave policies also apply to individuals who adopt a child. We offer a firm sponsored backup childcare center, subject to an employee co-pay, available for up to 20 days a year. We offer domestic partner benefits for same-sex and opposite-sex partners.

3. What is your firm's vacation policy?

The Firm has not established a formal "vacation leave" policy for legal staff employees. Rather, the Firm has articulated certain billable goal requirements, which should, nonetheless, permit individuals to take sufficient time for vacations and other personal time off, consistent with the legal staff employee's client responsibilities.

4. Do you have a flex-time policy?

Attorneys at every level are eligible to work flex-time, as appropriate.

5. Do you offer a sabbatical or leave-of-absence program? How many associates take advantage of this option on an annual basis?

Personal leave of absences are considered on a case by case basis.

Fitzpatrick, Cella, Harper & Scinto

1. What is your firm policy on maternity leave? Paternity leave?

The firm offers 12 weeks paid maternity leave, and we liberally allow associates to take additional unpaid time with health benefits. The firm does not have a paternity leave policy.

2. Do you offer any distinctive family-friendly options, such as adoption assistance or child care? Do you offer domestic partner benefits?

The firm offers health benefits to domestic partners, but does not yet offer child care options.

© 2007 Vault Inc.

3. What is your firm's vacation policy?

Attorneys receive four weeks vacation per year. If an attorney is unable to schedule vacation time, they may carry over five days of vacation, resulting in a maximum of 25 vacation days per year.

4. Do you have a flex-time policy?

We liberally allow our attorneys to adjust their hours.

5. Do you offer a sabbatical or leave-of-absence program? How many associates take advantage of this option on an annual basis?

We allow our lawyers to take a leave-of-absence. On average, we have less than five attorneys per year that take advantage of this option.

Foley & Lardner LLP

1. What is your firm policy on maternity leave? Paternity leave?

Foley & Lardner offers parental leave, which includes 4 weeks of paid leave for new parents who have completed one full year of service with the firm at the time of the leave; 8 weeks additional paid leave for biological mothers because of short-term disability; and an additional 12 weeks of unpaid leave for new parents (additional unpaid leave is granted on a case-by-case basis with approval by the firm's managing partner).

2. Do you offer any distinctive family-friendly options, such as adoption assistance or child care? Do you offer domestic partner benefits?

Foley reimburses qualified adoption expenses, as defined by the firm's policy, up to $5,000 for a new adoptive parent who has completed one full year of service with the firm at the time of the adoption. Foley offers Backup Care Options to support attorneys and staff who experience a temporary breakdown in their normal care arrangements - infants through elderly - and need to get to work. Through this benefit, firm members have access to experienced Backup Care Specialists 24 hours a day, 7 days a week. Foley also offers an Employee Assistance Program to support attorneys and staff who are in need of confidential, professional assistance. Foley offers same-sex domestic partner benefits.

3. What is your firm's vacation policy?

Less than 8 years of service = 3 weeks of vacation/year; 8 years or more of service = 4 weeks of vacation/year; maximum accrual is one year of vacation.

4. Do you have a flex-time policy?

Yes. Flexible schedules are available for associates, senior counsel and partners who are in good standing, upon approval of an acceptable proposal. Flexible schedules are to be tailored to meet the individual needs of attorneys and their practices.

5. Do you offer a sabbatical or leave-of-absence program? How many associates take advantage of this option on an annual basis?

Such arrangements are made on a case-by-case basis with approval from the firm's managing partner.

Visit the Vault Law Channel, the complete online resource for law careers, featuring firm profiles, message boards, the Vault Law Job Board, and more. www.vault.com/law

VAULT CAREER LIBRARY   761

Freshfields Bruckhaus Deringer

1. What is your firm policy on maternity leave? Paternity leave?

The period of maternity/special childcare leave for US based legal staff is up to 24 weeks. Special childcare leave refers to legal staff that takes on the primary and core care responsibility for a baby following the birth or adoption of a child. Full salary will be paid for a period of 12 weeks. In addition, if you have been an employee of Freshfields Bruckhaus Deringer for at least 15 months on the date your maternity/special child care leave commences, you will be entitled to half salary until the date of return up to a maximum of a further 12 weeks. If special childcare leave is not to be taken, we grant five days paternity leave around the time of birth of a child.

2. Do you offer any distinctive family-friendly options, such as adoption assistance or child care? Do you offer domestic partner benefits?

See above for leave following adoption . The firm pays 100% of benefits for domestic partners.

3. What is your firm's vacation policy?

26 days per year; may rollover up to 5 days and use by end of the first quarter of the following year.

4. Do you have a flex-time policy?

Informal; case by case

5. Do you offer a sabbatical or leave-of-absence program? How many associates take advantage of this option on an annual basis?

Informal; case by case

Fried, Frank, Harris, Shriver & Jacobson LLP

1. What is your firm policy on maternity leave? Paternity leave?

Various policy provisions are applicable for maternity leave and when combined, there is a total leave available of up to 6 months, with an extension option considered as needed. This leave is granted with full pay for the portion of time in which a disability is present and then also for an additional time period of up to 6 weeks designated as child care leave.

Paternity leave is offered for up to 6 weeks, essentially mirroring the 6 weeks of child care leave available in maternity situations.

2. Do you offer any distinctive family-friendly options, such as adoption assistance or child care? Do you offer domestic partner benefits?

We have a number of options available to attorneys here that are family-friendly. We offer fully paid back-up child careservices through a premier provider in our neighboring building, internal support groups for working parents and an employee assistance program that offers information and resources related to a wide variety of issues facing families.

Our maternity and child care policies contemplate and include paid time off for both men and women who are adopting.

We do offer coverage for domestic partners.

© 2007 Vault Inc.

3. What is your firm's vacation policy?

We offer attorneys 4 weeks of vacation with a carry-over provision.

4. Do you have a flex-time policy?

We offer attorneys a variety of options to consider as an alternative to our standard work schedule, including reducing the number of days scheduled to work within a week or limiting the number of hours scheduled during a work day. We are also are open to considering other arrangements as need be for attorneys to better balance their work and family life.

5. Do you offer a sabbatical or leave-of-absence program? How many associates take advantage of this option on an annual basis?

We certainly have situations where sabbaticals and leaves-of-absence are offered and utilized. We are not prepared at this time to release information on the number involved.

Gardere Wynne Sewell LLP

1. What is your firm policy on maternity leave? Paternity leave?

Maternity leave is treated like any other FMLA qualifying event ; associates recieve 100% paid leave for 12 weeks.

2. Do you offer any distinctive family-friendly options, such as adoption assistance or child care? Do you offer domestic partner benefits?

Domestic partner benefits are offered in the Group Long Term Care Policy.

3. What is your firm's vacation policy?

Associates receive two weeks paid vacation per year during their first three years of employment with the Firm and three weeks' paid vacation per year thereafter.

4. Do you have a flex-time policy?

The Flexible Hours Policy is intended to provide to Associates with responsibility for the rearing of children the option of working on a flexible hours program during certain limited periods of time while remaining eligible to return to the partnership track. The goal of the policy is to provide the opportunity to adopt a flexible hours program compatible with child-rearing responsibilities and with the needs of the Firm, while at the same time maintaining the opportunity for professional growth, experience, and career advancement.

5. Do you offer a sabbatical or leave-of-absence program? How many associates take advantage of this option on an annual basis?

No

Visit the Vault Law Channel, the complete online resource for law careers, featuring firm profiles, message boards, the Vault Law Job Board, and more. www.vault.com/law

VAULT CAREER LIBRARY   763

Gibson, Dunn & Crutcher LLP

1. What is your firm policy on maternity leave? Paternity leave?

Pregnancy disability leave is provided for the period of time that an attorney is disabled and unable to work as a result of pregnancy, for up to 90 days or until released from disability, whichever occurs first. This is normally a 6-8 week leave. provide up to 12 weeks of Family Leave/Child Care leave following the birth, adoption or placement for foster care of a child.

2. Do you offer any distinctive family-friendly options, such as adoption assistance or child care? Do you offer domestic partner benefits?

Domestic Partner Benefits are offered for same sex partners. Emergency Day Care is offered to attorneys.

3. What is your firm's vacation policy?

Non-Partner attorneys are able to take time-off with pay as they deem appropriate for rest and relaxation. This is not governed by a formal vacation policy, and time-off can be taken as the attorney deems appropriate, while meeting the needs and expectations of the Firm's performance guidelines and client needs.

4. Do you have a flex-time policy?

A part-time work schedule is available to associates and of counsel attorneys allowing them to work a less than full-time schedule due to family needs or other personal circumstances.

5. Do you offer a sabbatical or leave-of-absence program? How many associates take advantage of this option on an annual basis?

A personal leave of absence is available to attorneys.

Goodwin Procter LLP

1. What is your firm policy on maternity leave? Paternity leave?

An associate who gives birth is eligible for up to 12 weeks of paid leave and may be eligible for an additional 12 weeks of unpaid leave.

For paternity leave, an associate is eligible to up to 4 weeks of paid time off if the leave is taken within 6 months of birth. Additional time off, up to a total of 12 weeks , may be taken . An associate may use vacation time to receive pay for unpaid time off.

2. Do you offer any distinctive family-friendly options, such as adoption assistance or child care? Do you offer domestic partner benefits?

We have emergency child care facilities available on-site in Boston, NY and DC. We will be providing back up care for our new offices in California beginning this fall . We offer dependent care reimbursement accounts. Our EAP program offers assistance in finding resources for day care and elder care. Health Advocate provides resources for associates and family members for health care related issues.

© 2007 Vault Inc.

Domestic partner benefits are offered for health insurance, dental insurance, leaves of absence and for utilization of sick time. In CA, benefits are offered in accordance with CA law.

3. What is your firm's vacation policy?

We offer 4 weeks vacation per calendar year. An associate may carry over up to 5 unused vacation days into the next year.

4. Do you have a flex-time policy?

Associates may request a reduced work schedule or flexible hours.

5. Do you offer a sabbatical or leave-of-absence program? How many associates take advantage of this option on an annual basis?

We offer personal leaves of absence. We receive requests of approximately three a year .

Haynes and Boone, LLP

1. What is your firm policy on maternity leave? Paternity leave?

If an attorney has been with the firm for one year or more, she will receive 100% of salary for up to 12 weeks. Less than one year, she is able to use earned vacation to receive pay for time off. No policy for paternity leave.

2. Do you offer any distinctive family-friendly options, such as adoption assistance or child care? Do you offer domestic partner benefits?

No adoption assistance or child care options, but an employee will receive up to 12 weeks paid adoption leave. We do not offer domestic partner benefits.

3. What is your firm's vacation policy?

Less than 3 years - 10 days.

3 - 7 years - 15 days.

Beyond 7 years - 20 days.

4. Do you have a flex-time policy?

Yes.

5. Do you offer a sabbatical or leave-of-absence program? How many associates take advantage of this option on an annual basis?

Yes, we have a leave of absence program.

Visit the Vault Law Channel, the complete online resource for law careers, featuring firm profiles, message boards, the Vault Law Job Board, and more. www.vault.com/law

VAULT CAREER LIBRARY   765

Heller Ehrman LLP

1. What is your firm policy on maternity leave? Paternity leave?

Heller Ehrman policies provide up to four months leave for the birth parent who needs time off due to a pregnancy-related disability and/or post-delivery disability. Upon release to return to work, employees who are FMLA-eligible may take advantage of the firm's 16 weeks of FMLA for baby bonding. Any attorney who takes FMLA for baby bonding receives Parenting Pay at 100% compensation during the first six weeks of FMLA. For attorneys who adopt or foster, the same FMLA leave and Parenting Pay are available.

2. Do you offer any distinctive family-friendly options, such as adoption assistance or child care? Do you offer domestic partner benefits?

An employee who is not the birth parent and who is FMLA-eligible has the same leave of up to 16 weeks available as the birth parent. Any attorney who takes FMLA for baby bonding purposes receives Parenting Pay at 100% compensation during the first six weeks of FMLA. For attorneys who adopt or foster, the same FMLA leave and Parenting Pay are available.

3. What is your firm's vacation policy?

Pretax Dependent Care Reimbursement Program (Flexible Spending Account) and back-up dependent care: Memberships at dedicated back-up child care centers when regular care is unavailable. Back-up in-home care is also available for well children, mildly-ill children and adults/elderly. Yes, we offer domestic partner benefits.

4. Do you have a flex-time policy?

Associates who work full time accrue 20 days of vacation a year, up to a maximum of 30 days.

5. Do you offer a sabbatical or leave-of-absence program? How many associates take advantage of this option on an annual basis?

Heller Ehrman allows associates to work on a reduced or flex-time schedule. On a case-by-case basis, the firm considers part-time work schedules for associates caring for children under five years old. Usually, part-time associates work at least three days per week for up to a year; the firm adjusts their compensation accordingly. The firm will consider requests for longer periods of part-time work or for other part-time schedules for the purposes of child rearing.

Hinshaw & Culbertson LLP

1. What is your firm policy on maternity leave? Paternity leave?

Our maternity leave policy is 12 weeks in total, which is fully paid for partners. Our associates get 8 weeks paid. We don't have a paternity leave policy.

2. Do you offer any distinctive family-friendly options, such as adoption assistance or child care? Do you offer domestic partner benefits?

We do offer domestic partner benefits.

© 2007 Vault Inc.

3. What is your firm's vacation policy?

Partners receive 4 weeks per year.

Associates and Staff Attorneys policy goes as follows:

First Calendar Year (Summer Bar - July): 0 days

First Calendar Year (Winter Bar - February): 5 days accrued

Second Calendar Year: 10 days accrued

Third Calendar Year and Forward: 15 days accrued

4. Do you have a flex-time policy?

We do not have a flex time policy.

5. Do you offer a sabbatical or leave-of-absence program? How many associates take advantage of this option on an annual basis?

No, with the exception of personal leave.

We have a Associate Leaves of Absence policy which includes the following circumstances:

• The Family and Medical Leave Act of 1993

• Unpaid Personal Leave of Absence

• Jury Duty

• Bereavement Leave

• Military Leave - Short Term Training

• Military Leave - Extended Service

• Victims' Economic Security and Safety Act (VESSA) Unpaid Leave of Absence (Illinois Office Only)

Hogan & Hartson LLP

1. What is your firm policy on maternity leave? Paternity leave?

The firm's maternity and paternity leave policy allows new mothers to receive paid leave for the medical disability period after the birth of a child (normally six weeks for attorneys). Beyond the paid medical leave, we offer up to four weeks of paid job-protected family leave after the birth of a child. Upon request, associate employees may be out for a total of one year (includes paid and unpaid leave).

New fathers who are lawyers at Hogan & Hartson receive two weeks of paid paternity leave, and may receive two more weeks if they are the primary care giver.

2. Do you offer any distinctive family-friendly options, such as adoption assistance or child care? Do you offer domestic partner benefits?

Adoption

The firm provides up to $5,000 of financial aid per adoption to help employees with adopting children (with a cap of $10,000). After placement of an eligible child for adoption, attorneys are eligible for two weeks of paid family leave, which may be extended by two weeks of paid responsible caregiver leave.

Visit the Vault Law Channel, the complete online resource for law careers, featuring firm profiles, message boards, the Vault Law Job Board, and more. **www.vault.com/law**

767

Back up Child Care Center

The DC office Back-up Child Care Center enables lawyers and employees to manage their family obligations. The center is intended to provide back-up child care when regular child care arrangements are unavailable.

Since even the most reliable child care can fall through, a Hogan & Hartson employee can still come to work confident that her child will receive reliable care. "The center made it possible for me to come to work on dozens of occasions. My children enjoyed spending time with me during the commute and having lunch with me each day I could be productive at work because I knew they were safe and happy," noted one employee.

Life-Work Balance

Hogan & Hartson is consistently implementing new programs to create a working environment that meets the demands of working parents. We have developed initiatives that set us apart from our competition, including the Work Option Group; Alternative Career Tracks and Part-Time Options; the Sabbatical Program; the NY office Women's Working Group; the DC office Women's Steering Committee; formal mentoring and professional development programs; regular meetings for reduced hour attorneys; and panel discussions for all lawyers on life-work balance issues.

The firm does offer domestic partner benefits.

3. What is your firm's vacation policy?

The firm expects our attorneys to take their vacations. Attorneys are entitled to four weeks (20 days) for vacation during each full year.

4. Do you have a flex-time policy?

While lawyers have significant flexibility with their work schedules consistent with client needs, we have no expressed policy on flex time.

5. Do you offer a sabbatical or leave-of-absence program? How many associates take advantage of this option on an annual basis?

For more than 40 years Hogan & Hartson has institutionalized programs that provide our lawyers with opportunities to take breaks from the practices including a flexible approach to granting requests for a leave of absence and the Sabbatical program for partners.

Holland & Hart LLP

1. What is your firm policy on maternity leave? Paternity leave?

Disability Leave for Maternity: The period of disability for a normal pregnancy and delivery is presumed to be a minimum of eight weeks and, therefore, an associate may take eight weeks maternity leave with full compensation under this Policy without special certification from her physician. Certification of disability from the associate's treating physician is required for additional paid disability leave in excess of eight weeks under the firm's Short Term Disability Policy, which will be compensated at full regular base pay. Pregnancy-related disability leave in excess of 90 days will be governed by the firm's Long Term Disability Policy. Paternity Leave Benefits: Personal leave at full compensation for up to two weeks will be available to any male associate on the occasion of the birth or adoption of his child.

© 2007 Vault Inc.

2. Do you offer any distinctive family-friendly options, such as adoption assistance or child care? Do you offer domestic partner benefits?

Holland & Hart is pleased to offer group medical, dental, and life insurance benefits to qualified same sex domestic partners of eligible employees and Partners of Holland & Hart. Qualified same sex domestic partners are eligible for the same benefits available to covered dependents of eligible employees and Partners under the Medical/Dental and Dependent Life Insurance Plans (the "Plans"), with the exception of health care continuation coverage rights under the Consolidated Omnibus Budget Reconciliation Act of 1985, as amended ("COBRA"). Holland & Hart nevertheless has determined to offer qualified same sex domestic partners continuation coverage rights under the Medical/Dental Plan that are comparable to certain of the health care continuation coverage rights under COBRA upon the occurrence of certain events.

3. What is your firm's vacation policy?

Vacations for associates are computed on a fiscal year basis of July 1 through June 30.

Each new associate who joins the firm between July 1 and November 1 of the fiscal year will be eligible for a total of two weeks of paid vacation during that fiscal year.

At the beginning of the next fiscal year, and for each year thereafter, the associate will be eligible for a total of three weeks/fiscal year of paid vacation.

4. Do you have a flex-time policy?

Holland & Hart is committed to providing a flexible workplace that includes support for attorneys with disparate balances in their work and other life commitments. The firm recognizes that attorneys working on less than a full time basis can be just as committed to the practice of law and to the firm as their full time peers. The firm adopts the following policy in furtherance of its commitment to providing a supportive culture and professional advancement opportunities for those attorneys who, for a variety of personal reasons, choose to work in a part time arrangement. Ultimately it is the goal of this policy that each request for a part time commitment will be treated with flexibility and fairness to all attorneys, both part time and full time, and to the firm as an institution, in accordance with our Statement of Principles.

5. Do you offer a sabbatical or leave-of-absence program? How many associates take advantage of this option on an annual basis?

Personal leave without pay during periods when an associate is medically able to work may be requested from and granted by ASCOM after consultation with MCOM, provided that recommendations concerning leaves of greater than 30 days shall be forwarded to MCOM for final approval or denial. Personal leaves of 30 days or less may be granted by ASCOM.

Howrey LLP

1. What is your firm policy on maternity leave? Paternity leave?

Maternity: For the birth of a child, we offer 6-8 weeks disability, 6 weeks paid parental leave plus the use of PTO and/or unpaid leave. For the adoption of a child, we offer 6 weeks parental leave plus the use of PTO and/or unpaid leave.

Paternity: We offer 6 weeks paid paternity leave plus the use of PTO and/or unpaid leave upon the birth or adoption of a child.

Visit the Vault Law Channel, the complete online resource for law careers, featuring firm profiles, message boards, the Vault Law Job Board, and more. www.vault.com/law

VAULT CAREER LIBRARY   769

2. Do you offer any distinctive family-friendly options, such as adoption assistance or child care? Do you offer domestic partner benefits?

We offer emergency child care, family and parental leave, dependent child and domestic partner life insurances. We offer domestic partner benefits. Our EAP offers assistance in securing child care and elder care services.

3. What is your firm's vacation policy?

Associates receive 4 weeks annual sick/vacation leave.

4. Do you have a flex-time policy?

We have a part-time policy.

5. Do you offer a sabbatical or leave-of-absence program? How many associates take advantage of this option on an annual basis?

We do not have an official program, but would handle on a case-by-case basis.

Hughes Hubbard & Reed LLP

1. What is your firm policy on maternity leave? Paternity leave?

Maternity leave - 3 months paid

Paternity leave - 2 weeks paid

2. Do you offer any distinctive family-friendly options, such as adoption assistance or child care? Do you offer domestic partner benefits?

We have and EPA program

We offer back up child care paid by the firm.

We offer same sex domestic partner benefits

3. What is your firm's vacation policy?

Attorneys accrue 5 days at the end of each quarter, resulting in four weeks of vacation time per year. Unused vacation time can be carried over.

4. Do you have a flex-time policy?

Yes, but on a case-by-case basis only.

5. Do you offer a sabbatical or leave-of-absence program? How many associates take advantage of this option on an annual basis?

Yes, but on a case-by-case basis only. Fewer than 3 in any given year.

© 2007 Vault Inc.

Irell & Manella LLP

1. What is your firm policy on maternity leave? Paternity leave?

We have a twelve-week paid maternity leave and a four-week paid paternity leave, and attorneys often extend their leaves with additional time off.

2. Do you offer any distinctive family-friendly options, such as adoption assistance or child care? Do you offer domestic partner benefits?

We offer four-week paid leave for adoptive parents. As described below, several attorneys work a part-time schedule to accommodate family obligations. We offer domestic partner benefits.

3. What is your firm's vacation policy?

Associates who meet billable hours expectations are encouraged and expected to take vacation time, and the firm does not place a specific limit on the number of days that an associate may be absent from work for vacation.

4. Do you have a flex-time policy?

We don't have a flex-time policy, but we do have a flexible part-time policy. Part-time arrangements require individual approval and are tailored to accommodate the individual attorney and the firm. We have a variety of part-time arrangements, both short term and long term.

5. Do you offer a sabbatical or leave-of-absence program? How many associates take advantage of this option on an annual basis?

Leaves of absence for associates are arranged on an individual basis to address both the associate's and the firm's needs. We have a sabbatical program for partners.

Jackson Walker LLP

1. What is your firm policy on maternity leave? Paternity leave?

The Firm is committed to providing appropriate leave arrangements for maternity and paternity leaves.

2. Do you offer any distinctive family-friendly options, such as adoption assistance or child care? Do you offer domestic partner benefits?

No adoption or child care assistance offered at this time. No domestic partner benefits offered at this time.

3. What is your firm's vacation policy?

Vacation time is taken at the discretion of all professionals.

4. Do you have a flex-time policy?

The Firm's alternative work schedule program is determined by length of employment and practice group leaders and management's approval.

Visit the Vault Law Channel, the complete online resource for law careers, featuring firm profiles, message boards, the Vault Law Job Board, and more. **www.vault.com/law**

VAULT CAREER LIBRARY   771

5. Do you offer a sabbatical or leave-of-absence program? How many associates take advantage of this option on an annual basis?

The Firm will review requests for specific leave of absences and determine appropriate leave arrangements for such requests on a case-by-case basis.

Jenner & Block LLP

1. What is your firm policy on maternity leave? Paternity leave?

Jenner & Block combines a generous Short Term Disability program which when associated with the birth of a child and combined with Parental Leave provides female associates with up to 15 weeks of paid time off at 100% of their salary. During this leave period, the associate's billable hours are adjusted to compensate for the time-off from work. In respect to Parental Leave, specifically, all associates are eligible to take up to six (6) weeks of paid Parental Leave during any 12-month period upon the birth or adoption of a child, or the placement of a foster child. Parental Leave is available for spouses as well as same sex and opposite sex domestic partners.

2. Do you offer any distinctive family-friendly options, such as adoption assistance or child care? Do you offer domestic partner benefits?

Yes. One of the core values at Jenner & Block is to "Reward and Respect our People". This value is demonstrated through ongoing efforts to provide attorneys with work/life balance opportunities. With benefits such as a "Reduced - Time" policy, back-up child care and a generous Parental Leave program, Jenner & Block continues to support its attorneys in balancing the demands of family-care and child-rearing, with the demands of providing superior legal services to its clients. Additionally, the Firm's benefits and leave policy are available to both same sex and opposite sex domestic partners.

3. What is your firm's vacation policy?

Associate attorneys working full time hours may take up to three weeks (15 business days) of paid vacation annually. Jenner & Block provides nine paid holidays on an annual basis. Also, the firm's in-house travel agency is available to assist with vacation planning.

4. Do you have a flex-time policy?

Jenner & Block offers associates reduced/part-time work options relating to family-care and child-rearing, which consider the needs of the associate as well as the demands of providing superior legal services to its clients. Associates working on a reduced-time basis will be eligible for year-end bonus consideration, full benefit coverage, partner progression and will receive their annual review. Jenner & Block is not a firm that requires or encourages "face time." The firm has the technology to allow attorneys to work from home, as needed. This technology gives attorneys the flexibility to leave the office and still complete the document the client wants by morning.

5. Do you offer a sabbatical or leave-of-absence program? How many associates take advantage of this option on an annual basis?

While Jenner & Block does not employ a formal sabbatical or leave-of-absence program, the Firm does review requests for such leaves and considers them on a case-by-case basis. There have been instances when associates have been granted a leave-of-absence and have resumed their work at the Firm following the period of their absence.

© 2007 Vault Inc.

Jones Day

1. What is your firm policy on maternity leave? Paternity leave?

Paid medical leave of 8 weeks for routine childbirth (for mothers), 4 weeks adoption leave, 4 weeks paid family leave for associates (fathers or mothers).

2. Do you offer any distinctive family-friendly options, such as adoption assistance or child care? Do you offer domestic partner benefits?

We provide paid adoption and paid family leave in connection with adoption. Some form of back up child care is available in almost all offices. Domestic partner benefits? Yes.

3. What is your firm's vacation policy?

20 Days for Associates.

4. Do you have a flex-time policy?

Not as such. We have staggered schedules for some staff, and some informal flex arrangements for lawyers.

5. Do you offer a sabbatical or leave-of-absence program? How many associates take advantage of this option on an annual basis?

We do not have sabbatical leaves as such but we do have certain leaves of absence at discretion of firm. Many associates and others take advantage of paid medical and family leave. Leaves for other personal reasons do occur but are infrequent and we do not track the number.

Katten Muchin Rosenman LLP

1. What is your firm policy on maternity leave? Paternity leave?

Attorneys who have been at the Firm for at least one year are eligible for three months paid maternity leave or two weeks paid paternity leave. In certain circumstances, attorneys are eligible to take an additional three months unpaid maternity leave or 10 weeks unpaid paternity leave.

2. Do you offer any distinctive family-friendly options, such as adoption assistance or child care? Do you offer domestic partner benefits?

The Firm offers adoption benefits and free emergency child care. Attorneys who adopt a child are eligible for three months of paid leave provided that the attorney is eligible for short term disability and is the primary caregiver of the newly adopted child. During the Paid Child Care Leave, the Attorney continues to receive his or her salary or draw and all benefits. Eligible attorneys may seek an extension of child care leave for up to three additional months immediately following the Paid Child Care Leave. During this Extended Leave, the attorney does not receive any salary or draw, but continues to receive benefits. The Firm offers the same benefits for domestic partners as they do for spouses and children of married attorneys. However, due to government regulation, the Firm may not subsidize benefits for domestic partners.

Visit the Vault Law Channel, the complete online resource for law careers, featuring firm profiles, message boards, the Vault Law Job Board, and more. **www.vault.com/law**

VAULT CAREER LIBRARY   773

3. What is your firm's vacation policy?

The Firm has not established a formal vacation policy for Associates. Rather, the Firm has articulated certain work standards which should permit individuals to take sufficient time for vacations and other personal time off. There is no limit on Associate vacation (provided work standards are met). All Associates are encouraged to take regular vacations.

4. Do you have a flex-time policy?

Yes. The Firm recognizes that an individual Partner or Associate may decide that it is appropriate to devote time to the care of his or her family in lieu of a full time commitment to the Firm. The Firm, in turn, has developed a series of guidelines to attempt to accommodate the desires of such Attorneys to remain active professionals while working an alternative work schedule in connection with child care responsibilities.

5. Do you offer a sabbatical or leave-of-absence program? How many associates take advantage of this option on an annual basis?

Associates who have been at the Firm for five years and are in good standing are automatically eligible for a one-month, paid, sabbatical. For the sabbatical year, the Associate's annual billable hours requirement is adjusted downwards, but all bonuses are paid at the full year level. Every eligible Associate is encouraged to take advantage of the sabbatical. Approximately 6 to 8 Associates take advantage of the program each year.

Kenyon & Kenyon LLP

1. What is your firm policy on maternity leave? Paternity leave?

Associates are eligible for 3 months of maternity leave and an additional month of unpaid leave. (This runs concurrently with FMLA.) Although, we do not have a formal paternity leave policy, associates are eligible for up to four months of leave time under FMLA.

2. Do you offer any distinctive family-friendly options, such as adoption assistance or child care? Do you offer domestic partner benefits?

The firm provides back-up emergency daycare and coverage for domestic partners.

3. What is your firm's vacation policy?

Four weeks vacation.

4. Do you have a flex-time policy?

The Diversity Committee is presently exploring this option for possible implementation in 2008.

5. Do you offer a sabbatical or leave-of-absence program? How many associates take advantage of this option on an annual basis?

Three attorneys have taken sabbaticals in the past two years.

© 2007 Vault Inc.

Kirkland & Ellis LLP

1. What is your firm policy on maternity leave? Paternity leave?

Associates - Birth Mother:

Birth mothers receive at least 16 weeks paid leave. This is paid at full pay for the entire time. It consists of Paid Medical Leave with Short-Term Disability benefits and Paid Parental Leave. The Paid Medical Leave ends when the mother is recovered from childbirth; then 10 weeks Paid Parental Leave is in effect.

Associates - Adoption:

The primary caregiver receives 16 weeks paid leave. This is paid at full pay for the entire time. It consists of 6 weeks Paid Adoption Leave plus 10 weeks Paid Parental Leave.

Associates - Other Parent: Fathers, Adoptive Parents and Domestic Partners

They receive 10 weeks Paid Parental Leave. This is paid at full pay.

Partners

Partners receive up to 6 months paid leave of absence for the birth or adoption of a child. This is paid at full pay.

2. Do you offer any distinctive family-friendly options, such as adoption assistance or child care? Do you offer domestic partner benefits?

Kirkland offers:

• Medical, dental and vision insurance for domestic partners
• Backup child care
• Dependent Care Spending Account
• Nursing Mothers Program
• Employee Assistance Program
• The Parenting Link, a networking program for parents

3. What is your firm's vacation policy?

Associates accrue 15 work days per year during their first 3 years of service. After 3 years of service they accrue 20 work days. The maximum accrual is 25 days. Partners have no fixed vacation accrual schedule; they use vacation at their own discretion.

4. Do you have a flex-time policy?

Yes. Non-share partners and associates may request an alternate work schedule for personal or family reasons.

5. Do you offer a sabbatical or leave-of-absence program? How many associates take advantage of this option on an annual basis?

Kirkland provides Medial Paid Leave of Absence to associates for up to 6 months for any short-term disability that is certified by a health care provider. In addition, associates receive up to 6 weeks Paid Personal Leave to care for a family member who has a serious medical condition. these leaves of absence are paid at full pay.

Needless to say, Kirkland complies with the Family and Medical Leave Act of 1993 ("FMLA") and all state leave laws.

Visit the Vault Law Channel, the complete online resource for law careers, featuring firm profiles, message boards, the Vault Law Job Board, and more. www.vault.com/law

VAULT CAREER LIBRARY   775

Kirkpatrick & Lockhart Preston Gates Ellis LLP

1. What is your firm policy on maternity leave? Paternity leave?

All lawyers employed by the Firm are eligible for parental leave beginning on the first day of employment with the Firm. Parental leave is provided with respect to the birth or adoption of your child. Parental leave is separate from, and in addition to, any leave for which you may be eligible pursuant to short-term disability leave. Except where state laws require otherwise, parental leave may be taken for up to three months in duration.

The first six weeks of parental leave is paid leave. Any additional

parental leave is unpaid. Benefits continue during paid and unpaid parental leave, subject in all cases to the terms and conditions of the applicable employee benefit plan. Requests for additional unpaid leave after parental leave expires will be considered; however, benefits will not continue except where state laws require otherwise.

2. Do you offer any distinctive family-friendly options, such as adoption assistance or child care? Do you offer domestic partner benefits?

Yes. Back-up child care arrangements are available in certain offices.In addition, flexible spending accounts are offered and enable the participant to set aside funds for day care and adoption expenses on a tax-favored basis. Dom. Partner benefits - yes.

3. What is your firm's vacation policy?

Except where state laws require otherwise, K&L Gates does not have a rigidly defined vacation policy for attorneys, in recognition of the varying demands of its practice and the individual lifestyles of its lawyers. It has been generally accepted that annual vacations totaling 3 to 4 weeks are within the range of the Firm's expectations, subject to workload demands.

4. Do you have a flex-time policy?

Yes. At K&L Gates, we foster a culture that allows our lawyers to thrive professionally in the face of competing demands of firm and family life.

This culture is born of our broad and progressive Professional and Personal Life Integration (PPLI) initiative, the innovative cornerstone of which is our Balanced Hours program (BH program), launched in January 2006. We believe that the greater flexibility BH affords our lawyers helps us to create a work environment that ultimately improves client service while enhancing lawyer productivity, retention and morale.

5. Do you offer a sabbatical or leave-of-absence program? How many associates take advantage of this option on an annual basis?

No

Kramer Levin Naftalis & Frankel LLP

1. What is your firm policy on maternity leave? Paternity leave?

Maternity leave: Post-delivery disability leave (8 weeks); paid child care leave (4 weeks); sabbatical (5 weeks at the start of your fifth year of employment with the firm); some or all of her vacation (up to 4 weeks); and up to 3 months unpaid leave but all combinations cannot exceed 6 months. These options are available after being employed with the Firm for at least 1 year and in good standing.

© 2007 Vault Inc.

Paternity leave: Paid child care leave (4 weeks); some or all of his vacation (up to 4 weeks); and up to 3 months of unpaid leave. These options are available after being employed with the Firm for at least 1 year and in good standing.

2. Do you offer any distinctive family-friendly options, such as adoption assistance or child care? Do you offer domestic partner benefits?

We have back up emergency child care services and adoption leave similar to the paternity leave listed above. We also offer a dependent care plan which allows for certain childcare expenses to be reimbursed on a pre-tax basis. We offer full domestic partner benefits.

3. What is your firm's vacation policy?

Full-time attorneys are offered 20 days of vacation per year. Part-time attorneys are offered pro-rated vacation based on their work-week schedule.

4. Do you have a flex-time policy?

We do not have a flex-time policy.

5. Do you offer a sabbatical or leave-of-absence program? How many associates take advantage of this option on an annual basis?

We have a sabbatical program that offers 5 weeks of paid time off. The sabbatical is an option for an attorney during his/her 5th consecutive year of service with the Firm and is determined on a case-by-case basis. Vacation time can also be added to the sabbatical for a total of 9 weeks off. After the first sabbatical, an attorney is entitled to another sabbatical every subsequent 4th consecutive year.

Latham & Watkins LLP

1. What is your firm policy on maternity leave? Paternity leave?

Latham provides twelve weeks of paid maternity leave, subject to requirements of local law. Under the firm's Family Care Leave policy, a father or non-birthing mother may take up to twelve weeks leave to care for newborn or newly-adopted children.

2. Do you offer any distinctive family-friendly options, such as adoption assistance or child care? Do you offer domestic partner benefits?

Latham offers several distinctive family-friendly options including back up child care services to its attorneys as well as medical, health, life and long term care benefits to domestic partners.

3. What is your firm's vacation policy?

Associates are eligible for 15 vacation days per year.

4. Do you have a flex-time policy?

The firm offers reduced-time arrangements which allow its attorneys to balance personal demands with the demands of providing legal services to firm clients. Associates with reduced-time arrangements remain eligible for year-end bonuses and promotion.

Visit the Vault Law Channel, the complete online resource for law careers, featuring firm profiles, message boards, the Vault Law Job Board, and more. **www.vault.com/law**

VAULT CAREER LIBRARY   777

5. Do you offer a sabbatical or leave-of-absence program? How many associates take advantage of this option on an annual basis?

The firm provides generous paid and unpaid leaves of absence policies for associates. Leaves of absence are considered for a variety of reasons (including family care, childbirth/adoption, education and other personal reasons). The number of associates who take advantage of this option on an annual base varies from year-to-year.

LeBoeuf, Lamb, Greene & MacRae, LLP

1. What is your firm policy on maternity leave? Paternity leave?

We give three months maternity leave to the primary caregiver for the birth or adoption of a child. We give two weeks paternity leave to new fathers.

2. Do you offer any distinctive family-friendly options, such as adoption assistance or child care? Do you offer domestic partner benefits?

We do not have an official adoption assistance policy, but do allow attorneys time off if needed during the adoption process and of course the three months maternity leave for the primary caregiver. We do offer domestic partner benefits.

3. What is your firm's vacation policy?

All attorneys are entitled to 4 weeks vacation and three personal days.

4. Do you have a flex-time policy?

No

5. Do you offer a sabbatical or leave-of-absence program? How many associates take advantage of this option on an annual basis?

Nothing official, but we do allow attorneys to take a sabbatical or leave of absence (unpaid) if needed.

Linklaters

1. What is your firm policy on maternity leave? Paternity leave?

The Firm provides up to five paid days for new parents for the care of a new child by birth or adoption. The Firm will also provide up to an additional eleven paid weeks for the primary care giver. 'Primary Care Giver' is defined as the parental guardian principally responsible for the care of the child.

2. Do you offer any distinctive family-friendly options, such as adoption assistance or child care? Do you offer domestic partner benefits?

We offer domestic partner benefits for both same sex and opposite sex partnerships. The firm offers support and assistance for those applying for adoption in terms of providing references and information as required. The leave policy for adoption is as stated above.

© 2007 Vault Inc.

3. What is your firm's vacation policy?

All full-time employees are entitled to 22 days of vacation per calendar year. Summer associates do not receive vacation time during their 12 weeks of paid internship with the Firm.

4. Do you have a flex-time policy?

Yes, we do support flexible working arrangements which may be made available to all employees. There is no automatic entitlement and a clear case must be made and will be subject to the question of business need in all circumstances.

5. Do you offer a sabbatical or leave-of-absence program? How many associates take advantage of this option on an annual basis?

Employees who wish to have a leave of absence for non-family or medical reasons should apply, in writing, to the HR department, stating their reasons for the request. Requests for leave will be evaluated based upon the need of the individual and the Firm.

Lowenstein Sandler PC

1. What is your firm policy on maternity leave? Paternity leave?

At Lowenstein Sandler, for those attorneys who have worked at the firm for at least one year, the policies are: Maternity Leave: Three months paid and three months unpaid. Paternity Leave: As per the provisions of the Family Leave Act: up to 12 weeks unpaid leave.

2. Do you offer any distinctive family-friendly options, such as adoption assistance or child care? Do you offer domestic partner benefits?

Lowenstein Sandler offers back up childcare. Lowenstein Sandler does offer domestic partner benefits. The firm also recognizes civil unions. The firm does not have a formal policy with respect to adoption assistance.

3. What is your firm's vacation policy?

Lowenstein Sandler's vacation policy for attorneys: three weeks paid vacation time.

4. Do you have a flex-time policy?

There are currently fourteen attorneys at Lowenstein Sandler working on a part-time basis. The firm does not have a formal flex-time policy. These requests are handled on a case by case basis.

5. Do you offer a sabbatical or leave-of-absence program? How many associates take advantage of this option on an annual basis?

Attorneys have taken sabbatical/leaves of absence. Again, this is done on a case by case basis.

Visit the Vault Law Channel, the complete online resource for law careers, featuring firm profiles, message boards, the Vault Law Job Board, and more. **www.vault.com/law**

VAULT CAREER LIBRARY   779

Manatt, Phelps & Phillips, LLP

1. What is your firm policy on maternity leave? Paternity leave?

Maternity - up to 12 weeks Salary Continuation

2. Do you offer any distinctive family-friendly options, such as adoption assistance or child care? Do you offer domestic partner benefits?

Domestic Partner Benefits

3. What is your firm's vacation policy?

Attorneys are encouraged to take time off at their own discretion

4. Do you have a flex-time policy?

Yes

5. Do you offer a sabbatical or leave-of-absence program? How many associates take advantage of this option on an annual basis?

Yes

Mayer, Brown, Rowe & Maw LLP

1. What is your firm policy on maternity leave? Paternity leave?

The firm provides a 6 week paid parental leave to all new parents and mothers giving birth are eligible for medical leave under the firm's short-term disability policy.

2. Do you offer any distinctive family-friendly options, such as adoption assistance or child care? Do you offer domestic partner benefits?

The firm offers paid parental leave to adoptive parents (6 weeks as stated above). The firm offers domestic partner benefits as well.

3. What is your firm's vacation policy?

Attorneys accrue 4 weeks of vacation a year.

4. Do you have a flex-time policy?

We do not have a formal flex-time policy.

5. Do you offer a sabbatical or leave-of-absence program? How many associates take advantage of this option on an annual basis?

We do not have a sabbatical program, but associates may request a personal leave of absence when needed.

© 2007 Vault Inc.

McKenna Long & Aldridge LLP

1. What is your firm policy on maternity leave? Paternity leave?

Full-time, Part-time Regular and Part-time Special employees with at least 12 months' service at the time of birth or adoption of a child are eligible for up to 13 weeks of Parental Leave at a benefit equal to 100% of base salary at the time of the leave. This benefit is available to either parent, contingent on the employee's agreement to return to work as a Full-time, Part-time Regular or Part-time Special employee at the conclusion of the leave. The leave must be taken within the 12-month period following the birth or adoption of a child and should be used in 1-week increments. Requests for intermittent Parental Leave of less than 1-week increments will be considered.

2. Do you offer any distinctive family-friendly options, such as adoption assistance or child care? Do you offer domestic partner benefits?

We do not offer adoption assistance or child care on-site, but just this past month (March 1st) we rolled out Bright Horizons Family Solutions. This includes the Backup Care Advantage Program, which assists employees in balancing the competing demands of work and life. Employees can use the service when they need to be at work and their regular child or elder care is unavailable. This also includes the Priority Access Program, which gives employees priority access to full and part-time care at high-quality Bright Horizons child care centers on a space available basis (subject to other sponsoring clients and siblings of enrolled children).

3. What is your firm's vacation policy?

For our non-Partner attorneys, we offer Vacation time according to the schedule below:

Non-Partner Attorneys in Atlanta, Denver, Los Angeles, Philadelphia, San Diego, San Francisco and Washington accrue vacation time as follows:

Length of Service	Vacation Hours Accrued Per Pay Period		Vacation Days Accrued Annually
0-5 years	4.6875	15 days	
5+ years	6.25	20 days	

Non-Partner Attorneys in Albany and New York City accrue vacation time as follows:

Length of Service	Vacation Hours Accrued Per Pay Period		Vacation Days Accrued Annually
0-5 years	4.375	15 days	
5+ years	5.833	20 days	

4. Do you have a flex-time policy?

Flexible schedules may be permitted under certain circumstances. Any deviations from the normal work schedule must be approved and authorized by the Human Resources Manager/Office Administrator, as well as all supervisor(s). If the arrangement becomes a hardship on the supervising attorney(s)/managers or the firm, the employee will be expected to adjust his or her schedule back to the normal work schedule, Monday through Friday.

Visit the Vault Law Channel, the complete online resource for law careers, featuring firm profiles, message boards, the Vault Law Job Board, and more. www.vault.com/law

VAULT CAREER LIBRARY   781

5. Do you offer a sabbatical or leave-of-absence program? How many associates take advantage of this option on an annual basis?

The firm may provide unpaid personal leave to employees with at least 12 months service with the firm who need to take time off from work duties for compelling personal reasons when no other leave is applicable. The granting of a personal leave and any extension of such leave is allowed only in rare, emergency situations and is entirely at the firm's discretion.

Milbank, Tweed, Hadley & McCloy LLP

1. What is your firm policy on maternity leave? Paternity leave?

Paid disability leave (determined by individual's physician but typically 8 - 1 0 weeks) plus 4 weeks paid and up to 8 weeks unpaid child care leave. Child care leave (4 weeks paid and 8 weeks unpaid) available to mothers and fathers within 12 months of birth or adoption. Additional time, vacation or unpaid, can be taken as approved.

2. Do you offer any distinctive family-friendly options, such as adoption assistance or child care? Do you offer domestic partner benefits?

Primary child care providers offered the option of working a reduced work schedule for initial two months upon return to work. (Longer part-time arrangements also available.) We offer a number of family-friendly options including emergency back-up child care, a designated mothers room and same sex domestic partner benefits.

3. What is your firm's vacation policy?

4 weeks paid vacation

4. Do you have a flex-time policy?

Yes

5. Do you offer a sabbatical or leave-of-absence program? How many associates take advantage of this option on an annual basis?

We do not have a formal program although extended leaves are available on a case by case basis.

Mintz Levin Cohn Ferris Glovsky and Popeo, PC

1. What is your firm policy on maternity leave? Paternity leave?

The firm provides attorneys twelve weeks of fully-paid leave for birth mothers and eight weeks of fully-paid leave for fathers and non-birth mothers. Attorneys also may take four weeks of paid vacation time after their paid leave period. Finally, attorneys may take extended unpaid parenting leave of up to one year, during which they may continue to participate in our group health insurance plan.

2. Do you offer any distinctive family-friendly options, such as adoption assistance or child care? Do you offer domestic partner benefits?

Mintz Levin offers backup childcare either at high-quality childcare centers near the office or through professional, in-home babysitting services. We also provide access to 529 college savings plans that encourage families to prepare for the rising costs

© 2007 Vault Inc.

of higher education by providing federal income tax deferral as well as other tax benefits. The firm also sponsors a flexible spending account to provide employees the ability to pay for dependent care expenses with pre-tax dollars. We also provide access to various mortgage programs to assist attorneys in purchasing a home.

Mintz Levin operates on a broad definition of "family." We recognize that some employees in same-sex relationships are not permitted by law to marry and that other employees may choose not to marry. The Firm recognizes the value and significance of these relationships by extending our employment policies and benefits to our employees' partners, if they are "spousal equivalents," also known as "domestic partners." We have done so since 1993.

3. What is your firm's vacation policy?

Mintz Levin provides attorneys with four weeks of paid vacation each fiscal year.

4. Do you have a flex-time policy?

To demonstrate our long-standing commitment to and practice of havingflexible work arrangements, Mintz Levin recently adopted a formal policy on reduced hours, flexible hours, job sharing and telecommuting arrangements for attorneys.

5. Do you offer a sabbatical or leave-of-absence program? How many associates take advantage of this option on an annual basis?

Mintz Levin has a practice of allowing associates to take administrative leave to pursue outside interests or to address personal concerns.

Morgan & Finnegan, LLP

1. What is your firm policy on maternity leave? Paternity leave?

The primary caregiver may take 12 weeks of paid time off immediately following the birth or adoption of a child. This benefit runs concurrently with the benefits under the Family Medical Leave Act. The primary caregiver may extend the parental leave by taking his or her unused vacation. With advance approval from his or her supervising attorneys and the Executive Committee, the primary caregiver may take additional weeks of unpaid time off for a total maximum parental leave of 24 weeks. The primary caregiver is eligible for the Firm's associate and advisor bonus program on a pro-rated basis.

2. Do you offer any distinctive family-friendly options, such as adoption assistance or child care? Do you offer domestic partner benefits?

Dependent Care Flexible Spending Account

The Firm offers a Dependent Care Flexible Spending Account (also referred to as a Reimbursement Account).

Dependent Care: This reimbursement account enables you to set aside a predetermined amount of pre-tax dollars to cover eligible child care or adult care expenses while you are working full time.

Some examples would be nursery school, before school and after school programs, summer day camp.

3. What is your firm's vacation policy?

Associates can accrue up to four weeks of vacation time per year.

Visit the Vault Law Channel, the complete online resource for law careers, featuring firm profiles, message boards, the Vault Law Job Board, and more. www.vault.com/law

 783

4. Do you have a flex-time policy?

Case by case

5. Do you offer a sabbatical or leave-of-absence program? How many associates take advantage of this option on an annual basis?

No

Morrison & Foerster LLP

1. What is your firm policy on maternity leave? Paternity leave?

Our Maternity Leave Policy for attorneys provides for 90 days of paid maternity leave followed by 12 weeks of family care leave.

Our Paid Paternity Leave policy provides employees with 3 weeks of paid leave for an eligible father (or non-primary care giver parent in a marriage or domestic partnership) of a newly born child or a newly adopted child. If the employee is the primary caregiver, the paid leave is 4 weeks.

2. Do you offer any distinctive family-friendly options, such as adoption assistance or child care? Do you offer domestic partner benefits?

The firm's list of work/life policies and programs includes Flexible Work Arrangements, leave policies including Personal Leaves, Paid Paternity Leave, Paid Adoption Leave, Employee Assistance Program, Resource & Referral for all life events, Emergency Back-up Dependent Care, Prenatal & Lactation Program, Paid Community Service Day, Pre-tax Flexible Spending Accounts for Childcare and Healthcare, discounted Personal Banking Services and a scholarship program for children of staff employees.

Below are some further details on some of the programs listed above:

Our emergency Back-up Dependent Care Program is somewhat unique in that most of our U.S. locations have access to 2 services, a near-site backup child care center and/or an in-home backup dependent care service that can be used for either child or elder dependents. Employee can use either one or both.

We have a Prenatal & Lactation program for new and expecting parents. Employees can receive a free prenatal kit and access to a lactation consultation service called "Mothers at Work" that is 100% subsidized by the firm. Employees are also reimbursed by the firm for up to $200 for breast pump purchases. All of our U.S. locations have designated "Mothers Rooms" for nursing mothers who have returned to work while continuing to breastfeed.

Since 1994 we have offered coverage for both same-sex and opposite-sex domestic partnerships under the same terms as married couples in all benefit plans.

3. What is your firm's vacation policy?

Attorneys receive 3 or 4 weeks of vacation depending on seniority.

4. Do you have a flex-time policy?

Yes. Morrison & Foerster's Flexible Work Arrangements policy for lawyers allows for arrangements to be tailored based on the needs of the individual lawyer's unique circumstances, practice, and clients.

© 2007 Vault Inc.

5. Do you offer a sabbatical or leave-of-absence program? How many associates take advantage of this option on an annual basis?

While Morrison & Foerster does not offer a sabbatical program, our firm does on occasion approve personal leaves of absence. Each individual arrangement is reviewed on a case by case basis.

Munger, Tolles & Olson LLP

1. What is your firm policy on maternity leave? Paternity leave?

Our Firm maintains a flexible leave of absence policy for its associates. Following the birth or adoption of an associate's child, salary continuation is available for periods of up to four months for the primary caregiver (up to one month for the non-primary caregiver). Requests for lengthier unpaid personal leaves are considered on a case-by-case basis at the Firm's discretion.

2. Do you offer any distinctive family-friendly options, such as adoption assistance or child care? Do you offer domestic partner benefits?

MTO provides full insurance benefits to same-sex domestic partners of our attorneys and staff on the same basis as traditional spouses.

3. What is your firm's vacation policy?

The Firm allows associates considerable discretion in determining their working hours, subject to the needs of the Firm and its clients. As a result, there are no specific limits on the amount of vacation, sick or personal emergency time each associate may use during any given period. The Firm expects associates to take a reasonable amount of vacation time from year to year, but does not provide paid vacation, sick or personal time as a benefit.

4. Do you have a flex-time policy?

The Firm allows associates considerable discretion in determining their working hours, subject to the needs of the Firm and its clients. Any associate may request to work on a reduced time schedule. All reasonable requests will be given due consideration. A lawyer can make partner while working a reduced time schedule, though a reduced schedule may affect the amount of time it takes a lawyer to progress towards partnership.

5. Do you offer a sabbatical or leave-of-absence program? How many associates take advantage of this option on an annual basis?

We recognize that, at various points in their careers, our colleagues may need to reduce the number of hours they devote to their professional development within the firm in order to fulfill commitments and opportunities outside the firm. We are committed to supporting our colleagues in this regard. During the past three years, four associates have taken a leave of absence for reasons other than medical or parental responsibilities.

Nixon Peabody LLP

1. What is your firm policy on maternity leave? Paternity leave?

Maternity - The firm offers associates 12 weeks - 6-8 weeks disability pay; 4 weeks paid parenting leave. California: Same, plus additional paid 6 weeks of California Paid Family leave (benefit amount determined by state).

Visit the Vault Law Channel, the complete online resource for law careers, featuring firm profiles, message boards, the Vault Law Job Board, and more. www.vault.com/law

VAULT CAREER LIBRARY   785

Paid Parenting Leave - Following the birth or adoption of a child the firm provides four weeks paid parenting leave to either parent within three months following the birth or adoption of a child. The time may be taken intermittently or in a block of time and is in addition to any paid disability or income supplement payment. Paid Parenting Leave is provided to attorneys regularly scheduled to work 20 hours or more hours per week (either parent) following one year of service.

2. Do you offer any distinctive family-friendly options, such as adoption assistance or child care? Do you offer domestic partner benefits?

The firm has a number of family friendly benefits and policies in place to assist our employees as they welcome new children into their families. It also has a Domestic Partner Policy. These benefits and policies are described below:

Adoption Assistance: The firm's adoption assistance program grants up to $5,000 to employees to assist with expenses related to the adoption of a child.

Income Supplement Payment: While an employee is receiving pregnancy-related disability payments through either an employer plan or state plan, the firm provides an income supplement to assist with the difference between the employee's disability payment and regular salary.

Paid Parenting Leave: Following the birth or adoption of a child the firm provides four weeks paid parenting leave to either parent within three months following the birth or adoption of a child. The time may be taken intermittently or in a block of time and is in addition to any paid disability or income supplement payment.

Part-Time (Modified Work Arrangements) The Firm recognizes that at various times during a lawyer's career, circumstances may create a need or desire to work a reduced schedule and the Firm is committed to providing flexibility in its work arrangements. An attorney will be eligible for consideration for a modified work arrangement if the attorney: (1) has completed at least one year of full-time practice with the Firm; (2) has received evaluations reflecting very good performance, including consideration of whether the attorney has consistently satisfied the Firm's minimum standards for billable and non-billable hours; and (3) has the approval of his/her Practice Group Leader.

An attorney with a part-time/alternative work schedule will:

• receive a salary that fairly reflects the attorney's contribution to the Firm. For example, if the attorney is on an alternative work schedule that is 70% of the minimum billable hour expectation, he/she will be compensated at 70% of the full-time salary. Compensation will be reviewed at the same time and based on the same criteria as a full-time attorney.

• be eligible for participation in the Firm's Incentive Bonus Program in accordance with the terms of the program.

• Continue to receive the same benefits as a full-time attorney if they work at a 70% or more commitment (with the exception of vacation time, which is pro-rated).

• Alternative work schedule arrangements will not affect the basic eligibility of attorneys to be considered for partnership. The Firm's criteria for partnership will be applied to all attorneys uniformly regardless of any alternative work schedule arrangements.

Once parenting leave is complete, we offer an array of benefits to make the transition back to work as smooth as possible for our employees:

• Locked pumping rooms for nursing mothers;

• Generous sick and vacation policies;

• Subsidized back-up child care; and

• Alternative work arrangements (part-time).

© 2007 Vault Inc.

Domestic Partner Policy - The Firm endeavors in its employee benefit plans and human resources policies to treat a domestic partner or state recognized same-sex spouse the same as a different-gender spouse, to the extent permitted by federal law and insurance contracts. In general, the Firm's Benefits and Policies include coverage for a same or opposite sex domestic partner similar to coverage available under a Benefit or Policy that would apply to an employee's different-gender spouse.

3. What is your firm's vacation policy?

Vacation - All attorneys are eligible for four weeks vacation. Vacation is pro-rated for associates/counsel with reduced work commitment arrangements.

4. Do you have a flex-time policy?

The firm is currently reviewing adding a formal flex-time time policy. Current requests for flex-time schedules and full-time telecommuting schedules are reviewed and approved on a case-by-case basis. In addition, many attorneys and staff utilize flex-time on an informal or ad hoc basis.

The Firm recognizes that at various times during our employees' careers, circumstances may create a need or desire to work an alternative schedule. The Firm is committed to providing flexibility in its work arrangements, and recognizes that doing so will allow us to attract and retain top quality talent, committed to the profession, firm and our clients. Our alternative work schedules include employees working both part-time and flex-time schedules.

Alternative work schedule arrangements will not affect the basic eligibility of attorneys to be considered for partnership. However, attorneys who avail themselves of alternative work schedule arrangements may delay career progression and readiness for partnership status, since such arrangements may lengthen the time it takes to develop partner level lawyering skills, well-rounded legal experience and practice development/client relations ability and business, all of which are important to meeting the firm's criteria for election to partnership. The Firm's criteria for partnership will be applied to all attorneys uniformly regardless of any alternative work schedule arrangements.

Attorneys with an alternative work schedule will receive a salary that fairly reflects the attorney's contribution to the Firm. For example, if the attorney is on an alternative work schedule that is 70% of the minimum billable hour expectation, he/she will be compensated at 70% of the full-time salary. Compensation will be reviewed at the same time and based on the same criteria as a full-time attorney. Alternative work status attorneys are eligible for participation in the Firm's Incentive Bonus Program in accordance with the terms of the program.

5. Do you offer a sabbatical or leave-of-absence program? How many associates take advantage of this option on an annual basis?

Yes, the Firm offers an unpaid leave of absence to eligible attorneys. The firm recognizes that circumstances may arise in an attorney's career that may require an unpaid leave of absence beyond a period of paid disability or, accrued vacation and/or outside the scope of the Nixon Peabody's Parental Leave Policy for Counsel and Associates. An attorney will be eligible for an unpaid leave of absence if the attorney has completed at least one year of practice with the firm and has received evaluations reflecting very good performance. During a leave of absence, the firm will continue to provide the same level of contribution to medical coverage and life insurance. Vacation time will continue to accrue during the leave of absence.

On average, the firm has up 3-5 associates per year take advantage of the unpaid leave of absence. The majority of them do so for child care reasons.

Visit the Vault Law Channel, the complete online resource for law careers, featuring firm profiles, message boards, the Vault Law Job Board, and more. **www.vault.com/law**

VAULT CAREER LIBRARY   787

O'Melveny & Myers LLP

1. What is your firm policy on maternity leave? Paternity leave?

Our women lawyers can take up to 12 weeks paid maternity leave and men receive four weeks paid paternity leave. This leave applies to adoptive parents as well and to LGBT parents.

2. Do you offer any distinctive family-friendly options, such as adoption assistance or child care? Do you offer domestic partner benefits?

Yes, our family care policies include adoptions, for both opposite- and same sex couples. Our FSA (Flexible Spending Accounts) plans provide for pre-tax child care expenses. We also offer emergency back-up child care available in each office (through Bright Horizons). We offer domestic partner benefits to all employees - lawyers and staff. We began offering domestic partner benefits in 1996.

3. What is your firm's vacation policy?

Our associates in California and Washington, D.C. receive three weeks; and our counsel in those offices receive four weeks.. Our associates and counsel in New York receive four weeks and the associates in our international offices receive 160 hour per year.

4. Do you have a flex-time policy?

In recognition of the need for some of its attorneys to work fewer hours to attend to responsibilities outside of work, and to create a flexible workplace to retain its lawyers, we provides a progressive reduced workload policy. Associates are eligible to make partner while on a reduced workload. Our 2007 New Partner class consisted of three such partners. The policy is not limited to women with child-rearing responsibilities, and in fact, men have been successful on a reduced workload for reasons unrelated to childcare. Lawyers on reduced workload are reviewed annually, in the same way their full-time counterparts are reviewed. We pay our lawyers on reduced workload directly proportionately to their hours worked, and if a lawyer works more than his/her reduced workload target, he/she will be compensated for those additional hours. Lawyers on reduced workload are also eligible for a bonus that is directly proportional to the bonus a full-time associate would earn.

5. Do you offer a sabbatical or leave-of-absence program? How many associates take advantage of this option on an annual basis?

We have a leave-of-absence (LOA) program that is offered on a case-by-case basis. The number of associates that take advantage of the LOA program varies from year to year, but, on average, we have approximately 10-15 associates on leave at any given time.

Orrick, Herrington & Sutcliffe LLP

1. What is your firm policy on maternity leave? Paternity leave?

12 weeks Paid maternity leave. 10 days Paid Paternity leave. We offer the following family-friendly options:

2. Do you offer any distinctive family-friendly options, such as adoption assistance or child care? Do you offer domestic partner benefits?

We offer the following family-friendly options:

© 2007 Vault Inc.

Domestic Partner benefits

Back-Up Child Care Program

12 weeks Paid Adoption Leave

3. What is your firm's vacation policy?

CA - 15 days in first three comp classes, 20 days for all others. Cap on accrual at 30 days.

Outside CA - 20 days. Roll over to next year through 8/31

4. Do you have a flex-time policy?

The Attorney Alternative Work Arrangement policy would apply

5. Do you offer a sabbatical or leave-of-absence program? How many associates take advantage of this option on an annual basis?

Personal leaves-of-absence are handled on an ad hoc basis (i.e. no set policy). The associate must be in good standing to be considered. An average of about 5 associates take a personal leave a year.

Paul, Hastings, Janofsky & Walker LLP

1. What is your firm policy on maternity leave? Paternity leave?

Maternity Leave

Paul Hastings provides female associates on maternity leave up to six weeks (8 weeks for cesarean delivery) of disability pay, effective starting the birth date of the baby. This paid leave is supplemental to the short-term disability program.

Paternity Leave

Up to 10 regular work days for the birth or adoption of a child, for an employee who is not a primary caregiver.

2. Do you offer any distinctive family-friendly options, such as adoption assistance or child care? Do you offer domestic partner benefits?

Yes, Paul Hastings offers a special paid birth-bonding leave of up to eight weeks to Benefit-Eligible attorneys, who have a new-born or newly-adopted child and who have primary childcare responsibility, and up to ten regular workdays for the birth or adoption of a child to a Benefit-Eligible attorney, who is not the primary caregiver.

Paul Hastings also supplements the paid leave benefits of Benefit-Eligible female attorneys receive while they are receiving Firm-provided short-term disability benefits due to maternity to bring them up to full base pay. This supplement will extend for up to 6 weeks following the date of birth (8 weeks in the case of a cesarean delivery). This supplement will not be charged against any paid leave days.

Additionally, Paul Hastings offers back-up child care.

Yes, Paul Hastings offers domestic partner benefits.

Visit the Vault Law Channel, the complete online resource for law careers, featuring firm profiles, message boards, the Vault Law Job Board, and more. **www.vault.com/law**

VAULT CAREER LIBRARY   789

3. What is your firm's vacation policy?

Associates may take as much time off from work on regular business days as he or she wishes, with full pay, no effect on benefit plan participation, and no other adverse consequences. Time off may be taken for any reason, including vacation or other personal reasons, subject to the associate meeting his or her client obligations and those to the Firm/office/department/colleagues.

4. Do you have a flex-time policy?

Yes, Paul Hastings' policy establishes two categories of regular reduced/part-time schedules for associates, short-term status (3 - 6 months) and indefinite-term status.

5. Do you offer a sabbatical or leave-of-absence program? How many associates take advantage of this option on an annual basis?

Sabbatical

We do not have a sabbatical leave. Associate would request a personal leave.

Personal Leave

The Firm may grant an unpaid personal leave of absence for up to 60 days with proper approval where there are compelling reasons and no undue hardship to other employees or the Firm.

Charitable Involvement

Associates may take up to 5 days of paid leave, consecutively or incrementally, during a calendar year. Leave is not available for any event or activity for which the associate will receive remuneration of any kind from the charity or any other source. Application for leave will be approve at the Firm's discretion based on consideration including but not limited to business needs.

Paul, Weiss, Rifkind, Wharton & Garrison LLP

1. What is your firm policy on maternity leave? Paternity leave?

In the case of maternity, four weeks of paid parental leave is provided by the firm following short term disability due to pregnancy. In the event that the short term disability period following the delivery of a child is less than 8 weeks, the parental leave period will be extended so that the total time paid for disability due to pregnancy and for parental leave totals not less than 12 weeks.

All non-birth parents are eligible for a paid leave of up to four weeks, which includes the day of and any days taken immediately following the birth of the child, provided that the leave is taken within six months after the birth of the child, or the arrival in the attorney's home of the child who has been adopted. The four week period need not be consecutive, but all requests for split leaves are subject to departmental approval. Approval of paid parental leaves in excess of one per calendar year will be made on a case-by-case basis.

2. Do you offer any distinctive family-friendly options, such as adoption assistance or child care? Do you offer domestic partner benefits?

Yes. For new parents, we have an Infant Transition Program. Full-time child care is available at a Bright Horizons child care center blocks from our New York office without charge to the attorney for three months after return from parental leave. We also have back up emergency child care available for children up to 13 years old at Bright Horizons. In addition, through an arrangement with Caregivers on Call, we offer 24 hour, 7 day a week child care or elder care services at the attorney's home in the case of an emergency. We offer domestic partner benefits.

© 2007 Vault Inc.

3. What is your firm's vacation policy?

Associates are entitled to 20 days of vacation per year. In addition, associates may request an additional two weeks of unpaid time each year.

4. Do you have a flex-time policy?

Yes. Our flex-time policy (which we call an Alternative Work Schedule Program) is available to all associates. We do not require any length of service in order to qualify and no maximum time attorneys may remain on the program. Attorneys may request an alternative work schedule without stating a reason for their request - in other words, it is not limited to child care or family reasons. We have no requirement about how attorneys must structure their schedule... they can work fewer days per week, fewer weeks per month, or on a transaction by transaction basis. Finally each department has a partner who is the alternative work coordinator who is responsible for making sure that the schedule is working and that the associate continues to receive challenging and developmentally appropriate work assignments.

5. Do you offer a sabbatical or leave-of-absence program? How many associates take advantage of this option on an annual basis?

We have a flexible policy and allow leaves of absence on a case-by-case basis. In 2006, 11 associates took a non-parental leave of absence; in 2005, 9 associates did.

Patton Boggs LLP

1. What is your firm policy on maternity leave? Paternity leave?

The Firm recognizes that employees may desire or require an extended period of time off from work in connection with the birth of a child; adoption; or placement of a child for foster care. The Firm provides eligible attorneys 12 weeks of paid leave for primary care provider leave (previously "maternity leave") and 2 weeks paid leave for secondary provider leave (previously "paternity leave.") Associate attorneys are eligible to take additional paid leave through utilizing accrued Paid Time Off.

2. Do you offer any distinctive family-friendly options, such as adoption assistance or child care? Do you offer domestic partner benefits?

The Firm offers distinctive family-friendly options which include: Alternative Work Schedule Policy. This policy allows attorneys (at all levels throughout the firm) the opportunity to design their own flexible, individual, less than full-time work schedule. Two Billable Hour Tiers. The firm allows eligible attorneys to select from two different billable hour tiers. Domestic Partner Benefits. The firm offers domestic partner benefits for all benefit programs. Child Care. The firm offers emergency child care at some locations

3. What is your firm's vacation policy?

The Firm provides Paid Time Off (PTO) to allow eligible attorneys time away from work without the loss of compensation. PTO provides flexibility to use time off to meet personal needs, while also having individual responsibility to manage time away from work. Eligible attorneys accrue PTO at the rate of 30 workdays per year. The PTO balance is carried over from year to year. Attorneys may use accrued PTO to supplement the firm's paid leave policies, including for birth, adoption or placement for foster care.

Visit the Vault Law Channel, the complete online resource for law careers, featuring firm profiles, message boards, the Vault Law Job Board, and more. **www.vault.com/law**

VAULT CAREER LIBRARY   **791**

4. Do you have a flex-time policy?

The Firm has an Alternative Work Schedule Policy. This policy recognizes that attorneys may wish to work part-time or on an alternative work schedule basis, in order to balance family, personal responsibilities, and interests outside of the Firm with the demands of a professional career. This policy reflects the Firm's support for such arrangements. The policy is very adaptable to each attorney's situation or request and allows for individually-designed schedules, which include part-time, flex-time and other non-traditional work schedules or arrangements.

5. Do you offer a sabbatical or leave-of-absence program? How many associates take advantage of this option on an annual basis?

The Firm has a leave of absence program. Attorneys have used this program to take a leave of absence for many reasons, both personal and professional. Attorneys have taken leaves of absence to pursue volunteer opportunities, judicial clerkships, political campaign work, and pursuit of other professional and personal endeavors (i.e. authoring a book, travel, etc.). In the past year, 4% of associates have taken advantage of this option.

Powell Goldstein LLP

1. What is your firm policy on maternity leave? Paternity leave?

The Firm has maternity and parental leave policies. Our maternity policy allows for up to 3 months paid leave. An additional 3 months of unpaid leave can be taken with approval of the practice group leader. A total of 6 weeks parental leave is available for male attorneys within the first 3 months after the birth or adoption of a baby.

2. Do you offer any distinctive family-friendly options, such as adoption assistance or child care? Do you offer domestic partner benefits?

In the event of adoption, the primary care giver is eligible for up to 3 months paid leave. The Firm offers domestic partner benefits.

3. What is your firm's vacation policy?

The Firm does not closely monitor vacation time. Subject to client demands, each associate is strongly encouraged to take the full amount of vacation provided each year.

4. Do you have a flex-time policy?

Yes. The Firm strives to offer flexible working arrangements, to the extent possible, to those attorneys seeking to strike a more manageable balance between their personal and work commitments.

5. Do you offer a sabbatical or leave-of-absence program? How many associates take advantage of this option on an annual basis?

Yes. The Firm recognizes that associates sometimes have situations and/or responsibilities that will affect their work arrangements. Requests for a leave-of-absence or sabbatical are considered in light of the business needs of the Firms, its clients, and the attorney's individual practice group.

© 2007 Vault Inc.

Proskauer Rose LLP

1. What is your firm policy on maternity leave? Paternity leave?

Lawyers are eligible for up to eight weeks of paid leave for disability due to pregnancy, provided that they have been employed by the Firm for one year or more when the leave begins. In addition, lawyers who are primary care givers are eligible for up to eight weeks of child care leave at full pay following the birth or adoption of a child, while lawyers who are not primary caregivers may take up to two weeks of paid child care leave. Lawyers also may take any available vacation days and request additional unpaid leave following the birth or adoption of a child.

2. Do you offer any distinctive family-friendly options, such as adoption assistance or child care? Do you offer domestic partner benefits?

The Firm offers $5000 in adoption assistance, back-up child-care options, and domestic partner health benefits.

3. What is your firm's vacation policy?

Lawyers receive four weeks of vacation per calendar year, accrued at the rate of 1.66 days per month of service.

4. Do you have a flex-time policy?

The Firm provides flex-time/alternative work schedule options to its lawyers.

5. Do you offer a sabbatical or leave-of-absence program? How many associates take advantage of this option on an annual basis?

On a case-by-case basis.

Quarles & Brady LLP

1. What is your firm policy on maternity leave? Paternity leave?

Twelve weeks paid for maternity leave for mothers, six weeks parental leave for fathers, both which can be extended with use of vacation time. Associates can also take an additional 26 weeks off unpaid or work a reduce schedule for up to a year while still receiving FT benefits.

2. Do you offer any distinctive family-friendly options, such as adoption assistance or child care? Do you offer domestic partner benefits?

We offer domestic partner benefits, both same sex and opposite sex. Employee Assistance Program is available to the entire family and includes numerous work-life benefits including child care and elder care information and referral services, adoption information, financial consultation and traditional counseling. New parents receive a New Parent Packet which includes a gift and information about family benefits, dependent care and saving for college. Most offices have a "quiet room" for breastfeeding mothers. Our Phoenix office has an onsite backup childcare center.

3. What is your firm's vacation policy?

Three weeks.

Visit the Vault Law Channel, the complete online resource for law careers, featuring firm profiles, message boards, the Vault Law Job Board, and more. www.vault.com/law

VAULT CAREER LIBRARY

793

4. Do you have a flex-time policy?

Yes, the policy allows associates to work a reduce schedule for a proportionate salary. In addition full-time associates can set their own schedule so long as it works for clients and the practice group.

5. Do you offer a sabbatical or leave-of-absence program? How many associates take advantage of this option on an annual basis?

Leave of absences are typically tied to FMLA qualifying events and can be taken intermittently or as a block of time or as a temporary reduced schedule. Approximately 40 associates took leave in the last 12 months.

Quinn Emanuel Urquhart Oliver & Hedges, LLP

1. What is your firm policy on maternity leave? Paternity leave?

Maternity Leave: Four months.

Paternity Leave: Three days paid leave.

2. Do you offer any distinctive family-friendly options, such as adoption assistance or child care? Do you offer domestic partner benefits?

We offer domestic partner benefits. We have no formal programs regarding adoption assistance or child care.

3. What is your firm's vacation policy?

Three weeks per year.

4. Do you have a flex-time policy?

The firm does not have a set flex time schedule, but has been open to creating flexible work schedules when circumstances warranted doing so.

5. Do you offer a sabbatical or leave-of-absence program? How many associates take advantage of this option on an annual basis?

Sabbaticals and leaves-of-absence are allowed on a case-by-case basis. Numbers fluctuate each year. Both partners and associates have made use of these opportunities.

Reed Smith

1. What is your firm policy on maternity leave? Paternity leave?

[Soon to come]

© 2007 Vault Inc.

2. Do you offer any distinctive family-friendly options, such as adoption assistance or child care? Do you offer domestic partner benefits?

Reed Smith provides domestic partner benefits and has partnered with (and subsidizes the cost of) an off-site back-up daycare to provide daycare services for children at an affordable price.

3. What is your firm's vacation policy?

Reed Smith provides three weeks of paid annual vacation for full time Associates who are out of law school three years or less and four weeks of paid annual vacation thereafter.

4. Do you have a flex-time policy?

Reed Smith supports professional work/life balance through a variety of means, amongst them the following (but not limited to):

• Allowance of part-time and other alternative work schedules.

• Flexible leave of absence policies covering such matters as childbirth, care for sick family members, etc.

• Maintaining performance evaluation and compensation programs that incorporate the principle of proportionality of expectations, results and rewards, and administering the programs in a manner that assures that professionals working alternative work schedules are treated equitably;

• Providing or making available reasonable ancillary services (e.g., Employee Assistance Program, alternate child care referrals) that may assist with work/life balance.

5. Do you offer a sabbatical or leave-of-absence program? How many associates take advantage of this option on an annual basis?

Reed Smith does not have a sabbatical program.

Robins, Kaplan, Miller & Ciresi LLP

1. What is your firm policy on maternity leave? Paternity leave?

Our parental leave policy allows for 6 to 8 weeks paid disability leave as determined by a doctor for the birth mother. In addition, we offer 6 weeks paid parental leave that is available to either the mother or father upon the birth or adoption of a child. Personal leaves of up to 6 months are also available.

2. Do you offer any distinctive family-friendly options, such as adoption assistance or child care? Do you offer domestic partner benefits?

We offer sick child care where available. We also offer domestic partner benefits for medical, dental, and dependent life insurance. Domestic Partners are treated the same as a spouse under the policy.

3. What is your firm's vacation policy?

Attorneys are eligible to take up to three weeks of vacation per year.

4. Do you have a flex-time policy?

Requests for flex-time are handled on a case by case basis.

Visit the Vault Law Channel, the complete online resource for law careers, featuring firm profiles, message boards, the Vault Law Job Board, and more. www.vault.com/law

 795

5. Do you offer a sabbatical or leave-of-absence program? How many associates take advantage of this option on an annual basis?

Requests for sabbaticals or personal leaves of absence are handled on a case - by - case basis. In 2006, 22 associates were granted some form of leave.

Ropes & Gray LLP

1. What is your firm policy on maternity leave? Paternity leave?

Eleven weeks paid maternity leave, plus two weeks paid and 13 weeks unpaid child care leave for women. Two weeks paid plus 13 weeks unpaid child care leave for men.

2. Do you offer any distinctive family-friendly options, such as adoption assistance or child care? Do you offer domestic partner benefits?

Yes. Emergency day care; reduced-time schedules, maternity leave, child care leave, family care leave (which include adoptions); dependent care reimbursement accounts, and four tier medical, dental and vision coverage (individual + child(ren) coverage is available). Child care referral services are available through the firm's Employee Assistance Plan program.

Yes. Same and opposite gender domestic partners are eligible for insurance coverages.

3. What is your firm's vacation policy?

Associates earn 4 weeks of vacation (20 business days), and receive 11 holidays each calendar year. Up to 2 weeks of unused vacation may be carried over into the following year to be used in the first quarter of the year. Sick and personal days are available as needed.

4. Do you have a flex-time policy?

Yes. After 2 years of employment at the firm, associates (male or female) are able to work on a reduced-time schedule (either 60% or 80%) that is mutually agreeable to the associate and the firm.

5. Do you offer a sabbatical or leave-of-absence program? How many associates take advantage of this option on an annual basis?

Yes. The firm may grant personal leave to associates for compelling personal reasons for which parental, medical, or family care leave is not available. Personal leave is normally not granted for more than 26 weeks and will be paid or unpaid, in whole or in part, at the discretion of the firm.

Schiff Hardin LLP

1. What is your firm policy on maternity leave? Paternity leave?

The firm offers female attorneys 12 weeks of maternity leave and male attorneys 2 weeks of parental leave.

© 2007 Vault Inc.

2. Do you offer any distinctive family-friendly options, such as adoption assistance or child care? Do you offer domestic partner benefits?

In the case of adoption, the primary caretaker is allowed 4 weeks of leave. Attorneys may use their personal sick time for the care of children. Yes, domestic partner insurance has been an offering of our Firm for over ten years.

3. What is your firm's vacation policy?

Attorneys out of law school four years or less accrue three weeks of vacation per year. Attorneys out of law school more than four years accrue four weeks of vacation per year.

4. Do you have a flex-time policy?

We offer various part-time options.

5. Do you offer a sabbatical or leave-of-absence program? How many associates take advantage of this option on an annual basis?

We do not have sabbaticals nor do we offer paid leaves-of-absence other than medical and parental.

Schulte Roth & Zabel LLP

1. What is your firm policy on maternity leave? Paternity leave?

Eligible attorneys who are primary caregivers may take up to 12 weeks of paid and 12 weeks of unpaid leave upon the birth or adoption of a child. Eligible attorneys who are not primary caregivers may take 1 week of paid leave upon the birth or adoption of a child.

2. Do you offer any distinctive family-friendly options, such as adoption assistance or child care? Do you offer domestic partner benefits?

We do offer domestic partner benefits. We have emergency back-up child care available through an off-site program, Bright Horizons.

3. What is your firm's vacation policy?

Attorneys get 20 days of vacation each year. Ten of those days may be carried over automatically from one year to the next.

4. Do you have a flex-time policy?

We have people working on alternative schedules but we do not have a formal flex time policy at the present time.

5. Do you offer a sabbatical or leave-of-absence program? How many associates take advantage of this option on an annual basis?

Attorneys are eligible for a 4-week sabbatical after spending at least 5 years at the firm on a full-time schedule.

Visit the Vault Law Channel, the complete online resource for law careers, featuring firm profiles, message boards, the Vault Law Job Board, and more. www.vault.com/law

VAULT CAREER LIBRARY   797

Seyfarth Shaw LLP

1. What is your firm policy on maternity leave? Paternity leave?

Seyfarth Shaw is pleased to offer a paid maternity leave period of a total of 12 weeks, including any period of medical disability, to all female attorneys. A paid parenting leave period of 4 weeks will be available to all non-childbearing and adoptive parents. In addition to paid parenting leave, non-childbearing and adoptive parents may take an additional 8 weeks of unpaid child care leave. All employee benefits for which the attorney is otherwise eligible shall be maintained during parenting leaves of up to 6 months.

2. Do you offer any distinctive family-friendly options, such as adoption assistance or child care? Do you offer domestic partner benefits?

The Firm offers flexible spending accounts to assist with medical and dependent care expenses. The Firm offers domestic partner health benefits.

3. What is your firm's vacation policy?

Seyfarth offers varying amounts of vacation time, as determined by locale.

4. Do you have a flex-time policy?

We recognize the need for flexibility in the manner in which careers develop. Our alternate work arrangement provides that Associates are eligible for partnership track as long as they meet the partnership standards.

5. Do you offer a sabbatical or leave-of-absence program? How many associates take advantage of this option on an annual basis?

In addition to paid parenting leaves, the Firm offers unpaid child-care leaves, as well as leaves of absence and personal leaves. At any given time, approximately 3 out of 280 Associates are on an extended leave (more than 4 months).

Sidley Austin LLP

1. What is your firm policy on maternity leave? Paternity leave?

The Firm effectively provides associates with 12 weeks paid maternity leave and 4 weeks paid paternity leave. Additionally, if desired, unpaid leave and reduced work schedules are available.

2. Do you offer any distinctive family-friendly options, such as adoption assistance or child care? Do you offer domestic partner benefits?

The Firm offers 8 weeks paid adoption leave for a primary care-giver and 4 weeks paid adoption leave for non-primary caregiver. Additionally, if desired, unpaid leave and reduced work schedules are available. The firm also offers emergency back-up childcare through Bright Horizons. We offer benefits to same-sex domestic partners.

3. What is your firm's vacation policy?

The Firm offers associates 4 weeks paid vacation annually

© 2007 Vault Inc.

4. Do you have a flex-time policy?

Subject upon the needs of our lawyers and groups, our lawyers are treated as professionals and have flexibility in setting their schedule. Additionally, reduced work schedules are available.

5. Do you offer a sabbatical or leave-of-absence program? How many associates take advantage of this option on an annual basis?

The Firm does not offer a sabbatical program to its associates.

Simpson Thacher & Bartlett LLP

1. What is your firm policy on maternity leave? Paternity leave?

The firm provides a three-month paid maternity leave to women attorneys for the birth or adoption of a child, and makes available a three-month unpaid leave of absence immediately following the paid maternity leave period. The Firm also offers male attorneys a four-week paid paternity leave after the birth or adoption of a child, with the option of a three-month unpaid leave immediately thereafter.

2. Do you offer any distinctive family-friendly options, such as adoption assistance or child care? Do you offer domestic partner benefits?

The Firm offers access to a national network of high quality back-up care options for both children and elderly family members for all employees in its U.S. offices through Bright Horizons. The Firm maintains a lactation room for new mothers in each of its domestic offices to facilitate their transition back to work. The Firm's subsidized health and dental insurance includes spouses, same-sex domestic partners and children. The Firm offers employees dependent care pre-tax spending accounts.

3. What is your firm's vacation policy?

The firm provides full-time lawyers with four weeks of vacation time each calendar year. Part-time lawyers accrue vacation time on a pro-rated basis.

4. Do you have a flex-time policy?

The Firm recently adopted a revised flexible work arrangements policy which offers an expanded range of flexible work arrangements, including telecommuting, job sharing, and a program under which an attorney can work a 60% to 80% schedule. Currently, 33 attorneys participate in our flexible work arrangements program (27 of them work a reduced hours schedule).

5. Do you offer a sabbatical or leave-of-absence program? How many associates take advantage of this option on an annual basis?

Individual attorneys may request a leave of absence which must be approved by the appropriate assigning partner and the Chairs of the Personnel Committee. The number of attorneys who take a personal leave of absence varies from year to year.

Visit the Vault Law Channel, the complete online resource for law careers, featuring firm profiles, message boards, the Vault Law Job Board, and more. **www.vault.com/law**

VAULT CAREER LIBRARY   799

Skadden, Arps, Slates, Meagher & Flom LLP and Affiliates

1. What is your firm policy on maternity leave? Paternity leave?

Skadden's policy regarding maternity leave is a combination of several other policies, including disability leave, paid parental leave, paid vacation leave, and unpaid leave of absence. Although each pregnancy is unique, for a typical pregnancy an attorney generally receives 8 weeks of paid disability leave, followed by four weeks of paid parental leave. The attorney may then take any accrued vacation time to increase her paid time out of the office. In addition, the attorney may request an unpaid leave of absence of up to 6 months. Our parental leave policies are gender neutral and thus an attorney who is the non-primary caregiver for a child may take up to two weeks of paid leave, and an attorney who is the primary caregiver of the child may take a total of four weeks of parental leave. In addition, the attorney may request an upaid leave of absence of up to 6 months.

2. Do you offer any distinctive family-friendly options, such as adoption assistance or child care? Do you offer domestic partner benefits?

The firm offers emergency backup childcare through a membership with Bright Horizons. Firm personnel may choose between center-based care or in-home care when their regular care arrangements fail. In-home emergency eldercare is also available through Bright Horizons. Additionally, for attorneys returning from maternity leave, Skadden's NY office offers an Infant Transition program. This program allows the returning attorney mother to bring her infant to the Bright Horizon center located in our building for up to 3 months, with the goal of easing the transition back to work. In a further effort to ease the transition back to work, Skadden offers FRM (Flexible Return from Maternity). This program offers attorneys returning from maternity leave the flexibility of designing their own return schedule - either reduced hours or a combination of home and office days - during a defined period of time, not to exceed one year. Although the program is primarily designed to make it more feasible for women to return to work after the birth or adoption of a child, it may also be made available to men under appropriate circumstances. Same and opposite sex domestic partners are eligible for the same medical and dental benefits as those available to spouses of employees.

3. What is your firm's vacation policy?

Full-time associates earn 20 days of vacation each year. All attorneys are encouraged to take their accrued vacation each year, but are able to carry unused time to a maximum of 30 days.

4. Do you have a flex-time policy?

The firm has no formal flex-time policy, however Skadden attorneys have the flexibility to work outside the office when necessary. Through the firm's $3000 technology allowance, Skadden attorneys are provided with the resources to work remotely.

5. Do you offer a sabbatical or leave-of-absence program? How many associates take advantage of this option on an annual basis?

Leaves of absence of up to six months have long been available at Skadden. Recently, however, the firm implemented Sidebar, a program through which attorneys in good standing may take up to 3 years "off" from the firm with the expectation that they will return to Skadden at the end of that period, consistent with the needs of the firm and the department. An attorney may choose this course of action for any number of personal reasons, particularly the desire to spend more time with a child or aging family member.

The program encourages participants to remain connected with the firm. A partner is assigned to each participant to maintain contact and extend invitations to departmental events and CLE programs. The firm pays for continuing legal education and bar registration as part of the Sidebar program. If the participant is interested, there may be opportunities for ad hoc assignments.

© 2007 Vault Inc.

Steptoe & Johnson LLP

1. What is your firm policy on maternity leave? Paternity leave?

Maternity is treated like any other disability and falls under short-term disability benefits. Typically, after 6 months of service and with appropriate documentation from a treating physician, they are eligible for 6-8 weeks of disability at full pay.

2. Do you offer any distinctive family-friendly options, such as adoption assistance or child care? Do you offer domestic partner benefits?

Firm offers: Emergency Child Care in most office locations, Parental Leave and FMLA for time off during adoption process, Domestic Partner benefits.

3. What is your firm's vacation policy?

N/A

4. Do you have a flex-time policy?

No formal policy but flexible work schedules can be arranged with advanced authorization.

5. Do you offer a sabbatical or leave-of-absence program? How many associates take advantage of this option on an annual basis?

N/A

Stoel Rives LLP

1. What is your firm policy on maternity leave? Paternity leave?

The Firm provides a benefit of up to eight weeks of paid parental leave (leave taken to care for a newborn child, newly adopted child, or newly placed foster child) for a lawyer who has been employed for a period of at least 12 months and has worked at least 1,250 hours in the period immediately preceding the leave. For eligible employees, this paid leave will run concurrently with the first eight weeks of FMLA parental leave. When the lawyer who is eligible for the Firm's paid leave benefit is also eligible under state law for partial disability pay, the Firm will pay the difference between the disability pay and the lawyer's usual salary for the eight-week period. Paid parental leave is only available when taken in a single, continuous period that is completed within the 12 week period following the birth, adoption, or placement. If the lawyer on paid parental leave does not return to work, the lawyer is required to reimburse the Firm for the salary paid during such leave. In addition to providing the above-described paid parental leave, the Firm may, at its discretion, choose to allow salary continuation for a lawyer during other types of leave.

2. Do you offer any distinctive family-friendly options, such as adoption assistance or child care? Do you offer domestic partner benefits?

The firm offers domestic partner benefits.

The firm's parental leave policy (see below) applies to leave taken to care for a newborn child, newly adopted child, or newly placed foster child:

Visit the Vault Law Channel, the complete online resource for law careers, featuring firm profiles, message boards, the Vault Law Job Board, and more. www.vault.com/law

VAULT CAREER LIBRARY   801

The Firm provides a benefit of up to eight weeks of paid parental leave (leave taken to care for a newborn child, newly adopted child, or newly placed foster child) for a lawyer who has been employed for a period of at least 12 months and has worked at least 1,250 hours in the period immediately preceding the leave. For eligible employees, this paid leave will run concurrently with the first eight weeks of FMLA parental leave. When the lawyer who is eligible for the Firm's paid leave benefit is also eligible under state law for partial disability pay, the Firm will pay the difference between the disability pay and the lawyer's usual salary for the eight-week period. Paid parental leave is only available when taken in a single, continuous period that is completed within the 12 week period following the birth, adoption, or placement. If the lawyer on paid parental leave does not return to work, the lawyer is required to reimburse the Firm for the salary paid during such leave. In addition to providing the above-described paid parental leave, the Firm may, at its discretion, choose to allow salary continuation for a lawyer during other types of leave.

3. What is your firm's vacation policy?

The vacation policy applies to nonpartner and nonprincipal lawyers, including associates, of counsel lawyers, and staff lawyers. Vacation policies for partners and principals are detailed in the Partners Manual. A lawyer may take three weeks' annual vacation during his or her first six years with the Firm and four weeks' annual vacation thereafter. The Firm encourages all lawyers to take their vacation time each year. However, a lawyer may accumulate up to a maximum of two years' vacation accruals. Use of more than one year's vacation accrual within a six-month period is not permitted without approval of the PGL. Once a lawyer in his or her first six years accumulates six weeks of vacation, and once a lawyer beyond six years of service accumulates eight weeks of vacation, the accrual of additional vacation ceases until the lawyer uses accrued vacation. Regular vacations should be scheduled well in advance with the PGL so that workloads can be organized efficiently and to ensure effective client service. Regular vacation accruals for lawyers in their first through sixth years is calculated at the rate of 1.25 days multiplied by the number of months worked, for a total of 15 days per year. Thereafter, regular vacation accruals are calculated at the rate of 1.67 days multiplied by the number of months worked, for a total of 20 days per year. Unless otherwise required by law, unused vacation time that has been accrued since January 1, 2007 is not paid out on termination of employment. For reduced-schedule lawyers, accrued vacation is prorated by the percentage of the reduced schedule.

4. Do you have a flex-time policy?

We do not have a policy on flex-time, but we have had associates working flex-time schedules and we do our best to accommodate individual needs as they arise.

5. Do you offer a sabbatical or leave-of-absence program? How many associates take advantage of this option on an annual basis?

The firm has a sabbatical program. Most associates become partner before they are eligible for the sabbatical.

Sullivan & Cromwell LLP

1. What is your firm policy on maternity leave? Paternity leave?

S&C provides lawyers who are primary caregivers up to 6 months leave (3 months paid, 3 months unpaid) upon the birth or adoption of a child. Additional unpaid leave time is handled case-by-case. Paternity/childcare leave is up to 4 weeks paid and any additional unpaid paternity/childcare leave is handled case-by-case.

© 2007 Vault Inc.

2. Do you offer any distinctive family-friendly options, such as adoption assistance or child care? Do you offer domestic partner benefits?

S&C provides its US lawyers adoption assistance, which includes reimbursement up to $5,000 of expenses related to the adoption of a child under the age of 18. Covered expenses include adoption agency fees (both public and private), court costs and legal fees, transportation costs and unreimbursed medical expenses for the natural mother. Also, as noted above, substantial leave time is available in connection with the adoption of a child. S&C provides on-site emergency backup child care. S&C was one of the first firms to provide same-sex domestic partner benefits.

3. What is your firm's vacation policy?

Lawyers are entitled to 4 weeks paid vacation.

4. Do you have a flex-time policy?

The greatest strength of our Firm is the quality of our lawyers. To help provide meaningful career opportunities and accomodate the varying needs of our lawyers, S&C offers various flex-time arrangements. Flex-time lawyers are supported by a partner Flex-time mentor. We currently have 14 associates and 1 partner working flex-time schedules. The Firm first promoted a flex-time attorney to partner in 2004.

5. Do you offer a sabbatical or leave-of-absence program? How many associates take advantage of this option on an annual basis?

We do not have a formal sabbatical program, however, the Firm provides leaves of absence on a case-by-case basis. Last year, 10 associates took leaves of absence.

Thelen Reid Brown Raysman & Steiner LLP

1. What is your firm policy on maternity leave? Paternity leave?

Maternity leave is 12 weeks of paid time off and integrated with state disability where applicable. Paternity leave is 1 week paid time off. Primary caregivers (in the case of adoption, for instance) also get 12 weeks paid.

2. Do you offer any distinctive family-friendly options, such as adoption assistance or child care? Do you offer domestic partner benefits?

The Employee Assistance Program through Concern offers a variety of work/life benefits including adoption assistance. Back-up childcare is available through Bright Horizons. The firm offers benefits to qualified same and opposite sex domestic partners.

3. What is your firm's vacation policy?

Associates get 4 weeks paid vacation a year.

4. Do you have a flex-time policy?

We do have a part-time policy, but no official flex-time policy. Flex-time is allowed, however, contingent upon Practice Chair approval and business need.

Visit the Vault Law Channel, the complete online resource for law careers, featuring firm profiles, message boards, the Vault Law Job Board, and more. www.vault.com/law

VAULT CAREER LIBRARY   803

5. Do you offer a sabbatical or leave-of-absence program? How many associates take advantage of this option on an annual basis?

The firm does not have an official sabbatical or leave-of-absence program (outside of disability and maternity/paternity). Leave requests of this nature are reviewed on a case by case basis.

Thompson Coburn LLP

1. What is your firm policy on maternity leave? Paternity leave?

We offer 12 weeks of paid disability, including maternity leave. While we do not have a formal paternity policy, our male associates can work with their practice area leader to arrange for time off as needed and as approved.

2. Do you offer any distinctive family-friendly options, such as adoption assistance or child care? Do you offer domestic partner benefits?

We have a firm sponsored back-up childcare program and we offer domestic partner benefits.

3. What is your firm's vacation policy?

All associates are eligible for 3 weeks of annual vacation.

4. Do you have a flex-time policy?

Our associates have the flexibility to work from home and flex their in-office hours as needed.

5. Do you offer a sabbatical or leave-of-absence program? How many associates take advantage of this option on an annual basis?

We currently do not offer such a program.

Thompson & Knight LLP

1. What is your firm policy on maternity leave? Paternity leave?

The paid portion of the leave for a female associate who gives birth is 12 weeks, inclusive of any period of disability of the associate in connection with the pregnancy or childbirth. The paid portion of the leave for an associate whose spouse gives birth is four weeks. The paid portion of the leave for an associate who adopts a child is four weeks.

The maximum period of paid leave under this policy in any 12-month period is 12 weeks.

2. Do you offer any distinctive family-friendly options, such as adoption assistance or child care? Do you offer domestic partner benefits?

The Firm is currently in the process of deciding on the most suitable backup child care plan for our attorneys.

Thompson & Knight has contracted with a child care referral specialist organization to provide child care referral services for employees within the DFW metroplex. This service may be utilized by any employee who is in need of advice or assistance in arranging for suitable child care, for methods to use in evaluating child care quality, for determining competitive child care costs, and for answers or information concerning a variety of other issues regarding child care. The referral services and information are provided free of charge to the employee.

© 2007 Vault Inc.

The Firm also offers a Dependent Care Spending Account that allows eligible employees to set aside a designated amount from each paycheck on a pre-tax basis (maximum $5,000 annually) to reimburse themselves for the cost of dependent care.

Lastly, our parental leave policy covers children/dependents of domestic partners.

3. What is your firm's vacation policy?

Attorneys have no set number of vacation days or weeks.

4. Do you have a flex-time policy?

Yes. Thompson & Knight recognizes that some of our attorneys require flexibility in work schedules because of family or other personal needs. The Firm supports the efforts of its associates to balance personal and professional demands by providing flexible work arrangements. An associate will be eligible to request a flexible work schedule if the associate (1) has been employed by the Firm on a full-time basis for at least two consecutive years, exclusive of any leave, (2) received a meets expectations overall ranking on the last performance evaluation, and (3) the practice group can accommodate a reduced-hours schedule. A requesting associate has reasonable latitude in proposing a schedule that meets their needs and the Firm's needs. If the reduced hours commitment remains at least 75% of a full-time associate's minimum creditable hours, the associate's annual salary and bonus will be adjusted in proportion to the reduced commitment for annual creditable hours and the associate will receive proportionate credit for advancement toward partnership. If the reduced hours commitment is less than 75% of a full-time associate's minimum creditable hours, the associate's salary will be reduced more than proportionately.

5. Do you offer a sabbatical or leave-of-absence program? How many associates take advantage of this option on an annual basis?

A personal leave is an unpaid leave granted at the discretion of management during a given year. Leave may be granted for the following reasons:

• educational and developmental opportunities;

• exceptional personal circumstances;

• government or public office service; and

• other reasons deemed appropriate by the Firm.

On average, one associate each year takes advantage of this option.

Venable LLP

1. What is your firm policy on maternity leave? Paternity leave?

Venable calls this 'parent leave' and it is provided to new mothers and fathers. Parent leave provides paid leave for up to four weeks for lawyers who wish to take time off after the birth or adoption of a child.

2. Do you offer any distinctive family-friendly options, such as adoption assistance or child care? Do you offer domestic partner benefits?

Yes, Venable provides same-sex domestic partner benefits. Other family-friendly and work-life options include emergency back-up child care, long term care insurance options, personal health advocate services, an employee assistance program, and an on-site exercise facility.

Visit the Vault Law Channel, the complete online resource for law careers, featuring firm profiles, message boards, the Vault Law Job Board, and more. **www.vault.com/law**

VAULT CAREER LIBRARY   805

3. What is your firm's vacation policy?

New associates receive three weeks of vacation per year. Once an associate has been a member of any bar for three years, and with Venable for a year, the firm grants four weeks of vacation.

4. Do you have a flex-time policy?

For many years, the firm has honored requests from lawyers who seek to work a reduced schedule. A lawyer's personal decision to request a reduced schedule is unique, and the firm treats it as such - individually. Decisions to create a reduced schedule are based primarily on the department's ability to meet its clients' needs, among other factors. Compensation is reduced commensurately from what the lawyer would earn at a full-time level, and health care and other benefits remain available, as does eligibility to receive a year-end bonus.

5. Do you offer a sabbatical or leave-of-absence program? How many associates take advantage of this option on an annual basis?

Venable does not offer a sabbatical program. Occasionally, a lawyer may request a leave of absence for a variety of reasons. Each of these requests is reviewed individually.

White & Case LLP

1. What is your firm policy on maternity leave? Paternity leave?

Maternity/disability leave - from 12 to 26 weeks paid in full for maternity leave (depending on the Associates' length of service as well as pre and post natal medical condition). All Associates in NY, Washington DC, Florida, and Palo Alto Câlif. who have been with the firm for over 1 year, are eligible for 4 weeks of paid parental leave for the birth of a newborn or newly-adopted child.

2. Do you offer any distinctive family-friendly options, such as adoption assistance or child care? Do you offer domestic partner benefits?

Paid Adoption Leave (in the form of Paid Parental Leave - see above), Designated private pumping room for nursing mothers (New York, Palo Alto), Firm subsidized emergency back-up center-based and at home well/sick childcare, Firm subsidized back-up home-based elder care, pre-tax Dependent Care Reimbursement accounts, domestic (same and opposite sex) partner benefits

3. What is your firm's vacation policy?

North America - 4 weeks

4. Do you have a flex-time policy?

Yes. The Flexible Work Arrangement Program allows lawyers in the US offices to develop individualized work schedules on a gender and reason neutral basis. The program enables an attorney to shape and customize an appropriate work schedule, regardless of why they desire the alternative arrangement. In the London office, the Flexible Working Policy aims to have a formal process by which all London office employees may request a permanent change to their working pattern. Both programs formalize the implementation and evaluation process, providing clear guidelines for requesting an alternative work arrangement and ensuring a fair and consistent approach to the review and consideration of requests for flexible work arrangements.

© 2007 Vault Inc.

5. Do you offer a sabbatical or leave-of-absence program? How many associates take advantage of this option on an annual basis?

A sub-committee of associates in the New York office revised the New York Office Leave of Absence policy in late 2006. The revised policy permits an associate to request a leave of absence for personal or professional reasons for up to 6 months (may be extended). Associates who have been employed by the firm for 1 year and are in good standing are eligible to apply for a LOA. Associates continue to have email access during their LOA (access to other firm resources are determined on a case by case basis) and are assigned a LOA mentor.

Wiley Rein LLP

1. What is your firm policy on maternity leave? Paternity leave?

Maternity Leave: Following childbirth, Associates and Of Counsel are entitled to receive up to 10 weeks of paid Short Term Disability leave depending on tenure with the Firm. In addition, Associates and Of Counsel are entitled to two weeks paid child care leave upon the birth or adoption of a child. Associates and Of Counsel are eligible for 6 weeks of paid adoption leave if they are the child's primary caregiver. Under the DC Family and Medical Leave Act (FMLA), Associates and Of Counsel may take unpaid leave for a total of 16 weeks following the birth of a newborn child or a newly adopted child.

Paternity Leave: Associates and Of Counsel are entitled to two weeks paid child care leave upon the birth or adoption of a child.

2. Do you offer any distinctive family-friendly options, such as adoption assistance or child care? Do you offer domestic partner benefits?

We provide Emergency Back-up dependent care through Work Options Group both at day care centers and in-home. Associates receive 120 hours of backup care per year. We also provide benefits to domestic partners.

3. What is your firm's vacation policy?

Associates receive 20 days of vacation per year.

4. Do you have a flex-time policy?

The firm has associates, of counsel and partners who work on reduced time schedules. These arrangements are approved on a case by case basis by the firm's administrative committee.

5. Do you offer a sabbatical or leave-of-absence program? How many associates take advantage of this option on an annual basis?

The firm will consider extended personal leave for attorneys and consultants in compelling personal circumstances. We do not report any usage figures on this type of leave.

Williams & Connolly LLP

1. What is your firm policy on maternity leave? Paternity leave?

The firm offers three months of paid maternity leave. In addition, the firm liberally grants additional uncompensated leave beyond the initial three months, up to one year. Most frequently, associates have elected to extend their time off up to approximately six months. Maternity leave is also granted, on the same terms, upon the adoption of a child. The firm does not

Visit the Vault Law Channel, the complete online resource for law careers, featuring firm profiles, message boards, the Vault Law Job Board, and more. www.vault.com/law

VAULT CAREER LIBRARY   807

have a formal paternity leave policy. However, as discussed below, the firm has an unlimited vacation policy for associates, and male associates have taken extended vacation time after the birth of a child.

2. Do you offer any distinctive family-friendly options, such as adoption assistance or child care? Do you offer domestic partner benefits?

The firm has a number of policies and benefits that support our associates in pursuing their careers and enjoying and managing their family life. The firm has a part-time program that allows associates to work a 60% or 80% schedule, rather than a full time schedule. Associates receive credit for their part-time work, on the same pro-rata basis, toward the credited time necessary before consideration for partnership. The firm also has Employee Assistance Programs that offer support services to all employees in a wide range of areas, including adoption and elder care. The firm also offers health insurance benefits to domestic partners.

3. What is your firm's vacation policy?

Under the firm's policy, there is no set amount of paid vacation time for attorneys. As professionals, the firms expects attorneys to plan vacation time consistent with their obligations to their clients, their families, themselves, and the firm. With these varying factors, the firm anticipates that the amount of vacation an attorney will take will vary from year to year, but attorneys are encouraged to take four or more weeks of paid vacation a year.

4. Do you have a flex-time policy?

As discussed above, the firm has a part-time program for associates, which affords a great deal of flexibility. There are no set work hours for associates; accordingly, there is no "flex-time" policy. All associates are afforded substantial flexibility and independence, as professionals at the firm, to manage their day-to-day schedules.

5. Do you offer a sabbatical or leave-of-absence program? How many associates take advantage of this option on an annual basis?

The firm does not have a formal sabbatical or leave of absence program. Requests are considered on a case-by-case basis. Such requests have been granted, for example, to allow absences of up to one year for personal travel, political activity, and teaching. In addition, as noted above, the firm liberally extends maternity leave with an additional leave of absence.

Willkie Farr & Gallagher LLP

1. What is your firm policy on maternity leave? Paternity leave?

The parental leave policy of the Firm is divided into three leave periods: (1) disability leave, (2) paid child care leave, and (3) unpaid child care leave. Both of the child care leave portions of this policy (i.e., (2) and (3)) may be taken upon the birth or adoption of a child and are incremental to the period of disability leave associated with childbirth. These portions of the policy relate to the time necessary to adjust to the demands of a new child in the home and, therefore, are offered to both male and female associates in the Firm. Willkie offers 13 weeks of paid maternity leave and 6 months of unpaid leave in connection with the birth or adoption of a child. Willkie offers 4 weeks of paid paternity leave in connection with the birth or adoption of a child which can be taken up to 6 months after the birth or adoption.

2. Do you offer any distinctive family-friendly options, such as adoption assistance or child care? Do you offer domestic partner benefits?

Willkie does offer domestic partner benefits and back up child care.

© 2007 Vault Inc.

3. What is your firm's vacation policy?

Willkie offers 4 weeks of paid vacation in addition to personal and sick days.

4. Do you have a flex-time policy?

Yes.

5. Do you offer a sabbatical or leave-of-absence program? How many associates take advantage of this option on an annual basis?

We do not have a formal sabbatical or leave-of-absence program; however, we have, on a case-by-case basis, approved leave of absence requests.

Wilmer Cutler Pickering Hale and Dorr LLP

1. What is your firm policy on maternity leave? Paternity leave?

To care for a newborn or newly adopted child, lawyers may take parental leave for up to twelve consecutive months (three months paid) for the lawyer with primary childcare responsibility or up to three weeks (paid) for the lawyer with secondary childcare responsibility. Both parents may be regarded as "primary" as long as their leaves do not overlap. The Firm's share of premiums for medical, dental, disability and life insurance benefits continues without reduction for up to twelve months of a leave.

2. Do you offer any distinctive family-friendly options, such as adoption assistance or child care? Do you offer domestic partner benefits?

The Firm participates in backup/emergency day care programs located on-site in the Boston and Washington, D.C. offices and close to the New York office.

The Firm does not currently offer formal adoption assistance, although associates adopting a child are eligible for the same paid leave outlined above for maternity leave. In addition, associates are encouraged to work with our Employee Assistance Plan, which offers information and resources regarding adoption options at no cost to the associates.

The firm covers domestic partners under all benefit plans.

3. What is your firm's vacation policy?

Associates at WilmerHale are entitled to four (4) weeks of vacation per calendar year. For part-time associates, vacation entitlement is pro-rated. All associates are encouraged to take their vacation time each year. If an associate is unable to take all of his/her vacation time, up to two weeks of time may be rolled over to the following year.

4. Do you have a flex-time policy?

The Firm has a formal flex-time policy, which is intended to assist lawyers whose personal or professional circumstances or goals are best served by a schedule that is full-time but allows them to adjust their hours in the office. In many instances, such an arrangement responds to child-care needs, the illness of a family member, or comparable situations. However, the Firm will also consider, on a case-by-case basis, requests for flex-time arrangements to address other personal or professional circumstances or goals. Under the policy, a lawyer may adjust his or her regular office hours and/or work from home for up to 40% of the time (that is, the equivalent of two days a week). Both full-time and part-time associates are eligible for flex-time arrangements. Because a flextime schedule is not a reduced workload arrangement, there is no adjustment to an associate's salary or benefits.

Visit the Vault Law Channel, the complete online resource for law careers, featuring firm profiles, message boards, the Vault Law Job Board, and more. **www.vault.com/law**

VAULT CAREER LIBRARY   809

In addition, a flex-time schedule does not in itself affect an associate's eligibility for election to counselship or partnership, or the timing of that eligibility.

5. Do you offer a sabbatical or leave-of-absence program? How many associates take advantage of this option on an annual basis?

The Firm offers a three-month paid sabbatical to partners and senior lawyers (those on part-time are also eligible) after seven years of service as a partner or long-term counsel. This sabbatical, which may be taken without regard to purpose, has been used for work, writing, teaching, study, travel, and time with family, among other things.

Wilson Sonsini Goodrich & Rosati

1. What is your firm policy on maternity leave? Paternity leave?

Our leave policies meet or exceed all federal and state leave law requirements. We provide a combination maternity disability leave and baby bonding leave that typically lasts up to six months for female associates. New fathers may take bonding leave. Depending on length of service, the firm pays salary continuation for up to ten weeks for maternity disability (females only) and up to two weeks for baby bonding (male and female).

2. Do you offer any distinctive family-friendly options, such as adoption assistance or child care? Do you offer domestic partner benefits?

We do offer domestic partner benefits. We also offer a back-up childcare program.

3. What is your firm's vacation policy?

Associates accrue vacation at the rate of three weeks or four weeks per year, depending on length of service.

4. Do you have a flex-time policy?

The firm has a part-time policy that supports our associates who wish to continue their pursuit of a membership position and their relationship with the firm while reducing their work schedule to accomodate family needs.

5. Do you offer a sabbatical or leave-of-absence program? How many associates take advantage of this option on an annual basis?

The firm does not have a sabbatical program.

Winston & Strawn LLP

1. What is your firm policy on maternity leave? Paternity leave?

Winston offers its female associates 12 weeks of paid maternity leave. In addition, all associates are eligible for 12 weeks of unpaid paternity leave. We also offer additional unpaid leave on a case-by-case basis.

2. Do you offer any distinctive family-friendly options, such as adoption assistance or child care? Do you offer domestic partner benefits?

Winston offers emergency back-up child care services, dependent care flexible spending accounts, and a reduced hours work policy. We also offer domestic partner benefits.

3. What is your firm's vacation policy?

Winston treats its associates as professionals and permits them to manage their own schedules. All our attorneys are encouraged to find a healthy balance between their professional and personal lives, including taking time away from the office on vacation.

4. Do you have a flex-time policy?

Winston's reduced hours policy allows associates to work a part-time schedule and still progress toward partnership.

5. Do you offer a sabbatical or leave-of-absence program? How many associates take advantage of this option on an annual basis?

Winston offers associates personal and professional leaves on a case-by-case basis.

Visit the Vault Law Channel, the complete online resource for law careers, featuring firm profiles, message boards, the Vault Law Job Board, and more. www.vault.com/law

VAULT CAREER LIBRARY   811

Get the BUZZ on Top Schools

Read what STUDENTS and ALUMNI have to say about:

- Admissions
- Academics
- Career Opportunities
- Quality of Life
- Social Life

Surveys on thousands of top programs
College • MBA • Law School • Grad School

V ULT
> the most trusted name in career information™

Go to www.vault.com

Alphabetical List of Firms

Visit the Vault Law Channel, the complete online resource for law careers, featuring firm profiles, message boards, the Vault Law Job Board, and more. www.vault.com/law

VAULT CAREER LIBRARY 813

© 2007 Vault Inc.

Visit the Vault Law Channel, the complete online resource for law careers, featuring firm
profiles, message boards, the Vault Law Job Board, and more. **www.vault.com/law**

VAULT CAREER LIBRARY   **815**

Wondering what it's like to work at a specific employer?

Read what EMPLOYEES have to say about:

- Workplace culture
- Compensation
- Hours
- Diversity
- Hiring process

Read employer surveys on THOUSANDS of top employers.

V\ULT

> the most trusted name in career information™

Go to www.vault.com

About the Author

Brian Dalton

Brian Dalton is Vault's senior law editor. Prior to joining Vault, he was an associate at a New York City law firm. Before law school, he worked as, among other things, a football coach, French teacher and Peace Corps volunteer. He has a B.A. in history from Middlebury and a J.D. from Fordham.

Visit the Vault Law Channel, the complete online resource for law careers, featuring firm profiles, message boards, the Vault Law Job Board, and more. **www.vault.com/law**

VAULT CAREER LIBRARY   817

VΛULT

THE MOST TRUSTED NAME IN CAREER INFORMATION

Vault guides and employer profiles have been published since 1997 and are the premier source of insider information on careers.

Each year, Vault surveys and interviews thousands of employees to give readers the inside scoop on industries and specific employers to help them get the jobs they want.

"Fun reads, edgy details"
– FORBES MAGAZINE

"To get the un-varnished scoop, check out Vault"
– SMARTMONEY MAGAZINE

VΛULT

GO FOR THE GOLD!

GET VAULT GOLD MEMBERSHIP
AND GET ACCESS TO ALL OF VAULT'S
AWARD-WINNING LAW CAREER INFORMATION

◆ Access to **500+ extended insider law firm profiles**

◆ Access to **regional snapshots** for major non-HQ offices of major firms

◆ Complete access to **Vault's exclusive law firm rankings**, including quality of life rankings, diversity rankings, practice area rankings, and rankings by law firm partners

◆ Access to **Vault's Law Salary Central**, with salary information for 100s of top firms

◆ Receive **Vault's Law Job Alerts** of top law jobs posted on the Vault Law Job Board

◆ Access to complete **Vault message board archives**

◆ **15% off** all Vault Guide and Vault Career Services purchases

For more information go to
www.vault.com/law

V▲ULT
> the most trusted name in career information™

Use the Internet's
MOST TARGETED
job search tools.

Vault Job Board

Target your search by industry, function, and experience level, and find the job openings that you want.

VaultMatch Resume Database

Vault takes match-making to the next level: post your resume and customize your search by industry, function, experience and more. We'll match job listings with your interests and criteria and e-mail them directly to your in-box.

VAULT
> the most trusted name in career information™